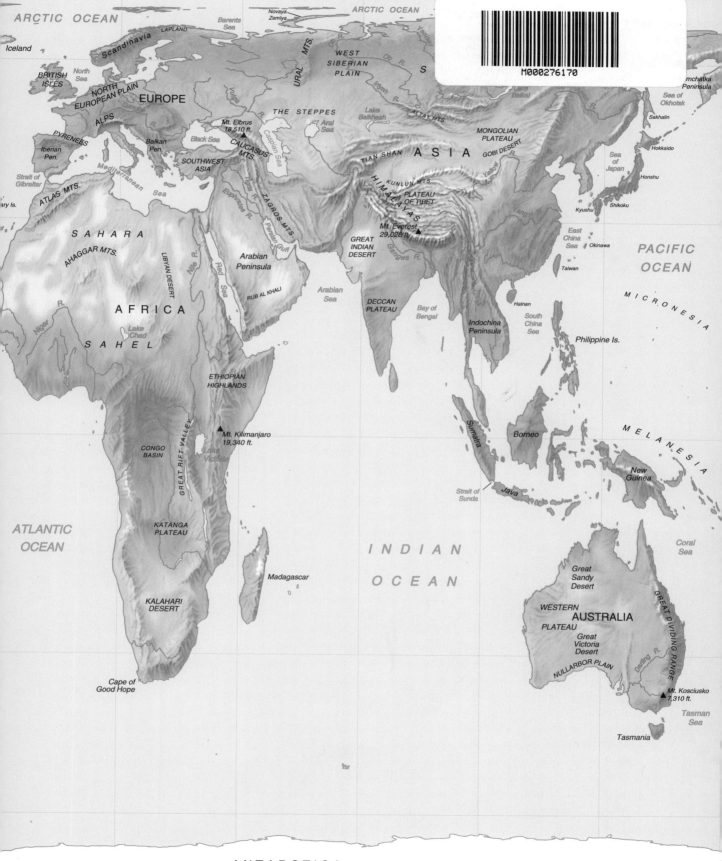

M000276170

ARCTIC OCEAN

ARCTIC OCEAN

Iceland

Novaya Zemlya

Barents Sea

LAPLAND

Scandinavia

BRITISH ISLES

North Sea

NORTH EUROPEAN PLAIN

EUROPE

URAL MTS.

WEST SIBERIAN PLAIN

Ob R.

Irtysh

S

Kamchatka Peninsula

ALPS

PYRENEES

THE STEPPES

Mt. Elbrus 18,510 ft.

CAUCASUS MTS.

Black Sea

Volga

Aral Sea

Lake Balkhash

ALTAY MTS.

MONGOLIAN PLATEAU

Lake Baikal

Sea of Okhotsk

Sakhalin

Sea of Japan

Hokkaido

Iberian Pen.

Balkan Pen.

Caspian Sea

SOUTHWEST ASIA

ASIA

TIAN SHAN

GOBI DESERT

Honshu

ATLAS MTS.

Mediterranean Sea

Strait of Gibraltar

ry Is.

ZAGROS MTS.

Tigris R.

Euphrates R.

KUNLUN MTS.

PLATEAU OF TIBET

Yellow

Kyushu

Shikoku

SAHARA

AHAGGAR MTS.

LIBYAN DESERT

Nile R.

Red Sea

Arabian Peninsula

Persian Gulf

HIMALAYAS

Mt. Everest 29,028 ft.

GREAT INDIAN DESERT

Ganges R.

Yangtze

East China Sea

Okinawa

Taiwan

PACIFIC OCEAN

MICRONESIA

AFRICA

SAHEL

Niger R.

Lake Chad

RUB AL KHALI

Arabian Sea

DECCAN PLATEAU

Bay of Bengal

Indochina Peninsula

Hainan

South China Sea

Philippine Is.

ETHIOPIAN HIGHLANDS

Sumatra

Borneo

MELANESIA

GREAT RIFT VALLEY

Mt. Kilimanjaro 19,340 ft.

Lake Victoria

CONGO BASIN

Strait of Sunda

Java

New Guinea

ATLANTIC OCEAN

KATANGA PLATEAU

Madagascar

INDIAN

OCEAN

Coral Sea

Great Sandy Desert

KALAHARI DESERT

WESTERN PLATEAU

AUSTRALIA

Great Victoria Desert

GREAT DIVIDING RANGE

Darling R.

NULLARBOR PLAIN

Cape of Good Hope

Mt. Kosciusko 7,310 ft.

Tasman Sea

Tasmania

ANTARCTICA

THE GLOBAL PAST

COMPREHENSIVE VOLUME

THE GLOBAL PAST

COMPREHENSIVE VOLUME

Lanny B. Fields
California State University–San Bernardino

Russell J. Barber
California State University–San Bernardino

Cheryl A. Riggs
California State University–San Bernardino

BEDFORD BOOKS 🙠 **Boston**

For Bedford Books

President and Publisher: Charles H. Christensen
General Manager and Associate Publisher: Joan E. Feinberg
History Editor: Katherine E. Kurzman
Developmental Editor: Jane Betz
Editorial Assistants: Thomas Pierce and Maura Shea
Managing Editor: Elizabeth M. Schaaf
Production Editor: Lori Chong Roncka
Production Assistants: Ellen C. Thibault and Ara Salibian
Copyeditor: Eric Newman
Proofreader: Paula Woolley
Text Design: Wanda Kossak
Photo Researcher: Carole Frohlich, The Visual Connection
Cartography: GeoSystems Global Corporation
Page Layout: DeNee Reiton Skipper
Indexer: Steve Csipke
Cover Design: Hannus Design Associates
Cover Art: Noh mask, "Ko-omote," first half of the sixteenth century (detail). Japan, Muromachi period.
 Courtesy of the Tokyo National Museum. Bodhisattva Avalokiteśvara (Bodhisattva of Compassion),
 mid–tenth century (detail). Bihar, eastern India. Marshall H. Gould and Frederick L. Jack Funds. Cour-
 tesy of the Museum of Fine Arts, Boston.
Composition: Ruttle, Shaw & Wetherill, Inc.
Printing and Binding: Quebecor Printing Kingsport

Library of Congress Catalog Card Number: 97–72370

Copyright © 1998 by Bedford Books
A Division of St. Martin's Press, Inc.

All rights reserved. No part of this book may be reproduced, stored in a retrieval system, or transmitted by
any form or by any means, electronic, mechanical, photocopying, recording, or otherwise, except as may
be expressly permitted by the applicable copyright statutes or in writing by the Publisher.

Manufactured in the United States of America.

2   1   0   9   8
f   e   d   c   b   a

For information, write: Bedford Books, 75 Arlington Street, Boston, MA 02116 (617–426–7440)

ISBN: 0–312–10332–8 (hardcover comprehensive vol.)
ISBN: 0–312–10330–1 (paperback Vol. 1)
ISBN: 0–312–10331–X (paperback Vol. 2)

On the Cover: The Japanese mask pictured on the front dates from the first half of the sixteenth century
and represents a precocious child or young woman. Actors used masks rather than facial expressions to
indicate character in the stylized and subtle form of theater called Noh. Noh drama appealed to the
sociopolitical elite, unlike the later Kabuki drama which appealed to the commoners. The Indian sculpture on the back represents the Bodhisattva of Compassion (Avalokiteśvara) and comes from the tenth
century. A *bodhisattva* is an enlightened being (Buddha) who chooses to stay on earth rather than go to
nirvana like other Buddhas. *Bodhisattvas* vow to help all other beings attain enlightenment and to
help them in need. This particular male *bodhisattva* was brought to China and revered as a female
bodhisattva named Guan Yin. Both genders were often depicted as fleshy beings associated with the
lotus flower favored by Buddhists.

On the Title Page: The Bayeux Tapestry is an important source of information about the Norman
conquest of England that began in 1066. This section of the tapestry, embroidered in France shortly after
the invasion, shows William the Conqueror's ship and standard as he and his forces set out to cross the
English Channel. Michael Holford.

*Acknowledgments and copyrights appear at the back of the book on pages 1119–1120, which constitute an
extension of the copyright page.*

Brief Contents

v

Contents

PART TWO
THE CONVERGENCE TOWARD EMPIRE 148

CHAPTER 7
The Greek Polis and the Roman Republic, around 800–31 B.C. 151

CHAPTER 8
The Greek Empire, the Hellenistic Age, and the Roman Empire, 359 B.C.–A.D. 476 183

CHAPTER 9
Early Civilizations in Nubia and Ethiopia, around 800 B.C.–A.D. 650 213

CHAPTER 44
World Integration   1095

Special Features

UNDER THE LENS

Maps

Preface for Instructors

In 1991, Lanny Fields, who had been teaching world history for more than ten years, wrote an article criticizing the books then available for this course, urging both publishers and professors to be bolder in their goals and methods for teaching a global history. This brief piece was published in *Perspectives,* the newsletter of the American Historical Association, where it came to the attention of an editor who had also been searching for a way to approach a course that was clearly growing. The conversations thus started branched out to include two more professors at California State University–San Bernardino; Cheryl Riggs, also in the Department of History, joined Lanny Fields to add her own experiences in the classroom and to strengthen a commitment to social and religious history. Russell Barber, an anthropologist-archaeologist, was recruited when it became clear that to write something "truly global" meant to move beyond what history alone could encompass; his research and understanding of other social science models has proved invaluable to the project. After the efforts of many years, we are pleased to present a book that is global in scope, practically structured, and designed with our students in mind.

As instructors in world history courses, we have found that the most difficult part of teaching these courses is finding a way to cover such a huge topic: deciding what to leave out, how to integrate diverse strands, and how to give the course shape. We have written *The Global Past* with this essential problem in mind and used a variety of approaches to make the text comprehensive and coherent and to help make the introductory world history course a valuable learning experience for students.

Truly Global Approach

From the beginning, *The Global Past* has been designed to provide truly global coverage of world history. Many world history textbooks were born

as Western civilization texts and expanded to incorporate sections on other parts of the world; these sections, however, are often poorly integrated into the textbook and overly brief. In contrast, these topics are given more extensive treatment in *The Global Past*—as their global significance demands—and are integrated into broader discussions throughout the book. The development and functioning of kingdoms before 1600 in sub-Saharan Africa, for example, is given an entire chapter and lays the historical context for a subsequent chapter on the African slave trade.

This broad geographical coverage gives students a better picture of the range of unique world events and encourages them to make comparisons that lead to insights about recurring patterns in world history. Indeed, comparison of events and processes in disparate places and times is an important theme of the book, a theme that is reinforced in the "Issue" chapters and in the special features.

Multidisciplinary Perspectives

Many disciplines have made significant contributions to the study of the human past, and *The Global Past* draws freely on anthropology, geography, and other social sciences to complement the insights of historians. Models and other intellectual tools of the social sciences help to frame discussions, making recurrent patterns more evident and understandable. Models are a widely misunderstood tool of the social sciences. A discussion on p. 17 explains to students that models are ideal constructs created by scholars and that real-world deviations from the expectations derived from models are revealing and frequently lead to new insights.

The presence of an anthropologist-archaeologist among the authors signals a commitment to examining human history before the existence of written records and in places where documents can be complemented with material evidence. The interests of modern archaeologists range from reconstructing past environments to exploring technological capabilities to explaining social change. *The Global Past* incorporates their findings throughout. Archaeological contributions are most obvious in chapters that discuss ancient times, such as those on human origins and the earliest civilizations, but they also enrich our understanding of more recent times and events, such as medieval reactions to the Black Death, plantation slavery in the Americas, the Industrial Revolution, and West African urbanization.

Balanced Coverage

In recognition that history is more than kings and battles, *The Global Past* explores political, economic, cultural, and social developments, attempting to provide balanced and integrated coverage. We have devoted entire chapters, for example, to such topics as "The American Exchange" (following the European voyages of discovery to the Americas) and "The Arts as Mirrors of the Modern World." Shorter treatments are integrated into chapters, linking political-economic events and cultural-social events. This recognition of connections between people, places, and different arenas of activity has been praised by reviewers.

A Variety of Special Features

A number of short sidebar essays are interspersed throughout the text to give students a sense of how people lived in the past, what their concerns were, and how historians interpret the past. These special features, which help to flesh out the coverage and provide a welcome change of pace, are of five types:

- "In Their Own Words," excerpts from primary sources, appear in every chapter. "*Haiku* Poetry and Commentary," for example, places *haiku* in the broader context of Japanese culture.
- "Paths to the Past," historiographic and methodological discussions, help students understand how historians know what they know. For example, "The Bog People" describes archaeological detective work on bog bodies found in Europe.
- "Encounters," narrative accounts of contacts between peoples, examine the places where cultures met. "The Sicilian Caterer," for example, discusses food catering in Sicily as a reflection of the interconnectedness of the ancient eastern Mediterranean.
- "Parallels and Divergences," comparisons of particular topics across time and space, examine similarities and differences between cultures. "China's Taiping Uprising," for example, compares this abortive revolution to the successful revolutions to which the chapter is devoted.
- "Under the Lens" boxes examine individual events, people, or objects in depth. "Paderewski and Polish Nationalism," for example, focuses on the work of one notable individual in a chapter that touches on nationalistic movements around the world.

Topical-Chronological Organization

As longtime teachers of the world history survey, we are well aware of the dilemma instructors face in such courses. On the one hand, students need to see the chronological pattern of history in order to organize all the information covered in a text of this size; on the other hand, students need to make connections *across* time in order to make the information meaningful. A textbook organized strictly according to chronology can, of course, become encyclopedic and mired in the minutiae of specific cases. One organized strictly according to topics, on the other hand, can obscure the basic and important temporal relationships that are central to understanding causality. *The Global Past* steers a middle course, maintaining a largely chronological structure in its ten parts while emphasizing important themes within each part in order to give the material coherence and meaning.

One of the great values of a topical treatment is its economy. Writing a truly global text means including sections often omitted in other books; providing balanced treatment of economic, cultural, and social history also adds length. The topical approach allows space for these essential elements while keeping the length of the book manageable; it is a way to emphasize important links without going into endless detail. It also encourages comparison, an important goal of this text. To make space for these new goals, we have scaled back on the traditional European coverage characteristic of the previous generation of world history texts. We hope instructors will agree that this tradeoff is more than compensated for in the truly global coverage that results.

The treatment of revolutions in Europe, Asia, and the Americas in a single chapter provides a good example. Grouping these varied events together draws students' attention to both their similarities and their differences. Further, the discussion of other revolutions can be shortened, since students will easily be able to see how they conform to the general pattern already established.

To give them coherence and thematic unity, each of the main parts of *The Global Past* closes with a brief chapter devoted to an issue—such as trade, empire, religion, or technology—that has shaped the events discussed in that part. These "Issue" chapters encourage students to step back and consider how events occurring in distant cultures connect to one another, and how they connect to events that occurred earlier and later in time.

Features to Assist the Student

The Global Past includes a variety of features to help students make sense of what they read, organize their thoughts, and study.

- An equal-area map at the beginning of each chapter, often with detail inserts, shows what geographical areas will be discussed in that chapter.

- 115 maps within the chapters are accompanied by detailed captions to encourage critical thinking.

- Full-color maps at the back of the book dedicate a two-page spread to each major geographical area and summarize the changes in each area over the period covered in the text.

- An outline at the beginning of each chapter helps students see how the topics covered relate to one another.

- Pronunciation guides, at the bottoms of text pages, give easy-to-read phonetic respellings for non-English words.

- Abundant, good-sized figures and charts are always accompanied by substantial captions to encourage critical thinking.

- Part and chapter timelines place significant events and processes in time, helping students recognize the chronological relationships within and between geographical areas.

- End-of-chapter summaries are ideal for study and review.

- Suggested readings at the end of each chapter offer carefully selected, annotated lists of classic, recent, and specialized studies for students to explore.

In addition to the full-color map appendix, *The Global Past* includes two other reference tools:

- a glossary of significant terms (which appear in boldface in the text), including pronunciation glosses where appropriate; and

- a full index, including cross-references, brief identifications, dates, and pronunciation glosses where appropriate.

Useful Ancillaries

Bedford Books has made available to the student three major ancillaries: a reader, a map workbook, and a study guide. The two-volume reader, *Reading THE GLOBAL PAST* (edited by Russell J. Barber, Lanny B. Fields, and Cheryl A. Riggs) is geared specifically to *The Global Past* and organized into similar parts. Each part offers an integrated set of readings organized around a critical theme of that part, such as the rise of civilization or the role of economics in empires. Most of the readings are primary sources such as travelers' accounts or political documents, but a few important secondary readings are included as examples of current historical thinking. Each part also contains a visual portfolio.

The two-volume map workbook, *Mapping THE GLOBAL PAST: Historical Geography Workbook* (written by Mark Newman at the University of Illinois–Chicago) gives students additional practice working with maps and analyzing the significance of geography in historical events.

The two-volume study guide, *Making the Most of THE GLOBAL PAST: A Study Guide* (written by Jay Boggis) gives students valuable practice in working with art, maps, timelines, outlines, summaries, essays, and test questions of all kinds.

Ancillaries for instructors help manage the formidable task of teaching an introductory world history course. An instructor's resource manual, *Teaching THE GLOBAL PAST* (written by Cheryl A. Riggs) offers summaries; sample syllabi; lecture suggestions; suggestions for student projects and paper topics; a general bibliography on teaching world history; a variety of references to books, films, and other teaching materials; tips for incorporating the other ancillaries; and more. A testbank (available in print, Macintosh, and Windows formats) offers multiple choice, true/false, fill in the blanks, short answer, reading art, and essay questions of graduated difficulty for all chapters. Color transparencies for maps and selected illustrations in the text allow instructors to focus on particular images in class. A unique *Audio Pronunciation Guide* lets instructors hear how unusual non-English words and phrases are pronounced, so they can speak confidently in class.

History has developed an increased awareness of how critical it is to study the totality of the human past: all arenas of human endeavor at all times and places. *The Global Past* will initiate students into that awareness as soon as they take their first survey course in world history.

Acknowledgments

It is trite but true to state that every book is a group effort; a textbook raises that statement to new heights. We have imposed on our colleagues at California State University–San Bernardino and elsewhere, regularly requesting information and comments. The School of Social and Behavioral Sciences at CSUSB and Deans Aubrey Bonnett and Ellen Gruenbaum assisted us by providing funds to facilitate the project.

At Bedford Books, Publisher Charles Christensen and General Manager Joan Feinberg have been both supportive and demanding, and their dedication to producing a quality book has been exemplary; Jane Betz has guided the text through its evolution; and Lori Chong Roncka has been responsible for its production. Carole Frohlich of The Visual Connection applied her skills and taste in researching the illustrations.

Louise Waller, formerly of St. Martin's Press, holds a special place in our gratitude. Her initial interest in and guidance of this project were very influential in shaping it, and we consider her an honorary author.

Finally, we extend our thanks to the various reviewers who read parts or all of the manuscript and shared their expertise and judgment with us. Not every comment was always welcome at the time, but it would be difficult to find one that did not ultimately help improve the text. We extend our thanks to that legion of reviewers: Roger Adelson, Arizona State University; Ruth Aurelius, Des Moines Area Community College; Norman Bennett, Boston University; Gail Bossenga, University of Kansas; Fritz Blockwell, Washington State University; Thomas W. Burkman, State University of New York–Buffalo; Captain Robert Carriedo, United States Air Force Academy; Ronald Coons, University of Connecticut; Captain Robert Cummings, United States Air Force Academy; R. Hunt Davis, University of Florida; Michael Fisher, Oberlin College; Vernard Foley, Purdue University; Robert D. Friedel, University of Maryland; Robert Garfield, DePaul University; Suzanne Gay, Oberlin College; Frank Garosi, California State University–Sacramento; Laura Gellot, University of Wisconsin–Parkside; Marc Gellot, University of Wisconsin–La Crosse; Marc Gilbert, North Georgia College; Christopher Gutherie, Tarleton State University; John S. Innes, Eastern Washington University; Doug Klepper, Santa Fe Community College; Gregory Kozlowski, DePaul University; James Krippner-Martinez, Haverford College; David Lelyveld, Columbia University; John Mandaville, Portland State University; C. Nicole Martin, Germanna Community College; David McComb, Colorado State University; Rebecca McCoy, University of Idaho; John Mears, Southern Methodist University; Gail Minault, University of Texas–Austin; David T. Morgan, University of Montevallo; Les Muray, Lansing Community College; Vera Reber, Shippensburg University; Donald Roper, State University of New York–New Paltz; Paul Scherer, Indiana State University–South Bend; James Shenton, Columbia University; Amos E. Simpson, University of Southwestern Louisiana; Leonard Smith, Oberlin College; Robert Tignor, Princeton University; Joseph Warren, Lansing Community College; Samuel Wells, Pearl River Community College; Allan Winkler, Miami University of Ohio; John Williams, Indiana State University; Marcia Wright, Columbia University. We would especially like to thank Marian Nelson of the University of Nebraska–Omaha and Robert Berry for their extensive help.

Lanny B. Fields
Russell J. Barber
Cheryl A. Riggs
San Bernardino, California
June 1997

THE
GLOBAL
PAST

COMPREHENSIVE VOLUME

THE HUMAN PAST IS OLD, VERY OLD. By 3 million years ago, recognizable human ancestors lived in Africa, and by 500,000 years ago they had evolved to have significant intelligence and cultural potential. By 100,000 years ago they had become biologically modern human beings like us.

From the achievement of biological modernity to shortly after 10,000 B.C., things stayed much the same for human beings, who lived in small groups of hunters and gatherers with simple organization. But populations slowly were growing, partly as a result of more favorable climatic conditions and partly as a result of expanded and refined technology that permitted human beings to earn their livelihoods more effectively. This growth would lead to more complex societies and eventually to civilizations, with their cities, complicated governments, and sophisticated technology. As children of civilization, we believe civilization to be the normal way of life; but if human existence were an apple, the period of civilization would be no thicker than its skin.

	SOUTHWEST ASIA	EGYPT	EASTERN MEDITERRANEAN
3000 B.C.	Sumerians	Archaic Egypt	
2500 B.C.		Old Kingdom	
2000 B.C.	Akkadians / Babylonians	Middle Kingdom	Minoans
1500 B.C.	Hittites	Hyksos / New Kingdom	Mycenaeans
	Assyrians		
1000 B.C.	Hebrew Kingdom		Phoenicians / Dorians
500 B.C.	Persian Empire		
A.D. 1			
A.D. 500			
A.D. 1000			
A.D. 1500			

PART ONE
EARLY TIMES

Part One of *The Global Past* takes you from our near-human and human ancestors to the earliest civilizations that developed around the world. Chapter 1 introduces concepts about the past and the study of it, concepts that will be used throughout the text. The vast period during which human beings evolved, as well as the cultural achievements of our early ancestors, is discussed in Chapter 2. Chapter 3 presents the idea of civilization, defining it and distinguishing it from other ways that human beings have organized themselves. The earliest civilizations of Mesopotamia, Egypt, and the eastern Mediterranean—including the first civilizations in the world—are discussed in Chapter 4. Chapter 5 treats the earliest civilizations of India and China, and Chapter 6 discusses the development of civilization in the Americas. Finally, Issue 1 probes trade, a powerful force in shaping civilizations.

INDIA	CHINA	MESOAMERICA	PERU	
				3000 B.C.
Indus Valley civilizations				2500 B.C.
				2000 B.C.
	Shang Dynasty			1500 B.C.
Aryans/Gangetic civilizations	Early Zhou Dynasty	Olmecs	Chavín	1000 B.C.
				500 B.C.
		Maya	Regional states	
		Teotihuacán		A.D. 1
				A.D. 500
			Wari Empire	
		Toltecs		A.D. 1000
				A.D. 1500

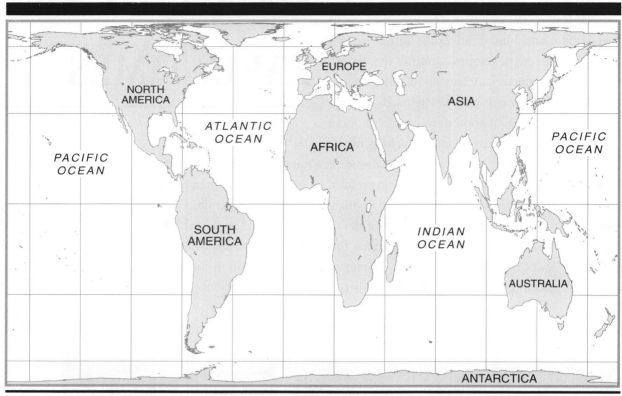

Some Calendric Equivalents. Around the world, different societies have developed various ways to keep track of time and label dates. This chart shows a few of those methods and how they relate to one another. The Hebrew, Chinese, and Mayan systems start with an ancient date and simply move forward; the Gregorian and Islamic calendars calculate forward and backward from a more recent reference point, hence requiring modifiers (B.C. and A.D. or B.H. and A.H.) to indicate whether a date is before or after the reference point. Dates have been converted to the Gregorian calendar throughout this textbook, but at least forty separate calendric systems have been used by the peoples discussed in The Global Past.

The Study of the Global Past

"*History*, n. An account mostly false, of events mostly unimportant, which are brought about by rulers mostly knaves, and soldiers mostly fools." So wrote Ambrose Bierce in *The Devil's Dictionary*, his cynical review of the human condition. Our knowledge of the past is necessarily flawed by the human failings of the scholars who study it—Bierce called historians "broad-gauge gossips"—but people nonetheless remain absorbed with the human past.

The Aztecs were fascinated by their Toltec forebears in Mexico and invented fictional links to them to legitimize their empire. Medieval Europeans elevated the ancient Greeks to a lofty status, using their philosophies as the basis for both social and scientific theories of the world; the medieval Roman Catholic Church even established a special dispensation for illustrious Greeks to be admitted to Heaven, despite the fact that they were not Christians. And in Japan and China, ancestor veneration and respect for one's predecessors have been basic and integral parts of everyday life for centuries.

Have these and other people been drawn to the past by a quaint and irrelevant captivation, by a pragmatic interest in exploiting earlier events to their own political advantage, or by an intellectual urge to understand how their age came to be? Probably all of these and many other factors have gone into every people's interest in the past, but every known society devotes itself to the perpetuation of its past in one way or another.

5

FIGURE **1.1** *George Washington and the Cherry Tree.* *Fictitious stories about famous people abound, such as the tale of George Washington as a child cutting down a cherry tree and honestly admitting his misdeed to his father. This anecdote has been used to teach children the value of honesty, but it was a fabrication itself, invented by Mason Locke Weems and recorded in his 1806 biography of Washington. Historians since then have tried to root out this false story, but its cultural value to Americans makes it unlikely they will succeed. This 1867 painting by John C. MacRae commemorates the event that never happened.* Corbis/Bettmann.

The academic study of the past draws upon this human interest in one's own history, both in the narrow sense of the ancestors of one's nation or ethnic group and in the broader sense of the ancestors of all people. But academic study distinguishes itself by its keen concern with accuracy and understanding. In the everyday world of the United States, it is a perfectly satisfactory story that young George Washington chopped down a cherry tree and was so honest that he told his parents. It serves as a model for children's behavior and helps foster patriotism by perpetuating a heroic image of one of its founders. The fact that the story is untrue in no way detracts from these purposes; in fact, a historically accurate account of the past might serve these purposes less well. The search for true accounts of the past and ways of understanding why events and processes occurred as they did, however, is the province of academic studies of the past and is the subject of this book.

WHY STUDY THE PAST?

If myths and folklore are more satisfying than the more complicated stories of the past that scholars produce, why bother with the scholarly accounts? There are several reasons.

Most scholars believe that we should be able to learn from the past. Of course events never really repeat themselves; after all, times and circumstances change, so the same event could never recur in just the same way and for just the same reasons. But certainly there are patterns to events.

For example, there have been dozens of cases in which a civilization has run short of resources, often with devastating effects. What are the common threads among the scarcity of wood in Great Britain of the seventeenth century, Ireland's food shortage during the potato famine of 1846, and the dearth of agricultural land and produce among the Central American Maya[1] of the eighth century? Can knowledge of these common threads help modern society cope with impending shortages of raw materials, such as energy sources or food? If studying the past helps us understand the range of ways in which people have met challenges and the relative success of those solutions, it may also help today's policymakers respond to the problems of the modern world in an informed manner.

Studying the past can inform us about the present in another basic way. Many conflicts and issues of any age are rooted in developments of earlier periods. The Cold War of the second half of the twentieth century would make little sense without an understanding of the Russian Revolution, the Stalinist era, World War II, and the Chinese Revolution. The Gulf War of 1991 and other regional conflicts of the latter half of the twentieth century would appear to be irrational squabbles without some understanding of the colonial history of the region and the creation of Israel, Jordan, Kuwait, and other states. The current economic woes of most Latin American countries would seem to be a product of mere mismanagement without knowledge of the colonial exploitation, external military pressures, and puppet regimes that form the background of the current governments. Earlier conflicts and friendships—sometimes in the quite distant past—often have profound effects on the politics of the modern world, and it is foolish to try to understand today's world without studying the world of yesterday.

The academic study of the past also can help us recognize fictitious accounts, concocted as justification for a particular political agenda. For example, Nazi Germany before World War II looked to historians, archaeologists, and anthropologists for reconstructions of the past population movements of different European ethnic groups. If ancestral Aryans (whom the Nazis argued were Germans) could be shown to have occupied

Poland or Russia, it was argued, this would be justification for a German reconquest of these "lost provinces." The reconstructions provided by the Nazi scholars were at best speculations, at worst pure fabrications; they were advanced as sound justifications for political policy, however, and required refutation by more reliable, less biased scholarship. If policymakers are to use knowledge of the past to help them make better decisions today, they must be scrupulously sure that their knowledge of the past is the most accurate possible. Critical scholarship can distinguish between the legitimate use of the past (to advise us about future policies) and the invention of a past to justify preconceived policies.

Perhaps most important, studying the past can inform us better about the human condition. Our personal experience is often so intense and so limited to our own country and period that it can blind us to the recognition that there have been other places and times with people whose lives have been just as full as ours with experiences, events, and crises. By studying the whole range of human experience—past and present—we are in a better position to understand the human world around us and, thereby, ourselves.

WHO STUDIES THE PAST?

Many people assume that the study of the past is the exclusive domain of historians. Historians, of course, are one of the major types of scholars who study the past, but they certainly are not the only ones. In fact, virtually all of the **social sciences**—the disciplines that study human culture and behavior—also have some stake in investigating the past. Political scientists may study ancient Greek ideas of democracy or the thinking of the architects of the French Revolution in order to better understand the historical underpinnings of today's conceptions of democracy. Economists may choose to study the social programs enacted in the United States during the Great Depression to gain insight into what course of action should be followed in subsequent depressions and recessions. But the social sciences most interested in the past—the disciplines that devote most or all of their attention to the past—are history, archaeology, and geography.

[1] **Maya:** MY yuh

History studies the human past primarily through the interpretation of documents. In the broad sense, a document is any written message, and historians may use such diverse sources as diaries, censuses, gravestone epitaphs, and notes written in the margins of books. Historians are interested in the whole range of human events and activities. In the past, however, most of historians' energies were spent in the study of political and sometimes economic issues, such as wars, revolutions, and struggles for power. Indeed, historical documents in many periods are predominantly concerned with these issues, making information on them more easily accessible to historians than information on the day-to-day activities of people. Nonetheless, historians in the past few decades have turned their attentions increasingly to **social history**, the study of everyday life in the past.

On the other hand, **archaeology** operates largely without recourse to documents. Instead, archaeologists study the human past primarily through material remains. These remains include the ruins of buildings and settlements, seeds and bones and other items that indicate the foodstuffs consumed by a people, imported objects that shed light on trade connections, and everyday items cast off after their usefulness has passed. In brief, archaeology studies the refuse left behind by past peoples. Archaeological remains are the clues that, after careful and thoughtful study, can be used to draw conclusions about everyday life. Archaeology is virtually the only window on the first many thousands of years of the human past, because the earliest writing was developed only a few thousand years ago. But even in examining the more recent past, archaeology can prove a valuable adjunct to documentary history.

The line between history and archaeology, drawn so sharply in the foregoing paragraphs, is really somewhat blurred. Historians sometimes draw on physical remains—especially art, architecture, and coinage—to help formulate and support their interpretations. Similarly, archaeologists may use documents when they are available. The difference between the two fields lies largely in the differing emphasis on either documents or physical remains. In this text, we will deal with the integrated study of the past, attempting to transcend the boundaries between history and archaeology.

Fortunately for those who study the past, documents and physical remains often provide com-

FIGURE 1.2 *Archaeological Remains at Pompeii.* *When Mount Vesuvius suddenly erupted in A.D. 79, it buried the ancient Roman city of Pompeii in volcanic ash and lava. People, dogs, and livestock were engulfed by these materials, sometimes caught in midstride, as was the case with these victims crawling up a stairway when overwhelmed by ash. Tragic events such as this one can create a record that reveals details in a manner unparalleled by most archaeological remains.* Soprantintendenza alla Antichita della Campania, Naples.

plementary information. Documents are relatively rich in detail, often providing a wealth of information on individuals, motives, and ideas. Physical remains, on the other hand, provide much more general information, often frustratingly lacking in detail. The conclusions drawn from physical remains often relate to material issues, such as economics and technology; scholars, however, can be very clever about interpreting the material clues and sometimes provide vivid reconstructions of social and ideological aspects of past **lifeways**, typical behaviors for a society. The physical remains that archaeologists examine usually are anonymous and can be related to no specific individual; in contrast, historians often can provide a name and personality to go with an individual involved in an event. Whereas the best written documentation frequently deals with the elite, physical remains frequently are best able to shed light on the everyday life of common people. Finally, while scholars must question the accuracy of the information in a document they study and the motives of its author, archaeologists normally can be assured that no one has manipulated ancient trash with an eye toward finding a favorable place in history.

Geography differs from history and archaeology in that it is defined by its theoretical focus, not its sources of data. To the geographer, the human past is of interest in terms of how people have used the planet's land and resources. The geographical perspective draws attention to the ways that human beings have exploited various resources (such as wood, food species, and minerals), how they have arranged their settlements over the face of the earth (both in relationship to resources and to one another), and how they have transported goods and communicated messages from one place to another. These interests can be addressed with either historical or archaeological data.

Is one of these approaches inherently better than the others? No, each can help solve one part of the puzzle of the past. Modern research tries to use these and other approaches in order to provide the fullest and most balanced possible picture of the past. In fact, most scholars of the past use interpretations of all the different types of evidence and draw on various approaches, calling the composite result "history." The problem of understanding the past is far too difficult to warrant restricting the tools available to solve it.

THE SOURCES OF INFORMATION ON THE PAST

The study of the past, if it is to have any credibility, has to be based on solid evidence. Scholars have three major sources of information on which they can draw to do their work: documents, oral accounts, and physical remains.

Documents

Documents are written records of all sorts. They typically are divided into primary and secondary sources. **Primary sources** are documents that have been written by a participant in the event, activity, or process described or analyzed. For example, an account of the assassination of Abraham Lincoln by a witness in Ford's Theater the evening of the killing would be a primary source, as would be the diary of John Wilkes Booth, the assassin. Clearly, any primary source might include biased reporting and even untruths, but it remains a primary source because it was written by participants or direct observers. Census reports, memoirs of an officer in the U.S. Civil War, and bills of lading for ships are all primary sources. Some primary sources are included as boxes in this textbook, under the heading "In Their Own Words."

In contrast, **secondary sources** are documents for which information is gathered from primary sources, analyzed, and digested, providing an interpretation of the event or process. A newspaper account of the Lincoln assassination, prepared by a reporter on the basis of interviews with witnesses but no firsthand knowledge, is a secondary source. This textbook also is a secondary source, because we, the authors, were neither direct participants in nor recorders of the events and processes discussed in it; rather, we have collected information from primary sources (as well as other secondary sources), selected those portions we have felt most important, and presented an integrated interpretation. Most scholarly books and articles are secondary sources. Most (but by no means all) secondary sources are written long after an event.

There are, of course, documents that do not fall easily into one category or the other. These works are neither primary nor secondary sources but are mixtures of both. For example, an explorer

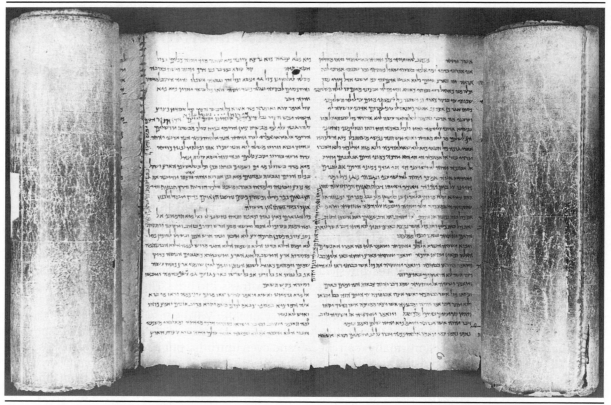

FIGURE 1.3 *Temple Scroll.* *Documents such as this one are the most important sources of information for historians. This document, one of the Dead Sea Scrolls, came to the attention of scholars in the 1950s after it had been found in a dry cave by desert nomads in Palestine. It is composed of well-preserved animal skin sewn into a twenty-seven-foot strip and describes the rights and duties of the king of Israel. It dates back to around 100 B.C.* Courtesy of Professor John C. Trever.

of sixteenth-century South America might have included in a book describing that continent both accounts of personal travels and experiences (primary) and stories heard from others (secondary); an attempt to reconcile these differing tales into a consistent interpretation (secondary) might also have been included.

Historians recognize the need to use both primary and secondary sources. Primary sources are preferred for the facts on which an interpretation is based. Those facts may have been restated in secondary sources, and, although it may be easier to use those restatements than to return to the primary sources, there is always a chance of distortion when information from a primary source is restated in a secondary source. Consequently, historians believe strongly that scholars should return to the original, primary sources to collect their

facts. Secondary sources, on the other hand, can provide valuable insights about how other scholars have interpreted particular facts and may serve as the embarkation point for new interpretations.

Primary sources, as noted previously, are not all equal in terms of their accuracy or completeness. In recognition of this, historians have developed a set of procedures often known as **source analysis**. Source analysis is concerned with two issues. First, is the document a legitimate example of what it is purported to be, or is it a fake or something other than what it is claimed to be? Second, to what degree should the document be believed? How accurate is it likely to be?

The first task, largely that of detecting fakes, is often a very technical one. Sometimes fakes are betrayed by physical characteristics of the documents. For example, the Horn Papers, alleged to be an eighteenth-century account of Euro-American settlers west of the Allegheny Mountains, were found to have been written with a metal pen tip, something that was not invented until about one hundred years after the supposed date of the writing of the Horn Papers. Types of paper, types of ink, styles of handwriting, use of vocabulary inappropriate to the time when a document was supposed to have been written, references to events that had not yet occurred—these and other clues have exposed documents as forgeries.

The second task, that of deciding to what degree a document should be believed, is more complex and less likely to yield so simple an answer. The historian must consider factors that affect either the writer's ability to observe and

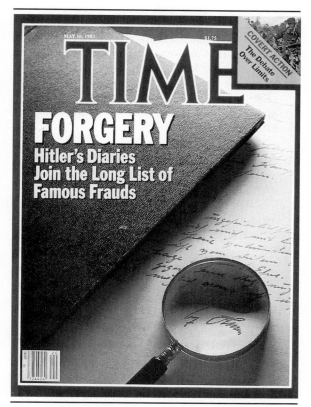

FIGURE 1.4 *Forged Hitler Diaries. Historians and other scholars are often wary of unauthenticated documents. In 1983, historians showed that a much-publicized diary of Adolf Hitler was a recent forgery, apparently contrived for economic profit. The methods of source analysis discussed in this chapter are the tools that historians can use to recognize such fakes.*
© 1983 Time Inc. Reprinted by permission.

understand the events transpiring around him or her or the writer's willingness to give a thoroughly honest account. These factors, considered together, constitute what historians call **bias**.

Bias is present in every account, regardless of how hard the writer tries to avoid it. Because all writers are limited by their experiences and preconceptions, they will see and interpret events in terms that make sense to them. Some writers have biases with limited impact on most of their reporting, and others are skilled at recognizing and overcoming much of their bias. The works of other writers, however, are sometimes permeated with biases that have profound effects on the reliability of what they report.

The biases and other circumstances affecting a document must be considered by a historian using that document. Consider, for example, a simple eyewitness account of the assassination of Abraham Lincoln. Was the witness physically in a position to observe the incident? (Factors such as the person's height, seat in the theater, and vision would affect the answer to this question.) Was the witness biased? (A Southern sympathizer would be expected to have a different emotional state from that of a Northern abolitionist at the sight of the assassination of the president, and this could shape a person's perception.) Did the witness have a vested interest in producing a certain sort of account? (If the story was being sold to a newspaper or magazine, there might be incentive to embellish details or create dramatic circumstances.) Had the witness read other accounts before presenting his or her account? Was the witness fluent in English and able to understand others' comments? Was the witness's account recorded shortly after the event, or had memory had time to fade? Are the claims of the accounts corroborated by other information?

These and similar questions have to be asked of every document or other account before the historian can decide which portions probably can be taken at face value and which are more likely to be distorted, fanciful, or simply untrue. Documents may have portions that are of little historical value because of their considerable bias, while other portions may be highly reliable. Source analysis attempts to identify these portions, but the nature of the problem is such that there can be scholarly disagreement about the reliability of a document or part of a document.

Historians often are faced with accounts of the same event by different observers, accounts that may not agree particularly well. The historian, then, must use source analysis to evaluate these accounts and try to establish which portions are probably accurate and which are not. Following are excerpts from various accounts of the death of Montezuma,[a] the emperor of the Aztec Empire in Mexico at the time of the Spanish conquest in 1521. These accounts, all describing the same event, underscore how divergent the information given in documents can be.

HERNANDO CORTÉS'S ACCOUNT

Hernando Cortés[b] led the Spanish forces against the Aztecs and wrote letters to Charles V, his king, about his successes. His second letter describes the capture of Montezuma and fierce fighting before the event described in the following passage:

> Montezuma, who with one of his sons and many other chiefs who had been captured at the beginning, was still a prisoner, asked to be carried to the roof of the fort where he could speak to the captains and the [Aztec] people, and cause the war to cease. I had him taken thither, and when he reached the parapet on the top of the fort, intending to speak to the people who were fighting there, one of his own subjects struck him on the head with a stone, with such force that within three days he died. I then had him taken out, dead as he was, by two of the Indian prisoners, who bore him away to his people; but I do not know what they did with him. . . .

SAHAGÚN'S AZTEC ACCOUNT

Bernardino de Sahagún,[c] a Spanish clergyman, collected native accounts of the conquest of Mexico in Nahuatl, the language of the Aztecs, and translated them into Spanish. These accounts were collected from Aztecs shortly after the conquest and presumably were altered minimally by Sahagún. After discussing the battles, the account describes how Montezuma and Itzquauhtzin[d] (a noble in Montezuma's service) mounted the roof and Itzquauhtzin harangued the Aztec crowd to surrender to the superior Spanish military might. The account continues:

> In the increasing outcry which followed, arrows fell upon the roof terrace. The Spaniards protected Montezuma and Itzquauhtzin with their shields so that the Mexicans [Aztecs] might not injure them. But the Mexicans were beside themselves with rage because the Spaniards had completely annihilated our brave warriors—had slain them without warning by treachery. . . . It was after another four days that the Spaniards threw the dead bodies of Montezuma and Itzquauhtzin out of the palace at a place called Teoayoc,[e] the stone turtle carving. As soon as they were recognized, men quickly took up Montezuma's body and carried it to Copulco,[f] placed it on a pile of wood, and fired it. The flames crackled and flared up into many tongues; the body seemed to lie sizzling, sending up a foul stench.

DURÁN'S AZTEC ACCOUNT

Diego Durán read a native account of the conquest, the *Chronicle X* (which since has been lost), and published his secondary account based on it in 1581. His account describes the battles and places Itzquauhtzin on the roof and stoned to death. He wrote:

> The *Chronicle* tells us that once the Spaniards had fled from Mexico [a temporary setback] and those who had remained behind [had] been killed, the Aztecs entered the chambers of King Montezuma in order to treat him more cruelly than they had dealt with the Spaniards. There they found him dead with a chain about his feet and five dagger wounds in his chest. Near him lay many noblemen and great lords who had been held prisoners with him. All of them had been slain shortly before the Spaniards abandoned the building.

---

[a] **Montezuma:** mon tuh ZOO muh
[b] **Hernando Cortés:** ehr NAHN doh kawr TEZ
[c] **Sahagún:** sah hah GOON

[d] **Itzquauhtzin:** eetz kwah OOT zihn
[e] **Teoayoc:** tay oh EYE ohk
[f] **Copulco:** koh PULL koh

Oral Accounts

Although written documents are the most important source for historians, **oral accounts** (stories and descriptions of the past preserved by word of mouth) also can be of considerable importance. For the study of events in the recent past, interviews with individuals who witnessed or participated in them can be invaluable. Oral accounts also can be of great value in the study of the history of nonliterate peoples (peoples who have no written language). In Nigeria, for example, oral histories have traditionally been kept by specialists who have memorized extremely long accounts and passed them on to the next generation. The fact that the same account, word for word, has been reported by different keepers of oral history suggests that the accounts may have been preserved with minimal distortion for several centuries and that they can be used (with appropriate source analysis) as a valuable source of precolonial history there. Similarly, among the Norse (Vikings), a literate people who maintained a strong oral tradition, the epics (histories) were kept by "singers" for whom the penalty of misremembering or altering a tale was death; with this strong incentive for accuracy, it appears that the Norse epics also were kept with great accuracy. The value of these epics as historical documents was demonstrated by their use in locating the archaeological remains of what is almost certainly Vinland, the famous Norse colony in North America.

Even in cases where an oral history has been distorted, elaborated, or exaggerated, it may be of use to the historian. In Hawaii, for example, accounts of native ruling dynasties are intertwined with mythology, and the rulers and gods merge. The myths, of course, are just as real and accurate as the history in the minds of the people who believe them, but to the historian, disentangling historically accurate and inaccurate information is a critical task. These accounts are the only ones available to the historian, and, despite the difficulty of separating accuracy from inaccuracy,

FIGURE 1.5 *Telling an Oral Account. In preliterate societies and sometimes in literate ones, accounts of the past have been preserved primarily in oral form. This has been true especially in Africa, where storytellers like the one shown in this photograph have preserved detailed accounts of events from centuries or even millennia earlier. Such accounts, of course, must be evaluated by source analysis (as must any source of information), but they constitute a valuable store of information about the past.* N. R. Farbman, *Life* Magazine, © 1947 Time Inc.

the careful analysis of these oral accounts has led to probable reconstructions of Hawaii's pre-European past.

Physical Remains

The final category of evidence that can be brought to bear on the study of the past consists of **physical remains**, material items left behind by past people and preserved. The study of physical remains is largely the province of specialists, though some types of physical evidence, such as architecture, can be studied without resorting to technical analysis. On the other hand, drawing conclusions about the trade networks of Iron Age Europeans, for example, requires identifying their artifacts and determining where they were manufactured, a process that demands special skills ranging from stylistic to chemical analysis. These special skills are part of the archaeologist's training, and most scholars in other fields must rely on their expertise for the interpretation of many archaeological remains. The accompanying box on bog people illustrates how archaeologists use their special skills to coax information out of physical remains.

Under the best of circumstances, the scholar studying the past will be able to use several of these types of information. Sometimes one type will be able to bridge gaps left by the others. Sometimes examination of a new class of information will lead to interpretations that conflict with traditional ones, leading to new insights or at least a critical reevaluation of traditional interpretations.

HISTORICAL FACT AND HISTORICAL INTERPRETATION

The preceding discussion of historical sources has referred to "facts" and "interpretations." Now we will explore the differences between them and discuss why both are critical to history.

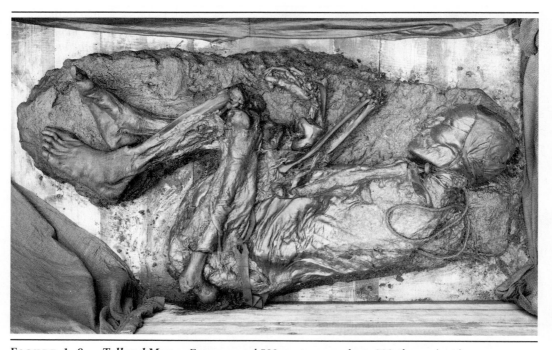

FIGURE 1.6   *Tolland Man.   From around 500 B.C. to around A.D. 800, the ancient inhabitants of Denmark periodically killed members of their society and placed their bodies in bogs, where the acidic water preserved them. This individual died about 2,000 years ago, having been stabbed, strangled, and beaten in the head. The exceptional preservation of the body permits us to know that the victim ate barley porridge for his last meal and had fingernails that were inconsistent with someone who did manual labor. This may have been a member of the elite sacrificed for religious reasons.*   National Museum, Copenhagen.

PATHS TO THE PAST

The Bog People

For centuries, Europeans have been cutting peat, a spongy mat of decayed plant fibers forming in bogs, and have used it for fuel. Occasionally, bog bodies have been found embedded in the peat. Remarkably preserved by the acidic bog water, these human bodies usually have intact skin, hair, organs, and clothing—materials that rarely are preserved in the archaeological record. These rare, archaeologically valuable bog bodies illustrate how archaeologists use physical remains to reconstruct the past.

Most bog bodies date to the Iron Age (about 1000 B.C.–A.D. 100), their age determined primarily through the use of radiocarbon dating, discussed in Chapter 2. In northern Europe, almost seven hundred bog bodies have been reported, although many were found before modern techniques of preservation or analysis were available, so the information about them is often scant. Much of the information that follows comes from the analysis of a recent find, the Lindow Man of England.

The mode of death of a bog person can be determined by searching for signs of disease or violence. The bog bodies are distinctive in the high degree of violence evident. Lindow Man is fairly typical, showing a chest wound (probably from a sword), a fractured skull, facial damage, and strangulation with a thong still around the neck. Other bog bodies also have slit throats. The number of violent acts committed against bog people has been called "murderous overkill," because any of the wounds would have been sufficient to cause death.

The bog people are anonymous, of course, but certain deductions can be made about them. Both men and women became bog people, and they were usually in their twenties or thirties at the times of their deaths. The bodies usually were naked or nearly so with no artifacts that could give an indication of a person's status in life. The fingernails, however, provide telltale clues. Modern laborers' fingernails have distinctive scratches and tiny splits in the ends; modern bank clerks, on the other hand, have smooth nails with few blemishes. Bog body fingernails have their closest parallels among bank clerks, suggesting that the bog people were individuals whose station placed them above the necessity of providing manual labor.

Of the bog bodies that have been fully analyzed, most seem to have died in the late spring. This is indicated by the species of pollen in the intestines. This pollen would have been in the air and consumed with food; its hard silica casings resisted digestion and remained intact in the body.

The last meal of the deceased also can be determined by analyzing remains in the intestine. In the case of Lindow Man, several types of grain were present. Electron spin resonance, a technique pioneered by physicists, revealed that the grains were heated to the temperature required for baking bread. Fragments of the grains indicate that part of the bread was burnt.

Taken together, these facts lead to an interpretation of what happened to these bog people. The number and nature of the violent acts committed against many of the bog people suggest that they were human sacrifices—ritually killed, then disposed of in the approved manner in a bog, perhaps in an attempt to ensure the springtime renewal. Those sacrificed were not commoners but rather members of the elite, perhaps nobility. Even the charring of the bread may be significant. During the Beltain festivals of seventeenth-century England, bread was distributed and the person who received a burnt piece by chance was referred to as being given to the gods as a sacrifice and was called "dead" during the rest of the ceremony. The Beltain festival probably was a bloodless carryover of an ancient Iron Age ritual that extended through much of northern Europe.

A **fact** is a description of an event or action that is generally agreed to be true on the basis of present evidence. It is a fact that Lincoln was shot while attending the theater; it is a fact that wheat and barley were the main foodstuffs in ancient Assyria.

Although facts are generally agreed upon, they can be reassessed with new information or ideas.

Domestic cotton, for example, once was believed to have originated in Africa and somehow to have arrived in South America several thousand years before Columbus. New information on the genetic structure of cotton, however, has revealed that there were independent domestications of wild cotton in Africa and South America. One fact has been discarded and replaced with a new one. Facts are our best approximations of truth, not truth itself, so it is understandable that the facts should change as our knowledge improves. It also is understandable that different scholars might have somewhat different conceptions of facts, depending on how they evaluate the sources.

At one time, many historians thought that history could and should concern itself only with facts. Leopold von Ranke[2] (1795–1886), a German historian, argued that historians should simply collect facts, which would speak for themselves. The history he argued for was straightforward and—though a little dry—unambiguous.

Unfortunately, von Ranke's approach suffered from a major flaw, one that has caused its rejection by modern scholars: The facts simply do not speak for themselves. In order for facts to take on any importance, someone must use them to create an **interpretation**, an inference that is consistent with the facts and extends knowledge beyond them by the use of logic, analogy, or some other method of reasoning. An interpretation provides some bit of understanding that otherwise would not have been possible, such as a cause, motivation, or consequence. A string of facts will lead to an interpretation only if the historian accumulating them states how they relate to one another and constructs an argument. Knowing all the facts leading to the beginning of World War I does not automatically provide any insight into why that war occurred; only by using those facts and general notions about how the world works (theory or philosophy) can the historian construct an interpretation of why the war began.

Distinguishing between a fact and an interpretation can be tricky, but the distinction is an important one. Facts are concerned primarily with actions and events, while interpretations are concerned primarily with causes, motives, and processes. It is a fact, for instance, that Abraham Lincoln was shot, but it is an interpretation that he was shot because John Wilkes Booth was a disgruntled Southern sympathizer, just as it is an interpretation that Lincoln's death made reconstruction in the South following the Civil War more harsh than it would have been otherwise. It is a fact that the government of ancient Egypt used military personnel to build the pyramids, but it is an interpretation to argue that the pyramids were a clever

[2] **von Ranke:** fahn RAHNG kuh

political stratagem to keep a huge standing army in readiness.

By their very nature, interpretations are more subject to differing opinions than are facts. Scholars may emphasize different facts or may approach their interpretation with divergent theoretical ideas about the world. Two scholars, for example, might accept the same facts regarding the Russian Revolution. The one who sees a nation as a set of factions competing with one another for power and resources will probably produce a very different interpretation from that of the scholar who sees a nation as a harmonious entity working for greater cooperation and unity. And, while new information sometimes can lay to rest all disagreements about the truth of a fact, differences of interpretation rarely, if ever, can be resolved so simply.

Interpretations are dependent on assumptions and rarely are subject to objective testing, but this statement should not be misconstrued to mean that all interpretations are created equal. Some interpretations are more likely than others to be correct because they accord better with the facts, they are more logically argued, or they are based on more reasonable assumptions. Bias, of course, can affect interpretation strongly.

Some of the most serious biases in historical reporting relate to race. Many European explorers of the sixteenth, seventeenth, and eighteenth centuries, for example, were committed to the notion that Europeans were superior to all other races; their accounts of other peoples were tainted accordingly. Many European explorers in Africa failed utterly to recognize the complexity of the governments that they encountered, largely because they were sure of the inherent "inferiority" of the Africans. These European accounts suffered from both inaccuracy and omissions, presumably because their writers expected nothing complex and simply never asked the appropriate questions. Chinese accounts of Southeast Asia and ancient Peruvian accounts of the peoples of the Amazonian jungles suffered from similar racial biases.

Gender is another area where serious biases have entered the documentary record. In most societies, men have been the primary leaders in politics, economics, religion, and scholarship. As a result, they have produced the vast majority of documents available to the historian, and these documents often suffer from gender bias. If women were believed (by men) to be delicate beings with no head for business, a male writer was likely to spend little effort describing women who headed businesses, because they would be considered merely aberrations from the norm. Similarly, arenas considered the province of women, particularly domestic life and household management, might be considered less interesting and therefore omitted from description. In some cases where women's lives were discussed by male writers, the resulting caricature speaks more to the writer's ignorance than to the actual state of affairs for women. As with racial bias, changing attitudes and recognition of the pervasiveness of such biases have made writers more aware of them in recent years, and at least some accounts show much less race and gender bias than in earlier times.

Recognizing the distinction between fact and interpretation is absolutely crucial to the successful study of history, and a large proportion of historical misinterpretation is the result of a confusion of the two. Facts are our best attempts to discover what really happened in the past; interpretations are the creations of scholars trying to understand the significance of the facts. Facts can be attacked only on the basis of whether or not they are true; because interpretations can never be proven or disproven, they can be criticized on the basis of whether they fit the facts and whether they follow in a reasonable manner from reasonable assumptions. Although facts are the building blocks of history, they are of limited value in themselves; they take on importance when they are used to support interpretations that provide insight into human activity in the past.

MODELS OF THE PAST

This text uses models to discuss empires, feudalism, and various other recurrent phenomena in history. A **model** is simply a picture of how or why a general process works. As with any picture, its creator decides which elements are important and how they fit together. So that the picture will be simple enough to be comprehended easily, minor elements may be omitted. The result draws our eye to relationships that are central and critical, stripping away details that camouflage what the

model-builder sees as the general pattern. Some models focus on how a process operates, and these are known as **descriptive models**; others focus on the motivations or underlying causes, and these are known as **explanatory models**. Both can be valuable in studying the past.

For example, we might construct a simple model to help us understand how recycling glass containers operates (Fig. 1.7). In our simple model, the collection of waste glass leads to recycling, which in turn leads to lowered cost of bottles and savings to consumers. Simultaneously, the collection of waste glass means that there is less litter on roadsides, and the costs of roadside trash collection are lowered. This simple version explains some of the benefits of glass recycling in general, but it certainly does not describe every case perfectly. In some communities, for example, roadside trash collection is carried out by volunteers, so there would be no appreciable savings; also, some container manufacturers might not pass the savings along to consumers. Still, the general pattern of the model can be expected to apply to most

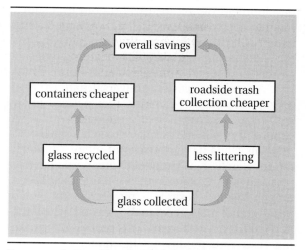

FIGURE 1.7 *Simple Model of Glass Recycling. A model is an ideal picture of a process, providing a way to conceptualize it, stripping away detail and reducing the process to simple relationships. This model of glass recycling shows how one action can be expected to lead to another, with causation indicated by arrows. However, not all the glass that is collected makes it to recycling, and a glass manufacturer may choose to increase profits rather than pass savings along to consumers. Recognizing such points where a model fails can help revise it.*

cases, and exceptions can be used to refine the model further.

The model can be extended at will. For example, you might be interested in who receives the financial benefit of selling glass to recyclers. It may be that more well-to-do people tend to discard glass with trash, while poorer people might collect the glass and sell it. As with any good model, this leads you to consider new angles to the phenomenon under study.

It is easy to see why models are so useful in examining processes that have occurred repeatedly in history. Each process has its own unique history—the people, places, and events that are the cast, stage, and play in the real-life drama; underlying these unique and fascinating specifics, however, lies a set of basic relationships. A model is an attempt to recognize those basic relationships and draw attention to them.

One important value of models is their ability to suggest general patterns that characterize a process wherever it occurs. Is there a single path to the development of empires? Are certain factors always necessary to their development? Some scholars believe that the same process (such as the development of empires) will unfold in a similar manner every time it occurs and that good scholarship will reveal these common patterns of history. Others are more skeptical, believing that each case is so distinctive that generalization is pointless. A model suggests a universal pattern, challenging scholars to examine that pattern in the light of specific cases. That examination may lend support to the model or may prove it wrong.

This leads us to the second major value of a model. Rarely does a model fit any particular case perfectly and explain it fully. A model inspired by French cases, for example, may be incomplete or narrow and may need to be revised when it is applied to Nigerian cases. This process of examining cases and modifying the model in response often produces a refined, improved picture of the process under study.

Models are common in social science, and you will see several discussed in this text. Whenever you examine a model, remember what it is. It is a proposal to be tested, an idea to stimulate your thinking, a deliberate oversimplification to aid in understanding. It is a form of interpretation, not fact. It is not crystallized truth, and it always must be subservient to facts.

TIME AND PERIODS OF HISTORY

All societies have recognized the passage of time. Some have focused on the periodic repetition of nature, as when day and night alternate or the seasons pass through their annual progression. Those societies have conceived of **cyclical time**, where a sequence of stages is seen as repeating forever. Other societies have focused on the sequence of days, one following another throughout time in a long line. Those societies have conceived of **linear time**, where time passes inexorably forward with no repetition or cycles. Most societies have recognized both concepts of time, sometimes focusing on one or the other for different purposes. Western society, for example, uses linear time concepts in its use of numbered years; it also uses cyclical concepts in the repetition of months and days or seasons within a year.

Calendars

Linear time requires some means of keeping track of time. Sometimes this has been accomplished by simply counting years in a ruler's reign ("in the fifteenth year of the reign of Tiberius Caesar"), but more often people have constructed a system of dates and years that form a **calendar system**. A calendar can be very simple or very complex, but it has to reconcile itself with the facts of astronomy. The earth takes slightly more than 365 days to revolve around the sun, and every calendar has to have years that approximate that figure, if a date is to continue to occur in the expected season over a long period of time. The exact length of the solar year is important, and, if we reckoned each year to be finished when exactly 365 days had elapsed, the Fourth of July would occur in the middle of winter after only about 700 years!

Most calendars use the same approach to this problem: They add one or more extra days to the year at regular intervals to compensate for the fractional day by which the solar year exceeds the approximation of 365 days. In the Western calendars and in English, the year with the extra day is called "leap year" and it occurs every four years, with very few exceptions.

From the historian's point of view, the major problem with calendars is that different societies

FIGURE 1.8 *Aztec Calendar Stone. Though not really a calendar in the modern sense, this artifact depicts the units that the Aztecs of Mexico used to keep track of time. The inner rings show the four previous cycles of the creation and destruction of the universe, as recorded in Aztec mythology. The next ring has twenty divisions, which could represent the twenty days of the Aztec month; since the Aztecs used base-twenty arithmetic, it probably had other symbolism as well. The calendar stone is made of volcanic rock and measures nearly fourteen feet across, weighing over twenty tons.* National Anthropological Museum, Mexico City. Paolo Koch/Rapho/Photo Researchers, Inc.

have used different ones. At least forty different historical calendars were adopted by civilizations around the world, and several calendars are still in use in the twentieth century. (Many of these contemporary calendars are used primarily for reckoning of religious rituals, as with the Hebrew and Chinese calendars. Others, such as the Islamic calendar, are used for everyday, secular timekeeping in several countries.) Local documents, of course, record events with the local calendar, and historians have to be careful to translate a date faithfully in order to see when an event fits into the broader world. An event might occur, for example, on 1 Hamal 1255 of the Borji calendar of Iran; that date might have to be translated into March 21, 1876 (Gregorian calendar, in use in most European countries), 25 Safar 1293 (Islamic calendar, in use throughout most of Southwest Asia), and March 8, 1876 (Julian calendar, in use in Russia), in order to place this event into the context of events in other countries. Most historians use the Gregorian calendar and convert dates to this standard.

Even in Europe, however, the use of a common calendar came late. The older Julian calendar had no leap years, and it was gradually supplanted by the more accurate Gregorian calendar, which incorporated leap years. Some places (such as Hungary, parts of Italy, and parts of Germany) adopted the more accurate Gregorian calendar in the sixteenth century, but others (including Russia, Lithuania, and parts of Greece) continued using the Julian calendar until the early years of the twentieth century. Different dates of adopting the Gregorian calendar led to confusing situations where adjacent cities might have dates that differed by up to two weeks. For example, the same instant of time was designated January 12, 1640 (London, England); January 4, 1640 (Dublin, Ireland); January 10, 1640 (Pisa, Italy); and November 28, 1639 (Moscow, Russia). Often, when a country decided to convert to the new system, it would adopt the date current in a neighboring country, sometimes necessitating that certain dates be skipped. For example, February 22, 1700, never existed in Norway, since this was in a skipped period.

Further complicating matters was the reckoning of the beginning of a new year. Traditionally,

England and its colonies considered the new year to begin on March 1, but in the eighteenth century, this was changed to the current January 1. George Washington, for example, was born on February 22, 1731; only in later years have we recalculated his birthdate by considering January 1 as the first of the year, moving his birthdate to 1732.

In the Western tradition, years are numbered. The starting point for this numbering is an approximation of the birth of Christ (Jesus of Nazareth), although the approximation probably is a couple of years off. All dates after that landmark are given in years since the birth of Jesus and are preceded by the letters "A.D." (*anno Domini*, Latin for "in the year of the Lord"). Some scholars prefer to distance themselves from the Christian implications of using "A.D.," and they use the letters "C.E." (common era) for the same meaning. Dates before the birth of Jesus are given in years before that event, as a number followed by "B.C." (before Christ); those who use "C.E." also will use "B.C.E." (before the common era) in place of "B.C." Finally, for convenience, dates with no letters following them are A.D./C.E. dates. So, A.D. 1371 is the same as 1371 C.E. or simply 1371; 551 B.C. is the same as 551 B.C.E. To simplify keeping chronological track, all dates in this textbook use the B.C./A.D. system.

Periodization

Historians and other scholars of the past typically use periods as basic units of analysis, so a few words about them are in order. A **period** is a span of time that scholars have defined for convenience. Ideally, conditions, events, and lifeways remained more or less similar during a period and were distinctive from preceding and succeeding periods. In reality, of course, the world has always been in a constant state of change, and no period has the kind of stability that such a description suggests. Nonetheless, a period sometimes is defined by momentous events that marked its beginning and end. The Cold War era, for example, may be defined as the period between the end of World War II (1945) and the collapse of the Soviet Empire (1989–1991). The period is marked by the political-military ascendancy of the Soviet Union and the United States as antagonistic superpowers, the absence of direct armed conflict between them, and the lack of a powerful common enemy.

Not all periods, however, are so easily defined. The European Renaissance, for example, has been defined by some scholars as the period after the Middle Ages when the arts and philosophy reoriented and great artists and thinkers developed.

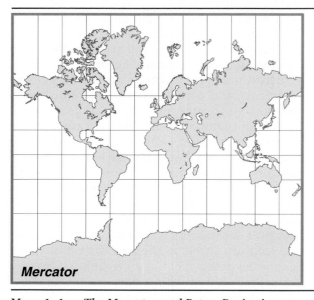

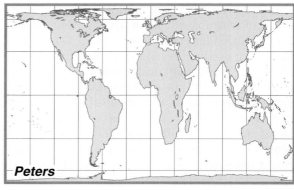

MAP 1.1 *The Mercator and Peters Projections Compared.* *Translating the spherical earth into a two-dimensional map requires distorting the size, shape, or relative positions of land masses. The Mercator projection (left) retains the relative shapes and positions of land masses accurately but makes lands nearer the poles* *appear larger than they really are; Greenland is far smaller than Africa, though they are depicted as about the same size on this projection. The Peters projection (right) accurately indicates the sizes of land masses, but it distorts their shapes.*

UNDER THE LENS

Maps and Map Projections

Just as we use calendars to keep track of time, we use maps to keep track of space. Essentially, a map is a picture of a piece of the world, presented more or less as it would be seen from the air. Although most people think of maps as unambiguous reflections of objective reality, a single place can be rendered very dissimilarly on different maps.

The first cartographic variable arises because the earth is round and a map is flat. Consequently, it is impossible to produce a map that does not incorporate some distortion in terms of shape, size, or relative placement of landforms. The mapmaker needs to select a **projection**, a systematic mathematical formula that provides rules for drawing the two-dimensional map from three-dimensional data. When a map of a very small area, like a town or city, is drawn, what projection is chosen matters little, because all will produce very similar maps. When a larger area is mapped, though, the inherent features of each projection begin to emerge and can affect the reader's overall impression tremendously.

The Mercator projection, for example, was devised in the sixteenth century for navigation. Consequently, it retains directions accurately, so that a straight line on a map in the Mercator projection can be followed by plotting a straight course in the real world. Unfortunately, retaining accurate directions means distorting size and shape of land masses, and Mercator maps make areas near the poles seem unrealistically large. The Peters projection, used for the world maps in this book, solves the problem of relative size, but it distorts the shape and relative position of land masses and would be difficult to navigate by.

Cartographers have to make a series of other choices about the maps they make. What should be included or excluded? What should be emphasized or downplayed? What should appear in the center of the map? All of these choices translate into impressions on the users of the map, and cartographers can manipulate those impressions. Consider, for example, the Mercator map of the world so frequently used. The projection makes northern continents inordinately large; western Europe usually is at the center of the map; and typically several European countries are labeled, whereas no African countries are. The impression the map conveys—intended or not—is that Europe is a huge continent, geographically central to the world, and filled with important places. Africa, in contrast, appears inordinately small, peripheral, and empty. The choices made by the mapmaker have created an image that the map user may uncritically accept.

Understandably, there is little agreement on what dates should be associated with this vague definition. Many scholars argue that the European Renaissance began around 1400 and ended around 1600, but others would expand those dates, compress them, slide them forward in time, or slide them back. Some of the disagreement revolves around the part of Europe that a scholar is most interested in or familiar with, because events took place at different dates in different countries. Part of the disagreement also develops from the vagueness of the definition. After all, who decides who was "great"?

Other periods, especially earlier ones, cause even greater disagreement. The European Iron Age, for example, is defined as beginning with the development of iron technology and often is associated with increased militarism and the development of militaristic local governments ruled by chieftains. The Iron Age is usually thought to have ended with the spread of larger-scale government, often coming from major states, such as Rome. The dates for the Iron Age in Europe usually are considered to be around 1000 B.C. to A.D. 100, but some scholars, arguing largely on the basis of Scandinavian societies, readily extend the ending date to A.D. 1000.

The underlying reason there is so much dispute about the delineation of periods is that they are analytical tools subject to the same disagreements as other interpretations. Just as scholars can disagree over the causes of the American Revolution, they can disagree over the dates for the European Renaissance. One scholar may focus more on

FIGURE 1.9 *Old Sarum from the Air. This hill rises from the Salisbury Plain of southern England, but it is not exactly a natural landform. Rather, it has been modified and enlarged by human activity to produce an easily defended site for a settlement. Old Sarum was built during Britain's Iron Age, around 500 B.C. Chronological periods like the "Iron Age" must be referred to with caution, as the same term can apply to considerably different spans of time in various parts of the world.* University of Cambridge Collection of Air Photographs/Richard Muir.

literature than on painting, another more on sculpture than on philosophy; and all may dispute which artists they believe were "great." Such disagreement may cause only minor problems within the discipline, because scholars are aware of the differing interpretations and expect some variations in the dates assigned periods by various interpretations, but it can be a source of great confusion for beginning students.

Although periods serve a valuable purpose in organizing history, they should not be thought of as "real" in the usual sense; they are creations of scholars, not natural divisions of time. Periods can even obscure essential continuities. No one ever went to bed in the Bronze Age and woke up the next morning in the Iron Age. Rarely is there an event so earthshaking that it virtually transforms life overnight, and one should expect great similarities between the beginning of one period and the end of the preceding one.

A final point about historical periods is that they cannot always be extended to places other than where they were originally defined. The Iron Age, for example, was originally defined in Europe, then applied successively to Southwest Asia, Egypt, India, sub-Saharan Africa, and East Asia. As the definition was applied farther and farther afield, it became less and less appropriate. The dates associated with the Iron Age in much of sub-Saharan Africa, for instance, are about A.D. 500 to 1750, nearly two millennia later than in Southwest Asia; in addition, the militarism that was a hallmark of the Iron Age in Europe and Southwest Asia (and to a lesser extent in India) was virtually absent in the Iron Age of Africa. As the "Iron Age" has been extended around much of Europe, Asia, and Africa, the concept has lost much of its utility. Similar criticisms can be made of other extensions of periods, such as the medieval periods in China, Korea, and Japan.

THE GLOBAL PAST AND RELATIVISM

The title of this text, *The Global Past*, indicates its emphasis on a planet-wide approach. Rather than restrict its focus to one or two continents—typically Europe and North America—this text treats peoples and countries from all over the world. Literally, it spans the human past from its beginning to today and on all the inhabited continents, as well as many islands.

Of course, selections have had to be made. Some areas have been omitted and others have received less attention than they warrant, but these compromises were necessary in the interests of keeping the text to a manageable size. The basic outline of the history of all major regions has been maintained, along with more in-depth treatments of places and issues that have had major impacts on the shape of the modern world.

This approach highlights comparisons between different places and times. In some cases, the text will point these out, but the student also

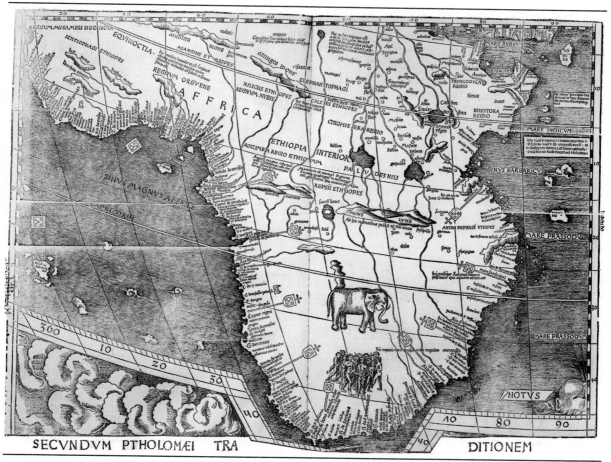

FIGURE 1.10 *Medieval European Map of Ethiopia. This map probably was drafted by John Ruysch in 1508, and it appeared in a republished edition of Ptolemy's* Geography. *The map depicts some recognizable features of northeastern Africa, but it incorporates errors and obsolete conventions that make it difficult for modern readers to use. Labels are in Latin and describe some fanciful places, such as "Troglodica regio" ("Region of cave-dwellers"). "Notus," or North, is in the lower right corner, not at the top as it would be on a modern map. Despite such difficulties and imaginative errors, maps like this one provide valuable information for scholars studying the past.* Waldburg-Wolfegg Princely Collection.

should be alert to thinking in these terms. Such comparisons are especially important in recognizing patterns of similar responses to similar conditions. Revolutions, resource shortages, incursions of aggressive neighbors, the spread of religious ideologies—all these classes of events and processes have common threads that unite them, and their analysis is one of the great opportunities of historical study.

But there also is a special responsibility that this approach demands. Human beings are particularly adept at **ethnocentrism**, the attitude that one's own ideas, values, culture, and cherished behavior patterns are socially, morally, or religiously correct and that all others are inferior. When learning about other people, ethnocentric attitudes can get in the way, leading to the condemnation of anything different or foreign. The whole point of studying a broad range of societies and countries is to learn from their diversity, to be able to see things a bit more through foreign eyes. Rejecting alien viewpoints out of hand defeats this purpose. **Cultural relativism**, the suspension of value judgments about other peoples and their ways, is important to the study of the past; it also is important to successful living in the modern, multicultural world. Certainly it is understandable to be shocked by genocide or social repression and to condemn it; but cultural relativism asks that we examine and understand the situation *before* we form our opinions. Cultural relativism does not require embracing the beliefs or value systems of foreigners or giving up one's own values. Rather, cultural relativism is the granting of respect to a society, people, or country, trying to see their world and behavior in their own terms, rather than simply rejecting all viewpoints but one's own. It is essential to the thoughtful consideration of the global past.

SUMMARY

1. Studying the past allows us to seek patterns of solutions to problems that may be parallel to modern problems, to learn the background of current world controversies, to recognize fictitious history tailored to support political policy, and to understand the diversity of the human condition.

2. Many disciplines study the past, particularly history (primarily concerned with documents), archaeology (primarily concerned with physical remains), and geography (primarily concerned with use of the land and spatial patterning). All provide valuable insights and should be used together to build a fuller understanding of the past.

3. Documents are subject to distortion and bias and must be evaluated before being accepted. Physical remains rarely give information on particular individuals yet frequently provide information on the everyday life of common people. Taken together, documents and physical remains form a stronger knowledge base than either alone.

4. Historical facts are generally accepted descriptions of what occurred in the past. Interpretations are arguments regarding the causes of, interrelationships among, or significance of several of those facts. Facts alone are of limited value to the study of history, because they say little about causes, motivations, or consequences; interpretations are valuable because they analyze that activity, but the same facts are subject to different interpretations.

5. A model is a simplified picture of a phenomenon or process that aids in understanding how or why it occurred. Models should be viewed as interpretations, not facts. Real cases that deviate from the model can point out its shortcomings, helping to refine it.

6. Calendars provide societies with a means of recording linear time. Although different calendars follow very different rules, a date in any one can be converted to a date in any other calendar. For convenience, historians divide the past into periods during which certain factors remain more or less consistent.

7. Cultural relativism is the notion that we should suspend our personal and moral judgments while trying to understand other peoples and their ideas.

SUGGESTED READINGS

Aveni, Anthony F. *Empires of Time: Calendars, Clocks, and Cultures.* New York: Basic Books, 1989. A detailed discussion of the variety of calendric and other time-keeping systems throughout history.

Brothwell, Don. *The Bog Man and the Archaeology of People.* London: British Museum of Natural History, 1986. An excellent, readable, and well-illustrated account of the analysis of Lindow Man and other bog bodies.

Rendell, Kenneth W. *Forging History: The Detection of Fake Letters and Documents.* Norman: University of Oklahoma Press, 1994. An entertaining and illuminating discussion of the methods used to detect fake documents.

Renfrew, Colin, and Paul Bahn. *Archaeology: Theories, Methods, and Practice.* London: Thames and Hudson, 1991. An excellent introduction to archaeological methods.

Shafer, Robert Jones, ed. *A Guide to Historical Method.* Third edition. Homewood, Ill.: Dorsey Press, 1980. A standard work on historiography (the methods of history).

Vansina, Jan. *Oral Tradition as History.* Madison: University of Wisconsin Press, 1985. A classic treatment of oral accounts; insightful, though not easy reading.

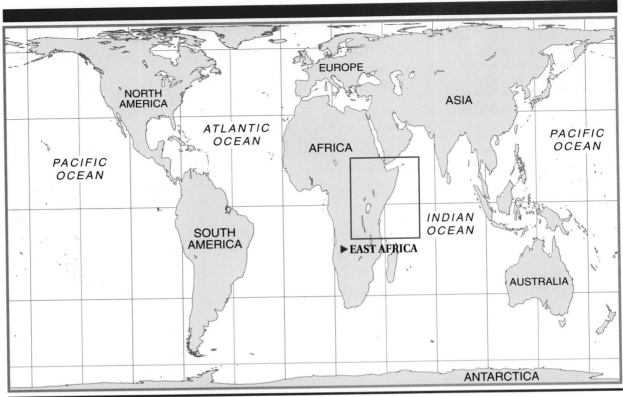

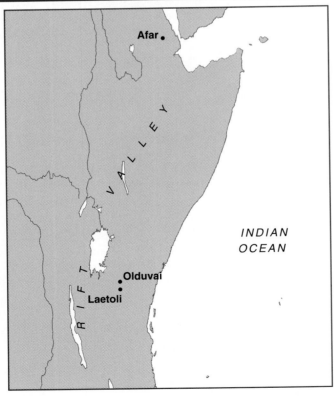

▶ **EAST AFRICA**

Beginnings
around 4,500,000–around 100,000 B.C.

On a hot summer day, Mary Leakey and other members of her archaeological expedition to the Laetoli[1] Beds of eastern Africa discovered footprints left by human ancestors who had died 3.5 million years before. A slight rain following a volcanic eruption had left damp ash that was the perfect medium for preserving tracks, and three of our forebears had trudged across the moist soil, one stepping in the prints of another and the third a bit off to the side. This is by no means the only evidence of these ancient ancestors, but it is perhaps the most dramatic.

As ancient as the Laetoli tracks are, they are comparatively recent in terms of the universe. Most astronomers place the beginning of the universe some 20 billion years ago. Geologists studying the earth date its beginning at 4.5 billion years ago, and paleontologists studying fossils conclude that life on earth began more than 3 billion years ago. Placed in this cosmic perspective, the human species is a newcomer to the scene, and the scant few thousand years of conventional history are merely a moment.

This chapter will trace the long journey from the earliest known human ancestors to today's human beings, focusing on the characteristics that make us distinctly human. It will also discuss the philosophical and technological developments that make it possible for scientists to investigate human evolution.

[1] **Laetoli:** ly eh TOH lee

FIGURE 2.1 *The Laetoli Footprints. Nearly 4 million years ago, a volcano in present-day Tanzania spewed out tons of dusty volcanic ash; within a few days, it rained slightly, turning the ash into a fine mud. Then, dozens of creatures—including three* Australopithecus afarensis—*wandered across this ash field, leaving tracks that subsequently were buried and protected by another layer of ash. These tracks are some of the earliest evidence of possible human ancestors.* John Reader/Photo Researchers, Inc.

THE SCIENTIFIC QUEST TO UNDERSTAND HUMAN ANCESTRY

Pondering human origins certainly is nothing new. People have been fascinated by the mystery of their own beginnings, and have created stories to explain them, probably for as long as they have had brains competent for the task. These stories became enshrined as myths, and every known religion and culture has at least one creation myth.

The scientific study of human ancestry began in Europe, where the Judeo-Christian tradition was dominant, so Judeo-Christian creation mythology, as recorded in the Book of Genesis in the Bible, was the starting place for scientific studies of human development. According to a myth recorded in Genesis, the earth and everything on it (including the first people, Adam and Eve) were created by God over the course of seven days. The Genesis myth certainly is explicit that human beings were created from clay, not modified from some other sort of organism, and it is explicit that only a week was required for the entire creation. Further, Archbishop James Ussher (1581–1656), a biblical scholar studying the chronology of the Bible, reasoned that creation took place in 4004 B.C. Though we now recognize this date to be in the very recent past, it was accepted as very ancient and therefore reasonable for the beginning of the universe by most Western scholars following its publication in 1654. Because Judeo-Christian myth was believed to be literally true by many European scholars, it seemed only sensible to use it as the basis for any scientific study.

The Great Shift in Worldview

Beginning in the eighteenth century, a succession of scientists began questioning the historical and scientific accuracy of the biblical creation myth. Geologists like James Hutton (1726–1797) and Charles Lyell (1797–1875) made convincing arguments that the earth was much older than Ussher's claim. Building on their conception of a long chronology, Charles Darwin (1809–1882) published *On the Origin of Species* in 1859. The central theme of this work is **biological evolution**, the concept that one species of plant or animal can (and did) change into another over long periods of time. Darwin argued that the great diversity of modern life all derived from a single, primitive, early species and that human beings evolved from ape-like ancestors.

Darwin's theory of evolution was grounded in the concept of **survival of the fittest**, the idea that individuals with traits that aid in their survival will live long enough to pass those traits on to their offspring. In contrast, individuals with maladaptive traits will be weeded out, because those traits will lead to their deaths before they have the opportunity to pass the traits on to offspring. In this man-

IN THEIR OWN WORDS

The Iroquois Creation Myth

Creation myths around the world often follow a common pattern: A god sees a void in the world and fills it with land, water, important plants and animals, and people, often creating them from some common material, such as dust or clay. Usually the mythically created world is familiar, with modern plants, animals, and cultural practices. One version of the creation myth of the Iroquois[a] Indians of northeastern North America has been perpetuated for centuries as an oral account. The version presented here was recorded by one of this book's authors in 1976 at the Tyendinaga[b] Reserve in eastern Canada.

> The world sprang up miraculously to form a place for the Great Spirit to live. The Great Spirit had to have existed before this time, but we have no knowledge of this earlier period. In order to populate the world, the Great Spirit created the diversity of plants and animals with which the Iroquois later would become familiar, as well as the hills and rivers that filled their lands.

[a] **Iroquois:** EE roh kwah
[b] **Tyendinaga:** ty ehn dihn AY guh

On one side of the world, the side where the Iroquois eventually would live, was a lake, beside which lived a woman and her daughter. They may have been truly people or spirits, but it is clear that they lived before the Iroquois of today. The mother instructed her daughter never to bathe in the lake, but she did so on one occasion and became pregnant with twins. The twins competed with one another to be born first, since that ensured greater spiritual power. While one twin [later called "the Good Twin"] outmaneuvered the other and was in position to be born first, the other [later called "the Evil Twin"] forced his birth through the mother's arm pit, killing her but succeeding in being born at the same time as his brother. The Good Twin created good things for the use of the Iroquois, such as corn, deer, and water; the Evil Twin created demons, snakes, and droughts to harass the Iroquois.

Creation myths such as this one provide a society with an explanation of how things began, as well as a place in a divine plan. As such, they promote cultural unity.

---

ner, nature rewards individuals lucky enough to have adaptive traits, whereas it penalizes all others with reduced likelihood of survival. Although Darwin never knew the exact mechanism through which traits were inherited, we now realize that genes, which are passed from parents to offspring during reproduction, carry the information that leads to the development of biologically inherited traits.

In the years following Darwin, science was won over to his theory of evolution and the idea of survival of the fittest. By 1900, virtually all scientists agreed that all modern forms of life came about gradually as ancient species evolved through intermediate species on the way to their modern forms. Human beings were seen as simply animals, though very special ones, shaped by natural forces over a very long time.

The story of Darwin's ideas is a complex one, and this is not the place for its detailed consideration. Here, the important point is that the middle part of the nineteenth century saw a major shift in the way in which most educated people viewed human origins. For a century or two prior to the work of Darwin and his colleagues, most Western scholars accepted some version of the Genesis story. This acceptance was an article of faith, based on a literal interpretation of the Bible. After Darwin, human origins were viewed as a scientific question, subject to reasoned debate and revision in light of new evidence or interpretations; the Bible was no longer considered the final authority on this question. This was a major shift in worldview that signaled a great change in Western society and opened up the scientific search for human ancestors.

The Search for Human Ancestors

Hutton, Lyell, and Darwin opened the door for scientists looking for tangible remains of the prehuman species that Darwin had predicted. A few fossils of premodern, humanlike creatures had been found in Europe prior to the publication of Darwin's theory, most notably the Gibraltar skull found in 1848 and the original Neanderthal skull found in Germany in 1856. These finds originally had been dismissed as pathologically deformed—but fully modern—bones; after Darwin, scholars began considering the possibility that they represented ancient human ancestors. The term **"missing link,"** referring to a human-ape that could bridge the gap between modern human beings and our proposed apelike ancestors, first appeared in the popular literature in 1879; its commonness after that date is an indicator of the public interest in the search.

The remains found, however, were unsatisfying as missing links, because they were decidedly more humanlike than apelike. (This is not surprising, as they were forms now recognized as quite recent.) A series of remains from Java found in 1891 by Eugène Dubois now are recognized as early, but criticisms kept these finds controversial until the 1930s. Before that time, two competing sets of finds promised to provide the long-sought missing link.

The first set of finds came from England, an unlikely spot for the evolution of a species whose nearest nonhuman relatives were from Africa. (In fact, Darwin had targeted Africa as the likely cradle of human evolution for just this reason.) In 1911, a clerk and amateur paleontologist named Charles Dawson brought into the British Museum of Natural History some fossils he reported finding in a gravel pit near the small town of Piltdown. They were oddly intermediate between human being and ape, and they were heralded immediately by the press and many scholars as the missing link. The Piltdown remains, however, were a false lead, the result of a clever hoax that would not be exposed unequivocally as fraudulent until 1954.

In 1924, a second set of remains was found in South Africa by Raymond Dart, a biologist. These remains proved to be among the earliest of our prehuman relatives to be found for the next half century. Dart named the creature, discussed later in this chapter, *Australopithecus*.[2] Although few people today believe Dart's creature to be a direct ancestor of modern human beings, it clearly is a close relative, and Dart's discovery—once the false lead of Piltdown was disposed of—led the search for human ancestors into sub-Saharan Africa, where it remains today.

Many modern researchers, including such well-known figures as L. S. B. Leakey, Mary Leakey, Donald Johanson, Glynn Isaac, and others, have devoted their professional lives to trying to unravel the tangles of the human evolutionary story. Although the tale is far from complete and many details are still in question, their efforts have pro-

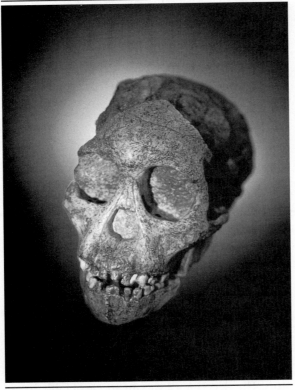

FIGURE 2.2   *The Taung Skull. Found in South Africa in 1924, this fossil turned scientists' eyes to Africa for possible human ancestors. The skull came from an* Australopithecus africanus *individual who died before reaching six years of age; babies and young children of all nonhuman primates resemble human beings more than older nonhuman primates do. Consequently, the Taung child skull misled scientists into expecting* Australopithecus *to be more humanlike than subsequent adult fossils indicated.*   John Reader/Photo Researchers, Inc.

[2] **Australopithecus:** ah strahl oh PIHTH eh kuhs

PATHS TO THE PAST

Dating Our Fossil Ancestors

Many of the dates assigned to fossils of our prehuman ancestors are very early and would have staggered Archbishop Ussher, or even Lyell. There are dozens of means of calculating these dates, but four methods are most widely used.

The simplest method of dating a fossil is to date the deposit in which it is found by **faunal succession**. As evolution progresses, different species in a line develop, become common, then die off. If the dates for the different species are well known—as they are, for instance, with wild pigs and antelopes—then a deposit can be dated on the basis of these species. The date of the deposit is the date of the fossils within it.

Another common method of dating is **potassium-argon dating**. A radioactive form of potassium, present naturally in volcanic rocks, produces the gas argon at a regular and known rate. The clock begins when a rock or volcanic ash is formed, and it is a simple matter to measure the argon and calculate the material's age. Potassium-argon dating of the volcanic ash layer in which the Laetoli footprints appeared, as well as dating of layers immediately over and under it, provided the date for the prints.

Radiocarbon dating works in a similar way, although its use is restricted to materials that were once alive, and its clock begins with the death of the organism. Although radiocarbon dating is extremely valuable for dating recent archaeological deposits, it is unreliable earlier than 70,000 years ago and is not useful for dating early prehuman fossils.

Finally, **paleomagnetic dating** sometimes is useful for dating fossils. The earth's magnetic north pole is slowly but constantly migrating, producing changing magnetic fields over the earth. Because magnetic fields are preserved in either burnt clay (as with a cooking fire) or natural clay deposits (as with a dried-out mud puddle or lake), these deposits can be dated by reading their preserved magnetic fields and comparing them with known magnetic fields at different dates.

All of these techniques, with the possible exception of radiocarbon dating, focus on dating the deposit in which the fossil is found, not the fossil itself. Often the fossil itself cannot be dated by any known technique, but fortunately dating its surroundings does the job equally well. None of these techniques is perfect, but their results usually are within 5 percent of being correct.

---

duced a general picture that probably will survive the challenges of future research and discoveries. Many of their conclusions have been made possible by the battery of scientific tools and techniques developed in the past decades, and these will support their ongoing efforts to learn more about our ancient relatives.

THE PATTERN OF HUMAN EVOLUTION

Human beings are members of the **primates**, the order of animals that also includes apes (such as gorillas, chimpanzees, and orangutans) and monkeys. The earliest primates occur in the fossil record around 70 million years ago, just before the extinction of the dinosaurs, and were small, rodentlike creatures. It was not until about 25 million years ago that monkeylike primates appeared, and primates resembling apes appeared only around 18 million years ago. These creatures are of great interest to anthropologists, but our concern here is primarily with the forms that were ancestral, or at least closely related, to human beings.

Early Ancestors and a Tentative Family Tree

The study of human evolution requires that we use a few specialized terms. A **hominid** is any member of the family that includes human beings. The technical definition of hominids focuses on anatomy, particularly dental anatomy, but it is suf-

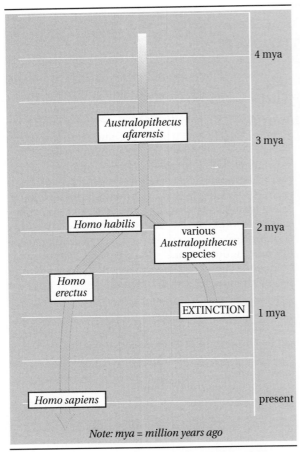

FIGURE 2.3 *A Reconstruction of Hominid Evolution. From a single ancestral line, hominids branched into two lines. The various species of* Australopithecus *grew more robust and adapted to eating inefficient high-fiber foods like leaves, eventually becoming extinct. The species of* Homo, *in contrast, used their intelligence to take advantage of a wide range of circumstances.*

ficient here simply to note that all hominids share some anatomical similarities and are related to one another. Hominids are divided into two major groups, *Australopithecus* and *Homo*. Each of these groups is a **genus**, a category of moderately closely related species. Modern human beings are members of the genus *Homo—Homo sapiens*,[3] to be precise. *Australopithecus* means "southern ape-man" and is the genus of the earliest known human predecessors.

Prior to about 5 million years ago, we have few fossil remains of hominids. It is conjectured that

[3] **Homo sapiens:** HOH moh SAY pee ehns

hominids developed around 15 million years ago, but preservation conditions for their fossils in the intervening 10 million years apparently were poor. Some anthropologists believe that during this period our ancestors were living and dying in forests, where acid soils rapidly decayed their bones. After 5 million B.C., the early hominid remains come from dry savannas, where bone preservation was better.

Figure 2.3 shows the relationships among hominids according to the most current reconstruction. Solid lines indicate an evolutionary line of descent, and blocked lines indicate extinctions. The evidence underlying this chart consists of several hundred fossils, most of them well or fairly well dated. Although there is disagreement among anthropologists about details of this family tree, the general picture has remained little changed for the past twenty years.

As the chart shows, there are two lines of hominids, sharing a common ancestor in *Australopithecus afarensis*. Just before 2 million years ago, the *Homo* line split off from the rest of the hominids and went on to become us; the *Australopithecus* line went on to produce several forms, all of which became extinct. Although there are occasional sensationalist reports that Bigfoot, a presumably mythical beast of northwestern North America, is a belated *Australopithecus*, there is no evidence that any of that line survived beyond 1 million years ago.

Lucy and the First Family

As the first clearly human ancestor, *Australopithecus afarensis* deserves special discussion. Fortunately, it is rather well known, thanks to a remarkable series of discoveries in Ethiopia by Donald Johanson in the mid-1970s. Johanson found and studied first a single well-preserved skeleton (nicknamed "Lucy"), then a group of well-preserved skeletons (nicknamed "The First Family"). These skeletons probably came from individuals who were killed and buried rapidly, perhaps by a mudslide, about 3.5 million years ago, preserving their skeletons.

The degree of completeness of the skeletons permits us to deduce a great deal about Lucy and her contemporaries. They were short, probably about four and a half feet tall, with bodies quite similar to our own. They walked upright with a nearly modern gait, not at all like modern apes.

FIGURE 2.4 *Lucy's Portrait. Lucy—Australo-pithecus afarensis—was a short creature with a body similar to ours and a more rugged, more forward-projecting face. We can reconstruct the contours of her face quite accurately from fossil bones, but the details of skin and hair cannot be inferred from fossils. It is proba-ble, however, that she had dark skin and more body hair than modern human beings.* Illustration by John Richards.
© by Weldon Owen Pty Ltd./Bra Bocker AB. Reproduced by permission of HarperCollins Publishers, Inc.

Their hands were very similar to our hands, with a thumb that could produce both delicate and pow-erful grips, though not exactly with the precision of modern human beings. Because only bones were found, no one knows about the skin color or hairi-ness of Lucy, but it is logical to assume that she was dark-skinned (because such coloring would have provided protection from ultraviolet poisoning in the sunny tropics) and may have had more hair than modern human beings (because that is the general pattern in primates).

Although the body of Lucy was more or less a scaled-down version of modern people, the head was quite different. The brain was much smaller, even when the body size is taken into account. The face also was very different, with a projecting mouth, a very flat nose, large ridges over the eyes, and a generally heavy cast. A useful oversimplifica-tion is that Lucy had the head of an ape and the body of a human being.

It is not easy to tell just how human Lucy was from the kind of evidence available, but some con-clusions are clear. Lucy and her cohorts used no tools (at least, none that have been preserved), built no houses, and had no fire. If Johanson's interpretation is correct, the First Family really is a kin group, traveling together at the time of their demise, but family groupings of different sorts are common among many modern nonhuman pri-mates. There is no way to know whether Lucy had language, but few if any anthropologists think that she did. Lucy appears to have been pretty nonhu-man in her lifestyle.

The Divergence of the *Australopithecus* and *Homo* Lines

Just before 2 million B.C., rapid evolution brought about an irrevocable split between the *Australo-pithecus* line and a new genus, *Homo*. At first, of course, the two lines showed only relatively minor differences from each other, but the two lines diverged radically as evolution proceeded.

Most of the *Australopithecus* line showed little major change, although some became more robust, particularly in their teeth and associated facial structure. At one time, it was thought that these changes meant that *Australopithecus* was getting larger or at least brawnier, but now it is clear that overall size remained more or less con-stant. The heavier teeth of some *Australopithecus* permitted a diet more specialized in leaves and

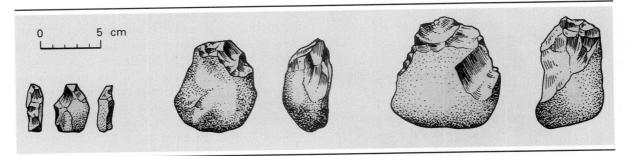

FIGURE 2.5   *Oldowan Tools.*   *These simple stone tools, invented by* Homo habilis, *were a major step in technology. There may have been earlier tools made of perishable materials, but Oldowan tools were rugged and required many decisions by their makers: selecting the correct stone, predicting where a blow would detach a flake, and matching the final product to a task. Nonetheless, they were much less complex than the later, highly patterned tools of* Homo erectus.   From Kevin Shillington, *History of Africa* (1989). Reproduced courtesy of Macmillan Press Ltd.

other vegetable matter that required extensive chewing. Brains remained about the same size.

The *Homo* line, on the other hand, was following a radically new direction. *Homo habilis*, the first of this line, was becoming slightly larger and developing a somewhat more delicate face—but the big changes were taking place inside the head, not outside it. *Homo habilis* was developing a larger brain.

A larger brain, in general, is disadvantageous. Large brains mean large heads, and a large-headed offspring and its mother are more likely to have serious difficulties during childbirth. In evolutionary terms, the gene that produces a large brain may be weeded out by the increased likelihood of death during childbirth. To outweigh this disadvantage, a large brain must confer some greater advantage. In the case of *Homo habilis*, that advantage presumably was intelligence.

Given the limited evidence regarding *Homo habilis*, we have few ways to infer its level of intelligence. Most scholars think that *Homo habilis* had no language, though solid evidence is lacking; we have no clear knowledge of home life or social activities. But, for the first time, we have evidence of technology.

Homo habilis made stone tools, known as **Oldowan tools**. Oldowan tools, named for the Olduvai[4] Gorge in Tanzania (eastern Africa), where they first were recognized, are moderately simple. They consist of a piece of stone with one to five

flakes removed from an edge by striking it with another stone, creating a sharp but irregular edge. Oldowan tools are revolutionary, because they are the first evidence of hominids' modifying the objects of nature to make them more useful; they show judgment in selecting a stone with the appropriate fracture and in being able to direct the blows so that the resulting sharp edge will be produced. One of the basic hallmarks of humanity—technology—was developing.

Homo erectus Becomes Human

By 1.6 million years ago, a new hominid had developed: *Homo erectus*. Although this form evolved out of *Homo habilis*, there appears to have been a period when both forms were in existence, just as Darwinian evolution would suggest, but *Homo erectus* outcompeted *Homo habilis*, which became extinct shortly thereafter.

Homo erectus was a natural outgrowth of its immediate ancestor. It was a bit larger (with modern or near-modern stature), less heavy in the face, and brainier. A *Homo erectus* on the subway or in the bus would be noticeable as unusual, but it probably would not be a cause for alarm.

Although *Homo habilis* showed sparks of intelligence, *Homo erectus* showed the full flame of intellect, developing several significant advances during its million-year existence. *Homo erectus* produced stone and other tools that improved on those of its predecessor in terms of effectiveness and ingenuity. Significantly, these were patterned:

[4] **Olduvai:** OHL doo vy

Tools of a similar kind were made to standardized, symmetrical shapes, showing a level of planning previously unknown. We also see the first use of fire, both for heating and for cooking. We see the first housing, both in caves and in constructed huts.

Another significant development of *Homo erectus* is cooperative behavior. For the first time, we have evidence that hominids coordinated their activities for their mutual benefit. At the archaeological sites of Torralba and Ambrona in Spain, *Homo erectus* hunted large game, including elephants. To do so must have required a number of hunters, and there is evidence that beaters, perhaps using fire, drove animals over cliffs and into swamps where they could be dispatched by hunters. Finally, there is evidence of butchering of the animals and removal of large quantities of meat, presumably for distribution to the families involved. Such a level of cooperation shows that *Homo erectus* recognized the benefits of sharing effort and rewards in a more profound way than other predators, and it shows the intellect necessary to communicate during complicated and coordinated activities, presumably through language.

Prior to *Homo erectus*, all hominids were found in Africa, the cradle of human evolution. With *Homo erectus*, however, hominids expanded out of Africa into diverse environments. By 500,000 B.C. or shortly thereafter, they were living in Africa, Asia as far north and east as northern China, Indonesia, Spain, England, and Germany. This spread certainly indicates that *Homo erectus* possessed the intellect necessary to solve the problems of new environments, particularly cold ones.

FIGURE 2.6 *Artist's Reconstruction of the Huts at Terra Amata.* *Some of the earliest constructed housing known is from this site in coastal southern France. Built by* Homo erectus *around 400,000 years ago, these huts were probably used over several years by a small group of individuals—perhaps fifteen people—during successive summers. Each hut was made of saplings lashed or woven together at their tops and wedged in place at their bases by rocks, resulting in a light oval structure with plenty of ventilation: perfect for summer on the coast.*
Illustration by David Bergen © Time Inc.

FIGURE 2.7 *A Cave Painting from Lascaux.* *Animals dominate the European cave art that blossomed around 23,000 B.C. The animal shown, probably a bison, has a spear driven into its body. The frequency of such depictions in this art has led many scholars to interpret it as part of a ritual designed to bring good fortune in the hunt. This painting from Lascaux Cave in France lies far underground and is accessible only after crawling through long tunnels and wading through an underground stream.* Sisse Brimberg and Norbert Aujoulat/NGS Image Collection. Photo by Norbert Aujoulat. Courtesy of Centre Nationale de Préhistoire, Périgueux.

Although they never have been found, clothing, needles for sewing it, and a host of other technological innovations must have been necessary for *Homo erectus* to have lived in the north.

Another implication of the spread of *Homo erectus* is that the species must have had a steady increase in population size. Normally a species with a stable population has little incentive to expand into less hospitable environments with which it is not familiar. The pressures of rising population levels, however, can encourage groups of intrepid individuals to set out in search of a less crowded locale. It also is possible that *Homo erectus* possessed the quintessentially human trait of curiosity.

Was *Homo erectus* human? There is no scientific definition of human, but *Homo erectus* certainly possessed many of the characteristics usually thought critical to humanity. At the very least, it represented a quantum leap toward humanity in the modern sense.

The Rise of *Homo sapiens*

Biologically modern human beings (*Homo sapiens*) evolved out of *Homo erectus* around or slightly before 100,000 years ago. The real question about

the evolution of modern people is not when or from whom, but where.

One school of thought, known as the **trellis theory**, argues that modern *Homo sapiens* evolved locally from preexisting *Homo erectus* populations. This would mean that modern Chinese were descended from Chinese *Homo erectus*, that modern Africans were descended from African *Homo erectus*, and so forth. This theory was first put forth in the 1930s, supported primarily by similarities between the teeth from *Homo erectus* remains in China and the teeth of modern Chinese. It had fallen into disfavor until recent discoveries at Yunxian,[5] in China, resurrected it. There, *Homo erectus* bones have anatomical traits in common with modern Chinese, suggesting an unbroken ancestry.

The opposing school of thought, dubbed the **"out-of-Africa" theory**, argues that the transition to modern *Homo sapiens* took place only once and in Africa. From there, modern people spread to the rest of the world, outcompeting earlier local hominids, who became extinct. Proponents of this view cite controversial evidence based on molecular biology that suggests that all modern people are

[5] **Yunxian:** yuhn SHEE ahn

descended from a single woman who lived as recently as 100,000 years ago. At this point, both theories are viable, though current anthropological opinion appears to favor the trellis theory.

Aside from the relatively minor cosmetic differences, *Homo sapiens* differs from *Homo erectus* primarily in intellectual capacities. Modern people have a larger brain and presumably greater intelligence, which may be reflected in improvements in technology and such. It is difficult, however, to know whether these improvements are because people are smarter or because there are more of

FIGURE 2.8 *Carved Venus. Nearly one hundred carved-stone Venus figures like this European example have been found. They were made across much of Eurasia between 30,000 and 15,000 B.C., but most are from Central Europe. They typically show large breasts, thighs, and buttocks, featureless faces, and fancy braided hairstyles. Emphasis on these female sexual characteristics suggests that these figures were used in fertility rituals. The Venus figures are some of the earliest evidence for religious activity and art production.* Jean Vertut.

them and they have been working at the problems longer. There are, however, two areas of endeavor in which modern human beings clearly outstrip *Homo erectus*: art and human burial.

Little or no art has survived from *Homo erectus*, consisting perhaps of a fossil shell with an X cut into it and a few similar items. In contrast, early *Homo sapiens* produced abundant expressions of art, including the famous cave paintings of Europe and the Sahara and the less famous—but equally impressive—Venus figurines of Europe and adjacent Asia.

Human burial is unknown for *Homo erectus*, yet early modern human beings practiced it regularly. At Shanidar Cave in Iraq, for instance, *Homo sapiens* skeletons from nearly 40,000 B.C. were found with clusters of pollen on them, indicating that flowers were interred with the dead. Tools and other artifacts occur sporadically in early *Homo sapiens* graves, probably offerings to assist the deceased in an afterlife. Early *Homo sapiens* burial practices suggest strong religious belief.

There is no evidence to prove that *Homo erectus* possessed the same capacity for abstract thinking as modern people. Both art and religion (and most early art probably was religious) demand considerable abstract thought, and *Homo erectus* might not have been mentally equipped for it.

HALLMARKS OF HUMANITY

Human evolution has produced a creature unlike any other on earth. Several features have contributed to this human uniqueness and have equipped human beings for their unparalleled accomplishments. These include:

—upright bipedalism;

—demographic potential;

—continuous sexual receptivity;

—intelligence;

—language; and

—technology.

Upright Bipedalism

Although human beings can crawl or climb, their most usual way of moving about is by walking on their legs. This stance, called **upright bipedalism**, characterized the earliest known hominids, as shown by the Laetoli footprints discussed at the beginning of this chapter. Bipedalism probably developed in response to the need to carry infants away from danger, but it also conferred the advantage of elevating the eyes to provide better vision on the savanna. Its greatest advantage, however, was realized only millions of years later, when tools were developed by *Homo habilis* and the hands were already free to use and carry them.

It is no accident that human hands are as flexible and versatile as they are. Freed from the need to carry the body around, they evolved toward other uses, particularly grasping and carrying of babies. This preadaptation made tools possible and practical immediately upon their invention. Without our hands, it is difficult to imagine any kind of developed human technology.

Upright bipedalism, however, brings its disadvantages. It has created considerable stresses in the lower back, often leading to injury, and human beings are slower and less efficient at walking and running than their four-legged competitors. Obviously, however, the adaptive advantages of upright bipedalism outweigh the disadvantages, because evolution favored the early bipedal hominids.

Demographic Potential

Compared with most animals, human beings have few young and invest a great deal in each one. Human beings mature much more slowly than most animals, so the learning period for each individual is long. This pattern of heavy investment in a few, slow-maturing young is called **k-selection**.

The implications of k-selection are several. First, a species with k-selection must be pretty successful to break even demographically. Given life expectancies and fertility in societies without modern medicine, a modern human being is unlikely to have more than five or six children. Some of these will die young, and others will survive but have no children. But to break even, an average of two children per family must survive to adulthood and reproduce; to have population growth, the average must be greater. These figures may sound unimpressive, but a cemetery from only a century ago will tell sad stories of infant deaths, epidemics, and other tragedies, underscoring the difficulties of maintaining human population levels.

Second, the long maturation period for children permits them to learn a great deal. Unlike some animals whose behavior is determined largely by instinct, human children learn most of their behavior. The system of learned behavior that is shared by a human group is called **culture**. Instincts are genetically programmed and take many generations to change through evolution, but culture can be changed quite rapidly, often over the course of a generation. The dominance of culture over instinct means that human societies are more flexible and able to adapt to changed circumstances faster and better than are creatures more ruled by instinct.

Finally, although many factors work against population growth in human beings, their fates are

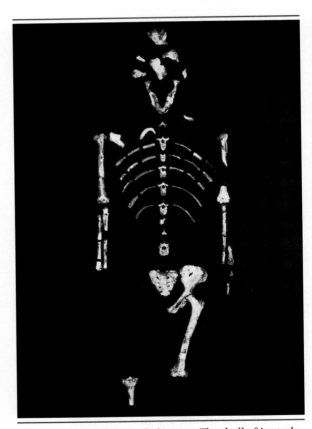

FIGURE 2.9 *Lucy's Skeleton.* The skull of Australopithecus afarensis *was attached to the spine underneath the brain case, the arms were too fragile for supporting weight continually, and the feet were specialized for the striding gait of bipedal walkers. These and other anatomical details confirm what was suggested by the Laetoli footprints: At this early date, nearly 4 million years ago, Lucy and her contemporaries were fully upright and bipedal. Modern human posture developed at an earlier period whose date we do not know.* Courtesy of the Human Origins Institute.

largely in their own hands. Unlike oysters, which simply spew their young into the ocean, human beings can use their culture to improve their success at survival. Paradoxically, while k-selection made it difficult for human beings to break even demographically, it also planted the seeds for the most dramatic population increases ever known, once the appropriate strategies of survival had been worked out.

Continuous Sexual Receptivity

Almost all animals have a limited breeding season during which all sexual activity takes place. Human beings, on the other hand, are continuously sexually receptive; that is, they can have sexual relations at any time and are inclined to do so. Consequently, the instinctual urge for sexual gratification probably encouraged early hominids to congregate into permanent groups—unlike most other animals, which gather together for the breeding season, then disperse again.

This distinctive characteristic, most anthropologists believe, is ultimately responsible for the prominence of the family among human beings. Although the specifics vary from society to society, every known human group has had some form of family. The family typically functions as a cooperative economic group, working for its communal survival, and is an important building block in most modern societies.

Intelligence

Intelligence is difficult to define and even more difficult to measure. The problems are considerable when the people being evaluated are sitting in front of you, but they become far greater when the subjects for evaluation are hominids who have been dead for millions of years.

Although there is no single, universally acceptable definition of **intelligence**, a working definition is the ability to learn, reason, and create. Given this definition, human beings clearly have greater intelligence than other animals. If we judge intelligence by its fruits, we also can rank hominid species. The *Australopithecus* species, with no tangible signs of intelligent behavior, would be at the bottom rung. *Homo habilis*, with crude tools and little else, would have ascended the first or second step of the ladder. *Homo erectus*, with its more complex technology, cooperative behavior, and

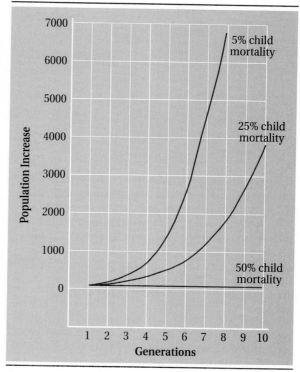

FIGURE 2.10 *Theoretical Rates of Population Increase.* *This graph shows the potential rate of population growth under differing estimates of the child mortality rate (the percentage of children who die before reaching maturity). Child mortality rates of 40 to 50 percent were common before 10,000 B.C.; modern world rates are around 5 percent.*

language, would be several rungs farther up, and *Homo sapiens*, with perhaps improved abstract thought, would be a couple of rungs above *Homo erectus*.

This ranking probably is adequate for our purposes, but there is an additional means of evaluating intelligence between species. Henry McHenry, an American anthropologist, has developed what he calls the **encephalization index**. Simply put, the encephalization index is a measure of the average brain size for a species, adjusted for its body size. (The latter adjustment is necessary because, all else being equal, larger animals have larger brains.) When the index is applied to living creatures, most animals measure in the 9 to 12 range, although chimpanzees and other apes have indexes in the low 30s; human beings measure in at 99.1—a huge increase over other animals. Table 2.1 (p. 40) shows that encephalization indexes produce about the same picture of relative intelli-

TABLE 2.1

Encephalization Indexes for Hominids

Hominid	Encephalization Index
Australopithecus afarensis	33.1
Other *Australopithecus* species	31–35
Homo habilis	51.1
Homo erectus	86.0
Homo sapiens	99.1

The encephalization index measures brain size in relation to body size. It provides a way to compare the intelligence of different species. Dogs, cats, mice, and most other mammals have indexes ranging from 9 to 12, and modern apes have indexes around 30 to 35. Comparing these figures to ones based on fossil hominids suggests that Australopithecus *had intellectual capabilities comparable to those of modern apes and that* Homo habilis *and* Homo erectus *had no modern analogue.*

gence for the hominids as did our ranking based on cultural accomplishments.

The importance of intelligence to human development cannot be overemphasized. By 100,000 years ago, all people throughout the world had developed intelligence comparable to that of modern human beings, and those abilities and skills were turned toward the development of survival strategies, the arts, mythology, social organization, and all the other aspects of culture. Intelligence is the key to language and technology, two other critical hallmarks of humanity.

Language

Language is the ability to communicate through the use of symbols; many linguists argue that the communication must be primarily verbal, although others disagree. The critical word in this definition is **symbol**, referring to an arbitrary marker that stands for something else. For example, "lemon" is a symbol for a yellow citrus fruit; there is no special reason why "bacon" isn't used to refer to that fruit, but it isn't—this is the nature of arbitrariness. On the other hand, a high-pitched scream in reaction to pain or a grunt while moving a piano is primarily instinctual, so these sounds fail the test of arbitrariness. By using symbols, human beings can create a limitless repertoire of messages, combining existing symbols in new ways or creating new symbols altogether.

As far as we know, no animals use language in nature. Their communication, instead, appears to be based entirely on **signs**, vocalizations that indicate meaning but are instinctual and therefore not arbitrary. When a chimpanzee, for example, hoots in a certain manner, it indicates danger. Because that hoot is instinctual, it is understood by chimpanzees who never have heard it before; all normal chimpanzees make the same hoot for the same meaning. The use of signs, in contrast to language, is limited to the relatively few messages that are part of the animal's instinctual repertoire. Chimpanzees, for example, have about thirty signs; rabbits have only about four. New or complicated messages, no matter how urgent or significant, simply cannot be communicated with signs.

Some captive gorillas and chimpanzees have been taught American Sign Language (ASL) by researchers and appear to communicate with hand gestures using grammar and other characteristics of language. There is disagreement over whether this is a true use of language or whether the animals are cleverly mimicking their teachers without any true understanding of the symbols. In any case, such possible use of language has never developed in nature and has resulted only from intensive and purposeful teaching on the part of human instructors.

The development and use of language permitted hominids to communicate a far wider range of messages than would have been possible before. This would have been highly useful in practical matters, such as the killing of elephants at Torralba and Ambrona and the distribution of their meat, and it also would have encouraged the development of personal interaction and friendships. Such relationships are characteristic of human beings and further strengthen family and group relationships, making the human social group more integrated and effective.

Technology

It is difficult to imagine human existence without technology. **Technology**, the production of material items, opens up avenues of human existence. Without it, human beings would be restricted to the relatively few parts of the world whose climate permits us to survive without clothes, fire, or other assistance. We would have to procure all our food from nature using only our hands and mouths, and these same hands and mouths would be our

FIGURE 2.11 *Koko Using Sign Language.* *Koko, the female gorilla in this photograph, has been taught to use American Sign Language, the language of hand symbols developed for the deaf. She has learned to express her wants, describe events, and inquire of her human custodians, but she has trouble dealing with topics in the future and with some abstract ideas. Without human intervention, no ape is known to have learned any language. Here, Koko does not read text; rather, she responds to the picture in the book.* Dr. Ronald H. Cohn/Gorilla Foundation.

only defense against wild animals and one another. Art and many other expressions of creativity would be out of the question.

Of course, technology has been part of the human heritage since the time of *Homo habilis.* Our intelligence permitted us to conceive of technological devices and techniques, and our upright posture and grasping hands permitted us to fashion and use them effectively. Since *Homo habilis,* we have continued to improve our technology and apply it to new problems. We shall see throughout this text that the relative advantage conferred by superior technology and the drive to secure resources to support this technology have been driving forces in the shaping of history.

AFTER BIOLOGICAL EVOLUTION

Biological evolution is an ongoing process with no goal or ending point, and we can be assured that human beings will continue to change. The rate of evolution slowed considerably, however, with the development of technology and social institutions. Lucy, for example, would not have lasted long on the dangerous African savanna if her vision had not been sharp. All three authors of this book, in contrast, would have suffered an unhappy fate

early if our survival had depended on our vision. Today we survive (and our genes are available for reproduction) because of eyeglass technology; 50,000 years ago we might have been supported by our community with the expectation that we would contribute to the group with activities that our limited vision would permit.

Nonetheless, biological evolution continues. A classic instance is **lactose intolerance**. Some adults develop cramps and diarrhea when they consume milk or milk products, whereas others can consume these foods with no ill effects. The difference is that those who develop problems have a genetic inability to produce the appropriate stomach enzymes to digest the sugar (lactose) in milk, which then passes to the intestines and wreaks havoc. This might seem like simply individual differences, but the distribution of lactose intolerance is closely related to where one's ancestors lived, and how long people there have kept cattle herds.

Prior to the development of **pastoralism**, the keeping of domesticated herd animals, milk was available to human beings only from one's mother, and that source was available only for the first few years of life. As a genetic encouragement to weaning, most children lose their ability to digest milk fully at about four years of age. The exceptions are lactose-tolerant children from societies with long traditions of dairy herds. The Fulani of western

		5 mya	
		–	
		–	Earliest known hominid fossils, 4.5 mya
Various *Australo-pithecus* species, 4.5–1.4 mya		–	
		–	
		4 mya	
		–	
		–	Lucy and the First Family, 3.5 mya
		–	
		–	
		3 mya	
		–	
		–	
		–	
		–	
	Homo habilis, 2.1–1.5 mya	2 mya	Earliest stone tools, 2.1 mya
		–	
		–	
Homo erectus, 1.6–.5 mya		–	
		–	Patterned stone tools, 1.2 mya
		1 mya	
		–	
		–	First use of fire, .6 mya
		–	Expansion to cold climates, .5 mya
		–	
Homo sapiens, 100,000 B.C.–present		–	
		present	First civilization, 3500 B.C.

Africa, for example, are pastoralists and have only 22 percent lactose intolerance; their neighbors, the nonpastoralist Ibo, have 95 percent lactose intolerance. Most people of Southwest Asian, South Asian, or European descent are lactose tolerant; most people of East Asian descent are lactose intolerant; and people of African descent can go either way, depending on their specific background. This patterning is all the more remarkable when one considers that lactose tolerance must have become common only in the past 6,000 or 8,000 years, the period after the development of dairy pastoralism.

Although biological evolution will continue, we should expect cultural change to be the primary way in which human beings of the future will adapt to their changing world. Since the attainment of modern capabilities around 100,000 B.C., human beings have changed primarily in their cultures. With the environmental improvement that accompanied the end of the glacial ages around 10,000 B.C., human beings began a steady and dramatic increase in their numbers, spreading to virtually all habitable niches. Within a few millennia of this change, developments that would lead to the rise of civilization were well under way.

SUMMARY

1. In the nineteenth century, scholars concerned with human origins shifted from a viewpoint based on scriptural revelation to one based on scientific philosophy. At this point, Darwin and others produced plausible theories and evidence to support human origins through evolutionary processes.

2. The earliest hominids are of the genus *Australopithecus* and existed in Africa by 5 million years ago. Although physically similar to human beings, they show no clear signs of culture.

3. The genus *Homo* developed around 2.1 million years ago in Africa, and its members show varying degrees of cultural behavior. *Homo habilis* used simple tools; *Homo erectus* used more advanced technology, fire, and cooperation to expand into cold climates; *Homo sapiens* may have greater ability for abstract thought than did *Homo erectus*.

4. There are two competing theories about the evolution of human beings. The trellis theory

argues that *Homo erectus* populations migrated to Asia around 500,000 B.C. and Europe a bit later, evolving locally into the modern races of *Homo sapiens*; the "out-of-Africa" theory argues that modern *Homo sapiens* developed only in Africa around 100,000 B.C. and migrated to the rest of the world.

5. As culture has become more prominent, human biological evolution has become less important. Most human adaptations in recent times have been cultural.

6. The hallmarks of humanity are upright bipedalism, demographic potential, continuous sexual receptivity, intelligence, language, and technology. These characteristics have permitted human beings to assume a unique position in their relation to the world and to one another. The biological potentials acquired through millions of years of evolution have left their mark on human events in the recent past and continue to do so.

SUGGESTED READINGS

Johanson, Donald, Lenora Johanson, and Blake Elgar. *Ancestors: In Search of Human Origins.* New York: Villard Books, 1993. A chatty discussion of one reconstruction of human evolution.

Leakey, Richard E., and L. Jan Slikkerveer. *Man-ape, Ape-man: The Quest for Human's Place in Nature and Dubois' "Missing Link."* Leiden, Netherlands: Netherlands Foundation/Kenya Wildlife Service, 1993. An enthralling account of the scholars who have built the modern picture of human evolution.

Rasmussen, D. Tab, ed. *The Origin and Evolution of Humans and Humanness.* Boston: Jones and Bartlett, 1993. A collection of *Scientific American* articles on various aspects of human evolution.

Walker, Alan, and Pat Shipman. *The Wisdom of the Bones: In Search of Human Origins.* New York: Knopf, 1996. An excellent and authoritative account; the best single work of its sort.

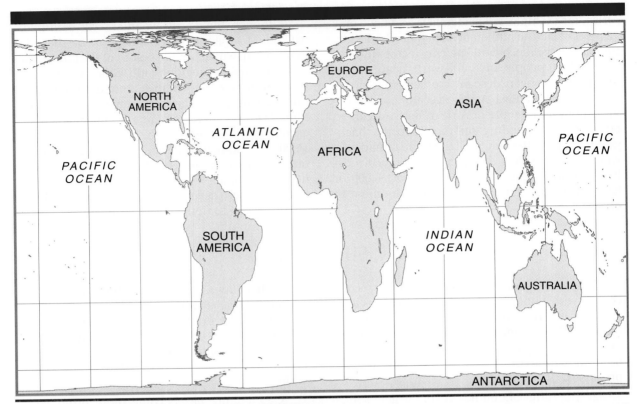

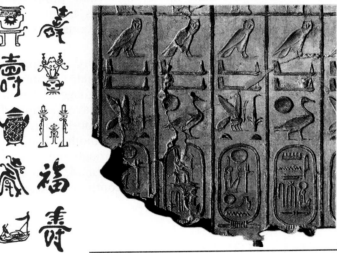

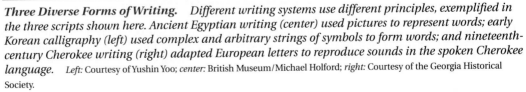

Three Diverse Forms of Writing. *Different writing systems use different principles, exemplified in the three scripts shown here. Ancient Egyptian writing (center) used pictures to represent words; early Korean calligraphy (left) used complex and arbitrary strings of symbols to form words; and nineteenth-century Cherokee writing (right) adapted European letters to reproduce sounds in the spoken Cherokee language.* Left: Courtesy of Yushin Yoo; *center:* British Museum/Michael Holford; *right:* Courtesy of the Georgia Historical Society.

Cultural Evolution, Complexity, and Civilization

A general definition of civilization: a civilized society is exhibiting the five qualities of truth, beauty, adventure, art, peace.

–ALFRED NORTH WHITEHEAD

This definition, by a British philosopher of the early twentieth century, equates civilization with all that is good; in common usage, the word carries a similarly positive meaning. An urbane sophisticate may be described as "very civilized," while an ill-behaved child may be urged to "act civilized."

In the study of the past, however, the term has a more neutral meaning, referring simply to societies that have developed a considerable degree of complexity. There is no implication that civilized people are any better or more moral or more intelligent than their noncivilized cousins. This chapter examines the general lifestyles of those who lived in the millennia before the development of civilization, which began around 3500 B.C. In addition, it explores the distinguishing characteristics of civilized societies and considers why it is useful to study these features.

THE IDEA OF CULTURAL EVOLUTION

Underlying the dichotomy between civilized and noncivilized peoples is the concept of **cultural evolution**, the idea that there is a general tendency over time for cultures to become more complex.

Increased complexity, of course, does not necessarily imply improvement or advancement, but simply a more tangled web of human interactions. This complexity is expressed in a wide variety of ways. More complex societies have a greater number of roles that their citizens can fill, with differences in occupations, wealth, social status, and political power. More complex societies settle in larger, more diverse groups that reflect the differences among the people that occupy them. More complex societies have advanced knowledge and skills, largely the result of the occupational specialization by members who have devoted great amounts of time to particular fields of endeavor.

Members of a simpler society, in contrast, are more like one another. Most or all have about the same degree of wealth and power, live in similar circumstances, and perform similar activities. An Amazonian rain forest farmer, isolated from any outside society, would live like most other Amazonian rain forest farmers in the essentials.

Stages of Cultural Evolution

Several models of cultural evolution are in use by social scientists, and most utilize **stages**, patterns of cultural characteristics that are common to societies of a similar level of complexity. Stages are artificial devices, created by scholars to help them catalogue and understand societies, and the model presented here uses four stages based primarily on political considerations: how a society allocates power.

The simplest stage of cultural evolution in this system is the **band**. Bands typically are small, with 30 to 200 people living together, deriving their food from hunting, fishing, and gathering of plant foods. Bands move with the seasons to take advantage of seasonally available foods. Although there may be division of labor according to gender, people of the same sex perform about the same range of activities. Men typically spend much of their time in hunting and making certain types of tools for their own use; women are more concerned with gathering plant materials for food and medicine and with domestic duties, such as preparing food and producing certain domestic implements. (These activities became women's work, probably because they were compatible with child care, itself a logical outgrowth of the biological function of breast-feeding infants.) Each family largely meets its own needs, although there are various communal tasks for which labor is pooled. Because everyone in a band is related, kinship links are very important. A family with plenty of food is likely to share with a family suffering a temporary shortage, because they can find some sort of kin relationship; a family that needs assistance in some task can expect to call on relatives for labor. Religion is personal, focused often on individual visions, but there is a shared body of belief. There often is no formal leader of a band, and no

TABLE 3.1
Typical Characteristics of Stages of Cultural Evolution

Stage	Size	Politics	Religion	Economics
Band	30–200	none	personal	hunter-gatherer; kin-sharing
Tribe	100–2,000	leader with persuasive power	kinship group–oriented	agricultural; kin-sharing
Chiefdom	1,000–10,000	leader with coercive power	priest-oriented	agricultural; class-oriented
Civilization	over 10,000	coercive leader with bureaucracy	state ideology	agricultural; class-oriented; occupational specialists

Most societies fit neatly into one or another of these stages, possessing all the defining characteristics. There are some exceptions, however, like the chiefdom-level hunting-gathering Native American groups of the northwest coast of North America. Similarly, the people of a region usually pass through the stages in sequence, beginning with bands, though there are exceptions to this generalization, too.

one has legitimate authority to compel obedience from another. War usually is rare for band-level peoples.

At the next level of complexity is the **tribe**. (This is a more technical usage than informally referring to an "Indian tribe," which may be at a band, tribe, or other stage.) The tribe typically is somewhat larger than the band, usually consisting of around 100 to 2,000 people. Tribes get most of their food through the growing of crops, although hunting and gathering may still be practiced. There are few or no occupations other than farmer, and everyone performs more or less the same activities. The need to tend their crops encourages them to settle in a single, permanent village—in other words, to be **sedentary**. There may be a formal leader, although he or she can lead only by example and persuasion; the leader has no power to enforce a policy. Societies at the tribe stage usually have limited involvement in warfare until population levels become high enough to create severe competition for agricultural land. Most religious responsibility is in the hands of kinship-based organizations that perform calendric ceremonies, many of which are to ensure good harvests.

More complex is the **chiefdom**. The chiefdom is somewhat larger than the tribe, consisting usually of 1,000 to 10,000 people, but it is distinguished by a radical shift in political power. The leader of a chiefdom, the chief, has true coercive power, the right to make a decision and forcibly implement it. In a band or tribe, a bad suggestion from a leader can be simply ignored; in a chiefdom, a chief's decision, good or bad, is enforced, sometimes against the will of the people. The chiefdom also has several layers of wealth, authority, and prestige, often with named classes. There frequently are many different occupations, although some people may continue the earlier path of the farmer who carries out a wide variety of activities. The trend toward the increasing importance of warfare in the tribe continues and intensifies with the chiefdom. Religion usually is in the hands of a priestly hierarchy, sometimes intimately linked with the government. Agriculture or pastoralism is almost always the economic base underwriting a chiefdom, although a few chiefdoms have been based on hunting and gathering.

The final stage of cultural evolution, **civilization**, further intensifies the occupational and sta-

FIGURE 3.1 *The King of Kuba.* *This photograph from the mid–twentieth century shows an African king in the splendor of his court. Even this late into the colonial period, the king retained great political, military, and economic power and paraded his status in his leopard skin, his expensive beaded ornaments, and his personal bulk. Such power and status are typical in chiefdoms such as Kuba.* Photo by Eliot Elisofon, 1947, neg. No. 22923. Eliot Elisofon Photographic Archives, National Museum of African Art, Smithsonian Institution, Washington, D.C.

tus differences among its members. It also possesses a number of distinctive characteristics, discussed at length later in this chapter. The concept of civilization, riddled as it is with connotations of superiority, is rejected outright by some modern scholars, but we will use it for reasons discussed at the end of this chapter.

If you examine one region, you usually will see a general trend that follows this band-tribe-chiefdom-civilization pattern over long periods of time. Sometimes, however, societies in a region skip over a stage, return to a stage previously abandoned, or stop at a stage before they reach civilization. These exceptions are fascinating and demand special attention, but they should not obscure the fact that the general model holds true most of the time. Most social scientists believe that population growth is at the root of cultural evolution.

The Population Trigger for the Agricultural Bomb

Human demographic potential was discussed in Chapter 2, where it was noted that human beings can increase their population levels through culture, adopting new lifeways to aid survival. In fact, they are so good at it that population pressures probably developed fairly early with the warming climates and improved conditions around 10,000 B.C. This meant that new ways of gaining food had to be found to support these increasing numbers of people.

Hunting and gathering was not a brutish or nasty way to procure food. Indeed, it required less labor and often provided a more reliable food supply than most forms of agriculture, and hunters and gatherers clearly had a more balanced diet that, given sufficient quantities of food, led to generally higher levels of health than most agriculturalists enjoyed.

The primary disadvantage of hunting and gathering, however, was that it could support only a limited number of people in a given area. Once people had reached the limit for their area, population levels would stabilize through increased mortality. On average, mothers bore about five children, yet only two could survive to replace their parents, if the limit of an area to provide food had been reached. Other children usually would die of diseases to which they were more susceptible because of hunger; in some societies, infanticide was practiced to ease the burden of providing for a larger family in hard times.

To put it in human terms, then, parents had to choose between the easier life of a hunter-gatherer and the more restrictive life of an agriculturalist. Hunters and gatherers realized that seeds germinate into plants, and there was no dramatic "discovery" of agriculture. Rather, parents decided that the increased efforts and lost freedoms of agriculture were an acceptable price for having more of their children survive.

Almost incidentally, choosing to become agriculturalists allowed their populations to grow to sizes and densities necessary for the development

FIGURE 3.2 *Aerial Photograph of Northern Mesopotamia Showing Irrigation Canals. This network of canals hints at how much effort is required to keep them operating and how they open land up to agriculture. Many of these canals are in identical positions to canals first constructed thousands of years ago.* Georg Gerster/Comstock.

of complex societies. Population pressure led to agriculture, which in turn released the brake on population levels, leading to greater numbers of people than ever before seen—and to greater cultural complexity. Once taken, the step to agriculture was normally irreversible, because the farmers had to settle in one place, and the wild food resources within traveling distance no longer would be sufficient to feed their increased numbers of mouths.

Irrigation agriculture warrants special attention. Agriculturalists in environments where water is scanty must use **irrigation**, the practice of bringing water to agricultural fields through canals or

THE CORE ELEMENTS OF CIVILIZATION 49

similar devices. Irrigation is very time consuming, with major labor investments in digging canals, as well as in repairing and cleaning them. Large-scale irrigation also requires special skills and organization for its effective operation. Efficient design of canals requires some engineering skill, because slopes must be steep enough to keep the water flowing yet shallow enough so that the canals will not be below the level of the fields by the time the water arrives. And irrigation always seems to lead to disputes over excessive drawing off of water upstream and the like; these disputes require adjudication by an individual or group.

The development of agriculture was fundamental to the development of complex society. Agriculture, sedentism, and population growth were partners in fostering the accumulation of goods, the development of different occupations and levels of wealth, and the need for stronger political leadership. The juggernaut of cultural evolution was gaining speed.

Why Some Cultures Never Developed Civilization

The previous paragraphs have discussed one possible trajectory of human evolution, where complexity continually increases; another possibility, of course, is that society in a region reaches a certain level of complexity and remains there. There are many reasons why this might happen. In the Kalahari Desert or along the Arctic coast, for examples, climate does not permit the development of agriculture, and populations large enough to lead to cultural complexity never developed locally. In some places, such as Panama and Costa Rica, local chiefdoms were conquered by the Spanish before they reached civilization. In still other places, such as the northwest coast of North America, chiefdoms were based on fishing in the exceptionally rich waters and were following a different track from those of most chiefdoms elsewhere.

It is important to recall that there is no reason why a society would want to evolve. Indeed, personal welfare was almost universally superior in the *less* complex societies. A member of a band traveled with the seasons, worked short hours, was healthy, and was not subject to the whim of a leader or government. Many personal freedoms were gradually surrendered on the road to civilization.

THE CORE ELEMENTS OF CIVILIZATION

Scholars, of course, vary somewhat in their ideas of which elements are essential to a definition of civilization. Nonetheless, there is consensus that some elements are crucial to the definition and always must be present, while others are sometimes important but more variable. This section discusses what we consider the six essential elements of civilization, and the section that follows discusses the variable ones.

The following are the core, invariable elements of civilization:

— dependence on agriculture;

— occupational specialization;

— class stratification;

— state government;

— long-distance trade; and

— urbanism.

Other characteristics (such as the presence of religion, art, tools, houses, and the like) could be included in this list, but, as discussed in Chapter 2, these really are characteristics of human existence, whether civilized or not.

Agricultural Dependence

To most people living today, getting food from the raising of plants and animals seems the normal thing to do, but this mode of food production has been in existence only for the past few thousand years, prior to which human beings got all their food from nature by hunting, fishing, and gathering.

The specifics of agriculture will vary from civilization to civilization. Civilizations of Africa, Europe, Asia, and the Pacific Islands, for example, had a wide variety of both plant crops and domesticated animals; in the Americas, on the other hand, civilizations had an equally broad range of plant foods but a more restricted range of domesticated animals. Pigs, cattle, sheep, goats, horses (originally food animals), chickens, ducks, geese, and other animals were common in civilizations in various parts of Asia, Africa, and Europe. In the Americas, far fewer animals were raised. The Maya, for example, had only dogs, ducks, and stingless bees, while the Inca had only dogs, guinea pigs (another food animal), and two domesticated animals of the camel family. Similarly, some civilizations have focused on grains, while others have gotten most of their calories from root crops.

Although the specifics of agriculture vary, all civilizations have developed some way of storing agricultural surplus. This is critical, of course, in seasonal environments, where crops grow poorly or not at all in the off season. It also is important elsewhere, because the amassing and control of agricultural surplus is one means that a government has of ensuring the loyalty—or at least control—of its people. For this reason, agriculture always has focused on crops that can be stored easily, usually in dried form.

Occupational Specialization

In early societies, each person was a generalist, shifting from one task to another in order to accomplish all or most of the jobs necessary for survival. Of course, certain members of a family or community would provide certain services for the whole group; this division of labor was especially common along sexual lines, with women's and men's tasks standardized within each society. But, in general, there was little specialization.

In civilizations, however, the situation was drastically different. Here, there was a great deal of **occupational specialization**, the division of labor into narrow jobs. In the precivilized Indus Valley of Pakistan in 4500 B.C., for example, a typical man produced stone tools, worked in the wheat and barley fields, built his own house, and butchered an animal for food when he was lucky enough to have meat; the typical woman raised children, prepared meals, and produced clothing. Two thousand years later, however, the development of civilization demanded much greater occupational specialization (at least for men) in the Indus Valley. By that time, a man might follow a career as a potter, a weaver, a butcher, a stone tool maker, or another specialist; he would ply his trade and hire other specialists to provide services at which he was unskilled. If he was a specialist farmer, he no longer made his own tools and perhaps did not even build his own house. In many societies, occupational specialization is far more marked for men than it is for women, many of whom have continued as generalists to the present day. Presumably,

the greater focus on the spectrum of domestic activities typical for women has demanded a greater breadth of activity for women than for men.

There is a certain efficiency to occupational specialization. A specialist typically is more skilled at a particular task than a generalist and may have specialized tools that would not be sensible investments for a generalist who performed that task only occasionally. Further, a specialist who devotes so much time to a task may, through practice, develop greater skill or new and more effective ways of performing that task.

From the point of view of the society as a whole, occupational specialization means that every specialist is dependent on every other specialist, because the generalist skills no longer are developed, especially in cities, where there are

FIGURE 3.3 *Chinese Capmaker. Civilizations spawn diverse and specialized occupations, such as the making of caps, shown here in an eighteenth-century depiction. Any society in which a person produces only a single type of ware has to rely on the cooperation and interaction of hundreds of specialists, each of whom produces and exchanges a single product.* From George Henry Mason, *The Costume of China* (London: W. Miller, 1800), Plate LI. Reproduced courtesy of the Harvard-Yenching Library.

An old vaudeville line, revived in Mel Brooks's film *History of the World—Part I*, says that "it's good to be the king." Certainly kings and emperors are at the top of the hierarchy of class stratification, and the rules surrounding their treatment point out their lofty position. The Aztecs ruled most of Mexico from 1300 to 1520, and their treatment of the emperor exemplifies this well.

The *Florentine Codex*, a book written by Aztecs just after the Spanish conquest, tells us how the ruler traveled.

> When the ruler went forth, in his hand rested his reed stalk which he went moving in rhythm with his words. His chamberlains and his elders went before him; on both sides, on either hand, they proceeded as they went clearing the way for him. None might cross in front of him; none might come forth before him; none might look up at him; none might come face to face with him.

The same work gives a hint of the splendorous clothing in which the emperor was clad:

> The cape with the serpent mask design, bordered with eyes; the cape with the conch shell design, bordered with eyes . . . the tawny colored breech cloth with the ocelot head; the ocelot breech cloth with a step design . . . the head band with two quetzal[a] feather tassels set off with gold, with which they bound their hair; a quetzal feather crest device set

[a] **quetzal:** KEHT zahl

IN THEIR OWN WORDS

It's Good to Be the Aztec Emperor

off with gold, which he wore upon his back . . . a golden arm band; golden ear plugs, which he inserted in his earlobes . . .

While the emperor was arrayed in gold, rare furs, and decorations incorporating feathers of the sacred quetzal bird, commoners were more likely to wear merely simple cotton breechcloths and capes.

Even the act of dining underscored the special nature of the emperor, as shown in this account by Bernal Díaz del Castillo,[b] a member of the Spanish conquering army:

> The great Montezuma had more than three hundred dishes prepared for him. . . . Everyday they cooked for him hens, turkeys, pheasants, partridges, quails, venison, marsh birds, hares, and rabbits and many kinds of birds and things that are reared in these lands. There are so many things that I would not soon finish telling you of them. . . . When he began to eat, they put in front of him a kind of gilded door so that they would not see him eating, and the four women withdrew and four important old gentlemen stood at his side whom Montezuma talked to and asked questions from time to time and as a great favor he would give each one of these old men a dish of what he liked best. . . . [When he was done] the same four women removed the tablecloths and came back to wash his hands, and they did it with great deference.

[b] **Díaz del Castillo:** DEE ahth dehl cahth TEE yoh

plenty of customers. There may be an incentive for individuals to become specialists, because they may be able to charge enough for their services so that they raise their standard of living. Because the community as a whole needs specialists' services, they are able to increase their charges, providing these charges do not become exorbitant.

Class Stratification

At its simplest, **class stratification** means that there are rich and poor people within a society; a slightly more complete definition is the condition

under which members of a society have differential access to resources and power. Each level of society is called a **class**, and many societies have names for the different classes. Among the Natchez Indians of Mississippi, for example, there were three named classes—the sun (the ruler), the nobles, and the stinkards (commoners)—each with its own set of rights and obligations. Once classes have been established, distinctive aspects of culture develop for the different classes; **elite culture** refers to the cultural elements distinctive to the upper classes, while **folk culture**, as used in this text, refers to the cultural elements embraced by the lower classes. Class stratification has been a part of most modern societies for so long that many students have difficulty imagining a class-less society, one in which such distinctions did not exist.

Class stratification is usually seen as an outgrowth of occupational specialization. If individuals have different occupations, it is a short step to income disparities, because those with more critical or difficult tasks can demand and receive greater compensation for their services. Trade flourished in a class-stratified society, because traders often were able to make great fortunes by taking chances in investment; at the same time, members of the elite were seeking expensive and rare items to demonstrate their wealth and importance. The power vested in the hereditary rulers of state governments permitted them to set themselves up as the highest class and to accentuate class differences by granting privileges and economic favors to their favorites.

State Government

All people have a need for some method of decision making, both to determine domestic policy and to deal with outsiders. There is, however, a wide variety of ways to perform these tasks, ranging from simply discussing them around a campfire to having elaborate dynasties or election systems. Civilizations are characterized by **state governments** (also known as **polities**): governments with strong leadership, a supporting bureaucracy, and a supportive ideology. These state governments can take many forms, from kingdoms to dictatorships to democracies.

In particular, state governments have coercive powers. That is, the leaders of a state government have the legitimate right to force citizens to conform to the will of the state. For example, if a citizen of seventeenth-century France was commanded to donate an estate to the king, that citizen could be legally forced to do so or suffer the consequences of refusal. Similarly, if a citizen of the United States decides not to pay taxes, that person can be forced to do so by the government or can be imprisoned. Because almost everyone alive today lives under a state form of government, these powers often seem basic to all political systems, but they really are a relatively recent development of the past few thousand years. To people living in a tribe or band, this power of the state to

FIGURE 3.4 *King Kamehameha II.* *This portrait of the last king of Hawaii was painted by an unknown artist in the early years of the twentieth century. Shown in European-style clothing, Kamehameha was the last of a line of divine kings who were attributed special powers and obligations by their subjects. Kamehameha had to avoid contact with certain categories of people who could pollute him, including women, low-class persons, and criminals. Eating food prepared by them, being touched by them, or (in some cases) even being seen by them would be spiritually dangerous.* Bishop Museum, The State Museum of Natural and Cultural History.

enforce its own dictates would be unreasonable and unacceptable.

Yet the coercive nature of state government is absolutely essential to a civilization. The greater numbers of people involved make simpler (and less forceful) forms of government ineffective. In living with so many other people, the individual must surrender many personal choices and freedoms for the good of the group. Of course, selfish and corrupt leaders also can take advantage of such a government to subvert its power for their own personal benefit.

The second characteristic of a state government is **bureaucracy**, a hierarchy in which officials represent the state and its ruler in many interactions. This also is the result of the size of a civilization. A smaller government (such as that of a chiefdom) might be able to operate with a single leader who would make decisions and deal with all governmental problems, but a civilization is simply too large for this option. A civilization must have officials to assist the leader in dealing with regional government, and they, in turn, must have their assistants to deal with local government, and so on. Many state governments, including most today, can involve significant percentages of the population in governmental roles somewhere within their bureaucracy.

The third defining characteristic of a state government is a state ideology to support it. The state ideology usually is a religion, but it also can be a more secular idea system, such as Confucianism in earlier China or Marxism-Leninism in many twentieth-century communist states. Whatever form it takes, the state ideology is distinctive to a particular state, serving to unify the people behind a common cause and to legitimize the state. The notion of independence of church and state is a recent idea, developing largely in the American and French revolutions of the eighteenth century. In contrast, most earlier civilizations have had their own distinctive religions, each with its characteristic gods, rituals, and mythology.

Sometimes, the religious and governmental officials are one and the same. Such a system, called a **theocracy**, usually recognizes a deity as the head of the government and a high religious official as the interpreter of that deity's will. A high priest (or, less commonly, high priestess) becomes the supreme worldly ruler under such an arrangement, merging priest and monarch and forging a direct and major link between government and religion. Ancient Egypt is an excellent example of this kind of a theocracy, where the supreme leader (pharaoh) was not only the head priest or priestess but also was considered divine in his or her own right, an earthly manifestation of a deity.

In nontheocratic states, the link is less direct but no less important. In those cases, the state ideology legitimizes the rulers, who frequently cite divine will as their ultimate source of power. It is critical to leaders that their positions remain unquestioned, and no higher authority could be invoked than that of the deities. The coronation of royalty in medieval Europe was conducted by religious officials, this practice growing directly out of divine underwriting of this royal authority.

Looked at even more broadly, a state ideology provides another function for a state government.

Unlike smaller-scale governments, state governments are often quite heterogeneous, incorporating diverse local factions that previously had viewed themselves as distinct. A common religion is an important way of promoting a sense of unity in a state that might otherwise risk dissolution. The Inca found religion a potent way of controlling ethnic groups within their empire, forcing them to adopt the Inca religion while allowing them to incorporate some of their own gods into the Inca pantheon. In this manner, a common bond was forged throughout the empire at the same time that the divine status of the emperor was confirmed.

Long-Distance Trade

Every society trades goods with its neighbors, often as symbols of their mutual good will. Civilizations, however, typically conduct large-scale trading operations at great distances. In part, this is in response to their greater ability to devote labor and resources to the activities necessary for this kind of trade. The mounting of a trading expedition begins with the amassing of goods to trade (and possibly the securing of loans to purchase the goods), an operation that requires up-front investment. Next, a team of skilled specialists must be assembled. They must be able to navigate to the intended distant place, to translate from one language to another, to defend the trading party from raiders and robbers along the way, to make judgments about values of goods, and to organize the entire operation. Finally, the organizers of the trade must accept the possibility that they will have to absorb big losses, because the risks in long-distance trade are usually great; but so are the profits.

Civilizations typically have had not only the means to mount long-distance trading operations but also the incentive. Many items procured through long-distance trade are luxury items to be used by a privileged class. Not only are the upper classes the only ones that can afford such exotica, but they can gain prestige from their ownership. Rare gems have been the privilege of the rich in most societies, and a jewel could serve as a symbol of the owner's status.

Although there have been cases of nonroyal entrepreneurs who have successfully negotiated major long-distance trading, until the past few centuries it typically has been controlled by a royal

FIGURE 3.5 *The Aztec* Pochteca. *The Aztec Empire of Mexico accorded long-distance traders,* pochteca, *a high status. The* pochteca *carried out trade over vast distances and also served as spies and government representatives. The top frame of this Aztec painting shows them meeting with a noble (on the left); the middle frame shows porters carrying parcels for the* pochteca; *the bottom frame shows a* pochteca *bargaining at the market.* Biblioteca Medicea Laurenziana, Florence.

family. Among the Aztecs of Mexico around 1300 to 1500, for example, there were *pochteca*,[1] a class of specialist traders employed by the government. They sometimes traveled well over a thousand miles from the Aztec heartland of central Mexico, including regular trips to Central America and possibly to the Mississippi Valley and what is now Arizona. These *pochteca* were a hybrid of diplomat, trader, and spy; they were feared and respected by their trading partners, and this fear and respect undoubtedly aided them in negotiations. The silk traders of Eurasia, sometimes royal and sometimes private, also mounted caravans that crossed thousands of miles of inhospitable terrain to link China and Europe.

Urbanism

Urbanism, of course, refers to the presence of cities, but the definition of "city" is not so easy as it sounds. Certainly, a city must be large, but are all large settlements cities? Further, how large is "large"? If the Athens of Aristotle were to be placed in the modern United States, it would be merely a small town, yet its importance in classical Greece was far greater than its small population (in modern terms) might indicate. What is needed is a definition of urbanism that does not rely exclusively on size, and such a definition comes from the discipline of geography.

As used in this text, **urbanism** refers to the condition in which the settlement system in a region meets the following conditions:

— some settlements are relatively large;
— the larger settlements have internal diversity, with rich and poor neighborhoods, commercial districts, and perhaps other zones; and
— the larger settlements serve as **central places**, places where people from surrounding communities go to procure goods and services unavailable in smaller settlements.

This definition, although more complex than some, emphasizes what is really important about urbanism. It is not merely the size of a settlement that matters, but what its relationship is to the entire region. The fact that Ur, the capital of ancient Sumeria, had an estimated population of more than 100,000 persons in 2200 B.C. is impressive, but the real significance of Ur is that it served

[1] *pochteca:* pohch TEH kuh

FIGURE 3.6 *Present-Day Teotihuacán, from the Air.* *The ancient Mexican city of Teotihuacán, one of the world's largest at its height in A.D. 700, had all the internal complexity of a modern city. Its central precinct was the most exclusive, with massive temples and palaces; nearby was a neighborhood of elite housing boasting courtyards and even fountains; farther away were industrial districts, warehouse districts, low-class neighborhoods, and slums. There were ethnic neighborhoods, too, such as "the Oaxaca barrio," where Oaxacan immigrants lived, practicing their religion and customs.* A. Moldvay/NGS Image Collection.

as an administrative, commercial, and religious center that controlled a vast area of what is now Iraq, with palaces for the rulers, great storehouses for grain, temples for worship, and craft centers for the manufacture of goods used over all of the Sumerian civilization.

Typically, **urbanization** (the development of cities) is a relatively rapid process. For example, at the ancient city of Teotihuacán[2] in central Mexico, the estimated population of 2,000 persons in 500 B.C. remained nearly constant until about 200 B.C. At that time, it swelled rapidly to 25,000 by 100 B.C., more than tenfold in a century; in the following 500 years, population increased another eightfold to nearly 200,000 by A.D. 400. This incredible rate of growth cannot be explained by the usual mechanism of **intrinsic growth**, the increase in popula-

tion as a result of families' having more than two children who survive to adulthood and become parents. To achieve this magnitude of population increase from intrinsic growth would require that every family more than double its size each generation, something that never has happened in recorded history. Instead, the growth of Teotihuacán must be attributed to the migration of people from the countryside into the city; indeed, during this period of intense growth at Teotihuacán, surrounding villages went into a population decline.

For many people, moving to the city meant abandoning their traditional kinship ties and support systems. Indeed, many left behind their families or disrupted their kin relationships, leaving themselves vulnerable to disaster with limited means of emergency help. Newly immigrated urbanites often found themselves among

[2] **Teotihuacán:** tay oh tee hwah KAHN

strangers, rather than among supportive family members who could help them through a lean time.

Why did country people wish to go to the city to live? Probably for reasons that are starkly similar to those of today. Life in the countryside was known to be hard, perhaps dull; for some people, rural farming had led to debt and even to loss of their land. The city, in contrast, was a vibrant place, full of good-paying jobs, excitement, and opportunities, especially in commercial and service occupations. Village farmers moving to Teotihuacán (or Ur or any other city) probably had visions of an improved life, perhaps a better job, and probably a higher standard of living. The fact that many were disappointed and found themselves trapped in the ancient equivalent of slums appears to have had little effect on the flood of immigrants into cities. The very factors at the heart of our definition of urbanism—the diversity of occupations, goods, and services in a city—probably have been directly responsible for the staggering growth of ancient and modern cities.

Although cities often develop as commercial centers, they usually gain other functions as well. State governments typically find them very handy as central places where administrative power can be concentrated, and religions usually find cities appropriate places to house their central hierarchies.

THE SECONDARY ELEMENTS OF CIVILIZATION

Although the six core elements discussed in the preceding section define civilization, many other elements often are present in civilization and are intimately linked to the core. Certain of these elements, called "secondary elements" in this text, are present in every civilization, but which ones are present will vary from case to case; relatively few civilizations will possess all the secondary elements.

There will be some disagreement among scholars about which elements belong in the set of secondary elements, but the following clearly are important:

— a developed transportation system;

— writing;

— standards of measurement (including currency);

— a formal legal system;

— a great art style;

— monumental architecture;

— mathematics;

— sophisticated metallurgy; and

— astronomy.

Developed Transportation System

The earliest human beings walked along trails blazed by animals, carrying their goods on their backs or in their hands. This mode of transportation proved adequate for millennia, and it is still important in many places. Civilizations, however, often have made improvements to facilitate the movement of people and goods. Without such transportation improvements, a civilization might experience difficulty moving troops to establish internal order or repel intrusion, moving commodities that were produced in one area for use elsewhere, or moving vital diplomatic information rapidly.

Many improvements have been in terms of vehicles. The development of boats is lost in prehistory, but early agriculturalists clearly used them. The ongoing technical improvement of boats has resulted in faster, more manageable, more stable, and larger vessels.

Much later than boats, wheeled vehicles were developed in Eurasia and Africa. The earliest evidence for such vehicles comes from the ox-drawn wagons of Sumeria and the later horse-drawn war chariots; human beings have drawn carts at most periods, too. In the Americas, the wheel was known in some areas but never was used for vehicles, and human or pack-animal labor was used for transportation.

In a sense, the animals that pulled vehicles were developed by human invention, because they were domesticated animals, modified from their wild forms by selective breeding. Although strength and stamina clearly were important considerations, docility must have been primary, especially in Africa and Eurasia, where many of the wild progenitors of draft animals were vicious and dangerous beasts. In the Americas, only a single draft animal was developed, the llama of Peru, and that was used for carrying bundles but never for drawing vehicles.

FIGURE 3.7 *Wheeled Toy from Ancient Mexico.*
This pottery toy from Veracruz is nearly 3,000 years old and still rolls on its tiny, axled wheels. While people in the Americas were well aware of how a wheel could work—as this toy shows—they chose not to utilize it. This choice may reflect the dense rain forests and steep mountains in which the earliest American civilizations developed, as well as the shortage of animals that could be domesticated for pulling carts. © Justin Kerr 1987.

A second approach to improving transportation is to improve the route over which a vehicle passes. Graded and paved roads, bridges, and causeways through wetlands can vastly improve the speed and ease with which goods and personnel can be moved. The Roman road system is particularly well known and admired, but the Incan, Chinese, and Persian road systems were equally sophisticated and perhaps more impressive because of the rugged nature of the lands traversed.

A final way to attack the problems of land transportation is through improved organization. The Inca, for example, employed a system of runners (*chaski*) and support facilities that permitted a message or light parcel to cross the empire rapidly. Each *chaski* would run only a few miles to the next way station, where his message or parcel would be passed on to the next *chaski*, covering hundreds of miles in just a few days.

Writing

The idea that spoken language could be converted into a written form and preserved is such a revolutionary idea that it took true genius to conceive of it. Some forms of writing are **alphabetic**, using a limited number of symbols to represent the component sounds of a language. English is alphabetic and uses just twenty-six letters (and a few punctuation marks) to produce all of its messages. In contrast, some other forms of writing are **ideographic**, wherein each symbol represents an idea, irrespective of the pronunciation of the spoken word. (Chinese and Mayan writing systems are largely ideographic, although each also incorporates some phonetic [pronunciation-based] elements.) Ideographic writing has many more symbols than alphabetic writing, often thousands of characters.

Writing has developed in many places around the world. In many cases, a preexisting written language that was developed in another place served as a model for imitation, but it appears that writing developed independently in at least three places in antiquity. Curiously, the motivations behind the development of writing in each of these places seem to have been different.

The earliest system of writing developed in Sumeria around 4500 B.C. This system apparently began as an ideographic system that soon was modified into **cuneiform**,[3] an ideographic system with some alphabetic (or syllabic) elements that is discussed in more depth in Chapter 4. It was developed primarily to keep track of business accounts among the traders of Sumeria.

Independently, writing developed in the Shang Dynasty of China around 1500 B.C. This writing was largely phonetic, though there also are pictographic (picture-writing) and ideographic elements. Our earliest evidence of this writing suggests that it developed as a medium for religious-divinatory expression. (Chinese writing is discussed further in Chapter 5.)

Again independently, the Maya of the third century and their immediate predecessors in eastern Mexico developed a system of glyphic writing that is neither alphabetic nor ideographic but a mixture of the two. Mayan writing's primary purpose was to glorify rulers and nobles on monuments dedicated to them, and it is discussed further in Chapter 6.

[3] **cuneiform:** koo NAY ih form

FIGURE 3.8 *Three Babylonian Recipes. Writing permits a society to commit its knowledge and ideas to a durable medium, passing it along to the future. This clay tablet from Babylon in Mesopotamia is in the Akkadian language, recorded with cuneiform script. It gives recipes for goat stew, bird stew, and braised turnips. All were heavily seasoned with leeks and onions.* Yale Babylonian Collection.

Once writing developed, regardless of the initial function, it proved useful for a wide spectrum of purposes. Curiously, some civilizations never developed writing, notably those of Peru.

Standards of Measurement

A traditional builder can estimate lengths by eye, just as a barter system may work perfectly well using no more sophisticated or standardized measure than "some." But a larger-scale society needs a more accurate and standardized system of weights and measures. An Aztec tax levy required a particular amount of corn or cotton, just as a Babylonian merchant expected to get a consistent amount of wheat for his *shekel*. Further, monumental architecture demands standardized units of measure, both for planning and construction.

Only disaster could have followed if several beam-cutters for a Chinese temple had measured the lengths of their beams in multiples of their own forearms or, worse yet, if they simply had guessed at length.

Most civilizations used standardized units of measure for length and volume, and many had standardized units of weight. Less common were units of time, the best known of which is the hour, ultimately based on Sumerian astronomy (filtered through Egypt) and the sundial.

A special case is the standardized unit of currency. Money usually derives its value from one of two characteristics: its natural rarity or the labor that goes into its production. The use of gold as a standard for currency in recent times and the use of cowrie shells as money in interior Africa (far from the ocean where the mollusk lives) are examples of rarity-based money. Examples of labor-based currency are the shell beads (*wampum*) used by the Iroquois and Algonquian[4] Indians of northeastern North America; the shells occurred locally in great abundance, but the value of *wampum* came from the great deal of work required to laboriously grind out the beads. Early civilizations typically used rarity-based currency, particularly metals. Later, however, they frequently switched to labor-based currency, possibly to permit the government to produce greater quantities of money to cover its debt.

Formal Legal System

Small-scale societies display a high degree of shared values and attitudes about what constitutes proper behavior and what should be done about departures from that standard. Larger-scale societies, on the other hand, have more diversity of opinion and greater possibilities of avoiding punishment for a transgression, because one can simply move to another community where no one knows of the wrongdoing. Under these circumstances, a formal legal system with a code of laws and sometimes with police and judges to enforce them emerges.

The most famous and one of the earlier of these formal legal systems was established by Hammurabi[5] of Babylonia in the eighteenth century B.C. Hammurabi actually revised the codes of

[4] **Algonquian:** al GOHN kee uhn
[5] **Hammurabi:** hawm oo RAH bee

Libit-Ishtar, Ibi-Sin, and Ur-Nammu, all earlier judges of Sumeria, making two contributions. First, he adapted the codes for the three-tiered social system of Babylonia, which differed from that of Sumeria, which had only two legal classes. Second, unlike earlier local codes, Hammurabi's code served as a model for judges throughout Babylonia. (See "In Their Own Words" in Chapter 4 for more discussion.)

Formal legal systems appear to never have been in force in the earliest civilizations of a region. Rather, they seem to have developed several centuries later, after the civilization has had sufficient time to identify its problems.

Great Art Style

The term **great art style** refers to an art style that occurs over a broad area and is the dominant style, often the only style other than family-based folk art. A great art style typically—though not always—occurs in public settings and is associated with a state government and state religion. Despite the way it sounds, the term conveys no value judgment of what is or is not "great" art.

A great art style can help unify a civilization by providing a commonality throughout the geographical extent of the civilization. At the same time, its grandeur often serves to enhance the prestige of the rulers, and its usual focus on religious and dynastic themes aids in legitimizing the government and its leaders.

In some cases, great art styles are very easy to appreciate, as with the socialist-realist poster art associated with the Russian Revolution. These images were realistic and powerful, evoking the strength and importance of workers. Such art styles provide a rallying point for sympathies. In contrast, some great art styles are obscure and mysterious to all but the initiated elite. An example of this latter type of great art style is the Chavín[6] style of Peru, around 1200 to 100 B.C., in which figures are formed of out-of-place body parts and intertwine with one another in a complex mass that is very difficult to interpret. This difficulty probably made the priests especially important, because only they were privy to the arcane truths and events represented by the art.

Some civilizations had no great art style, as was the case with the Inca and, according to some

[6] **Chavín:** chah VEEN

scholars, the Roman Empire. These civilizations instead incorporated aspects of the styles of neighbors and conquered peoples into an eclectic and composite—though sometimes disharmonious—style.

Monumental Architecture

Monumental architecture simply refers to large and impressive buildings and similar structures erected at public expense. Although the concept is simple, the execution is not. The production of monumental architecture demands many technical and organizational skills usually available only in civilizations, and the costs for labor and materials could be extravagant and beyond the means of less complex societies.

Unlike simpler architecture that can be planned without extensive engineering skills, monumental architecture requires professional planning. The mechanical stresses involved in large buildings can be quite extreme, and small deviations from a plan can result in major problems for a large structure, sometimes affecting its stability.

No lesser a logistical problem is organizing the workforce. Assuming that sufficient funds have been allocated, the task of assembling and maintaining a workforce sufficient to build a monumental structure is daunting. Every worker must be fed; if workers are paid, someone must do the calculating of wages and distribution of pay; housing for the workers must be established; various other needs must be met, sometimes including such items as clothing, medical care, female companionship for male workers, and spiritual comfort. Organizing such an effort and keeping it organized over a period of years is no small task and requires a large force of administrators, accountants, quartermasters, and the like.

The materials for monumental architecture often were special, selected for their unusual appearance or their special structural characteristics. For example, many polished limestone blocks that faced the great pyramids of Egypt came from the Libyan and Arabian hills, hundreds of miles distant, because suitably beautiful stone was not available locally. The colossal stone heads of the Olmecs of eastern Mexico were rafted and hauled over 100 miles through jungle in order to provide a sufficiently hard stone for the preparation of huge portraits of the Olmec rulers.

FIGURE 3.9 *The Bayon. Eight hundred years ago, the Khmer civilization flourished in what is now Cambodia. To proclaim the grandeur of their cities and their deities, Khmer rulers built massive temples, some so large that they are termed "temple-mountains." The one shown here, the Bayon, has fifty-four towers and a central spire, all rising majestically from the jungle. Such monumental architecture enhances the stature of a society, its rulers, and its deities.* Wilbur E. Garrett/NGS Image Collection.

Monumental architecture can serve many purposes. The pyramids of Egypt were primarily monuments to and resting places for dead royalty. In contrast, the Mayan pyramids of eastern Mexico, Guatemala, Belize, Honduras, and El Salvador were primarily raised platforms to support temples for worship. The massive temples that flanked the main streets of Teotihuacán were used for religious ceremonies, but many scholars feel that their main function was to impress visiting traders.

But these and other examples of monumental architecture had a common underlying purpose: They aggrandized the deities, the rulers who represented them, and the civilizations over which they ruled. As such, they were impressive reminders to the commoners, to internal political rivals, and to visiting representatives of foreign powers. They served as tangible proofs of the legitimacy of the state and its associated religion, as well as its awesome power.

Although monumental architecture was erected with public funds, the edifices were not necessarily open to the public. Many monuments were visited only by a select few of the elite classes. Mayan temples and their counterparts at Teotihuacán were forbidden to the commoners, and some were accessible only to the highest of the nobility and priestly classes. Indeed, massive Mayan temples that might have taken hundreds or thousands of workers many years to complete were designed for use only by the favored few, as evidenced by interior spaces that could accommodate no more than ten or twenty people at a time.

Mathematics

Many small-scale societies have had very limited mathematics, often merely counting of the one-two-three-many variety. Civilizations, on the other hand, have greater need for a developed mathe-

PATHS TO THE PAST

Building an Egyptian Pyramid

Egyptian pyramids are magnificent examples of monumental architecture, longstanding symbols of ancient engineering skills. They served as memorials to—and often burial places for—pharaohs and a few other important officials. These monuments were huge: The Great Pyramid is 754 feet along each side and 481 feet high, covering an area of 13.1 acres. All the pyramids had the familiar shape of four triangular sides tilted together to form a point at the top, and many had internal chambers and passages, mostly for the storage of treasures or of the bodies of the deceased. These are impressive monuments, but how difficult were they to build? Careful analysis of ancient Egyptian documents and artifacts, coupled with experimentation by archaeologists, has provided answers.

There are six basic steps to building an Egyptian pyramid. First, because such a massive structure requires bedrock to rest upon, workers—including slaves, hired laborers, and soldiers—had to remove the sand and loose rock on the surface and level the bedrock to receive the pyramid foundation. This, as well as other Egyptian stoneworking, was accomplished primarily with stone hammers, copper chisels, and a great deal of labor.

Second, the area had to be surveyed so that the pyramid could be laid out facing the cardinal points (north, south, east, and west), with equal sides. The surveying tools for this were known from canal building and consisted primarily of the *merkhet* (a bar and plumb line used for measuring the angle of a star or the sun above the horizon), the *bay* (a sighting rod with a notch in its top), and a calibrated measuring cord (for measuring distances). With these three instruments, some ingenuity, and some knowledge of arithmetic and elementary geometry, a surveyor could achieve the accuracy shown in the positioning and construction of the pyramids.

Third, while the first two steps were going on, crews were quarrying the limestone for construction and transporting it to the construction site. The transportation was primarily via the Nile River, which, during flood, was within a mile of the pyramid sites. After that, the stones were hauled along a temporary construction road by human labor, using sledges (heavy platforms with runners like those on modern sleds), ropes, perhaps rollers (wooden poles over which blocks were pulled), and a great deal of labor. Experiments have shown that these techniques are fully workable.

Fourth, at the site itself, the stones were cut into shape and smoothed. This was done primarily with copper chisels and stone hammers, although sand abrasives probably were used sometimes. Although some early scholars speculated that ancient Egypt had some "lost secret" for tempering copper to make harder tools, there is neither evidence nor need for this explanation: Experiments with copper tools have shown them equal to the task of working the soft limestone used for the pyramids.

Fifth, the shaped stones had to be raised to their proper positions and placed there. Fanciful ideas have been advanced of machines ranging from the quaint (a catapultlike wooden frame that would have swung a block into place) to the bizarre (spacecraft assisting the ancient Egyptians for reasons that presumably were known only to the space aliens). More likely, the blocks were hauled up earthen ramps that were laboriously built to where the stones were needed, then removed. Both the huge interior blocks and the smaller exterior blocks were apparently brought to their places in this way.

Sixth and finally, the pyramids may have been painted. Although we are accustomed to thinking of the pyramids as the gleaming white of their limestone facings, several analyses of materials on their surfaces have suggested the possibility that they may have been painted brightly as a final step. Scaffolds would have supported painters on the sloping and slippery pyramid faces.

How difficult was it to build an Egyptian pyramid? The principles and skills involved were not incredibly complex, at least in terms of modern standards, and we certainly need not resort to "lost secrets of the ancients" or to space aliens to understand how the construction took place. On the other hand, the scale of the task was daunting, and the construction was carried out within fine tolerances, as with the less than one-half-inch variation for the basal level of the Great Pyramid. We must admire the ancient builders who brought together skills, planning, organization, and labor to produce some of the greatest monuments of their day.

matics. Both commercial trade and tax collection for a state government require arithmetic as a means of calculating and recording figures. Monumental architecture demands enough sophistication in geometry and arithmetic to calculate angles and lengths and to accurately estimate amounts of materials needed. Astronomy requires skills in analyzing number series. For the most part, early civilizations focused on mathematical procedures that facilitated practical tasks, rather than on theoretical concerns. We have little idea of how sophisticated mathematics was in preliterate civilizations or in civilizations whose writing has not been deciphered, although the presence of monumental architecture may provide a clue that it was moderately well developed.

Sophisticated Metallurgy

The set of skills, practices, and knowledge that relate to the working of metals collectively is known as **metallurgy**. Metals have been in use in various parts of the world for the past 10,000 years, but early usage was based on very simple principles and limited understanding. For example, the most common early metal use consisted of taking native copper (copper found in pure form) and hammering it into shape without the use of heat. Although this practice produced a workable tool or attractive ornament, it was limited by the rarity of native metals, the restriction to soft metals like copper, the relative crudeness of the product, and the impossibility of mass production.

The sophisticated metallurgy of many civilizations goes beyond these simple practices. More advanced techniques include smelting (the rendering of ores to derive pure metals from compounds), alloying (the mixing of different metals to produce a metal with characteristics different from those of any of its components), casting (producing shaped objects by melting metal and pouring it into a mold, where it hardens), plating (the production of a thin layer of one metal on another, usually a precious metal on a less valuable one), annealing (heating and gradually cooling a metal to reduce internal stresses and make it harder and more durable), and other techniques.

In Europe, Africa, and Asia, metallurgy was considerably more developed than in the Americas. Much of the impetus for this greater development was military. The development of bronze in

what is now Turkey around 3000 B.C. was a turning point in Eurasian metallurgy. Bronze, an alloy of copper and tin, was harder than other available materials and could be formed easily into weaponry, giving its possessors an immediate edge over their enemies. From this time, Eurasian metallurgy focused largely on improving weapons, leading finally to iron and steel.

In the Americas, the range of known metallurgical techniques restricted artisans to using relatively soft metals, such as gold, silver, and copper. As a result, ornaments were the focus of metallurgical work, and metal tools had only limited importance in technology.

Astronomy

Early civilizations saw astronomy very differently from modern ones. Although modern scholars conceive of astronomy as a theoretical science, their earlier counterparts saw it as a craft that supported practical activities with major impacts on daily life. One of astronomy's greatest impacts in ancient civilizations was in terms of maintaining the calendar, a critical task for scheduling religious rituals. The other major impact was in the practice of **astrology**, the prediction of the future on the basis of the alignments of stars and planets. Both ritual scheduling and astrological prediction were important activities in most ancient civilizations.

Before the development of civilizations, small-scale societies used simple astronomy, largely to predict a few simple yearly events. Foremost among these were the equinoxes (when sunlight and darkness are of equal duration) and the solstices (the days with the shortest and longest duration of daylight). These "four corners" of the solar year mark the beginnings of the four seasons in the modern Western calendar, and their importance to changing seasons was not lost on other peoples.

But the astronomy of early civilizations went much further. Ancient Egyptians, basing their reasoning on the dates when the star Sirius rose above the horizon, realized that leap years were needed to adjust the calendar to account for the fractional part of a day exceeding 365 days per year. Zhou[7] Dynasty astronomers in China predicted solar eclipses, although not flawlessly, as shown by a document from 1311 B.C. that notes one such

[7] **Zhou:** JOH

FIGURE 3.10 *Stonehenge.* *Built on a grassy plain in southern England, Stonehenge was begun around 2800 B.C. and was finished by 1500 B.C. The structure was apparently a combination of temple for religious rituals and astronomical observatory for viewing (and perhaps predicting) celestial events. Lines of sight along stones' edges produce shadows and light shafts that shift with the seasons, permitting the recognition of the vernal equinox and other potentially significant astronomical events. These in turn triggered seasonal rituals and astrological predictions.* Christopher Chippindale.

eclipse occurring "on the wrong day." Assyrian astronomers compiled a list of rising times for the planet Venus and apparently could predict future risings. Further, ancient astronomers could apply some of their knowledge to building, as at Chichen Itzá,[8] a Mayan city in Mexico. There, at the spring and autumn equinoxes, the shadow of a railing falls on a stairway of a temple to form the undulating body of a snake that terminates at the bottom of the stairway with a sculpture of a snake's head.

These are impressive successes of ancient astronomers, but we should not ascribe more knowledge to them than is warranted. Much of their knowledge was gained by relentless observation and record keeping, rather than by scientific understanding. Babylonian astronomers had some knowledge of lunar eclipses and their recurrence, but they attributed them to the moon deity's doing battle with demons, not to the geometrical and physical explanations of modern science. Given the calendrical and astrological purposes of early astronomy, scientific explanation of the modern sort simply was irrelevant.

INTERRELATIONSHIPS OF THE ELEMENTS OF CIVILIZATION

As no doubt has been obvious in the reading of this chapter, the elements that characterize civilization are not independent of one another. Rather, they are intimately related to one another, with the development of one leading to the development of others. It is easy to create various models of how these elements interrelate, although there is no guarantee that such a plausible picture will be accurate.

One possible model for interrelating the elements of civilization begins with population pressures that lead to the agricultural dependence that kicks off the process. The increased food supply permits population increase, which in turn encourages urbanism and long-distance trade. Urbanism and trade lead to increased occupational specialization and class stratification; some scholars believe that it also leads directly to a state

[8] **Chichen Itzá:** CHEE chehn eet ZAH

government. The establishment of the state is followed by a state religion, a great art style, and a legal code; state support, in combination with occupational specialization, leads to monumental architecture, developed transportation systems, sophisticated metallurgy, mathematics, and astronomy. Writing develops out of some combination of occupational specialization, trade, and the aggrandizing of rulers.

Probably the best explanations of the development of civilization recognize that there are many processes taking place simultaneously and that there is no simple sequence of events or set of causes and effects. The best explanations also probably are directed toward specific cases, rather than toward discovering any single cause of the development of civilization in all places. The differences among Peru and China and Egypt and India are so great that no recognizable pattern may characterize them all.

UTILITY OF THE CONCEPT OF CIVILIZATION

The discussion earlier in this chapter noted that some scholars find the civilization concept so flawed that they reject it outright. Now that we have discussed the concept at some length, is it worth using?

We believe that it is, though it carries some liabilities. The concept of civilization grew out of a kind of judgmental and ethnocentric scholarship that few scholars of today would endorse. We hope history and related disciplines have matured to a stage where the term no longer will be used with these implications.

But the concept emphasizes a basic distinction that is useful in the study of the human past: There are fundamental differences between simple, small-scale societies and complex, large-scale societies. Those relatively complex societies, which we call "civilizations," have a different and faster pace of development and change; they are stimulated by economic and political competition; and a greater diversity of events and processes shapes their futures. The smaller-scale societies, in contrast, have a slower pace of change; they have fewer and less complicated factions; and the lifestyles and life histories of their members are more alike. All of these factors distinguish civilizations from other human societies.

We believe these differences to be basic and important, but the line between civilized and noncivilized societies should not be drawn too starkly. In reality, societies lie along a continuum of complexity. At one end of the continuum lie the small-scale, less complex societies, and at the other end lie the highly complex ones. Although there will be no controversies regarding the societies near the ends, some societies in the middle may pose difficulties in classification. The wise student will remember that it matters little how one categorizes those borderline cases; what really matters is an understanding of how that society was organized and developed. After all, the concept of civilization was invented by human beings as a convenience to help understand human diversity; it has no independent existence, and it is meaningless to search for the answer to whether or not a society is "truly" a civilization.

SUMMARY

1. Cultural evolution is the general pattern of change that has occurred over long periods of time in most places throughout the world, where societies become more complex, particularly in terms of different roles for their members and advanced knowledge and skills.

2. The underlying cause of most cultural evolution probably is population growth, which leads to agriculture, which in turn leads to a wide variety of developments.

3. One model of stages of cultural evolution defines bands (hunter-gatherers with little leadership), tribes (agriculturalists with leadership by example), chiefdoms (agriculturalists with coercive leadership), and civilization.

4. Civilization is defined by six core elements: agricultural dependence, occupational specialization, class stratification, state government, long-distance trade, and urbanism. Secondary elements are common but not universal among civiliza-

tions: a developed transportation system, writing, standardized measurement, a formal legal system, a great art style, monumental architecture, mathematics, sophisticated metallurgy, and astronomy.

5. The elements that characterize civilization are intimately interrelated, with one element encouraging the development of others.

6. Societies that are not civilizations are simply smaller-scale societies that have been able to survive successfully without resorting to the more complex strategies of civilizations, many of which place restrictions on their citizenry.

SUGGESTED READINGS

Lamberg-Karlovsky, C. C., and Jeremy A. Sabloff. *Ancient Civilizations: The Near East and Mesoamerica*. Second edition. Prospect Heights, Ill.: Waveland Press, 1995. An accessible comparison of the origins of civilization in Southwest Asia and Mesoamerica.

Renfrew, Colin. *Approaches to Social Archaeology*. Edinburgh, Scot.: Edinburgh University Press, 1984. An influential discussion of theories and models of cultural evolution.

Sabloff, Jeremy A., and C. C. Lamberg-Karlovsky, eds. *Ancient Civilization and Trade*. Albuquerque: University of New Mexico Press, 1975. A collection of classic scholarly articles on the role of trade in civilization.

Tainter, Joseph A. *The Collapse of Complex Societies*. Cambridge, Eng.: Cambridge University Press, 1988. A scholarly examination of the processes that bring about the collapse of civilizations, drawing on different world examples.

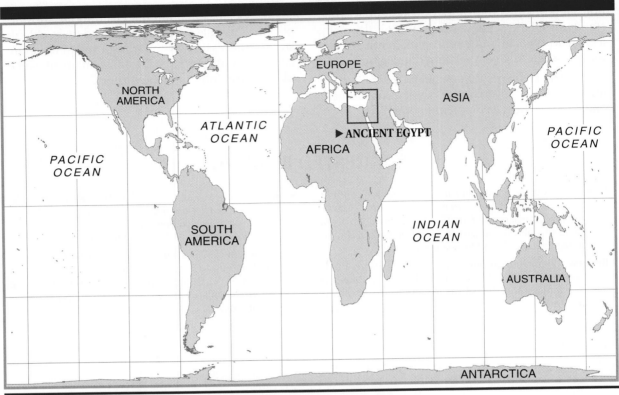

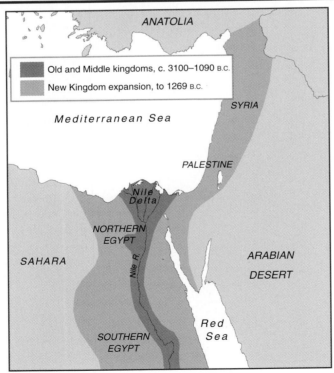

Old and Middle kingdoms, c. 3100–1090 B.C.

New Kingdom expansion, to 1269 B.C.

▶ **ANCIENT EGYPT**

Southwest Asia, Egypt, and the Eastern Mediterranean

around 3500–331 B.C.

The young man stood up, rubbed his aching lower back with his hands, and kicked at the parched ground. Rain had been scarce, causing river levels to drop and irrigation ditches to dry up. If moisture didn't come soon to the shriveling plants, the entire crop would be dead. He made up his mind to spend the next day traveling with other farmers from his area to the nearby city, where they could pay the priests to offer a special sacrifice to Ishtar, the fertility goddess. He believed that her intervention with Enki, the water god, would appease whatever insult had caused the god to withhold the precious life fluid. Perhaps Enki would allow the water to flow again in the mighty rivers.

Approximately 8,500 years ago, agriculture developed in Southwest Asia and Egypt in the Tigris-Euphrates[1] and Nile river valleys. The turn from a hunter-gatherer society to an agriculturally based society produced the opportunity for the development of civilization, as discussed in Chapter 3. Growth toward urbanization first occurred in the river valley of southern Mesopotamia (roughly modern Iraq and Kuwait) and in Egypt. Some larger urban centers could support extensive long-distance trade, massive building projects, and armies to protect them. Scholars call these centers **city-states** and identify them by the cities' names. Eventually, several city-states negotiated treaties or conquered their neighbors, resulting in the development of kingdoms that placed several cities under central authorities. Several kingdoms divided Mesopotamia, but Egyptian city-states

[1] **Tigris:** TY grihs; **Euphrates:** yoo FRAY teez

67

merged into two large kingdoms (in the north and south). Egyptians eventually moved toward unification, finally encompassing the entire river valley civilization in one large kingdom. Unification was often a fleeting phenomenon in Mesopotamian history; a few kingdoms expanded into **empires** (states that control large areas that incorporate societies culturally different from themselves).

The impact of large-scale agricultural production and the growth of urban centers also influenced labor practices and gender roles. In sedentary agricultural societies, the rate of child-bearing increased to as frequently as possible to ensure that enough surviving children could help with chores and tend fields. Women needed to be engaged in labor compatible with the needs of child rearing; their work had to be relatively safe and easily interruptible, like textile production and food preparation. Men's occupations remained outside the home as farmers, artisans, and merchants, who sometimes traveled long distances to sell their goods; while they were traveling with the caravans, however, their wives sometimes managed their business interests.

The religious practices of ancient peoples in Southwest Asia, Egypt, and the eastern Mediterranean also changed after the development of wide-scale agriculture. They developed formal ritualistic practices to manipulate the actions of nature deities who they believed controlled wind, rain, and agricultural cycles and war deities who defended their cities. Rituals became increasingly complex, necessitating a priestly class to memorize and perform them. In many areas of Southwest Asia, Egypt, and the Mediterranean, new deities were introduced through conquest and migration. When one city conquered another, the subjects often identified the conqueror's deities with existing ones, intertwining the myths until the divinities became indistinguishable.

Scholars call the worship of many deities **polytheism**; in some cities, hundreds of deities were worshiped. The worship of deities residing in natural forces and objects such as wind, groves of trees, and mountains is called **animism**. The practice of attributing to deities such human characteristics as human form or temperament is **anthropomorphism**. Agricultural communities focused their worship on fertility goddesses, while city populations predominantly worshiped male sky gods that were said to afford the city protection and guide warriors in battle.

FIGURE 4.1 *Pazuzu, the Assyrian Wind Demon. Pazuzu's fierce features (the body of a lion, snarling lips, a scorpion's tail, and wings) reflect the fear Mesopotamians had of the violent and destructive winds that came howling through their lands. High winds blew dirt and debris that damaged crops and buildings, causing great human distress and sometimes financial ruin. Mesopotamians believed Pazuzu's countenance to be so menacing that pregnant women wore his image around their necks to scare off demons that might threaten the unborn baby's health.* Louvre © R.M.N.

MESOPOTAMIA: THE LAND BETWEEN THE RIVERS

Mesopotamia contained many city-states with long histories of independence. The city-states included the cities and the surrounding supportive villages and farms, united under a single government. Just like those who lived within the city walls, those who lived several miles away in smaller villages identified with the city—trading there, paying taxes, and attending religious functions. Farmers of the Mesopotamian city of Uruk, for example, lived within the city walls and walked an hour or so to their fields nearby. As the city grew in population and area, from approximately three and a half to ten miles in radius, outlying villages and fields were incorporated to supply the city's needs, and farmers participated in civic affairs.

The climate and unpredictable behavior of the Tigris and Euphrates rivers also figured in everyday life in Mesopotamia. The rivers' headwaters, located in mountainous regions of modern Turkey, swelled in periods of heavy rainfall, causing floods that ravaged irrigation systems and crops downstream. The Tigris, in particular, caused severe damage to buildings and populations, as well as to agriculture. The rivers, not easy to navigate, often hampered trade. Yet the spring floods also left replenishing deposits of nutrients, and people found it practical to cultivate near the rivers and their tributaries. As a result, the periodic devastation had to be endured.

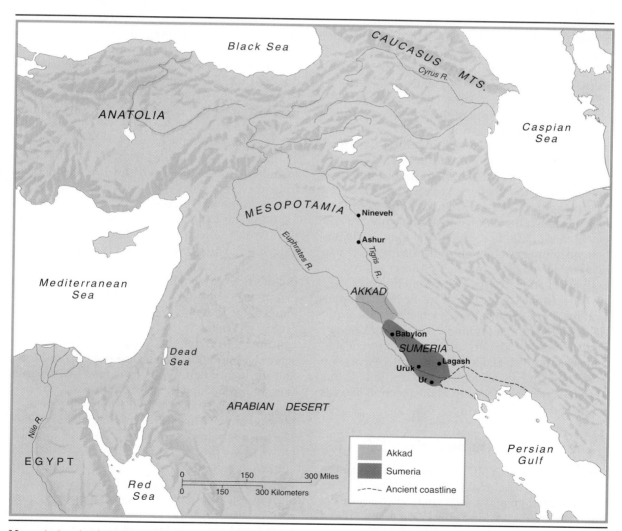

M A P 4 . 1 *Ancient Mesopotamia, around 3500– around 2100* B.C. *The Mesopotamian civilization developed in Sumeria and its culture spread from the Tigris River to the eastern Mediterranean seaboard through conquest first by the Akkadians and then by other empires; Uruk, Ur, and Lagash were three of the first city-states. The flat topography of this area allowed for conquering peoples to move fairly rapidly through the region.*

Although kings are often portrayed in scenes of conquest and triumph, much of the surviving Mesopotamian great art depicts Mesopotamian kings' relationship with their deities. Reliefs on temple walls and in palaces featured mythological scenes. Statues and figurines of deities resided in each household to protect and give favor to the family within. Artisans shaped sacred vessels in gold and silver for priests to perform a variety of complex rituals. Musical instruments were highly decorated and used to perform sacred songs.

As Mesopotamian city-states grew and demand for greater public works increased, efficient political organization became essential. The growth of government, therefore, paralleled urban growth. Initially, cities were ruled by councils, usually composed of wealthy elders. Eventually the role of king developed, particularly because of increased hostilities between cities that encouraged people to look to a strong military leader. The king's authority grew out of three primary responsibilities: military, civic, and religious. The king's military responsibility gave him authority to lead the army against enemies and to defend the city against attack. The king's civic responsibility gave him authority to raise taxes, to care for the people's well-being through public works, and to keep the peace through the enforcement of customary and newly developing law codes. The king's religious responsibility gave him authority as high priest to oversee all religious practices. The king's role as high priest and lawgiver legitimized his rule.

The earliest city-state wars in Mesopotamia resulted from skirmishes over fertile land, water rights, and control of trade routes. The lack of naturally occurring barriers accommodated repeated attacks and raids, resulting in the loss of lives and property; captives became slaves, and the victors invested energy and wealth in the erection of walls for protection.

The Sumerians, around 3500–2350 B.C.

Civilization began in Sumeria, in southern Mesopotamia. Eventually, through long-distance trade, migration, and a series of later conquests of the area by larger kingdoms, Sumerian culture extended far beyond the borders of the Tigris and Euphrates rivers into major parts of Southwest Asia. A study of the Sumerians, then, serves as a good example of Mesopotamian civilization in general.

By 3500 B.C., Sumerian city-states had emerged. Three of the major cities, Uruk, Ur, and Lagash, constructed massive walls for protection. By 3000 B.C., Sumerian cities had an average of several thousand people; in 2700 B.C., Uruk housed around 50,000 people, not including those in its seventy-six satellite villages. The wall around the city measured more than six miles in circumference. The city of Ur had a population of about 30,000 people. A monumental structure called a **ziggurat**, a tiered temple near the center of the city, loomed over the entire area as a reminder of the divine presence and of the city's power. The ziggurat functioned as an administrative, religious, and market center. By 2500 B.C., approximately 500,000 people inhabited Sumeria, the majority of whom lived in cities.

Sumerians were agriculturalists and pastoralists. The fields yielded two annual harvests of wheat and barley (to make into bread, beer, or porridge). Women and children tended small household gardens of onions, leeks, cucumbers, and legumes. Sheep supplied wool for clothing, as well as milk, cheese, and mutton. The diet also included various fish from the rivers and dates from the palm trees that lined irrigation canals. Excess commodities could be traded at market, if anything was left after paying taxes; one Sumerian poet wrote, "You can have a lord, you can have a king, but the man to fear is the tax collector."

The Sumerian long-distance trade network included only neighboring cities at first but expanded eventually to include the Iranian Plateau, the Indus Valley, and the eastern Mediterranean. Traveling by rafts, sailboats, and overland caravans, merchants bartered grain and wool for scarce commodities such as lumber and stone, and for luxury items such as carved ivory combs from India and lapis lazuli from Iran.

Sumerian cities followed the pattern of most Mesopotamian cities in developing their polities. The open terrain of Sumeria left the cities vulnerable to raids and periodic conquests. Originally, council members governed each city-state, but during periods of emergency they elected a specific war leader called a **lugal**, meaning "great man." Because of accelerating hostilities in the region and the people's dissatisfaction with the council, the *lugal* remained in office for increasingly longer periods of time until the position finally became permanent. As his authority solidified, the *lugal*, now a king, gained the right to

FIGURE 4.2 *Ziggurat of Choga Zambil. Located in the southwestern part of modern-day Iran, the site contains structures that date back to around 1250 B.C. Close examination reveals a four-tiered ziggurat as well as the ruins of the city near its base and a portion of the city wall. In some ziggurats, the ground level was used as a market center and storage area for taxes paid in goods. The second level consisted of apartments for officials and meeting rooms, and the third level housed the royal family. The fourth and highest level was the temple area, where sacred rituals were performed. This massive monumental architecture demonstrates a complex government that could raise taxes to support the engineers, stone masons, and laborers needed to complete such a building project.* Georg Gerster/Comstock.

name his successor, usually his son. This was the origin of Mesopotamian **dynastic succession**, a succession of rulers from the same family.

Sumerians developed a bureaucracy to regulate and record the collection and distribution of tax monies and to keep records concerning trade. Scribes, an important part of this bureaucracy, originally came from aristocratic families that could afford to educate their sons. This record keeping spurred the development of cuneiform writing.

The Sumerian pantheon included more than 3,000 deities who had responsibility for every aspect of life, including plows, carts, and the production of beer (of which there were nineteen varieties). Sumerians believed that the deities created humans to be their servants; if humans did not perform their functions properly, the deities would destroy them. Two of the major deities of Mesopotamia were the goddess Ishtar and the god Enki. Through the centuries, Ishtar's myth changed and became associated with various other goddesses. She is primarily identified as a fertility goddess but is also a goddess of love and war. Enki's name in the ancient Sumerian language means "lord of the earth," but he was usually depicted as the god of the ever-precious life source: water. Sumerians fashioned a complex cosmology that viewed the heavenly bodies, air, earth, and water as the most important forces.

The deities required constant consultation and worship; consequently, the temple played a significant role in the life of the city. The priests and priestesses, in addition to performing rituals there, interpreted the deities' desires by reading animal entrails and observing natural phenomena

Figure 4.3 *Cylinder Seal.* *Cylinder seals (left) were an early form of writing in Meso-potamia, most designed with drawings of different commodities or scenes of deities that were then rolled over clay (right) to produce a record of a transaction or of a prayer against illness or calamity. Other seals endorsed such legal documents as contracts or tax records. The cylinder seal could be used over and over again. This seal depicts the Sumerian sun god, rising over a mountain, and the goddess Ishtar, shown with wings. In the center is Enki, the god of wisdom and water.* Courtesy of the Trustees of the British Museum.

for signs. The large tracts of land belonging to the temples supported the priestly class, and priests frequently rented tracts out. A portion of every farmer's harvest was a tax dedicated to the temple. The excess enabled the priests to distribute grain to widows, orphans, and needy families. Payments for special services, such as a private ritual or a visit to a temple prostitute (often a part of fertility rituals), also subsidized the temple economy.

Sumerian society consisted of a three-tiered class stratification: the elite, free subjects, and slaves. The elite included the king, his officials, the royal family, the high priests and priestesses, and the wealthiest landowners and merchants. Many elite estates outside of the urban center could become as large as small cities, with artisan work-shops that produced goods for trade, great fields for food production, and dormitories for the many servants, artisans, and slaves. A typical house of the elite in cities had multiple stories with numer-ous rooms, and the entire structure was white-washed.

The free subjects were farmers, artisans, scribes, and the lesser merchants, priests, and priestesses. For the most part, free subjects lived modestly in small one-story houses in the city or in rented houses on large estates. Clay pottery consti-tuted household crockery for the majority of sub-jects. Some farmers owned small pieces of property that barely supported a family.

People became slaves in various ways. War captives, subjects forced to sell themselves to pay their debts, and those convicted of crimes became slaves. Some men sold wives and children to keep themselves out of debt slavery. As in most ancient forms of slavery, **manumission** (freeing of a slave) occurred frequently. A Sumerian slave could engage in trade and business enterprises, borrow money, and marry a free subject.

Sumerians used cosmetics to beautify them-selves, which may have been a sign of status. Both elite men and women adorned their eyes with paints and used charcoal as an eyeliner. Most elite women and some men painted their faces white and their lips and fingernails red, and men wore highly stylized false beards. Oil was used for cleansing the body, and the body and hair were perfumed.

Clothing in Sumeria consisted of wool wraps for men, who went barefoot and bare-chested. Women wore a fitted dress or drape, with their hair in braids or pulled back with a headband or small hat. Women spun, wove, and sewed the clothing at home. On large estates throughout Mesopotamian history, owners organized servant or slave women into small cloth-manufacturing groups that produced enough cloth to export. Later in Mesopotamian history, different clothing styles spread through long-distance trade. Eventually men abandoned the wrap in favor of woven tunics.

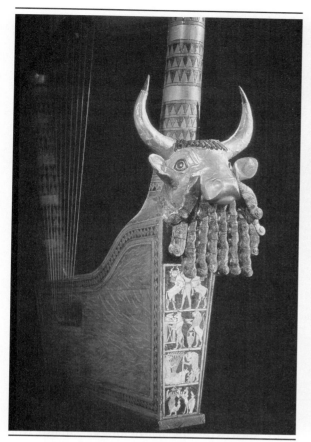

FIGURE 4.4 *Sumerian Lyre.* *This Sumerian lyre depicts a sacred bull, symbolic of strength and fertility. The bull is fashioned from gold, and its beard from lapis lazuli, a deep blue gemstone. Musicians would wash their hands before performing ritual hymns; one such hymn to the Sumerian goddess Ishtar says, "They play songs for [Ishtar] to rejoice the heart."* Boltin Picture Library.

FIGURE 4.5 *Sumerian Priestess.* *This statue of a priestess shows the common practice of lining the eyes and eyebrows with a dark color. The woman's elaborate hairpiece includes a long woolen covering, typically worn by women of the nobility. She also wears a traditional woolen wrap, a skirtlike garment that was used by both sexes.* Courtesy of the National Museum, Damascus.

Women participated in the economies of Sumerian cities, although in limited ways. They could own property (but most land remained in the control of men, because property generally passed from father to son). In some cases women controlled the making of cloth and sent it with their merchant husbands to supplement the family income. There are later records of Mesopotamian women demanding that their husbands send them the money their cloth brought at market. Women also engaged in other businesses and exclusively produced the most popular drink, beer.

Gender roles became increasingly fixed as the civilization developed. Women's responsibilities remained primarily in the household; the majority of women spent hours gardening, weaving, or grinding on stone grinders. Specialization of labor led to mass production by male workers. Male artisans produced pottery, jewelry, and various wood products. Other male occupations included smithing, which produced bronze castings, and construction, which erected the first arches out of wedge-shaped bricks.

Formal legal codes were developed not only to assist in controlling crime and establishing order but also to clarify family relationships and property rights. A husband (with support from his family) paid a bride-price to the father of the bride. A man who broke his engagement forfeited his bride-price. If the engagement was broken off by the woman, the man received twice the worth of

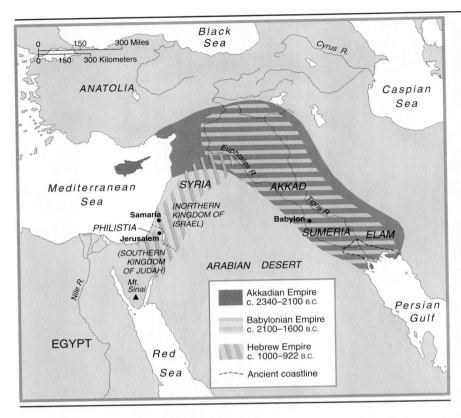

MAP 4.2 *The Akkadian (around 2340–around 2100 B.C.), Babylonian (around 2100–around 1600 B.C.), and Hebrew (around 1000–922 B.C.) Empires.* The Babylonian Empire under King Hammurabi (reign dates 1792–1750 B.C.) stretched from the Persian Gulf to the borders of Syria. The Akkadian Empire encompassed Sumer, Elam, the various territories between the Tigris and Euphrates rivers, Syria, and Southeast Anatolia. The ancient Hebrews expanded this empire to the Euphrates River during the reign of King David, around 1000–961 B.C., but lost that territory by 922 B.C. The remaining lands were broken into two kingdoms: Israel and Judah.

the bride-price. Whether or not they could read it, both the bride and the groom signed a marriage contract that enumerated conditions, such as the duties of each as husband and wife and the division of property in a divorce settlement. Women were subject to their husbands and fathers, and women who bore no children could be divorced.

Sumerian ingenuity also contributed to the advancement of technology. Farmers invented the plow, which initially demanded two people: one to push and one to pull. The adoption of bronze metallurgy revolutionized farming because the stronger, heavier bronze-tipped plows created deeper and straighter furrows in which to plant; this replaced the less-productive scattering technique (tossing the seed onto the ground). Eventually, ox-drawn plows increased productivity, because they could cut deeper into the soil and cultivate more land at a quicker pace. The discovery of the wheel allowed for greater amounts of goods to be transported in long-distance trade, because merchants could move significantly more material by cart than on pack animals. Cuneiform writing preserved myths and legends in early liter-

ature, such as the epic tale of King Gilgamesh, who set off on a journey to learn the secret of eternal life, and the story of the great flood.

Political Conquest, Migration, and Change in Southwest Asia

Sumerians warred among themselves for more than half a millennium until 2350 B.C., when they succumbed to their Akkadian[2] neighbors from central Mesopotamia, led by King Sargon. In a series of sweeping campaigns, the Akkadians united all of Mesopotamia into a large kingdom ruled through Akkadian governors. On several occasions of conquest in global history, the conquerors adopted the culture of those they conquered, and the Akkadians were among the first known to do so. After their adoption of Sumerian culture, the Akkadians spread it beyond southern Mesopotamia into all areas of their political and economic influence. After approximately a cen-

[2] **Akkadian:** ahk KAY dee an

tury, the Akkadians fell, inaugurating a period of upheaval during which the Sumerians regained political control over their cities. The resurgence soon ebbed, however, and Sumeria never regained political power, although its culture lived on in the lives of other Southwest Asian peoples.

FIGURE 4.6 *Hammurabi's Code.* *The top of this seven-foot stela shows King Hammurabi receiving the code of law from Shamash, the powerful sun god, seated on his heavenly throne. The first section of cuneiform writing describes Hammurabi as having been chosen by the deities to lead the peoples of Mesopotamia, thereby giving sacred justification to Hammurabi's conquests and legitimizing his reign. The rest of the stela is inscribed with the entire code of Hammurabi. Stelae like this were placed at major crossroads around the empire so that all people would see Hammurabi's relationship with the deities and accept his law.* Louvre © R.M.N.

It was not until the rise of another people, the Amorites, that a unified Mesopotamia again emerged. The migration of Amorites, out of the Arabian desert area, occurred sometime between 2000 and 1600 B.C. Most of these Amorites ended up in Mesopotamia, and one group established its capital at the ancient city of Babylon, from which they received another name—Babylonians. Another Amorite group may have been the tribal Hebrews, the religious ancestors of modern Jews.

The Babylonians conquered Sumeria during the kingship of Hammurabi (reign dates 1792–1750 B.C.). Under Hammurabi, Babylon became the seat of a mighty kingdom through a network of treaty alliances and opportunistic treaty breaking. Law codes had become increasingly complicated, reflecting the complexity of the growing Mesopotamian civilization. Hammurabi established a new law code that synthesized the various law codes of the peoples he ruled, helping to establish a uniformity of law in the area. He placed multiple large stones with engraved laws at important trade crossroads to attest to the legitimacy of his rule. Hammurabi legitimized his law code through the traditional declaration that law comes from the gods through their representative, the king. The law code reveals much about how the society operated. These ancient Mesopotamian laws form a legacy of jurisprudence that became the foundation of modern legal systems.

The Babylonians also contributed to the study of mathematics; working in arithmetic, geometry, and algebra, they used both base-ten and base-sixty number systems. Their mathematical contributions included calculation close to the true value of pi, the 360° circle, and methods for computing square roots. Today we continue to use their numerical system of twenty-four-hour days and sixty-minute hours. By 1590 B.C., however, the Babylonian kingdom suffered invasion by peoples east of Mesopotamia, reducing its influence and precipitating its decline.

The tribal Hebrews may have moved into Mesopotamia first, then relocated to Palestine, or migrated directly into Palestine. In any event, their culture was heavily influenced by Mesopotamia; their holy writings include a similar flood story to that found in the Sumerian legend of *The Epic of Gilgamesh.* Hebrew tradition professes a westward migration from Sumeria perhaps around 1900 B.C. or as late as 1600 B.C.; scholars are unsure of the

IN THEIR OWN WORDS

The Law Code of Hammurabi

King Hammurabi of Babylonia issued a law code in the eighteenth century B.C. The stone panel on which 282 laws were carved stood nearly eight feet high and shows Hammurabi receiving the laws from a god. The laws reflect the social and economic realities of Mesopotamian life. Many scholars believe that several of the laws demonstrate an attempt to curb abuses and injustices perpetuated by the nobility, whose wealth gave them power. The laws reveal a society divided into social groups, and the code distributes justice by social status. Within the same social level, equal payment is exacted on the pattern of "an eye for an eye and a tooth for a tooth." A payment system is employed for retribution between the social levels. Many abuses existed because victims of crimes could not always prove their cases.

The following are examples of Hammurabi's code. Review each selection, asking yourself what issues are being addressed, what status are the persons involved, and what punishments are given.

1. If a man brings an accusation against another man, charging him with murder, but cannot prove it, the accuser shall be put to death.

4. If he bears [false] witness concerning grain or money, he shall himself bear the penalty imposed in that case.

5. If a judge pronounces a judgment, renders a decision, delivers a verdict duly signed and sealed, and afterward alters his judgment, they shall call that judge to account for the alteration of the judgment . . . and he shall pay twelvefold the penalty in that judgment; and, in the assembly, they shall expel him from his seat of judgment . . .

22. If a man practices robbery and is captured, that man shall be put to death.

23. If the robber is not captured, the man who has been robbed shall, in the presence of god, make an itemized statement of his loss, and the city and the governor . . . shall compensate him for whatever was lost.

55. If a man opens his canal for irrigation and neglects it and the water carries away an adjacent field, he shall pay out grain on the basis of the adjacent field [the field's yield].

129. If the wife of a man is caught lying with another man, they shall bind them and throw them into the water. If the husband of the woman wishes to spare his wife, then the king shall spare his [subject].

142. If a woman hates her husband and says, "You may not possess me" . . . and if she has been careful and without reproach . . . she may take her dowry and go to her father's house.

195. If a son strikes his father, they shall cut off his hand.

196. If a man destroys the eye of another man [of equal status], they shall destroy his eye.

198. If he destroys the eye of a client [one of lesser status] or breaks the bone of a client, he shall pay one *mina* of silver.

199. If he destroys the eye of a man's slave or breaks a bone . . . he shall pay one-half his [the slave's] price [because the slave's worth is diminished].

221–223. If a physician sets a broken bone for a man or cures a sprained tendon, the patient shall [pay] five *shekels* of silver . . . a client pays three *shekels* . . . a slave's owner pays two *shekels*.

229. If a builder builds a house for a man and does not make . . . [it] sound, and the house . . . collapses and causes the death of the owner . . . the builder shall be put to death.

date. Portions of the Hebrew tribes may have moved into Egypt, perhaps as a result of a famine.

Early Hebrew law demonstrates Mesopotamian roots and resembles Hammurabi's law code in particular. These laws appear in the first five books of Hebrew holy writings, the Torah, and are comparable to the code of Hammurabi. Later laws (including the Ten Commandments) were developed after the exodus from Egypt and are less specific, focusing on an ethical code of behavior, such as "You shall not commit murder" and "You shall not steal." These laws, unlike the more specific ones, usually did not spell out particular retributive punishments in the code but were open to interpretation by judges. These later laws, usually called Mosaic law after the lawgiver Moses, do not wholly replace the earlier laws but demonstrate a general evolution toward abstract legal concepts, indicative of what was evolving throughout Southwest Asia.

Hebrew government experienced several stages of development. At first, the Hebrew tribes formed a confederacy loosely organized under tribal judges, who commanded during limited military crises and who provided arbitration in settling intertribal disputes. One of the judges was a woman named Deborah. The Hebrews turned to kingship around 1025 B.C., however, to provide skilled military leadership and to unify the tribes during their wars to conquer Palestine and to defeat the Philistines, who had migrated into the coastal area about 1175 B.C. Slowly, power passed from those chosen to lead by their merit to dynastic succession.

A treaty limiting the neighboring Philistines to the coastal strip, in combination with territorial expansion, brought the Hebrews a large kingdom during the reigns of David (reign dates around 1000–961 B.C.) and Solomon (reign dates 961–922 B.C.). The kingdom stretched from the Euphrates River to the Red Sea and played a significant part in the long-distance trade network of the region. The kingdom split under Solomon's sons into northern and southern kingdoms, both of which were then conquered by expansive empires. The northern kingdom fell in 722 B.C. to the Assyrians, and its population either relocated or assimilated into the invading culture. The southern kingdom succumbed to the New Babylonian Empire in 586 B.C., and many of its population were taken to Babylon as captives to ensure their obedience.

The king, his officials, and the priests were the traditional interpreters of divine will, but another figure in Hebrew society, the **prophet**, claimed great authority. A prophet was a person called by the god—regardless of station—to act as his representative. Prophets were not always accepted, but, nevertheless, they played a significant role in society, acting as a counterbalance to the king's authority and often challenging it.

Hebrews defined their relationship with the deity as a **covenant**: a contractual agreement between their god, Yahweh,[3] and themselves. Increasingly, city-states in Southwest Asia had

[3] **Yahweh:** YAH way

FIGURE 4.7 *The Torah.* *This painting depicts a Hebrew reading the Torah, or Jewish law, which was the expression of the covenant between the Hebrews and their god, Yahweh. Early Jews believed their laws came directly from Yahweh, just as Mesopotamians believed Hammurabi's code came from their deities. The individual books that made up the Torah were written on sheepskin scrolls that were read from right to left as the documents were unrolled. The priests in early Hebrew society were responsible for interpreting the Torah to the people, and when they failed to fulfill their responsibility, prophets denounced them. Over time, the Torah has come to include all of the Jewish sacred writings.* Yale University Art Gallery, Dura-Europos Collection.

chosen one particular god or goddess as its **patron deity**. The people believed this deity lived in the local temple and protected their city. They still practiced polytheism, but the patron deity became dominant locally, and the people believed they were the chosen people of that deity. The Hebrew covenant was similar to other cities' relationships to patron deities, but for the Hebrews "covenant" meant exclusive worship of their god. This attitude eventually developed from a belief of Yahweh's superiority over all other deities to **monotheism**, the belief that only one god exists. The idea of monotheism was not unique to the Hebrews; Egyptians, New Babylonians, and Persians experimented with monotheistic ideas, but only Hebrew practice of it has survived until the present. Hebrew monotheism also became the foundation for two later monotheistic religions, Christianity and Islam.

The covenantal relationship affected the Hebrew worldview. Hebrews believed that time was linear rather than cyclical (which was the prevailing Southwest Asian worldview) and that time would end when Yahweh's purpose for creation had been fulfilled. In addition, the covenant undergirded the egalitarianism inherited from their tribal past that assured the equal treatment of all free male Hebrews under the law. (The society was patriarchal, and law focused on male relationships.) This placed the king in a quite different position from that of kings like Sargon or Hammurabi. In Hammurabi's law code, social status frequently determined punishment or payment, but Hebrew society held every free male, even the king, equally subject to the laws of the covenant.

EGYPT: THE GIFT OF THE NILE

Egypt has been described as the gift of the Nile; the Nile River was the civilization's lifeblood. Its regular, mild flooding aided the development of an effective irrigation system and yielded rich deposits of silt. The Nile flooded between July and October (draining northward from the southern mountains) when spring rains swelled its East African tributaries. The peoples near the river exploited the waters and silt deposits for their agriculture. As farming intensified around 5200 B.C., the stable climate and relative geographical isola-

tion led to a civilization that lasted for thousands of years.

Early Egypt is usually divided by scholars into two major areas, northern and southern. In southern Egypt, natural reservoirs allowed villagers to plant grain and irrigate fields. The high agricultural yield soon led to urbanism, and, at about the same time Mesopotamian city-states were developing (around 3500 B.C.), Egyptian civilization emerged. The cooperative irrigation efforts between local villages led to trade agreements that became the basis of provincial areas called **nomes**, governed by **nomarchs**. Unification of the upper Nile culminated about 3300 B.C., when a single king ruled the entire upper area. In contrast to Mesopotamia, Egypt did not develop a competitive city-state system before unification.

FIGURE 4.8 *Egyptian Tomb Mural. This mural gives an idea of the abundance of foods available in the Nile River Valley. The servants prepare for a banquet that will include fresh grapes, pomegranates, lotus plants, cucumbers, and figs. The banqueters will also feast on eggs, fish, ducks, pigeons, and geese. Depictions of the variety of foods found in Egypt were common, often demonstrating the wealth of the individual in whose tomb the mural appeared.* Erich Lessing/Art Resource, N.Y.

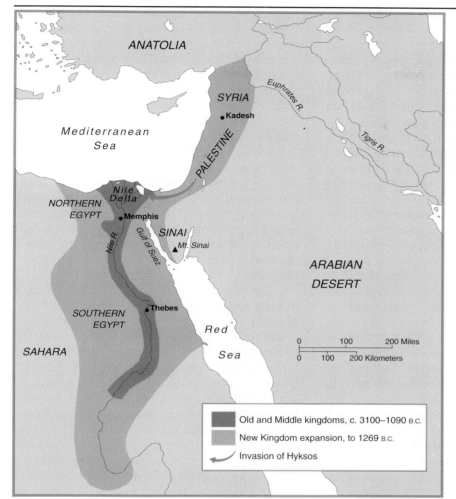

M A P 4 . 3 *Ancient Egypt, around 3100–1085 B.C. Egyptian civilization began along the Nile River Valley around 3500 B.C., eventually uniting into one polity by around 3100 B.C. During the New Kingdom Era, 1570–1085 B.C., Egyptians established an empire, conquering territory as far north as Syria.*

The delta area, or northern Egypt, experienced a slightly different development from that of its neighbor to the south because of different geographical conditions. Less urbanized, the area was marshy and pocked with swamps where crocodiles and hippopotami competed with human beings for limited habitable land. Early inhabitants consisted of herders and their cattle, as well as some persevering farmers.

The Egyptian diet was varied. As in Mesopotamia, grain crops became the mainstay of the Egyptian diet, providing the staples of bread, beer, and porridge. Fruit included grapes, dates, and pomegranates, from which wine could be produced. The Nile teemed with various kinds of fish that Egyptians enjoyed fresh, salted, or dried. Various animals supplied meat and milk products. The table of a wealthy Egyptian might be laden with various vegetables (like lentils, cucumbers, melons, and various gourds) flavored with herbs or honey. In later periods, trade brought in new foods, such as chickpeas. Egyptian agriculture usually produced more food than was needed for the population because of the favorable climatic conditions.

Labor in Egypt followed the seasonal rise and recession of the Nile waters. Between July and September, when the water rose, no work could be done in the fields. Many farmers, criminals working off punishment, and slaves provided labor for construction and maintenance of monumental building projects. When the flood waters crested, only the boundary stones could be seen across the fields. Occasionally they would dislodge, and the moving of a field marker to one's own advantage was considered a serious crime. After the flood waters receded in October, farmers broke up large clods of earth and began plowing with ox-drawn plows. Workers sowed seeds, and sheep and goats followed behind, trampling in the seeds. Poorer farmers received seed and the use of draft animals from the government to ensure a good crop.

During the growing season, October to February, irrigation canals continued to supply farmers with water as the ground dried out. The technology of a *shadouf*[4] (an upright support with a swinging lever to lift something) allowed a bucket to be lowered into the canal. The full bucket was then raised by a weight at the other end of a pole.

In February, the harvest began. Tending the crops was mostly a male occupation, but harvesting included women and children. Men cut wheat and barley with flint-bladed wooden sickles; later, the straw was collected to make mats or bricks. Draft animals carried the grain to a threshing area, and, after cattle loosened the grain by trampling on it, women tossed the material into the air to separate the grain from the chaff. Scribes recorded the amount harvested, and tax collectors took the government's portion to state granaries. Tax rates reflected the level of flooding; a good flood meant high yields. Canal repair occupied the farmer's time after the harvest until just a few weeks before the Nile's flood cycle began again.

Political unification of northern and southern Egypt resulted from the exportation of southern Egypt's political organization into the northern area. The process of unification is shrouded in legend. Traditional Egyptian folklore credits King Menes of southern Egypt with the political consolidation. (King Menes may be a composite of several heroic kings.) Whatever the process, unification came by about 3100 B.C. The Nile flowed northward, allowing its current to carry traders who had designed ships for long-distance trade into the northern area. The winds blew southward, allowing for sails to carry the traders homeward. This ease of movement on the river encouraged travel and trade between the two areas and encouraged unification.

Prior to unification, nomarchs claimed a semi-divine authority that evolved from their great houses resting in proximity to the temple of the patron god of the city. Traditionally the nomarch interpreted the will of the god. As unification occurred, the myths of the gods justified rule by one powerful king-nomarch: **pharaoh**.[5]

As Egypt united politically, so did it unite religiously. Egyptians worshiped over two thousand gods, and many deities and their myths amalgamated. The patron god of southern Egypt was Ra, and the nomarchs claimed to be the sons of Ra. The patron god of northern Egypt was Amon. With unification, the two deities eventually fused into the one high god, Amon-Ra,[6] whose incarnate son was pharaoh, ruler of all Egypt. The pharaoh, now a god-king, differed from Mesopotamian kings who merely represented the city's patron god. Upon the pharaoh's death, he became the ruler of the underworld, and his heir became the new pharaoh.

The rule of law developed differently in Egypt from the way it did in Mesopotamia. In Mesopotamia, law passed from the god to the king or, in the case of the early Hebrews, to a chosen representative. But the Egyptian pharaoh, as god incarnate, embodied all authority; everyone listened when the pharaoh said, "I have spoken it," for the pharaoh's words constituted law. Egyptian law was probably the first egalitarian law, and women could give testimony and bring suits. Unlike early Mesopotamian law, punishments did not reflect social status, and there seem to have been few complaints of bribery or favoritism. In a system similar to that of modern U.S. law, the accused was presumed innocent until proven guilty. The law demanded retribution for theft or property damage several times the original value. Other punishments included beatings, hard labor, exile, and mutilation. Tomb robbing, murder, or treason resulted in a death sentence.

The pharaoh dictated all policy and cared for the Egyptians as if they were children. The pharaoh instructed when to plant and when to harvest according to the Nile flooding pattern. Any disaster might call the pharaoh's legitimacy into question and, thereby, threaten the dynasty. The pharaoh, like the Mesopotamian kings, supervised the irrigation system, the granaries, and the temples. Yet, realistically, the pharaoh could not single-handedly rule the entire kingdom, and

[4] *shadouf*: shah DOOF

[5] **pharaoh**: FAIR oh
[6] **Amon-Ra**: AH muhn ray

so a hierarchy of authority emerged. The farther from the pharaoh's gaze, however, the greater the independence of the bureaucrats.

The chief administrators of the bureaucracy collected taxes, supervised public works, directed military campaigns and a police force, acted as chief justices, and managed artisans for the pharaoh's needs. Duties also included supervising the great royal estates and granaries. All officials in the bureaucracy lived well, often on large estates.

Egypt was divided into provinces run by the local nomarchs, who occasionally challenged centralized control through independent alliances or who emerged as powerful founders of new dynasties after the reign of a weak pharaoh. Among other duties, nomarchs levied and collected taxes assessed for the monumental architectural projects. They worked with the bureaucratic officials (who often carried large sticks as an inducement) sent to represent the pharaoh at tax time. The pharaoh controlled almost all the land and allocated its use to priests and nobility, but he occasionally gave land to temples and important officials. This land usage later developed into freeholding or private ownership that eventually hampered central authority.

The pharaohs were usually male, but a few women ruled during regencies. The pharaoh became divine upon marriage; the wife was a princess or queen and, therefore, a member of the royal family, often a sister or half-sister. In artwork, aristocratic women were often pictured equal in size to their husbands, showing their important social status in the community. A woman could not hold government offices but could take over duties while her husband was away on official business.

Women in Egypt owned property, which they could control and dispose of as they wished, and land often passed through the female line. Men brought a house and two-thirds of a marriage fund to the union. Women contributed a dowry, furnishings, and one-third of the marriage fund. In a divorce, the wife received one-third of the marriage fund and custody of the children (who received the other two-thirds of the fund for support). Her personal property and dowry remained in her control (as did any personal debts).

Gender roles in Egypt were similar to those in Mesopotamia. The most common labor for women consisted of food preparation, spinning,

FIGURE 4.9 *Beer-brewing around 2500 B.C. This woman is in the process of forcing fermented grain through a sieve to make beer. Grain, a mainstay of the Egyptian diet, was used to make bread as well as beer, the most common drink. As in many early societies in Southwest Asia, Egyptian women were solely responsible for baking and brewing.* Egyptian Museum, Cairo.

weaving, and managing the household. Many women had careers, however, in various trades. Flax was grown for the production of linen, and some estates had servant women in workshops producing linen for market. Other trades included nursing, hairdressing, housekeeping, and performing (as musicians, dancers, and acrobats). As in Mesopotamia, brewing was exclusively done by women. Men worked as launderers, mat weavers, artisans, and in out-of-doors tasks like hunting, fishing, mining, building, and farming (the last of these being the most common occupation). The occupation of scribes allowed for the most social

PARALLELS AND DIVERGENCES

The Written Word: Cuneiform and Hieroglyphics

The impact of the written word in human history is immeasurable; writing enabled the preservation of ideas, values, and information beyond the memories and lifespans of individuals. Myths and epic tales were preserved for future populations, political and economic transactions were recorded, and laws were posted. The earliest known experimentation with writing occurred in Sumeria and Egypt. Both of these systems experienced a number of developmental stages, using increasingly more complex and abstract symbols.

Sumerian writing began about 3300 B.C. with pictorial representations primarily associated with financial record keeping by scribes. These first records consisted of numerical representations. As record keeping became more complex, pictographs, symbols for the actions and commodities involved—a shaft of wheat, a bundle of barley—were used. These pictographs were written vertically on clay tablets with sharp reeds.

Sumerian writing underwent several changes. For now-unknown reasons, the pictographs began to be recorded on their sides in about 3000 B.C. Perhaps it was discovered that fewer smudges occurred when writing horizontally from left to right and placing them on their sides somewhat preserved the vertical tradition. Whatever the reason, the pictographs, now less recognizable, became more stylistic. By about 2400 B.C., another significant change occurred: Scribes changed from using sharp reeds to wedge-shaped tips. This new style is called cuneiform by scholars after a Latin word meaning "wedge-shaped." The new cuneiform writing demanded even more abstract symbolism, and therefore the pictograph fell into obscurity.

Egyptian hieroglyphics developed by about 3300 B.C. Egyptian writing, however, took a somewhat different path from that of Sumerian writing. Some hieroglyphs, called **ideographs**, meant entire words or complex ideas, and some hieroglyphs came to represent phonetic sounds. The ideograph and phonetic styles began about 2900 B.C. and developed rather rapidly into a form that used only script. Many of the older hieroglyphs remained in use, so an Egyptian text, therefore, might contain both hieroglyphs and script. Egyptians developed a paperlike substance, perhaps as early as 3100 B.C., from the pulp of the papyrus plant, which grows plentifully along the Nile. The writing instrument was a reed, cut at an angle and dipped into black or red ink.

The uses for writing proliferated throughout Egyptian history. The earliest examples of writing correspond to the more mundane political and economic activities of urban living. Records of tax payments, king lists, and supply inventories head the list. As the use of writing increased, more diverse applications developed in religious and professional life. Individuals wrote prayers and left them in temples, and priests formalized rituals. Inscriptions of stories and myths adorned statues of individuals and deities. It became increasingly common to record and post legal codes, preserve medical records, and produce school texts for mathematical methods and scribal vocabulary. Great deeds of kings and pharaohs were recorded, biographical stories of important nobles written, and the various records of statecraft assembled. In addition, many explanations of the activities of deities and humans served as decoration and captions to beautiful paintings on household walls and tombs.

mobility; peasants who could afford to sent sons to school in hopes that they might find employment with a rich official. One royal scribe encouraged an apprentice to work hard by describing other, less desirable occupations: "The washerman's day is going up, going down. All his limbs are weak . . . the maker of pots is smeared with soil . . . the cobbler mingles with vats. His odor is penetrating. His hands

are red . . . ." Most scribes were men, but some women were court and temple scribes and officials.

The social structure of Egypt consisted of five basic classes. The three elite classes consisted of the royal family, who were officials and supporters at the court, the priests and priestesses, and the wealthy nobility. Scribes, lesser nobility, bureaucratic officials, and artisans filled the fourth class, and peasant farmers the fifth. By about 1570 B.C., two additions completed the social structure: professional soldiers and slaves (a consequence of military expansion). Wealthy nobles lived in beautiful houses with courtyards and many servants. No merchant class existed in the earliest period, because all trade was controlled by the pharaoh. Some social mobility persisted throughout Egyptian history, however.

Egyptian great art styles changed little over the centuries. The most popular painting style depicted daily scenes and myths on tomb and temple walls. These paintings portrayed dinner parties, hunting excursions (a favorite pastime of the wealthy), entertainments, and individuals, and were often accompanied by hieroglyphic texts explaining the art's content. Art also illustrated the complex rituals in texts of *The Book of the Dead*, a guide to the afterlife originally compiled around 2100 B.C. Egyptian artists crafted jewelry made from gold, gems, and glass beads. Other artists created statues, many depicting the pharaoh or Egyptian deities. The pharaohs' tombs were packed with beautiful gold and precious stone artifacts (which helps explain the attraction of tomb robbing over the centuries).

With unification and a relatively stable environment, the Egyptians perceived their existence as secure and harmonious and the idea of change as evil. Of course, change could be observed in Egyptian society, yet the stability of the Nile, unification, and isolation during the earliest centuries led to a worldview that life should be unchanging. Some major changes that did occur can best be recognized by a brief review of the three major eras in Egyptian history.

The Eras of Egypt, around 2700–1090 B.C.

Egypt has a long history of independence, and its noteworthy longevity is attributed to its stability and relative isolation. Scholars now know that thirty-one dynasties existed; they are grouped into four major divisions with intermediate periods during times of social and political upheaval. These divisions help us organize the long chronology of Egyptian history. Little documentary evidence survives from 3100 to around 2700 B.C., at which time records become more prolific and a clearer picture of Egyptian civilization emerges. For this reason, we will focus on the three eras

called the Old Kingdom, the Middle Kingdom, and the New Kingdom, spanning from around the year 2700 B.C. to 1090 B.C.

THE OLD KINGDOM, AROUND 2700–2200 B.C. The most striking phenomenon of the Old Kingdom period, besides unification and the growth of bureaucracy, was the construction of the pyramids. Whereas Mesopotamian ziggurats centered on economic, governmental, and religious activities, the pyramid served only as a tomb for early Egyptian pharaohs. The devotion of this architectural project to the eternal preservation of the remains of a single person demonstrates the power and religious authority of the Old Kingdom pharaohs. Only the pharaoh and those entombed with him to serve him in the underworld enjoyed an afterlife. Scholars estimate that roughly 2.5 million tons of limestone were hewn between 2700 B.C. and about 2600 B.C. to construct the tombs. Pyramid construction was abandoned after the Old Kingdom period in favor of smaller projects, however, because the pharaoh's authority waned under political and economic challenges. By about 2100 B.C., the afterlife became more egalitarian and eventually was extended to all social levels, in part due to the pharaohs' decreasing credibility.

The Old Kingdom ended with a series of devastating droughts that undermined the pharaoh's credibility. A later chronicler wrote, "Everything is filthy: There is no such thing as clean linen these days. The dead are thrown into the river. People abandon the city and live in tents. . . . Pharaoh is kidnapped by the mob." A series of pharaohs, all of whose legitimacy was thrown into doubt because of the continuing drought, took the throne. Twenty years saw twenty pharaohs. In 2200 B.C., a civil war among the nobility left Egypt open to intrusion by outside raiders and subject to local control.

THE MIDDLE KINGDOM, 2050–1800 B.C. Not until 2050 B.C. did a new dynasty regain control from the local nomarchs. The pharaohs of the Middle Kingdom forced recentralization and identified themselves as the saviors of the people. One pharaoh boasted that he gave charity to the destitute and to orphans and elevated the poor in status, which gave him broader political support. This political philosophy by pharaohs resulted in more local public reclamation projects, rather than the great pyramids of the Old Kingdom era.

FIGURE 4.10 *Pyramids.* *This aerial view attests to the immense size of the tomb and temple complex constructed at Giza. Built as tombs in the Old Kingdom Era 2700–2200 B.C., the pyramids stand as monuments to the power of Old Kingdom pharaohs. The ancient Greek historian Herodotus estimated that 100,000 workers labored for over twenty years to complete the tomb of Cheop (left). The tomb of Chephren (center) retains its original limestone cap. The pyramid on the right is the final resting place of Mycerinus; the three small structures to its right are probably the tombs of his immediate family. The Great Sphinx (lower right), with the body of a lion and the head of the pharaoh Chephren, is eighty yards long and twenty-two yards high but is dwarfed by the size of the pyramids. After 2200 B.C., monumental architecture changed to temple construction. This change reflects the religious shift in Egyptian society from a focus on pharaohs and their afterlife to a focus on the general population and its salvation.* John Ross.

The Middle Kingdom period experienced a surge in trade that linked the Nile with Southwest Asian trade routes. One dynasty engaged in commercial activity with Syria, Crete, and Nubia; this created a great network of long-distance trade and cultural exchange. The beginning of a merchant class developed in this period as trade expanded and the pharaoh's absolute control over the economy diminished.

Nomarch rivalries led to another civil war that heralded a second intermediate period. The final blow came with the invasion of the Hyksos[7] from the area of Palestine about 1700 B.C. Little is known

about the Hyksos, who ruled Egypt until around 1570 B.C. They adopted Egyptian culture and political structure, ruling as pharaohs and continuing traditional political organization. The Hyksos also contributed to Egyptian culture, such as bronze technology that improved instruments of war and agriculture. Native Egyptians, however, resented Hyksos overlordship and retaliated with revolts and resistance. Eventually, a new dynasty (the eighteenth) defeated the Hyksos and established an empire in the New Kingdom era.

THE NEW KINGDOM, 1570–1090 B.C. The pharaohs of the eighteenth dynasty engaged in a policy of military expansion. No longer interested in the

[7] **Hyksos:** HIHKS ohs

FIGURE 4.11 *Egyptian Royal Family, Fourteenth Century* B.C. *This limestone carving of Akhenaton and Queen Nefertiti holding their children is in stark contrast to the earlier art of Figure 4.8. The warm, less idealized depiction of the royal family is indicative of the new art style that Akhenaton encouraged. The rays shine down to bring the breath of life from Aton, the new monotheistic deity introduced by Akhenaton. Although the worship of Aton did not survive, the use of realism continued in Egyptian art.* Bildarchiv Preussischer Kulturbesitz.

smaller trade network of earlier dynasties, the Egyptians pursued control of the lucrative trade routes of their former conquerors, the Hyksos. Having adopted Hyksos bronze weaponry and chariots, Egypt soon dominated the peoples of Palestine. In expanding beyond their cultural borders, Egypt had created an empire.

The fourth ruler of the eighteenth dynasty was a woman, Hatshepsut (reign dates 1496–1490 B.C.). At the death of her husband, a six-year-old son succeeded, and the queen became regent. The young prince could not resist Hatshepsut's authority, and she soon declared herself pharaoh, justifying her rule by claiming divine parentage from Amon-Ra. Palace priests supported her rise to power for their own political interests. Hatshepsut's reign focused on trade rather than on military expansion; she initiated a major trading expedition that met with almost universal success. But soon the adult prince deposed her and immediately tried to obliterate her name from all records and return her policies of commerce to policies of aggression.

Expansion that had hammered out an empire in the fifteenth and early fourteenth centuries B.C. halted under the pharaoh Amonhotep IV (reign

dates 1367–1350 B.C.), who followed an isolationist foreign policy to allow internal political and religious reorganization. Amonhotep IV abandoned the traditional polytheism headed by Amon-Ra, whose chief priests located in Thebes[8] held great power and wealth. Amonhotep IV favored monotheistic worship of an obscure god, Aton. Neither animistic nor anthropomorphic, Aton represented an abstract concept of deity symbolized by the sun disk and its rays. By Amonhotep's sixth reigning year, he renounced his name and changed it to Akhen*aton*. Many ancient kings and pharaohs incorporated a god's name into theirs to demonstrate legitimacy, so *Amon*hotep became Akhen*aton* ("to be pleasing to Aton"). He built a new capital, which liberated him from the traditional political influence of the priests of Amon-Ra. This served both the spiritual and political agendas of Akhenaton.

During Akhenaton's reign, many changes took place. New art styles broke onto the traditional artistic stage. No longer was the pharaoh depicted in expressionless or disinterested remoteness. Akhenaton's body was reproduced in all its flabby

[8] **Thebes:** THEEBZ

glory, and one depiction shows the pharaoh affectionately kissing his child. Another change hit closer to Egyptian sensibilities; all Egyptians were instructed to worship only Aton, and Akhenaton was Aton's sole interpreter, thereby ensuring his control over all religious practice and the demise of priestly power. Akhenaton destroyed Amon-Ra's temples, but the outraged priests led many commoners in secret worship of the traditional deities; ill will toward the pharaoh boiled beneath the hot Egyptian sun. A corrupt bureaucracy capitalized on the pharaoh's decline in popularity by gaining control of the administration.

Monotheism proved too difficult to accept, and soon after Akhenaton's death his young heir, Tutankh*aton* (reign dates 1352–1344 B.C.), changed his name to Tutankh*amon*[9] (nicknamed by moderns "King Tut"). His name change signaled the restoration of polytheism, and the worship of Amon-Ra returned to the palace at Thebes. During his short reign, under the approving gaze of the priests, he tried to obliterate Akhenaton's name from the lists of pharaohs and to reverse his policies (similar to what had occurred after Hatshepsut). Isolationism gave way to renewed interest in foreign affairs.

Egypt's interests clashed with those of the Hittites, who conquered parts of Mesopotamia, Syria, and Palestine between 1400 and 1200 B.C. They intruded upon Egyptian territories during Akhenaton's isolationist rule. The reign of Ramses[10] II (reign dates 1290–1224 B.C.) heralded the decline of Egypt's military grandeur. Ramses failed to defeat the intrusive Hittites, but he managed to curb their invasion of Egypt. In 1269 B.C., the two kings signed "The Treaty of the Gods," which effectively halted expansion attempts. The protracted years of warfare and bloodshed had proved to be too costly for both aggressors.

After Ramses II, the authority of the pharaoh declined. Maintaining the military and engaging in grandiose temple projects depleted the treasury, and the priestly class increasingly opposed dynastic control. Egypt lost its empire by about 1085 B.C. and suffered through invasions, including conquest and temporary rule by the Nubians. Egypt finally fell to the Persian Empire in 525 B.C. after a series of invasions from the northeast.

EXPANSIVE EMPIRES

Throughout Southwest Asian history runs a checkerboard pattern of conquests and raids by expanding kingdoms. The Hittites, Assyrians, and Persians are representative examples of states that expanded into empires as they moved beyond their cultural borders. Each had its own history and important cultural contributions, but what brought these states into prominence were their innovations in military techniques, which permitted conquest and control of large areas, and in social and political structures, which maintained their vast holdings.

The Hittites, around 1700–around 1200 B.C.

The people called the Hittites had developed by about 1700 B.C. an empire in what is now modern Turkey. They were part of the large Indo-European migration that relocated peoples into India, Greece, and Southwest Asia around 2700 B.C. The king, chosen because of his military abilities, ruled as first among equals in the warrior society. A council of elders from among the nobility advised the king.

Expansion intensified in 1525 B.C. under the able chief Telepinush,[11] who led the evolution of Hittite kingship from a war leader of a chiefdom to a judicial and legislative monarch over an empire. He issued edicts similar to those of Hammurabi and established a clear path of succession and regulation of behavior to inhibit power struggles. The Hittites moved southward into northern Mesopotamia against the powerful kingdom of the Mitanni under the command of Suppiluliuma[12] (reign dates 1372–1334 B.C.). After conquering the Mitanni, Suppiluliuma turned toward Syria, taking several smaller kingdoms. The Hittite realm by 1353 B.C. had only one rival in size and power— Egypt. The recently widowed Egyptian queen offered an alliance with Suppiluliuma; the alliance was to be cemented by her marriage to one of his sons. Suppiluliuma distrusted the queen, and his diplomatic delays eventually lost him the chance

---

[9] **Tutankhamon:** toot ahngk AH muhn
[10] **Ramses:** RAM seez

[11] **Telepinush:** tehl eh PIHN oosh
[12] **Suppiluliuma:** SOOP ihl OO lee OO mah

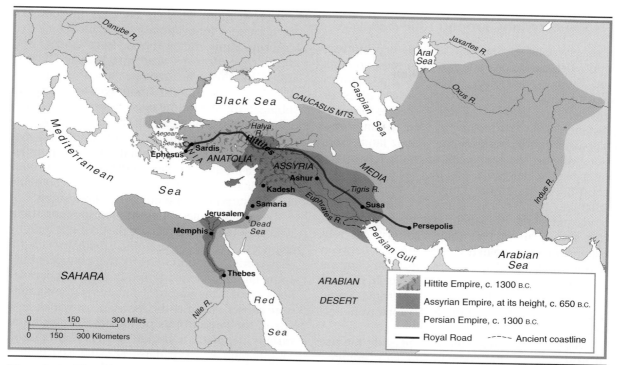

M A P 4 . 4 *The Hittite (around 1700–around 1200 B.C.), Assyrian (around 1300–626 B.C.), and Persian (559–331 B.C.) Empires.* *The Hittites migrated into Anatolia around 2700 B.C. and expanded into an empire by around 1700 B.C.; their expansion south was halted at Kadesh by the Egyptians. Assyrian expansion united Mesopotamian and Egyptian civilizations during the seventh century B.C. The Persian Empire controlled its vast territory with local governors called satraps, who ruled with semiautonomous authority. The Persian road system from Persepolis to Ephesus also served to unite the empire.*

to govern Egypt through his son. The Hittite Empire continued to expand, however, and grew to 260,000 square miles by 1334 B.C.

Hittite expansion relied heavily on iron weaponry and innovations in the use of chariots. Iron weapons were stronger and cheaper to make than those of bronze used by their enemies. Hittite chariots carried a driver and an archer, as did most chariots, but also one shield bearer, who could protect the other two in the heat of battle. Spoked wheels and an axle placed in the rear made the Hittite chariot more maneuverable, and specially trained horses gave it speed. Iron weaponry, chariots, and military use of horses revolutionized warfare in Southwest Asia.

The Hittites controlled their empire by setting up vassal kingdoms that allowed the local royal houses to rule in exchange for taxes and military support against Egypt. Their law extended to this web of vassal states, replacing the older Hammurabic law code; the newer laws focused less on retribution and more on restitution of property. Hittites often extended their interests through diplomacy, preferring negotiation and treaties to costly military conquest. These practices resulted in elite support in the local areas.

Overextension and preoccupation with fighting the Egyptians resulted in the weakening of Hittite control, however. Egypt's formidable resistance under Ramses II finally stopped Hittite aggression southward. Other Indo-Europeans who had been migrating into the area now known as Turkey caused disruption in the Hittite homeland. The Hittite Empire finally collapsed by about 1200 B.C., after devastating raids created political instability that left a vacuum of central authority throughout the region. The vacuum was soon filled by the Assyrians.

The Assyrians, around 1300–626 B.C.

The Assyrians' fertile lands, excellent pasturage, and cities on major trade routes in Mesopotamia led them to establish many trading colonies beyond their borders. The Assyrian city of Ashur enjoyed the prosperity of a major center for long-distance trade, particularly in textiles, limestone, alabaster, marble, and copper. Their lands were not easily defended; this left them open to attack by aggressive neighbors, and they fell under Hittite control. As the Hittite Empire declined around 1300 B.C., the Assyrians regained control of their lands and reorganized their aristocracy into a warrior society to protect their territory. Assyrian expansion soon created a large empire. Between about 1300 and 626 B.C., the Assyrian Empire gained some territories and lost others. In the seventh century B.C., the Assyrians defeated Egypt, and, for a short time, both civilizations were unified under Assyrian rule.

Assyrian military science, especially the use of iron, became the standard for later empires. Assyrians, like the Hittites, used iron weaponry, and it gave them a distinct advantage over the bronze weapons of their enemies in southern Mesopotamia. Innovations in equipment included battering rams, heavy bows, long lances, and armor. They effectively used horsemen and heavily armed infantry. The Assyrians used any means available to accomplish their goal of complete subjugation: Men of the cities were dismembered or burned alive, and even in those cities that surrendered to the approaching army, officials met the same fate. Assyrians often relocated populations as a punitive measure and as a means to control resistance. Assyrian methods convinced many cities to surrender with little or no opposition.

Assyrian armies, often numbering more than 200,000 soldiers, marched on paved roads built by engineers. The well-maintained roads provided a relay communication network that connected the entire empire. The roads also transported populations around the empire. Conquered populations were conscripted into the Assyrian army, making it one of the largest of its period, and relocation of various populations helped to maintain control. King Sargon II (reign dates 722–706 B.C.) built a new capital in 713 B.C. and wrote that he populated it with various "peoples of the four quarters, of

FIGURE 4.12 *Ashurnasirpal II at the Hunt. Hunting was a major pastime of kings and soldiers during periods of relative peace, as it honed fighting skills and used many of the same tactics as warfare. This relief carving is of Ashurnasirpal II, king of the Assyrians. Soldiers form an enclosure by interlocking their shield arms and drive the lions toward the king; the charioteer positions the chariot so that the king can take aim and kill the lion—a feat which bears witness to Ashurnasirpal's power and skill as a commander.* Courtesy of the Trustees of the British Museum.

strange tongues and different speech." It is estimated that as many as four million people may have been relocated.

The Assyrian great art style also reflected martial values. Reliefs depicted their kings in battle or hunting. Ashur, their patron deity, mandated that the king defeat Assyria's enemies, and the hunting scenes personified the warrior king, who, through the hunt, protected his people from the ravages of wild beasts. Hunting was also used as a means for military training during periods of peace. The Assyrian art style parallels Egyptian art and biography, in which pharaohs always defeated their enemies.

Like others before them, the Assyrians adopted cuneiform writing and compiled previous law codes and knowledge in order to assimilate the wisdom of their subjects. In the city of Nineveh, they built a great library that contained many tablets on such topics as religion, biography, and astronomy produced by the various peoples they ruled. They also developed a system of placing locations on maps that is similar to the modern system of longitude and latitude.

Although the Assyrians dispersed the conquered populations throughout the empire to weaken resistance, the empire eventually succumbed to a typical difficulty of overextended empires: the inability to perpetuate control over subject peoples. In 626 B.C., the last expansive Assyrian king died and Assyria's enemies united under the leadership of the New Babylonians and the Medes to defeat Assyria. After Assyria's defeat, the empire was devoured by the victors, especially New Babylon, which became a formidable empire itself.

The Persians, 559–331 B.C.

The ancestors of the Persians were part of the Aryan migration of around 2000 B.C. that wandered from the Eurasian steppes into India and Southwest Asia. They eventually settled in a land they called Parsa (Persia), next to the Persian Gulf in southern Iran. During the empires of the Hittites, of the Assyrians, and of their neighbors to the north, the New Babylonians and the Medes, the people of Persia remained in a tribal organization.

Persia rose to prominence against its Medean overlords under the growing power of Cyrus (reign dates 559–530 B.C.), who claimed the title of King of Kings (or emperor) and succeeded in uniting the various Persian groups into a political threat. Cyrus exploited the political unrest within the Medean bureaucracy and army through alliances with several key Medean leaders. On the day of battle, the leaders of the Medean army defected to the Persians, bringing the army with them, and Cyrus carried the day without the necessity of battle. The Medean army remained critical to Cyrus's successes. Diplomacy was a tactic Cyrus would use again.

Cyrus expanded northeastward onto the Iranian plateau, enveloping the kingdom of Lydia, and challenged Greek colonists on the coast of Ionia. Cyrus finally turned his attention to the last remaining empire in the area—New Babylon. The city of Babylon was the focus of a wealthy trade network that stretched through Syria into Palestine and the Mediterranean. The city boasted a population of more than 200,000 people. The city walls were so thick that two rows of houses and a street wide enough for a chariot rested comfortably at their tops. In 539 B.C., Cyrus was able to enter the city of Babylon without firing an arrow because he claimed he would reinstate the patron deity, Marduk. Marduk's worship had been prohibited when the New Babylonian king flirted with monotheism. As Cyrus approached Babylon, he professed himself the avenger of Marduk, and the great bronze doors of the Ishtar gate swung open. The people of the city threw garlands at Cyrus's feet, and the New Babylonian Empire was no more.

Cyrus based his administration upon the policy of using local authority and the relocation of displaced populations to their homelands, like the Jews from the southern Hebrew kingdom (Judah) who had been captives in Babylon. He divided the empire into twelve provinces called **satrapies**, with a ruling **satrap**,[13] or governor, appointed from the Persian aristocracy. Local administration fell under the satrap, who was encouraged by the presence of imperial troops to remain loyal. Codified laws and the standardization of taxes, 20 percent of the annual yield, gained Cyrus a reputation for fairness and consistency. Standardization of currency and weights and measures helped to stimulate long-distance trade. The collection of tariffs,

---

[13] **satrap:** SAY trap

commercial taxes, and tribute brought massive wealth to the royal treasury; Babylon supplied 33 tons of silver annually and India nearly 12 tons of gold. Cyrus's policies of diplomatic sensitivity tended to keep his subjects loyal, and this helps to explain the longevity of Persian rule over such a vast and diverse empire.

Conquest continued under Cyrus's son, Cambyses[14] (reign dates 529–522 B.C.). He conquered part of Egypt in 525 B.C., but expansion ended when he was unable to rule as effectively as his father. Persia was soon in rebellion and Cambyses died returning home. The Persian Empire returned to expansionist policies after the successful seizure of the imperial throne by Darius I (reign dates 521–486 B.C.), who conquered as far as the western bank of the Indus River. The Persian Empire now stretched from the Indus River to modern Turkey and southward, encompassing Egypt.

With secure borders in the eastern portion of his empire, Darius I turned his royal gaze westward toward the lucrative grain trade coming from the Black Sea into the Aegean Sea. Darius's plan to envelop these Greek commercial routes was thwarted by the Macedonians in 514 B.C. The Persian Empire, however, lasted another 200 years, until Alexander of Macedon conquered Persia in 331 B.C.

The vast highway network, inherited from the Assyrians and expanded by the Persians, enhanced both trade and communication among all the major cities in the Persian Empire. The caravans traveling the road system were protected in most areas, particularly on the 1,700-mile royal road between Susa and Sardis. The royal road had more than 100 inns located along its route, with about a day's journey between them. The Greek historian Herodotus[15] (whose words inspired a motto for the U.S. postal system) said of the royal messengers who traveled the road network, "Nothing stops these couriers from covering their allotted stage in the quickest possible time, neither snow, rain, heat, nor darkness."

Persian religion had a profound influence on the development of world religions. It is also a good example of a unifying ideology in an empire. Zoroastrianism, based upon the revelations of a visionary, Zoroaster,[16] was another experiment with monotheism. Ahuramazda, an all-powerful, wise creator-god, is locked in a cosmic battle with the forces of darkness. The dualistic nature of the contest between good and evil threatened the religion's monotheism, but Zoroastrians believe that Ahuramazda will eventually win this war. Humanity, which must choose to which side its allegiance is given, engages in a moral struggle that mirrors the cosmic battle. This religious perspective contributed to the age's ethical development in law and human behavior as it spread throughout the empire. It profoundly influenced the captive Hebrews in New Babylon, who were codifying Mosaic law, and inspired new concepts of heaven and hell that eventually were incorporated into Christianity and Islam. Zoroastrianism appealed to individuals rather than to particular polities or culture groups; anyone who followed the ethical tenets stated in the holy writings (Avesta) was given the rewards of righteousness from Ahuramazda.

SEAFARING PEOPLES OF THE EASTERN MEDITERRANEAN

The peoples of the Mediterranean were similar to those of many agricultural societies in Southwest Asia. Because of the topography of their regions, however, they harvested the seas and developed vast shipping networks that transported goods around the Mediterranean. Three of the most prominent of these peoples were the Minoans,[17] the Mycenaeans,[18] and the Phoenicians.[19]

Although the Mediterranean initially served as a barrier, discouraging invaders to the island, the people who occupied the island of Crete (called Minoans) perfected seafaring technologies as they exploited fishing beds in natural harbor areas and along the coast from around 2000 B.C. Minoans soon traversed the eastern Mediterranean and established trade colonies for business with the various island and coastal populations they encountered. The trading network brought wealth, which they invested in great palaces, aqueducts, and harbor improvements. Minoans created in their wall paintings some of the most beautiful

---

[14] **Cambyses:** kam BY seez
[15] **Herodotus:** hur RAHD uh tuhs
[16] **Zoroaster:** ZAWR oh ahs tur

[17] **Minoans:** my NOH uhnz
[18] **Mycenaeans:** my seh NEE uhnz
[19] **Phoenicians:** foh NEE shuhnz

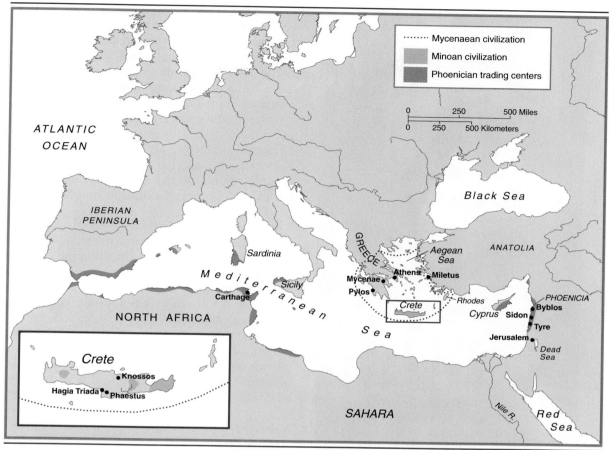

MAP 4.5 *Minoan (around 2200–1550 B.C.), Mycenaean (around 1600–1150 B.C.), and Phoenician (around 1000–146 B.C.) Civilizations.* *Minoan civilization developed on the island of Crete, where palace complexes housed goods at Knossos, Phaistos, and Hagia Triada for trade throughout the eastern Mediterranean. The Mycenaean civilization encircled much of Greece and the Aegean Islands by 1250 B.C. Mycenaeans often raided Minoan ships laden with goods bound for Aegean ports. The Phoenicians became a seafaring people, establishing colonies throughout the Mediterranean, disseminating their alphabet along with their trade goods.*

representations of sea and shore life of the Mediterranean world. Popular motifs included athletic games, picturesque landscapes, dolphins playing in the sea, and animals from much of the Mediterranean. Examples of Minoan artisans' handiwork have been found all over the eastern Mediterranean. Their jewelry, pottery, stone and ivory carvings, and other exports adorned the bodies and palaces of early kings and peoples.

Mycenaeans, northern neighbors in Greece, began to interlope in Minoan economic interests and seized many Minoan colonies in the Aegean. Their encroachment benefited from a great nat-

ural disaster, the volcanic eruption on the island of Thera (seventy miles north of Crete) in 1450 B.C. The resulting tidal wave hit the coastal area of Crete, destroyed harbor areas, killed thousands, and devastated the bulk of the Minoan fleet. Not long after, the island fell to the Mycenaeans.

The Mycenaeans had moved into the area of Greece during the Indo-European movement flowing from the area of the Black Sea and Central Asia in the second millennium B.C. They mingled with the local population, and, over the centuries, the two peoples became one. These invaders brought skills of horse handling and charioteering to the

FIGURE 4.13 *Minoan Priestess. The art of the Minoan civilization does not include portrayals of warfare. Instead, the walls at the palace at Knossos are covered with geometric designs, flora and fauna, and figures engaged in religious and everyday activities. This scene comes from a room that was probably used as a house shrine room. The woman wears a large earring and is dressed in brilliantly colored clothing similar to those depicted on fertility statues. Her face is made up with red lips and cheeks and outlined eyes and eyebrows. She moves toward a group that surrounds a seated goddess (not shown). Scholars believe that she may be a priestess performing a ritual; whatever was in her hand has been obscured.* Archaeological Receipts Fund (TAP Service).

area. Because of its topography, few places in Greece are more than a few miles from water, and the Mycenaeans soon turned to sea trade. They learned much from the great Minoan commercial centers, but the mentor relationship changed after the volcanic eruption at Thera. The Mycenaeans competed with the trade network of Egypt until shortly after 1400 B.C.; by 1350 B.C., they had subjugated the Minoans and interloped in the waning Egyptian commerce. Mycenaeans then became lords of the sea, and the distinction between trade and piracy disappeared. They often seized cargo from rivals' ships and sold it at non-Mycenaean ports.

Mycenaeans traded many goods, especially bronze items. The Minoans taught the Mycenaeans how to make and work bronze; farmers adopted it in agrarian technology, artisans used it for tools (hammers and carving knives), and warriors used it for weapons and armor. The king of Pylos controlled more than four hundred bronzesmiths in that one urban center. The Mycenaean pattern of trading and raiding worked well during periods of unimpeded commercial activity. But between 1300 and 1200 B.C., unrest in Egypt, Palestine, and the Anatolian Peninsula diminished Mycenaean wealth because of the interruption in trade and the shortage of cargos to confiscate.

The decline of the Mycenaeans has been hotly debated by historians because little archaeological evidence remains and almost nothing survives in Greek folklore. The Dorians (as they came to be called) probably migrated into southwest Anatolia, southern Greece, and Crete and mixed with or scattered their populations. They reintroduced pastoralism into the area, and their rural lifestyle replaced the urbanization of the Mycenaean period. Dorians populated much of the Greek mainland by about 1000 B.C. Other factors also influenced Mycenaean decline, such as interruption of long-distance trade during the Hittite Empire's collapse, overcultivation of lands for cash crops, and internal warfare.

The Phoenicians occupied the eastern coastal Mediterranean area now known as Lebanon, tending their sheep and crops as other Southwest Asian peoples had done. Many settled between the Mediterranean Sea and the mountains, turned to trade, and established port cities by about 1000 B.C. The mountain forests held the rich natural

EGYPT	MESOPOTAMIA	EASTERN MEDITERRANEAN		

			—	Copper tools used widely, c. 3500 B.C.
Ancient Egyptian Kingdom, c. 3500–1085 B.C.	Mesopotamian city-states, c. 3500–2350 B.C.		**3500 B.C.** — — —	
			3000 B.C.	Bronze technology spreads, c. 3000 B.C.
			— — —	
			2500 B.C. —	
	Akkadian Empire, c. 2340–2100 B.C.	Minoan Civilization, c. 2200–1550 B.C.	— —	
	Babylonian Empire, c. 2100–1600 B.C.		**2000 B.C.** —	
			— —	Hammurabi, king of Babylon, reign dates 1792–1750 B.C.
	Hittite Empire, c. 1700–1200 B.C.	Mycenaean Civilization, c. 1600–1150 B.C.	— **1500 B.C.**	Iron technology in use, c. 1500 B.C.
			—	Akhenaton, pharaoh of Egypt, reign dates 1367–1350 B.C.
	Assyrian Empire, c. 1300–626 B.C.	Dorians, c. 1200–800 B.C.	— — —	
	Hebrew Empire, c. 1025–922 B.C.	Phoenician seafaring, c. 1000–146 B.C.	**1000 B.C.**	Carthage becomes center of Phoenician trade, c. 900 B.C.
			— — — —	

resource of cedar trees. These great cedars of Lebanon, prized throughout Southwest Asia and Egypt, often grew to 135 feet, making them ideal for masts and planking on shipping vessels and as building materials for wealthy kings and nobles in the sparsely forested interior areas.

Phoenicians soon dominated eastern Mediterranean trade by building a network of independent city-states at Tyre, Sidon, Byblos, and Arvad. They seized the opportunity to exploit the rest of the Mediterranean commercially and established a trade network that spread to Cyprus, North Africa, Sicily, Sardinia, and the Iberian Peninsula. By the seventh century B.C., Carthage (in North Africa), the most important Phoenician colony, dominated the Mediterranean. Phoenician commercial activities contributed to navigational and maritime technologies. They populated the sea with both merchant vessels and fast warships, which carried battering rams that could pierce the hulls of enemy ships with their bronze tips. Phoenicians could navigate by night using astronomy, yet they usually sailed in the safety of daylight. They used watchfires—an ancient form of lighthouse—at high points on shore during the night to help ships navigate safely into harbor.

Phoenician trade in the eastern Mediterranean eventually declined. By 900 B.C., Assyrians were threatening the eastern Mediterranean coastal areas, and Phoenician ships were confiscated for warships. As the Assyrians invaded the cities, the center of Phoenician trade shifted to Carthage, which dominated central Mediterranean trade until 146 B.C.

SUMMARY

1. Agriculture set the stage for the development of civilizations in Southwest Asia and Egypt. Polytheism was the prominent form of religion, but the Hebrews and Zoroastrians developed monotheism, which was long lasting.

2. The societies of Southwest Asia endured the ebb and flow of developing kingdoms and expanding empires whose religious ideology justified expansion under a divine mandate, while Egypt moved toward unification under relative isolation. Culture was often spread through conquest and during periods of migration.

3. In both Sumeria and Egypt, writing developed in response to political and economic needs.

4. In Southwest Asia and Egypt, women generally played minor parts in political history. Men worked in various professions and were the primary focus of law codes; women worked in the home and in some professions, and they were both property owners and property themselves.

5. The power of kingship varied: Southwest Asian kings' authority derived from their close relationship with the patron god, and the Egyptian pharaohs' authority derived from their divine nature. In Egypt, law came from the pharaoh's pronouncements. In Mesopotamia, law came from the deities through the authority of the king. The Hebrews perpetuated egalitarianism, placing even their king under the law of the covenant. Changes in Hebrew laws paralleled similar changes taking place in other legal codes, for example as abstract concepts like the Ten Commandments replaced more specific laws on retribution.

6. The introduction of iron and chariots revolutionized warfare. Hittites, Assyrians, and Persians made innovations in the governance of large territories that helped to establish and control extended empires.

7. Seafaring among the peoples of the eastern Mediterranean served as a conduit for the exchange of goods and ideas and as inspiration in the exploration of unknown coastal areas. Commercial activity inspired innovation in seafaring technologies.

SUGGESTED READINGS

Aldred, Cyril. *Egyptians*. Revised edition. London: Thames and Hudson, 1987. A cultural and political history of Egypt.

Gurney, O. R. *The Hittites*. Revised edition. New York: Penguin, 1990. A good overview of the history of the Hittites.

Harden, Donald B. *The Phoenicians*. Harmondsworth, Eng.: Penguin, 1971. A study of the Phoenicians and their colonization of the Mediterranean through archaeological and literary evidence.

Kramer, S. N. *The Sumerians: Their History, Culture, and Character.* Chicago: University of Chicago Press, 1971. A standard treatment of Sumerian civilization.

Oppenheim, A. Leo. *Ancient Mesopotamia*. Second edition. Chicago: University of Chicago Press, 1977. A review that centers on the Babylonian and Assyrian peoples.

Orlinsky, H. M. *Ancient Israel*. Second edition. Ithaca, N.Y.: Cornell University Press, 1960. A brief but thorough review of ancient Hebrew history.

Taylor, Lord William. *The Mycenaeans*. London: Thames and Hudson, 1983. A review of Mycenaean history and culture.

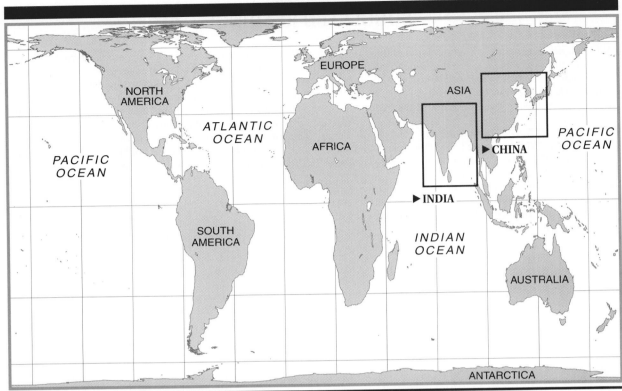

EUROPE

ASIA

NORTH
AMERICA

ATLANTIC
OCEAN

AFRICA

▶ CHINA

PACIFIC
OCEAN

PACIFIC
OCEAN

▶ INDIA

SOUTH
AMERICA

INDIAN
OCEAN

AUSTRALIA

ANTARCTICA

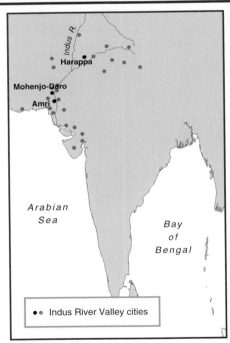

Indus R.

Harappa

Mohenjo-Daro
Amri

Arabian
Sea

Bay
of
Bengal

•• Indus River Valley cities

▶ INDIA

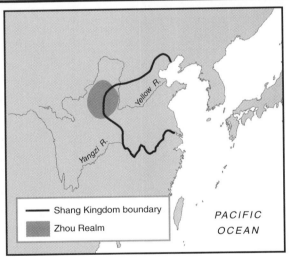

Yellow R.

Yangzi R.

—— Shang Kingdom boundary

▨ Zhou Realm

PACIFIC
OCEAN

▶ CHINA

Early River Valley Civilizations of South and East Asia

around 2500–around 700 B.C.

The Chinese king mused in the divining chamber. His army was to fight a great battle in three days, and he needed counsel from the spirit of his dead queen. What a splendid warrior she had been! Never once had she lost in battle, and many regarded her as the goddess of battle. What would she say to him? The solemn diviner readied the oracle bone to receive the answer to his question.

Near the end of the Shang Dynasty, religion featured prominently in the lives of the Chinese rulers. Religion became and remained important for the people of China and India, beginning in the early third millennium B.C.

Civilizations emerged in the river valleys of South and East Asia only shortly after the development of civilizations in Mesopotamia and Egypt. In South Asia, civilization arose in the Indus Valley; elements of that civilization fused with elements carried from immigrants from Central Asia, forming the first of a series of civilizations in the Ganges Valley.[1] In East Asia, civilization arose independently in the Yellow River Valley.

INDUS VALLEY CIVILIZATION, AROUND 2500–AROUND 1750 B.C.

Early nomads periodically inhabited the Indus floodplain during harsh winters. Around 5000 B.C., people in the lowlands began practicing settled forms of agriculture, and villages dotted the

[1] **Ganges:** GAN jeez

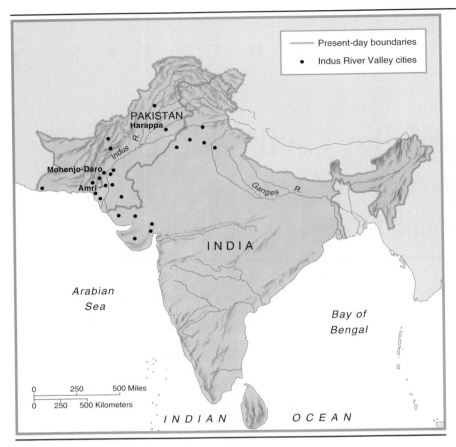

MAP 5.1   *Indus Valley Civilization, around 2500– around 1750 B.C.*   The earliest civilization in India lay in the northwestern part of the subcontinent. Although the major cities of Mohenjo-Daro and Harappa were three hundred miles apart, they were laid out in a similar plan. This suggests either overall political unity or a common cultural pattern of urban organization and development.

Indus River banks. The excavated Amri Village archaeological site reveals a twenty-acre village with homes of mud brick. Amri villagers used a wheel to fashion pots decorated with geometric patterns. They hunted elephants, tigers, bears, boars, and deer. They also fished in the Indus River waters. Another excavation site reveals that the villagers grew wheat and barley, used flint blades, and raised domesticated sheep, goats, and cows.

Over the next two millennia, floodplain dwellers in larger villages or towns mass produced ceramics decorated with geometric patterns. These and other products were traded over long distances and brought modest prosperity to the larger communities. In the following centuries, many villages, like Amri Village, doubled in size. Houses were built from adobe brick with interior courtyards, often according to a common design. Archaeological remains from Amri Village and other sites demonstrate the continued evolution of villages, the development of intensive agriculture, the mass production of ceramic wares, and the improvement of metallurgical techniques to produce copper and, eventually, bronze vessels. Thus, many of the preconditions for civilization emerged in the Indus Valley.

From these and other sites we may conclude that the improving agricultural conditions caused the rapid growth of local populations and the development of civilization. Population densities in the Indus Valley reached a critical mass sometime after 3000 B.C., and urbanization emerged. In addition, the increasing grain yields supported these cities of people, like artisans, who engaged in specialized labor other than agriculture. The geographic expanse of the Indus Valley civilization covered areas from present-day eastern Iran to the western coast of India.

Mohenjo-Daro, a walled city of 35,000 to 40,000 people, rose according to a construction plan with a central citadel that towered nearly fifty feet. This wall measured about three and one-half miles along its perimeter. People in the

FIGURE 5.1 *The Great Bath at Mohenjo-Daro.* *The excavated ruins of the Great Bath at Mohenjo-Daro indicate the use of ritual cleansing in early Indian cultures. The bath's network of running water and covered drains also supported private bathing rooms. Today, Hindu temples use bathing steps built along the river banks for the purpose of ritual cleansing. Atop the brick structure of the Great Bath is a Buddhist ruin (upper right), built over 2,000 years later.* Josephine Powell.

Indus Valley used furnace-baked bricks for walls and major buildings, while sun-baked ones could be found in homes. These individual urban dwellings usually had interior courtyards around which families organized domestic life.

Because of Mohenjo-Daro's proximity to the Indus River, which tended to flood, the city was destroyed by the rampaging river, and, each time, a new city was built from the flood ruins. An extensive community sewer system that drained houses with indoor plumbing suggests a highly effective government. A major building in Mohenjo-Daro, perhaps a bathing complex, shows the value that Indians placed on water to clean and purify. Ritual bathing likely became a central part of religious life, as it remains in India today. Irrigation networks helped transform the Indus Valley civilization's agricultural base to yield even larger grain surpluses.

Indus Valley people harvested a wide variety of crops. They grew grains like wheat (the main grain staple), barley, millet, and sorghum and stored them in granaries on raised brick floors that permitted air circulation beneath and retarded mildew. They also ate dates, lentils, and peas.

Artisans lived and worked in special sections of the Indus Valley cities. Metallurgists forged copper and bronze implements, ranging from agricultural tools to weapons to ceremonial pieces. Bronze female figurines indicate that Indian artisans skillfully employed complex casting techniques. Potters also created ceramic utensils, such as drain pipes and terra cotta ornaments. They also fashioned miniature bullock carts and miniature ships for decorative purposes. Cotton appeared at this time in India, and the Indus people wove and dyed its fibers. These textiles became important trade items not only within the Indus Valley but also across Southwest Asia.

Long-distance trade, a major occupation of the Indus Valley people, transported commodities such as timber and cotton throughout the Indus region and as far as Mesopotamia and Central Asia. There was an especially robust trade with Sumer from around 2300 B.C. to around 2000 B.C., through which the Indians imported tin and precious stones. Local trade within the Indus floodplain flourished after the standardization of weights and measures, although some scholars argue that increasing trade volume created the need to standardize.

The organization underlying these activities suggests some kind of controlling political force or perhaps a common pattern of urban development throughout the Indus Valley. The regularity found in these cities indicates governments given to careful organization and planning. The massive citadels and other large buildings, including one in Mohenjo-Daro that may have been a palace, hint at centralized polity. Indus cities likely employed officials, including tax collectors, city planners, water control experts, and scribes, and they also supported merchants and artisans. Similarities among the dwellings and establishments of the merchants and artisans have caused most scholars of ancient India to argue for a **guild**, an organization of merchants and artisans based on specific trades and crafts that works for communal political, economic, and social interests. More should be learned about these elements of the Indus Valley civilization if its undeciphered language is decoded.

Recovered artifacts suggest that the Indus people worshiped animals and venerated a female deity, which may be seen in the large numbers of statues, jewelry pieces, and other relics. Many figurines are female with enlarged breasts and genitals prominently displayed, suggesting the worship of a fertility goddess. In Mohenjo-Daro, one unusual piece is a multi-faced figure surrounded by animals and seated cross-legged in a yogi posture. These features have caused some to speculate that this represents an early form of Shiva, an Indian deity later associated with animals.

Among the most intriguing and elusive remnants of the Indus Valley civilization are small square seals. Merchants and others may have used these rectangular artifacts to mark and thereby identify their property. Seal surfaces might have been covered with ink and pressed on one's possessions, or perhaps a seal impression might have been left on a piece of soft clay or wax. The Indus Valley seals contain pictographic signs that may be the names of merchants.

FIGURE 5.2 *Horned Figure of Mohenjo-Daro.* *The figure in this artifact is seated in a yoga position with arms resting on crossed legs, a meditation position still in use among Hindus and Buddhists today. Various creatures surround the figure, suggesting that this was a deity of animals, similar to Shiva in later centuries.* John C. Huntington.

The Indus Valley civilization flourished around 2500–1750 B.C., although some cities emerged earlier and others lasted a few centuries longer. Over time, the major cities declined. An imaginative interpretation of the archaeological evidence highlights catastrophic flooding induced by earth movements associated with earthquakes. Other scholars argue for a more gradual process as overfarming or overgrazing of the surrounding lands may have contributed to erosion, flooding, and decline. In areas where irrigation networks predominated, centuries of evaporating irrigation water may have left large amounts of salt or alkali residues, reducing the land's ability to sustain agriculture. Further, some have noted that accelerated cutting of trees for firewood removed a major energy source for brick makers and others. The continued clear-cutting of trees may have increased the amount of water runoff and overwhelmed the irrigation systems. Other scholars have argued that rainfall declined in the Indus region; one river in the northeastern Indus Valley ran dry, for example. Most likely some combination of these factors led to the civilization's decline.

Many of the Indus Valley civilization's cultural and social practices, like animal-centered worship and the yogic traditions of physical exercise and meditation, emerged in the Ganges Valley and other places. Water has been regarded as holy throughout Indian history, and the segregation of peoples along occupational and kinship lines persists in cities.

ARYAN MIGRATIONS AND EARLY SETTLEMENTS, AROUND 1400–AROUND 700 B.C.

Mountain barriers often limited extended contact and interactions between the peoples of India and other areas, while internal obstructions, like dense jungles, slowed the spread of groups across the Indian subcontinent. The Himalayan, the Hindu Kush, and the Pamir mountain ranges formed a kind of semipermeable alpine wall in the northeast and northwest of the Indian subcontinent. Although these ranges inhibited extensive interchanges between the Indian and Chinese civilizations, they did not act as impenetrable barricades. Mountain passes afforded access to determined peoples. Around 1400 B.C., an immigrant group called the Aryans crossed the mountains into India and migrated slowly across the region. After 1000 B.C., the Aryans reached the Ganges River Valley, an area of dense forest and jungles. Only with the mass production and use of iron tools, along with a climatic shift to less rainfall, did the Ganges region yield to widespread Aryan settlement. (See Map 5.2 on p. 102.)

The Aryan homeland was probably in the southern part of Central Asia. Some Aryans migrated toward Mesopotamia, and others moved through the Hindu Kush passes or across the Persian plateau into South Asia. In fact, the Aryans are part of a larger series of migrations of Indo-Europeans into broad areas of the vast Eurasian land mass; even today, most peoples in Europe and India speak languages that have evolved from a common tongue. The Aryans' warlike ways permeated their religious and poetic works, which were carefully transmitted by successive generations. Aryans herded cattle, sheep, goats, and

FIGURE 5.3   *Vedic Ritual of the Fire Altar.* Brahmans *have presided over many rituals during the last 3,000 years, one of the most important and enduring being the Fire Altar Ritual. The Vedas outlined the proper way to conduct the highly detailed, sometimes weeks-long ceremonies; as ritual experts, the* brahmans *directed such activities, thereby maintaining their elite social position.*   Courtesy of Adelaide de Menil, 1975 © The Film Study Center, Harvard University.

horses. (The horse had been domesticated by pre-Aryan groups, but it had not been used in warfare.)

Because the Aryans gradually moved across India in a process that took centuries, Aryan social, religious, economic, and political practices changed through a process of cultural interaction and diffusion. The Aryan language, for example, borrowed many words from local peoples, and the Aryan religion adopted existing indigenous spiritual techniques, like yoga. Over the centuries, the resulting synthesis became Indian rather than Aryan or Gangetic.

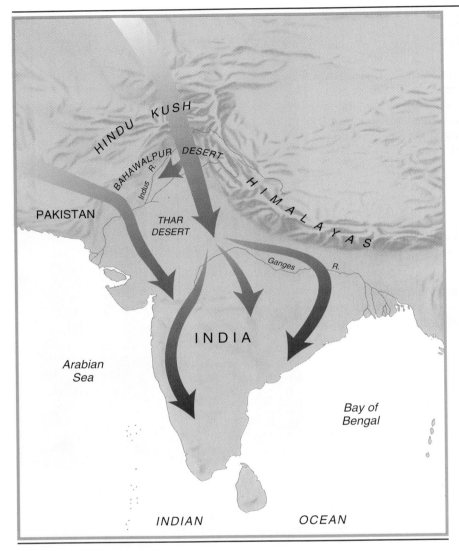

MAP 5.2 *Aryan Migration into India, around 1450–around 700 B.C.*
The Aryans migrated from Central Asia and from the Iranian plateau into the Indian subcontinent. They spread slowly over the subcontinent until about 700 B.C., mixing with the indigenous peoples.

Knowledge of the Aryans comes largely from the four **Vedas**,[2] a series of religious and ceremonial writings transmitted orally until they were transcribed around 500 B.C. Rituals performed by the Aryan priests, the **brahmans**, formed the core texts of the four main Vedas. The oldest and most venerable of the Vedas, the Rig Veda, consists of more than 1,000 poems. Rhyme facilitated memorization for the *brahmans*, the guardians of textual accuracy. These hymns praised deities like the bearded and powerful Indra, who loved to eat, drink, and fight. Often carrying a thunderbolt or wielding a great bow while riding in a chariot, Indra won all battles.

[2] **Vedas:** VAY duhs

Indeed, Indra may remind us of the Greek god Zeus or of the Norse deity Thor, both of whom hurled thunderbolts and were powerful among an anthropomorphic pantheon of deities.

Society

Although Aryan religion and society were strongly influenced by men, women sometimes played important roles. Men became the priests, and the dominant deities were male, some of whom had multiple wives. Men ruled hierarchies, including kingdoms and their own households. Women usually lived with husbands and were supposed to be subservient to them. Men worked in the fields, while women often wove textiles at home. After

1000 B.C., better harvests and population growth in the Ganges Valley spurred the need for more complicated political systems. A more rigid social and political organization developed, and this brought men even greater power.

Although society stacked the cards against women, there were exceptions. Women in the higher social groups accomplished many notable things. At least twenty women are listed as authors of parts of the Rig Veda, one of the holiest works in Indian literature. Some others received an education and became authorities on parts of the Vedas.

Many women in upper-class households could read and write. On occasion, a woman might even address an assembly of political leaders that advised the ruler on a variety of issues.

From 1000 to 700 B.C., women of elite groups enjoyed certain advantages usually denied to women of later times. A woman might choose a husband, and she was responsible for managing the household. She also could move relatively freely in the local society. Women at all social levels likely wove textiles, and the income from that endeavor often proved sufficient to

PARALLELS AND DIVERGENCES

Indo-European Connections

Students, teachers, and scholars are sometimes fascinated by the congruences between Indian and European languages, pre-Christian religions, and mythologies. Given the great distance between the two Eurasian civilization centers, the similarities are even more surprising. One factor in their relationship is the common origin of many Indo-European peoples. Around the beginning of the second millennium B.C., a movement of Central Asian tribal groups commenced. They spoke related dialects and had broadly similar social structures and religious systems. Some passed into the Indian subcontinent; others settled in Greece or other parts of Europe. Successive waves of tribes continued their expansion for the next millennium.

One clear similarity between Indians and Europeans is language. As long ago as the 1780s, Sir William Jones discovered significant linguistic bonds between the Persian, Indian Sanskrit, German (and its derivative language, English), and Latin (and its derivative language, Spanish), and he posited a single Indo-European language family. Different forms of the English word *father* illustrate Jones's discovery:

—German   *vater*

—Sanskrit   *pitar*

—Persian   *pedar*

—Latin   *pater*

—Spanish   *padre*

Another congruence concerns religion. As noted in this chapter, the Aryan deity Indra resembles the Greek Zeus and the Norse Thor. All employ thunderbolts as weapons and preside over other deities who have anthropomorphic attributes. These similarities suggest that early Indo-Europeans had common religious beliefs.

An additional similarity is the general likeness of the ancient Greek epic poem the *Iliad* and the Indian epic the *Mahabharata*. Both poems depict panoramic battles, warrior values, heroic acts, and interventions by impatient deities. The ancient Greek epic poem the *Odyssey* and its Indian counterpart the *Ramayana* depict the travels of their heroes, each of whom is an ideal ruler. Sita, Rama's abducted wife, is the ideal wife, loyal despite numerous temptations. Likewise, Penelope, Odysseus's wife, exemplifies loyalty to her husband, who has been absent from his homeland for two decades. Both husbands return when their wives are in the midst of being forced to decide among suitors. In each case, the disguised hero strings his bow, which only he has the strength to string, and dispatches the suitors with a volley of arrows.

Although the similarities are striking, a major point is that each epic, religion, or language is translated into a particular cultural context over time. The *Iliad* examines war, bravery, and honor, focusing on the battles themselves and the personal qualities of the warriors. The *Mahabharata* spends considerable time on political intrigues and combat, but it also contains lengthy passages that teach values like duty, honor, and courage. It further espouses important spiritual ideas. Yet both works have long provided examples for moral living to young and old alike.

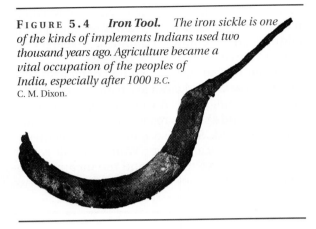

FIGURE 5.4 *Iron Tool.* *The iron sickle is one of the kinds of implements Indians used two thousand years ago. Agriculture became a vital occupation of the peoples of India, especially after 1000 B.C.* C. M. Dixon.

enhance their standing in the family or to support them if they lived alone.

Aryan society had strict regulations and hierarchical patterns. Atop the social pyramid were the priests (*brahmans*), followed by the warriors (*kshatriyas*[3]) and the merchants, farmers, and other commoners (*vaishyas*[4]); at the bottom were menial workers and indigenous peoples (*shudras*[5]). This ranking system was formulated in the time before the eighth century B.C. and may have developed out of a simple hierarchy based on skin color, with the lighter Aryans of the three highest categories holding higher status than the darker local people.

Politics and Iron

Early Aryan polities evolved into city-states and often were based on kinship ties, with the *raja*, the ruler who dominated the group's decision-making process, at the top. *Brahmans* acted as key advisors and officials. Additionally, the *raja* often consulted either with a council of elders or with household heads. These individuals and bodies limited the power of the *raja*. During the first half-millennium B.C., city-states appeared in the Ganges Valley, and they often fought one another. Gradually, however, a few kingdoms emerged from these wars, although no unified Gangetic state developed in this era.

Another key development was the mastery of iron metallurgy. Once the Aryans accomplished this sometime after 1000 B.C., they soon mass produced weapons to arm the soldiers of the city-states. Aryans also tipped their plows with iron and made iron axes to clear the previously resistant forests in the Ganges Valley. This cluster of changes transformed agriculture, leading to larger grain supplies and a growing population density. At the same time, the conditions were ripe for the development of long-distance trade from the city-states and kingdoms to other parts of Asia.

The effort needed to make weapons and iron tools on a large scale taxed the resources of the city rulers. Iron had to be mined, and that process involved finding, organizing, and supplying a large number of people. The iron ore often needed processing, and the iron itself had to be fashioned into tools and weapons.

Elite Culture

Indian civilization boasts two preeminent literary works: the *Mahabharata*,[6] the world's longest poem, with nearly two hundred thousand lines, and the *Ramayana*,[7] an epic about the legendary hero Rama. The *Mahabharata* describes great tribal wars, including heroics and treachery amid ferocious battles. The Indian epics have long remained popular in India as well as in many Southeast Asian countries, including Indonesia, Cambodia, Vietnam, and Burma. The Thai monarchy still refers to itself as the Rama house.

YELLOW RIVER CIVILIZATION, AROUND 1500–771 B.C.

Mountains, jungles, and deserts usually inhibited human penetration into China. The South China Sea and the East China Sea also limited early contact with non-Chinese peoples. There was little contact in the northeast, because there were no significant invaders to trouble seriously the Chinese living there. The north, however, lacked natural obstacles to human ingress. There was, of course, the Gobi Desert, but it did not completely prevent various nomadic groups from invading China.

China's relative isolation from the rest of Asia may have meant that without the ability to directly

---

[3] *kshatriyas:* KSHAH tree ahs
[4] *vaishyas:* VAY shee ahs
[5] *shudras:* SHOO druhs
[6] *Mahabharata:* mah hah BAH rah tah
[7] *Ramayana:* RAH mah yah nah

ENCOUNTERS

Southeast Asian Food Contributions to Early Asian Civilizations

Early forms of agriculture appeared in Southeast Asia. Settled life was found in the areas of present-day Vietnam and Thailand. The people there were developing from a society based on hunting and gathering to one more settled and agricultural. Archaeological finds in the Spirit Cave in Thailand reveal a wide variety of food products like yams, rice, and domesticated chickens. During the period from around 4000 to around 2500 B.C., agriculture became more complex. New domesticated animals came into use, including the pig.

Over time, Southeast Asia played a vital role in the transmission of plants and animals to other parts of Eurasia. Rice is native to Southeast Asia and possibly to East Asia, and it spread to become the dominant grain harvested in much of East Asia and a major foodstuff in South Asia. Pigs and chickens were transported across the Eurasian land mass, and both became important food sources to the Chinese and other East Asian peoples. The pig especially has been a prized domesticated animal, not merely for its meat but also because it could be raised on the scraps and waste products of human consumption. A later Chinese writer noted that the pig was a miniature fertilizer factory. Pigs and chickens were transported west to India and then to Mesopotamia and beyond. The water buffalo originated in Southeast Asia and played a major role in China as a beast of burden and as a foodstuff. Taro, a tuber, was carried by people across Southeast Asia and then to the islands of the Pacific, where it became a major food source for the Polynesians, the Melanesians, and the Micronesians.

compare themselves with the peoples of other great civilizations, the Chinese viewed themselves as superior to all others. The Chinese name for China, Zhong Guo[8] ("the Central Kingdom"), reflected this self-perception. Although most peoples view themselves as superior to outsiders, China was unique in developing a long-sustained supreme self-confidence that lasted into recent times.

Mountains within China also had important consequences. The Qinling[9] Mountains were a watershed. South of these mountains, nearly forty inches of rain fell on average annually; north of the Qinling Mountains, average annual rainfall totaled in the ten-inch range, and aridity inhibited the development of agriculture in that part of the Yellow River Valley. Numerous mountain ranges slowed easy communication from one area to another; this promoted regional differences, for example in spoken dialects and cooking styles.

Ethnic diversity was a fact of ancient Chinese history, as in India. Despite the diversity, the unification of the Chinese written language in the third century B.C. gave successive governments an elite cultural base with common features. In addition, the relatively large number of Chinese aided their successful efforts to assimilate non-Chinese peoples. Those peoples who refused to be so assimilated were either destroyed or forced to live outside the Chinese settlements. These policies ensured the political and ethnic dominance of the Chinese.

Agriculture appeared in China by the sixth millennium B.C. For a long time, scholars believed the Yellow River to be the sole center of early agricultural life in China, but recent archaeological discoveries have altered this perspective. In Southeast China, one site dates the early cultivation of rice at around 5000 B.C., and archaeologists have found another major agricultural area along the coast.

We will focus, however, on the Yellow River area, especially on the area of Banpo Village near the present city of Xian.[10] Fishing and hunting dominated the early years of life in Banpo (around 4500–around 4000 B.C.), but farming and animal husbandry soon became major sources of food for the villagers. Millet, a grain that could weather long periods of little rainfall, was the primary foodstuff. Chinese in Banpo also knew how to spin, weave, and sew. Debris

[8] **Zhong Guo:** joong GWAH
[9] **Qinling:** CHIHN lihng

[10] **Xian:** shee YAHN

FIGURE 5.5 *Banpo Village Excavation Site.* *Banpo villagers made and used an assortment of clay pots. Some were used for grain and seed storage. Others were used to hold the remains of deceased children. A moat surrounded the village, probably for defense against wild animals and predatory humans.* China Pictorial Photo Service.

from several kiln sites reveal that the Banpo people fired pottery and decorated these pieces with images of animals and fish and geometric designs. Domesticated animals included the dog and the pig. The Banpo lifestyle was essentially peaceful, as discussed generally for early tribe-level peoples in Chapter 3.

By the third millennium B.C., a cluster of developments soon brought cities and centralized polities into being. Agriculture became more widespread and led to larger populations, as well as surpluses with which to feed the cities. Bronze metallurgy needed the organization of large numbers of people by a controlling force. City rulers, feeling the necessity to defend themselves against encroachment on their farmlands, organized armies and built huge earthen walls surrounding the urban centers. Unlike that of Banpo, this society was stratified with a ruling group, a pattern of Chinese civilization that began around 2000 B.C.

Two mythical cultural heroes indicate important Chinese ideals. Huangdi[11] ("Yellow Emperor"), an imaginary figure assigned to the early centuries of the third millennium (about 2700 B.C.), was said to have established monarchical rule, fought with non-Chinese peoples, and spread Chinese culture. In Chinese culture,

Huangdi holds a position akin to that of Rama in Indian culture. Both monarchs ruled fairly and lived heroically; they defined the ideal king for their respective peoples. Another moral exemplar, Yü (late third millennium B.C.), tamed the flood-prone Yellow River. He personifies the dedicated official. While directing a long-lasting water control effort, the digging of a channel for the Yellow River to reach the sea, not once did Yü take time out to return home. A popular Chinese saying noted that "We would be fish if it were not for Yü." Later, Yü supposedly founded China's first dynasty, Xia[12] (traditional dates 2205–1766 B.C.), but most scholars consider Xia to be mythical. Hence our attention will center on the successor Shang Dynasty, which began around 1500 B.C.

The Shang Dynasty, around 1500–around 1050 B.C.

Although traditional accounts have supported Shang's existence, material evidence supporting the actuality of the Shang came to light only around 1900. These remnants, along with other materials, confirmed the Shang's existence. Thirty Shang monarchs ruled, and succession passed from brother to brother or from father to son.

[11] **Huangdi:** HWANG dee

[12] **Xia:** shee YAH

POLITICS. Shang life revolved around walled cities. Inside one capital at Anyang (which may have covered an area of about ten square miles) lay the king's palace. In addition, about one dozen royal tomb complexes, residences of the aristocracy, government buildings, and dwellings of officials and artisans existed within the city. The planned city was laid out in a grid pattern along a north-south axis similar to that found in the Indus cities. The surrounding area included a religious center, an ancestral burial ground, and a hunting preserve.

Hunting provided sport, food for the royal table, and a means for training the armed forces. To surround game on large hunting preserves stretching over many square miles, the monarch and other members of the elite would have to coordinate the massed movement of mounted horsemen and perhaps charioteers. Subsequently, the hunted animals would be forced into a restricted area where they could be killed.

The Shang kingdom also included affiliated territories, the subordinate rulers of which received their titles and authority to rule from the Shang monarch in exchange for their recognition of his overlordship and promise to aid him when the realm came under attack. Such leaders usually came to the capital on a regular schedule, bearing tribute (often valuable products native to the affiliated area). On the other hand, the monarch recognized the affiliated lord's right to rule and aided him in times of conflict. Beyond the core area and affiliated lands lay the places where other ethnic peoples dwelled. The rulers of these places traded and sometimes warred with the Chinese.

SOCIETY. Shang society included an aristocracy, officials, merchants, artisans, peasants, and slaves (usually war prisoners, especially those who were non-Chinese). Some social mobility and mixing occurred. Women usually submitted to men in political, social, and economic matters, yet some aristocratic women transcended these social limitations. In the mid-1970s, an excavated Shang tomb revealed the remains of Fu Hao[13] (Lady Hao), who lived around 1300 B.C. She was a wife of King Wuding. Like her husband, Fu Hao acted as a diviner in the religious practice of seeking the spirits' views on various important matters. Hundreds of bronze pieces, bone artifacts, and

[13] **Fu Hao:** foo HOW

FIGURE 5.6 *Jade Figurine from the Fu Hao Tomb.* *This small carved piece demonstrates the sophisticated level of Shang artisanry. It also shows the sitting posture characteristic of early East Asian cultures and suggests the subordinate status of servants. The hooked portion at the rear may be an artistic extension of the figure's sash.* Institute of Archaeology, Beijing.

jade items were recovered from her tomb. Evidence suggests that Fu Hao commanded an army, garnered a reputation of military invincibility, and served as an official.

Some oracle bone inscriptions reveal that after Fu Hao's death, the king implored her spirit to aid in his battles. Although aristocratic women like Fu Hao were not commonly active, she was not unique. Fu Jing (Lady Jing), another wife of Wuding, led armies and played an active political role in government.

Other Shang tombs have provided social information about the aristocrats through lavish burial chambers with numerous grave goods. The scale of the funeral complexes suggests that the monarchs and other aristocrats could command large populations, including slaves, to work on these elaborate monuments. They also indicate a highly stratified society. Some tombs held the remains of people who had been killed and interred with the aristocrat, and there may have been a relationship between the numbers of people killed and the status of the aristocrat who was buried in the tomb. Chariots buried along with horses show a new and important weapon of the Shang era. The idea for these chariots came from Central Asia.

ECONOMY. Agriculture was the basis of the Shang economy. In the Yellow River Valley, millet was the key grain harvested; in the south, rice became the staple crop. Most Chinese worked in agriculture and produced enough of a crop surplus to support large cities and growing numbers of people.

Metallurgy reached sophisticated levels during the Shang era. Bronze pieces included not only tools and weapons but also ceremonial items that were exchanged between the monarch and the lords of the affiliated states during their ceremonies of pledging loyalty. Indeed, it seems likely that the ruling elite valued the ceremonial bronzes more highly than the bronze implements.

ELITE CULTURE. One glory of Shang China was the development of a sophisticated elite culture. Thanks to generations of dedicated archaeologists, a rich variety of artifacts has been recovered in the twentieth century. Most prized are the Shang ceremonial bronzes. Artisans perfected the techniques necessary to produce beautiful bronze items with surfaces so malleable that incisions carved on them could be made with remarkable ease. To achieve that result, the artisans experimented with alloys of copper, lead, tin, antimony, arsenic, and zinc. All bronze surfaces available for decoration were covered by intricate designs representing animals, birds, mythical creatures, gods, or human beings. Some weighed nearly one ton.

Shang religious practices are reflected in the monumental structures near the cities and in the practice of divination. Members of the Shang elite respected their dead ancestors and frequently called upon them for blessings and approval. Kings built impressive temples to their forebears and regularly visited these sites to perform ceremonial acts announcing victory in battle, a bumper harvest, or the birth of a son and heir. Other subjects of veneration included cultural heroes, celestial bodies, and natural objects, such as mountains.

Members of the Shang elite believed in a paramount diety, the Lord on High, and regularly requested its blessings or guidance on proposed actions. To divine the future, they used animal bones and turtle shells. The normal divining process began with preparing the shells or oracle bones by cleaning and drying them. Then the diviner scraped away the bone or shell until it was thin. After asking the Lord on High his question, the diviner placed a heated piece of metal on the thin surface. The high temperature would crack the bone or shell, and the diviner would interpret the cracks (the Lord on High's answer) and relay the message to the questioner. Diviners kept the divination artifact, often with the question, answer, and result written on the surface.

The oracle bones also tell us about the other key Shang contribution, the development of a written language. Since its development more than three millennia ago, the written word has become more important than the spoken word. The origins of the written characters predate by centuries the practice of divination. Crude markings, which may have reflected ownership or some form of record keeping, are found on artifacts recovered at the Banpo site. Certainly these efforts became more regularized and complex over succeeding centuries. In the Shang era, extant evidence associates writing with divination. From the 200,000 recovered oracle bones, scholars have reconstructed a written language containing 3,000 characters. Of these, about 800 have been deciphered. Many characters evolved from pictures (pictographs), others represented ideas (ideograms), and most combined a pronunciation indicator with a part that suggested the meaning of the character. Eventually 214 of these "parts" became key components of the written characters

FIGURE 5.7 *Bronze Mask of the Shang Dynasty.* *The stylized facial features of this piece demonstrate the skill of Shang metal workers. This bronze mask was apparently used for decorative purposes and probably was not worn.* Asian Art and Archeology.

for literate Chinese. For the first thousand years, the characters developed regional and local variations. Only in the late third century B.C. did writing become standardized. Because regional variants of spoken Chinese became mutually unintelligible dialects over time, the unified characters gave a cultural cohesion that helped overcome the geographical and ethnic diversity.

THE LAST DAYS OF THE SHANG DYNASTY. According to historical documents, the last Shang monarch terrorized his subjects, and once he even drank wine from a cup made from the skull of an opponent. (This was a common practice in many parts of the world.) In what was a caricature of excess, hostile sources described him as a giant of a man who drank a lake of ale and ate a forest of meat. At the same time, evidence indicates that slaves revolted against the king and their other overlords.

Seeing an opportunity, successive leaders of Zhou,[14] a western affiliated state, carried out an extended campaign against Shang. At long last, around 1050 B.C, the Zhou state's army approached the Shang capital, where the Zhou captured and executed the hapless Shang king.

The Early Zhou, around 1050–771 B.C.

The Zhou Dynasty (around 1050–around 256 B.C.) arose in a strategic region that produced many of China's early dynasties. Although little is known about its first centuries, Zhou gained an honored reputation among later Chinese.

THE EARLY ZHOU GOVERNMENT. The dynastic founders included outstanding and revered figures, like the Cultured King (reigned before 1050 B.C.), who long pondered the overthrow of the Shang monarch. The motivation for his plans is hard to determine, given a paucity of documents, especially of those showing the Shang perspective. The Cultured King's eldest son, the Martial King (reign dates around 1050–around 1043 B.C.), defeated the Shang army and placed two of his brothers in charge of the Shang heartland. After a few years, the Martial King died and left a young son as his successor. The two brothers who ruled the Shang realm revolted against

FIGURE 5.8 *Shang Oracle Bone. Having been used to divine the future, this bone was etched with a record of the event, giving us an example of early Chinese writing. The inscription on the left begins, "On the day,* jia chen, *a great and violent wind struck, . . . the moon was eclipsed. . . ." Diviners were important in Shang society and were usually members of the royal family.* From Joseph Needham, *Science and Civilization,* Vol. I, op. p. 84. Courtesy of Royal Asiatic Society.

their nephew, and former Shang officials joined the rebels. The boy monarch and government faced a serious crisis.

Members of the Zhou elite appointed another brother of the Martial King, the Duke of Zhou (lived in the eleventh century B.C.), as a regent, and he swiftly sent a force that crushed the uprising. To forestall future unrest, the Duke of Zhou resettled members of the Shang elite to places where they could be controlled. For his actions as well as for refusing to take power for himself, the Duke of Zhou has been revered by later philosophers.

To justify their conquest of Shang and to legitimize their own government, the Zhou rulers developed the idea of the **Mandate of**

[14] **Zhou:** JOH

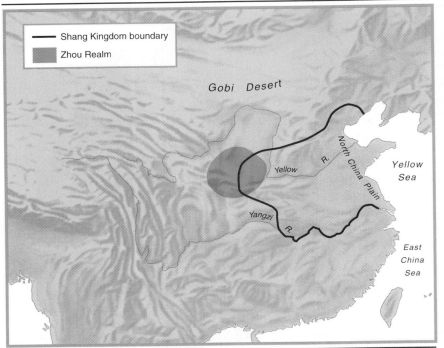

MAP 5.3 *Yellow River Civilizations, around 1500–771 B.C.* The key Chinese civilizations developed in the Yellow River Valley of northern China, with the Shang in the east and the Zhou in the west. Zhou conquered Shang in the eleventh century B.C. by seizing and maintaining control of the mountain passes and rivers that served as natural defenses.

Heaven, a concept that justified rebellion in certain cases. "Heaven" was a name for a Zhou god who conferred upon a dynastic house the right to rule because of its virtuous behavior. Heaven could also assist a challenger, if the existing house had become corrupt and the new house was virtuous. Zhou claimed that Shang lost the Mandate and that this justified the change of regime. In fact, the Zhou god, Heaven, replaced the Shang deity, the Lord on High, and politics was henceforth equated with moral conduct.

The Martial King established a legal code to regulate the people. In addition, the monarch and many of his officials often traveled the realm to monitor lower officials.

THE DECLINE OF ZHOU: DECENTRALIZED POLITICS.
The early years of Zhou saw effective government from the center, but gradually monarchs became less competent. One striking example of royal misrule came in 771 B.C., when threats from nomads north and northwest of the capital forced the creation of a warning-fire system. Lighted fires were a signal to bring armies from nearby garrisons. Enraptured by one of his wives, the frivolous king amused her by lighting the warning fires. The royal couple gleefully watched as the defensive forces arrived only to learn of the false

alarm. After a few false alarms, a legitimate nomadic attack came, but when the fires were lit, the rescuers refused to come and the capital fell. Whether or not this account reflected the whole story of the fall of the capital to outside forces, the remaining Zhou influence dissipated when the capital was moved a few hundred miles to the east.

Along with ineffective Zhou monarchs, geographical elements aided the decline of the central authority. The area of North and Central China was simply too large to administer effectively. Realizing this problem and following a general Shang political strategy, Zhou rulers created a series of states in their claimed territories and appointed rulers there. The appointments received confirmation in an elaborate ceremony during which the subordinate lord pledged loyalty to the king and obedience to his commands. They became his **vassals**, subordinate lords who loyally aided their king in exchange for lands and privileges. When the central polity lost its effectiveness, these territorial leaders gained some measure of independence.

Below the king was a hierarchical aristocratic order. The most important group comprised the blood relatives of the ruling house. Subordinate to this elite in social rank were vassal groups, which ruled smaller territories and had little royal blood. They often fought for the higher lords or served as officials.

Artisans and a few merchants worked in these urban centers but occupied a middle social rank. Those who worked the land were bound there for fixed periods. If they were mistreated, however, it was easy and common for them to flee elsewhere.

Agriculture grew more important with the rise of **manorialism**, a self-sufficient economic system centered on a lord's household and with some agricultural workers bound to the land. The growing trend was for local areas to produce as much as possible to meet their own needs. **Serfs**, rural folk who farmed the lord's land and who found themselves tied to it, worked their portions; collectively, all serfs tilled a central section for the lord's subsistence. Most of the harvest went to the lord, and the remainder was allocated to the serfs.

This system came to be known as the **well-field system** because the plots resembled the

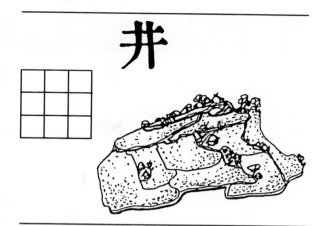

FIGURE 5.9 *Well-Field System. Based on* jing, *the Chinese word for "well" (top), this schematic (left) illustrates the gridlike farming system developed in Early Zhou China. All land belonged to the lord, who rented each outer section to a peasant family. The center plot was collectively farmed by all families and its harvest went to the lord. In practice, the well-field ideal was adapted to the natural topography of the land (right).* Left, right: From Ray Huang, *China: A Macro History* (Armonk, N.Y.: M. E. Sharpe, Inc.), an Eastgate Book © 1988. Reproduced with permission.

IN THEIR OWN WORDS

Daily Life as Seen in Chinese Poetry

Early Chinese poetry, the *Book of Songs*, reveals much about the lives of ordinary people. In that sense, it can serve as a source for the study of social history in ancient China. In one poem written more than 3,000 years ago, for example, the common folk ordered their lives about the calendar:

> In the tenth month the cricket goes under my bed.
> I stop up every hole to smoke out the rats,
> Plugging the windows, burying the doors:
> 'Come, wife and children,
> The change of the year is at hand.
> Come and live in this house.'
> . . . .
> In the ninth month we make ready the stack-yards,
> In the tenth month we bring in the harvest,
> Millet for wine, millet for cooking, the early and the late,
> Paddy and hemp, beans and wheat.
> . . . .
> My harvesting is over,

Go up and begin your work in the house. . . .

Gender issues were sometimes revealed in Chinese poetry of the same period:

> Mat over mat, bamboo on rush
> so it be soft, to sleep, to wake in hush,
> from dreams of bears and snakes?
> . . . .
> Bears be for boys; snakes, girls.
> Boys shall have beds, hold scepters for their toys,
> . . . .
> bellow when they would cry
> . . . .
> Small girls shall sleep on floor and play with tiles,
> wear simple clothes and do no act amiss,
> cook, brew and seemly speak,
> conducing so the family's quietness.

Boys slept on beds, while girls slept on the floor; this indicates the subordination of women in Chinese society. Girls were expected to behave and speak quietly, whereas boys might bellow when they cried.

SOUTH AND EAST ASIA

Indus Valley Civilization, c. 2500–c. 1750 B.C.

Aryan migrations, c. 1750 B.C.

Shang Dynasty, c. 1500–c. 1050 B.C.

Age of Vedas, c. 1200–c. 750 B.C.

Early Zhou Dynasty, c. 1050–c. 771 B.C.

Iron Age, c. 1000 B.C.

2500 B.C.

2000 B.C.

Fall of Mohenjo–Daro, c. 1750 B.C.

Founding of Shang, c. 1500 B.C.

1500 B.C.

Martial King conquers Shang, c. 1050 B.C.

1000 B.C.

Duke of Zhou reconquers Shang, c. 1042 B.C.

Fall of Early Zhou, 771 B.C.

Chinese character for "well" (*jing*), which looks similar to a tic-tac-toe schematic. Because this period of Chinese history saw the decline of larger cities that brought the widespread practice of subsistence farming, the population level likely stayed near that of the Shang era.

We know little about the women and children of this time. One source of our information about gender hierarchy is the *Book of Songs*, a diverse collection of music from all social groups. Each song provides a brief look at the lives and concerns of the Chinese people. The book shows a dominant male order with women clearly subordinated. Men worked in the fields, while women wove in the homes. This division of tasks based on gender lasted for centuries and extended even to traditional ceremonies in which the monarch plowed and his consorts wove.

Early Zhou elite culture continued some earlier traditions and added new practices as well. Shang divination practices, for example, vanished, but bronze making continued, although the Zhou pieces seemed to lose the complexity and malleability of their Shang predecessors. The Zhou rulers kept documents from the time of the dynasty's founding; these long resided in archives until their recovery and editing. Other glimpses of Zhou elite culture come from the popular *Book of Songs*.

SUMMARY

1. The Indus Valley civilization lasted for centuries and boasted cities with standardized patterns, including brick-built houses, effective drainage systems, and efficient grain-storage areas. A combination of factors brought about the civilization's decline, including excessive deforestation, recurrent flooding induced by earthquakes, salt accumulation, overgrazing, and a prolonged dry spell.

2. The Aryan peoples came into India and slowly moved across the northwest until they reached the Ganges River Valley. They brought chariot warfare. Their religious system, led by the *brahmans*, was described in the Vedas. The Aryans held themselves apart from and over the local peoples, yet a synthesis of Aryan and local culture gradually emerged.

3. Two key epic poems, the *Ramayana* and *Mahabharata*, reflected and influenced Indian political as well as religious ideas.

4. The Shang people built a civilization in the Yellow River Valley of China. It manifested elements of civilization, such as long-distance trade, cities, a writing system, and metallurgy.

5. The Shang polity, a loose confederation of aligned states, was a monarchy. Society was dominated by aristocrats, including a few women who fought in battles and ruled some areas. Elites developed a writing system and a process of predicting the future by using oracle bones. They also supported the production of sophisticated artifacts of bronze, bones, and precious stones.

6. The Shang fell to the Zhou, another Chinese group, who brought a new dynasty and a short-lived but more centralized government. After a few generations, however, political decline and the development of a manorial economic system led to Chinese decentralization.

SUGGESTED READINGS

Allchin, Bridget, and Raymond Allchin. *The Rise of Civilization in India and Pakistan.* Cambridge, Eng.: Cambridge University Press, 1982. A standard treatment of the Indus Valley civilization.

Chang, K. C., ed. *Shang Civilization.* New Haven, Conn.: Yale University Press, 1980. A classic examination of the archaeology of the Shang Dynasty.

Hsu Cho-yun and Katheryn Linduff. *Western Chou Civilization.* New Haven, Conn.: Yale University Press, 1988. A standard analysis and presentation of early Zhou history.

Thapar, Romila. *Ancient India.* Delhi: Oxford University Press, 1992. Interpretive essays about ancient India.

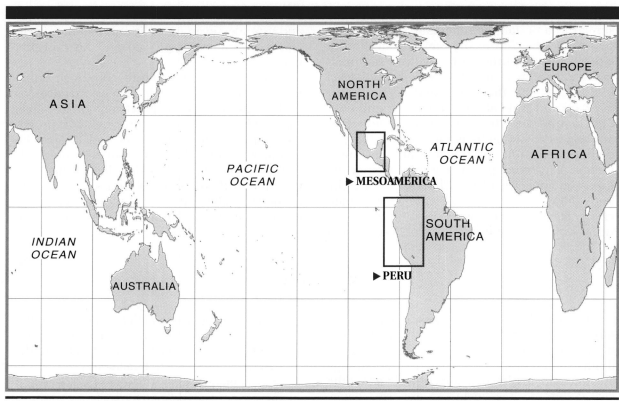

ASIA

PACIFIC
OCEAN

INDIAN
OCEAN

AUSTRALIA

NORTH
AMERICA

EUROPE

ATLANTIC
OCEAN

AFRICA

▶ MESOAMERICA

SOUTH
AMERICA

▶ PERU

Gulf of
Mexico

Valley
of
Mexico

Mayan
Lowland

Olmec
Heartland

Usumacinta R.

PACIFIC
OCEAN

▶ MESOAMERICA

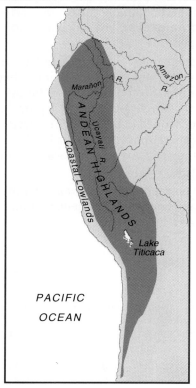

Marañón

Amazon
R.

Ucayali R.

ANDEAN HIGHLANDS

Coastal Lowlands

Lake
Titicaca

PACIFIC
OCEAN

▶ PERU

C H A P T E R **6**

The Development of Civilizations in the Americas

The earth's longest winter was ending. After five million years of cold weather, the climate finally was warming, and winters were getting shorter. Somewhere in northeastern Asia, people were going about their business — hunting game, sewing clothing, and preparing meals. They were unaware that they soon would become the first human colonists in a new world: the Americas.

When these immigrants, whose descendants became known as American Indians, came to the Americas sometime after 43,000 B.C., their arrival constituted the first population movement into the western hemisphere. Following this initial peopling, the Americas developed essentially independently of Africa, Asia, and Europe. Although there were a few sporadic contacts earlier, the voyage of Christopher Columbus in 1492 established the first sustained or significant contact between the two hemispheres. Despite their isolation from each other, the two halves of the world followed similar patterns of development that led to the development of civilization in various places. This chapter discusses that development in the Americas to about A.D. 1300, placing greatest emphasis on artifact-rich Mexico and adjacent areas; later developments are treated in Chapter 16.

In the period before 1300, few societies in the Americas had any system of written language. The major exceptions were the civilizations of Mexico and adjacent Central America, where writing began by 500 B.C. and perhaps a few centuries earlier. Even there, however, the vast majority of writings are lost to us. Although books were produced in much of this area, many of the older ones have been destroyed by natural processes over the centuries. More recent books, those still extant at the time of the Spanish conquest, often were searched out and destroyed by the Spanish as works of the devil; a reasonable guess is that the *conquistadores* burned or otherwise destroyed several thousand books (more than a thousand different titles) in Mexico alone.

One upshot of this paucity of documents is that most of the information we have about ancient American peoples has been derived from archaeology. The earlier peoples of the Americas had no writing, and the writing of some literate societies of later periods cannot be deciphered. When documents or inscriptions have survived and can be translated, however, their contributions have been incorporated into this chapter.

THE PEOPLING OF THE AMERICAS AND EARLY CULTURES

Separated from the rest of the world by the Atlantic and Pacific oceans, the American continents were not part of the spread of *Homo erectus* described in Chapter 2. Indeed, they were among the later parts of the earth to be colonized by human beings, and the only human remains that have been found in the Americas are of biologically modern *Homo sapiens.*

The Great Migration

Biological evolution is a slow process, and the time elapsed since the first immigrants came to the Americas is short. Consequently, one might expect the descendants of these immigrants—today's American Indians—to share many traits with people living in their old home, the source area for the migration to America. By far the closest similarity lies between American Indians and the inhabitants of Siberia in northeastern Asia. The two groups have literally hundreds of distinctive traits in common, including shovel-shaped incisors (an anatomical form of the front teeth, found only rarely among other human groups), characteristic

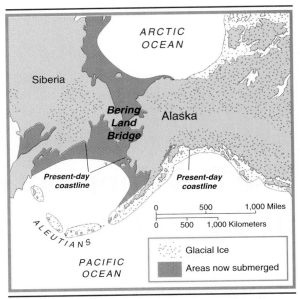

MAP 6.1 *The Bering Land Bridge. Lowered sea levels created a land link between Siberia and Alaska in the area that today is covered by the water of the Bering Strait. This land bridge appeared several times between 43,000 and 15,000 B.C. and was at times over one thousand miles wide. It provided the route for the first people to enter the Americas.*

blood proteins, and skeletal details. When dealing with genetics, it always is possible that a trait developed twice independently by chance, but the probability is billions to one against it. There is little doubt of the common ancestry of Asians and American Indians.

The Americas are separated from the other continents by water on all sides. However, the Bering Strait, which separates Alaska and Siberia, is only about 90 miles wide today. In some earlier periods, however, the colder climate caused huge amounts of water to freeze into glaciers, lowering the sea level and turning the Bering Strait into the **Bering Land Bridge**, a vast stretch of dry land connecting North America and Asia. We know that various animals crossed over the land bridge—mammoths (a now-extinct kind of northern elephant), for example, evolved in Eurasia and then migrated to the Americas—and people made the crossing, too. The Bering Land Bridge was an inviting place, offering milder winters and more resources than Siberia, and the immigrants probably moved gradually onto it, eventually crossing over into America without even realizing it. When the climate warmed again and the land submerged, they were stranded on the American side.

Modern scholars agree that the first human entry into the Americas took place via the Bering Land Bridge between about 43,000 and 10,000 B.C., but there is considerable controversy about the specific date of the crossing. This is not surprising, because the most crucial archaeological data for settling the issue lie under 120 feet of water in the Bering Sea, an area essentially inaccessible to archaeologists. It is clear that there were four major periods when the Bering Land Bridge was available, the earliest beginning at 43,000 B.C. and the most recent ending about 10,000 B.C. Correlating the possible crossing dates with the earliest known sites, most archaeologists believe that the first immigrants entered the Americas between 33,000 and 14,000 B.C.

Lifeways of the Earliest Americans

Unfortunately, we know less than we would like about the first Americans. The earliest archaeological sites are small and have a limited range of materials in them, principally because perishable items of wood, leather, and even bone usually have disappeared over the millennia. Most of what remains are stone tools, with occasional bones or seeds from food waste. On their basis, a general picture of these early Americans, called **Paleo-Indians**, has emerged.

The Paleo-Indians lived, for the most part, in small bands that consisted usually of about 30 to 100 people. At some seasons or for special activities, more than one band might come together, or the band might split into smaller family units. Paleo-Indians hunted, gathered, and fished for all their food, typically using a broad range of the foodstuffs available locally.

Paleo-Indians lived in a world in which many of the huge mammals of the glacial period had not yet become extinct. On the North American plains, for example, mammoths, prehistoric horses, and giant bison roamed, while mastodons (another extinct type of elephant) crashed about in swamps, and a wealth of other large animals occupied a variety of habitats. It is clear that Paleo-Indians hunted both mammoths and bison, sometimes killing them singly and sometimes driving bison herds over cliffs for mass killing. The hunting of game of this size with stone-tipped spears must have been dangerous in the extreme.

FIGURE 6.1 *Folsom Bison Excavation.* *In 1926, a local cowboy discovered a huge bison skeleton in a ravine in southwestern New Mexico. He recognized that the spearhead embedded in the bones meant that human beings must have been contemporary with this ancient beast. The archaeologists who later excavated the site found abundant evidence to confirm his conclusion. The left foreground of this photo is the area in which both bones and stone tools were found, confirming that American Indians had been in the Americas since ancient times.* Photo by Frank M. Figgins. Courtesy of the American Museum of National History.

In the past, archaeologists were very taken with the hunting of big game by Paleo-Indians, and some argued that these large animals formed the mainstay of the Paleo-Indian diet. This conclusion perhaps is understandable, given that many of the sites excavated early on were kill sites of these large prey, but recent evidence suggests that large game may have played a much smaller role in Paleo-Indian life than previously believed. Archaeological sites such as the Shawnee-Minisink site in New Jersey have re-vealed the other side of Paleo-Indian diet: squirrels, rabbits, fish, berries, and wild grain seeds. At sites like this one, prosaic foodstuffs formed the entire diet, and big game did not appear at all. Many archaeologists now believe that in most areas big game was an occasional element of Paleo-Indian meals but hardly everyday fare.

The big game, except for the smallest species of bison, became extinct mostly between 11,000 and 9000 B.C. Many archaeologists believe that human hunting may have played a part in those extinctions (although there is no evidence that Paleo-Indians ever hunted most of the species that became extinct), but there were other momentous processes going on at the same time. The world was becoming warmer, the glaciers were receding from the northern areas of North America, and vegetation all over the Americas was changing. These changes must have played a major role in the extinction of the big game, probably a greater role than human predation.

Around 8000 B.C., tool styles changed in the Americas, and archaeologists consider this date the end of the Paleo-Indian Period, which was replaced with a series of regional foraging traditions. With the exceptions of warmed climate, extinction of big game, and changed tool styles, however, lifeways continued much as in the preceding millennia.

NUCLEAR AMERICA

Two places in the Americas clearly developed civilization in antiquity: one in Mexico and adjacent Central America, and one in Peru and nearby areas. These areas are the ones that, throughout American prehistory, have been in the forefront of innovation and change. They were the earliest in the Americas to develop agriculture and the earliest to develop complex societies, and many would argue that they were the only areas where civilization emerged. Many ideas and practices that developed in these areas then diffused into other parts of the Americas. Because of this, these two areas collectively are termed **Nuclear America**, composed of Mesoamerica and Peru.

As a culture area, **Mesoamerica** is defined as the geographical area where certain distinctive cultural traits are or were present. Obviously, the boundaries of this area have varied over the centuries, but basically it consists of the area of the modern countries of Mexico, Guatemala, and Belize and adjacent portions of Honduras and El Salvador. In the past several thousand years, this area has shared a number of cultural characteristics, including corn-squash-beans agriculture, pyramids as bases for temples, a glyphic writing system, a similar calendric system, a distinctive ball game, and human sacrifice. The list could be elaborated; indeed, a recent compilation of defining characteristics of Mesoamerica listed seventy-eight cultural traits. What is important for our purposes is that the various regions of Mesoamerica shared knowledge and many ideas and practices, making the culture area as a whole a reasonable unit to examine.

Peru, when seen as a culture area, consists of the highland and coastal portions of modern Peru, as well as adjacent highland and coastal areas of Ecuador, Bolivia, and Chile. A few of the defining cultural characteristics of this culture area are corn-bean-potato agriculture, terraced fields, prominent sun gods, and mummification of the dead. As with Mesoamerica, Peru had its regional variations, but there was an overall pattern of similarity.

Although the area between Mesoamerica and Peru had some elements in common with these areas, the differences are great enough to warrant this intermediate area's being considered not part of Nuclear America. Indeed, the difficulties of travel in Panama and some other intermediate areas must have restricted direct land contact between the two parts of Nuclear America. Yet there is evidence that such contact occasionally occurred, presumably by coastal sea travel. The only linguistic relatives of the Tarascan language of western Mexico are found in South America, and several food plants domesticated in one area were transported to the other at various times in prehistory.

PARALLELS AND DIVERGENCES

The Amazing Chili

The chili pepper was one of the first plants to be domesticated in America, indeed in the world. Its use in the Americas spread to any place it would grow, and after Europeans brought it back to their homelands, its use spread rapidly in Europe, Africa, and Asia. Today, inhabitants of Ethiopia, Indonesia, western China, India, Thailand, and a host of other places have integrated chilis into their diet, sometimes with searing results. Indeed, the incorporation has been so complete that most of these people will tell you that chilis always have been part of their cuisine.

The initial attraction, doubtless, was the taste. Chilis vary tremendously, from the pungent bell pepper to the excruciatingly hot *habanero*.[a] Each adds its distinctive flavor, dominating or not at the discretion of the cook. Chilis can cover the flavor of food that is a bit spoiled, although this probably would have been of little advantage in the tropics, where spoiled food needs to be recognized and discarded, rather than consumed anyway. Chilis also have the ability to retard spoilage; capsaicin, the component that burns the mouth, has even direr effects on many bacteria, and a dish laced with chili is more likely to survive room temperature storage than one without.

An additional factor that may have favored the use of chili is conceptions of folk medicine. Most peoples in the world have some notion of heat balance in the body. Too much or too little heat can cause illness. (This concept is embedded in the English term "a cold," meaning a mild disease.) In these societies, foods that can restore balance by heating or cooling the body are valuable, and a strong chili certainly can restore body heat. We have no idea whether ancient Mexicans and Peruvians had this type of conception of disease, but it may be significant that virtually all of their modern descendants do.

Finally, chilis are good for you. They contain high concentrations of vitamin C, more than seven times that of oranges. Even small amounts of chili contain useful quantities of vitamin C, a nutrient that might have been difficult to get without chilis. Of course, ancient Americans had no way of knowing of this benefit, except possibly by the observation that chili eaters were less likely to contract scurvy, the vitamin C deficiency disease, than those who abstained.

[a] *habanero:* ah bah NAY roh

THE RISE OF AGRICULTURE

The basic characteristics of agriculture and current explanations of why it has developed around the world were discussed in Chapter 3. To put it briefly, agriculture permits people to produce more food than do hunting and gathering, but it ties them to a single place and demands that they spend much more time working for their suppers.

The Chronology and General Nature of Agriculture in Mesoamerica

The process and details of agricultural development in Mesoamerica are much better known than are those in Peru, largely because more research has been directed toward Mesoamerica. Agricultural development in Mesoamerica followed two paths, one in the dry highlands of central Mexico and another in the moist coastal lowlands of eastern Mexico, Belize, Guatemala, and Honduras.

The earliest known domesticated plants in highland Mesoamerica appear about 6500 B.C. These include squash, chili peppers, avocados, and corn, with cobs only the size of a child's little finger. The wild progenitors from which these plants were developed came from a variety of zones and regions, but they are found together archaeologically, indicating that they had been brought together by the early agriculturalists. At this early stage of agriculture, people were expending little energy on cultivation; they planted the crops, then continued on their long-established seasonal movements for hunting and gathering. If the crops had done well when they returned to the area at harvest time, so much the better; if not, they could survive off wild foods.

From 6500 to 2300 B.C., Mesoamericans increased their reliance on agriculture. The variety of crops increased with the addition of various kinds of beans, new species of squash, and pumpkins. An import from Peru, cotton, also was grown in some quantity, and it is unclear whether it was used for its fiber in weaving, for its oily seeds as food, or (most probably) for both. Corn was being improved during this period and, by 3000 B.C., was nearly the size of an adult's thumb. Although agricultural produce had provided only about 5 percent of the diet in 6000 B.C., it had increased to about 40 percent by 4500 B.C. and to 85 percent by 3000 B.C. As agriculture's importance increased, farmers became sedentary, staying in one place to tend their crops.

From 2300 B.C. onward, virtually all peoples in central Mexico and many other portions of highland Mesoamerica were fully dependent on agriculture and lived sedentary lives in villages. Over time, new crops were domesticated and old domesticates were improved. By 700 B.C., experiments in irrigation were beginning, and sophisticated irrigation systems probably were in use by 300 B.C. By this time, agriculture had taken firm hold of highland Mesoamerican society.

The path to agriculture in lowland Mesoamerica was considerably different. There, year-round moisture and warmth created an endless growing season perfect for starchy root crops, especially **manioc** (widely known by its Spanish name, *yuca*[1]). Manioc roots cannot be stored very well after harvesting, but they can be kept in the ground until needed. They provide a delicious and calorie-rich starch similar to potatoes, but there is a catch. Until the development of recent forms, all manioc has had large quantities of oxalic acid, a poison, in its roots. This poison can be removed easily by grating the root, soaking it in water to leach out the oxalic acid, and cooking the grated manioc. Because manioc roots do not preserve well archaeologically, the earliest evidence of their use comes from small obsidian blades used for grating them. The blades are known from around 4000 B.C., but it is possible that earlier use of manioc has left behind no recognizable remains.

Around 1200 B.C., maize from the highlands first appeared in the lowlands. Although not terribly well adapted to the moist soils of the lowlands, corn rapidly became popular and eclipsed manioc in importance. Other highland domesticates also came into the lowlands, and shortly after this date the lowland diet began to more closely resemble the highland diet.

The Chronology and General Nature of Agriculture in Peru

As noted previously, evidence on the development of agriculture is far less well known in Peru than in Mesoamerica. It is clear, however, that a fairly extensive set of plants was domesticated and cultivated by 5000 B.C., and many believe that the roots of Peruvian agriculture extend back earlier. Among the domesticated crops were some distinctive Peruvian species, including **quinoa**[2] (an important grain from the amaranth plant) and potatoes, a staple of the later Peruvian diet; there also were some crops domesticated independently in both Mesoamerica and Peru, including corn, beans, and chili peppers. The Peruvian versions of these latter crops, however, were different from their Mesoamerican cousins in subtle ways. Early Peruvian corn, for example, was sweet corn (the kind eaten on the cob in today's United States) and had a high sugar-to-starch ratio; early Mesoamerican corn, in contrast, was the popcorn type, with a low sugar-to-starch ratio.

Unlike Mesoamericans (who domesticated virtually no animals), early Peruvians domesticated a few animals, especially the llama and alpaca (camel-like animals raised for food, wool, and pack carrying) and the guinea pig (a food animal). Compared with Eurasia and Africa, however, Peru domesticated few animals, none of which affected the way of life to the extent livestock transformed most of Eurasia and Africa.

The Significance of Agricultural Development in the Americas

The primary significance of the development of agriculture in the Americas, of course, is that it provided a base for the development of larger, denser, sedentary populations, some of whom would launch the developments leading to civilization. There are, however, several other significant aspects.

[1] *yuca:* YOO kuh

[2] **quinoa:** KEE nwuh

FIGURE 6.2   *Ancient Inca Road.* *Segments of the massive Inca road network survive in many parts of modern Peru, Bolivia, Chile, and Ecuador. Here, a modern Aymara woman of Bolivia trudges along an Inca road, with its paved surface, raised curbs, and gentle slope. She leads one alpaca (a relative of the llama) and herds others. Alpacas provide soft, strong hair that is spun into thread and used in weaving textiles today, just as it has been since around 1500 B.C.* Hans Sylvester/Liaison International.

First, both in Mesoamerica and Peru, the early domesticated crops are derived from wild ancestors that came from widely scattered habitats. This means that agriculture, in a real sense, had no single point of origin, nor was it developed by a genius who first conceived the idea. Rather, different plants were experimented with in many areas, and the more successful experiments were passed from hand to hand, eventually becoming established as staples.

Second, there were some exchanges of crops between Mesoamerica and Peru. Common beans, popping corn, and perhaps chilis passed from Mesoamerica to Peru; cotton, lima beans, sweet corn, and probably jack beans came in return. This is significant, because although one society can, say, reinvent a similar pottery style by chance, plants with identical or near-identical genetic makeup cannot be developed independently. Consequently, we have unequivocal evidence of early contact between the two areas of Nuclear America, though we have no idea how it may have come about or how frequent it was. That these crops were unknown until much later in the area between the two halves of Nuclear America supports the idea of sea contact between Mesoamerica and Peru.

Third, both in Peru and Mesoamerica, domesticated foods were balanced and complementary. They were balanced in terms of agriculture, as corn, squash, and beans, planted in rotation in the same field, will replenish nutrients used by the others, keeping the soil fertile for long periods. Even more significant from the viewpoint of the development of civilization, the major staples of Nuclear America provided a nutritionally balanced diet that could support healthy life without major consumption of meat. This may help explain why American civilizations never developed the range of domesticated animals that their counterparts in Africa and Eurasia did. Also, because draft animals almost always have been first domesticated for food and then assigned labor duties, the dearth of domesticated food animals may account for the absence of draft animals and the concomitant lack of wheeled vehicles in the Americas.

Fourth and finally, the successful American staple foods were easily stored. Corn and beans dry easily, and the harder squashes keep well. Potatoes at first appear to be an exception, but ancient Peruvians preserved them by freeze-drying—exposing them to the frigid temperatures of glaciers in the high Andes peaks, producing a hard, nutty, and easily stored foodstuff through controlled freezer burn. This ability to store food is critical in seasonal environments, but it has an even more far-reaching implication. Stored food can be warehoused, and if a government controls that supply of food, it controls its people. It may be significant that in the Mesoamerican lowlands the advent of corn—the first storable staple there—corresponded exactly to the development of Olmec society, the first complex society in Mesoamerica.

ceremonial centers and the art and architecture within them. The centers were carved out of the jungle and apparently were used only seasonally, maintained the rest of the year by a small staff, perhaps composed of priests. We do not know what rituals went on there, but they must have been extravagant, if the scale of the centers themselves is an indication.

The ceremonial center at La Venta is the best known. The site is laid out with geometric regularity along a north-south axis, with an accuracy that suggests some skill at engineering and perhaps astronomy. At one end of the site, the Olmecs erected a huge pyramid of clay and earth, more than 300 feet high, with ridged sides. There are several rectangular clay-and-earth mounds, court-

THE GROWTH OF CIVILIZATION IN MESOAMERICA

As noted earlier, two major zones are particularly important in the study of Mesoamerica, because civilization developed there: the dry highlands of central Mexico and the moist lowlands of eastern Mexico and Central America. Each of the dozens of regions had its own complex developments and interactions with other regions, but we will restrict our treatment to four societies, two from the lowlands and two from the highlands.

The Olmecs, around 1200–around 400 B.C.

Olmec society developed around 1200 B.C. along the coast of the Gulf of Mexico, in the modern Mexican states of Veracruz and Tabasco. Of the four Mesoamerican societies discussed here, only the Olmec sometimes is considered not to be a civilization. Although the Olmecs possessed many of the elements of civilization, they may not have had the overall complexity that is implied by that concept. Theirs was, however, the first complex society in Mesoamerica, and they set the pattern for their successors. They made a deep and lasting impression on all Mesoamerican civilizations to follow them.

The primary Olmec characteristic that has earned them a place in history is their creation of

FIGURE 6.3 *Olmec Colossal Head.* *These enormous sculpted stone heads probably depict Olmec kings. All share certain characteristics, particularly flattened noses, broad faces, lips whose outline is more or less trapezoidal, and a leather helmet. Each has additional characteristics, however, such as scars, gapped teeth, big ears, or closely set eyes that make it unique. These individual traits suggest that the heads are portraits of real individuals rather than stylized monuments to a single individual or to a class of individuals.* Richard H. Stewart/© National Geographic Society.

UNDER THE LENS

The Mesoamerican Ball Game

The Mesoamerican ball game, variously known as *pelota* or *pok-ta-pok*, was widespread in Mesoamerica and distinctive to the Mesoamerican culture area. Other versions of the game are known in the prehistoric Caribbean, in the North American Southwest, and in northeastern South America, where it probably originated.

The game was a team sport, as were many pre-Columbian sports. The rules, court, and equipment varied over time and from culture to culture, but the basics were similar. The ball was made of hard, solid rubber, about the consistency of a modern truck tire, and was the size of a modern softball or a little larger. The court was generally rectangular, I-shaped, or H-shaped; goals typically consisted of rings on the side walls, or of the area between two uprights in the "end zone." The object of the game was to propel the ball into the goal without the use of the hands or, apparently in some places, the feet. Art showing the game in progress often shows players, all male, knocking the ball with a hip. In some places, players wore padding or special guards; in others they were exposed directly to the battering effects of the ball. Needless to say, injuries were many and scores were low; in some places, the game ended with the first score.

The game, while clearly having a recreational function in some areas, was primarily a ritual. In some places, winning players were sacrificed; in others, losers were; in still others, all players lived to compete again. There are records of betting on ball games, and in some places successful players were able to claim the clothing of spectators, sometimes inducing spectators to flee the court at the scoring of the winning point.

The Mesoamerican ball game never became widely popular among Europeans, who widely adopted other Indian games like lacrosse. The Mesoamerican ball game, however, may have been the inspiration for the Spanish Basque *pelota*, a game that appeared in the seventeenth century, a few decades after *conquistadores* returned to Spain. The game was played with teams, and the object was to hurl a hard leather ball through a ring set high on a wall. Europeans had almost no team sports before the sixteenth century, and most of those they did have seem to have been borrowed from the American Indians.

---

yards between them, a fence made of stone pillars set into a mudbrick wall, and several series of pavements composed of colored stone blocks forming jaguar faces. Among these structures, all of which are related to one another in the strictest geometrical manner, are various pits containing offerings of jade axes and other precious materials; many mounds also contain offerings. Large statues, including the colossal heads discussed in the following paragraphs, were distributed through the site. La Venta had no ball courts for playing the ceremonial Mesoamerican ball game; other Olmec ceremonial centers, however, had ball courts, and ceramic figures of ball players have been found at La Venta and elsewhere. (Jade, jaguars, and the ball game all were associated with the gods in later Mesoamerica.)

The entirety of these ceremonial centers bespeaks a society that could marshal a good deal of labor to produce monumental architecture in honor of the gods. Not only was a huge amount of labor needed just to build La Venta, but the individual components sometimes required extra effort. The immense carved heads, for example, were made of basalt, a hard volcanic rock that does not occur naturally near La Venta. To obtain it, the Olmecs removed blocks from quarries 70 miles and farther away; the blocks, some weighing 12 to 15 tons, must have been floated down the Usumacinta River, then moved overland the half mile or so to their ultimate location. Only then could the long job of carving a hard stone with a stone chisel of equal hardness begin.

The **colossal heads**, as these sculptures are known, range in size from about 6 to 9 feet high. They probably represented Olmec rulers, and the twenty-five or so of them known may have represented the rulers of a single dynasty. The heads share common characteristics, particularly the baby face, the leather helmet, the broad nose, and the trapezoidal mouth. Yet each has an individuality, complete with scars, blemishes, or gapped teeth, that has led many scholars to believe they are portraits of individuals, not simply conventionalized images.

A later myth links jaguars and babies through a mating between a jaguar and a woman. The baby produced by this union devoured its mother while nursing, then went on to become the first ruler of the land. Are these baby-faced rulers the embodiment of that myth? Many scholars think so, especially because other Olmec art shows **were-babies**, babies with fangs, jaguar paws, and helmets, sometimes devouring their mothers while nursing.

Recent research has begun the decipherment of Olmec writing, which now appears to be ancestral to the better-known Mayan writing. Perhaps the translation of inscriptions on monuments will provide more information about this little-known people.

The Olmecs possessed many of the elements of civilization discussed in Chapter 3. They carried on long-distance trade and created monumental architecture and a great art style; they apparently had writing; they had class stratification, occupational specialists, and considerable technological skill. On the other hand, some important characteristics of civilizations were absent. They had no cities, and the vast majority of their population lived in small villages; they probably were not a state and were more likely governed through a chiefdom. In the spectrum of societies, they were at the very edge of civilization.

The end for the Olmecs came around 400 B.C. Most evidence suggests that the Olmecs quietly changed into the ancestors of the Mayan civilization that succeeded them in the lowlands, but there are disturbing hints that the end might not have been so gentle. A few colossal heads have broken noses and other damage that may suggest vandalism, and some scholars believe that a conquering people may have defaced the images of the previous rulers to underscore the change in rulership. There is, however, no other evidence of violence or conquest.

The Olmecs remain enigmatic, largely because of how little we know of their life beyond the ceremonial centers. It is clear, however, that many of their characteristics became embedded somehow in the traditions of Mesoamerica and kept cropping up in later civilizations. The ball game, the importance of the jaguar, the erection of pyramids, the use of glyphic writing—these and other traits have made many scholars view Olmec society as an ancestral culture that set the tone for all Mesoamerican civilizations to come.

FIGURE 6.4 *Olmec Jade Sculpture of a Jaguar Baby. Much Olmec art focuses on babies, jaguars, and warriors, often showing a mixture of features. In this carving, for example, a mother holds a baby with a characteristic pudgy face and body, but with a nose shaped more like a jaguar's; the baby is also marked with a jaguar glyph. Other sculptures show babies with fangs or military helmets. It is believed that the dynasty of Olmec kings was linked to jaguars in mythology.* Lee Boltin Picture Library.

The Maya,
around 200 B.C.–around A.D. 800

After the disappearance of Olmec society, rapid changes took place for the Indians of the Guatemalan jungles. Around 200 B.C., these changes brought about the Mayan civilization, the successor of the Olmecs in lowland Mesoamerica. Mayan culture persisted through the Spanish conquest, but this discussion will focus on the civilization—formally known as "Classic Maya"—that flourished until around A.D. 800.

FIGURE 6.5 *Mayan Mural at Bonampak.* *This reconstruction of a wall painting from the Mayan city of Bonampak, painted by Antonia Tejeda, faithfully reproduces the detail originally recorded around* A.D. *800. The king stands in the center of a raised platform, flanked by counselors, high priests, and nobles. A war captive sprawls on the steps before him, stripped of regalia, his ear ornaments torn from his earlobes. Other captives are arrayed beside the central one, some bleeding and one shown only as a severed head. Victorious warriors of Bonampak are in full regalia below. These sacrifices (and the war to secure captives for sacrifice) were to confirm the designation of the heir to the throne at Bonampak.*
Peabody Museum, Harvard University.

There can be little argument that the Maya were a civilization, possessing the core elements of civilization. They were agriculturally dependent, using sophisticated farming techniques; they focused on plant crops, but they also raised ducks and stingerless bees. They carried on long-distance trade over broad portions of Mesoamerica and into the Caribbean. They lived in cities ruled by state governments. They had a variety of specialized occupations and a rigid class system.

The Maya also possessed many of the secondary elements of civilization. A state religion, a great art style, and monumental architecture helped legitimize the government. A complex system of **sacbes**,[3] earthen roads raised above the surface of the jungle floor, connected major cities. A formal legal system governed the adjudication of disputes. The Maya had writing that seems to have been derived from an earlier Olmec writing system, moderately sophisticated astronomy, mathematics that permitted massive engineering projects, and standardized measures.

The Mayan civilization was not politically unified. Indeed, it consisted of a series of competing, often belligerent city-states, each ruled by its own monarch. True, there were alliances and several attempts at empire, but the single city and the villages surrounding it were the basic political entity. In the fourth century A.D., the Tikal[4] city-state conquered the neighboring city-state of Uaxactún[5] and held it for a few decades, but the captured

[3] **sacbes:** SAWK bayz

[4] **Tikal:** TEE kahl
[5] **Uaxactún:** wah shawk TOON

lands were lost within a generation; the Dos Pilas[6] city-state built a modest empire in the seventh century, though its conquests were lost within a century. The peace that archaeologists once thought reigned over the Maya was mythical; the Mayan city-states, like city-states elsewhere, were fighting with one another on a regular basis, sometimes nearly constantly.

Although Mayan rulers and diplomats usually were men, women played a crucial role in politics, because the political legitimacy of a ruler was based on the political station of both parents. By A.D. 645, for example, Dos Pilas was expanding and was threatened by neighboring city-states. Some years later, the king of Dos Pilas sent his daughter, Lady Wak-Chanil-Ahaw, to Naranjo,[7] another nearby city-state, to revive its royal house, creating an ally for Dos Pilas. Naranjo had been defeated in recent wars, and its royal house had little status until Lady Wak-Chanil-Ahaw married into it. She religiously revivified the city by spilling blood from her tongue, a sacrifice that was thought to open the spiritual channel between Naranjo and the gods. She ruled Naranjo until 693, when her son became king at the age of five, and in all likelihood remained a powerful regent over the child king. During her reign and that of her son, Naranjo effectively acted as an ally of Dos Pilas, facilitating its imperial ambitions.

The unity of Mayan civilization was cultural, not political. Although different city-states surely felt themselves quite distinct from one another, they really were very similar in ideology, technology, and way of life. Their mutual antagonism was rooted in both their competition for scarce resources and their religion, which demanded captives for sacrifice.

The environment of the Mayan lowlands is basically jungle with little variation from one spot to another. The soils, although moderately fertile, are easily exhausted by tillage, and the traditional method of clearing the jungle by fire only reduced their fertility. The corn-squash-beans agriculture of the Maya was reasonably productive, but there were many mouths to feed, and agricultural shortfalls may have contributed to the ultimate demise of the Maya.

The Maya, unlike their Olmec predecessors, were urban. The focal point of a city-state was a

[6] **Dos Pilas:** DOHS PEE lahs
[7] **Naranjo:** nah RAHN hoh

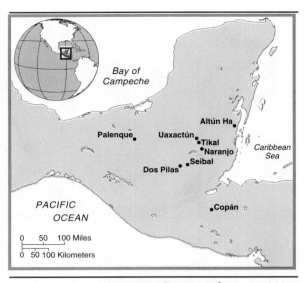

MAP 6.2 *Mayan Cities.* *Between about* A.D. *300 and 700, a few dozen Mayan cities were distributed over the lowland rain forests of eastern Mexico and adjacent Guatemala and Honduras. Resources like good agricultural soils, water, and building materials were spread over the land quite evenly; consequently, these cities were located primarily with an eye to limiting territorial disputes with neighboring cities.*

city with large numbers of people, diverse urban zones, and the typical hierarchic relationship with its satellite villages. It once was thought that these cities were ceremonial centers, because they seemed to consist mostly of temples and palaces. Then it was recognized that the common people lived in the vast areas surrounding the grand stone buildings of the city centers in thatched huts that left only faint archaeological traces. Current estimates of the sizes of various Mayan cities range from around 10,000 to 60,000 people, with additional people in each city's hinterland (the villages served by and politically subservient to the city).

The central portion of a Mayan city was a splendid collection of monumental public architecture. Lining the streets were stone pyramids crowned with temples made of limestone, which was sometimes partially or entirely painted with bright colors. The king and his close relatives occupied a palace complex in the central area. A moderately sized city might have twenty-five temples and pyramids as well as several ball courts, some shrines to gods, **stelae** (large stones with low-relief carvings on their flat surfaces), and the palace. **Plazas** (flat open areas between buildings) and courtyards completed the typical roster of components for the central city.

While the king and his retinue lived in the palace, the commoners were relegated to simpler housing outside the central city. Common houses were wood-framed with grass or similar material forming a thatch for walls and roof; each usually was on a low mound to keep its floor dry in wet weather. This simple housing, though impoverished by royal standards, was well ventilated and easily cleaned. In fact, it seems to have produced more healthful conditions than the palaces—the skeletal remains of commoners show that their general level of health was higher than that of the elite.

The whole system and the splendor of the elite was supported, of course, by the commoners. The corn that fed commoner and king alike was grown by the commoners, the grand buildings were constructed by commoners (following the direction of engineers, of course), and the various industries were carried on by the commoners.

The king and the nobles formed one class, and the commoners formed the other. Commoners could not aspire to become nobles or rulers; a commoner would live as a commoner, marry another commoner, and die a commoner. But not all kinds of commoner were alike. Among the commoners, for example, feather workers had higher status than agricultural laborers. Although feather workers typically had somewhat greater wealth than farmers, the primary difference lay in social recognition by the community, which valued the production of feathered headgear for royalty more highly than the growing of corn.

Elite Mayan women shared the grand lifestyle of elite men, but they usually were less prominent in politics and trading. They were expected to propitiate the gods by participating in certain types of sacrifice, including piercing their tongues and other body parts. As elsewhere in Mesoamerica, the Maya regarded the act of weaving as the essence of being a woman, and elite women were expected to spend considerable amounts of time

FIGURE 6.6 *Palenque.* *The Mayan city of Palenque rises out of the rain forest on a hill in southeastern Mexico. The city center included the royal palace with its tower and subterranean rooms (center), the Temple of Inscriptions with the tomb of King Pacal (left), ball courts (just out of the picture to the right), and dozens of other temples. The road visible at the rear left is an ancient one that leads to the remains of agricultural fields and commoners' housing. Before clearing and reconstruction by archaeologists, Palenque appeared as a series of jungle-covered hummocks with only an occasional piece of masonry protruding.* Charles M. Gordon/West Stock.

FIGURE 6.7 *Lady Xoc Offering a Sacrifice.* *The Mayan nobility were required to sacrifice to the gods in various ways, including the spilling of their own blood. This early eighth-century carving from a building facade at Yaxchilán shows Lady Xoc, the queen, running a rope through a slit cut in her tongue, part of a celebration for the birth of a son to the king by another wife. The bloody rope would then be placed in a bowl and burned or otherwise conveyed to the gods, while Lady Xoc would have a vision. Standing over her is her husband, King Shield-Jaguar, who carries a staff in the form of the Tree of Life; block writing at the top and left margins explains the scene. The faces have been eroded by natural processes but originally showed fine detail.* British Museum © Justin Kerr.

weaving. We currently know little about how involved women became in Mayan commerce.

Among the Mayan elite, at least the scribes and some of the nobility were fully literate. Their glyphic writing resembled a series of blocky pictures. Most surviving Mayan writing appears on stelae, the walls of monumental buildings, or painted pottery, often from royal tombs. These writings usually glorify the ruler and his dynasty, sometimes giving information about political

alliances. Information on the commoners, general histories, myths and religious rituals, and the like are not recorded in these sources. Paintings sometimes show scribes writing on paper or parchment, and a broader range of information doubtless was recorded on materials that have disintegrated over the centuries.

Extant Mayan archaeological remains proclaim the importance of religion. Temples, ball courts, godly representations, and ritual equipment are prominent at all the large sites. In part, of course, this reflects which segments of Mayan life produced durable and recognizable articles, but the conclusion is inescapable that a state religion dominated life, at least for the elite. Habitations of commoners housed small and simple female figurines, suggesting to many scholars that a female fertility cult was important to the nonelite.

Mayan religion recognized dozens of universal deities, plus dozens more of local gods and goddesses, including a patron for each city-state. The gods stood in a hierarchic relationship to the king that was similar to the relationship between the king and the nobles. Essentially, the deities rewarded the people of a city-state so long as the proper sacrifices were made to them. These sacrifices took several forms, including the sacrificing of prisoners of war, self-inflicted ritual bleeding on the part of members of the royal family or priests, the building of temples or other monumental architecture in honor of a deity, and the burial or destruction of precious items. All of these forms of sacrifice are depicted in Mayan art.

The moderately even distribution of similar economic resources throughout the Mayan lowlands made local trade less critical than in some places. Salt, scanty in the largely vegetarian diet of the Maya, was necessary for life but available only on the coast and constituted one of the few important items of trade within the Mayan lowlands. But the absence of essential resources—particularly obsidian and basalt—made trade with the outside imperative. **Obsidian**, the delicate volcanic glass required for the fancy and exquisitely sharp Mayan tools, occurred only in the highlands of Mesoamerica; basalt, the hard volcanic rock used for corn-grinding stones, also occurred only in the highlands. Salt, obsidian, and basalt, probably more than any other products, were responsible for long-distance trade among the Maya.

Mayan civilization lasted for nearly a millennium, although individual city-states came and

IN THEIR OWN WORDS

Mayan Glyphs

The Maya carved written messages on stone facings of buildings, painted them on pottery, drew them on the pages of books, and incised them on bone. Scholars had been unable to read these inscriptions until breakthroughs in the past few years. Recent translations have opened a new window on the Mayan world.

Mayan writing was a combination of pictographs (symbols that depicted the item being referred to), phonetic symbols representing syllables, and ideographs. Phrases were produced by combining these elements, and there often were several ways of writing the same word or phrase. These phrases were combined to produce sentences, usually in the following pattern: time of action, verb, direct object, subject. Sentences could merely describe the action of an associated picture or could present abstract religious and philosophical ideas.

The illustrations below are Mayan glyphs that show how words and phrases were formed. The first glyph shows the head of a big cat and could represent the jaguar, margay, ocelot, or any other large feline. The second glyph combines this basic element with a phonetic glyph to clarify that a jaguar is meant. The Mayan word for jaguar was *balam*, and the *ba* element to the left of the basic element indicates that the intended meaning begins with *ba*, eliminating all other big cats, as none of them was designated by a word beginning with *ba*. Similarly, the third glyph shows the basic glyph with a *ma* suffix (indicating a word ending with *ma* or *m*), and the fourth glyph shows phonetic glyphs preceding and following the basic element. The fifth glyph shows "jaguar" constructed entirely from phonetic glyphs. The symbolism could become very obscure, because the base element could be replaced with another whose pronunciation was similar.

The following text is an excerpt translated from the inscriptions at the Temple of the Foliated Cross in the Mayan city of Palenque.[a] The text links the ruler of Palenque to his mythical forebears, lending him legitimacy. It is presented in the order it was written by the Mayan carver, and editorial notes are in square brackets.

Thirty-four years, 14 months [20-day Mayan months] after God K had been born and then 2 *baktuns* [800 years] ended on February 16, 2325 B.C. On that day, Lady Beastie [First Mother of the Maya], Divine Lord of Matawil, manifested a divinity through bloodletting [i.e., created a god by spilling some of her own blood in self-sacrifice]. It had come to pass on Yax-Hal Witznal in the shell place at the Na-Te-Kan [places within the sacred precinct of the Palenque; "the shell place" refers to the feet of Pacal, the father of Lord Chan-Bahlum], on November 8, 2360 B.C. [this date was recorded wrong and should have been A.D. 622], 2947 years, 3 months, 16 days later. . . . On the next day, the Mah-Kina-Bahlum-Kuk Building [a temple at Palenque] was dedicated in the house of Lord Chan-Bahlum [the king of Palenque at the time the inscription was carved], Divine Palenque Lord. On the third day Lord Chan-Bahlum, Divine Palenque Lord, he let blood with an obsidian blade [spilling his own blood in self-sacrifice]; he took the bundle [received an offering] after it had come to pass at the Waterlily Place [the royal palace of Palenque]. . . . Forty-nine years, 6 months, 4 days after he had been born and then he crowned himself, Lord Chan-Bahlum, Divine Palenque Lord, on January 10, 692.

[a]**Palenque:** pah LEHN kay

balam

ba - balam

balam - ma

ba - balam - ma

ba - la - m(a)

From Linda Schele and David Friedel, *A Forest of Kings: The Untold Story of the Ancient Maya* (New York: William Morrow and Company, Inc., 1990), p. 52. Reproduced with permission.

went with time. Between 700 and 800, however, the civilization collapsed rapidly. The cities were abandoned; the state governments collapsed; monumental architecture and great art no longer were produced; knowledge of the calendar, writing, mathematics, and other fields of learning was lost. The Mayan did not simply exchange one government or art style for another: They radically changed their entire way of life, abandoning civilization altogether. At the same time, the population of the Mayan lowlands seems to have plummeted, eliminating the elite and drastically reducing the rest of the Maya. What was the cause of this catastrophe?

There is no shortage of suggestions. Earthquake, hurricane, and epidemic have been suggested, but no evidence supports the existence of any of these natural disasters. Invasions from the highlands, peasant revolts, and ecological failure all have their scholarly supporters, and all have some evidence to support them. Although the jury is still out on why the Maya collapsed, the possible explanation that follows incorporates several of the causes cited here.

Agriculture in the Mayan lowlands had certain intrinsic limitations, particularly the lowering of soil fertility with use. This problem is not amenable to a technological solution; the only answer is to increase fallowing periods and open more land, requiring greater labor expenditures. A people faced with a dwindling food supply brought on by steadily increasing population and perhaps a few bad harvests logically should devote increased labor to developing farmlands.

But, from the Mayan point of view, the appropriate response would have been different. Because the gods were unhappy, they had to be propitiated with sacrifices. Kingly sacrifices could be accomplished with relative ease (unless one was the king), requiring no major reallocation of labor; captives for sacrifice and temple building, however, meant the investment of commoner labor, either as soldiers or as construction workers. In short, most of the ways to meet a crisis required siphoning labor away from agriculture—precisely at the time that it required more labor. The diverting of labor from agriculture to warfare and the construction of monumental architecture can be seen in the last years of the Mayan cities. Again and again, the grandest and most numerous temples are from the period just before the collapse, and evidence of warfare is strongest for this period, too.

FIGURE 6.8 *Mayan Encountering Highland Mexican.* *This detail from a scene decorating the rim of a Mayan pot shows a visit by a highland Mexican (perhaps from Teotihuacán) to the Mayan city of Tikal. Ethnic Maya are shown with distinctive features: sloping noses that descend from the forehead in an unbroken line, foreheads that slope backward markedly, and pendulous lower lips. Highland Mexicans, in contrast, are depicted with more vertical foreheads, noses that angle outward from the plane of the forehead, and thinner lips. Headdresses and other clothing styles differ, too. Such encounters appear increasingly in Mayan art just before the Mayan collapse.* From Linda Schele and David Friedel, *A Forest of Kings: The Untold Story of the Ancient Maya* (New York: William Morrow and Company, Inc., 1990), p. 162. Reproduced with permission.

These practices would make the crisis more acute. As less and less food was available, the commoners would suffer the most, because the food redistribution system emanated from the king and the hierarchic system guaranteed that the nobility would be fed. Conditions would degenerate in a rapid spiral, and faith in the gods could be damaged severely. At this point, the commoners could be on the brink of violent uprising.

An additional factor has to be added to the mix. Around 650 to 700, Mayan art increasingly depicted highland Mexicans. This evidence, along with the increased presence of pottery and other goods from the highlands, suggests that trade or other contact was increasing. Outsiders could have actively supported the violent overthrow of governments, perhaps in hope of moving into the resulting power vacuum themselves; alternatively, they could have contributed inadvertently to the upheaval by undermining faith in the Mayan pantheon. The fact that the fall of Mayan cities traveled from west to east, with the earliest collapses nearest the highlands, suggests that highlanders were somehow involved.

Either way, the Mayan commoners eventually ousted their kings and nobles. Without the elite to operate the complex machinery of a Mayan city-state, it ground to a halt. Redistribution of food broke down, and the cities were abandoned in favor of villages that grew their own food locally. The call for engineers, scribes, and other occupational specialists disappeared. Despite its problems, the Mayan city-state had organized laborers for efficient agricultural production, and without that guidance, food supplies diminished, causing a drop in population. The delicate balance of the city-state, once upset, caused the disappearance of elite Mayan culture and major disruptions in commoner culture.

This plausible explanation is currently held by many archaeologists, but it is unlikely to be confirmed or rejected by the written Mayan record, which seems to be mute about the end of the Mayan civilization. In the northern parts of the Mayan lowlands, particularly the Yucatán Peninsula, Mayan culture persisted to the time of the Spanish conquest in the sixteenth century, albeit in a less complex form and minus many of the attributes of civilization.

Teotihuacán, around 100 B.C.–around A.D. 700

Perhaps the most dramatic case of urbanism in the Americas comes from Teotihuacán and its environs in the central Mexican highlands. Prior to about 200 B.C., only small villages existed in the area that would become Teotihuacán. In the next century, perhaps 25,000 people were attracted to the new city, and their numbers would swell to around 70,000 people by A.D. 150. By around A.D. 400, as many as 200,000 people lived there.

The growth of Teotihuacán, as with most cities, was at the expense of its neighbors and competitors. Not only were rural areas depleted of much of their population, but the rival city of Cuicuilco[8] was depopulated to the point of near-abandonment.

What was the attraction of Teotihuacán? Initially, there probably were two lures. The growth of the city itself was one, because huge numbers of laborers were required to build it. Second, the city was situated next to and controlled the Pachuca quarries, a rich source of fine obsidian, a stone that was traded throughout Mesoamerica. The quarrying and especially the flaking of that obsidian into tools and weapons was a specialized job that presumably would have brought financial reward with it. The volume of Pachuca obsidian found at great distances from the quarries suggests that the obsidian trade was a major boost to Teotihuacán's economy.

As the city was established, other attractants developed. Because the nearby villages had been nearly depopulated, an agricultural force of some size was drawn from Teotihuacán itself. Agriculture was based on sophisticated and massive irrigation systems that kept production levels high and may have stimulated the growth of a powerful government to administer them. The city became a trade center for a wide range of products, including pottery, stone tools, ceramic figurines, and shell beads; production areas within Teotihuacán have been identified archaeologically. All of these jobs would have attracted immigrants, even if not all of them were to find good jobs and actually better themselves.

Teotihuacán can be likened to Washington, D.C., and the comparison is apt in many ways. Traveling through Washington, the visitor sees the hustle and bustle of a major city. There is an abundance of monuments dedicated to important individuals, and the layout of the city is designed to awe the visitor. Although there is much beauty and elegance, there are poor sections of the city, and most of the inhabitants lead quite modest lives. Every one of these statements would have been true of Teotihuacán in its heyday, and a modern visitor might find Teotihuacán exotic yet strangely familiar.

Teotihuacán was laid out on a north-south grid, as were most Mesoamerican cities. At the city center, at the intersection of the two largest avenues, was the most imposing and ornate architecture. Here were dozens of stone pyramids topped with temples to the gods, dominated by the huge Temple of the Moon and the even larger Temple of the Sun. Nearby was the Ciudadela,[9]

[8] **Cuicuilco:** kwee KWEEL koh

[9] **Ciudadela:** see oo dah DAY luh

FIGURE 6.9 *Archaeological Map of Teotihuacán.* *This map shows the remains of the central precinct of Teotihuacán. Dominating the area is the massive Pyramid of the Sun, with the temple at its apex; it was one of the largest structures in the Americas before the twentieth century. Surrounded by various pyramids, temples, and palaces, the Pyramid of the Sun was located in an elite zone accessed via the Avenue of the Dead. This street, the largest and most important in the city, passed before dozens of examples of imposing monumental architecture.* From Rene Millon, *Urbanization at Teotihuacán, Mexico*, Vol. I, Part 2. Reproduced with permission.

probably a palace for rulers and certainly elite housing for someone. Across the street from the Ciudadela was the Great Market Place, a huge plaza flanked by buildings that may have been warehouses.

Farther from the center of town were the less prestigious areas. Commoner housing in the early days of the city was small and wood-framed, but beginning about 300, public housing projects were initiated. Large multifamily housing structures built of masonry—we would call them apartment buildings today—were constructed in this period. Many were low-cost housing, with small rooms and in poor neighborhoods; these tended to be the larger housing structures, one of which had 176 rooms. Middle- and upper-class housing also was erected, presumably for the growing ranks of suc-

cessful merchants, petty officials, and industrial specialists. This more elegant housing had fewer units per building and often was decorated with murals. Some such housing even had fountains in internal courtyards.

Building at this scale, of course, required careful attention to practical demands. Storm drain systems, sewage disposal, and trash removal all had to be planned and carried out by the central government.

The central government of Teotihuacán, unlike those of the Mayan city-states and many other Mesoamerican civilizations, is not portrayed prominently in art, unless in unrecognized symbolic representations. Coupled with the fact that the script at Teotihuacán has not been deciphered, this means that our knowledge about government there is limited. It is clear that Teotihuacán was a city-state and that it had no empire, although it apparently had considerable political influence in foreign lands throughout Mesoamerica. There may have been dual rulers, one primarily concerned with domestic affairs and business, the other (at least after 500) concerned with warfare. Although temples and religious art are everywhere in Teotihuacán, one is left with the impression that religion—like government—served as an organizational mechanism to promote commercial enterprise. In fact, it has been argued that the impressive religious architecture of Teotihuacán was designed to inspire admiration in visitors, in hopes of extracting better deals from awe-struck traders.

After about 300, Teotihuacán was the uncontested leader in trade in Mesoamerica. Goods produced there could be found throughout Mesoamerica, and foreign goods were common in Teotihuacán. Foreigners themselves were prominent in Teotihuacán, and there were neighborhoods whose goods, burial practices, and art reflected the tastes of their foreign occupants. These foreign enclaves may have been permanent trading stations, ghettos, or consulates.

Around 650, Teotihuacán was thriving. Business was good, there were no signs of internal strife, and the size and military power of the city discouraged attacks from outsiders. But disaster was about to strike. A huge fire in 716 enveloped the northern end of the city, destroying poor and middle-income neighborhoods, some industrial areas, and some commercial districts. There appears to have been some selective looting and perhaps arson, but it generally is believed that this was incidental to an accidental disaster. There are no signs of external attack, no signs of rioting or mass death, no signs of violence directed at the ruling elite. But the great fire marks the beginning of the decline of Teotihuacán as a city and the center of a vast trading network.

The city continued to be occupied for a few decades before it finally was abandoned, but abundant signs indicate that this was not the Teotihuacán of old. New construction nearly halted, and old buildings were not always well maintained. The trade of Teotihuacán's goods was drastically diminished, as evidenced both at home and abroad. The population plummeted; by 750, the population was so small that it may have consisted merely of squatters who had moved in to live on the ruins of the city.

With the demise of Teotihuacán there was no clearly dominant power in the highlands. There were several cities, each with its local sphere of power, but none that could consistently outcompete the others either in military or economic terms.

The Toltecs, around A.D. 900–around 1200

The Toltecs had their own unique writing system. Scholars today cannot decipher it, but as we move into this more recent period, we can consult oral tradition and other historical sources available at the time of the Spanish conquest and written down then. In this sense, the Toltecs may be considered the first "historical" civilization in the Mexican highlands about which we have a broad range of oral and written information.

The versions of Toltec history that have come down to us are sometimes conflicting and confusing. Some of this doubtless arises from the differing meanings of "Tollan,"[10] the name of the ancient Toltec capital. The word means "place of the reeds," but it was a common place-name, and several places have borne it, probably including Teotihuacán. Consequently, the oral traditions of the Toltecs probably are conflated with accounts of other peoples.

The Toltecs generally were mythologized by their descendants as a great people, taller than people of today and better-looking. They were said to excel in learning and the arts and even to possess lost arts, such as making cotton grow in colors or growing gigantic ears of corn. Small wonder that such wonderful people were always well fed, happy, and wealthy. This legacy of good press made claiming Toltec ancestry so desirable that versions of Toltec history clearly were manipulated by later peoples who created fictional kinship links to the Toltecs, legitimizing claims to land or political power.

The central series of events in Toltec oral tradition is the conflict between Quetzalcóatl[11] and Tezcatlipoca.[12] Both of these legendary gods and the

---

[10] **Tollan:** TOHL ahn
[11] **Quetzalcóatl:** keht zahl KOH aht
[12] **Tezcatlipoca:** tehz kawt lee POH kuh

events ascribed to them may refer to priests dedicated to their worship. The most popular version of the story has Quetzalcóatl, the feathered serpent, in conflict with Tezcatlipoca, the god of war. Quetzalcóatl abhors human sacrifice and favors the sacrifice of butterflies and flowers, but Tezcatlipoca, in keeping with his bloodthirsty patronage, demands human blood. After a series of conflicts, Tezcatlipoca defeats Quetzalcóatl by luring him into public drunkenness, a humiliating sin. Quetzalcóatl then leaves Tollan and goes eastward to the Gulf of Mexico, where he either sets himself on fire and ascends to the heavens as the Morning Star (Venus) or floats eastward on a raft of serpents, prophesying that he will return to conquer his people. In the meantime, Huémac,[13] a follower of Tezcatlipoca, has become king.

Clearly, this is not straightforward history, and gods and people have become intimately blended in a mythic account. Many interpreters feel noteworthy that Quetzalcóatl is associated with the peoples to the north of the Valley of Mexico, while Huémac is associated with the peoples to the south. Allegorically, this may represent a struggle between dynasties or alliances, represented by gods. Alternatively, they may represent different religious factions or even the religious versus the secular factions of the government. Further complicating the interpretation is the suspicion that Quetzalcóatl's distaste for human sacrifice, a long-established institution in Mesoamerica, may have been a post-Spanish elaboration in the face of Christianity — placing words that condemned human sacrifice in the mouths of Mexican gods themselves. In any case, the interpretation of the account is anything but simple.

Historical accounts certainly have been kind to the Toltecs, granting them a favorable position and a great empire. Archaeological evidence, on the other hand, suggests that theirs was merely a modest state, perhaps a small empire. The town of Tollan was founded around 650 and was small until around 900. At that point, it appears to have gained some measure of control of the Pachuca obsidian deposits that had helped make Teotihuacán rich. It expanded to a city of 30,000 inhabitants at its peak, with another 30,000 persons in satellite towns and villages surrounding it. Although the city's buildings had a distinctive architectural style, the city was unplanned and not

nearly as impressive as Teotihuacán. Its political control appears never to have extended beyond the northern half of the Valley of Mexico and adjacent areas to the north. In fact, it can reasonably be considered merely one of two or three competing regional powers, none of which was successful at extending its influence broadly.

Were it not for the myths surrounding Tollan and the Toltecs, they would not stand out from their contemporaries very strongly. As we shall see in Chapter 16, however, later peoples found it politically imperative to trace themselves back to the Toltecs to legitimize their power.

THE GROWTH OF CIVILIZATION IN PERU, AROUND 4000 B.C.– AROUND A.D. 1300

The geography of Peru is dominated by the Andes Mountains, some of the highest and most rugged in the world. The highlands of Peru are cut by valleys, where human occupation is focused, and contact between valleys has always been limited by the difficulty of movement. On the coast lies one of the driest deserts in the world, and settlement was largely restricted to river valleys, where irrigation supported agriculture. These twin obstacles—dry desert and impassable mountains— have served to isolate Peruvian regions more strongly than in most areas, and the result has been a series of highly regional cultures. Only during exceptional periods have there been unifications, and they typically have been moderately brief, doubtless because of the difficulties of maintaining necessary transportation and communication systems.

Details of events that occurred in ancient Peru are far less well known than in Mesoamerica, largely because the Peruvians never developed a system of writing to record their own history. In the truest sense, ancient Peruvian civilizations were prehistoric.

Chavín

The first unification of Peru spans from about 1200 to 300 B.C. and is called Chavín. In many respects, Chavín archaeology is much like Olmec archaeology. It is known mostly from ceremonial centers

---

[13] **Huémac:** WAY mahk

FIGURE 6.10 *Chavín Sculpted Head.* *Chavín artists depicted the human form in various ways, one of the most striking being rows of large heads set into walls. About three feet in diameter and attached to the wall by projections in the rear, these heads from the site of Chavín de Hauntar in Peru bear a slight resemblance to Olmec colossal heads from Mexico. Archaeologists interpret pain, paralysis, or rapture in the lines of these Chavín faces, and the material in the nose may depict wads of hallucinogenic snuff. Such heads are found only at Chavín ceremonial centers.* Ric Ergenbright.

that exhibit a great art style incorporating monumental architecture. Some motifs and themes of the art are even similar, such as oversized portrait heads and prominent jaguars, prompting some scholars to speculate that there may have been some contact between Mesoamerica and Peru at this time. Finally, Chavín, like the Olmecs, demonstrates by its works that the society was stratified, with some form of elite that could command great amounts of labor.

But here the similarity ends. While the Olmecs formed a culture focused in a single region, Chavín had a discontinuous distribution that covered nearly all of Peru. To state it differently: Chavín seems to have been an overlay that bridged across various Peruvian cultures, not a culture itself.

Chavín is best conceived of as merely an art style and (probably) an associated religion that spread throughout Peru and was adopted by communities of very different cultures.

Perhaps the easiest way to conceive of Chavín is to compare it to modern-day Roman Catholicism. Catholic churches everywhere have similar statues, paintings, and architecture, reflecting generally similar (though not necessarily identical) beliefs and practices. Catholic churches in Brazil, Hong Kong, and Lithuania will be similar, especially in terms of the physical items that could survive for future archaeologists; but the everyday lives and cultures of people in Brazil, Hong Kong, and Lithuania are very different from one another. In essence, the Catholic Church can be seen as an

FIGURE 6.11 *Gate of the Sun at Tiahuanaco.* *Tiahuanaco, a major city of the Wari Empire, is believed by some scholars to have been the imperial capital. Today, this gate seems isolated on a windy Bolivian plain, but around A.D. 1000 it was part of the ceremonial complex of a thriving city. The gate stands nearly ten feet high, carved from a single slab of volcanic stone. At the top is the sun god, with radiating headdress and a staff in each hand; beside and below him are a series of bird-headed figures. Nearby are several religious buildings, including a subterranean temple with small sculptured heads set into its walls. The wall heads, staff god, and bird-people may derive from Chavín mythology.* Mireille Vautier/Woodfin Camp & Associates.

overlay onto different world cultures, just as Chavín can be seen as an overlay onto different ancient Peruvian cultures.

Conceiving of Chavín as a cultural overlay of this sort can explain how one region might have a strong Chavín presence, complete with a major ceremonial center, while a neighboring region might have virtually no Chavín presence. There is no evidence that there was a political wing of Chavín or any kind of central religious administration. Consequently, it is most reasonable to view Chavín as the result of a diffused idea, not a unification in the usual sense.

In the centuries following Chavín, regional societies continued following their several trajectories. Some quite complex societies developed, ones with massive irrigation systems and probably state-level governments; these were the first Peruvian civilizations. Technology, particularly metal-lurgy and civil engineering, saw a great deal of development, and several of these societies produced massive monumental architecture.

The Wari Empire

The first political unification of Peru came around A.D. 700 and lasted until about 1100. This is the Wari Empire, also known as the "Huari" or "Tiahuanaco"[14] Empire. There is disagreement about where the empire originated, with Peruvian and Bolivian archaeologists both claiming the heartland for their home countries. Regardless, in a few decades the empire came to control about two-thirds of the Peruvian area, including both highland and coastal areas. It is believed to have spread primarily by conquest.

[14] **Tiahuanaco:** tee uh wahn AH koh

PERU	MESOAMERICAN HIGHLANDS	MESOAMERICAN LOWLANDS		
Paleo-Indian Period, c. 43,000–c. 8000 B.C.			**14,000 B.C.**	Initial entry of people into the Americas, between 43,000 B.C. and 15,000 B.C.
			–	
			12,000 B.C.	
			–	
			10,000 B.C.	Rapid climatic warming, c. 10,000 B.C.
			–	
			8000 B.C.	Big game extinction complete, 8000 B.C.
Regional foraging traditions, c. 8000–c. 2300 B.C.			–	
			6000 B.C.	Beginnings of agricultural experimentation, c. 6500 B.C.
			–	
			4000 B.C.	Sedentary villages in Peru, c. 4000 B.C.
			–	Agricultural dependence, c. 3200 B.C.
			2000 B.C.	Sedentary villages in Mesoamerica, c. 2300 B.C.
			–	
Chavín, c. 1200–c. 400 B.C.		Olmecs, c. 1200–c. 400 B.C.		
Regional States, c. 1300 B.C.–c. A.D. 700	Teotihuacán, c. 100 B.C.–c. A.D. 700	Maya, c. 200 B.C.–c. A.D. 800	**A.D. 1**	
Wari Empire, c. A.D. 700–c. 1100	Toltecs, c. A.D. 900–c. 1200		–	Teotihuacán fire, A.D. 716 Maya collapse complete, A.D. 800

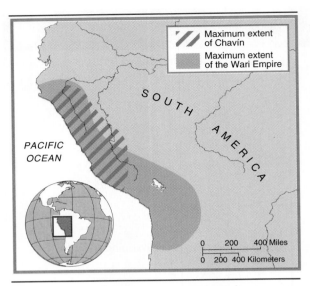

MAP 6.3 *Chavín and the Wari Empire.* *In the second millennium* B.C., *Chavín produced the first cultural unification of large parts of Peru. After the breakdown of Chavín, regional cultures dominated Peru for almost 2,000 years, until the Wari Empire achieved another unification in the first millennium* A.D. *While Chavín was largely limited to religion and art and was present only at some settlements within its range, the Wari Empire was comprehensive, controlling the political, economic, and social aspects of all communities within its territory.*

Wherever Wari extended its imperial hand, great changes took place. The empire was urban, and new planned cities sprang up across Peru, usually with the distinctive Wari style of architecture, emphasizing monumental buildings, closely packed structures, and carvings of the sun god. Great emphasis was placed on water control and on extending the range of cultivated lands through efficient irrigation systems, probably to support a growing population. The deities of Wari appeared everywhere the empire went, suggesting the existence of a state religion. The general similarity of Wari cities at this time has suggested to many scholars that the Wari central government was not only strong but also dedicated to imposing its stamp, perhaps forcibly, on subject peoples. Certainly the art reflects a concern with militarism that was rooted in earlier cultures but seems to have blossomed in the Wari Empire.

After the breakup of the Wari Empire, regional cultures again dominated. Many, but not all, of these had a state-level government, complex irrigation systems, and urban settlements. Some of the kingdoms known from historic Peru, such as the Chimú of the northern coast, were founded in this era. Only the Inca, treated in detail in Chapter 16, would unify these diverse polities into a single empire.

SUMMARY

1. The Americas were first peopled by immigrants from northeastern Asia who became American Indians. The exact date of the migration is unknown, but it probably took place between 33,000 and 14,000 B.C. via the Bering Land Bridge.

2. Agriculture developed independently in several areas of the Americas, particularly in Mesoamerica and Peru, which together make up Nuclear America. A variety of staple crops (especially maize, squash, and beans) provided a nutritional base that required little or no meat, and domesticated animals never were important in the Americas before Columbus.

3. Nuclear America preceded the rest of the Americas in the development of complex society.

4. In Mesoamerica, the Olmecs were the first complex society, though there is disagreement over whether this society should properly be considered a civilization because it probably lacked both the state and urbanism. They were succeeded in the lowlands by the Maya civilization, with its city-states, monumental architecture, and developed writing.

5. In the Mesoamerican highlands, Teotihuacán established its vast commercial base in the largest city of the Americas in the first millennium. It was succeeded by the Toltecs, a group important in mythic history but modest in reality.

6. In Peru, geography encouraged regionalism that was punctuated only by unusual periods of unification. Chavín provided an ideological unification, and the Wari Empire provided the first political unification.

SUGGESTED READINGS

Coe, Michael D. *Breaking the Maya Code*. New York: Thames and Hudson, 1992. An account of Mayan writing for the nonspecialist.

Matos Moctezuma, Eduardo. *Teotihuacán, the City of the Gods*. New York: Rizzoli, 1990. A well-illustrated and accurate portrayal of Teotihuacán.

Miller, Virginia E., ed. *The Role of Gender in Precolumbian Art and Architecture*. Lanham, Md.: University Press of America, 1988. A collection of essays on gender and the arts in Mesoamerica and South America.

Moseley, Michael E. *The Incas and Their Ancestors: The Archaeology of Peru*. New York: Thames and Hudson, 1992. A textbook summary of ancient Peru.

Weaver, Muriel Porter. *The Aztecs, Maya, and Their Predecessors: Archaeology of Mesoamerica*. San Diego, Calif.: Academic Press, 1993. Widely used textbook on ancient Mesoamerica.

Trading in the Early United States. Benjamin Hawkins, U.S. Indian Agent in South
Carolina about 1800, trades iron agricultural tools with Creek Indians in return for agricultural produce. Unidentified artist, *Benjamin Hawkins and the Creek Indians,* circa 1805. Oil on canvas, 35 7/8
x 49 7/8 inches. Greenville County Museum of Art, Greenville, S.C. Gift of The Museum Association, Inc., with funds
donated by Corporate Partners.

Trade and Exchange

People have been trading items with one another for a very long time, possibly since before the biological evolution of fully modern human beings. The essential characteristic of trade is that two people agree to swap items, but there are many variations on how and why the exchange takes place.

For example, you may have a surplus of tomatoes in your garden, while a neighbor may have extra cucumbers. You can trade tomatoes for cucumbers to mutual benefit. This form of trade, where one useful commodity is exchanged for another, is known as **barter** and often is viewed as an early kind of trade. Although it is true that this kind of trade was among the earliest, it persists today, both in garden-level exchanges and in trade between major governments.

Alternatively, trade can take place with some unit of currency as its medium. When you buy cucumbers from a supermarket, for instance, you pay for them with paper money or coins (or some substitute, such as a credit card, debit card, or check). The use of currency lends convenience to the transaction, because you need not haul, say, a cartload of fish to the market to pay for your vegetables. Currency also permits a greater level of stability in pricing, because the currency maintains a generally constant value, while the value of tomatoes or apricots may fluctuate wildly, depending on the season, the weather, and other factors. Trade that uses currency usually is called **purchase**.

Purchase became a major mode of trade in most places as societies became more complex.

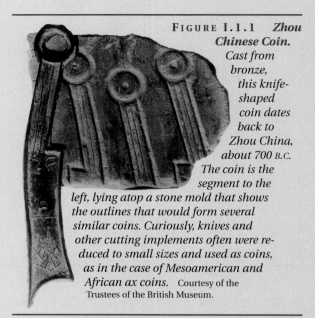

FIGURE I.1.1 *Zhou Chinese Coin. Cast from bronze, this knife-shaped coin dates back to Zhou China, about 700 B.C. The coin is the segment to the left, lying atop a stone mold that shows the outlines that would form several similar coins. Curiously, knives and other cutting implements often were reduced to small sizes and used as coins, as in the case of Mesoamerican and African ax coins.* Courtesy of the Trustees of the British Museum.

The nature of currency has varied greatly over space and time, including such diverse monetary units as cowrie shells (Africa, Asia, and elsewhere), blankets (North America and Central America), coins (Europe, India, China, and elsewhere), paper money (China and elsewhere), and cacao beans (Central America).

ECONOMIC AND NONECONOMIC TRADE

Just as modes of trade have varied, so have the motivations behind trade. The type of trade that most people think of first is **economic trade**, for which the underlying motivation is obtaining an otherwise unavailable item. Economic trade probably was practiced at least by 70,000 B.C. in Africa and Europe; we know this because large quantities of high-quality stone for tools are often found in archaeological sites at considerable distance from the origin of the stone, distances greater than people would be expected to have traveled under normal circumstances. Probably the stone passed through several hands before it reached its ultimate destination. Such economic trade became very important in later times, as with the obsidian trade in Bronze Age Europe and Mesoamerica and with the salt trade in China and Europe.

In contrast, some trade takes place not because the participants are anxious to obtain products from one other but because the act of trading serves to cement friendships and other ties. This kind of trade is known as **noneconomic trade**. For example, traditional Indians of the Amazon River Basin in Brazil who meet and wish to show friendly intentions will give one another arrows. The arrows from one group are scarcely different from those of the other, but the act of trading indicates the individuals' close and amicable feelings toward one another. Most people in modern North America exchange presents at holidays, and, although they rarely think of it as trade, it is another example of noneconomic trade. Although noneconomic trade is very important in small-scale societies, it has only a limited role in more complex societies.

THE CONSEQUENCES OF ECONOMIC TRADE

Some of the outcomes of trade are immediately apparent, but others are a bit less obvious. The most important of the consequences of trade fall into five categories:

—obtaining goods;

—obtaining ideas and information with the goods;

—carrying disease germs from one place to another;

—developing reciprocal political relationships with trading partners; and

—modifying the status of the traders.

Obtaining goods is the most obvious of the results of trade. Short-distance trade, whereby neighbors trade with neighbors, may help a community make it through a hard time. Over a series of good years, that community may have accumulated goods or currency that neighbors traded for surplus food when they were having poor harvests. Later, if the community has a bad harvest of its own, it has items to trade with its neighbors to obtain much-needed food. Over many years, the entire region benefits from the lessening of the impact of famine through trade.

Trade within a kingdom or empire often became enormous, permitting a state to provide most of its needs internally and thereby decrease its reliance on outsiders. The Maya, for example, required salt as a supplement to their overwhelmingly agricultural diet, and the easiest way to get it was by evaporating sea water on the coast. An extensive fleet of vessels carried this salt up and down the coast, and bearers carried it over the sacbe roads into the interior. Other routes brought from the highlands to the lowlands hard stone for grinding stones and obsidian for cutting tools. Those kingdoms that controlled all of these resources within their borders and could transport them throughout their domain were at a competitive advantage over their neighbors, not having to fear economic pressure.

Goods obtained through long-distance trade, until the dramatic transformation of transportation in the nineteenth century, could not be perishable, because the time required to import them was so long. As a result, long-distance trade focused primarily on nonfood products and a few durable foodstuffs, such as spices. Many of the items obtained by long-distance trade were of such rarity and cost at their destination that they were used only by the wealthy. Indeed, some were recognized status symbols, such as lapis lazuli, a blue gemstone imported into ancient Mesopotamia from Iran. The silks that were imported into India, Arab lands, and medieval Europe from East Asia were worn only by the rich.

Sometimes, however, items obtained by long-distance trade transformed a society, as in the case of basalt traded into the Mayan lowlands (discussed in Chapter 6). The Mayan lowlands have no hard stone to make grinding stones, and without grinding stones, dried corn could not be effectively processed for eating. The importation of basalt, a hard stone, permitted the production of grinding stones and the efficient milling of corn, in turn allowing the Maya to base their economy on the more efficient corn grain, rather than on roots.

But traders brought back more than merely the goods in their packs. As traders became familiar with the people they traded with, the traders came to know the people's way of life, their ideas, their culture. Often they had to live long periods among these foreign people, and sometimes they picked up new concepts, new ways of doing things, and new tastes. These they carried home, where the items sometimes became popular. Medieval European traders with the Arab world brought back styles of music, tastes for certain spicy dishes, new words and phrases, and new clothing styles.

Perhaps the most unexpected import to accompany long-distance trade was germs. No one until the last century or so had any understanding of germ theory, and traders did not fully comprehend the hazards they risked by traveling to foreign lands. A trading party often would consist of hundreds of people, and a few almost certainly would be infected with some contagious disease. Upon arriving at their destination, they would unwittingly spread germs to local people, few of whom were likely to have much natural

FIGURE I.1.2 *Peppercorn Harvest. Long-distance trade was restricted to nonperishable items of considerable value, such as spices. Here, fourteenth-century native workers in the Andaman Islands, off India, harvest the small berries that will become black pepper, while an Arab trader looks on and nibbles a berry to test its flavor.* Bibliothèque nationale, Paris.

FIGURE I.1.3 *Plague in Naples. Micco Spadero in 1656 painted this graphic portrayal of the horrors of being caught in a plague. Slaves with hooks are dragging bodies to mass graves, and litter bearers carry those stricken but not yet dead to hospitals. The germs that caused these plagues often were transmitted by trade or other long-distance inter-action.* Museo Nazionale, Naples/Alinari/Art Resource, N.Y.

resistance. An epidemic might accompany the arrival of a trading company, and the company's return home could be equally disastrous, bringing back another set of exotic germs. The great plagues of Europe have been linked to increased trading contacts with Asia, and the devastation of Native American populations was largely the result of contact with diseased traders and others from Europe.

If countries have no trading relationships with one another, most of their dealings are likely to be hostile. Neighbors are in competition for borderlands, for resources, and for political or military superiority. But trade can change all that. The fortunes of your country may become linked to those of your trading partners, and anything that hurts them also hurts you indirectly. Consequently, the establishment of a trading relationship often leads to some form of political alliance. If trading is so crucial to the welfare of two countries that they cannot survive without it, political alliance is practically imperative.

On the other hand, trade can have a less benign aspect. If the trade is critical for your country yet not for your trading partner, your country is likely to find itself in a politically weak position and probably will become dependent on your partner. The ascendancy of Spain over Portugal in the scramble for colonial holdings in the sixteenth century was, in part, a result of their respective positions in trading relationships. One or more countries also can use trade as a weapon against other countries.

Finally, the status of the traders as individuals often was changed by their success in commerce. Successful trading expeditions often brought great financial success to the traders or to those whose backing financed the expeditions. Sometimes these were individuals or companies, in which case the entrepreneurs often became very wealthy, such as with colonial fur-trading companies in North America. More often, the state controlled the trade, as in ancient Egypt and Mesopotamia, and the state or royal houses grew more wealthy and powerful. In general, successful trading has led to greater disparities between the wealth of the rich and the poor. In some cases, however, such as under the Roman Empire and in seventeenth-century Europe, trading has contributed to the growth of a middle class. In still other cases, as in China, merchants sometimes grew wealthy but maintained a low social status.

TRADE ROUTES

Successful trade requires efficient routes over which commodities can be transported. The ideal trade route provided rapid, safe, and inexpensive passage of goods between trading partners, but not all would-be traders were favored with such

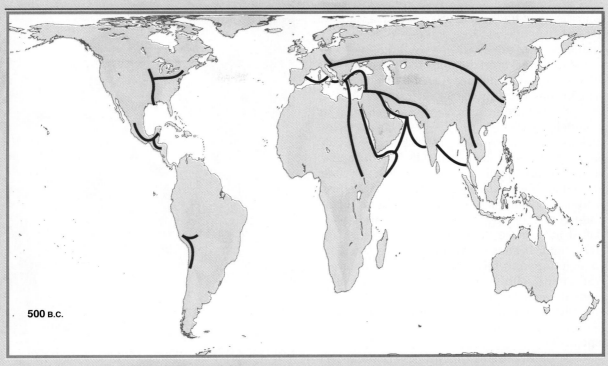

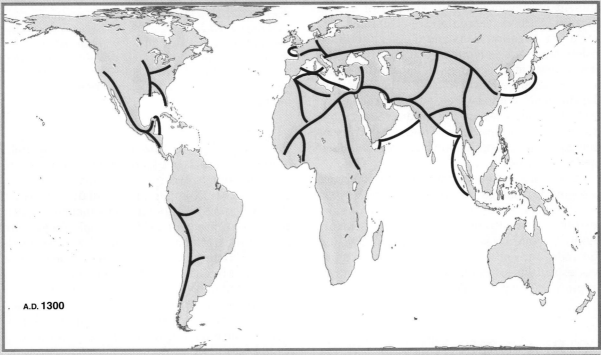

MAP 1.1.1 *Major World Trade Routes of 500 B.C. and A.D. 1300.* Established trade routes avoided difficult terrain and especially dangerous areas, providing travelers with relatively safe passage and few surprises. People living along these trade routes supplied provisions and services to travelers, often prospering greatly.

From 500 B.C. to A.D. 1300 there is a great similarity of the major world trade routes, demonstrating how the benefits of a known trade route were not readily abandoned in favor of another. Many routes, however, became longer or added branches, reflecting an overall expansion of trade during this period.

routes. A good trade route was as much a valuable natural resource as were mineral ores, salt, or timber.

The optimal overland trade route should be as direct as possible, minimizing the distance traveled. In addition, it should avoid obstacles that will slow the passage or increase its danger, such as mountains or swamps. Similarly, human obstacles, such as notorious bandits and toll barriers, should be avoided. Technology available for land transportation, until quite recently, could carry only limited amounts of weight, so points for reprovisioning food and water were critical along a land trade route. Finally, because few traders were skilled at locating themselves in relation to the stars (and because few maps were accurate enough to permit this, anyway), it was important that a trade route be easy to follow. River valleys often fit many of these criteria, and trade frequently followed them when possible. Needless to say, once a good route was discovered, it was used repeatedly.

Sea routes became important with the development of substantial ships capable of oceanic voyages. Earlier sea routes were along coasts, because navigation skills and the need to reprovision small vessels required that land be in sight at all times. Later, when vessels became larger and more seaworthy and when celestial navigation and the magnetic compass became well known, sea trade routes cut across the oceans. Such routes usually followed prevailing winds and currents, though hazards to navigation, both real and imagined, were avoided.

Countries and peoples with good trade routes had great advantage over others and often prospered. Cities along trade routes often became wealthy by provisioning caravans or extracting tribute for safe passage, indirectly profiting from the trade; a city at the junction of two trade routes was especially fortunate. Wars were fought and empires built in part to control trade routes.

OTHER FORMS OF EXCHANGE

Although the term "trade" is reserved for cases of partners' mutually agreeing to swap items, other kinds of interaction share similarities with trade. These fall under the general category of **exchange**, any process whereby goods pass between part-

FIGURE I.1.4 *Nubians Rendering Tribute to Egypt.* *This mural shows Nubian porters bringing a variety of goods to Egypt as tribute. A linked chain of gold rings, a leopard skin, and a live baboon are prominent in the scene, along with less easily identified food, feathers, and exotic wood. This painting comes from the tomb chapel of Sebekhotep, an Egyptian treasurer, and dates from about 1400 B.C.* Courtesy of the Trustees of the British Museum.

ners, even if goods flow in one direction only. Trade, of course, is one kind of exchange, but there are many others. Piracy, raiding, and banditry, for example, result in goods circulating broadly, though certainly without the agreement of all partners. A Mycenaean pirate, for example, might seize goods from a Minoan vessel, then sell those goods at an Egyptian port. They then might be shipped aboard a Mycenaean vessel, which in turn might be captured by Minoan pirates, who sell the goods at a Minoan port, completing the circle.

An especially significant form of exchange is **tribute**, the rendering of goods to a powerful individual or state by a subordinate. Some governments in Mesoamerica, for example, received so much tribute from conquered states and subordinate allies that these goods became an expected part of the annual income of the state, one that was factored into the calculation of taxes and other revenue-raising programs. Although the subordinate state rarely received any material goods in exchange, it still benefited, because the powerful government to which it rendered tribute made a valuable ally against mutual enemies.

The flow of ideas has been prominent in some periods, also, and that often is considered exchange, as well. This textbook uses that extended meaning when discussing such periods of intense movement of ideas as the Roman imperial era and the spread of Islam.

Historians sometimes overlook the importance of these other forms of exchange, yet they can be quite significant. It has been estimated, for example, that as much as half of the exchange of goods in the seventeenth-century Caribbean took place through mechanisms other than trade, and certainly the exchange of ideas has been an important factor in many historic periods.

TRADE AS A CATALYST FOR CHANGE

Many scholars have seen long-distance trade as a major force in the development of civilization. In the past, several theories have discussed trade as the primary cause of increased complexity, but modern theorists prefer to be a bit more cautious, typically considering trade one of several factors that acted together to transform society.

Some of this caution grew out of a recognition that there are preconditions to long-distance trade. First, you need a product. Sometimes that product can be collected easily, but usually it needs to be manufactured or otherwise processed, and that requires certain technical skills and a workforce. Second, you need a society that is orga-

nized in such a manner that it can carry out trade expeditions. This means that personnel can be supported by specialist farmers while they are away on expeditions, producing no food for themselves. It also means that someone is in a position of sufficient authority to be able to organize the expedition and all that goes with it. Third, you need a society that has sufficient differences in wealth so that an individual, a company, or the government can invest the resources needed to mount the expedition, because the reward will be reaped only after the expedition is successfully completed. Goods need to be accumulated for trade, material wants during the expedition must be met, and some personnel may require compensation before the expedition is completed. The investor also has to be prepared for the possibility of a total loss and must have sufficient funds to be able to survive it.

The band-level societies described in Chapter 3 simply could not have engaged in long-distance trade of this sort, because they lacked the expertise and organization required. Rather, only societies that already were moving toward greater complexity (as a result of increasing population pressure and additional factors) could participate in long-distance trade. Once they engaged in such trade, however, they would be changed by it. Individuals with some wealth might become much wealthier; a political organization could become much stronger; occupational specialization and technical skills required in producing the commodity could develop further. Just as a catalyst facilitates a chemical reaction but does not cause it, trade was important in encouraging the ongoing process of evolving cultural complexity in early civilizations and their immediate predecessors.

SUGGESTED READINGS

Earle, Timothy K., and Jonathan E. Ericson, eds. *Exchange Systems in Prehistory.* New York: Academic Press, 1977. A set of provocative and timeless essays on models of trade.

Sabloff, Jeremy A., and C. C. Lamberg-Karlovsky, eds. *Ancient Civilization and Trade.* Albuquerque: University of New Mexico Press, 1975. A collection of classic essays on the role of trade in the origin of civilizations.

Torrence, Robin. *Production and Exchange of Stone Tools: Prehistoric Obsidian in the Aegean.* Cambridge, Eng.: Cambridge University Press, 1986. An excellent summary of extant models of trade, coupled with a thorough regional case study.

U P TO THIS POINT, *THE GLOBAL PAST* has emphasized primarily the earliest development of civilization around the world. Some of those civilizations adopted a type of government that brings several different peoples together under its aegis: an empire. Although empires existed in these early periods, they were relatively few and small. Part Two focuses on the several large empires that developed around the world in the first millennium B.C.

One of the great incentives to form an empire is economics. By controlling another people, a state can exact tribute or taxation, which can constitute a significant portion of its revenues. Perhaps even more important, an empire controls a wide range of environmental and production zones, giving it easy access to a broader variety of resources and commodities than any available to a smaller state. This may be why empires often expand along trade routes. Such factors allow an empire to rely less on foreign trade to support its needs, reducing the likelihood of its becoming politically subservient to a foreign power.

In most of the cases discussed in Part Two, empires were established through military action, meaning that the coalition formed in an empire is often fragile. If several peoples are united by the sword, they may simply wait until the sword wielder becomes weak, at which time they can defect from the empire and reestablish their independent governments. There seems to be a powerful tendency for

	GREECE	ROME	NUBIA	
2000 B.C.			Egyptian colonies	Kerma
1500 B.C.			Egyptian colonies	
1000 B.C.				
	Lyric Age		Kush	
500 B.C.	Classical Age	Etruscan Rome		
		Roman Republic	Meroë	
	◄ Alexander's Empire			
A.D. 1	Hellenistic Age	Early Roman Empire		
		Later Roman Empire		
A.D. 500				
A.D. 1000				

PART TWO

THE CONVERGENCE TOWARD EMPIRE

regional states to form out of the debris of a collapsed empire. In fact, one way of seeing history is as an alternation between vast interregional empires that unite many peoples and small, regional states, each dominated by a single people. Parts Three and Four will explore this pattern further.

A final consequence of an empire often is the establishment of a sphere of interchange, in which goods, foodstuffs, and ideas pass among the empire's component peoples. The impact of such an exchange typically far outlasts the political unity of the empire.

In Part Two, Chapters 7 and 8 discuss Greece and Rome, polities whose histories were linked by abundant cultural contact and which followed similar trajectories that led to expansive empires. Chapter 9 treats the Kush and Axum civilizations of Northeast Africa, each an empire for at least part of its span. Chapter 10 moves to India, discussing the Maurya and Gupta empires, and Chapter 11 treats the rise and fall of the Qin and Han empires, the first empires of China. Finally, Issue 2 discusses a general model of the formation, internal stresses, and collapse of empires.

ETHIOPIA	INDIA	CHINA	
			2000 B.C.
			1500 B.C.
			1000 B.C.
			500 B.C.
Pre-Axumite Period		Warring States Period	
	Maurya Empire		
	Regional states		◄ Qin Empire
		Early Han Empire	A.D. 1
Axum			
	Gupta Empire	Later Han Empire	
			A.D. 500
			A.D. 1000

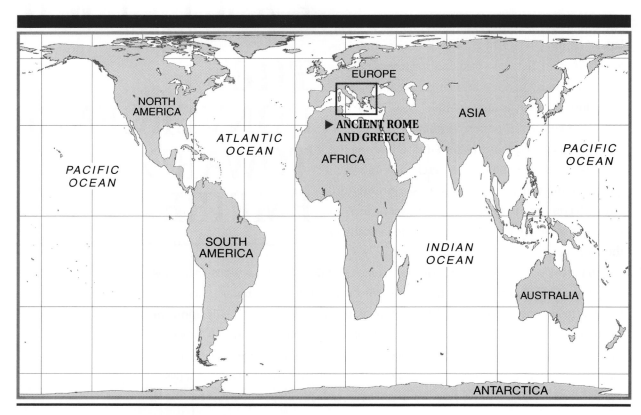

EUROPE

ASIA

► ANCIENT ROME
AND GREECE

NORTH
AMERICA

*ATLANTIC
OCEAN*

AFRICA

*PACIFIC
OCEAN*

*PACIFIC
OCEAN*

SOUTH
AMERICA

*INDIAN
OCEAN*

AUSTRALIA

ANTARCTICA

GAUL

ETRURIA

Adriatic Sea

Corsica

● **Rome**

Sardinia

*Tyrrhenian
Sea*

Mediterranean

Sicily

N. AFRICA

Sea

► **ANCIENT ROME**

MACEDONIA

*Aegean
Sea*

LYDIA

*Ionian
Sea*

Peloponnesus

● **Athens**

Crete

Mediterranean   Sea

► **ANCIENT GREECE**

The Greek Polis and the Roman Republic

around 800–31 B.C.

I sing of arms and of a man [Aeneas]: his fate had made him fugitive; he was the first to journey from the coasts of Troy as far as Italy. . . . Across the lands and waters he was battered . . . and many sufferings were his in war . . . until he brought a city into being and carried in his gods to Latium; from this have come the Latin race, the lords of Alba, and the ramparts of high Rome.

—VIRGIL, *The Aeneid*

The Aeneid, an epic by the Roman poet Virgil, is a story that demonstrates the great affinity Romans had for Greek culture, because they believed the founder of their city was Greek and that Greek culture was their own heritage. Greece and Rome faced similar challenges in their development and had many common characteristics. Chapters 7 and 8 discuss how each society governed itself and developed a definition of citizenship, how each responded to internal sociopolitical pressures, and how each dealt with expansion. It is important to pay attention to those instances where common challenges were met with different responses. This chapter will review Greek history from the ninth century to the fourth century B.C., covering what scholars call the Lyric and Classical periods. Roman history will be examined from early development under Etruscan control through the inception and demise of the Roman Republic, 509 to 31 B.C.

DEVELOPMENT OF THE GREEK CITY-STATE

Scholars know very little about Greece during the period between around 1200 and 800 B.C. because much of Greece experienced de-urbanization, and consequently minimal documentary evidence has survived. During this elusive historical period, Greek culture began to diffuse to the Aegean Basin, and, by about 800 B.C., the cultural unification of Greece was under way.

Early Greek communities supplied the population with shelter, defense, and a market for local trade. An **acropolis**, a higher area, served as a gathering place for safety against raids. People also came to an **agora**, a central market area similar to the Mesoamerican plaza, to barter goods and exchange news. The agora was a busy place, teeming with fixed and movable stalls. Sandal makers, potters, tanners, and bronzesmiths peddled their wares. A "fast food" meal could be purchased from one of the street vendors, as in large cities of today. Much like farm laborers today in the American Southwest, poor men met in a designated area hoping for a day's hire by a citizen who needed some extra workers. Slaves could be purchased in the agora, as well. The agora also housed courts, where aristocrats argued legal particulars and settled disputes.

In most cases, the rural areas and urban settlements that surrounded the acropolis and agora eventually evolved into city-states. The Greek city-state was called a **polis** (the plural is **poleis**[1]). Each polis jealously guarded its independence, and, ideally, every free male who belonged to a kin group and who owned land within the geographical area of the polis held citizenship there. A citizen's identity came from the polis. Generally, because the polis was originally populated by kin groups, Greeks resisted allowing outsiders to become citizens. When long-distance trade expanded, immigrant merchants paid higher taxes than citizen merchants. Later, laws often allowed the purchasing of citizenship, but the expense prohibited many from obtaining it. In any commercial center, however, citizens of many poleis might be seen selling their commodities and arranging future transactions.

At the same time as the development of the polis, a new style of warfare emerged that affected social and legal conditions. The older style of aristocratic warfare was no longer practical, and a citizen army developed under the leadership of local aristocrats. Each citizen-soldier, a **hoplite**, became a cog in a massive human machine called a **phalanx**,[2] a block of infantry soldiers consisting of as many as one hundred men lined up in rows as many as eight deep. As time passed, phalanx soldiers demanded better economic conditions, less arbitrary justice, and a vote in a citizen assembly in exchange for their invaluable defense of the polis and the personal wealth of the aristocrats. This change in warfare caused an important move toward the concept of citizens' rights.

Greek political history is a checkerboard of various government structures, such as monarchy, oligarchy, tyranny, and democracy. By about 750 to 600 B.C., monarchy gave way to **oligarchy**, rule by a few influential members of the elite in a council. Early oligarchy was usually based on a hereditary aristocracy rather than on wealth. Over the generations, the inherited influence of these aristocrats tended to support their own interests at the expense of citizens of the lower classes. With continued growth in trade, however, bloodlines offered less political influence and the oligarchy's membership shifted to the wealthy elite.

Tension between the oligarchy and other citizens remained common. Between 675 and 600 B.C., it was not unusual to see a polis develop a **tyranny**, originally meaning the usurpation of rule by an individual with widespread popular support. A tyrant was usually brought into power by citizens in opposition to oppressive oligarchical control. This individual promised reform to the hoplites or offices to the merchants. Several tyrants saved poleis from civil war and rebellion, often proving effective in steering the ship of state. Unfortunately, the outcome sometimes exchanged aristocratic oppression for tyrannical oppression after only a few months or years of reform; this is the condition that corresponds to the English meaning of the word "tyrant."

Other reformers replaced oligarchies or tyrants with democracies. A **democracy** is government in the hands of all its citizens or their elected representatives. In many poleis, two factions

---

[1] **poleis:** POH lee ihs

[2] **phalanx:** FAY langks

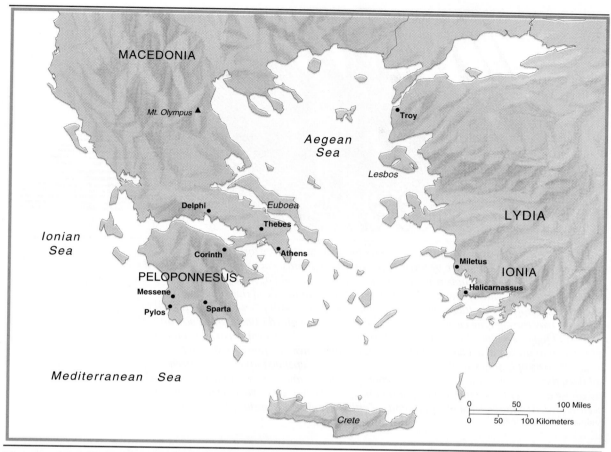

MAP 7.1 *Major Poleis of Ancient Greece.* *The Peloponnesus is the large southern area that was dominated by Sparta and was more rural than the area to the north of the isthmus, where the large poleis of Athens, Thebes, and Delphi were found. Lands north of Delphi were also more rural, in part because of the terrain, while Delphi, one of the most sacred sites in ancient Greece, was believed to be the center of the earth. Here the oracle temple of Apollo attracted many people from all over southwestern Asia and southeastern Europe, who came to consult the god on personal and political affairs through the young virgin who acted as a medium.*

developed: the oligarchs and the democrats, who constantly competed for control of the city.

Two examples of Greek political development are Athens and Sparta. Athens's history depicts the typical development spurred by the factors discussed, while Sparta's development demonstrates the exception.

Athens: The Typical Pattern

The polis of Athens dominated the surrounding countryside; as many as two hundred various-sized villages were incorporated into the city-state.

Athens's early government was an oligarchy, consisting of a council of aristocrats called the **Areopagite**,[3] a name derived from where they met—the Areopagus or "hill of Ares," the war god. This council met yearly and elected nine **archons**,[4] officials who ran the day-to-day government. The archons consisted of a chief judge and six lesser judges, an official in charge of priestly functions, and a war chief. In addition to the Areopagite Council and archons, the Citizens' Assembly met

[3] **Areopagite:** air ee OH pah gyt
[4] **archons:** AWR kahnz

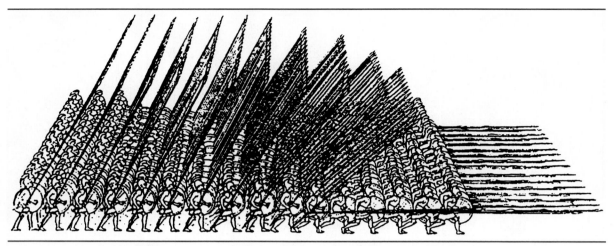

FIGURE 7.1 **Phalanx Warfare.** *Hoplites lined up in phalanx form, ready to fight, protected by helmets, and, later, by breastplates and shin guards. Each hoplite wore a sword strapped at the waist for hand-to-hand combat and held a shield in the left hand and a pike in the right. The left side of the shield covered the exposed right side of the man standing next to each hoplite. In battle, each phalanx moved as a unit, with pikes raised, as it tried to wedge its way through the enemy line. The phalanx that remained intact gained advantage and could fight as a block in hand-to-hand combat; this kind of warfare was much more effective than unorganized bands of men charging each other. The phalanx system required large numbers of hoplites, and because defense of the city depended upon these citizen-soldiers, they often demanded social and economic reforms and the right to redress oligarchical abuse of power before they would consent to fight. The hoplite threats to boycott battles eventually led to the concept of equal rights of citizens and to the world's first democracies.*
Andromeda Oxford Limited.

when summoned by the archons on matters relating to diplomacy and warfare.

The move toward a democracy in Athens was actually the result of social unrest. Many Athenian citizens had fallen prey to aristocratic abuses, as when aristocratic interests were protected in the law courts to the detriment of other citizens. In 620 B.C., reform took shape through the efforts of a lawgiver named Draco, who was the first to write down Athenian law. Penalties under Draconian law were severe; even small offenses resulted in the death penalty. By the sixth century B.C., aristocratic abuses were common again. Both rich and poor agreed that peaceful reform was preferable to violence, and two lawgivers, Solon and Cleisthenes,[5] initiated reforms through the office of archon. The particulars of many of the reforms remain historically obscure, but scholars are aware of several economic and social innovations. Many poorer farmers had sold their property and, in extreme

cases, themselves into slavery because of repeated poor harvests brought on by droughts and decreasing yields from the exhausted soil. As a consequence, these farmers became ineligible to fight in the phalanx. In 594 B.C., Solon arranged for the purchase of many former citizens' freedom from slavery and enacted laws to cease the practice of using one's person as collateral for debts. Solon also made judicial and governmental policies less prone to aristocratic abuse by giving the poor redress in popular courts. In a one-time action, all free adult males living in Athens became members of the Citizens' Assembly, regardless of whether they owned land or were immigrants. To thwart the power of the hereditary oligarchy, Solon dissolved the old kinship groups and created four new fictive kinship groups determined by wealth. He then created a new ruling Council of One Hundred (made up of elected members from each new kinship group) to govern the city.

Solon's reforms broke the stranglehold of the old aristocracy in Athens, yet they did not yield

[5] **Cleisthenes:** KLYS thah neez

FIGURE 7.2 *Athenian Acropolis. The polis of Athens developed around the Acropolis, a high rocky area that afforded a good view of the surrounding terrain and was a defendable position against attacks. The ruins that crown the Acropolis date from building projects of the fifth-century B.C. period of Athenian dominance, and eventually became the models for Classical Greek architecture and sculpture. The most famous building, the Parthenon (seen here in the center of the Acropolis) was a temple dedicated to Athena, patron goddess of Athens. It measures about 228 feet by 101 feet and is constructed of marble, with eight columns on each end and seventeen on each side. The inner room that once housed a gold-and-marble statue of Athena had a two-tiered colonnade running along the sides and around the back of the statue. Other statues depicted scenes from the myths of Athena. (See also the close-up of a relief from the Parthenon in Figure 7.6.)* Robert Harding Picture Library.

long-lasting results. No land reforms accompanied the laws against debt slavery, and poverty soon led to the enslavement of poor citizens again, as the laws against using oneself as collateral increasingly were ignored. Additionally, Solon's establishment of wealth instead of heredity as the litmus test for power did not change oligarchical rule; it merely created a different ruling elite in the Council of One Hundred.

By 508 B.C., Athens was forced again to chose a reforming lawgiver, Cleisthenes, to settle social unrest. The ruling elite refused to allow new immigrants to participate in government, so many wealthy merchants living in the city had inferior legal status. Many poor farmers had sold themselves into slavery again. Cleisthenes created demes,[6] new political districts based on where one lived. Cleisthenes disbanded Solon's Council of One Hundred and created a new one. Its membership consisted of fifty elected members from each of ten newly formed fictive kinship groups composed of all economic and social levels from the demes. This created a Council of Five Hundred, whose members were elected on a yearly basis. An administrative subcouncil was then elected from the new Council of Five Hundred to do the daily work of the government. This was democracy in action, because even poorer farmers could be

[6] **demes:** DEEMZ

elected to the Council of Five Hundred and the subcouncil. Yet it did not take long for government's time-consuming work to become a low priority for the small farmers whose farms required their continued presence. Although elections continued, Athenian government again fell into the hands of the wealthiest citizens, who could afford to be absent from their estates or businesses.

Athenian democracy had occurred as a direct result of the need for social reform. Reforms were not long lasting, and, although Athens remained a democracy for most of its history, the wealthy were able to dominate it with patronage and the buying of votes.

Sparta: The Exception

Spartan history is singularly different from that of Athens and all other Greek poleis. During the seventh and sixth centuries B.C., Sparta engaged in a period of expansion and aggression. Most other Greek poleis sent out colonists or incorporated nearby territories that had space for expansion by making their inhabitants citizens. Sparta, however, conquered its western neighbor, Messenia, whose fertile lands could yield enough grain to feed the expanding Spartan population. The Messenians became **helots**, members of an inferior status, who were not slaves but were restricted in their rights and constantly guarded by Spartan soldiers.

Around 650 B.C., the helots revolted, and Sparta, greatly weakened by the uprising, almost lost its domination of them. This was a turning point in Spartan history; Sparta's fear of another helot revolt resulted in a complete reorganization into a rigid hierarchy. Helots remained at the bottom. Allies of Sparta were politically free but obligated to serve with the Spartan army when called. In Sparta, only males who had reached the age of thirty and had been born of two Spartan parents could be citizens. At any given time, there were approximately five to ten helots for every citizen, and defense became the driving force in Spartan society.

Sparta had a mixed government consisting of monarchical, oligarchical, and democratic elements that made it unique in Greek political history. Spartan governmental reforms retained monarchy in the two-king system, because it was believed that two kings met the need for a balance of power to thwart tyrannical abuse. The kings led the army in battle, policed the helots, performed rituals, and exercised judicial functions. The Council of Thirty, consisting of the two kings and twenty-eight retired soldiers, prepared legislation for the Citizens' Assembly and performed judicial functions. Five overseers, one elected to represent each of the five districts of Sparta, performed the daily work of government, oversaw the kings in their responsibilities, negotiated foreign policy, and presided over the Citizens' Assembly. The Citizens' Assembly included a gathering of all citizens (including the Council of Thirty and the overseers); its duties were to ratify council legislation, declare war, and impeach recalcitrant kings. This created a balance of political power in Sparta.

Harkening back to an ancient legendary lawgiver, Lycurgus, the Spartans justified their military society and their suppression of the helots through the enforcement of their idea of justice. They saw the helot revolt as a sign that they had abandoned the ancient traditions based upon good law, and they devoted their lives to the protection and promotion of their polis, making civic duty the mainstay of Spartan life. Consequently, Sparta, with no merchants of its own and no private ownership of land until the fourth century B.C., engaged in little commerce.

Spartans lived a regimented life wherein individualism was punished with exile or death to preserve the common good. Spartan babies were examined at birth to determine their strength and health; if they were sickly they were exposed to the elements and allowed to die. In Sparta, exposure was a state decision rather than a parental one. Female babies were less desirable, but those who were strong and might survive to produce more children were allowed to live. This practice of infanticide by exposure occurred throughout Greece as well as in some other cultures and served to limit the financial burden of unduly large families and to control sex ratios.

Young Spartan boys trained in athletics and military tactics when they were removed to barracks life at the age of seven. The military communal living limited personal freedoms. Spartans could marry at the age of eighteen years but had to continue living in the barracks; conjugal visits had to be made by stealth. Young men continued practical military training as hoplites in the army until they were granted full citizenship at thirty years of age, when they could live at home (though they continued to have meals at the barracks). Re re-ment finally came at age sixty, when the vet an became eligible for election to the Council.

Women were also trained in athletics and vere given a mandate to serve the state by producing strong sons. Spartan women had a reputation for being outspoken and militaristic; they often lined the road as the hoplites marched out of the bar-racks on their way to war, and one mother is said to have challenged a son to "come back with your shield or on it!" The Spartan who dropped his shield and fled the battle disgraced his family and polis and probably would not make it home alive. But the Spartan who marched home or returned among the revered dead gave his mother and family great honor.

FIGURE 7.3 *Spartan Woman. This bronze statue represents a young Spartan woman performing gymnastics, in which both girls and boys were trained. Spartan women enjoyed more social freedoms than most other Greek women, because Spartans believed that outspoken and authoritative women challenged men to live up to their responsibilities. Stories circulated about Spartan women chastising weak or lazy men and hooting at the losers at competitive athletic events. Because hoplites were often called away into battle, women were expected to protect the polis from enemy attack. A story is told of a king invading in 275 B.C. from an area northwest of Greece and his reluctance to attack Sparta. He was aware that the city would be defended only by Spartan women, children, and old men, but the women's reputation for battle gave him pause.* National Archaeological Museum, Athens/Archaeological Receipts Fund (TAP Service).

LIFE IN ANCIENT GREECE

The geography of Greece and the entire Aegean area had a profound effect upon Greek society. Very few cities are more than a dozen miles from the coast, because most of the interior regions are mountainous. The earliest communities found themselves somewhat isolated by these natural barriers, resulting in a strong sense of self-sufficiency and local kinship identity that later inhibited Greek political unification. Coastal trade brought the various communities into contact with one another, but local citizens generally discouraged extension of citizenship to immigrants from other areas.

By 800 B.C., Greek farmers left their cities to work in the fields during the day and returned at night. This pattern lasted until the commuting time to newly cultivated and often remote fields became prohibitive, forcing those in the outlying areas to live on their land. Social structure then focused on the *oikos,*[7] or household, which consisted of the family, land, slaves or tenants, buildings, and livestock of a single farmer. Each self-sufficient *oikos* produced and maintained most of what the family needed. As a matter of fact, the Greek word for the management of a household is *oikonomia*, from which our English word "economy" is derived.

Farmers produced many crops for the family's table and for exchange. The primary dietary crops were grain, grapes, and olives, from which bread, wine, and oil could be produced. Fruits and vegetables included grapes, figs, lentils, and leeks; honey was gathered to sweeten many dishes. Fish and shellfish were consumed fresh or dried. Goat milk was drunk or turned into milk products like cheese. Most meat came from wild game,

[7] *oikos:* OY kohs

including deer and boar, which adorned only holiday banquet tables. Farmers did not practice crop rotation for soil replenishment but let fields lie fallow to regenerate the soil. Oxen pulled the plows, designed merely to scratch into the limited topsoil of the region, and farmers followed, scattering the seed.

The Greek Social Structure

The social structure consisted of aristocrats, commoners (peasants, artisans, and laborers), and slaves. In early Greece, the wealthy aristocrats and peasant farmers lived in similar housing and engaged in the same types of employment. Housing was designed around a courtyard, giving maximum security with a surrounding wall (usually windowless). As a matter of fact, burglars were called "walldiggers" because of this construction, which forced them to tunnel through the outer wall to rob the occupants. Aristocrats tilled the soil in early Greek society; owning land and performing manual labor was the ideal. Odysseus, the hero of the Homeric epic *The Odyssey*, was known for being able to plow a straight furrow—a sign of a good farmer. As cities grew and political power became centralized, however, wealthy aristocrats participating in government or practicing law remained in the cities, leaving their estates in the hands of trusted servants.

Commoners and slaves comprised the largest percentage of the population. The peasant farmers tended to own land in hilly areas or in less fertile sections. Those farmers too poor to own land worked parcels of aristocratic lands as tenants for a portion of the yield. Urbanites worked as artisans or day laborers. Those who fell into debt or were captured in war became slaves. Most slaves were treated well as house servants or field laborers, but some slaves had to engage in dangerous work, like mining silver. Other slaves were highly educated doctors, teachers, and merchants. Manumission was frequent and often came in the form of a gift in a will or as the result of a slave's personal economic prowess; city slaves often engaged in commercial enterprises for their wealthy owners. A merchant class developed about the seventh century B.C., when increased long-distance trade brought greater wealth to the cities.

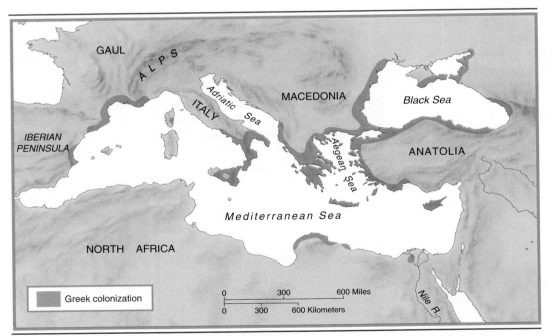

MAP 7.2 *Greek Colonization.* *This map shows the areas colonized by Greek poleis around the Mediterranean basin. The Greek trade network was based on ethnic ties between poleis and colonies; this alliance assured lower prices for all Greeks dealing with Greek traders. In addition, poleis with numerous colonies enjoyed a favored trade status with their colonies. Athens, for example, was able to support building programs and the fine arts and to employ some of the best educators in Greece for their children.*

FIGURE 7.4 *Greek Colonial Trade.* *Greek colonies dotted the coastal areas of the eastern Mediterranean Sea, bringing great wealth to the poleis that originated them. Athens, Corinth, and Thebes established many colonies. This platter comes from a Greek colony in modern-day Libya. The large figure on the left checks the weight of a shipment of juice from the silphium plant, which was used for medicine and flavoring foods. A scribe makes notes on the transaction as the goods are assembled. The containers are stored under the flooring. The presence of weights and measures signifies their importance in the transaction; merchants often carried their own weights to ensure fairness.* Bibliothèque nationale, Paris.

Gender Roles

Gender roles developed in Greek society much as they had in other early civilizations. Women's contributions to family life focused on child rearing and household duties. Aristocratic women were often in charge of large households with a multitude of servants and sizeable budgets to manage. In the humblest hovel and the wealthiest villa, women wove cloth. As a matter of fact, some Greek myths associated the creative acts of procreation and weaving. Women also participated in society as priestesses or prostitutes, and the priestesses held a highly respected position in Greek religion. Greeks believed that women were more spiritual and less intellectual than men. The priestesses for the Oracle of Apollo at Delphi were selected from among the girls of local families and were chosen for their propensity toward erratic and ecstatic behavior. Aristocratic men engaged in political and legal professions, but most men worked as farmers, laborers, artisans, craftsmen, and merchants.

Children were welcomed into the family, but the father (except in Sparta) had the authority to choose life or death for any child deemed unsuitable or too expensive to raise. (Girls were considered more expendable.) Children were socialized in their gender roles from an early age, and wealthy families formally educated both young boys and girls in reading, writing, singing, and playing instruments. In their teen years, girls continued their domestic educations, while boys progressed to studies in mathematics, poetry, philosophy, music, and gymnastics.

A favorite male pastime was frequenting a public gymnasium, consisting of pools, steam baths, and a sandy area for sports. Athletic activity was an important part of Greek society because Greeks admired a well-toned body as well as an educated mind. Formal games became sources of pride and honor for those cities whose athletes won prizes in competitions. Athletes were honored with tax exemptions, permission to wear purple (a sign of prestige), and often a statue. Besides creating a diversion, these competitive sports kept the citizen army in good physical condition; wars were frequent between the fiercely competitive and independent poleis.

Trade and Colonization

In the eighth century B.C., Greek trade and colonization expanded, profoundly affecting Greek society. The limited arable land and overcultivation were always problems for Greek farmers, forcing the importation of numerous goods, particularly grains from Egypt and the area of the Black Sea. Many cities sent out large groups of people to establish new colonies to relieve the

ENCOUNTERS

The Sicilian Caterer

By the fifth century B.C., Athens had achieved its status as the leader in Greek elite culture. While Athenians of earlier periods had focused on feasts dedicated to the gods, these now were eclipsed by more secular social dining. Dining at the earlier feasts to the gods had been a rigid affair, with diners seated at communal tables. Social dining in the later period, on the other hand, was more relaxed, with the diners typically reclining on couches in what was referred to as the "Sicilian style." This term is telling, because the Athenian banquet of this period owed much to Sicily, the island immediately to the south of the Italian peninsula.

Greek city-states had established colonies in Sicily beginning in the eighth century B.C.; the most famous was Syracuse. These essentially independent colonies had retained many aspects of Greek culture, but they also had absorbed certain Sicilian ways, especially in terms of food and dining. Sicilians, by all reports, enjoyed their meals and regarded them as an opportunity to delight the senses. Well-to-do Sicilians ate reclining, often with flowers arranged around them. Meals consisted of small amounts of many dishes, often prepared with exotic ingredients and served with sauces.

In part through connections with the Sicilian colonies, Athens imported this style of dining. The thick, unsauced slabs of roasted meat that had graced earlier Greek tables were replaced with daintier dishes that were prepared, not merely cooked, and dressed with sauces. Wealthy Athenian diners often festooned themselves with garlands of flowers while reclining "Sicilian style."

There was, however, another, more direct route by which Sicilian cuisine and dining habits made their way to Athens. Although everyday meals were prepared by a household's servants, special dinner parties with guests usually were catered, and the most sought-after caterers were Sicilians. Archestratus[a] was a famous wandering gastronome who would stoop to exercising his culinary skills when his funds were running short; Mithraicos[b] was so famous for his cooking skill that Plato discussed him in *Gorgias*; and there were two caterers named Heraclides.[c] All of these caterers were from Sicily, and there must have been many other less famous caterers whose names have been lost. Those mentioned here are known because they wrote cookbooks describing how dishes in the Sicilian style should be prepared; alas, none of the books has survived.

Hints at the Sicilian style of cuisine survive, however, and it seems to have contained a great many fish dishes. Combinations rare in today's cooking appear to have been common then, such as fish baked with cheese and vinegar. The Mediterranean was—and is—justly famous for its fresh fish, and the seasonings probably were to satisfy Sicilian tastes, not to disguise old fish.

Food historians have a saying that the French learned to cook from the Italians and that the Italians learned to cook from the Greeks. This is a convenient oversimplification, but it emphasizes the fact that there was a great deal of contact between regions and many influences that shaped the cooking of any single region. The Mediterranean was a small place, and people and ideas—like fish—circulated freely.

[a]**Archestratus:** ahr keh STRAY tuhs
[b]**Mithraicos:** mihth RAY cohs
[c]**Heraclides:** hair ah KLY deez

pressure of population growth and to improve trade. Colonies were sent eastward to the coast of modern Turkey (called Ionia), northeastward to the Black Sea, westward to Sicily and southern Italy, and even as far west as the coast of Spain. Greeks traded primarily olive oil and wine for staple foods and wood, along with luxury items. The colonists took Greek culture and attitudes with them, often displacing indigenous peoples through war. They did intermarry with local people, but they kept Greek lifeways dominant. The new colony usually had very close economic and religious ties to the originating polis, but like the polis at home, it remained politically independent.

Increased trade with colonies and other peoples of the Mediterranean shores brought wealth to many citizens. Conversely, catastrophic loss from poor business ventures or speculation could ruin a family economically and politically. Land remained the preferential basis of wealth, however, and many wealthy merchants purchased large tracts of land to legitimize themselves. Aristocrats disdained those who gained wealth through trade, but many provided financial backing to slaves to establish businesses, while themselves remaining silent partners.

A CENTURY OF GREEK CONFLICT

Greek poleis fought frequent wars of aggression and defense among themselves. Sometimes the oligarchy of one city supported the oligarchy of another city against tyrants or democratic reformers. Through all these conflicts, however, there remained the basic idea that all poleis should remain self-governing and independent of any non-Greek power. A series of events, however, threatened Greek society between 490 and 404 B.C., resulting in a century occupied mainly with war and conflict.

The Persian Wars, 490–479 B.C.

Greek poleis infrequently united in a common effort, but they did so to defend Greece from the Persians. By the sixth century B.C., the huge Persian Empire became interested in the lucrative Greek trade along the western coast of modern Turkey, threatening the Ionian cities there. After swallowing up the smaller nearby kingdom of Lydia in 546 B.C., Persia soon encroached on the Greeks in the region. The Ionian cities revolted against Persia in 499 B.C., with only nominal help from the European mainland Greeks. This conflict initiated long-term hostilities between Greece and Persia. When Persia's King Darius I invaded Thrace in 490 B.C., the Persian Wars (490–479 B.C.) began. Some Greek poleis had surrendered to the Persians, but others allied in a common effort to defeat Persian aggression. Athens soon emerged as the leader of the allied effort. After their defeat in 479 B.C., the Persians retreated from the Aegean, and a new era in Greek history unfolded as Athens exploited its leadership role.

Athenian Dominance, 479–431 B.C.

The city of Athens had established several colonies on the Ionian coast and had developed a fleet of merchant ships that became a significant factor in naval engagements with the Persian fleet. Naval victories during the Persian Wars proved the effectiveness of a standing fleet against Persian invasion. In the aftermath of the wars, Athens insisted on the continuance of a well-maintained fleet, which Athens would manage but the allies would fund. Athens soon dominated the **Delian League**, a coalition for the common defense and the liberation of any Greeks who remained under Persian control. A treasury, housed on the island of Delos, was established to accomplish this. Athens forced each polis to join the coalition on its liberation from Persia.

Athens's overlordship of other league members and financial control of the treasury soon threatened traditional Greek independence. Any threat of withdrawal from the coalition was met with force, and allies were treated as subjects. At the same time, because of its access to all ports, Athens enjoyed unprecedented commercial expansion and corresponding economic growth. Democratic Athens increasingly meddled in the political affairs of other poleis and dominated the Greek economy. The future of Athenian power seemed secure when the treasury was moved from Delos to Athens in 454 B.C. Athens had been severely damaged in the Persian Wars, and the money used to rebuild the city came from the league's funds.

The Peloponnesian Wars, 431–404 B.C.

Athens's dominance of the Delian League led to widespread unrest among the poleis. Hostilities with Persia came to an end in 449 B.C. with the signing of a peace treaty between the two antagonists. Athens continued to block secession from the Delian League, even though there was no longer a need for an organization for the common defense. The allies, realizing that they were actually subjects of Athenian interests, turned to rebellion. Sparta and its allies had resisted Athenian overlordship and had not joined the Delian League. Sparta took this opportunity to crush Athenian power and led the rebellion against Athens. The wars were fought in two major periods (431–421 B.C. and 415–404 B.C.), with an uneasy

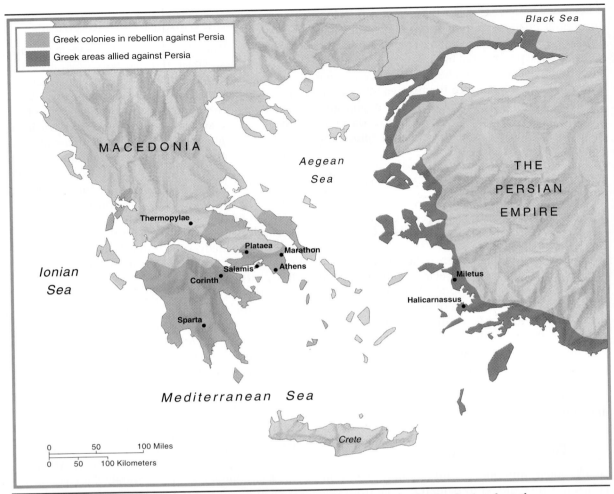

MAP 7.3   *The Persian Wars, 490–479 B.C.   During the Persian Wars, the Greek colonies along the coast of modern Turkey were threatened by the encroachment of the Persians. Many of the poleis finally were taken over or were forced to accept pro-Persian governments. They soon rebelled, calling on aid from their Greek homeland. However, not all areas in Greece joined the alliance of poleis against Persia. Greeks rarely came together in political or military unity; each polis fiercely guarded its independence. During the Persian Wars, the powerful states of Athens and Sparta supplied commanders to lead the Greek alliance. The three major land battles of the Persian Wars occurred at Marathon, Thermopylae, and Plataea. The last and most significant naval battle, near Salamis, launched the Athenians into naval dominance.*

peace between them. By 404 B.C., Athens lay defeated, its walls demolished and its citizenry demoralized. Unconditional surrender placed the city in the hands of a tyrant backed by Sparta, but Athens overthrew the tyranny and regained its independence; democracy finally returned to Athens by the winter of 403–402 B.C.

The end of the Peloponnesian Wars did not mean peace for Greece. Skirmishes between poleis continued for a generation, which even saw the Persian emperor arbitrate local disputes. The tradition of polis independence discouraged Greece from uniting politically, and the history of Greece from this point until the rise of Macedonia in the north is the history of each individual polis.

GREEK PHILOSOPHY AND THE ARTS

Ancient Greek history is often divided into several ages based upon periods in artistic and intellectual history. The Lyric, the Classical, and the Hellenistic

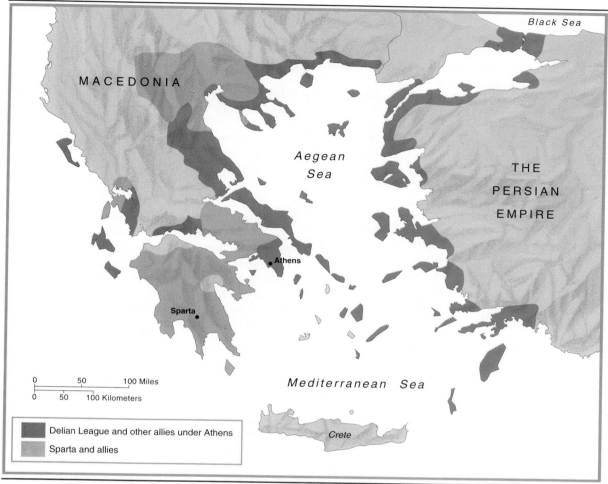

MAP 7.4 *The Peloponnesian Wars, 431–404* B.C. *The two major antagonists in the Peloponnesian Wars were Sparta and Athens. Athens led the Delian League, which developed after the victory over Persia in 479 B.C., for the common defense of Greeks against any future Persian attack. Sparta and many of its allies had never joined the Delian League and resented Athenian overlordship in Greece. As the map demonstrates, most of Athens's strength rested on alliances developed along trade routes. Athens had used the Delian League as a means to further its dominance of shipping lanes; Sparta, on the other hand, gained allies from among the more rural areas.*

ages are periods of innovation in the arts and philosophy. We will discuss the Lyric and Classical ages in this chapter and the Hellenistic Age in Chapter 8.

The Lyric Age, around 800–around 500 B.C.

The Lyric Age includes some of the earliest literature of European civilization. The word "lyric" is used because early Greek poetry and epic stories were sung and often accompanied by musical instruments, usually the lyre. Through oral accounts, the Greeks kept alive many of the stories about the Mycenaean age that later emerged in the heroic epics *The Iliad* and *The Odyssey*. Their composition is attributed to Homer, but they are actually a compilation of legends by many storytellers of the eighth century B.C. These stories of heroic deeds and individualism became the foundation for Greek education. Greek boys, particularly aristocrats, were schooled in these two classics and committed long passages to memory. Each city-state claimed a heroic founder from *The Iliad*, and

IN THEIR OWN WORDS

Odysseus and Aeneas

Heroes played significant roles as models for behavior in Greek and Roman society. The Greek myths, reflecting on their Mycenaean forebears, recounted numerous adventures and deeds that inspired the youth of the Lyric and Classical ages. Roman myths also instructed many young, aspiring aristocratic boys to greatness as they heard or read about the deeds of the heroic past. Two such awe-inspiring heroes were Odysseus and Aeneas.

Odysseus was brave, astute, and enterprising. His cunning led to lies on occasion, but his prudent counsel and valor in battle made him the perfect mix of heroic ideals for Greek youth. Odysseus's life entertained as well as inspired; his experiences in *The Odyssey*, the story of his ten-year trek back to his homeland after fighting with other Mycenaeans at Troy, proved to be the most popular of Greek adventures. In this selection, his intellect liberates him and his men from the cave of the Cyclops.

The Cyclops [who had been blinded by Odysseus earlier] . . . sat down in the entrance himself, spreading his arms wide, to catch anyone who tried to get out with the sheep . . . but I was planning so that things would come out the best way . . . combining all my resource and treacheries . . . and as I thought, this was the plan that seemed best to me. There were some male sheep, rams, well nourished, thick, and fleecy. . . . Silently I caught these and lashed them together. . . . I had them in threes, and the one in the middle carried a man, while the other two went on each side, so guarding my friends. . . . There was one ram, far the finest of all the flock. This one I clasped around the back, snuggled under the wool of the belly, and stayed there still, and with a firm twist of the hands and enduring spirit clung fast to the glory of this fleece, unrelenting. . . . [The Cyclops] felt over the backs of all his sheep . . . but . . . did not notice how my men were fastened under the breasts. . . . Last of all the flock the ram went out of the doorway . . . and when we had got a little way from the yard and the cavern, first I got myself loose . . . then set my companions free, and rapidly then, and with many a backward glance, we drove the long-striding sheep, rich with fat, until we reached our ship.

Romans believed that Aeneas, the founder of their city, came from the ancient Greek city of Troy. Aeneas had traits similar to Odysseus's, those of bravery, honor, and intelligence. Young Romans learned from Aeneas that duty to the state remained paramount and that honor came with loyalty. In the following selection from *The Aeneid*, Aeneas has traveled into a sacred cavern that leads to the underworld of spirits. Aeneas's dead father tries to convince Aeneas to do his duty and found the city by showing him the spirits of future Romans waiting to be born. The passage explains that it is Rome's destiny to conquer and rule the world.

Now turn your two eyes here, to look upon your Romans, your own people. Here is Caesar . . . and Pompey . . . who could leave to silence you, great Cato? . . . who can ignore the [Gracchus brothers]? . . . For other peoples will, I do not doubt, still cast their bronze to breathe with softer features, or draw out of the marble living lines, plead causes better, trace the ways of heaven with wands and tell the rising constellations; but yours will be the rulership of nations, remember, Roman, these will be your arts: to teach the ways of peace to those you conquer, to spare defeated peoples, [and to] tame the proud.

---

their nostalgic reverence for the heroic Mycenaean Age gave them a sense of unity, cultural superiority, and tradition.

The Lyric Age also produced prominent poets who wrote for the enjoyment of an increasingly sophisticated, literate clientele. One of these was Sappho (born about 612 B.C.), who lived on the island of Lesbos. Sappho grew up a typical Greek girl from a wealthy family; when she was old enough, she married a husband suitable to her station, and they had a daughter. But Sappho's life changed following the untimely death of her husband. In ancient Greek society, most poets and intellectuals were male. Sappho overcame this masculine predominance and established a circle of women who were devoted to one another and to their love of poetry. The Greek philosopher Plato, normally uninterested in women's contributions, lauded Sappho's poetry, as did the scholars of following centuries, who named her one of the Nine Lyric Poets.

Many intellectuals from Greece traveled to participate in the artistic atmosphere of Lesbos. Sappho's poetry praises the feminine, and she

FIGURE 7.5 **Sappho.** *Sappho is depicted on a vase commemorating her fame as a lyric poet. Much of her work was viewed as depraved and was destroyed in later centuries by the early Christian Church. No complete poems of Sappho remain, but quotations from her poems, preserved in other writers' works, attest to her talents. During the Lyric Age, when Sappho wrote, Greeks came in contact with several other cultures from around the eastern Mediterranean and as far north as the Black Sea. It has been argued that interaction with these peoples led to a movement toward individualism in philosophy and literature and away from the older Homeric constructs. Sappho's lifestyle, portrayed in her poetry, was less tolerated than male homosexuality and demonstrates great individualism for this period.* Staatliche Antikensammlung, Berlin.

wrote love poetry about her relationships with many of the women who resided in her community at Lesbos (from which modern English derives the term "lesbian"). Homosexuality in ancient Greece was considered an appropriate expression of sexuality, and bisexuality was common. Although most Greeks thought a heterosexual relationship was the ideal (because it produced children to inherit property and prestige), they believed that experimentation made one a better partner. Elders were expected to teach younger partners of the same sex the sensual arts. Many selections of Greek poetry and plays treated sexuality as a driving force to be enjoyed, romanticized, and even joked about.

Philosophy, the pursuit of wisdom or knowledge, also blossomed in Greece's Lyric Age. Greek philosophy originated on the Ionian coast as a consequence of the interaction between Persians and the Ionian colonists; the intellectual challenge of meeting a new and different culture instigated Greek investigation into physics (the study of the natural world) and cosmology (the study of the origin and properties of the universe). The science and mathematics of southwestern Asia and Egypt challenged the older religious myths of these colonists. The Olympian deities had been associated with natural phenomena: The sun was Apollo's chariot; thunder and lightning were rages of Zeus. Now Greek intellectuals began asking different questions regarding how the universe functioned and how nature worked. They did not stop believing in their traditional anthropomorphic deities but removed them to a distant, uninterested role in the operation of the universe. The ancient cosmology of the Olympian myths gave way to such practical knowledge as recognition of tides and sea currents, greater understanding of weather patterns, and new techniques in agriculture.

The Classical Age, around 500–around 338 B.C.

The Classical Age was a period of warfare but also one of artistic and intellectual development. The wealth of Athenians attracted artisans and philosophers. Wealthy Athenians patronized the arts, and Classical Athens became a center for intellectual and artistic development.

Greek sculpture and architecture flourished under private and public patronage. Idealization

FIGURE 7.6 *Poseidon, Apollo, and Artemis.* *This relief from the eastern side of the Parthenon depicts three Olympian deities seated on their thrones. On the left is Poseidon, god of earthquakes and the sea, who was worshiped by sailors. The center figure is Apollo, the god associated with music, archery, prophecy, medicine, and philosophy. Many people traveled to the sacred city of Delphi, where Greeks believed Apollo spoke through the oracle of the temple. Seated at the right is Artemis, Apollo's sister, the goddess associated with uncultivated areas, like forests where wild beasts lived. She is described in myth as a lion among women and a hunter. Greeks worshiped her as a birth goddess, believing she brought fertility to men, women, and fruit trees and that she protected the unborn. She was particularly popular among the peoples living in the large rural areas of the Peloponnesus. This relief is a fine example of the style of sculpture during the productive period of fifth-century Athens.* Erich Lessing/Art Resource, N.Y.

of the human body became the focus of Greek sculpture in marble and bronze. Every city proudly displayed statues of anthropomorphic deities, prominent citizens, and favorite athletes. Building projects increased, and their architectural designs included multiple columns topped with different ornate designs. The buildings of the acropolis were constructed under the public works projects of Pericles (495–429 B.C.), the archon and most prominent political leader of Athens during its period of dominance. The **Parthenon**, the temple of Athena on the acropolis, was decorated with painted relief sculpture.

In addition, Greeks wrote poetry, drama, and histories. Poetry continued to idealize love and war. Athenian dramatists, like Sophocles (496–406 B.C.), were producing plays concerning such notable topics as the mutual rights and responsibilities of the individual and the state, the powerful dilemma of good and evil, and the psychological struggles of human relationships. Such plays became vehicles with which to delve into the public and private lives of Greek citizens. The tragic and comic plays produced during the Classical Age have served as inspiration for dramatists of later centuries. There are few poets from Sparta; those who did write often penned stories about military life. Spartan virtues focused on bravery, duty to country, and self-denial. One Spartan poet glorified bravery with these words, "Let him [a Spartan hoplite] not stand beyond the range of the missiles, for he has a shield. Rather let him go near and slay his warrior foe, wounding him at close quarters with long spear or sword."

Herodotus[8] (484–425 B.C.) and Thucydides[9] (460–400 B.C.) wrote about the major conflicts of the age. Herodotus wrote a history of the Persian Wars but also digressed, filling pages with interesting mythic tales, customs, and events from various cultures. Thucydides, an Athenian commander and later exile from Athens during the Peloponnesian Wars, composed a more focused account of that conflict. His analysis, as well as details of battles and political rivalries, enlightens our understanding of Greek society during that period.

Sophists, itinerant paid instructors, developed a new style of teaching that was focused not upon the traditional values of the epics of Homer but upon the more practical instruction of how to advance in the professions of politics, law, teaching, and play writing. This was particularly true in the subjects of politics and law, where they taught the art of argument, **rhetoric**. Sophists focused upon winning the legal battle and supplied an argument for either side of an issue, regardless of the moral judgment of "right or wrong." By the mid–fifth century B.C., most sophists followed their fortunes to Athens, where their emphasis on rhetoric met with opportunities in the hire of young aristocrats primed for legal careers or with the commoner in the street who might be elected to the democratic council or argue for himself in a court of law.

Philosophy continued to challenge traditional thinking in the Classical Age. Socrates (469–399 B.C.) taught many students in Athens, but Socrates was not a sophist. He vehemently disagreed with

the sophists' style of argumentation and situational morality and with their accepting payment for teaching. Like the sophists, however, Socrates did engage in dialogue with Athenian citizens, frequently questioning members of the Council, the archons, and other officials in public. This technique often infuriated and embarrassed those in leadership, as his probing questions demonstrated their ignorance. This behavior led his enemies to arrest him on charges of corruption and treason. After being convicted and sentenced to death, Socrates took poison (the usual means of execution for a citizen of his status) and died in 399 B.C. The Athenian democracy had executed a philosopher over the issue of freedom of speech.

Plato (427–347 B.C.) studied under Socrates and is the primary literary source for our knowledge of him. Like Socrates, Plato insisted upon clarity of thought and precise definition. He founded a school near Athens to teach his philosophy. Plato's political theory criticized democratic government; Plato believed that only the philosophically enlightened should have the responsibility of governing. Plato argued that government should be entrusted to individuals who have gone beyond the mere experiences of everyday life and who have achieved greater knowledge about the eternal principles of truth, beauty, and morality. These individuals' entire lives should be spent in the pursuit of higher knowledge and practical training. A leader, therefore, is not found among the wealthiest or most popular but is the one who despises wealth because of its baseness and who rejects pride because of its vanity. Such a leader would be a philosopher-king, a man incorruptible, truly indifferent to the usual accolades of the world.

Aristotle (384–322 B.C.) was Plato's most famous student and was the philosopher who invented formal **logic**, the methodology of systematic reasoning to discover truth. For Aristotle, no myth or revelation could produce as much knowledge as correct conclusions based upon accurate observation. Knowledge comes from the investigation of the causes of things, and Aristotle categorized four causes as a means to organize knowledge. Studying these causes leads to wisdom, which results in proper moral behavior. Aristotle's political philosophy led him to say that people are political animals. He saw human social

---

[8] **Herodotus:** hih RAHD uh tuhs
[9] **Thucydides:** thoo SIHD ih deez

evolution passing from birth and solitude to inter-action and learning in the family, to membership in the clan, to participation in the tribe, to the nat-ural culmination of life in the polis. At the school that he founded, he studied more than 158 differ-ent constitutions, both Greek and foreign. Upon completing his analysis, Aristotle began to catego-rize the political systems into subgroups of monar-chy, oligarchy, democracy, and others. Aristotle also studied biology and first arranged it into clas-sifications. He applied his systematic use of obser-vation and logic to order the particulars of nature and human experience.

Philosophers such as Plato and Aristotle are recognized for their persistence in trying to formu-late moral political philosophies based upon ethics. Their contributions significantly influenced later political theory and philosophy, and their cosmologies laid the foundation for future specu-lation on the nature of the universe. Their cosmo-logical theory of the earth as the center of the universe, for example, remained prominent in Western thought through the fifteenth century A.D.

THE EARLY HISTORY OF ROME

The Roman civilization developed from a small group of villages along the Tiber River by about 1000 B.C. and grew into an empire that enveloped much of the Mediterranean by 31 B.C. By about 600 B.C., the Etruscans, from lands just to the north-west, controlled the city of Rome and several of its neighboring cities. Rome rebelled against the Etruscans, finally winning its independence in 509 B.C. The study of Roman history is usually divided into three general eras: the Etruscan (around 600–509 B.C.), the Republic (509–31 B.C.), and the Empire (31 B.C.–A.D. 476). Chapter 7 covers the his-tory of Etruscan Rome and the Republic, and the Roman Empire is discussed in Chapter 8.

Etruscan Rome, around 600–509 B.C.

The city of Rome gradually came under the politi-cal control of the Etruscans, whose twelve inde-pendent city-states flourished in the seventh and sixth centuries B.C. By around 600 B.C., an Etruscan monarch held the political reins of the city. Etruscan cities became important commercial centers for the Greek colonists from southern Italy, and the city of Rome continued to grow under Etruscan control. During Etruscan control, a restructuring of Roman society occurred.

The restructuring was similar to the changes made in Athens under Solon and Cleisthenes: The three original hereditary kin groups of the city were replaced with twenty-one regional fictive kin-ship groups, four urban and seventeen rural. The reason for the reorganization seems to have been for levying taxes and taking the census. As a result, old kinship loyalties were broken, and new Etruscan and immigrant families became influ-ential.

The military probably reorganized under the Etruscans, although scholars still are unsure of the date when this occurred. Instead of fighting in clan blocks, soldiers mustered in **centuries**, groups of one hundred men. In times of emergency, the cen-turies would assemble together in a designated place. The assembly came to be called the Centu-rion Assembly. Membership in the centuries depended upon property ownership, paralleling development in Greece. Citizen-soldiers, like the hoplites of Greece, became the mainstay of the army.

Much of Etruscan culture influenced the Romans. The deities Jupiter and Juno were Etruscan and only later took on some characteris-tics of their Greek counterparts, Zeus and Hera. The Etruscans had used the Greek alphabet, which the Romans adopted and adapted, until it became the alphabet used by later European languages. Roman men also used the Etruscan toga, a white gown that became a symbol of citizenship status. Etruscans introduced Romans to long-distance trade with Greek colonists in southern Italy, a rela-tionship that would eventually bring the Romans into the Mediterranean Sea trade network.

In the last years of the sixth century B.C., Etruscan monarchies outside of Etruria began to crumble. The customary date of the expulsion of the last Etruscan monarch from the city of Rome is 509 B.C., the traditional date for the founding of the Roman Republic.

The Republic, 509–31 B.C.

After the Etruscans were expelled, the Romans had to design a government. The political system was based upon the idea of government in public

FIGURE 7.7   *Etruscan Mural.*   *This wall painting demonstrates the highly decorative art style of the Etruscans as found in the houses and tombs of the wealthy. Tomb painting usually depicted such events as banquets and funerals. Music was an important part of these Etruscan rites; lute and harp players accompany singers, and dancers perform the formal funeral dance for the occupant of the tomb. Etruscan wealth came from the cultivation of rich soils and from trade with Greek colonies, where Etruscan artists came into contact with and were influenced by Greek art. Etruscan art styles lived on in Roman art forms, particularly in Roman wall painting and architecture.*   Scala/Art Resource, N.Y.

hands; Romans literally called the powers of government "public things." Romans hated the idea of monarchy and awarded leadership of the military to two army commanders, called **consuls**, who were elected yearly. Consuls held the power to command and coerce the troops and to execute the law. This division of power was similar to Sparta's choice of a two-king system to thwart the rise of a tyrant.

In addition, the elders of elite families within the city had acted as an advisory council, called the **Senate**, to the Etruscan king. Although the Senate had no formal legislative power, the consuls usually took its advice and sought its consent because elders were traditionally leaders in Roman society. The Senate emerged as a formidable body during the Republic because of the extension of this familial influence. Family lineage continued to play an important role in Roman political history.

A distinguished career gave the family prestige that translated into political opportunity; a respected family name could elevate a young politician into the heady circles of power politics.

The Centurion Assembly, mentioned earlier, met when called by the Senate. It elected the consuls and other officials from among candidates handpicked by the senators from their own families. As in Greece, the aristocrats continued to manipulate the outcome of elections. In times of emergency, the Centurion Assembly would be called to prepare for war.

As time passed, new offices and groups developed within the governmental structure, all controlled by powerful families. Although democratic elections were held, Rome was essentially governed by an oligarchy in the form of the Senate. Romans called their government *Senatus Populosque Romanus*, "the Senate and People of Rome."

MAP 7.5 *Expansion of the Roman Republic, to 264 B.C.* *Roman conquest of central Italy brought Roman interests into conflict with established Greek colonies in southern Italy, called Magna Graecia. The Romans had drawn up treaties agreeing not to interfere in the politics or with the trade of southern Italian Greeks, provided they did not ally with any of the tribal peoples or cities falling to Roman expansion in the north. Once these areas were subdued, however, Roman interests turned to the south and Sicily. Roman ships were seen in the Gulf of Taranto near Tarentum in 282, a breach of the treaty that initiated hostilities with the Greeks. By 272 B.C., Magna Graecia was under Roman domination and soon Roman expansion into Sicily would spark the first war with Carthage.*

LIFE IN THE ROMAN REPUBLIC

Roman farming was little different from that of many civilizations. Oxen were raised and employed as draft animals. There was a variety of soil types in the area, so a variety of plows developed; some larger plows dug furrows in deep, rich soils, and other lighter plows scratched through the thinner layers of topsoil. Farmers rotated their crops and used animal dung or lentil crops to replenish the nutrients in their fields—unlike the Greeks, who replenished fields by leaving them fallow. These innovations led to higher annual production. Pigs, cattle, and sheep supplied meat; cattle and sheep supplied milk by-products. Olives were made into oil, grapes into wine, and grains into breads and porridges. The daily diet of the early Romans also included cabbages, turnips, and beans.

Family life and gender roles were also similar to those in Greece. Men were farmers, artisans, and laborers; wealthy men were occupied with the business of government. Only men were citizens. One of the most important roles for men was service in the Roman army. Every citizen between the ages of seventeen and forty-five spent a total of sixteen years in the Roman army, but service to the state could extend to twenty years in an emergency. These sixteen years were not usually served consecutively in the early Republic, and, because it was a citizen army, not everyone was called to fight at the same time. Usually armies consisted of about 20,000 troops. At first, fighting close to home did not significantly interfere with farming responsibilities. As the Republic expanded in later years, however, troops were forced to spend longer periods away from family and farms, and many became impoverished and lost their property. Because citizenship was a requirement for fighting in the army, loss of property resulted in ineligibil-

FIGURE 7.8 **Roman Family.** *This sarcophagus portrays a Roman family dining; the husband reclines and the wife plays music while the children romp with a pet dog. Slaves bring food, perhaps prepared with ingredients from as far away as the Black Sea or North Africa. Common dinners might include lamb, mackerel, or sowbelly cooked in salted tunafish brine. They might also feast on sliced eggs, leeks, ripe apples, or figs. As tomatoes were not imported into Italy until many centuries later, any dishes requiring a sauce used* liquamen, *made from the entrails and juice of cooked fish (which had a taste similar to anchovy paste). The normal drink was wine, usually watered down.* Vatican Museum.

ity to serve. Aristocrats, however, found that army service functioned as a ladder of opportunity for political advancement. Military offices were actually offices of state, and those with successful military careers garnered political power as well.

As in the Greek households, Roman women ran the business of the home. Women were engaged in the typical occupations of weaving and child rearing, and nonelite women attended wealthy women, serving as maids. A funerary inscription from Rome gives insight into the domestic lives of most women: "Here lies Amymone,[10] wife of Marcus, best and most beautiful, worker in wool, pious, chaste, thrifty, faithful, a stayer-at-home." Women also participated in Roman life as prostitutes and priestesses. Romans had fewer priestesses in their state cults than did the Greeks, but one of the most important religious functions of early Rome fell to the vestal virgins, who lived in the temple and tended the eternal hearth-flame of the goddess Vesta.

In the Republic, both women and children were literally under the hand of the husband or father, who had the power of life and death over them. Roman women did not even have personal names. A man usually had three names: a first or given name, a family name, and a clan name (Gaius Julius Caesar, for instance). Each woman bore the feminine form of her family name (such as "Julia" for the family of Julius). Women of the same name, living at the same time were designated by a number or the title of "the older" or "the younger."

Children were educated by their parents; there was no state-supported education, as there was in Greece. Most of the population remained illiterate, but wealthy parents saw to the formal education of their children. The mother had the responsibility of basic education until her children reached about seven years old, when a tutor (usually a slave) took over or the children were sent to small private schools, segregated by gender. Girls' formal education ended at about twelve or thirteen, after which they continued to be instructed in women's

[10] **Amymone:** ah MEE moh nay

UNDER THE LENS

Gods and Goddesses of Greece and Rome

Both Greeks and Romans were polytheistic. The primary deities tended to be anthropomorphic in both societies. Greeks often sculpted their gods and goddesses, but Romans less frequently portrayed their deities.

By the eighth century B.C., Greeks had developed the genealogy of deities. The origin of the deities, first written by a poet named Hesiod, was also a system of the origins of the universe. The entire system of deities is too complicated and contradictory to relate, but out of the copulation of these deities comes the pantheon of the twelve Olympian deities, named after their home on Mount Olympus. Each Greek polis had a particular deity as its patron and observed important religious ceremonies on that deity's behalf. Before the development of new cosmologies based on the four elements of air, water, fire, and earth in the sixth century B.C., belief in these anthropomorphic deities served to explain the origins of all things. People identified deities with particular functions, and with the personalities given in the myths, they emerged as topics of interesting and entertaining stories, as well as explanations for cosmic events. Zeus, the father of the deities, was associated with war, weather, and luck. Demeter was a goddess associated with agriculture and marriage. Apollo was the god of youth, music, poetry, and philosophy, and he was associated with the sun and enlightenment. Athena was goddess of wisdom and art as well as the patron deity of Athens.

After the introduction of formal philosophy in the sixth century B.C., belief in these deities often diminished among the intellectual elite, but the general population continued to worship them,

giving offerings and sacrifices at their temples. Old traditions are not easily given up. Little change in religious practice occurred until about the third century B.C.

The Roman religious experience was significantly different from that of the Greeks, who tended to be conservative in their beliefs. Instead of fearing the whims of their deities or ignoring them as many Greek philosophers did, the Romans viewed themselves as being in harmony with the will of their deities. Meticulous ritual kept them in a proper relationship with the myriad deities adopted throughout the years of expansion.

Roman religion, however, had less of a fixation on mythology, and few stories emerged. The deities were forces that wielded great power, but no priestly class developed to perform complicated rituals. Priestly functions were the business of the state and remained in the hands of political leaders; the chief priest, or ***pontifex maximus,*** was an elected position within the Roman government. Household deities also were piously revered after the example of Aeneas, who risked his life to bring the household deities out of burning Troy.

A major deity of Rome, Vesta, the goddess of the hearth, had no statue representing her in the city's temple. Vesta's hearth was the symbolic hearth of the city of Rome. A few girls between the ages of six and ten years were chosen to become vestal virgins, remaining in the temple's service until the age of thirty, at which time they could leave and marry. Each Roman household had a parallel responsibility, and the young girls and women of the household remained responsible for tending their home fires.

work. Boys continued their education to become participants in civic duties.

Romans originally worshiped animistic deities, but, after they came into contact with Etruscans (whose pantheon of anthropomorphic deities was similar to that of the Greeks), their religious attitudes changed. They adopted the Etruscan deities to their pantheon, and as they expanded throughout Italy and, eventually, into Mediterranean areas, they adopted conquered

peoples' religious practices as well. Over the centuries, Romans developed an ever-expanding list of officially acceptable deities to worship, believing that these deities would protect and strengthen the Republic if Roman citizens continued to worship them. The adoption of deities also aided in assimilating conquered peoples into the Republic.

The social structure initially featured three classes among Romans: the wealthy aristocratic class of **patricians**, the commoner class of **ple-**

beians, and slaves. In Roman society, you were born into the patrician or plebeian class and usually married within your class. The patricians acted as patrons to the client plebeians, who depended upon them for political favors, intercession in judicial matters, and help in times of emergency. Patronage in the Republic was similar to that of Greece. Plebeians supported their patrician patrons in elections to offices, while remaining ineligible themselves for influential positions because of their lower social status. As in many other societies, slaves were those who had fallen into debt and those who had been captured in war. The determination of aristocratic status and commoner status shifted from birth to wealth during the fourth century B.C., during a period of social reform.

EXPANSION DURING THE ROMAN REPUBLIC

Decades of upheaval followed the expulsion of Etruscan kings, as Rome and other city-states fought as allies to ensure that the Etruscan threat remained checked. Roman defense and trade interests led to warfare with their former Italian allies, and fragile alliances for mutual defense slowly deteriorated as the Romans expanded into neighboring territories. By the end of the third century B.C., with few exceptions, the Republic's military expansion caught all of Italy south of the Tiber in its political net.

Political control balanced upon a unique system of alliances that became the backbone of the

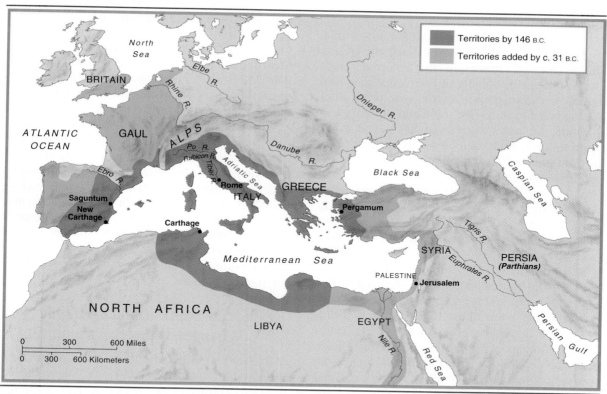

MAP 7.6 *The Roman Empire. Rome created an empire once it moved beyond its cultural area outside of Italy. By 146 B.C., Romans had acquired Carthaginian territories, including much of northern Africa, the southwestern coast of Europe, the coast of the eastern Adriatic, and Greece. By around 40 B.C., the Romans had conquered the interior of western Europe, most of modern Turkey, and the eastern coastal area of the Mediterranean Sea. Not long after, in 31 B.C., Egypt would also fall to Roman expansion. The Roman Empire then encircled the Mediterranean Sea, prompting them to call that body of water* Mare Nostrum, *"our sea." This encircling of the Mediterranean initiated a unified trade network that blossomed under the political unity of Rome.*

future Roman Empire, and the success of these alliances rested on new definitions of kinship as an element of citizenship. The award of citizenship was essentially the awarding of a Roman name, a holdover from the vestiges of clan membership prior to Etruscan restructuring. To have a Roman name meant that you were a member of a Roman family and deserved certain rights as a citizen. When Romans extended the rights of the Roman name to the people of a conquered city, the new citizens tended to remain loyal to the Republic because of the privileges attached. There were levels of citizenship, however, and those born of parents from the city of Rome enjoyed superior rights. Citizens of lesser status bore the majority of taxes and responsibilities but were better off than those without fictive kinship ties. The extension of the Roman name was significantly different from the Greek tendency to withhold citizenship from outsiders.

This expansion enriched the Republic's trade and created a military machine. Each city granted limited Roman citizenship also received special trade status with the city of Rome, but they were not allowed to negotiate treaties with other cities. All roads led to Rome for trade and diplomacy. In addition, the cities were required to send troops upon request, and this increase in the availability of thousands of citizen-soldiers to augment the centuries ensured that the Republic's army could win battles or wars by sheer numbers, regardless of skill. Enemies of Rome had difficulty defeating the Republic's army because an inexhaustible number of troops holding the Roman name were available from all over Italy.

Dominance also extended to independent allies of the Roman Republic with some differences; they did not receive citizenship, and their governments were allowed to continue ruling under the Republic's protection, as long as the local aristocrats remained loyal to Roman interests. The Republic's expansion into southern Italy was very different from Greek colonization. Greek colonies were populated by citizens who demanded political independence from the originating polis. They enjoyed a favored trade status but not compulsory political dependence. In Italy, cities had to submit to Roman political and economic supervision.

The Republic's trade interests moved beyond the Italian peninsula with three opportunistic wars fought with the city of Carthage, the Phoenician colony in northern Africa (264–146 B.C.). The Punic Wars, so called after the language of the Carthaginians, began when the Roman Republic challenged Carthage's dominance over commercial activities in the western Mediterranean. The battles that ensued demonstrated the tenacity of the Roman army. Three wars were fought (264–241 B.C., 218–202 B.C., and 150–146 B.C.) and, in the end, a siege by the Roman army ended in Carthage's complete destruction. The city was looted, then razed, the population killed or enslaved, and the territory annexed by the Roman Republic.

The Punic Wars actually brought the Roman Republic into an empire as it moved outside of its cultural base in Italy. The Romans took control of the western Mediterranean and continued expansion that took them northward into Gaul and eventually to England. Eastward expansion into Greece and Southwest Asia was initially a retaliation against the Macedonian monarch for aiding Carthage during the Punic Wars. Victory in the Macedonian Wars (215–146 B.C.) and the Syrian War (192–189 B.C.) brought Greece, most of modern Turkey, Syria, Palestine, and the Aegean Islands under Roman control. By the first century B.C., Egypt also fell to Roman rule, when Roman political rivalries drew the Egyptian queen into war. The Roman Empire then encircled the Mediterranean.

The new territories became Roman provinces and had a significant impact on Roman society. Land was available for economic exploitation and redistribution. The extension of the Roman name was awarded only selectively to peoples in the new provinces so that politicians in Rome could exploit the territories for higher taxes and personal investment opportunities.

Social, Political, and Economic Changes during Expansion

As in Greece, social conditions led to major tensions and reforms. Many plebeian soldiers who left their small farms for long periods to fight in foreign wars found themselves in financial distress when they returned. In addition, expansion had created an increase in wealthy plebeian traders, who wanted access to the privileges of the aristocratic patrician class. The first social conflict came in 494 B.C. after plebeian soldiers had experienced their first protracted absences from their farms while fighting against neighboring cities. Additionally, wealthy plebeian traders (many of them familiar with Greek democratic ideas through their trade contacts) aspired to participate in the governance of the Republic. The desperate plebeian farmers, spurred by the wealthy plebeians, marched out of the city and refused to fight in its defense. They organized themselves and demanded that the patricians recognize their elected representatives, **tribunes**. This plebeian boycott led to the formation of an assembly of plebeians called the Council of Plebeians, which enacted its own legislation. The Senate recognized the Council of Plebeians but maintained control through the process of giving advice to the council's members and consent to the council's actions before they could be recognized as law.

Reform came slowly, and, when grudgingly given by the patricians, its effects finally opened the door to power for wealthy plebeians and to occasional land reform for debtors. By 367 B.C., a law was enacted that each year at least one of the elected consuls must be a plebeian, breaking the exclusive hold of patricians on the consulship. Wealthy plebeians now could gain as much political prestige as patricians, and the traditional familial prestige could be inherited by plebeians, too. Henceforth, the distinction between wealthy plebeians and patricians diminished, and a new aristocracy based on wealth was formed that included both (much like the new ruling class in Athens under Solon's reforms).

The policy of expansion exacerbated the financial difficulties of the common farmers in the Republic. Because of the protracted wars fought in Spain, North Africa, and Gaul, many soldiers found themselves returning home after the campaigns to bankrupted farms. During the Second Punic War, Hannibal's soldiers fed off Italian farms and destroyed what they could not consume, leaving devastation in their wake. At the same time, increased trade from the new territories enriched the aristocrats, who bought these forfeited lands and used slave labor to farm them. The disenfranchised soldiers had little or no means of employment, and because many lost their property, their sons were no longer eligible for service in the army. In the second century B.C., while the Roman Republic was expanding geographically and trade was enriching many, the army was experiencing a manpower shortage, and the poor were becoming

FIGURE 7.9 *Voting in Republican Rome.* *One of the significant changes in Roman politics was the initiation of the secret ballot in 137 B.C., which allowed lower-class Romans to vote without interference from the fiercely competitive Roman aristocracy. The aristocracy then moved from intimidation to bribery to ensure election to high office or passage of legislation. Later, when the optimate and populares parties emerged in Rome, each party spent large sums of money buying up votes among the poor and destitute. This coin shows the process of balloting. This citizen marked a piece of wood with a v, which represents an affirmative vote (v being the first letter of the Latin phrase meaning "as you propose").* Bibliothèque nationale, Paris.

destitute. Land reform came only sporadically through the Council of Plebeians, whose leadership was now part of the elite.

The poor found two brothers to champion social reform. Tiberius and Gaius Gracchus[11] challenged the ruling oligarchy by trying to force through reform legislation, like providing land for retiring soldiers so that their heirs would be eligible for military service. In 133 B.C., Tiberius, knowing that his initiation of reform could win him the gratitude of plebeian veterans and future success in elections, manipulated the vote in the Council of Plebeians to force land reform. Primarily concerned with how the reforms would affect their personal finances, the senators panicked, and violence broke out in the council meeting between

[11] **Gracchus:** GRAK uhs

Tiberius's supporters and those who were backed by senators. In the end, Tiberius was killed, along with many of his supporters. Using greater political sensitivity ten years later, his brother, Gaius, successfully introduced some reforms but eventually met the same end. Reforms came, but they only temporarily contained the discontentment. The oligarchy could not look beyond its own self-interest for long, and, consequently, the movement for reform initiated by the Gracchus brothers led to an atmosphere wherein new political parties emerged.

The **optimate**[12] party consisted of traditionalists who supported aristocratic control through old family alliances and senatorial contacts. The **populares**[13] party consisted of those who garnered the citizens' votes in exchange for reforms and grants. It was the same political game of patronage, but the old guard had competition from ambitious young politicians who saw that entitlements (giving away bread and arranging for circuses for entertainment of the urban poor) could buy them needed votes. The Gracchus brothers had inadvertently discovered a new political modus operandi: They could bypass the old oligarchy and use the mass vote of the poor to win elections and pass legislation. From now on, the optimate and populares factions rivaled for political control, creating a new ruling class of about two thousand wealthy, competitive politicians.

The Impact of Expansion on Roman Elite Culture

Expansion increased the trade and revenues flowing into the city of Rome and allowed many merchants and politicians to become extremely wealthy. Many used their buying power to purchase even more land, the traditional source of wealth. Large estates began to specialize in certain lucrative cash crops, such as grapes and olives. After Carthage's defeat, Italy became the major producer of wine and olive oil for Mediterranean trade. In addition, large estates also could support the grazing requirements of cattle, which provided leather, meat, and cheese. Slowly, as expansion continued around the Mediterranean, and, as cash crops became more popular in Italy, the Republic increased imports of basic commodities and regional products. The economic result was a greater fiscal gap between the wealthy and the increasing number of poor, who were reduced to trading their votes for patronage and handouts.

Roman engineering developed massive building projects. A vast system of aqueducts carried water to thirsty citizens. It has been estimated that more than 220 million gallons of water per day came over the aqueducts into the city of Rome, furnishing fountains, public bathhouses, and households. Aqueducts employed the use of another engineering design, the arch. Romans had cut down most of the tall timber, and finding trees large enough for beams in large buildings proved difficult. The arch was a good engineering solution; it could support massive amounts of pressure, and Roman architects found it more stable than a flat beam in the new architectural styles of vaults and domes. The refining of arches and the development of concrete enabled some of the Republic's most memorable architectural accomplishments.

Romans linked their city and their newly won territories together with a system of roads built during the late Republic and continuing through the Empire period. The Via Appia[14] was built around 312 B.C. and, as a major thoroughfare into the city, brought thousands of ox-drawn carts loaded with harvests and goods into the city. Both slaves and soldiers worked on the massive road network; each road was first surveyed and then layered with sand, lime concrete and stone, more sand, and, finally, stone blocks set with concrete. Small gaps were filled with flint and pebbles to create a relatively smooth surface. These durable roads can still be seen in many places throughout Europe. They remained invaluable to trade, troop transport, communications, and travel.

Many members of the Roman elite enjoyed listening to political orations and reading the opinions of popular writers. Public speaking remained a means to fame, and successfully arguing legal cases often led to a promising political career. Cato the Elder (234–149 B.C.) argued in public addresses for preservation of traditional Roman values of austerity and patriotism in the face of newly imported foreign (particularly Greek) ideas infiltrating the Republic during its expansion. He complained of lax moral behavior, economic extravagance, and increased freedom of women.

---

[12] **optimate:** AHP tih mayt
[13] **populares:** pahp yoo LAHR es

[14] **Via Appia:** VEE yah AHP pee ah

FIGURE 7.10 *Ruins of the Roman Forum. Rome's forum was at the heart of the ancient city of Rome, in an area that developed into a government and market center with many buildings, temples, and shops. The architecture of the forum was duplicated in most of the areas that the Romans conquered. The phrase "all roads lead to Rome" came from the idea of the Golden Milestone in the center of the forum, where all roads to Rome converged. No chariot traffic was allowed in this bustling area, but hundreds of people, buying and selling goods and on their way to official business, crowded the lanes. It was in one of the buildings of the forum that the Senate presided and great speeches were delivered by Roman orators such as Cicero. This was also where Gaius Julius Caesar met his death at the hands of assassins in 44 B.C.* Dan Budnik / Woodfin Camp & Associates.

He was elected to a position that gave him the authority to enact reforms to improve moral behavior and curb economic excesses.

Cicero (106–43 B.C.) became the most famous of Rome's orators during the Republic. Although not born to wealth, he received support from a wealthy Roman entrepreneur who financed his career in politics. His individual talent for public speaking soon took him to the forefront of the Republic's elite. Fifty-eight out of more than one hundred of his speeches survive, as do eight hundred of his letters. These documents reveal to us the typical lifestyle of the successful politician of the Republic. Cicero's luxurious and cultured life included ownership of a mansion in the city of Rome and at least eight country houses. Several of the country houses were large villas, richly furnished with wall paintings, floor mosaics, and Greek art. Like many of his day, he studied and followed the tenets of the school of Greek philosophy called **Stoicism** (the belief that knowledge and wisdom are virtuous and that a virtuous person lives in harmony with nature). Romans were not known for their own philosophical treatises but readily adopted Greek concepts. Cicero accepted the Stoic idea that no person should tyrannize another, and all should treat one another generously, because all humans have equal personal value. The reading of Stoic moral philosophy in Cicero's treatises influenced later Western thinkers down to the present day. The late Republic's politics were volatile, however, and Cicero found himself embroiled in the rivalries of a civil war; he died trying to escape execution in 43 B.C.

THE END OF THE ROMAN REPUBLIC

The Republic of the second century B.C. was essentially an empire, still governed by a political structure that was more in tune with the needs of a city-state. Rampant mismanagement of conquered territories persisted and was infrequently criticized by anyone with enough influence to change policies. Individuals desiring only to advance politically gained reputations that brought prestige and power. Eventually they retired into the Senate, where their personal accomplishments determined senatorial rank. Each retiring government official coveted the title "First Man of the Senate."

Power shifted from the Senate to consuls. Because of continuing battles in Gaul and in North Africa and a reluctance by the Senate to institute long-lasting debt relief, the property qualification for the army was dropped. This action opened the door for the creation of a professional standing army. Landless men could serve, and, upon retirement, their consuls requested that the Senate and Council of Plebeians award them severance pay in land, usually in one of the new territories. This innovation alleviated the habitual shortage of troops but also shifted troop allegiance to the consuls and away from the state, essentially making soldiers clients of the consuls. Consuls soon discovered that the army and not the Senate could dictate who would win elections and advance up the political ladder.

Ambitious consuls used foreign wars to satisfy their own appetites for greater prestige and wealth. Abuse of authority even led consuls to march their armies into Rome and place the city under dictatorial power. In 88 B.C., rivalry between two consuls, Marius (157–86 B.C.) and Sulla (138–78 B.C.), resulted in Sulla's marching his army into the city of Rome and declaring martial law. The majority of the Senate backed Sulla, an optimate, against Marius, a populares. Sulla received dictatorial power—full legislative, military, and financial control—and executed Marius's supporters. In 81 B.C., Sulla enacted legislation prohibiting any future commander from bringing troops into Rome. Although Sulla restored control to the Republic after he gave up his dictatorial powers and retired in 79 B.C., the precedent was set.

FIGURE 7.11 *Caesar.* *Statues like this figure of Gaius Julius Caesar were often used for propaganda in ancient Roman society. Shown in the carefully chosen dress and pose of a commander, this statue demonstrated the military authority of Caesar to all who viewed it. Each commander in Rome was given authority to lead his troops; this authority was called the* imperium *and the commander was called the* imperator. *The nature of the command determined the amount of* imperium. *Consuls held greater* imperium *than any other commander except a dictator, who held supreme* imperium. *When Gaius Julius Caesar became Perpetual Dictator, it meant he would hold supreme* imperium *for life. This is in part why his enemies assassinated him; they were fearful of this kind of military power because it reminded them of a king's power.* Alinari/Art Resource, N.Y.

In the middle of the first century B.C., the precedent was repeated during a rivalry between Gaius Julius Caesar (100–44 B.C.) and Pompey (106–48 B.C.). At first they formed an alliance with Crassus, another politician. The alliance was called the First Triumvirate and served as a means to gain mutual support. When Crassus died, however, the alliance disintegrated into rivalry because Julius Caesar was a populares and Pompey was an optimate. Civil war finally broke out in 49 B.C. Caesar began the war when he decided to illegally cross the Rubicon River, the border of the province of Gaul, and march his army to Rome. By the end of 45 B.C., Caesar held Rome and established himself as dictator. Pompey was dead and the Senate was cowed.

Caesar enacted many reforms for the betterment of the general population, including land grants for the resettlement of thousands of the impoverished to new territories. He remained unable to pacify the optimate party in the Senate, however, and he infuriated many of his populares supporters by enlarging the Senate from 600 to 900 members with Germanic representatives from the province of Gaul. In 44 B.C., he accepted the title of Perpetual Dictator, and his enemies interpreted this as a move toward monarchy. In secret meetings they conspired against him, and, on the Ides of March (March 15), 44 B.C., Caesar was assassinated on his way into the Senate.

Roman politics never reverted to the system of government of the early city-state. After the death of Caesar came another period of civil war and reorganization under the subtle brilliance of Caesar's nephew, Octavian. Like his uncle, Octavian gained singular control of the political structure. The formal end of the Republic came with the defeat of Octavian's last rival at the battle of Actium in 31 B.C., but, in a sense, the Republic died with Caesar's last gasp in 44 B.C.

GREECE AND ROME COMPARED

The histories of Greece and the Roman Republic demonstrate their unique experiences in global history, yet they exhibit some similar basic social and political developments. In the polis period of Greek history, roughly 800 to 338 B.C., and in the Roman Republican period, roughly 509 to 31 B.C., the peoples of Greece and Rome experienced social and political pressures that precipitated reorganization.

Greek and Roman cultures developed in strikingly similar ways.

— Both societies originated as city-states.
— Both societies viewed kinship (the family or clan structures) as the basis for political development.
— Both societies slowly moved away from a hereditary aristocracy toward one based on wealth.
— Changes in warfare and expansion resulted in social pressures that led to the development of limited citizens' rights and reforms.
— Both societies had a form of patron-client relationship, in which the wealthier citizens provided protection in exchange for political support.
— Both societies often had social unrest when the patron relationship was abused or ignored.

Although there were many similarities, there were also many differences between Greek and Roman development.

— As each society experienced growth, the Greeks usually sent out colonies that remained independent, with jealously guarded citizenship, while the Romans usually conquered and gave citizenship to foreign peoples.
— Greek political history usually moved through several styles of government, including monarchy, oligarchy, tyranny, and democracy, as social pressures dictated. Rome experienced monarchy under the Etruscans but rejected it in favor of oligarchy. Many aspects of the Republic's government were democratic, but its political history is really the history of the ruling class. Finally, the Republic succumbed to imperial control after years of civil war.
— The Athenian attempt at economic and political dominance led to Greek rebellion, while Roman control of neighboring areas of Italy led to empire.

ROME		GREECE		
			800 B.C.	Cultural unification of Greece, c. 800 B.C.
		Lyric Age, c. 800–500 B.C.	–	
			–	
			–	
			–	
			700 B.C.	Greek colonization expands, c. 700 B.C.
			–	
	Age of Tyrants, c. 675–600 B.C.		–	Greek Helots revolt, c. 650 B.C.
			–	
			–	Sappho, Greek poet, born 612 B.C.
			600 B.C.	
Etruscan control of Rome, 600–509 B.C.			–	
			–	
			–	
			–	Cleisthenes forms a democracy in Athens, 508 B.C.
			500 B.C.	
Roman Republic, 509–31 B.C.	Roman expansion, c. 500–31 B.C.		–	Roman council of Plebeians formed, 494 B.C.
		Athenian domination of the Delian League, c. 479–431 B.C.	Classical Age, c. 500–338 B.C.	–	Sophocles, Greek philosopher, 496–406 B.C.
			–	
			–	
			400 B.C.	
			–	
			–	Plebeians eligible Roman for consulship, 367 B.C.
			–	
			–	Romans build Via Appia, c. 312 B.C.
			300 B.C.	
			–	
			–	
			–	
			–	Cato the Elder, Roman statesman, 234–149 B.C.
			200 B.C.	
			–	
			–	
			–	
			–	Cicero, Roman statesman, 106–43 B.C.
			100 B.C.	
			–	
			–	
			–	Battle of Actium, 31 B.C.
			–	

SUMMARY

1. The geography of Greece contributed to attitudes of exclusiveness and independence. Citizenship was originally based on kinship. Oppressive aristocracies had to yield to demands for citizens' rights in order to get hoplites to fight for their cities and defend the wealth of aristocrats.

2. There was a variety of governing forms, including oligarchy, tyranny, and democracy. Athenian democracy is an example of political reformers' restructuring government to meet the citizens' needs. Sparta is a singular example of reorganization into a military state that employed elements of monarchy, oligarchy, and democracy, creating a mixed government.

3. Greek society originally consisted of three classes: aristocrats, commoners, and slaves. A merchant class developed as long-distance trade expanded. By about 800 B.C., the polis developed around the agora.

4. Greek gender roles mirror those of many early civilizations: Men were primarily farmers, and women were weavers and caretakers for children.

5. Many Greek poleis sent out colonies that were associated with the originating polis through trade and religious observance. The expansion of long-distance trade brought new wealth to many families.

6. The fifth century B.C. was a century of conflict marked by the Persian Wars, Athenian dominance, and the Peloponnesian Wars.

7. The Lyric and Classical ages of Greek history were fertile artistic periods. Sappho was an important poet from the Lyric Age, and new styles in sculpture and literature flourished under increased patronage in the Classical Age. Philosophers of both periods challenged old ways of thinking.

8. The city of Rome fell to the political control of the Etruscans. A rebellion expelled the Etruscan king and established the Roman Republic in 509 B.C. The Republic's government was basically oligarchical, ruled by the Senate, with consuls in charge of the army.

9. Roman society had three classes: aristocratic patrician, commoner plebeian, and slave. Social reform in the fourth century B.C. made the distinction between patrician and plebeian less significant. A new class system emerged based on wealth rather than birth.

10. The Republic was a period of great geographical expansion. The Punic Wars resulted in empire, and the Republic continued to expand into western Europe, southeastern Europe, Palestine, and Egypt.

11. Expansion and constant warfare brought about plebeian boycotts for land reform and increased opportunities for political advancement. Sociopolitical pressures created a two-party system of optimates and populares.

12. Romans built roads to connect their territories and aqueducts to bring water from long distances. The elite took advantage of the increased wealth resulting from the Republic's expansion and patronized the arts.

13. Roman governance disintegrated into competitions between rivals that finally ended in civil wars and assassination. The Republic ended in 31 B.C.

SUGGESTED READINGS

Boardman, John, Jasper Griffen, and Oswyn Murray, eds. *Greece and the Hellenistic World*. Oxford History of the Classical World Series. New York: Oxford University Press, 1988. Good coverage of social history, philosophy and the arts, and political history.

Boren, Henry C. *Roman Society*. Second edition. Lexington, Mass.: D. C. Heath, 1992. A general cultural history of Rome.

Frost, Frank. *Greek Society*. Third edition. Lexington, Mass.: D. C. Heath, 1987. A short but informative history of Greece, with special sections on the Greek people.

Grant, Michael. *The History of Rome*. New York: Charles Scribner's Sons, 1978. A standard history of Rome.

Green, Peter. *Ancient Greece*. New York: Thames and Hudson, 1979; reprint, 1989. A well-illustrated history of Greece for the general reader.

Lefkowitz, Mary R., and Maureen B. Fant. *Women's Life in Greece and Rome*. Second edition. Baltimore: Johns Hopkins University Press, 1992. A primary sourcebook, full of insights into women's lives in ancient Greece and Rome.

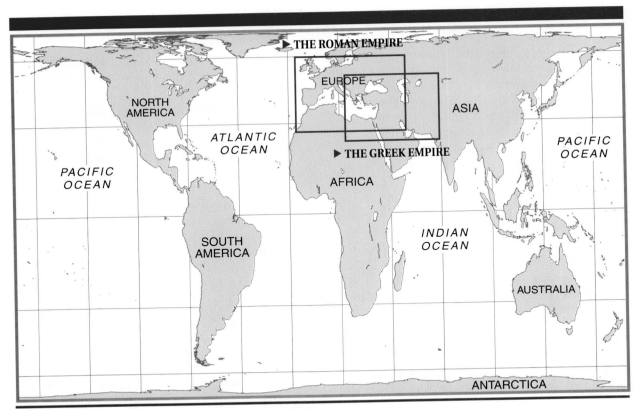

▶ THE ROMAN EMPIRE

▶ THE GREEK EMPIRE

EUROPE

ASIA

AFRICA

NORTH AMERICA

SOUTH AMERICA

AUSTRALIA

ANTARCTICA

ATLANTIC OCEAN

PACIFIC OCEAN

PACIFIC OCEAN

INDIAN OCEAN

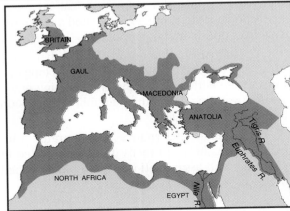

▶ THE ROMAN EMPIRE

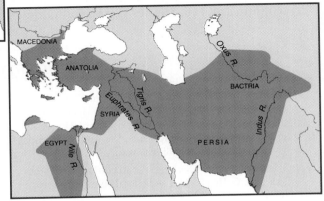

▶ THE GREEK EMPIRE

The Greek Empire, the Hellenistic Age, and the Roman Empire

359 B.C.–A.D. 476

You must now at last perceive of what kind of a universe you are a part, and the true nature of the lord of the universe of which your being is a part, and how a limit of time is fixed for you, which if you do not use for clearing away the clouds from your mind, it will go and you will go, and it will never return.

–MARCUS AURELIUS

This quotation from the writings of Marcus Aurelius (reign dates 161–180), a Roman emperor, shows us the blending of the Greek and Roman cultures. Marcus Aurelius followed Stoicism, a Greek philosophy popular in the Roman Empire. This chapter examines Greek expansion and empire, the Hellenistic Age, and the Roman Empire, with an emphasis on the cultural interaction between conquerors and indigenous peoples.

THE GREEK EMPIRE, 359–323 B.C.

After 479 B.C., Greeks were always mindful of the potential for another Persian war, and their fear of Persian attack led them to discussions on reorganizing a coalition for common defense. A leader in this movement spoke eloquently in favor of Philip of Macedon (reign dates 359–336 B.C.) as the natural military commander of the coalition. The opposition, however, warned against what they viewed as Philip's imperialist intentions. The poleis remained indecisive, with frequent eruptions of violence over the issue. Soon Philip held all of Greece, and, after his untimely death, his son Alexander conquered Persia.

Macedonian Greece, 359–336 B.C.

Macedonia, located in southeastern Europe, developed politically differently from the rest of Greece. The peoples of the area formed a patchwork of independent tribal principalities with strong kings instead of the poleis common in the rest of Greece. Macedonians were less urbanized than their southern neighbors, and other Greeks considered them barbarous and uncouth cousins. While the rest of Greece evolved toward urbanization, Macedonia did not develop the central administration necessary to support urban economic development. Macedonian tribes spent a considerable amount of time on border security. During a period of relative peace, unification was finally achieved under Philip II, whose exploits earned him a reputation for military skill and leadership far beyond Macedonia.

Philip II had forged a strong, loyal, professional army during his political career, and through diplomacy and warfare he gained a foothold in northern Greece. A war over the governance of the polis of Delphi, which housed the very popular and lucrative Oracle of Apollo, brought Philip and his army into central Greece. The poleis of Athens and Thebes united against his invasion, but the union crumbled when confronted by his superior military expertise. After his victory, Philip offered generous terms for peace, particularly to Athens, and managed to set up a coalition that united all Greek poleis into one uneasy confederacy under his authority. Shortly after the establishment of the confederacy and on the eve of beginning a campaign against Persia, Philip of Macedon was assassinated.

Philip's young son Alexander (reign dates 336–323 B.C.) took the helm of government. Although only nineteen years old, Alexander already was known as a brilliant commander of Philip's cavalry. Alexander soon redrew the map of Greece and Southwest Asia and thus received the

accolade "the Great." Alexander's attentions first focused on crushing Greek uprisings against Macedonian rule. By the spring of 334 B.C., Alexander was ready to pursue his father's plan to liberate the Greek poleis in the Turkish Peninsula from Persian control. He left a trusted friend and troops behind to maintain his interests in Greece and Macedonia and attacked Persia. He never returned; his conquests kept him occupied until his death in 323 B.C.

Alexander's Conquests, 334–323 B.C.

Alexander engaged the Persian army in the northern Turkish Peninsula and then moved southward in a series of victorious campaigns. In 333 B.C., he fought the Persian king Darius III, who retreated from the battlefield when he realized that the

FIGURE 8.1 *Alexander as Egyptian Pharaoh.*
This Egyptian coin depicts Alexander wearing ram's horns, a symbol of power and authority throughout Southwest Asia, including Egypt. Alexander took the title of pharaoh, the incarnate son of Amon-Ra and the religious and political leader of all Egyptians. Egyptian subjects transferred their loyalty to Alexander and helped support his defeat of the Persian king, Darius. This coin was minted as a propaganda aid to demonstrate Alexander's authority as the conqueror and new king of Egypt. Ptolemy, one of Alexander's generals, seized Egypt as his own kingdom after Alexander's death in 323 B.C., setting up the Ptolemaic dynasty that reigned until 31 B.C. The Ptolemies also used coinage to depict their authority. Gift of Mrs. George M. Brett. Museum of Fine Arts, Boston.

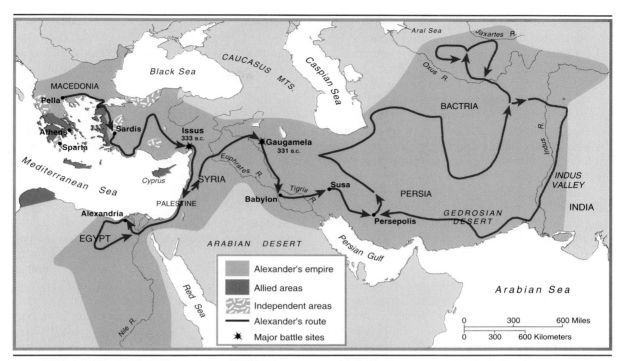

MAP 8.1 *Alexander's Empire.* *Between 333 B.C. and 323 B.C., Alexander had conquered most of Southwest Asia. Because of the rapidity of his conquests, Alexander was given the accolade of "the Great." Throughout European history, Alexander remained a hero to military leaders.*

Greeks were winning the day. This victory allowed Alexander to move southwestward along the Mediterranean coast, subduing cities in Palestine and liberating Egypt from Persian control. The Egyptians, already in a state of rebellion against Persia, hailed Alexander as a liberator and acclaimed him pharaoh. While in Egypt, he designed the city of Alexandria on the Mediterranean coast, one of several cities Alexander founded that bore his name.

By 331 B.C., Alexander left Egypt in pursuit of Darius. Going into the interior of Persia, Alexander systematically subdued numerous Persian cities, where vast treasures were stored. Darius was defeated again in 331 at the battle of Gaugamela[1] and fled a second time, only to be assassinated by his second in command, Bessus. When Bessus engaged Alexander in 330 B.C., he fared no better than his predecessor. Upon Bessus's capture, Alexander had him brutally killed in retaliation for assassinating his king.

With this victory, Alexander pressed on from the coast of the Caspian Sea and finally reached the Indus River Valley. Alexander forged ahead, penetrating the Punjab region, but his troops, exhausted, homesick, and fearful they might never return, demanded he halt the advance. For three days Alexander sulked in his tent, but then accepted the will of his army and began the return to Persia. The travail on the retreat route down the Indus River and then along the Indian Ocean and the Persian Gulf nearly caused Alexander's first defeat, as sickness and difficult terrain impeded the army's progress. Returning to Babylon after traveling more than 20,000 miles, his soldiers were fewer in number but full of stories about their conquests and the exotic Indian subcontinent.

The Problem of Governance in the Greek Empire

As of 330 B.C., Alexander was the king of kings, an emperor over a vast domain stretching from Greece and Egypt to the edge of the Indus River. The conqueror made few structural changes in the old Persian government; its subjects were used to changes of rulers and hardly noticed the minimal

[1] **Gaugamela:** gow geh MEHL ah

reorganization at the top. The only major innovation separated the military authority from the fiscal structure in western territories, creating a centralized financial administration to ensure that tribute payments did not disappear into the pockets of local commanders and troops. In Egypt, Alexander basically governed through traditional systems as pharaoh, and in Greece he remained the king of Macedonia and the head of the Greek confederacy. Maintaining control over such a vast territory with diverse peoples proved difficult.

The Greek Empire did not survive Alexander's early demise from an infection in old wounds complicated by heavy drinking, but even Alexander probably could not have held the empire together. The problems went beyond the mere governance of a vast territory; the greatest obstacles lay in very basic traditions of Greek culture. Macedonian troops viewed their kings as first among equals, and other Greek troops continued to resist the concept of empire at the expense of their poleis' independence. Finally, Greeks continued to view their culture as superior to all others and socially segregated themselves from indigenous peoples. Alexander's attempts to unite all the peoples of his empire failed to overcome these deeply rooted beliefs.

Alexander had initiated a campaign of integration between the Greek military and local peoples within the empire. This was done with various levels of success. He brought Persian cavalry into his army and began to train young Persians in the Macedonian style of warfare. Alexander also encouraged social integration; he married into the Persian nobility and forced his highest officers to marry Persians as well. One story tells of Alexander at a mass wedding banquet; as he mixed water and wine for drinking (dilution was a common practice), he announced that just as the wine and water mixed, so did the blood of the peoples. Although the marriages produced children, the families tended to perpetuate Greek lifestyles over indigenous customs because the fathers were Greek.

Alexander adopted both the Persian and Egyptian styles of kingship, with their ceremonies and royal costumes. He insisted that his commanders prostrate themselves before addressing him in court, as the Persian subjects traditionally did. Adoption of such ceremonies angered and alienated his Macedonian officers, who had enjoyed his close camaraderie and trust. He increasingly gave audience to Persian advisors over his Macedonian generals. When Alexander declared himself divine, in the tradition of all pharaohs of Egypt, he insisted that even his Greek troops accept him as deified, thus further distancing him from them and from his Macedonian heritage.

These cultural innovations were too much for the Greek sense of superiority over the other peoples of the empire and Greek attitudes toward kingship; troops reacted with disdain and rebellion at Alexander's promotion of a divine emperorship. By 324 B.C., Alexander again found himself facing a mutinous army. Many of the troops wanted to return to their homelands or demanded greater rights. At the same time, the Greek poleis were straining to regain their independence. Persian subjects also had reservations; many of the governors chosen from Persian nobility resisted reorganization and mismanaged their territories. Upon Alexander's death in 323 B.C., the empire disintegrated into rival territories. A successor had not been named, and the ambitious, battle-hardened veteran officers of his campaigns engaged in a geographical tug of war for the next fifty years.

THE SUCCESSOR STATES, 323–31 B.C.

By 272 B.C., three commanders emerged as the inheritors of most of the Greek Empire. Ptolemy,[2] a trusted friend of Alexander since boyhood, established a dynasty that held Egypt until it fell to the Romans in 31 B.C. Another commander, Seleucus,[3] successfully took Babylon in 311 B.C. and established himself as the dynastic ruler of the heartland of the old Persian Empire. He added Syria, Palestine, and Mesopotamia to his holdings, and his successors governed a Seleucid[4] Empire until Rome conquered much of the area in 62 B.C.

Macedonia and Greece were another matter. The third commander, Antigonus, returned to Greece and established the Antigonid dynasty, which tried to control the constantly rebelling

[2] **Ptolemy:** TAHL uh mee
[3] **Seleucus:** sih LOO kuhs
[4] **Seleucid:** sih LOO sihd

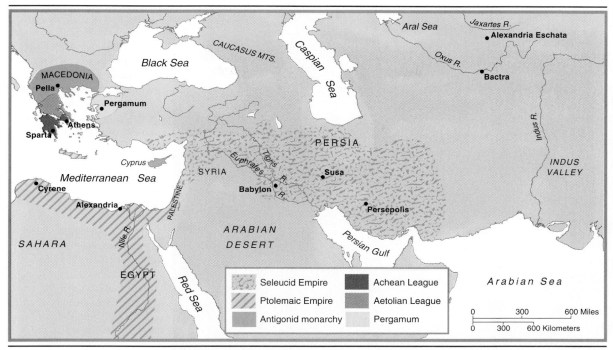

MAP 8.2 *Successor States.* *The Greek Empire did not survive Alexander's death in 323 B.C. Although his generals fought for control of various areas, no one was able to unite these territories again until the rise of Islam in the seventh century A.D. In the end, three successor states survived and two Greek defensive leagues developed.*

poleis. A philosopher of the period, Diogenes, requested that he be buried face down because, "in a little while, what is down will be up." This sentiment reflects the upheaval during the struggle to retain Macedonian overlordship of Greece. Defensive leagues were established against the Antigonids, with the innovation of multi-polis citizenship to strengthen the alliance. Nevertheless, many rivalries and the continued promotion of polis independence led to conflict. By 200 B.C., Greek embassies had appeared in the Roman Senate begging for help against Macedonian aggression. The Romans, who harbored a grudge against the Macedonian king for aiding Carthage during the Second Punic War, mounted a campaign against Macedonia that finally concluded with a peace settlement. The Greek poleis were declared free at the Isthmian Games in 196 B.C., and the thunderous response of the spectators is said to have killed a flock of birds flying overhead. Little did the Greeks realize that their continued requests for assistance to intervene between feuding poleis would bring Romans permanently into Greece. By the first century B.C., most of the territory of the three Hellenistic successor states had succumbed to Roman occupation, and the history of Greece became entwined with the history of the Roman Empire.

THE HELLENISTIC AGE, 323–31 B.C.

Greeks had been calling themselves **Hellenes** since about the seventh century B.C., and scholars have named the era from 323 to 31 B.C. the Hellenistic Age because of the spread of Greek culture, **Hellenization**, across Southwest Asia and the Mediterranean basin. To a large degree, the process of Hellenization remained an urban phenomenon, because most Greeks who populated the cities remained culturally separated from the surrounding rural countryside. In a sense, Hellenization was a veneer.

FIGURE 8.2 *Hellenistic Theater.* This Greek theater was constructed on a hillside in Pergamum, a city on the coast of the Anatolian peninsula. It demonstrates the importing of Classical Greek architecture into Hellenized areas. Drama was a significant part of social life in all Greek cities, much like the cinema in American culture today. The hillside construction provided acoustical advantages: As the players spoke their lines, the sound would rise up to even those seated at the very top of the theater. This theater shared the acropolis of Pergamum with a temple to Zeus and the royal palace of the kingdom of Pergamum. Elizabeth Steiner/German Archaeological Institute, Istanbul. Courtesy of National Geographic Society Image Collection.

Hellenistic Cities

In most of the successor states, the rural areas absorbed little of Greek culture, and the Greeks of the urban centers remained aloof from many local customs, preferring their Greek heritage. It was the cities that were the conduits of intellectual and social interaction. In the cities, members of the ethnic elites often adopted Greek culture, including dress, mannerisms, and education. Local peoples tended to become bilingual, while most Greeks spoke only their own language. No common calendar prevailed, and no common body of law governed the cities until after the Hellenistic Age. The larger, more integrated Hellenistic cities, like Alexandria, eventually overcame Greek prejudices, and the indigenous elite found equal opportunities for advancement and political power.

The city of Alexandria, in Egypt, is perhaps the best example of a Hellenistic city. Alexander the Great laid out the city on a grid pattern, and the new city became the capital of Egypt. It grew into an unusually large city and became a regional administrative center, with residents from Palestine, Syria, Arabia, Babylon, and elsewhere in southwestern Asia. The most famous structures of Hellenistic Alexandria were the lighthouse and the museum-library. Temples, gymnasia, and theaters in the city were constructed in the Greek style.

In the Hellenistic Age, life changed significantly for elite women but little for those in other classes. Elite Hellenistic women had more access to wealth than their Classical Greek predecessors, as Greeks amassed fortunes from increased trade and power over new territories. More and more of the wives of statesmen participated in political intrigues. Some women became monarchs in two of the Hellenistic kingdoms that emerged after Alexander's death, becoming role models for other elite women. The most famous was probably Cleopatra VII, queen of Egypt. The Hellenistic Age opened formal education to elite women, who participated in intellectual movements of the day.

Wealth was the friend of opportunity; conversely, poverty was the companion of failure. Large slums surrounded the city centers. The feeling of belonging, so paramount in the kinship ties of the polis, gave way to feelings of displacement and disorientation. As a result, people tended to band into groups for personal identity. These groups were professional guilds and religious cults that gave a sense of security in an increasingly alienating social environment.

The Hellenistic Exchange

Although perhaps not as significant as later exchanges, like the Islamic, Mongol, and American exchanges, many kinds of cultural exchange occurred during the Hellenistic Age. For example, both plants and animals were part of the exchange. Greeks transplanted their olive trees and grapevines into new areas. One of Ptolemy's officials transplanted 300 fir trees onto his Egyptian estate, and, in another instance, palm trees were sent to Greece for planting. In addition, local spices were added to Greek perfumes. Parks and zoos housed animals exotic to Greeks but common to local peoples. Ideas also formed a part of the Hellenistic exchange, as philosophies and religions found new audiences. Mystery cults, for example, were a new expression of the powers of ancient deities, and religions like Judaism and Zoroastrianism found new adherents among various Hellenistic populations.

Food was a significant part of the exchange. Veterans of Alexander's campaigns returned to Greece with a variety of new foods they had encountered. Foremost among these, in the eyes of Greeks, were onions from Egypt and shallots from Phoenicia. The heatlike sensation these vegetables produced in the mouth was believed to spur the "martial ardor" of soldiers, making them more valiant in battle. These vegetables, therefore, were used as a kind of strategic weapon. Another import brought to Greece through Alexander's campaigns was sugar from India, known at that time as "solid honey" or "Indian salt"; it was very rare in Greece and used only for medicine. More commonly used was the lemon, introduced from Persia or India, also by the Alexandrian veterans.

Ease of travel helped the exchange of goods. The Persian road system was improved, with more inns and water supplies available to weary, thirsty travelers. The Persian road system was linked to the extensive silk-road trade, bringing silk (in both raw form and as finished cloth), skins, and spices westward and taking wines, linen, horses, and pomegranates eastward. Trade increased through-

out Southwest Asia, and, although there were few technological innovations in shipping, larger ships carried greater amounts of goods. Larger port facilities, breakwaters to protect ships, and more warehouses were constructed. In some cases, improving port facilities was necessary for the increase in numbers and size of the ships.

The foods coming into Greece through trade were numerous. *Foie gras*, the enlarged liver of a force-fed goose, was an Egyptian delicacy that was introduced to Greece in this period, just as cumin seed was introduced as a seasoning from Syria. Cheesecakes were popular among Greeks, and various regional styles from all over the eastern Mediterranean were available at urban Greek bakeries, often prepared by bakers from the city where the recipe originated.

Hellenistic Arts and Sciences

Education of elite Greek men in Hellenistic cities continued, consisting of the teaching of basic grammar, math, music, and traditional mythologies from age seven to about fourteen years. From fourteen to about eighteen years, more sophisticated language studies began and were augmented with geography and the study of Homeric epics. At eighteen, schooling centered on the gymnasium, where athletics and advanced literature were the focus. Many of the larger cities' gymnasia had their own libraries and provided lectures on literature for their members. Finally, the wealthiest individuals were tutored in philosophy and rhetoric. In part, the extensive schooling in traditional Greek culture preserved Greek tradition for Greeks living far from the poleis. These young aristocrats then became the officials of the royal courts. Anyone who wanted access to the Greek elite had to become Hellenized.

Hellenistic literature focused on new interests and developed new styles. In each of the successor areas Greek historians wrote local histories. For example, several histories of Egypt and Babylonia were produced. Many literary works attest to the amount of travel during the Hellenistic Age. Megasthenes, a Seleucid diplomat, journeyed to the court of the emperor of India and returned with a journal of his impressions.

Several Greek philosophical systems flourished and spread throughout southwestern Asia and the Mediterranean. Many of the new schools were influenced by the exchange of ideas prevalent in Hellenized cities. The new ideas challenged older beliefs and systems, resulting in major reorientations in philosophy. To a certain extent, philosophical exposition focused on ethics and the art of living in the increasingly complex, cosmopolitan societies.

Many philosophers focused on finding the best way to live happily in "these trying times" and then taught it. The philosophy of **Epicureanism**, based on the philosophy of Epicurus, had begun in the fourth century B.C. Epicureans argued that human pleasure was the purpose of life but not in excess, for excess brings about an imbalance that in turn produces unhappiness. In the later Hellenistic and Roman Empire periods, however, the Epicureans withdrew into indifference, finding balance and tranquility in their image of life as a garden. The philosophy's tenet, "eat, drink, and be merry, for tomorrow we die," did not originally encourage irresponsibility, only the enjoyment of life. **Stoicism**, which also began in the fourth century B.C., concluded that human happiness lay in adhering to the laws of nature. These laws led

ENCOUNTERS

Mystery Cults

Mystery cults were part of the Hellenistic exchange, spread by merchants and soldiers as they traveled the expansive empires. The more intimate identity with the city-state had disappeared in the vast, impersonal empires, leading to feelings of isolation, helplessness, and abandonment. Individuals often asked for personal intervention from a traditional deity, but deities seemed indifferent to the sufferings of humans. The state required only that the rituals be performed; belief in the deity was not mandatory. Because of this political and religious detachment, personal devotion soon found expression in the private mystery cults of Southwest Asia.

The name "mystery cult" comes from the initiation ceremonies of the cults. Often thrilling, sensual, and dramatic, they represented the mysteries of the universe, and, as a consequence, the initiation rituals were kept secret by cult members. The mystery-cult deities were amalgamations of older deities from Southwest Asia, and their theologies presented them as more receptive than traditional Greek deities' myths to the personal needs of the population. Archaeological evidence, literature, and architecture help scholars to interpret some of the practices of mystery cults, such as baptismal rites and sacred meals. Mystery cults often provided for their widows and orphans and gave charity, but only to their own membership. Some cults were too expensive to participate in or were gender-exclusive. Two very popular cults were those of Isis from Egypt and Mithras from Persia.

The mystery cult of Isis evolved from the ancient Egyptian state cult of Isis and Osiris. By the Roman Empire period, the cult was highly Hellenized, with statues and temples of Greek design. Isis was increasingly identified with the powers of all deities and was named "O Thou of Countless Names." Worshipers came to her for miracles, advice, and the promise of eternal happiness. The cult had secret initiation rites and purification bathing in waters from the Nile. The more public rituals included the reenactment of Osiris's resurrection, with its dances, music, and processions. The cult was very popular, although rather expensive, and it attracted many wealthy women.

Another example is the cult of Mithras. Its ancient antecedents were in Persian religion, in which Mithras represented light, truth, and salvation. In the Roman Empire, Mithras was associated with the Roman sun god and had the additional identity of a victorious warrior over the forces of evil, which made the cult popular among Roman soldiers. Mithraism spread throughout the Roman Empire, particularly from the second century, and shrines have been found in Syria, Asia Minor, Spain, central Italy, western North Africa, and Gaul, as well as along the Rhine and Danube rivers.

Mystery cults that promised eternal life were extremely popular; if this life were a trial, the next might be a reward. While intellectuals tended to turn to ethical philosophies for purpose in life, the general population worshiped the deities who demanded moral behavior and who rewarded that behavior with salvation and resurrection.

F I G U R E 8.3 *Realism in Hellenistic Art. A move toward portraying figures more realistically in Hellenistic sculpting is evidenced in this depiction of a young jockey on a racehorse. Absent is the idealized formality of the Classical Greek style, abandoned in favor of demonstrating the drama of the race. The young boy grimaces as he struggles to retain his balance on a horse straining to its full stride.* National Archaeological Museum, Athens/ Archaeological Receipts Fund (TAP Service).

humanity to self-control and performance of duty rather than to the mere pursuit of pleasure. According to Stoicism, wisdom is the goal of life, and a wise individual conforms to the natural laws instituted by the god of reason. True happiness, Stoics believe, can be found in distinguishing between what you can and what you cannot control.

Older schools, such as **Skepticism** and **Cynicism**, continued to find followers in Greece and elsewhere. Skeptics believed that nothing could really be known. They advocated that there is no ultimate pattern by which to order one's life; therefore, nothing really matters. In order to maintain peaceful coexistence, however, they maintained that moral behavior is based on the normal conventions of the polis. Most Skeptics argued against the luxury and material wealth that long-distance trade brought to Greece. Cynics often wandered around Greece calling for a return to the simple life of the early polis. They idealized the life of poverty, wearing only rags and eating only what was given to them.

Science and mathematics advanced during the Hellenistic Age. Archimedes[5] calculated the approximate value of pi, and Euclid[6] presented theorems on plane and solid geometry. Astronomy is a kindred discipline to mathematics, and many individuals contributed to both fields. One Greek developed the hypothesis that the stars and the sun were fixed bodies and that the earth revolved around the sun. There were also advances in stargazing; optical aids were invented that resulted in the production of star maps, for example. Eratosthenes,[7] a geographer, produced near-accurate calculations of the circumference of the earth and, with less accuracy, the size of the sun and moon and their distance from earth. Many of these ancient scholars were also inventors, creating ingenious mechanical devices, such as steam-driven toys, water clocks, water pumps, and war machines.

THE EARLY ROMAN EMPIRE, 31 B.C.–AROUND A.D. 200

Scholars have associated the beginning of the Roman Empire not only with geographical expansion but also with the political career of Gaius Octavian Caesar (reign dates 31 B.C.–A.D. 14), who transformed the political structure of Rome essentially into an imperial dynasty. Like Alexander, the nineteen-year-old Octavian was a prodigy; unlike Alexander, his expertise lay not with his military

[5]**Archimedes:** ahr kuh MEE deez
[6]**Euclid:** YOO klihd

[7]**Eratosthenes:** ehr uh TAHS theh neez

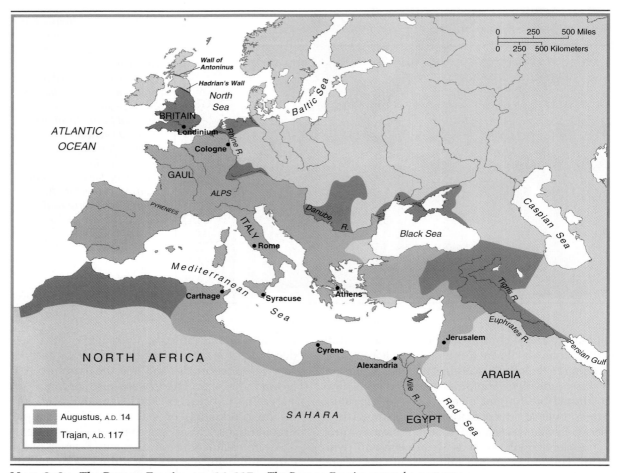

MAP 8.3 *The Roman Empire, A.D. 14–117.* *The Roman Empire covered a vast area that encircled the Mediterranean Sea. Augustus warned his successors not to expand the size of the empire, cautioning that it would become too difficult to defend. The expansion that followed Augustus's death brought the empire to its greatest size under Trajan in A.D. 117. Augustus's fears had been well founded; the northern borders in particular became difficult to defend when migrations began at the end of the second century.*

skill but in his keen administrative talent. Octavian created a system of governance, called the principate system, that ran the Roman Empire until about A.D. 200.

The Principate System

Octavian was the nephew and adopted heir of Julius Caesar. His inheritance included the wealth, clients, military loyalty to the name of Caesar, and family prestige garnered by his illustrious uncle. Marc Antony, Caesar's trusted colleague and a consul, described the young Octavian as that boy "who

owes everything to his name." Octavian, who had been educated and resided in Greece, traveled to Rome to collect his inheritance. The young Octavian began his political career as a minor player, but history was to write a different chapter for the inexperienced but talented junior statesman.

After Julius Caesar was assassinated, government once again dissolved into party politics and military rivalry. Octavian (having inherited Caesar's influence with the army and his wealth) immediately realized that he could not defeat the popular Marc Antony, who had joined forces with another of Caesar's commanders, Lepidus. Octavian agreed to an alliance with them, called the Second Triumvirate, and the Senate commissioned the Triumvirate to rewrite the constitution and to restore the Republic through dictatorial powers. After a purge of 300 senators and as many as 2,000 of their enemies' supporters, Octavian and Antony forced Lepidus into retirement and soon revived their rivalry.

When Octavian's forces defeated Antony and his ally, Queen Cleopatra of Ptolemaic Egypt, in 31 B.C., the dictatorial powers fell solely into the hands of Octavian. Octavian reduced the size of the army from about 300,000 to about 140,000 troops, what he considered a manageable and affordable size. To help ensure peace in the provinces, imperial soldiers serving there received land, and indigenous troops were awarded citizenship on retirement. Octavian diminished the official membership of the Senate from 1,000 to 600 members, whom he alone chose by means of his dictatorial powers. By 27 B.C., Octavian's political grip was secure enough for him to declare the Republic restored. Not wishing to make the same mistake as his uncle Julius Caesar in appearing to want to be king, Octavian returned the dictatorial powers the Senate had bestowed earlier. A hand-picked and cowering Senate, however, clamored for his continued service to the state. The Senate awarded him the honorific title of Augustus, "Venerable One," which gave Octavian significant moral credibility and religious prestige. Thereafter, he abandoned his family name and chose to use Augustus only.

Although no longer holding dictatorial authority, Octavian nevertheless retained power through amassing traditional offices and honorific titles. He eventually secured superior authority over the consulships, tribunate power over the Council of Plebeians, and governing authority over lucrative provinces. He continued as *pontifex maximus*, the head of Roman religion, and received the honorific title of "Father of the Country." Augustus consolidated the legislative, military, financial, and religious powers into one-man rule, under the title of emperor. Because of the efficiency of the forty-four year rule of Augustus and the reluctance of both the Senate and Roman citizens to return to the chaos of highly competitive military rivals, the emperorship became a traditional hereditary position within the Roman state. With all direct descendants dead, Augustus placed his son-in-

FIGURE 8.4 *Roman Statue of Augustus.* *This statue depicts the emperor as* pontifex maximus, *chief priest of Roman religion. The style is reminiscent of Classical Greek statuary; Romans copied many famous Greek sculptors and many of the Greek statues in museums today are Roman copies of Greek originals. This particular statue is important for two reasons. First, its depiction of Augustus demonstrates his role in Roman religion. The Romans believed that proper worship through the state cults kept the empire safe under what they called "the peace of the gods"; the emperor was accountable for maintaining the "peace of the gods" because he was* pontifex maximus. *Second, Augustus gained politically by having himself portrayed in this manner because it gave the aura of religious legitimacy to his rule.* Alinari/Art Resource, N.Y.

law, Tiberius, as consul and adopted him as his legal heir to what essentially was a dynastic throne.

Augustus's political astuteness essentially established an imperial monarchy in Rome based on traditional titles and offices. Scholars call this structure the **principate system**. At the death of Augustus in A.D. 14, Rome encircled the Mediterranean, holding northern territories from England to the Rhine and Danube rivers, eastern territories from the Balkans and Greece to the Turkish Peninsula and Palestine, and southern territories from Egypt to Libya and Numidia on the coast of North Africa.

The Principate after Augustus, A.D. 14–211

After the death of Augustus, the principate system continued under Augustus's heirs, the Julio-Claudians. The dynasty ended with the death of Nero because he had no heir. From 68 to 69, Rome was thrown into a year of civil war as military rivals fought to gain the emperorship. The Senate did not try to regain its Republican-era power; because governance operated through the well-established bureaucracy, there was little impetus to change the system as it had evolved. The military supported effective emperors and assassinated ones whom they believed to be incompetent, often hailing popular commanders as new emperors. Consequently, the power and loyalty of the army slowly became a linchpin in the machinery of emperor selection and succession.

Emperors of the late first and second centuries continued to rule the vast empire through an effective administration, a comprehensive legal system, and competent people. In later years of turmoil and emperor assassinations, the business of empire continued to be conducted efficiently by the vast bureaucracy because purges were restricted to only the highest levels of government. Across the empire, the administration tolerated as much local autonomy as possible to discourage resentment and resistance. As long as peace was maintained, there was little interference in daily lives.

The second century once was called the "Golden Age" of Rome because of the relative peace and political stability between 96 and 192. During the second century, emperors were chosen and adopted by their predecessors on the advice of the Senate and with the support of the army. Edward Gibbon, an eighteenth-century English historian, wrote that second-century Rome was the ideal century and place in which to live in all of human history because of the Senate's role in the selection of emperors, the vast wealth of the empire, the relative peace, and the expanded bureaucracy.

Some scholars today hesitate to call the second century a "Golden Age," however, because its wealth and peace basically were enjoyed by only

FIGURE 8.5 **Triumphal Arch.** *This arch was constructed to honor the major accomplishments of Emperor Trajan during his reign; it was built around A.D. 117. Such arches were often constructed to demonstrate the great deeds of rulers and generals. They also served as imperial propaganda. Most people could not read, so men of power would pay artists and sculptors to depict heroic deeds on coins or in reliefs on arches. This particular view is the side of the arch that faces the city of Benevento, in southern Italy.* Alinari/Art Resource, N.Y.

UNDER THE LENS
Roman Law

The history of the Roman legal tradition is a long one, and Romans recognized law as an extraordinarily important development in their society. Virgil wrote *The Aeneid* in the first century B.C. In it, he clearly demonstrates the Roman attitude toward law when he writes that other societies have their arts and great learning, but the Roman contribution to humanity is justice and protection of the weak. Romans believed their destiny was to rule other peoples.

As early as the third century B.C., Roman professional jurists (not jury members, but teachers of Roman law) had attended Roman courts as qualified specialists, giving counsel to the elected officials and judges, who usually were not well versed in legal tradition. This innovation limited the arbitrariness of jurisprudence, and a tradition of consistency in law developed. Because the jurists were not advocates for either side in disputes, their competent interpretations usually were trusted by both parties.

Roman citizenship and law were complementary elements in Roman society. By the first century B.C., Rome was an empire with the ideology that Roman law was preferable to local legal traditions, and, as many groups in the provinces gradually gained citizenship rights, they held a vested interest in the success of the state. The benefits provincials received when enfranchised helped to curtail resistance and rebellion. In the first century, the Judean Christian missionary Paul chose to be transported to Rome for trial, as was his right as a Roman citizen. All in all, Roman law was an effective social organizer.

An important development for noncitizens arose in 242 B.C. with the establishment of a special office for cases involving at least one foreigner or noncitizen subject. With this alteration, Roman law moved from a civic legal structure, in which only citizens were addressed, to a universal legal structure that included all inhabitants of the ever-growing Roman state. The commercial, political, and social structures evolving during expansion brought about the need for this special office, and a new tradition of "the law of the nations" emerged. Romans were not entirely unique in this development; other polities (such as China) had created special legal definitions for noncitizen merchants and other foreign peoples living within their borders, but the Roman experience continued beyond merely defining specific commercial relationships. The "law of the nations" evolved into a legal system based on principles believed by Roman jurists to be universally applicable and universally acceptable. This universalist approach to dealing with the various peoples of the empire has been identified as the basis for the concept of international law in Western civilization.

The Roman legal system, however, did not establish a consistently fair and just legal structure. Ideally, jurists would be impartial, judges would come to fair decisions, and justice would prevail. But Roman courts fared no better than the legal courts of the twentieth century. Some professional jurists remained blinded by their own sympathies to oligarchical interests, and political circumstance frequently created an atmosphere tolerant of either apathetic neglect or extreme prejudice on the part of the officials who adjudicated.

---

the elite. Although the bureaucracy was efficient, many local bureaucrats were corrupt. Most of the provinces' lower classes suffered from having to pay more taxes than they owed and from little, if any, protection from bands of thieves. The empire's borders were extended during the second century (something that Augustus had warned against), an effort that proved expensive and yielded little political or military advantage. It increased the length of the defensive line, creating too sparse a military presence for effective protection. In fact, the **pax Romana**, the Roman peace established during Augustus's reign, had begun to crumble as early as 161, when the borders began to collapse. In 170, a military defeat in Venice saw that city burned, and it was not alone in this experience. Defensive walls had to be constructed to help impede the progress of enemy raids across northern borders. A civil service was employed that allowed nonmilitary personnel to work in the bureaucracy, freeing military officers for empire defense but raising the cost of administration. As the end of the second century approached, the added costs of defending the borders and the reorganization of the bureaucracy created a heavy tax burden for the lower classes.

THE LATE ROMAN EMPIRE, AROUND 200–476

As the third century dawned, the Roman Empire faced military and economic crisis. A military monarchy replaced the principate system by 211 in response to threats to the borders. The empire recovered in the fourth century under a political and military reorganization that stabilized its borders. Although the reorganization was not long lasting, it set the stage for the future division of the empire into two areas, the Western Roman Empire and the Eastern Roman Empire or Byzantium.

The Third-Century Crisis

Economic instability fed the flames of destruction in the third century. Coins were minted with debased metal, taxes were increased and collected from fewer and fewer farmers able to pay them, spiraling inflation ate away at those least able to maintain themselves, and the poor continued to file into the cities, expecting the state to support them as it had in the past. In order to keep the urban poor under control, the state had to distribute grain and bread at enormous cost. Much of the land near Rome had been turned into large aristocratic estates that grazed sheep and produced cash crops for trade. Aristocratic landowners remained wealthy and refused to offer land redistribution to ease the crisis. The small farmers persisted, as they had during the Republic, but their numbers diminished and they produced less. Consequently, greater amounts of grain had to be imported from Egypt and the Black Sea area than ever before.

In addition, the dispossessed, desperate, and unemployed population was riddled with crime and demanded reform. Emperors often appeased the Roman citizens with various entertainments, including gladiatorial games and the ever-popular chariot races. As entertaining as these events must have been, they were expensive to maintain on a regular basis. They became less frequent and ultimately were unsuccessful in pacifying the increasingly desperate population.

Rome previously had held its borders secure with troops and alliances with friendly Germanic tribes to the north. As early as the first century, many Germans had integrated into the Roman Empire through acculturation and service in auxiliary units within the army. But in the third century, Germans amassed in the borderlands were too numerous to assimilate, and the rise of the Persians again in the east threatened the security of the eastern border defenses. In 212, the emperor issued a decree that awarded citizenship to every free male living within the empire, permitting a conscription to increase the numbers available for military defense. The Persian Empire attacked and captured thirty-seven Roman cities. In 244, the Roman emperor was captured while fighting against Persia and was forced to act as a footstool when the Persian king mounted his horse. With the increase in German migration and raids and with the attacks on the eastern borders, the empire faced the serious crisis of a two-front war. Troops had to be transported and serviced, so the military crisis inflated the economic crisis.

The military and economic crises paved the way to political chaos. As the armies panicked because of emperors' failures to gain victory in the field, assassination and rebellion broke out. A clear military monarchy arose during the Severi dynasty (193–235), replacing the ineffectual principate system and its semblance of titles and senatorial power. The Senate was reduced to a toothless, ineffectual body. An emperor who marched with his army in the field, however, could hardly keep the peace in the cities through the necessary hands-on administration of economic reforms. Within forty-two years, the Severi dynasty fell to anarchy; the next forty-nine years saw twenty-two emperors. The empire had to reform or collapse.

The Empire's Revival

The reform came with the able leadership of Diocletian (reign dates 284–305), who was proclaimed emperor by the army in 284. The key to stability resided in the army's loyalty. Diocletian retained the troops' loyalty by securing the Roman Empire's borders through administrative and military reforms. In addition, the savior motif of the mystery cults was popular, and Diocletian offered himself as a savior figure to the people.

REFORMS. The emperor could not be everywhere at once; he could not be in the cities working on bureaucratic and administrative reform and, at the same time, out in the field leading the troops against Germanic or Persian invaders. Because it

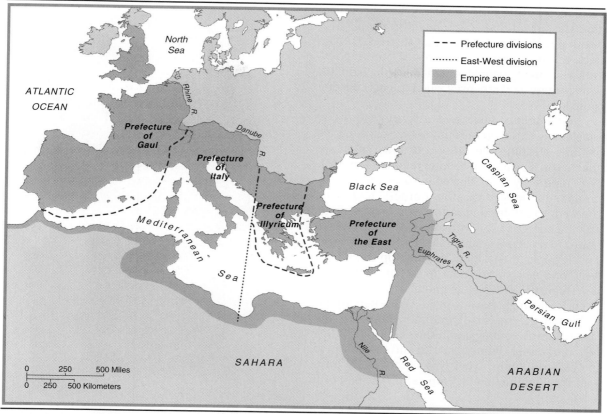

MAP 8.4 *Diocletian's Division of the Empire, A.D. 284–305.* *Diocletian divided the Roman Empire into two administrative territories and four prefectures (military areas defended by one of the four armies). Each of the rulers of the empire, two Augusti and two Caesars, was responsible for a prefecture's defense. This division saved the empire from border collapse during a two-front war.*

was apparent that power had to be shared, in 286 Diocletian split the empire into two administrative units in order to govern more efficiently. The division was basically between the eastern and western parts of the empire. Diocletian chose a colleague, who remained subordinate to him, to rule the west, while he remained in the east. Each of the two administrators took the title of Augustus, but Diocletian retained ultimate authority.

The military reform included another innovation in the hierarchy of authority. Under each Augustus would be a commander called a Caesar. The result was two Augusti and two Caesars, each of the four with control over an army that could mobilize quickly and move swiftly to areas of hostility. The sharing of authority among four confederates also allowed for a balance of power that temporarily impeded rebellion.

Diocletian also instituted economic and social reforms to reverse the effects of the second and third centuries. In 301, he introduced an edict on prices and wages that tried to curb the rate of **inflation**, the rapid increase in prices that causes a decline in purchasing power. Diocletian legislated against raising prices during times of crisis, considering it treason to do so. He also encouraged military officials to requisition supplies as a portion of the soldiers' pay to reduce the need to distribute coin.

Tax reforms were also introduced in an attempt to make taxation uniform and to increase revenues. A head tax, initiated on everyone living in the empire, raised badly needed revenues. The traditional land tax levied a tax on each tax district, which included several individual fields. More and more people were fleeing the rural areas for the protection of the cities or of a neighboring aristocrat. This meant that fewer and fewer people were left to pay the tax owed for that district. Diocletian's response was to stabilize the land-tax revenues by forcing people to remain on the land. (Of course, many still ran away when the tax collector came.)

The administrative and military reforms of Diocletian shored up the empire for a short period of time. Dividing the army into four parts was effective in slowing the disintegration of the Western Empire. By 305, Diocletian assessed that the immediate danger on the borders had been checked, so he decided to force the new system's order of succession to work. Each Augustus was to retire, then each Caesar would be promoted to the vacant Augustus position, opening up the Caesar level for a new commander to be chosen by each new Augustus. The system had merit and, in a different time, might have worked. Diocletian underestimated the power of tradition, however, and civil war broke out again. In the end, Constantine held the Western Empire (in 312) and soon invaded the Eastern Empire, where his victory in 324 once again unified the Roman Empire into the hands of a single ruler.

CONSTANTINE. Like Diocletian before him, Constantine (reign dates 312–337) had to deal with a two-front war and economic problems. Diocletian's system, with its four armies, was very costly, essentially creating two bureaucracies and four military budgets. Constantine decided to pull the bureaucracy under one administration again. He credited all his victories to the Christian god, and, in a bold move to unify the population and to settle internal disputes, Constantine made Christianity one of the state religions. Appearances remained important, however, and Constantine carefully continued to use the symbol for the sun god on his coinage. By maintaining a dual relationship, Constantine demonstrated his alliance with a traditional god of Rome, while also endearing himself to a growing population of Christian subjects. Scholars still debate the sincerity of Constantine's conversion, but the sociopolitical impact remains significant.

With Constantine's patronage of Christianity, persecution of Christians ceased, and many members of the elite converted in order to gain political advantage. Christians, who saw Constantine's conversion as a sign from their god to support the

FIGURE 8.6 *Bust of Constantine.* *The heavenward gaze on this bust of the emperor Constantine has a propaganda purpose similar to that of the statue of Augustus as* pontifex maximus *(Figure 8.4). After the assassinations during the third century, it was politically even more important for an emperor to be perceived by the army as having spiritual authority and divine right to rule. Beginning with Diocletian, emperors claimed a new status as special friend to a Roman deity that protected them and guided their policies. Diocletian professed Jupiter as his friend and Constantine claimed both Sol Invictus (the Unconquerable Sun God) and the Christian God as his friends, which can be seen in much of the imperial art produced during his reign. This bust demonstrates Constantine's spirituality as he gazes heavenward for direction from one of the deities, a posture not lost on the army or the general population.* The Metropolitan Museum of Art. Bequest of Mrs. F. F. Thompson, 1926. 26.229.

empire, could now enthusiastically participate in the army. Some Christians had been in the army prior to this, but now patriotism became popular, as they fought and prayed for their Christian emperor alongside non-Christians. A common ideological motivation to protect and preserve the empire produced stability.

Constantine abandoned the western capital of Rome for a well-defended city, which he named Constantinople (modern Istanbul). Like Alexandria in Egypt, Constantinople became an intellectual, religious, and economic center, as well as the eastern capital. The city's walls and geographical location formed an imposing defensive system. Situated on a promontory, the city was bordered by water on three sides, making siege almost futile.

Diocletian's division of eastern and western administration was revived after Constantine's death in 337. One-man rule returned for the last time under Emperor Theodosius, who died in 395. By the dawn of the fifth century, Diocletian's east-west division had become permanent.

The Fall of Rome

"The fall of Rome" is a commonly used phrase describing the decline of Imperial Roman culture in the Western Empire. The Eastern Empire continued and evolved into a new state, called Byzantium (which will be discussed in Chapter 17). Scholars today recognize that the fall of Rome was a process that took centuries and had several causes.

Germanic migration into the Western Empire was a significant cause of change. By the fourth and fifth centuries, Germanic migrations occurred so rapidly and in such large numbers that both Germanic and Roman cultures changed; there was not enough time for the Germans to be absorbed. Other Germans raided or conquered large portions of the Western Empire.

As time passed, Roman aristocrats increasingly fled the overcrowded, chaotic cities for the countryside, where they could live in relative safety on their self-sufficient estates. Many displaced people also fled to these large estates, where aristocratic landlords protected them against tax collection, conscription into the Roman army, and invasion by hostile Germans. These people then worked the land for a portion of what they produced. Other small farmers exchanged a portion of their yields to the same aristocratic neighbors in return for protection against tax collection. Slowly, in the west, political and social disintegration continued under German migration, and eventually the Western administration collapsed entirely. Germanic tribal kings filled the administrative void by extorting yearly payments in exchange for protection and peace. In later centuries, the large aristocratic holdings became the manors of the Middle Ages, with the descendants of the small farmers attached to the land as serfs.

When a German king, Odovacar,[8] finally deposed the last Western emperor in 476, hardly anyone noticed or cared. Yet even this German king wanted to be identified with Roman culture; he sent the imperial insignia to Constantinople and informed the Eastern emperor that he would rule the west under Eastern overlordship. In actuality, Odovacar ruled the west as he did any Germanic territory, independent of Eastern control or interest.

Those areas that tried to remain independent of Germanic control were the cities and the surrounding countrysides that supported them. Rome had experienced devastating raids. Cities' populations decreased, with many officials abandoning the ship of state. With no imperial or local administration, citizens (often the poorest) turned for guidance to the only surviving urban authority, the Christian bishop. The Christian Church had in place a bureaucracy that could assume the secular duties. Consequently, many bishops, including Rome's, became secular as well as religious leaders, thereby filling the political vacuum.

By the late fifth century, the once-vast Roman Empire was essentially gone. Byzantium, which encircled the eastern Mediterranean territories until the Islamic invasions of the seventh century, prospered until Constantinople fell to the Ottoman Turks in 1453. The Western territories lay either in the hands of Germanic kings or were islands of independence.

LIFE IN THE ROMAN EMPIRE

Augustus had secured the borders of the empire, consolidated Roman administration, and established throughout the Mediterranean a cohesive trade network that had brought peace and stability in the first century A.D. The Roman road network behind the ramparts not only allowed troops to move swiftly into areas of hostilities but also provided trade routes linking the smaller towns to the economic activity of the growing empire. The vast empire became a conduit for the exchange of commodities and culture between provincial peoples and Romans.

[8] **Odovacar:** OH doh vah cawr

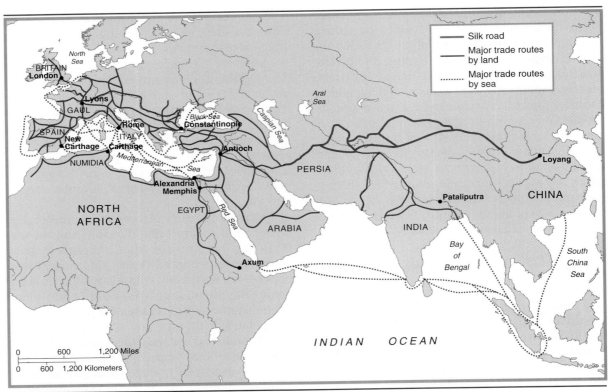

MAP 8.5 *Major Trade Routes around A.D. 200.* The Roman Empire encircled the Mediterranean Sea and exploited it as a highway for the exchange of goods. Outside the Mediterranean basin, Roman ships sailed from Africa to India, then to Malaya and Java and, by the second century, to China. During the Han period, the silk road was opened and connected empires in China, India, and Central Asia with the Roman Empire. Goods were carried from one end of the empire to the other—for example, hides, tin, and wool from Britain might be exchanged at the same market as glass, carpets, and ivory from India and spices and silk from China.

The Roman Exchange

Traditional commercial products, previously unavailable commodities, styles, and ideas coursed through the Roman Empire and its trading partners in great volumes, forming the **Roman exchange**. The Roman exchange was a significant aspect of life in the Roman Empire, developing rapidly as a result of the pax Romana.

The vast trade network and relative ease of travel linked the eastern caravans and southern shipping up the Nile to the northern and western Mediterranean all the way to the Black Sea settlements in the northeast and England in the northwest. Trade traveled overland in wheeled carts and by mule. In some cities, especially Rome, wheeled traffic had to be limited or restricted to nighttime because of the volume of traffic. (Still, the noise in the streets must have disturbed many a sleepy citizen.) Most trade, however, moved by riverboat or ship, because water transport was quicker and accommodated larger loads. In addition, commerce within the Roman Empire was facilitated by a common currency and low customs duties for goods moving between provinces.

The founding of new towns and the occupation of established cities in provinces enhanced stability and helped cultural exchange throughout the empire. Often beginning as military outposts, small market towns arose around the safety of the Roman forts and legion headquarters, and many of these eventually developed into urban centers that traded with local populations. Stationing troops away from their homelands was a policy that tended to keep rebellions down and assured that local soldiers would not have to fight their kinsmen. This policy exposed them to new ideas and lifeways; many soldiers married local women (who had their own languages and styles of cooking and clothing). On retirement, soldiers most often remained on the lands awarded them in the provinces where they had spent much of their careers. Soldiers who returned to their homelands brought back a patchwork of novel ideas, ranging from mystery cults to foreign words to new ways of making rope.

The love of exotica and a prosperous Roman elite stimulated trade with places outside the empire, too. Ivory from Axum, aromatic silphium gum from Hungary, perfumes and incense from India, silk from China, and rare foods made their way to the homes of wealthy Romans in Italy and abroad. In return, trading partners received Roman goods, as exemplified by a Roman silver goblet that made its way through the Egyptian trade route all the way to Meroë, in Africa.

Not all aspects of exchange resulted in benefit. Germs often traveled with those journeying from one part of the empire to another. In the second century, troops on campaign in Persia with Marcus Aurelius returned to the Italian peninsula carrying deadly contagion. The resulting epidemic devastated parts of the Italian population.

Life in the Roman Provinces

Of the approximately 100 million people within the empire at the time of Augustus, at least 75 percent lived in the provincial territories. Life in provincial towns consisted of a mixture between local customs and Roman practices, contributing to Roman exchange. For example, **Romanization**, the emulation of Roman ways, occurred among many local people, especially elites who desired social, political, or legal advantages. Sometimes Romans awarded citizenship (which included the right to wear the Roman toga, a sign of citizenship) to members of the local elite who supported Roman occupation. Romanization in Britain, for example, meant that local Britons adopted such aspects of Roman-style cooking as using the newly imported Roman bread oven, cooking hard-boiled eggs, seasoning their dishes with fish sauce, and relishing dainty pastries. The Germanic peoples who migrated into the Roman Empire in the first

century came south for peace and opportunity. They became Romanized over the centuries and lost most of their Germanic culture. These Germans became citizens, wore Roman dress, and spoke Latin, and their descendants even became emperors.

Many provincial cities adopted the Roman recreation of bathing. Bathers would oil themselves and then clean away the sweat and dirt by running special scrapers across their skin. The water was heated by furnaces or naturally by hot springs, then pumped under the rooms and into the baths. These bathhouses served as centers for rest and relaxation, as well as conduits for gossip and news from abroad. A courtyard for games and exercise served patrons' needs as well. The baths were very popular, being inexpensive and free for children. Men and women often shared the same bath areas, but some public bathhouses limited women to morning hours, with men attending in the afternoons.

Roman entertainments also made their way to the provincial areas. Citizens and townspeople enjoyed plays, poetry readings, gladiatorial fights, animal hunts, and acrobatic displays. Exotic wild animals for the arenas included crocodiles from Egypt, lions from Mesopotamia, leopards from northern Africa, and bears from Scotland. Large arenas for racing and major sports were called **circuses**. Entertainments in circuses included boxing and chariot racing. In Rome, the Circus Maximus could accommodate 25,000 spectators. In provincial areas, circus patrons were fewer but just as enthusiastic. Chariot races were attended by hundreds of excited fans, many of whom lost great amounts of money betting on the outcome. Chariot racing was an expensive but significant business, run by private entrepreneurs, similar to major-league team owners today. Racers became heroic figures, often being memorialized in mosaics and statues, and the competition between rival cities' teams often resulted in riotous violence.

Similar to the Hellenistic rural areas, the rural provincial areas at first felt little impact from Roman occupation, because administration and trade occurred in either forts or urban centers. As time passed, however, the retired Roman soldiers farming their lands brought Roman ideas to rural households, particularly in the western parts of the empire. Wealthy Romans often purchased large amounts of land and built Roman villas, where

FIGURE 8.7 *Chariot Race.* *The action and excitement of the popular chariot races is shown in this mosaic; many mosaics immortalize the names of the talented charioteers who achieved fame and fortune. Chariot racing was extremely dangerous, and thousands of drivers lost their lives competing for a share of the considerable bets placed on them and their horses. The track was an elongated circular surface; terraced seating was built of stone or cut into a hillside that surrounded the track. Around the center of the track ran a small wall to ensure that head-on collisions were avoided, with a break in the wall for attendants to run onto the track and remove crashed chariots and mangled men and horses before another chariot collided with the wreckage. Inside the center area, counters moved stakes with color-coded balls to keep track of the completed laps of each charioteer, who wore the corresponding colors.* Cliche Ch. Thioc, Musée de la Civilisation Gallo-Romaine, Lyon.

they lived an idyllic lifestyle that held little resemblance to that of the hardworking farmer who eked out a living to pay Roman taxes. Many of the wealthiest villas had hypocaust heating (hot air pumped under a raised floor), tiled roofs, multiple rooms, glazed windows, plastered and painted walls, and mosaic-tiled floors. Villa living became a sign of wealth and power throughout the empire.

Many temples were erected in the provinces, and, in the usual manner of Roman religious inclusiveness, local deities were adopted into the official list of Roman religions. Among the state cultic practices that were exported from Rome was that of Roma, the patron goddess of the Roman state. Augustus encouraged his own veneration in a state cult, particularly in the eastern part of the empire, where there was a tradition of divine kingship. Augustus imitated Alexander by encouraging subjects to see him as divine. Mystery cults from the eastern provinces found their way into the city of Rome and into the western provinces, brought by tourists, merchants, and military personnel.

Life in the City of Rome

Citizens in the capital city became inundated with new ideas and goods, and the population swelled with artisans and merchants from around the empire. Roman city life improved somewhat during the empire period, but living in any city presents certain problems. Augustus had divided the city into fourteen districts, each with minimal self-governance and personnel who doubled as police and firefighters. Augustus and Agrippa (one of his commanders) had buildings inspected and repaired, initiated public works projects, and established a board of works to enforce building codes. Crime and fire always caused concern in the densely populated city, which had been mostly destroyed by a catastrophic fire in A.D. 64. Consequently, large portions of the city were rebuilt in stone.

Most citizens lived in overcrowded apartment complexes. It was common to throw waste into the streets below, often with devastating results. The satirist Juvenal complained, "See what a height it is to that towering roof from which a potsherd comes crack upon my head every time that some broken or leaky vessel is pitched out of the window!" Others complained about the poor living conditions. One slum landlord confessed that two of his buildings had collapsed, and in another the walls were all cracked. Not only the tenants but even the mice had left.

Buildings snuggled against one another, and windows, opened for a breath of air, invited in all the bustling noise of the city's streets. One poet bewailed the racket: "There's nowhere a poor man can get any quiet in Rome. . . . The laughter of the passing throng wakes me and Rome is at my bed's head." The city streets bulged with stalls, whose merchants each tried to outsell the competition. Vendors sold food to wide-eyed tourists, and street entertainers, many of them women, performed for enough money to buy their daily bread.

The elite of the city fared somewhat better than the apartment dwellers. Their houses, which were built around a courtyard, placed bedrooms in quieter areas off the street. Wealthy men and women were very style-conscious, wanting to demonstrate their status by wearing the newest imports from around the empire. As hairstyles became increasingly elaborate, many depended on wigs to give their hair height. Slaves attended the elite women, helping them with their elaborate hairstyles, dressing them in the newest fashions, and adorning them with layers of jewelry. Those who criticized the opulence of Rome's wealthy citizens often complained that servants and slaves wasted too much time grooming their masters and mistresses.

Some of the elite women had indirect political influence. Numerous wives and mothers throughout Roman history influenced the political careers of their husbands and sons, but few were able to hold power themselves. Emperor Claudius's wife, Agrippina the Younger, ran the empire as Claudius (reign dates 41–54) became increasingly incapacitated by infirmities. Agrippina maneuvered her thirteen-year-old son by a previous husband into the line of succession over Claudius's own younger son. In 54, when the young Nero became emperor, her image was placed on coins with his.

By the first century B.C., elite women had gained control over lands through inheritance or, sometimes, through private investment from

FIGURE 8.8 *Nero and Agrippina. Coinage was an important tool in Roman society; not only was it used as commercial exchange but its decoration served as a means for propaganda. This coin's obverse side shows Emperor Nero and his mother, Agrippina, who married Emperor Claudius after Nero was born. Although her husband was in line for the imperial crown, it is rumored that Agrippina poisoned him and married her uncle Claudius to make Nero his heir. Her influence is demonstrated in her appearance on this coin, minted soon after Nero's ascension to the throne in A.D. 54. Other women had been placed on coins but Agrippina is depicted on this coin as Nero's equal, demonstrating her desire to be empress and co-ruler. The writing around the edge of the coin identifies her as the emperor's mother. Nero arranged her death in 59.* Museo Nazionale, Naples.

funds under their own control. Augustus enacted restrictive laws to limit fiscal independence of women. In addition, harsh laws were passed against the promiscuity of elite women, whose sexual liberation surpassed even that of the prostitutes. Augustus's daughter, Julia, had created such a public spectacle of herself by entertaining multiple lovers that he banished her from Rome. Augustus was concerned also with elite women who were refusing to marry or who chose to abort pregnancies because their condition limited participation in social functions.

ROMAN ARTS AND IDEOLOGIES

The people of the Roman Empire adopted many of the Hellenistic arts, religions, and philosophies, contributing their own styles and intellectual speculation to them. There were many people traveling around the empire on business and for pleasure. Multiple belief systems, like peoples, rubbed elbows in the bustling Hellenistic cities of the eastern Mediterranean and soon found their way into the western territories. Not everyone thought that Roman occupation had a positive effect, as identity with their ancestral heritage was submerged in the vast, impersonal bureaucratic society. Many individuals frequented astrologers to reassure them or sought miraculous cures and interventions to ease their physical and emotional suffering. Others searched for meaning in life by pursuing personal enlightenment and salvation in the varied philosophies and mystery cults available.

Roman Arts

It is difficult to categorize art during the Roman Empire into one great art style, because a variety of local expressions continued. Certain decorative styles (such as mosaic floors and mural wall paintings) did become widespread, as the Roman elite decorated their provincial homes in Roman styles. Romans continued the use of arches in public works, such as the aqueducts, temples, and amphitheaters throughout the entire breadth and width of the empire.

Roman art, in turn, was heavily influenced by local styles; for instance, Romans adopted Greek techniques and forms in architecture and sculpture. In Egypt in the late second century A.D., painting mummy portraits became common. The portraits were painted on wooden boards and then wrapped and placed with the mummy at the time of burial. In addition, it became popular to paint murals or panels of scenes from epics and myths on walls in elite homes.

As with many governments, art served the propaganda purposes of the emperors. Many of the reliefs on columns and arches commemorated military or political themes. Emperors and high officials used sculpture to portray their power or benevolence. Roman coins are another example of art propaganda. Almost all emperors commemorated events or advanced policies on the coins that passed through their subjects' hands.

Literature during the Roman Empire was as eclectic as the various cultural areas of the empire. The most prolific writers were rhetoricians, philosophers, and historians, many of whom were Greek educators. One significant contributor to Roman history was the late-first-century historian Tacitus, who wrote several histories. The Jewish historian Josephus wrote a history of a Jewish revolt (A.D. 66–73) and a twenty-book history of the Jews from the Creation to A.D. 66, immediately before the outbreak of the revolt. Later Roman historians included many Christians who wrote about the relationship between the empire and the new religion. The most productive author may have been Plutarch (42–126), whose writings were widely read works in the empire. His *Parallel Lives of the Famous Greeks and Romans* brought not only Greek history to interested Romans but also Roman history to Greek readers. Roman biography enjoyed great popularity in the second century through the scandalous pen of Suetonius, whose biographies of the emperors exposed every rumored tidbit about their behavior. Many incorrect perceptions persist today because his work has been uncritically accepted as fact.

Ovid (43 B.C.–A.D. 17) was one of the few Roman poets who received wide acclaim in their own time. He abandoned the Roman profession of politics to write poetry. By A.D. 8, he became the leading poet of Rome, although he was later banished for some unknown reason by Augustus. His poetry included such topics as the art of love, cosmetics, the art of seduction, and intrigue. He also wrote a fifteen-book collection of Classical Greek stories and Southwest Asian legends.

Other Roman literary works include the satires of Juvenal and Petronius from the first and early second century. Juvenal detested the Hellenization of Rome and attacked what he considered to be depraved behavior among the elite. Petronius, a novelist, wrote one of the most popular and scandalous novels of the Roman Empire period, *The Satyricon*. In it, he mocked the lavish lifestyle prevalent among the elite in Rome and ridiculed popular Greek love romances of the day.

Roman Philosophies

Older philosophies (such as Stoicism and Platonism) took on newer applications and had revivals. Seneca (4–65) was a Stoic philosopher who wrote several plays that included maxims for moral behavior according to the Stoic virtues of patience and duty. Stoicism took on a religious tone under the able pen of the freed slave Epictetus (55–135). In his works, Epictetus stressed that all men were brothers (he didn't include women) and that human nature contained some of the divine nature of god. Plotinus (205–270) initiated a revival of Platonism called Neoplatonism in the third century. Plotinus brought the contemporary interest in salvation to the philosophy, making it analogous to the popular mystery cults of the period. Plotinus argued that the Ineffable One first created the Mind, where all the ideas resided. The Mind then created the World Soul, which in turn created individual souls who fell into material existence in bodies. Neoplatonism's development coincided with the development of Christian theology, and many Christian thinkers adopted Neoplatonic vocabulary and imagery. Some equated the Ineffable One, Mind, and World Soul with the Father, Son, and Holy Spirit of the Christian Trinity.

Religions in the Roman Empire

Romans were polytheistic and adopted into their pantheon conquered peoples' deities, the most powerful of which were officially listed as state deities. Usually Romans demanded that the state deities be worshiped in order to preserve "the peace of the gods." Romans were very religious and did not want to offend their deities with neglect. When famine or disease ravished local areas, citizens stoned or jailed nonworshipers, believing that the deities were punishing everyone because these individuals were being lax in worship. Mystery cults became popular in the empire and

FIGURE 8.9 *Domestic Scene. The walls of Roman aristocratic houses were often decorated with colorful murals depicting Roman architectural styles and scenes of flora and fauna, myths, and everyday life. In this mural from Pompeii, three women and a child are shown in a household scene.* Alinari/Art Resource, N.Y.

IN THEIR OWN WORDS

The Eruption of Mount Vesuvius

In the long history of the globe, many natural disasters have proven deadly to plant and animal life. Floods, earthquakes, and volcanic eruptions continue to demonstrate nature's power over humanity today. The eruption of the volcano on Mount Vesuvius, southeast of Naples, is an example of such devastation. On August 24, A.D. 79, the life of one young man named Pliny[a] changed forever. Although Pliny was across the bay of Naples and watched the eruption from afar, he and his mother experienced the accompanying earthquakes and gagged on the pumice and ash. The following excerpts from his letters to the historian Tacitus are a lasting historical record of the horrors of that day:

> It was not clear at that distance from which mountain the cloud was rising . . . its general appearance can best be expressed as being like an umbrella pine, for it rose to a great height on a sort of trunk and then split off into branches. . . . Sometimes it looked white, sometimes blotched and dirty, according to the amount of soil and ashes it carried with it.

Pliny's uncle quickly boarded a ship and accompanied the local fleet across the bay to aid in the rescue of those in danger from the eruption, an act of heroism from which he never returned. During the rest of the day and into the night, Pliny and his mother huddled together as the earthquakes continued and as Vesuvius belched flames and ash into the air. As buildings came tumbling down, they tried to evacuate the town to safety.

> Once beyond the buildings we stopped, and there we had some extraordinary experiences which

[a]**Pliny:** PLIH nee

thoroughly alarmed us. We also saw the sea sucked away and apparently forced back by the earthquake: at any rate it receded from the shore [a tidal wave] so that quantities of sea creatures were left stranded on dry sand. On the landward side a fearful black cloud was rent by forked and quivering bursts of flame, and parted to reveal great tongues of fire, like flashes of lightning magnified in size.

Pliny then describes the panic of the citizens.

> You could hear the shrieks of women, the wailing of infants, and the shouting of men; some were calling their parents, others their children or their wives, trying to recognize them by their voices . . . then darkness came on once more and ashes began to fall again, this time in heavy showers. We rose from time to time and shook them off, otherwise we should have been buried and crushed beneath their weight. . . . At last the darkness thinned and dispersed into smoke or cloud; then there was genuine daylight, and the sun actually shone out, but yellowish as it is during an eclipse. We were terrified to see everything changed, buried deep in ashes like snowdrifts.

Pliny and his mother later learned the fate of his uncle.

> My uncle decided to go down to the shore and investigate on the spot the possibility of any escape by sea, but he found the waves still wild and dangerous. . . . He stood leaning on two slaves and then suddenly collapsed, I imagine because the dense fumes choked his breathing by blocking his windpipe. . . . When daylight returned on the 26th . . . his body was found intact and uninjured, still fully clothed and looking more like sleep than death.

---

spread from the eastern Mediterranean area to England. In addition, the emperor's cult demanded that citizens pour out a libation to the emperor's image, an offering of drink comparable to a national pledge of allegiance. Failure to respect the emperor in this way resulted in treason charges.

JUDAISM. The basic tenets of Judaism were discussed in Chapter 4. Judaism was a very old religion by the time of the Roman Empire and was tolerated by Romans because of its ancient heritage. Romans believed that the Jewish god deserved respect because of the numerous victories recorded in ancient Hebrew histories. Romans did not want to anger such a powerful god. Jews, however, were monotheistic and refused to worship the Roman state deities. Jews also demanded that the Romans not violate the sanctity of their temple by polluting it with the presence of unbelievers. Most of the time Romans did not enter the temple area, and the **Sanhedrin**,[9] the religious council and highest seat of Jewish justice, was allowed to run the temple without Roman interference. The Jews were given an exemption from worshiping all state deities, including the practice of pouring out the libation to the emperor. During the Roman occupation, some Romans converted to Judaism, but most of the time the Roman soldiers and officials lived in an uneasy peace with the Jewish population.

Jews came under attack by the Romans for political reasons in the mid–first century A.D. Many Jews resisted Roman occupation of Palestine and continually harassed the provincial governor and his troops. In 66, a group of Jewish freedom fighters took a fortress on the plateau of Masada from the Roman garrison stationed there. By 70, the Romans decided that the continuous unrest and rebellion had to be quelled or they might lose Palestine to the rebels; the Romans could not allow an independent state to control a portion of the Mediterranean's lucrative coastal trade network. Finally, after a six-month siege in 73, the Romans took the fortress back. When they breached the wall, they found the fortress burned and all but one woman and five children dead. The Jews of Masada had chosen suicide to mar a Roman victory. During this uprising, Jews endured the destruction of the temple in Jerusalem, the confiscation of holy articles (including the Ark of the Covenant), and the dispersion of many of their people to other provincial areas.

CHRISTIANITY. During Tiberius's reign, the new religion of Christianity emerged out of Judaism in Palestine. Christians were followers of Joshua ben Joseph of Nazareth (whose Hellenized name was Jesus, which is the common name used today), who they believed was the Jewish messiah, or savior. Jesus' followers claimed that he was crucified by the Roman governor of Judea to placate some of the Jewish religious leaders. They also believed that Jesus was resurrected from the dead after three days. The movement gained popularity in the first century, inspired by the preaching of Jesus' closest followers, the twelve apostles.

The twelve apostles were men, but Christian tradition attests to several women as loyal followers of Jesus and leaders in the early movement. Many women, like Phoebe and Olympia, achieved official status in the Christian Church as deaconesses, although their role usually remained limited to the instruction of women and the care of the sick. There is evidence to suggest that Christian widows, who were supported by charitable funds, formally organized into a group that had certain responsibilities during the liturgy. Many wealthy women became patronesses of important theologians, like Jerome and John Chrysostom.[10] Several women became prominent theologians in what later became heretical movements, but other women were recognized as martyrs, saints, and ascetics to be emulated by both men and women.

Christianity's message of salvation and loving one's neighbor soon spread to many cities within the empire, becoming more and more popular. Christians came to believe in a Trinity, with the Jewish god as Father, Jesus as the incarnate Son, and the love expressed between the two as the Holy Spirit. In following centuries, Christians philosophically argued that the three entities constituted not three gods but one god with three personalities.

The Christian religious structure gradually developed into a formal hierarchy. Deacons and deaconesses helped the priests and administered communal funds. The priests presided over local house churches, performing religious rites such as baptism and the sacred sacrificial meal. The bishop remained responsible for teaching, preaching, and correctly interpreting the developing doctrine. As time passed, each urban center retained only one bishop, who supervised all priests and deacons. Bishops gathered in councils and debated correct interpretations of scriptures and philosophical constructs, eventually determining correct doctrine for all Christians.

At first, Christians considered themselves Jews; they claimed the same right as the Jews of exemption from practicing the rituals of the Roman state cults. Christians and Jews, however, had a serious dispute over monotheism. Because

---

[9] **Sanhedrin:** san HE drihn

[10] **Chrysostom:** KRIH saws tuhm

FIGURE 8.10 *Political Graffiti in Ancient Rome.* *Romans often used graffiti to communicate their opinions of current events. A popular second-century novel,* The Golden Ass, *told of a hapless young man who was magically turned into an ass because of his bad attitude and disrespect of religion. Through his experiences he learned the value of religion and was returned to human form, after which he joined the mystery cult of Isis. Soon "ass" became a popular slur for people considered unethical or impious. Romans believed that both Jews and Christians were asinine in their refusal to worship the traditional Roman deities or participate in mystery cults. In this picture the scrawled message reads "Alexamenos adores his god." It is the earliest known rendering of the crucifixion of Jesus. In this instance, both the crucified Jesus and his devotee are the objects of ridicule.* Alinari/Art Resource, N.Y.

Christians were soon barred from worshiping in the Jewish temple or synagogues, the Romans demanded that Christians participate in the state cults, particularly that of the emperor. Most Christians refused to recant their beliefs, and most Romans refused to recognize a mere mortal who had died a criminal's death as a deity worth worshiping. Thus began the persecution of Christians within the empire; their deaths, from the Roman point of view, were justified through the Christian failure to observe religious obligations. As a result, Christians were forced to worship their god in secret or face persecution and martyrdom.

As time passed, Romans learned that they had little to fear from the Christians; many citizens realized that family members, neighbors, and even wealthy aristocrats were Christians. Part of the new religion's appeal was its similarity to many of the mystery cults that had become popular during the Hellenistic Age. When Constantine became the first Christian emperor of the Roman Empire, he made Christianity an official state religion. Constantine's conversion, edicts of tolerance, and favorable tax laws for Christians made the new religion politically and economically popular. The religion also became popular in part because someone of any class or station could join, and anyone, whether a member or not, could receive charity during times of crisis. In addition, many of the intellectual elite had previously rejected the low social status and assumed illiteracy of Jesus and most of his followers. Christian theologians, however, soon were able to overcome these intellectual objections when they adopted Greek philosophical constructs and vocabularies. Christian theological development focused increasingly on philosophical issues and less and less on the stories and miracles of Jesus.

Christian leaders also adopted organizational structures from Roman culture. For example, Christian churches were grouped into dioceses, sectors that paralleled the Roman tax districts of the same name. In addition, many titles and offices of the Roman government eventually fell to bishops, who defended their cities and dioceses as the empire disintegrated in the late fifth century A.D. For example, the bishop of Rome became "duke," "defender of the city," and "pontiff" (high priest).

By the end of the fourth century, Emperor Theodosius made Christianity the only legal religion in the empire, but non-Christian religious practices persisted. Christianity's popularity continued to grow, however, and, by about the fifth century, approximately 60 percent of the population of the empire was Christian.

A COMPARISON OF THE GREEK AND ROMAN EMPIRES

The peoples of the Greek Empire and the Hellenistic Age (359–31 B.C.) and the Roman Empire (31 B.C.–A.D. 476) shared analogous problems and challenges. In some cases, both Greeks and

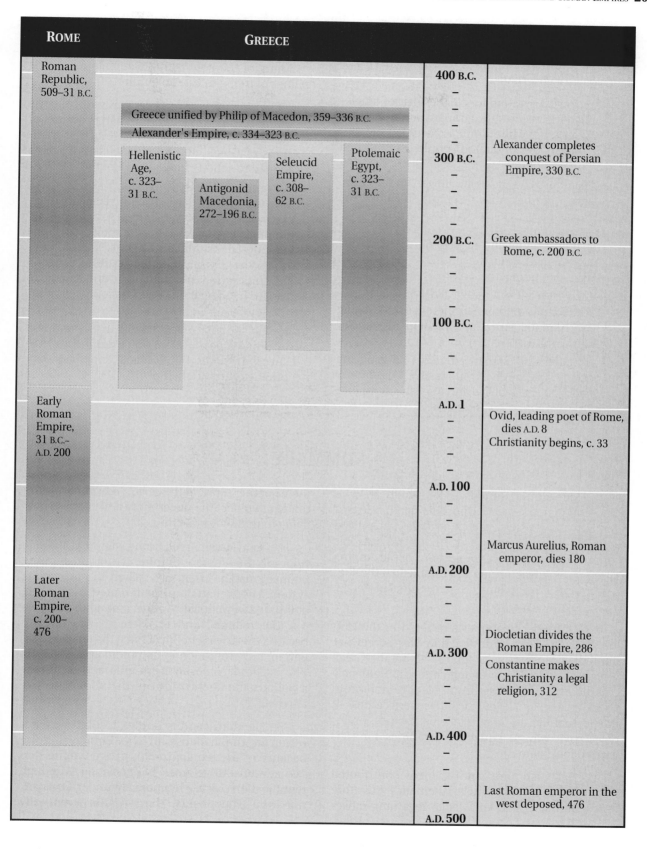

ROME	GREECE		
Roman Republic, 509–31 B.C.		**400 B.C.**	
	Greece unified by Philip of Macedon, 359–336 B.C.		
	Alexander's Empire, c. 334–323 B.C.		
	Hellenistic Age, c. 323–31 B.C. / Antigonid Macedonia, 272–196 B.C. / Seleucid Empire, c. 308–62 B.C. / Ptolemaic Egypt, c. 323–31 B.C.	**300 B.C.**	Alexander completes conquest of Persian Empire, 330 B.C.
		200 B.C.	Greek ambassadors to Rome, c. 200 B.C.
		100 B.C.	
Early Roman Empire, 31 B.C.–A.D. 200		**A.D. 1**	Ovid, leading poet of Rome, dies A.D. 8 / Christianity begins, c. 33
		A.D. 100	
		A.D. 200	Marcus Aurelius, Roman emperor, dies 180
Later Roman Empire, c. 200–476		**A.D. 300**	Diocletian divides the Roman Empire, 286
			Constantine makes Christianity a legal religion, 312
		A.D. 400	
		A.D. 500	Last Roman emperor in the west deposed, 476

Romans responded similarly to them, and at other times they pursued very different paths.

Many of the similarities involved citizenship and styles of governance.

—Greeks slowly abandoned the idea of single-polis citizenship and adopted multiple-polis citizenships, while Romans awarded citizenship to many conquered peoples that formed a unitary polity.

—Alexander's conquests swallowed up the entire Persian Empire, and his empire included the diverse cultures of the Greeks, Egyptians, Persians, and others. Roman expansion devoured the Italian peninsula, most of northern Europe and England, and the entire Mediterranean basin, including the cultures of the Greeks, Egyptians, North Africans, and Germans.

—Alexander and Roman emperors used existing governmental structures to help administer their empires.

—Alexander and Roman emperors adopted the eastern style of divine monarchy. (Alexander's Greek subjects rebelled, but Augustus's emperor cult set a precedent for succeeding emperors, like Diocletian.)

Many of the contrasting elements reveal the realities of trying to rule an empire.

—Expansion under Alexander was swift, and the empire's life was short, in part because of Alexander's death and because of the traditions of Greek culture. Augustus's long reign helped to solidify the Roman Empire.

—Alexander's military expansion was successful, but the empire lacked a universal ideology necessary for survival. Roman expansion into empire began under the Republic, as Rome conquered its Italian neighbors. After conquest, the granting of Roman citizenship, good administration, Roman law, and access to wealth by indigenous elites encouraged internal stability.

—Hellenistic culture tended to remain dominant in urban areas of Alexander's empire and the successor states, but Romans tended to adapt other cultures to their own.

SUMMARY

1. Macedonia united under Philip II, who then conquered Greece. Upon his death, Alexander overthrew Persia and created a vast, short-lived empire. After Alexander's death in 323 B.C., his commanders competed for portions of the empire. Three emerged victorious and established the successor states of Ptolemaic Egypt, Seleucid Persia, and Antigonid Greece.

2. Alexander's conquests ushered in the Hellenistic Age. Cultural interaction was somewhat limited because Greeks tended to retain Greek ways, but Hellenistic exchange brought many new commodities and ideas from eastern lands into Greek areas. The Hellenistic cities were centers of intellectual life. In larger Hellenistic cities, prejudices gave way to equal opportunities for Hellenized local elites.

3. Hellenistic arts and sciences contributed important works, like new mathematics, literature styles, and scientific knowledge regarding movements of the stars and the earth. New philosophies tended to reflect the uncertainty and concern over living in multicultural cities.

4. Octavian emerged from civil war as the sole ruler of the Roman Empire. Through cunning political maneuvering, he created the principate system. The Roman Empire after Augustus became embroiled in political rivalries among the emperors, the military, and the Senate. The military became the driving political force through assassination and promotion of emperors as early as 68. The pax Romana began to crumble, and eventually a military monarchy replaced the principate system by 211.

5. The third-century border hostilities did not result in the collapse of the Roman Empire because of the reorganization of the empire into two administrative areas by Diocletian. Although reunification existed temporarily under Constantine and Theodosius, the division eventually

became permanent in 395. This division foreshadowed the end of the Roman Empire and the evolution of two autonomous societies, the Western Roman Empire and the Eastern Roman Empire; the latter developed into the Byzantine culture.

6. The Roman exchange saw massive amounts of commodities and various ideas move across the vast empire, affecting both Romans and indigenous populations. Many individuals became Romanized, and many Romans adopted lifestyles of the indigenous populations among whom they lived. Life in the Roman provinces reflected the Roman exchange. Many soldiers retired in the provincial areas, where they influenced and were influenced by local peoples and customs. Rome became a bustling city, full of immigrants, tourists, and merchants.

7. Roman arts and philosophies adopted many Hellenistic styles. Although there was no single great art style, many works of art and literature were produced. Older philosophies enjoyed revivals in the Roman Empire.

8. Roman religious ideas respected the ancient Jewish god, but political hostilities eventually led the Roman government to destroy the Jewish temple and disperse large numbers of Jews throughout the empire. Christianity emerged from Judaism, and Constantine became the first Christian Roman emperor and moved Christianity onto the official list of tolerated Roman religions.

SUGGESTED READINGS

Adkins, Lesley, and Roy Adkins. *Introduction to the Romans.* Secaucus, N.J.: Quintet Publishing Limited, 1991. A short, beautifully illustrated review of Roman culture.

Bury, J. B., and Russell Meiggs. *A History of Greece to the Death of Alexander the Great.* Fourth edition. New York: St. Martin's Press, 1975; reprint with revisions and corrections, 1991. A standard history of Greece.

Ferguson, John. *The Heritage of Hellenism: The Greek World from 323 B.C. to 31 B.C.* In Geoffrey Barraclough, general ed., *History of European Civilization Library.* London: Thames and Hudson, 1973. A good review of Hellenistic culture.

Fox, Robin Lane. *The Search for Alexander.* Boston: Little, Brown, 1980. A study of the life and the impact of Alexander.

Grant, Michael. *History of Rome.* Englewood Cliffs, N.J.: Prentice Hall, 1978. An older but still valuable standard history of Rome.

Jones, A. H. M. *The Decline of the Ancient World.* New York: Longman, 1996. A review of the fragmentation of the late Roman Empire.

Koester, Helmut. *Introduction to the New Testament.* Vol. 1: *History, Culture and Religion of the Hellenistic Age.* Philadelphia: Fortress Press, 1982. A study that examines religious concepts in the Hellenistic Age.

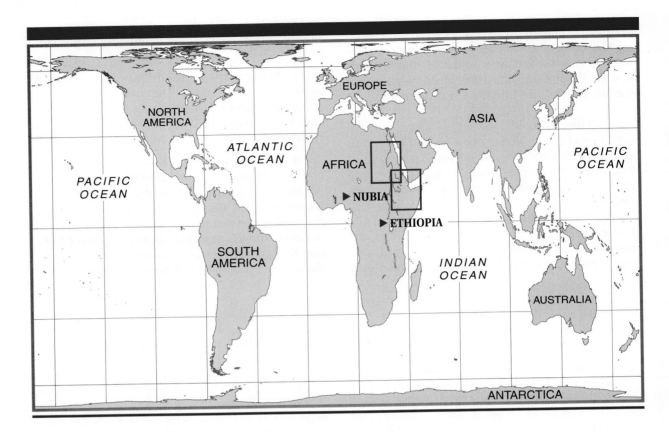

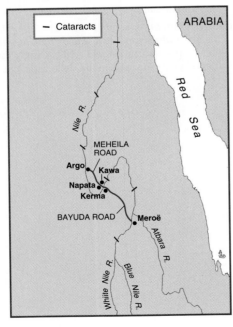

▶ **NUBIA**

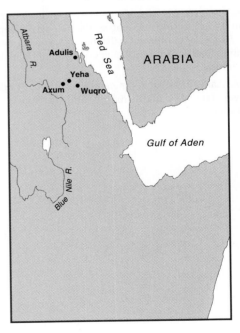

▶ **ETHIOPIA**

Early Civilizations in Nubia and Ethiopia

around 800 B.C.–A.D. 650

Around 2200 B.C., a group of Egyptian explorers scratched their names at the highest point they ascended the Nile. Whether they returned to Egypt and reported to the pharaoh is unknown, but no record of their expedition other than these fragile graffiti has survived. Within a few hundred years, a civilization would develop in the land these Egyptians visited, a civilization that briefly would eclipse and rule Egypt itself. This was one of three great early civilizations of northeastern Africa.

In northeastern Africa, to the south and southeast of Egypt, lay the regions of Nubia and Ethiopia, where the earliest African civilizations outside of Egypt arose. From early times, the people of Nubia and Ethiopia had had contacts with civilizations to the north, and long-distance trade led to the creation of local Nubian and Ethiopian elites, which in turn led to full-blown civilizations. The development of complex societies in other parts of Africa took place somewhat later and is treated in Chapter 15.

EARLY CIVILIZATION IN NUBIA: KUSH AND MEROË, AROUND 800 B.C.–AROUND A.D. 400

The Nubian region lies due south of Egypt, upriver along the Nile River in what today is the Sudan. During the period approximately between 800 B.C. and A.D. 400, this region was dominated by local civilization in the form of states called Kush and Meroë.[1] These states developed largely because of Nubia's favorable location for trade.

Nubia's great virtue was its location along the only reliable route between Egypt and tropical Africa before the development of the domesticated camel and caravan routes across the Sahara. The hostility of the land away from the river made this corridor very narrow indeed, and all trade had to pass through the region's riverside communities, placing the people along it in a prime position to become brokers in trade between Egypt and resource-rich areas to the south. That position was strengthened by the cataracts of the Nile, six series of rapids that were difficult and dangerous to navigate with a boat, forcing traders to carry goods by land.

Although Nubia grew prominent as an intermediary in trade between sub-Saharan Africa and Egypt, Nubia itself was not blessed with great material resources. The Nile's banks supported only a narrow strip of lush vegetation, while areas away from the river were predominantly hot and dry desert. The only land with agricultural potential lay directly along the Nile, and irrigation was necessary to grow crops there. Modest amounts of gold, iron, and other minerals constituted Nubia's only notable natural resources.

Evidence for early civilization in Nubia comes from both documents and archaeology. Unfortunately, many of the documents are written in a locally developed alphabet and language that modern scholars have not yet deciphered. Consequently, most of our knowledge comes from archaeology and Egyptian writings about Nubia. The domination of documentary evidence by Egyptian sources may engender a bias toward stressing the connection between Egypt and Nubia.

Kerma: A Rehearsal for Civilization, around 1800–around 1600 B.C.

Twice Egypt extended its political sway over parts of Nubia, controlling them as colonies. From around 1900 to 1700 B.C., Middle Kingdom rulers held northern Nubia; again from about 1600 to 1100 B.C., New Kingdom rulers extended their rule over northern and central Nubia. While some scholars believe that these colonies were meant to be buffers protecting Egypt's southern frontier, most believe they were designed to control the lucrative Nile trade.

Near the end of the earlier period of Egyptian control, around 1800 B.C., a local society developed in central Nubia. Named "Kerma" after the major city in its territory, this society distinguished itself in terms of trade for the next two hundred years. The city of Kerma itself was walled and had a variety of large structures associated with it. Near the city were two (or more) ***deffufas***,[2] massive towers constructed of mud bricks with fired brick facings. Within these structures, archaeologists have found abundant evidence of the manufacture and storage of goods. They also have found many Egyptian-style seals, placed on containers during shipment to ensure that they were not tampered with, and fragments of various goods manufactured in Egypt. The evidence seems clear that the largest structures in Kerma were devoted to the trade of goods and—to a lesser extent—their manufacture, probably an indication of the importance of these activities to the city.

Unfortunately, little else is known about Kerma. A major cemetery has been excavated, and one tomb has yielded what appear to be at least 322 sacrificial victims interred with several elite persons. This suggests that there was substantial class stratification at this date. It also underscores the local element in Kerma, because human sacrifice was not practiced in Egypt at this period.

At one time it was thought that Kerma was really an Egyptian colony, and scholars even wrote about a hypothetical "viceroy of Egypt." Now it is known that the viceroy never existed and that Kerma was an independent Nubian development that traded with Egypt and borrowed freely from its culture. Kerma developed during a weakening in Egypt's hold on the area around 1800 B.C.; and as soon as Egypt reasserted its control around 1600 B.C., Kerma was unable to withstand the hostile attentions of a powerful foreign civilization and yielded to Egypt its control of the Nile trade. Kerma dissolved as a political entity.

According to our limited current knowledge, we probably should not consider Kerma a civilization. Although it possessed the agricultural dependence, class stratification, and long-distance trade

---

[1] **Meroë:** MAYR oh eh

[2] ***deffufas:*** duh FOO fuhz

FIGURE 9.1 *The Western Deffufa at Kerma.* *Begun around 1800 B.C., this structure was used for many centuries and was the most important religious building in Kerma. The deffufa (temple) was massive but had very little space inside, most of its volume being composed of masonry. It was remodeled dozens of times, and in its final form the only open interior area was composed of a narrow passage with a sanctuary and a stair to the roof, where rituals presumably were conducted. Virtually nothing is known of the nature of these rituals.* T. Kendall.

that are core characteristics of civilization, it apparently operated with a chiefdom-level government and may have had little occupational specialization. But Kerma remains significant as the first Nubian experiment in complex society and the control of trade, a rehearsal of sorts for what was to follow with the Kush and Meroë kingdoms.

Kush: Nubia Asserts Itself, around 800–around 400 B.C.

Around 1100 B.C., Egypt's internal politics weakened its political situation so much that colonial control of the Nubian region collapsed. The power vacuum initially was filled by a series of local chiefs, each with a territory. Nubia had been under Egyptian control for most of the previous 800 years, and the power of Egyptian culture was demonstrated when the installation of chiefs required the approval of the Egyptian priests of Amun.

By around 800 B.C., the divided power of the chiefs came to be vested in a single king, establish-

ing the Kush kingdom, the first indigenous state government in the region. The capital and principal city of Kush was Napata,[3] a colonial town of the old Egyptian regime. Kush's kings were crowned in Napata, at a major temple there. Although evidence is largely lacking, most scholars also suspect that Napata was the focus of Kush's trade, because it lies at the intersection of the Bayuda[4] Road (the land route to the city of Meroë, a major population center) and the Meheila[5] Road (the land route to Kawa and Argo, two more large population centers). In addition, Napata lay just downstream of the Fourth Cataract, at an ideal spot for the reloading of boats with goods that had been carried around the rapids.

During the Kush period, gold mining probably developed in Nubia, and some scholars believe that this was the underpinning of Kushite development. Gold is of little value, however, unless there

[3] **Napata:** nah PAH tah
[4] **Bayuda:** by OO duh
[5] **Meheila:** mah HAY luh

FIGURE 9.2 *King Shebaka of Kush. Identified by the Egyptian writing on his belt, King Shebaka reigned over Kush in the late eighth century B.C. He is shown in a posture distinctive to Egyptian art: rigidly symmetrical and frontal, kneeling in offering to the gods. The eyes, face, and garments show a strong Egyptian cast. The statue is about six inches high and cast in bronze.* National Archaeological Museum, Athens.

is someone to buy it, and presumably trade with Egypt would have been critical to the development of a gold industry.

The state government that ruled Kush was headed by an Egyptian-style divine king who claimed descent from Egyptian gods, particularly Amon. The kings were absolute monarchs with great power over their subjects and in death were memorialized with opulent tombs. King lists trace rulership for most of the Kush period, though there are some inconsistencies within them.

The king and related nobles formed the elite and lived in major cities. Most of the rest of Kush society consisted of commoners who either tilled fields and lived in modest villages or performed manual labor in the cities. An intermediate class in Kush is ill documented, but presumably there was at least a small class of skilled artisans who made luxury goods consumed by the elite and engineers who produced monumental architecture.

The major cities of Kush consisted of monumental temples, palaces, and government buildings (especially warehouses) within a central precinct, surrounded by densely packed houses, which in turn were encircled by a defensive wall. In a style that incorporated both Egyptian and local Nubian characteristics, the monumental buildings were made of both mud bricks and large stone blocks, requiring considerable engineering expertise. The simpler housing consisted mostly of single-room dwellings made of mud bricks with a porch to the rear where cooking and other household activities took place. Because the city walls were limited in diameter, population growth led to more and more commoners living outside the walls.

For a brief period, Kush conquered and ruled Egypt, establishing a short-lived empire. In 712 B.C., Kushite forces installed Shebaka,[6] the king of Kush, as the first pharaoh of Egypt's twenty-fifth dynasty. During the twenty-fifth dynasty, there was a return to Egyptian styles of architecture and art that had been current 1,500 years earlier, and some old temples were copied precisely in new locations. This turning to ancient models extended into the copying of ancient texts, and Kushite copies of some Old Kingdom Egyptian records provide our only copies of ancient documents. Historians have developed no satisfactory explanation for why a Kushite government would emphasize ancient Egyptian forms so strongly, but it may relate to an attempt to legitimize its rule.

Weakened by internal conflict and external assault, Egypt had been easy prey for its Kushite conquerors. But the Kushite military was not sufficiently powerful to protect Egypt from invasion by foreign conquerors; indeed, their weapons were primarily of bronze and no match for the iron weapons of contemporary Southwest Asian militaries. The first of the conquests of this period was

[6]**Shebaka:** sheh BAH kah

by the Assyrians in 667 B.C., and this dispossessed the twenty-fifth dynasty, ending Kush's brief rule outside Nubia. The Assyrians made no effort to penetrate Nubia, however, and the Kush state continued to rule there.

Meroë: Nubia Consolidates Its Position through Trade, around 400 B.C.–around A.D. 400

Around 400 B.C., Meroë began to supplant Napata as the first city of Kush. Though kings continued to be crowned at Napata, their palaces and courts were about 100 miles south in Meroë. Governmental administration was focused in Meroë, and burgeoning trade was controlled from there. In part, this shift may have been to place the capital in a position less vulnerable to military incursions that were constantly threatening the northern parts of Kush in this period; it may also have been in response to river fluctuations that threatened agricultural productivity in the north. Some scholars continue to call this kingdom "Kush," while others designate it as a separate kingdom called "Meroë," a policy we follow here. Our inability to read Meroitic writing prevents us from knowing whether contemporary Nubian writers recognized a distinction.

In general outline, Meroë was much like Kush. Divine kings continued to trace ancestry to Egyptian gods and rule absolutely; governmental hierarchies still carried out the king's wishes throughout the kingdom; the pattern of settlement persisted, with walled cities housing many people, while others lived in villages and produced food by farming and raising animals. There were, however, significant changes in Meroë.

In the forefront of change was the increased volume of trade and diversity of products traded. The Nubian region was now a major conduit of gold, ivory, slaves, and other goods going to Egypt. In return, manufactured goods came from Egypt. Many of these were luxury goods for the elite, including a Roman goblet of silver and a gold ring inscribed in Greek, both found at Meroë. Everyday goods for commoners also came into Nubia through this trade, including wine, pottery, and clothing. Most evidence indicates that goods flowing from Meroë were predominantly raw materials, while goods returning were mostly manufactured items. This pattern has become common in modern times, as developing countries supply resources for developed countries to process and return to them.

A second major change was the expansion of iron working. Although iron working in Nubia dates back at least to Kerma, the output was greatly expanded in the Meroë kingdom. Meroë itself, as well as other cities, accumulated high mounds of slag around its edges, testimony to the quantities of iron that must have been produced. There are no signs of technological breakthroughs or greater usage of iron in Meroë of this period, so presumably the increase in output was in response to expanded exportation. Traditional views of Meroë see large quantities of iron traded to the south of Nubia, although some scholars cite the lack of evidence for this and are skeptical. If Meroë had been a major exporter of iron implements, this

FIGURE 9.3 *Hinged Armlet of Queen Amanishakheto of Meroë.* *This jewelry, designed to be worn on the upper arm, is made of gold inset with bits of fused glass (at that time a rare and precious material). The central figure on the armlet is a winged goddess reminiscent of Egypt, but the surrounding geometric ornamentation is distinctly Meroitic. This and other gold jewelry overlooked by looters in Queen Amanishakheto's tomb suggest that she was a wealthy and powerful queen.*
Victor R. Boswell Jr./ NGS Image Collection.

would have increased the amount of exported finished goods, improving its balance of trade.

Another significant change is unequivocal evidence for an expanded middle class. Cemeteries consisted of graves with elaborate monuments for the elite and simple graves for the commoners, but for the first time there are graves intermediate in complexity and cost. This probably means the beginnings of a middle class, perhaps emerging from the more skilled artisans, scribes, and petty government officials.

Elite women also improved their status in Meroë. Women began taking increasingly important roles in government; some women, such as Queen Amanitere,[7] served as ruling monarchs. Our evidence is limited to the elite, and there is no evidence revealing whether middle-class and commoner women also had expanded roles in society.

Finally, population was growing rapidly. One result was that the limited agricultural land of Nubia was insufficient to support the number of farmers. As a result, many sought jobs in the cities, leading to a major increase in urbanization. Cities were becoming more numerous, larger, and more densely settled.

Meroë itself was typical of the larger Meroitic cities. In earlier Kush times, the city wall had enclosed most of the city; by the time of Meroë, the wall encircled merely the central precinct, with its monumental palaces and temples made of mud brick, a bath, and servants' quarters. All other development was outside the wall, including a densely packed mass of houses for all but the small elite. The huge iron slag piles at the edges of many cities took up space needed for housing, polluted water supplies, and increased problems of flooding and erosion.

Some population pressure was relieved by the development of the **saqia**,[8] an ox-powered water wheel to lift water from the Nile to agricultural fields. The northern parts of Nubia had been only scantily populated since around 700 B.C., because a long-term fluctuation of river level appears to have made previous irrigation technology ineffective there. With the invention of the *saqia* around A.D. 100, these areas were opened up, and their rapid resettlement between A.D. 100 and 300 suggests that good land was hard to find elsewhere.

The Nile's banks in northern Nubia were lined with striplike agricultural villages in later Meroë times, around A.D. 200 to around 400, and a few fortified towns on hilltops administered the area.

Despite the development in northern Nubia, the Meroë kingdom crumbled by around A.D. 400. The reasons are not entirely clear, but the camel may be, in part, implicated. About 100 B.C. seminomadic desert peoples adopted the domesticated camel (camels had been domesticated earlier in southern Asia), and from this time onward, their raids on Meroë settlements became more frequent and intensive. There also are hints, discussed later in this chapter, that the Axum state may have invaded parts of Meroë. Either of these explanations could account for diminishing trade and fortified hilltop towns in northern Nubia in the later years of the Meroë kingdom.

Another intriguing possibility may relate to the demise of Meroë. The pattern of fortified administrative towns and prosperous villages in northern Nubia is in marked contrast to the pattern of rich cities and poor agricultural villages seen in the south. Although no documentary evidence supports the idea, some archaeologists have suggested that the northern pattern is out of keeping with a divine kingship, where commoners are expected to accept their poverty so that the king or his representatives can live in the opulence they warrant. Instead, they suggest, northern Nubia may have effectively seceded from Meroë and been ruled by a series of local warlords. Although this suggestion might explain certain aspects of the evidence, it is difficult to accept this interpretation without further support.

In any case, about A.D. 400 various poorly known local kingdoms, not unlike the domains of warlords discussed in the preceding paragraph, supplanted Meroë. By the sixth century, these were consolidated into the Christian Nubian kingdoms.

Kush and Meroë as a Civilization

Kush and Meroë form a cultural continuum, and, unlike Kerma, they clearly fit the core criteria for civilization. They inherited Kerma's agricultural dependence, long-distance trade, and class stratification, and they developed unambiguous occupational specialization, a state government powerful enough to establish a brief empire, and urbanism.

---

[7]**Amanitere:** ah mahn ih TAY ree
[8]*saqia:* SAH kee uh

FIGURE 9.4 Saqia. *The ox-driven water wheel that permitted the expansion of Meroë into northern Nubia continues in use today. This photograph shows a man goading oxen into turning an axle, which transmits its power through gears to lift irrigation water from wells.* Michael S. Yamashita.

In addition, they possessed many of the secondary elements of civilization. Noteworthy among these are their metallurgy (especially as it related to iron), writing, monumental architecture, state religion, great art style, and sophisticated transportation system based largely on the Nile River. The monumental architecture suggests mathematical and engineering skills, and the prominence of trade suggests standardized units of measure, although only limited archaeological evidence supports this suggestion. Many of these elements seem to have been outgrowths of the long-distance trade on which Nubian civilization was based or the aggrandizement of the elite who controlled the trade.

The Relationship of Egypt to Kush and Meroë

The Egyptian heritage of Kush and Meroë is obvious, particularly in the arena of religion. Most of the gods and goddesses to whom temples were

dedicated were Egyptian, including Amon, Isis, and Apis. Some temples, such as the temple at Jebel Barkal, were built by Egyptians themselves during their occupations of Nubia, while others were built along similar lines by Nubians after the end of the Egyptian occupations. Much of the painted and low-relief sculpted art that adorned the walls of the temples and other monumental buildings was similar to Egyptian art, with its emphasis on static images, limited perspective, and frontal or silhouette depictions of persons.

The debt to Egypt also was evident in the conceptions and treatment of Nubian royalty. The rulers of Kush and Meroë were divine kings and queens; their leadership was legitimized by their descent from Egyptian deities, and their claim to power was indisputable. In life, rulers assumed Egyptian names and trappings, and many of the luxury goods in their palaces were designed and manufactured in Egypt. In death, monarchs were buried in elaborate tombs, sometimes patterned after the pyramids and mastabas of Egypt, and were accompanied by goods of Egyptian pattern.

Figure 9.5 *The Royal Cemetery at the City of Meroë.* *The large pyramids in the final resting place of the kings and queens of Meroë reflect Egyptian influence. This cemetery was in use through most of the span of the kingdom of Meroë. In recent times, some of the small pyramids have been restored and new shrines have been built by Nubian Muslims out of reverence for what they consider as a holy place.* Michael S. Yamashita.

Kush and Meroë, of course, exercised selection in their adoption of Egyptian models for religion and royalty, rejecting or modifying them in some cases. The Egyptian pantheon was augmented with local Nubian gods, particularly Apedemak,[9] the lion god. Many Nubian temples incorporated features unknown in classic Egyptian architecture, including mazelike corridors with ramps connecting different stories. The paintings and sculptures decorating monumental buildings were largely Egyptian in style, yet somewhat different in content. For example, in the Temple at Naqa, Queen Amanitere is depicted wearing a Nubian-style wrapped skirt and brandishing a sword over her head in a very un-Egyptian manner. Ruling queens of Nubia apparently exercised more power than most female Egyptian pharaohs and were not required to wear false beards, as were their counterparts in Egypt. Despite such differences, it is clear that elite culture was heavily influenced by Egypt.

[9] **Apedemak:** ah PEH deh mak

Why did the elite of these early Nubian civilizations take on so many Egyptian characteristics? There probably were many reasons. Part of the answer lies in the political legitimation to be gained by adopting divine kingship on the Egyptian model, especially given the cultural and political links between Nubia and Egypt before 1000 B.C. Another part lies in the Kush rule of Egypt under Shebaka, a period when those links were strengthened greatly. But much of the answer probably lies in the trade relationship between Egypt and Nubia. Large-scale trade between Egypt and Nubia began with Kerma, and, at this time, Nubia was Egypt's untutored country cousin. Settlements in Kerma were smaller, governments were less powerful, the gap between the elite and the commoners was narrower, and the trappings of wealth and power were less grand. It is little wonder that the emerging elite of Kerma looked to a neighbor for a model of how a sophisticated elite should conduct itself. (This pattern has repeated itself in many times and places around the world, as one society emulates another that it believes to be more worldly or sophisticated; a good example is the emulation of French manners and cooking by eighteenth-century North Americans.) It probably is this self-conscious creation of an elite culture in early Nubian civilization that made Egypt's stamp so prominent.

FIGURE 9.6 *Queen Amanitere of Kush.* *This low-relief sculpture from the Lion Temple in the city of Naqa depicts Queen Amanitere of Kush as a warrior queen, carrying swords and flanked by a fierce lion. The style of depiction draws heavily on Egyptian art, with its profile view, conventions of facial depiction (especially the shape of the eyes), the queen's jewelry (including a snake ornament on her forehead), and the Egyptian hieroglyphics above her right forearm. Her attire and martial attitude, however, are distinctly Kushite.* From Graham Connah, *African Civilizations*, p. 44, fig. 9.6. Reproduced by permission of Cambridge University Press.

EARLY CIVILIZATION IN ETHIOPIA: AXUM, AROUND A.D. 50–650

To the east of Nubia lies the region of Ethiopia consisting of the modern countries of Ethiopia and Eritrea. Beginning around A.D. 50, the kingdom of Axum[10] was the first civilization of Ethiopia.

The region of Ethiopia is dominated by its highlands. Rising thousands of feet above the near-equatorial desert, the highlands provide rich environments with adequate rain and pleasant temperatures. To the northeast, they slant rapidly down to the Red Sea. Soils in many parts of Ethiopia are rich, but there is limited mineral wealth. This environment molded the Axum kingdom.

Information about Axum comes from a wide variety of sources. The Axumites developed a written language, **Ge'ez**,[11] that can be read by modern scholars, and they also wrote in Greek and in a form of Arabic. Although paper documents from Ethiopia are not known until the thirteenth century, earlier coins and stone buildings yield many valuable inscriptions written by Axumites. Also, foreign writers discussed Axum at length. Finally, archaeologists have excavated at several of the major sites.

The Pre-Axumite Period, around 500–around 100 B.C.

Long before the rise of the Axum kingdom, Ethiopians had become sophisticated agriculturalists, adopting crops domesticated elsewhere and domesticating some of their own, including coffee, *tef* (a milletlike grain), okra, and perhaps one kind of eggplant. From this base the Ethiopian population grew, protected from outside attack by mountain barriers.

The Pre-Axumite Period developed around 500 B.C., but there is little solid information about how it came into being. The use of southern Arabian writing is an indication that ties to southern Arabia were strong. Some scholars believe that South Arabians crossed the Red Sea and ascended the highlands, thus spurring the development of

[10]**Axum:** AKS oom
[11]**Ge'ez:** ghee ehz

UNDER THE LENS

The Afrocentric Interpretation

Beginning in the 1970s, some scholars have argued for an **Afrocentric** interpretation of history, wherein Africa is seen as the primary location of important innovations that subsequently spread, coalesced into Western civilization, and were adopted around the world. This interpretation challenges the more widely held view that Western civilization developed primarily through southwestern Asian and European inputs, with contributions from Africa, eastern Asia, the Americas, and elsewhere.

Some Afrocentric ideas are nearly universally rejected among scholars. These include claims that steel and birth control were invented in Africa and spread to the rest of the world, that Africans discovered the Americas, and that Ludwig von Beethoven was an African. Our concern in this box is not with unlikely suggestions such as these, which we see as obscuring the argument of Afrocentrism.

A far stronger argument for Afrocentric interpretation is presented by Martin Bernal. In his *Black Athena*, he developed a complicated argument that derives Greek civilization—and ultimately Western civilization—from black Africa. Reduced to its basics, his argument is that Egypt was "essentially African," relating more to sub-Saharan African cultures than to its neighbors in the Mediterranean and southwestern Asia; further, he argues that Egypt colonized Greece, taking it from its barbaric past into civilization and founding Western civilization, which later would spread around the world. Hence, Africa was the seat of the development of world civilization. He calls this model of development the "Revised Ancient Model," emphasizing his claim that it was accepted by the ancients; the alternative explanation, seeing ancient Greece as a melting pot of eastern Mediterranean and local influences, is called the "Aryan model," emphasizing its purported racist overtones.

Why have traditional scholars come to such radically different interpretations from Bernal and the other Afrocentrists? According to many Afrocentrists, it is because the traditional scholars either are racists or are captive to racist ideas that they learned in traditional history. The critics of Afrocentrism suggest that the reason lies in the weaknesses of the Afrocentric argument.

Many of the facts accepted by Afrocentrists are in question. Bernal, for example, states that he has determined 20 to 25 percent of all Greek words to be of Egyptian origin; linguists see almost no Egyptian origins in Greek, which is of the Indo-European family, not the Hamitic family of Egyptian. Bernal also argues that Greek art resembles Egyptian art; art historians see few such similarities.

Although these facts may or may not be in error, a deeper criticism of Afrocentrism is that it searches for *the* place from which Western civilization spread. The authors of this text argue that Western civilization was woven out of diverse threads from many places, including Africa, Asia, and Europe, and that no single homeland can be found. Because of this, we reject Afrocentrism, Eurocentrism, or any other "centrism" that argues for focusing undue attention on the contributions of one people and (by implication) paying less attention to the contributions of the rest of the world.

---

the Pre-Axumite kingdom; others argue that the link to southern Arabia was based on trade and stimulated a local development. In the southern Arabian writing the Pre-Axumites used, they referred to themselves as the "kingdom of D'MT." (In common with ancient Hebrew, this writing omitted vowels, so the true name might have been something like "D'Meta.")

The Pre-Axumite kingdom was urban, with a major city at Yeha.[12] There, archaeologists have found a temple to Almouqah[13] (the local moon god), elite tombs, and a stepped pyramid of unknown function. All of these were made of masonry and, though by no means so massive as the later Axumite architecture, qualify as monumental. The people used iron and bronze and may have obtained the bronze through trade. The Pre-Axumites of Yeha may have had a state, although many scholars believe the "kingdom of D'MT" was really a sophisticated chiefdom. Pre-Axumite soci-

[12] **Yeha:** YAY hah

[13] **Almouqah:** ahl MOO kah

FIGURE 9.7 *Early Axumite Writing. This stone altar from the first century A.D. shows a man on a camel, identified by the writing beneath as Ha'anum, son of Du-zu'd. The inscription is written in the Ge'ez script and bears similarities to writing from South Arabia.* British Museum/Michael Holford.

ety, in many ways, was analogous to Kerma in Nubia, because each had many of the primary elements of civilization but probably did not have state-level government. Each also paved the way for the emergence of the civilization that followed.

Around 100 B.C., the Pre-Axumite kingdom disappeared under unknown circumstances. Shortly thereafter it was replaced by a more extensive, powerful, and important polity: Axum.

The Rise of Axum

After the fall of the Pre-Axumite kingdom, Ethiopia was ruled by a multitude of small, local chiefdoms. Around A.D. 50, several of these welded together under the **nagashi**, an individual who led several clans. This group was the core of the Axum state,

and the *nagashi* became the king. From this beginning, the Axum kingdom expanded to become the Axum Empire, absorbing (sometimes forcibly) smaller polities at the fringes of its realm. These groups often maintained their distinct ethnic status, although, as the Axum state expanded, those near the center were likely to become assimilated into generalized Axumite culture.

Throughout its span, the Axum Empire was primarily agricultural, in that the majority of its people lived in villages and towns, farming or raising livestock for a living. The variety of altitudes in the highlands provided many microclimates, so a great variety of crops could be grown within walking distance of most communities. The only major limitation to agriculture was scarcity of water in some places, and terracing and irrigation solved that. Although there are records of occasional famines, the Axum Empire seems to have suffered hunger less frequently than most of its neighbors.

The Axum Empire was built on a strong agricultural base, but long-distance trade was what made it an important civilization. Land trade through the rugged highlands of Ethiopia was difficult and costly, though it was carried on to some extent. The Red Sea coast of Ethiopia (now Eritrea), which provided an economical link to major sea routes, was much more widely used. By A.D. 65, the Axum Empire had extended its domain to include portions of the coast, notably the city of Adulis. Adulis had been developed by the Ptolemaic Egyptians, but the Axum Empire expanded the harbor and improved its facilities in the last years of the first century A.D. With its sheltered harbor at Gabaza and its fine facilities, Adulis was an excellent place for vessels to stop; equally important, it lay along the Red Sea route that connected Egypt and the Mediterranean with Arabia, Persia, and India. From this point onward, Axum's fate was tied to foreign trade.

There was something of a power void in Red Sea trading following the fall of Egypt to the Roman Empire in 31 B.C., and Axum was one of the states that took advantage of the situation. Its excellent harbor, government-supported trade, and keen interest in trading made it a strong competitor in the field, and the profits from this trade are what permitted the Axum Empire to develop.

The city of Axum apparently was the first capital of the Axum state. Like Yeha before it, the city of Axum had been a religious center before it became a major political center. A divine king

FIGURE 9.8   *Ethiopian Meal.*   *There are few known pictures of everyday Axumite life, and none that show people eating. It is clear, however, that many modern Ethiopian eating habits developed in the Axum Empire. This eighteenth-century Ethiopian illustration depicts table manners that probably extend unbroken from Axum to contemporary Ethiopia. At the right, a woman is shown making* injera, *a spongy and flexible bread, from a millet-flour batter. In the center, men use the* injera *to grasp bits of a stewlike dish from their bowls, eating wrapper and stew together.*   British Library Orient 723/Courtesy of the Harvard University Library.

serves in both the religious and political worlds, and a religious center brings an aura of authority that makes it an appropriate secular capital.

Axum as a Functioning State

The Axum state was ruled from at least the second century A.D. by an absolute monarch called "the king of kings." This was more than merely a colorful title, because the administration of provinces was delegated to local kings who owed allegiance and tribute to the king of kings in the city of Axum. Axum was an empire.

In pre-Christian times, the king was considered divine: the son of Mahrem, the god of war. After the fourth-century official conversion of the Axum Empire to Christianity, the king's legendary parentage was shifted to King Solomon and Queen Balkis of Sheba (modern Yemen in southern Arabia). Within the Christian setting, this was as close to divinity as possible, and it underscored Axum's special relationship to southern Arabia, discussed in the following paragraphs. King lists exist for the Axum Empire, though they have gaps.

Beneath Axum's emperor and other members of the royal house were at least two classes. By 300 or so, a middle class had developed, consisting of artisans, government officers, and skilled workers. Below them were commoners—mostly rural peasants and urban laborers. There also apparently were slaves, though we know little of the details of their status.

Although there were many cities in the state of Axum, the city of Axum was the largest and probably the most complex. Like almost all Axumite cities, it had no fortifications surrounding it, but it had a unique feature: a central precinct devoted to the royal family and their retainers. In this area were the palace, governmental administration buildings, military garrisons, and a religious center. Outside of town, two **stela parks**, elite cemeteries with tall stones as markers, housed royal tombs. Surrounding the central precinct were industrial areas and houses. The population of the city of Axum at its height is estimated at between 10,000 and 20,000 people.

Trade ranged far and wide, by both land routes and sea routes. The Axum Empire is known to have had extensive trading relations with Rome and its eastern provinces (including Egypt), southern Arabia, India, and Sri Lanka. Trade was highly regulated to benefit the royal house. There were royal taxes on imports into the Axum Empire, as well as on goods that passed through its port on the way to other destinations; these were collected at a posh customs house at Gabaza, the port installation for Adulis. Certain goods were under royal monopoly, and although their nature is unknown, it is almost certain that they were items that returned high profits.

Documented imports into the Axum Empire include iron, other metals, fabrics (including silk), clothing, perfumes, glass, and ceramics. The Axumite elite seasoned their foods with imported spices, cooked it in imported vegetable oils, and washed it down with imported wine; they used sugarcane from Southwest Asia, though it is unknown whether it was used as a food or as a medicine. Documented exports include a variety of materials for jewelry and art, including ivory, gold, obsidian, emeralds, and tortoise shell. Other exports include exotic medicinal items, such as rhinoceros horn and hippopotamus teeth; spices, perfumes, and slaves were other important exports. The Roman Empire was a market for certain popular "African exotica" that were funneled through Axum: monkeys for pets, other live animals for fighting in the arenas, and exotic foods for Roman tables. The Axum Empire had a healthier balance of trade than Kush and Meroë, with a mix of raw materials and finished products among both imports and exports.

The Axum Empire apparently was always alert to an opportunity to expand its trade. According to Procopius, a contemporary Roman writer, ambassadors from the Eastern Roman Empire had little trouble convincing King Kaleb of Axum to attempt wresting the silk trade away from Persia around 520. The Axum Empire's geographical location, however, was at the edge of the silk trade network, putting it at a disadvantage and dooming its attempt to failure.

In return for the rewards it reaped for its elite, the Axum Empire guaranteed traders safe passage. This required a significant military, which probably already existed, since the origin of the Axum state may have involved military action, and certainly its maintenance did. Rebellions of subject polities sometimes occurred, particularly during the confusion at the succession of a new king, and

coin inscriptions inform us of the zeal with which the military put them down. Military garrisons guarded the city of Axum and other settlements. The general lack of archaeological evidence of warfare throughout the Axum Empire is impressive, and walled settlements were rare, suggesting that the capable Axumite army served as a successful deterrent to internal warfare. The importance of the military, particularly in the establishment of the Axum state, probably was symbolized by the descent of the pre-Christian king from the god of war.

Although Axum and Meroë were rivals, the Axum Empire's military might probably was not directly responsible for the fall of Meroë in Nubia. In an inscription dating to around 340, King Ezana[14] of Axum claimed that he had conquered lands to the west along the Nile, and some historians have interpreted this statement as referring to Meroë. The date may be a little early but is approximately appropriate. The problem with this interpretation is that there is little or no evidence for it in Meroë. Ethiopian goods appear with no greater frequency there after this date (they actually drop off somewhat), and there are no evidences of conquering invaders. There are at least five major branches of the Nile to the west of Ethiopia, and Ezana's claim, if true, probably refers to the conquest of some local polity along one of those branches.

Military action in southern Arabia is less ambiguous. Axumite troops occupied Sheba in the sixth century. In 570 they made an unsuccessful attack on Mecca in Arabia. This was the year of Muhammad's birth, and the failure of a Christian army to take the holy city would later take on great symbolic significance in the Islamic world.

The conversion of the Axum Empire to Christianity began around 330. At this date, Frumentius (an Axumite leader known by this Latinized name) was ordained first bishop of Axum, and King Ezana's well-orchestrated conversion followed shortly thereafter. A public baptism, initiating Ezana into Christianity, was advertised in advance and attended by throngs. The conversion of the elite was rapid, and pre-Christian state and royal symbols were replaced. Coins formerly had a disk and crescent on them, representing the sun god and moon god; these motifs were replaced with a cross. The pre-Christian royalty were buried in

[14] **Ezana:** eh ZAHN uh

IN THEIR OWN WORDS

Ezana's Account of His Nubian Victories

This account, written by Emperor Ezana of Axum around 340, describes his victories beyond the western edge of his empire. Clearly, this was in the Nile region, but was it Meroë? Some scholars consider the Seda River of this document to be the White Nile branch of the Nile and the Takkaze River to be the Atbara River, in which case the conquests would be in Meroë; others, however, suggest that the Seda may be the Blue Nile branch, in which case these conquests probably were to the east of the kingdom of Meroë.

Through the might of the Lord of All[a] I took the field against the Noba,[b] when the people of Noba revolted, when they boasted, and the Noba said, "He will not cross over the Takkaze," when they did violence to the peoples Mangurto and Hasa and Barya,[c] and the Blacks[d] waged war on the Red[e] Peoples and a second and a third time broke their oath and without consideration slew their neighbors and plundered our envoys and our messengers whom I had sent to interrogate them, robbing them of their possessions and seizing their lances. When I sent again and they did not hear me and reviled me and made off, I took the field against them. And I armed

[a] **Lord of All:** the Christian God
[b] **Noba:** Nubians
[c] **Barya:** tribal peoples within the Axum Empire
[d] **Blacks:** dark-skinned people
[e] **Red:** light-skinned

myself with the power of the Lord of the Land and fought on the Takkaze at the ford of Kemalke. And thereupon they fled and stood not still, and I pursued the fugitives twenty-three days, slaying some of them and capturing others and taking booty from them, where I came, while prisoners and booty were brought back by my people who marched out, while I burnt their towns, those of masonry and those of straw, and seized their grain and their bronze and their dried meat and the images in their temples and destroyed the stocks of grain and cotton, and the enemy plunged into the river Seda, and there were many who perished in the water, the number I know not, and as their vessels foundered, a multitude of people, men and women, were drowned. . . . And I arrived at the Kasu,[f] slaying some and taking others prisoner at the junction of the rivers Seda and Takkaze. And on the day after my arrival, I dispatched into the field the troops of Mahaza and the Dawawa and Falha and Sera[g] up the Seda against the towns of masonry and straw. . . . My people returned safe and sound after they had taken some prisoners and slain others and had seized their booty through the power of the Lord of Heaven. And I erected a throne at the junction of the rivers Seda and Takkaze, opposite the town of masonry which is on the peninsula.

[f] **Kasu:** a Nubian people
[g] **Sera:** more tribal peoples within the Axum Empire

---

subterranean tombs with tall stone stelae over them in special cemeteries in the city of Axum; Christian royalty were placed in above-ground tombs on a hill outside the city. The legendary ancestry of the king, already discussed, shifted from pre-Christian gods to biblical figures.

The rapid conversion of Axumite leadership, many historians believe, was prompted by political and economic reasons. As will be discussed later, the Axum Empire had strong ties with the Roman Empire, which had recently become a Christian empire. Axumite leaders well may have felt that sharing religion would assist the formation of alliances with Roman traders. Whatever the motivation, Axum was one of the earliest states to adopt Christianity.

As was usual in many places that adopted Christianity in this era, conversion of commoners, especially in the more rural provinces, went more slowly. Despite royal encouragement, conversion went so slowly that the king found it necessary to sponsor activities by Syrian Christian missionaries in rural Axum as late as the early fifth century.

Axumite Christianity was **monophysite**. That is, it held that Jesus Christ had a single, unitary nature, not the dual natures of man and god that mainstream Christianity claimed. Monophysite churches were common in this period, centered on the eastern Mediterranean and northeastern Africa. A council of Christian bishops declared this view heretical in 451, creating a rift between Ethiopian and mainstream Christianity.

FIGURE 9.9 *Pre-Christian and Christian Axumite Coins.* *These coins are from the fourth-century reign of King Ezana; both bear his image. The pre-Christian coin (left) is from the early part of his reign and displays the disk and crescent that symbolize the sun god and the moon goddess respectively. The coin on the right was minted after Ezana's conversion to Christianity and replaces the earlier symbols with the Christian cross. Ezana's religious conversion was a major event in the history of the Axum Empire, and it was commemorated in literature, songs, and art.* Left: Courtesy of the Trustees of the British Museum. *Right:* Courtesy of the Institute of Addis Ababa, Ethiopia.

Axum as a Civilization

Axum possessed all the core elements of civilization. Its agricultural base supported a state government that developed into an empire; long-distance trade financed the government and the elite of the class structure. Occupational specialists produced items to fuel trade and provided services for other specialists. The city of Axum dominated an urban hierarchy that extended throughout the Axum Empire.

In addition, most of the secondary elements of civilization, many of which have been touched upon in the preceding pages, also were present in Axum. These include metallurgy, a state religion, a well-developed transportation system, and writing. Monumental architecture and coinage warrant a bit more discussion here.

Axumites designed and erected many works of monumental architecture. Reflecting cosmopolitan influences in the Axum Empire, designers gave some buildings Greek or Arabian elements, while others have such distinctively Axumite elements as wall recesses and low-relief geometric designs carved into stone faces. The Axum Empire primarily derived its great art style, symbols, and trappings for the elite from within, borrowing only occasional elements from neighboring countries.

Perhaps most unusual of the Axumite monuments are the immense stelae that mark royal tombs in the stela parks. Some of these are the largest single-piece sculptures ever made. They are tall, slender stones, carved to imitate windows and doors and conventionally described by the number of "stories" the carving makes them appear to have. The tallest known is 13 stories, measuring more than 108 feet high yet only about 9 feet wide. The stone for these stelae was quarried locally, reducing the hazards of long-distance transport of such long and narrow pieces of stone. Nonetheless, the engineering skills and organization needed to transport, work, and raise these enormous and unwieldy stelae were considerable.

FIGURE 9.10 *Stela from Axum.* *The death of a member of the Axumite royalty was an event of great importance, and the deceased was interred in a special royal cemetery that included many stelae. These stelae were tall and narrow, with carved surfaces that resembled the doors and windows of a house. Carved from a single stone, the stela shown rises seventy feet and is carved to depict ten "floors." Dating to about A.D. 600, this stela is the only one that is still upright.* Werner Forman/Art Resource, N.Y.

Axumite coins have been mentioned as sources for inscriptions, but their place in Axumite civilization is important, too. Axum was the first African state other than Egypt to mint coins, doing so from about 270 onward. Presumably the Axum Empire's mercantile orientation made coinage an important item, and Axumite metallurgical skills made it practical. Axumite emperors took the opportunity to place political slogans and symbols on coins, fortifying their position. Axumite coins were used regularly in southern Arabia, Syria, Meroë, and the Roman Empire.

Unlike Kush and Meroë, Axum was a vibrant part of the Greco-Roman world. Far from a provincial backwater, it took a significant role in political relationships between major countries. Indeed, in the late third century, Mani, the noted Persian historian and theologian, placed Axum in powerful company as one of the four great empires of the world, along with Rome, Persia, and China.

The Decline of Axum, around A.D. 600–650

From the beginning it was clear that the Axum Empire would rise or fall with its trade. In good times the Axumites had profited from their membership in a commercial network that linked countries on three continents, but they were trapped in that network when new networks developed, excluding the Axum Empire.

Between around 600 and 650, the Axum Empire went into a rapid decline from which it never recovered. Imports dwindled, the port languished, and royal coffers were depleted. Even the long-time capital city may have shifted. In 630, King Ashama ibn Abjar[15] was buried not in the city of Axum as had been all of his predecessors but at Wuqro,[16] to the southeast. This may indicate that the religious glue holding together the Axum Empire was coming undone. Finally, in 650, the Axum state was conquered by Gudit, a woman chief of the Agau tribe, and the old Axumite territory was divided into local rulerships.

During the rise of Axum, the Roman Empire had been politically ascendant. Its powerful military had claimed a huge empire, and its efficient political machinery had administered it. On the eastern side of the Red Sea, the Roman Empire and

the Axum Empire had come to an alliance of sorts, based on common economic interests. Axum exported certain goods to Rome, particularly the so-called African exotica: rare animals, unusual foods, and strange medicines. The effort by ambassadors from the Eastern Roman Empire to channel the silk trade through Axum was merely an attempt to expand an existing trade link.

But Persia and its Arab allies were on the opposite bank of the Red Sea, poised to challenge the Roman-Axumite alliance. In the early seventh century, the Axum Empire sent troops to southern Arabia, probably in an unsuccessful attempt to thwart the efforts of Persian troops there. In the meantime, Persian assaults were weakening the Eastern Roman Empire, and Arabs allied with Persia finished the conquest in 642. At this point, a critical market for Axum's goods closed and military rivals were strengthened. Concurrent with its commercial woes, the environment of Axum was suffering from misuses. Environmental degradation depleted critical resources, creating problems in supplying luxury goods for trade as well as food for local consumption. The upshot was the destruction of Axum's commercial power and the rapid end of the state.

THE COMMERCIAL BASIS FOR THE EARLY CIVILIZATIONS OF NUBIA AND ETHIOPIA

Kush, Meroë, and Axum shared a commercial basis for their prosperity. They were situated in favorable locations along transportation routes, and their agricultural bases were strong enough to support economies focused on trade. To a certain extent, their fortunes were linked. Many scholars believe that the opening of Adulis as an Axumite port hurt Meroë's economic welfare, and some believe that this was an important contributing factor to the breakup of Meroë.

It may have been inevitable that the Axum Empire would dominate the trading competition. Its position gave it access to the sea and areas beyond sub-Saharan Africa, such as Arabia and India. Meroë, on the other hand, was restricted to the sub-Saharan trade that made its way down the Nile. Axum's stronger economy also made it more

[15] **Ashama ibn Abjar:** ah SHAH mah ihb uhn AB jahr
[16] **Wuqro:** WOO kroh

PATHS TO THE PAST

Environmental Degradation at the City of Axum

Smog and acid rain may be recent problems, but the actions of ancient peoples also damaged their environments. A study by the geographer Karl Butzer has examined some of the unanticipated and negative effects that resulted from use of the environment at the city of Axum.

Soils record amazing detail about the environment during their formation, and their careful analysis can reveal details of climate, vegetation, and human land use. Butzer looked at soils around the city of Axum and teased out their story through careful analysis. The chronology of Axum has been revised since his study, and this summary adjusts his dates in light of more recent findings.

At around 100 B.C., a marked climatic change took place in the Ethiopian highlands. The rainy season, formerly three to four months long, nearly doubled to about six months. The total amount of rain falling per year increased considerably, meaning that more water was available in and on the surface of the ground. This resulted in a near doubling of the growing season, so that two crops—rather than one—could be harvested in a normal year. It also meant that most locales could accomplish this result without irrigation. The result of this change was an increase in the food supply, followed by steady population growth.

This climatic pattern persisted for several centuries, during which time the city of Axum reached its peak population. By about 500, however, problems began to set in. Catastrophic erosion began occurring, sometimes denuding entire hillsides to the bedrock. Most of this erosion was in the form of sediments washing gently down a slope, but some of it was in mudslides, occasionally burying parts of the outskirts of the city of Axum.

The erosion was only a symptom of the greater problem: overuse of the land. Even at only 14 degrees above the equator, the city of Axum's elevation of about 6,700 feet above sea level kept the climate cool, and firewood must have been a critical commodity. Add to this the need for wood to build houses and to cook food, and the city's 10,000 or more inhabitants must have used a good deal of wood. In so doing, they cut too many trees from their forests, opening up soils to erosion.

The consequences were several. First, of course, wood had to be cut at increasing distances from the city of Axum, increasing the cost of procuring it. Also, forest-dwelling animals were driven farther away. The cost to the ecosystem undoubtedly was much broader, but two species were very important to the Axumites. The civet cat, a forest-dwelling carnivore, has strong scent glands that produce **civet**, a musky substance used in perfumes. This was one of Axum's exports, but it would have been increasingly difficult to procure after 500. Similarly, elephants would have retreated from these cleared areas, making ivory harder to obtain for export.

Finally, around 600, the climate changed again, decreasing the reliability of rainfall. After this date, total amounts of rainfall diminished, though rain increasingly fell in a few big storms that spawned flooding and erosion. The forest had difficulty reestablishing itself under these conditions, and the decrease in usable farm land meant that people had difficulty producing enough food for themselves.

These problems were not the cause of the Axum Empire's fall, but they were significant problems that the empire would have had to face if it had survived long enough. As it was, the successors to Axum were left with scars that have not yet entirely healed. Human beings are naturally intrusive to environments, building cities and establishing high concentrations of people. Only with the greatest care can they avoid degrading the environment that supports them.

of an equal trading partner with countries to the north, dealing in both raw materials and finished products.

Kush and Meroë were shaped by a complex interplay of local factors and external contact with civilizations that served as models. Although they derived some inspiration from Egypt and southern Arabia, they were not mere copies of those civilizations. No amount of instruction about urbanism, for example, will induce a society to live in cities unless it has the population levels, economic development, and political organization to permit it.

NUBIA	ETHIOPIA		
		2000 B.C.	
		–	
Egyptian colonies, c. 1900–1700 B.C.		–	
Kerma, c. 1800–1600 B.C.		–	
		–	
Egyptian colonies, c. 1600–1100 B.C.		**1500 B.C.**	
		–	
		–	
		–	
		–	
		1000 B.C.	
		–	
		–	Shebaka installed as Kushite pharaoh of Egypt, 712 B.C.
Kush, c. 800–400 B.C.		–	Kushites ejected from Egypt by Assyrians, 667 B.C.
		–	
		500 B.C.	
	Pre-Axumite Period, c. 500–100 B.C.	–	
Meroë, c. 400 B.C.–A.D. 400		–	
		–	
		–	Adoption of domesticated camel, c. 100 B.C.
		A.D. 1	
	Axum, A.D. 50–650	–	Axum expands to coast, 65 *Saqia* invented, c. 100
Rapid settlement of northern Nubia, A.D. 100–300		–	
		–	Axum begins minting coins, 270
		–	Ezana converts to Christianity, 331
	Conversion to Christianity, A.D. 330–450	–	Ezana conquers lands to west, 340
		A.D. 500	
		–	Unsuccessful Axumite attack on Mecca, 570
		–	Conquest and dissolution of Axum, 650
		–	

SUMMARY

1. Trade between Egypt and sub-Saharan Africa encouraged the development of the Kush and Meroë kingdoms in Nubia. They were preceded by the Kerma culture, which may have been a sophisticated chiefdom and apparently was not a civilization. Kush and Meroë meet the criteria for civilization.

2. Around 800 B.C., about three centuries after Egyptian withdrawal from its Nubian colony, the Kush kingdom developed; Meroë developed out of Kush. Trade intensified throughout the span of Kush and Meroë.

3. Kush and Meroë were states with divine kings who traced their ancestry to the Egyptian gods. Many of the elite symbols of these kingdoms were adopted from the Egyptians whose colonies had ruled much of the area for nearly 800 years and who formed their most important trading partners. In addition, Kush's conquest and half-century rule of Egypt cemented the Egypt-Nubia ties.

4. The Meroë kingdom disintegrated, perhaps under military pressure from camel-mounted desert raiders or from Axum. It was replaced by local chiefdoms. The rise of Axum may have sped the fall of Meroë—either directly, through military action or, more likely, through superior geographical position and the luring away of trade.

5. The Pre-Axumite kingdom probably was an urban chiefdom, though little is known about it.

6. The Axum kingdom developed in Ethiopia, also under the stimulus of trade; it rapidly developed into the Axum Empire. The Axum Empire focused its commercial attentions on the Red Sea trade and had a strong partner in the Roman Empire.

7. The Axum Empire was ruled by a divine monarch, an emperor who delegated power to subordinate local kings, who in turn rendered him tribute. Regulations ensured that the divine monarch would profit greatly by trade.

8. The Axum state had a strong military that ensured domestic peace and safety to traders and conquered new areas to become part of the Axum Empire.

9. The Axum Empire officially became a Christian state around 330. The elite converted rapidly, though rural peasants took much longer. Conversion probably aided the Axum Empire's economic alliance with the Roman Empire.

10. Axum was a society meeting the criteria for civilization. It was a major power and exerted considerable influence in politics beyond its borders.

11. The Axum Empire declined and disintegrated as changes in political relationships between countries destroyed its commercial basis. The alliance between Persia and some Arab groups was successful at overcoming the Roman-Axumite alliance. Supply problems created by environmental deterioration aggravated Axum's commercial problems.

SUGGESTED READINGS

Adams, William Y. *Nubia: Corridor to Africa.* London: Allen Lane, 1977. (The 1984 reprint has an updated introduction.) Classic treatment of the Kush and Meroë civilizations.

Bernal, Martin. *Black Athena: The Afroasiatic Roots of Classical Civilization.* Two vols. New Brunswick, N.J.: Rutgers University Press, 1987, 1991. Presentation of Bernal's Afrocentric interpretation.

Butzer, Karl. "Rise and Fall of Axum, Ethiopia: A Geo-Archaeological Interpretation." *American Antiquity* 46(3) (1981):471–95. Technical treatment of Axum's historic environmental degradation.

Connah, Graham. *African Civilizations: Precolonial Cities and States in Tropical Africa: An Archaeological Perspective.* Cambridge, Eng.: Cambridge University Press, 1987. A good general treatment of African civilizations other than Egypt.

Munro-Hay, S. C. *Aksum: An African Civilisation of Late Antiquity.* Edinburgh: University of Edinburgh Press, 1991. A popular account of Axum and the author's excavations there.

Trigger, Bruce. *Nubia Under the Pharaohs.* London: Thames and Hudson, 1976. General treatment of Egyptian colonies in Nubia and their possible successors.

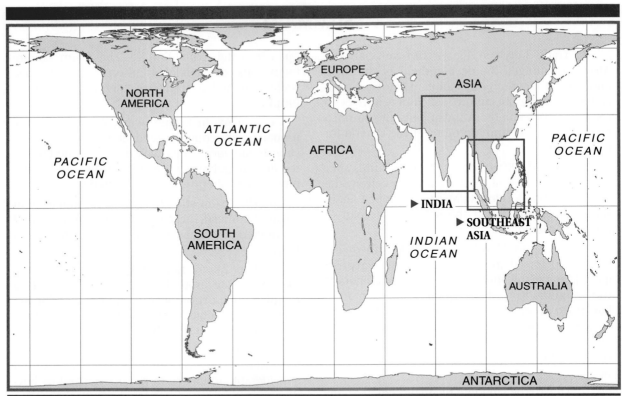

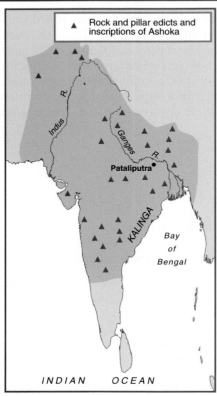

Rock and pillar edicts and inscriptions of Ashoka

Indus R.

Ganges R.

Pataliputra

KALINGA

Bay of Bengal

INDIAN OCEAN

▶ INDIA

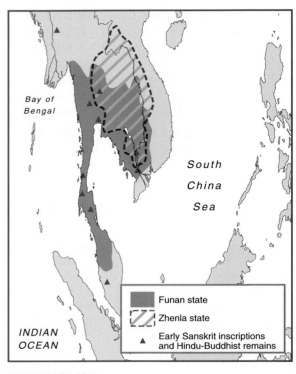

Bay of Bengal

South China Sea

INDIAN OCEAN

Funan state

Zhenla state

Early Sanskrit inscriptions and Hindu-Buddhist remains

▶ SOUTHEAST ASIA

Indian Empires, Society, Ideology, and Regional Influence

around 500 B.C.–around A.D. 600

The Indian emperor had wielded enormous power for years. His stooped shoulders testified to the heavy burden he had borne, and he wished to retire to a life of ascetic discipline far away from the burdensome world. His son could rule effectively, expanding the vast realm already conquered. Yes, it was time. The Jain priest smiled and offered the white robe, and the two men set off to join their fellows on a journey to the south.

This Jain story recounts the fate of Chandragupta, a mighty Indian emperor who abandoned his throne for spiritual treasures. In this chapter, we will examine the interplay of politics, society, ideology, and international influence in the early imperial age.

In this era, Indians fashioned two major empires, the Maurya and the Gupta, that united significant regions of the subcontinent. Each used religion to govern culturally diverse subjects. Buddhism spread throughout Central, East, and Southeast Asia, while many Southeast Asians adopted aspects of Hindu culture.

At the same time, Indian society grew more complex, and a caste system developed that was largely based on occupation and strictly regulated group interaction. Indian rulers regarded agriculture as an essential part of the economy and also encouraged trade. Both were important revenue sources for Indian governments.

THE MAURYA EMPIRE, AROUND 320–AROUND 180 B.C.

Over the centuries after 1000 B.C., small states began to appear in the Ganges River Valley. By the sixth and fifth centuries B.C., regional kingdoms with complex bureaucracies appeared and lasted for decades. In the late fourth century B.C., the first empire emerged, united the Ganges region, and used it as a base from which to expand westward and southward. At its height, the Maurya[1] Empire united and ruled much of the Indian subcontinent.

Origins and Early Empire

Significant economic and social developments underlay the founding of the Maurya Empire. The introduction and spread of iron axes and plows in the Ganges River Valley during the first half-millennium B.C. helped develop an agricultural economy. By the sixth century B.C., agricultural villages became key sources of tax revenue for states. Over time, villages also became socially stratified, and artisans began producing wares for urban markets. As cities grew, artisans and merchants organized themselves into guilds that managed trade and other matters. By the fifth century B.C., coinage, letters of credit, and promissory notes reflected widespread economic activity and stimulated further growth.

The founder of the Maurya Empire, Chandragupta Maurya (reign dates around 320–around 301 B.C.), came from an elite family of the warrior caste. He founded a dynasty that ruled for nearly 150 years. Specifically, Chandragupta ruled for decades after usurping power from an earlier monarch, and that state in the central Ganges region provided a base for conquering the entire river valley and expanding west to the Indus region. A key aim of these policies was to gain control over important trade routes. Indeed, the prosperity of Maurya rule lay in the lucrative trade taxes.

Bureaucracy had been a feature of earlier political life, and the system Chandragupta inherited was complicated. Most government bureaus dealt with financial matters or control of the people and the lands. Manufacturing enterprises were supervised by a board of officials. Tax collection was a vital state concern, and the tax on agricultural land usually averaged between one-quarter and one-half of the annual harvest. Commercial activities also received the attention of a bureau. A census and statistics bureau kept the state informed about the population and the yields of mines and other government properties. Another board oversaw the upkeep of public lands and facilities. A separate governmental unit handled military affairs. The infantry numbered in the tens of thousands. Thousands more served in the cavalry or worked in the elephant force.

Pataliputra,[2] the imperial capital, possessed a palisade with nearly 600 towers and was several times larger than Rome in the second century A.D. The circumference of the city wall measured 21 miles, and a wide and deep moat further protected the capital.

Security matters became an obsessive concern for the Maurya emperor and went far beyond the physical defense measures of the palisade and moat. A vast network of spies and informers also provided security in the capital and a check on the bureaucracy. These informers included clerics, students, merchants, ordinary subjects, and prostitutes.

The empire was subdivided into districts approximating the earlier tribal and regional boundaries. Significant areas received the close attention of government officials, including trusted military commanders and kin of the monarch. Often, if a region handed over its tax revenues, the central government left it alone.

Though published long after the fall of the Maurya state, the *Treatise on Financial Gain* presents a political philosophy that probably originated in Chandragupta's era. Largely written by Kautilya, one of Chandragupta's most effective officials, it underwent many revisions. Begun around 300 B.C., the *Treatise* opens with a section on the education and training of a monarch, who was to be ever watchful and trust no one. The ruler had to be attentive to messengers and listen to the advice of his officials, who represented the will of his subjects. Finally, the emperor was warned to control his desires, like greed and lust, because these "enemies" could lead to trouble.

---

[1] **Maurya:** MOH ree ah

[2] **Pataliputra:** pah TAH lee put rah

One section urged that officials be carefully selected and supervised. Only trusted and capable people should be given the top positions. Because humans are subject to changeable moods and bad habits, they must be closely and continually monitored. The emperor should also see that his officials do not form cliques, because they would form alternate power centers.

The *Treatise* stressed the protection of the monarch's subjects. The monarch had to control crime by implementing and maintaining an effective police force. Furthermore, he had to see that the legal codes either deterred criminals or punished them; thus, crime prevention rested with the ruler, who enforced the laws through harsh penalties.

Some of our information about the government and society of Mauryan times comes from the diary of a Greek ambassador, Megasthenes. It indicated the hierarchical nature of Indian society. The royal family members formed the top social group, with the *brahman* priests beneath them in the social scale. Farmers came next, then herders and soldiers.

Chandragupta ruled ably; he established the empire and left a stable system for his successor. The tradition recounted at the start of this chapter has Chandragupta abandoning his throne and dying in the south. Little is known about Bindusara[3] (reign dates around 301–around 273 B.C.), the second emperor, who expanded the empire's borders southward. Bindusara left the throne to one of his elder sons, who did not reign for long.

The Age of Ashoka

The youngest of Bindusara's sons, Ashoka[4] (reign dates around 269–around 232 B.C.), was not heir to the throne. He revolted against his ruling brother, causing a civil war that killed many, including all but one of Ashoka's brothers. After coming to power, Ashoka started a war with Kalinga, a southeastern state, for control of its land and sea trade routes. The carnage from the campaign brought much death, injury, and imprisonment. Remorseful, Ashoka attempted to rule more humanely, employing Buddhist ideas.

[3]**Bindusara:** bihn doo SAH rah
[4]**Ashoka:** ah SHOH kah

FIGURE 10.1 *Carved Pillar from Ashoka's Era. Ashoka had carved pillars like this one placed around his empire. They contained accounts of his reign and gave his subjects commands regarding proper behavior. Today, they are important primary sources of information about the Maurya Empire.* Archaeological Survey of India. Courtesy of the India Office Library, London.

Ashoka is a significant figure in Indian history, because he established a Buddhist-inspired humanistic philosophy to guide his government and his subjects. He changed his grandfather's harsh ideology of conquest to one more appropriate to ruling humanely. Ashoka modified the traditional concept of **dharma**—the cosmic law of truth and proper conduct. He emphasized the ethical content of *dharma*, turning it into an idea of morally guided living. Because Ashoka ruled a vast empire of culturally diverse subjects and believed that they must be united in service to the state and one another, he also promoted *dharma* as a policy of social responsibility. People were exhorted to be truthful, compassionate, and morally upright. The village leader collected taxes, and the household head properly ordered the family. All were to help others, especially the less fortunate.

Ashoka created a cohort of trusted officials (Dharma Officers) who traveled the empire investigating the conduct of local officials. These officials had the authority to rectify injustices and punish errant bureaucrats. This effort extended the monarch's hand into his realm and gave people a sense that the state could correct its own mistakes. Of course, it also reflected Ashoka's centralized control of his empire. In another effort to humanize his rule, Ashoka ordered a general revision of the legal code to weed out poorly conceived, unjust, and harsh laws. Attention was given to prisoners to see that they were not treated too harshly. Laborers and slaves received special consideration from Ashoka, who protected their interests. Behind these efforts lay the conviction that taking care of the social welfare of all people brought social stability.

Ashoka established an extensive public works system. There were public treatment centers for the sick and establishments for the care of animals. Medicines were free. Travelers rested in the shade

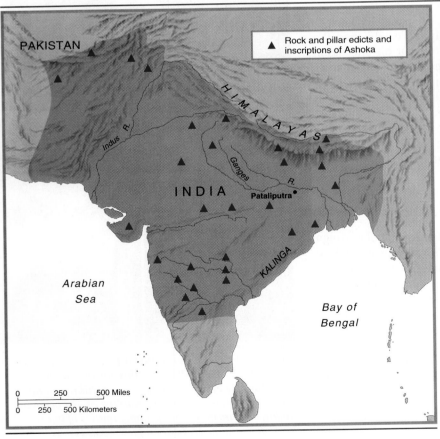

MAP 10.1 *India in 240* B.C. *This map shows the vast empire ruled by Ashoka near the end of his reign. The territory includes much of present-day India, Bangladesh, and Pakistan. Only in the eighteenth century would India again be so united. Ashoka's rock edicts are found all over his empire.*

IN THEIR OWN WORDS

A Carved-Rock Edict of Ashoka

Soon after Ashoka came to power, he ordered the carving of stones to provide permanent messages to his subjects, including his own descendants. A major theme within these stelae relates to *dharma*, the concept modified by Ashoka to mean correct behavior and helpfulness to others. The edict here also notes Indian relations to other states along and beyond its borders.

When he had been consecrated eight years, the Beloved of the Gods . . . [Ashoka] conquered Kalinga. A hundred and fifty thousand people were deported, a hundred thousand were killed, and many times that number perished. Afterwards . . . the Beloved of the Gods very earnestly practiced *dharma*, desired *dharma*, and taught *dharma*. On conquering Kalinga, the Beloved of the Gods felt remorse, for when an independent country is conquered, the slaughter, death, and deportation of the people is extremely grievous. . . . What is even more deplorable to the Beloved of the Gods, is that those who dwell there whether . . . householders who show obedience to their superiors, obedience to mother and father, obedience to their teachers and behave well and devotedly toward their friends, acquaintances, colleagues, relatives, slaves, servants—all suffer violence, murder, and separations from their loved ones.

The Beloved of the Gods believes that one who does wrong should be forgiven. . . . And the Beloved of the Gods conciliates the forest tribes of his empire, but he warns them that he has power even in his remorse, and he asks them to repent, lest they be killed. . . .

The Beloved of the Gods considers victory by *dharma* to be the foremost victory. And . . . [he] has gained this victory on all his frontiers . . . where reigns the Greek king named Antiochus, and beyond the realm of that Antiochus in the lands of the four kings named Ptolemy, Antigonus, Magas, and Alexander; and in the south over the Cholas and Pandyas as far as Sri Lanka. . . .

What is obtained by this is victory everywhere, and everywhere victory is pleasant. This pleasure has been obtained through victory by *dharma*, yet it is but a slight pleasure, for the Beloved of the Gods only looks upon that as important in its results which pertains to the next world.

This inscription of *dharma* has been engraved so that any sons or great grandsons that I may have should not think of gaining new conquests. . . . They should only consider conquest by *dharma* to be a true conquest, and delight in the *dharma* should be their whole delight. . . .

of banyan trees planted by the state along the major roads, and they ate mangos from other state-planted trees. Wells for public use were dug.

Ashoka had come to power as a mature adult who shrewdly created a public relations bureau that interpreted celestial apparitions to enhance his august image. Ashoka had edicts announcing his ruling philosophy carved in rock, some of which survive. (They cover a vast area from Afghanistan to South India.) Ashoka enjoined his subjects to obey their parents and to be truthful and compassionate with others. People were instructed to avoid killing animals; to set an example, the number of meat dishes on the royal dining table was sharply limited. The policy of not killing animals severely curtailed the animal sacrifices

prescribed by the Vedas, thereby reducing the income of the brahmans who relied on these sacrifices for their livelihoods.

Apart from the blossoming of Buddhism through Ashoka's patronage, elite culture flourished. Sculptures decorated the capital's Buddhist temples and shrines. Architecture prospered under a monarch who knew that monumental art powerfully advertised his imperial image.

Around 232 B.C., Ashoka died after decades in power, and rivalries and conflicts erupted among many claimants to the throne. At the same time, distant regions began to assert their independence; like the Roman Empire, the Maurya Empire split into eastern and western parts. The great national expenditures for the government, the army, and the building ventures also declined with the continued warfare. Divisive tendencies overwhelmed the state, and, for the next half-millennium, India fell prey to invaders and to a time of regionalism (around 180 B.C.–A.D. 320), as will be seen in Chapter 14.

THE GUPTA EMPIRE, A.D. 320–550

After this period of disunity, India's next empire, the Gupta, united the two northern river valleys and much of North India, beginning in the fourth century A.D. Gupta monarchs based themselves in the Ganges River Valley because of its significant economic base and association with the heartland of the Maurya Empire. As the Mauryas favored Buddhism, the Guptas supported Hinduism. Because of this royal patronage, Hindu arts, literature, and architecture flourished. In addition, Hindu priests benefited from this support and their own commitment to their religion's growth.

Origins and Early Empire

Agriculture and trade formed the Gupta economic base. The first rulers built irrigation systems, including canals fed by rivers and lakes, to promote and maintain high agricultural yields. Because the Gupta tax on agricultural land was a percentage of annual harvests, increasing the crop yields also expanded state revenues. Farmers who worked on fields irrigated by these waterworks also paid additional taxes. Internal and long-distance trade increased.

Like Chandragupta Maurya, Chandra Gupta I (reign dates 320–335) used a policy of marriage alliances and military conquest to forge an empire of long duration and relative prosperity. Control of land and sea trade routes in the north gave added financial resources to support a large bureaucracy and army. Additionally, the Guptas permitted significant local autonomy as long as taxes were paid. This reduced the financial burden at the imperial level, although the widespread practice of **tax farming**, the selling of tax-collecting authority by the state, led to abuses. Chandra Gupta I's heir, Samudra Gupta, ruled from 335 to 375. During that

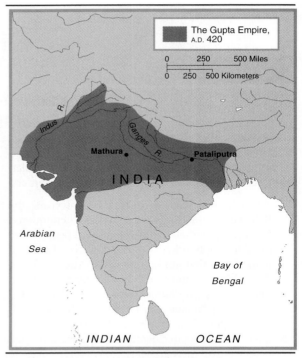

MAP 10.2 *The Gupta Empire in A.D. 420.*
Gupta rule was largely confined to northern India and included the Indus and Ganges river valleys. The area was smaller than that controlled by Ashoka, but it provided great wealth to the Gupta treasury by helping to support artisans and artists who worked for the state.

forty-year span, he brought northern India under the Gupta sway and expanded his empire's borders southward.

The Age of Chandra Gupta II

The forty-year reign (375–415) of Emperor Chandra Gupta II was a time of political stability and artistic growth. Some of our knowledge of the court life and general society of this era comes from the diary of a Chinese traveler, Faxian,[5] who came to India on a six-year Buddhist pilgrimage (405–411).

According to Faxian, Chandra Gupta II's capital was a place of wealth and peaceful policies. Neither capital nor corporal punishment existed there. Faxian also praised the harmonious living of the people, who enjoyed freedom and practiced

[5] **Faxian:** fahs YEHN

religious tolerance. In addition, the state provided hospital care for all.

The state's ability to provide significant social services for the urban populations came not only from taxes on agriculture and commerce but also from other sources. Chandra Gupta II relied on substantial income from royal monopolies on salt and minerals, on gold and silver workshops, and on mills that produced prized textiles.

Artisans and merchants organized into guilds; and apart from economic benefit, these organizations provided significant means of controlling their members. Each had its own regulations, banner, dues, ranking hierarchy, and profit-sharing methods. Guild rules had the force of law for members. Marriage opportunities for artisans, disputes between guild members, work rules, and funeral arrangements occupied guild leadership. Looking after the interests of orphans and widows of members also became a major guild concern. Thus, from the Gupta perspective, guilds controlled significant numbers of people and provided welfare benefits.

During the Gupta era, the imperial court fostered achievements in the arts, especially in literature. Sanskrit became the dominant literary language in northern India and remained so for centuries. Many commentaries were written on ancient Indian classics, like the Vedas, and a major collection of folk tales, *Panchatantra*,[6] depicted talking animals, charming its Indian readers. Audiences in Southwest Asia, Africa, and Europe also delighted in these tales, thus demonstrating the primacy of Indian arts in other countries. Writing poetry was a major preoccupation at the court of Chandra Gupta II, himself a poet and dramatist. Poetic competitions awarded prizes for all kinds of word play, including puns and epigrams.

The most significant literary form of the Gupta era was drama. Many playwrights composed Sanskrit plays, and imperial attitudes fostered a positive image of court life and insisted that tragic endings and themes be omitted. Kalidasa[7] (lived in the fifth century), one of India's great writers at this time, was a court dramatist. His position in Indian literature has been favorably compared with that of England's William Shakespeare. Kalidasa's extant seven plays, all written in Sanskrit, reveal a dramatist of great craft. The play *Shakuntala*[8] shows the writer's skill in creating characters of humane manners or courtliness; these reflected the values of the Gupta court. Kalidasa also eloquently described the beauty of both humans and nature in his plays and poems.

Architecture and sculpture, especially that associated with Hindu and Buddhist temples, flourished. Hindu temples began to be built around the time of the Gupta Empire, partly to counteract the religious influence of Buddhist communities. Each Hindu temple was dedicated to a single deity such as the popular Vishnu or Shiva, who were represented by sculptures with human features as well as by more abstract symbols. Buddhist sculpture reached high levels of realism, and Buddhist temples were decorated with colorful frescoes and intricate, highly detailed wood carvings.

Intellectual life also flourished in universities across northern India. Students came from all over Asia to study in schools like Nalanda University, where Indian astronomers and mathematicians made discoveries that spread across Eurasia. One astronomer posited a round earth that rotated on

FIGURE 10.2 *Gold Coin of the Gupta Empire.*
This coin represents the only known portrait of Emperor Chandra Gupta II. Depicted as an archer, he wears a halo that suggests divine status. This coin is also a fine example of Indian artisanship of the Gupta era.
Los Angeles County Museum of Art, gift of Anna Bing Arnold and Justin Dart.

[6] *Panchatantra:* PAHN chah TAHN trah
[7] **Kalidasa:** KAH lee DAH sah
[8] *Shakuntala:* shah KUN tah lah

FIGURE 10.3 *Relief Carving of Vishnu.* *This colossal sculpture of the Gupta era depicts Vishnu in one of his forms, the boar. He has just rescued the Goddess of the Earth from the Serpent King of the Sea. This is one of the earliest major Hindu relief carvings, and shows many carved devotees of the Hindu deity.* Archaeological Survey of India.

an axis; this individual also solved problems using quadratic equations and negative numbers. Others discovered zero, developed place value ordering of numbers, and calculated the value of pi with accuracy.

Able rulers kept the Guptas in power for another century after Chandra Gupta II's death, but the huge cost of defending the ever-vulnerable northwest frontier depleted the treasury. Although the Gupta Empire collapsed in 550, the development of Hindu arts continued.

INDIAN SOCIETY

The Indian subcontinent is home to diverse social groups, and Indian history has seen a wide range of solutions to the ordering of its peoples. Caste, class, and gender are three significant groupings of Indians in the period under consideration.

Caste in the Imperial Age

Two social classification systems existed in India during the imperial age. One system was the traditional ***varna*** structure of the Aryans (the four-group model discussed in Chapter 5). Another was the ***jati***, a system defined by one's birth and pollution. One aspect of pollution is one's job and another is one's birth. We will treat both as caste systems. A **caste** is a hierarchical system of categories that determine one's status, occupation, rights, and duties. Usually, little mobility among castes occurs, because physical characteristics, such as darkness of skin, were different for each caste. Although some historians use caste in a specific way to mean only the *jati* system, we will apply caste to both the *varna* and *jati* systems.

The *varna* castes achieved a general acceptance among the elite early in the imperial age. The *brahmans, kshatriyas,* and *vaishyas* generally were the Aryans, and the *shudras* were the darker-skinned indigenous peoples. Another group was the outcastes, or pariahs; its members were conceived of as being outside the caste system and beneath the lowest caste member—consequently, they were shunned even by *shudras*. This status stemmed from the outcastes' willingness to work at menial and polluting tasks, such as waste removal. According to this reasoning, the outcastes were unclean and therefore unworthy of incorporation into the *varna* system.

UNDER THE LENS

Nalanda: An Important Indian University

During the Gupta era, a Buddhist university was established in the city of Nalanda. One of many universities in India at that time, Nalanda University boasted at its peak three separate libraries and eight colleges. Several thousand students attended Nalanda at a time, some of whom came from states in other parts of Asia, including Sri Lanka, Indonesia, Korea, and China. Perhaps only 30 percent of those who applied were admitted after taking rigorous entrance examinations. The university was funded by various endowments (some from foreign countries), grants, and the assigned revenues of 200 villages.

Students studied a variety of subjects, including religion, philosophy, logic, and grammar. More than 1,000 teachers lectured to students or led discussions at Nalanda University. Many teachers were Buddhist monks; others were Hindus, indicating the tolerant religious atmosphere of the Gupta era. Nagarjuna, one of the great Buddhist scholars, taught at Nalanda.

At Nalanda and other places, Indian mathematicians built on earlier mathematical work and developed the rudiments of algebra. They worked out a number system of nine digits and zero, all of which we use today and which is mistakenly called the arabic numeral system. Indian mathematicians also calculated the value of pi to nine decimal places, solved quadratic equations, explored trigonometry, and approached the discovery of calculus.

Indian scientists affiliated with Nalanda University proposed an atomic theory of matter, and Indian physicians knew the workings of the nervous system and its relation to the spinal cord. The medical course, which originally took eight years to complete, was reduced to six years. It included both theoretical and practical subjects, including operating on patients to set bones and deliver babies. Indian doctors also treated ailments with a large variety of drugs.

Many Indian discoveries passed to Southwest Asia and Africa through the Muslims, who referred to mathematics as *Hindisat* or the Indian art. Islamic mathematicians regularly employed the Indian system of numeration in their calculations. Muslim astronomers relied on Indian conceptions of the universe in developing Islamic astronomy. In the eighth century, Muslim rulers invited Indian physicians to organize hospitals in Persia, indicating the international prestige accorded Indian medicine.

Nalanda University played a significant role in the development of science and the humanities in India. It inspired the foundation of other centers of higher education, producing some of India's greatest scholars, who perpetuated a tradition of independence of thought and freedom of criticism. Nalanda University was in decline by the thirteenth century, when its libraries and educational facilities perished in the fighting caused by invaders.

FIGURE 10.4 *Ruins of Nalanda University.* *This picture of Nalanda University conveys a sense of its immense size. Nalanda was an international university and monastery with several libraries and colleges. For centuries, Nalanda faculty instructed students from all over Asia in mathematics, medicine, astronomy, and the humanities.* Martin Hürlimann.

The *jati* classification system of castes seems to have developed in the Ganges River Valley and slowly spread across India. Over time, thousands of *jati* (occupational groups similar to guilds) formed. Occupations that involved the taking of life, such as hunting, fishing, and butchering, polluted an individual. Similarly, dealing in the necessary removal of dead bodies brought pollution. Thus, social interaction among *jati* was strictly limited so that less-polluted castes were not contaminated. Marriage, for example, was limited to partners from one's own *jati*. Both the *varna* and *jati* systems became increasingly rigid over time, prohibiting nearly all movement from one caste to another.

Class in the Imperial Age

Imperial society revolved around three groups: an upper class, an intermediary class, and a lower class. The top class included the royal family members and their kin, plus various courtiers, high officials, and their families. The intermediary class contained middle and lower officials, as well as merchants and financiers. At the bottom were artisans, peasants, and others, including slaves.

The imperial government brought forth a ruling class of larger numbers and social diversity. Preimperial rulers generally came from the *kshatriyas* and were supported by the *brahmans*. As governing became more complex, *kshatriya* and *brahman varna* members ruled together. In addition, clerks and tax collectors were two new groups that joined the ruling class. Political influence depended on one's special talents, for example in the ability to complete administrative tasks.

Money lenders and prosperous landlords became a significant social and economic force in the imperial age. With the rise of trade and the expansion of agriculture, financiers often made fortunes lending money. Over time, some of these wealthy people helped imperial governments manage their own financial issues; a few even loaned money to monarchs. Landlords also gained economic prestige in the communities, and some parlayed their influence into tax-farming ventures by the Gupta age. They purchased the right to collect tax revenues and often used devious means to amass far more than the prescribed amount, keeping the excess for themselves.

Lower social classes represented the largest segment of India's population in the imperial age.

FIGURE 10.5 *The Sacred Thread of Caste.* *This thirteenth-century sculpture shows the sacred thread of the upper caste draped over the left shoulder of the figure, and under the right arm. Such emblems marked upper-caste members, keeping them distinct from other castes.* Courtesy of Robert Fisher.

The peasant village spread throughout the Ganges area and from there, with government prodding, to frontiers. As peasants grew in number, tax revenues based on their labor became vital to state finances. Although Kautilya warned against excessive taxes in his *Treatise*, the number and amount of taxes in Maurya times heavily burdened peasants. Later, under the Guptas, the picture of urban prosperity depicted by Faxian gave way to a harsher reality for peasants, who paid heavy taxes and labored for the state during the nonagricultural season. Corrupt and ravenous tax collectors often brought added misery for peasants in late Gupta times, many of whom responded by either revolting or fleeing.

Gender Matters

Men and women had distinct social identities and economic functions in the imperial age. Men generally dominated, while women remained subordinate to men. During the imperial age, however, gender practices sometimes changed significantly.

Indian men began the imperial age at the top of various social groups. They headed households, ruled and administered *varna* and *jati* castes, performed most of the work outside the home, and created most elements of elite culture. Exceptional women might exert social influence, but most did not.

Women of the social and political elites experienced a declining array of choices regarding their lives during the imperial era. At the time of the Maurya Empire, some elite women not only read and wrote but also commented on important religious works like the Vedas. Part of the reason for this was that the accepted marriage age for young Maurya women was in their late teen years, and women had time to be formally educated. By the time of the Gupta Empire, the marriage age dropped to the low teens for women, and this meant that their educations under the supervision of their parents ceased, reducing opportunities for young women.

Women sometimes enjoyed better treatment in religious institutions than in other social groups. In some lower social classes, female deities, including mother goddesses, were popularly worshiped, and women usually served as priestesses for these religions. Buddhism's rejection of the existing social system meant that many women became nuns, and the great majority came from the social elite. Individual women were prominent, as in early Buddhism, but ceased to wield influence after a few centuries. In other countries where Buddhism spread, nuns enjoyed a high status.

INDIAN IDEOLOGIES

All three major Indian religions—Jainism, Buddhism, and Hinduism—began before the imperial age. All three became deeply embedded in Indian society and contributed greatly to Indian history. Buddhism and Hinduism were patronized by emperors and benefited from these associations. The **Upanishads** (discourses speculating about the

FIGURE 10.6 *Mother Goddess Figure of the Imperial Age.* *This striking figure is evidence of worship of female deities during the imperial era. While much attention was given to Hindu and other deities, many commoners were comfortable worshiping local deities. This figure was discovered in North India.* Courtesy of the Government Museum, Mathura.

nature of reality and appended to the Vedas) were also composed before the imperial age, but these texts never formed the basis for a religion.

Common to these religions are the concepts of *karma* and reincarnation. Indians believed that **karma** is the residue of actions by an individual, and it attaches to one's soul. Some actions leave good *karma* and others leave bad *karma*. Taking of life and dealing in human waste, for example, are considered polluting, which provides a rationale for low caste rankings. Once *karma* is removed by spiritual enlightenment, the soul reaches an ideal state and ceases to be reborn after the death of the body. **Reincarnation** is the belief that people have past lives and will have future lives, each time the soul of the dead person is reborn. The soul's reincarnated form is determined by the amount and nature of the *karma* the soul accumulated in its previous lives.

Spiritual Unrest in the Sixth Century B.C.

During the sixth century B.C., intellectual questioning brought a significant transformation of the ideological landscape. Domination by *brahmans* had long been established through the priestly *varna*, yet many people were dissatisfied with the power and wealth of these priests and with the rigid rituals they espoused. Within several decades, a group of thinkers created the elements of Jainism, the basis of Buddhism, and the foundation of the Upanishads. What brought forth this dynamic intellectual ferment?

Scholars have offered many reasons for the serious questioning in India and in many other parts of the world during the sixth century B.C. Some have pointed to the breakup of tribal loyalties and the development of settled urban life. Change occurred in the appearance of more complex and less personal governmental agencies. People seemed less likely to know their local officials personally.

In India, a variety of factors may have led to the acceptance and spread of new religious ideas. Newly prosperous merchants, for example, felt discriminated against by the *brahmans*. Some historians have emphasized a growing disenchantment by *kshatriyas* and others with *brahmans*, who demanded large fees for performing the Vedic rites. Some scholars have suggested that the extension of the caste system triggered local resistance and prompted questioning of institutions and their underlying assumptions. Many religious leaders responded to the basic perception of impermanence and illusion, giving different solutions. In fact, no one reason has proved acceptable, and a combination of explanations seems reasonable.

The Upanishadic Tradition

Scholars generally accept the view that commentaries on the Vedas began around 1000 B.C. The first group of writings, the Brahmanas, expounded upon ideas in the Vedas and stressed the impor-

tance of the kings and priests for political and social stability. Brahmana commentaries developed over the succeeding three centuries.

As noted previously, in the seventh and sixth centuries B.C. spiritual seekers left their homes and sought solitude as well as answers to questions about the nature of the universe and the place of human beings within it. From these came the poetic and religious dialogues known as the Upanishads.

The authors of the Upanishads accepted the Vedas, including their sacrifices and special religious chants. In fact, the 108 Upanishads are included as a part of the Vedas. The Upanishads constitute late additions to the nearly 1,000 years of Vedic religious development.

The Upanishads greatly extend the spiritual thinking of the Indians. One major tenet of these works is that each human has a soul, a spiritual entity seeking union with the omnipresent spirit essence. This union is hampered because the senses serve the body by seeing and interpreting a world that is an illusion.

How does one realize that such illusions blind the soul? One learns through the guidance of a spiritual teacher or by reading the Upanishads. Thereafter, the seeker must begin an arduous process of meditation and spiritual discipline.

Assuming that one approaches the goal of knowing the two realities, what then? The final knowing of the Upanishadic teachers is that the soul and the omnipresent spirit essence are one. This spiritual realization means that one's remaining task is to shed the bodily form so that upon death the individual soul merges into the cosmic soul.

Mahavira and the Jain Response to the Life of the Senses

One sixth-century spiritual seeker, Vardhamana Mahavira (around 540–around 468 B.C.), ardently followed a path toward release from the bonds of the sensate world. Born into a politically elite family in the Ganges River Valley, Mahavira lived an ordinary upper-class life for his first thirty years. Then he experienced a personal crisis that caused him to abandon his worldly life and seek a different meaning of existence. This path occupied the next twelve years; during that time, Mahavira became less encumbered by social convention and

cation (acts of fasting, enduring pain), because Mahavira believed the senses and the body imprison the soul. Because life's ultimate quest is liberation from pain, suffering, and ignorance, the body and the sensate world hinder success. In fact, Jains believe that suffering, willingly undertaken, eliminates existing karma that binds the soul from release.

One unique aspect of the Jain worldview offers a vision of a universe fully alive in its manifestations. This perspective sees souls everywhere as part of a spiritual nomenclature. The first category of creatures has six senses: sight, taste, touch, smell, hearing, and intelligence (mind). Included are humans, gods, monkeys, horses, pigeons, and snakes. Another category has four senses (touch, taste, smell, and sight) and lacks intelligence and hearing. Some representative beings are flies, wasps, and butterflies. A fourth category, two-sense creatures (those of touch and taste), includes worms and leeches. One-sense beings (those that have touch) are vegetable bodies (trees), earth bodies (stones, minerals, jewels), water bodies (rivers, seas, rain), fire bodies (lights, flames, lightning), and wind bodies (gases and winds of all kinds). For Jains, life is in all matter and all things are revered.

Ahimsa (causing no harm to and revering living souls) developed at the time of Mahavira. It may have originated with Jains or with Buddhists; our sources do not offer definite proof. Nevertheless, Jains became ardent adherents of the *ahimsa* lifestyle. *Ahimsa* means not merely avoiding physical injury to all creatures—for example, turning the other cheek when struck—it means not verbally abusing creatures. In fact, *ahimsa* covers even intended actions: A person's having violent thoughts is the same as his or her doing violence toward another creature. Jains believed that one must guard against one's thoughts and live a carefully circumscribed life or face eternal soul bondage.

Some Jain monks followed Mahavira's path of nudism and self-mortification in keeping with the tenets of *ahimsa*. If any clothing were permitted, it was a cloth covering the mouth to prevent unwary beings from entering the mouth and being killed. Jains might also be seen stepping carefully or carrying brooms to gently sweep the path before them. These Jains did not light fires at night, because moths or other beings might perish in the

FIGURE 10.7 *Bahubali, a Jain Saint. This example of Jain sculpture is over fifty feet tall and depicts one of the first Jains to reach enlightenment. Bahubali was so long immersed in meditation that plants grew around him, encircling his legs and arms. This art clearly depicts the Jain value of being in harmony with nature.*
S. Nagaraj/Dinodia Picture Agency.

material needs. He threw off his clothes and practiced acts of self-denial, such as fasting or eating the barest minimum of food necessary for survival. Ultimately, Mahavira determined that death by starvation would bring release of the soul and its passage into the perfect peace of paradise, a place of no karmic activity. He believed that any action, including eating, would kill other beings and cause bad *karma*. Mahavira became the founder of Jainism.

Jains (from *jina*, meaning spiritual warrior or self-conqueror) practice determined self-mortifi-

PARALLELS AND DIVERGENCES
Eating Implements

Throughout traditional India and many other places around the globe, food usually was eaten with the hands. In other places, implements of one sort or another were used. People raised to use eating implements often view the eating of food with the hands as distasteful and potentially unclean, though there always is a developed code of etiquette that rules the use of the hands, as fully as in the traditions with implements. Conversely, those accustomed to using their hands often find eating with implements dangerous-looking and barbaric.

There are four main modes of transporting food to one's mouth. The oldest and most widespread is the use of the hands. All peoples use the hands to some extent, but Indian, Arab, and most African traditions employ this primary mode of eating. Second, some people modify hand eating by adding an edible sheet, pieces of which are torn off and used to envelop loose food. Examples are in Ethiopia, where a supple bread called *injera* is used, and Mexico, where corn tortillas serve the same purpose. Third, some peoples use chopsticks, slender rods serving as extensions of the fingers to grasp chunks of food; their traditional use is in East Asia. Finally, the knife-fork-spoon toolkit of Europe can be used to cut, spear, and scoop food. The spoon has been used by most societies, although sometimes only as a serving implement.

At one level, any approach serves the desired end: The food finds its way to one's mouth. In addition, each allows a way to distinguish sophisticated from rustic diners. A refined Indian diner, for example, eats only with the right hand, because the left is ritually unclean and is used for defiling but necessary hygienic functions. The hand should be held palm downward in eating, and one mouthful should be chewed and swallowed before the next is eaten. Failure to follow this etiquette labels the eater a boor.

At another level, however, the mode of eating reflects a delicate balance among ecology, values, and tastes. Under Jainism, foods were primarily vegetables cut into small pieces. They could be eaten without additional implements, and, because they were prepared lukewarm, the hand would not be burned. Traditional Jains did not have reusable plates because of the implied lack of cleanliness; instead they placed their food on leaves, which could be disposed of after each meal.

Chopsticks, on the other hand, developed partly from a fuel shortage in China. Cooking with fast-burning grasses, the most readily available fuel, required that food be cut into small pieces and stir-fried briefly at high temperatures. Implements were needed because of the extreme heat. Rice was cooked into a sticky mass that could be easily grasped with chopsticks, while smaller morsels could be transferred from bowl to mouth with a scooping motion.

Finally, the knife and fork developed as eating implements in Europe, because that region favored heavy meat consumption, and meat tended to be roasted in large chunks. Rather than cutting up a slab of meat before serving and risking its cooling, the diner carved it one slice at a time. The fork appeared in medieval times, but it frequently was replaced by the hand or a knife.

---

flames. They begged for their daily food and water so that they would not take life in preparing food. They also preferred to eat vegetables, and a few, like Mahavira, starved themselves to death.

Other Jain monks wore clothes, and, although they accepted Jain doctrines, they did not go to the lengths of the other group. All Jains rejected Hindu texts, like the Vedas, as sole sources of the truth. By rejecting the Vedas as the authoritative texts governing one's life, Jains made each individual responsible for personal spiritual development. In this way, Jains appealed to urban groups like the merchants, who rejected their low *varna* status. In fact, many Jains became merchants and bankers, and some grew wealthy. Others promoted learning by collecting and disseminating books, including non-Jain works, because Jains practiced toleration of diverse ideas and practices. Because they appreciated education, Jains contributed to India's mathematical discoveries, to developments in astronomy, and to the study of languages. Mahavira encouraged storytelling, and some Jains wrote in the local vernacular languages. They helped develop India's rich regional languages.

Siddhartha and Buddhism in the Imperial Age

Like Jainism, Buddhism rejected the authority of the Vedas. Unlike Jainism, Buddhism has many sects and three major subdivisions. For a variety of reasons, however, Buddhism ultimately disappeared in India, its homeland.

Prince Siddhartha Gautama (around 563–around 480 B.C.) lived a life similar to that of Mahavira, his contemporary. Both came from the warrior *varna*, and both lived without experiencing significant suffering until around the age of thirty years. Stories about Siddhartha were not written until after his death; therefore, knowledge about his life has remained suspect. Buddhist tradition claims that Siddhartha Gautama, who resided only within his father's royal domain, took a series of trips on which he saw seriously ill people, dead people, and an ascetic who followed the path of spiritual seeking. The combined experiences are said to have shaken Prince Siddhartha to the foundation of his being and offered him a path to spiritual insight. He spent nights of sleepless questioning and decided to abandon his wife, son, and father, the king. Like Mahavira, Siddhartha began a quest for the meaning of existence.

Within six years, Siddhartha tried varied spiritual disciplines, including self-mortification practices. Siddhartha ate the bare caloric minimum to sustain life and briefly followed the starvation way. Near death, he suddenly halted this regimen and resumed a life-nurturing diet. Moreover, he announced that he would follow a path of moderation, which he called the "middle way"—not indulgent and not ascetic.

Apart from a moderate asceticism, meditation became the way by which Siddhartha became enlightened. Meditation had been long practiced by Indian ascetics and became a key discipline in Buddhism. Basically, meditation quiets the chattering mind. Buddhists believe that when one becomes skilled at meditation, spiritual knowledge may erupt into the consciousness, including the basic perception of the world's impermanence. Siddhartha meditated and saw his past lives and their connection to his present life; he then knew the meaning of existence. At that time, he became enlightened, seeing life as it truly was, in all of its interconnectedness. Siddhartha became the **Buddha**, the one who is enlightened.

After this experience, the Buddha walked to a nearby park and preached a sermon that presented the famous **Four Noble Truths**, a key basis of Buddhism:

— First Truth: Life is suffering.

— Second Truth: Suffering has a cause.

— Third Truth: The cause is desire.

— Fourth Truth: Desire and suffering may be eliminated by following the **Eightfold Path**, composed of correct views, correct aspirations, correct speech, correct conduct, correct livelihood, correct effort, correct mindfulness, and correct meditation.

FIGURE 10.8 *Fasting Siddhartha Gautama.*
This sculpture from northwestern India shows Siddhartha Gautama following the extreme asceticism of some spiritual traditions. He eventually abandoned this path and sought moderation in all things. This ethic became the cornerstone of most Buddhist sects and earned Siddhartha the title Buddha, meaning "enlightened one." The sculpture vividly captures the results of disciplined food deprivation.
Courtesy of the Central Museum, Lahore.

The Four Noble Truths provide a perspective with which to view life and a way to eliminate suffering. "Life is suffering" means that the universe is in constant flux or change, but people fail to recognize its essential nature. Instead, they seek permanence by desiring attachments, like spouses, children, and material things. These, however, give only a temporary sense of permanence. Humans may become ill, they die, or they may not follow the path we wish them to. In other words, all relationships have pain and will ultimately be severed by time and death. By eliminating these attachments and the desire for permanence that underlies them, one is freed to completely adhere to the Eightfold Path, becoming a monk or a nun.

The preliminary step to the Buddhist goal is enlightenment, seeing the world as impermanent. After that, one must live an exemplary life like that of the Buddha, who preached for the more than four remaining decades in his life. Finally, when death comes to the enlightened, correct-living person, one enters *nirvana*. Literally meaning "blowing out," like the flame of a candle, *nirvana* signified the state at which existence ceases. In other words, one is no longer reborn; one has been extinguished, and that is all. Centuries later, *nirvana* became heaven, especially in Mahayana Buddhism.

Buddhism remained a small sect of traveling ascetics who performed spiritual disciplines and accepted food and drink from people. In the monsoon season, they lived in sheltered dwellings, and soon permanent residences, monasteries, appeared. This community of monks followed a lifestyle that included chastity, *ahimsa*, and poverty, thus eliminating the worldly attachments. Soon, these monasteries, among the first in history, became centers of learning and discipline.

Nearing death, the Buddha left a final message for his disciples: He told them to be their own lamps, to be their own refuges. The Buddha implied that adherents should rely on themselves rather than on external sources. They should strive vigilantly and hold firmly to truth. After the Buddha died, sectarian differences emerged among his followers. Buddhism remained a modest movement in India until the time of Emperor Ashoka, who promoted Buddhist missionary activity.

The history of Buddhism in India centers on thinkers who elaborated on the already sophisticated Buddhistic treatment of psychology. Nagarjuna[9] and Vashubandhu[10] developed treatises on reality and how the mind perceives it. They wrote *sutras,* prose or poetic treatises about some issues in Buddhism.

Buddhism ultimately disappeared in India as it spread across Asia. One reason may be that Buddhism regarded all humans as capable of being enlightened in a single lifetime. This perspective went against the Indian belief that members of the lowest caste would have to live an exemplary life merely to be reincarnated into a higher caste. Buddhism tolerated Hinduism and had no ritual specialists of its own. It stressed a monastic life and detachment from society. It gradually waned as a religion.

Beginning in the fourth century A.D., Hinduism experienced a revival. Hindus borrowed from other ideologies; Shankara, a key Hindu thinker of the ninth century, used Buddhist ideas in his own system of belief. Incorporation of borrowed ideas blurred the distinctions between Hinduism and Buddhism and aided in Buddhism's extinction in India. Shankara also founded many Hindu monasteries. Finally, Hindu temples competed with Buddhist and Jain monasteries that were involved in trade, especially trade with Central Asia. Often with the aid of local governments, Hindus attacked and destroyed Buddhist monasteries. Jainism was strong enough to withstand the persecutions; Buddhism was not.

The Development of Hinduism

Hinduism developed in India over a long period from around 500 B.C. to around A.D. 500. It was closely associated with *brahmans*, ritual specialists who relied on the Vedas for their ritualistic knowledge. *Brahmans* wandered across India spreading their beliefs and gaining converts. In addition, Hindu temples and monasteries became tightly connected with society. Hindus were also accepting of local deities.

Many deities formed the Hindu pantheon. One early god, Indra, represented the warring nature of the Indo-Europeans but lost his importance as Aryan society evolved. When ruling

[9] **Nagarjuna:** nah GAHR juh nah
[10] **Vashubandhu:** VAH shuh BAHN dhuh

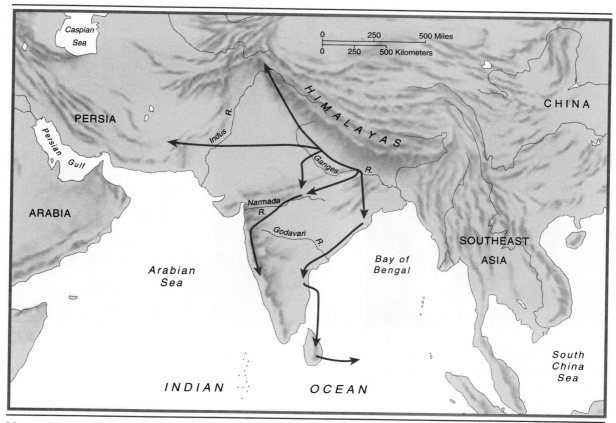

MAP 10.3 *The Spread of Buddhism after 250 B.C. Ashoka played a major role in spreading Buddhism in India and surrounding areas. Tamraparni (modern-day Sri Lanka) became an important Buddhist center. From there, Buddhism was spread throughout Southeast Asia by missionaries and merchants.*

became more important, Varuna, a deity associated with order and justice, assumed a larger role. A stable political order grew more attractive to the rajas (rulers). During the imperial era, two other deities, Shiva and Vishnu, assumed prominent places in Hinduism. Shiva was probably an indigenous, non-Aryan deity, while Vishnu was originally an unimportant Aryan god.

Hindus, who believe that Shiva, the Mighty Lord, in his manifestation as a fierce destroyer controls life and death, represent him wearing a necklace of skulls. He also is seen as a naked ascetic, typically depicted with a third eye in the middle of his forehead. This is the mystic eye or the eye of wisdom, important to the yogis and other spiritual adepts. One common symbol representing Shiva is the phallus, which stands for his fertility aspect. In another guise, Shiva is lord of the animals and is associated with the Indus deity mentioned in Chapter 5.

Vishnu represents the supreme being from whom the universe emanates. In addition, he is the preserver of life. Two of his incarnations are Rama and Krishna. The Krishna form is one of the most popular avatars in Hinduism. According to Hindu lore, Vishnu, in his preserver role, saved the world from destruction numerous times. Hindus also believe that Buddha was an incarnation of Vishnu.

A cluster of developments, including the establishment of temples and the worship of local and regional deities, fused into Hinduism during

FIGURE 10.9 *A Carved Hindu Temple. This eighth-century Kailasha Temple was carved 100 feet down into the rock at Ellura in South-Central India. It shows the skilled artisanry and massive resources available to Hindu monarchs, even after the imperial era.*
Victor Kennet/Reproduced courtesy of Thames and Hudson Ltd.

the first millennium A.D. Some national and regional governments granted land and other resources to *brahmans* in exchange for political support. Gupta emperors were especially favorable to the *brahmans*, and many temple complexes were founded in the capital region as well as in the empire.

Hindu temple priests interacted with local leaders and their communities. Deities of these settlements, for example, became more firmly tied into the Hindu pantheon, and, because of the linkages of exchange between villages and clusters of villages in a region, a popular local deity might become venerated throughout the region. Krishna, a regional god, evolved into his paramount identity in this way. Thus, deities were woven into a religious tapestry of great complexity and diversity.

Vishnu, Shiva, and Krishna became three significant Hindu deities. Krishna's main temple at Mathura in northern India attracted devotees from all over the region. Temple priests demanded that adherents be loyal to the deity; thus, religious devotion meant faith in and salvation from a god. Hinduism became India's most important religion.

IMPERIAL INDIA'S REGIONAL IMPACT

India long enjoyed trade relations with Eurasia and Africa. The origins of economic ties date at least to the third millennium B.C. In later periods, products from India were popular in the Seleucid, Roman, and Axum empires. The influence of India, however, went beyond trade goods. Mathematics and astronomy strongly attracted attention in many lands, and Buddhism and Hinduism exerted a great amount of influence far beyond India's borders. Southeast Asian countries particularly enjoyed close relations with Indian governments and used Indian ideas and religions to bolster their political systems.

Trade and Other Relations with Regions West and North of India

Since the third millennium B.C., Indians traded extensively with peoples of Asia and Africa, and Indian products remained popular with Persians,

Egyptians, Greeks, and Romans. Later, when Arabs reached the borders of India and even briefly settled in the Indus Valley, Indian products contributed to the Islamic exchange that will be discussed in Chapter 12.

Diplomatic contacts also flourished from the imperial era. Chandragupta Maurya enjoyed peaceful relations with the Seleucids, after he stopped their eastward advance. Ashoka sent ambassadors to parts of Asia in the third century B.C., and diplomacy aided peaceful relations in the Maurya and Gupta eras.

Buddhism slowly spread to the north and northwest beginning with Ashoka, who sent Buddhist missionaries to other Asian lands. The conversion process advanced partly through missionary and merchant contacts into Central Asia. In the first century A.D., Central Asian rulers in India played a key role in the spread of Buddhism into Central Asia and China. As will be seen in Chapter 14, Buddhism slowly took root in China,

and many monks and Buddhist students came to India, the home of Buddhism, in later decades and centuries.

India's Impact on Southeast Asia

More than trade linked the peoples and governments of Indian and Southeast Asia (Indochina). Certainly, ships and merchants plied the coastal waters of South and Southeast Asia. We have even seen in Chapter 5 that rice and various animals (particularly chickens) came from Southeast Asia into the Indian subcontinent during prehistoric and early historic times. In later centuries, the flow of trade continued in both directions.

Large Indian ships bearing cargo reached Southeast Asian ports by the time of the Maurya Empire. They used the seasonal winds to sail to the Isthmus of Kra on the Malay Peninsula, transported the trade items across the narrow land strip, and loaded their wares on waiting ships.

FIGURE 10.10 *Relief of an Indian Ship.* *This carving attests to the maritime skills of Indians who ranged far across the Indian Ocean. During the imperial era, many sailors, merchants, and priests brought goods and ideas from India to Southeast Asia.* Courtesy of Robert Fisher.

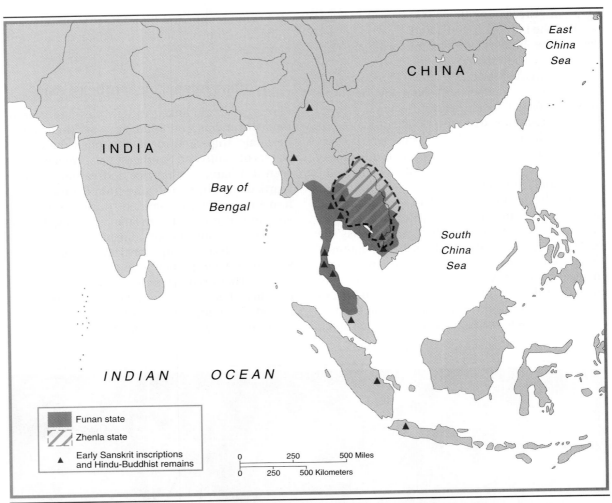

MAP 10.4 India's Relations with Southeast Asia. *Both mainlanders and islanders in Southeast Asia had extensive trade contacts with Indians. Nearly all such trade occurred through maritime activity. Cultural influence came slowly and may be seen in the Sanskrit inscriptions on Hindu-Buddhist artifacts.*

Then, they made landfall near the Mekong River Valley. The return trip needed the shift of the winds that usually took months to occur. During the interim, the Indian merchants and others lived in the Mekong River region. Even though the Maurya Empire fell in the second century B.C., trade with the Southeast Asians continued.

During the first and second centuries A.D., two things caused a heightened Indian commercial interest in Southeast Asia. The Roman emperor Vespasian banned the export of gold coins from the Roman Empire, and this forced Indian rulers, who needed gold for various purposes, to seek new

supplies. At the same time, chiefdoms in the Mekong River Valley united under a single rule that the Chinese called Funan. This kingdom commanded the Mekong trade route, a major one between India and China.

Two popular stories, perhaps historically inaccurate, symbolize the growing Indian and Southeast Asian relationship. The first tale concerns a traveler, Kaudinya, who arrives in the Mekong River Valley by sea. He marries a local princess, then establishes a dynasty. A later account gives the same name, Kaudinya, to an Indian *brahman* who marries a princess and begins ruling with her.

INDIA

Spiritual unrest leads to founding of Upanishadic tradition, Buddhism, and Jainism, sixth and fifth centuries	**500 B.C.**	Birth of Buddha, c. 563 B.C.
		Birth of Mahavira, c. 540 B.C.
	400 B.C.	
	300 B.C.	Chandragupta founds Maurya Empire, c. 320 B.C.
Maurya Empire, c. 320– c. 180 B.C.		Ashoka ascends throne, c. 269 B.C.
		Kalinga War ends, 261 B.C.
		Beginning of Buddhist missionizing, c. 250 B.C.
	200 B.C.	Fall of Maurya Empire, c. 180 B.C.
Regional Indian states, 180 B.C.–A.D. 320	**100 B.C.**	
	A.D. 1	
	A.D. 100	
	A.D. 200	
	A.D. 300	Nalanda University founded, c. 320
Expanded patronage of Indian elite arts, 320–650	Gupta Empire, 320–550	Chandra Gupta II begins reign, 375
	A.D. 400	Faxian travels in India, c. 405–411
		Kalidasa writes plays, c. 450
	A.D. 500	Fall of Gupta Empire, c. 550
	A.D. 600	

This story notes that he changed local rules to be in accord with Indian practices. What the tales show is the influence of Indians on Southeast Asian governments.

Archaeologists also know that in the early part of the first millennium A.D., Funan rulers welcomed Indian trade and *brahman* advisors. The monarchs adopted the Indian title "Varman" (meaning armor or protection by a deity) as a part of their dynastic names. They followed the Indian calendar system, they used parts of the Indian legal system, and they worshiped the Hindu deities Shiva and Vishnu. Thus, local people, likely Khmers,[11] incorporated elements of Indian culture into their own. In that sense, India's impact on Southeast Asians parallels China's impact on East Asians.

Material evidence shows that there was extensive trade between countries around the Indian Ocean in the first millennium. In one manufacturing center controlled by Funan, for example, scholars have found Roman medallions and Iranian coins. Much jewelry was fashioned there from diamonds, gold, sapphires, rubies, jade, and opals. Many raw materials had to be brought from other parts of Asia.

When Funan declined, a second state also known by a Chinese name, Zhenla,[12] rose in the same area. The elite of this successor state regularly used Sanskrit to write their names. The Zhenla monarch worshiped Shiva, and the elite built temples to Shiva to curry favor with their sovereign. Thus, Indian religious practices helped bind the ruling elite. Indian *brahmans* advised Zhenla rulers, and eventually a school for the study of the *Treatise*, the Indian manual of politics, was founded in the capital. Gupta architectural styles graced the large buildings of Zhenla. Although Sanskrit was used for rituals, Khmer remained the vernacular language.

Buddhism spread across Southeast Asia. In Ashoka's age, it crossed the strait into Sri Lanka, the teardrop-shaped island off India's southern tip. Gradually, the Sri Lankans began sending missionaries into the parts of Southeast Asia today known as Burma (Myanmar), Thailand, Cambodia, Laos, and the islands of Indonesia. Then, mainland peoples like the Mon-Khmer group that settled in the river valleys of Southeast Asia often converted to Buddhism; many of their descendants still follow this faith today. Tolerant embrace of Buddhism permitted the enfolding of the older animistic practices into the Buddhist fabric. Other states in Southeast Asia experienced strong influences from Indian culture. Dancers in modern Java and Bali still perform versions of the Indian epics, and temples in the Hindu style are found on both islands.

SUMMARY

1. Chandragupta Maurya seized control of a state and used its bureaucracy and army to fashion an empire. The imperial ideology is reflected in a later text, the *Treatise on Financial Gain*.

2. Ashoka, the third Maurya emperor, seized power in a bloody civil war and fought another war. Thereafter, Ashoka changed state policy from conquest to rule and humanized his polity by modifying *dharma*, a Buddhist and Indian religious concept, to mean ethical and social responsibility. People lived more easily, but Ashoka failed to provide long-term stability.

3. After a five-century interim the Guptas imitated the Mauryas and built a prosperous state. Hinduism flourished.

4. The *varna* system of the Vedas declined during Ashoka's age and largely gave way to the *jati* caste system of kinship communities tied by economic benefit. Merchants and peasants contributed greatly to the economic well-being of imperial states.

5. In the sixth century B.C., spiritual and social unrest led some to found major Indian ideologies: Jainism, Buddhism, and the Upanishadic tradition.

6. Upanishadic thinkers explored the nature of the universe and the place of humans within it.

[11] **Khmers:** kuh MAIRZ
[12] **Zhenla:** JEHN lah

7. Mahavira developed Jainism to seek release from life. Jains rejected the Vedas and embraced *ahimsa*, a way of life revering living souls and causing no harm to them.

8. Siddhartha Gautama founded Buddhism on the Four Noble Truths. Buddhism became a religion that stressed meditation and *ahimsa*.

9. Hinduism developed from ideas and practices associated with the Vedas, from devotion to Shiva and Vishnu, and from the building of temples by Gupta monarchs.

10. India influenced many peoples through trade, ideas, and religions. Southeast Asians welcomed Indian goods, as well as *brahmans* and Buddhist monks, who advised their rulers. Law codes, calendars, and rituals followed in their wake. Shiva, Vishnu, and the Buddha were venerated by some Southeast Asians.

SUGGESTED READINGS

Auboyer, Jeannine. *Daily Life in Ancient India.* London: Morrison and Gibb Limited, 1965. A description of life in the early imperial era of Indian history.

Embree, Ainsley, ed. *Sources of Indian Tradition.* New York: Columbia University Press, 1988. A significant selection of Jain, Buddhist, Upanishadic, and Hindu sources and commentaries upon them.

Thapar, Romila. *Asoka and the Decline of the Mauryas.* Oxford, Eng.: Oxford University Press, 1961. A classic treatment of the reign of one of India's greatest rulers.

Wolpert, Stanley. *A New History of India.* New York: Oxford University Press, 1993. A standard history of India.

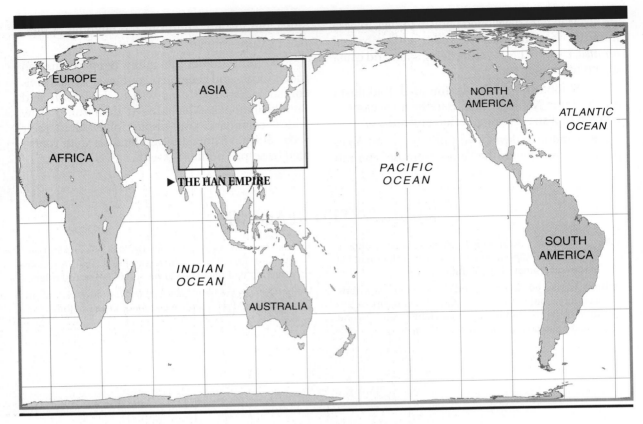

► THE HAN EMPIRE

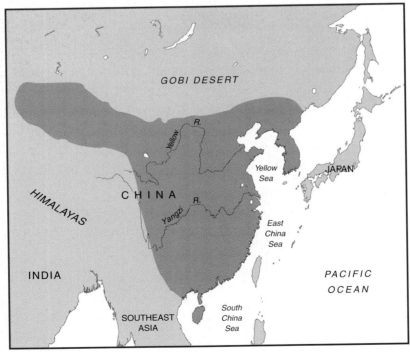

► THE HAN EMPIRE

China: From Feudalism to Empire

770 B.C.–A.D. 220

A Chinese philosopher once dreamed he was a butterfly. In that dream, the butterfly flitted from place to place, doing butterfly things. When he woke, the philosopher did not know whether he was himself or whether he was a butterfly, dreaming he was a philosopher.

This story from the Warring States Period, an age when iron helped transform life in China, has charmed readers and inspired poets, artists, and movie directors. In this chapter, we shall see how the appearance of iron and the consequences of its widespread use in the seventh century B.C. improved agricultural production, stimulated population growth, and brought about the rise of large cities. Feudalism faded before the metal plows and iron weapons. Gone too were the chariot-driven aristocratic warriors, made obsolete by peasant-conscript armies. To support these large military forces, governments mobilized their human and material resources as quickly and as efficiently as possible. Leaders adopted a centralized political system with a chain of command emphasizing strict obedience. Failure to adopt this effective but harsh political method meant defeat and annexation by larger states. Eventually, China was united by emperors who ruled empires, dominating East Asia.

LATE ZHOU: THE DECLINE AND FALL OF FEUDALISM, 770–221 B.C.

The loss of the western capital in 771 B.C. symbolized the impotence of the Zhou ruling house. Although nearly all other rulers paid lip service to the Zhou kings, royal commands were ignored. Many states, both powerful and weak, were ruled by dukes. In respect for tradition, the Zhou title of king remained solely for the Zhou sovereign's use until around 300 B.C. During the succeeding decades (770–670 B.C.) the existing local governments warred with one another with increasing ferocity. Of perhaps two hundred or more states, fewer than a dozen survived by the seventh century B.C. Because the Zhou state had no political might with which to bring stability, the more powerful states tried to impose peace. But power shifts among states threatened stability.

In the late fifth century B.C., a major state (Jin) in the central Yellow River Valley broke into three parts. This event began an era (403–221 B.C.) known as the Warring States Period, when a few mighty governments engaged in warfare on a massive scale. Decentralized feudal polities had long since fallen to more centralized regimes.

Economic and Social Change in the Warring States Period

A cluster of developments transformed Chinese agriculture and led to widespread social and economic change. The making of bronze and iron agricultural tools, the use of manure as fertilizer, the employment of cattle as draft animals, and the introduction of plows permitted farming of new lands and better use of existing fields. Grain yields per land unit increased significantly and brought the surpluses to support larger populations and larger cities. As the urban centers grew, merchants

FIGURE 11.1 *Early Chinese Plow. The plow shown in this stone relief from southwestern China of the Late Han era is similar to plows used centuries earlier. The draft animal is probably a water buffalo, although humans sometimes provided the labor. Iron-tipped plowshares transformed Chinese agriculture and life throughout the imperial age.* Werner Forman/Art Resource, N.Y.

and artisans became more numerous. Social mobility, upward and downward, became commonplace.

As seen in Chapter 5, the Chinese developed the techniques of bronze metallurgy in their earliest cities. Yet the overwhelming use for bronze was only in ceremonial pieces and weapons. By the fifth century B.C., employment of bronze and iron agricultural tools had spread from the Yellow River Valley to other regions of China. Around the same time, the Chinese began replacing some human labor with cattle used as draft animals. These changes enabled farmers to work a wide variety of soils, thus increasing the amount of land under cultivation. Scholars do not know exactly when the Chinese developed techniques of iron metallurgy, although some archaeological finds suggest its appearance as early as the seventh century B.C. By about 500 B.C., the Chinese made iron agricultural tools and, over the next centuries, began mass producing iron implements that helped transform agriculture. Farmers either purchased iron plow tips or rented them from the state governments.

New techniques of political control also permitted officials to gather and direct large numbers of people in public works projects. One effort was a canal in the state of Qin.[1] The monarch of a rival state sent his hydraulic engineer, Zheng Guo,[2] who promised the Qin ruler bountiful harvests from the irrigated lands. They schemed to entice the Qin monarch to waste his state's human and material resources on the extravagant water control effort. Qin laborers using iron shovels and other tools began digging the hundred-mile-long canal. Later, Qin spies learned of the deception. Summoned before the Qin ruler, Zheng Guo noted how the Qin state efficiently absorbed the expenditures of resources. He reiterated his promise of immense wealth, and the king kept him. After eight years the canal was completed and irrigated large tracts of land. The Zheng Guo Canal, along with a second major hydraulic project in the southern Qin territory, reduced fears of drought-induced famines.

Water projects like these brought even larger agricultural reserves, which fed the burgeoning cities. Trade grew and some merchants became wealthy, though most peasants struggled to produce enough to pay their taxes and to provide for their families.

[1] **Qin:** CHIN
[2] **Zheng Guo:** JUNG gwaw

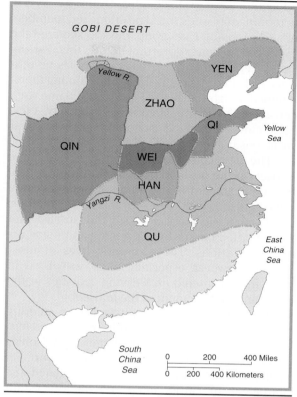

M A P 1 1 . 1   *China in 250 B.C.: The Warring States. Around 250 B.C., China was divided into seven warring states. They ruled much of northern and north central China (the Yellow and Yangzi river valleys). The Qin state in the northwest conquered the other states in a unification war lasting from 230 to 221 B.C. It also conquered additional territory in the south, extending China's boundaries farther than ever before. China's southward expansion continued for centuries.*

The Chinese also built road systems linking the cities. Peasants made the roads, constructed hydraulic works, erected city walls, and put up the barrier walls at the borders. As the flow of goods increased, one major problem limited the growth of trade. Because China lacked a system of standard axle lengths, the ruts of one warring state's roads often stopped the movement of another state's carts. Consequently, merchants spent much time reloading their trade goods at a state's border.

Many factors undermined the traditional social structure. The old aristocracy failed to meet the challenges of new political systems that needed the services of the best-qualified people.

Education began challenging birthright as the determinant of one's social position, and members of a low-ranking elite group, the *shi*, acquired the expertise to enter government. By the Warring States Period, many *shi* replaced nobles as officials. Artisans, especially the leaders among them, attained a high social and legal status. Some were considered to be equal to officials in society. A few merchants prospered economically, yet their social position remained low.

The new conditions in the cities had some impact on the position of women. Although they never became officials, some women became skilled artisans with their own social designations. One woman became a successful industrialist after she inherited her husband's mining and metallurgical operations. The economic lives of most women, however, especially those who lived in rural areas, centered on weaving activities in the home and management of the household.

Feudalism could not withstand the withering demands of all-out warfare, and decentralized feudal polities succumbed to the large states. Nobles could not effectively raise and long support the small personal armies that had dominated the campaigns of earlier eras. The manor system described in Chapter 5 could not compete with the newly emerging individual landholding system. Furthermore, large centralized states could control the labor armies that built the massive irrigation networks.

Chinese Intellectual Culture

The transformation of society and the economy created the material prosperity to support larger numbers of scholars, including writers and philosophers. Monarchs and officials, for example, sponsored scholars who published literary anthologies.

During this age (around 500–230 B.C.), two poetry collections appeared. Although the *Classic of Songs* was compiled in the sixth century, its songs had been sung for centuries. Poignant love songs of simple yet vibrant verses inspired later poets. Another collection, the *Songs of the South*, contained poems attributed to Qu Yuan,[3] an exiled official of the third century B.C. During travels across luxuriant southern lands, Qu Yuan com-

posed songs lamenting his misfortune. He tired of his exile and drowned himself, and Chinese annually remember him in Dragon Boat Festivals.

Prose blossomed. The *Classic of Documents*, a collection of early Zhou writings, appeared along with a basic chronicle of the Lu state (*Spring and Autumn Annals*). Both were associated with **Confucianism**. Perhaps the most significant development in prose, the essay, expanded into a sophisticated genre.

Confucianism representative of *shi* aspirations has been the most significant philosophy in Chinese history. Founded by Confucius (551–479 B.C.), the son of an aristocratic warrior, Confucianism stressed a human-centered, moral-based life. Orphaned at an early age, Confucius acquired an education and a profound love of learning. Nurturing a lifelong ambition to transform the corrupt political culture of his state, Confucius joined the government but fell from power before he could effect significant change. In his remaining years, Confucius taught disciples how to govern subjects, families, and themselves. Although Confucius considered himself a failure, generations of Chinese have been profoundly influenced by his writings.

A vital part of Confucius's teachings concerned ritual. He came from a group of aristocrats who mastered various rituals used in government. These experts were sometimes called upon by political leaders to advise them about the correct procedures of enthronement. Confucius took that sense of ritual and broadened it to include the rituals of one's daily life. Eating, sleeping, walking, conversing, parenting, and other daily activities were assigned proper ritual forms. By wholeheartedly following these mannered ways, one would live morally. Confucius believed that monarchs, officials, husbands, wives, parents, and children all must do the right things in their lives. For Confucius, ritual showed a way to social harmony and stability.

Although Confucius taught practical military subjects like archery and chariot driving, he believed that education should teach people to be good. He not only developed a teacher-student relationship but also defined the content of education. Students studied and practiced loyalty, humaneness, sincerity, and **filial piety** (honoring one's parents).

The Confucian ideal type, the **gentleman**, embodied all of these traits. The Chinese charac-

[3] **Qu Yuan:** CHOO ywahn

FIGURE 11.2 *Illustration of Filial Piety.* *Made in Sichuan, this painted lacquer basket was discovered at the site of a Chinese city in Korea. The Chinese conquered and ruled Korea for centuries, beginning in the second century B.C. The figure on the extreme left is a parent receiving homage from children. The closed sleeves and slight bow of the first child show respect and obedience. A similar scene may be seen with the fifth and sixth figures from the left. Chinese and East Asians regarded filial piety as a person's most important obligation.* R. B. Fleming.

ters for "gentleman" originally meant "son of a lord" in the feudal period. In that sense it connoted a birthright. Confucius, to be in accord with the social changes taking place and to meet the needs of his students, transformed the gentleman into one of noble character, not necessarily noble birth. The gentleman treated people humanely, and the Confucians encapsulated this sentiment with the saying, "Do not do unto others as you would not have them do unto you." This maxim is similar to Christianity's Golden Rule: Do unto others as you would have them do unto you. The gentleman aided weak and poor people. Ideally, the gentleman reviewed and criticized his daily actions. Finally, he radiated moral force. In the company of others, his personality compelled imitation of his actions. Thus Confucius hoped to change the political culture of his state, and later Confucians hoped that a few good men could transform any ailing government.

The gentleman showed loyalty to superiors, friends, and family. Confucians believed that people had to be loyal: Subjects had to obey their rulers, children their parents, and subordinates their superiors. Over time, the Confucians elabo-

rated the concept of loyalty and its corollary, obedience, into a hierarchical system of five relationships:

— ruler-subject,
— parent-child,
— husband-wife,
— elder sibling–younger sibling, and
— elder friend–younger friend.

The person on the left side of the relationship dominated the one on the right, and superiors had to care for subordinates. The person on the right side of the relationship obeyed or showed loyalty to the one on the left.

Filial behavior impressed the Confucians, who saw the family as the basic social unit. A well-ordered family meant social and political stability. If a parent died, the children mourned their loss, usually for twenty-seven months. Every dutiful son had to produce a son to carry on the family name. Through a cohesive family structure, Confucians offered rulers social stability.

The hierarchical social order also gave each person a place and an identity. One consequence was the elaboration of an ideology that reinforced the subordination of women. Indeed, it was said that a woman's father, husband, and son dominated her sequentially in her life stages. When she married, she moved to her husband's house, which usually meant living with her in-laws. Filial piety required that she obey her parents-in-law. The most difficult relationship involved mother-in-law and daughter-in-law, because both competed for the affection of the son/husband. Wives who enjoyed their husbands' open attentions often faced the ire of their mothers-in-law.

The tough-minded side of the Warring States politics is seen in the **Legalists**, philosophers and bureaucrats who espoused a statist political theory. Legalist thinkers and officials believed that government must be powerful militarily and economically. In the Warring States Period, survival demanded harsh laws enforced by the toughest punishments. Therefore, the Legalists believed that people often behaved badly and needed to be kept under the most strict control. The all-powerful Legalist state had to suppress all who undermined its interests, including scholars, who lived off the production of others and who carped incessantly against government. Confucian scholars took a different view of the state. Most agreed that some laws were necessary, but only for the uneducated. They vehemently opposed restrictions on morally upright scholars. Confucians also believed that government should nurture the people, while Legalists insisted that subjects obediently serve the state.

Daoism was another Chinese philosophy that became popular in the Warring States era. Daoism has a mystical, intuitive component, unlike either Confucianism or Legalism. In addition, Confucianism developed near the original heartland of Chinese civilization, preserving many of its elements. Legalism developed in the northern frontier, reflecting the harshness of border life. Daoism flourished in the south, harmonizing with the lush landscapes there. The two main Daoist thinkers are Lao Zi[4] (around the sixth century B.C.), who wrote the *Dao De Jing*, and Zhuang Zi[5] (around 340–around 280 B.C.), who wrote *Zhuang Zi*.

Daoists employ symbols to help explain their way. **Dao** literally means a path or way; metaphorically, it signifies the totality of everything or the

FIGURE 11.3 *Lao Zi Riding an Ox.* *Legend says that late in his life, Lao Zi became tired of the human world and traveled west. As he left China, a gatekeeper implored Lao Zi to leave behind something of value. In response, Lao Zi wrote the* Dao De Jing; *the scroll shown here may be this work. Riding effortlessly on the animal without using reins illustrates the Daoist ideal of acting in harmony with nature.* National Palace Museum, Taipei, Taiwan, Republic of China.

universe. On another level Dao is the origin of all things; it is, however, unknowable. One Daoist passage states that "The Dao that can be spoken about is not the true Dao." It can be ascertained only in nonrational ways, and to give it a name—even Dao—is to limit it. Thus, we come to the ultimate human paradox: talking about something about which we cannot speak. The third level of Dao is a

---

[4] **Lao Zi:** LOW dzuh
[5] **Zhuang Zi:** joo AHNG dzuh

path or way of life that one travels to a higher plane of being.

Daoists ridiculed the Confucian education and behavior codes, which Daoists believed hindered people from living naturally. Daoists hated offensive warfare and fought only when given no other choice.

Some scholars divide Daoism into **Contemplative Daoism** and **Purposive Daoism**. Contemplative Daoism, the most mystical and anarchistic philosophy in China's intellectual culture, asserts that the best government is no government and that the best social conventions are no social conventions. This form, not unlike the mystical tradi-

tions of India, stresses looking within oneself and seeing the natural world in a holistic way. For example, in looking at a tree one sees the leaves, branches, trunk, and roots; the Daoists would say that the person misses the totality of the tree. When we analyze the tree into its component parts, we miss the essence of the tree. The ideal type in Contemplative Daoism, the **immortal**, possesses magical attributes, subsists on simple foods (no meat), drinks dew from plants, flies, and cannot be destroyed.

The Purposive Daoists, unlike the Contemplative Daoists, believe in limited government. They also differ from the Contemplative Daoists in that

UNDER THE LENS

Chinese Perspectives on Yin/Yang *and* the Five Elements

The Classical Age's concepts of *yin/yang* and of the Five Elements merit focused attention. Although ancient texts from the first half of the first millennium B.C. mention *yin* (dark) and *yang* (light), their appearance as part of an interpretative perspective occurs only late in the third century B.C. The same may be said of the Five Elements system. We will examine each perspective and see the resulting integrated view of the human world.

Ancient Chinese saw certain alternating symmetrical patterns in natural cycles like the day and the year. Days had dark (*yin*) and light (*yang*) times. The years also had times when the daylight periods were more lengthy and times when the night grew longer. Each increase of light brought a decrease by dark and vice versa. Other polarities like cold/hot and wet/dry were added to the *yin/yang* analytical framework.

By the third century B.C., societal components were included in the *yin/yang* schema. *Yin* became viewed as passive, and the vagina was *yin*'s sexual symbol. *Yang* became seen as active, and the penis was its sexual symbol. In a broad sense, men were linked with more active traits, while women were labeled with passive aspects. All of this reflected the perspective of the dominant patriarchal culture.

Yin/yang analysis may be applied to medicine. If one has a fever (too much heat or *yang*), medicine with a *yin* nature must be ingested to bring the body back into balance. Other illnesses may be diagnosed

as reflecting too much bodily *yin*, so *yang* medicines will be prescribed.

The Five Elements system also became an elaborated perspective in the third century B.C. The Five Elements are Earth, Fire, Water, Metal, and Wood. In general, one element overcomes another, but no unilinear hierarchy is determined. In addition, the Chinese associated each element with a dynasty, a color, and other things. During the Zhou era, Fire dominated, and its corresponding color was red. Later, the Five Elements system was further elaborated to correspond to things such as a major organ, a season, a cardinal point on the compass, a note on the musical scale, and so forth. One scholar has noted that this organizing scheme paralleled the growth of the imperial bureaucracy and its organization of the empire.

China's Five Elements perspective resembles the system of correspondences of the Hopi Indian tribe of Arizona. The Hopi base their system on the four directions. Each direction has a specific, corresponding color, cloud pattern, lightning formation, tree species, type of obligation, and so forth. When the Hopi construct their religious altars, they combine materials like corn and colored sand, each of which stands for a specific concept. A whole panoply of concepts, therefore, can be visually arrayed and connected to give thanks to the spirits and to request future favors. Both the Chinese and Hopi ways signify attempts to understand and interpret the natural world.

they favor minimal social regulation. Purposive Daoists shun combat situations, but if forced to fight, they will employ all available means to win. Some martial arts employ Daoist ways. Purposive Daoists believe that aggressive people cause resentment in others, so they counsel quietude and patience in one's relationships.

Another condition of the intellectuals' creative lives stemmed from the leisure time they enjoyed to formulate their ideas. Indeed, they lived off the manual labor of others. This material prosperity enabled the support of a large leisured class that created elite culture, a class that the Legalists despised.

THE QIN EMPIRE, 221–207 B.C.

During the eighth and seventh centuries B.C., the Qin state appeared in western China. Natural defenses helped protect the Qin region, but intensified large-scale warfare threatened ruin. Soon a traveling strategist, Wei Yang[6] (around 390–338 B.C.), gained the confidence of the Qin ruler and launched a program that transformed his government into a great power.

Wei Yang developed a centralized Qin polity. He implemented a series of laws enforced by punishments and rewards, and then he imposed these regulations on all except the ruler. Wei Yang divided the state into **commandaries** (large administrative districts similar to provinces) and appointed officials, accountable to the monarch, over them. This system of central authority permitted Qin rulers efficiently to raise and supply large armies that regularly defeated enemy forces.

Wei Yang's successors added techniques of statecraft to improve Qin's government. They gathered statistics about demographics, agriculture, mines, tax revenues, and expenditures. Job descriptions were written in order to find the best-qualified people, and a merit-rating system evaluated their performance. The Qin bureaucracy effectively ruled a powerful state that awed its rivals.

Agriculture received favored treatment in economic planning. Wei Yang believed that farming was the foundation of political and military power, and he promoted individual landowning, as well as the abolition of the manorial feudal system. The government lent or rented iron farm tools to peasant farmers. Wei Yang lauded the peasants as hardworking, loyal subjects and denounced aristocrats and other groups (like scholars) as lazy, disloyal idlers. During the Warring States Period, Qin officials harassed scholars and killed many aristocrats who unsuccessfully challenged the government.

Wei Yang's reforms contributed to the Qin state's growing power. In a campaign against the powerful state of Zhao,[7] during the Battle of Changping (260 B.C.), the Qin army trapped a large opposing army. After receiving assurances of good treatment, the Zhao commander surrendered. Nevertheless, the Qin force annihilated the unarmed enemy troops. The Qin state gained a reputation for ruthlessness.

King Jeng (259–210 B.C.) of the Qin state gathered talented advisors who devised stratagems such as bribing officials in the enemy states. The unification wars began in 230 B.C. and lasted for nine years. In one campaign, a river was diverted against a state capital's wall and destroyed it. The last warring state fell in 221 B.C., and King Jeng ordered national celebrations to inaugurate a peaceful era. He also commanded his advisors to choose a new royal title, because "king" seemed unworthy. These men, along with their ruler, settled on "emperor." King Jeng became the First Emperor of the Qin Empire.

Below the emperor, three officials presided over the bureaucracy, supervising record keeping, military affairs, and lower officials. Next came nine bureau chiefs who handled the key decisions and directives of their agencies. All received orders directly from the emperor, who monitored their labors.

The Qin government imposed a unified, centralized rule and an administrative system of commandaries on the conquered territories. Three officials ran a commandary: a military commander, a civil official, and an inspector who watched all. Subcommandary officials toiled in this chain of command and passed their reports to the appropriate commandary officials. All obeyed the central government, which hired and fired them.

Officials standardized weights and measures, money, written characters, axle lengths, and laws. Laws in particular extended everywhere in a mas-

---

[6] **Wei Yang:** WAY yahng

[7] **Zhao:** JOW

FIGURE 11.4 *The Great Wall. This view of the Great Wall shows it snaking across the mountains of northern China. Technically called the Long Wall, the edifice shown here was built in the fifteenth century by laborers of the Ming Empire. During the Qin era, it deterred the Huns; in the Ming era, it deterred the Mongols. The wall was also meant to hinder Chinese from traveling and carrying Chinese technology away with them.* Henri Cartier-Bresson/ Magnum Photos.

sive social engineering experiment that outlawed local customs and unnecessarily angered the newly conquered peoples. An early Zhou official once noted, "Never change local customs of conquered peoples, or they will resent it and you." As we have seen elsewhere, the Romans, Mauryas, and Guptas permitted a great deal of local autonomy in their empires. But the strong militarist orientation of Qin rulers led them to demand that local customs conform to Qin practices.

Large-scale public works projects began before the final unification in 221 B.C. China's northern frontiers were vulnerable to incursions by nomads. In preimperial times, various northern states erected walls to protect themselves. The Qin Empire built a 2,000-mile-long barrier, using the surviving walls and adding new sections. This effort took much labor and resources, but it

defined the border between nomads and agriculturists. The wall system was intended to slow, rather than stop, attacks. Once warned, the Qin army could mobilize and repel invaders. The Great Wall as it exists today was built in the fifteenth century. The emperor also built scaled-down replicas of palaces and mansions from the states conquered by his armies. He ordered architects and engineers to defeated states, and they returned with drawings of prominent dwellings. A road network also linked the new regions with the capital.

Many Qin policies reflected a concerted effort to bring security both to the state and to adversely affected social groups. During the unification wars, the Qin regime moved rich and powerful families to the capital region. One historian claimed that 120,000 families were forcibly shifted there. The Qin government uprooted more of its subjects by forcing them to settle frontier areas. The great Qin highways may have carried as many as a million of these forced settlers. Another security matter came with the disarmament of the people. All had to turn in their weapons, some of which were recast into statues or bells.

Peasant farmers received good treatment, for the emperor decreed that landless people could acquire previously vacated or virgin land. Apparently the supply of labor available to the Qin state greatly increased, because the monarch abolished the labor tax of thirty days' labor owed to the state. About the same time, plentiful grain supplies enabled him to give a tax rebate. Each village

FIGURE 11.5 *The First Qin Emperor.* *This painting shows the Qin ruler presiding over the burning of the books and the execution of scholars. Completed late in the imperial era, it mistakenly assumes that both events happened at the same time. The earliest account records these events as happening a year apart. The marring of the ruler's face shows the hatred with which he was regarded by scholars of later generations.* ET Archive.

received an amount of grain and a few animals. This action is one of the few tax rebates in world history.

To advise him about key policies and other matters, the emperor gathered a brain trust. Earlier kings had assembled large numbers of intellectuals, and the First Emperor emulated these forerunners. In 213 B.C., the monarch invited his imperial academicians to a banquet during which a Confucian criticized the centralized rule. He argued for a return to the Zhou feudal system with kingdoms established in frontier areas and ruled by blood relatives who could aid the government in troubled times. The emperor ordered officials to deliberate on the proposal and approved a chief minister's petition recommending that privately owned books, except those concerned with medicine, agriculture, and divination, be burned. Most of China's classics disappeared in flames. Unfortunately, the copies of all banned and permitted works stored in the Imperial Library also burned a few years later.

The year following the book-burning, the emperor learned of a treasonous speech by two academicians. Suspecting similar sentiments by others, he ordered the interrogation of court scholars. As a result, 460 academicians died, and a like number were forced to toil on the Great Wall project. For these two transgressions, scholars have long reviled this monarch.

Because he lived in fear of assassination, the First Emperor led a secretive life. He never slept in the same room on successive nights. When he walked on the palace grounds, walled pathways hid him, and he traveled in covered carriages. Although the First Emperor feared for his life, he often traveled around his beloved realm. On imperial tours, he ascended sacred peaks to sacrifice animals to local deities. A downpour interrupted one such ascent, and, grateful to a sheltering tree, the monarch ennobled it. On another sortie, he punished a mountain spirit that thwarted his progress by denuding the mountain, painting some of its rocks red, the color that convicts wore.

The First Emperor's last trip took place in 210 B.C. Accompanied by Hu Hai[8]—his favorite son—and by key officials, the imperial party meandered through southeast and coastal China. When the entourage stopped by the sea, the emperor con-

[8] **Hu Hai:** HOO hy

PATHS TO THE PAST

Did the Qin Empire Burn Books and Bury Scholars?

We saw in Chapter 1 how historians analyze and interpret sources in order to understand an event. Here, we will examine accounts in *The Historical Records*, written by Sima Qian around 100 B.C. In recent years doubt has been cast on the infamous events of 213–212 B.C., when the Qin Empire supposedly burned books and executed 460 imperial academicians.

The 213 B.C. event centered on an imperial banquet, at which an academician criticized the government. The First Emperor commanded his officials to debate the speech, and a top official proposed burning most books in private hands.

But not all historians accept this account. They note that although Sima Qian lamented the loss of literature, there is no condemnation in his biography of the official who urged the emperor to burn the books and who should have been denounced for that destruction. In fact, this minister is ranked at a level of the greatest officials. Another discrepancy in the record concerns the lack of punishment for the offending academician, who should have been a logical target for reprisal. The same account alleged that the Qin state permitted people to keep possession of works on divination. Because divining could have been used to predict the fall of a government, works of divination would presumably have been burned.

A skeptical view has been taken of the alleged punishment of nearly 1,000 academicians. *The Historical Records* offers a conversation between two academicians who slandered the emperor, then fled. The ruler learned of the verbal attacks and launched an investigation of all academicians. Eventually, the history alleges, 460 scholars perished and more were punished by being sent north to work on the Great Wall. How would Sima Qian have been able to reconstruct a conversation between two academicians who lived more than a century earlier? They would have taken great pains to speak in guarded ways. It is difficult to imagine that a plot encompassing more than 900 scholars could have existed. These officials had advised their sovereign on various matters. In short, they rendered the Qin Empire invaluable service long after the 212 B.C. date.

One modern scholar using this kind of textual analysis has concluded that some of Sima Qian's negative accounts of the Qin Empire are later additions by scholars who hated the First Emperor of the Qin Empire. If true, this perspective shows *The Historical Records* in a different light. It also suggests that understanding of the Qin Empire has been obscured by the smoke of deliberate intent.

Whether or not one agrees with a particular scholar's interpretation of an event, new ideas or perspectives may be uncovered by subjecting a document to rigorous analysis, including focused questions. This constant probing and examining opens historians to exciting vistas of discovery.

tracted a fatal disease and succumbed. Far from the capital and in unfriendly territory, the top officials, Hu Hai, and the dead monarch's servants conspired to hide the death and plotted to elevate Hu Hai, instead of the presumed heir apparent, to the throne. This plot commenced a significant political struggle that eventually toppled the Qin Empire. To maintain the ruse that the emperor lived, trusted servants brought food, clothing, and other necessities to the covered imperial carriage. The hot weather intensified the death stench, so the plotters masked it by placing a cartload of dead fish nearby. Upon reaching the capital, the conspirators commanded in the emperor's name that his heir apparent commit suicide. The young man dutifully obeyed "his father's orders." Only then did the plotters announce the emperor's death and Hu Hai's immediate ascension to the throne.

Preliminary work on the First Emperor's tomb had commenced when that monarch had assumed power in 246 B.C. When he finally died in 210 B.C., tens of thousands of people hastily completed the tomb complex. A detachment of clay soldiers, horses, and vehicles symbolically guarded the First Emperor's burial place. More than seven thousand life-size soldiers modeled on an elite-guard detachment lay buried there until their discovery and excavation in the mid-1970s. Bronze soldiers, horses, and a carriage have also been recovered. The central tomb lies beneath a large artificial hill. Inside the mound rests a palace with a gigantic relief map of China and river channels through which mercury once coursed. (Mercury rivers flowed into a mercury sea upon which floated the First Emperor's sarcophagus.)

The collapse of the Qin government came rapidly. Hu Hai resumed work on dormant construction projects and commissioned a special guard of 50,000 soldiers. Discontent with the government, resentment about the labor projects, and anger about the changing of local customs caused the unrest. Deteriorating weather contributed to the Qin state's demise. Recent scholarship suggests that a volcanic eruption in Iceland thrust a massive amount of volcanic material into the atmosphere and altered weather patterns in the northern hemisphere. Extant Chinese texts note heavy and prolonged rainfalls. Not only would the deluge have provoked floods, it would have destroyed crops and brought famine.

Whatever the circumstances, uprisings began. Although Qin armies defeated the early rebels, more successful anti-Qin efforts proliferated. One imperial messenger brought news of additional challenges to an irritated Hu Hai, who had the messenger killed. Subsequent "positive" reports meant that the Second Emperor had lost touch with his realm. At the same time, a general purge crippled the top government levels as Hu Hai's former teacher and trusted advisor eliminated political rivals. The tutor assassinated the Second Emperor and elevated a grandson of the First Emperor. The new monarch soon killed his "patron." While these sordid events consumed elite figures, a rebel force broke through the capital region's southern defenses and captured the hapless grandson.

The Qin state's collapse should not mask its achievements. An administrative structure like that of the Qin Empire, with top officials each supervising a clearly delineated area of government, served successive imperial polities. The Qin

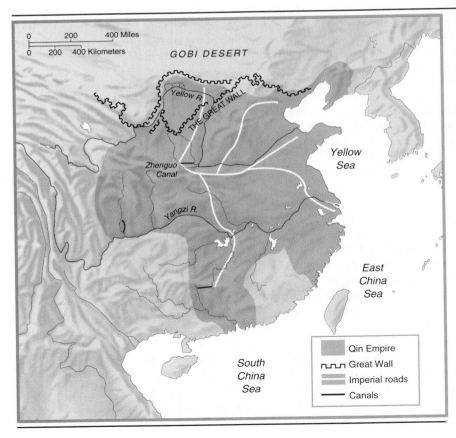

MAP 11.2 *The Qin Empire in 210 B.C. The Qin road system linked many far-flung parts of the empire with the capital. The Great Wall is also indicated, as well as three major canals: the two northernmost were used primarily for irrigation and the southernmost was used primarily for transportation. Effective communication and transportation were essential to the empire's well-being.*

FIGURE 11.6 *Figures from the Qin Emperor's Tomb.* *Excavations in the 1970s uncovered part of the vast remains of the First Qin Emperor's burial site. Construction of this complex began more than thirty years before the emperor died. Terra-cotta figures of warriors are arranged in rows, and each has an individual face. A few smaller bronze figures, like this horse-drawn cart, have also been found. The artisanry testifies to the cultural splendor of China's first imperial age.* Cultural Relics Publishing House.

legacy of standardization provided cultural and political cohesiveness. By erecting the Great Wall, the Qin government finished delineating the boundaries between the northern nomads and the Chinese agriculturalists.

THE HAN EMPIRE, 202 B.C.–A.D. 220

The Han Empire has been regarded as a defining era in Chinese history, and the Chinese people during this time often called themselves the "People of Han." During that time, Chinese power dominated many parts of East Asia, and Chinese influence held sway over Koreans, Vietnamese, and other Asians. In addition, some of China's most important historical works were written in the Han imperial period.

The Early Han Empire, 202 B.C.–A.D. 9

Although Early Han emperors adhered to the Qin political structure, they lessened its tax and service burdens on the people. This permitted society to recover from the disastrous wars and famine of the

Qin era. Around 120 B.C., however, the Martial Emperor revived costly public works projects and expansionist military campaigns. His successors contented themselves with ruling more humanely and seeking pleasure.

POLITICAL DEVELOPMENTS. In the last years of the Qin Empire, some peasants ignited the first unsuccessful challenge to the empire. Although it failed, an aristocrat and a commoner led new rebellions. The aristocrat regularly defeated the Qin forces and proclaimed himself dictator, naming the commoner as the King of Han. Within months, Liu Bang,[9] who was the king of Han, seized the former Qin capital and declared war on the dictator. During the years of civil war (206–202 B.C.), Liu Bang selected outstanding people to command his armies and to run his government. He held the strategic center and ultimately won, founding one of China's great empires, which lasted for four centuries. Therefore, Liu Bang became the First Emperor of Han.

Liu Bang softened the Qin laws, lowered taxes, and lightened the people's burdens, because, as a commoner, he knew their travails. He controlled

[9]**Liu Bang:** LYOH BONG

the Qin heartland and other populated areas while installing his top military commanders as kings of distant realms. By 195 B.C., the First Han Emperor replaced these kings with his kin to secure the dynasty. Gradually the military nature of the new government assumed a more civilian character, something that the Qin monarchs failed to do. The First Han Emperor needed the Confucians' ritual expertise for the enthronement rites that gave him legitimacy, and some Confucians entered government service.

Succession worried the new emperor. At one point he favored a son by a concubine over his empress's son, the acknowledged heir apparent. Because Empress Lu frequently gave sage advice to her husband and often acted courageously, she earned the ruling elite's support. When the emperor tried to replace the heir apparent, their opposition dissuaded him. Before he died in 195 B.C., the emperor named Empress Lu as regent for their son, who was still a minor.

Empress Lu (reign dates 195–180 B.C.) ruled through minors and followed her husband's policies of relaxed rule and mild laws to give the common people relief from years of war, disease, and suffering. Fearful that the population might not recover from its terrible losses, she decreed that single women of childbearing age be taxed five times more heavily than other adults. Empress Lu provided a steady ruling hand, and when she died, another son of the First Han Emperor succeeded.

Some Chinese historians have reviled Empress Lu by exaggerating her negative traits and de-emphasizing her significant contributions. If she had been politically inept, the Han state would have collapsed. Because most of these historians adhered to Confucian ideals, they may have reflected the Confucian bias against females. Nearly every woman who ruled endured negative assessments by these historians.

Like the Qin capital, Changan, the capital of the early Han state, became a vibrant city for tens of thousands of Chinese. The city was laid out on a grid pattern according to the four cardinal directions; the streets inside the city ran along north-south or east-west lines. Palaces took up a significant fraction of land inside the city, and an armory was built between the two main palaces located in the southern part of Changan. The city walls, which were built after the two palaces, were constructed using the conscript and convict labor of both men and women. These walls of rammed earth were about 40 feet high and 40 to 50 feet wide at the base. Nine markets served the city, and records of the day describe various activities in Changan, including the existence of city youth gangs, each with its own distinctive color of clothing. Most of Changan was in place by 180 B.C.

The next two reigns (180–141 B.C.) continued the policies of low state expenses and minimal taxes. Some scholars have asserted that the light government hand reflects a commitment by monarchs to Contemplative Daoist beliefs that the best government rests easily on the people. Frequent decrees solicited nominations of honorable people to be officials. One problem—the peripheral kingdoms that had been created in the early years of the empire—exploded around 155 B.C., when kings who nursed personal grudges or ambitions to rule the empire revolted. After a few worrisome weeks, the Han armies prevailed, and the central government reduced or abolished the larger and more dangerous kingdoms.

Because Liu Che,[10] the Martial Emperor (reign dates 141–87 B.C.), succeeded to the throne as a minor, others made decisions for him early in his reign. His grandmother, for example, promoted Daoist ideas that were prominent at this time. Another early decree favored Confucian scholars, because it asserted that people who espoused other philosophies could not hold high positions. By the first century A.D., Confucianism had become the orthodox ideology of the empire.

The reign of Liu Che is significant because during this time Han power dominated Central and East Asia. Interest in distant lands grew. Zhang Qian,[11] a diplomat, went west to gather knowledge and to seek alliances with friendly states. After many years, Zhang Qian returned—without diplomatic treaties, but with much knowledge. His mission set the foundation for Chinese trade and intercourse with other peoples. Han armies invaded the western lands of what came to be called Chinese Turkestan, and, despite heavy casualties, Chinese influence prevailed. Other armies conquered Korea and Vietnam. The costs of these campaigns demanded new resources.

The Han state took a variety of measures to cope with the rising costs of its expansive foreign policy. Iron and salt monopolies began when the

[10]**Liu Che:** LYOH CHUH
[11]**Zhang Qian:** JONG chee YAHN

IN THEIR OWN WORDS

Peasant Life in Early Imperial China

Life for the common folk was often quite difficult, as may be seen in a memorandum sent by Chao Cuo,[a] an official, to his emperor around 160 B.C. Perhaps a bit of rhetorical emphasis may be found in the document, but the sometimes horrible living conditions are, in fact, vividly portrayed.

If the people are poor, then depravity follows. Poverty originates in insufficiency; insufficiency originates in not farming. If the people do not engage in farming, they will not be attached to the land. If they do not become attached to the land, they will leave their native places and regard their families lightly. . . .

A wise ruler says that this is so. Therefore he urges people to devote themselves to farming and mulberry culture. He lowers taxes and enlarges stores in order to fill the granaries against [the time of] floods and droughts. . . .

Pearls, jade, gold, and silver cannot be eaten in case of hunger, nor can they be worn in case of cold. Yet people value them because of the emperor's use of them.

They [peasants] till the land in spring, hoe in summer, harvest in autumn, and store in winter. [Besides,] they have to cut wood for fuel, work in the government buildings and render labor service. In the spring, they cannot escape the wind and dust; in the summer, they cannot escape the heat; in the autumn, they cannot escape the chilling rain; and in the winter, they cannot escape the cold. Throughout the four seasons, they do not have a single day of rest. Furthermore, their private expenditures for parting with those who are leaving and for welcoming those who are coming, for consoling the bereaved, visiting the sick, caring for the orphans, and bringing up the young, all have to be defrayed from that income. . . . Collections are urgent, taxation exorbitant; and the taxes are collected at no fixed date. Orders issued in the morning have to be executed in the evening. Those who have something sell it at half price, those who have nothing have to borrow at 100 percent interest. Hence there are people who have sold their land, their houses, their wives and children in order to pay their debts [taxes]. . . .

The picture, of course, details a life of desperate poverty, and the monarch took measures to help the poor. A few decades later, however, taxes rose to levels where people became so impoverished that some revolted against the state.

[a]**Chao Cuo:** CHOW swohw

---

government licensed the production, distribution, and sale of salt and iron to a few people. Liu Che imposed burdensome taxes on commerce, and the peasants suffered from additional levies. Frontier soldiers farmed to defray garrison expenses, and this military colonist system became a regular policy of successor states.

Despite the glories of Liu Che's reign, his expansionist and statist policies impoverished merchants and peasants alike. Great unrest troubled the empire, and it took harsh measures to crush incipient uprisings. Court maneuvers, including charges of witchcraft leveled at the empress, compelled her adult son, the heir apparent, to attack those who influenced his father. Both mother and son perished in the ensuing struggle. On his deathbed, a saddened Liu Che created a Regency Council of trusted advisors to supervise his infant son and successor.

Although limited prosperity and stable rule continued for a few decades after Liu Che's reign, serious decline set in after 49 B.C. A major problem of reduced revenues developed because Liu Che had rewarded outstanding officials with tax-free estates. As these estates expanded, key revenue sectors disappeared and increased the burden on peasants, many of whom fled to the tax-exempt estates. A vicious cycle of rising taxes shrank the tax base and caused tax revenues to decline. The financial crisis precipitated a political crisis.

Despite the many problems facing the political elite, members of the Wang[12] clan benefited

[12]**Wang:** WONG

from the long life of Empress Wang (reign dates 49–33 B.C.). When her husband died, she became empress dowager and regent for her young son and outlived several reigning emperors. She never dominated the government in the manner of Empress Lu. Each new monarch under Empress Dowager Wang had to act like an obedient, filial child to this matriarch. Through successive reigns she appointed her clan's members to key posts. One, Wang Mang, amassed power, usurped the throne, and proclaimed a new dynasty (A.D. 9–23).

Wang Mang limited landholding, abolished tax-free lands, lowered taxes, reinstituted the monopolies, pushed currency reforms, and mounted aggressive campaigns against the northern nomads. The tax reforms alienated elite groups. A massive rupture in the Yellow River dike system killed many and made beggars of others, who turned to banditry and rebellion. One rebel group, the Red Eyebrows, named for distinctive red markings they painted over their eyes, overwhelmed Wang Mang's armies, took the capital, and assassinated him. After a civil war, a Han relative ascended the throne in A.D. 25.

SOCIAL AND ECONOMIC DEVELOPMENTS. Han society developed in the relatively relaxed atmosphere of the Early Han period. Social mobility took place, as demonstrated by several top officials who came from the commoner ranks. By the first century B.C., ennobled aristocrats had passed their titles and property to their heirs. As we have noted, these tax-free estates unduly burdened governments. Han society included many social gradations: aristocrats of royal blood, ennobled aristocrats, officials, commoners, and slaves who served the government and private citizens alike.

Agriculture was recognized by the state as the dominant economic form. Not only did the state resume the practice of lending or renting iron agri-

FIGURE 11.7 *State Burdens on the Peasants.* *This stamped brick illustrates a familiar scene: paying taxes. The bowed peasant pours his grain before the tax collector, who is seated with accounting slips in his hands. The subservient posture of the peasant suggests that he is bowed under the weight of his obligation. His simple clothes also contrast with the official's finery.* Courtesy of the Chinese Cultural Center of San Francisco.

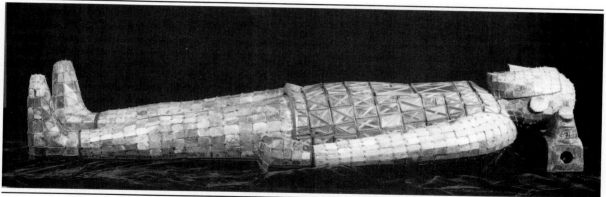

FIGURE 11.8 **The Han Jade Princess.** *This burial suit for royalty of the Early Han Period was discovered in the 1970s. Jade was believed to inhibit bodily decay, and for this reason jade pieces were sewn into an enclosing suit for the body. Princess Dou Wan died in the second century B.C. Her headrest is similar to ones used as pillows for sleeping.* Robert Harding Picture Library.

cultural tools, but some officials also identified farming experts who were sent at public expense through areas to disseminate their expertise and to increase production. By the second century of Han rule, monarchs had established large public granaries to be filled in times of surplus and drawn upon in times of shortage.

Manufacture and commerce prospered. Iron foundries proliferated in Han times, and, although many establishments were privately owned, the state also supported these works. The monopolies of iron and salt during the time of the Martial Emperor were highly unpopular, because they drove up prices. Later the state abolished the monopolies only to reestablish them a short time after. Trade grew dramatically after 120 B.C. with the opening of western trade routes to Chinese merchants, and many Chinese goods circulated through most of Eurasia. Although merchants traded lacquerware, iron products, precious jewels, and other items, silk provided the greatest profits. In fact, the two western routes across the formidable deserts (the Gobi Desert and the Tarim Basin) were appropriately named the silk roads.

ELITE CULTURE. Many different forms of literature developed in the Early Han period. The dominant literary genre was the prose poem, a form that combined lengthy prose and poetic passages. The Han era saw the perfection of the prose poem in the hands of a succession of capable writers.

Another Han literary development came in the area of bibliography under the leadership of a Han prince who categorized the imperial holdings.

History writing set a pattern of excellence that was imitated for centuries. Sima Tan,[13] the Grand Historian of Han, began a general history of China. The project passed to his son, Sima Qian,[14] who chose castration over death when punished for angering the Martial Emperor. The son lived to fulfill his father's dying wish that the history be completed. The work, *The Historical Records*, is a masterful, comprehensive treatment of two thousand years. Written in a graceful, elegant style, it contains a half-million written characters. It accurately dates events and long-deceased rulers. Although Sima Qian sometimes embellished things for dramatic effect, scholars have admired his methods of weighing evidence.

Confucianism survived the Qin oppression to become the favored ideology of Han. We have seen the promotion of Confucian books and scholars during the Martial Emperor's reign. Successive monarchs gathered Confucian worthies and excluded followers of other traditions. Wang Mang, the usurper, even based his reforms on an ancient Confucian work. A key Confucian thinker, Dong Zhongshu[15] (179–104 B.C.), reworked Confucian

[13] **Sima Tan:** SEE mah TAHN
[14] **Sima Qian:** SEE mah chee AHN
[15] **Dong Zhongshu:** DOONG joong shoo

ideas into a framework suitable to an empire. He posited the existence of three interrelated levels of the universe: the realm of Heaven, the realm of Humanity, and the realm of Earth. These realms joined in the monarch. If the state governed well and people prospered, Heaven and Earth gave favorable signs. Conversely, when a ruler became tyrannical, negative portents occurred: An earthquake might devour a city (such an event is recorded) or a comet might light the sky. (Chinese first recorded Halley's Comet during the Han Empire.) Thus, "bad" rulers felt admonishment from natural forces and human critics. The interpretation of portents gained favor across East Asia.

The Late Han Empire, A.D. 25–220

For about a century after the Han emperor ascended the throne, peace and prosperity were the norm for most Chinese. After A.D. 120, corruption began to become widespread, and factional politics weakened the imperial court. Large-scale uprisings weakened the imperial system, bringing warlords into power in many parts of China.

POLITICAL DEVELOPMENTS. Political control slowly returned to the Han Empire after the usurpation of Wang Mang and the massive revolts that toppled him. Korea remained under Chinese

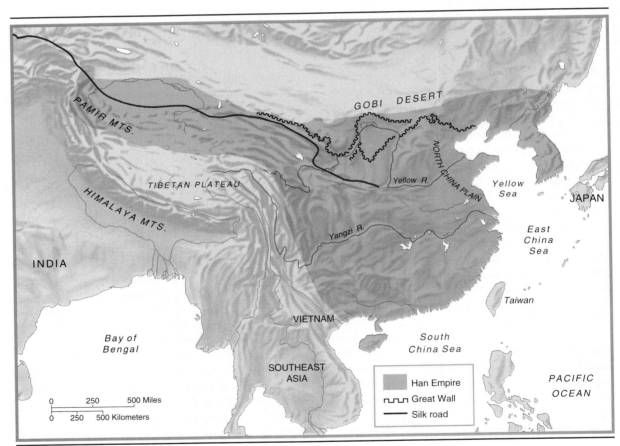

MAP 11.3 *The Han Empire in A.D. 120.* *This map shows the greatest extent of the Han Empire, which controlled parts of Korea, Vietnam, and Central Asia. The silk roads came under Chinese jurisdiction and carried Chinese wares westward, some eventually arriving in Rome to the delight of wealthy Romans, who prized Chinese silk. Land trade was a major revenue source for Chinese rulers, who paid much attention and wealth to keeping land routes under their control.*

FIGURE 11.9 *Flying Horse of Late Han.* *This bronze sculpture captures the great speed and pride of the horse. To emphasize the flying ideal, the horse's hoof rests on a soaring bird. Power and grace are combined in this excellent example of Chinese artisanry from centuries ago.* Robert Harding Picture Library.

domination, but Vietnam rebelled under the Trung sisters, whose fragile government fell to a new Chinese campaign around A.D. 50. The Chinese armies also returned to Central Asia and remained there until nomads pushed them back.

The first monarchs of the Later Han Empire ruled effectively. They selected able officials and presided over stable and prosperous times. Over time, the decline of the monarchs permitted the interaction of three key political groups: the empresses and their families, the court officials, and the **eunuchs** (castrated boys and men). Eunuchs influenced politics in Chinese history. Men were needed to guard the women's quarters of the inner palace, but the monarch did not wish to have virile males there because they might impregnate his empress. Yet, eunuchs did gain influence by supporting strong-willed empresses or by befriending heirs apparent.

The last effective ruler was Empress Deng[16] (reign dates 106–121), who ruled as regent for her infant son and who relied on the significant political influence of her family. When the child died, she kept power as regent, ruling for another child

[16]**Deng:** DUHNG

successor, and during her tenure the country enjoyed general tranquility. Several of her family members held key political posts. After her death, power came into the hands of other prominent families that produced empresses. Eunuchs also gained prominence through their close ties to monarchs and their control of key government and military posts. Officials opposed the other groups. Despite continual friction among the factions, a customary practice of balancing alliances kept each group from becoming too powerful.

Stability was shattered when warlords gained control late in the second century. These military figures rose during the Yellow Turban Revolt of 184. The Yellow Turbans lived in communities with healers or "miracle workers." These peaceful centers sprang up in the 170s and 180s, but the Han government saw the Yellow Turbans as subversive because they were tightly organized groups of thousands, some of which carried weapons for self-defense. In 184, a Han military campaign against the Yellow Turbans triggered a major uprising. The corruption-ridden Han forces disintegrated before the fierce attacks of the enemy. Military power soon shifted to regional armies and their commanders, who defeated the rebels.

FIGURE **11.10** *Zhang Heng's Seismoscope.* *This cutaway view of an adaptation of Zhang Heng's seismoscope shows how the mechanism was designed to work: The central weight shifted with any movement and caused the dragon's jaws to release a ball, which fell into the frog's mouth and thus indicated the line of an earthquake's seismic wave. Placement of several of these devices would allow the scientist to plot the quake's epicenter. The piece is an example of Chinese technological development nearly two thousand years ago.* Science and Society Picture Library.

Eventually, the commanders became warlords who challenged the central government. One warlord seized the capital and destroyed the political system. His successor captured the last hapless Han monarch and terminated the dynasty in 220.

ELITE CULTURE AND SOCIETY. Daoism changed during the Han era from a philosophy accessible to a tiny elite into a popular religion. This metamorphosis began in the Early Han when Lao Zi became a Daoist divinity. Soon a myriad of divine beings, including the Stove God, who symbolizes Daoist experimentation with alchemy to discover elixirs of immortality, were recognized.

Religious Daoists became interested in health issues, seeking to prolong their lives by a variety of practices. Cinnabar was the preferred elixir of longevity because its bright red color seemed to connote health, vitality, heat, and happiness. Ingested cinnabar was a poison, however, and shortened life. Daoists also experimented with diet, exercise, and breathing techniques to prolong life.

Many patterns and trends described for the Early Han era continued after A.D. 25. Although aristocratic families perished in the wars that toppled Wang Mang, the new government created an aristocracy that dominated society and politics. In fact, some great clans persisted into an era of division (220–589) that followed the Han period. One's education, especially when tied to government service, afforded privileges and honors. Individual elite women, some of whom were educated, played important political and cultural roles, although females generally were subordinated to men.

SOUTH AND EAST ASIA

		Zhou king moves capital, 770 B.C.
	700 B.C.	
Chinese feudalism, to 403 B.C.		
	600 B.C.	Iron used in China, c. 620 B.C.
Origins of Confucianism, Daoism, Legalism	**500 B.C.**	Confucius begins teaching, c. 500 B.C.
	400 B.C.	
		Wei Yang starts reforms in Qin state, 356 B.C.
	300 B.C.	
Qin ▶ Empire, 221–267 B.C.		Founding of Qin Empire, 221 B.C.
	200 B.C.	Founding of Early Han Empire, 202 B.C.
Early Han Empire, 202 B.C.–A.D. 9	**100 B.C.**	Conquest of Korea, Vietnam, and Central Asia, 111–100 B.C.
	A.D. 1	End of Early Han, 9 Founding of Late Han, 25
Wang ▶ Mang's rule, A.D. 9–23		
Late Han Empire, A.D. 9 – 220	**A.D. 100**	Invention of paper, 105
		Yellow Turban Revolt, 184
	A.D. 200	Fall of Han Empire, 220

The Han era was a dynamic time for economic development. Agriculture continued to dominate the Chinese economy, and agricultural specialists were employed by the state to share their expertise with other farmers. In essays, they discussed planting techniques, new tools, and new seed varieties. Manufacturing continued, and the mass-production techniques for iron and steel greatly improved. Chinese trade grew, especially in Chinese silks, which were in demand all across Eurasia. The famed silk roads were conquered by the Martial Emperor and remained in Chinese hands through much of the era.

Zhang Heng[17] (78–139), a prose poem master and a noted scientist, designed instruments to facilitate the observation and display of heavenly bodies. He invented the first seismograph and mastered diverse mathematical branches. Cai Lun,[18] a eunuch and member of the inner court around A.D. 100, invented paper. The method he employed yielded a writing surface that could be inexpensively fashioned and widely distributed. Not only did it transform state business, but books became lighter, easier to handle, cheaper, and more widely read.

Imperial veneration of Confucius grew, and the sage's family home became a national shrine. Little original thought characterized Confucianism at this time. The most significant work came from a skeptical rationalist, Wang Chung[19] (27–97), who debunked myths and superstitions. He ridiculed the art of divining the future. Wang Chung pioneered in the effort to base arguments on observation and reasoned discourse.

SUMMARY

1. The Zhou state entered 770 B.C. in a weak condition and remained so until the mid–third century B.C., when it was conquered.

2. The Late Zhou era, 770–256 B.C., is overlapped by the Warring States Period, 403–221 B.C. The Qin Empire united and ruled China from 221–207 B.C. The Han Empire endured for four centuries but also saw a failed attempt at usurpation by Wang Mang.

3. China experienced a transformation from the seventh to the third centuries B.C. The two major forces of prolonged warfare and iron technology drove this change and brought the demise of Chinese feudalism.

4. Warfare on an increasing scale forced states to mobilize their economic and human resources. Most successful states moved to a centralized political system.

5. Bronze and iron plow tips, along with manure fertilizing, led to more plentiful grain supplies and larger populations. Iron weapons changed the nature of warfare. Central governments employed armies of workers to build massive hydraulic projects to improve crop yields.

6. Aristocrats failed to adapt to the profound changes and lapsed into insignificance or disappeared. Peasants became individual landowners, and merchants became more prosperous. A few successfully entered politics.

7. Confucianism developed an ethically based educational system along with a way to rule an empire. Legalism offered a path to military success through central rule and merit-based office holding. Daoism appealed to people who devalued social conventions and sought spiritual solace in private.

8. In the fourth century B.C., the Qin state used the Legalist system to conquer its rival states and forged an empire. It standardized laws, money, weights and measures, and written characters. It also built a road system linking key regions with the capital and the Great Wall. The founder's death and hapless rule of his successor coupled with widespread discontent toppled the Qin Empire.

[17] **Zhang Heng:** JONG huhng

[18] **Cai Lun:** SY lwuhn
[19] **Wang Chung:** WONG chee UHNG

9. The Han Empire emerged from the civil wars, and able monarchs ruled lightly and permitted the people to recover. Decades later, Liu Che conquered parts of Korea, Vietnam, and Central Asia, but the costly wars nearly toppled his rule.

10. Decline weakened the monarchy and precipitated a usurpation by Wang Mang, who failed to reform the Han system. New uprisings enabled a Han family member to reclaim the throne. The Late Han lasted for two centuries.

11. Many elements of elite Chinese culture developed in the Han era. Two historians wrote major works. Prose poems reached an apex of development. Science and technology also flourished.

SUGGESTED READINGS

Bode, Derk, ed. *The Cambridge History of China.* Vol. 1. Cambridge, Eng.: Cambridge University Press, 1986. A synthesis of scholarship on early imperial Chinese history.

DeBary, William, ed. *Sources of Chinese Tradition.* New York: Columbia University Press, 1960. A standard collection of sources and commentary for Chinese history.

Durrant, Stephen. *The Cloudy Mirror.* Albany: State University of New York Press, 1995. A recent study of the philosophy of Sima Qian, the Grand Historian of the Han Empire.

Hsu Cho-yun. *Han Agriculture.* Seattle: University of Washington Press, 1980. A study of Chinese agriculture.

Riches from a Han Emperor's Tomb. *Rows of life-sized ceramic soldiers from the tomb of the first Han Chinese emperor underscore the military might and orientation of the empire.* China Pictorial Service.

Empire

All thys were of hys anpyre.

—ROBERT OF GLOUCESTER

In this first known written usage of "empire" in English, Robert used the term in 1297 to indicate an extensive territory made up of formerly independent states. The word also carried the connotation of supreme power, reflecting its genesis in *imperare*, the Latin verb meaning "to command."

Our modern usage of "empire" is similar to Robert's: a state that controls a large area, incorporating into itself previously independent societies that view themselves as culturally different from the controlling society. Stated differently, an empire is a politically unified state in which one people dominates its neighbors. This domination usually is by military force, but a number of other means of control can come into play, including religion, diplomacy, and trade. **Imperial** simply refers to an empire. The core idea of empire—the domination and political control of its neighbors by a single state—has occurred to would-be emperors in many places and times around the world.

Why do empires develop in some places and not in others? What are the consequences for states that become imperial? Why do empires eventually crumble? This chapter presents a model that tries to answer these questions. In thinking about this model, remember that models are not necessarily "true" in every detail but that they are interpretations created by scholars. Models serve

281

as simplified versions of reality, helping us see a general pattern. The details that don't fit the model can help us refine it for future use, pointing out shortcomings and additional factors of importance.

THE CONRAD-DEMAREST MODEL OF EMPIRE

In an attempt to understand better the development and fall of empires, Geoffrey Conrad and Arthur Demarest recently have produced a model. Both Conrad and Demarest are specialists in Latin American civilizations, and their examples and inspiration came primarily from the last of the major pre-Columbian American civilizations, the Aztec of Mexico and the Inca of Peru. Nonetheless, their model is designed to apply to empires in all places and all times.

The Rise of Empires

Many earlier models of the imperial process proposed a single cause for the development of empires; greedy leaders, stressful environmental circumstances, and population pressure have been common suggestions. The Conrad-Demarest model takes a different approach. Rather than claiming that all empires developed in response to the same singular condition, Conrad and Demarest argue that empires arose out of many causes, working together and intimately linked with one another. They draw a distinction between the preconditions of empire (conditions that are necessary to support an empire but not sufficient to bring empire about) and critical causes (factors that, in the presence of the preconditions, will spark the development of empire). The preconditions are factors that might permit or encourage the development of empire as an effective solution to societal problems, but not every society that is characterized by these preconditions will develop an empire. The critical causes, according to the model, are those that actually bring about empire and are distinctive to the few societies that become imperial.

As Conrad and Demarest see it, the primary preconditions of empire are six: high agricultural potential, an environmental mosaic, state-level government, several states with none clearly dominant, mutual antagonism among those states, and adequate military resources.

Environmental factors, according to the Conrad-Demarest model, are preconditions. Good agricultural potential, for example, is critical, because an expansionistic society without good land probably will be unable to support the initial conquests necessary to begin building an empire. In addition, a region with a mosaic of different environmental zones will be more conducive to the birth of empire than one with more or less even resource distribution. Each zone in an environmental mosaic has distinctive resources and potentials, and they are wedged in among one another. A society whose control extends over only one of these zones must trade with its neighbors or in some similar manner obtain the materials that come from other zones. The empire, on the other hand, gains great advantage by controlling many of those zones, reducing dependence on trade, increasing self-sufficiency, and increasing the ability to weather a bad year when some (but not all) of the zones have limited production of food or other necessities. In pre-Columbian Mexico, for example, major empires developed in the central highlands, where there is a marked environmental mosaic; in the eastern lowlands, where the environment is more uniform, successful empires never developed.

Conrad and Demarest also consider aspects of demography in relation to the development of empire. They reject the simple argument that empires develop when population becomes too great in an area and its inhabitants are forced to expand. (This argument, incidentally, often has been used as a justification for expansion by would-be conquerors, as with Adolf Hitler's doctrine of *lebensraum* ["living space"] during World War II.) Instead, Conrad and Demarest argue that population levels typically are manageable before the establishment of empires. Indeed, empires often institute programs designed specifically to promote population increase, often to produce soldiers to fuel the military engine that runs the state. The Aztecs, for example, actively encouraged women to have large families, and women who died in childbirth were promised deification as *mociuaquetzque*[1] goddesses and an afterlife in the

---

[1] *mociuaquetzque:* moh see yoo KEHTZ kay

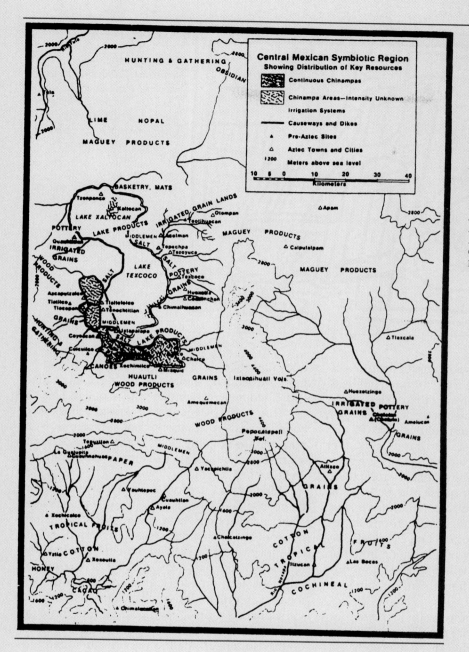

FIGURE I.2.1 *Central Mexican Environmental Mosaic.* Central Mexico, the heartland of the Aztec Empire, was composed of various environmental zones, each with different resources and potentials. By controlling several such zones, the Aztec rulers enhanced the developing empire's wealth and access to vital resources. From Geoffrey W. Conrad and Arthur A. Demarest, *Religion and Empire: The Dynamics of Aztec and Inca Expansionism* (New York: Cambridge University Press), 1984. Reproduced with permission.

supreme heaven normally reserved for warriors who died in battle. Indeed, mothers were perceived as special warriors in the struggles for empire. Ironically, gross overpopulation appears to be a result of empire, not a cause.

The Conrad-Demarest model also considers economic motivation as a precondition to the development of empire. Once a state is successful at conquest, booty or tribute will follow, and those can be very major contributions to that state's economy. The leaders, of course, receive the bulk of this windfall, but wise rulers will redistribute some of this wealth to others immediately below them in the hierarchy, who in turn will distribute some of it to those below them, and so forth. This redistribution can be in the form of rewards for meritorious service, outright gifts, public works, or tax rebates. The redistribution of wealth helps

FIGURE I.2.2 *Death of an Aztec Woman. This Aztec drawing shows a woman who has died in childbirth and become a* mociuaquetzque *goddess. Her body is locked up and protected for four days by her family to prevent the removal of body parts for use as charms to give warriors courage in battle. A link between childbirth and warfare is also seen in the belief that spirits of women who died in childbirth shared the heaven otherwise reserved for warriors killed in battle.* Detail from the *Codex Florentino.* Courtesy of Biblioteca Medicea Laurenziana, Florence.

involve everyone, regardless of rank, in the fruits of conquest and empire, assuring continued political support. And, because the wealth trickles down through the established hierarchy, it helps reinforce the system of social and political ranking.

Conrad and Demarest also argue that the absence of a dominating competing state is a precondition to the rise of empire. Such a strong state would be in a position to quash the aspirations (and the soldiers) of a small state that was seeking empire, and it would be in its best interest to do so. The power vacuum that Conrad and Demarest see as critical to the nurturing of a fledgling imperial power ensures that a state with imperial intentions can develop without interference from a superior military power.

Finally, out of this antagonistic jockeying for power a successful imperial power must develop considerable military might. This could be based on large armies, superior equipment (including new weapons, such as iron spears or jet fighters), sophisticated strategy, or improved organization. A combination of these factors would be most effective.

The model has accumulated a substantial number of preconditions, many of which seem important. Why are they only preconditions? Because one can find plenty of examples of societies that met all of these preconditions and yet never developed empires, including Shang China, Old Kingdom Egypt, and the Greek poleis. This has led Conrad and Demarest to consider these preconditions as necessary but not sufficient to support empire building. They wanted to isolate the spark that lights the fires of empire and conquest, and they believe it to be ideology.

Ideology, as used in this model, refers to that complex of ideas and philosophy that directs one's goals, expectations, and actions. It can include religion, but it also can be secularly based, as with a political theory like communism. The ideology that will make a state successful at the empire business, according to Conrad and Demarest, will focus on glorifying the military and fostering the individual's feeling of identification with the state.

The ideology of some preimperial states, no doubt, is more attuned to these factors than others, but the Conrad-Demarest model suggests that a nascent imperial power can rework its ideology to emphasize these features. The Aztecs, for instance, elevated one god in their pantheon to the status of the most important: Huitzilopochtli,[2] the god of war. The cult of Huitzilopochtli glorified warriors, encouraging young nobles to participate

[2] **Huitzilopochtli:** hweet zee loh POHCH tlee

FIGURE I.2.3 *Human Sacrifice to Huitzilopochtli. This reproduction of an Aztec drawing shows a priest, at the top of the temple stairs, grasping and tearing out the heart of a person whose chest has been slashed open. At the base of the stairs, relatives collect the body of an earlier sacrifice whose remains have been hurled down the stairs. These sacrifices were to Huitzilopochtli, the war god, to ensure continued imperial success in battle. Being sacrificed was a great honor, often actively sought by Aztecs.* British Museum/Fotomas Index.

in the winning of empire. The Aztecs also expanded the existing institution of human sacrifice, bringing it to a scale previously unknown. The world would cease to exist if the sacrifices were not made in sufficient numbers, and the major way to procure sacrificial victims was through warfare; therefore, warfare, the fulcrum of Aztec empire building, was necessary as an ongoing institution. The Aztec people were inundated with propaganda, a technique in use by many societies, both ancient and modern, urging them to do their share in the noble cause of the furtherance of the empire. In short, by manipulating ideologies, the leaders of the successful Aztec imperial state produced a population that felt a duty and a desire to support the drive for empire.

According to the Conrad-Demarest model, therefore, many small states may have the preconditions of empire. They may have good agricultural land that is part of a larger environmental mosaic; they may covet the wealth of their neighbors; there may be a power vacuum that has created a panoply of antagonistic, belligerent states; and they may have considerable military power. But all this will not be enough if a state's ideology does not endorse and justify warfare and expansion. Many states might profit from an empire, but few are able effectively to establish it.

The Conrad-Demarest model is attractive in its ability to integrate several factors into an explanation of the rise of empires. Unlike explanations based on simple assertions—for instance, that a state's leaders were greedy or that the military establishment was strong—the Conrad-Demarest model, although it does not quarrel with those assertions, goes further. It tries to explain why some states that had greedy rulers and strong armies became the seats of great empires, while others were absorbed into someone else's empire.

There are, however, limitations to the Conrad-Demarest model. Although it recognizes the importance of environmental differences in resource endowment, other models place the role of trade more centrally. Further, probably because their model was inspired by American examples, Conrad and Demarest do not consider certain factors that were important in Eurasia and Africa but not in the Americas. Particularly, they do not consider the development of superior iron weaponry and subsequent domination of neighbors by one people, such as the example of the Hittites and Assyrians. Nor do they address **pastoralism** (specialized livestock herding) and its implications for some Eurasian and African empires, such as the Mongol and Songhai.

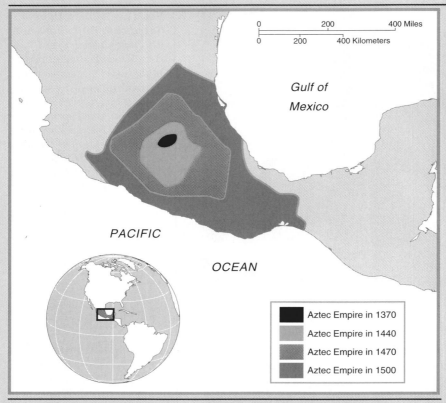

MAP I.2.1 *Growth of the Aztec Empire.* *The Aztec Empire expanded rapidly through conquest, threat, and diplomacy. From 1440 onward, the size of the empire approximately doubled every generation. Such rapid growth is predicted by the Conrad-Demarest model of empire formation, but it is unsustainable for long periods.*

Gulf of Mexico

PACIFIC

OCEAN

Aztec Empire in 1370
Aztec Empire in 1440
Aztec Empire in 1470
Aztec Empire in 1500

The Fall of Empires

If the factors discussed earlier produce empires, what do Conrad and Demarest believe causes the downfall of empires? Exactly the same factors. As they see it, the ideological and other conditions that are necessary for the establishment of an effective empire will eventually consume that empire.

An ideology that supports warfare and conquest will drive an imperial power farther and farther from its homeland and central power base. The need for captives to sacrifice, for heathens to convert, or for peoples to dominate persists long after the empire has expanded to a point where further conquest is economically counterproductive. As imperial armies travel farther from home, they face a host of difficulties: unfamiliar terrain (where conventional tactics might be ineffective), long and fragile supply lines, difficulties of reinforcement, and communication problems. Distant states that are incorporated into the empire become especially difficult to govern, because dis-

tance from the imperial heartland increases the costs and problems of controlling local rulers. As the cost of conquest goes up, the profits often go down: The richest states near home already have been conquered, and states farther removed may be less wealthy. In addition, the difficulties of transporting booty back to the capital become overwhelming. Alexander's Greek empire presents a classic example of expansion beyond the point of practicality. In such a case the pragmatic reasons for conquest are gone, but the ideology that demands it remains.

In the meantime, other aspects of imperial expansion also are souring. State-supported efforts to increase population, if successful, now may be creating a real problem. Just at a time when more effort is needed to increase production of food and other necessities in order to support the domestic front, warfare becomes more expensive, draining resources. If this situation continues, domestic shortages might erode faith in the ideology, which in turn might lead to class or regional conflicts, perhaps even to revolt.

The only hope for the survival of the empire, according to the Conrad-Demarest model, lies in an ideological change. The ideology that underlies empire building, once the erosion of faith begins, must be modified so that continued expansion is unnecessary. A less militaristic, less aggressive ideology might allow the empire to redirect its energies toward domestic problems. The establishment of such a new ideology, however, would be no easy matter, especially given that subject states would notice the change and might interpret it as weakness, perhaps staging uprisings at inopportune moments. According to this analysis, empires are inherently unstable, a conclusion supported by their generally short duration.

The Conrad-Demarest Model in Brief

Models are simplifications, and they can be summarized as a few principles. The Conrad-Demarest model can be reduced to the following principles:

1. Necessary preconditions for the rise of empire are:
   a. state-level government;
   b. high agricultural potential of the environment;
   c. an environmental mosaic;
   d. several small states with no clearly dominant state (a "power vacuum");
   e. mutual antagonism among those states; and
   f. adequate military resources.

2. The primary reason a state succeeds in empire building is an ideology supporting personal identification with the state, empire, conquest, and militarism.

3. The major results of empire are:
   a. economic rewards, reaped especially in the early years and redistributed to the elite and often to all levels of the citizenry; and
   b. population increase, often supported by the government and its ideology.

4. Empires fall because:
   a. the ideology of expansion and conquest fuels attempts at conquest beyond practical limits;
   b. failure to continue conquest indefinitely and to continue to bring its economic fruits home erodes faith in the ideology that supports the empire; and
   c. rebellions topple the empire.

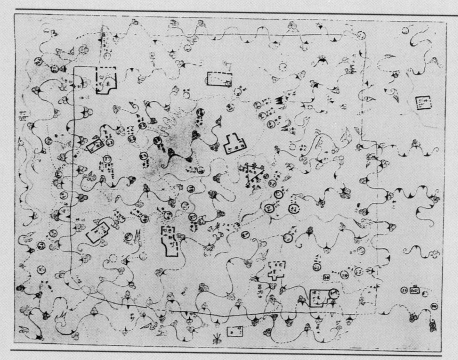

FIGURE I.2.4 *Han Chinese Map.* *This second century* B.C. *map, one of the earliest surviving from China, shows mountains (circles), rivers (wiggly lines), and military defenses (angular boxes). Chinese maps of this period may have been devoted exclusively to military functions, since contemporary documents mention them only in that context.* Wen-wu, Beijing.

APPLYING THE CONRAD-DEMAREST MODEL

As with most models, the Conrad-Demarest model sounds appealing when presented in the abstract or when applied to a case that was used as inspiration for the model. The examples presented here are mostly from the Aztecs, and they support the model. The real test, of course, is whether the model can help us understand a new case.

The Qin and Han empires, as discussed in Chapter 11, unified central China for the first time. Out of the power vacuum produced by centuries of turmoil and disunity during the Warring States Period, the Qin state and its successor, the Han state, emerged as powers that could forge an empire by conquering previously independent states. The two empires formed a continuum sometimes called the Qin-Han Empire, which will be examined here in light of the Conrad-Demarest model.

The core states of the Qin-Han Empire possessed all the necessary preconditions suggested by the Conrad-Demarest model. The preimperial Qin state was in a region of great agricultural potential, yet the environmental mosaic of China left it lacking resources found in neighboring regions. The Warring States Period established a series of mutually antagonistic states, several of which had considerable military power yet none of which was clearly dominant. With these preconditions met, the spark necessary to ignite imperial expansion, according to Conrad and Demarest's model, was ideology.

During the short-lived Qin Empire and the early years of the Han Empire, emperors predominantly followed Legalist philosophy, advocating militarism, conquest, and unification. The emperor whose warriors carved out much of the early Han Empire by conquest was not nicknamed "the Martial Emperor" because of pacifist inclinations. This ideology glorifying the military fits well with the predictions of the model.

The Qin-Han Empire reacted to imperial success much as predicted by the Conrad-Demarest model. This empire took advantage of its control of various zones in the environmental mosaic through the **ever-normal granary system**, a system whereby the government collected grain from all over the empire into warehouses and redistributed it to the people as it was required. This system pooled the produce of various regions, creating a more or less constant total supply, regardless of the agricultural success of any zone in the mosaic.

The emperor received massive material benefit in tribute, spoils of war, and commerce, once the sources for goods were controlled. The emperor then distributed some portion of that wealth. Much of that redistribution was directed through the official hierarchy, from the emperor through officials and eventually to the people. Public works, for example, normally were announced to the people by local officials, who took care to be sure it was clear that the emperor ultimately was the source of this munificence. There also were general gifts to the people on special occasions, such as the reaching of adulthood for a royal heir; these gifts usually consisted of wine, meat, or (more rarely) money. All these gifts, as well as the more ostentatious rewards reserved for top advisors and officials, helped cement the Han people together with the emperor in whatever endeavors he undertook.

Although Legalist philosophy was dominant at the Qin-Han court during the period of initial expansion of the empire, Confucianism gradually arose as a competitor. There was a period when the two vied for the emperor's support, but Confucianism eventually became the dominant philosophy of the Han Empire.

Confucian philosophy, in Han hands, evolved in a manner that elevated the emperor. Han scholars, such as Dong Zhongshu, extended Confucian thought to incorporate the concept of emperor (a notion invented in China centuries after Confucius's death). Dong developed the formula that was to characterize the Han version of Confucian political philosophy: "to subject the people to the emperor, and the emperor to heaven." This fit nicely with the Han conception of the emperor as the "son of Heaven," an official title: As a divine-right ruler, his will was inspired, perhaps informed, by the gods. The only sensible course for a devout mortal was total obedience to the emperor.

The Legalist philosophy of the Qin Empire is exactly the militaristic type of ideology that the Conrad-Demarest model predicts for the rise of empire. Elements of that philosophy were domi-

SUGGESTED READINGS **289**

nant during the period of greatest expansion of the early Han Empire. After that, the Confucian philosophy, although not militaristic, provided a different kind of ideological underpinning for the empire. Confucians stressed ritual and persuasion over might to maintain imperial rule; they often spoke out against expansionist military campaigns. A glorification of militarism was unnecessary in the later Han Empire, because the glorification of the emperor superseded it: If the emperor decreed military action, it was, by definition, the will of the gods and therefore appropriate.

In short, the Qin-Han Empire fits Conrad and Demarest's suggestion that a long-lived empire will modify its ideology to reduce dependence on militarism. The Qin Empire failed to make an ideological transition and fell within fourteen years. The Han Empire successfully made the transition to an appropriate ideology and lasted four centuries.

Has the Conrad-Demarest model improved our understanding of the Qin-Han Empire? Certainly it has drawn attention to factors that probably were important in the formation and functioning of the empire. It has helped us see how diverse practices, such as the ever-normal granary system, fit into the imperial system. Finally, it has drawn attention to a potentially significant factor for future research: the role of imperial government in Qin-Han population increase. The frustratingly fragmentary evidence could be seen as supporting a state-sponsored population increase, but more research will be necessary in order for us to see whether that conclusion is justified.

SUGGESTED READINGS

Carneiro, Robert L. "Political Expansion as an Expression of the Principle of Competitive Exclusion." In Robert Cohen and Elman R. Service, eds. *Origins of the State: The Anthropology of Political Evolution*. Philadelphia: Institute for the Study of Human Issues, 1978, pp. 205–23. Presents an alternative model for the development of empires, based on ecological and economic factors.

Conrad, Geoffrey W., and Arthur A. Demarest. *Religion and Empire: The Dynamics of Aztec and Inca Expansionism*. New York: Cambridge University Press, 1984. The book-length origin of the model discussed here.

R EGIONAL STATES HAVE BEEN PERHAPS the most common political form in history. It is easier to rule a small territory than a large one, especially if the larger entity includes more than one ethnic group. Because of this, empires have traditionally been inherently unstable, and their declines can lead to regionalism. Often, regional and local states preceded large kingdoms and empires, and occasionally they succeeded empires that collapsed.

To explore these aspects of regionalism, we have devoted Part Three to times when regional states flourished. We will examine the evidence in Asia, Africa, and Europe as we formulate answers to various questions. What is the relationship between trade and the development of regionalism? How do people reorganize their political structures when imperial bureaucracies weaken?

Chapter 12 examines the rise of Islam from Muhammad's visions in a desert town to a religion commanding the allegiance of people on three continents. The Islamic Empire expanded so far and so rapidly that its initial political unity broke down, although sociocultural unity persisted and grew. Chapter 13 explores

	ISLAM		EUROPE
200 B.C.			
A.D. 1			
A.D. 200			
A.D. 400			
A.D. 600		Early Middle Ages	
	Umayyad Caliphate		
A.D. 800		Abbasid Caliphate	
	Islamic regionalism		
A.D. 1000			
		Central Middle Ages	
A.D. 1200			
		Late Middle Ages	
A.D. 1400			
A.D. 1600			

PART THREE

THE RISE OF REGIONAL STATES

European history from the collapse of the Western Roman Empire to around 1450. Despite serious challenges from outside and within, regional states created political stability, economic prosperity, and artistic development. Chapter 14 discusses regional states of South, Southeast, and East Asia and shows how their governments were increasingly linked by maritime trade. Chapter 15 probes the histories of sub-Saharan African states and finds both diversity and similarity of political forms there. Once again, trade seems to have been an impetus to the rise and fall of larger states. Issue 3 develops the concept of feudalism, a sociopolitical structure common during times of regional states. Feudalism was a response to collapsing empires or governments in many parts of Eurasia.

ASIA				AFRICA		
Indian regionalism						200 B.C.
						A.D. 1
	Chinese regionalism	Japanese regionalism	Regionalism in West and Central Africa			A.D. 200
						A.D. 400
	Regionalism in Southeast Asia		Regionalism in East Africa			A.D. 600
Indian regionalism						A.D. 800
				Regionalism in Southwest Africa		A.D. 1000
						A.D. 1200
						A.D. 1400
						A.D. 1600

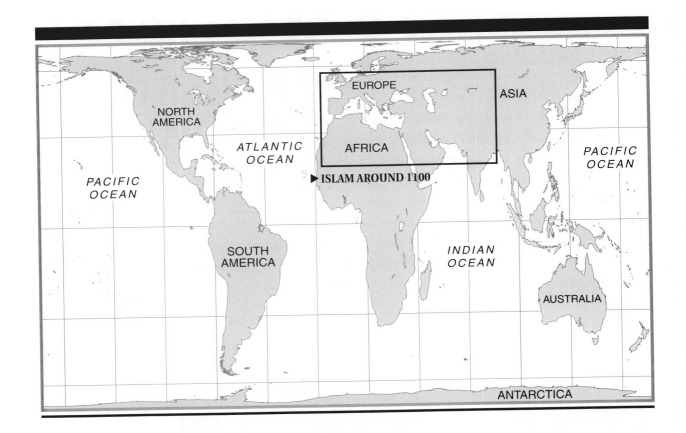

► ISLAM AROUND 1100

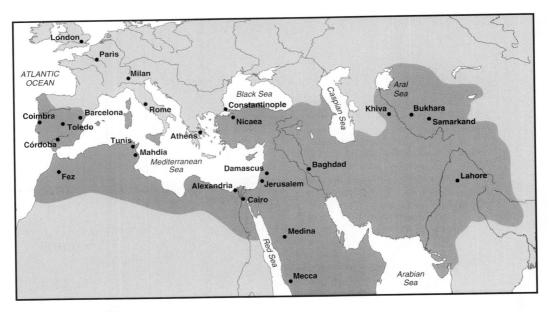

► ISLAM AROUND 1100

Islamic Expansion and Regionalism

622–1258

Rumi was dead. People from all over central Turkey came to the funeral of this scholar and mystic, who for decades had danced and sung in praise of Allah. His joyous enthusiasm infected many in and around the mountain town where he lived. Now they came to mourn and celebrate Rumi's passing and his reunion with Allah. Muslims, Jews, and Christians attended, because Rumi spoke to everyone.

This anecdote about a thirteenth-century Islamic thinker and poet shows the respect and affection with which he and many like him were held. In the seventh century, Islam developed as a religion, expanding through parts of Asia, Africa, and Europe, and Islam's success also sowed the seeds of regionalism. Although some of Islam's spread came through military conquest, much resulted from peaceful conversion by Islamic mystics (Sufis) and traders. "Muslim" is the name for a follower of Islam. For two centuries, the vast realm of Islam was politically tied together rather loosely. Centralized rule weakened, and regional patterns asserted themselves. Nonetheless, common religious adherence and general social practices, including a legal system, held Muslims together.

In this chapter, we will examine the rise, expansion, and regionalism of the peoples who were united by Islam. We will discuss the various factors that propelled these processes and explore the consequences of the Islamic Empire's early development. **Dar al-Islam**, or the Islamic world, connected Asia with Africa and Europe. People of diverse ethnic groups and occupational backgrounds embraced Islam and shared certain beliefs and practices, like daily prayers while facing toward Mecca, the home of the most sacred Muslim shrines. Muslim travelers visited places like Ghana in western Africa, Samarkand in Central Asia, and Canton in southern China, where they usually were welcomed warmly by their fellow believers. Foodstuffs and ideas also traveled to most areas of Eurasia and Africa, where they enriched people's lives.

THE EARLY DECADES OF ISLAM: MUHAMMAD AND THE FOUR CALIPHS, 622–661

At the center of Islam's beliefs are the revelations received from the god **Allah** by Muhammad ibn Abdullah (around 570–632). Muhammad grew up as an orphan, eventually marrying a wealthy widow with connections to merchant families of Mecca, an oasis-city at the western edge of the Arabian Desert. Around the age of forty years, Muhammad began having a series of religious experiences that changed not only his life but also those of millions around the globe. He became the prophet for a religion that developed into a political system.

Before addressing the rise and expansion of Islam, we should examine the environment into which it came.

Pre-Islamic Society

Mecca straddled key trade routes that ran between Africa and Asia; consequently, merchant families of Mecca gained extensive knowledge about the outside world. They remained independent of the imperial power struggles of the Byzantine Empire with the Sassanian[1] Empire and negotiated a working arrangement with tribal groups to permit Meccan caravans to travel peacefully through their territories.

Pastoral tribes lived in Arabia's harsh desert terrains, which were punctuated here and there by oases or by the occasional city, like Mecca. Tribal politics included consultative decision making at councils where men and (more rarely) women were able to express themselves; in this way, people were made to feel a part of the system. Thus, tribal leaders could count on the loyalty of their members. Tribes traded with settled peoples or sometimes raided wealthy merchant caravans by employing swift cavalry attacks. Occasionally, women fought alongside men.

Although Muslims view Islam as the universal religion, they believe that Judaism and Christianity also had prophets. Adam, Moses, and Jesus, for example, were prophets of God, stating or restating the first tenets of Islam in the eyes of Muslims. Thus, Jews and Christians were "Peoples of the Book" even though from the Muslim perspective they had strayed from Muhammad's true teachings. In addition, some Christians and Jews who converted to Islam did so because they felt that Muhammad's teachings were natural outgrowths of Christianity or Judaism.

Muhammad's Role and Legacy

The visions and voices that provided the essential message of Islam began to come to Muhammad in a cave to which he retreated from time to time. A pious man, Muhammad often took solitary retreats into the nearby mountains to receive, Muslims believe, messages from Allah through Gabriel, the messenger angel. One central theme of these revelations was that Allah had chosen Muhammad as his prophet and desired him to preach the message of submission to Allah. The word "Islam" means submission.

Gradually, Muhammad gathered followers and enemies. His disciples adopted his message of social justice and charity, especially to orphans and widows. As the message spread, merchant oligarchs who ruled Mecca vehemently opposed the new religion, which challenged their political and financial well-being. They threatened Muhammad and his tiny band. At the same time, people in Medina, around 250 miles to the north, invited Muhammad, who had gained a reputation for honesty, to mediate internal disputes there. Muhammad and his followers fled Mecca and arrived in Medina, where they spread Allah's message. This move, known as the ***hijra***[2] (migration), took place in 622 and is the beginning date of the

---

[1] **Sassanian:** sah SAHN ee ehn

[2] ***hijra:*** HEEJ rah

Muslim calendar, which is still followed in many parts of the world. By mediating disputes in Medina, rendering judgments, and receiving delegations, Muhammad served as both administrator and prophet of Islam.

Muhammad ruled Medina, using it as a base from which to unite the tribes and peoples of Arabia. The prophet's charismatic manner attracted a wide following, and his evolving political statecraft brought him great personal respect. Several caravans from Mecca were attacked by the Muslims, and the Meccan merchants retaliated; Muhammad won many of the battles against the armed forces from Mecca. Eventually, the leaders of Mecca could not stem the growth of Islam and the consequent undermining of their own power. When Muhammad returned to Mecca, the city capitulated. Mecca became the religion's spiritual center, while Medina became a political and administrative capital of the new Islamic state. By 632, Muhammad had united the Arabs, exercising both political and religious influence over them.

Central to Islam are its five pillars or basic tenets:

— belief in the oneness of Allah and Muhammad as Allah's prophet,

— prayer five times each day,

— the giving of charitable contributions,

— fasting from sunrise to sunset during the holy month of Ramadan, and

— pilgrimage to Mecca at least once.

Muslims were thought to go to paradise if they followed these tenets or to suffer punishments if they failed to uphold them.

Muhammad also forged an alliance between urban merchants and tribal leaders. He used networks already established by Meccan merchant families, expanding them to include important tribes. Both tribal leaders and merchants played a role in the planning of Islam's initial expansion and contributed to evolving social egalitarianism.

Islam's First Crisis and Expansion

The religion of Islam and its government faced a serious crisis after Muhammad died in 632, but Islam continued to expand dynamically. Some Muslims who had submitted because of Muhammad's charismatic personality abandoned their new faith. Other figures, jealous of Muhammad's success, claimed to be prophets, hoping to wrest some followers from Islam.

Responding to these challenges, the close, early followers of Muhammad selected one of their own, Abu Bakr,[3] as **caliph**, the religious and political successor of Muhammad. Abu Bakr declared that none could leave the religious community. Military force gave strength to the caliph's words; the divisions soon closed, and the threatening prophetic challenges faded.

At the same time, the caliph ordered that the spiritual messages of Allah to Muhammad be gathered into the **Qur'an**,[4] the Holy Book of Islam. The Qur'an, written in Arabic, reached its final form around the middle of the seventh century and has remained unchanged over the succeeding centuries, although various commentaries on it have appeared.

The next three caliphs followed the direction of the first caliph and presided over a rapid expansion of the Islamic state, spreading the religion as Muslims went throughout Southwest Asia and into North Africa. The remarkable early growth of Islam resulted from the able direction of experienced urban leaders, combined with the formidable mobility of the nomads. For example, the use of cavalry forces meant that the Muslims rode far into the territory of the enemy before effective resistance could be mounted. Often these Arabs were aided by the large number of other Arabs living in Palestine, Iraq, and Syria; they collaborated in taking control of various governments. Once the Sassanian Empire fell to the Muslims, vast resources commanded by that agrarian state came under their control. Thus, a combination of military factors, organizational skills, and resources proved formidable.

Another driving force behind the Arabs' success was the desire to take wealth from the conquered peoples and redistribute it to members of the Islamic community. This process was designed to create the de facto economic equality promised by the Qur'an and Muhammad, yet some of the distributions were deemed unfair and triggered opposition movements. The **Shi'a**,[5] one of the most prominent of the dissident groups, fought for

[3] **Abu Bakr:** ah BOO BAH kur
[4] **Qur'an:** KOOR ahn
[5] **Shi'a:** SHEE ah

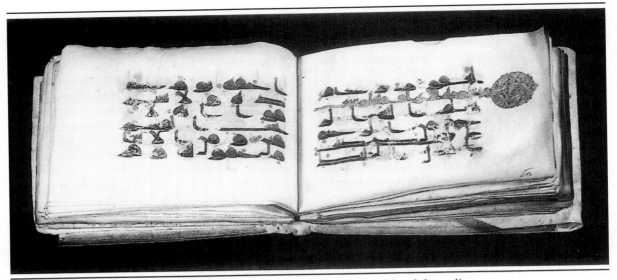

FIGURE 12.1 *Early Qur'an with Kufic Script.* *Calligraphy is considered the earliest and among the most important of the Muslim visual arts. An accomplished calligrapher exemplified discipline of mind and hand, as well as the idea of the cultured individual. The Kufic style of calligraphy is most associated with the Qur'an, since Kufic was the first form of Arabic used to write the words of Allah. The Kufic text here dates from the mid–seventh century.* Courtesy of Biblioteca Ambrosiana, Milan.

power in the name of Ali (the fourth caliph) and his descendants. Ali had been assassinated in a succession crisis, and most Shi'ites claimed that his killing had interrupted the clear succession from Muhammad.

A major factor in the Islamic state's early success was the unity it forged. A tribe's primary loyalty was directed to the caliph, the head of the religion and of the state. A general loyalty superseded tribal allegiances and brought widespread unity. At the same time, the early caliphs' charge to reconquer those Arabs who had abandoned the faith brought coalitions of Islamic forces drawn from various tribes.

A major alliance of Syrian tribes soon joined forces with the Muslims and played a vital part in the Islamic state's expansion. Syrians long had preyed on the caravans plying the trade routes of their region, and they had religious and economic motives for converting to Islam. With Syrian assistance, much of the early Islamic expansion followed the trade routes of the entire region. These confederations brought conflict with the Sassanian and Byzantine empires. Soon, the Sassanian Empire fell to the Muslims, and the Byzantine Empire was severely weakened.

As with all wars, loss of life resulted. Zealous Muslims took to heart the Qur'anic injunctions of

jihad,[6] or struggle to make the world Islamic. Some interpreted *jihad* to mean military struggle, but many others took *jihad* to mean persuasion. Both were important in the spread of Islam. Early Muslim warriors sought booty. They sometimes slaughtered urban peoples, who were despised by nomadic warriors. Women and children might be carried off as slaves.

Thus, the first four caliphs also presided over a military expansion of Muslims far beyond the borders of Arabia, creating an Islamic empire. This growth transformed Islam into a transregional religion, one that united diverse peoples across a wide section of Southwest Asia and North Africa.

THE UMAYYAD AND ABBASID CALIPHATES, 661–1258

During the nearly six centuries of the Umayyad[7] and Abbasid[8] caliphates, expansion continued along with the development of artistic pursuits. Islam spread across Africa and into Europe and deep into India and reached the borders of China.

[6] *jihad:* jee HAHD
[7] **Umayyad:** OOM ee yahd
[8] **Abbasid:** ahb BAH sihd

The blending of Arab, Persian, and Indian ideas, literary forms, and art styles enriched courtier and commoner throughout the Dar al-Islam.

The Umayyad Caliphate, 661–750

Damascus became the Islamic Empire's capital. The ruling Umayyad clan had been an important Meccan merchant group specializing in trade with Damascus. Although Mecca and Medina remained religiously important to Muslims, Damascus, a major urban center and the nexus of vital trade routes from Asia and Europe, dominated Dar al-Islam's political and economic affairs. From Damascus, Umayyad caliphs directed operations in Africa, Europe, and Asia.

The rise of Damascus as the political center of the Islamic Empire brought a challenge from factions in Medina and Mecca, who resented the shift away from Arabia and their own loss of influence in shaping policy. Fighting erupted and finally ended with victory for the Umayyads and their supporters. Dynastic succession became a regular feature of the Damascus and successor empires. Damascus's strategic location facilitated its role as nerve center of the Umayyad Empire.

Early eighth-century Umayyad caliphs or emperors attempted a series of reforms in order to secure long-lasting political and fiscal stability, but their efforts were undermined by continuing sectarian social unrest. Centralizing policies kept the caliphate's control of officials at all government levels, and the caliphs gave income from state lands to military leaders who promised to use the funds to support and equip themselves and an agreed-upon number of soldiers. The incessant need for trained military personnel forced succeeding Muslim rulers to extend this land policy

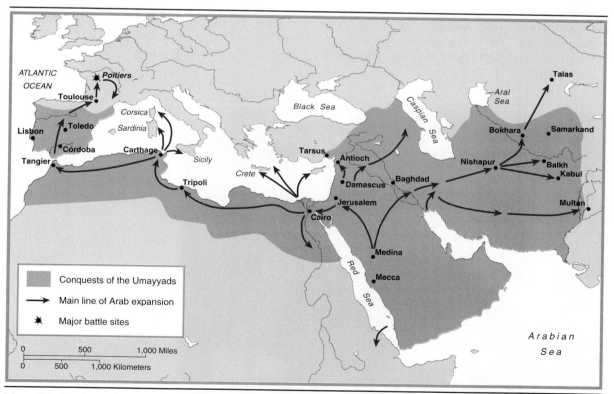

M A P   1 2 . 1   *Dar al-Islam around 750.* *Arab Muslims expanded rapidly across trade routes in Asia, Africa, and Europe, reaching the Atlantic and Indian Oceans in less than a century after Muhammad's death. Cities usually fell to conquest while the rural folk were converted, generally by peaceful means. Much of the southern Mediterranean Sea became a place of commerce for Muslim merchants. These early Islamic centers often became bases for later expansion across Africa, Europe, and Asia.*

over widespread areas. Gradually, state control lagged, and revenue from these state lands came under the complete charge of military officers. This reduced the amount of tax revenues and made the warriors semiautonomous, leading to decentralized rule in later eras.

Although Umayyad caliphs borrowed from Byzantine traditions and practices, they also put an Islamic stamp on their rule. Byzantine political institutions, like absolute monarchy, were used by the Umayyad caliphs, who adopted and adapted court rituals and bureaucratic institutions as necessary. Another Byzantine pattern adopted by the Umayyad caliphs was the patronage of artists. During the time of Abd al-Malik (reign dates 685–705), Arabic was introduced as the administrative language. The caliph also introduced a new style of coinage that replaced human figures with words proclaiming in Arabic the oneness of Allah and Muhammad as the prophet. Islam forbade pictorial representations of Muhammad.

The Umayyad rulers directed the expansion of Islam across North Africa and far into Spain. Arab fleets sailed the Mediterranean Sea to conquer Cyprus and many North African cities. Arab forces that conquered the Nile River Valley pushed westward and soon came into contact with Berbers, nomadic peoples of North Africa, many of whom converted to Islam. In part because of the strong nomadic component in the Arab forces, an Arab-Berber alliance emerged. By 710, Muslims crossed the Strait of Gibraltar into Spain. Within five years, much of Spain had fallen to the combined forces, who were increasingly referred to as **Moors**, North Africans of mixed Berber and Arab parentage. Parts of Spain remained under Muslim control until the fifteenth century, and Spanish Muslims traded extensively with Christian Europeans.

Arab military forces also moved eastward into India and northeastward into Central Asia. By 711, an Arab fleet had taken several cities in the Indus River Valley, and an army marched overland to extend the conquests up the valley. Although Muslim control of the Indus Valley was weak, it provided trade links with the core region of the Islamic Empire and gave important benefits to Muslims in terms of trade goods and ideas.

Just as eastern expansion brought Persians and Indians under the Islamic Empire's control, so the northeastern push brought Turkic peoples into

FIGURE 12.2 *Mosaics of the Great Mosque of Damascus.* *These mosaics from the early eighth century are part of an artistic tradition dating back to the Roman period, showing the absorption and adaptation of techniques by the Islamic artists and artisans. The walls of the mosque are decorated with architectural motifs, while the arcade (the supporting column arches) are decorated with trees. The trees are realistically portrayed, reflecting a careful study of nature.* Photo by J. E. Dayton/Reproduced courtesy of Thames and Hudson, Ltd.

FIGURE 12.3 *Great Mosque at Kairouan, Tunisia.* *This seventh-century mosque was a site of pilgrimage and the first major Islamic monument built in North Africa. Shown are the prayer hall, domes, and facade, lined with columns taken from other, pre-Islamic structures. The use of columned interiors may have been both structurally necessary and a borrowing from other architectural traditions, but Muslim architects used them in religiously and artistically unique combinations. This mosque was rebuilt in the ninth and tenth centuries.* George Rogers/Magnum Photos.

the Muslim realm. Persian and Turkish joined Arabic to become major languages in Dar al-Islam.

Muslim monarchs frequently ruled the Islamic realms with mild policies. They basically left the existing social systems intact when indigenous customs did not interfere with Islamic practices. Muslims retained the tax rates of former monarchs or sometimes reduced them. In some cases, therefore, peasants found their tax obligations less under Muslim rulers. One assessment levied by most Islamic monarchs was a head tax on nonbelievers, and its rate was generally assessed according to the nonbeliever's wealth. The tax provided an economic incentive for non-Muslims to convert, while favorable treatment for Muslim merchants brought additional conversions among the

traders. Because merchants and artisans were respected and taxed moderately, trade generally improved, benefiting rulers and subjects alike. Islamic stress on works of charity resulted in government and private monies for helping organizations like foundling homes.

Ineffective rule by later Umayyad caliphs and widespread tribal unrest undermined the caliphate. Corruption by the caliphs provoked unrest among the Shi'ites and others, while ambitious tribal groups plotted to overthrow the Umayyads. A coalition of opposition forces led by the Abbasids claimed the caliphate position and launched a serious revolt in Mesopotamia. Within a short time, the Abbasid rebels ousted the Umayyads from power. The Abbasid Caliphate

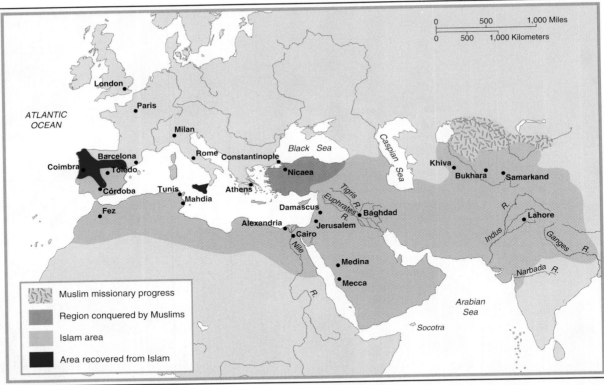

MAP 12.2 *Islam around 1100.* *Although military conquest continued to add new territory to Dar al-Islam, much of the religion's spread came from missionary activity. Sufi mystics were especially effective in spreading the teachings of Muhammad. The great expanse of Dar al-Islam, however, proved difficult to rule from a single center. Eventually regional centers emerged and vied for political dominance.*

rose in Mesopotamia, farther east and nearer the geographic center of Dar al-Islam. Eventually, the Abbasids located their capital in Baghdad, near the heart of their support base.

The Abbasid Caliphate, 749–1258

Early Abbasid caliphs enjoyed the varied pleasures of a lavish urban lifestyle. Baghdad, even more than Damascus, became a vibrant intellectual center where ideas from ancient Greece were treasured and developed and where scholars from Persia, India, and Egypt interacted with one another. Finally, Baghdad symbolized a widespread urbanization that saw the appearance of cities like Cairo, Basra,[9] and Toledo in diverse parts of Dar al-Islam. An unintended consequence of the shift of the Islamic Empire's capital farther east

[9]**Basra:** BAHZ rah

was the growing difficulty of maintaining control of the western regions in North Africa and Spain. Indeed, some Umayyads fled to Spain, established an independent caliphate there, and ruled into the eleventh century.

The growth of cities in Mesopotamia, of course, increased the demand for agricultural produce and spurred improvements of yields per land unit, largely through more intensive cultivation of the land. At the same time, a massive land reclamation project in southern Mesopotamia took most of the ninth century to complete. In order to have labor resources to clear the land and work on sugarcane plantations, landowners imported hundreds of thousands of sub-Saharan African slaves. Abuses of these workers provoked an uprising that lasted from 869 to 884.

Although the Abbasid caliphs ruled effectively until the tenth century, their far-flung empire eventually proved too difficult to govern, both at the core and at the periphery. Political challenges came from formerly conquered groups, like the Persians and Turks, who maintained and manipulated the existing political structure for their own purposes. The great expanse of Dar al-Islam challenged centralization, with the result that the decline of the Abbasid caliphs mirrored increasing local rule. Regionalism gradually replaced centralization in the Islamic world. Tax revenues declined as many private estates were taken off the tax rolls. Economic weakness accelerated political decay, and the last Abbasid caliph succumbed to a Mongol army in 1258 (see Chapter 19). Regionalism had fully replaced control from Baghdad or from any other major city.

THE BIRTH OF ISLAMIC CULTURE

The Islamic religion inspired many artists to create works of art, and Muslim rulers patronized artisans and architects to develop works of beauty and majesty. As the immense wealth of the realm poured into the Abbasid coffers and trade flourished, Baghdad prospered. **Mosques**, the Muslim places of worship, were built in monumental style with large buildings and great courtyards to encompass the faithful. The minaret tower also made its appearance in Baghdad and became a major element of the mosque complexes. Stucco decoration reached a high level and adorned official buildings. These stylistic patterns were soon replicated throughout the Islamic world.

Knowledge was sought by the Abbasid caliphs and their officials. Works in Sanskrit, Greek, Persian, and other languages were translated into Arabic and furthered rational inquiry. Mathematicians built on the fundamental work of Indians and Greeks to explore the field of algebra. The Indian numeration system and concept of zero passed to Muslims and from them to the Christian Europeans. Medicine was diligently studied by scholars who translated the Classical Greek studies.

Astronomy and astrology occupied the attention of some Islamic thinkers. Many astronomical texts from India and the Mediterranean were translated and carefully studied. Al-Khwarizmi[10] (died around 850) synthesized Greek, Iranian, and

[10]**Al-Khwarizmi:** ahl KWAR ihz mee

FIGURE 12.4 *Chess Piece from the Abbasid Caliphate.* *Chess originated in India as a game of strategy and warfare. This ivory piece with an official atop an elephant reflects Indian chess pieces of similar design. Instead of kings and queens typical of European chess figures, Asian chess pieces usually portrayed kings and chief ministers.* Bibliothèque nationale, Paris.

Indian astronomical knowledge with his own discoveries and helped establish the reputation of Islamic astronomy. Chinese rulers, for example, invited Muslim astronomers to their courts.

Arabic language and literature benefited from the patronage of the Abbasid caliphs. Qur'anic Arabic became the vehicle for new forms of poetry and prose, including essays, didactic writings, and historical writing. Grammar was a field of diligent study because the interpretation of Qur'anic passages depended on an accurate understanding of word order, usage, and meaning. In addition, with the spread of Islam among the subject peoples through religious conversion, Arabic became the language of rulers and ruled alike.

Written Persian evolved into a significant literary language during the Abbasid era. Often called "New Persian," the language developed from the

In 1244, Shams Tabrizi and Rumi forged a friendship that transformed Persian mystical poetry into direct, erotic idioms. Both men, the former a wanderer who took any job and the latter a scholar and teacher, sought union with the divine. In the famous story that follows, we can see how Shams was a disciple to a basket maker and worked as a mason, two occupations associated with Sufism. We can see how artisan networks supported Sufis. Rumi's disciples founded the Mevlana Order of Dervishes, a Sufi group devoted to dancing as a mystical practice. Whirling dervishes and Sufis played a significant role in the peaceful spread of Islam.

IN THEIR OWN WORDS

Shams and Rumi: Two Sufi Mystics

Shams wandered the world looking for a companion, a friend on his level of attainment. Sometimes, for three or four days he would be lost in mystical awareness. Then he would take work as a mason, or a mason's helper, to balance his visionary bewilderment with hard physical labor. When he was paid, he would always contrive to slip the wages into another worker's jacket before he left. He never stayed anywhere long. Whenever students began to assemble around him, as they inevitably did, he would excuse himself for a drink of water, wrap his black cloak around [himself], and be gone. . . .

Shams arrived in Konya sometime in the fall of 1244. He took lodging at an inn, pretending to be a successful merchant, a seller of sugar, though in his room there was only a broken water pot, a ragged mat, and a headrest of unbaked clay. He fasted continually, breaking it once every ten or twelve days with bread soaked in mutton broth.

Shams was a disciple of a certain basket maker in Tabriz, Ruknaddin Sanjabi, but he traveled all over the region to find and hear the deepest teachers. . . . One day as Shams sat at the gate of an inn, Rumi came riding by on a donkey, surrounded by a crowd of students. Shams rose and took hold of the bridle, . . . "Tell me! Who was greater, Muhammad or Bestami?" "Muhammad was incomparable among the prophets and saints." "Then how is it he [Muhammad] said, 'We have not known You [Allah] as You should be known,' while Bestami cried out, 'How great is my glory!'" Rumi fainted when he heard the depth the question came from and fell to the ground. When he revived, he answered, "For Muhammad the mystery was always unfolding, while Bestami took one gulp and was satisfied." The two tottered off together and were closeted for weeks and months at a time in that mystical conversation called *sohbet*.

Rumi's disciples feared the fascination of their teacher with Shams, and, eventually, they forced Shams to leave. Rumi, however, sent his son to bring the mystic back. Later, Shams disappeared a second time and for good, and Rumi wrote poems expressing his abject grief at his friend's departure. Rumi also wore mourning clothes, including a hat and black cloak that are now customary among modern followers of the dervish sect.

---

ninth to the eleventh centuries from Middle Persian, and came to include words from other languages, including Arabic. New Persian began as a means to disseminate popular poetry and evolved into an elite vehicle to express more subtle and complex ideas. Rudaki[11] (died around 940) built on existing Arab and Persian poetic traditions and is seen as the first New Persian poet. His poetic style is regarded as combining freedom and simplicity of expression with nobility of theme.

Hadith,[12] a collection of accounts of Muhammad and early Islamic personalities, became a treasured source of information. Preachers mined it for stirring tales with which to delight people, and scholars interested in legal matters used it as a basis to develop legal theories.

Although the Abbasid Empire fell into decline and eventual destruction at the hands of the Mongols in 1258, Islam continued to flourish. Sufi mystics traveled alone or in company to rural areas

[11] **Rudaki:** ruh DAKH ee

[12] **Hadith:** HAH deeth

and new lands, spreading the message of Islam. Sufis played a major role in Islamizing the countryside by performing attention-getting feats of mental and physical control. They often built mosques in the towns or communities where they resided, and these places of worship were also used for other activities. Many Sufi tombs became venerated places of pilgrimage for Muslims.

In parts of Africa, wandering scholars, judges, and saints carried Islam from place to place, establishing educational centers and mosques in places where they resided. People in the community often converted to Islam and enjoyed the varied benefits they believed this faith bestowed.

ISLAMIC SOCIETY

Muhammad and the Islamic religion significantly affected Islamic society. Muhammad established the norms and traditions of Islamic law, using them as a means to regulate society by delineating the standards of accepted behavior. Although social hierarchies existed within the Islamic Empire, all people were equal before Allah, and all were to be given status according to law. Through Muhammad, Allah also decreed that orphans and poor people be given good treatment and charity when necessary. Islam also provided for the favored treatment of women, especially in comparison with other religions and social traditions.

Islamic Law

Muhammad himself played a significant role in rendering verdicts in legal matters, and, because of his reputation for integrity, fairness came to be an important matter in law. Judges and lawyers attempted to tie their decisions to the injunctions given in the Qur'an. Four main schools of law emerged in the first Islamic centuries, and judges usually had to claim adherence to one school's avowed perspective on legal interpretations. In addition, a legal opinion was often formulated by connecting it with a previous ruling. General acceptance of the new decision by one or more schools depended on the persuasiveness of the legal reasoning and its being written in Arabic. There was no system of appeals for legal decisions, and only a mistake made by a judge was grounds for another judge to reverse a decision. Within the

mainstream of legal thought, this tradition and process allowed for stability but permitted some adaptation to changing conditions. At the same time, other legal traditions grew up in the far reaches of the Islamic world.

Many early legal scholars came from merchant families, and they attempted to represent their business interests in the face of officials who asserted absolute state power to order and run society. Merchant judges and scholars created Islamic law as an expression of the responsibility of people for their own lives and for the ordering of society. Thus, the community as a whole gained an

FIGURE 12.5 *Islamic Law and the Family. Law in Dar al-Islam had a significant impact on political, economic, and social life. This manuscript illustration shows a judge settling a dispute between father and daughter. Often a father had a higher standing in law, but women, in fact, generally received fairer treatment under Islamic law than they did under most other legal systems in the world at the time of early Islam.* Bibliothèque nationale, Paris.

FIGURE 12.6 *Mamluk Hunting Scene. From their origins as slaves, the Mamluks became the rulers of parts of Africa and Syria for centuries, beginning in the mid–thirteenth century. This basin, inlaid with silver and gold, shows Mamluk emirs and their servants in a detailed hunting scene.* Louvre © R.M.N.

autonomous standing that over time undermined the legitimacy of imperial authority. This legal tradition strengthened the religious community and weakened strong monarchies, often causing them to negotiate rather than dictate.

Merchant influence on Islamic law also may be seen in its emphasis on contractual matters. Great respect for contracts gained currency in legal cases, and people were held to the letter of a contract in business or in social affairs like marriage. When a case involved general principles, tradition usually prevailed, except when a contrary point emerged from a contract between two parties. Then, the contract usually prevailed. This gave stability to economic relationships and facilitated trade.

Social Classes

Islamic society was organized in a hierarchical manner, with members of the royal family and aristocracy at the top. In addition, officials and merchants formed an intermediate class, and urban laborers and peasants constituted the lower classes. Slaves usually languished at the bottom of Islamic society. We will consider merchants, artisans, and slaves.

One of the most significant contributions of the merchant class was to help develop and preserve a degree of flexibility in Islamic society. Islamic government had its share of officials from various social levels, and merchants played vital political roles from Islam's inception. Furthermore, by helping to create an autonomous legal system that recognized contracts as significant, merchants permitted a variety of social groups to be free from arbitrary administrative rulings. This process allowed for legal flexibility and forestalled a bureaucratically imposed social structure.

Artisans also played a vital social role beyond their economic contributions. Certainly, artisans organized themselves into guilds to provide social stability and regular work. Later Sufi brotherhoods formed around artisan guilds. These organizations also provided for social interaction among spiritual seekers who lived in communities of likeminded mystics. Sufi missionaries who were connected to a specific brotherhood often helped spread Islam by peaceful means.

Slaves played significant roles in Islam's history, and they were used primarily as soldiers, agricultural workers, house servants, and concubines. Because Islam forbade the enslaving of Muslims, the great majority of slaves came from outside the

Islamic realm. Many male slaves served in Islamic armies, and a few gained political power. The Mamluks, for example, were slave-warriors who ruled Egypt from the mid–thirteenth until the early nineteenth century.

Family and Gender Issues

As with nearly all societies we have studied, men were socially dominant; yet women in Muslim society had certain rights and a position somewhat different from their counterparts elsewhere. Marriage was recognized in Islamic law as a contract between the husband and wife. Although a husband was permitted to have four wives, each was legally regarded as equal to the others. All children of these unions were considered legitimate. Birth control measures were accepted in marital relations, but the husband could not interrupt the sexual act because doing so denied his wife her own pleasure. Judges recognized the equal participa-

tion of male and female in the creation of a child. The wife was regarded as more than a mere vessel for male seed, as was believed in many societies before 1500. Usually, unless another arrangement was spelled out in a marriage contract, the husband had legal guardianship of children.

Concubines were a class of slaves that had a special position in Islamic society, and, although they were treated as property, these women had certain rights. Once impregnated by her owner, a concubine could not be sold to another, and she was freed when he died. One concubine married a caliph, and two of their sons became caliphs. Some concubines had property, and any child of a slave-master union was legally recognized and free. Many concubines became educated and were accomplished dancers, poets, and storytellers.

Social forces permitted some women to assert themselves, especially in Islam's early history. Because of the more egalitarian nature of early Islamic society, some women played active roles.

FIGURE 12.7 *Harem Wall Painting. This reconstruction of a ninth-century wall painting depicts the intricate and precise harem dance, one of the entertainments available to the political elite in early Dar al-Islam. The original painting, with its Eastern-style figures, decorated the harem quarters of Jausaq Palace in Samarra.* Staatliche Museen zu Berlin—Preussischer Kulturbesitz, Museum fur Islamische Kunst.

Kahdijah,[13] Muhammad's first wife, also assumed a vital position in Islam's founding, choosing him as her husband and becoming his first convert and strongest supporter. After Kahdijah's death, A'isha,[14] another wife of Muhammad, became a significant political figure. Because she came from a powerful family, A'isha's opinion carried great weight. She supported various factions in succession disputes, helping her candidate to gain power. She also was the source for many stories about Muhammad. As Islamic political control spread to Damascus and Baghdad, however, older traditions of covering and secluding women began to dominate social life. A'isha, for example, donned the veil in her later years.

THE ISLAMIC EXCHANGE

The hemispheric nature of Islam with its spread to India, the borders of China, the civilizations of Africa, and the Iberian Peninsula of Europe brought a dramatic exchange of goods, technologies, foodstuffs, and ideas. Trade usually flourished in Dar al-Islam as Muslim merchants traveled the trade routes of Eurasia and Africa. Muhammad himself appreciated the value of commerce to a society and government, and his orientation characterized most of his political successors.

Mechanisms of Exchange

People took goods and ideas across Dar al-Islam by a variety of ways, including proselytizing, traveling, and trading. We have seen how Sufis took Islam to areas over much of the eastern hemisphere, and they carried other ideas along with their religion. Many Muslims faithfully made the *hajj*, the pilgrimage to Mecca, at least once in their lifetimes, and this resulted in a large number of people who traveled. In addition, the *hajji*, the Muslim pilgrim, met and associated with others who had made the journey to Arabia. This resulted in exchanges of ideas and information across Dar al-Islam from West Africa to India. Itinerant scholars and judges also frequently traveled not only for the *hajj* but also for adventure and the spreading of their religion. Some ended up at the courts of

[13] **Kahdijah:** kah DEE jah
[14] **A'isha:** AYH shah

caliphs, and others found employment at schools or translation centers, like the one at Toledo in Spain. These intellectuals played a major role in the spread of ideas in the eastern hemisphere.

Trade provided the greatest vehicle for the transmission of goods and ideas. For centuries, Muslims dominated the land routes across Central Asia, and only in the thirteenth century did the Mongols seize these avenues from the Muslims. The Mongols admired the Muslims' financial skills and placed them in charge of commerce in Central Asia. Water routes in the Mediterranean Sea, the Red Sea, and the Arabian Sea were filled with Arab ships. In fact, there was a large amount of commerce on water between Muslims and Chinese.

Paper

One of the things the Chinese passed on to the Muslims was the knowledge of making paper. Paper making played a variety of roles throughout the Islamic world. In the mid–eighth century, Chinese artisans who knew how to make paper were captured by Muslims in Central Asia, and, by the end of that century, paper-manufacturing works could be found in Baghdad. Knowledge of paper making reached Spain by the beginning of the tenth century, and with paper came a greater appreciation for the written word and a spread of literacy among the higher classes. At the same time, the ease of manufacture and relative inexpensiveness of the process guaranteed a larger reading audience and a spur to learning.

In West Africa, the spread of paper making and the use of paper often paralleled the movement of Islam. Oral tradition played a major role in African religion, but, because the Qur'an was written, Islam had seemingly limitless longevity. When paper making spread from North Africa into West Africa, along with it came authorities on the written word, scholars who included judges, teachers, and students. They formed the core of believers and founded institutions that firmly anchored Islam into society. In the thirteenth and fourteenth centuries, Islamic schools appeared all across western Africa and across much of central Africa.

During the thirteenth century, Muslim Turks brought paper-making technology and paper when they invaded northern India. After the establishment of a Muslim government over parts of the north, the use of paper spread across the subcon-

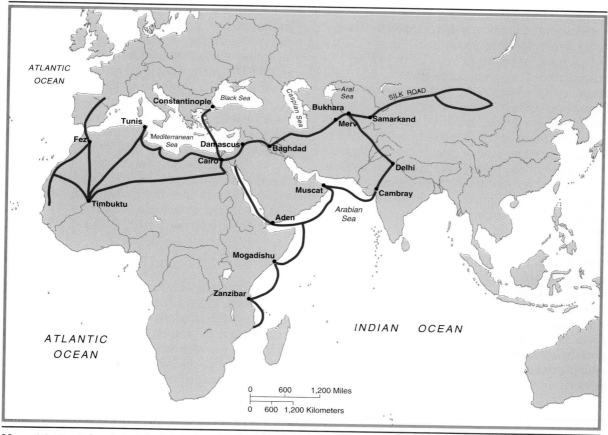

MAP 12.3 *Islamic Trade Routes around 1200.* Muslims controlled many of the major trade arteries in Central and Southwest Asia by 1200. Peoples, products, and ideas went by these and other routes across Asia and Africa. Merchants played an important role in the spread of Islam in Africa and around the Indian Ocean. Europeans eagerly traded with Muslim merchants, especially in Spain and the Mediterranean basin.

tinent. There the diffusion came by choice rather than through forced acceptance, because people preferred the cheaper and easier-to-use paper to the palm leaf, which previously had served the same function. At the same time, the widespread availability of paper meant that Indian and other governments could increase the number of reports and information about their jurisdictions. Control often increased with the amount of accountability demanded.

Foodstuffs

From the eighth through the thirteenth centuries, there was a rapid diffusion of agricultural products, especially from India to other parts of Asia, Africa, and Europe. Dar al-Islam, which bordered

on or controlled parts of these areas, helped bring about the spread of these items, some of which greatly affected local and regional economies.

Grain staples, including new varieties of wheat and rice, came into Southwest Asia and Africa. Because these crops could grow in the hot months, when the agricultural fields would otherwise lie dormant, planting them facilitated double-cropping agriculture. This spread economic prosperity and supported larger populations, promoting the growth of cities. Certain foodstuffs needed large amounts of water, and Muslim farmers were forced to develop or improve irrigation techniques. Cisterns and underground canals reduced water evaporation and improved supplies, while water-lifting devices and techniques improved the delivery of water to the fields.

Sugarcane, bananas, sour oranges, lemons, watermelons, cucumbers, and spinach were regularly eaten by Muslims. In addition, European Crusaders, many of whom lived in Southwest Asia for most of their lives, grew accustomed to the varied cuisines there. When they returned home, some ingredients and recipes came with them. Norman Sicily was another place where Muslims and Christians interacted; it was a gateway on the road to Europe for many new vegetables that enhanced diets. Most of the people who ate the foods from the south came from wealthy or otherwise prominent families; common folk seldom could afford the expense of incorporating almonds or spinach into fare for their tables.

Cane sugar became a major elite foodstuff and preservative. Although employed in small quantities for flavoring, sugar was also used in the preserving of fruits, especially oranges and lemons. Preservation of other foods or seasoning dishes was helped by the addition of spices like cumin, coriander, and cinnamon. Color became an important enhancement to a feast, and saffron was added to many preparations to give a yellowish-golden hue.

The Islamic exchange also extended beyond Europe. Rosewater came into Christian Europe from the Muslim areas and was used in a variety of ways. It not only enchanted the palate of the diner but also gave off a pleasant aroma to charm a discriminating nose. Rosewater served both Arabs and Europeans as a medicine, prescribed as a favored treatment for fevers. Once the Europeans established colonies in the Americas, they took along those southern foodstuffs that were difficult to grow in the relatively inhospitable climates of northern Europe. Sugar found a comfortable home in the Caribbean area, rice flourished in the Carolinas, and oranges benefited from the favorable growing conditions of Brazil.

Ideas and Practices

The great number of travelers on the highways of Dar al-Islam carried a variety of ideas and practices with them. Rashid al-Din, a Persian historian of the thirteenth century, spent time in China as an advisor to the Mongols. As a physician, he was impressed by the specialized knowledge of anatomy developed over the centuries by Chinese

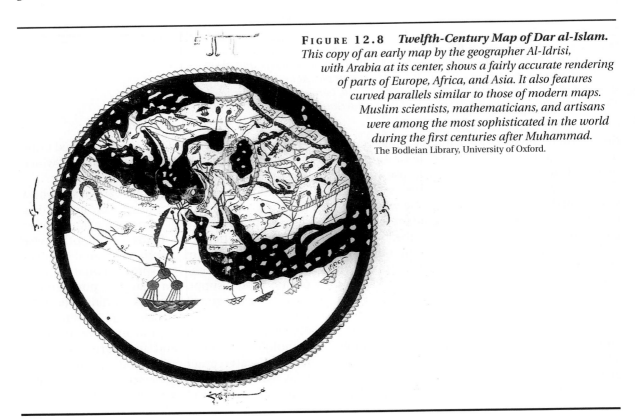

FIGURE 12.8 *Twelfth-Century Map of Dar al-Islam.*
This copy of an early map by the geographer Al-Idrisi, with Arabia at its center, shows a fairly accurate rendering of parts of Europe, Africa, and Asia. It also features curved parallels similar to those of modern maps. Muslim scientists, mathematicians, and artisans were among the most sophisticated in the world during the first centuries after Muhammad.
The Bodleian Library, University of Oxford.

medical practitioners. During his visit, Rashid al-Din had a major Chinese anatomy text translated into Arabic, and he carried it home, from where it eventually reached Christian Europe.

Muslim Spain also benefited from ideas and practices that came from other parts of the Islamic world. Use of the water-wheel arrived from Syria, while the information on how to build underground canals passed from Persia.

THE INTELLECTUAL HERITAGE OF ISLAM

Early in the rise and spread of Islam, Muslim rulers supported artists, writers, scientists, and other intellectuals. Education was highly prized, and generations of scholars and students benefited from the growing body of knowledge transmitted from other parts of the hemisphere, as well as from the synthesis of Muslim-discovered ideas and technologies with those from Greece, Persia, and India. Libraries were founded in most large cities, and some became scholarly research centers. During the ninth century, for example, Muslims founded Al-Azhar, a university in Cairo that became famed for its scholarly endeavors. When Europeans began establishing universities, Al-Azhar was one model for some of their institutions.

Mathematics was a subject of intellectual pursuit for many Muslims. Because they inherited much of Greek and Hellenistic mathematics and because they came into contact with Indian mathematicians, Muslims were able to synthesize and develop old and new branches of mathematics. We have already seen that the Muslims adopted and adapted the Hindu numeration system for their own purposes, and we know that this fundamental way of presenting mathematical ideas enriched European thought. Al-Khwarizmi, an outstanding Muslim mathematician, made discoveries in geometry and arithmetic by improving on the discoveries of his predecessors. He developed the field of algebra by combining Greek geometry with Indian arithmetical discoveries. Al-Khwarizmi's translated writings were used by European thinkers in their own mathematical studies.

Ibn Sina,[15] also known as Avicenna (died around 1037), came from Bukhara in Central Asia.

[15]**Sina:** SEE nah

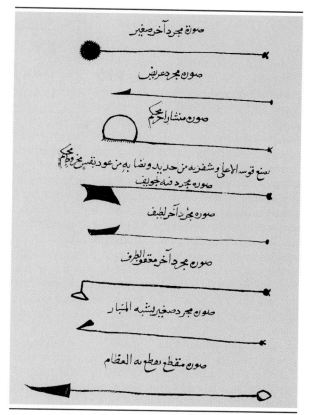

FIGURE 12.9 *Surgical Instruments of Islamic Spain.* *These illustrations are from an encyclopedia of medicine written in the tenth or eleventh century by Abu az-Zahrawi, a Spanish physician. Az-Zahrawi designed and drew his own surgical instruments, including the scrapers, scalpels, hooks, and forceps shown here. Some of these implements were used in Az-Zahrawi's obstetrical practice. His work was translated into Latin in the twelfth century and gained great attention in other parts of Europe.* The Bodleian Library, University of Oxford.

He mastered several intellectual disciplines and traveled to Baghdad to further his education. In the realm of philosophy, he helped establish the foundation of Persian philosophical inquiry by writing a short encyclopedia in Persian. Ibn Sina prided himself on his successful synthesis of the universal insights of philosophy with the discoveries and interpretations of Islamic prophecy. In addition, Ibn Sina's medical knowledge drew the attention of physicians because he and other Muslim physicians incorporated the discoveries of Galen and other Greeks in their own medical writings. Ibn Sina wrote a medical encyclopedia used throughout Dar al-Islam and published in Europe in the sixteenth century. Other medical texts by Ibn

ENCOUNTERS
Ibn Battuta: World Traveler

Abu Abdallah ibn Battuta[a] (1304–1368), who lived in an era later than that covered by this chapter, journeyed farther afield than any other Muslim of his era. Ibn Battuta left his home in Morocco and went to Mecca, like many Muslims. Yet he also ventured throughout Dar al-Islam from extreme northwestern Africa and southwestern Europe to India and Central Asia. Once he traveled to the southeastern coast of China and wandered through many islands of present-day Indonesia. Scholars have estimated that he logged around 73,000 miles, a distance far greater than any other known traveler until the sixteenth century. Because of his significant "wanderings," an official account of his trips was ordered by Ibn Battuta's monarch, and that document forms almost the sole basis of our knowledge about him. It also tells us much about Dar al-Islam in the fourteenth century.

Born in North Africa, probably to moderately wealthy parents, Ibn Battuta studied law, a subject that made him welcome in nearly all parts of the Islamic realm. Because lawyers and judges were in constant demand, Ibn Battuta found employment readily enough. Having such a background and training also meant that Ibn Battuta consorted with members of the social elite on his journeys, and because most of the places he visited had long been under Islamic rule, Ibn Battuta's ideas, customs, and moral outlook found a resonant echo in the people and groups with which he interacted. Faces and clothing may have differed greatly, but the intellectual discourse and values underlying the social interaction showed a remarkable similarity. Ibn Battuta traveled among his peers, who were often friendly familiars rather than exotic aliens.

Central to his journeys were pilgrimages to Mecca, the holy city of Islam, and Ibn Battuta made several *hajjs* in his lifetime. In Mecca, Ibn Battuta met and socialized with a great variety of people, most of whom enjoyed elite status in their homelands. One individual contact afforded Ibn Battuta a chance to work in India, because at that time a Muslim government ruled over part of North India. Ibn Battuta took up the offer and ventured to India, where he worked for some years. Additional travel in India convinced Ibn Battuta that he must visit China, a place spoken of in glowing terms. Resigning from his post, the restless traveler made his way to the eastern coast of India and booked private passage to China, where he stayed for some months. Leaving East Asia in the mid-1340s, he eventually returned to Mecca and finally home.

Ibn Battuta's remaining years were spent in travels to West Africa and Spain. Finally, the last days of this remarkable adventurer were spent as an official in a regional administrative post, while a younger scholar was assigned to write a travel journal in collaboration with Ibn Battuta. It took two years and flowed in the style of travel literature that was common for that day in the western part of Dar al-Islam.

Ibn Battuta had much in common with Marco Polo, the famed European traveler. Indeed, both men journeyed far and served as officials in distant lands. Yet Marco Polo moved as a stranger among unfamiliar peoples, while Ibn Battuta usually felt intellectually and socially at ease with his peers. Ibn Battuta, who traveled much farther than Marco Polo, was a valued member of the global Islamic elite, and his extensive journeys show the elite cultural unity of Dar al-Islam.

[a]**ibn Battuta:** IH buhn bah TUH tah

Sina and his fellow physicians were translated into Latin as early as the twelfth century and remained valuable resources for Europeans for half a millennium. Muslims established pharmacies and medical schools, and rulers required that prospective doctors pass state medical examinations before they could be certified to practice medicine.

Muslims played a significant role in the transmission of many Greek manuscripts of which Europeans were ignorant. In the twelfth century, for example, European scholars who visited Muslim cities, like Toledo in Spain, returned with several texts of Aristotle. They learned about Aristotle's writings on physics and metaphysics. Because Aristotle's ideas had long been admired in Europe, these manuscripts created a sensation in various intellectual circles and enriched the discussions and writings of European thinkers.

ISLAM

First four caliphs, 622–661

Umayyad Caliphate, 661–750

Abbasid Caliphate, 749–1258

Islamic regional-ism c. 900– c. 1600

	Muhammad's birth, c. 570
600	
	Hijra to Medina, 622
	Assassination of Ali, fourth caliph and head of Shi'a, 661
700	
	Arab fleet captures Indus Valley cities and Arab forces enter Spain, c. 710
	Paper making in Baghdad, c. 752
800	
	Death of Al-Khwarizmi, mathematician and astronomer, c. 850
	African slave uprising begins in Southern Mesopotamia, 869
900	Al-Azhar Mosque and School founded, c. 910
1000	
	Death of Ibn Sina, philosopher and humanist, c. 1037
1100	
1200	
	Rumi and Shams meet, 1244
	Fall of Abbasid Caliphate to Mongols, 1258

UNITY AND DIVERSITY

Although Dar al-Islam encompassed a vast realm by the thirteenth century, it was fragmented politically. The rapid conquests during the early decades after Muhammad's death could not be held together over the following centuries.

The unity of Dar al-Islam stemmed from Muslims' adherence to a range of common religious and social practices. Believers prayed to Allah five times a day, knew that Muhammad was Allah's prophet, and practiced charitable acts whenever possible. They submitted to Islamic law and were judged when they failed to follow it. After the first centuries of Islam's appearance, travelers, including pilgrims, could go from place to place in Dar al-Islam and feel comfortable talking with their Muslim brothers and sisters who lived thousands of miles away.

Despite these similarities, great diversity could be found in the Islamic world. Political differences were perhaps most apparent. Factional infighting characterized Islam from the beginning and continued to plague various caliphates. Another problem stemmed from the great distances between areas over which Islam held political sway. Communication necessary to run a centralized polity soon broke down, fragmenting administrative control. Thus, the unity of Islamic states was sundered, leading to regionalism. The destruction of the Baghdad Caliphate in 1258 by the Mongols caused the few remaining allegiances to a universal polity to dissolve.

SUMMARY

1. Muhammad, a merchant, experienced a series of spiritual messages telling him to convey Allah's message to all people. His religion of Islam began in Arabia, and his death sparked a drive to carry Islam's message to distant places. The subsequent fusion of religious and political elements transformed Islam into an empire.

2. Within half a century, Damascus fell to the Islamic advance. It became the center of the Umayyad Caliphate and directed further expansion. The Umayyads, a Meccan merchant family, illustrate one dimension of Islam's debt to merchants.

3. By the mid–eighth century, the Abbasid caliphs took over leadership and built Baghdad as their capital. Ideas and practices from the Greeks and Persians enriched Arab thought and brought about the first of many intellectual syntheses.

4. Islamic society developed a more flexible social structure, because merchants were determined to remain independent of autocratic domination. Merchants played a vital role in the development of Islamic law and society unencumbered by political manipulation. Artisan organizations sometimes served as centers where Sufi mystics interacted. Slaves became a vital part of Islamic society.

5. Families were subject to Islamic law, and the equal rights of a husband's wives were recognized. Individual elite women sometimes became politically important, although the seclusion of women became widespread when traditional patterns asserted themselves.

6. Islam was spread primarily by Sufi spiritual leaders who converted millions by their ardor, ethical living, and amazing feats. Eventually Dar al-Islam stretched from the Atlantic Ocean eastward to the Pacific Ocean and included Indonesia, part of the Philippines, and India.

7. The expanse of dominion that touched most of the eastern hemisphere's great civilizations, along with Muslim receptivity, brought an Islamic exchange of goods, foods, and ideas that benefited hundreds of millions of people.

8. Islam's intellectual impact stimulated thinkers and practitioners in Africa, Europe, and Asia. It set the basis for additional discoveries across continents and centuries.

9. Despite many factors favoring unity within Dar al-Islam, the vast political realm proved impossible to govern. Unified rule broke down, leading to regionalism and localism.

SUGGESTED READINGS

Adas, Michael, ed. *Islamic and European Expansion.* Philadelphia: Temple University Press, 1993. Interpretative essays on Dar al-Islam, especially after the tenth century.

Donner, F. M. *The Early Islamic Conquests.* Princeton, N.J.: Princeton University Press, 1981. A classic treatment of the early decades of Islam.

Hodgson, Marshall. *Rethinking World History.* Ed. Edmund Burke III. Cambridge, Eng.: Cambridge University Press, 1993. A collection of important essays by a major scholar of Islam.

Hourani, Albert. *A History of the Arab Peoples.* Cambridge, Mass.: Harvard University Press, 1991. A standard history of the Arab peoples before and after Islam.

Shah, Idries. *Sufi Studies.* New York: Dutton, 1973. Essays on the development of Sufism.

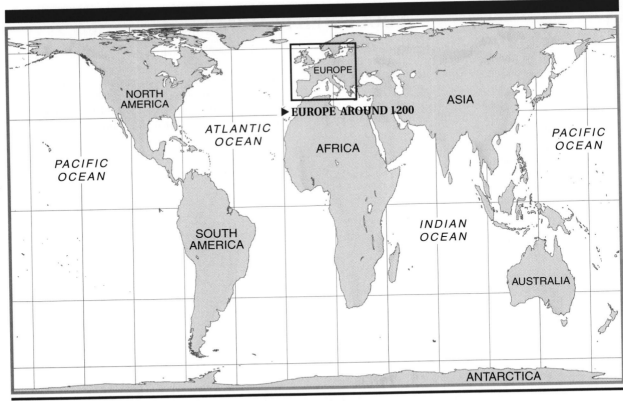

EUROPE

▶ EUROPE AROUND 1200

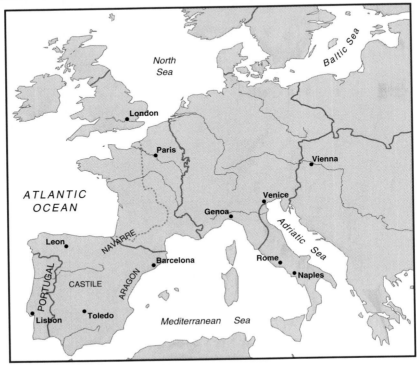

▶ EUROPE AROUND 1200

The European Middle Ages

around 500–around 1450

Many people have heard of the fearless King Arthur and his Knights of the Round Table. Arthur was probably a sixth-century British king, and oral tradition has preserved little more than his name. A twelfth-century poet created the imaginary kingdom of Camelot and cast Arthur as a tragic hero to entertain the courts of Europe. Although the knightly adventures are entertaining, little of the King Arthur story—or much of popular belief about the Middle Ages today—is real history.

Scholars call the era in Europe from around 500 to around 1450 the medieval period, or the Middle Ages. The geographic area that most scholars identify as medieval Europe encompasses roughly central, western, and northwestern Europe. The various peoples that populated medieval Europe synthesized a new culture around 500, as a result of the Roman exchange discussed in Chapter 8. This new European culture consisted of Greco-Roman, Germanic, and Christian elements. Europe coalesced only briefly into an empire, during the reign of Charlemagne. Christianity was fostered by kings in their areas, and the papacy during the Central Middle Ages tried, with little lasting success, to develop a universal sovereignty over all of Europe. Medieval contributions to art, architecture, literature, economics, statecraft, religion, and agrarian technology had a profound impact on later European civilization.

THE EARLY MIDDLE AGES, AROUND 500–AROUND 1050

Slowly, Germanic kings who had migrated into the disintegrating Western Roman Empire conquered and unified large territories into regional kingdoms across Europe. In each kingdom, the Germans settled on farms and estates, where their warrior-elite intermingled with the ecclesiastical and Roman aristocrats. This blending of Roman, Christian, and Germanic societies under regional Germanic kings created the basis for a new European culture.

The Rise of the Franks and the Carolingian Empire

The history of early medieval culture is dominated by the rise of the Franks, a Germanic people who eventually turned the regional kingdoms of central Europe into a unified empire. When King Clovis converted to Christianity and was baptized in 496, the Franks became closely allied with the pope in Rome. Other central European peoples at this time were either non-Christian or had converted to a sect of Christianity called Arianism, which defined Jesus as more human than divine. Clovis supported Roman missionary efforts within his expanding territory. As the subject peoples converted, they acknowledged the legitimacy of the Christian Frankish king's rule. Competition between Roman and Arian Christianity added to the Germanic political rivalries, as adherents tried to conquer and convert one another.

MAP 13.1 *Germanic States of the Early Middle Ages around 500. Germanic peoples migrated into the Western Roman Empire's territories during the fourth and fifth centuries. This map shows where the major folk movements ended by around 500. With these migrations came the opportunity for Germanic, Greco-Roman Classical, and Christian elements to synthesize into a new medieval culture in Europe.*

The kingdom of the Franks grew in size and influence. The Frankish Merovingian[1] dynasty kept control of the expanding territories through a loose network of regional bureaucrats. The Merovingian kings, however, slowly weakened as expansion ceased in the seventh century. The royal family was soon impoverished because of the customs of dividing inheritance equally among sons and awarding land gifts to loyal warriors. Royal impoverishment undermined royal authority over the kingdom. The Carolingians,[2] one regional bureaucratic family, emerged as rivals to the Merovingians through careful land management and through territorial expansion that brought in new wealth. In 732, a Carolingian named Charles Martel led the Franks to victory against invading Muslims from Spain. This victory essentially ended Muslim expansion farther into Europe and gained the gratitude and loyalty of many Franks to the Carolingian family. Charles's son, Pepin[3] the Short (reign dates 751–768), challenged the right of the weak Merovingians to rule the Franks. After gaining papal approval for his actions, Pepin deposed the Merovingian king, and a papal emissary anointed him the new king of the Franks.

Pepin soon traveled to Rome to defend the papacy against threats of Lombard invaders. While Pepin was there, the pope again crowned him king of the Franks to solidify their alliance and to reiterate Pepin's legitimacy as a Christian king and not a usurper. The pope, fearing that Pepin would establish himself in Italy as king of the newly conquered territory, narrated the folk story of Emperor Constantine's having given this western territory to the papacy. In imitation of Constantine, Pepin granted the pope political jurisdiction over much of central Italy, forming the Papal States. The alliance between the Franks and the papacy initiated a new missionary surge during the reign of Pepin's son, Charlemagne.

It was during the reign of Charlemagne[4] (reign dates 768–814) that the Franks extended their holdings over most of Europe. The Carolingian Empire, which was established by Charlemagne, took decades to achieve and was won at the cost of much bloodshed. Charlemagne ruled his empire through a network of warriors in the tradition of Germanic culture. In earlier Germanic chiefdoms there had been a close relationship between the king, who had been seen as a gift giver, and his warriors, those who had fought for him and who had received his gifts in exchange for their loyalty, advice, and political support. This loyalty was based upon a Germanic friendship structure, the **comitatus**,[5] which compelled kings to rule in consultation with their warriors.

Charlemagne allowed his most trusted warriors to govern large regions of the empire and, using the comitatus structure as justification, demanded a personal oath of allegiance from them. The warrior-governors accepted Charlemagne's rule because it resulted in the acquisition of lands and treasures, and governors often needed the military support of other elite warriors in times of regional rebellion.

In addition, Charlemagne kept administrative control through bureaucratic envoys who usually traveled in pairs. One secular person (to consult with Charlemagne's warriors) and one person from a religious order (to consult with church officials) assured that revenue was raised, military support was garnered, and Christianity was established. They also reminded the distant and sometimes reluctant warrior-elite not to waver in their allegiance, lest they face the revenge of Charlemagne's loyal warriors. Because many of these envoys lived in their assigned regions for long periods of time, there was always a tendency for the envoys to fall under the influence of the regional governor.

Charlemagne also extended royal law to territories he conquered beyond the Frankish homeland, using both Germanic and Roman structures. These laws regulated interpersonal relationships and defined responsibilities to the crown and to the Christian Church. In a law of 802, Charlemagne states:

> Let no one, through his cleverness or astuteness, dare to oppose or thwart the written law, as many are wont to do, or the judicial sentence passed upon him, or to do injury to the churches of God . . . but all shall live entirely in accordance with God's precept, justly and under a just rule. . . . And let the [envoys] themselves make a diligent investigation whenever any man claims that an injustice has been done to him by anyone. . . .

[1] **Merovingian:** mair oh VIHN jee an
[2] **Carolingians:** cair oh LIHN jee anz
[3] **Pepin:** PEH pihn
[4] **Charlemagne:** SHAHR leh mayn

[5] **comitatus:** koh mee TAH toos

FIGURE 13.1 *Fall of Pampelona.* *This scene on Charlemagne's tomb in Aachen depicts him defeating the Saracens (a term used for any Muslim or Arab in the Middle Ages) who held the city of Pampelona, in northern Spain, in 778. The hand of the Christian God, at the top of the picture, is seen striking down the defensive walls of the city. Charlemagne's defensive wars against the Saracens set up a buffer zone, called the Spanish March, between Muslim Spain and his empire. Throughout the Middle Ages, Charlemagne was hailed as a hero and model for good kingship because of his military prowess and his administrative talents.* Bildarchiv Foto Marburg/Art Resource, N.Y.

Charlemagne modeled his reign on the tradition of Christian emperors. For example, he followed Pepin's policy of supporting missionary activity throughout the empire. At Charlemagne's request, the papacy had sent him copies of church liturgies and practices so that he could initiate uniform practices and establish schools for the education of clergy within the realm. He encouraged Christian intellectuals from diverse areas to reside at his court, and their presence inspired cultural innovation and renewed interest in education and Greco-Roman ideas.

At the end of Charlemagne's reign, western and central Europe were part of a single empire. Charlemagne employed Christianity to help unify the empire ideologically and used the services of scholars to help educate his bureaucracy. As long

as he continued expansion, the empire prospered economically and politically; new territories brought wealth and lands to distribute to his loyal warriors.

Charlemagne came to the aid of the papacy during a dispute in Rome between the pope and rival political factions within the city, adjudicating the dispute and ruling in favor of the pope. In doing so, he judged the pope and returned him to the papal throne. Later, on a return visit to Rome, Charlemagne was crowned Western Roman Emperor by a grateful pope on Christmas Day, 800, during holy services. With this action, the pope resurrected the imperial crown and set a new precedent of popes making emperors. Charlemagne accepted the title but also retained the title of "King of the Franks and Lombards." Charlemagne's action of judging the pope and reinstating him and the pope's action of crowning Charlemagne set the precedent for the controversies over authority between popes and monarchs in later medieval history.

By 804, the Carolingian Empire ceased expansion, causing economic and political instability reminiscent of the Merovingian period. With the end of military expansion came the end of large land grants, both of which not only threatened the king's control but also lessened the acquisition of wealth. Although Charlemagne enforced some unity through the strength of his own personality and expertise, and his control of the comitatus, the empire was at best a loosely aligned network of territories bound by loyalty and land gifts. The long-term consequence was the disintegration of the empire. Louis (reign dates 814–840) was not the warrior or administrator that his father, Charlemagne, had been. He had great difficulty controlling the warrior-elite of his realm, some of whom were his sons.

The rivalries between Louis's sons plunged Europe into decades of violent warfare. The sons rebelled in the last years of Louis's reign, fighting over territories and titles, and a settlement was not made until three years after Louis died. In the Treaty of Verdun of 843, Europe was essentially divided into three regional kingdoms: the old western lands of Francia[6] (which for the sake of clarity we will call France), eastern Francia (which again for clarity we will call Germany), and a long narrow strip between the two that also extended to include Italy, whose king also held the imperial crown. Eventually, the imperial title and the territory of Italy fell into the hands of the king of Germany. The kingdom division of this period foreshadowed the early modern map of Europe, and the battles of Louis's sons over territory between France and Germany were inherited by generations of French and German peoples.

The Eighth-, Ninth-, and Tenth-Century Invasions

In the eighth, ninth, and tenth centuries, Europe experienced invasions and migrations that contributed to political fragmentation within the embryonic kingdoms. Magyars[7] from eastern

[6] **Francia:** FRANK ee uh
[7] **Magyars:** MAG yahrz

Europe, Muslims from Spain and North Africa, and Vikings from Scandinavia invaded into the disintegrating empire with such ferocity that the newly formed kingdoms were unable successfully to resist the multidirectional onslaught.

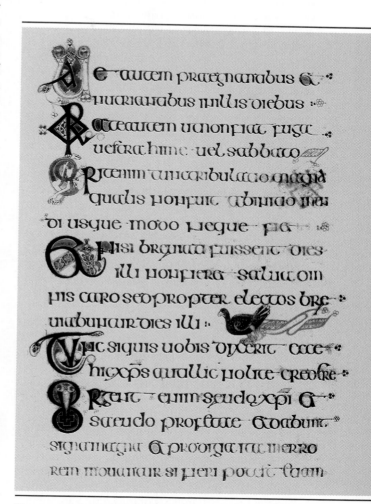

FIGURE 13.2 Book of Kells. *An illuminated manuscript of the Christian gospels produced by Northumbrian Celtic monks around 800, the* Book of Kells *is highly decorated with geometric figures, fanciful beasts, and human portraiture. This page shows some of these decorative features, in particular the script developed by these monks. After the Northumbrian writing style was imported to the Carolingian court of Charlemagne, it became known as Carolingian miniscule. Prior to this time, Latin was written in all capital letters with no spaces between words, making it very difficult to read. The innovation of lowercase letters spread throughout Europe and is still in use today, including in the English language.*
Trinity College Library, Dublin.

UNDER THE LENS
Medieval Renaissances

Scholars today recognize that medieval Europe saw a series of **renaissances**, which were artistic periods when Greco-Roman styles were emulated and synthesized with local techniques to create new styles. Five major periods of renaissance have been recognized in the medieval period: the Northumbrian Renaissance of the seventh century, the Carolingian Renaissance of the ninth century, the Ottonian Renaissance of the tenth century, the more widespread Twelfth-Century Renaissance, and the Italian Renaissance of the fourteenth century. The Twelfth-Century Renaissance is examined more fully in the context of the Central Middle Ages in this chapter.

The renaissance in Northumbria (a region in northern England) was occasioned by the importation of Greco-Roman arts to northern English monasteries in the seventh century. Artistic innovation produced a style of manuscript illumination (the decorating of a manuscript) of geometric design, a new script style, vernacular epic poetry, and a new style of architecture. One of the Northumbrian intellectuals of the day, Bede (died 735), wrote on a variety of subjects, including textbooks for monks. His best-known literary work is the *Ecclesiastical History of the English Church and People.* He also wrote a book on natural philosophy. Bede used the astronomical knowledge of the day to develop principles of timekeeping and dating, most specifically the A.D. system explained in Chapter 1.

Many ideas from Northumbria were exported by Alcuin[a] (735–804) and other monks to the Carolingian Empire, which was experiencing its own period of artistic innovation under Charlemagne. Charlemagne and Alcuin set on a course of education that raised the literacy standards of the empire, for members of both the clergy and the Carolingian nobility. Einhart, one of Charlemagne's biographers, wrote *The Life of Charlemagne* in the tradition of Roman biography. The new Northumbrian script evolved into Carolingian minuscule, a script that employed both upper- and lowercase letters that allowed for easier reading. Perhaps the most notable Carolingian scholar was John Scotus Eriugena[b] (810–877), who translated numerous philosophical texts from Greek and who was also an original thinker and scholar. Eriugena wrote a successful synthesis of Neoplatonism and Christian theology in the work *On Nature*, which was essentially a natural philosophy. Architecture also blossomed at Charlemagne's court. Carolingian architects built the palace in Aachen[c] on the model of Hagia Sophia,[d] the famous church in Constantinople. Under Charlemagne, schools were opened to address the illiteracy of the clergy and monks, and scholars focused on correcting translations and preserving traditional Christian theology. The educational foundation of this period directly facilitated the later development of the major schools and universities that became the intellectual centers of Europe in the twelfth to the fourteenth centuries.

The Ottonian Renaissance climaxed in the last three decades of the tenth century in Germany under the emperors Otto II (reign dates 973–983) and Otto III (reign dates 983–1002). Many scholars and artists flocked to the Ottonian court. Monasteries received significant endowments that supported theologians, teachers, and writers. Gerbert (940–1003), a monk who later became Pope Sylvester II, journeyed to Spain and returned with books and ideas on Islamic science. He also studied astronomy, Greco-Roman literature, logic, and mathematics. Gerbert was perhaps the first medieval European to import Arab knowledge into medieval intellectual circles.

[a]**Alcuin:** AL koo ihn
[b]**Eriugena:** AIR ih yoo GAY nah
[c]**Aachen:** AWK awn
[d]**Hagia Sophia:** HAW jee uh soh FEE uh

Kings were unable to defend against raids in several places at once because of the invaders' mobility. This created the need for local responses to attack. Consequently, regional lords were given or took over many royal responsibilities and usurped royal rights; this was particularly true in France, where the king was unable to stem the tide of Viking raids in the north and Muslim raids in the south. One story tells of a monastery in France that moved from the mouth of a river farther inland, only to be attacked again the following year. The monastery relocated several times, but each time

Vikings found and attacked it. Finally, the monastery moved hundreds of miles into eastern territories and the following year was wiped out by a Magyar raid coming from the east.

In Germany, invasions resulted in periods of decentralization but also periods of centralization under strong monarchs. Weak monarchs in the ninth century prompted the rise of five prominent nobles from the five traditional tribal areas, who reinstated the Germanic custom of kings ruling with a council of warriors. These five nobles eventually became rival princes, and whenever the monarch was weak, they threatened to usurp royal authority, sometimes even forcing an imperial election that placed one of them on the throne. Stronger monarchs, however, forced centralization policies on the five princes. One example of effective centralization occurred under the leadership of Otto I (reign dates 936–973), who instituted a period of monarchical control that witnessed the defeat of invading Magyars in 955.

As emperors, German kings were also responsible for the protection of Italy, and many emper-

ors, including Otto I, crossed the Alps to defend Italy and the papacy against various threats. Italy remained under imperial rule, but because of the geographical obstacle of the Alps, succeeding emperors found it difficult to maintain Germany and Italy in a tight alliance. Whenever the emperor was in Italy, the German nobles tended to usurp authority, and whenever the emperor was in Germany, the papacy and the Italian cities pushed for independence. The empire of Germany and Italy, which in the twelfth century became known as the Holy Roman Empire, endured more in name than in reality. Italian coastal cities built fortifications against Muslim raids and employed naval power to check Muslim dominance of the western Mediterranean. The Papal States continued under the power of the pope, but the political governance of Italy was increasingly under the influence of local families within powerful, fortified cities.

Muslims and Vikings were not just raiders but also settlers in Europe. Muslims had been in Spain as early as the seventh century and had traded with their neighbors to the north long before they

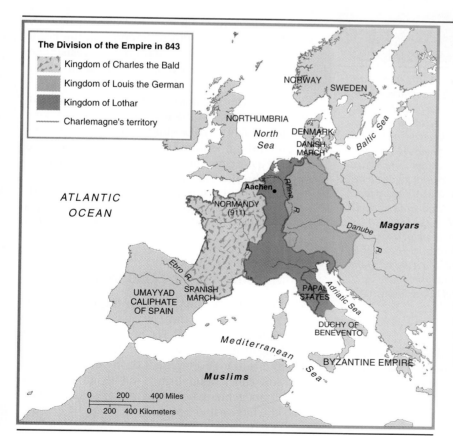

MAP 13.2 *The Carolingian Empire and Its Division in 843.* *This map shows the extent of the Carolingian Empire under Charlemagne and his son, Louis. Louis lost control of the empire to three of his sons, who continued to wage war after his death, until a treaty was established in 843. The Treaty of Verdun split the empire into three kingdoms under a tenuous imperial title held by Lothar. Eventually Lothar's kingdom collapsed, a result of Viking invasions as well as the intermittent fighting between the kingdoms. Its territories were divided between Charles the Bald and Louis the German's successors, and the imperial title fell to the king of the Germans.*

FIGURE 13.3 *Viking Carving.* *This stone was found in Sweden and is carved with the symbols for a memorial to a Viking warrior. From carvings like this, scholars have learned about Viking attitudes toward death and afterlife. In the center of the carving is a ship on its journey to Valhalla, the Viking heaven, with the souls of brave warriors. Viking kings often were buried or burned in their ships, which were fully loaded with their possessions for use in the afterlife. At the bottom of the carving is the dead warriors' homeland, including the village they are leaving behind. At the top of the carving, two warriors fight another warrior approaching Valhalla on horseback. At the entrance the rider is met by a Valkyrie, a handmaiden of the war god Odin. The duty of the handmaiden is to lead the brave warrior into Valhalla and to Odin, the chief Viking deity.* ATA, Sweden.

fought with Charles Martel in 732. Goods acquired through piracy and raiding were traded downstream or across the sea. Vikings moved down the Dnieper and Volga rivers into the Black Sea area. They set up a trading center in Kiev and exchanged goods with traders from Europe and Southwest Asia. Vikings or Muslims, after raiding one coastal city, often sailed farther down the coast to exchange goods with merchants in the next city. It was through these two groups that Europe was able to exchange many goods and ideas with traders from the eastern Mediterranean.

Eventually, the Vikings were able to establish a settlement in France at the mouth of the Seine River. The Vikings had used the area as a wintering base, typically raiding upriver during milder weather. The French king, Charles the Simple, struck an agreement with the Vikings to refrain from further raids in exchange for governance of the territory as a vassal of the king. The Viking chief, Rolf, agreed, and Normandy was established.

Vikings successfully conquered and settled in the northern and central sections of England and soon held Ireland as well. Heretofore, England had been a loose confederation of small Anglo-Saxon kingdoms that cooperated under the ambiguous authority of a commander-in-chief. Four of the kingdoms dominated England before the Viking raids, but, with the Viking invasion in the ninth century, all the major areas fell except the southern kingdom of Wessex, which emerged as the home base for English consolidation and resistance. Although England recovered independence for a short time under the able leadership of Wessex's King Alfred (reign dates 871–899), a second wave of invasion resulted in the establishment of a Viking empire of Norway, Denmark, and England. The empire did not endure beyond the first ruler, and by 1042 a descendant of Alfred had taken back the English throne. The result of Viking invasions in England was the opposite from Europe's experience; instead of decentralization and political regionalization, England experienced unification under a single monarchy.

Feudalism and Manorialism

By the tenth century, the synthesis of Greco-Roman, Germanic, and Christian elements was completed. This synthesis and the regionalism resulting from three centuries of invasions contributed to the development of the political organization called feudalism and the jurisdictional land-management system of manorialism, named after the large estates or manors.

Feudalism in Europe was the political system by which kings tried to rule, without bureaucracies, through regional leaders who gave military support and loyalty in exchange for **fiefs** (gifts of land that included manors) to use for their own support and enrichment. Upon taking the oath of loyalty to the king, the leader became a vassal and assumed legal authority over the lands and the people living on them. The relationship between the vassal and lord was contractual and developed into a pattern of rights and obligations of vassals. Charlemagne had laid the foundation for feudal relationships in Europe through his policies of land granting and oath taking. The level of feudalism varied throughout Europe.

Vassals were responsible for local governance, the collection of taxes, the establishment of courts, and the maintenance of the peace. Many powerful vassals received or usurped royal rights, such as the building of castles, the minting of coins, and the collecting of taxes and fees. As long as the vassal remained loyal to the king, there was little monarchical intervention in regional affairs. Strong kings occasionally attempted to reassert central dominance, but when an ineffectual king came to the throne royal power was usually weakened again.

Manorialism was most common in northern France and parts of England but was rare in Scandinavia, northern Germany, the southern coastal areas of France, and Italy. The lands of medieval manors were farmed by peasants or serfs. A peasant was merely a farmer who worked family-owned land or worked for the lord of a manor; a **serf** was a farmer who lived on the fief and was not free to leave. Serfs owed a variety of manorial obligations, such as a certain number of hours per week laboring for the lord directly. Peasants sometimes worked on manors for wages but were free to leave the manor and travel to towns or other manors for work. Usually they did not move because social conditions were such that travel and relocation were very difficult.

Although feudalism and manorialism began in the Early Middle Ages, their structures continued into the thirteenth century in many areas of medieval Europe. Remnants of feudal society persisted into the fifteenth century and beyond in social mannerisms and class attitudes, in part because poets and other writers of the Central Middle Ages idealized the lives of knights in literature.

THE CENTRAL MIDDLE AGES, AROUND 1050–AROUND 1350

By 1050, Europe was engaged in economic expansion, political recentralization, and new artistic creativity. Political centralization under monarchies also supported growing bureaucracies, and more individuals within the population gained access to political power. The economic prosperity brought new patronage of the arts and another medieval renaissance period.

Commercial Expansion and Its Consequences

Commercial activity expanded rapidly in the years between 1050 and 1300, as towns and cities grew in size and population and as trade further developed commercial exchange. Trade with Byzantine and Muslim areas increased in Italy, where Italian merchants soon challenged the dominance of Muslim traders in the Mediterranean and opened central and western Europe to luxuries such as pepper, sugar, cinnamon, and silk. In northern Europe, areas like Flanders were developing into mercantile centers. The Flanders wool trade with England, the Rhineland, and the Baltic Sea area supported the largest European textile production in the twelfth century, supplying most of Europe and beyond. Many areas specialized in particular commodities for export under commercial alliances and consequently increased the importation of goods they no longer locally produced.

Long-distance trade increased the need for capital, and early banking developed and investments accelerated as profit margins soared. Risks were tremendous, but a commercial venture could return as much as a 100 percent profit. Kings generally encouraged the commercial activities of the cities, seeing the opportunity for taxes and revenues independent of feudal lords' claims.

As a result of the increased commercial activity, several fundamental changes took place within European society. A middle class of merchants and artisans emerged, creating new social and political pressures. A monied economy developed, and the right to mint coins became a closely guarded prerogative of kings and great lords. Peasants who remained on manors increasingly received wages

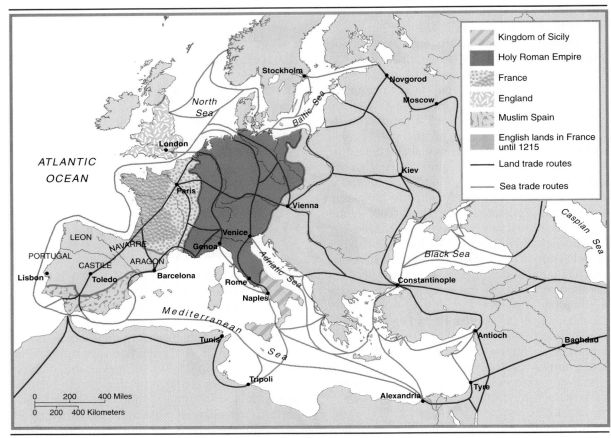

MAP 13.3 *Europe around 1200. Medieval Europe was heavily engaged in long distance trade by 1200, as shown in this map. Tin and wool from England and citrus, leather, and honey from Portugal and Spain were traded for dried fruits and almonds from North Africa. Slaves, timber, grain, honey, and furs came to markets from territories north of the Black Sea. Central European furs, metals, and wine were traded in Italian markets for olive oil and goods imported from Southeast Asia, such as carpets, glassware, and spices. At the same time goods traveled the trade networks, ideas were exchanged among merchants and travelers throughout the Mediterranean area.*

for their labor or paid rents for their fields. During the twelfth century, kings gradually replaced the vassalage military obligation with money payments called "shield money," hiring mercenary soldiers instead of calling up retainers. Kings also employed paid professionals in ever-growing bureaucracies.

The Twelfth-Century Renaissance

More commercial wealth created opportunity for greater patronage of the arts in the twelfth century, creating what scholars describe as the Twelfth-Century Renaissance. Schools and universities

developed, new literary styles became popular, philosophers and theologians argued fine points of law and physics, and innovations in art and architecture appeared.

In the twelfth century, education became increasingly important. Most students had traditionally come from the aristocracy, but education was a path to social mobility. Students from the various social levels attended monastic schools, where talent and skill determined opportunity. In addition, wealthy merchants sent younger sons to schools, some of whom returned to the family businesses and others of whom became bureaucrats or entered teaching. The growing bureaucracies of both royal and ecclesiastical administrations called for talented, educated individuals who could produce deeds and wills, conduct government surveys, keep financial records, and record legal proceedings. Europe moved from an oral, memory-based society of oaths to a society of paper, pen, and ink. Many who could not read or write chose to employ the educated to record their legal transactions.

Both secular and religious schools gave students a liberal arts education. Such an education was identified as the seven subjects of astronomy, geometry, arithmetic, music, grammar, rhetoric, and logic. Each student also chose one specialty area in church or civil law, medicine, or theology. Many universities became associated with particular disciplines because of their faculties' reputations; the University of Bologna (in Italy), for example, specialized in law.

Student life in the Central Middle Ages had many commonalities with student life today; one student pleaded in a letter home:

The city is expensive and makes many demands: I have to rent lodgings, buy necessities, and provide for many other things that I cannot specify. Therefore, I beg you, [father], that by the prompting of divine pity you may assist me, so that I may be able to complete what I have so well begun.

The father replied to his wayward son:

I have recently learned that you live dissolutely, preferring play to work and strumming your guitar while others are at their studies.

Increasing literacy among aristocratic men and women led to the production and patronage of secular and devotional literature. Lyric poetry, epic stories, romance poetry (inspired by the

IN THEIR OWN WORDS
Hildegard of Bingen

Hildegard of Bingen (1098–1179) was a poet, dramatist, musician, composer, scientist, mystic, biographer, counselor to the famous, and abbess. In her own day, she was well known and revered. Numbered among her many correspondents were various kings and ecclesiastical authorities, including Frederick I, the Holy Roman Emperor. In one treatise on physics, Hildegard describes medicinal properties of more than three hundred herbs, metals, stones, and minerals. In another treatise on causes and cures, she delves into nutrition and metabolism. Her advice to individuals was to engage always in balance in life, just as (in her view) the cosmos is perfectly balanced. In her visionary literature, she focused on cosmology and the centrality of humanity in creation; as she saw it, each individual is a microcosm of the created world and is intricately bound to nature.

The following selection is taken from one of her works in which she describes a vision of God, the creator, as a divine flame. Her poetic prose is a good example of the beauty of medieval literature.

I am the highest fiery power, who has enkindled every spark that lives and breathes. . . . I distinguish all things as they are, surrounding the circle of the world with my superior wings; that is, flying about it with wisdom, I have ordered it rightly. And I, flaming life of the divine substance, flare up above the beauty of the plains, I shine in the waters and blaze in the sun, the moon, and the stars, and with an airy wind, as if by an invisible life which sustains the whole, I arouse all things to life. For air lives in freshness and flowers, the waters flow as if they were alive. The sun, too, lives in its light, and when the moon wanes it is fired anew by the light of the sun, just as if it lived again; the stars also grow clear in their light as if [they] were living. . . . And so I, the fiery power, lie hidden in these things, and they themselves burn by me, as the breath unceasingly moves the man, like a windy flame in a fire. All these things live in their essence and were not devised in death, for I am Life. And I am Reason, and have the wind of the resounding Word through which every creature has been made, and I have given my breath to all these things so that none of them is mortal in its kind, for I am Life. I am Life whole and entire, not cut from stone, not sprouted from twigs, not rooted in the powers of a man's sex; rather all that is living is rooted in me. For Reason is the root, and in it blossoms the resounding Word.

FIGURE 13.4 **_Twelfth-Century University._** *Universities became more numerous during the Central Middle Ages. A university education consisted of the seven liberal arts, with opportunities for graduate work in theology, philosophy, medicine, and law. This twelfth-century Italian woodcarving shows a variety of students; some wear religious garb while others are dressed in the popular secular clothing of the day. The fact that they all have books suggests that this is a graduate class—probably a class on law.* Alinari/Art Resource, N.Y.

ideals of courtly love), personal letters, autobiographies, and genealogies became increasingly popular. Many aristocratic women became patrons of the troubadour poets in the courts of the twelfth century. French lyric poetry crossed the channel from France to England through the patronage of Eleanor of Aquitaine (1122–1204). Eleanor had supported troubadour poetry at the court of her first husband, King Louis VII of France. Upon her marriage to King Henry II of England, Eleanor became a significant patron of poets and musicians in England. A few women produced lyric poetry themselves, such as the twelfth-century countess Beatriz, who wrote about an unrequited love in this poem:

> I've lately been in great distress
> over a knight who once was mine,
> and I want it known for all eternity
> how I love him to excess.
> Now I see I've been betrayed
> because I wouldn't sleep with him;
> night and day my mind won't rest
> to think of the mistake I made . . .

William IX, Count of Poitou (1071–1127), teased his peers with this little gem that parodied the popular lyric poetic style:

> I'll make some verses just for fun
> Not about me nor any one,
> Nor deed that noble knights have done
> Nor love's ado:—
> I made them riding in the sun
> (My horse helped, too) . . .

The growing middle class enjoyed stories that bawdily poked fun at social mores and tales of clever, humanlike animal characters who outwitted opponents. These genres became increasingly popular among the general population. Geoffrey Chaucer (1340–1400), a famous English poet, amused many English with the delightful parodies of personalities in his *Canterbury Tales.*

Philosophy, theology, and medieval science were intertwined in the entire Middle Ages. Religion supported investigation into the rational order of the universe, and theologians populated the ranks of early scientists. Medieval science was called natural philosophy, and for most natural philosophers, faith and reason were inseparable, because God was seen as the divine architect of the universe. This use of one's reason to develop faith and an understanding of the created universe during the twelfth century was called **scholasticism**. Astronomy, mathematics, medicine, biology, and botany were several of the areas of medieval intellectual pursuit that laid the foundations for modern science.

Throughout the Twelfth-Century Renaissance, many scholars consulted Greek and Roman works and embraced Muslim knowledge. New thought was not threatening to theology but opened up the cosmos to closer scrutiny and better understanding of how the Christian God was thought to order the natural world. In the twelfth century, some Greco-Roman philosophical and scientific works were brought into medieval Europe through contact with Muslim traders and intellectuals. This access to Greco-Roman and Muslim works on physics, mathematics, astronomy, astrology, and medicine led to a surge of intellectual activity that created a deluge of writings.

Scholastic thought continued into the thirteenth century. The monk-scholastic Thomas Aquinas[8] (1225–1274) had an immense effect on the development of European physics as well as that of Christian theology. Aquinas was a natural philosopher who accepted the scholastic principle that reason enhanced the revelation found in Christian theology. He argued that a proposition is valid only if it is argued from the facts found in the natural world. One famous argument is his "proofs for the existence of God," in which he rationally argued that all things must have a cause. He observed that in nature everything that moves does so because of some action upon it. If one logically moves backward through each movement and action, one will eventually get to the first mover, or the uncaused cause. Aquinas concluded that the first mover must be the creator of the universe.

Perhaps the most visual representation of the Twelfth-Century Renaissance is the parallel development of Gothic architecture and the realistic style of sculptural decoration that became popular in twelfth-century cathedral building. One scholar has noted that more stone was quarried for building churches, abbeys, castles, hospitals, and town halls in medieval France than for the pyramid and temple building of ancient Egypt. The structural engineering of these stone edifices remains remarkable even in light of today's standards. The curved arches and thicker walls of Romanesque architecture in the eleventh and early twelfth centuries gave way to the ever-increasing height and delicacy of the Gothic style in the twelfth and thirteenth centuries. Rib-vaulted ceilings and pointed arches allowed ever-narrowing pillars to support greater and greater heights. The Gothic style permitted multistoried walls with stained-glass windows that bathed the immense interior in light. The incentive was to attract the eye to move from ground level heavenward; and even today most people, upon entering a cathedral for the first time, look up.

The building boom was, in part, a result of increased commercial wealth. The cathedrals were funded through donations and increased taxes,

FIGURE 13.5 *Gothic Church.* *This example of Gothic architecture is Westminster Abbey in London, England, built in the early thirteenth century in the French style. Most churches were built in a cruciform shape with chapels at the end of each transept; at the far end of this church is a typical chapel area with a large stained-glass window. The high altar was usually placed where the cross intersects. This view is a good example of a long nave, bordered by huge interior columns that support the rib-vaulted ceiling, common to Gothic architecture. The large windows of the exterior walls bathe the nave with light, as seen here reflecting on the floor.* Edwin Smith.

and many guilds donated labor or money for special projects, like windows that featured typical guild scenes. The likenesses of wealthy merchants and aristocrats often could be recognized in the faces of stained-glass figures. These edifices were

[8] **Aquinas:** uh KWY nihs

viewed with great pride; any city that supported a cathedral saw an increase in the local economy when pious pilgrims spent money on food, lodging, and souvenirs. Sometimes the masses of people inside the cathedrals were so great that the clergy could hardly go about the business of daily services.

Regional Monarchies

The trend in centralization during the eleventh century resulted in the growing power of the monarchy within England and France. After a brief revival of imperial power in the twelfth century, thirteenth-century Germany experienced a resurgence of the authority of the five princedoms at the expense of imperial power, and the imperial crown was increasingly subject to the older tradition of election. In Spain, Christians expelled Muslims and established the Christian kingdom of Castile.[9]

Generally, increased royal administrative responsibilities gave rise to bureaucratic governments. Royal law and **canon law**, church laws regulated by church officials, continued to develop in opposition to local feudal customs of law, giving greater uniformity and control of judicial practices. Conflict shifted from the battlefield to the courtroom. Chanceries (secretarial offices) grew in size and output, creating the need for larger numbers of highly educated personnel.

England had developed somewhat differently from Europe after 1066, when Duke William of Normandy conquered England. William brought French feudal customs of vassalage with him to England, but regionalism did not occur. William retained many Anglo-Saxon political traditions that reserved significant monarchical influence in local areas. In England, all levels of vassals owed direct allegiance to the new king over their loyalty to their immediate lords. William carefully awarded noncontiguous lands to his vassals in order to frustrate independence and regionalism. Thus, the concept of the community of the realm (similar to Charlemagne's comitatus) developed, perpetuating the idea of king and great vassals ruling the kingdom for mutual benefit. Denied regional independence, vassals developed a vested interest in cooperating with the crown to assure the safety and success of the entire realm. Because

of this, England moved toward a centralized system of government.

When King John (reign dates 1199–1216) lost his French holdings during a war with the French king in 1215, his English vassals forced him to sign the **Magna Carta**, or Great Charter, which reiterated traditional English aristocratic rights to participate in the rule of England. Many of John's English vassals also had lost their French properties, and they wanted to limit John's ability to act without their approval. In the vassals' opinion, John had abused his monarchical authority by taxing his subjects without their consultation, by challenging the papacy over selection of a new archbishop of Canterbury, and by developing policy without the consent of his great vassals. Because of these actions, the Great Council of the Realm (the traditional English council of great vassals who advised the king) was able to knot up the purse strings of the English monarch. John could not raise taxes without the council's consent. English political history is essentially the history of the tension between monarchical interests and the interests of the great lords of the realm.

The French experience was somewhat different. Although French kings traditionally had been weak from the ninth to around the twelfth century, the monarchy gradually recovered its authority in the following centuries. Effective governance under several talented kings led the French crown toward centralization and soon placed royal rights over those of aristocrats. The Estates General (consisting of clergy, the first estate; nobles, the second estate; and townspeople, the third estate) was called to meet only at the king's desire. The capture of the English king's French territories made the French crown exceedingly wealthy and powerful again. For the first time in centuries, the French king was wealthier than the major vassals of France. The monarch continued centralization policies, and, unlike the English Council of the Realm, the French Estates General had no control over taxation.

In Spain, the European defeat of Muslims who had held parts of that country since the early eighth century resulted in the establishment of the Christian kingdom of Castile. By 1085, the Muslim city of Toledo fell to the Christians and remained an important center for the exchange of goods and ideas. During the twelfth century, several Christian kingdoms in northern and central Spain estab-

[9] **Castile:** KAH steel

FIGURE 13.6 *French Illuminated Manuscript. Illuminated manuscripts were often used for portraiture in the Middle Ages. These portraits are of Blanche of Castile, regent of France from 1226 to 1234, and her young son, Louis. The two figures below probably represent the abbot who had this manuscript prepared and the scribe who did much of the work—it was typical to portray important individuals who had commissioned a work as well as those who had prepared it. The scribe on the lower right writes with a quill pen in his right hand, while his left hand holds a knifelike instrument used to scrape off dried ink when a mistake was made. The scraping often caused abrasions on the vellum, and sometimes even holes that obscured the text.* The Pierpont Morgan Library/Art Resource, N.Y.

lished themselves and pushed the Muslims farther south. At times, Muslims and Christians allied against other Spanish Christians in the competition for territory. In 1212, the papacy declared a crusade against all Muslims in Spain, and a united, multinational Christian army invaded the south, expanding Castile and the Christian kingdoms of Aragon and Portugal. By 1300, the only Muslim presence was the small kingdom of Granada, which was eventually taken over by Castile. Former Spanish Muslim territories were populated quickly with relocated Christian peasants. The two kingdoms of Castile and Aragon eventually united into

the single kingdom of Spain, and Portugal remained a separate kingdom.

Women were not traditionally rulers in the Central Middle Ages, but several exercised significant political influence. Mothers of young kings served as regents during their sons' infancies. Blanche of Castile (1188–1252) married a French king and reigned as regent for eight years after his death. During her regency, Blanche defeated a vassal rebellion. Many years later King Louis IX left for Southwest Asia on crusade, again leaving France in the able hands of his mother, Blanche. Many daughters of kings were given in marriage to princes to solidify alliances or, as inheritors of large estates, to consolidate territories. Eleanor of Aquitaine, the patroness of medieval literature and music, controlled wealthy lands that were coveted by her second husband, Henry II of England.

THE LATE MIDDLE AGES, AROUND 1350–AROUND 1450

By the Late Middle Ages, many changes had taken place across Europe. Monarchs were developing strong central authority within their realms, and economic and artistic growth persisted. But new problems soon forced additional changes in the map of medieval Europe and engendered new religious attitudes.

Late Medieval Politics

Late medieval monarchs continued to challenge regional lords for control of their realms and engaged in war with their neighbors as they tried to expand their territories. In Spain, the marriage of Ferdinand of Aragon to Isabella of Castile in 1469 effectively united most of the Iberian Peninsula under one monarchy. By 1492, the small Muslim state of Granada fell to the Spanish kingdom, leaving only Portugal independent.

In England, the continuing tension between royal and aristocratic rights pitted the elite against a king in need of funds to fight the French. The Hundred Years War (1337–1453) between France and England was the result of years of English claims to French territories. To finance the war the king was forced to grant concessions of legislative rights for fiscal support of his policies. The English king was still unable to untie the purse strings of England.

In France, the Hundred Years War created economic and political instability. The war was fought on French soil, and the devastation to property and life was enormous. Political instability threatened the monarchy; for a short time in 1356, the Estates General came under the control of a cloth merchant from Paris, after the king had been captured by the English. Royal rights were usurped, as the Estates General took over the royal privileges of legislation, taxation, and administration in regular meetings. Within another year, the French peasantry rebelled for two weeks until an aristocratic

and urban coalition put down the rebellion. This chaotic dissolution of law and order led to renewed support of royalism, and the long-term result of the rebellion was the loss of an opportunity for cooperative governance between the crown and the Estates General. French monarchs compromised with the aristocracy and the middle class by appointing leaders from these classes to its growing bureaucracy.

French kings were unable to stem the tide of the English onslaught and devastation of French lands. Finally, with the aid of a pious young Joan of Arc, the king was able to rout the English and turn the tide in favor of France. Joan was captured and stood trial on trumped-up charges of heresy and witchcraft. She was subsequently burned at the stake by the English. But because of Joan's successes and inspiring example, the Hundred Years War came to an end with a French victory in 1453.

Italy and Germany experienced the same kinds of internal struggles that England and France had endured, but no central, unifying political entity emerged. The Holy Roman Empire endured under regional disputes. Italy remained dominated by regional jurisdictions, and rival factions vied for regional leadership. Many cities retained their independence and grew wealthy in the lucrative Mediterranean trade.

Death and Disillusionment

As the Middle Ages came to an end around 1450, the European population had been profoundly affected by demographic, social, and economic changes. Wars and plagues disillusioned and devastated the population. Many of these changes gave way to economic recovery that spurred new commercial and intellectual activity.

Several wars marred the peace during the Late Middle Ages, including wars between rival Italian city-states, wars between Christians and Muslims in Spain, and the Hundred Years War. The Hundred Years War had held northwestern Europe hostage; the social, economic, and human toll left a mark that was not soon erased from memory. The devastation to the English and French economies was incalculable. The war also interrupted commerce to and from most other areas of medieval Europe, affecting the local economies.

As a consequence of simultaneous plagues from 1347 to 1349, the European population was ravaged, trade and commerce were virtually stopped in many areas, and whole towns and villages effectively disappeared forever. Europeans named the plagues the "Black Death." A series of intermittent plagues followed the Black Death in the years from 1361 to 1407, and, when the diseases had run their course, more than 20 million people had died. Occasionally plagues returned from the fifteenth to the nineteenth centuries. The Black Death influenced artistic styles; many graphic scenes of plague victims, mass burials, skeletons, and the "Grim Reaper" (death personified) became common in artists' work. There was a spectrum of reactions, from religious fanaticism to atheism. The horrors of disease and destruction psychologically crippled much of western Europe.

War and plagues created a shortage of labor, which, ironically, benefited many who survived in the form of higher wages. In some areas, serfs were relieved of obligations in order to entice them to stay and work; in other areas, serfdom became even more oppressive. Many landowners changed to commercial enterprises (like wool production) because they were more lucrative. This dislocated some people whose families had farmed the acreage for generations. Although the plagues devastated urban populations, they had a greater impact on rural peoples because entire village populations were ravaged. Many cities saw an increase in population as the rural dispossessed relocated in urban centers. Many remained unemployed because of a lack of special skills or because guild members and town leaders reserved jobs for their own members. During the second half of the fourteenth century, there were various outbreaks of violence as social tensions exploded.

Recovery

Several pockets of medieval Europe had not suffered the devastation of intermittent warfare, and a few isolated rural populations had escaped the worst onslaught of the plagues. Some commercial centers, particularly in the far north, continued to prosper at the expense of rival centers that had not fared so well. By the mid–fifteenth century, as the Hundred Years War came to a close, many of the

FIGURE **13.7** *Grim Reaper.* *The Late Middle Ages were fraught with death and disease. Many popular apocalyptic texts were illustrated with depictions of the Grim Reaper, or Death. Death was often shown as a triumphant warrior, striking down the innocent, the heedless, and the sinful without regard for social station or age. Many responded to their uncertain futures either by losing their faith entirely or by becoming more religious.* Giraudon/Art Resource, N.Y.

areas that had suffered the most were also recovering from their recessions.

Many innovations of the Late Middle Ages had profound effects on European recovery. New technologies in ship building helped to open up the New World to Europeans in need of funds to reinvigorate their economies. A by-product of increasing literacy was the demand for more books. New technologies produced better paper, and wood-block carvings were perfected and used to stamp artwork on the numerous and more cheaply produced devotional books. The manuscript illumination of the Early and Central Middle Ages was too expensive for mass production, and wood-block printing inspired the adoption of the Asian technology of movable-type printing, which soon revolutionized society. Gunpowder, developed in China, was a new technology in the Late Middle Ages. In the later era of the Hundred Years War, its use with cannon led to new architectural advances in wall defenses. Soon, individual foot soldiers were carrying guns into battle.

While much of western Europe was still experiencing a slow recovery, Italy was in the beginning of an economic expansion and cultural revival of Greco-Roman styles called the Italian Renaissance. Less affected by war, disease, and the resulting economic devastation, Italian cities continued to take advantage of commercial opportunity throughout the Mediterranean Sea. The new wealth and new ideas that inspired the Italian Renaissance would soon cross the Alps and help stimulate the recovery of late medieval Europe.

EVERYDAY LIFE

The general population of medieval Europe continued to rise until around the middle of the fourteenth century. City populations of 25,000 to 50,000 were not uncommon, and a few major centers, like Paris, could boast of populations around 100,000. Scholars estimate the entire European population by 1300 to have been about 70 to 80 million, an increase from the approximate total of around 26 million in 600. Although urbanization and commercialism grew at a rapid pace from 1050 to 1300, most Europeans, like most peoples of the world, lived in rural areas. The mean family size in cities was 3.9 and in the country 4.8.

Rural Life

Each manor consisted of the lord's manor-house, a village, fields, an orchard, and buildings for special tasks. Each farmer worked his own strips in the various fields as well as a portion of the lord's strips (see Figure 13.8). The produce from each strip was divided between the farmer and the lord according to each farmer's obligation. All produce from the lord's strips was retained by the lord. As time passed, occupational specialization increased on the manors; smiths, bakers, shepherds, and other artisan specialists worked full time at their occupations for the benefit of the entire manor population in exchange for other farmers tilling their strips.

The lords of the manor were also the lords of manorial law. Each lord held a manorial court where villagers could make complaints against their neighbors or where the lord could pronounce punishments or exact payments. Usual proceedings included complaints of negligence of required duties, charges of petty theft, and typical lord-villager transactions, as the following notations from a manor court demonstrate:

> Hugh Free appeared asking for clemency because his beast was caught in the lord's garden; Roger Pleader appeared with a suit against Nicholas Croke explaining that neither he nor his [kin] killed Nicholas's peacock; Gilbert Richard's son paid five shillings for a license to marry.

Some farmers lived as peasants in nonmanorial communal villages. The villages were small agrarian communities of several huts surrounded by fields not subject to feudal control. These villages often developed around secure locations, like castles, or in ecclesiastical districts where stone churches offered protection. Many such villages came under manorial jurisdiction during times of crisis. As in the manorial system, nonmanorial farming was a cooperative effort; tools, draft animals, and plows were too expensive for a single peasant to own. Law was established by a village council, and the necessity of mutual dependence gave incentive for quick settlement of disputes.

Many agricultural innovations and new technologies led to increased productivity and improved quality of life. The three-field system divided the land into three major field areas, where planting was done by rotation. Each season, farm-

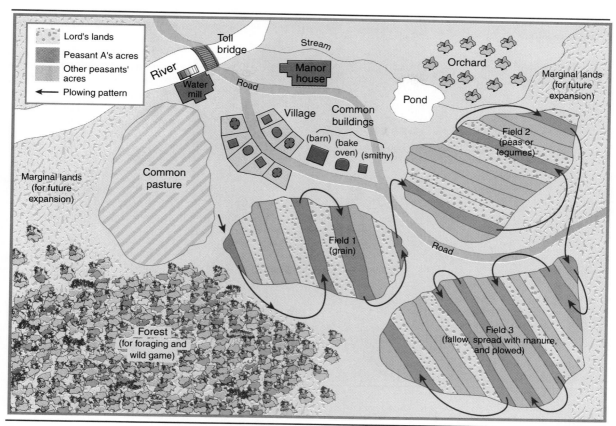

FIGURE 13.8 *Medieval Manor. Serf and peasant farmers tilled fields divided into long, alternating strips that made plowing easier by eliminating the need for tight turns with plow and oxen. Individual farmers often owned some animals and equipment, but more typically, almost everything on the manor belonged to the lord: the common bakery, the orchard, the pond or stream and the fish in it, the forage area, and everything else needed to work a self-sufficient farm. The marginal lands near the manor held wild game, but those who hunted without permission were charged with poaching. Each farmer had to pay the lord, in goods or in labor, for the use of any equipment or special service—even for picking apples from the orchard.*

ers planted crops in two fields and let the other lie fallow, allowing nature to replenish the nutrients in its depleted soil. Careful planning and the spreading of manure helped to bolster the yield per acre, which in turn yielded surpluses. In addition, the introduction of new harnessing techniques, the heavy-wheeled plow, and iron plow tips resulted in increased cultivation in the heavy, rich soils of Europe. Water mills and windmills led to increased productivity. All of these factors increased the food supply and resulted in a healthier and growing population.

Villages and manors were successful only when families worked together for the benefit of all. Women and older children toiled alongside their husbands and fathers on the farms, and in their spare time children played with their toys: tops, play swords, wooden tricycles, and dolls. Everyday life consisted of rising early and laboring long hours tilling in the fields, tending animals, or working at any of the other myriad chores associated with farm life. Next to their huts, most farmers had small vegetable plots that required their attention after their village or manor obligations were complete.

Medieval women had varied employment. In order to supplement income, peasant women often hired out to other manors if laborers or

FIGURE **13.9** *Feudal Agriculture.* *These miniatures from a fourteenth-century manual on agriculture depict the seasonal chores of feudal life. Each scene features a monthly task associated with different crops, animals, and regions.* Giraudon/Art Resource, N.Y.

maids were needed. Women, whether aristocratic or poor, were responsible for the preparation of food in the household. They also managed the household and cared for children, servants, and many of the family-owned animals. They frequently were the healers and midwives. Aristocratic women often ran the manors when their husbands and sons were absent because of feudal obligations. These women instructed the overseers on how to run the manors and kept the financial records, collecting rents and payments and procuring supplies not produced on the manor.

By the end of the Early Middle Ages in the eleventh century, many marginal lands were coming under development, trade towns were growing into cities, and most local economies were thriving. Economic growth was the result of new technologies that led to greater production on village communes and manors, and the surpluses for trade benefited both farmer and lord. The growing village and manorial populations often meant relocation for some peasants, because many villages and manors were landlocked by their neighbors and could not expand to accommodate the increasing numbers. Cultivation of marginal lands

drew excess population from settled areas, and lords of new manors enticed laborers by establishing more liberal manorial conditions. Some lords had to ease their control to keep peasants and serfs from running away in search of better opportunities elsewhere.

Urban Life

From around the twelfth to the fifteenth centuries, opportunities for employment proliferated. Many artisans from the village communities and manors relocated to the growing towns, particularly smiths, bakers, tanners, and others who could sell their goods or services. They joined merchants, who traded goods from as near as the manor down the lane to as far away as China.

Towns and cities that developed and prospered on feudal lands were given charters from the lords who held jurisdictional authority. The charters were essentially contracts of operation that spelled out the obligations of the towns and cities to the lord and the lord's responsibility to the town. Eventually, many towns extracted charters that gave them greater freedom. Usually the town was awarded the right of self-governance in exchange for yearly payments.

Town governance was organized around the guild system. Each profession, artisan or merchant, had a guild. The shoemaker guild, for instance, licensed, set prices, and generally regulated all shoemakers in the town. Shoemakers (like all artisans, bankers, and merchants) were located on the same streets: Shoemaker Street, Baker Street, and so on. Every shoemaker had to be a member of the guild, paying dues and performing guild responsibilities. Guilds permeated all aspects of urban life, from the workplace to recreation. They gave donations to churches, often paying for chapels, stained-glass windows, and upkeep. The building of a cathedral was usually a boon to a town, giving carpenters, stonemasons, cloth makers, candle makers, and many others employment for centuries. Guilds helped with funeral expenses and supported widows and orphans. Elected representatives, almost always the wealthy and influential from each guild, formed an urban council responsible for justice, trade laws, and negotiations with the lord. Towns and cities gained these freedoms sometimes in cooperation with investment-hungry lords and, at other times, through violent riots or with the help of mercenaries hired to fight for the town's cause.

Many women played important roles in the towns and cities. As mentioned earlier, some were artisans themselves. Some women found employment as goldsmiths, cloth makers, and various other professions that required periods of training and apprenticeship. Many a wife worked with her husband and continued the family business after his death, directing apprentices just as the husbands, the mastercraftsmen, had. These women inherited membership in the guilds. Single women also had the right to own property and establish businesses. By the thirteenth century, many aristocratic women and wealthy merchant women were engaged in long-distance trade ventures. One English woman lost her cargo to Spanish pirates; upon learning of her loss, she filed a lawsuit and gained royal permission to seize Spanish cargo at English ports until the loss was repaid.

MEDIEVAL CHRISTIANITY

During the Christianization of medieval Europe, the Christian Church extended its bureaucracy, focusing on uniformity. Monastic houses served as spiritual retreats and educational centers. Liturgical practices became universal, the parish system was fully developed, the seven sacraments were regularized, and sacred law was codified. The papacy in the early eleventh century was still primarily a regional power with little political influence beyond Italy. This slowly changed from the eleventh through the thirteenth centuries as popes

FIGURE 13.10 *Florentine Guilds.* *On the feast day of Saint John the Baptist, the citizens of medieval Florence proceeded to the cathedral to honor the saint and to display their civic pride. This scene on a painted chest shows thirty-nine-foot-high banners, embroidered with the symbols of numerous guilds and hung from houses along the processional route. Among those represented by such associations were wool makers, furriers, doctors, druggists, and sword makers; in all, about seventy-three guilds functioned in the city. Some of the more prominent groups were highly political, controlling commercial regulations as well as magisterial concerns.* Scala/Art Resource, N.Y.

who were trained as lawyers brought the bureaucracy under closer papal scrutiny. These popes organized and instituted reform within the ecclesiastical hierarchy.

Although medieval Europe was predominantly Christian, various religious minorities were present throughout the period. The largest group of non-Christians consisted of Jews, who had been present in western Europe since the first century. Christian theology forbade persecution of Jews, but most of them found living in Christian Europe dangerous, if not deadly. Periodically, many Jews were attacked and beaten, killed, or expelled from territories because angry mobs believing that Jews had murdered Jesus wanted to retaliate. In some cases, kings and bishops protected Jews and gave them sanctuary; in other cases they instigated the attacks for personal gain. Often, Jewish businesses were bankrupted, confiscated, or destroyed.

Some areas of medieval Europe were more accepting of religious and intellectual differences. The Norman kingdom of Sicily and southern Italy was well known for its religious tolerance of and openmindedness to non-Christian ideas. The kingdom was a playing field of artistic, intellectual, and social exchange. For most of medieval Europe, however, the Christian worldview dominated, and there was no concept of the separation of church and state.

Monasticism

Monastic houses played a key role in medieval society. Men and women took vows of poverty and chastity in their personal lives and pledged obedience to the abbots and abbesses, who headed the monasteries and nunneries. Most lived lives of prayer and hard work. Many monasteries and nunneries supported the poor in their local areas through donations and alms. Monks divided their days between farm labor and prayer. As some monasteries became centers for learning and monks spent less time in the fields, the need for agricultural laborers increased. These monasteries often hired day laborers or housed peasants who agreed to live a semimonastic lifestyle without taking the formal vows.

Nuns also lived lives of prayer and work. Nunneries hired laborers or produced sewn or woven items. Some nuns served as nurses in aristocratic households or in monastic infirmaries. Many nunneries were endowed by the families of wealthy aristocratic women or by retired aristocratic widows who donated their own wealth to the nunnery. Most early monasteries and nunneries were constructed in close proximity, with the abbot as the joint head, but some abbesses wielded great power too; Saint Hilda governed the joint nunnery and monastery at Whitby (in northern England) in the seventh century. Because women could not be priests, some nunneries maintained a priest to officiate at the liturgical services. The priest, in these circumstances, came under the authority of the abbess (except in judicial matters concerning church law). The number of double houses (consisting of a monastery and a nunnery) headed by abbesses was greatly reduced in the twelfth century under the reform movement.

Education had traditionally been reserved for members of religious orders and the aristocracy. Many monasteries became centers for learning; in the Early Middle Ages they had been the preservers of Greco-Roman literature. Because of monastic education, many monks were advisors or administrators in the kings' bureaucracies. Nuns were also highly educated and contributed to manuscript copying and illumination. Some nunneries became famous for their expertise in illumination and calligraphy. Nuns were expected to read the scriptures, the works of early theologians, biographies of saints and founders of their order, and the rules of their order.

Feudalization of the Church

The Christian Church was not immune to the feudal development of Europe. Many church lands fell into the hands of kings and great lords, who then made bishops vassals and granted the church properties as fiefs. Many of these fiefs were cathedral towns, some of which were great centers of trade. Scholars call this process the **feudalization of the church**. Because bishops were lords, they held feudal rights within their own fiefs and executed justice in their own religious law courts. When kings had regained control over the judicial practices within their realms, these ecclesiastical courts retained their independence. Criminal clergy were not to be tried in the king's court because the clergy were under the authority of their religious superiors. Kings bristled at this independence, and they increasingly took over the appointing of bishops and abbots rather than allow a traditional local election. This allowed kings to regain jurisdiction over the church properties within their realms. Bishops often married and they fathered children, but these offspring did not have legal rights to inherit church lands. Therefore, on bishops' deaths the lands reverted to kings, who could keep tight control over the wealth. Many younger relatives of kings and great lords became bishops to ensure a close allegiance and to keep control and wealth in the family.

Monasteries also became feudalized under abbots who were also vassals. During the invasions of the Early Middle Ages, monastery lands gained protection from kings or powerful lords. Abbots soon were granted the monastery as a fief and became feudal lords, with the same feudal obligations as any knight: support, loyalty, and military service (which was filled by hiring mercenary knights). Every monastery was a self-sufficient enterprise, often bustling with activity. Most had large agricultural lands that were cultivated to support the monastery. Many monastic grounds became the sites for local or regional fairs for the exchange of goods and gossip, and some towns developed around monastic grounds. Because individual monks took vows of personal poverty, all the income of highly productive monastic lands went into the communal wealth of the monastery, making it a desirable fief. Many younger sons of aristocratic families were groomed to become abbots.

Reform Movements

By the mid–eleventh century, concerns over the abuses within monasticism and the feudalization of the church spurred reform movements. Reform was not a new phenomenon; particular reforms of liturgies and practices had been supported by early medieval popes. Apprehension over the buying and selling of ecclesiastical offices, the common practice of marriage among clergy, and feudal obligations by ecclesiastical officials led many lay people and clergy alike to support reforms to eliminate such activities.

In monasteries and nunneries, reformers called for withdrawal from worldly affairs and the return to the spiritual discipline of poverty, chastity, and obedience. Within monasticism, those who had chosen the spiritual life as adults often desired a more austere, devoted religious life than those who had matured within the walls of the monastery. Many aristocrats had placed young children in monasteries and nunneries for education and religious training that someday might benefit the family. Aristocratic women often retired into nunneries after their husbands died—this was to escape having to remarry, and not for religious reasons. Laxity and, sometimes, outright antimonastic behaviors permeated many of the monasteries and nunneries. To accomplish monastic reform, several reformers turned to secular benefactors.

LAY REFORM. Lay reform included land grants to churches, monasteries, and nunneries that were free of feudal obligations and statutes against lax practices. As early as 909, Duke William of Aquitaine gave lands for a new monastery at Cluny, which led to the establishment of many monasteries free of feudal obligations. Other reform monasteries sprang up across Europe on donated marginal lands or in areas where devout laity supported reform. Reform ideas spread throughout medieval society at large. Pious individuals read devotional literature, helped erect magnificent cathedrals, and joined pilgrimages. Lay reform gave birth to an entire movement of lay piety, discussed in the following section.

MONASTIC REFORM. In addition to the Cluniac monks, the Cistercian and Carthusian monastic reformers focused on austere lives, limiting the comforts of the monasteries. In some cases, the austerity became so severe that monks and nuns died of poor diet and the cold. The reformers focused on a return to a life of devout prayer and tried to stem the corrupting tide of monastic wealth that caused laxity. Many great reform monasteries and nunneries, however, became communally wealthy as a result of their early austerity, because more people donated lands and wealth to them and the economic successes of their lands brought in revenues. Others refocused their attention from a devotion to prayer to a devotion to intellectualism and became known as great theological centers and libraries. There was a constant trend toward reform because of the countertrend toward permissiveness and disillusionment.

Toward the end of the Central Middle Ages, a new monasticlike movement created a different avenue for spiritual life. The Franciscans and Dominicans, for examples, lived communally but did not take the vows of the monastic orders.

FIGURE 13.11 *Saint Francis and Saint Dominic.* *This sculpture depicts an imaginary meeting of Saint Francis (left) and Saint Dominic (right). Saint Francis was famous for his work among the poor and sick, representing the embodiment of Christian charity and love. Saint Dominic was known for his intellect and his work among heretics, representing the embodiment of Christian faith and doctrine. Both figures had a profound effect on medieval Christianity as founders of major religious movements who participated in the reforms of the late medieval period.* Mansell Collection © Time Inc.

Instead of separating themselves from the world, they served it by caring for the sick and the destitute and by preaching against heresy. Franciscans were particularly associated with the ministries to the sick and the poor, Dominicans with education and preaching. Women's houses remained closely associated with men's. Saint Francis himself supervised the women's counterpart to the Franciscans—the Poor Clares, established by Saint Clare, a devoted follower of Francis.

PAPAL REFORM. Papal reform centered on the concept of ecclesiastical jurisdiction and the independence of church officials within kings' realms. The issue of independence was primarily played out in the confrontation of the pope with the Holy Roman Emperor and kings who tried to resist the reformation of feudal relationships within the church. Papal reformers established decrees that challenged the tradition of **investiture**, the proce-

dure whereby secular lords chose ecclesiastical successors and awarded them the symbols of holy office. The papal view held that secular lords should not control church lands through choosing friends or relatives as ecclesiastical officials, nor should they invest spiritual authority. The imperial and monarchical views held that the divine right of royal authority allowed for investiture. Because most bishops were feudal lords over vast church lands, the king wanted to retain control over them. At this time, from one-quarter to one-third of Europe's lands were church lands, and kings' loss of control over these territories would have had serious economic and political ramifications for the realms.

The issue came to a head during the Gregorian Reform, led by Pope Gregory VII (reign dates 1073–1085), and the imperial reign of Henry IV (reign dates 1056–1106). Each man insisted that he held authority over the other. Gregory excommunicated Henry and deposed him. Henry ignored Gregory's decrees to stop investiture and deposed Gregory. The issue of supremacy that had been introduced by the pope's crowning Charlemagne in 800 was fought out between the two men with no real resolution during their lives. Eventually (between 1107 and 1122), several compromises were reached between popes and monarchs. Bishops were elected and then invested by other bishops, but the king or emperor retained the right to veto any candidate up for election. In reality, the king's veto power permitted a series of choices until his candidate was chosen.

Tension between secular and religious authority continued to plague medieval culture. Many reforming bishops and popes tried to eliminate monarchical encroachment on church properties, church tithes, tax monies, and judicial responsibilities. As a result of the Gregorian Reform, the papacy entered into European political affairs as popes tried to gain control of church properties and religious functions within the kingdoms and regional boundaries of medieval Europe.

Popular Piety

Reform movements helped incite a widespread religious revivalism among medieval commoners that is usually termed popular piety. Popular piety reflected an atmosphere of devotion and emotionalism that led to a focus on spirituality. Pilgrimages became more common, interest in the healing powers of holy relics became widespread, and a faith in miraculous intervention became a bastion against the harsh realities of earthly life. None of these was new, but they became intensified.

Another result of popular piety was the change in attitude toward Jesus and Mary. Earlier representations primarily pictured Jesus as the second person of the Trinity, the divine Christ, judge of the world. In this atmosphere, there was more focus on the humanity of Jesus, the lover, comforter, and healer. The representations of Christ the king gave way to the suffering, bleeding Jesus with whom humanity could empathize. A focus on the Virgin Mary (mother of Jesus) also became popular, giving women a more positive image. As men saw themselves redeemed by Jesus from the sins of Adam, women gained a model in Mary that liberated them from the sins of Eve. Chastity became the idealized state for women, inspiring more women to become nuns. One legend circulated

FIGURE 13.12 *Fourteenth-Century Crucifix. During the Late Middle Ages in Europe, popular piety helped to spur emotionalism in the practice of Christianity. One result of the increased emotionalism was a tendency to portray Christ less as the king of heaven and more as a suffering servant. While earlier crucifixes tended to show Jesus in a triumphal pose with a golden crown, this fourteenth-century crucifix demonstrates the Passion of a suffering Jesus on the cross. People seemed to relate better to a god that could share the heartaches and travails of human life, and scenes of Jesus' life and death became more common in religious art. This is also the period during which artists designed works to commemorate the fourteen stages of Christ's Passion and death, later known as the stations of the cross. Like the suffering Jesus shown here, the stations were designed for devotional purposes, particularly for those who could not read devotional literature.* Bildarchiv Foto Marburg/Art Resource, N.Y.

ENCOUNTERS
The Crusades

The Crusades of medieval Europe were Christian holy wars against Muslims in the western and eastern Mediterranean and against heretics within the interior of Europe. Crusades were a product of pilgrimage mentality, personal greed, and feudal knighthood. Liberating early Christian holy lands in Southwest Asia from nonbelievers or Christian territory from heretics inspired crusaders—knights, peasants, and even children—to take up the cross and sword and go on a pilgrimage to save souls and lands for Christ. The promise of land and wealth inflamed many Europeans, from kings to lowly squires, to strike out on the long and arduous journeys toward hostilities that they believed would result in immeasurable rewards.

The initial endorsement by the pope to attack Muslims in Palestine was in response to pleas from the Byzantine emperor, whose territory Muslims had conquered, and from the general European population to control fighting between groups of knights. Trained for fighting, and in the absence of wars to occupy them, knights often broke the peace. Efforts to restrain them from pillaging and plundering Europe were unsuccessful, until the call from the Byzantine emperor in 1095 to aid against the Muslim invasions of Byzantine lands gave a focus for knightly energies. Pope Urban II seized the opportunity and preached in support of the first crusade.

There were many crusades, some successful in their outcome, most devastating to crusader and enemy alike. Some crusaders never reached their goal; thousands died along the way or finally dispersed. Several European kings—including Henry II and Richard I from England, Philip II from France, and Emperor Frederick I (who died on the way while taking a bath in a river)—set out on crusades. One crusade was sidetracked to Constantinople, where the crusaders became embroiled in local politics. Crusaders who arrived in Palestine fought bloody battles against Muslims that horrified even the combatants. In some cases, the Roman Christians could not distinguish Muslims from Jews or eastern Christians, and they tended to kill everyone indiscriminately. Crusader states were established and governed by European lords. Although continuously defended by knights, the area could not withstand reconquest by Muslim forces. By 1291, the crusader states were abandoned.

The crusades in Europe and in Southwest Asia had a significant economic impact. Towns and cities on the crusader routes enjoyed economic booms as crusaders and pilgrims traveled through. The crusaders returned home with stories of the various peoples they had encountered and with many relics and sacred art objects that soon adorned the cathedrals of Europe. There were enough pieces of the "true cross" of Jesus purchased to build an entire cathedral. The crusader states established travel routes that brought nonmilitary pilgrims from Europe. Pilgrims returning home introduced new foods, new ideas, and technology, all of which helped to stimulate exchange between the eastern and western Mediterranean.

The military orders of the Teutonic Knights, the Knights Templar, and the Hospitalers attacked heretics in Europe and non-Christians on the border of eastern Europe. In some areas, particularly in parts of Germany, the military orders received vast estates and became very wealthy, powerful forces challenging royal authority. Crusades against heretics were fought in a variety of ways—by military orders fulfilling their vows against heresy, by kings and aristocrats feeding their hunger for lands by confiscating territories, and by Dominicans acting as papal inquisitors.

---

that told of God's receiving complaints from the Devil because Mary's merciful tenderness was allowing too many of the damned into heaven. Intense personal piety and devotion also led to larger numbers of men and women entering the monastic life. The strength of these new devotees' faith was matched by the increasing frequency of mystical experiences.

Popular piety often veered from the formal theological introspection of the church hierarchy and intellectuals. The bishops were responsible for the spiritual care of all souls, the supervision and education of all priests, and the eradication of all heresies within the diocese. Because of their responsibilities these bishops tended to be less tolerant of new ideas than the Christian intellectuals. Many bishops, however, allowed lay preachers (not ordained) within their dioceses but closely scrutinized what was being preached. Lay preachers were encouraged to enter the church schools and to adhere to established church doctrine; some agreed, and some refused. The tension between official doctrinal belief and individual inspiration sparked many disagreements between the institutional church and the popular pietists.

Medieval popular piety sometimes led lay preachers to espouse ideas that had no basis in medieval science or theology. An example is the Cathar belief that Jesus did not have a real physical body or that the creator God of the Old Testament was evil for trapping souls in physical bodies. Many lay preachers attacked ecclesiastical abuses that they thought should have been reformed, while some bishops exposed major theological errors in popular preaching. Sometimes because of arrogance on the part of ecclesiastical officials and sometimes because of obstinacy on the part of lay preachers, disagreements became violent.

The rise in popularity of lay preachers led to a concern by church officials over the issue of religious dissent. Many tolerant bishops encouraged lay preachers' efforts to reach the poor and the displaced. When a question of competency arose, however, ecclesiastical officials usually performed an inquiry, or **inquisition**, into what was being taught or preached. These were usually minor investigations limited to local interests. By the 1230s, however, the papacy saw a need to establish consistency in questioning and punishment and formed the formal papal inquisitional system. Most medieval inquisitions resulted in dismissal of charges or a few years of imprisonment.

Papal Monarchy

The monarchical paradigm of centralization in the Central Middle Ages was used by the papacy as a model for its own organizational development. The closest thing to papal dominance was the period of papal authority from roughly the end of the twelfth century to the end of the thirteenth. Scholars refer to this development as the **papal monarchy** because the papacy had established a central administrative bureaucracy that rivaled those of kings. The papal chancery more than doubled its output almost yearly; thousands of letters passed from Rome to various cities within Europe. Taxes from church lands and donations increased papal wealth, which helped to support the growing papal bureaucracy and the papal missionary activities. The papal court was established as the last court of appeal for the courts of Europe, increasing

the number of visitors to the holy city of Rome. The pope had been elevated from a regional ruler and general spiritual advisor to a universal political authority competing with monarchs for the loyalty of Christian subjects. The height of papal power came during the reign of Innocent III (reign dates 1198–1216). Innocent III intruded on the election of a Holy Roman Emperor, challenged a French king's divorce, and forced King John of England to become a papal vassal.

Continued papal intervention in secular affairs after Innocent III gradually led to disillusionment with papal spiritual leadership. Popular piety and reform movements continued to examine practices of Christianity, which included the actions of the papacy. During the pontificate of Boniface VIII (reign dates 1293–1300), the English and French kings actively resisted papal interference in their affairs. Pope Boniface pressed papal claims farther than ever, but the more pressure he exerted, the more resistance he encountered. After a period of papal residence in Avignon, under the protective eye of the French crown, the papacy never again achieved the political influence of Innocent III's day. From the fourteenth century, the papacy gradually became a political puppet of rival factions in Italian politics. Increasingly, trust was placed in the hands of ecclesiastical councils and assemblies under strong monarchical influence. Christian governance was becoming regional.

New Theologies

The devastation of war and plagues in the Late Middle Ages led to religious questioning and sparked new intellectual speculation. The fourteenth century produced numerous mystics, both men and women, who argued that to know God one must turn away from natural philosophy and toward purely spiritual exercises. Theology continued to be systematized, and rational explanations of the universe increasingly gave way to theories of the incomprehensibility of God. The new theology of nominalism taught that any knowledge of the divine was so minute and limited that rational inquiry was ineffectual in its ability to fathom the universe. Intellectual speculation tended toward a separation between inquiry concerning the natural world and inquiry concerning the divine realm. This philosophical split foreshadowed the divergent paths of early modern science and theology.

EUROPE

		Early Middle Ages, 500–1050	—	
			—	
			600	
	Northumbrian Renaissance, seventh century		—	
			—	
			—	Bede dies, 735
	Carolingian Renaissance, ninth century		800	Charlemagne crowned Western Roman Emperor, 800
Viking, Magyar, and Muslim invasions, ninth and tenth centuries			—	Cluny, reform monastery, founded, 909
			—	
			1000	
		Central Middle Ages, 1050–1350	—	Pope Gregory VII issues decree against lay investiture, 1075
	Twelfth-Century Renaissance		—	
			—	Hildegard of Bingen dies, 1179
			1200	Eleanor of Aquitaine dies, 1204 / King John of England signs Magna Carta, 1215
			—	
			—	
Black Death, 1361–1407	Hundred Years War, 1337–1453	Late Middle Ages, 1350–1450	—	
			1400	Geoffrey Chaucer dies, 1400
			—	
			—	
			—	

SUMMARY

1. The Early Middle Ages was a synthesis of Greco-Roman, Germanic, and Christian societies. The Franks eventually conquered most of medieval Europe and established the Carolingian Empire, ruled by Charlemagne.

2. After the eighth-, ninth-, and tenth-century invasions by Muslims, Vikings, and Magyars, Europe developed regional kingdoms. As areas experienced further regionalization, feudalism and manorialism became more common. The entire medieval period saw the ebb and flow between localization under vassal authority and centralization under royal authority.

3. The people in the Central Middle Ages experienced commercial expansion and economic growth. During the Twelfth-Century Renaissance, literacy increased and intellectual speculation spurred new ideas. New styles of literature and architecture reflected economic growth as urban centers patronized the arts. National monarchies developed bureaucracies that challenged vassal localism.

4. In the Late Middle Ages, Europe experienced both destruction and innovation. Several kings gained greater control of their realms and expanded their territories. Those who survived plagues and wars often found greater economic opportunity. Recovery came with a reinvigorated European economy.

5. Rural life was centered on the manor. New technologies resulted in surplus production and occupational specialization, which in turn led to better health, longer life, and increased opportunities in rural and urban life. Towns took on self-governance through representative guilds.

6. Monasticism was a significant part of medieval European society; many monasteries were houses of learning. Religious and secular leaders led reform movements, and popular piety inspired religious revivalism but sometimes led to heresy. The papal monarchy emerged out of papal reform against investiture but could not sustain universal authority over the Christian society. Wars and plagues led to religious questioning and new theologies.

SUGGESTED READINGS

Epstein, Steven A. *Wage, Labor, and Guilds in Medieval Europe.* Chapel Hill: University of North Carolina Press, 1991. A fresh examination of labor and associated themes in the Middle Ages.

Hanawalt, Barbara A. *Growing Up in Medieval London.* Oxford, Eng.: Oxford University Press, 1993. A highly readable study of what childhood and parenting were like in medieval England.

Hollister, C. Warren. *Medieval Europe.* Seventh edition. New York: McGraw-Hill, 1994. A very informative and entertaining review of medieval Europe.

Russell, Jeffrey Burton. *A History of Medieval Christianity.* Arlington Heights, Ill.: Harlan Davidson, 1968. A standard history of medieval Christianity, with emphasis on the tension between established order and spiritual reform.

Shahar, Shulamith. *The Fourth Estate: A History of Women in the Middle Ages.* Translated by Chaya Galai. New York: Methuen, 1983; reprint, New York: Routledge, 1994. A study of the various roles of women in medieval Europe.

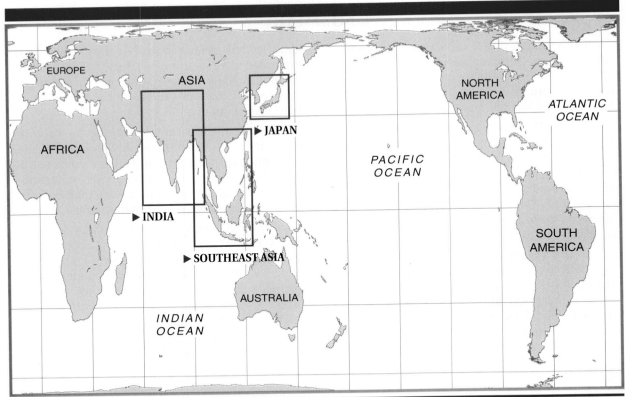

EUROPE

ASIA

AFRICA

NORTH
AMERICA

ATLANTIC
OCEAN

►JAPAN

PACIFIC
OCEAN

►INDIA

SOUTH
AMERICA

►SOUTHEAST ASIA

AUSTRALIA

INDIAN
OCEAN

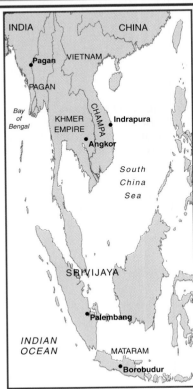

INDIA

CHINA

Pagan

VIETNAM

PAGAN

Bay
of
Bengal

KHMER
EMPIRE

CHAMPA

Indrapura

Angkor

South
China
Sea

SRIVIJAYA

Palembang

INDIAN
OCEAN

MATARAM

Borobudur

►SOUTHEAST ASIA

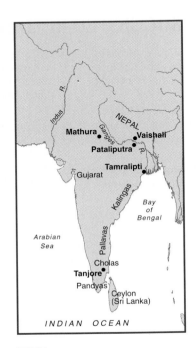

Indus R.

NEPAL

Mathura

Ganges

Vaishali

Pataliputra

R.

Tamralipti

Gujarat

Kalingas

Arabian
Sea

Pallavas

Bay
of
Bengal

Cholas

Tanjore

Pandyas

Ceylon
(Sri Lanka)

INDIAN OCEAN

►INDIA

Hokkaido

Sea
of
Japan

KOREA

Honshu

Kyoto

Kamakura

Nara

Ise Shrine

Shikoku

PACIFIC
OCEAN

Kyushu

►JAPAN

Regionalism in South, Southeast, and East Asia

around 180 B.C.–around A.D. 1450

The Japanese warrior grew nervous. To whom should he give his loyalty? Many of his friends supported the regional lord, Minamoto Yoritomo, but others supported leaders elsewhere. It was confusing to have so many different great warlords. The breakdown of imperial power had caused problems for simple folk like himself.

Regionalism was a common development in Asia, and regional governments frequently emerged with the decline or collapse of imperial governments. In Japan, an emerging feudal system demanded the allegiance and subordination of local warriors to a regional military lord.

In previous chapters pertaining to Asia, we focused on empires and the factors that led to their unification and decline. Here we will examine the appearance of regional states in southern, southeastern, and eastern Asia to probe elements that promoted regionalism and localism. Two additional themes, the spread of religion (Buddhism, Hinduism, and Islam) and the role of maritime trade in state building, will be explored.

REGIONALISM IN INDIA, AROUND 180 B.C.– AROUND A.D. 1100

Northern states dominated coverage of India in Chapters 5 and 10; in the period under consideration here, the south became politically significant. Not only did southern states raid northward, but

345

they also controlled much of the maritime trade along the Indian coastline and fostered their own elite culture.

Northwestern India

After the collapse of the Maurya Empire, invaders from Central Asia and Persia created instability in the Indus region. Some conquered and ruled Gandhara, in a part of the Indus Valley where Buddhism had long been established. By the second century B.C., artists in Gandhara produced a new art style, most notably represented in sculpture. The Gandhara sculptures of Buddhas and Bodhisattvas displayed elements of Greek artistic realism that contrasted with the more "Indian" figures from Mathura, a major artistic center farther east. Greek influence came from descendants of Greeks who had settled in the Indus Valley in the fourth century B.C. Mathura works show Buddhas with non-Greek features dressed in *dhotis*, traditional Indian loincloths.

Invaders—like the Kushanas, a Central Asian people—fought to control a key trade route that snaked across northern India. The Kushanas settled in western India, where they adopted Indian names and practices of the warrior caste. The Kushanas forged a government that controlled some of northern India but were unable to extend their control to the south.

By the first century A.D., the Kushanas adopted Buddhism and patronized artists and artisans who continued to develop impressive sculptural and other art forms. The Kushanas also maintained close links to their Central Asian homeland. In the third century, the Kushana state suffered a fatal defeat at the hands of the invading Persians and disappeared.

From the fifth to the eighth centuries, other groups invaded India from the north and west. Tribes of Huns, peoples from Central Asia, invaded northwestern India in the fifth and sixth centuries, causing great political instability. Beginning in the eighth century, Arab fleets and armies also conquered parts of the Indus Valley. These events set in motion a long process of the introduction and slow spread of Islam throughout much of India in succeeding centuries.

The northwestern and western parts of India also experienced social change caused by invasions from Central Asia. As new invaders displaced

FIGURE 14.1 *Standing Buddha from Mathura. Mathura, in northern India, became a major center of Buddhist sculpture in the era of regionalism (around 180 B.C.–around A.D. 1450). This standing figure portrays the serenity of the Enlightened One, dressed in the traditional Indian robe. The circular array behind the figure represents the aura of light emanating from the Buddha, not unlike the halos around holy figures in Christian art.* National Museum, Delhi.

an existing government, they absorbed the ruling groups or pushed them south. Continual infusions of peoples enriched the regional societies, showing the continued social flexibility of the Indian caste system.

Northeastern India

After Gupta rule collapsed, the next major ruler, Harsha (reign dates 606–647), used the Ganges Valley as a base. Harsha conquered a vast territory and brought changes that perpetuated Indian regionalism.

Harsha never controlled the trade routes in the northwest and consequently ruled with fewer financial resources than the Guptas, who had controlled the Indus Valley. Instead of paying his officials with money, Harsha often gave them land. Like the Gupta emperors, Harsha was obliged annually to donate land or other forms of wealth to Hindu temples, according to customary practice.

Because these church lands were untaxed, they deprived the state of essential revenues.

At the same time, Harsha expanded the **samanta system,** the granting of semiautonomous rule to recently conquered territories and their rulers. The Guptas had permitted some local control, but Harsha could not afford a large central bureaucracy. Consequently, he maintained local political elites, providing that they swore loyalty to him.

Harsha's shift of his capital from Pataliputra to Kanauj, farther west in the Ganges Valley, had the unintended consequence of promoting regionalism in the long term. This move permitted the eventual growth of autonomous kingdoms in and around the Ganges Delta during times of political weakness of the central government. Successors to Harsha maintained Kanauj as the capital and permanently lost control of the east.

Although Harsha adhered to Buddhism, he tolerated Hinduism, including practices that he

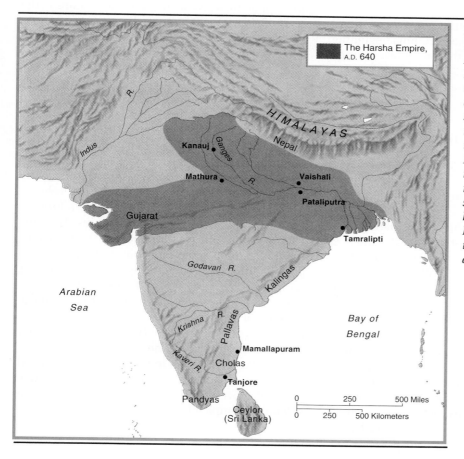

MAP 14.1 *Regional States in India around 640. Although much of northern India was united under the rule of Harsha, the rest of India was divided into regional states. For the remaining centuries until 1500, regionalism was the dominant theme in Indian history. The Pallavas, the Cholas, and the Pandyas ruled parts of the south in succeeding centuries, each being temporarily dominant. Intraregional trade continued to flourish despite political division.*

The Harsha Empire, A.D. 640

personally disliked. Harsha supported Buddhist priests and Buddhist art, and he also supported Hindu temples and their *brahmans*. The practice of **suttee**, the suicide of widows on the funeral pyres of their husbands, had appeared among members of the Hindu elite. When Harsha's widowed sister faced this ordeal, the monarch intervened to spare her a fiery death. He spoke against *suttee* but did not legislate against it, unwilling to antagonize powerful Hindu leaders.

Many features of Harsha's administration remind one of the system of Charlemagne in Europe. Neither ruler could afford large bureaucracies and so resorted to the expediency of permitting local rulers much autonomous control over their domains. Harsha and Charlemagne also granted land to subordinates in exchange for oaths and acts of loyalty. In addition, Harsha and Charlemagne aided religions by generous donations and other pious acts. Many of these actions eventually undermined the central government and led to regional rule in the decades after the deaths of Harsha and Charlemagne.

Muslim raiders and conquerors from Central Asia drove deep into northeastern India beginning in the eleventh century. By the thirteenth century, one group established the Delhi Sultanate in north-central India and used it as a base from which to expand southward.

Southern India

Southern Indians usually stopped invasions by northern states. Geography played a key role in that resistance, as mountain ranges blocked easy access inland and along the coast.

From the second century A.D., many states rose in the south and vied for political dominance. Three of these states, Pandya, Pallava, and Chola, developed long-lived polities, although at times one of these three dominated the others. Indeed, much of the time, decentralized rule followed feudal patterns similar to those in Zhou China and medieval Europe: Land was granted to subordinates in exchange for loyal service, and the manor or landed estate became a system for managing agriculture. One similarity with Europe but difference from Zhou China was the practice of donating tax-free land to religious institutions. In both Europe and India, these practices reduced state revenues.

People in southern India added a third kind of caste system to the other two caste structures, and all became fully established in the south. The latest division of castes in the south was based on geographical factors: the hill-people caste, the plains-people caste, the desert-people caste, the forest-people caste, and the coastal-people caste. Each of these five divisions comprised various occupational groupings, among them farmers, boat makers, and hunters.

Another feature in the south was the place of women in politics, elite culture, and the economy. Female rulers were not uncommon in the south, and succession occasionally passed from one woman to another. Princesses often received excellent educations, and some served as diplomatic emissaries. Elite women wrote poems; Vijavanka,[1] for example, was favorably compared to Kalidasa, the great poet and dramatist of the Gupta court. Women also worked alongside their husbands as artisans and merchants, although their individual contributions often went unrecognized. Some planted, weeded, and harvested grains in the paddy fields, too.

Arts and scholarship in southern India reflected a variety of factors, including patronage from monarchs, merchants, and devout believers. Many Hindu temples in the south had universities attached to them, and students not only learned Sanskrit grammar and Hindu philosophy, but they also studied law, medicine, and astronomy. Others wrote major poems, plays, and essays. Indeed, the corpus of writings in the many southern languages is vast. Tamil, an indigenous language unrelated to the Indo-European language family, developed into a major literary language of southern India.

Religious art, especially sculptures depicting Hindu deities, thrived in the south. Monarchs there sponsored exceptional pieces in the eleventh and twelfth centuries. One of the most famous sculptures is a bronze cast of Shiva dancing. This dance of life represents the dual nature of Shiva, the creator and destroyer, two necessary elements of universal existence. Hindus believe that destruction of the old is necessary before the creation of the new, which in turn must be destroyed to be created anew. The piece combines a dynamic sense of movement with delicate beauty and is a splendid example of southern art.

[1] **Vijavanka:** vee jah VAHN kah

FIGURE 14.2 *Shiva as Lord of the Dance.* *Produced in southern India during the eleventh century, this copper sculpture shows the major Hindu deity, Shiva, performing the dance of creation and destruction. In one hand he holds a drum, symbolizing sound, or creation, and in another he holds the fire that will destroy that which was created. Shiva dances within a circle of fire, reflecting the cyclical and never-ending nature of the processes of creation and destruction. The figure crushed beneath his foot is a demon representing ignorance.* Nataraja: Siva as King of Dance, South India, Chola period, 11th century. Bronze, H. 111.5 cm. © The Cleveland Museum of Art, 1996, Purchased from the J. H. Wade Fund, 1939. 331.

Temple building became a major form of religious devotion in the south, and many places boasted major temple complexes. In the eighth century, Pallava rulers and merchants patronized construction of numerous temples, and Pallava artists and architects set the pattern for temple building not only in southern India but also in Southeast Asia.

The affluence of the merchants testifies to the importance of trade among cities in southern India. India's maritime trade also grew through the entire first millennium A.D. Merchant guilds formed in the manner we have seen elsewhere and controlled their members' lives. Monarchs appreciated the significant revenues from trade that flowed into their coffers, and they undertook a variety of measures to promote trade.

The Chola government's growing dominance in the tenth and eleventh centuries reflected its participation in Indian Ocean trade. Two monarchs, Rajaraja I (reign dates 985–1014) and Rajendra I (reign dates 1014–1044), built the foundation of Chola power by taking control of trade routes, especially those along the two Indian coasts. In addition, Rajaraja I began a major raid on Sri Lanka, and Rajendra I completed its conquest. They also took control of the major islands off the eastern coast of India. In the eleventh century, maritime rivalries between the Indians and Malays of Southeast Asia led to a major naval campaign launched by the Chola state. The Indians devastated the Malay kingdom that controlled most of the shipping between India and China.

Despite the significant revenues emanating from trade, the bulk of Chola financial resources came from the land. The core area of Chola lay in the Kaveri River Valley, a fertile region whose complex hydraulic system built over the centuries provided two rice harvests each year. In the core area, relatively strong state control lay in the people,

PARALLELS AND DIVERGENCES

Economic and Political Uses of Temples

Asian temples and monasteries served economic and political functions, as well as religious ones. They provided ways to focus economic activities of people near where they resided. Some regional temples and monasteries acquired sufficient influence to play significant political roles.

Indian temples often became economic centers. In southern India, for example, temple complexes employed large numbers of artisans to craft and repair sculptures, bronze works, and murals. Hewn blocks of granite formed the temple base and superstructure. Peasants also worked the agricultural lands owned by the temples, and some temples used the services of temple prostitutes, who plied their trade for the complex's economic well-being, as well as for religious rites like symbolizing nature's fertility. Many religious centers amassed great sums of money and lent some out to devotees.

Chinese Buddhist monasteries also benefited from the largess of faithful followers. Some monasteries developed pawn shops, banks, and credit unions, and many Buddhist temples also became large landowners. Chinese governments tended to look less favorably upon successful monasteries and sometimes forced them to return their lands to tax rolls. Peasants who worked these estates were also forced back into taxpaying. Indian monarchs tended to see monasteries as opportunities for economic and political support, paying close attention to establishing influence over them.

Southern Indian and Javanese temples also served direct political and religious purposes. The massive temple complex at Tanjore, the Chola capital, was completed early in the tenth century, impressing visitors and subjects with the ruler's political might. Similarly, Borobudur (a symbolic replica of India's holy Mount Meru) in central Java encompasses nine terraced tiers in a vast area. The artistry suggests Javanese mastery of Indian sculptural techniques but may also indicate the presence and active employment of Indian artisans. Whatever the origins, the immediate effect upon an observer is one of awesome majesty.

Japanese monarchs well understood the political influence of Buddhist monasteries. One emperor in the eighth century remarked that he could not control the throw of the dice, a local river that regularly flooded, and the warrior monks of nearby temples. He later moved the capital from Nara to Heian to get away from politically powerful monasteries. Civil and military leaders later appreciated the political influence of large temple complexes and helped persecute religious leaders who threatened the positions of the established sects.

---

but, in regions more distant, the pattern seen in Harsha's realm appeared. Local autonomy was permitted in exchange for loyalty and regular revenues flowing to the capital.

Within the south, patterns of regionalism and localism emerged similar to those of Europe and Asia. Overall unity was never achieved in the south, because one state ruled in competition with other governments. As in Europe, Zhou China, or Japan, there existed a feudal-like practice wherein a subordinate person pledged support to a dominant person in exchange for land. Revenues from trade, especially maritime commerce, gave monarchs sufficient funds to induce local rulers to remain loyal. When monies from these sources dried up, central control usually broke down completely. Thus, Indian regionalism resembled its European and East Asian counterparts.

REGIONALISM IN SOUTHEAST ASIA, AROUND 600–AROUND 1450

Some peoples of Southeast Asian states, including Funanese and Vietnamese, have been considered in Chapter 10. Our focus here will be on the Malays, Burmese, and Thais, all of whom were strongly influenced by Indian culture.

Island and Peninsular Southeast Asia

From the sixth to the fifteenth centuries, except for the time when the Chola state controlled trade in the eastern Indian Ocean, Malays generally dominated the maritime trade that ran from India to

China. Their ships and crews handled the bulk of goods that came through the sea lanes between southern and eastern Asia. At the same time, rulers of Malay states developed complex ruling systems that united and integrated river-valley and plains economic systems. As with the Indians, central to the successful policies of the Malay monarchs was the use of revenues from maritime trade to strengthen their control over different economic regions and skillful adoption of ideas and terminology from Indian religions. The Indian word **maharaja** ("great ruler") carried political and religious significance for Malays. Buddhist priests and Hindu *brahmans* traveled the Southeast Asian sea lanes and spread their religions throughout southeastern and eastern Asia. Muslim merchants and missionaries followed the same routes and converted Malays in later centuries. Malay peoples inhabited the coastal areas of the Malay Peninsula, as well as the islands of Indonesia. The mainland Malays did not develop independent states, but the islands of Sumatra and Java became the centers of two contrasting governmental systems. The former supported maritime-based governments, and in the latter many agriculture-based polities developed.

Much of Southeast Asia's early trade with India was handled by the Funanese people of mainland Southeast Asia. In the fifth century, members of the elite in southern China responded to the loss of access to the silk-road trade by sending trading missions to Southeast Asia. Malays jumped at the

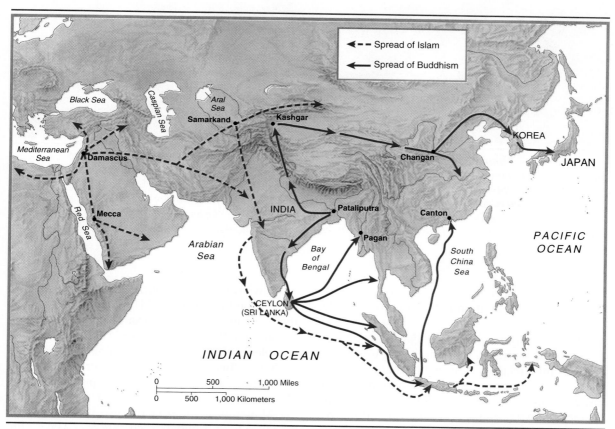

MAP 14.2 *The Spread of Islam and Buddhism, 200 B.C.–A.D. 1450.* *Islam and Buddhism followed similar land and maritime routes when they spread through Asia. Although conquest was important in the early spread of Islam, later conversions came largely through missionary activities, especially in Southeast Asia. Trade routes were crucial avenues for the transmission of both Islam and Buddhism. East Asia remained largely Buddhist, while other parts of Asia often became increasingly Islamic.*

FIGURE 14.3 *Temple Complex at Borobudur.* *The architectural design of this immense Buddhist temple at Borobudur in Java reflects the steps on the path to nirvana. On the lower levels, relief and sculpture show the earthly life of desires, while the middle terraces portray the life and spiritual education of the Buddha. At the summit is an unfinished sculpture of Buddha, demonstrating the formless world of spiritual enlightenment. Thus, the temple symbolizes the Buddhist vision of the world, leading to knowledge beyond desire and form.* Georg Gerster/Comstock.

opportunity, ignoring Funan as a way station to China and gradually dominating maritime trade with China.

In the seventh century, Srivijaya,[2] a state on the island of Sumatra, formed an empire with a strong commercial basis. A key element in Srivijaya's expansionist drive was the development of a port city and its use as a base for maritime trade. Upland products like timber were brought downriver and were sold or shipped overseas. Soon, Srivijaya extended its sway over peoples of other river valleys, first on the Sumatra coast and then on the Malay Peninsula.

Srivijaya monarchs borrowed from Indian culture, using Buddhism and Hinduism to legitimize their rule in Sumatra. For example, Srivijaya leaders adopted the title of *maharaja* and built temple complexes throughout their realms. In addition, both Buddhism and Hinduism were tolerant of indigenous religious cults and permitted the absorption of local deities into their pantheons.

Monarchs from Srivijaya also used maritime revenues to consolidate their rule over Malays on Sumatra and the Malay Peninsula. They lavishly endowed religious centers to gain and maintain support of the local people. Tax revenues, especially from maritime sources, were returned to the local temples in the form of annual religious dona-

[2] **Srivijaya:** shree vah JY yah

MAP 14.3 *Southeast Asian States around 1200. Many states flourished in twelfth- and thirteenth-century Southeast Asia, some prospering along the major trade routes between China and India. No one state or ruling group was able to unite either mainland or archipelago Southeast Asia. Buddhism was the dominant religion in this region until 1200, but thereafter gave way to the advance of Islam (spread by missionary and commercial efforts), especially on the islands.*

tions. The Srivijaya rulers also demanded that subordinates swear allegiance in exchange for continued rule of their domains, and failure to remain loyal brought military action and curses on the heads of recalcitrant leaders. A combination of fear and Srivijaya largess generally kept political harmony and stability.

Central Javanese kingdoms vied for influence and control of the agricultural lands. During the eighth century, the Sailendra[3] dynasty established itself in central Java and grew strong enough to build a massive temple complex at Borobudur, completed early in the ninth century. Borobudur displayed Buddhist artistic motifs, reflecting the power of Sailendra monarchs who admired Indian culture. About the same time as the completion of Borobudur, Sailendra monarchs negotiated a political alliance with the Srivijayans that linked the river valley and plains economies. The combined resources helped both semiautonomous

states and enhanced their maritime trade with China and India, which endured until the eleventh century, when the Cholas devastated the Srivijaya port cities and precipitated a two-century decline.

East Javanese kingdoms that rose and fell from the eighth to the fourteenth centuries formed and adopted Hindu- and Buddhist-inspired elite culture. By the fourteenth century, Muslims appeared in the waters of Indonesia and made inroads among the merchants, the courtiers, and the commoners. Islam had a growing impact on the Malays and spread through the Indonesian archipelago and into the southern Philippine Islands.

Other Southeast Asian States

A basic tension existed between peoples who lived in the hills and those who inhabited the river valley lowlands in many states of Southeast Asia. Lowlanders often came into a river valley and forced existing settlers out. Many refugees settled in the hills and mountains, where they eked out

[3] **Sailendra:** sy LEHN drah

FIGURE 14.4 *Ananda Temple at Pagan, Burma.* *Pagan became an important political and religious center in Burmese history. This temple, constructed in the eleventh century, captures the ornate splendor of Burmese Buddhism; it is still in use today.* Archaeological Survey of India.

livings by hunting and gathering. The Miao, Yao, Karens, Shan, and other hill peoples were thought of as savages by the sedentary lowlanders, who used force and discriminatory policies to maintain political dominance over them.

The Irrawaddy and Chao Praya river valleys supported agriculture-based local governments during the first millennium A.D. Historical records say little about these peoples, but it is known that they actively traded with Indian merchants and adopted Indian institutions.

Beginning in the ninth century, the Burmese peoples began moving from southern China into the Irrawaddy River Valley. Pagan,[4] a city in the middle of the Irrawaddy River Valley, became the capital, lending its name to a powerful Burmese state that unified most of the basin. The rulers of Pagan built thousands of Buddhist temples, many

[4]**Pagan:** pah GAHN

of which still enchant visitors today. Some temple complexes became politically influential and successfully lobbied for favorable treatment from authorities.

In the tenth century, the Burmese rulers of Pagan began to develop an interest in maritime commerce because of the massive trade in the Bay of Bengal region and because the land route into China had been closed to them. A port city on the Irrawaddy River welcomed Indian, Malay, and a few Chinese ships and merchants beginning in the eleventh century. By the twelfth century, a major maritime trade center emerged and played a significant role in trade between Southeast Asians and Indians. After the collapse of the Pagan state in the thirteenth century, chaos reigned as other peoples moved south from China in the wake of the Mongol disruptions. Only in the sixteenth century did a new Burmese government control much of the former Pagan realm. One result of expansion of the new states from the sixteenth century was conflict with the Thais.

Like the Burmese, the Thai[5] people began moving south from China and took a different route that eventually left them in the lower reaches of the Chao Praya River. This migration, which began in the twelfth century, accelerated in the aftermath of the Mongol conquest of China's southwest. Soon, the Thais became the dominant group in the central lower river valley and established a capital at Ayuthia.[6] Eventually, many Thais converted to Theravada Buddhism. As the Ayuthia government grew powerful, it expanded Thai influence to the south and east. In the north and west, the Thais had to fend off attacks by the Burmese. Although the Burmese never established permanent control, they hastened the decline and collapse of the Ayuthia government.

Thai artists achieved great success in creating Buddhist statues, and the architecture of the Thai temples combined graceful sloping roofs with ornate temple decorations. These sculptures frequently had full-fleshed arms and legs that revealed curves of a sensual nature. A famous reclining Buddha at Ayuthia has long attracted both faithful Buddhist pilgrims and admiring travelers.

CHINESE REGIONALISM, 220–589

This section will focus on Chinese regionalism in a time of general political division, economic turmoil, and social conflict. Despite these unsettling conditions, writers and artists produced literature, literary criticism, calligraphy, and philosophy. Perhaps the political fragmentation and social upheaval allowed for a loosening of obligations imposed on individuals by governments, families, and clans.

Political Developments after the Third Century

When the Han Empire fell in 220, it was succeeded by three regional kingdoms, each of which was based in a self-contained economic area. The northern state, Wei,[7] united the Yellow River Valley and controlled a large sedentary population. The southeastern state, Wu, occupied much of the Lower Yangzi Valley, especially the agriculturally productive Yangzi Delta area. The southwestern kingdom, Shu, ruled the Upper Yangzi Valley. Although Wei managed to conquer and temporarily rule all three regions, it soon collapsed, and not until the late sixth century did a government reunite China.

The conquest and rule of northern China by non-Chinese peoples in the fourth century shocked many elite Chinese. How could the nomadic "barbarians" have wrested away the Yellow River Valley and the North China Plain? Some elite families remained in the north and accommodated themselves to the alien rulers, while others fled south of the Yangzi River.

The Huns, a branch of the Xiongnu[8] nomads, first overran Yellow River cities in the early fourth century. Non-Chinese peoples had often been encouraged to settle in the border areas, as long as they agreed to pay taxes, nominally follow Chinese practices, and help defend the frontier areas against nomadic raiders. Some Chinese abused their non-Chinese subjects and caused an uprising that weakened China's defenses and permitted the Huns to wrest control of the north from Chinese hands.

Various governments ruled north and south of the Yangzi River. In the north, for example, one Hun tribe conquered, ruled for one or two generations, and was then tossed out by another tribe. The loss of life in the often brutal campaigns was enormous. Economic activity was frequently disrupted as rulers either drove away the Chinese peasants or enslaved them. The Yangzi River Valley was colonized by refugees from the north. Local non-Chinese were chased away, absorbed, or exterminated by these peasant farmers, and agriculture, villages, towns, and temples were established. Soon a governmental administrative apparatus, including tax collectors, followed. The land was fertile, and the milder climate provided for a wider variety of crops and larger yields. Eventually, maritime trade between Chinese and Southeast Asians developed.

---

[5]**Thai:** ty
[6]**Ayuthia:** ay YOO thee yah

[7]**Wei:** way
[8]**Xiongnu:** sheeyahng nuh

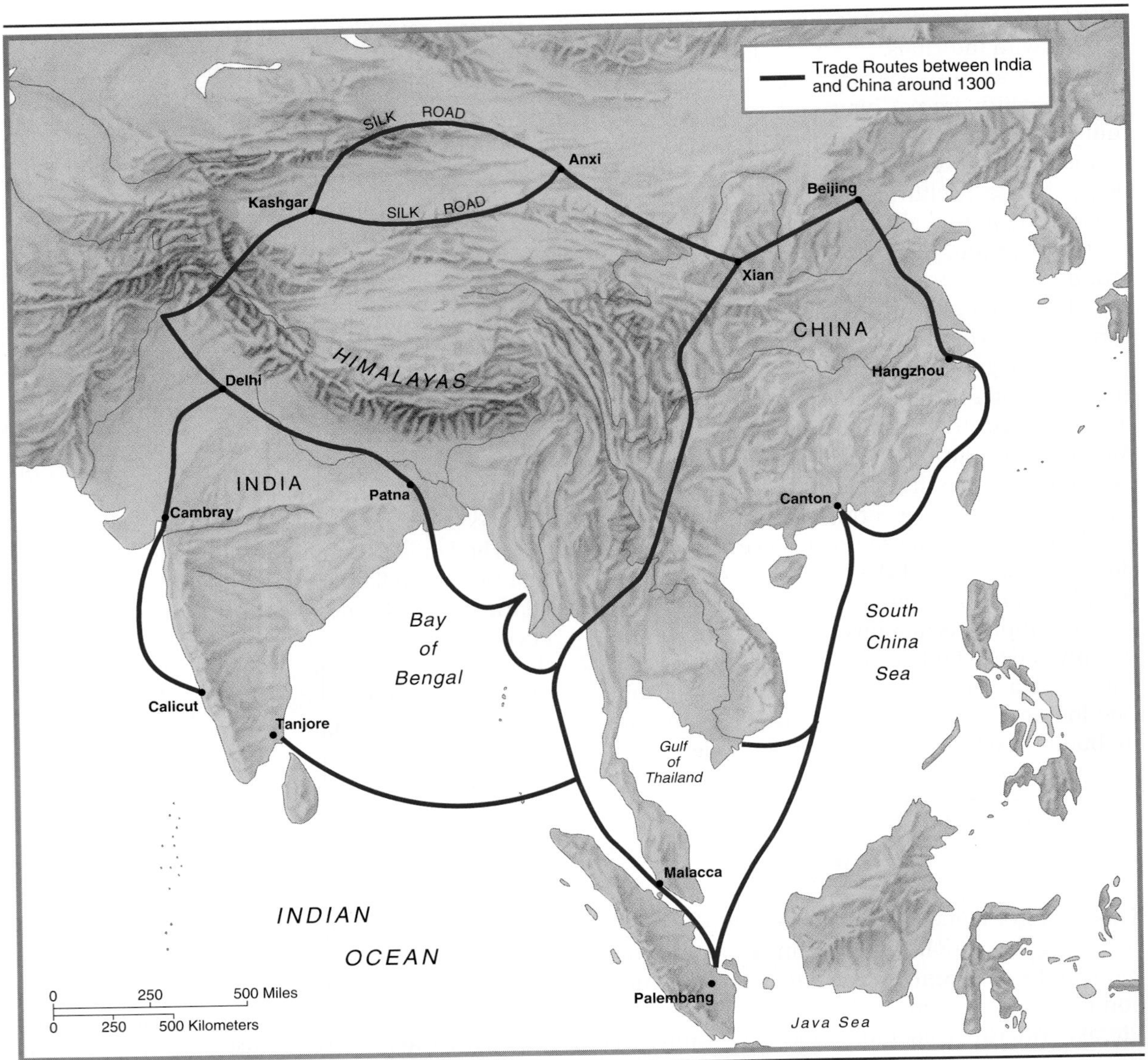

MAP 14.4 *Trade Routes between India and China around 1300.* *Following the Mongol conquest of much of East and Central Asia, support of commercial activity and the favoring of merchants by Mongol rulers stimulated trade across Eurasia. Bustling with trade venturers, both land and maritime routes were increasingly traveled during the period of regionalism, becoming even more crowded by 1300.*

Confucianism in the Regional Era

Confucianism, a system of ideas and practices that stressed family values, became more appreciated during the time of regionalism because it helped promote social stability. In northern China, after the conquests of the nomads, many extended families survived the vicissitudes of political turmoil because of their substantial social and economic resources. One key for social stability, as these families soon learned, was to inculcate Confucian values that stressed a tightly knit family structure. Social cohesion meant an increased chance of surviving alien governments that sometimes persecuted ethnic Chinese.

Confucian ideas benefited not only elite families but also certain regional rulers, who appreciated the sociopolitical aspects of Confucianism when carefully guided by the state. Time-tested Confucian values like filial piety, harmony, loyalty, and sincerity could be reinvigorated by a united local polity. Social stability could be strengthened because cohesive families tended to stay united no matter what political or economic pressures they faced. Regional monarchs appreciated a Confucian ideology that inspired attitudes of obedience in subjects and officials. Stable social conditions and loyal officials were results that appealed to all rulers.

Buddhism's Adaptation to Chinese Conditions

Buddhism arrived in China by land routes from Central Asia and by water routes from Southeast Asia from the first through the seventh centuries. It did not become popular, however, until the fall of the Han Dynasty in the third century. Buddhism gained influence through missionary activity and an accommodation effort by priests who wished to make it more appealing to the Chinese. For example, to overcome Chinese discomfort with Siddhartha Gautama (the Buddha), who abandoned his family to seek the meaning of life and suffering, new Buddhist scriptures emphasized that one could be a good Buddhist as well as a devoted hus-band, father, and son. These efforts were successful, and, by the early sixth century, it is estimated that China had about 30,000 temples and nearly 2 million monks and nuns. Buddhism was the religion of perhaps 90 percent of the northern Chinese. Many Chinese in the south also embraced Buddhism.

Some Buddhist monasteries possessed large land tracts and laborers to work them. These tax-free estates represented a liability to governments, which occasionally confiscated lands and forced religious people back onto the tax rolls. Of course, the interrelationship between religious activity and economic development was not peculiar to China. It may be seen also in Europe, India, and Southeast Asia.

Arts and Philosophy

The period of Chinese regionalism saw the continued development of the arts and philosophy. Chinese poetry became increasingly influenced by Buddhism, and poets often extolled the beauty of the natural landscape. Literary criticism first appeared, and long-lasting categories of literature were firmly established. The success of Buddhism provoked Daoists to imitate successful ways of the foreign religion.

FIGURE 14.5 *Education of Noblewomen. Attributed to Gu Kaizhi, a famous artist who lived in the fourth century, this painting is from a silk handscroll depicting the practice of teaching noble-women proper etiquette. Additionally, many elite women were taught to read and write. The seal marks on the painting indicate its changing ownership over the centuries.* Courtesy of the Trustees of the British Museum.

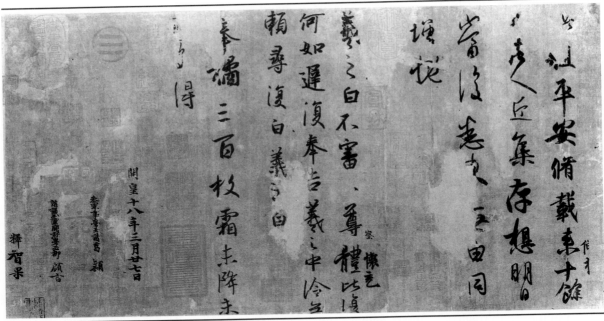

FIGURE 14.6 *Calligraphy of Wang Xizhi.* *Generally regarded as China's greatest calligrapher, Wang Xizhi created this example of decorative writing sixteen centuries ago. Calligraphy, which Chinese scholars practiced as a mental and artistic exercise, was a means by which character could be judged.* National Palace Museum, Taipei, Taiwan, Republic of China.

Literature is often regarded by Chinese scholars as the most important Chinese artistic form, and poetry is the most influential literary genre. The period under consideration is filled with important literary works, and one of the finest poets was Cao Zhi[9] (192–232), son of the founder of the Wei state. Cao Zhi was not in line to succeed to the throne, so he spent his days composing beautiful verse. Two significant poets, Tao Yuanming (365–427) and Xie Lingyun[10] (385–433), lived about midway through the era. Tao Yuanming was an official who became disgusted with bureaucratic life and returned home to live out his days as a gentleman farmer. Many of his poems celebrate the simple pleasures of rural life:

> I planted beans at the foot of the southern
>   mountain.
> Weeds flourished, but my bean shoots were few.
> I get up at dawn, work to clear away the tangle;
> Wrapped in moonlight, I shoulder my hoe
>   and come home.

The path is narrow, grass and trees tall:
The evening dew wets my clothes.
Wet clothes—they're not worth the worry
Just so my hopes aren't disappointed!

The line about shouldering his hoe and heading home is one of the most famous in Chinese literature. Xie Lingyun's poems espoused Buddhist ideas and extolled the beauties of nature.

Literary criticism became well established with the appearance of the first treatise on the subject, written by Liu Xie[11] (around 465–around 532). This work set forth categories and standards by which to judge literary pieces, and it examined the history and development of Chinese literature. Liu Xie's work is still regarded as a major reference of literary analysis.

Calligraphy received a powerful boost from Wang Xizhi[12] (321–379), who was considered China's greatest calligraphic master. Calligraphy meant various things to scholar-artists. Writing Chinese characters from memory helped focus the

[9]**Cao Zhi:** sow jur
[10]**Xie Lingyun:** sheeyeh lihng yoon

[11]**Liu Xie:** leeyoo sheeyeh
[12]**Wang Xizhi:** wahng shee jur

mind, and artists appreciated the close linkage between the sweep of one's cursive script and the lines of paintings. The Chinese also believed that one's handwriting revealed one's inner mind and character. Wang Xizhi's writing style became so highly prized that some of it was carved into stone.

Daoism's unfettered social philosophy attracted some adherents in the third and fourth centuries. These eccentrics protested the rigid forms of correct social behavior demanded by the Confucians, yet they also were escaping the dangerous times in which they survived by seeming to be foolish. One interesting group of third-century Daoist eccentrics was known as "The Seven Sages of the Bamboo Grove," a group of drinkers who enjoyed one another's company. One sage delighted in startling his houseguests by appearing in the nude. Another would roll his eyeballs until only the white parts showed, a favorite way to interrupt a boring conversation. Many of the "Sages" were competent poets and musicians who attracted attention for their entertaining verse.

Daoists competed with Buddhists, who successfully spread Buddhism in China. Daoist monasteries built in the era of regionalism were established to counter the influence of Buddhist monasteries. Daoist monks studied Daoist alchemy and philosophy. They also used their medical knowledge to cure people, at the same time proselytizing to their patients. Leaders of the two religions commenced a bitter rivalry that endured for centuries. In the sixth and seventh centuries, one attempt to bridge the chasm between Buddhism and Daoism resulted in the development of Zen Buddhism, a sect that combined Daoist and Buddhist elements.

JAPANESE REGIONALISM, AROUND 250–1333

Japanese leaders sought to create a powerful state, but they had to overcome strong economic and social factors that supported regionalism. Military conquest and the borrowing of Chinese political institutions helped create centralized rule. But court power struggles brought new families into the political arena, and the creation of private estates provided the economic basis for regionalism and feudalism.

Economic and Religious Factors

Although rudimentary agriculture had developed in the first millennium B.C., intensive agriculture came to Japan from mainland East Asia in the third century B.C. Paddy-field rice growing a few centuries later significantly increased grain yields. A village became the economic center for local peasants who lived there and farmed the surrounding paddy fields. Villages had walls to protect their inhabitants and to emphasize their separateness from other communities. Supporting this identity was the collective worship of a local deity, a ***kami***,[13] usually connected to fertility. Sometimes villages united into village networks for mutual protection. Over time, powerful clans gained control of village clusters and increased their influence. One such clan-village cluster and its *kami* were appropriated by the Yamato clan.

Before the sixth century, Shinto, Japan's indigenous religion, never developed an organized priesthood or a complex theology. Instead, it retained strong animistic elements, believing that natural objects were alive and worthy of veneration. Rocks as well as trees were thought to have life and should be appreciated. Shinto also possessed strong shamanistic traits because shamans—intermediaries who communicated with the spirit world—became essential to interpreting the will of the *kami*. In that sense, the head of the Yamato clan was also the head priest of Shinto.

The Yamato clan identified itself with the sun goddess, a potent deity among the Japanese people. The sun has figured prominently in the name "Japan" (place where the sun rises) and on many flags. Eventually, the myth developed that the Yamato emperor was a descendant of the sun goddess herself.

After the imperial system became relatively centralized in the seventh century, agricultural lands were taken over by the state. This public-land program began to be undermined in the succeeding century when private estates, ***shoen***,[14] were recognized by the central government. Over the course of time, more and more *shoen* were granted to individuals or to religious temples. By

[13] ***kami:*** kah mee
[14] ***shoen:*** shoh ehn

the twelfth century, *shoen* provided the economic support for several court factions. Military leaders, relying on the *shoen* system, declared independence from the imperial system and created a parallel political structure based on private estates.

The Imperial Age, around 250–858

We have already seen the early formation of the Japanese state by the Yamato family. Here our attention will center on the adoption of Chinese institutions to gain control of the rural population.

Although various Japanese monarchs conducted diplomatic relations with China in the early centuries of Yamato rule, the intensive period of borrowing from China came after 587, when Soga no Umako, head of the Soga clan, became the only court leader by ousting rival clans. Rather than assume power as the founder of a new dynasty, Umako manipulated the existing structure by placing pliant rulers on the throne. He also followed a common practice of marrying women of one's own clan to Yamato men in the hope that a male offspring of such a union would later ascend to the throne. This pattern was repeated many times in Japanese history.

IN THEIR OWN WORDS

Famine in the Japanese Feudal Age

Daily life in twelfth-century Japan was vividly portrayed by Kamo no Chomei in his work *An Account of My Hermitage*. Written in 1212, it presents the author's views and descriptions of everyday affairs in the imperial capital of Kyoto. The breakdown of imperial rule brought regionalism and severe economic problems. Long-distance trade collapsed during the fighting and resulting social chaos. This particular passage describes a famine of 1181 and 1182 and reflects Kamo's ardent Buddhist beliefs.

. . . there was a dreadful drought and famine that lasted for two years. Spring and summer brought drought, autumn was marked by typhoons and floods, one misfortune followed another so that none of the various types of grain ripened properly. . . . As a result, the people in the different provinces either abandoned their lands and migrated to other regions or left their homes and went to live in the mountains. . . .

It was customary for the capital to depend on the countryside for all its needs, and once supplies of provisions ceased to come in, the inhabitants found it impossible to live in their usual style. In desperation they brought out one after another of their various treasures, asking so little for them that they were all but throwing them away, but even then they could find no buyers. On the rare occasions when a transaction was arranged, gold counted for little, while grain was the prized item. Beggars lined the roadside, the sound of their pitiful cries dinning in one's ears.

So the first year came to an end, and it was expected that the new year would bring a return to normalcy. But instead epidemics broke out, adding to the suffering, and relief seemed nowhere in sight. People were now dying of hunger, and each day their plight worsened; they were like fish trapped in shallow water. . . . Beside the walls of the buildings and along the roads, the bodies of those who had starved to death were beyond count. Since nothing had been done to remove them, the stench soon filled the city, and the sight of them as they decayed was often too ghastly to look at. . . .

The woodcutters and other poor people by this time no longer had the strength to deliver firewood to the city, so persons with no other means of support broke up their own houses and peddled the wood in the markets. But as much wood as a man could carry did not bring enough to sustain life for a single day. Strangely enough, among the wood I saw bits of metal foil attached. When I investigated, I found that some people, lacking any other resort, were going to the old temples, stealing Buddhist images, ripping out the furnishings in the sacred halls, and breaking them up for firewood. Truly I was born into an age of defilement and evil to be witness to such heartless acts!

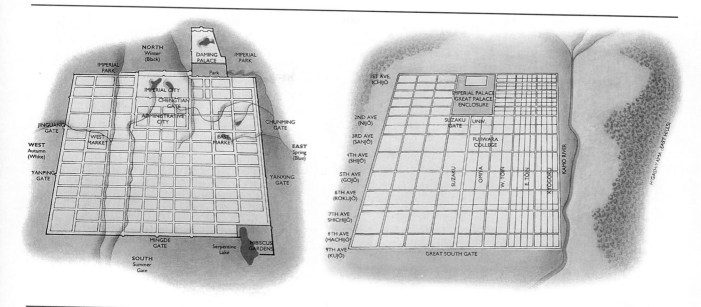

FIGURE 14.7 *The Japanese Capital at Kyoto. Like its predecessors, Kyoto, or Heian kyo (right), was built on the model of the Chinese capital, Changan (left). The imperial palace is located in the north-central part of the city, as the North Star is placed in the night sky. Streets are laid out on a grid pattern and run north-south and east-west.* From *Cradles of Civilization: China* (Norman: University of Oklahoma Press). Reproduced with permission.

Soga no Umako, Empress Suiko [15] (reign dates 593–627), and Prince Shotoku formed a ruling team that promoted borrowing institutions and ideas from the Chinese. One major development was the adoption of Buddhism as the religion not only of the Soga clan but also of the court. In the sixth century, Buddhism was introduced to the Japanese by a Korean monarch who desired a diplomatic and military alliance with the Japanese. By the eighth century, Buddhism became the state religion, and Buddhist temples were built in regional centers.

Although the Soga clan was ousted from power in 645, the borrowing from China continued. Many Japanese went to China on diplomatic and educational missions, and several students who stayed in China later became major reform leaders. The high point of Japanese borrowing came in the eighth century. During that time, the Japanese implemented a Chinese-style law code and established a bureaucracy. A replica of the Chinese imperial capital was built at Nara and another at Heian, [16] but the city was laid out on a smaller scale. The Japanese also wrote Chinese-style poetry and used Chinese characters to write their own language. Two histories of Japan, the *Kojiki* (*Record of Ancient Matters*) and *Nihon Shoki* (*History of Japan*), followed Chinese historiographical models.

Modification of Chinese institutions and practices also occurred. The Japanese, for example, added a religious bureau to the state because the monarchs were regarded as *kami* descended from the sun goddess. Japanese-style poetry was collected in an anthology, the *Collection of Myriad Poems*. It featured poems with Japanese themes by poets like Kakinomoto Hitomaro, one of Japan's great poets. An interesting feature of the *Collection of Myriad Poems* was the inclusion of anonymous poems, including many attributed to commoners. Because these people could not write, poets likely wrote down the oral compositions.

[15] **Suiko:** sooee koh

[16] **Heian:** hay yahn

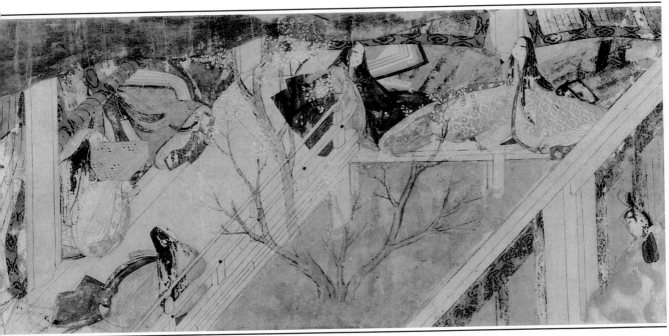

FIGURE 14.8 *Scene from* **The Tale of Genji.** *The oldest complete novel written any-where in the world,* The Tale of Genji, *by the Japanese Lady Murasaki, is also considered to be one of the finest. Illustrations of the events of this famous book appeared soon after it was written in the first quarter of the eleventh century. This scene shows women playing* go, *a game of strategy based on an older Chinese game. Despite their cloistering by Japanese society, many aristocratic women acquired both cultural skills and education.*
The Tokugawa Art Museum, Nagoya.

The Aristocratic Age, 858–1160

The Fujiwara clan played a vital role in the development of the Japanese central government. After the mid–ninth century, members of that family garnered a succession of titles and power that created a family dictatorship. Marriage politics in the pattern of the Soga clan also played a crucial role in the ascendancy of the Fujiwara because certain of its female members married the Yamato emperors and princes. When the marriage system broke down, the Fujiwara could fall back on its domination of two regency posts. Along with a handful of other prominent aristocratic families, the Fujiwara dominated the imperial court.

At the same time that this sociopolitical process unfolded, an economic trend undermined the imperial system. The Fujiwara gained control of many *shoen* estates and isolated them from the imperial land-tax system. This process encouraged other families to create their own economic bases, especially in frontier areas.

Apart from the important aristocratic families that lived in the imperial capital, members of the social elite away from the capital dominated their respective areas. Like the gulf that separated the courtier aristocrats from the regional nobility, the provincial nobility lived far above the social level of the common folk. Noblewomen usually were much freer to own property. They were treated with respect because they might marry into a higher social level and thereby elevate a family's status.

In all cases, land served as the economic base undergirding social prominence. Estates provided revenues to the imperial government, to the local religious temple, and to the local socially elite families. Commonly, services were exchanged for access to revenues from land parcels.

Buddhism took new forms in the aristocratic era. The essential tendency was the spread of Buddhism to the common folk. Prior to the tenth century, Buddhism's complex message remained difficult to comprehend and generally inaccessible to ordinary Japanese, so a few priests began to emphasize faith rather than an esoteric knowledge of scriptures. Soon, Buddhist priests actively sought conversions in rural towns and villages, and singing and dancing often accompanied the proselytizing efforts of the more charismatic priests. At the same time, efforts were made to accommodate Shinto. *Kami* guarded Buddhist temples, and many Buddhas were interpreted as Shinto gods.

An indigenous Japanese literature matured in the Aristocratic Age. Writing Chinese-style poetry gradually declined, and native Japanese genres assumed more importance. Perhaps the most striking development was the Japanese novel, which reached a high degree of sophistication in the hands of Murasaki Shikibu (around 978–around 1015), an aristocratic woman who came from a minor branch of the Fujiwara family. Lady Murasaki wrote *The Tale of Genji*, a work that many scholars believe is Japan's greatest novel.

The Tale of Genji concerns the life and loves of a fictional imperial prince, Genji. At another level, it is the account of the imperial court: its values, its social life, and its varied activities. It reflects court patronage of the arts. The novel also contains hundreds of poems and quotations from Chinese and Japanese history; many additional poems are original. All of this suggests the vast learning and creative power of Lady Murasaki, who was a member of the court and the daughter of a midlevel Japanese official.

Architecture also reached a high level of development. One wooden structure, the Byodo-in (Phoenix Hall), still stands as a testament to the impressive building expertise of its architects. Built in the tenth century, the Byodo-in, which housed a sculpture of the Buddha, was constructed in graceful lines and accompanied by a reflecting pond.

The Development of Feudalism, 1160–1333

The breakdown of the central government accelerated with the rise and dominance of the military families. Indeed, the appearance of a new system of local power based on mutual and reciprocal allegiances led to the establishment of Japanese feudalism. The prevailing governmental structure was the **shogunate**, a military overlordship headed by a *shogun*; it ruled in tandem with the Japanese monarchy, in an uneasy relationship.

The second half of the twelfth century in Japan was dominated by the power struggle between two military families, the Minamoto and the Taira.[17] Both had been established in provinces far away from the imperial capital, and court factions used the two families to provide military muscle. By the mid–twelfth century, however, power had shifted from the aristocratic families to the military houses. Between 1156 and 1185, the Taira and Minamoto vied for political supremacy, and the Taira initially prevailed. Each warrior house not only relied on branch houses whose members were blood kin, but they also used coalitions of other warrior families to increase their own strength. The warrior, a professional fighter, lived and died by the sword. A more familiar name for the warrior was **samurai**, meaning "the one who serves."

The Taira family preferred to work within the imperial system and, like the Soga and Fujiwara, married its women to the Yamato men. Taira revenues centered on *shoen* estates and maritime trade. By 1180, a Taira infant was placed on the throne, even though he was clearly a figurehead ruler. A disaffected imperial prince called on Minamoto warriors to fight the Taira, and the five-year Gempei War (1180–1185) commenced. By the end of the conflict, the Taira family had been destroyed, and Minamoto Yoritomo (1147–1199), head of the Minamoto family, had established a separate governmental system that became known as the Kamakura Shogunate.

Minamoto Yoritomo was one of Japan's most significant political figures because he did not choose to work within the imperial structure but opted to establish a separate government that handled the affairs of the military class. Because Yoritomo lacked the experienced personnel to govern all of Japan, he agreed to maintain the imperial system. To the warriors who offered him allegiance, Yoritomo gave land taken from the Taira and their allies. The land-based manor system underlay the interlocking web of personal relationships of warrior chiefs and their vassals. Unlike in the European and Chinese feudal systems, but similar to southern Indian feudalism, Japanese peasants were not tied to the land in serfdom.

[17] **Taira:** ty rah

Figure 14.9 *Minamoto Yoritomo.* *The founder of Japan's first shogunate, Minamoto Yoritomo is shown wearing formal court robes and not his military attire. Rather than directly involving himself in the affairs of the imperial court, Yoritomo created a separate administrative structure to handle warrior affairs, a policy that helped usher in the feudal age of Japanese history.* Tokyo National Museum.

Once established, the shogunal government weathered a series of crises, including the deaths of Yoritomo and his sons. Power passed to the Hojo family, a house of loyal retainers tied by marriage to the Minamoto. By early in the thirteenth century, Hojo regents ruled the shogunate in place of the Minamoto family. Perhaps the most able Hojo regent was Hojo Yasutoki (reign dates 1224–1242). Yasutoki brought a vigorous personal style to the post, and he forged an alliance with able subordinates to provide an effective administrative team. Consensus politics became a major part of Japan's political culture in the Hojo regency and remains important even today. Among Yasutoki's accomplishments was the supervision of the publication in 1232 of the *Joei*[18] *Law Code*, a set of guidelines and precedents for handling legal disputes. This document became the handbook for generations of judiciary members who staffed one of the most sophisticated trial systems in the world. The *Joei Law Code* was used in Japan as late as the nineteenth century.

Hojo regents provided effective government and justice for the Japanese people. In times of famine, for example, government rice stores were made available to the suffering people, and taxes were reduced or canceled for the most severely effected areas. One regent ardently followed Zen Buddhism.

Two Mongol invasion attempts helped undermine Hojo rule. As a result of two typhoons and fierce local resistance, both campaigns failed, and Japan was spared the onus of Mongol rule. Yet the *samurai* demanded rewards in land and money that the Hojo leaders could not deliver. Afterward, the government declined, falling in a time of social chaos in the fourteenth century.

Two major Buddhist sects, Zen and Nichiren,[19] became influential in the first phase of shogunal rule. Zen stresses strict discipline in the training of its adherents, and it places great emphasis on meditation. Nichiren Buddhism was named for its founder, Nichiren (1222–1282), who believed that Japan would become the center of "true" Bud-

[18] *Joei:* joh ay

[19] **Nichiren:** nee chee rehn

dhism, namely his own sect. Both Zen and Nichiren Buddhism appealed to some *samurai*, and each has remained important in Japanese life.

Zen had developed in China and had appeared in Japan prior to the twelfth century but had failed to take hold. In the 1100s, Japanese priests went to China and brought back their own interpretations of the Zen message. In the thirteenth century, some Hojo regents sponsored the building of a Zen center in Kamakura, the shogunal capital. With this patronage, Zen spread among the warriors, who valued its emphasis on discipline in a natural environment. Zen offered a way of coping with the horrors of battle and death, which were common occurrences in a *samurai*'s daily life. Along with Zen teachings and practices from China came tea, to which the Japanese became devoted.

Nichiren Buddhism argued that Buddhism had reached its highest form in Japan and asserted that the *Lotus Sutra*, a major Buddhist work, was its true text. Sincerely reciting the name of the *Lotus Sutra*, in fact, was said to grant the reciter a chance at salvation. Nichiren quarreled with other religious leaders and certain officials, resulting in his suffering persecution that helped increase his following. The Nichiren sect cultivated the warriors, many of whom liked its message.

Literature flourished in the early feudal age. Prose essays developed under the discipline of stylistic masters like Kamo no Chomei, who in 1212 wrote the much-admired *An Account of My Hermitage*. Women like Lady Nijo wrote memoirs, a major genre of the Warrior Age. She was a member of the aristocracy and was the concubine of a reigning monarch. Her *Confessions of Lady Nijo* was prized as an important social document.

MAP 14.5 *Japan around 1200.* The island of Honshu was where most significant political activity took place in the historical era. Nara was the capital for much of the eighth century; Kyoto was the capital until the late twelfth century. The Ise Shrine, dedicated to the sun goddess Amaterasu, is situated fifty miles east of Nara. After 1180, Kamakura became the capital of the warrior government set up by Minamoto Yoritomo. The Minamotos' political dominance was ensured by 1185.

FIGURE 14.10 *Japanese Teapot.* During the feudal age, the Japanese developed the tea ceremony, a formal ritual activity. It usually involved very simple but precise action, suggesting harmony and serenity in a time of political uncertainty. When samurai *entered a tea house, they were obliged to leave their swords outside. The implements of the tea ceremony often were modest, but this seventeenth-century teapot is made of gold.* The Tokugawa Art Museum, Nagoya.

ENCOUNTERS

The Tea Ceremony

Tea is one of the most widely consumed beverages in the world, having been adopted by most societies around the globe. No one knows exactly where or when the tea plant was domesticated, although it clearly was somewhere in the area near the Southwest Chinese border. The first written record of tea comes from about A.D. 350, and it became a major tribute item four centuries later in the Chinese Empire. Tea came to Japan in 729 as a gift to Emperor Shomu, probably from the Chinese court. It spread to Southwest Asia through the Mongols, who had in turn adopted its use from the Chinese. The British became aware of tea through their contacts in China, and the drinking of tea in England and Europe began in the seventeenth century. Indeed, early English colonists in Massachusetts emigrated from England before tea drinking had become common there, and, when tea was introduced to Massachusetts, some were unfamiliar with how to prepare it and tried eating the leaves on bread. Tea was introduced to India by the English in the eighteenth century.

At various times, tea has been prepared in myriad ways. In addition to simply boiling or steeping the leaves, it has been flavored with substances like sugar, milk, salt, ginger, flowers, citrus peel, flour, butter, and fruit juices. The most common way of preparing tea in China and Japan, the areas with the longest tradition of tea drinking, however, is simply to brew it with hot water.

The first tea tax in China was imposed by the ruler in 780, but tea had not yet attained its eventual status of cultural symbol. To help elevate it, tea merchants later hired a poet, Lu Yu (1125–1210), to write a book popularizing it. His *Classic of Tea* made a point appreciated by Buddhist, Daoist, and Confucian alike: The simplicity and beauty of a well-ordered tea ceremony reflected the harmony and flow that ideally ordered the universe. Lu Yu's work presented essays on the pleasures and benefits of tea drinking, the proper method of preparation, the twenty-four utensils whose use he advocated, and practices for the formal presentation of tea.

From that time, the spread of tea has been accompanied by some version of the tea ceremony. The Mongols adopted elements of the ceremony and passed them to the Arabs and others to the west; the English adapted their version from that of China. Almost everywhere that tea is drunk, rules of etiquette order its consumption.

But nowhere else has such a formalized tea ceremony developed as in Japan. The tea practices that arose in the thirteenth century later grew into a showy and elaborate ceremony. The rise of Zen Buddhism and its philosophy of simplicity, however, made these ostentatious practices less appealing, and a major revision of the tea ceremony took place in 1588. Sen no Rikyu, an expert on the tea ceremony, reduced the ceremonial clutter to seven rules. He redesigned the physical setting of tea drinking, advocating a small tearoom and use of the simplest—but most elegant—of implements. The tenor of the tea ceremony was to be one of contrived tranquility. The modern Japanese tea ceremony continues this tradition.

The versions of tea drinking in China, Japan, and elsewhere, however, were adopted only by the elite or by those who aspired to that status. Less well-to-do folk typically consumed their tea with little or no ceremony, and much tea was drunk in commercial teahouses that were gathering places particularly for men. There they ate light foods, drank tea, relaxed, and chatted; the teahouses served much the same social function as the British pub or the American bar. Women were more likely to congregate at home, eating snacks, drinking tea, relaxing, and talking. In these informal, nonelite settings, the philosophical symbolism of the tea ceremony was largely absent, and the rules of etiquette—so much as they were known—were relaxed or ignored to maximize the pleasure of the event.

Japan experienced long eras of political division, not a few of which also saw chaos erupting from battles and campaigns of great ferocity. Yet these times of weak rule also witnessed the continuance of cultural forms produced by elite persons.

Women played even more active roles in the production of literature from these ages. A variety of Buddhist sects also appeared, and some appealed directly to the common folk. Buddhism's popular appeal helped keep it vibrant.

INDIA	SOUTHEAST ASIA	JAPAN	CHINA		
Indian regionalism, c. 180 B.C.– c. A.D. 320				200 B.C.	Fall of Maurya Empire, c. 180 B.C.
				A.D. 1	Buddhism in China, A.D. 57
			Chinese regionalism, 220–589	200	Chandra Gupta founds Gupta Empire, 320
		Imperial Age, c. 450– c. 850		400	Buddhism in Japan, c. 550
Harsha's rule, 606–647	Srivijaya-Sailendra Era, c. 650– c. 1100			600	Harsha begins conquest of North India, c. 606
	Burmese settle in Irrawaddy River Valley (Pagan Era), c. 800– c. 1350	Aristocratic Age, c. 850– c. 1160		800	Building of Borobudur temple in Java, ninth century
					Rajaraja I ascends to throne in Chola, 985
Chola state (south), c. 1000– c. 1300				1000	Indian fleet destroys Srivijayan navy, 1025
					Minamoto Yoritomo becomes *shogun*, 1192
		Development of feudalism, after 1180		1200	Nichiren founds new Buddhist sect, c. 1250
				1400	

SOME CAUSES AND CONSEQUENCES OF REGIONALISM

Regional tendencies frequently asserted themselves in Asia. Economic factors, like changes in trade and land management, played significant roles in the downfall of centralized polities. On occasion, feudalism resulted from the breakdown of political unity and the assertion of local interests. Despite the disappearance of centralized governments, most forms of art continued to flourish because of patronage from nonmonarchical elements, like merchants and temple priests. In addition, the weakening of the social fabric sometimes promoted social experimentation and an appreciation for ideologies that engendered social stability.

Economic developments strongly contributed to the collapse of imperial governments in Asia. Trade, especially long-distance trade, became inextricably linked to the fate of some states. The regime of Harsha aspired to duplicate the grandeur of his Gupta predecessors, but unlike them Harsha never controlled the trade routes running through the Indus River Valley. Similarly, loss of the silk-road trade contributed to the decline of the Han Empire, helping to foster regionalism in China. Maritime trade revenues increased dramatically after the sixth century and provided southern Indian and Southeast Asian monarchs with monies to purchase local rulers' loyalties. Conversely, when these funds dwindled, control outside the core areas weakened.

Land management assumed a large role during these times. The development of private estates became the first step toward regional rule, because landlords usually succeeded in reducing or eliminating tax liabilities associated with their lands. Harsha gave land to officials and to temples, thereby accelerating regionalism. Temples owned large tax-exempt estates throughout Asia and deprived the state of important tax revenues.

Feudalism appeared in Japan during the time of regionalism. Not only did feudalism result from the breakdown of central authority, but it also emerged from the development of private estates. The decline of a dynasty sometimes resulted in the weakening of central control. At the same time, local control of private-estate revenues enhanced regional power groups. Monarchs who aspired to retain some form of unity used money and loyalty oaths to win support from lower levels. Minamoto Yoritomo insisted that subordinates faithfully serve their military leaders. Again, fear of a strong ruler and interest in rewards facilitated these feudal relationships.

Social controls enforced by states, clans, and families may be undermined or broken during the social upheaval accompanying an empire's collapse. During these eras, social experimentation, like that of the Seven Sages, sometimes occurs. The absence of normal social controls may lead to the development of new forms of literature or to the embracing of foreign religions, like Buddhism or Hinduism.

SUMMARY

1. When the Maurya Empire of India fell around 180 B.C., local and regional rule began in India. In the northwest, many states were founded by invaders who promoted Buddhism. In the northeast, Harsha became a major ruler in the seventh century. He promulgated policies that weakened his government and encouraged regionalism.

2. Southern India saw the rise and fall of many states, some of which depended heavily on agriculture and some of which based themselves more on trade, especially maritime commerce. Monarchs and merchants supported artists who produced spectacular sculptures and massive temple complexes. Hinduism became progressively more common there in the eighth and ninth centuries.

3. The Malay people often controlled the ocean waterways of Southeast Asia. On Sumatra and Java, societies based largely on maritime trade, Buddhist motifs became popular and are seen in the massive temple complex of Borobudur.

4. On the Southeast Asian mainland, the Burmese and Thai peoples migrated along major river valleys and displaced earlier peoples, some of

whom were forced into the mountains. The Burmese, like the Thais, adopted Theravada Buddhism. Both the Burmese and the Thais built governments that promoted Buddhist ideas and warred against each other. Temple-building projects took place in both areas and saw the development of distinctive Burmese and Thai artistic styles.

5. Chinese calligraphy, literary criticism, and poetry continued to develop in the era of Chinese regionalism.

6. The uncertain Chinese political climate from the third through the sixth centuries highlighted the importance of family networks to stand against or bend with difficult governments. Confucian ideas that supported a strong family system continued to be favored among the Chinese social elite.

7. Japanese villages became key economic units with the development of paddy-field agriculture in the third century. Clan networks gained control of the villages and increased their political influence. In the seventh and eighth centuries, Yamato monarchs implemented a modified Chinese imperial system that turned private land holdings into imperial lands.

8. The Japanese aristocratic and feudal eras saw the appearance of private estates that supported hierarchical allegiances and responsibilities. Thus, Japanese feudalism's rise came from the collapse of imperial rule. Minamoto Yoritomo played a key role in building feudalism.

9. Buddhism became accessible to the Japanese commoners with a stress on faith in the Buddhist message. In the feudal age, Zen and Nichiren Buddhism reached out to the warriors.

SUGGESTED READINGS

Devahuti, D. *Harsha*. Oxford, Eng.: Clarendon Press, 1970. A classic biography of a major figure in Indian history.

Needham, Joseph. *Science and Civilization in China*. Vol. I. Cambridge, Eng.: Cambridge University Press, 1954–84. A multivolume history of Chinese science and elite culture.

Tarling, Nicholas, ed. *The Cambridge History of Southeast Asia*. Vol. I. Cambridge, Eng.: Cambridge University Press, 1993. A collection of essays about early Southeast Asia.

Thakur, V. K. *The Historiography of Indian Feudalism*. New Delhi: Commonwealth Press, 1989. An examination of prominent theories about the development of Indian feudalism.

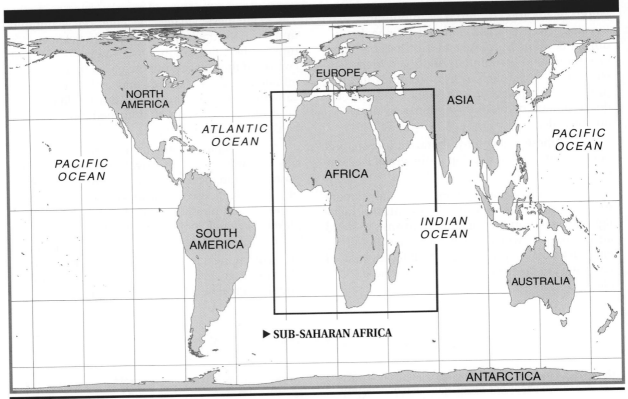

▶ SUB-SAHARAN AFRICA

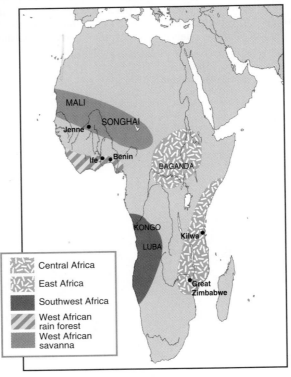

▶ SUB-SAHARAN AFRICA

Regional Kingdoms of Sub-Saharan Africa

around 200–around 1600

On his head he wears gold-embroidered caps covered with turbans of finest cotton. He gives audience to the people for the redressing of grievances in a hut, around which are placed ten horses bedecked with gold caparisons. Behind him stand ten slaves carrying shields and swords mounted with gold....

A Moorish scholar from Spain wrote these words to describe the majesty of the king of Ghana, a West African state, in 1067. Most of Africa south of the Sahara Desert was ruled by similar kings by this date.

One of Africa's historically most significant features is the Sahara, the largest desert in the world and one of the driest. Prior to 10,000 years ago, the Sahara was much wetter, and paintings on rock faces show that people, hippopotami, and other animals that need considerable amounts of water thrived there. Subsequently, however, the region has dried progressively, forcing out large-scale human habitation and forming a barrier that by 5000 B.C. stretched across the continent, separating North Africa and its Southwest Asian and European neighbors from the remainder of Africa.

The area south of the Sahara, known collectively as **sub-Saharan Africa**, had a wealth of indigenous states whose development often was stimulated by trade. These states varied greatly in size, with the smallest kingdoms having only a few thousand citizens and the largest having populations over one million. Regional states were the general rule, but a few empires developed and were successful for a time. Largely cut off from the rest of the world, these states developed a distinctive African stamp.

Nestled among the sub-Saharan states, often in lands less suitable to successful agriculture, were a variety of band-, tribe-, and chiefdom-level societies. These societies typically interacted with the states, particularly through trade, but they were basically autonomous.

None of the sub-Saharan states or other societies developed writing, so documentary evidence is limited largely to their later history, particularly after the development of large-scale commerce with Arab and North African Muslims around 700. Archaeology can offer some assistance in reconstructing the earlier periods, but archaeological research in sub-Saharan Africa is made difficult by poor preservation of remains and too few archaeologists studying such a vast area. Thus, little is

known archaeologically about many regions, and no region is known so well as comparable areas of the other inhabited continents. This means that our knowledge of detailed events and processes in many areas is frustratingly incomplete.

SETTING THE STAGE FOR SUB-SAHARAN AFRICAN CIVILIZATION

Most of human evolution took place in Africa, as discussed in Chapter 2. By 30,000 B.C., Africans had spread to most of the corners of the continent. The reason for that spread lay largely in the success of their adaptation: Success led to larger populations, which in turn led to the search for new lands to support the overflow.

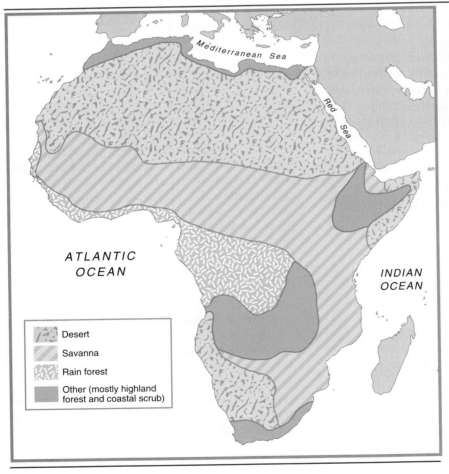

MAP 15.1 *Environmental Zones of Africa.* *Most of Africa is desert or savanna. Oases, coasts, and river valleys in the arid lands are moister than other areas. Trade between environmental zones was an important factor in African state formation.*

UNDER THE LENS

The Banana Staple

Bananas were domesticated in India and came to Africa with the inventory of Asian crops that arrived around A.D. 200. Several types appear to have arrived at about the same time, including both sweet bananas and their starchier cousins, plantains. Most peoples that grow bananas use them sparingly in their diet, often as sweets. But several African societies have developed a special relationship with bananas, relying on them for a major portion of their nutrition.

Bananas present both advantages and challenges to those who rely heavily on them. On the one hand, they can be an incredibly productive crop, yielding more food per unit area planted than any other crop available in Africa until the 1500s; they also provide a good nutritional base with a moderate caloric content and a good range of vitamins and minerals. But there are three drawbacks. Bananas require a great deal of water, a resource scarce in much of East Africa, where bananas first were introduced; they are finicky about the climate they will grow in; and they deplete soil fertility. This means that they can be grown effectively only in areas with appropriate climate and by people ready to devote the labor required to irrigate them and use manure as fertilizer.

After becoming established in some of the coastal communities along East Africa, the banana was carried into the interior by agriculturalists who had managed to procure cuttings for their own horticultural experiments. The earliest inland record of bananas is in Kenya about 250, around the Mount Kenya region. From there, they were carried eastward through some very inhospitable terrain until they arrived at the foot of Mount Kilimanjaro in present-day Tanzania, where they found a perfect setting.

There, the ancestors of the modern Chaga people applied traditional agricultural practices that included irrigation and manuring, and the result was phenomenal production. Eventually, they abandoned the yams that previously had been their mainstay to focus entirely on bananas. From there, the package of crop and cultivation practices spread to other places with appropriate climate throughout sub-Saharan Africa.

One of the places where bananas became a staple is in the Baganda kingdom of Uganda. The Baganda people prepared (and still do) a dish called *matoke*[a] that can be varied infinitely but has a consistent pattern. To make *matoke*, peel your bananas and wrap them in banana leaves, then steam or boil them. After they have been cooking about an hour and are very soft, mash them. To complete your *matoke*, mix the mashed bananas with cooked fish, or meat, or vegetables, or fruit, or seasonings. The more prosperous the diner, the more sumptuous the additions, but the banana remains the basis. For most Baganda, *matoke* is the main dish at every meal.

[a] *matoke:* mah TOH kee

In later periods, most Africans relied primarily on domesticated plants and animals for their food; this reliance permitted them to have greater control over their food supply and to increase the total amount of food. Local domestication of various plant foodstuffs began around 5000 B.C. or a bit earlier, a date comparable to that of domestication in Eurasia and the Americas. Black-eyed peas and cowpeas were local domesticates that provided protein. Sorghum (a grain), several types of millet (another grain), African rice, African yams, and *ackee* (a starchy fruit) were African staple crops that fueled the expansion of the sub-Saharan African population. Other local crops, such as watermelon, coconut, many kinds of vegetable greens, and sesame, also were domesticated locally and filled out the culinary roster. Later, around A.D. 200, domesticated crops from India and Southeast Asia began appearing on the east coast of Africa and spread throughout sub-Saharan Africa. These included Asian yams, taro, and bananas, crops that could thrive in zones where African domesticates were less successful. Finally, various highly productive American crops, including peanuts, manioc, corn, and chilis, were introduced to sub-Saharan Africa by the Europeans in the sixteenth and following centuries. While plant foods always have provided the bulk of

African foods, meat also was available from early times in the form of domesticated cattle, goats, and guinea fowl. All of these crops and animals were integrated into a subsistence economy that was able to provide for large and expanding populations.

Iron was critical to the development of complex society in many parts of Africa. Tropical grasses that formed thick root mats essentially prevented cultivation with stone hoes, but iron implements could cut through the roots effectively, permitting the spread of large-scale agriculture to the vast African grasslands. The traditional viewpoint among archaeologists has been that the technology of working iron came to sub-Saharan Africa from outside, probably from Southwest Asia. In recent years, however, increasing information has muddied the picture. Clearly, West Africans were making and using iron by at least 500 B.C., a date previously thought a millennium too early. This technology may have been imported from outside or invented locally, but current evidence is inadequate to determine which.

By A.D. 200 or so, two processes appear to have coincided. First, iron making and using became popular in sub-Saharan Africa and spread over much of the continent. All of this technology followed similar patterns, and it is believed to be linked. Second, certain pottery styles began appearing in widely separated parts of the continent, and trade items became more common everywhere. Many scholars interpret this pair of phenomena as evidence of the **Bantu expansion**, the spread of Bantu-speaking peoples over most of sub-Saharan Africa, bringing their distinctive artifacts, iron technology, language, and culture with them. Some scholars, however, believe it more likely that this evidence signals the development of widespread trading links across Africa that were stimulated by the development of and commerce in iron. Regardless, this event is the final stone that paved the way for sub-Saharan African civilization.

As this chapter will show, civilizations developed in most parts of sub-Saharan Africa by the period between 200 and 1200, maybe earlier in some places. Certainly they all possessed the core elements of agricultural dependency, state government with its extended bureaucracy, urbanism, long-distance trade, class stratification, and occupational specialization. Many also possessed vari-ous of the secondary elements of civilization, including monumental architecture, a great art style, currency, and metallurgy. As noted earlier, no sub-Saharan African civilization developed writing, so we are dependent primarily on archaeology (and scanty oral tradition) for information on the period before 500, but there has been precious little archaeological research in that period. As a result, we are currently unable to determine how far back in time some of these civilizations reach.

WEST AND CENTRAL AFRICA

The environment of western and central Africa consists of three broad bands, extending from west to east. In the north is the Sahara Desert, with little rainfall or vegetation; **oases**, islands of lush vegetation usually fed by a spring, are the only places where human settlement has developed in the Sahara in the past several thousand years. Immediately to the south of the Sahara is the **savanna**, a semiarid grassland with occasional trees. Water is more abundant here, occurring in springs, seasonal and permanent rivers, and groundwater trapped in the soil; this zone also has abundant iron supplies, which were tapped by its occupants. Of all the zones, the savanna was the most densely populated. Finally, to the south of the savanna is the **tropical rain forest**, a dense tangle of trees and undergrowth with abundant—sometimes over-abundant—water. The tropical rain forest poses three major challenges to human settlement: diseases that thrive in its saturated soils, transportation through tangled vegetation, and land clearance for agriculture. Despite these drawbacks, the tropical rain forest saw the development of several kingdoms.

The Rise of Civilization in West Africa: Jenne, around 200–around 700

At one time, historians saw the kingdoms of western and central Africa as direct outgrowths of contact with Arab traders around the year 700. This was understandable, because they could base their conclusions only on documents, and the documents were written by the Arabs after 700. The

FIGURE 15.1 *Jenne Warrior. This sculpture portrays a warrior or possibly a founding ancestor. The rich ornaments indicate that the individual is a member of the elite. The statue is about two feet tall and made of terra-cotta, lightly fired clay; its exact date is not known.*
Photo by Franco Khoury. National Museum of African Art,
Eliot Elifson Photographic Archives, Smithsonian Institution.

absence of earlier written evidence led scholars to believe that sub-Saharan civilization was inspired by, if not directly copied from, the Arabs who first recorded it. In recent years, however, a revolution has occurred in the interpretation of how these kingdoms developed, largely based on new archaeological finds. It now is clear that at least one region of West Africa had a functioning civilization by A.D. 200, centuries before the Arab trade commenced.

The story begins at the city of Jenne,[1] in the southern part of what is now the Mali Republic. The settlement of Jenne began around 300 B.C., but at this point it was merely one village among many in West Africa. By A.D. 200, however, the settlement had grown greatly, and, although precise estimates are not available, the population of Jenne probably was more than 10,000. Part of a settlement hierarchy, Jenne was urban.

Jenne's early urbanism is significant because there is no evidence of trade with areas north of the Sahara. There are abundant indications of trade within West Africa but no items traceable to Nubia, the Sudan, Egypt, or other parts of North Africa. This means that external stimulus cannot be invoked to explain the rise of Jenne.

Jenne's location at the southern edge of the savanna provides clues that may explain its development. This edge of the savanna has greater rainfall than areas farther north, providing more reliable agricultural yields to support a large population. Archaeological remains at Jenne show that the diet of its inhabitants was dominated by African rice, which grew well in the rich soils along the Niger River at Jenne. In addition, the inhabitants raised cattle and either sheep or goats and supplemented their diet of domesticated foods with wild plants and animals. This strong base permitted Jenne to invest in trading expeditions southward into the rain forest, probably initially trading surplus agricultural products for salt, a desperately needed necessity for agriculturalists with no access to the sea or its resources. Later, Jenne provided a broad range of products to the rain forest towns, including gold, iron, and ivory. In return, Jenne received salt, wood, dried fish, and perhaps slaves. Jenne's position at the southern periphery of the savanna, though poor for the

[1] **Jenne:** ZHEHN eh

trans-Sahara trade, was perfect for the savanna-forest trade.

While most of our knowledge of Jenne comes from later periods, archaeological evidence and oral tradition provide some peeks into life in early Jenne. Society was divided into tiers, with a small elite and a great mass of commoners; it is unknown whether slaves existed at this date. The elite were buried in tombs cut into bedrock, accompanied by platters of food, vessels of drink, and ornaments of various kinds. In later times, servants were sacrificed in the tombs, but there is no evidence of this in early Jenne. Markets apparently were held in the city on fixed days of the week, and farmers and others from areas around the city would bring their produce for sale or barter. In the early period at Jenne, there is no evidence of the use of currency.

Jenne is the only urban community of its sort known at this date in western or central Africa, but our present state of knowledge is admittedly poor. On the basis of available evidence, it seems to have possessed a state government, urbanism, and the other core criteria for civilization. Was it truly the isolated case that some scholars believe it to be, or is archaeological knowledge so incomplete that other contemporary civilizations remain unrecognized? There is no way at the moment to know, but there are intriguing hints that Jenne may have been the center of only one among several such early urban societies.

Later West and Central African Kingdoms: The Northern Stimulus, around 700–around 1600

Around 700, the first Muslim traders established commerce between the northern savanna regions of western and central Africa and their home bases north of the Sahara. This contact was permitted by two factors. The first was the camel, domesticated and used for several centuries in North Africa but not used south of the Sahara; the second was the gradually expanding fund of information on the Sahara, its routes, and its oases. By this date, the dangerous trial-and-error process of exploring the desert had revealed reliable knowledge that permitted caravans to advance from one oasis to the next all the way across the Sahara with limited danger of getting lost or running out of supplies.

By the 900s, trade between sub-Saharan Africa and the Muslim world was substantial and regular. Cloth, salt, steel swords, glass, and luxury goods flowed south, while gold, slaves, ostrich feathers, fine leathers, and fancy woods passed northward. The expansion of West and Central African commerce with the advent of the Dar al-Islam market fit nicely with the trade systems that had been set up earlier.

The **cola nut** held a special place in this trade. Indigenous only to sub-Saharan Africa, the cola nut was (and is) often chewed before a meal to stimulate appetite and digestion; sometimes it was powdered and used as a condiment during the meal. (This is the same cola nut that formerly flavored cola soft drinks.) It is a mild stimulant, and its significance lies in the fact that it is the only stimulant permitted strict Muslims. Consequently, when Arabs developed a taste for the cola nut, West Africa profited as its only source.

The trans-Sahara trade transformed western and central African kingdoms. Gold had been mined and worked in West Africa using indigenous technology since at least 800. With the coming of the Muslim trade, a new and profitable market opened, spurring increased production. Many other items that had some value locally were greatly desired in the north, and far higher prices could be charged the Arabs. This spurred the development of larger cities, a more powerful elite, greater class stratification, and stronger governments.

Another major change brought by the Arab and North African traders was Islam. Prior to this time, sub-Saharan Africans practiced religions based on polytheism and animism. After the coming of the Arabs, Islam spread widely in sub-Saharan Africa, especially in the savanna zone. While examples of forced conversion are known, they apparently were rare. This makes sense, because the Muslim intruders usually were a small, militarily negligible body, unable to force their hosts into anything. Far more common was voluntary conversion.

For certain groups, converting to Islam had important practical advantages, some of which have already been discussed in Chapter 12. Given a choice, Arab and North African merchants preferred to deal with other Muslims. Perhaps more important, Islam provided a code of ethics for traders of vastly different cultural backgrounds,

FIGURE 15.2 *Jingereber Mosque of Timbuktu.*
Timbuktu was a major trading center of West Africa.
Situated at the edge of the Sahara Desert, it provided
services to caravans and travelers who made the diffi-
cult crossing from the north, and served as a locus of
exchange for goods that originated farther south. With
the trade and travel across the Sahara came Islam. This
mosque, built as a house of Muslim worship around
1350, is one of the oldest still standing in West Africa.
Courtesy of Jean-Louis Bourgeois.

enabling them to interact with trust and shared expectations and providing explicit ritual sanctions if ethical rules were broken. Islam assisted African and Arab merchants in dealing with one another, facilitating interregional trade.

Islam spread through most West and Central African kingdoms in a predictable manner. First to convert were the merchants, because they had the greatest incentive as well as the greatest contact with Muslim outsiders. Next to convert were the rulers, whose conversions usually were state events, with carefully planned ceremonies and speeches. As merchants gained greater wealth, they and the rulers came to share power to a greater extent, forming an elite that was further removed from the commoners. This distance was reflected both in social interactions and in habitations, as rulers and merchants came to live in a quarter of the city separated from the rest of the populace. The commoners themselves were the last to become Muslims, and their conversion sometimes was inspired by a charismatic Sufi preacher or the desire to avoid being captured and made a slave (because a Muslim could not be legally enslaved by another Muslim). In many cases the conversion of commoners was nominal only, and traditional religious practices continued little changed. Conversion of a people was not always complete, and sometimes a royal edict was required to convince the commoners of the good judgment of converting to Islam.

Later West and Central African Government and Civilization, around 700–around 1600

Throughout most of West and Central Africa after 700, government was similar. The so-called **Sudanic-type state** was ruled by a divine king, usually mythically descended from the creator god. This king had absolute authority over his subjects, and he was attributed divine characteristics. Particularly, he was believed to have no need to eat, and the smuggling of food into the palace, its preparation, and his consumption of it were guarded with secrecy. The king's status meant that he had contact with commoners rarely and only under ritually regulated circumstances. As a divine being, the king could not die a natural death, so he was ceremonially strangled or poisoned when near death. A king's successor was determined partly by descent and partly by the will of the titled officials who had attended the previous king.

The Sudanic-type state was highly bureaucratic. The king appointed a wide variety of officials, the most important of whom almost always were the Queen Mother, the Queen Sister, two or three Great Wives, and four Advisors (usually male). The Queen Mother, of course, was an office filled by the accident of being the mother of the king; there usually was room for choice of the Queen Sister, because any king might have several sisters; the Great Wives and Advisors were selected primarily for their wisdom and judgment. This system is distinctive in that it reserved many pivotal

IN THEIR OWN WORDS

The Court of Mansa Musa

Kanka Musa, whose name was prefaced by the respectful term, "Mansa," was the emperor of Mali in the early fourteenth century, near the end of the empire's height. He became famous for the opulent *hajj* that took him, an enormous entourage, and magnificent and precious art to Mecca for a pilgrimage. Ibn Fadl Allah al Omari,[a] a contemporary Egyptian scholar, collected information on Musa from a friend in Mali and published the following account of the splendor of the imperial court at Niani. Note the combination of African and Muslim symbols and elements.

The sultan [ruler] of this kingdom presides in his palace in a great balcony called *bembe* where he has a great seat of ebony that is like a throne fit for a large and tall person; on either side it is flanked by elephant tusks turned towards each other. His weapons stand near him, being all of gold—saber, lance, quiver, bow, and arrows. He wears wide trousers made of about twenty pieces of material which he alone may wear. Behind him there stand about a score of Turkish or other pages that are bought for him in Cairo [in Egypt]; one of them, at his left, holds a silk umbrella surmounted by a dome and a bird of gold; the bird has the figure of a falcon. His officers are seated in a circle about him, in two rows, one to the right and one to the left; beyond them sit the chief commanders of his cavalry. In front of him there is a person who never leaves him and who is his executioner; also another who serves as a spokesman between the sovereign and his subjects, and who is named the herald. In front of them again, there are drummers. Others dance before their sovereign, who enjoys this, and make him laugh. Two banners are spread behind him. Before him they keep two saddled and bridled horses in case he should wish to ride.

[a] **Ibn Fadl Allah al Omari:** IB uhn FAH duhl AHL uh ahl oh MAHR ee

---

advisory positions for women, something rare in state-level governments. Both men and women, chosen primarily for their abilities, composed this inner circle of advisors. This approach to government differs markedly from a strictly hereditary system of the sort found in many states elsewhere.

The government also supported a hierarchy of local officials, including provincial and district chiefs and other local administrators. Their primary duties were:

— raising tribute to support the opulent lifestyle of the king and his court;

— gathering commodities for long-distance trade, some of which was carried on under royal auspices; and

— seeing that royal edicts and wishes were carried out throughout the realm.

Kings gathered artisans to create works in the great art style that developed. Bronze castings of the West African kingdoms are particularly well known, probably because they survived the centuries well and became favorites of early-twentieth-century art collectors in Europe and North America. Other media were important, however, and art included carved wooden sculptures, ivory carvings, cast gold, featherwork, and painted leather.

West and Central African kings directed great public works projects; few are still archaeologically visible, because they were made with unfired mud that served well in its time but has disintegrated over the centuries. Some known monumental works include royal tombs cut into bedrock, groups of large standing stones serving to mark elite burials, walled palaces, mosques, and great walls surrounding cities. Royal patronage also supported irrigation and drainage projects that permitted the growing of substantial surpluses of foodstuffs.

Political History in West and Central Africa

Little can be said about the political history of this area before documents. After the coming of the Arabs, it becomes much better known, and the picture becomes even clearer following the coming of the Portuguese and other Europeans after 1440.

Our first evidence, around 800, indicates that there were a great number of independent polities throughout the savannas of West and Central Africa. Most of these were small kingdoms with a central city or town and outlying towns and villages, usually with populations running in the tens of thousands. These kingdoms could be considered city-states comparable to those in Europe, Asia, and Central America.

An exception to this pattern was Ghana, an inland empire centered on the western portion of present-day Mali. Oral tradition states that Ghana had twenty kings before the time of Muhammad (around 600), and it is unclear how early the kingdom and empire may have begun or what was its process of formation. The Ghana state was destroyed by the Almoravids, a Berber group from North Africa bent on converting the Ghanaians to Islam and controlling the trans-Saharan trade. In 1054, the Almoravids captured critical trading centers in the north of Ghana, weakening that state enough so that it toppled by 1077. Almoravids held some kind of control over Ghana for a brief time, but by 1100 they had lost it. Ghana, however, had disintegrated and could not reunite itself, and for the next century the area was composed of many small states.

Around 1200, another empire developed, larger and richer than Ghana. The Mali Empire was centered on the city of Niani[2] in the old Ghana Empire and incorporated all that Ghana previously had controlled. Mali extended its empire beyond the borders of the old Ghana state in all directions, including westward to the Atlantic Ocean. Much of this extension was through military conquest, and therein lay the seeds of Mali's destruction. Mali's military was overextended, and it was tolerated by subject states only so long as it provided protection under which trade could proceed. When it failed in this purpose, however, these conquered states felt no ties of loyalty and seceded or joined rival empires. As more states defected from the empire, Mali was weakened and less able to fulfill its duties as protector. The empire began eroding by 1320.

The chief state to benefit from Mali's weakening was Songhai,[3] situated to the east of Mali. Once part of the Mali Empire, Songhai was an early defector that began building its own empire by around 1350. Most of the defector states from Mali became part of the Songhai Empire, either imme-diately or after a period of independence. Songhai relied on diplomacy as much as military action to build its empire, and this resulted in greater loyalty among its subjects. At its height in 1515, Songhai was the largest sub-Saharan African empire, with a population numbering well over one million. Songhai's rich province of Hausaland was lost after its local ethnic group staged a successful revolt there; subsequent internal dissension further weakened the Songhai Empire. In 1590, following civil strife over imperial succession, Moroccan forces conquered and occupied Songhai.

All of the states and empires discussed so far are from the savanna zone, but states also developed in the tropical rain forest zone. Here, Islam and its literary tradition took little hold, so most of our early information comes from archaeology.

FIGURE 15.3 *Queen Mother of Benin and Attendants. This cast bronze sculpture from the eighteenth century focuses on the Queen Mother with her large headgear and rich ornaments. She is surrounded by women servants, who themselves were probably nobles. In many sub-Saharan societies, the Queen Mother was one of several powerful female advisors to a king. This sculpture comes from Benin, in the coastal rain forest of West Africa.* Metropolitan Museum of Art, Gift of Mr. and Mrs. Klaus G. Perls, 1991.

[2] **Niani:** nee AHN ee
[3] **Songhai:** SOHNG HY

FIGURE 15.4 *Procession at the Court of Benin.* *Benin became rich through participation in the slave trade with Europeans. This seventeenth-century Dutch engraving shows the king of Benin on horseback, surrounded by musicians, attendants, and tame leopards; soldiers and nobles, also on horses, follow. Pictured leaving the palace, whose turrets are surmounted by brass ornaments in the form of birds, the procession is probably headed to a shrine where a ritual will be performed.* From Olfert Dapper, *Beschreibung von Afrika*, first published in Amsterdam in 1670.

Current information suggests that settlements in the forest zone were modest villages prior to around 600. By around 850, a handful of archaeological sites, such as Igbo Ukwu, show evidence of larger size, greater wealth, and the presence of an elite. Such sites contain some traded items from the Arabs, although their numbers are few, and most archaeologists believe they came there through trade links with the savanna kingdoms. Little is known about the government or economics of these early communities, although some scholars believe they were chiefdoms.

One point is clear: The development of large and complex polities came later to the forest than to the savanna. In fact, the rise of complexity par-

allels quite closely the rise of the large-scale trade networks of the savanna kingdoms to the north. It may very well be that the interregional trade carried on by Ghana and other states in the savanna led them to seek commodities from the forest communities; this, in turn, may have stimulated the development of a wealthy class that gained power and came to lead the forest communities.

Good evidence for kingdoms begins to appear by 1200, with the development of the Ife[4] state; shortly thereafter, Benin,[5] the other major state in the forest zone, also originated. Both Ife and Benin

[4] **Ife:** EE fay
[5] **Benin:** beh NEEN

had sophisticated royal courts and an extravagant cast-bronze sculptural tradition. The wealth of these states resulted directly from their control of trade between the coast and the savanna.

In 1440, the Portuguese began trading for slaves with the forest kingdoms of West Africa. Under this stimulus, these kingdoms expanded in size and power as they accumulated wealth from the European slave trade over the next centuries. While slavery had existed in West Africa centuries before and had expanded under Islam, its intensity increased and its nature changed markedly when the Europeans became involved. This event marked a turning point in the history of West and Central Africa.

EAST AFRICA

East Africa from present-day Somalia to Mozambique can be viewed as two great zones: the coast and the interior. From around 700 to 1600, coastal East Africans lived radically different lives from those of their interior cousins, yet the two were intimately linked by the ties of economy.

Coastal East Africa and the Indian Ocean Trade, around 700–around 1600

The coastal zone of East Africa is a narrow strip, scarcely five miles wide and more than a thousand miles long. The zone is generally favorable for human occupation, presenting a variety of food and other resources. But the most desirable point about the coast, at least from the 700s onward, was its accessibility to ships plying the trade routes of the Indian Ocean.

The east coast of Africa is only about 1,600 sea miles from India and closer still to Arabia. (In contrast, the west coast of Africa is about 3,000 sea miles from the nearest part of Europe.) Further, winds and currents between Africa and Asia are seasonal and they reverse direction every six months, making travel easy and relatively safe. (In contrast, the west coast was made inaccessible by contrary winds and currents that could not easily be overcome with maritime technology available before the fifteenth century.) Given this geography, it is little wonder that coastal East Africa had extensive contacts with Asia far earlier than coastal

West Africa had contact with Europe. Some of those early contacts on the eastern coast were discussed previously in terms of imported crops around 200, but even more pervasive contacts developed by 700.

The Axumites and contemporary southern Arabs had established some trade contacts with the coastal peoples of East Africa by around 300, but these were sporadic and limited. Around 700, the volume of trade between Asia and coastal East Africa increased considerably. Arabs, Persians, Indians, and Malays are documented as visiting the coast for trade, and Chinese may have done so as well. Ivory, tortoise shell, incense, spices, gold, iron, amber, slaves, ambergris (a fragrant secretion from whales, used in perfume making), and other perfume oils were major exports from East Africa; in return, Asia sent ceramics, soapstone pots, cloth, beads, and glass. Anxious to take advantage of this commerce, Africans developed cities and towns along the coast specifically as ports of trade. Many of these ports were preexisting villages, but some were new and located in areas that had excellent harbors but insufficient resources to provide food for a community.

As a result of this trade, the elite of these coastal communities became wealthy. They expended some of their wealth on fancy tombs and houses made of stone, and some of their houses even had indoor toilets. Meanwhile, other inhabitants, principally dock workers, fishermen, laborers, and servants, remained poor and continued living in the mud-and-thatch huts that had previously been the universal type of housing. Some of these settlements took on Arab or Persian names, and the local language—Swahili—adopted many Arabic words. Islam became the dominant religion, at least among the elite, and mosques were built. A recent archaeological survey has located 173 coastal settlements with stone structures for the elite.

It perhaps is not surprising that at one time scholars believed these to be Arab colonies, outposts set up in a foreign land to facilitate trading. Certainly the number of Arab characteristics is great, but the documents, oral history, and archaeological evidence all agree that these coastal settlements were local African developments, encouraged by trade.

Kilwa was one of the two or three largest of the coastal settlements. Gaspar Correa, a member of Vasco da Gama's Portuguese crew, wrote an account of his visit to Kilwa in 1514, in which he describes that place:

> The city is large and is of good buildings of stone and mortar with terraces, and the houses have much wood works. The city comes down to the shore, and is entirely surrounded by a wall and towers, within which there may be 12,000 inhabitants. The country all round is very luxuriant with many trees and gardens of all sorts of vegetables. . . . The streets of the city are very narrow, as the houses are very high, of three and four stories, and one can run along the tops of them upon the terraces, as the houses are very close together; and in the port there are many ships.

Correa focused his description on the elite portions of town, and Kilwa is noted for having a larger elite section than other port communities. We can be sure, however, that there was another side to Kilwa, where common people and slaves lived simpler lives in houses made of thatch and mud.

The form of government along the East African coast varied from place to place. In some cities and towns, authority was vested in a council of lineage heads; in others, local rulers were elected, and some of these were able to convert their positions into hereditary ones, leading to de facto kingship. In at least some cases, an Arab or Persian accepted a position as ruler, presumably a

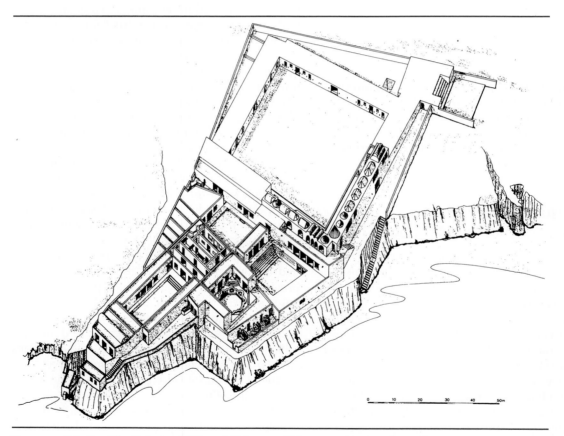

FIGURE 15.5 *The Palace of Husuni Kubwa.* *This reconstruction, drawn by an archaeologist who excavated there, shows the magnificent palace of Husuni Kubwa, constructed by the Mahdalis, a dynasty of rulers of Kilwa on the eastern coast of Africa. Trade with Arabs, among others, enriched this community and especially its rulers, who in the fourteenth century converted some of their wealth into this cliff-top palace overlooking the northern coast of Kilwa Island. The octagonal structure in the center foreground is a swimming pool, and the square depression to its right is a reception court with hundreds of niches for oil lamps. The largest structure, at the top of this drawing, was a warehouse for precious Mahdali goods waiting to be traded.* From *A Thousand Years of East Africa,* The British Institute in Eastern Africa. Reproduced with permission of the Institute.

compromise candidate when local factions could not agree. Rulers typically continued to live in their own houses, making them a bit more fancy by adding sculpture or other ornamentation. Each of these governmental systems was extended only to a single community, and there is no evidence of any attempt to incorporate several communities into a single polity. Not until the conclusion of the Portuguese conquest of the East African coast around 1640 would the region be united under a single government.

The Interior of East Africa, around 1150–around 1600

The settlements along the East African coast traded over great distances, and some of their inhabitants reaped the rewards in the form of wealth, but their economic success would have been impossible without the interior. Most of the people of this zone lived a more modest life than those we have discussed previously in this chapter, living in small villages with limited class stratification. One of their contributions to the coast was in providing food and other necessities not always available in the quantities required to support the coastal cities and towns. Some of these small-scale societies specialized in animal herding, others focused on agriculture, and still others practiced both. A second contribution of these peoples to the coastal lifestyle was in supplying many of the materials the coastal people traded with foreigners, particularly ivory and slaves. In return, they received salt, shell and glass beads, cotton cloth produced in the coastal towns, and perhaps some of the fancy cloth imported from Asia.

One exception to this characterization stands out starkly: Zimbabwe.[6] The ancient Zimbabwe state (around 1150–around 1600) in the highlands of present-day Zimbabwe (formerly Rhodesia) was centered on a major city, usually termed "Great Zimbabwe." This city consisted of several massive circular buildings of stone, as well as areas of thatched huts. The stone buildings have attracted a great deal of attention because of their size. The largest had an exterior wall of stone nearly 800 feet long, more than 15 feet thick, and about 31 feet high; this amounts to about 50,000 cubic feet of masonry. Put into perspective, this is enough masonry to face an Egyptian pyramid measuring more than 200 feet at the base of each side. Further, the stone blocks are very finely cut and set together closely with mortar, reflecting high building standards.

Great Zimbabwe is the largest of the settlements of the historic Zimbabwe state, with an estimated population of 10,000 to 12,000 persons within its walls, but there also are nearly 200 other sites known that have similar stone structures. These cities and towns are generally believed to be regional centers under the capital at Great Zimbabwe. In addition, there are many village sites with no stone architecture of the sort that surrounds the larger settlements, representing the smallest unit in the settlement hierarchy. This clearly is an urban system.

The Zimbabwe state probably developed shortly before 1150, perhaps with an original capital at Mapungubwe,[7] shifting to Great Zimbabwe around 1250. While there are no documents to guide interpretation, oral history and archaeology suggest that the ancestors of the modern Shona people built and lived in Great Zimbabwe.

The great wealth of Zimbabwe is reflected both in its architecture and in some of the artifacts that have been found there. Persian bowls, Chinese ceramics, Southwest Asian glass, shell and glass beads, and a coin minted in Kilwa, all found at Great Zimbabwe, indicate wealth. They also point to the apparent source of that wealth: extensive trade with the coastal settlements.

Zimbabwe controlled areas rich in gold, and gold was perhaps the most sought-after commodity the coastal towns had to offer Asian traders. Evidence of Zimbabwean gold mines and processing areas have been found, and some historians believe that a fifteenth-century Portuguese account referring to gold mines in the kingdom of Butua may refer to Zimbabwe.

Little is known regarding the government of Zimbabwe. The assumption usually is that it was a state with a king and lesser district chiefs. Many scholars believe that trade was a royal monopoly, and some believe that the king was a hereditary ruler identified as the descendant of a god. These conclusions are supported by oral traditions, but there are no documents to corroborate them.

In the seventeenth century, Portuguese control of the East African coast became greater, and it began to extend inland. At the same time that its

---

[6] **Zimbabwe:** zihm BAHB way

[7] **Mapungubwe:** mah puhn GUHB way

FIGURE 15.6 *Great Enclosure at Great Zimbabwe.* *This aerial photograph shows the central portion of the archaeological site of Great Zimbabwe in the interior of eastern Africa. The Great Enclosure encircles an area of about 100 acres, believed to have been used largely for religious rituals and elite housing. Archaeologists estimate that 18,000 persons might have lived at this site, and nearly 200 similar though smaller sites are known. Great Zimbabwe was at its height in the first half of the second millennium.* Courtesy of the Department of Information, Rhodesia.

coastal partners were in the process of being conquered by a foreign power, for reasons presently unknown, Zimbabwe collapsed. First the gold trade languished, then the urban system broke down, and shortly thereafter elite culture at Zimbabwe disintegrated.

SOUTHWEST AFRICA

The southwestern portion of Africa, largely comprised of what is today Angola, has undergone tremendous environmental change in the past few centuries, largely as a result of human activity. Consequently, the present environments are not representative of those that would have been exploited by southwestern Africans at the time

when states were first developing. Along the coast was a narrow, relatively moist strip; in the northern and southern parts of the interior was savanna; and between the savanna zones, in the central interior, was a zone of dense tropical rain forest. In the far south, the savanna graded into the inhospitable Kalahari Desert.

Agriculture became prominent in Southwest Africa sometime after A.D. 500, probably around 800. By 1000, it was practiced in all zones except the driest and those that were the most densely forested. Important crops were mostly derived from parts of Africa farther north and included sorghum, millet, yams, bananas, peanuts, and sugarcane. Fish were widely used in areas along the coast and fertile rivers, and land animals provided protein elsewhere.

Southwest Africa diverges from most of the rest of Africa in its degree of internal diversity. In most parts of Africa, the various peoples followed more or less similar lifestyles, changing in parallel over time as conditions in the region changed. In Southwest Africa, however, some peoples became intensive agriculturalists and developed states; others adopted agriculture but retained egalitarian political systems; still others retained hunting and gathering as the primary components of their subsistence. Some of these choices may be explained as reflecting the limitations or possibilities of the environment, but others seem to relate to other, as yet unrecognized, factors.

The Development of Early Southwest African Kingdoms, around 1000–around 1600

Those peoples who developed kingdoms in Southwest Africa followed more or less the same pattern of political development. In most parts of Southwest Africa, men heading lineages were also recognized to have a special relationship with the land. These individuals, known as **lords of the land**, simultaneously were leaders of their kinship groups and priests who dealt with spirits that inhabited various spots in their lineage territories. As some lineages prospered and their populations grew, lords of the land began to augment their kinship-religious duties with expanded political and economic powers. Prosperous lineages meant increased revenues for the lords of the land, who administered lineage finances; lords of the land became increasingly liberated from ordinary duties, and their image as special individuals grew. Eventually, they were wealthy and powerful and were revered as leaders in politics, as well as in religion and kinship. At this stage, some would declare themselves leaders of related lineages, deposing other lords of the land by political maneuvering or by force of arms. As this occurred, several villages would be united under a single coercive leader, who began acquiring an entourage of counselors, judges, ambassadors, and courtiers.

Probably the earliest of the Southwest African kingdoms was Luba in the interior southern savannas. According to oral tradition, the kingdom of Luba was founded by Kongolo, a lord of the land who subsumed several lineages into his own, appointing their former leaders as subordinates who, with his consent, could rule their lineages in

FIGURE 15.7 *Elite Grave from Luba. The Luba kingdom of southwestern Africa was characterized by the same sort of class stratification known throughout sub-Saharan Africa. This grave from the Lake Kisale region provides evidence of the wealth and high status of its occupant. The elaborate ceramic bowls were produced only for use in burials and probably contained food; the various iron weapons befit the warrior status of the elite male; finally, the ivory and iron jewelry indicate that this is the grave of a member of the elite. Graves such as this date from the eighth and ninth centuries.* Pierre de Maret, Africa Museum, Tervuren, Belgium.

his absence. Kongolo and his subordinate leaders were permitted to own slaves, although apparently no one else was permitted to do so. The system has been considered feudal by some scholars, because each level of the hierarchy delegated authority to the level below it, unless a crisis necessitated cooperative behavior to support the king. The Luba kingdom probably was formed between 1000 and 1100.

On the southern coast of Southwest Africa, another kingdom formed around 1200. This was the famous Kongo kingdom. Although not the largest or most powerful of the states in this region, it is the best known because of abundant oral tradition and sixteenth-century Portuguese accounts describing it. According to oral tradition, the Kongo state developed slowly, perhaps over a century or more beginning around 1200, as various lords of the land amalgamated their power to form a single king. Because Kongo is so well documented, we shall describe it as an example of kingdoms in Southwest Africa.

The Kingdom of Kongo, around 1200–around 1600

The king of Kongo usually inherited his position, probably from his father, although royal inheritance sometimes passed through female lines, in which case a king would inherit by virtue of being the son of the king's sister. There was no rule that the eldest son should be named king, and a group of nine to twelve electors had to select which son would become the new king. Rarely, they would be forced to go outside the royal family to select a king, if they judged all hereditary candidates to be incompetent.

The king had considerable, though not absolute, power. He was able to declare war, open or close trade routes, appoint governors and other officials, and collect taxes, but in all these tasks he was overseen by a council. The king and council maintained a delicate balance of power. On the one hand, the council could countermand a royal decree; on the other hand, the king appointed the council and could disband it or remove specific members. The system encouraged cooperation, because either of these actions would destabilize the country, laying it open to outside invasion from its neighbors, a constant threat.

The king ruled over a series of provinces, but each of these had its own governor who carried out everyday administration. Governors came into power by various mechanisms, most apparently inherited from when they were independent lineage territories. These included election by the people with the king's confirmation, inheritance from one's father, and royal appointment. Governors received salaries from the king, who was the only authority able to collect taxes. Beneath the governors were hereditary village chiefs, who also probably received stipends.

Banza was the capital city of Kongo, and it reportedly housed many thousands of people within its encircling stone walls. It served as a fortress to protect the king in times of trouble, as the control center for the trade between the coast and interior, and as a religious center (because the king was considered divine and retained important ceremonial obligations).

At Banza, the king held court. Seated on a ceremonial stool, wearing a headdress and bracelet of copper or ivory, and holding a tax purse, the king was surrounded by symbols of his various religious and secular roles. We know little about court life, only that several officials remained with the king at most times to serve his needs as soon as he voiced them.

The lifeways of the common people of Kongo are poorly known. Clearly, most people were farmers living in small villages spread throughout the kingdom. Along the Atlantic Ocean and some stretches of rivers, small villages were dominated by fishing, although it is unknown whether men, women, or both sexes worked in this occupation. It is known, however, that those who fished also produced pottery for trade. In addition, there were miners, metal workers, makers of **raffia** (a fabric made of palm fiber), salt manufacturers, and merchants. Each of the occupations probably had a traditional status associated with it.

It appears that much, perhaps all, trade was controlled by the king. *Nzimbu*[8] (a type of cowrie shell) were the official currency of Kongo; currency from neighboring states, including cross-shaped copper ingots and squares of raffia, probably also was accepted. Major articles traded included salt, iron, copper, woven goods, and pottery. It is clear, however, that this trade linked the coastal and interior sections of Southwest Africa but did not extend significantly beyond the region. While only limited archaeological study has been devoted to

[8] *Nzimbu:* NZIHM boo

FIGURE 15.8 *Dutch Delegation at the Court of Kongo.* *This Dutch engraving from 1642 depicts Dutch traders kneeling before the king of Kongo, a major kingdom of southwestern Africa. Courtiers in elite dress stand beside the seated king. There are several European items in this engraving: the chandelier hanging above the king, the king's leather boots, and a miniature cross dangling from the king's left elbow. These items probably were special gifts bestowed on the king by European traders, but it is possible that they were added by the engraver as artistic flourishes. The Latin inscription above the king's throne, which reads "Sir Alvare, King of Kongo," was almost certainly invented by the artist.* From Olfert Dapper, Beschreibung von Africa, Amsterdam, 1670.

this region, virtually none of the exotic products of long-distance trade have been found in Southwest Africa.

The family in the Kongo kingdom was largely oriented around the mother's line. It is probable that the basic family unit was the extended family, with sisters, their husbands, and children living together in a single house. Among the aristocracy, marriages were important political devices, because a series of good marriages could ally a man with several powerful lineages and propel him into a favorable position for a royal appointment.

Religion in Kongo, as throughout Southwest Africa, was local polytheism. Islam penetrated to this area only in the fifteenth century, and then not

as a serious competitor to local faiths. There were no commercial incentives to convert to Islam in Southwest Africa, because there was no major or direct trade with Dar al-Islam. In addition, the divine nature of the king might have been undermined by the introduction of a new religion, so it is unlikely that rulers—the typical leaders in national conversion—would have been inclined to support this new religion.

Trade, Civilization, and Southwest Africa

Southwest Africa stands apart in one respect from the other regions of Africa that have been discussed in this chapter: Its development received

PATHS TO THE PAST

The Recognition of Segmentary Opposition

Prior to the 1930s, British colonial administrators frequently complained that Africans were "capricious" or "unpredictable" in their political alliances. On one occasion, a village might carry on a violent feud with a neighboring village, but a few days later, the two might fight side by side against a coalition of more distant villages; the following month, all of these combatants might unite to fight the British. What the colonial administrators failed to realize was that these shifting coalitions were reflections of a widespread African approach to political organization.

In the early 1930s, E. E. Evans-Pritchard, a British anthropologist, was asked by the British colonial administrators of the Anglo-Egyptian Sudan to investigate this phenomenon and try to explain it. Evans-Pritchard spent two years with the Nuer tribe of the Sudan, and its members explained to him the workings of **segmentary opposition**.

The principle underlying segmentary opposition is simple. Each person is a member of a series of hierarchic groups, mostly based on kinship and village residence. The simplest element is a family within a village; next is the village itself; then comes a series of progressively larger groups consisting of ever-larger coalitions of villages; finally comes the entire Nuer tribe. In any conflict—violent, judicial, or otherwise—a person's loyalty rightfully is owed to the largest group that can array itself against the antagonist. In an argument over my neighbor's dog, the conflict involves my family against my neighbor's family; if someone from a neighboring village steals something from me, the conflict is seen as my village against the neighboring village. If my antagonist comes from a village that is involved in a high-level coalition opposing a similar coalition that includes my village, these coalitions would be the stage for the conflict. Finally, outsiders could find the entire Nuer tribe marshaled against themselves in a conflict. A person's political loyalties in a segmentary system were not simply to the state; rather, they were owed to a series of nested entities culminating in the chiefdom or state.

When Evans-Pritchard published his findings on segmentary opposition, colonial administrators began to understand previously baffling events. The Nuer, for example, were perennial enemies with the neighboring Dinka, constantly conducting feuds and raiding against each other; this enmity was underscored by mythological tales explaining their differences. Consequently, the British in the late nineteenth century believed they could count on Dinka aid to conquer the Nuer but were astonished when the Nuer and Dinka united unsuccessfully to resist British incursions. In reality, the Nuer and Dinka saw themselves as enemies when in mutual conflict and as allies when in conflict against a common enemy.

Scholars since the 1930s have realized that many states in sub-Saharan Africa were organized around the principle of segmentary opposition, permitting them the flexibility to quarrel yet effectively unite, depending on the circumstances. As so often is the case, behavior that seemed irrational was merely based on unfamiliar principles.

---

no significant stimulus from trade with distant places. While West Africa began its development of complexity with Jenne and before the advent of significant outside trade, the rise of trade with Dar al-Islam spurred growth in the savanna; at the same time, savanna-forest trade (and the later European slave trade) stimulated growth in the forests. Similarly, the Indian Ocean trade was crucial to the rise of complexity in East Africa. In Southwest Africa, however, there was no ready access to trade routes with foreign traders from distant lands, and trade within this area was sufficient to promote the development of civilization.

Trade is a potent force in stimulating complexity, and it matters little whether the trade is with far-away lands or with nearby ones.

SIMILARITY AMID DIVERSITY IN SUB-SAHARAN AFRICA

This chapter has focused on only a few of the many civilizations that flourished throughout sub-Saharan Africa. We have not touched on the Mongo, the Loango, the Mande, the Bachwezi, the

WEST AND CENTRAL AFRICA	EAST AFRICA	SOUTHWEST AFRICA		
Jenne, 200–700			**200**	Asian crops arrive in East Africa, spread of iron metallurgy, and Bantu expansion begins, c. 200
			–	Arab and Axumite trade with East Africa, c. 300
			400	
			–	
			–	
			600	
			–	Inception of Arab trade in West Africa, c. 700
			800	Agriculture becomes important in Southwest Africa, c. 800
			–	Arab trade becomes common, c. 900
		Luba Kingdom, 1000–1600	**1000**	
			–	Conquest of Ghana, 1077
Mali, 1200–1400	Ife and Benin, 1200–1600	Great Zimbabwe, 1150–1600	Kongo Kingdom, 1200–1600	**1200**
			1400	Portuguese open slave trade in West Africa, 1440
			–	American crops arrive in West Africa, c. 1500
			1600	

Mossi, and many others with long and important histories. The sampling of societies discussed in this chapter, however, shows two major patterns in sub-Saharan African civilizations.

On the one hand, there is great diversity from place to place. Certainly the stone cities and towns of the East African coast would not be confused with the wood-mud-grass houses of villages in Southwest Africa. The details of culture, mythology, and language differed from place to place, and these differences formed the basis by which individuals identified with their societies.

On the other hand, probably more than on any other continent after the development of civilization, there is an essential similarity, largely political, among sub-Saharan African civilizations. Characteristics of government typically shared by these civilizations are:

— a state whose ruler has strong but rarely absolute power;

— an institutionalized system of confirming royal succession, so that an inept or undesirable heir in line to the throne by virtue of heredity can be excluded from leadership;

— a broad and institutionalized system of advisors; and

— an unusually high degree of formal political participation on the part of women.

All of these characteristics tend to have made these governments more responsive to a broad range of opinion within the realm, presumably better serving the people. None of these governments had full consent of the governed, but all had a greater element of responsiveness to public interests than many of their counterparts elsewhere.

These political similarities may be rooted in the Bantu expansion, the result of a single political form spreading out from a center of dispersal and then changing only gradually and slightly over the centuries, resulting in parallel structures. Alternatively, they may be the result of convergence, as different societies found the same solutions to the common problems of survival in the generally semiarid lands south of the Sahara. The answer must await more and better archaeological study of the period before A.D. 200.

SUMMARY

1. There were many regional states and a few empires in precolonial sub-Saharan Africa. Many of these were urban civilizations.

2. African civilization was based on agriculture using both locally domesticated and imported crops. Trade was an important spur to the development of civilization in many places.

3. Iron technology allowed the expansion of agriculture into African lands previously unavailable for farming. The Bantu expansion may have carried iron technology with it.

4. In West and Central Africa, early states such as Jenne developed largely through trade within sub-Saharan Africa.

5. Following the inception of trans-Saharan trade with the Arabs and Muslims, West and Central African states developed stronger governments, more pronounced class stratification, and larger urban systems. Also, many adopted Islam, largely because of the economic advantages.

6. The Ghana, Mali, and Songhai empires were civilizations of the savanna zone of West Africa. Forest states in West Africa, such as Ife and Benin, developed into civilizations somewhat later than the savanna states.

7. In coastal East Africa, settlements took advantage of trade with Asia and other lands along the rim of the Indian Ocean to develop a local elite and considerable wealth. While they sometimes took on the trappings of Arabia, they were indigenous African developments.

8. In interior East Africa, most peoples were at the tribe or chiefdom level. Zimbabwe, however, was an urban state that traded gold with the coastal settlements in order to support a powerful elite.

9. In Southwest Africa, kingdoms such as Luba and Kongo developed out of lineages. They were stimulated by the growth of trade within the region but—unlike other parts of Africa—not by interregional trade.

SUGGESTED READINGS

Connah, Graham. *African Civilizations.* Cambridge, Eng.: Cambridge University Press, 1987. A good treatment of the archaeological evidence regarding sub-Saharan states.

Fage, J. D., and Roland Oliver, gen. eds. *The Cambridge History of Africa.* Eight vols., each with a volume ed. Cambridge, Eng.: Cambridge University Press, 1975–85. A basic source.

Sherratt, Andrew, ed. *The Cambridge Encyclopedia of Archaeology.* New York/Cambridge, Eng.: Crown Publishers/Cambridge University Press, 1980. An excellent overview of the civilizations discussed in this chapter, focusing on the archaeological evidence.

Summers, Roger. *Zimbabwe: A Rhodesian Mystery.* Johannesburg, South Africa: Thomas Nelson and Sons, 1965. A popular treatment of Zimbabwe by a competent professional archaeologist; most useful for details on the discovery and early (mis)interpretation of the site.

UNESCO. *General History of Africa.* Eight vols., each with a volume ed. Paris: UNESCO, 1981–88. (Also reprinted by various publishers.) A very detailed treatment, especially focusing on the role of Islam in Africa; volumes III and IV are especially useful.

Shogun's *Vassal*.   *In this detail from a thirteenth-century scroll, a Japanese vassal (center) reads aloud the document that describes his rights and privileges over a territory granted to him by the shogun. The household reacts with pleasure and anticipation at the wealth and social status that this land will bring them. If this territory were large enough, the vassal could divide it into smaller estates and grant it to subordinates, who would then become his vassals.*   From the Eshi no Soshi (scroll), painting on silk, 13th century. Sakamoto Photo Research Laboratory, Tokyo.

Feudalism

I, John of Toul, affirm that I am the vassal of the Lady Beatrice, countess of Troyes, and of her son Theobald, count of Champagne, against every creature living or dead, excepting my allegiance to Lord Enjourand of Coucy, Lord John of Arcis, and the count of Grandpré. If it should happen that the count of Grandpré should be at war with the countess and count of Champagne . . . I will aid the count of Grandpré [myself] and will aid the count and countess of Champagne by sending them . . . knights. . . .

—JOHN OF TOUL

This excerpt comes from a document in which one medieval knight tried to work out the potentially conflicting obligations of serving more than one lord at a time. Many medieval knights had multiple obligations of service in feudal France, which was one of the most complex feudal structures in the world.

In Issue 2, we saw how models can be used to help us make comparisons and contrasts on a global level, and in this issue we will present a model of feudalism in order to compare several examples of empires or kingdoms that transformed to regional control. As with any model, generalizations sometimes camouflage the experiences of specific societies, but there is an advantage to these generalizations because they can help us see patterns and trends that are similar around the world. In feudalism's case, we can see how some overextended polities tried to maintain control over their territories.

THE FEUDAL MODEL

Feudalism is a decentralized sociopolitical structure in which a weak monarchy attempts to control the lands of the realm through reciprocal agreements with regional leaders. Some scholars do not like the term "feudalism" because it has been traditionally used to compare the history of medieval feudal France with the histories of other regions of the world, using Europe as the model, which limits the kind of comparisons one can make. If the term's definition takes on a more generic meaning, then European feudalism no longer acts as the paradigm by which other feudal systems are judged but becomes one among many feudal structures to study. In this issue we will use feudalism to examine several societies that experienced similar political episodes of regionalism in their histories.

The characteristics of a feudal society are:

—a decentralized administration indicative of weakened monarchical control (including an ineffective or nonexistent bureaucracy);

—regional leaders (members of an aristocratic warrior-elite) who receive land for use (economic exploitation, such as the collection of taxes, and jurisdictional authority, such as law courts, over large territories); and

—the receipt of these lands in exchange for loyalty oaths and military support of the monarch.

Feudalism usually emerges when a monarchy does not maintain central control over the realm. An example might be when empires expand to include vast territories that a monarch cannot easily control, resulting in the empire's breaking into regions with regional governance under a weak monarch. The breakup of an empire does not always end in feudalism but sometimes leads to a complete political collapse and the growth of new polities out of the remnants of the old. Feudalism, however, exists only in the presence of a nominal central ruler with limited power. If a monarch attempts centralization, regional leaders usually resist the efforts at encroachment onto their spheres of influence, sometimes resulting in hostilities that lead to a usurpation of the throne by a regional leader.

Feudal states include a system of land management wherein a monarch awards land use to a subordinate regional leader in return for a pledge of loyalty and military support. Additionally, the regional leader acts as a local governor, collecting taxes and tributes, maintaining judicial authority, and organizing local military units. The lands received are populated by peasants or commoners whose production financially supports the regional leader. In some cases, regional leaders reapportion lands to their own loyal followers, who become leaders of smaller areas; this process is called **subinfeudation**. In times of war, the monarch calls on the feudally obligated regional leaders (the aristocratic warrior-elite) to assemble with their vassals and fulfill their obligations of military aid. Regional leaders frequently take advantage of destabilization, occasionally engaging in rivalries or in challenges that end in outright rebellion. If the regional leader does not remain loyal to the monarch, theoretically the lands might be forfeited and granted to another, but only if the ruler is powerful enough to command his other regional leaders to fight on behalf of the monarchy.

FEUDAL SYSTEMS

Chinese, European, and Japanese societies all produced periods of feudalism. The feudal era in China dates from around 900 to around 400 B.C., in Europe from around A.D. 900 to around 1100, and in Japan from around A.D. 1200 to around 1600. Of course, because feudalism influences social structures and customs, many feudal elements continued to exist in these societies well after these dates. In each area, feudal relationships ebbed and flowed with the political tides of centralization and decentralization. A general review of Chinese, European, and Japanese histories reveals that their feudal structures were essentially the same and that a basic pattern of land use in exchange for military service is certainly present within the three societies.

China

The Late Zhou era (900–400 B.C.) was a period of decentralization in Chinese history. Our knowledge of these times is fragmentary, so we cannot precisely say how reciprocal relationships evolved and whether they extended much below the highest aristocratic level. Zhou rulers controlled their

FIGURE I.3.1 *Rebellious Vassals. Warfare in the Han Dynasty had changed little since China's feudal era. Occasionally, vassals seeking greater territories or privileges rose up against monarchs and their loyal vassals, as seen in this woodcut based on a second century A.D. carving. When ruling forces were defeated, dynasties changed or independent polities emerged. When loyal troops were victorious, rebel vassals lost both their lands and their lives, leaving their families dispossessed and orphaned.*

Stone Rubbing
from the Wu family shrine, Chiahsiang, Shantung. From *Chin-shih-so.* Photo by Eileen Tweedy.

territories through their regional leaders, consisting of old allies and kinsmen. Similar to the earlier Shang Period, kinship was sometimes fictive or arranged through marital ties. A ceremony existed that included the presentation of handfuls of dirt, representing the lands awarded, for oaths of loyalty and promises of support. The exchange of land for loyalty fits the feudal model.

In periods of strong rulers, those whose allegiance was suspect were forced to migrate to areas of dependable loyalty. When Zhou rulers remained relatively strong, they had control of their landed aristocrats, but when the monarchy became weak, they lost revenues, resulting in less tribute to the Zhou treasury. In addition, the landed aristocrats became increasingly hostile toward the ruler and one another.

In the Early Zhou Period, an embryonic bureaucratic system had been created. Administrators served as clerks and overseers, keeping records and performing as advisors or department heads for regional leaders, as well as for the monarch. A skilled professional bureaucracy was developing and becoming an important aspect in Chinese government. Yet, after a few generations, and certainly by the ninth century B.C., central power dissipated, and the local lords wielded considerable independence of the monarchy. The loss of central authority by the Zhou monarchy and the loss of bureaucratic control fit the pattern of the feudal model.

Allied regional leaders defeated the Zhou ruler, and, although the Zhou dynasty continued under weaker successors, warring persisted as regional leaders fought among themselves. Central power all but evaporated; similarly to the French royal lands in the European feudal period, the lands directly under the control of the Zhou ruler shrank to include only the capital and its supporting rural lands. China then entered the prolonged Warring States Period (403–221 B.C.), when regional leaders engaged in deadly rivalries, vying for power and influence. Eventually the regional leaders abandoned the imperial structure, leading China out of feudalism. Private ownership of land replaced the feudal practice of awarding land for military support, and regional leaders developed state bureaucracies to govern their territories.

Europe

Aspects of Roman and Germanic practices and customs from roughly A.D. 500 contributed to European feudalism, but the feudal structure emerged after the invasions of the ninth and tenth centuries spurred decentralization and regionalism, particularly in France. Feudalism in Europe, therefore, was part of an evolving process and was

FIGURE I.3.2 *Land Grants.* *This castle in Yorkshire, in northern England, was a manor granted to a loyal vassal. The castle is located in the center of the estate, the village spreads out along the road, and the fields surround the castle and the village. This organization reflects their interrelationship between the lord and the peasants: In feudal society peasants worked the land and produced the wealth that sustained the lifestyle of the vassals.* Aerofilms, Ltd.

closely associated with the Germanic custom of the king as gift giver.

In general, European feudalism consisted of the awarding of lands, called **fiefs**, to regional leaders by the king, who received oaths of loyalty and military support in return. The one who granted land was a lord, and the one who received land was a vassal. A fief could include large agricultural lands (and the peasants and serfs who worked them), towns, villages, or even church properties. The vassal was expected to support the lord's interests on and off the battlefield. In return, the lord represented the vassal before the law or in social matters, such as arranging marriages. Vassals usually fell under the legal jurisdiction of their lords. European feudalism was a complicated system of rights and privileges, as well as of land use.

The reapportionment of granted lands by the regional lords became very complex over time. Lords sometimes acquired additional lands and wealth by making themselves vassals of other lords. The feudal network, therefore, was not only a vertical hierarchy but also a horizontal entanglement of relationships (as is evidenced in the example of John of Toul at the opening of this issue). Any lord could be the lord of many vassals and simultaneously be a vassal of many lords. The idea of **liege lord**, one who had a greater feudal claim,

gave vassals a means to choose which lord to serve if competing demands were claimed. Although European feudalism became increasingly complex, it conforms to the basic feudal structure.

The granting of fiefs was carefully orchestrated with family and kin groups. Many regional vassals kept tight control of lands by giving fiefs only to family members or to the church, whose bishops, abbots, or other ecclesiastical officials could not leave church lands to heirs. A formal ceremony, similar to that in China, was performed that signified the process of becoming a vassal. This ceremony involved the action of paying homage to the lord, signifying the lord's authority over the vassal. If the fief had been held by one family for several generations, the tendency was to view the fief as a hereditary right.

Although feudal customs continued to dominate much of medieval European history, monarchs pressed for centralization in the eleventh century and supported growing bureaucracies that regained control of revenues and governance.

Japan

In Japan there was a long-lived practice of the warrior-elite class giving out lands in exchange for gathering a group of retainers who owed loyalty

FIGURE 1.3.3 *Investiture Ceremony.* *This thirteenth-century work depicts the ninth-century emperor Charlemagne in the traditional posture of granting privileges to a vassal. The vassal kneels before the king; his weaponless hands, positioned in prayer, are a sign of submission. Traditionally, a clod of dirt or a banner was presented to symbolize the territories awarded to the vassal. A sword, representing the vassal's military obligation to his monarch, might also be given.* Bibliothèque nationale, Paris.

and service to their lord, an arrangement that directly compares to the feudal model. Early Japanese aristocratic society was organized around a clan structure with subordinate social and economic groups bound to the clans through fictive kinship ties. From the seventh to the twelfth centuries, Japanese monarchs and aristocrats borrowed the Chinese political system and imposed it on their subjects, but this system eventually disintegrated.

By the twelfth century, a warrior-elite supplanted aristocrats on some lands and created its own governmental structure. Aristocrats had taken advantage of a decentralized landholding system by appointing their own agents as overseers of land parcels. These agents collected rent monies from peasants who tilled the plots. In exchange, the aristocrats gave power to these subordinates to collect the rents and fees from the tillers. This system was essentially a bureaucracy. The warrior-elite, however, ended this bureaucracy and gained economic and jurisdictional control of their own regions. They then founded the shogunates, three successive regional leaders' families that controlled Japan through ineffective emperors from the twelfth through the nineteenth centuries.

During that time, a whole series of reciprocal relationships involving loyalty oaths and obligations evolved that follow the pattern of the feudal model. **Daimyo**, retainers of the *shogun*, further subdivided lands among their own retainers, the *samurai*. This pattern of subinfeudation was very

similar to Europe's, but *samurai* usually served only one *daimyo*.

Central control by the warrior groups was strong in the thirteenth century, but the Mongol invasions of the 1270s and 1280s severely weakened this feudal system because the retainers who responded to the *shogun*'s call to defeat the invading Mongols were not given lands in reward for their successful efforts. Because Mongol lands were distant from Japan and the operation was defensive, there was no conquered territory to award to feudal retainers. This lack of reward weakened the *shogun-daimyo* relationship. The first shogunate fell some decades later, in 1333. The next shogunate was impotent in terms of control, and this impotence led to the regional wars of 1467 to 1568. During the third shogunate in the seventeenth century, more and more *samurai* moved off their lands and lost economic control of their territories. This process of relocation essentially ended feudalism in Japan as centralization reemerged.

FEUDAL-LIKE SOCIETIES

There are many examples of societies that manifested one or more of the characteristics of feudalism, particularly weak monarchical control or a type of strong regionalism. A society cannot be feudal, however, without tension between royal privilege and local autonomy. The Early Shang

Figure I.3.4 Samurai.
This daimyo *(center top) has assembled the vassals of his territories—the* samurai. *Many* samurai *were actually clansmen of the* daimyo, *who was in turn the vassal of the* shogun. *In many feudal societies, vassalage followed family lineage, which helped to keep land grants intact and provided a base of support when challenging lords or monarchs.*
Stephen Turnbull/Japan Archive.

Period and the Early Zhou Empire in China, the Harsha Empire in India, the Byzantine Empire in southeastern Europe, and the Carolingian Empire in western Europe had relationships of vassalage and land management, but the rulers retained central bureaucratic administrations that impeded regional leaders' power in local areas.

Feudalism does not include those areas where no central authority exists and lands and power are vested solely in regional aristocrats, even if one regional leader dominates an alliance of several regional leaders. After the breakup of the Mongol Empire, the monarchy toppled and independent allied states appeared. Some societies had strong regional alliances dominated by one regional leader but never developed a monarchy or central authority. Scholars identify the states that demonstrate some of the characteristics of feudalism but not all as being feudal-like.

FEUDAL CODES

Examining the codes of behavior from feudal China, Europe, and Japan helps us to see how feudal relationships and responsibilities work. In part, these codes were products of the particular social customs and warrior mentality. All warriors are bound in some way to their superiors by oaths of loyalty. The Chinese warriors were bound by a code of honorable or righteous behavior, ***li***, which under Confucian influences evolved into the virtues of the Chinese "gentleman." European knights were bound by a code of suitable behavior, **chivalry**, that encouraged the ideals of honesty, courtesy, and defense of the defenseless. The Japanese *samurai* were bound by a code of self-denial, indifference to adversity, and generosity to the less fortunate; in later centuries this code would be formalized as the ***bushido*** code. In each case, local customs and the lord's expectations influenced the codes.

Loyalty to one's superior was central to feudal structures in all three areas. The Chinese warrior was expected to travel many miles to attend the investiture ceremony, where allegiance and loyalty were pledged. Religious overtones helped to solidify the monarch's authority in the minds of the participants. It was not until later in the Warring States Period that regional leaders refused to go to the capital and participate in the ceremony. In Europe, as in China, a ceremony of investiture humbled the vassal in the presence of the lord. Kings expected their vassals to kiss their feet as an act of submission. In Japan, *samurai* were pledged to the service of their lord with extraordinary devotion.

They were never to question the instructions of their lord and were expected to shield him on the battlefield. The Japanese lord could even order the death of a *samurai* by ritual suicide.

In each feudal structure there was a variety of attention paid to the prescribed practices. But codes of behavior were not enough to control heavily armed warriors from taking advantage of the very people they were pledged to defend. Knights errant frequently broke the peace of Europe, for example, and their constant rivalries, in part, prompted religious leaders to initiate the First Crusade in order to establish peace. Like the legendary Robin Hood of England, Chinese knights errant championed the downtrodden and frequently challenged bureaucratic authority. Their exploits were popular in Chinese literature. Masterless *samurai* frequently bullied the local peasant populations and sometimes quarreled among themselves until violence settled the dispute. Loyalty to one's lord was usually observed when lords were able to dominate their retainers, but, when relationships changed, lords were increasingly unable to demand obedience. Often the oath taken was only as solid as the armor of the lord who demanded it.

COMPARING FEUDAL STRUCTURES

By comparing the feudal structures of China, Europe, and Japan, scholars can gain insight into how states have coped with decentralization and regionalism. General patterns can be used to create a model, which can then be used to study other societies facing similar challenges.

By definition, the basic characteristics of the model have to be found in all examples. In each of these cases, weak monarchies led to regionalism, and land was exchanged for the military support and loyalty of regional leaders to stop disintegration into smaller independent polities. Why would regional leaders retain a weak monarch? Comparison of the examples suggests one answer might be in the key characteristic of loyalty. Regional leaders often recognized the legitimacy of keeping weak monarchs through religious tenets of divine right of rule. In China the monarch ruled through the Mandate of Heaven, in Europe Christian monarchs ruled by the grace of God, and in Japan the *shogun* received legitimacy from the god-emperor.

In applying any model to a set of specific circumstances, however, instances of dissimilarity will be observed; the states studied here developed feudal practices that were not exactly alike. In European and Japanese feudalism, complex subinfeudation helped to organize and maintain several levels of the warrior-elite. In contrast, China probably did not develop an elaborate practice of subinfeudation; the feudal relationship remained at the highest aristocratic level. Unlike Chinese and Japanese feudal disputes, which led to periods of warring regions, European feudal disputes retreated from the battlefield into the emerging court system as monarchs regained central administration.

SUGGESTED READINGS

Bloch, Mark. *Feudal Society.* Two vols. Trans. by L. A. Manyon. Chicago: University of Chicago Press, 1961. This seminal work, first published in 1940, is still a standard on medieval feudalism.

Duus, Peter. *Japanese Feudalism.* Third edition. New York: Knopf/Random House, 1993. A standard work on Japanese feudalism.

Gernet, Jacques. *A History of Chinese Civilization.* Trans. by J. R. Foster. Cambridge, Eng.: Cambridge University Press, 1985. A general history of China.

Herlihy, David. *The History of Feudalism.* New York: Harper and Row, 1970; reprinted, London: Humanities Press, 1992. This primary sourcebook's selections clearly show elements of the European feudal structure.

Varley, H. Paul, Ivan Morris, and Nobuko Morris. *Samurai.* New York: Delacorte, 1970. A review of the Japanese *samurai* structure.

PART THREE EXAMINED REGIONALISM IN MANY parts of the world. Part Four will explore the resumption of empire building after times of regionalism in the Americas, Europe, and Asia. Political ambitions and desire for wealth propelled rulers to extend their domains far beyond their homelands. In fact, the new empires controlled larger areas than those discussed in Part Two. Control and expansion of trade routes brought commercial growth and economic prosperity on an unprecedented scale. Much of Eurasia and Africa was linked by a vibrant and thriving trade network that exchanged goods, technologies, ideas, and diseases at levels greater than ever.

Chapter 16 presents the empires of the Aztecs and Incas, governments that ruled vast areas. The Aztecs and Incas effectively integrated their subjects politically and economically into their empires. Europeans conquered these territories in the early sixteenth century. Chapter 17 examines the Byzantine Empire and assesses some of the reasons for its unusual longevity. The empire's domination of trade routes coming from Eurasia and Africa helped provide the economic foundation

AMERICAS	EURASIA-AFRICA

400
500 — Byzantine Empire
600
700
800
900
1000
1100
1200
1300
1400 — Aztec Empire
1500 — Inca Empire
1600

for the political longevity of the Byzantine state. Chapter 18 studies the reestablishment of imperial rule in East Asia. It also examines the unprecedented economic growth in China and the social changes generated by increasing economic opportunities. Chapter 19 analyzes the contradictory nature of the Mongol Empire, a state that was founded with great violence but one whose rulers encouraged commercial activity. The Mongols helped promote a trade network with sea and land routes linking Europe, Asia, and Africa. Economic prosperity affected many in these lands until a catastrophic epidemic effectively dampened transregional trade, causing political decay and economic bankruptcy.

PART FOUR

THE REEMERGENCE OF EXPANSIVE SOCIETIES

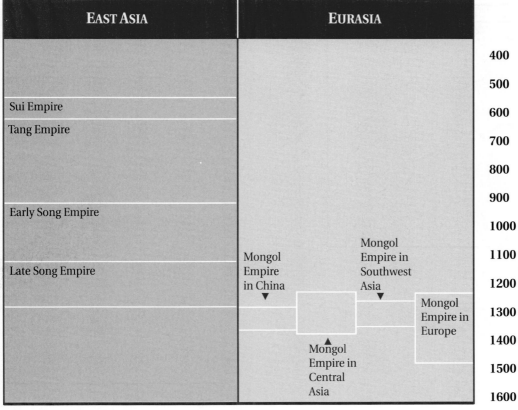

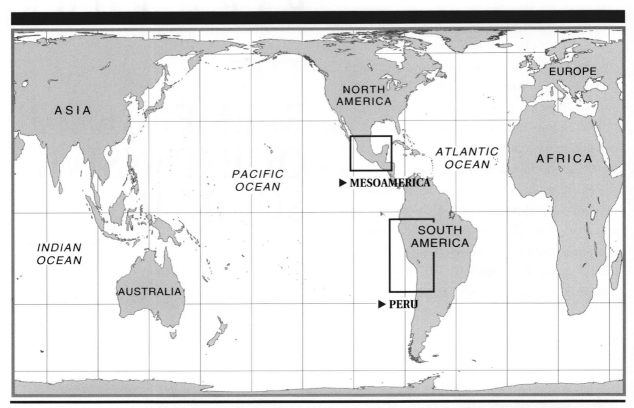

ASIA

EUROPE

NORTH
AMERICA

ATLANTIC
OCEAN

AFRICA

PACIFIC
OCEAN

► MESOAMERICA

INDIAN
OCEAN

SOUTH
AMERICA

AUSTRALIA

► PERU

AZTLÁN

Gulf of
Mexico

Culhuacán   Tenochtitlán
         Tlaxcala

Usumacinta R.

PACIFIC
OCEAN

► MESOAMERICA

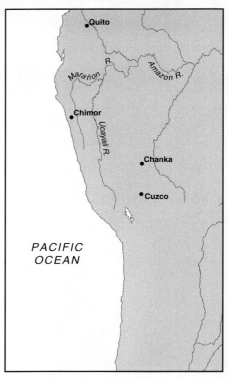

Quito

Marañón   R.   Amazon R.

Chimor

Ucayali R.

Chanka

Cuzco

PACIFIC
OCEAN

► PERU

The Americas on the Eve of European Contact

around 1300–1532

Under the rising full moon and clear skies of October 11, 1492, Guacanagarí, the chief of the Caribbean island of Guanahani, gazed out over the ocean surrounding his realm. Unbeknownst to him, Christopher Columbus and a boatload of sailors were anchored beyond his vision. The next morning, they would come ashore and greet the local Indians, changing forever the course of history. What were the Americas like on that sultry night as Guacanagarí peered into the twilight?

This chapter focuses on the latest societies of the Americas before contact with Europeans, ones that arose isolated from the rest of the world and were functioning entities at the time of European contact. It relates an essentially American story, and Europeans enter into it only as the agents truncating the Native American tradition.

The Nuclear American civilizations discussed here, those of the Aztecs and Incas, were among the most complex of pre-Columbian civilizations. They were surrounded by many other civilizations. Similarly, the North American societies treated here, the Iroquois, Hopi, and Navajo, are only a few of the many North American Indian groups extant in the sixteenth century.

THE AZTEC EMPIRE, 1325–1521

The Valley of Mexico, the site of present-day Mexico City, saw the rise and fall of Teotihuacán, the Toltecs, and many other peoples and states prior

FIGURE 16.1 *Tenochtitlán in 1519.* At the eve of the Spanish conquest, the Aztec capital of Tenochtitlán was a bustling city built around a central religious precinct, shown in this reconstruction. The Great Temple in the center had two stairways, one dedicated to Huitzilopochtli (the war god) and the other to Tlaloc (the rain god); other gods had separate temples or shrines within temples. David Hiser/Photographers Aspen.

to A.D. 1300. This rich environment encouraged the growth of population and accumulation of wealth, allowing states to develop and expand. The richest, most powerful, and most expansive of the pre-Columbian states of the Valley of Mexico was the last: the Aztec Empire.

From Aztlán to Tenochtitlán

The Aztecs did not originate in the Valley of Mexico. Rather, they began somewhere in the north, in a place they mythically designated Aztlán. While the location of Aztlán is not known exactly and has been claimed for such unlikely places as present-day northeastern New Mexico and southern Wisconsin, it almost certainly was somewhere in northwestern Mexico, probably around Durango. The people of Aztlán were not yet known as Aztecs and went by a number of names, including "Mexica,"[1] which they called themselves. They were part of a larger category of northern peoples collectively known as Chichimecs.

The Chichimecs were mobile tribes that lived by hunting, gathering, farming, and raiding. While some scholars claim them to have been at the tribe

level, most believe that the Mexica were a chiefdom at this point. The Chichimecs had been in contact with the Valley of Mexico since the time of Teotihuacán, whose northern colonies and mining communities were raided almost constantly by the warlike Chichimecs.

The Mexica migration was demanded by Huitzilopochtli, a god who spoke through his priests. Oral histories, written down in the fifteenth or sixteenth century, place the departure from Aztlán in 1111 and the arrival in the Valley of Mexico in 1325. The long trek was marked by incessant privations and hostilities with the peoples through whose land they passed. Wherever the Mexica stopped temporarily, they built a temple dedicated to Huitzilopochtli, suggesting that their travel was perhaps more in the nature of conquest.

Legend states that Huitzilopochtli told the Mexica priests that they would recognize the proper place to settle by an eagle perched on a prickly pear cactus, a sight they finally saw in the Valley in Mexico. They settled there and founded their capital, Tenochtitlán,[2] meaning "place of the fruit of the prickly pear cactus." This mythic found-

[1] **Mexica:** meh SHEE kuh

[2] **Tenochtitlán:** teh nohch tee TLAHN

ing is pictured on the Mexican flag. Archaeology tells us that the Mexica founded short-lived settlements in the northern parts of the Valley of Mexico in their early years there and that Tenochtitlán was founded around the date indicated in the mythic history.

The Valley of Mexico was far from empty of people when the Mexica arrived. Immigrant Chichimecs of other tribes had swollen the already large population of the region, and the Mexica were not welcomed by the inhabitants. The Mexica were seen as competitors demanding land, and their military prowess was not lost on the local rulers. Further, the Mexica had customs that alienated their neighbors. One notable example occurred in 1325, when the daughter of Coxcox,[3] king of the neighboring state of Culhuacán,[4] was to wed a Mexica noble. The woman arrived at the Mexica city, and, under command from Huitzilopochtli, priests sacrificed her and removed her skin to be worn by a priest. Many Mesoamerican peoples sacrificed people, but even the Mexica rarely sacrificed a royal bride, and, when her father arrived the next day, he was understandably shocked. In his anger, Coxcox led his warriors against the Mexica, who were forced to move on.

By 1345, the Mexica had refined their diplomatic skills. They realized that they were feared by their neighbors, and they used their reputation to their own advantage. Through a skillful combination of treaties and warfare, the Mexica carved out their place in the Valley of Mexico, developed their capital city, and established their political control of the area. With this process they came to be known as the "Aztecs," and upon this basis they built the Aztec Empire.

Aztec Society

The Aztecs had only a short history of intensive agriculture. In their Chichimec past, they had practiced agriculture as an adjunct to hunting and gathering, but their new life in the Valley of Mexico demanded a greater food supply than the old ways could provide, so they developed new means of producing food. Mostly they adopted agricultural crops and techniques already in use in the Valley of Mexico. Of paramount importance were **chinampas**, fields formed by dredging nutrient-rich mud

[3] **Coxcox:** KOSH kosh
[4] **Culhuacán:** kool hwah KAHN

from lake bottoms and forming fertile artificial islands by piling it in shallow water. *Chinampas* were very important to the Aztecs, who had been forced into areas with large numbers of lakes. The labor investment for *chinampas* was great, but so was the return: Aztec *chinampas* provided as much food per unit area as any agricultural technique known today. And in addition, *chinampas* were a self-sustaining system that required no fertilizing, irrigation, or flushing to remove salts deposited by irrigation. Largely forced into this labor-intensive strategy by the shortage of arable land, the Aztecs developed one of the most efficient forms of agriculture known anywhere in the world.

Religion permeated every aspect of Aztec life, especially for the elite. The Aztecs had many gods, chief of whom was Huitzilopochtli. Other important gods included Quetzalcóatl and Tlaloc (the rain god), both inherited from Teotihuacán and the Toltecs. These and other gods competed with one another for human attention, and all demanded sacrifices. Many of these sacrifices consisted of destroying inanimate objects, killing animals, or simply letting the blood of priests, but some of them required killing human beings. While human sacrifice was practiced by most Mesoamerican civilizations, the Aztecs conducted their sacrifices at a scale previously unknown, sometimes sacrificing thousands of people in a multiday ritual.

The reason underlying human sacrifice was simple: The gods were thought to demand sacrifices in return for continued well-being. The sun required blood to continue its transit; the seasons required blood to return on schedule; less important needs could be satisfied by a sacrifice of flowers or inanimate objects. But most important, the universe itself was renewed every fifty-two years, at the end of each calendric cycle, and failure to provide the proper sacrifices at this dangerous period could result in total destruction of the sort that had occurred several times before, according to Aztec mythology. Because of this context, sacrifice was considered an honor. Some people volunteered, others were selected on the basis of their merit, and warriors captured in battle—particularly valiant or noble ones—often were sacrificed. In fact, this need for captives probably was one incentive for the near-constant warfare that characterized Aztec history.

FIGURE 16.2 *Modern* **Chinampa.** *In order to support their vast capital, the Aztecs needed to increase the agricultural productivity of the surrounding area. To do so, they developed* chinampas, *gardens made by piling mud into the shallow waters of Lake Texcoco, on which the island city of Tenochtitlán was built. Still in use, these* chinampas *increased the amount of land available for cultivation and created some of the most fertile farmland anywhere. Though sometimes called "floating gardens," they were firmly anchored to the lake bottom.* David Hiser/Photographers Aspen.

As well as sacrifices, the gods needed imposing places dedicated to their worship, and the temple-pyramids served this purpose. Clearly descendent from earlier Teotihuacano temple-pyramids, these huge stone edifices had temples on their tops, and this is where sacrifice and other devotions took place, including divination and the reading of omens. The scale and majesty of these pyramids awed the Spanish *conquistadores* who beheld them.

The gods also legitimized the hierarchy that permeated Aztec society. At the top were the nobles, viewed as descendants of Quetzalcóatl and sharing in his divine nature, and rulers could come only from this class. At the top of the noble class were the ***tlatoani***,[5] the monarchs ruling cities and surrounding regions, and the Aztec emperor. Upon the death of a *tlatoani*, candidates would be named from the eligible family, and then the candidate deemed most capable would be elected by male nobles. This combination of hereditary kingship and election was established by Acamapichtli,[6] the first Aztec monarch.

The primary roles of noblewomen seem to have been as wives and mothers. The ideal noble-

[5] ***tlatoani:*** tlah toh AH nee
[6] **Acamapichtli:** ah kah mah PEECH tlee

woman was said to be respectful of her husband and unintrusive into his affairs. She was supposed to be quiet and decorous, and she was supposed to be a skilled weaver who practiced her art as a symbol of her domestic role. A woman in childbirth was thought of as a warrior of sorts and, if she died during the birth, was eligible for the heaven otherwise reserved for warriors who died in battle.

Beneath the *tlatoani* and other nobles were various categories of commoners, also in a hierarchy. Near the top were merchants and artisans, and below them were agriculturalists, laborers, and slaves. Slave status usually was acquired by selling oneself into slavery and was open to both men and women.

While slavery status was permanent, it was not passed on to one's children, and it was not particularly onerous. People selling themselves into slavery would be paid a certain amount one year before the slavery commenced; after that year, they became slaves, and their labor was controlled by their owners, who had certain obligations to them in terms of support. Slaves could own property (including other slaves), marry, and retain most of their legal rights. Most individuals selling themselves into slavery were impoverished, often from gambling, and used their payment to settle debts.

The Aztecs used art as one means of differentiating the different classes. **Sumptuary laws**, regulations stating what clothing and ornaments could be worn legally only by members of a certain class, provided a means by which a person's class immediately could be identified. Feather headdresses, for example, were reserved for the *tlatoani*. These magnificent constructions, often five or more feet high, were built on wooden frames and might contain 20,000 brightly colored feathers from tropical birds; some were so ornate and large that servants were needed to help support their massive weight.

One of the most highly valued arts was poetry. All elite men were expected to be skilled orators; in fact, *tlatoani* translates literally as "speaker." Nahuátl,[7] the language of the Aztecs, was much given to metaphor, and Aztec poetry pondered the meaning of life, the beauty of flowers, and the anguish of leaving one's home upon achieving

[7] **Nahuátl:** nah HWAHT

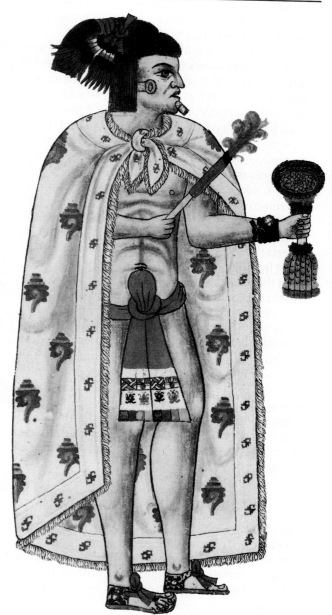

**FIGURE 16.3 *Noble Aztec Headdress.* *The social position of an Aztec man was indicated by clothing and other symbols. The noble shown in this Aztec illustration wears a fancy but modest headdress in keeping with his station in life. The* tlatoani, *in contrast, wore a huge feather headdress mounted on a wooden frame, featuring rare feathers of the quetzal bird, attached with glue made from orchid roots and bound with hammered gold spacers and studs.* Bibliothèque nationale, Paris.

adulthood. Poetry and human sacrifice may seem incongruous to the modern reader, but they were perfectly harmonious to the Aztec elite.

Writing was a skill shared by most nobles and by those commoners whose profession demanded it. The written Nahuátl language was glyphic, so it looked like a series of pictures, each of which referred to a particular concept. The Aztecs, however, had no fixed rules regarding glyph order, and a certain amount of experience and creativity was necessary to read a passage. The Aztecs wrote books on society, morality, accounting, administration, poetry, science, and many other subjects, but most were destroyed by the Spanish during the conquest. Fortunately, a few have survived, as have some copies of earlier books with notes by Spanish priests that explain how these texts should be read.

The lifeways of commoners were less varied than those of the elite. Most commoner men were farmers or laborers; most commoner women ran a household and might also be weavers or physicians. For most of these commoners, the ***calpulli***,[8] or residential unit, was the major orienting point. The *calpulli* was a district of a community, where land was held at least partly in common. *Calpulli* provided certain institutional services, including schools (for boys only) and temples. In addition, *calpulli* elected local officials and conducted taxing, censuses, and public works. For commoners, the *calpulli* was the most accessible level of government.

Politics and the Aztec Empire

The Aztecs passed gradually from a local state to an empire. The founding of the Aztec royal house was in 1372, when Acamapichtli ascended to the throne, justifying his legitimacy through the lineage of his mother, a princess of Culhuacán. Because *tlatoani* were elected, the Aztec rulership could and often did pass from brother to brother; women were excluded from rulership. As the Aztecs came to dominate the Valley of Mexico and beyond, the *tlatoani* of Tenochtitlán gradually became the Aztec emperors.

At its height just before 1520, the Aztec Empire extended from the Atlantic to the Pacific, from northern parts of present-day Guatemala to the northern edge of the central highlands of Mexico.

[8] ***calpulli:*** kahl POO lee

Although a few pockets of resistance successfully held out against the Aztecs, most notably the Tarascans on the west coast, most peoples within this area clearly were under Aztec domination.

The Aztecs integrated peoples who had been brought into the empire by military or diplomatic means. Conquered peoples were permitted to retain their own religion and government, but they took on obligations to the Aztecs. First, they had to provide tribute to the emperor. This tribute was explicitly specified in documents originating in Tenochtitlán and might consist of a mixture of everyday items (corn, cotton cloth, and animal hides) and luxury items (tropical feathers, cacao, and turquoise). Second, conquered peoples were expected to serve as allies in future wars. Third, they were expected to worship the central gods of the Aztecs, in addition to their own traditional gods. Finally, they were expected to contribute individuals for the human sacrifices required by Mesoamerican religions.

For many conquerors, establishing a stable empire is the primary goal, permitting the conqueror to reap the material benefits of conquest. While the demand for tribute shows that material benefit was important to the Aztecs, they had another need to fill: captives for sacrifice. Consequently, the Aztecs did not wish to consolidate their conquests to the point that further warfare would be unnecessary. Indeed, Tenochtitlán and Tlaxcala, a neighboring state, conducted ritualized warfare regularly for the express reasons of training troops and mutually obtaining captives for sacrifice.

The Aztec military was equipped with spears, arrows, swords with obsidian blades and tips, slings, and clubs, and was finely trained in their use. They wore cotton armor, which was very effective against most of these weapons. They were organized into military companies, some of which were based on *calpulli* and some of which were elite forces. Although books on tactics have not survived, warfare of the Aztecs clearly demonstrates that they had well-developed tactical theories.

In addition to their military strength, the Aztecs used ***pochteca***, merchants who also served as diplomats and spies. The *pochteca* traveled widely outside the empire, because foreign trade was their specialty. While conducting their trade, they gathered information of potential military

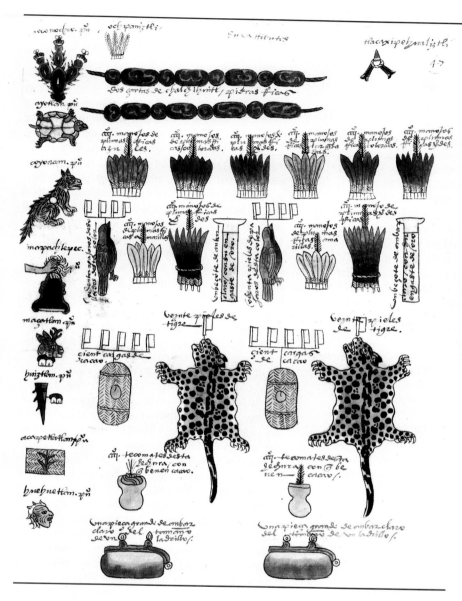

FIGURE 16.4 *Aztec Tribute List.* *The central imperial government of the Aztecs kept track of the tribute obligations of dependent allies through written documents. This copy of a tribute list was made just a few years after the Spanish conquest and shows some of the items rendered as payment, including jade beads, bundles of exotic feathers, cacao beans, and jaguar skins. The small feathers and flags projecting upward from the objects are Aztec glyphs indicating numbers; the images in the vertical row on the left are the names of tributary states; the Spanish writing is a sixteenth-century translation.* The Bodleian Library, University of Oxford.

value and sometimes negotiated with foreign powers. Once an area was conquered, their job was done; what had formerly come to Tenochtitlán as trade would then come as tribute. While the ideal *pochteca* was decorous and self-effacing, front teeth filed to points must have presented a fearsome appearance to potential trading and diplomatic partners, enhancing the *pochteca*'s reputation for being dangerous.

Montezuma II was elected to the posts of *tlatoani* of Tenochtitlán and Aztec emperor in 1502. By all accounts he was a generally able ruler,

extending the boundaries of the empire and maintaining the operation of the state. In 1519, a force of Spanish soldiers commanded by Hernando Cortés landed in eastern Mexico, bent on the conquest of Mexico. The Aztecs, of course, had no idea that the Spanish existed, and the sudden appearance of strange people in their territory was unsettling; this was especially true because rumors were circulating that the Spanish were gods, perhaps the Quetzalcóatl and his divine retinue, who myths said would return from the east someday. The Spanish advanced, collecting disaffected peoples

A few of the Aztec books, called **codices** (singular, **codex**), have survived intact, and one of these is the *Florentine Codex*. Named for the city where it was preserved after the conquest, the *Florentine Codex* discusses many aspects of Aztec life, including proper behavior, religious rituals, and professions. It was dictated to Spanish scribes in the Aztec language and written in Roman letters; a Spanish translation, marginal notes, and illustrations (some with Aztec writing included) were then added. The translated excerpts that follow describe a few of the sacrifices and divining practices that preceded the departure of a major trading expedition. They provide an insight into how thoroughly religion and trade were interwoven in the Aztec mind.

IN THEIR OWN WORDS

Merchants in the Aztec Empire

And when they [the merchants] were about to set out, then they sought a good day sign—One Serpent . . . One Crocodile, or One Monkey, or Seven Serpent.[a] The vanguard merchants who had read the day signs knew on which one they would set out. And when it was the day before they would set out on a good day sign, thereupon they once and for all washed their heads with soap and cut their hair here in Mexico. And all the time that they went traveling in Anauac, nevermore did they wash their hair with soap [or] cut their hair.[b] They only bathed up to their necks, not submerging in water; all the time they traveled abstaining. And when night had fallen, when the time of blowing shell trumpets[c] arrived, thereupon they began cutting lengths of paper. . . . Then they painted it with liquid rubber. They impaled the [lump of] rubber on a spit; thereupon they set it on fire. As it continued to burn, so they painted. And thus did they paint the paper: they gave it lips, nose, eyes. It resembled a man. Thus did they make a representation of the fire [god]. [After cutting other paper representations of gods] all their offerings were arranged together in the middle of the courtyard, whereupon they entered their home [and] stood before the fire. There they beheaded a quail [to honor the fire]. When they had beheaded it, thereupon, with pointed obsidian blades, they pierced their ears, or they pierced their tongues. When the blood already flowed, they took it with their hands [and] said, "*Teonappa*,"[d] when they cast it into the fire. Thereupon they spattered the papers with it. . . . Thereupon he [the merchant] offered the paper to the fire. As he offered it, then he took white copal [incense] . . . then he inserted it among the papers so that it would blaze up well. And he stood watching it closely as it burned, taking good care of it. If the paper only smoked, when it did not burn well, he was much frightened. There he saw that perhaps a sickness would somewhere go to seize him. But if it burned quickly, so that it crackled [and] popped a great deal, he was greatly pleased thereby. He said within himself, "He hath been good to me, the master, our lord.[e] I shall indeed reach the place where I am to go." And when they had assembled indeed all the loads, they thereupon arranged them on carrying frames; they set one each on the hired burden-carriers to carry on their backs: Not very heavy, they put on only a limited amount. . . . Then they went forth [and] proceeded straightaway to the boats. None entered the women's quarters, neither did they turn back [or] look to one side. If perchance he had gone forgetting something, he might no more come to take it, nor might they still go to offer it to him. No longer could he do it. Neither did even one of all the old merchants [and] merchant women go following them. When one turned back they thought it an omen of evil—sinful; they regarded it as dangerous. In this manner did the vanguard merchants depart.

[a] These dates in the Aztec calendar were considered particularly auspicious for travel.
[b] This was a departure from normal behavior, because the Aztecs viewed personal hygiene and cleanliness as very important.
[c] Shell trumpets were sounded in Aztec cities at dusk.

[d] This word, although not fully translatable, begins with a root meaning "god."
[e] Referring to a patron god.

of the Aztec Empire with them as allies, and marched on Tenochtitlán. After initial setbacks, the Spanish captured Montezuma; his apparent capitulation alienated his subjects, and he died under mysterious circumstances—perhaps murdered by the Spanish, perhaps killed by his own people. (This mystery is examined in the "In Their Own Words" box in Chapter 1.)

By this time, the Aztecs had elected Cuitlahuac[9] as the new *tlatoani*, and he was able to rally his forces to drive the Spanish from the city. The success was only short lived, however, because Cuitlahuac and many other Aztecs had been infected with smallpox and died within a few months. The Spanish laid siege to Tenochtitlán and captured it in 1521, sacking it and massacring huge numbers of its inhabitants. This effectively crushed the Aztec Empire.

How could a force of only a few hundred Spanish conquer a major empire? Certainly Montezuma's initial vacillation was a factor. Spanish military technology also was superior to that of the Aztecs, and the horse gave the Spanish an advantage, but the most important factors probably were goals and disease. The Spanish were fighting a war of killing and conquest; the Aztecs were trying to take captives. Each was practicing war as experience dictated, and the ensuing interaction favored the Spanish. And perhaps most important, the Spanish brought smallpox and other germs with them, inadvertently but effectively destroying huge numbers of the Aztecs and mortally disrupting their society. Pockets of resistance held out for almost seventy years, but effective native rule of Mexico ended in 1521.

THE INCA EMPIRE, 1438–1532

At about the same time that the Aztecs were coming to dominate Mesoamerica, the Incas were rising in Peru. After the collapse of the Tiahuanaco Empire about A.D. 1100, Cuzco was one of the many regional kingdoms of Peru that took its place. In the four centuries that followed, Cuzco expanded to control the largest empire in the pre-Columbian Americas. From its position high in the Andes, Cuzco governed the Empire of Tawantinsuyu[10]—"Land of the Four Quarters"—commonly called the Inca Empire. (**"Inca"** accurately refers to the ruler of the empire, not the empire itself or its people, but we will follow the common practice of using "Inca" to describe the empire and people; the leader will be called the "the Inca emperor.") Because the Incas had no writing, events before the coming of the Spanish are based on legendary history and archaeology.

The Cuzco State Becomes the Inca Empire

Protected by mountains, Cuzco was a small and undistinguished state in southern Peru following the breakup of the Tiahuanaco Empire. Around 1438, Cuzco was ruled by a monarch named Viracocha.[11] Chanka, a neighboring state, was emboldened by Viracocha's weak response to their challenges and attacked Cuzco. Most of Cuzco's allies waited to see the outcome before committing themselves, and Viracocha and his heir abandoned the city to seek refuge in the mountains. Another of Viracocha's sons rallied the soldiers of Cuzco, who repulsed the Chanka, chased them to their homeland, and conquered them. The son was proclaimed the new ruler and assumed the name Pachacuti.[12] Pachacuti was a relentless conqueror, and within a few decades he and his heirs led military expeditions that extended the realm of Cuzco from Ecuador to northern Chile.

Of course, diplomacy went hand in glove with warfare. The Inca emperor had a standard course of action when he wished to bring a new state into the empire, as exemplified by the conquest of the Masqo.[13] The ruler first sent spies to ascertain the condition of the Masqo state, especially its military strength and alliances. Then he sent emissaries to the ruler of Masqo, offering gifts and privileges if Masqo voluntarily would become part of the empire. When the Masqo ruler refused, the Incas tried to woo away his allies, isolating Masqo. Only if a state still refused to join the empire would military action be taken against it.

[9]**Cuitlahuac:** kweht lah HOO ahk

[10]**Tawantinsuyu:** tah wahn tihn SOO yoo
[11]**Viracocha:** veer ah KOHCH uh
[12]**Pachacuti:** pah chah KOO tee
[13]**Masqo:** MAH skoh

The military forces of the Inca Empire were equipped and organized similarly to those of their enemies. Important weapons were clubs, slings, bows and arrows, and spears; leather armor and helmets were used by at least some soldiers. As the Incas absorbed conquered peoples, the ranks of the Inca armies swelled, so that they usually outnumbered their enemies in later years of the empire.

The Incas used both humane and brutal measures as alternatives in dealing with conquered peoples. They generally had a reputation for fair treatment of prisoners and conquered peoples. Typically, at the conquest of a state, prisoners were set free and leaders were given gifts, reducing any incentive to fight on indefinitely. Further, the local government usually was incorporated into the imperial government, and leaders often retained their positions under the changed circumstances. Such humane practices reportedly encouraged states and individuals to surrender to the Incas. These humane actions were more a matter of practicality than morality. In this way, an initially small state was able to extend dominion over a huge area, sometimes conquering states far stronger than it and generally avoiding exhausting its resources in protracted military actions.

But the Inca Empire was capable of drastic and brutal expedients: When regions persisted in rebelling, their populations could be relocated, often hundreds of miles away in a radically different environment. The challenges of survival became so great that political unrest was quelled. Sometimes this system of population relocations was applied immediately to a conquered province if it was felt that uprisings might be forthcoming; sometimes groups from established parts of the empire were relocated to newly conquered regions to serve as model citizens.

The Inca approach to empire building was very different from that of the Tiahuanaco Empire, which preceded it. While Tiahuanaco imposed its stamp heavily on conquered states, the Incas left them as intact as possible, using existing governmental organizations. Rather than recast a region, the Incas simply added it to the ever-growing imperial organization. The only requirements for a new province were four: It had to incorporate Inti[14] (the Incas' sun god) into its pantheon, it had to

Figure 16.5 *Inti, the Inca Sun God.* *Inti, depicted here in a woven tapestry from around 1450, was the supreme god of the Incas. His role in the maintenance of the universe was considered paramount, his worship was mandatory for any peoples entering Inca territory, and his likeness appeared throughout the Inca Empire.* British Museum/Photo by Derek Witty.

submit to the rule of the Inca emperor, it had to render tribute to Cuzco, and it had to participate in the economic exchange system controlled by the imperial government at Cuzco. In return, Cuzco extended imperial military protection, provided preferential trading agreements, and incorporated gods of conquered peoples into its ever-expanding pantheon.

Such a massive empire, especially in such rugged territory, required an efficient transporta-

[14] **Inti:** EEN tee

tion and communication system. The Inca roads and *chaski* (runners), discussed briefly in Chapter 3, provided this. The empire built thousands of miles of paved roads, hundreds of suspension bridges spanning dizzying chasms, and hundreds of staircases cut into the steep sides of mountains. *Chaski* were state employees who carried messages or small packages rapidly, each runner traveling only a couple of miles to the next. Slower transportation of bulkier items was over the same routes, using llamas or people as carriers. As elsewhere in the Americas, no wheeled vehicles were used; indeed, the steep slopes and stairs of many Inca roads would have prevented their safe or efficient use.

The Inca Empire was extremely successful, but it had a serious weakness: succession of the emperor. Rulers and their families were viewed as direct descendants of Inti, and only they were eligible for consideration as emperor. (To ensure divine blood, members of the ruler's family were permitted to marry only their siblings.) From within the royal family, however, any male could serve as the Inca emperor. In early times, the emperor designated his own successor, and that candidate was confirmed by the **ayllu**,[15] a kind of cabinet of nobles appointed by the ruler to advise him. As time went on, however, this system became unwieldy. Rulers tended to take more of the authority of appointing a successor, yet several emperors died unexpectedly in their youth and had designated no successor. These instances led to factionalism and civil war, factors that facilitated the Spanish conquest of Peru in the sixteenth century.

Inca Society

Inca society was based on the same food crops as its predecessors: potatoes, quinoa, corn, beans, and chilis. What changed under the Incas was the way these crops were distributed throughout the empire. In earlier periods, people ate foods that were available locally. If possible, a community farmed at different elevations to take advantage of the different climates and range of crops that could be grown; this agricultural strategy is called **verticality**. The Incas carried verticality one step farther, moving crops considerable distances over

[15] **ayllu:** EYE yoo

FIGURE 16.6 *Inca Bridge over the Apurímac River. The Andes are dissected by thousands of deep gorges between mountains, and the Inca road system had to provide ways to cross these efficiently. A common solution was to build bridges like the one shown here, a suspension bridge made of rope spun locally from grass fiber. This Inca bridge, and dozens of others like it, has been maintained for the last five centuries by local villagers.* Loren McIntyre.

the excellent roads and allowing people in the coastal deserts of the north to eat highland foods.

This was not the only economic difference between the Inca Empire and its predecessors, nor even the most important. The Incas practiced public ownership and administration of land, and all production was viewed as the property of the state. Consequently, that production was gathered together, then redistributed by the state according to what it saw as need. On the one hand, this was a

FIGURE 16.7 *Inca Coca Users.* *The coca bush, from whose leaves cocaine is refined, is native to the Andes. The Incas and their predecessors used coca leaves as a drug. The leaves were chewed with lime, which was kept in a small dipping bottle dangling from the larger container for leaves, shown in this sixteenth-century drawing. The Inca government used coca as a tool of control, fostering addiction among miners and other state laborers engaged in particularly grueling work. The drug made the workers less susceptible to pain and incapable of serious uprisings.* Institut d'Ethnologie, Musée de l'Homme.

benign system, because it meant that a regional crop failure would have little effect on that region's inhabitants; surpluses from elsewhere could take up the slack. On the other hand, it was a powerful agent of control by the Inca government, which could withhold food from an area in order to force compliance with its policies.

The Inca Empire controlled the labor of its citizens. Most of the time, people were expected to go about their regular tasks, but for about one month out of a year, healthy men were obliged to contribute their time for the good of the state; this is known as **corvée labor.** *Corvée* labor was used primarily for military service and the construction of public works, such as roads. Sometimes *chaski* served under *corvée* labor.

Coca, the plant from which cocaine is extracted, grows abundantly in the Andes, and its production was controlled by the state. Men were allocated a modest amount of coca leaves for personal use, and most men seem to have been moderate in their use of it, though art occasionally depicts a glassy-eyed man with a wad of leaves in his mouth, apparently an abuser. Larger allocations were distributed to workers in particular industries, especially mining, to help them endure pain and increase their output.

As could be expected, given the nature of Inca conquest, religion varied tremendously from place to place. There were, however, a few commonalities. First, Inti was worshiped everywhere; this was necessary if the divine nature of the Inca emperor was to be acknowledged. Second, in most areas, there was a cult of the dead. Ancestors were revered, burial places were accorded special importance, and many corpses were wrapped and placed in such a manner that they became mummified. Third, human sacrifice took place, although on a small scale, particularly the sacrifice of children, whose youth was thought to ensure that they were uncorrupted by the vices of maturity.

An excellent example of the diversity of society and religion within the Inca Empire is the acceptance of homosexuality. In the deserts of the northern coastal part of the empire, the Chimú[16] people were a late addition to the Inca Empire, conquered only in the late fourteenth century. The Chimú not only tolerated homosexual behavior but required it in certain priestly rituals. Their mythology

[16]**Chimú:** chee MOO

PARALLELS AND DIVERGENCES

Human Sacrifice around the World

The Spaniards who chronicled their entry into the Americas were shocked by the human sacrifice they encountered, especially in Mexico and parts of the Caribbean and South America. They considered such practices to be proof of the natives' debased nature and evidence that they worshiped the devil. What they didn't realize was that human sacrifice at one time or another has been prominent in a wide range of societies on every inhabited continent, including the Spaniards' own Europe. Historically speaking, human sacrifice should be seen as a relatively common practice, not something restricted to a few aberrant societies.

As usually defined, human sacrifice is the killing of a person as part of a religious ritual. Peoples practicing human sacrifice usually have considered the victim an offering to a deity. Accordingly, the person offered must be a desirable, perhaps noble, person, certainly not a despised individual. Contrary to the popular impression, sacrificed individuals rarely were killed against their will; rather, as with the Christian martyrs under Roman persecution, dying in this prescribed manner was often seen as an honor that ensured one a place in heaven or its equivalent. Among the Aztecs, even captives taken in battle probably were honored by their sacrifice, because they worshiped the same gods and subscribed to the same general beliefs as the Aztecs.

The roster of societies that have practiced some form of human sacrifice is impressively long. The Sumerians sacrificed servants and others at the death of a king, and the sacrifices were buried with the king. The ancient Hebrews and their Phoenician neighbors sacrificed human beings in beseeching gods for favors or in atonement for great sins. People of the Roman Empire, especially under the influence of mystery cults, sacrificed people, as did those of ancient Egypt, Hindu India, first-millennium Japan, Zhou China, the Benin and Dahomey kingdoms of Africa, Polynesian kingdoms in Hawaii and New Zealand, Cahokia of pre-Columbian North America, native Australia, and Borneo. Europeans practiced human sacrifice as late as the medieval era, and the bog bodies discussed in Chapter 1 are an example of human sacrifices. The roster of societies practicing human sacrifice is so great that it cannot be viewed merely as an aberration.

Why has human sacrifice been so common? Probably the answer lies in the relationship that most societies have with their deities, who can be compelled—or at least encouraged—to provide something if the people who worship them perform the correct activity with the proper attitude. If a community is willing to give up one of its best to sacrifice, how can a god or goddess refuse them a favor? Sacrificing one person is thought to produce a divine obligation to stop the plague, to bring rain, or to send away the invaders. Sometimes the victim has been seen as a scapegoat, absorbing the wrongdoing of the entire community and cleansing it, but the essential petition to the deity remains the same.

---

included many examples of homosexual, transvestite, or androgynous deities, and their art commemorated these myths and rituals, often in graphic detail. In contrast, along the southern coast of the empire, homosexuality was generally frowned upon, certainly was not integrated into religious activities, and appears to have been relatively uncommon.

Through most of the Inca Empire, ceremonial centers with little or no permanent population served as centers for worship. In the highlands these featured temples made of huge, irregularly cut stones fit together very precisely; in the lowlands, temples were made of mudbrick. Many of the ceremonies were for the elite only, but commoners also made pilgrimages to these shrines.

The Inca approach to empire building did not encourage the development of a great art style. Indeed, provinces were encouraged to continue their traditional art styles, and representations of Inti around the empire took many forms.

Inca social structure was based on a hierarchy that placed the emperor and his family at the top, other nobles immediately below, and commoners

FIGURE 16.8   *Inca Architecture from Machu Picchu.*   *Inca architecture throughout the highlands shares several distinctive characteristics. The wall at the left shows large blocks, carefully shaped so that they fit together with essentially no crevices between them; sometimes the blocks are six or more feet across. The peaked roof in the background is that of a brewing house where* chicha, *a corn beer, was made and sold. Machu Picchu is located on the eastern, rainy side of the Andes, and the peaked roofs help to keep the town dry during the rainy season.*   Mireille Vautier/Woodfin Camp & Associates.

far below them. Beneath the commoners were **yanakuna,**[17] a status usually translated as "slaves," though little is known about them. The scant information we have on women suggests that they had very little political or economic power and were expected to find their primary roles as wives and mothers.

An Experiment in Private Ownership

While land in general was owned by the empire, the Incas did experiment with the private ownership of property. Beginning around 1480, members of the nobility who had rendered special service to the empire were granted tracts of land in part of the Urubamba[18] Valley, near Cuzco. This healthful and pleasant area became a playground for the elite.

There is considerable disagreement about how to interpret this phenomenon. Some scholars believe that the land awarded the nobles was theirs to use but not to own. Others believe it was given to them outright, an outgrowth of the practice of royal gift giving, originally restricted to llamas, clothing, and other valuable items. Wives also were distributed according to this system.

[17] **yanakuna:** yah nah KOO nah

[18] **Urubamba:** oo roo BAHM bah

This experiment in private ownership may be significant, because it may mean that the Incas were moving toward a new economic system. But the Spanish conquest cut short whatever course they would have followed, and we will never know what the outcome would have been.

The Spanish Conquest

In 1527, the Inca emperor died, leaving two sons to compete for his position: Waskar in Cuzco and Atahualpa[19] in the northern city of Quito. The ensuing civil war ended in 1532, when Atahualpa's forces succeeded in killing Waskar in battle. By this time, Spanish forces under the command of Francisco Pizarro had landed on the coast of Peru. Within the year, the Inca Empire fell.

The excellent Inca communication system alerted Atahualpa to the presence of the Spanish before they even landed, and Atahualpa called to military service all able-bodied men near the Spanish landing site. This was partly to expand his own army, and partly to prevent disaffected regions from allying with the Spanish. Probably because their numbers were small—around 200 horsemen—the Spanish were permitted to penetrate the easily defensible passes surrounding Cuzco, and they entered the Inca capital.

At a confrontation, Atahualpa demanded that the Spanish return everything they had plundered on the trip to Cuzco. The Spanish refused and the next day lured Atahualpa and 2,000 of his top officials into an ambush, where Atahualpa was captured and the officials were, in the words of a *conquistador*, "killed like ants." Cuzco, while the nerve center of the empire, had a total population of only around 10,000 people, and there were no senior officials left to take command. Atahualpa was executed, and a puppet ruler was installed by the Spanish. In the course of a few hours, the back of the Inca Empire was broken, a consequence of its highly centralized imperial power structure.

As in Mesoamerica, the last empire of Peru was founded only shortly before the Spanish conquest. Far from entrenched in its ways, it was actively experimenting with new systems of economic organization and was grappling with the difficulties of royal succession. This empire, which so impressed the Spanish, was but in its infancy when it was strangled.

[19]**Atahualpa:** ah tah HWAHL pah

NATIVE AMERICAN SOCIETIES IN NORTH AMERICA

In the year 1500, there were more than 800 languages spoken in North America and about 1,000 different peoples. This level of cultural diversity was at least comparable to that in Eurasia at the same period and may have been greater, so it is impossible to select a few examples that do justice to that diversity. Nonetheless, the following treatment discusses four societies from three major culture areas of North America. There were no North American societies in this period that were urban states, so there were no civilizations. The three societies presented here exemplify the levels of complexity in this period.

The Eastern Woodlands: The Iroquois

The vast area to the east of the Mississippi River and along its western banks was characterized by dense forests and is known as the Eastern Woodlands. Except in the far north, where the growing season is too short, all societies here based their existence on maize-squash-beans agriculture, and all were at the tribe or chiefdom level. An example is the Iroquois.

The Iroquois are a group of closely related peoples living in and around New York State and the Canadian province of Ontario. The Iroquois way of life developed around 1050, spurred largely by the advent of a new form of corn that matured faster than its predecessors, allowing greater and more reliable yields and agricultural dependence. Settlement shifted to the fertile flood plains along rivers, and warfare increased as competition for these limited lands developed. Fortified towns developed as a response to increased hostilities.

Also as a result of this, five of the Iroquois tribes formed around 1300 a confederacy under Hiawatha. (Hiawatha probably was a real person who was instrumental in the formation of the confederacy, but later elaborations have transformed him into an almost superhuman hero.) This confederacy bound the tribes together in peaceful alliances and ensured their cooperation against outsiders. Later, in 1722, a refugee tribe from North Carolina was added to the confederacy, reforming it into the Six Nations of the present day. The Iroquois confederacy oversaw a highly efficient military organization, lauded by one English colonial

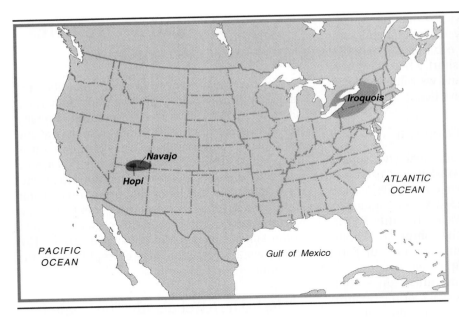

MAP 16.1 *Locations of Iroquois, Hopi, and Navajo.* *These tribes are only three of the nearly one thousand tribes that inhabited North America just before the arrival of Europeans.*

governor as the most powerful military force in North America in the 1750s.

But the Iroquois confederacy was more than a military machine. It also was a political system that provided for diplomat-ambassadors, elected chiefs, and a council whose members were elected by their tribe and made decisions for the confederacy as a whole. The confederacy had a body of rules and laws that organized its political functioning and guaranteed various rights to its citizenry.

While the Iroquois had no writing, they produced pictorial belts made of **wampum**, shell beads of different colors that were strung together in such a way that they formed pictures. The pictures served as memory aids, commemorating historic events and recording treaties. The exchanging of these belts at the time of a treaty or other agreement with a foreign power sealed the transaction, much in the same way that signing a written treaty or shaking hands might in other cultural contexts.

The Iroquois vested considerable power in women, who were the primary owners of land and were the focus of kinship organizations that were central to everyday life. They had the right to express views in the council; they also had the right to vote for office holders, though they were not normally permitted to hold elected office.

Iroquois religion was largely in the hands of kinship groups and voluntary societies that held ceremonies at fixed calendric dates. Six thanksgiving festivals, for example, were held at regular times of the year. The Planting Festival, held around May, was to bless the seeds of corn, squash, beans, and sunflowers that were being planted; the Strawberry Festival thanked nature for providing these first fruits of the warm months; the Harvest Festival in autumn welcomed the harvesting of the corn and its storage for the year. These and other ceremonies were organized and conducted by individuals as members of voluntary societies; there were no priests or similar full-time religious practitioners. Male and female healers, using both spiritual and herbal remedies, conducted healing rituals as needed.

As a major military power, the Iroquois were successful at resisting European domination for some time, though their ranks were decimated by European diseases. Their alliance with the English and their defeat in the American Revolution led to the downfall of the Iroquois in the United States, where they were reduced by harsh treaty settlements and vigilante attack.

The Southwest: The Hopi and the Navajo

The Southwest is characterized by arid and semi-arid lands, particularly in the states of Arizona, New Mexico, Colorado, and Utah. This area was populated both by band-level hunter-gatherers and by tribe-level agriculturalists in this period.

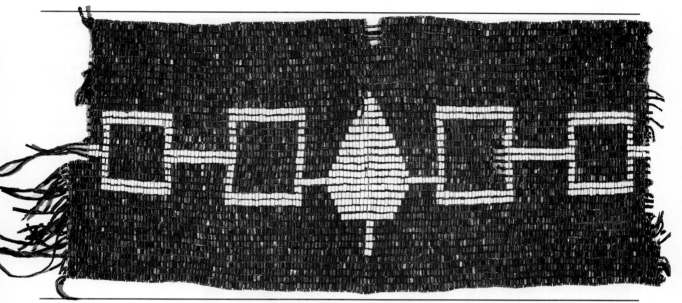

FIGURE 16.9 *Iroquois Wampum Belt.* *The Iroquois used beaded belts to commemorate and seal agreements. This belt, known as the Hiawatha Belt, records the original founding of the League of the Iroquois, the banding together of five tribes into a confederacy for mutual cooperation. Made of shell beads, it may date from as early as 1300. The squares represent four of the five tribes of the Iroquois, and the central figure represents the Onondaga tribe, whose territory is geographically central. The Onondaga symbol is interpreted both as a tree (representing the peace shared by the League members) and a heart (representing the central position of the Onondaga).* New York State Museum. Acquired May 24, 1927, by bequest of Emma Treadwell Thacher of Albany, N.Y. Courtesy of Chief Irving Powless Jr., Onondaga Nation.

The Hopi[20] are an example of tribe-level agriculturalists. Farming on the dry mesas where the Hopi lived was a laborious and precarious practice. A bad year could spell disaster, and bad years could be expected every seven to ten years.

To even the odds a bit, the Hopi took several precautions. First, they hand-watered their crops, because no streams large enough to support irrigation existed in their lands; this practice ensured that crops would receive sufficient water in all but the worst of times. Second, they established reciprocal relationships among villages, so that a village with a poor agricultural return one year could receive aid from a neighbor with better luck; another year, when fortunes were reversed, the aid would be returned. Third, the Hopi continued to hunt and gather foods as adjuncts to their diet. In bad years, these foraged foods would form a greater part of the diet. Finally, the Hopi had an

agreement with the spirit world to ensure rain in response to ritual devotion. If rain did not materialize, clearly, as the Hopi saw it, the ritual had been performed poorly.

This agreement was based on the belief that there were mutual obligations between the Hopi and the spirits. If the Hopi performed rituals properly, the spirits were obligated to bring rain; this rain, in turn, obligated the Hopi to perform the rituals, completing the cycle. The rituals were not prayers requesting that the spirits provide rain; nor were they magic forcing them. Rather, the spirits were seen as equals with the Hopi in the sense that they, too, had social obligations that bound their actions. Men conducted (and still do conduct) the ceremonies privately in underground rooms called *kivas*.[21]

Hopi population levels remained moderately low, never high enough to outstrip the available

[20] **Hopi:** HOH pee

[21] *kivas:* KEE vuhz

FIGURE 16.10 *Great Kiva at Aztec Ruins.* *The Hopi consider their* kivas *sacred places that may not be photographed; however, this reconstruction of a prehistoric non-Hopi kiva from northern New Mexico embodies all the main characteristics of a Hopi* kiva. *The round, sunken room had a bench along its periphery where participants could sit facing the* sipapu, *a symbolic connection to the spirit world.*
George H. Huey

agricultural land; and the Hopi rarely engaged in warfare. Their multiroomed masonry houses (*pueblos*), sometimes reaching two or three stories high, look as if they might have been designed as defensive structures, but more likely they were designed for protection from the harsh seasonal temperatures of the region.

Living around the *pueblos* of the Hopi and other tribes were the Dene.[22] These relatively recent immigrants to the Southwest arrived from the north sometime after 1000 and led a nomadic way of life at the band level. They hunted and gathered their food without recourse to agriculture and lived in insubstantial houses designed to be used only for a night or two. Different groups of the Dene became the modern Apache and Navajo.[23]

The results of the European arrival in the Southwest were very dissimilar for the Navajo and *pueblo*-dwelling peoples (like the Hopi). Spanish missionaries focused their attentions on the *pueblo* dwellers, because they were sedentary and the establishment of a mission that exploited

Indian labor was practical. This meant that most *pueblo*-dwelling tribes had intensive missionary contact, resulting in rapid depopulation from disease, rapid modification of traditional religious and social systems, and, in some cases, virtual reduction to slave labor. The Hopi were one of the few *pueblo*-dwellers to escape most of these consequences, because their land was dry and at some distance from the rivers around which the Spanish concentrated their efforts. Of the twenty-three *pueblo*-dwelling tribes, only two were so lucky.

The Navajo fared very differently. As nomads, they avoided the most injurious Spanish attentions, adopting Spanish traits they found desirable and simply moving away if less desirable ones were being forced on them. Their most significant adoption from the Spanish was sheep raising. This pastoralism was based on domesticated sheep that had strayed from Spanish flocks or had been taken by Navajo raids. The sheep provided meat, an important adjunct to Navajo subsistence, and encouraged the Navajo to live in base camps, where limited farming was practical. The wool from the sheep formed the basis for weaving, an important occupation of Navajo women to this

[22] **Dene:** DEE neh
[23] **Navajo:** NAH vah hoh

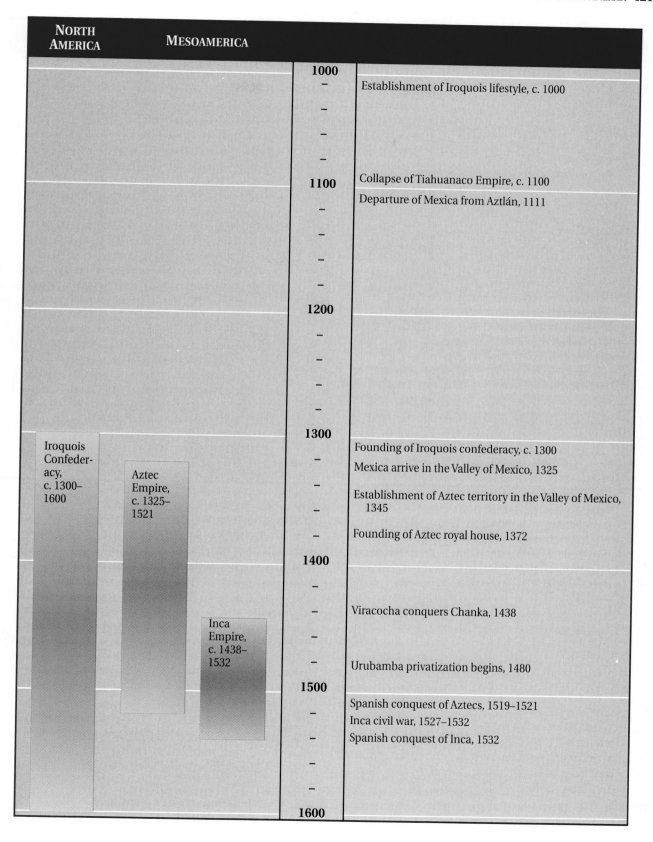

NORTH AMERICA	MESOAMERICA		
		1000	Establishment of Iroquois lifestyle, c. 1000
		1100	Collapse of Tiahuanaco Empire, c. 1100
			Departure of Mexica from Aztlán, 1111
		1200	
		1300	Founding of Iroquois confederacy, c. 1300
Iroquois Confederacy, c. 1300–1600	Aztec Empire, c. 1325–1521		Mexica arrive in the Valley of Mexico, 1325
			Establishment of Aztec territory in the Valley of Mexico, 1345
			Founding of Aztec royal house, 1372
		1400	
	Inca Empire, c. 1438–1532		Viracocha conquers Chanka, 1438
			Urubamba privatization begins, 1480
		1500	Spanish conquest of Aztecs, 1519–1521
			Inca civil war, 1527–1532
			Spanish conquest of Inca, 1532
		1600	

UNDER THE LENS
The Hopi World Order

The Hopi view of the world and the place of the Hopi within it was founded in three basic principles: the bipartite universe, reciprocity with the spirits, and the system of correspondences. From these principles, the Hopi derived their basic moral, religious, and social order.

The Hopi recognized that there were two independent but similar worlds, one for the living Hopi and one for the spirits; this is the **bipartite universe**. The worlds were opposite to each other, so that summer in the spirit world was winter in the Hopi world, night in the Hopi world was day in the spirit world. In some manner, things in one world could transform into the other. The Hopi believed that after death, a person's spirit went to the spirit world to become a **kachina**[a] and that at birth, a baby was invested with a spirit that had been a *kachina*. Similarly and importantly, the *kachinas* had an essence (parallel to Hopi blood) called ***navala***, which could migrate to the Hopi world and become rain, that much-needed commodity for desert farmers lacking rivers that could be harnessed for irrigation.

[a] ***kachina:*** kah CHEE nah

The spirit world and the Hopi world were related to each other by mutual obligations: **reciprocity with the spirits**. The Hopi were obligated to perform rituals for the *kachinas* (because the *kachinas* had provided *navala* in the form of rain), and the Hopis' rituals obligated the *kachinas* to continue providing *navala*. The cycle was neverending, as rain obligated the Hopi to perform the rituals, which in turn obligated the *kachinas* to provide the rain, and so forth. Without a full complement of properly performed rituals, the Hopi could expect only drought and death.

Finally, the **system of correspondences** was a complex symbol system that related cardinal directions, colors, types of clouds, ritual items, lightning, plants, animals, and many other things. The color for north, for example, was identified with forked lightning, yellow sweet corn, and butterflies, among others. The use or reference of any of these things during a ritual could stand for any of the others to which it corresponded. As a result, a collection of items on an altar could represent a complex series of relationships, prayers, and requests to the *kachinas*. This Hopi view of the world developed centuries ago and persists today among traditional Hopi.

day. Weaving also permitted many Navajo to enter the cash economy in the nineteenth century, when Euro-American markets developed after the coming of the railroad. Despite various episodes of clashes and mistreatment by European and American governments, these adaptations permitted the Navajo to thrive. In the past three centuries, they have transformed from a small group to the most populous Indian tribe in North America.

SUMMARY

1. The Aztecs descended from a seminomadic tribe that migrated to the Valley of Mexico around 1300.

2. Through a series of military and diplomatic maneuvers, the Aztecs established a large empire. Warfare maintained and expanded the empire, as well as providing captives for religiously mandated human sacrifice.

3. Aztec society was highly hierarchic, with nobles who were believed to be descended from gods. This hierarchic nature permeated Aztec life, affecting one's legal, economic, social, and political fortunes.

4. The Aztec Empire was conquered by the Spanish in 1521, largely as the result of the plummeting Aztec population owing to newly introduced diseases and the desertion of Aztec allies to the Spanish.

5. The kingdom of Cuzco in Peru expanded into the Inca Empire, also through warfare and

diplomacy. The Incas permitted newly conquered peoples to retain their ways of life and even their governmental hierarchies as they were incorporated into the Inca Empire, producing a heterogeneous empire.

6. The Incas generally rewarded rulers and states with gifts for surrendering to them. They also sometimes relocated large groups of people for imperial security.

7. The Inca Empire vested property ownership primarily in the government. *Corvée* labor, food redistribution, and population relocations were aspects of governmental control. The government also provided massive public works. A late experiment in private ownership was cut short by the Spanish conquest.

8. Leadership succession was a weakness of the Inca Empire, and the Spanish conquest was facilitated by a civil war over royal succession.

9. North America had a wide variety of societies at the time of European contact, including those of the Iroquois, Hopi, and Navajo. None of these had urban states.

SUGGESTED READINGS

Anderson, Arthur J., and Charles E. Dibble, ed. and trans. *Florentine Codex.* Monographs of the School of American Research, #14 (in 13 parts). Santa Fe, N.M.: The School of American Research and the University of Utah, 1951–81. An annotated translation of this important codex, written by Aztec scribes shortly after the Spanish conquest.

Baudin, Louis. *A Socialist Empire: The Incas of Peru.* New York: Van Nostrand, 1961. The classic Marxist interpretation of the Inca.

Berdan, Frances F. *The Aztecs of Central Mexico: An Imperial Society.* New York: Holt, Rinehart and Winston, 1982. A brief, readable, authoritative summary of Aztec society.

Brundage, Burr Cartwright. *Empire of the Inca.* Norman: University of Oklahoma Press, 1963. A general treatment of the Incas from the historical perspective.

Gillespie, Susan D. *Aztec Kings: The Construction of Rulership in Mexica History.* Tucson: University of Arizona Press, 1989. A feminist perspective on early Aztec history.

Kissam, Edward, and Michael Schmidt, trans. *Poems of the Aztec Peoples.* Ypsilanti, Mich.: Bilingual Press/Editorial Bilingüe, 1983. English translations of many Aztec poems.

Sturtevant, William C., ed. *Handbook of North American Indians.* Fifteen volumes. Washington, D.C.: Smithsonian Institution, 1978–present. The best single reference on North American Indians, containing authoritative articles with good bibliographies. To date, about two-thirds of the volumes have been published.

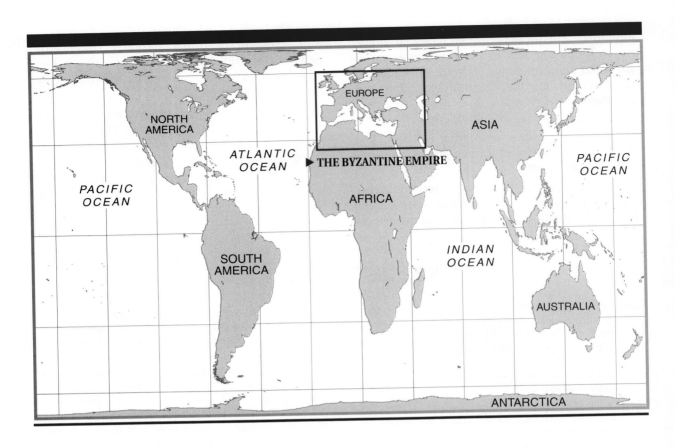

▶ **THE BYZANTINE EMPIRE**

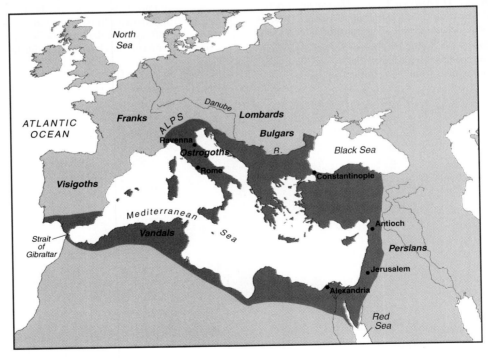

▶ **THE BYZANTINE EMPIRE**

The Byzantine Empire

around 450–1453

"The Golden Horn," observed a sixth-century writer, "is always calm." The bay of the ancient city of Byzantium acquired this name from the shape of its harbor and the commercial wealth that filled the purses of the city's citizens. In 330, Constantine renamed the city Constantinople (today called Istanbul) and established it as the new capital of the Roman Empire. Constantinople later became the seat of a new empire, which scholars have named the Byzantine Empire, after the original city of Byzantium.

The Byzantine Empire evolved over time, so a date of origin is difficult to identify. Some scholars date the empire as early as 330, when Constantine named Constantinople the new capital. Other scholars prefer the date of 395, which ended the last unification of the Roman Empire under Theodosius, or that of 476, when the last Western Roman Emperor was deposed by a German conqueror. Still other scholars prefer to see the origins of the Byzantine Empire from a nonpolitical perspective. Significant social, religious, and artistic differences between the western and eastern portions of the Roman Empire had existed long before the permanent political separation in the fifth century. It is perhaps best to recognize that the Byzantine Empire evolved from the previous Roman polity and accept a general date for its inception of around 450.

BYZANTINE SOCIETY

The Byzantine Empire is the longest-lasting empire in history, surviving well over 1,000 years. The various territories of the empire had long, illustrious histories before the fourth century. Many of the societies that you read about in Chapters 4, 7, and 8 occupied the same geographical areas.

Geography and Demography

The Byzantine Empire covered a vast territory. At the height of its power in the sixth century, the empire encompassed Greece, the Balkans south of the Danube River, Anatolia, Palestine, parts of North Africa, and the islands of the eastern Mediterranean and the Aegean seas. In addition, large portions of the earlier Western Roman Empire were reconquered by the Byzantine Emperor Justinian (reign dates 527–565), including much of Italy and southern Spain. Between the years 450 and 1453, the Byzantine Empire won and lost large portions of these areas.

Over the centuries, the Byzantine Empire was home to millions of ethnically diverse people. A conservative estimate places more than 30 million persons in the empire in the sixth century. The distribution approximated 8 million in Egypt, 9 million in the easternmost territories (Syria, Palestine, and parts of Mesopotamia), 10 million in the area of modern Turkey, and 3 to 4 million in the Balkans. Demographic shifts due to border hostilities from about the mid–seventh century to about the mid–ninth century caused some de-

MAP 17.1 *The Byzantine Empire at Its Height.* *Under Justinian, the empire reached its greatest expanse by 565 A.D. A major campaign to reconquer western European territories was undertaken, achieving temporary results in some areas. By the end of the seventh century, eastern and southern Byzantine territories began to fall to Muslim invasions.*

urbanization. Many cities in Thrace, Greece, and the area of modern Turkey ceased to exist or survived only as small towns. Some urban centers relocated to safer sites.

Life in the Empire

The ideological link that provided unity for the empire was a religious one. Missionary activity had spread Christianity throughout the Roman Empire in the second century. When Emperor Theodosius declared Christianity the empire's only legal religion at the end of the fourth century, its influence as a unifying instrument became central to succeeding rulers. One monk, upon arriving in Thrace from an eastern territory in the ninth century, was challenged to prove he was a friend and not an enemy. His reply cited not his citizenship but rather that he, like his parents, followed the Christian faith. At the same time, belief in many different religions continued in private life. The practices of Judaism, Islam, Zoroastrianism, and local religious customs could be observed in any major urban center. Although animosity and persecution sometimes occurred against minority Christian sects that had been declared heretical, such as the Monophysites, the sects were tolerated when tolerance was politically expedient.

Generally, the lives of local people throughout the empire continued in much the same way as they always had in the centuries prior to the Byzantine Empire. Farmers plowed and harvested their fields, artisans made and sold their wares, the elite controlled wealth and wielded political influence, and imperial officers collected taxes and tried to keep the peace. Urban and rural living ebbed and flowed according to the economic and political factors of each generation.

Peasant life remained basically stable in the Byzantine Empire. In the fourth century, many farmers did not have free status, and others retained various levels of freedom. Sources show that there existed a variety of peasant statuses between the tenth and twelfth centuries. By the thirteenth to the fifteenth centuries, this pattern had not changed very much. There were certainly periods when peasants became serfs of great aristocrats or specific places where they were subjected to aristocratic control, but these patterns were not universal. The village community, made up of free landholding peasants, continued throughout Byzantine history. Usually these communities had relative independence from aristocratic control and governed themselves.

The merchants were the economic backbone of trade around the empire. Merchants bought and sold goods, sometimes as agents of the state and sometimes as independent traders. Some merchants became very wealthy, but merchants generally remained low on the social scale and were not allowed to hold important political offices. Seventh- and eighth-century deurbanization significantly reduced the number of merchants. By the eleventh century, however, urban renewal again stimulated merchant activities throughout the empire. Many merchants of Constantinople gained in wealth and social prestige, becoming a powerful political group within the city. Political power, however, was never sustained by merchants in most Byzantine areas. Many women in the thirteenth to the fifteenth centuries were merchants, retailing in cloth, beauty aids, and some foods. One Muslim source noted that the majority of artisans and sellers in the city of Constantinople were women.

BYZANTINE POLITICAL HISTORY

The Byzantine Empire inherited a system of law and an imperial structure from its Roman predecessor. Expansion concentrated on recapturing the Western Roman Empire's territories, and much of Justinian's efforts and the empire's resources were spent in Italy. During most of Byzantine history, emperors and armies fought to defend the far-flung borders of the empire, sometimes losing significant amounts of territory. Changes in administrative policies, however, prolonged the Byzantine Empire until 1453.

Byzantine Law

The early legal structure of the Byzantine Empire was inherited from Greek and Roman antecedents. Laws, however, were not systematically organized, and judges had no consistency in interpreting the law; many times inconsistencies surfaced, much to the frustration of those trying to adjudicate disputes. Several attempts at reconciling diverse

IN THEIR OWN WORDS

A Twelfth-Century Byzantine Market

Great markets constituted the heart of the trade centers in the Byzantine Empire. When the market commenced, great excitement ran through attenders of all ages. New clothes, jewelry, prepared foods, and fresh produce awaited the willing purchase of the marketgoers. The following excerpt is from an anonymous writer of the twelfth century. Although the work is fictional, this description of a market in Thessalonike in the territory of Macedonia reveals how these markets must have looked.

It is the most considerable . . . [market] among the inhabitants of Macedonia. Not only would the local population assemble there, but people from everywhere and of every sort would arrive. Greeks come from every place, as well as the neighboring tribes of . . . [Bulgars] who live as far as the Danube and the land of the Scythians, and the inhabitants of Campania, Italians, Spaniards and Portuguese, and Celts from beyond the Alps. . . . I for one . . . had until now no personal experience of the event and knew about it only from hearsay. So I desired to be a spectator of this sight and see everything without exception. With this purpose I climbed a hill located nearby and, sitting there, could observe the . . . [market] with ease. It looked like this: Tents of merchants were pitched in two lines facing one another. The lines ran a long distance, leaving between them a broad lane that allowed for the rush of the crowd. . . . Other tents were set up off this lane. They also formed lines, but not very long ones, as if they were the short legs of a crouching reptile. . . .

Looking down from my hill I saw all kinds of fabric and thread . . . of men's and women's garb produced both in Boeotia [Greece] and in the Peloponnese and carried on commercial ships from Italy to Greece. Also Phoenicia [Lebanon] sent many an object; Egypt and Spain . . . produced the best implements. Merchants brought all these things directly from their countries to old Macedonia and [Thessalonike]. But the Black Sea sent its produce first to . . . Byzantium and therefrom it was brought here and adorned the [market]. Numbers of horses and mules carried their load from there.

interpretations and pulling the myriad legal pronouncements together into collections had failed. Emperor Justinian, however, appointed a commission to create a new, authoritative law code, the *Codex Justinianus*. Shortly afterward, he commissioned a work to codify the works of Roman jurists. These and other legal reviews became known as the *Corpus Juris Civilis* (528–535), which was the foundation of law codes in most of Europe after the eleventh century.

Increasingly, Christianity influenced Byzantine law, as the church grew in size, wealth, and influence. The patriarch of Constantinople wielded great authority over legal practice. As Christian morality became the accepted pattern of behavior for the empire, Christian influence upon legislation increased, and civil law and canon law began to converge; this was similar to the influence of Islamic law in Muslim areas. Church courts remained independent of imperial courts, and the patriarch's court reserved the right of appeal of civil court decisions.

Emperors and Empresses

During Byzantine history, both the emperors and the empresses engaged in pomp and pageantry at court to demonstrate their elevated status and to display the emperor's religious authority. The foundation of imperial authority lay with past Roman emperors, but much of the Byzantine imperial persona came from Hellenistic and Christian influences that gave emperors even greater spiritual authority than their predecessors.

Solemn ceremonies and impressive pageantry created an ambience of otherworldliness and conferred power on the person of the emperor. The royal apparel for official occasions consisted of a long white tunic of silk with a purple cape, decorated on both sides with embroidered gold cloth. The imperial crown held precious jewels, such as pearls and rubies. One envoy to the court of a tenth-century Byzantine emperor observed the imperial grandeur. If his account is to be believed, he entered the great hall escorted by eunuchs and approached the emperor, who was seated on a magnificent throne. Mechanical birds sang and lions roared as the diplomat approached. After he prostrated himself three times before the emperor (a mandatory ritual), he looked up and saw that the throne and the emperor had ascended to the ceiling. He was forced to finish his interview peering heavenward. Other accounts by visiting Muslims describe beautiful Persian carpets, golden candelabra hung from silvered copper chains, and floors covered with ivy, rosemary, and roses. As one crossed the floor, perfume from crushed leaves and petals filled the room. Such theatrics dramatically conveyed magnificence and might.

Since the time of Constantine, Byzantine rulers viewed themselves as representatives of Christ, given divine authority to govern the Christian empire. Because of the political theory of divine selection, dynastic succession was not guaranteed to an emperor's heir. Selection was made by the army, the Senate of Constantinople, or the citizenry of Constantinople, each operating as a divine agent. In the later centuries of the empire, however, family succession became more common.

Imperial legitimacy came from the basic understanding that the emperor was chosen by the Christian God. Divine will, however, could turn against an emperor as surely as it favored his ascension to the throne (which was made painfully clear when usurpations were successful). Palace intrigues, plots, and assassinations fill the pages of Byzantine history during times of political crisis. Nearly one-half of Byzantine emperors died violently or fled to safety in monasteries. Most of those killed were poisoned, stabbed, or decapitated by rivals to the throne. One poor victim's head was publicly displayed on a pike. Another suffered multiple attacks to his person: He was chained and beaten, his teeth were knocked out with a hammer, one of his hands was cut off, he was paraded through Constantinople on a sick camel (symbolizing weakness, poverty, and humil-

FIGURE 17.1 *Emperor Justinian.* *This mosaic portrait of Justinian and his civil and ecclesiastical officials is found in the sixth-century Church of San Vitale in the city of Ravenna in northern Italy. Its place of prominence near the altar reminded worshipers of the emperor's exalted status in Christian society and of Justinian's claim of political authority over the city. Ravenna was one of the cities captured by the Byzantines in their reconquest of western territories during Justinian's reign. Eastern emperors after Justinian continued to claim the city as part of their empire until the conquests of Charlemagne in the eighth century.* Scala/Art Resource, N.Y.

iation), he had boiling water thrown in his face and one of his eyes plucked out, and he was finally hung up in the Hippodrome (a large arena used for sports) for even more torture. After pleading for relief, he was mercifully run through with a sword.

Emperors controlled many lands, incomes, and other material resources of the Christian

FIGURE 17.2 *Emperor John Cantacuzene.*
This portrayal of Emperor John Cantacuzene demonstrates his religious authority during a 1351 council of Eastern Orthodox bishops and monks. Although their religious power was often challenged by patriarchs, many emperors convened and directed council meetings, thereby influencing the development of church doctrine. Bibliothèque nationale, Paris.

church. They often determined ecclesiastical staffs or appointed bishops, including the patriarch of Constantinople. Emperors also called for or presided over church councils, at which they tried to impose their theological views. Emperors could not determine Christian doctrine by themselves; that could be accomplished only by bishops meeting in specially called church councils.

Empresses also played significant roles in the administration of the empire, albeit in more subtle ways, such as through regencies. Most empresses minted their own coins and controlled their own attendants, and they maintained parallel courts composed of elite women. Not every imperial wife gained the title of empress in the fourth and fifth centuries, however. Sometimes the title was given to an emperor's mother or sister instead of his wife.

Emperors' brides often came from distant lands as diplomatic ties wedded the interests of states together. By the twelfth century, wives gained the title of empress more consistently as dynastic succession regularly passed from father to son. Because of this, regencies became more common as young emperors waited to take the reins of power.

Although power usually resided in the emperor, or in the empress as regent, there were occasions when empresses ruled in their own names or influenced laws. Three examples are Irene (reign dates 797–802), Zoë (co-empress, 1042), and Theodora (co-empress, 1042; reign dates 1055–1056), all of whom ruled for brief periods. Irene began her rule as regent of her young son, between 780 and 797, but at his maturity she took the throne after blinding and deposing him. During the co-reign of the sisters Zoë and Theodora, the sale of offices was abolished and many people were elevated into the Senate. Decrees of the empresses demonstrate their influence in the running of the Byzantine state.

Empress Theodora (497–548), not to be confused with the co-empress Theodora, is perhaps the most famous empress in Byzantine history. A former actress, she married Emperor Justinian in 527. She endowed many churches, monasteries, orphanages, and hospitals. Her influence on Justinian's rule is hard to evaluate, but her participation in stemming the Nika Rebellion (see p. 439) suggests a relationship with significant influence. In addition, artifact inscriptions suggest equal reverence for both Justinian and Theodora. She received many letters from kings, one of whom she had instructed to write directly to her for matters to be placed before the emperor.

Byzantine Bureaucracy

A vast, effective bureaucracy aided the monarch in administration of the empire. Although its size fluctuated according to political necessity, the bureaucracy lasted throughout Byzantine history. Similarly to Muslim cities, most early Byzantine cities had governing councils that worked with imperial officials. In contrast to the Muslim councils, the councils of Byzantine cities were populated by wealthy local landowners instead of merchants.

Bishops also participated in the regulation of cities, because the local churches over which they

FIGURE 17.3 *Empress Theodora.* *Empress Theodora is depicted in similar fashion to her husband, the Emperor Justinian. Located on the wall opposite Justinian's portrait (Figure 17.1) in the Church of San Vitale, this mosaic demonstrates the imperial authority of the empress. Theodora is posed with her attendants in a mirror image of Justinian and his officials. Some scholars interpret the role of Theodora's court staff as a mirror bureaucracy that aided Justinian in governing the empire.* Bildarchiv Foto Marburg/Art Resource, N.Y.

presided usually possessed large amounts of land. As lack of participation in city councils plagued the late-sixth-century cities (because council members became personally responsible for tax payments to the state), bishops gradually filled the political gap, dispensing justice and raising taxes, sometimes functioning as governors.

Imperial Expansion

Justinian's armies had recaptured portions of what had been the Western Empire in the early sixth century. Belisarius, Justinian's able general, had put down a rebellion in North Africa in 534 and in the next year conquered Sicily and Dalmatia. Between 535 and 540, Belisarius wrestled Italy from the Germans, and Byzantine forces retook parts of Spain by 550. Continued fighting over Italy lasted until the capitulation of the Germans in Italy

in 555. It looked as if the Roman Empire would be resurrected.

By the end of the sixth century, however, most of Italy had fallen under the control of the Germanic Lombards. Byzantine emperors continued to claim authority over the western territories, and a Byzantine official residing in the northern Italian city of Ravenna claimed to govern the west in the name of the emperor. Most Italian cities were islands of independence fighting against Lombard encroachment. Because of border threats elsewhere in the Byzantine Empire, little aid was forthcoming.

The Empire under Siege

Throughout Byzantine history, raids and conquests threatened or redrew the empire's borders. Numerous invasions by different tribal groups from areas in Europe and Asia disrupted trade. In some cases, diplomacy brought peaceful resolution, but usually hostilities resulted in more bloodshed and territorial loss. Significant regional losses ensued under the conquests of the Arab Muslims and the Crusaders, but Byzantine resiliency maintained a smaller, yet still vital, Byzantine state. The final onslaught came from the conquering Ottoman Turks, but Byzantine influence continued to live in the cultures of the conquerors.

Although Justinian's period was one of expansion, he also dealt with raids on the northern and eastern borders of the empire. Raiders across the lines of defense along the Danube penetrated as far south as the Peloponnesus in Greece. The Persian Sassanians clashed with eastern imperial forces and gained control of Egypt, Palestine, and Syria for a brief time. Justinian responded to the multiple onslaught by reorganizing the administrative structure of the empire into provinces in order to give greater control to the central government. In the provinces, he secured the frontier areas with large fortified encampments from which the army could defend the borders. The reorganization saved the empire from conquest.

In the seventh and eighth centuries, continuing hostilities saw the loss of territory and another reorganization. The Byzantine Empire could not hold on to its farther eastern and southern provinces and, finally, lost them permanently to the Arab Muslims. Another reorganization of the empire's administration replaced the provinces and focused on smaller areas called *themes*,[1] old areas of land organization. The *themes* were now administered by generals exercising both military and civil power under the direct control of the emperor. The *theme* system allowed for greater military response to attacks on the borders. As time went on, the number of *themes* increased; by the mid–ninth century, there were more than twenty *themes* in existence, and, by the eleventh century, great landowners controlled some of them.

Arab Muslim conquest of some coastal areas broke the naval dominance of the eastern Mediterranean by the Byzantines, but trade continued to flow between Byzantine and Muslim areas. Constantinople itself was besieged twice by Arab Muslims in the seventh and eighth centuries but did

not fall. In addition to Arab Muslim conflicts, Pepin the Short conquered most of the areas in Italy that had been captured by the Lombards or by Justinian. Pepin established the Papal States and set up an alliance with the pope. This loss of Italian territory essentially ended Byzantine imperial claims over the papacy; the pope increasingly turned to the Franks rather than to the Byzantines for military help.

During this same period, Bulgar forces (people from the territory along the northern border) repeatedly crossed the Danube and continued their raids into the next two centuries. The highly successful Byzantine dynasty of Macedonian emperors (857–1056) dealt with the brunt of these invasions. Basil II, the Bulgar-slayer (reign dates 976–1025), eventually stopped the Bulgar invasions; in 1014, he crushed the enemy's army and took between 14,000 and 15,000 prisoners. He blinded ninety-nine in every hundred, leaving one to guide his fellows back to their home territory. Basil then annexed Bulgaria, placing the entire Balkan population under imperial control. Basil had also achieved an alliance with the Russians, who had been threatening the empire in the tenth century. In 988, Russia's Prince Vladimir sealed a treaty by being baptized and marrying a Byzantine princess.

Various border skirmishes continued to stress the empire, as hostile peoples crossed the borders in the eleventh to the thirteenth centuries. In 1095, western Christians were called upon to aid in retaking Christian holy lands from the Arab Muslims at the request of the patriarch of Constantinople. The lands were retaken but not given back to Byzantine leaders; instead, Crusader States were established. In the late twelfth century, wayward European Crusaders under the influence of Pope Innocent III and Venetian economic interests set out for the holy lands on the Fourth Crusade. They soon became embroiled in Byzantine politics and ended up conquering Constantinople in 1204. Roman Catholics sat on the thrones of the Byzantine emperor and the patriarch. Only three areas of the empire retained independence from the crusaders: Nicea (on the west coast of Turkey), Epirus (on the west coast of Greece), and Trebizond (on the northeast coast of Turkey).

Crusaders held Constantinople for almost six decades. Niceans and Bulgars joined forces against their common western enemies and continually

---

[1] *themes:* THEHM ehs *or* THEEMZ

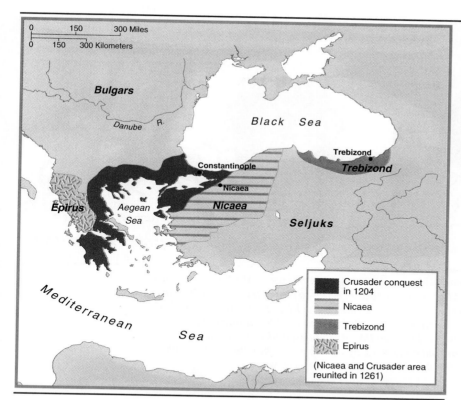

MAP 17.2 *Byzantine States around 1215.* Medieval European crusaders' invasions and Muslims' conquests broke the Byzantine Empire into regional states by 1215. In the mid–thirteenth century, the areas that had fallen to the European crusaders were reunited with the Nicaean state under one polity.

harassed them. Within a little more than fifty years, the coalition finally expelled the westerners from the sacred city. In 1261, Michael VIII established a new dynasty in Constantinople and reunited parts of the Byzantine Empire.

The expulsion of the crusaders, however, did not restore the Byzantine Empire to its former glory. Much of Constantinople lay in ruins, not only from the sacking and looting of 1204 but also from lack of maintenance. By the thirteenth century, the Italian commercial centers of Venice and Genoa held important economic routes, and Constantinople could not regain its economic footing. Michael VIII continually had to defend his diminished Byzantine Empire against western retaliation by the crusaders and the encroachment of the Serbs.

In the fourteenth and fifteenth centuries, the Byzantine Empire continued to be plagued by border skirmishes and a dire threat to its territories in Anatolia. The vigorous new state of the Ottomans was on the rise in the east, and Ottoman soldiers had captured most of the territory of Anatolia from the Byzantines by 1340. In another fifteen years,

the Ottoman Turks had gained a toehold in Europe. Parts of Thrace fell to them in the 1360s and most of Greece soon afterward.

The final assault occurred in 1453, when the Ottoman sultan, Mehmed[2] II (reign dates 1451–1481), laid siege to Constantinople with more than 80,000 troops. Emperor Constantine XI defended the city with 7,000 soldiers and twenty-six warships. The physical defenses of the city were formidable, but Mehmed had plans. He also had 120 ships with which to patrol the coastal waters. To circumvent the defensive chain stretched across the entrance to the Golden Horn, Mehmed had seventy of his vessels moved overland on rollers and then launched into the harbor to attack the north end of the city. Several of his forward observers spied out the wall defenses, and, with this information, Mehmed directed engineers to lay mines at strategic places and aim cannonballs to knock down the remaining walls. Gunpowder technology was the undoing of Constantinople's legendary walled defenses. The Byzantine Empire

[2] **Mehmed:** MEH mehd

FIGURE 17.4 *Muslim Defeat of Byzantine Army.*   *In this scene, Muslim Turks defeat a retreating Byzantine force. The Muslim cavalry was superior to that of most Byzantine horsemen, who often lost territory to Muslim cavalry advances. The Byzantine Empire controlled many trade routes, and competitive states (especially Muslim) tried to capture Byzantine territories to extend their trade networks. When Dar al-Islam expanded into Anatolia, it competed with Byzantine religion and economics. By 1215, parts of the empire had fallen to invaders or were split into regional kingdoms.*   Biblioteca Nacional, Madrid.

finally breathed its last as the emperor died with his troops in the final defense of the city; it had taken seven weeks for Constantinople to fall.

The Empire's Longevity

From the sixth to the fifteenth centuries, the Byzantine political structure experienced several organizational and administrative changes and aspects of governance underwent significant realignments as the empire adjusted to changing political conditions. The ability of Byzantine emperors and officials to remain flexible in their administration of the empire contributed significantly to its survival in the face of large territorial losses.

Emperors also changed socioreligious policies in attempts to defend the empire. For example, Monophysites (who had been deemed heretics by a church council in 451) were tolerated during periods of Persian and Arab invasions so as to keep them loyal to the empire and allow them to be conscripted into the army. Many Monophysites in Egypt and Syria, however, welcomed the Muslim conquerors as liberators from Byzantine policies.

CONSTANTINOPLE, THE SEAT OF EMPIRE

Constantine chose the site of the old city of Byzantium for his new capital for several reasons. It already functioned as a major commercial center, it sat strategically at the mouth of the Bosporus Strait, and it lay bordered on three sides by water, offering almost impenetrable protection when fortified. The city lasted as the Byzantine capital for almost the entire history of the Byzantine Empire, and, in many ways, the imperial city is a microcosm of Byzantine society.

The Imperial City

Because Constantinople lay at the crossroads of major overland trade routes, the city itself was a hub of activity. Although the official language of the city was Greek, as many as seventy-two languages could be heard as travelers wove their way through the throngs of people, carts, and animals along the twelve-foot-wide, two-mile-long main street of the teeming city. Constantinople resembled many major trade centers; the streets were crowded with shops and open-air bazaars, whose vendors barked out their bargains to passersby. Moneychangers guarded tables full of bags of foreign and local coins to exchange. Street entertainers added to the noise and confusion of the streets, where pickpockets and petty thieves probed at loose purses.

An incredible range of commodities could be found in the city. By the time of Justinian, silk was being produced by local silkworms, descendants of the first worms smuggled into Constantinople as eggs from China. Beautifully brocaded silk garments caught the eyes of many people, but few could afford them. Gold and silver ornaments, religious statues, and other trinkets tempted the traveler to part with some hard-earned money. Food stalls abounded, filled with exotic smells and delicacies from the various homelands of the colorful faces in the crowd. More traders and merchants entered every hour through the Great Golden Gate at the west end of the city; here merchants from

the Adriatic coast and northern Greece arrived with their treasures.

The public works of Justinian were probably the most ambitious in the city's history. Projects during the early Roman Empire had included the erection of aqueducts to ensure an adequate water supply for the city, Roman baths to accommodate the citizens' desire for relaxation and entertainment, and the Hippodrome to stage public spectacles similar to those in the Colosseum or Circus Maximus of Rome. Constantine's construction projects had included many church buildings and a forum. Justinian's projects rebuilt sections of the city that had been destroyed in a fire and further fortified the city against enemy attack. Triple walls, 13 miles in circumference, protected the city; in some places these walls measured 25 feet in width. Multiple watchtowers held soldiers who scrutinized the approach of caravans and ships and observed travelers approaching the fifty gates of the city. A moat protected the only side of the city that was accessible by land, and a great

FIGURE 17.5 *Chariot on Silk. This seventh-century silk textile depicts a charioteer driving his horses in a race, perhaps in the Hippodrome in Constantinople. Elaborately designed textiles such as this found their way along the numerous trade routes far beyond Constantinople. The introduction of silkworm eggs from China into Constantinople allowed for local production that drove the price of silk merchandise down, making it more affordable to Europeans.* Musée du Moyen Age (Cluny), Paris, France. Giraudon/Art Resource, N.Y.

FIGURE 17.6 *Hagia Sophia.* *This photograph of Hagia Sophia (Greek for "Holy Wisdom") gives a representative view of the vast interior, especially the height of the dome of this cathedral, built in Constantinople under Emperor Justinian and completed in* A.D. *537. One can imagine kneeling near the figures on the floor near the center of the picture and sensing the reverence that the architecture instills. The row of windows near the base of the dome creates an ethereal effect when sunlight floods the room and incense floats toward the ceiling.* Bildarchiv Foto Marburg/Art Resource, N.Y.

chain impeded unwanted ships in the Golden Horn.

Justinian's most celebrated building project, however, was the rebuilding of Hagia Sophia ("Holy Wisdom"), a church nearly destroyed by a fire in 532. The new edifice soared 180 feet, overshadowing the other churches of the city, and spread more than 100 feet across. It was the largest domed building in the world at that time. Ten thousand workers toiled six years to complete the project, and the result was magnificent. The rather bulky exterior belies the beauty of an interior flooded with light. Forty windows at the base of the dome allowed the sun's rays into the building from any angle, and the effect made it seem as if the dome floated in the air, as if a gift from heaven. Rose-colored dawns cast an ethereal light throughout, and a huge silk hanging depicting Christ

between the saints Peter and Paul shimmered in the light. The interior of the building was decorated with more than twenty tons of silver, the dome was covered in gold, and mosaics depicting various saints and religious figures adorned the massive walls and ceilings, complementing the marble surfaces. Tradition says that upon entering the church for the first time, Justinian exclaimed, "I have surpassed you, Solomon!" (alluding to Solomon's construction of the great temple of Jerusalem). After serving several centuries as a mosque, today Hagia Sophia is a museum.

Hagia Sophia held thousands of worshiping citizens and pilgrims. On Easter Sundays, the emperor himself participated in an impressive procession through the streets to the church, preceded by attendants dressed as the twelve apostles. The emperor wore a white robe, and, as he came into view, the population prostrated themselves in reverence to him. Here was Christ's representative on earth and the successor to Constantine, who had called himself the thirteenth apostle.

Imperial laws and restrictions governed trade in the city. Magistrates enforced strict import and export regulations on all raw materials and finished products. Some foreign merchants were limited to a certain number of days in the city, to help protect local merchants and control the markets. Certain dyes, especially royal purple, were restricted for use by only the imperial household. Restrictions applied to many professions as well. For example, butchers could not go outside the city to buy their goats, sheep, or pigs directly from herdsmen; they were forced to purchase them from a designated seller inside the city. They then butchered and sold what they had purchased for the day. Punishments for infractions of the restrictions on trade included expulsion from one's guild, flogging, or banishment.

Twenty-two guilds organized and controlled the workers of the city. In contrast to the independent guilds of Europe, Byzantine guilds came under the direct authority of the city's prefect (an imperially appointed official), who acted as chief justice, chief of police, and chief trade regulator. Each guild then supervised its own members, setting wages and work hours. This helped maintain strict price and supply controls. As with European guilds, each specialty was restricted to a particular area or block in the city. Grocers and others who sold perishable goods remained the only exception; they were allowed to set up business in various neighborhoods.

Because the city was a major trade center, myriad professions existed to employ the working population. The many artisan professions included metalworkers, shipbuilders, candlemakers, bakers, potters, and perfumers. Merchants sold the completed goods in the city's shops or exported them to faraway places. Most workers were men, but many women worked in the imperial silk factory and other textile-producing workshops. Fishing, working the docks, and providing menial labor filled the time of those on the lower end of the social scale. Slaves were imported from central and northern Europe and from Africa to be domestic servants, land workers, and workshop laborers.

Private Life in the City

The city of Constantinople enjoyed times of population growth and endured periods of plague in its lengthy history. From the sixth to the thirteenth centuries, the city's population numbered about one million people. Of these, some were the fortunate wealthy, who lived in relative comfort. Constantinople had no space for expansion, so excess population migrated to suburban areas that developed near the city, such as the northern shore of the Golden Horn. Most of the citizens lived in neighborhoods that were cramped and unsanitary. Alleys and narrow streets functioned as waste-disposal areas that often bred disease, which occasionally developed into epidemics that killed thousands.

The poor depended on the gifts of pilgrims and priests, and the homeless often found shelter in public spaces. Frequently those who had died during the night had to be removed before business could commence the next day. Following in Greek and Roman traditions of public charity, Justinian tried to remedy the predicament with a decree that distributed as many as 80,000 loaves of bread to the hungry every day. His public works projects, in part, were initiated to put the unemployed back to work.

Recreation could be found in various places around the city. The public baths afforded a place for rest and relaxation for all classes. As in Rome, people gathered there to exchange gossip, informally establish business ties, and meet new friends. The heat of the summer months often drove citizens to the baths more than once a day. The Hippodrome, by far, was the most popular place for entertainment, and everyone was admitted free of charge. The emperor and his subjects shouted encouragement to their champions in the competitions held there. In the early Byzantine Empire, chariot races offered the most popular sport. Animal fights and lighter entertainments by clowns, jugglers, and dancers also delighted the crowd between major events. Torture and executions of capital offenders also occasionally drew the curious to the Hippodrome, as did the emperor's speeches and heated political debates. By the early thirteenth century, crusaders from Europe amused the citizens with jousts between mounted knights. If the citizens wearied of the city noise and the roars of the Hippodrome crowd, they could walk the spacious parks and gardens found throughout the city.

Clothing indicated a person's social status, as in many places of the world. Within the city, various sects and professions wore distinctive clothing or colors. Two rival factions in the city wore characteristic bits of cloth on their shoulders to identify them as Green Party or Blue Party members, not unlike the gangs of Han Empire China and modern North America. The factions began as clubs associated with the Hippodrome, where they led the cheering fans of the green and blue teams. Members of these groups also acted as bodyguards to the emperor, for which they wore distinctive Hun-style clothing: cloaks and shoes, large-sleeved tunics gathered at the wrist, and a particular hairstyle, cropped in the front and long and flowing in the back. Rich merchants and citizens could afford the new styles, especially the silk clothing, so popular in Constantinople; their horses even sported embroidered saddlecloth. Long, elaborately decorated coats replaced Roman togas among the elite by the sixth century. Silver and gold threads woven into brocaded fabrics adorned the bodies of the wealthy, while ornate jewelry of silver and gold, mounted with precious gems, decorated their necks, arms, and hands. In contrast to the elite with their high fashions, commoners and slaves continued to wear knee-length tunics cinched at the waist.

Life in the city encompassed a broad spectrum of lifestyles. Some ethnic groups or religious sects lived in segregated neighborhoods; Jews were not allowed to live within the city walls but found shelter in the suburb north of the city. Most elite and merchant house construction centered on a courtyard, with windowless walls facing the street. Poorer houses consisted of multiple-story apartment buildings (sometimes nine stories high) that offered cramped quarters for multiple-family living. Food variety in families' diets was determined by wealth. Dried, cured, or fresh meats could be purchased, but few poor families could afford much meat. Fruits, such as apples, pears, grapes, figs, and melons, could be purchased from the markets in the city. Shoppers also found vegetables, such as cabbage, leeks, cucumbers, onions, and carrots. Elite dishes were flavored with honey, pepper, and cinnamon. Every household, large or small, helped consume the tons of fish from the bulging nets of fishing ships each day. Pastoralists supplied the milk products used in many house-

holds. A common dish for both rich and poor families consisted of a mixture of fish, cheese, and vegetables cooked in a casserole.

Most women in Constantinople experienced less freedom than men. Except for the empress, they could not attend the exciting sports events at the Hippodrome. Women could not participate in processions or parades or engage in the many public political debates and protests. All women, including the empress, were required to cover their heads and faces in public, in similar fashion to women in Muslim society. Women did control the households, however; whether the household was large or small, all domestic arrangements came under the authority of the wife and mother. Wealthier women employed servants or owned slaves to assist them in keeping the home comfortable. In poorer homes, younger girls learned domestic chores by working alongside their mothers.

Women were mentioned frequently in Byzantine law, and, during Justinian's reign, several changes in Byzantine law affected women. Wives could own property of equal value to their dowries, which, in some cases, was a considerable amount. In addition, widows retained the right to be guardians of their children, thus, in certain circumstances, controlling vast amounts of family wealth. Justinian complained that Constantinople housed too many brothels, staffed by young girls and innocent women enticed from rural areas, and he outlawed all houses of prostitution in the city. His edicts may have slowed prostitution but did not eliminate its practice. Divorce could be filed by a woman if her husband did not consummate the marriage within two years, made false claims of adultery against her, held her captive, or was unfaithful to her. A wife could not obtain a divorce for any other reason. Justinian did not accept mutual consent as grounds for divorce. These divorce laws, however, were repealed by Justinian's successor, who recognized them to be unpopular.

Children belonged to both fathers and mothers, particularly after Justinian issued his law code. Although the law limited the ages for marriage to fourteen years for boys and twelve years for girls, many families arranged marriages by the time the children were four or five years old. Sons of artisans were expected to follow in the same professions as their fathers. Children of concubines, as in Muslim society, received legal status and limited rights of inheritance.

FIGURE 17.7 *Danielis, a Wealthy Byzantine Woman.* *Danielis was a very wealthy Byzantine widow who lived in the ninth century. Her control of her own wealth demonstrates the financial freedom women enjoyed under Byzantine law. She was a sponsor and supporter of a young politician named Basil, who in A.D. 867 became Emperor Basil I, founder of a new dynasty. Her close association with the emperor gave her influence in Byzantine society. Basil made her son, John, an official in his bureaucracy. When John died, Danielis left most of her great wealth to Leo VI, Basil's son and successor. In this drawing, Danielis visits Basil and presents him with gifts.* Biblioteca Nacional, Madrid.

The Nika Rebellion

Social unrest often exploded into riot and revolt in the city during periods of heavy taxation and economic distress. Tax payments took the form of gold from city dwellers and produce from rural-area dwellers. During Justinian's war with the Persians, taxes were increased to pay for the expenses of combat and interruption of trade. In January 532, rioting broke out at the instigation of the Greens and the Blues, who had gained some popular political influence. The disturbance began in the Hippodrome and spread to the streets and throughout the city. Shouts of "Nika!"[3] ("Victory!") filled the afternoon air as the proponents organized into a mob ready to fight for tax relief.

The Nika Rebellion incited full-scale looting that destroyed many businesses and ignited widespread fires that damaged many buildings, including the imperial palace. Soon the rebels were calling for a new imperial election, and the situation became desperate as the nephew of a previous emperor was elected by the crowd. Justinian wavered, considering whether to flee the city. It may have been Empress Theodora's persuasion that convinced him to stay, and he finally mobilized his army to his defense. Under Justinian's direction, the army wrested the city from the rebels and attacked and massacred nearly 30,000 of them in the Hippodrome. Justinian rebuilt the city after the Nika Rebellion; the construction projects put many unemployed people to work and helped calm political tensions.

BYZANTINE ECONOMY

The Byzantine economy centered on agriculture and trade. Agriculture was the mainstay of revenues for the government and supplied local people with the basic commodities for survival.

[3] **Nika:** NY kah

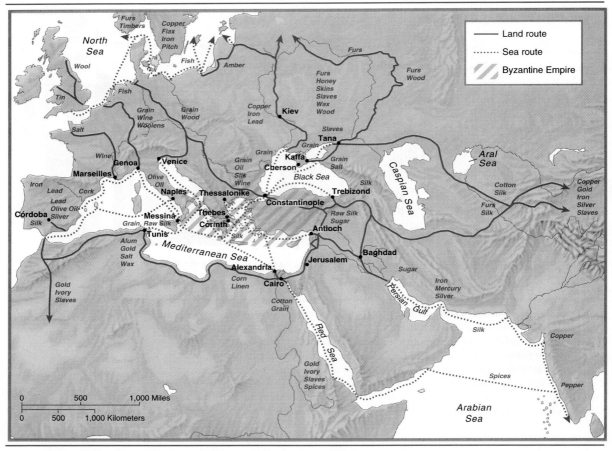

MAP 17.3 Byzantine Trade. *Byzantine trade served as a link between the European trade network and East Asian and Indian trade networks, with Constantinople as its hub. Silks, jewels, precious metals, sugar, and spices from eastern areas were brought along the silk road and spice routes to exchange for slaves, wood, honey, woolens, and grain from European areas.*

Trade took many merchants across the empire on their way to domestic markets in ships and along caravan routes. Few foreign trading expeditions were sent by the Byzantines, whose almost ideal placement at the crossroads of Eurasia and Africa afforded them a wealth of trade goods.

Landholders consisted of the state, the Christian Church, and individuals. Some landholders held large estates that rivaled the aristocratic villas of the Western Roman Empire or the manors of medieval Europe; poor farmers had small landholdings and could barely eke out a living. Some of these impoverished farmers became tenants of wealthier landowners. They were similar to the serfs of medieval Europe: They remained tied to the land that they worked and fell under the legal jurisdiction of the landowner. One-third of tenant harvests went to pay imperial taxes, leaving only two-thirds to pay rent to landlords and to meet all other expenses. Heavy taxation prompted many tenant farmers to abandon their allegiance to the Byzantine Empire when enemy soldiers invaded their territories. From the seventh to ninth centuries, border hostilities caused the breakup of large landholdings. By the tenth century, most farming was done by free farmers with small landholdings.

Most domestic trade was conducted in the major market cities of the empire, Constantinople, Thessalonike,[4] and Trebizond, where goods from various places were brought for sale. Generally, domestic trade was significant. Wine, oil, wool,

[4] **Thessalonike:** THEHS uh LOHN eh kah

metals, marble, timber, and finished products, such as cloth and leather goods, were exchanged at the major market cities. Local networks of trade between the empire's urban centers and rural areas supplied the subjects with various staples. The volume of trade between urban centers was greater in the eastern territories than it was in western areas, which tended to be more self-sufficient.

Long-distance trade was a central component of the Byzantine economy, and the location of major trade cities made the empire a natural center for the passage of goods moving between Europe and Asia. Long-distance trade brought spices, jewelry, and other products from China, Persia, and India as well as aromatics from Axum and rhinoceros-horn medicine from sub-Saharan Africa. Other items, such as grain, wine, honey, wax, furs, skins, gold, iron, ivory, and slaves, came from Europe and Africa. In addition, many raw materials came into the empire that then were transformed into finished products and later exported. Byzantine glassware, for example, was highly prized; emperors often sent pieces as gifts to foreign rulers. Goods moved overland from their places of origin into the empire through trade stations in Persia or north of the Caspian Sea into the Black Sea area. Water routes from Southeast Asia transported goods across the Bay of Bengal, the Arabian Sea, and either the Persian Gulf or the Red Sea into ports in Southwest Asia.

Byzantine trade fluctuated, depending upon the political circumstances and general economic conditions. The collapse of Axum in 650 cut off one area of trade from the Byzantines. The political and military reverses of the mid–seventh to mid–ninth centuries, which caused deurbanization in the empire, helped create a decline in the volume of trade. By the tenth century, lessened hostilities led to a revival of urbanism and trade after nearly three centuries of decline. Significant commerce between Dar al-Islam and the Byzantine Empire increased the number of available goods, slaves, and revenues. The eleventh and twelfth centuries experienced significant growth as urban centers sprawled and Italian markets flourished. Egyptian sources show that Byzantine products, such as brocades and finished furniture, became increasingly popular in Egypt.

In the thirteenth century, the Byzantine trade network experienced serious decline because of the competition of Italian trade networks, which controlled exclusive access to the markets of central and western Europe. The Italians regulated Byzantine exports of food and raw materials to the west and the imports of finished products of Italian and French cloth. By the fourteenth century, Byzantine trade, although still extensive, remained subsidiary to the growing Italian network. The fourteenth-century conquests of Byzantine lands by Ottoman Turks further challenged Byzantine trade. As with other empires we have reviewed, decline in trade and political disintegration often coincided.

Interregional trade treaties helped regulate the flow of goods around the empire, and some peace treaties had clauses attached to them that determined trade relations with neighboring polities. These documents established agreements on trade sites, terms of exchange, and certain privileges for merchants (like duty exemptions). A clause in the peace treaty of 562 with Persia, for example, specified that all trade be done at specific stations. Sometimes clauses designated where and for how long foreign merchants could reside in the cities. In 907, a treaty with the Russians specified that their merchants in Constantinople be housed at St. Mamas, a monastery in the southwestern section of the city, be permitted to receive supplies for six months, and be exempt from duties. The treaties with Italian cities were primarily commercial. The first was with Venice in 992, followed by treaties with most of the other Italian maritime centers.

FIGURE 17.8 *Byzantine Currency.* The Nomisma *coin of the Byzantine Empire was so stable that it became the currency of choice of most merchants in the Mediterranean Sea trade from around the tenth to the thirteenth centuries. Europeans used the coin, calling it a bezant. Devaluation of coins was often a major factor in the interruption of trade networks, and merchants preferred to be paid with currency they could trust.* British Museum/Photo by Derek Bayes.

Italian merchants enjoyed many privileges that others did not, including free access to many markets.

One major component of Byzantine trade was the stability of its coinage. The *Nomisma*, a Byzantine coin, became the preferred medium of exchange from Central Asia to western Europe. While its gold content fluctuated somewhat over the centuries, the coin remained a standard on which users could confidently rely. The eighth-century English historian Bede, wanting to demonstrate the purity of a local princess, described her as "pure as a bezant."

BYZANTINE CHRISTIANITY

Between the fourth and the seventh centuries, Christianity became entrenched as the major religion of the Byzantine Empire. Patriarchs (bishops) of Jerusalem, Antioch, Alexandria, Rome, and Constantinople emerged as leaders of the church. When Arab Muslim conquests of Byzantine territories came to include the cities of Jerusalem, Antioch, and Alexandria, the remaining patriarchs of Constantinople and Rome became the two most prominent Christian leaders. The patriarch of Rome (the pope) became the head of the western Christian church, and the patriarch of Constantinople became the leader of eastern Christians. The presence of powerful Christian emperors who also claimed spiritual authority, however, created a competition for control over the eastern church. The relationships between the patriarchs of Constantinople and the emperors were a mixture of mutual support and rivalry. The emperor often convened councils and intervened in spiritual matters, while the patriarch frequently intruded in imperial affairs and plotted with officials against the monarch. At most times, however, both worked for the mutual benefit of the Christian religion.

The Eastern Orthodox Church

Christians in the Eastern Roman Empire developed some theological perspectives and liturgical practices that differed profoundly from those of the Western Roman Empire. Religion is, above all, a cultural expression, and as the two halves of the empire diverged culturally down different paths, so did the Christian faith develop disparate practices in the two areas. A few examples of the variation in practices will help to explain the 1054 **schism**, a religious split caused by irreconcilable differences of opinion. The consequence of the schism was the formation of two major branches of Christianity: the Roman Catholic and the Eastern Orthodox.

Some examples of the practices that separated Christians are found in social attitudes, rituals, and theological opinions. For example, Byzantine men began abstaining from shaving in the seventh century, as beards became popular throughout the society. Beards were associated with manliness; emperors from the fourth century on increasingly wore beards, and beards at court distinguished powerful officials from court eunuchs. Byzantine monks always wore beards after biblical and monastic tradition. The shaving off of a beard came to be a severe punishment for any Byzantine man. By the eleventh century, the beardless Europeans were thought to be effeminate; clearly, beards translated into a matter of pride for Byzantine men. Some bearded Byzantine priests even refused to offer the bread and wine of the sacred meal to shaven (that is, western) communicants.

Another distinction between eastern and western Christianity was that of language. The traditional language of theology had been Greek. During the Roman Empire, the official language had become Latin, but many theologians continued to write in Greek. As time passed and the breakup of the Roman Empire commenced, western theologians came to accept Latin as their theological language. Byzantine theologians came to regard Latin treatises as unworthy of serious consideration because of translation difficulties in expressing the nuances of theology. Many of the theological arguments that led to the 1054 schism occurred as a result of misunderstandings because of language difficulties.

Many liturgical rituals differed between the two areas and clashes occurred over territorial control. One difference in ritual was the calculation of the celebration of Easter. The Council of Nicaea in 325 named the date for Easter as the first Sunday after the first full moon after the spring equinox (which tied it to the traditional celebration of the Jewish Passover feast). Differences between the dating of Easter, which falls sometime between March 21 and April 25, developed because Byzantines used different computations of astronomical tables. For example, Easter might be celebrated in Italy on April 18 and in Constantinople on April 25. (A discrepancy between the days of celebration still exists today.)

A major clash concerning territorial control erupted in the ninth century, challenging the traditional Byzantine view of the equality of patriarchs. The patriarch of Constantinople had been deposed by the Byzantine emperor, who placed Photius (his secretary) on the patriarchal throne. The pope objected and claimed the right to depose Photius and any priests who had supported him. This assertion of papal supremacy over the patriarch deeply offended many easterners and had a profound effect on strained relations between eastern and Roman Christians.

The most serious of the differences, however, were theological. The best example is the addition of the clause "and the Son" to the Nicene Creed (a statement of faith adopted from the First Council of Nicaea in 325), which was repeated by Christians at most worship services. The western church had added the clause to help explain the meaning of the Trinity. The Byzantine Christians agreed with the theology of the clause but objected on the grounds that language could be neither added to nor subtracted from the creed. The clause caused a conflict that reverberated throughout Christendom. Even the Byzantine emperor joined the fracas and had the original creed carved on silver tablets. The "and the Son" clause played a significant role in the theological arguments that led to the formal schism in 1054. Today, the clause remains a major stumbling block to Christian reunification.

The schism between eastern and western Christianity created the Roman Catholic Church in medieval Europe and the Eastern Orthodox Church in the Byzantine Empire. Each side claimed that it held the correct interpretation of scripture and was heir to Christian tradition. The very titles suggest this: The word "catholic" means universal and the word "orthodox" means correct belief. By the time the European crusaders entered Byzantine territories in the late eleventh century, great animosity already existed. The conquest of Constantinople by crusaders for a short time in the thirteenth century exacerbated the enmity of each side for the other.

Eastern Orthodox Monasticism

Christian monasticism began in the Eastern Roman Empire and continued to be a significant element of Byzantine Christianity. Although monasticism had originated with hermit monks in the eastern deserts, it soon became an urban phenomenon; one-third of the approximately 1,000 monasteries and nunneries were located within

FIGURE 17.9 *Greek Island Monastery. This is the Simonopetra Monastery on Mount Athos, an island off the Greek coast. There are many monasteries on the island, placed there because of its remoteness. The monasteries were built into steep cliffs that impeded access in order to preserve the seclusion of the monks living there. In the eleventh century, all women (and female animals) were banned from the island to keep the monks from being distracted by thoughts about sex and to preserve their spiritual focus. The ban remains in effect today.* Otis Imboden/ NGS Image Collection.

Constantinople. The population of these monasteries ranged from as few as three monks to as many as several hundred. The hermit attitude of renunciation of the world, however, continued in remote monasteries, such as those on Mount Athos. The ethnic diversity of the empire led to distinctive ethnic monasteries.

As with the monasteries of Roman Catholic Europe, Eastern Orthodox monasteries often owned extensive properties and contributed to the intricate trade system and economy of the empire. Some monasteries received special economic privileges from the state. They could inherit properties from private citizens, they remained protected against confiscation by covetous neighbors, and they could rent out their lands to farmers without paying new taxes. Monastery properties grew substantially in the tenth century. Some monks tried to curb the growth, fearing that the resulting wealth would tempt the monks from their spiritual duties. One emperor tried to restrict the purchase of new lands in 964, but monasteries continued to expand. In an attempt to redistribute monastic wealth and increase state revenues, emperors in the fourteenth century granted some monastic lands to soldiers as payment for their services.

Unlike their Roman Catholic counterparts, Eastern Orthodox monasteries did not establish particular orders, such as Benedictines or Cistercians. Each monastery remained under its own rule (which was patterned on generally accepted practices), and individuals exercised a level of autonomy. In contrast to the western model of monks' vowing obedience to their abbots, eastern monks frequently moved from monastery to monastery or out into hermitage, away from the community. Also in contrast to European monasteries, Byzantine monasteries did not develop a special focus on becoming educators, although intellectual pursuits did appeal to many monks. Much of the literature of the early Byzantine Empire, such as accounts of the lives of the saints and wise sayings of the desert hermits, came from the monasteries. Monks and nuns formed the majority of the educated in the ninth century. Scholars have estimated that 50 percent of Byzantine scribes in the tenth and eleventh centuries were monks. Literacy, of course, facilitated the reading of prayers and scriptures.

Eastern Orthodox monasteries, like their Roman Catholic counterparts, ran hospitals and orphanages in addition to performing various charitable services. Refugees found safe haven within their walls during times of political upheaval, and beggars and the dispossessed received food and clothing. Many monasteries also offered housing to pilgrims on the way to holy sites and housed prisoners living out sentences of banishment for their crimes.

Byzantine monasteries became great patrons of the arts, although monks usually did not produce visual art themselves. Manuscript illumination did not become a monastic occupation, as it had in western Christianity. Some of the best examples of Byzantine silver and gold vessels, visual art, and textiles were produced by artisans for monasteries. Architects and artists were usually imported to build and decorate the churches and residence halls.

Monasteries remained the primary residence for those seeking a spiritual life of prayer and devotion to God. Many Christian mystics experienced their spiritual encounters with the divine in monasteries, and many of their writings contributed to the development of Eastern Orthodox tradition.

BYZANTINE ELITE ARTS

Patronage of the arts in Byzantine society came primarily from the state and the Eastern Orthodox Church; significant patronage by individuals did not come until about the fifteenth century. The unique Byzantine style was influenced by Classical Greek, Roman, and Hellenistic literature, philosophy, and visual art. By the sixth century, Christian motifs and genres dominated the art of the empire.

Literature

Byzantine literature inherited styles from previous generations. With the advent of Christianity, some dramatic forms were abandoned because of their topics, which were perceived as immoral (such as the poetry of Sappho from ancient Greece). Poetry, as well, became attached to ritual in the form of hymns. The writing of sermons and wise sayings of holy individuals offered the reader a selection of devotional materials. Histories of various military and religious events became popular. Between about the mid–seventh century and the beginning of the ninth century, very little literature was produced beyond theological treatises.

Literature adopted an encyclopedic focus in the mid–ninth century, when compilations became popular. Many technical works dealt with the administration of the empire, such as military textbooks, treatises on taxation, documents on the imperial system, and law textbooks. Religious works continued to be produced, especially idealized biographies of saints' lives, **hagiographies**.[5] Other works included collections of Classical Greek and Roman literature.

A famous twelfth-century historian named Anna Komnene[6] (1083–1153) was the eldest daughter of an emperor. She wrote a history of her father's reign that scholars have found most helpful in analyzing the twelfth-century empire. During this same period, a new genre developed in literature that discussed the dual nature of good and evil in every individual; many characters showed attributes of both heroes and villains. Stories and poems about sex, chastity, and romance written by professional novelists and poets rather than government officials or monks entertained the literate of the empire. Hagiographies went out of style in this new literary climate.

From the thirteenth to the mid–fourteenth century, Byzantine literature experienced a revival of hagiography and a new pessimism in the representation of history—no great surprise since the empire was under much political and economic stress. Western literary styles had been imported into the area through the Crusader States in the twelfth and thirteenth centuries, and their influence appears in thirteenth-century Byzantine works. During this period, several intellectuals began translating Latin texts into Greek. Some traveled to Italy, where they translated into Latin Greek texts, especially philosophical works, that they had brought with them. Many of these intellectuals tried to preserve the ancient Classical Greek and Roman styles, a practice that may have helped to stimulate the Italian Renaissance.

Philosophy and Theology

Byzantine philosophy was closely associated with Christian topics. The philosopher and the monk had a lot in common; they both loved wisdom and both disciplined themselves to live a moral life. As with all Byzantine intellectual traditions, philoso-

phy inherited and adopted Greco-Roman and Hellenistic traditions. In addition, philosophical speculation benefited from the Byzantine exchange, particularly that of Islamic philosophy. Christian theologians of the first four centuries A.D. gave Byzantine philosophers paradigms for what they saw as the "true" philosophical life: martyrdom and monasticism.

The prominent Byzantine philosopher John of Damascus (675–749) divided philosophy into two main branches: theoretical and practical. Theoretical philosophy consisted of physics, mathematics, and theology, and practical philosophy included ethics, economics, and politics. His division served as the basis for the study of philosophy in the Byzantine Empire. A Neoplatonic revival heavily influenced Byzantine philosophy, particularly through the works of John of Damascus. John is a good example of a Byzantine Christian philosopher; he wrote many polemical works, including some against Islam and heresies, as well as sermons, hymns, moral tracts, hagiographies, and biblical commentaries.

Eleventh-century philosophy benefited from a focus on education. For example, at the University of Constantinople (begun around the mid–eleventh century), the school of philosophy was headed by an influential teacher, Michael Psellos (1018–1081?). Psellos drew on a diverse offering of sources in his classes on philosophy, and he assembled topics from them in a short encyclopedia. Some of Psellos's works, as well as those of many of his successors, analyzed Aristotle's ethics, physics, and logic. In his classes, Psellos stressed physics, which he taught was created by God but functions according to the laws of nature. This conception left little room for miracles.

The eleventh to the mid–thirteenth centuries witnessed renewed interest in the philosophical works of Plato and the Neoplatonists, especially within Christian intellectual circles. Earlier mystical writings, such as those of the sixth-century mystic Pseudo Dionysius[7] the Areopagite, also became popular again. His works on mysticism were the most influential Christian writings on Neoplatonic ideas.

After the fall of Constantinople to crusaders in 1204, the focus of Byzantine philosophical activity shifted to Nicaea. A group of philosophers gathered there; their polemics covered all the subjects

[5]**hagiography:** HAW jee AHG ruh fee *or* HAY gee AHG ruh fee
[6]**Komnene:** kohm NEHN ay

[7]**Dionysius:** DY oh NIHS ee uhs

UNDER THE LENS

The Iconoclastic Controversy

Byzantine Christians venerated **icons** because they were the images of holy people, even Christ himself. One would not throw away or deface an icon, for example, because it represents the subject of its art. Like the stories of the saints in the hagiographies, the images inspire virtue; some described them as "silent writing," and in this sense, their destruction would be like ripping up a Bible or defacing the Qur'an. Icons are still produced today in Eastern Orthodoxy, and the attitude toward them is still one of respect.

In the eighth century, a controversy arose over the practice of venerating icons in the Byzantine Empire. Many individuals thought that people were worshiping the icons instead of giving them special respect; these objections were based upon older traditions of not making or worshiping false idols. The issue fixed particularly on making images of Christ and then spread to other images; some denounced the practice and asserted that it should be stopped. Several bishops condemned icons in the early eighth century, and their views fueled a formidable movement.

Emperor Leo III (reign dates 717–741) supported the movement and issued in 726 an edict demanding the destruction of a famous icon of Christ on a gate in Constantinople. The citizens rioted. Nevertheless, the **iconoclasts**, icon destroyers, gained momentum. By 730, Leo III deposed the dissenting patriarch of Constantinople and issued a decree demanding the destruction of all icons. In the ensuing years, hundreds of thousands of icons were destroyed. This destruction significantly defaced holy places because icons covered the walls, screens, and altars of every Eastern Orthodox Church and monastery. Almost every household also had icons used for daily devotionals, and placards with icon images were often carried in processions and parades. Many Monophysites applauded the emperor's decree, believing that Christ did not have a human body, and therefore no image of him could be made. Many monks, the most ardent defenders of icons, were forced to whitewash the images in their churches and monasteries; those who refused to do so were prosecuted.

In the following decades, other emperors continued iconoclastic policies. One emperor called a local council to condemn icon veneration as satanic. The issue extended beyond painted images and challenged the perception of the saints. Veneration of saints' relics was questioned as inappropriate, but this issue did not result in relic destruction. Many **iconophiles**, venerators of icons, who lived in isolated areas continued their practices; the farther away from the capital one lived, the less one observed the decree.

The iconoclastic controversy contributed to the hostilities between eastern and western Christendom that ended in the schism of 1054. A decree prohibiting religious images also was sent to the pope. Because there was a different artistic tradition in western Christianity that did not include veneration of icons, western Christians failed to understand the objection to simple representations of Christ and the saints. Heated debates between popes and Byzantine patriarchs and emperors commenced. The papacy was threatened if it did not comply, which helped to convince the pope at that time that the Franks were better allies than Byzantine emperors.

Although theological issues were at the heart of the controversy, scholars argue that economic and political motivations also spurred Leo III to act. Leo and succeeding emperors used the excuse of iconoclasm to confiscate monastic properties of those monasteries whose monks refused to comply with the decree; these monasteries continued to function under state control. Some scholars argue that the emperor needed to reassert his authority over the church, which might be accomplished by deposing the patriarch and forcing compliance with the decree. The iconoclastic controversy lost momentum in the ninth century as some emperors gave sympathetic support to iconophiles and finally ended with a formal compromise that icons were constructive representations of holy individuals. Icons are still a significant part of Eastern Orthodoxy today.

of philosophy. They particularly argued over the virtues and vices of Aristotle's ideas versus those of the Neoplatonists. Toward the end of the Byzantine Empire, the debate of first-century Christians about the relationship of Greek philosophy to Christianity rose again. The debate raged on, and the discipline of philosophy became suspect to many Byzantine intellectuals who came to believe there should be a separation between the disciplines of Greek philosophy and theology.

Visual Arts

The visual arts of the Byzantine Empire were rendered in such media as textiles, manuscript illustration, metalwork, painting, and mosaics. Many earlier styles and subjects influenced Byzantine arts, as did the exchange of styles with conquerors and peoples on the borders. A unique element of Byzantine religious art was the expected attitude of the viewer to the object; the artist was secondary to the religious person depicted. In addition, artistic style tended to remain consistent, and model books and artisan tradition served to keep the styles uniform.

Some changes did occur stylistically in Byzantine art, especially in painting during the eleventh to the fifteenth centuries. Scenes of everyday life appear in the eleventh century, augmenting the dominant religious themes and imperial portraits of preceding centuries. By the eleventh and twelfth centuries an attempt to display more emotion can be observed in paintings. New ideas influencing artists in the thirteenth century significantly altered the previous 150 years of Byzantine art, in part because of patronage by local officials. Uniformity of the previous centuries gave way to new expressions as the empire came to an end.

FIGURE 17.10 *Virgin of Vladimir. Icons decorated Byzantine churches and monasteries and were venerated during liturgical services. The Russian city of Kiev adopted Eastern Orthodoxy, which embraced iconographic art. This twelfth-century icon of the Virgin Mary and baby Jesus is from Constantinople. It was eventually taken to Russia, where it became one of the most famous icons of Russian Orthodoxy, known as the Virgin of Vladimir.* Sovfoto.

SUMMARY

1. The Byzantine Empire evolved out of the Eastern Roman Empire and soon developed a uniquely Byzantine culture. The empire at its height encompassed Greece, the Balkans up to the Danube River, the Turkish Peninsula, Palestine, parts of North Africa, and the islands of the eastern Mediterranean and the Aegean seas. The population of the empire in the sixth century has been estimated at more than 30 million people.

2. Christianity became the ideological link that united the Byzantine Empire. Everyday life in the empire remained largely unchanged as farmers, artisans, merchants, and others continued to live in much the same ways as those of previous generations.

3. Byzantine law was codified during Justinian's reign in the *Corpus Juris Civilis*, which became influential beyond the borders of the

EURASIA-AFRICA

Byzantine Empire, 450–1453

Justinian's Expansion, 527–565

Religious themes dominate, c. 650–c. 800

Iconoclastic controversy, 726–842

Secular themes become more prominent, c. 800–1453

Crusaders control parts of Byzantine Empire, 1204–1261

400

600

800

1000

1200

1400

Constantinople named the capital of the Roman Empire, 330

Justinian rebuilds Hagia Sophia, 532
Corpus Juris Civilis completed, 535

Russia's Vladimir I cements relations with Constantinople, 988
First commercial treaties with Italian cities, 992

The schism of the Eastern Orthodox Church and the Roman Catholic Church, 1054

Anna Komnene dies, 1153

Constantinople conquered by Ottoman Turks, 1453

empire. The Christian Church influenced Byzantine law, and the patriarch's court functioned as the court of appeals.

4. Emperors and empresses played significant roles in the empire. Although emperors were thought to have been chosen by divine will, they were actually selected by the army, the Senate, or the citizens of Constantinople. Most empresses maintained parallel courts with elite women and influenced the policies of the emperors. Some empresses ruled for brief periods.

5. Many border raids disturbed the peace of the empire between 450 and 1453. Muslims conquered the eastern and southern portions of the Byzantine Empire, and crusaders conquered Constantinople in 1204. The Ottoman Turks conquered Constantinople in 1453, ending the Byzantine Empire.

6. Reorganization of the imperial administration into provinces occurred under Justinian. This system was replaced with the *theme* organization, which enabled better defense of the empire.

7. In 330, the city of Byzantium was chosen as the capital and renamed Constantinople by Constantine. Many ethnic groups populated the city, which was the hub of an extensive trade network. Many public works were erected by Justinian, including Hagia Sophia, the impressive church. Constantinople had formidable defenses: a three-wall system, water on three sides, and a moat that impeded the only land access.

8. Citizens numbered about one million in the city of Constantinople. All citizens could attend public recreation areas, such as the baths and gardens. Some women held control over vast fortunes and, if widowed, over their children. Social unrest broke out as the Nika Rebellion in 532, when the citizens of Constantinople looted and burned the city, after which Justinian ordered 30,000 rioters to be massacred in the Hippodrome.

9. The economic foundation of the Byzantine Empire was agriculture and trade. Both domestic trade and long-distance trade moved raw materials and finished products throughout the empire and beyond. Muslim and Italian competition inhibited Byzantine trade, and, after the thirteenth century, the empire never regained its extensive trade network.

10. Christianity remained the religion of the empire, and heresies were sometimes tolerated for political reasons. The Byzantine Empire's Christians developed different practices, rituals, and theologies that eventually brought them into conflict with western Christians. The pope and patriarch excommunicated each other in 1054, creating the Eastern Orthodox Church and the Roman Catholic Church. Monasticism was an important element of Eastern Orthodoxy. Most monasteries were patrons of the arts; monks usually hired artisans to build and decorate their churches and monasteries.

11. Patronage of the state and the church increased the production of Byzantine art. Literature, philosophy, and visual arts inherited Classical Greek, Roman, and Hellenistic antecedents, yet a distinctive Byzantine style developed. Christianity had great influence on the arts, supplying religious themes for expression.

SUGGESTED READINGS

Browning, Robert. *Justinian and Theodora*. New York: Thames and Hudson, 1987. An examination of the reign of Justinian and the influence of Theodora.

Haussig, H. W. *A History of Byzantine Civilization*. Trans. by J. M. Hussey. New York: Praeger Publishers, 1971. A thorough coverage of the Byzantine Empire.

Mango, Cyril. *Byzantium: The Empire of New Rome*. New York: Charles Scribner's Sons, 1980. A standard review of Byzantine history.

Meyendorff, John. *Byzantine Theology*. Second edition. New York: Fordham University Press, 1979. A standard work on Eastern Orthodoxy.

Rice, Tamara Talbot. *Everyday Life in Byzantium*. New York: Barnes and Noble, 1994. An informative review of life in the Byzantine Empire, especially in the early centuries.

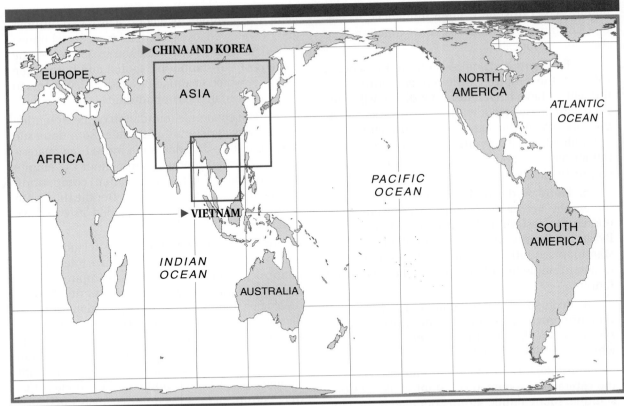

► CHINA AND KOREA

► VIETNAM

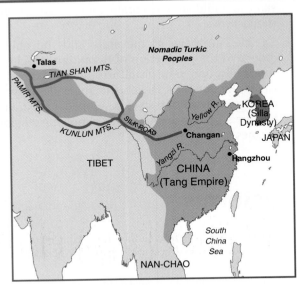

EUROPE

ASIA

AFRICA

NORTH
AMERICA

ATLANTIC
OCEAN

PACIFIC
OCEAN

► VIETNAM

INDIAN
OCEAN

AUSTRALIA

SOUTH
AMERICA

Talas

TIAN SHAN MTS.

PAMIR MTS.

KUNLUN MTS.

SILK ROAD

Nomadic Turkic
Peoples

Yellow R.

Changan

Yangzi R.

CHINA
(Tang Empire)

TIBET

KOREA
(Silla
Dynasty)

JAPAN

Hangzhou

South
China
Sea

NAN-CHAO

► **CHINA AND KOREA**

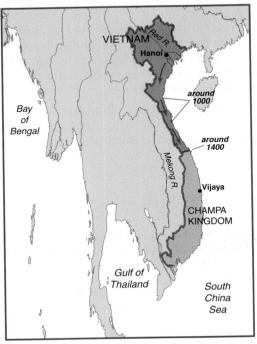

VIETNAM

Red R.

Hanoi

around
1000

Bay
of
Bengal

Mekong R.

around
1400

Vijaya

CHAMPA
KINGDOM

Gulf of
Thailand

South
China
Sea

► **VIETNAM**

Empires and Other States in East Asia

589–1279

The Song Chinese naval commander confidently surveyed the enemy's fleet. Although outnumbered in ships and sailors, he had two secret weapons. One was a small number of paddle-wheel ships that could travel rapidly, terrifying people who could not discern the cause of the propulsion. The Chinese admiral also had tested gunpowder weapons of great destructive power. Both weapons would help him defeat this rival navy.

This account recalls a naval battle wherein Chinese ships smashed an invading force in 1161. It also suggests the success the Chinese had in adapting technological discoveries to military affairs, helping to fuel empire building.

In this chapter, we will see how the Sui dynastic house reunited China. Reestablishment of a centralized, bureaucratic state gave the political strength to conduct an expansionist foreign policy, including an attempted reassertion of Chinese domination over the Korean Peninsula and Central Asian trade routes. Later, several elements of China's domestic market flourished, and its maritime commerce, especially with Southeast Asia and South Asia, improved. While the Koreans and the Vietnamese ultimately became independent, they used their own versions of Chinese political and cultural forms to establish strong and stable polities.

CHINA REUNIFIED: THE SUI AND TANG EMPIRES, 589–907

Sui[1] and Tang[2] power dominated East Asia for nearly two centuries, before decline and internal crisis forced a redirection of imperial energies to internal matters. These two regimes harnessed their subjects by creating a stable government staffed with individuals chosen by a civil service examination system.

The Sui Empire, 589–618

The Sui Empire lasted only three decades but had significant achievements. It reunited China permanently, inaugurated an effective political recruitment system, strengthened central control over regional and local officials, reestablished strong frontier boundaries, and created a solid economic base.

The long national division began to come to an end in the 580s, when General Yang Jian[3] (reign dates 581–604) usurped power in one of the northern Chinese states. He slowly consolidated his position and expanded his conquest of North China. In 589, after a long period of planning, the conquest of South China began. Sui partisans made and distributed tens of thousands of leaflets denouncing the southern monarch. A combined land and river attack began in Central China, passed through the Yangzi River gorges, and continued to the river's mouth. The Sui fleet numbered in the thousands, including large ramming ships. Once the waterborne effort was victorious, the land defenses crumbled, and the captured southern monarch was sent north to the Sui capital, where he peacefully lived out his life in exile.

Most of Yang Jian's activities were devoted to building a powerful government and consolidating unified rule over the north and the south. He was a skilled judge of talented people and an empire builder, but he was given to fits of temper (he once beat a man to death with a horse whip). Because he came to power by a palace coup, Yang Jian grew suspicious of everyone, including his sons. Yet for

[1] **Sui:** SWAY
[2] **Tang:** TAHNG
[3] **Yang Jian:** YAHNG JEE yahn

FIGURE 18.1 *Shrine to the Amida Buddha. Cast in 593, this bronze Amida Buddha illuminates the importance of Buddhism for the Sui Empire. Aiding those who called on him for help, protected by guardian deities, and surrounded by adoring animals, the Amida Buddha gained a widespread following in China, especially among the poor. Over the next century and a half, Buddhism became the dominant religion of China, uniting northerners and southerners as well as upper and lower classes.* Gift of Mrs. W. Scott Fitz. Courtesy of the Museum of Fine Arts, Boston.

all his faults, Yang Jian was a strong and successful monarch who monitored his officials by requiring them to write regular reports about their actions. He knew that only through the reestablishment of a centralized, bureaucratic administration would the unity last, but he paid a stiff price in personally having to read mountains of reports.

One of Yang Jian's most reliable and astute advisors was his wife, the Sui empress Dugu Jielo, who shared her husband's political vision, his tough-minded governing style, and his thrifty ways. She insisted on his not having other wives and was a sole partner in marriage as well as a chief advisor in politics. One of her major political acts was to persuade her husband to name her second (and favorite) son, Yang Guang (reign dates 604–618), as heir apparent.

Yang Jian established uniform practices for government and society. Weights and measures were standardized once again, and laws were codified. Standardized written tests were given to prospective office holders in order to find the most capable people. Begun in 589, this practice commenced the establishment of a civil service examination system. Administrative offices were thus staffed by capable individuals who owed their positions and loyalty to the monarch. To prevent regional and local officials from building local power bases, Yang Jian refused them permission to serve in the areas of their birth. To ensure that officials were honest and efficient, inspectors were regularly dispatched to distant places. These "eyes and ears of the ruler" became an indispensable administrative tool.

Buddhism, the personal belief system of Yang Jian, was used by the Sui leaders as a unifying force because it was established pervasively in both North and South China. Imperial support of monks and temples throughout the empire brought a measure of assurance to people in South China. Yang Jian also supported Confucianism because it stressed loyalty, honesty, and hard work by Confucian-trained officials. Because Confucianism stressed family unity, it helped foster social stability.

Building projects consumed much Sui attention and resources and contributed to the long-term economic well-being of the Chinese people. Roads connecting distant parts of the empire were built or resurfaced. The capital, Changan, was con-structed near the site of the previous imperial capital and was laid out on a north-south grid, measuring about six miles east to west and more than five miles north to south. Rebuilding of the Great Wall began in the north.

Yang Jian spent his last years without the empress, who died of natural causes. When the ruler became ill in 604, Yang Guang, the heir apparent, may have killed his father in order to facilitate the transition. Yang Guang's early years saw a continuation of his father's policies: Civil service examinations were held, building projects continued, and able government followed. One project was the construction of the Grand Canal, a waterway system connecting the Yangzi and Yellow river systems and, more important, two vital

FIGURE 18.2 *Emperor Yang Guang on the Grand Canal.* *Dragon boats plied the Grand Canal in the Sui era, carrying Emperor Yang Guang and his courtiers. These multideck ships relied on sails or human labor to move. This eighteenth-century painting captures the lively activity on the major north-south waterway linking key economic areas. Although the labor and material resources of the empire were heavily taxed to produce the canal, the long-range vision of Sui monarchs provided some of the means to keep the empire united.* Bibliothèque nationale, Paris/ET Archive.

economic centers. Thus, economic unity underlay political unity, and water transport flourished in a network of canals and natural waterways.

Yang Guang continued an expansive foreign policy against Eastern Turks and Koreans, but, although he was successful against the former, he failed miserably against the latter. Campaigns against the Koreans were mounted in 612, 613, and 614. Each was a military disaster stemming from strong Korean resistance, unfavorable weather conditions, and formidable logistical problems. The heavy taxes to supply these campaigns brought the Chinese people to starvation levels and prompted revolts that spread over much of North China. The massive building projects and cruel treatment of laborers caused widespread hatred of the state. Defeat also depressed the monarch, who submerged his sorrows in sensual pleasures. By 618, large parts of the empire were under rebel control, and the Sui Empire passed from the scene. Its legacy of unity was passed to its successor state, the Tang Empire.

The Early Tang Empire, 618–762

The Chinese people have a saying, "Qin–Han, Sui–Tang." It means that the short-lived Qin state (221–207 B.C.) accomplished much that was inherited by its successor state, the Han Empire, just as the short-lived Sui Empire left a significant heritage to the Tang state. The Tang Empire is important in another way: Its great power and prestige in East Asia caused its political system and cultural patterns to become models—followed with modifications—for the Koreans, Japanese, and Vietnamese.

The Tang Empire was founded by an aristocrat, Li Yuan (reign dates 618–627), who took command of a rebel force to maintain some influence for his family and for a major section of the Sui political elite. Within a year, Li Yuan's forces, some of which were led by his sons, defeated the major rebel contenders. The Tang Empire was proclaimed, and the founder inherited and modified the Sui institutions.

FIGURE 18.3 *Tang Era Woman Riding.* *Tang artisans were famed for their colorful ceramic ware. This piece depicts a woman riding the solidly built horse typically represented in the fine arts of the seventh and eighth centuries. Especially in the early decades of the empire, elite women often rode on horseback. A few, such as Empress Wu, also wielded considerable power in the imperial administration.* Laurie Platt Winfrey, Inc.

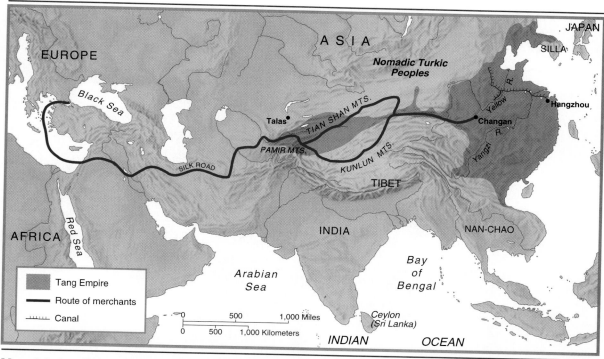

MAP 18.1 *China around 750.* *The Tang Empire occupied the largest amount of territory under Chinese rule in East and Central Asia until the eighteenth century. At its greatest extent in 750, the Tang Empire controlled the famed silk roads and permitted Chinese merchants to trade directly throughout Central Asia. Control of these roads was lost soon after the Talas River Battle in 751, significantly reducing income for the Tang court.*

Li Shimin,[4] the second son of the emperor, became increasingly hostile to his brother, the heir apparent. Li Shimin, a brilliant commander, formed a group of skilled advisors. In 627, the hostility between the two brothers led to bloodshed, when Li Shimin's allies plotted an ambush of the heir apparent within the palace walls. Li Shimin soon dethroned his father and became the second Tang emperor (reign dates 627–649).

Li Shimin pacified the frontiers, revised the law codes, consulted widely among his officials, and presided over an efficient administration. Like the Sui founder, Li Shimin controlled his officials by meticulously reviewing their mandated reports. Top officials were commanded to sleep in their offices in shifts so that the monarch might consult them when necessary. By the end of his reign the nation was peaceful and prosperous.

[4]**Li Shimin:** LEE SHER mihn

Only three women in Chinese history exercised direct political power, and one was Empress Wu (627–705). Wu began her court life as a minor concubine in Li Shimin's inner palace. When he died, she—along with other childless court women—was sent to a nunnery, and on one occasion the new emperor visited that holy place and became infatuated with his father's concubine. Wu was brought to the palace and eventually displaced the reigning empress. As imperial consort, Empress Wu not only provided male heirs, but she also aided her husband in ruling when he suffered from declining eyesight. Over time, she became the de facto ruler and purged her political rivals. At the time of the emperor's death, her son succeeded to the throne, and Wu ruled as a regent for her sons until she usurped power for herself.

In 690, Empress Wu proclaimed herself emperor (a title reserved for men), and to ensure her succession she had long prepared popular

FIGURE 18.4 *Relations between Chinese and Central Asians.* *China developed a series of complex relations with the states and peoples of Central Asia. This line drawing of the Song era depicts the Tang general Guo Ziyi receiving the homage of Uighur Turks. General Guo had served with these soldiers in Central Asia, and later, when Uighur armies threatened China, the general went unarmed into the enemy camp. Guo's former allies paid homage to him and later supported the Tang monarchy in its bid to regain power. The drawing also illustrates the Chinese ideal of foreign powers submitting to a culture that leads by moral force rather than by force of arms.* National Palace Museum, Taiwan, Republic of China.

opinion by granting amnesties and tax relief to various groups. She used the examination system to select a new generation of officials who were capable as well as personally loyal to her. At the same time, the aristocrats' strong grip on power was undermined. Despite the fact that purges were undertaken to cow or eliminate opponents, China was generally tranquil. After Wu had been in power for several years, old age and senility led to her forced retirement.

Xuanzong[5] (reign dates 712–756), the next major ruler, was an able monarch, and during the first three decades of his rule, he presided over a vigorous administration staffed with effective officials. Thousands of musicians, artists, and poets performed their tasks at the emperor's command. It was a prosperous time, during which Chinese armies roamed as far west as Central Asia beyond the famed silk roads.

Scholars have noted that the highlight of this age was reflected in poetry, because three of China's greatest poets wrote during this time. For centuries, poetry had remained the most prestigious of the literary genres, and scholars who circulated in the capital used their poems to introduce themselves to potential patrons. Wang Wei, a nature poet, also became a painter who founded a school of painting. Li Bo cultivated an eccentric persona, one linked with drinking and carousing. Du Fu often wrote lyrics of biting social commentary that partly reflected his own impoverished circumstances.

[5]**Xuanzong:** SHOO wahn zoong

Dynastic crisis owing to multiple causes nearly toppled the empire in the 750s. Declining revenues, a result of tax evasion, had grown to significant proportions, and the existing funds no longer supported the emperor's court. Central to this fiasco was the breakdown of the land-tenure system that had been in effect since Sui times. People were ignoring imperial laws and avoiding taxes by bribing officials. Another element in the fiscal crisis was an imperial ego that demanded more and more expensive entertainments and luxurious living at a time of reduced tax receipts.

IN THEIR OWN WORDS

Poetry of China's Three Masters

Tang Xuanzong's era produced significant poets, including Wang Wei, Li Bo, and Du Fu. Wang Wei (699–759) has been revered for his poems of natural settings, especially mountains:

Bamboo Lodge

I sit alone in the dark bamboo grove,
Playing the zither and whistling long.
In this deep wood no one would know—
Only the bright moon comes to shine.

My Retreat at Mount Zhungnan

In my mid-age I loved greatly the Path,
In late years I made my home by the Southern Hill.
When the spirit moves, I often wander alone
Among lovely scenes known only to myself.
I ramble where the stream ends,
Then sit and watch the clouds rise.
Occasionally I meet an old man in the woods,
So we talk and laugh without thinking of going home.

Li Bo (701–762) came from Southwest China and became adept in the martial arts. Li Bo loved to drink, and a story (probably untrue) has a drunken Li Bo adrift in a river leaning out of his watercraft to embrace the moon's reflection in the water. The boat capsized and the poet drowned. Li Bo often followed a Daoist path, and, like Wang Wei, he loved mountains:

Summer Day in the Mountains

Lazily I wave a white feather fan,
And lie naked in the green forest;
I hang my cap on a crag,
My bare head sprinkled by the pine wind.

Du Fu (710–770) tried for much of his adult life to get an official position. His ambitions played a tragic role in Du Fu's family life as reflected in his lines:

My old wife stays in a strange land,
Our ten mouths separated by wind and snow.
Who would have left them long uncared for?
So I went home to share their hunger and thirst.
Entering the door, I heard a loud wail;
Our youngest boy had died of starvation.
. . . .
Ashamed I am to be a father
That the lack of food should have caused his death.

Perhaps because of his own suffering, Du Fu's poems expressed great concern with the suffering of the common people and a strong Confucian anger about their troubles:

The silk that was bestowed at the vermilion court
Came originally from some poor shivering women;
. . . .
Inside the vermilion gate wine and meat are stinking;
On the roadside lie the bones of people frozen to death.

The vermilion gate and court meant the imperial palace. And the rotting wine and meat show the luxurious palace in the time of Emperor Xuanzong, when tens of thousands lived in the imperial palace complex of the forbidden city.

The contrasting scenes of poor people and sumptuous court life show Du Fu to be a moralist critic of his government at a time of failing imperial power. The poor, however, suffered both in prosperous and in impoverished times. The poetic tone shifted from a love of the natural environment for its particular beauty to a stark portrayal of a government feeding on its people.

The frontiers had also become increasingly unstable, and this instability undermined the state's aura of invincibility. In 751, a Muslim army defeated the Chinese at the Talas River in Central Asia. Coupled with this reversal was the northward expansion of the Tibetans, who cut off China's access to the silk roads and deprived the government of the lucrative revenues from western trade. In the southwestern part of the empire, a Thai army inflicted a serious defeat in 754 on the Tang frontier forces. General An Lushan, who commanded a significant frontier army in the northeast and could count on the support of other northern frontier commanders, also rebelled. By themselves, any one of these uprisings or defeats would not have been decisive, but over a five-year period, the cumulative effect shook the Tang state to its foundations.

The An Lushan Uprising (755–763) nearly toppled the Tang Dynasty. Rebel forces marched rapidly toward the capital but were stopped by the defenders at the major eastern pass leading into the metropolitan region. One chief official, in what must have been one of history's great blunders, ordered the defenders to attack the stymied rebels. The engagement led to a total defeat for the imperial forces and opened the capital to the rebels. The emperor, his favorite concubine, her cousin, and a few courtiers fled to the south. The palace guard blamed the mistress and her cousin for the debacle and threatened to mutiny unless they were killed, and the emperor reluctantly complied with his guards' demand.

After many difficult years, the rebels were defeated and the ruling house was restored, yet circumstances after the restoration were quite different from those of earlier times. For example, the tax base had shrunk dramatically, and many areas of the empire had passed out of the central government's control. Before 755, Chinese rulers were more confident and expansive; now they became more wary and introspective. The aristocracy played a smaller role in politics. The scholar-official who earned a position in the government by passing a series of civil service examinations became a major political, cultural, and social player. Buddhism was weakened after a series of purges, and Confucianism emerged as the dominant ideology for both the state and the scholar-official.

The Late Tang Empire, 763–907

Beginning in 780 and lasting for about four decades, a series of effective Tang monarchs recaptured some of the lost court power and influence. They quelled new rebellions and reclaimed some measure of imperial authority over distant provinces, and the dynasty seemed to rebound. During that time some major historical works appeared, and the beginning of a reinterpretation of Confucianism surfaced. Significant writers included Han Yu (768–824), who developed a form of prose called the **Ancient Style**, which demanded that essays be clear, lucid, and simple in contrast to the more florid style of the writers of his day. The Ancient Style soon became the prevalent writing method.

By the early ninth century, several factors combined to weaken imperial influence. The later monarchs failed to lead effectively and found themselves the pawns of court factions. Another factor in the decline of the court was the growing power and eventual dominance of the eunuchs. One emperor tried to rally soldiers to slay the eunuch leaders, but the plot was discovered and crushed. With the decline of imperial rule came the dominance of local military leaders, who became semi-independent warlords and fought with one another for dominance.

In the mid–ninth century, Buddhism was dealt a serious blow. The reigning monarch believed that the monasteries were too large and, because they were tax exempt, that large amounts of potential tax receipts were unavailable to the state. In addition, tens of thousands of potential taxpayers were working for the monasteries. From 841 to 846, a series of court decrees closed hundreds of monasteries, led to the confiscation of their properties, and returned their monks and nuns to the tax rolls. In addition, thousands of gold, silver, and other metal statues were melted down. These actions severely weakened the economic foundation of Buddhist influence.

Late in the century, a major uprising left the Tang state reeling. During the ten years of fighting, nearly all of the remaining imperial forces evolved into warlord units similar to the armies at the end of the Han era. By 907, the last Tang leader was ousted, and a brief period of division and turmoil gripped China.

The period of division between the Tang and Song[6] dynasties (907–960) was a time when non-Chinese peoples ruled parts of North China and artistic development flourished. During this relatively brief time of political fragmentation, intense political rivalries developed.

THE SONG EMPIRE, 960–1279

Scholars have been fascinated by the contradictions of the Song period. Some have argued that the Song Empire's military weakness permitted the north and eventually all of China to be conquered and ruled by non-Chinese. Yet others have asserted that the Song Empire also established a powerful economic base that maintained independence and kept non-Chinese groups like the Mongols at bay for decades. The government, staffed by civil service appointees, ran smoothly and oversaw a long era of political stability.

Early Political Stability, 960–1127

Most of the early Song monarchs were effective rulers, and they presided over a centralized, unified bureaucratic state. Key to government stability was a group of officials who attained their positions by passing a series of rigorous examinations. Numbering in the thousands, officials who passed these tests were the majority of bureaucrats, providing a loyal, hardworking, talented workforce that was united in Confucian outlook. Despite several efforts at reform and growing political factionalism, the general tenor of rule was stable and efficient.

In 960, General Zhao Guangyin[7] (reign dates 960–978) overthrew his ruler, and for the next two decades he and his successor brother established the Song Empire (960–1279). Determined to avoid challenges from his own top officers, Emperor Zhao invited them to a banquet, thanking them but remarking that he felt uneasy on the throne. Emperor Zhao added that he feared being toppled by one of those in attendance, and when the drunken officers professed their loyalties, the emperor proposed that they all retire the next day.

Yet in safeguarding the throne, the army lost most of its experienced commanders. The transfer of the best units from the frontiers to the capital also forestalled challenges from ambitious generals, but the lack of stable northern borders plagued the founder's successors.

Many top Song officials were outstanding writers. Underlying elite cultural development was the growing use of printing, first by government, then by private interests. **Block printing**, the carving and inking of text on a wooden surface to reproduce many copies, was perfected during the Song era. Tang artisans had first used block printing for Buddhist scriptures. In the Song era, editions of the classical Confucian texts, the standard histories, and new works of literature were printed. Inexpensive books became generally available, sparking great interest in scholarly endeavors.

Su Shi[8] (1036–1101), who came from an illustrious family—his father and brother were talented prose and poetry stylists—has usually been regarded as the outstanding Song poet. Much in the manner of Li Bo of the previous dynasty, Su's poems often had a carefree air:

> Spring night—one hour worth a thousand gold coins;
> clear scent of flowers, shadowy moon.
> Songs and flutes upstairs—threads of sound;
> in the garden, a swing, where night is deep and still.

Political tragedy overtook Su Shi because of his opposition to court policies. He was exiled to Hainan Island in the distant south, and, although a tropical paradise not unlike the Hawaiian Islands, Hainan was far from Chinese civilization. Exile there was a cultural if not physical death sentence.

The poet Ouyang Xiu[9] (1007–1072) wrote in the eleventh century. Not only were his poems widely praised, but Ouyang's prose was admired even more because he further perfected the Ancient Style begun in the Tang era. Beyond poetry and prose, Ouyang devoted considerable attention to philosophy and the writing of histories, one of which was the *New Tang History*.

The greatest historian of the Song era was Sima Guang[10] (1019–1086). By his time, most of the

---

[6] **Song:** SOHNG
[7] **Zhao Guangyin:** JOW GWAHNG yihn

[8] **Su Shi:** SOO sher
[9] **Ouyang Xiu:** OH yahng SEE yuh
[10] **Sima Guang:** SEE mah GWAHNG

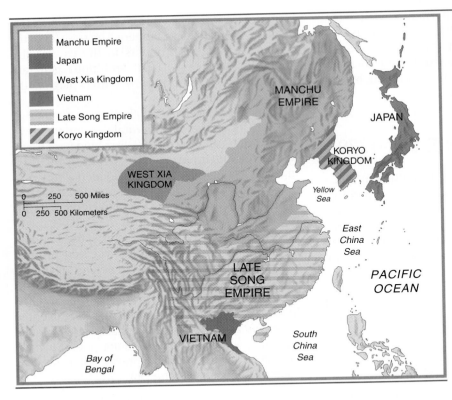

MAP 18.2 *East Asia around 1200.* *The territory under Chinese control was significantly reduced after the invasion of the Manchus in 1127. Vietnam had become an independent state in the tenth century, and Korea was ruled by the Koryo dynasty. The West Xia Kingdom had been established by Tibetans in the tenth century, ruling much of Northwest China. All of these states existed in an uneasy balance of power until the Mongol invasions of the thirteenth century.*

official histories were dynasty-centered, and although such divisions of time are natural in one political perspective, they are limited in the broader chronological sweep. Sima Guang undertook a monumental effort, the writing of a chronological history from 403 B.C. to A.D. 959. It was titled *Comprehensive Mirror for Aid in Government* and was admired not only for its factual accuracy but also for its balanced, objective assessments.

Confucianism received much attention and energy from Song scholars. Not only did Ouyang Xiu reinvigorate Confucius's ideas, but also major Confucian thinkers interacted to lay the groundwork for the grand reinterpretation of Confucian philosophy in the next century. A key influence for this development was Buddhism, which offered a metaphysical interpretation largely foreign to Confucian thought.

The Late Song Era, 1127–1279

Conquest and rule of North China by invaders forced the Song state to move south. Although it controlled much less territory than its predecessor state, the Late Song government established a stable political order and a rather prosperous economy before succumbing to the Mongols in 1279. The military capabilities of the new government have been derided by some scholars, yet the Late Song government resisted the Mongols for four decades.

The government revived the use of paper money and the payment of taxes in currency. Officials also encouraged the development of local and regional trade. Some manufacturing took place in cottage industries rather than in large-scale manufacturing centers, but other industries were state-run, including the salt and porcelain industries.

In philosophy, new interpretations of Confucian ideas were synthesized into a system called Neo-Confucianism. The scholar Zhu Xi[11] (1130–1200) integrated the strands developed by earlier thinkers into one coherent system. Zhu Xi also interpreted the basic works of Confucius and his successors, and he wrote many historical commentaries. Although Zhu Xi was a political opponent of the government during his own time, his

[11] **Zhu Xi:** JOO shee

ideas and interpretations became the official view by the fourteenth century. In order to pass the imperial examinations between 1313 and 1905, scholars had to use Zhu Xi's ideas.

Landscape painting remained fascinating for many Chinese artists in Late Song times. Both professional and scholarly painters followed their Early Song predecessors in concentrating on the landscape style, which had developed earlier. Natural settings have captivated Chinese; Wang Wei of the Tang created many admired landscapes. Ma Yuan (who flourished in the thirteenth century) mastered the landscape form in which human beings are tiny within the great expanse of mountains and lakes. Ma Yuan followed the tradition of presenting nature and people in a harmonious relationship. This kind of painting continued into Mongol times and beyond. Chinese also continued painting still lifes, portraits, and cityscapes.

After long battles with the Mongols, who persistently tried to conquer the south, the Song government succumbed in 1279. Fierce resistance brought the Mongols' vengeance against southern cities and discrimination toward southern scholars who sought positions in the Mongol government. The extensive land holdings of the Chinese empires of Sui and Tang had been lost, and all lands north and south of the Yangzi River fell to the Mongols, with the result that no territory remained under Chinese control in the last two decades of the thirteenth century. Instead, the non-Chinese Mongols ruled an empire that spanned from eastern Europe to Korea; that development is examined in Chapter 19.

Scientific and Technological Developments

A cluster of discoveries and applications came in the Song era, many of which were publicized in print. Some discoveries came because of government interest and support, while others developed from private inspiration.

The measurement of time was vital to the Chinese emperor and his bureaucrats. For example, the monarch insisted that all peoples who sought diplomatic relations adhere to the Chinese calendar (and, presumably, China's view of the world). Highly reliable star charts were produced in the Song era, and one astronomer invented a mechanical clockwork. It was in the form of a water-driven

FIGURE 18.5 *Chinese Medicine. Traveling doctors treated rural patients during the Song era. Although the introduction of exams and licensing of practitioners brought sophistication to Chinese medicine during this time, much medicine was practiced by doctors who went from village to village. This scene depicts a peasant needing to be held down while he receives treatment. A physician's assistant looks on, awaiting instructions.* National Palace Museum, Taiwan, Republic of China.

clock tower that rotated a wheel linked by gears to a celestial globe that mapped the sky. The whole apparatus moved at precise, regulated intervals.

Chinese astronomers knew of the regular periods of Halley's comet and described sunspots long before anyone else did. In 1054, the Chinese recorded the great nova explosion in the Crab Nebula. They noted the appearance of the gold-colored "guest star" and observed it through the twenty-seven days of its visibility. By that time, their accurate calculations measured the solar year at 365.2445 days, which is only four minutes off modern measurements.

Medical knowledge was also greatly advanced in the Song period. Chinese physicians carefully studied the patterns of epidemics and persuaded politicians to promote good hygienic practices.

Pharmacology benefited from the widespread use of drugs, and physicians systematically collected the results of their treatment of diseases. Numerous illnesses were described and catalogued with the recommended treatments, and this information was published by block-printing methods for distribution to government medical offices. Although the first recorded dissection of a human cadaver occurred in China during the first century A.D., the systematic study of human anatomy occurred during the Song era. The book *Diagrams of Internal Organs and Blood Vessels* was compiled and printed early in the twelfth century. Eventually it became available to Rashid al-Din, a Persian physician and historian who was serving in China and carried the work home, whence it passed to Europe.

CHINA'S ECONOMIC DEVELOPMENT, 589–1279

From the sixth to the twelfth centuries, China's economy changed dramatically, reaching a level of development similar to that of Europe in the eighteenth century. Not only did agricultural production expand, but crop specialization and trade intensified as well. Commerce generally blossomed both domestically and regionally; an East Asian and Southeast Asian network of expanded commercial relationships developed by the late thirteenth century. At the same time, mass manufacturing produced enormous quantities of products for the state and for trade. China seemed poised on the edge of what modern economists refer to as self-sustaining economic growth.

Chinese Agriculture

The Sui and Tang monarchs sought to maintain control of the peasants and landlords through a policy forbidding private landownership. Rights to the land were granted to subjects by the state in fixed allotments. Regular censuses were taken, and the lands were redistributed based on demographic changes. Taxes and service obligations (labor and military) were also determined according to land allotments and census findings. The system worked, from the state's perspective, until the mid–eighth century, when it collapsed during the An Lushan Uprising. From that point, private landowning became the dominant agricultural pattern, and a landlord class gradually emerged by the Song era.

Private markets contributed to the commercialization of agriculture. After the mid–eighth century, a weakened Tang state lost control of markets, and private markets began to appear. Gradually, through improved distribution systems and wider circulation of coinage, the commercialization of agriculture grew. By Song times, some local districts turned to crop or product specialization. In the southeast, for example, farmers produced only fruits like oranges or lychees for export and had to trade these products for rice and other staples. Others grew timber for commercial markets.

By the Song era, the Chinese had mastered the **paddy-field method** of growing rice—wet-field rice cultivation by the use of dams, irrigation ditches, sluice-gates, and the treadle water pump. Enormous amounts of labor and financial resources were used to prepare the paddy fields. Rice was a staple in Central and South China, and the paddy-field method allowed for yields that were three times greater than those obtained by conventional methods. In addition, Chinese farmers experimented with growing different varieties and strains of rice to develop more productive and disease-resistant yields.

Agriculture's development had a significant impact on other economic and social sectors. The familiar pattern of a dozen or so agricultural villages served by a market town began in Tang times, expanded in the Song era, and continued into the twentieth century. In addition, growing agricultural prosperity and productive capacity permitted Chinese cities to enlarge to one million or more persons, largely through the spread of suburbs outside city walls.

Commercial Expansion

The Tang imperial system of state-controlled trade through the establishment of governmental markets ultimately gave way to a mixed system of state-run and private markets. Early in Sui and Tang times, Chinese monarchs attempted to dominate the exchange of goods to limit the numbers of wealthy merchants, to forestall hoarding, and to control prices. This system remained in place until the mid–Tang era, when the An Lushan Uprising

FIGURE 18.6 *Rice Paddy Farming. Large rice yields prompted farmers to pursue the paddy-field method, which depended on water-control techniques, especially pumping. This painting shows human and animal power being used to transfer water between fields.* © Wan-go Weng.

greatly weakened the imperial court. Private markets grew up and slipped out of government control, although officials still licensed trade officials and worked with merchant and artisan guilds and associations to ensure regularity and fairness of market sales.

Sui and Tang emperors also attempted to open and maintain the land trade routes between China and Central Asia. The second Sui monarch, Yang Guang, spent a vast amount of money to secure the allegiance or acquiescence of western tribes that controlled the silk roads, achieving limited success by his diplomatic effort. The second Tang emperor, Li Shimin, directed the westward expansion of Chinese military forces that brought the silk roads under direct control, as they remained until the defeat of the Chinese army at the Talas River Battle in 751. The loss of trade routes after that date reduced Tang government revenues, leading to declining state control over commerce.

Another element in commercial growth was the improvement in transportation. Here again, the state played an essential role in the upkeep of roads and bridges, although privately built roads also came into existence. One area of development was the public building of canals and related transportation waterways. Water transport was a cheap and efficient way to convey goods. At least 40,000 vessels of various sizes plied the Grand Canal, and, by Song times, more than 30,000 miles of connected inland waterways interlaced heavily populated sections of Central China. Boat-building techniques improved, and Chinese craft effectively sailed on inland and maritime waters. Chinese ships used iron nails, waterproofing, buoyancy chambers, nautical compasses, and a variety of technical design elements in their construction and operation by the twelfth century. In fact, travelers in East, Southeast, and South Asian waters usually preferred to take Chinese vessels because of their technological superiority.

Fiscal measures gradually developed to keep pace with the burgeoning commercial growth, especially after the fall of Tang. Tang officials could not make enough coins to keep in circulation, but the Song government oversaw improved mining operations and ore extraction for silver and copper to produce sufficient coinage for the economy. Song copper coins were regularly used in Korea, Japan, and Vietnam by the twelfth century. In addition, the Song government expanded the printing of paper money backed by government reserves. Bills of transfer and exchange also were used, and deposit shops issued checks for people who placed bullion in their establishments. Monetary devices were as important to commerce as blood is to the body.

The Development of Manufacturing

The Chinese increased their emphasis on manufacturing to produce large quantities of iron and steel. By the onset of the eleventh century, 100,000 to 150,000 tons of those materials were produced annually, and most were used in making weapons and armor for the armed forces. Mining of other metals, like copper, also increased dramatically in the Song era. Production of porcelain ("china") also grew extensively in the Song period.

The state ran many manufacturing centers, partly because of the enormous funds and sup-plies needed. Deforestation in much of northern China forced the Chinese to use coal and coke to fuel blast furnaces. The water transport system that linked major economic regions to the capital also provided for a relatively inexpensive means to carry finished products.

The textile industry, largely privately run, benefited from technological developments to improve production. By the eleventh century, water-powered machines spun hemp thread. In addition, a spinning wheel with multiple spindles and driven by a foot treadle spun cotton thread. A cotton gin was developed to facilitate the separation of cotton seeds from cotton fibers. And by the twelfth century, a silk-reeling machine had been perfected and placed in production. It saved labor costs and replaced many women workers.

Despite the development of an impressive economic base that annually produced more than 100,000 tons of iron and steel, North China was overrun by Manchus (called Ruzhen) early in the twelfth century. The Manchus initially had little use for such industrial operations and permitted them to rust away.

ENCOUNTERS
The Talas River Battle of 751

In the mid–eighth century, two expanding peoples, the Arabs and the Chinese, met and fought in Central Asia. The Arabs came from Southwest Asia and confidently expected to defeat all challengers. The Chinese were retracing the steps of earlier Chinese expeditionary forces into Central Asia and expected to be triumphant, like their predecessors of eight centuries earlier. The Arabs won, and many far-reaching trends were started by this watershed event.

The Chinese force dispatched by Tang Xuanzong had conquered the famed silk roads and pushed beyond the formidable Central Asian mountain ranges to the Talas River. In 751, the Chinese army, led by a Korean, Gao Xianzhi, met a grievous defeat and suffered the loss of most of its forces. The Talas River defeat forced Chinese forces to regroup hundreds of miles to the east. Yet Tibetan forces closed off China's corridor route to the silk roads and other western points. China's attention drew ever more toward domestic matters and toward the South China Sea. For more than a millennium no army dispatched by a government of China reclaimed the silk roads.

China's defeat sparked many developments in Eurasia. Many Chinese were captured by the Arab-led force, and one scholar noted that through these prisoners of war, China's expertise in the manufacture of paper passed throughout Eurasia, being spread by Muslims. The Central Asians and Arabs benefited from these technologies, which later passed along to the Indians, Africans, and Europeans. Presumably these developments facilitated the spread of knowledge and the growth of the intellectual elite.

Islam had been expanding rapidly in many directions during the previous century, and the Arab-led force had been dispatched by the Umayyad caliph in Damascus. Although the Arabs did not capitalize on their victory by settling in Central Asia, Islam became deeply rooted there several centuries later.

FIGURE 18.7 *Song Naval Warfare.* *The rear section of this boat is for steering and propulsion; the front, stacked with gunpowder-filled weapons, could be detached and set adrift toward enemy vessels, to explode with devastating effect. Gunpowder, invented in the tenth century, was seldom used in warfare until the twelfth century. Firearms and cannons were not developed until the next century.*
From the *Wu bei zhi* (Records of military preparations), 1621.

ELEMENTS OF CHINESE SOCIETY

In this period, significant social changes occurred in China. Political control and social influence slipped from the aristocrats to the landlords, while the peasants retained their position of second on the social scale. Artisans and merchants were commoners. By the twelfth century, some landlords were becoming merchants and manufacturers in order to earn money and to support their families. Neo-Confucianism was hostile to independent women and enforced the belief that all women should be under some form of male control. When Neo-Confucianism spread to Japan and Vietnam, for example, the position of Japanese and Vietnamese women worsened. Ethnic minorities also suffered from discrimination by the Chinese people.

China's Social Classes

China developed an ideology of a four-class social system by the second century B.C. The four (scholars, peasants, artisans, and merchants) were positioned in hierarchical order with the scholars at the top and the merchants at the bottom. By the Song era, this social classification remained, but the components of the scholar elite had changed.

Both the Sui and Tang empires were dominated by scholars who came from the aristocracy. Great aristocratic clans from Northwest China had provided the leadership for the rise to power of both the Sui and Tang dynasties. As a reward for their support and continued allegiance, the rulers maintained official lists and rankings of the elite families and clans. In addition, government officials frequently came from these families, who educated their sons to follow the Confucian code. Although the examination system began earlier, the ***yin* privilege**, the exemption of high officials' sons from the civil service examinations, maintained an aristocratic character in officialdom.

Several factors, however, worked against permanent aristocratic social and political dominance. Empress Wu, for example, reduced the influence of the northwestern clans by favoring candidates from Northeast China. In addition, Chinese law fostered an equal division of property among male heirs. This worked against the long-term stability of great clans, because of the splitting of land over several generations. Many great clans also disappeared in the wars of the eighth, ninth, and tenth centuries.

The growth of the examination system as a major recruitment instrument by the state, especially in the Song era, also had important social consequences. For nearly a century, many Song officials were scholars who used the *yin* privilege to maintain their families' political and social predominance. Most lived in the capital and served as a social and political elite there. By the mid–eleventh century, however, restriction of the *yin* privilege, success of southerners in the examination system, and political purges destroyed most of the families' and clans' political and social influence.

By the twelfth century, many scholarly families firmly established themselves in their local areas. In doing so, they responded to the reduction in the number of scholars being taken into the government. Some became landlords, teachers, market superintendents, or merchants. Many scholarly merchants took advantage of their writing and mathematical skills to benefit from the burgeoning economy. Eventually, scholars became an unofficial governing class beneath the lowest level of normal bureaucratic activity.

Peasants were socially high but economically low. Peasants remained second on the social scale, a position that meant little to their daily lives. Although enterprising peasants might escape the daily struggles for survival, the vast mass of peasants toiled in the same conditions as their ancestors.

Artisans and merchants were excluded from the examination system until the Late Song period. Artisans, although often highly skilled, were usually illiterate and did not take the exams. Their technical knowledge might be passed on to sons or apprentices, but they did not build large family or clan networks. They received a certain amount of social largess from their guilds, which were often organized along kinship lines. Merchants also formed guilds and trade networks, sometimes accumulating fortunes but having little social standing or political power.

Gender Issues

Men dominated all aspects of public life in China; they became officials, produced most artistic works, performed most economic tasks outside the home, and presided over social institutions, including the family. Their social position was recognized by law; it was relatively easy for a man to divorce a woman and extremely difficult for a woman to divorce a man.

Exceptional women certainly attained limited recognition in histories and other works. The first empress of the Sui era and Empress Wu of the Tang period played key political roles. Lady Yang effectively acted the part of Emperor Xuanzong's favorite concubine in the mid–eighth century, but she has been remembered as causing the emperor's downfall. Li Qingchao[12] wrote beautiful poetry in the Song period.

[12] **Li Qingchao:** LEE CHEENG chee yow

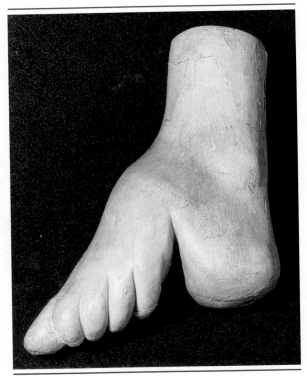

FIGURE 18.8 *Footbinding. Women endured footbinding to satisfy men's desire that they possess unnaturally small "lotus" feet. This cast conveys the ideal foot, doubled on itself into the tiniest size possible. This practice spread throughout all classes and involved a years-long process that caused excruciating pain. A woman's suitability as a marriage partner was jeopardized if she did not conform to this standard. In China's male-dominated society, where women had few options besides marriage, the ideal of the bound foot lasted for a thousand years.* Wellcome Institute Library, London.

Commoner women often lived under control of men throughout their lives. Perhaps the most infamous practice was footbinding, the prevention of the natural growth of women's feet through tight binding. Men thought the tiny feet to be erotic, helping to create a centuries-long fashion. Elite women initially and, eventually, women of the lower classes suffered permanent crippling. Over time perhaps one billion women suffered from this custom. Widows increasingly were expected not to remarry, and they either lived with their in-laws or returned home without prospect of marriage. Women wove at home and handled a variety of domestic chores, like the pickling of foods for preservation. They also toiled in a variety of occupations, especially those associated with the silk industry. But they lost jobs to machines that could do the work of many and at cheaper cost. Women not only were bound by foot wrappings; their lack of education and inferior status bound them to men.

Ethnic Minorities in China

China has had a long and significant experience with ethnic minorities. In times of prosperity and strong government, foreign merchants and other aliens received good treatment from the Chinese. They often resided in foreign enclaves of major cities, including the capital, and even established temples where they worshiped their deities. From the sixth to the thirteenth centuries, however, the Chinese expanded from north to south and treated non-Chinese with assimilation, encapsulation, or expulsion measures.

Because of their larger numbers the Chinese believed that they could intermarry with and absorb ethnic minorities. Large numbers of Manchu people, for example, were ultimately assimilated by the Chinese people. When conquering a new region, the Chinese sent in colonists, many of whom married the non-Chinese. At the

PARALLELS AND DIVERGENCES

The "Other" before 1600

Most societies have designated one or more social groups as deserving of contempt and discrimination. Often racial, ethnic, or caste groups, these unfortunates were seen as the antithesis of the rest of the societies in which they resided. In recognition of this, modern social theorists have come to call such groups "the other."

Chinese and Mesoamericans, for example, used the term "dog" to symbolize contempt for another group. Chinese characters employed to write the names of non-Chinese people sometimes contain a component that means dog. Because the dog was a beast and had negative connotations to the Chinese, their use of its name indicated their utter contempt for the non-Chinese peoples. Similarly, when the Aztecs first moved into the Valley of Mexico, indigenous peoples sometimes referred to them as *chichimecs* or "sons of dogs." This pejorative usage, however, took on a more favorable tone when the Aztecs became powerful.

The Japanese also had at least two kinds of "others." One was the Ainu[a] people, a North Asian people. For centuries, the Japanese fought the Ainu and pushed them out of Honshu. Many Ainu died in these campaigns, and those who escaped to the northern island of Hokkaido eventually were forced to live away from the Japanese. In the sixteenth century, however, the local Japanese warlord who had jurisdiction over the Ainu developed a policy of tolerance that lasted for three hundred years. Rather than subjugate and annihilate the Ainu chiefdoms, the feudal lord took a peaceful approach to relations, emphasizing conciliation and non-interference in Ainu life. By the nineteenth century, the Japanese government continued the previous policy, treating the Ainu as a principal asset to the northern island. Throughout, the Ainu were regarded with sympathy and humanity.

The *eta,*[b] members of a Japanese caste group, were forced to live in ghettoes attached to towns or cities. The *eta* performed socially useful but degrading occupations, like butchering, leather working, burying human bodies, and waste removal. Because Shinto beliefs excoriated "polluting" activities, like waste removal, people who performed these tasks suffered religious condemnation. Only in the nineteenth century were the *eta* granted legal equality. The Koreans had their own outcast group whose members performed similar useful societal functions.

Low caste members in India and Jews in Europe also suffered discrimination despite the fact that they performed necessary social or economic jobs. Members of India's low castes frequently handled "polluting" tasks such as removing dead bodies. Jews provided financing opportunities to Christian merchants, officials, and monarchs because Christians were forbidden by their religion to participate in usury. Both groups suffered religious discrimination, including being forced to live in ghettoes.

[a]**Ainu:** EYE noo

[b]*eta:* EH tah

same time, the Chinese established Confucian schools and encouraged members of indigenous elites to study there. The Koreans and Vietnamese resisted assimilation, despite their borrowing of Chinese culture and institutions.

Encapsulation occurred when ethnic groups were driven into the hills and then were surrounded or encapsulated by the Chinese, who took over the nearby lowlands that were more suitable for agriculture. The Miao and Yao peoples of South China suffered encapsulation, a fate they and other ethnic minorities faced in parts of Southeast Asia, too.

In Southwest China, expulsion was often a familiar pattern for dealing with ethnic groups. Both the Burmese and Thai peoples, for example, had polities along the Chinese frontier and on occasion raided or destroyed Chinese settlements. In the Song era, when the Chinese moved farther south, the Burmese and Thais were forced out of their homelands and migrated to Southeast Asia.

KOREA CREATES AN INDEPENDENT STATE

Geographical elements have played a key role in the history of Korea. Near both China and Japan, Korea has long suffered from the expansionist tendencies of both countries. One effective long-term Korean strategy was to ally with the Chinese and adopt some Chinese state institutions to govern themselves.

China has influenced Korea for more than two millennia. During the Warring States Period (403–221 B.C.), for example, Chinese refugees from the unification wars fled to territory where Koreans lived. In the late second century B.C., Chinese armies conquered and ruled parts of Korea for four centuries. Three Chinese districts in Korea later succumbed to Korean forces, but the fourth, Lolang, remained in Chinese hands until A.D. 313. After the Koreans regained control of their peninsula, three kingdoms emerged, and they contended with one another for domination of the peninsula.

Japan also fought with the Koreans because of competing trade and diplomatic interests. Some historians have asserted that the Japanese long held a toehold colony, Mimana or Kaya, on the peninsula. According to ancient Japanese chroni-

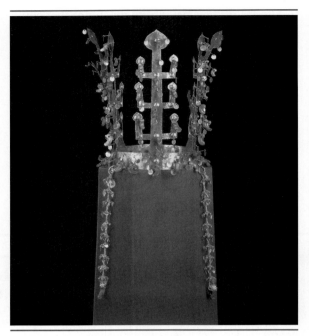

FIGURE 18.9 *Korean Crown. Korean artisans produced dazzling pieces, including this seventh-century crown recovered from a Silla tomb in southeastern Korea. Made of cut sheet gold and jade pieces, the highly stylized elements of its design seem to represent trees and antler shapes that were especially striking when illuminated. Silla monarchs united the peninsula and ruled for centuries.* National Museum of Korea, Seoul.

cles, several semihistorical figures, including the legendary Japanese Empress Sujun, invaded or conquered parts of Korea. Whatever the facts, there has been a long and often contentious relationship between the Koreans and Japanese.

In the sixth and seventh centuries, the Chinese, Koreans, and Japanese began to interact in many ways. In the sixth century, Koreans and Japanese crossed the strait between them, bearing gifts and information, and much of Japan's early knowledge of China came from Korea. Buddhism came from China via Korean monarchs, who tried to impress the Japanese in the hope of forging an alliance against the other kingdoms.

In the seventh century, growing Chinese military power threatened Korea, when the second Sui emperor unsuccessfully tried to conquer it. The second Tang emperor also failed to impose Chinese rule on the peninsula. The third Tang emperor and Empress Wu attempted several campaigns in Korea. In 661, Chinese and Japanese naval forces fought a battle near the Kumgum

River because both sides wanted to dominate the peninsula. The Japanese suffered a major defeat and retreated to their islands.

China seemed victorious and prepared to take Korea, yet the Korean king rallied his people against Chinese rule, and by 668, the beleaguered Chinese forces were forced to abandon their conquests. The Korean monarch proclaimed his rule over Korea and adopted some Chinese political and cultural forms that had proved effective in ruling large populations. The dominance of the Korean aristocracy, however, meant that many Chinese institutions, like the examination system, were ignored or significantly modified. The new Silla[13] Dynasty lasted until 918, when it was replaced by the Koryo Dynasty. The Koryo monarchs ruled with a modified Chinese system with many indigenous practices. The dynasty briefly resisted the Mongols but finally capitulated, surviving until 1388.

VIETNAM CREATES AN IMPERIAL AND EXPANSIONIST STATE

Like the Koreans, the Vietnamese people endured Chinese rule and often rebelled against their overlords. In the tenth century, under the leadership of patriots, the Vietnamese threw off the Chinese yoke and established a powerful polity.

Successive Vietnamese governments, like those in Korea and Japan, freely borrowed from the Chinese and modified various practices to suit themselves. Centralized rule wielded by scholar-officials, who had to pass a series of civil service examinations, became the norm. These political and social elite members, like their Chinese counterparts, wrote Chinese-style poems in the Chinese language. In addition, like Chinese Confucians, Vietnamese scholars promoted values of filial piety, loyalty, and humane behavior. They occupied the top rung of the Chinese-style social scale and praised the Vietnamese peasants, who occupied the second rung. Vietnamese merchants, like their Chinese counterparts, suffered the scorn of scholars and officials.

The Vietnamese government embarked on a long-range expansion southward. The Vietnamese conquered various states along the southern borders and annexed them. From the tenth to the thirteenth centuries, the Vietnamese fashioned an empire stretching hundreds of miles beside the South China Sea. A key part of this expansion was the resettlement of Vietnamese peasant villages long distances from their original homes in the north. The strong village cohesiveness and peasant militancy in defense of their new lands facilitated this process. As the distances between the Vietnamese capital and the southern frontiers lengthened, a desire for local autonomy was enhanced. Under weak monarchs, this regionalism led to the weakening of the Vietnamese Empire.

Both the Chinese and Mongols attempted to conquer Vietnam in later times but failed. The Mongols launched three unsuccessful invasions of Vietnam; each withered before tropical diseases

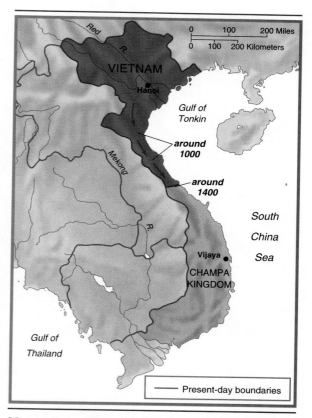

MAP 18.3 *Vietnam's Southward Expansion, to 1400. Vietnamese monarchs and peoples expanded southward steadily between the tenth and thirteenth centuries. Mountains to the west confined the migration to the coast and river plains. The Vietnamese assimilated many other cultures in their march south.*

[13] **Silla:** SHEE yihl ah

CHINA	KOREA	VIETNAM		
			–	
			–	
			–	
				Yang Jian unites China, 589
Sui Empire, 589–618			**600**	
Tang Empire, 618–907			–	Yang Guang's last Korean campaign fails, 616
	Silla Dynasty, 668–918			Korea is united, 668
			–	
			–	An Lushan Uprising begins, 755
			800	
			–	
			–	Gunpowder invented in China, c. 900
	Koryo Dynasty, 918–1388		–	Vietnam gains independence, 969
Early Song Empire, 960–1127		Ly Empire, 969–1408	**1000**	
			–	Ouyang Xiu born, 1007
			–	Manchus overrun northern China, 1127
Late Song Empire, 1127–1279			–	
			1200	Zhu Xi dies, 1200
			–	
			–	Vietnamese defeat Mongols, 1287
			–	
			1400	
	Le Empire, 1428–1802		–	
			–	
			–	

and guerrilla resistance by the Vietnamese. In the 1280s, Tran Hung Dao, a hero to later generations of Vietnamese patriots, commanded the successful resistance to the Mongols.

The Chinese failed to impose permanent control, while the peoples south of Vietnam could not resist the steady encroachment of Vietnamese influence. Vietnam has sometimes been called by scholars the "Lesser Dragon," meaning that it is a smaller version of China. Certainly, in its Chinese-style institutions and expansive foreign policy, that designation is apt.

SUMMARY

1. After a lengthy period of division, Yang Jian, a general in a northern Chinese kingdom, usurped the throne, pacified the north, and soon conquered South China. The Sui Empire lasted for nearly three decades and established the basis for a unified Chinese state. Among the unifying elements were the Grand Canal, an examination system, and the promotion of Buddhism.

2. The Sui Empire fell after failing to conquer Korea, and the Tang Empire succeeded to power. The Tang emperors expanded their control of Central Asia and conquered many tribes. The Tang Empire also saw the rise of an exceptionally talented trio of poets, Wang Wei, Li Bo, and Du Fu, who left an enduring poetic legacy. During the second half of the Tang era, regional warlords wrested control from the central government.

3. Following a brief time of disunity, a northern general, Zhao Guangyin, usurped power, pacified the north, then conquered the south. The Song Empire never aspired to the imperial legacy of the Han, Sui, and Tang empires, but it effectively ruled the central area of the Yellow and Yangzi river valleys. Key to the strength of the Song Empire's success was a polity resting firmly on an imperial examination system that selected talented scholars who mastered the ideas of Confucianism.

4. The Song era also saw the appearance of a sophisticated economic system of large-scale industrial manufacturing, high levels of agricultural productivity, and significant levels of commercial activity. The considerable technological advances of the eleventh century were aided by the use of printing to spread knowledge. The conquest of the north by non-Chinese aborted this development.

5. Although the four-class system (scholars, peasants, artisans, and merchants) remained in effect, the scholar class changed in social content. Aristocrats were eventually replaced by local landlord scholars. China's ethnic minorities endured a variety of discriminatory policies, including assimilation, encapsulation, and expulsion.

6. Since around 100 B.C., Korea had been influenced by China, experiencing four centuries of direct Chinese rule. After ousting the Chinese, the Koreans formed three regional governments that were united through conquest in the seventh century. Both the Chinese and Japanese had attempted to control parts of Korea but failed. Korean independence meant some use of political institutions and ideas borrowed from China.

7. The Vietnamese threw off a millennium of Chinese control in the tenth century and followed some Chinese practices. The Vietnamese commenced a long era of southward imperial expansion.

SUGGESTED READINGS

Ebrey, Patricia. *The Inner Quarters*. Berkeley: University of California Press, 1993. An interpretation of women's roles in the Song imperial period.

Hall, John, ed. *Japan before Tokugawa*. Princeton, N.J.: Princeton University Press, 1986. Essays about feudal Japanese society and its economic foundation.

Lee, K. B. *A New History of Korea*. Trans. by E. Wagner. Cambridge, Mass.: Harvard University Press, 1985. An important interpretative history of Korea.

Lo, W. W. *An Introduction to the Civil Service of Sung China*. Honolulu: University of Hawaii Press, 1987. A look at the examination system and its impact on China's social system.

Woodside, A. B. *Vietnam and the Chinese Model*. Cambridge, Mass.: Harvard University Press, 1968. A classic study of Vietnam's cultural relations with China.

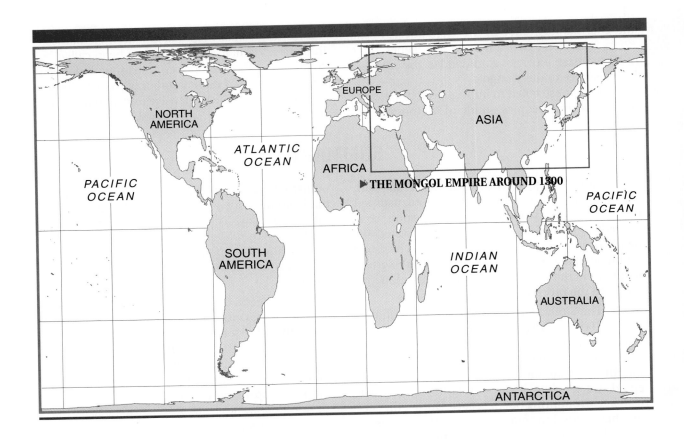

THE MONGOL EMPIRE AROUND 1300

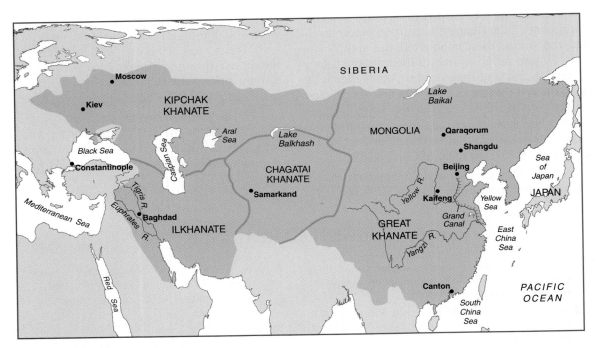

▶ THE MONGOL EMPIRE AROUND 1300

The Mongol Empire: Ascendancy, Domination, and Decline in Eurasia

1206–1480

The Korean navigator trembled before the Mongol general. A great storm was coming, and it would threaten the invasion fleet. Thousands of Mongols were beginning to push off the beachhead and threaten a full-scale rout of the Japanese defenders. The Mongol commander scowled and ordered the fleet to stay anchored another day.

This scene in 1274 recounts the beginnings of the great disaster that thwarted one thrust of Mongol imperial expansion. A typhoon struck the Mongol ships and killed tens of thousands, saving Japan from Mongol rule. Although failing to conquer Japan, the Mongols won and ruled an empire stretching across much of central Eurasia.

Civilizations have traditionally been based in cities. Some Mongol leaders, however, retained a nomadic lifestyle even as other Mongols built an empire. They originated in the Asian **steppe**, the grasslands of Inner Asia (Manchuria, Mongolia, and eastern Turkestan). Although Mongol nomads usually distrusted settled peoples, they traded with agricultural peoples who lived generally south of Mongolia. In the thirteenth century, under the leadership of a great warrior, Chinggis[1] Khan (sometimes spelled Genghis Khan), the Mongols swept south, east, and west to conquer much of Asia and part of Europe. In the process they fashioned one of the largest empires in history. At the same time, because the Mongols united much of

[1] **Chinggis:** JIHNG guhs

East, Central, and Southwest Asia and because they favored merchants, land-based commerce flourished as never before. The reuniting of China also revived a vast maritime trade stretching from the South China Sea to the Indian Ocean and the Red Sea.

In this chapter, we will examine the rise of the Mongols and survey their rapid defeat of numerous states in Asia and Europe. In Eurasia, only the Indian subcontinent, the area of Europe west of the Danube River, and Siberia escaped the great Mongol army. We will look at the Mongol leadership, the war machine, and the administrative system that permitted the Mongols to control a vast domain. Then we will survey the polities and societies of the four regions they ruled: East Asia (China, Mongolia, and Korea), Central Asia, the Kipchak Khanate (Russia and the adjacent eastern steppelands), and Southwest Asia (Persia). The Mongols destroyed a Central Asian civilization in their rise to imperial rule, yet they effectively preserved long-established civilizations in East and Southwest Asia.

CHINGGIS KHAN AND THE RISE OF THE MONGOLS

Temujin[2] (around 1162–1227), who is better known by his title Chinggis Khan ("Illustrious Leader of the Mongols"), united the various clans and tribes that dwelled in the area known today as Mongolia. For the purpose of simplicity, we will refer to this man as Chinggis Khan throughout this chapter, even though the title was not claimed until 1206. Chinggis Khan came from a noble tribal family, and the unification effort occupied much of his adult life. Despite many setbacks, Chinggis Khan gathered a group of talented followers and united his tribe. Warring followed, but the military skills of Chinggis Khan helped unite the peoples of Mongolia.

Before examining the great conference of leaders that assembled in 1206 to recognize Temujin as Chinggis Khan, we should survey the peoples he subdued early. The great majority herded sheep, cattle, camels, yaks (shaggy-haired oxen), and horses. Their diet featured beef, mutton, and milk.

[2]**Temujin:** teh MUH jeen

One favored drink was fermented mare's milk. Because the Mongolian nomads tended herds, they had to move from pasture to pasture in a regular fashion in order to prevent overgrazing. In addition, they feared the vagaries of weather that might bring drought and an end to the herds' food supplies or animal diseases that might swiftly destroy a herd. The mobile life prevented storage of quantities of goods that could ease the ravages of the elements.

Hunting supplied food to supplement the daily diet. The hunt was conducted like a military operation, as various units of a tribe surrounded a

FIGURE 19.1 *Mongol and Horse.* *The cavalry was a key element of the Mongols' success. A close relationship to horses was cultivated from childhood, and strict attention was paid to their proper use and well-being. The combination of well-trained riders and dependable horses gave the Mongol forces superior speed and maneuverability over most of the armies they encountered. This Chinese painting captures the relation of rider and horse as an archer stops to retrieve the animal he has brought down. Mongol archers were skilled at firing long distances and from the saddle.* Louvre © R. M. N.

game-filled area where disciplined maneuvering herded the creatures into a killing zone. Chinggis Khan used these activities as war games and severely punished leaders who failed to play their assigned parts.

The horse was significant in the Mongol conquest, and the Mongol cavalry represented two millennia of improvement in the use of the horse in warfare. Mongols learned to ride horses at a young age, and they quickly became expert riders. They earned the reputation of enduring great privation during a campaign and were said to be able to ride for ten consecutive days, eating while in the saddle. In one campaign in eastern Europe, Mongols rode about fifty miles per day.

The constant warfare between tribes before 1206 often became fierce. In the manner of his predecessors, Chinggis Khan might kill all of the adult males from a defeated tribe in order to forestall a possible retributive strike at a later time. If allowed to live, warriors from tribes were often conscripted and interspersed among the main military units. Women, especially attractive ones, could expect to be taken as wives by victorious men; even married women who might be pregnant could be subject to this practice. Sons born soon after coming into a new father's tent generally experienced the same treatment accorded his biological children.

Women of the Mongol upper class sometimes asserted themselves politically. Chabi,[3] the main wife of Khubilai[4] Khan, became a major advisor to her husband. The second wife of one khan played a masterful political role in a succession dispute and served as regent for her son. Other aristocratic Mongol women effectively administered vast personal domains. And a few women fought alongside men in battle.

Although the overwhelming number of people united by 1206 spoke Mongol, some traced their ancestry to other ethnic groups, like the Turks. When Chinggis Khan met with the dignitaries of the Mongols in 1206, he decreed that the spoken Mongol language (previously unwritten) be written down in a Turkic script, a practice that is still followed.

In 1206, a great gathering of the tribal leaders and members of the political elite proclaimed Chinggis Khan to be the preeminent Mongol ruler

[3] **Chabi:** CHAH bee
[4] **Khubilai:** KOO bih lay

FIGURE 19.2 *Mongol Battle Scene. This Persian miniature depicts a young Chinggis Khan riding into battle accompanied by his mother (in white). Mongol elite women sometimes played active political roles and fought alongside their sons, fathers, or husbands. Chinggis's father, a chieftain, was killed when the future khan was still a boy, and another family seized tribal leadership. Widow and children existed for the next few years on the fringes of society, until Chinggis began his rise to power.* © United Nations Educational, Scientific and Cultural Organization (UNESCO), Paris.

and then pledged to follow him with absolute obedience. To solidify his position, which was based on a succession of military and political victories, Chinggis Khan promoted the religious interpretation that he was the choice of Tengri, the Mongol deity; he was said to have granted Chinggis Khan the power to conquer the world. To give a more permanent base for Mongol unity, Chinggis Khan

FIGURE 19.3 *Relics of Chinggis Khan.* *The nomadic Mongol peoples of Central Asia kept their property ready for frequent moves. Their dwellings, called* yurts, *were comprised of a portable, cylindrical framework made of willow that supported a felt or skin covering. This 1930s photo taken in Inner Mongolia shows the* yurt *that holds the relics of the Great Khan, revered by Mongols for centuries.*   Peabody Museum, Harvard University. Photo by Owen Lattimore.

also compiled and proclaimed the **Yasa**,[5] a binding legal code taken from Mongol customs, ancestral traditions, and additional decrees promulgated by the new monarch. For example, the annual hunt was strictly regulated by the *Yasa*. Another major innovation commencing in 1206 was the establishment of a relay postal or message system, like the American Pony Express. This communication network carried important messages rapidly from one part of the realm to another and became renowned across Asia.

Certainly an element of good fortune accompanied Chinggis Khan's successes. Many of the enemy states he conquered had ineffective rulers or had been weakened by internal problems. Yet, fortune aside, Chinggis Khan became a skilled military commander, and he possessed the great talent of identifying outstanding individuals and

placing them where their assets benefited him most. Finally, as the events of 1206 indicate, Chinggis Khan possessed effective organizational abilities. The Mongol government and its army would conquer and hold sway through much of Asia for generations.

THE CONQUEST AND RULE OF CHINA AND KOREA

Chinggis Khan began a major invasion of Chinese territory in 1211, and the collapse of the last Chinese resistance took place in 1279. During the interim, although Mongol attention was often diverted elsewhere, the Mongols periodically returned to renew their military campaign. One Mongol ploy was an appeal for the Jidan people to revolt against the Manchus, who had conquered

[5] **Yasa:** YAH sah

and ruled the Jidan. The Jidan, a group ethnically kindred to the Mongols, responded favorably to the Mongol call in that part of China. As seen in Chapter 18, parts of North China had long been under foreign domination, and in that sense the Mongols were another group seeking to control China.

The Conquest of North China

By 1215, the Mongols had advanced across North China to the city that eventually became known as Beijing. Beijing, like most large cities, was walled, and siege warfare was needed to capture the city.

FIGURE 19.4 *Jidan Funerary Mask. The Jidan people came from Northeast Asia and ruled Northeast China for almost two centuries. This death mask of bronze and gold shows an artistic style more North Asian than Chinese, the result of a conscious effort of the Jidan to retain their ethnic identity against Chinese influences. While in possession of Northeast China, rather than use the Chinese language, they created a new writing system to record their own language. The Jidan were ethnically related to the Mongols and some Jidan later served Chinggis Khan and his successors in ruling China and other states.* From *Empires Beyond the Great Wall: The Heritage of Genghis Khan* (Natural History Museum of Los Angeles County, 1994). Courtesy of the Zhelimu League Museum, Inner Mongolia Autonomous Region, People's Republic of China. Photo by Marc Carter.

The Beijing siege endured for months and infuriated the impatient Mongols, who, in more than thirty days of pillage and looting, killed large numbers of Chinese and Manchus after the city fell to them. This massacre also may have shown the Mongol fear of a possible counterattack from the large numbers of people who dwelled in cities. Later, when a small Mongol force returned to their steppe pasture to the north, they slaughtered their captive Chinese prisoners. Some have argued that the Mongols did not wish to be slowed by the horseless Chinese, while others noted that the Mongol escorting party might have feared an uprising by the large number of captives. Later, the Mongols used terror in the form of wholesale massacres to awe their enemies, and several cities surrendered to the approaching Mongols rather than face widespread killing. The campaigns in North China continued with little pause until the Manchus were defeated in 1234.

The Campaigns of Khubilai Khan

It took another forty-five years before South China fell to the Mongols in 1279, leading to the Mongol Empire (1279–1368), because the Late Song Empire put up a strong resistance to the nomads. Khubilai Khan (1215–1294), a grandson of Chinggis Khan, presided over the conquest and ruled over most of East Asia until his death in 1294. He was a remarkable ruler of China because he attempted to straddle both the Mongol and Chinese elements in his armies and government. Khubilai Khan understood that while China might be conquered on horseback, it had to be ruled in the traditional manner of bureaucratic control developed during the previous few centuries. Consequently, Khubilai Khan invited Chinese scholars and officials into his administration, but because he did not wish to rely solely on the Chinese, he also invited people like Marco Polo, the European adventurer, to serve in his government. The non-Chinese were given the designation of "Colored-Eye People," presumably because the irises of their eyes bore colors other than the dark brown common to the Mongols.

Khubilai Khan also attempted to further expand through conquest the boundaries of his domain. In that way, he faithfully adhered to his grandfather's admonition to conquer the known

UNDER THE LENS
Yehluchucai:
A Jidan Advisor
to Chinggis Khan

The Mongols' nomadic origins made them suspicious of urban centers and agrarian societies. Chinggis Khan developed a strict code of laws to guide and bind the Mongols, but he and his successors needed to rely on others for advice and techniques for ruling large agrarian states.

Yehluchucai[a] came from a noble Jidan family whose men long had served the Manchus ruling North China. Yehluchucai's father reached the top level of the government, and his son could have relied on the *yin* privilege to avoid taking the imperial exams. Being a proud man, Yehluchucai decided to forgo the *yin* privilege and prepared for the exams. The year he took them, Yehluchucai ranked number one in the empire and thereby merited a choice government position, in which he served for a few years. Then the Mongols attacked the city in which the young Jidan lived. The carnage of the siege and the subsequent Mongol slaughter of many residents compelled Yehluchucai to seek refuge in a Buddhist monastery. Within three years, he attained spiritual enlightenment, and because of his Jidan heritage (tribal kinship to the Mongols), Chinggis Khan summoned him.

[a] **Yehluchucai:** YEH loo CHOO sy

In the initial meeting, the Jidan's frank manner and impressive figure caused Chinggis Khan to seek his counsel. Over the years, Yehluchucai often interceded on behalf of conquered peoples by asking that they not be killed. Many survived because of Yehluchucai's skillful pleas, and perhaps his greatest success came in the 1230s.

As more of northern China came under Mongol control, the Mongol leaders debated about what to do with the vast lands under their possession. One faction argued for turning the territory into a pastureland, which would have necessitated slaughtering millions of Chinese. Yehluchucai and others argued that by taxing the people instead of killing them, the Mongols could gain all of the riches that they desired. Yehluchucai also reckoned an amount that could be garnered by levying a tax. Ögödei permitted Yehluchucai to implement the proposal, and the tallies squared with the estimates. Millions of lives were spared by Yehluchucai's clever arguments. Shortly thereafter, he became a major advisor to the monarch. Over time, Yehluchucai brought in many Chinese officials and organized a Chinese-style administration that became a basis for the Chinese system finally implemented under Khubilai Khan after 1260.

---

world. In addition, the continued campaigning provided the ever-restless Mongol warriors outlets for their energies; better to have them focused outward, Khubilai Khan's thinking went, than plotting some kind of internal uprising. Besides, new conquests meant new chances for glory and booty from the defeated peoples.

Khubilai Khan twice attempted to conquer Japan. In 1274, more than 30,000 warriors and support personnel sailed from Korea to Japan. After the Mongol landing on the southern island of Kyushu, fierce resistance by Japanese *samurai* slowed the invaders. A typhoon smashed the hapless fleet and wrecked the Mongols' hope for a victory. A combined Mongol and Chinese fleet with around 150,000 people launched a second invasion in 1281 and was ravaged by another typhoon. Khubilai Khan called off a third effort in the mid-1280s.

Further campaigns were launched against Southeast Asian states by Khubilai Khan. In the 1280s, two major invasions attempted to annex Vietnam, but resistance by the Vietnamese was too strong. (An earlier Mongol invasion of Vietnam had been thwarted by heat, insects, and tropical diseases.) A Mongol armada sailed to the islands of the Southeast Asian coast, including Java, but this campaign also failed to take its military objectives.

Despite the string of defeats along the periphery of the Asian mainland, Khubilai Khan remained in firm control of China. There he laid the foundation for a rule lasting nearly one century. One major legacy was the rebuilding of the Grand Canal, which permitted Khubilai Khan and others to ship grain from the prosperous south.

China under Khubilai Khan's Successors

While violent court intrigues occupied the Mongols, the local Chinese populace experienced moderate rule. In fact, much power passed into the hands of educated Chinese landowners who acted as unpaid officials, often keeping order and mediating in clan or family disputes. This quasi-administrative system characterized Chinese society until early in the twentieth century and enabled governments to rule tens of millions of people with a mere 20,000 officials.

The Mongols appreciated the artisan and merchant classes, two groups that in theory languished at the bottom of the Chinese social scale. Artisans were organized and protected by the state, and they were exempted from certain taxes. In addition, the state allocated them rations of food, clothing, and salt. Physicians, too, were seen as artisans and favorably treated. They worked in imperial hospitals and practiced Islamic as well as

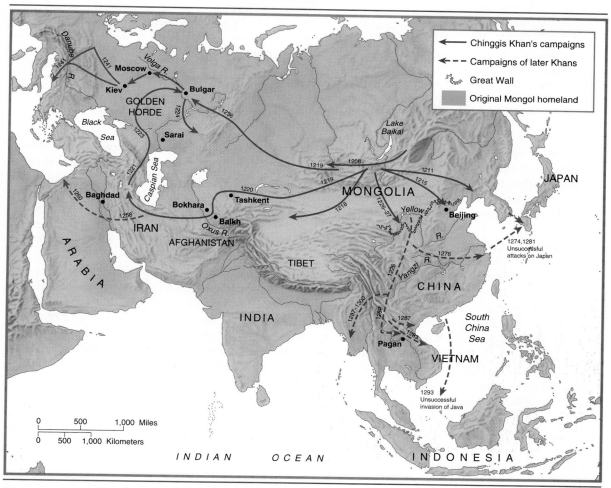

MAP 19.1 *Campaigns of the Mongol Khans, 1206–1300. Mongol forces ranged across much of Asia and parts of Europe. Naval expeditions did not achieve the success of the land campaigns, which—with the exception of those waged against the Mamluks and Vietnamese—were usually victorious.*

FIGURE 19.5 *Mongol Naval Battle Scene.* *While attempting two unsuccessful invasions of Japan, the Mongols fought several naval engagements. This Japanese painting shows a Mongol vessel being boarded by* samurai, *bearing swords and wearing layered armor. Japanese* samurai *tended to prefer individual combat, while the Mongols usually fought in group formations.* Imperial Household Collection, Kyoto/Laurie Platt Winfrey, Inc.

traditional Chinese medicine. Merchants were accorded high status all over the Mongol realm and were eligible for state loans at the low annual interest of 10 percent. For this reason and others, domestic and international commerce mushroomed.

Artistic forms flourished during Mongol rule. A new poetic form that was closely tied to folksongs dominated versification during the Mongol era. Storytelling became a popular art form in the Chinese cities as professionals plied their narrative trades, sometimes for days or weeks in one neighborhood. The books used by the storytellers occasionally became the foundation for the emergence of Chinese novels. Opera developed, and more than 150 play manuscripts still exist. They were written in colloquial Chinese, reflecting close ties to the common people. Painting, especially in the landscape genre, closely followed the tradition established in the previous Song era and reached new levels of expression in the hands of a few Chinese masters, like Zhao Mengfu,[6] whose canvases inspired generations of artists in China, Korea, and Japan.

[6]**Zhao Mengfu:** JOW MEHNG foo

Khubilai's successors did not always share his preference for ruling from the cities, and some of them reverted to the traditional Mongol nomadic life. During the first half of the fourteenth century, Mongol factions representing the sedentary and nomadic lifestyles contended at the imperial court, and some rulers were assassinated after only a few months in power.

In 1368, the Mongol government fell to a Chinese rebellion led by a commoner. Those Mongols who survived the terrible battles of the 1360s returned to the steppelands north of China and contented themselves with periodic sorties into the agrarian domain they once ruled. Never again did the Mongols conquer China.

The Conquest of Korea

Korea, like China, fell to the Mongols in the thirteenth century. Although the initial invasion began in 1218, it took the Mongols until the late 1250s to subdue the tenacious Korean people completely. The Koryo Dynasty (935–1392) had long ruled Korea and was in a weakened state when the Mongols swept into the peninsula. The Mongols could lay waste to the cities, but they could not persuade the Korean monarch to surrender. Indeed, the royal family fled to an island off the coast and stayed there for many years despite numerous Mongol efforts to entice them to return. As long as there was a focus of Korean resistance, guerrilla fighters harassed the nomads.

In 1259, the last opposition to the Mongols disappeared and an accommodation was negotiated with the Korean court. In exchange for tribute items, like clothing, horses, and animal skins, the Koreans were permitted much local autonomy. On occasion, the Mongols demanded and received Korean soldiers to fight in their wars, especially during the failed invasions of Japan, and, in the large military campaigns, units from parts of Eurasia fought alongside Mongol soldiers.

Korea also became a base from which the invasions of Japan were launched. Each invasion severely drained the resources available in Korea and led to great suffering. Pleas from the Korean monarch persuaded Khubilai Khan to cancel plans for a third invasion. From that time until the mid–fourteenth century, when Mongol rule collapsed in much of East Asia, the Koreans were treated mildly by their nomadic overlords.

DEVASTATION AND RULE IN CENTRAL ASIA, 1219–1370

In 1219, much of Central Asia was ruled by a polity headed by Ala al-Din Muhammad, a Muslim ruler (shah), who had once planned to conquer China. After seeing that the Mongols had begun their invasion of North China, the shah sent observers

FIGURE 19.6 *"Autumn Colors on the Zhiao and Hua Mountains." Zhao Mengfu (1254–1322) excelled at painting landscapes, such as this scene of a marshy plain of willows, boats, and scattered houses, backed by hills covered in fall color, dated 1295. Zhao was related to the ruling family of the Song Empire and briefly retired when the Mongols took over. Responding to an appeal from Kubilai Khan, he returned to court life. Zhao was criticized by fellow Chinese as a collaborator, but this did not deter him from lending his considerable prestige to the group of artists serving the Mongols.* National Palace Museum, Taiwan, Republic of China.

PARALLELS AND DIVERGENCES

The Reliance of Pastoralists on Settled Peoples

Nineteenth-century anthropologists argued that pastoralism was a less complex way of life than agriculture and that pastoralists developed at an earlier date in human prehistory. Modern archaeology, however, has shown that pastoralism is the most recent form of subsistence to evolve, appearing only after agriculture has become well established in a region. Studies of historic and modern pastoralists indicate that herding simply cannot produce the quantity and especially the diversity of products needed to ensure survival; pastoralists always rely heavily on farmers.

Herders produce mostly meat, milk and milk products, and fiber from their animals' coats. They may supplement their herding with the hunting of wild animals and the gathering of wild plants, but their primary emphasis must be on their herd animals. A major problem, of course, is that they must limit the number of animals slaughtered to ensure that their herds remain large, so a meat surplus is rare; in fact, most pastoralists do not produce enough meat to keep themselves alive, if that were the only food they relied on. The demands of their animals force them to move regularly for fresh pasturage, so pastoralists have little opportunity to grow crops to supplement their food supply.

Instead, pastoralists typically obtain major portions of their food and other goods from nearby agriculturalists. Much of this is obtained by trade, because farmers usually relish the meat and cheese supplied by the pastoralists and will trade quantities of their agricultural produce for these products. In addition, wool and other pastoralist products can be traded to the sedentary farmers and urbanites for goods otherwise unavailable to the herders.

In some periods, pastoralists also have used their mobility and endurance to superior military advantage, seizing desired goods by raiding. As a result of trading and raiding, some pastoralists became quite wealthy, and some settled down in older age, opting for the less strenuous life of the city. This reliance on settled peoples has led one anthropologist to refer to pastoralists as "part-societies," recognizing that they could not persist without their sedentary economic partners.

The Mongols viewed empires with suspicion because they were convinced that the Chinese and others cheated them. Mongols hated the tolls and fees at their borders and bristled at the violations of Mongol-Chinese agreements. City folk were not to be trusted and perhaps were to be eradicated. Had the Mongol attempts been more concerted and successful, the Mongols would have found their own way of life threatened. Pastoralists soon realized that raiding could be conducted only in a limited manner, being sure to skim only some wealth from settled peoples; if weakened too much, agriculturalists could not have supported the pastoralists. In short, successful pastoralists have contented themselves with being traders and limited predators.

to ascertain the power of this new military group. Chinggis Khan also learned of his formidable neighbor and wanted to establish friendly relations with the shah. With that in mind, the Mongol leader dispatched diplomats to offer a friendly alliance between the ruler of the west and the ruler of the east. Soon thereafter, a wealth-laden caravan under Mongol protection arrived in one of the eastern cities of the shah's realm. A subordinate of the shah killed a Mongol envoy and confiscated the convoy's goods, and the shah did not repudiate the action of his official. Chinggis Khan and his successors regarded this action as a personal affront and swore vengeance against the offending state and its ruler. In 1219, Chinggis Khan headed a large invasion force that probably numbered over 100,000 soldiers. Over the next two years, the Mongols systematically destroyed Ala al-Din Muhammad's Central Asian empire and hounded him all across his lands. Although they failed to capture him, they did make his life thoroughly miserable.

The campaign had all of the elements of most Mongol invasions except that the destructiveness seemed to go beyond the usual limits of Mongol warring. To derive the maximum effectiveness of

FIGURE 19.7 *Ruins of the Citadel of Herat. During their conquest of Central Asia, the Mongols destroyed many cities and settlements. To avoid army casualties, Mongol forces usually spared cities that surrendered without resistance, while the inhabitants of those that resisted were massacred as a warning to others. Reports claim that only twenty-five people survived the attack on the citadel of Herat in Afghanistan, built on the site of a fort raised by Alexander the Great.* © 1992 John Adderley.

the arrayed armies, the Mongols relied on strict discipline to maneuver so that all units converged on a designated place at a given time. When the Mongols lost an important leader or a prince to an enemy, they warred without mercy. One city in the southern part of the shah's empire managed to kill one of Chinggis's grandsons. The town was taken, the inhabitants were slaughtered, the buildings were burned, and the surviving urban structures were pulled down. Resistance to the Mongols continued. When another city fell after a long siege, all of its men, women, and children were beheaded and each group's severed heads were formed into a separate pyramid. On at least three occasions, after the Mongol forces withdrew, a trailing Mongol force suddenly returned and killed all those who had returned or left their hiding places. It became a common practice of Mongol warfare for soldiers to single out artisans in a town, spare them from death, and march them off to service, usually in the Mongol homeland. When Samarkand fell in 1220, around 30,000 artisans and engineers were spared. By the end of this campaign little remained of the vibrant civilization there.

Rule over the Central Asian lands passed to the eldest son of Chinggis Khan. Prosperity slowly returned to towns and cities because many vital trade routes passed through them. A key stretch of the Mongol post road also went through Central Asia, and many travelers and couriers visited scenic or otherwise famous sites.

THE KIPCHAK KHANATE AND THE DOMINATION OF RUSSIA, 1221–1480

Russia had no major leader when the Mongols arrived in the 1220s. The government of Kiev (around 900–1240) had long since passed its prime and disintegrated into warring princely factions. Some Kievan princes went north and northeast to settle the vast forest areas there. Indeed, the wooden houses and buildings in many northeast towns and villages resembled the log dwellings across the North American frontier of the eighteenth and early nineteenth centuries. Russia, in fact, in the early decades of the thirteenth century, was a patchwork of independent principalities and city-states that stretched west to east from the Baltic Sea to the Ural Mountains and north to south from the White Sea to the Black Sea.

The initial Mongol thrust in 1221 was more of a scouting expedition by two of Chinggis Khan's able commanders. They had trailed Ala al-Din Muhammad, the fugitive Central Asian sultan, to the Caspian Sea area, and, after assuring themselves that he had perished, they decided to cross the Caucasus Mountains and explore the northern reaches of the steppe. News of their plundering in the kingdom of Georgia and elsewhere gave Russian princes time to mobilize a large army to meet them. Outnumbered, the Mongols used a ploy that had often worked in the past. They charged the Russian positions and then broke off the attack to take flight. Like many other Mongol opponents, the Russians could not resist chasing the fleeing cavalry. After an extended ride, the Mongol forces swung around and were joined by hidden forces that entrapped the pursuers. The enemy was annihilated, and the Mongols returned to finish off the remaining forces. Fortunately for the Mongols, the rivalries among the surviving Russian princes brought counterattacks in a piecemeal fashion. Soon the Russians were severely defeated, and the Mongol army heeded the command of Chinggis Khan to return to Central Asia.

The Conquest of the Bulgars, Kipchaks, and Russians

The second main incursion into Russia came around fifteen years later when a large Mongol army, numbering perhaps 120,000 soldiers, attacked. Batu,[7] another grandson of Chinggis, headed this expedition accompanied by many key Mongol leaders and princes, including representatives of the lines of Chinggis Khan's four sons. It was a carefully planned major thrust into Europe and relied heavily on intelligence gathered by merchant-spies.

The first attack came against Bulgars, who lived along the Volga River and who had served as a buffer between the Russians and the steppe peoples. By autumn 1236, the Mongols destroyed the Bulgars and rebuilt their capital. Some Bulgars fled to Russia, where they were granted asylum.

A second expedition along the Volga targeted the Kipchak people, who were a loose confederation of Turkish tribes. After a brief, hard-hitting attack, the Kipchaks were defeated, and many joined with the Mongols in their attacks against the Russians. When the Mongol leader, Batu, established his domain, the Kipchak component of his subjects inspired the name Kipchak Khanate for this section of the Mongol Empire.

With most of the Volga River Valley secured, the Mongols turned to the Russians. Once again, because of internal rivalries, Russian leaders failed to lay coordinated defensive plans. The initial operation went through the winter of 1237 and 1238 and brought the towns and cities of the northeast under Mongol domination. The usual thorough destruction was conducted throughout the area, and only the city-state of Novgorod in the northwest was spared because a spring thaw undermined cavalry operations. Batu then spent the next year and a half resupplying men and materials as well as defeating remnant opposition forces in the south.

By 1240, the Mongols resumed their march toward Kiev and then into eastern Europe. One Mongol commander wished to spare Kiev from utter destruction and offered peace terms. The defenders replied by executing the Mongol envoys. This infuriated the Mongols, who gathered their entire attacking force before the city. The fight was ferocious and ended in Mongol victory. As might

[7] **Batu:** BAH too

Ha cōqui ſtrēt en lannīc ſeignoꝛ·oꝛ·ꝯ·ꝑ·m·

ſont mlt engꝛignoꝛs mā ꝯrēt homes qui ſauoiēt nocr ʒ ceaux entrerēt

FIGURE 19.8 *King Bela of Hungary Facing the Mongols.* *On April 10, 1241, a Hungarian force led by King Bela was defeated by the Mongols, under Batu Khan. In this European-painted scene, Batu, grandson of Chinggis Khan, faces the Hungarians at the bridge over the Sajo River, captured with the aid of artillery barrages. The Mongol forces conquered most of eastern Europe (southern Poland to the Adriatic, at Bosnia) and were on the brink of invading the west when the death of the Great Khan in December 1241 sent Batu back east to help select a successor.* Osterreichische Nationalbibliothek.

be expected, the city suffered great destruction, including the ravaging of tombs of Russian saints and dignitaries, whose bones were exhumed and scattered on the streets. The Mongols then rode toward the heart of Europe.

The Attack on the Hungarians

Hungary, the main target in Europe, was ruled by an otherwise capable monarch who was so unwise as to execute some Mongol envoys. That action, as well as the king's refusal to surrender the Kipchaks who had fled from the Mongols, assured the Mongol invasion of his land. At the same time, to protect their northern flank, the Mongols launched a strike by a force of about 30,000 men into Poland and Bohemia. That expedition saw fierce fighting, including one savage encounter during which the

Mongols severed the ears of their slain enemies. Nine bags of ears were collected as war trophies. Several other Mongol units advanced through the Carpathian Mountains into Hungary in a coordinated effort. The decisive battle, in April 1241, brought utter defeat for the Hungarian monarch, who fled to the Adriatic Sea. He was pursued by a detachment of Mongols who arrived at the Mediterranean seacoast but could not follow the monarch to his island retreat. Some months later in Mongolia, the death of the Great Khan (head of the Mongols) Ögödei[8] (1229–1241) forced a withdrawal of the Mongol armies from Europe. They never returned to the western campaign. Instead they withdrew to the Volga steppe region, where Batu established his headquarters. From there, he

[8] **Ögödei:** OOH geh day

IN THEIR OWN WORDS
Humanitarian Elements of Mongol Rule

People may think of Mongols as barbaric, but they also had humanitarian traits. Warfare, of course, has caused great suffering throughout history, but the Mongol rulers seemed unusually destructive of life and property. Our view of the Mongols comes from others because the Mongols never wrote about themselves.

One perspective is provided by the historian Ala-ad-Din Ata-Malik Juvaini (1226–1283), who records some humanitarian acts of Mongol rulers, especially Ögödei Khan. Juvaini actually held mixed views about the Mongols, who destroyed much of his beloved Persian culture. In his *History of the World-Conqueror*, he discusses Mongol atrocities and mentions their humanitarian deeds. In the following selections, we can see how Ögödei treated commoners.

A poor man, who was unable to earn a living and had learned no trade, sharpened pieces of iron into the shape of awls and mounted them on pieces of wood. He then sat down where the retinue of the Khan would pass and waited. The Khan caught sight of him from afar and sent one of his attendants to him. The poor man told him of the weakness of his condition, the smallness of his property, and the largeness of his family and gave him the awls. But when the messenger saw his clumsy awls, . . . hardly . . . worth a barleycorn, he thought them unworthy of being presented to the Khan and so left them . . . and [returning] told what he had seen. The Khan ordered him [to go back and] bring all the awls that the man had with him. . . . taking them in his hand he said: "Even this kind will serve for herdmen to mend . . . seams . . . with." And for each awl he gave the man an [ingot of gold or silver].

A poor man came to his court with ten thongs tied to a stick. He opened his mouth in prayer [for the Khan] and stood at a distance. The royal glance fell upon him and when the officers inquired about his business, he said, "I had a kid [goat] in my household. I made its flesh the sustenance of my family, and out of its hide I fashioned thongs for the men-at-arms, which I have brought with me." The Khan took the thongs and said: "This poor fellow has brought us what is better than goats." And he ordered him to be given a hundred ingots and a thousand head of sheep. And he added that when this was consumed, [the man] should come again, and he would give him more.

An Indian woman with two children on her back was passing by a gate. The Khan, who had just returned from the country, caught sight of her and ordered the treasurer to give her five ingots. He took them to her at once, but put one in his pocket and gave her only four. The woman noticed that one was missing and pleaded with him to give it to her. The Khan asked him what the woman had been saying. He replied that she was a woman with a family and was uttering a prayer. The Khan then asked, "What family has she?" "Two small orphans," replied the treasurer. The Khan went to the treasury and ordered the woman to be summoned. Then he commanded her to take every kind of clothing that pleased her fancy, as many embroidered garments as a rich and wealthy man would wear.

---

and his successors demanded that the Russians render various services common to subject peoples elsewhere in the expanding empire.

Mongol Administration of Russia

The Great Khan Möngke[9] (reign dates 1251–1259) ordered a census of the Russian population in the 1250s for tax and service purposes. This was part of a general effort by Möngke to maximize the employment of the empire's human and material resources. The initial population count commenced in 1257 and expanded to all areas by 1260. Some evidence suggests that the Mongols imposed agricultural and commercial taxes on the Russians, although it is unclear what rates were demanded. In addition, the Mongols divided the population into administrative units for conscription purposes, with each unit responsible for supplying a certain number of soldiers when called upon.

When ruling Russia, Mongol leaders like Batu relied heavily on local Russian princes who col-

[9]**Möngke:** MEHNG keh

lected taxes and then remitted them to the capital, Sarai. Initially, the khans demanded that princes appear at regular intervals so that they might renew their pledges of allegiance to the khan, and sometimes the Russians accompanied the tax revenues. The Mongols permitted much self-government. Indeed, one reason for the rise to power of the Moscow princes in the fourteenth century was their use of excess funds collected for the Mongols to finance local building and other projects. Moscow sovereigns continued to curry favor with their Mongol overlords, so that they might benefit from being the khan's officials.

In the late fourteenth century, one Moscow prince, Dmitri, briefly challenged Mongol domination by refusing to acknowledge Mongol overlordship. In addition, an army of a Central Asian leader who claimed descent from Chinggis Khan attacked the Kipchak Khanate and inflicted serious damage upon it. Several tribal confederations broke off to form the Kazan Khanate, the Siberian Khanate, and the Crimean Khanate. By 1480, the Kipchak Khanate's weakened condition enabled the Moscow prince Ivan III to renounce Mongol overlordship and resist the efforts of a Mongol army to punish him. In that campaign, the Crimean Mongols aligned with Ivan III.

Mongol rule in Russia brought many political changes to the Russian people. Initially, great destruction devastated the land and its peoples. One chronicle of the time said that after the Mongols passed through, no one was left to mourn the fallen. Yet their relatively lax ruling policies permitted the growth of local administration and the consolidation of power by the Moscow princes. The extended era of peace permitted a rebound and some material prosperity among the nobility and the merchants. Mongol rulers often preferred hunting to ruling; their soldiers were splendid warriors but ineffective administrators.

THE MONGOLS IN SOUTHWEST ASIA, 1258–AROUND 1350

Southwest Asia was composed of a multitude of polities at the time of the Mongol invasion and conquest in the 1250s. The Abbasid Caliphate, which had loosely ruled over the Islamic world for centuries, and the Saljuq[10] Turks, who had long dominated the Persian lands, were in a weakened state when the Mongols arrived. In fact, much of the area was in the hands of petty rulers who fought one another and vied for control of larger domains.

In the mid-1250s, the Mongol leadership decided to subjugate Southwest Asia, which had experienced haphazard Mongol rule, much in the manner of the great campaign of the 1230s and 1240s in Russia and eastern Europe. Command of the operation was given to Hülegü,[11] one of the Great Khan's younger brothers. In addition, all Mongol and allied sovereigns were expected to supply specified numbers of men or supplies. Failure to respond signaled disloyalty and invited swift retaliation by the Mongols.

Hülegü took a long time in arriving in Persia, the first focus of his conquest, because his large force of more than 100,000 needed time to cross rivers and traverse difficult mountain ranges and other natural obstacles. Hülegü's army also traveled with large siege machines that could not be quickly or easily transported.

Once in Persia, the commander began probing the formidable mountain fortifications of the Ismaili sect (popularly known as the Assassins). This group had long been identified as a major obstacle to unification of the region, and, over the succeeding months, castles and other forts of the Ismailis were systematically destroyed. Other Mongol forces began conquering parts of Persia to the south.

After subduing the Ismaili sect, Hülegü conquered the Abbasid Caliphate. In the normal pattern of the Mongols, smaller towns around the great capital, Baghdad, were first taken and plundered, and then came the assault on the capital itself. As they had done on many previous occasions, the Mongols built a wooden palisade surrounding the capital to keep the townspeople from escaping. In addition, Hülegü drove many captives ahead of the attacking forces to break the will of the besieged as well as to minimize the attackers' losses. Once the city fell in early 1258, the slaughter began, and some sources note that part of the savage killing came from Georgian units of the Caucasus Mountains region that fought alongside the Mongols. These Georgian soldiers avenged

[10] **Saljuq:** sehl JUHK
[11] **Hülegü:** HOO leh guh

FIGURE 19.9 *Mongol Siege of Baghdad.* *Baghdad fell to Mongol forces under Hülegü in 1258, ending the Abbasid Caliphate. The Mongols built a wall around the city to prevent escape during the siege, in which the caliph and over 500,000 inhabitants were killed. The conquerors later made pyramids of the heads of slain inhabitants to deter further resistance to their rule.* Bibliothèque nationale, Paris.

themselves on their former Muslim overlords. As in previous conquests, artisans were spared; most of them were rounded up for the long trek to the Mongol capital, Qaraqorum.[12]

Mongol forces ranged over most of Southwest Asia and even managed to take Damascus for a brief time. Their ability to maintain a lasting presence along the eastern Mediterranean coast was continually frustrated by the rulers of Egypt. In the seesaw fighting for the extreme western part of Southwest Asia, the European monarchs and the European crusaders, who controlled some cities and areas, refused to cooperate with the Mongols against their common Muslim enemy.

[12]**Qaraqorum:** kah rah KOHR uhm

Hülegü and his successors ruled Persia, Mesopotamia, and parts of the Caucasus region for nearly a century. The economy of Persia and the surrounding territories was devastated in the thirteenth century by the Mongol conquest and the Mongols' harsh taxation policies. Warfare, famine, and disease sharply reduced the population, which slowly recovered to pre-Mongol levels in the last decade of the thirteenth century. There was some influx of Turkish and Mongol settlers, but they lived in nomadic communities and had little effect on either agriculture or urban life.

From the 1290s to the mid-1330s, there was a spurt of economic growth, especially in agriculture and trade. Owing to the adoption of lighter taxes, small-scale peasant landholding increased and helped to promote agricultural prosperity. Cities gradually became active economic centers, though nothing in commerce or agriculture reached the levels of pre-Mongol times. Trade routes running through much of Asia lay in the control of the Mongols, and the increased commercial volume also improved the fortunes of artisans and merchants in Persian cities. Chinese products once again reached Persia, and Persian traders and advisors often traveled to China.

The arts experienced some interruption with the destruction of the great cities of Southwest Asia. Poetry, which had long flourished under previous governments, went into decline after the Mongols arrived. This was largely linked to the poets' loss of elite patronage, as well as to the urban devastation. Nevertheless, certain forms that included mystical poetry continued under the Mongols.

The Mongols supported the writing of historical works in an attempt to immortalize themselves. Certain Persian Muslim historians are key sources for our knowledge of the Mongol era; Juvaini and Rashid al-Din (1247–1318) deserve special mention. Both men served in Mongol administrations; Juvaini came from a long line of top government officials in Central Asia, while Rashid al-Din was a physician. Juvaini's history contained highly polished prose and poetry. Written in pieces over the span of a decade, this history has been an invaluable source of information about the Mongols because of the variety of people Juvaini knew. Rashid al-Din wrote long after the Mongol conquest, and his style lacks the flair of Juvaini's. Rashid al-Din's major historical work, however, developed from a wide range of sources. He assembled a resource team of two Chinese scholars, a Buddhist monk from South Asia, a spe-

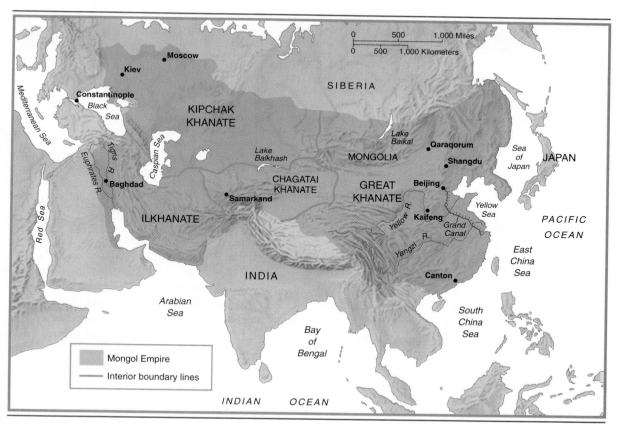

MAP 19.2 *The Mongol Empire around 1300.* *The empire became so large that it broke into four khanates centered in Persia, Russia, Central Asia, and East Asia. Despite this division, trade continued to flow smoothly across Eurasia.*

FIGURE 19.10 *Persian Perspective on the Mongols.* *After their state was overrun by the Mongols, some Persians wrote or painted what they saw or heard of the atrocities committed by the conquerors. This manuscript illustrates one prisoner being executed with arrows, while others are buried alive, head down. While many kinds of brutality were inflicted by the Mongols, fear, rumor, and imagination may have played a role in creating this scene, and others.* Chester Beatty Library and Gallery of Oriental Art, Dublin.

cialist on Mongol tribal traditions, and a European traveler. Thus, perhaps more than any previous scholar, Rashid al-Din conveyed a Eurasian perspective, ranging far beyond the geographic limits of Islam.

Mathematics and science continued to flourish in the Mongol period. A few Persian mathematicians explored algebra and trigonometry, following in the footsteps of their Muslim predecessors. The Persians laid the foundation for important mathematical discoveries in later times. Astronomy also benefited from the erection of an observatory by Hülegü, who was interested more in astrology than in astronomy. The observatory provided a place for the gathering of astronomers and facilitated their continued scholarly research, which reached new heights.

THE MONGOL EXCHANGE

The Mongols exploded across Eurasia in the thirteenth century and united a vast area of the Eurasian landmass while providing nearly unprecedented security for merchants and travelers. At the same time, Mongol fleets patrolled the sea lanes of the East China Sea and the South China Sea, thereby facilitating maritime trade between India and China. The growth of the China market added a vital piece to the puzzle of Eurasian trade. South China's trade, both internally and externally, flourished prior to the Mongol conquest. The Southern Song government, for example, opened nine Chinese port cities to maritime trade. Thereafter, once the cities recovered

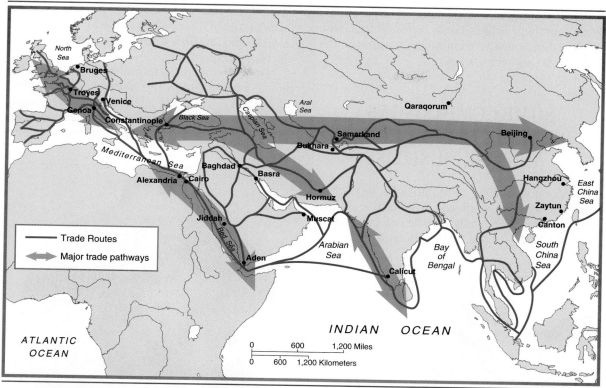

MAP 19.3 *The Mongol Empire and Trade around 1340.* The Mongol exchange *benefited from the growth of land and maritime trade across Eurasia and parts of Africa. Mongol leaders favored merchants and actively promoted commerce. As a result, caravans traversed the silk roads and convoys of merchant ships plied the seas and oceans off Asia and Africa. The volume of trade was unparalleled until the seventeenth century.*

from the destruction of warfare, the increase of commerce accelerated. It was aided by the Mongol appreciation for trade and merchants. A reunited China became a major exporter and importer, thus becoming a significant impetus to a burgeoning trade that brought hemispheric prosperity until the mid–fourteenth century. Europeans sent furs, grain, and merchants eastward. Indeed, the inter-mixing of people, goods, ideas, and diseases created the basis for what may be called the Mongol exchange.

One great benefit of the Mongol unity was the increased trade between regions of Eurasia. Like most nomadic groups that needed to exchange goods in order to survive, the Mongols promoted trade and supported merchants who traveled from place to place in search of profitable exchanges. European merchants, like Marco Polo and his

uncles, as well as Muslim merchants traveled to China in pursuit of business profits and adventure.

Traders, soldiers, and officials served in distant parts of the Mongol Empire. Russians fought in China, while Chinese, Turks, and Persians worked in places like Mongolia, China, and Russia. Some of these subjects returned home with new ideas and ways of doing things. Marco Polo governed an area of southern China and returned to Venice with tales of coal being used as a fuel and paper currency being employed as a major exchange medium.

Knowledge of the compass and of gunpowder technology, along with many other technological wonders, moved from east to west, with the compass arriving in the 1200s and gunpowder reaching Europe in the 1300s. Some in the Islamic world gained access to the compass and gunpowder, but it was the Europeans who employed the compass to aid in their explorations overseas and who employed gunpowder technology to enhance the power of state governments.

SOME COMPARISONS BETWEEN THE MONGOLS AND THE MUSLIMS

Both Mongols (1200s) and Muslims (600s and 700s) rapidly conquered vast areas of the eastern hemisphere in their early decades of power, and there are some fruitful comparisons to be made

about their rule and legacies. After a century or more of rule in their domains, the Mongols settled in, while the Muslims continued to expand, generally by peaceful means.

Despite the devastation brought about by their conquests, both the Mongols and Muslims adopted many political institutions of their newly conquered subjects. Certainly, the Mongols used terror as a means to cow their enemies, and cities

FIGURE 19.11 *Astronomical Chart of the Mongol Era.* *Mongol leaders in Southwest Asia employed many scholars from among conquered peoples, drawing on the rich resources of the Muslim scientific tradition. This constellation chart comes from a Persian manuscript written by Nasr al-Din Tusi, a famous astronomer and mathematician. Tusi not only survived the invasion of his homeland but went on to achieve high office, build an observatory, and write many important works in his various fields of expertise. Although Mongol leaders were more interested in astrology than astronomy, both continued to flourish under foreign rule.* Reproduced by permission of the Harvard-Yenching Institute.

FIGURE 19.12 *Yuan Dynasty Vase.* *This vase was created around 1350 by Chinese artisans working under Mongol rule. During this time, potters were encouraged to increase production of their wares, resulting in new techniques, new levels of sophistication, and new markets. White pottery, which was the most popular, included vases, dishes, and figurines that could be painted and glazed or incised with decorative patterns. Widespread distribution of this work was facilitated by the stimulation of trade during the era of the Mongol exchange.* Victoria and Albert Museum.

EURASIA

1100		Chinggis Khan born, c. 1162	
1200	Mongol rule of Central Asia, 1219–1370	Kipchak Khanate, 1221–1480	Chinggis Khan proclaimed leader of the Mongols, 1206 Mongol campaign in Central Asia begins, 1219 Fall of Baghdad to the Mongols, 1258
Yuan Empire, c. 1260–1368		Mongol rule in Southwest Asia, 1258–c. 1360	
1300			
			Mongol rule ends in China, 1368
1400			
			Ivan III defeats Mongols and ends their rule of Russia, 1480
1500			

that resisted Mongol demands suffered grave population losses. Although losses did accompany the Muslim conquests, terror was more sporadic. Muslims generally left irrigation systems alone, while the Mongols destroyed them in parts of Central Asia. Once in power, both groups tolerated local religions, although Muslim rulers imposed special taxes on nonbelievers. The Mongols realized that winning the local religious leaders' support through tax exemptions and other means facilitated rule over the common people.

Muslims continued to spread their religion long after their initial conquests, unlike the Mongols. In that sense, the peaceful expansion of the religion of Islam continued over the centuries and the miles of land and sea. Judges, merchants, and Sufis roamed over continents and found converts from the western Pacific to the eastern Atlantic basins. Dar al-Islam was a realm of sociocultural unity that the Mongol domain never achieved. Indeed, Mongols in Southwest and Central Asia often adopted Islam, Christianity, and Buddhism as their own religions.

Both Mongols and Muslims appreciated trade and presided over eras of significant commercial growth. Chinggis Khan usually favored merchants and artisans because he understood the benefits of business ventures. Muhammad and many members of the Muslim ruling class were themselves merchants and pushed Islamic expansion along long-distance trade routes. Muslim merchants were often favored by Islamic governments spurring trade and encouraging non-Muslim business people to convert. Unity in the Mongol and Muslim empires also created the stability and peace necessary for successful commercial ventures.

The Mongol and Islamic exchanges brought many ideas, foodstuffs, and textiles to diverse parts of the hemisphere. Muslim astronomers served Chinese, Indian, and Arab monarchs. Chinese paper makers found a home in Baghdad, and from there paper making and its use spread across Dar al-Islam. Gunpowder was taken by the Mongols into Southwest Asia and from there passed to Europe. All regions eventually were transformed by this technology.

Perhaps the greatest difference and permanent legacy related to religion. The Mongols were tolerant of the religions of others. The Muslims ardently practiced their faith and carried it everywhere they went. Today, hundreds of millions of Muslims reside in Eurasia and are a living testimony to the enduring legacy of Islam. Mongols either assimilated into the societies that they ruled or returned to Mongolia, where their descendants still reside.

SUMMARY

1. Mongol unity came in 1206, when Chinggis Khan was proclaimed the leader of the Mongols. At that time, he also gave the Mongols a law code and began working on a courier system to transmit messages rapidly throughout his empire.

2. China was a major target of Chinggis Khan, whose campaign against it began in 1211. The conquest of North China concluded in 1234, and all of China fell into Mongol hands by 1279. With the example of Khubilai Khan, the Mongols came to rule China like traditional monarchs, although one faction preferred to maintain a nomadic identity.

3. Mongol factional strife in China led to a weak government, and revolts in the mid–fourteenth century finally toppled the Mongols there.

4. Central Asia fell to the Mongols in 1221 after a bitter struggle that shattered the urban civilization there. The Mongols often deliberately employed terror as a weapon to facilitate their conquests in Central Asia and elsewhere. Rule over Central Asia passed to one line of Chinggis's sons and lasted for over a century.

5. Russia fell to the Mongols during a three-year campaign marked by frightful massacres. Control passed to Batu, the leader of the expedition, and the Mongol rule lasted for more than two centuries.

6. Local rule was encouraged by the Mongols and permitted the growth of influence by the Chinese gentry landlords and the Moscow princes.

7. Persia and the rest of Southwest Asia endured successive invasions by the Mongols from the 1220s through the 1250s. Although Mongol conquest and rule initially devastated the region's people and economy, some return to pre-Mongol

prosperity occurred from the 1290s to the 1330s. History writing expanded owing to Mongol patronage, and some forms of poetry flourished.

8. Despite the destruction caused by many Mongol invasions, the rule brought peaceful conditions and the growth of trade. A Mongol exchange between Asia and Europe occurred, and goods, technologies, and foodstuffs spread across that vast domain.

9. The Mongols came from the steppelands of Asia and followed a nomadic lifestyle, spurring the development of civilization in much of Eurasia.

SUGGESTED READINGS

Boyle, John. *The Mongol World Empire, 1206–1370*. London: Variorum Reprints, 1977. A classic examination of the Mongol realm in light of Eurasian politics and society.

Cleaves, Francis, trans. *The Secret History of the Mongols*. Cambridge, Mass.: Harvard University Press, 1982. An accurate translation of and insightful commentary on a major source of Mongol history.

Dardess, John. *Conquerors and Confucians*. New York: Columbia University Press, 1973. A classic interpretation of the Mongol rule of China.

Luc, Kwanten. *Imperial Nomads: A History of Central Asia, 500–1500*. Philadelphia: University of Pennsylvania Press, 1979. A standard look at the geopolitical context of Central Asia and the Mongol role within it.

Rossabi, Morris. *Khubilai Khan*. Berkeley: University of California Press, 1988. An examination of later Mongol rule in East Asia.

Buddha. This cave-temple carving of the Buddha is nearly forty-five feet tall and was commissioned by the Wei emperors, who ruled China from the fourth to the sixth century. The artistic style shows the Buddha with Asian features, demonstrating the acculturation of Buddhism in China. The earliest known Buddhist community in China dates from around A.D. 65; scholars believe Buddhism followed the silk road and the southern sea routes to Asian territories. George Holton/Photo Researchers, Inc.

World Religions and Their Spread

At the end of the tenth century, Vladimire I of Russia faced a religious quandary. People in his realm practiced myriad polytheistic customs that helped to impede cultural uniformity and remained in stark contrast to the cohesiveness of the neighboring monotheistic states. Vladimire chose eastern Christianity over Judaism, Islam, or western Christianity primarily because of the close commercial ties his realm enjoyed with the Byzantine Empire and the diplomatic advantages the conversion would bring to his court. Vladimire was baptized, married the Byzantine emperor's sister, and commenced the conversion of his subjects to eastern Christianity in 988. This conversion of Russia is one example of how world religions spread.

A religion becomes a **world religion** when it gains significant numbers of adherents across broad geographical expanses. The world religions of Judaism, Hinduism, Buddhism, Christianity, and Islam all moved across continents and into new cultural areas, where they were adopted and adapted by new peoples.

The effects of the dissemination of world religions are numerous. As a religion spread beyond its point of origin, its structure, theology, and practice often changed as believers integrated it into their own cultural perspectives. In addition, the religion affected the society to which it came, sometimes changing or altogether eliminating local practices. In this chapter we will examine the ways in which world religions spread and discuss some of the consequential effects of their spread.

THE WAYS IN WHICH RELIGIONS SPREAD

Religions spread as a result of conquests and coercion, missionary activities, migrations, and trade and cultural interactions. Expansion of a religion as a result of conquest may coerce or encourage a subject population to accept a new religion or entice the conquerors to adopt a new religion. Dissemination through missionary activity entails a concentrated effort to persuade indigenous people to convert. Transporting a religion through migration brings it to new areas, as individuals carry their religion with them when they move. Finally, the spread of religion through trade and cultural interaction occurs whenever people of different cultures meet and exchange ideas and customs. Some combination of these four factors was almost always present in the spread of the world religions under examination here.

Conquest and Coercion

Because many peoples consider their belief system superior to those of others, conquerors sometimes desired to spread their religion to those they conquered. In addition, forced conversions helped the new regime to organize and control the subdued population through ideology. A unified belief system was more efficient for maintaining control and legitimizing rule. Uniform belief helped to ensure an obedient population, and kings and emperors often claimed to rule through divine mandate.

Examples of the spread of religion through violence or coercion are relatively rare, but cases can be identified. During the seventh-century Muslim expansion, there were incidents of forced conversion as the Arabs swept through Southwest Asia. In addition, Spanish *conquistadores* compelled many indigenous people in Mexico to convert to Christianity, and Portuguese colonists in

FIGURE I.4.1   *Conversion.*   *Conversion was often a matter of political or social circumstances rather than a result of personal choice. In this scene from medieval Europe, King Clovis is baptized by a Christian missionary. Soon after Clovis's conversion and baptism, hundreds of his subjects were also baptized. As the Franks conquered new territories in Europe, they demanded that local populations convert to Christianity. This gave Frankish kings, like Charlemagne, a religious ideology to unite the realm and the religious sanction to rule by the grace of God.*   Musée Condée, Chantilly/Laurie Platt Winfrey, Inc.

Asia forced Hindus to convert to Christianity. Monarchs often used coercion to convert their populations in order to unify them. When the Sui monarch reunited China through conquest in the late sixth century, he championed Buddhism as a way to link the peoples of the north and south together with one ideology. Germanic kings, like Clovis and Charlemagne, forced their tribes to convert to Christianity because it gave them divine right of rule and helped establish hereditary succession.

Conquerors were also converted when they came in contact with the cultures of their subjects. If the indigenous religion unified the polity and aided in governance, monarchs benefited by converting. By the eleventh century, Turks had conquered the Arabian territories of Syria and Palestine, as well as a large portion of Persia. Islam, already entrenched in these areas, spread to the conquerors, and the Turks became Muslims. Hun conquerors of northern China converted to Buddhism through their use of Buddhists in the government, and Mongol conquerors of Southeast Asia soon adopted Islam through contact with the Muslim population there. The adoption of Islam aided in Mongol rule.

Missionary Activity

In addition to conquests, missionary activity has contributed significantly to the spread of world religions. A **missionary** is a person who purposely sets out to preach, teach, and persuade individuals or groups to consciously accept the belief system or theology of the religion. This kind of activity is called **proselytizing**. Most world religions have included some element of proselytizing.

Although Buddhism is found throughout the world today, its main geographical focus has been in Central, East, South, and Southeast Asia, and it owes its spread largely to missionaries. This development began during the time of Ashoka, who commanded Buddhist priests to carry the message of the Buddha to distant lands in the third century B.C. Buddhism then spread to the rest of India, to Central Asia, to China, and to Southeast Asia. Missionaries used a variety of techniques, including illusion, singing, and dancing, to convey the potency of their message.

Missionaries, mostly monks, took Christian belief beyond the geographical area of ancient Palestine, spreading Christianity among Greeks, Romans, and other peoples of the Mediterranean region in the first to the fourth centuries A.D. Various missionary activities continued to expand Christianity to medieval Europe in the fifth and sixth centuries and beyond. Missionary activities later extended to Arabia, India, China, and the Americas. When some Europeans arrived in China on trading expeditions, they met Asian Christians whose ancestors had been converted by early missionaries.

Islamic missionary activity followed the roads of conquest and trade. Most proselytizing centered on the cities, and missionary activity in the countryside occurred at a slower pace. Wandering Sufi mystics spread Islam throughout Africa, Europe, and Asia, sometimes moving into unconquered territories by themselves. These itinerant missionaries expanded Islam far beyond the borders of Muslim states. Most conversions to Islam were the result of missionary activities.

Not every world religion has a tradition of proselytizing. Judaism traditionally did not support missionary activity, although some people did convert to Judaism in different periods and in different places when they came in contact with Jews. Some Roman intellectuals became Jews while living in Palestine during the Roman Empire. Most conversions to Judaism arose from marriage.

Migration

Significant numbers of peoples throughout the centuries migrated into new areas, resulting in the spread of religious practices to the newly adopted homeland. Immigrants often settled in neighborhoods where they felt more comfortable among those who shared their cultural heritage. As they interacted with the indigenous population, ideas and customs dispersed. Descendants sometimes moved away from ethnic neighborhoods into the surrounding population, spreading their religious heritage through social contact and marriage.

Migration was closely linked with cultural interaction because it offered two opportunities for exchange: It exposed both the indigenous and the migrating populations to each others' religious practices. One example of this is the Jewish **diaspora**, the forced migration of a people. Thousands of Jews were forced to relocate from Palestine to the city of Babylon in the sixth century B.C., where

FIGURE I.4.2 *Joden Savannah. Jews relocated to many areas of the globe during periods of persecution and expulsion. In northern South America, near the banks of the Surinam River, a state called Joden Savannah (the Jewish Savannah) was carved out of the forest by emigrating Jews. The central community was named Jerusalem-on-the-River, in memory of the ancient Jewish homeland. As depicted in this nineteenth-century drawing of a storefront, the Jewish community traded with indigenous peoples. The Jews also established farms that produced sugar, coffee, and cotton.* Beth Hatefutsoth, The Nahum Goldmann Museum of the Jewish Diaspora, Tel-Aviv.

they intermarried with local people. Jewish theology was influenced by local cosmology, and, when Jews migrated back to their homeland in Palestine, they brought some Babylonian ideas with them. Another diaspora occurred in A.D. 70, when the Romans broke up a rebellion in Palestine; some migrated westward to Europe and others eastward to territories of Southwest Asia or southward to parts of Africa. Some moved to Ethiopia, where indigenous people converted to Judaism, producing a large Jewish population there, the Felasha. In the following centuries, Jews migrated into the Turkish Peninsula, an area where various peoples from Central Asia came in contact with them. In India, the cities of Calcutta and Bombay also had

numerous Jews, who were mostly immigrants from Baghdad. The Jewish populations are largest in Europe, and some scholars argue that most European Jews are descendants of Khazar emigrants to eastern Europe.

In addition, other world religions spread into new areas through migration. Hindus migrated to Southeast Asia, sometimes moving their entire families when they found employment as advisors to the Khmers of Southeast Asia. Christian migration occurred in significant numbers during and after the centuries of European colonization. Many Muslim scholars, teachers, administrators, and judges followed Sufi missionaries and traders into Africa. An example of this is the settlement of

Timbuktu, on the bend of the Niger River in West Africa, which originated around 1100 as a commercial center but by 1400 had become an important Muslim intellectual center.

Trade and Cultural Interaction

The spread of religion through trade and cultural interaction is the most complex of the four factors in the spread of world religions. Although it was closely linked with conquest, missionary activity, and migration, occasionally cultural interaction alone brought conversion. Cultural interaction occurs when travelers, such as merchants or immigrants, bring their religious practices with them into an area. One very important factor in the decision to convert is the perception of the status of the persons in the religion. The politically powerful and the wealthy, such as traders and rulers, were the most likely to serve as models.

Perhaps the most significant catalyst in the spread of world religions was that of trade. Merchants facilitated the spread of religion as they followed the trade routes throughout the globe. Trade, coupled with migration, spread Judaism to China, where a group of Jews resided in the capital city of Song China after receiving permission from the emperor to build a synagogue there. Buddhist merchants from India actively traded in the cities of Southeast Asia and carried their religious practices with them, converting many people. In Dar al-Islam, non-Muslim merchants often converted because an injunction in the Qur'an regarding moral behavior and social interaction made commercial contacts easier and more lucrative for Muslims. In other states, many peoples came into contact with Islam as Muslim traders and merchants traversed the trade routes. Conversions to Islam in Southeast Asia and in sub-Saharan Africa, for example, were primarily the result of the growth of trade. From the eighth century on, Islam spread rapidly along the various trade networks of the fourteenth and fifteenth centuries.

Conversion to a new religion was often a practical economic or political decision. Some Jews in Europe converted to Christianity so that they could protect their property from anti-Jewish mobs or own land. Muslim law forbade the ownership of Muslims as slaves, and conversions in West Africa became common as indigenous people tried to avoid being sold as slaves to Muslim traders. Many people in the Roman Empire converted to Christianity, especially in the first five centuries A.D., because of the unrestricted charitable services offered by Christians to the poor. After the conversion of Constantine in the fourth century, Christians were awarded tax exemptions, and priests were even given monetary grants. People also converted to Islam to avoid the sometimes oppressive taxes on nonbelievers. An intriguing example of mass conversion comes from the eighth century. The king of Khazar (located roughly between the Caucasus mountains and the Volga River) adopted Judaism as the state religion in 740. Many scholars have speculated that this conversion was prompted for political ends. The

FIGURE I.4.3 *Pagoda Mosque.* *Islam traveled with Muslim traders into many areas of the world. In China, Muslims took control of major western trade routes during the eighth century. Converts to Islam employed the local architecture when constructing their mosques. Many pagoda mosques can be found today in northwestern China.* China Features, Beijing.

Khazar state was situated in a strategic military and commercial position, and Byzantine and Muslim interests threatened Khazar independence; one Khazar princess had married a Byzantine emperor to help cement political relations. Khazars may have converted to Judaism to unify the state with a single ideology that was distinct from that of its closest neighbors, making it more difficult to assimilate the Khazar population.

Many people have converted to a new religion for cultural reasons, sometimes because they admire those who practice the religion. Koreans and Japanese in the fourth and sixth centuries, for example, converted to Buddhism because they believed it came from China, and they highly respected Chinese ways. When the Emperor Constantine converted to Christianity, many members of the Roman elite converted in order to gain political advancement. In the Americas, some indigenous peoples living close to European settlements gave up their traditional lifeways and became Christians when they accepted European cultural practices and technology. Some Romans converted to Judaism because they believed monotheism to be more logical than polytheism.

WHEN RELIGIONS AND SOCIETIES MEET

The effects of new religious ideas entering a society often involved changes both in the society and in the practice of the religion. Local customs were blended into religious practice, and social behaviors frequently changed to accommodate the new religious sensibilities. Certain kinds of rituals and attitudes affected lifestyle changes. Particular kinds of clothing were adopted, new foods or the abstinence from foods was introduced, and the prohibition of alcohol or the ritualistic consumption of alcohol was initiated.

Adopting and Adapting New Religions

The adoption of a new religion sometimes met with resistance, affecting how it was integrated with local custom. Buddhism had a difficult time being accepted by the Chinese because of translation problems and social differences. Because Siddhartha Gautama had left his family in order to

seek the meaning of existence, Chinese who believed in loyalty to one's family deplored his actions. Also, in China pork is a favorite food, and many Chinese dishes use it as an ingredient. Muslims, however, are forbidden to eat pork. This cultural barrier caused a serious conflict with Chinese acceptance of Islam. As a consequence, there are few Muslims living in the traditional pork-raising areas of southern China but many more Muslims who populate the traditional sheep-raising western areas. Buddhism sometimes encountered cultural resistance to its promotion of vegetarianism because the consumption of meat was associated with high status and affluence in China, Korea, and Japan.

Often, the culture changed the religion. The prominence of militancy in Japan changed Buddhism, which had initially stressed nonviolence. The warrior-monk became a familiar figure in Japanese politics by the eighth century and caused much bloodshed until the sixteenth century, when the militant sects were destroyed. Zen Buddhism appealed to *samurai* warriors, and Zen priests developed the Japanese martial arts of *karate* and *judo*.

In most cases of the spread of world religions there has been at least some level of adoption or adaptation of ideas and practices. This blending has created new customs and rituals. Some Japanese practiced Buddhism and Shintoism at the same time, mingling elements of both into their daily practices. Originally, December 25 was celebrated by peoples in the Roman Empire as the winter solstice, and, in the fourth century, Christians adopted the date to celebrate Jesus' birth. The adoption of the non-Christian festival date allowed the observance to continue among a population reluctant to abandon a popular festival and transformed this local custom into one of the most celebrated of Christian holy days. The Chinese were influenced by Buddhist ideas, such as the notion of reincarnation. In eastern Mexico, native populations incorporated their own religious beliefs into Christianity, and many native religious elements continue in the practice of Christianity there today.

Syncretic Religions

In some instances a new religion will form, using elements of both the earlier, traditional religion and the newly introduced religion. Such a religion

FIGURE 1.4.4 **The Last Supper.** *Many religions were influenced by the new cultures with which they came in contact. This scene, portraying the passover meal just prior to Jesus' crucifixion, is a common theme in Christian art. The disciples are gathered around the table in traditional poses, but the food is more appropriate to South American palates than to Jewish diets of the first century* A.D. *or to European Christians. The platter holds a guinea pig, a delicacy to Andean Indians.* South American Pictures.

is called **syncretic**, and an excellent example comes from the Iroquois of the Great Lakes region of Canada and the United States. This example will be given fuller review in order to demonstrate the process of forming a syncretic religion.

Prior to the American Revolution, the six tribes of the Iroquois confederacy thrived. But the Iroquois had allied with the British in the American Revolution, and they received the harshest treatment of all loyalists after the British defeat. Their lands were reduced, orchards were chopped down in retribution, and their livelihood was generally restricted. These disasters led to a tailspin of despair, alcoholism, and general breakdown of the

traditional moral order. By the end of the eighteenth century, the Iroquois were a pale reflection of their former selves, living their lives in what one scholar has termed "slums in the wilderness."

Then, in 1799, an Iroquois named Handsome Lake had the first of several religious visions. In narrating the first vision, Handsome Lake described angels in the form of Iroquois men in ceremonial dress who came to him and instructed him as to the role he was destined to play in the rebirth of the Iroquois people. He was to be a prophet, to instruct the people in morals, and to lead them back to a path of righteousness and prosperity. Those who rejected his message would be relegated to a smoky, hot damnation. Later visions provided more detail about how the Iroquois should reform themselves, what rituals were most important, and what spirits would assist the Iroquois in their victory over circumstances.

Handsome Lake became a well-known prophet of and preacher to the Iroquois. His fame as a preacher became so great that Iroquois traveled far by foot to hear him speak, and his charisma attracted thousands of adherents. He had four main visions before his death in 1815, and from these visions he developed a new religion that drew its inspiration jointly from traditional Iroquois religion and from Christianity.

In general, Handsome Lake advocated the return to practices based on traditional Iroquois values, particularly advocating that Iroquois abstain from alcohol, witchcraft, birth control, gossiping, and domestic violence, all of which had been on the rise in the dark years following the end of the American Revolution. In addition, Iroquois were encouraged to be industrious in seeking work to support their families and in maintaining tribal lands to form a haven against European culture. Handsome Lake advocated adopting a few European ways, mostly regarding education and agricultural technology, but he strongly rejected commercialism and profit, private ownership, and gambling.

In some cases, Handsome Lake's views were adopted so fully that the tribal government enforced his moral code. The primary sanctions against violating this morality, however, came from Christianity. Jesus was one of the spirits that appeared to Handsome Lake, and he and other spirits described a hereafter that had a lovely, restful glade for good Iroquois and a smoky, fiery pit for the bad—clearly the visions of heaven and hell in contemporary Christianity. Sinners, if they repented and wanted to avoid the scorching eternity of hell, could be forgiven after public confession. Confession, heaven, hell, Jesus, and angels all were Christian elements that had no equivalent in earlier Iroquois religion.

Handsome Lake had several disciples, and they preached his teachings after his death. For some years, the religion he preached was practiced by many Iroquois as simply a revised version of their traditional faith, but, around 1840, it was formalized into the modern church called "Longhouse Religion." The name comes from the ceremonial building where many services are held, and the cross that appears inside it speaks eloquently to the merger of the Iroquois cross formed by the junction of the sacred four directions and the Christian cross on which Jesus was crucified. Longhouse Religion is practiced today by perhaps a quarter of the Iroquois.

TOLERANCE AND INTOLERANCE IN WORLD RELIGIONS

Many theological, economic, and political factors affect whether a society will exercise intolerance or encourage tolerance of other religions. In some instances intolerance was the result of monotheism or the idea of holy war. In other instances it was a result of cultural bias. Religious tolerance fostered peace within an empire that included people of diverse religious practices. Tolerance also enabled trade to flow without interruption.

Some theological intolerance stemmed from monotheistic religions' exclusivity. Polytheistic religions, such as Hinduism and Buddhism, typically have no theology that impedes the acceptance of other religious practices, so adherents had no compunction about being intolerant or forcing conversions. According to ancient Jewish tradition, Jews were forbidden to intermarry with non-Jews and often discriminated against those who did. In medieval Europe, Jews were frequently subjected to violence, in which their businesses, their homes, and their lives were destroyed. Jews in many European cities were also forced to live in **ghettoes** (an Italian word that means the Jewish section of a city).

Intolerance was sometimes a consequence of wars of conquest by conquerors who believed in the superiority of their religion and believed that they were fighting a holy war. When ancient Jews conquered the area of Canaan in ancient Palestine, they believed that it was necessary to eliminate non-Jews in order to keep their religion pure from what they saw as contamination through cultural interaction. When Muslims expanded into India during *jihad* (Muslim holy war), they destroyed or defaced many Buddhist and Hindu temples and statues. One raiding party destroyed the university at Nalanda in 1193. Christian crusaders from medieval Europe conquered the Palestine area in a holy war to extract ancient Christian sites from Arab Muslim control. In all these examples, holy war was the extreme expression of intolerance.

In many areas, however, tolerance of a variety of religious practices prevailed. Muslims tolerated both Jews and Christians as "people of protection" or "people of the book," referring to the scriptures shared by the three monotheistic traditions. Jews and Christians were tolerated but not given equal status in Muslim countries. In contrast to other areas in Europe, the Muslim city of Toledo, Spain, in the tenth century tolerated Judaism and had more than 10,000 Jewish citizens. Many non-Muslims found living under Islamic law tolerable but converted anyway for financial or social advantages. In the twelfth century, toleration of Jews and Muslims was a policy of the Norman kings of Sicily, in part because of trade connections. Also, several Christian missionary societies worked against the political and social exploitation of the European colonizers in the seventeenth and eighteenth centuries because they believed the practices violated Christian principles.

SUGGESTED READINGS

Chadwick, Henry, and G. R. Evans, eds. *Atlas of the Christian Church*. Oxford, Eng.: Equinox, 1987. A well-illustrated history of the development and spread of Christianity.

Faruqi, Isma'il Ragial, and David Sopher, eds. *Historical Atlas of the Religions of the World*. New York: Macmillan, 1974. A good review of world religions, with excellent maps.

Fisher, Sydney, and William Ochsenwald, eds. *The Middle East: A History*. Fourth edition. New York: McGraw-Hill, 1990. A history of the spread of Islam within the broader context of Dar al-Islam expansion.

McManners, John. *The Oxford Illustrated History of Christianity*. New York: Oxford University Press, 1990. A general history of Christianity in all parts of the world through the twentieth century.

Monroe, Charles R. *World Religions*. Amherst, N.Y.: Prometheus Books, 1995. A good general survey of major religions and philosophies.

THE PRECEDING PAGES HAVE TRACED THE HUMAN STORY from some millions of years ago to around A.D.1500. They have scrutinized some periods and peoples, and they have examined others more lightly. Even this vastly simplified version of the past is very complicated, and it is easy to get mired in the details, losing sight of the main currents of development. Part Five tries to place this vast period in perspective, searching out patterns and trends over time. It draws attention to events that are the last gasps of a changing order and other events that foreshadow the modern era to come.

Chapter 20 looks at this period from the focused perspective of science and technology. How well were the processes of the natural world understood? How skilled were people at harnessing the natural world to control them? How much did science and technology influence each other?

Chapter 21 examines the broad sweep of human existence, focusing on issues that have had profound effects in shaping the world. Oriented around the growth of population as a long-term and consistent trend, this chapter links many developments to their demographic basis. How has the inexorable growth of human population affected history? How have people met their obligations to increasingly demanding governments? What role has trade played in the unfolding of human history? How have people's self-conceptions and allegiances changed in response to a more complicated world? And, finally, how much environmental degradation have human beings wreaked on their planet?

Medieval European Farming. *Around the world, technology has transformed everyday life. This four-teenth-century illustration shows a medieval European farmer using a horse-drawn harrow to till a field. The domestication of animals and the use of iron tools (the blades of the plows and harrows used to turn the soil and the blades of the scythes used to harvest grain) increased productivity. In the background, a scarecrow dressed as an archer guards a planted field.* Giraudon/Art Resource, N.Y

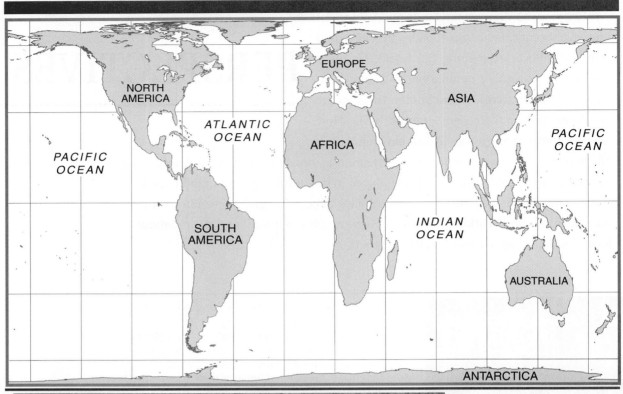

A Traditional Blacksmith from Ghana. *Using a bellows to raise the heat of his fire, a blacksmith shapes iron in a manner that can be traced back many centuries.*
Larry Burrrows, *Life* Magazine, ©Time Inc.

C H A P T E R **20**

Technology and Science
Before 1500

A sweaty blacksmith, skin caked with soot, heats his iron to a dull red. He murmurs a prayer, then slides a willow sapling among the coals and tosses on a small cup of bull urine. He nestles the iron into its fiery bed, confident that it will be strong.

For centuries, practical technologists such as this blacksmith followed arcane procedures to control the fashioning of products. Occasionally, accident or ingenuity sparked a new discovery, with widespread impact.

Historians often focus on political, military, and economic events. The expansion of a state into an empire, the conquest of neighboring lands, the creation of a middle class—developments like these sometimes dominate history texts, but it is important to remember that many of these changes were made possible by new technology. Some of these critical technological developments have been discussed in the previous chapters, including irrigation, iron, paper, and gunpowder. This chapter will investigate some of these and other technological feats further and will consider the relationship between technology and science in the period before 1500.

THE RELATIONSHIP BETWEEN TECHNOLOGY AND SCIENCE

Technology and science seem so enmeshed today that many people think of the two as an inseparable pair, but a major distinction can be drawn

509

between them. As used in this chapter, **technology** is the study of making devices that serve a purpose; **science**, on the other hand, is the quest to understand phenomena, to learn how things work and the reasons behind their operation. Technology is interested only in making something that serves a purpose, regardless of whether the principles behind the device are understood; science is concerned with knowledge, both general principles and specific facts. Technology is interested only in *whether* a device operates; science is interested in *how* and *why* things operate. Technology is applied; science is theoretical.

This distinction, of course, has not always been made by historic societies. Medieval Europe, for example, made less of a distinction between science and technology, considering both to be aspects of natural philosophy; Islamic science in this period fused science, technology, and religion together into a single category of knowledge; and other societies have had their own unique ways of conceiving of the relationship between applied and theoretical activities.

Historians of science, too, differ in how they conceive of science and technology. Some distinguish between science and technology on the basis of goals, as we do here; others distinguish on the basis of methodology; still others focus on whether practitioners reached conclusions similar to those reached by modern science. One school of thinking suggests that any distinction made between science and technology is misleading, because the overlaps are so great. All of these viewpoints lead to valuable insights, but we believe that seeing science and technology as distinguished by their goals will help point out a broad pattern in this period.

The magnetic compass provides an example of the dichotomy between science and technology. It was well known by the twelfth century in China and most of Eurasia that a piece of magnetite ("lodestone") would always point southward if suspended by a string or floated on a tiny raft in a bowl of water. How to make and use the compass—the domain of technology—was firmly established. For about a century, however, why the compass worked—the domain of science—was considered mysterious. In the thirteenth century, scholars in Europe and China seized upon the scientific issue and attempted to explain magnetism. Although these thirteenth-century attempts invoked different principles from those involved in the modern explanation established by physics in the nineteenth century, they still are scientific, because they tried to explain systematically why the magnetic compass operated.

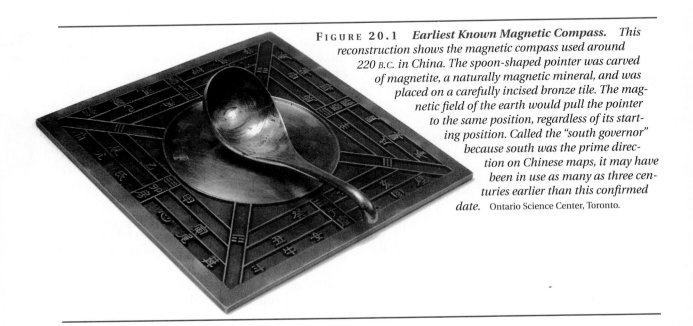

FIGURE 20.1 *Earliest Known Magnetic Compass. This reconstruction shows the magnetic compass used around 220 B.C. in China. The spoon-shaped pointer was carved of magnetite, a naturally magnetic mineral, and was placed on a carefully incised bronze tile. The magnetic field of the earth would pull the pointer to the same position, regardless of its starting position. Called the "south governor" because south was the prime direction on Chinese maps, it may have been in use as many as three centuries earlier than this confirmed date.* Ontario Science Center, Toronto.

EXAMPLES OF TECHNOLOGICAL INNOVATION

From the thousands of examples of technological discoveries before 1500, a few cases illustrate some of the common threads that run through them and the diversity that separates them.

Domesticated Plants and Animals

We do not normally think of agriculture and pastoralism as technological achievements, probably because we usually focus on the great changes in human behavior that came about with these modes of subsistence. Nonetheless, new and improved devices were involved: the crops and livestock themselves. We have discussed agriculture at some length in Chapter 3, and here we focus only on aspects relating directly to science and technology.

Recall that "domestication" refers to the act of genetically modifying a plant or animal from its wild ancestor so that it will be more useful to human beings. The first corn plants had only a few tiny seeds and required a long growing season;

they were modified for greater production and more rapid maturation. The first wheat plants had seeds with brittle connections to their stalks, meaning that much grain was lost in harvesting because it fell to the ground at the slightest movement of the plant; they were modified to produce a tough connection that would withstand the rigors of harvesting. Hundreds of other crops have been transformed to increase their production, improve their quality, or modify their growing requirements so that they can be grown in a wider range of environments.

Even more critical were the modifications that had to be made in domesticating animals. While a corn plant with only a few kernels might have been a nuisance, it was not dangerous. Cattle or swine with the aggressive temperament and nasty disposition of their wild ancestors, however, were quite another matter. Most of the animals that have been domesticated for human use were quite savage in the wild, and it would have been critical to tame them before they could become a major part of human economies. Taming individual animals would have been time consuming and only imperfectly effective, because the aggressive behavioral traits were instinctual.

How did early domesticators go about modifying their crops and livestock? Because all early

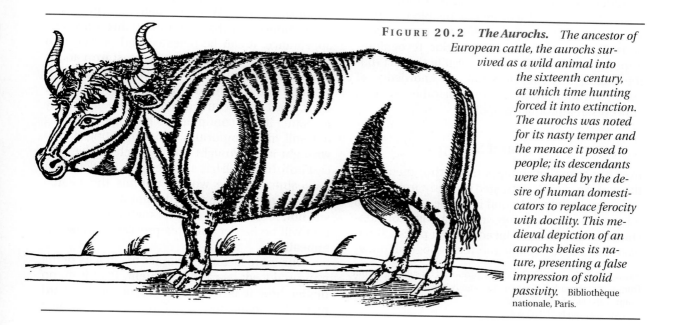

FIGURE 20.2 *The Aurochs. The ancestor of European cattle, the aurochs survived as a wild animal into the sixteenth century, at which time hunting forced it into extinction. The aurochs was noted for its nasty temper and the menace it posed to people; its descendants were shaped by the desire of human domesticators to replace ferocity with docility. This medieval depiction of an aurochs belies its nature, presenting a false impression of stolid passivity.* Bibliothèque nationale, Paris.

domestication took place long before writing, we must rely upon indirect evidence. It may be reasonable to assume that modern hunters and gatherers might have a similar knowledge of plant and animal breeding to that of the earliest domesticators. The twentieth-century !Kung[1] of Southwest Africa eat *magongo*[2] nuts, the fruit of a wild tree, but they normally consume only the smaller nuts. The larger nuts are thrown into ravines, where the greater moisture encourages their germination. As the !Kung say, the bigger nuts are likely to produce trees that produce bigger nuts. Similarly, various hunters might have tried to kill the most aggressive of wild animals, arguing that removal of such animals from a population would make animals in future generations less hostile and easier to hunt.

All hunters and gatherers have recognized that offspring will resemble their parents, among plants and animals, as well as people. This is an example of scientific recognition, because it invokes a general principle to explain why something happens. Presumably, early domesticators used scientific recognition to see that the plants and animals with the most desired traits were bred for the next generation, while those with unwanted characteristics were killed before they could reproduce.

Probably the practical knowledge of inherited traits was discovered as it related to people, then extended to animals, then to plants. Alternatively, it may have been discovered as people observed the results of their propagation of plants or animals. Either way, it was a scientific recognition important for domestication, despite the fact that these early domesticators had no knowledge of genes, chromosomes, heredity, or other modern concepts of reproductive biology.

Iron and Steel

Iron has many advantages over other metals for the making of tools. If treated properly, iron can be very hard and durable, and it can be sharpened to a keen edge. In addition, iron is a common substance and can be produced in most places. But it also has some significant technological draw-

[1] **!Kung:** KUNG, preceded by a click produced by sucking air out from under the sides of the tongue; many Westerners pronounce the word without the click.
[2] ***magongo:*** mah GOHNG goh

backs: It requires a more sophisticated process for refining than do the other metals that were commonly used for tools in antiquity (copper, tin, zinc, lead, silver, and gold), and it will be soft, malleable, or brittle if not treated properly. Before going into the historical aspects of iron making, we shall review the technological factors that are involved in its manufacture.

Iron on our planet occurs almost exclusively as **ore**, compounds in which the metal is chemically bonded to other elements. (The exceptions are mostly meteorites that have struck earth while passing through space, and they were used to make ornaments before iron was used for tools.) Before the iron from ore can be used, the other elements must be removed by smelting. Copper or lead ores can be smelted at low temperatures, of the sort obtained in a hot campfire, but iron ores require a much higher temperature. To obtain this temperature, air must be pumped onto the fire through bellows or some other mechanism, increasing the oxygen concentration and the heat of combustion. In addition, only certain fuels will attain the necessary temperature, notably hardwood charcoal.

Once the iron ore has been smelted, the impure iron is allowed to run out of the smelter, forming a rocky mass called the **bloom**. This bloom can be refined further simply by hammering it when hot, mechanically forcing the glassy impurities from it. When enough impurities have been removed so that the iron attains a metallic appearance, it can be reheated and poured into molds. This form of iron is called **cast iron** and is useful for some purposes, such as cauldrons, but it is brittle and soft, making it of little use for most tools. Cast iron can be made more useful by reheating it and continuing to hammer it, driving out still more impurities and converting it into **wrought iron**. Wrought iron is much harder than cast iron, but it still has a tendency to brittleness or malleability. If the worker pounds the heated wrought iron into the desired shape and plunges it, still hot, into water to cool it rapidly, the resulting iron will be harder still; this process is known as **annealing**.

One more factor determines the quality of the iron produced: its carbide content. Pure iron, no matter how it is treated, is not a terribly hard metal. But small amounts of iron carbide, formed by the chemical bonding of iron and carbon, produce **steel**, a much harder and more useful substance. Hence, to produce harder iron—steel—the smelter must introduce free carbon into the iron while it is molten or at least heated to a high temperature.

This is an impressive suite of techniques that must be controlled to produce high-quality iron tools. High-temperature fires are needed in the smelting; free carbon must be introduced into the molten iron; the iron must be cast, then wrought; and finally it must be annealed. To make matters worse, few of these techniques could be borrowed from earlier metallurgical practice because metals used earlier had different characteristics and required different treatment. Quenching hot copper or bronze rapidly in water, for example, actually makes it softer and less useful.

The earliest smelting of iron appears to have taken place in Anatolia, around 2000 B.C., about the time of the Hittite rise to power there. From this start, iron smelting spread around the eastern Mediterranean—to India, to Europe, and eventually to the Americas after Columbus. The Chinese began making iron around the seventh century B.C.; theirs was probably an independent invention of iron-making technology. African iron making may have been either invented independently or carried from India by traders.

Our best documentary information on early iron making comes from Southwest Asia and, later, Europe. There, literature tells us that swords often received names and were thought of as having individual characteristics, almost like personalities. Literature from *The Odyssey* onward describes the particular attributes of specific swords, and one of the more fabled swords, the Excalibur of Britain's King Arthur, was described as "a most excellent sword." These descriptions were not just literary contrivances of the authors or delusions of the warriors. Indeed, different weapons varied greatly in their qualities, largely related to the quality of the metal from which they were made. For iron swords, the critical variables usually were the amount of iron carbide in them and the techniques employed by their makers.

Contemporary accounts of early iron making are understandably rare, because the iron makers wished to retain their trade secrets. We do know, however, that there were many procedures in-

FIGURE 20.3 *Forging a Samurai Sword. The early forging of edged weapons of iron was attended in most places by complicated rituals that lay somewhere between magic and science, and Japan was no exception. This painting from the sixteenth century shows several Japanese swordmakers performing the range of operations necessary—including prayer—to produce a good samurai sword. While the men make swords, a woman makes tea.* Werner Forman/Art Resource, N.Y.

volved that to the modern mind seem unrelated to the manufacture of iron. Hittite blacksmiths, for example, were required to abstain from sexual activity with women before making a sword. Their contemporaries in Mesopotamia had incantations that had to be recited during the making of the sword, as did thirteenth-century Japanese smiths. And almost everywhere there were seemingly useless additions to the smelting vessel or the bed of coals where the iron was heated for hammering. The recitation of an incantation might serve the practical purpose of ensuring that a process lasts a certain amount of time, but most of these actions seem better explained as attempts to infuse the

---

UNDER THE LENS
Recipes for Fine Iron

Detailed accounts of iron working in premedieval times are rare. Most iron workers were illiterate, and their work was judged degrading and was unlikely to catch the attention of the literate elite. Further, there was little incentive to write down detailed accounts, because many of the practices were trade secrets, jealously guarded rather than indiscriminately advertised.

From later periods, however, after time had erased much of the secrecy associated with iron working, there are many accounts of how to produce the best iron. Most of these are excellent examples of how physics and metaphysics blended in early science.

An example comes from medieval Poland. A remarkable ninety-two-page poem extolling iron and its makers was published around 1598 by Walenty Roździeński,[a] a Polish smith. This work, the *Officina Ferraria*, includes explanations for the mechanisms by which the quality of the iron can be controlled. A few quotations illustrate that physical and magical mechanisms were considered to control the process.

> Certain tests, they say, show that the iron of no other country [than Spain] is sharper. It is obviously the water in which the smiths quench the iron that

brings this about. . . . The iron here has an especial substance, but the water is stronger than iron itself; quenching in it increases the sharpness of the iron.

Modern physics tells us that the strength of iron is related to how quickly it is annealed ("quenched"), not some special property of the water in which it is quenched.

> In Styria also they dig ore with the property of yielding both steel and plain iron; but steel has to be smelted twice, while iron is smelted only once.

The carbide content—the discriminating feature between iron and steel—resides not in the ore but in the carbon introduced, in this case, during the second smelting. And in discussing the Polish ore from Nikwa, Roździeński notes that steel can be made from it, but only if the smith uses "charcoal from young pine trees, since charcoal from other kinds of wood won't do." The young pines, with their greater sap content, presumably burned slowly enough to liberate free carbon that could incorporate with the iron to produce steel.

> In olden times some elves . . . used to haunt forges. . . . Those forgemasters whose forges they haunted had great luck, everything went well for them, almost according to what they had in mind, both in the craft of ironwork and in everything else.

[a]**Walenty Roździeński:** vah LEHN tee ROHZH dzee EHN skee

---

iron with the perceived characteristics of a particular material.

An example of these actions is the so-called **green withy**[3] **smelting** of pre-Roman Britain. In this process, fresh twigs of willow and similar plants ("withies") were added to the molten iron shortly before it was poured out. In this manner, the withies would burn just sufficiently to yield free carbon that converted the iron to steel. From the point of view of the iron makers, however, the withies were important for their mystical properties, giving the resulting iron flexibility, like the willow from which the withies came. This connection, of course, makes no sense in terms of modern scientific conceptions, but it clearly is a scientific

[3]**withy:** WIHTH ee

explanation. It seeks a general principle that explains *why* a procedure works.

Shortly after Southwest Asia was developing iron technology, so was China. There, wrought iron was being produced by the seventh century B.C., cast-iron tools by the sixth century B.C., and steel by the second century B.C. Unlike in Southwest Asia, Europe, or Africa, iron working in China very rapidly attained mass production, largely because the required technological elements already existed and needed only to be brought together. Efficient furnaces that could be used for iron smelting had been developed for the manufacture of fine pottery, bellows had been used in bronze casting, and fluxes (agents to reduce the melting temperature of something) were known from ceramic manufacture.

Chinese iron making also followed scientific principles, although those principles again were different from modern ones. For example, swords were classed according to the number of "refinings," that is, how many times their iron had been folded and hammered together when heated. Texts inform us that contemporary Chinese believed that swords with greater numbers of refinings were stronger, yet the physical principle underlying their strength related to their carbide content, which is essentially unrelated to the number of refinings.

Wherever iron was made, its quality improved over time. In any area, the earliest iron was the most variable, including pieces that were scarcely usable. With time, however, the softest and most brittle pieces became less common, and the finest iron was superior to that of a generation before. This pattern is evidence that the iron makers were attentive to the results of their procedures, adjusting their techniques when they saw improvement. At the same time, however, there is little evidence that theoretical, scientific understanding of iron metallurgy kept pace.

Although iron in most areas became an incredibly important material shortly after the onset of its use, especially for military purposes, there is no evidence that scholars took much interest in it during this period. This may relate to the traditional status of blacksmiths from India through Southwest Asia, the Mediterranean, and Europe. While recognized as critical to society, blacksmiths were viewed as degraded as a result of their profession. In India, ironworkers formed one of the lowest castes, and less rigid social systems elsewhere relegated them to similar lowly positions. Perhaps scholars were reluctant to show interest in such an undervalued subject.

Ships and Shipbuilding

The oldest known archaeological remains of a boat come from northern Europe about 12,000 years ago. However, water transportation is known to be much older. The peopling of Australia 50,000 or more years ago must have been accomplished by boats of some sort, because there never was a land bridge connecting Australia to Asia. These early boats, however, presumably were small and simple, probably rafts or dugout canoes. Such simple conveyances would have been suggested the first time someone saw a log or a mat of vegetation floating down a river, and they would have required little genius or special skill to develop.

Later vessels, however, became larger, particularly as long-distance trade burgeoned and these ships became the vehicles for much of that trade. All of the ancient civilizations with access to waterways achieved a certain level of shipbuilding skill, but the Greeks stand out as particularly capable. Given the geography of Greece, with its long and convoluted coastline and almost all of its ancient population along the sea, it is not surprising that ancient Greeks relied heavily on maritime transportation. In addition, their large population and limited agricultural base forced them to trade with the outside world for food.

Ships of the Greek Classical period were of two types, named for their shapes: long ships and round ships. **Long ships** were long and narrow, with a typical length-to-width ratio of 10:1. Such ships were fast, yet they had great difficulties weathering storms and had limited space on board. (The space was so limited that there were neither stores nor galley, so the ship had to send its crew ashore twice daily to forage for meals.) Used almost exclusively for military purposes by governments or pirates, these warships were equipped with a bronze ram at the prow and were propelled by one or more banks of rowers. The most effective of these long ships, the **trireme**,[4] had three banks of rowers and could attain speeds of approximately 8 to 10 miles per hour for prolonged periods and spurts up to nearly 15 miles per hour. Triremes typically were about 120 feet long and carried a crew of around 170 rowers and 30 officers and marines.

The other principal type of ancient Greek ship was the **round ship**, which was much broader, usually with a length-to-width ratio around 4:1. This made it less sleek than its long ship cousin, and it was much slower. On the other hand, it had much more space on board, so it was used primarily as a trading vessel. An added virtue of its squat shape was its ability to survive stormy weather, especially if it was fully burdened and rode low in the water. Round ships usually were considerably larger than long ships, often running 150 to 200 feet in length. Powered by sails exclusively, round ships averaged about 4 miles per hour.

[4]**trireme:** TRY reem

FIGURE 20.4 *Greek Trireme. This full-scale replica of a Greek trireme was produced as part of an experiment to assess the difficulties of making and using such a long ship. A full complement of rowers propelled this vessel in the Mediterranean Sea. The experiment showed that the trireme was less seaworthy and more fragile than documentary records had suggested.* Trireme Trust, Courtesy of John Coates.

The Greeks experimented widely with ship design. One experimental vessel built in the third century B.C. was reported to have been more than 400 feet long and to have carried more than 4,000 rowers. This mammoth vessel survived its initial tests, but it was so difficult either to power or maneuver that it was kept permanently in port as a monument to Ptolemy IV, the Greek ruler of Egypt who had commissioned its construction. Other experiments, less ambitious but more practical, produced innovative arrangements to increase the number of rowers, improved steering systems, and assembled masts and sails in ways that permitted sailing farther away from the direction of the wind. Some of these were successful and were incorporated into future designs, while others were mercifully forgotten.

At the same time that shipbuilders were developing the Greek fleets, scholars were exploring the physics of water pressure and buoyancy. The most noteworthy and influential of these was Archimedes[5] (287–212 B.C.), whose interest in the subject is traced in a story recounted by his contemporaries. Archimedes was entering his bath in a public bathing house and sloshed water out of the tub. Suddenly recognizing that the amount of water displaced was equal to the volume of his body, he rushed home to work on his idea, shouting *"Eureka!"* ("I have found it!"). Unfortunately, he neglected to clothe himself and was remembered ever after for his famous nude dash through Syracuse.

Archimedes studied how water was displaced by solids immersed in it, how density affected whether a solid would float or sink, and how the shape of the lower portion of a floating solid

[5]**Archimedes:** ahr kih MEE deez

affected its stability. Another of his studies examined the relationship between the length of a lever and its efficiency. All of these areas of study could have been directly applicable to shipbuilding, and Archimedes even used examples of oars and masts to discuss his principles of leverage. Nonetheless, these scholarly findings were never translated into improved vessels. Archimedes' discoveries were the closest ancient Greeks came to bridging the gap between scholarly science and applied technology, yet even he didn't use these principles to improve Greek shipbuilding.

Why were these revolutionary and potentially valuable insights not applied to the practical world of shipbuilding? The answers lie partly in the division of labor, partly in economics, and partly in the philosophy of ancient Greece. First, the shipbuilders were of a vastly different class from Archimedes, and probably few or none ever read scholarly discussions of science or took part in discussions of it. They most likely were unaware that Archimedes' principles even existed.

Second, some of the improvements that Archimedes' findings might have prompted were of little benefit to the Greek economic system. Improving the efficiency of delivering power from rower to oar to vessel was not a major concern, because labor was abundant and cheap. Slave economies are not always attuned to labor-saving devices or machines that use power more efficiently. In fact, such devices sometimes have been considered dangerous, because they threaten to idle huge numbers of slaves, giving them time to contemplate rebellion.

Third, ancient Greek philosophers made a major distinction between material things and essential things. Codified by Plato but really existing before him, this distinction held that you could hold a real rock (a material thing), but that the essence of "rockness" was a concept that could be treated only in thought. Plato's famous analogy was that we see only the shadows thrown onto the wall of the cave by something passing between a fire and the wall. The shadow is the material thing; the unseen body that casts the shadow is the essential thing.

By definition and inclination, Greek scholars dealt with essential things. Their discussions, therefore, were on a logical plane, dealing with general principles, and there was a general disdain for application of those principles to everyday things, even for most empirical testing. Their preferred mode of operation was to ponder a problem, come up with a logical explanation, and then move on to another problem. Hero, probably a contemporary of Archimedes, actually conducted a few experiments in the physics of water pressure, but he was a rare exception, and his conclusions had no more effect on shipbuilding than those of his colleagues.

Gunpowder

The first explosive to be successfully produced and used, gunpowder is simply a finely ground mixture of three common substances: charcoal, sulphur, and saltpeter. Charcoal can be produced anywhere there is wood; sulphur can be mined from most volcanic deposits; and saltpeter can be either mined or scraped from the bottom of dung heaps or from old mortar, where it forms naturally. Chemically speaking, the sulphur serves to instigate a reaction, because its flash point is low and it can be set off by a low-temperature flame. The heat released from the burning sulphur then forces the saltpeter to liberate oxygen, which supports the ignition of the charcoal to a high temperature. These joint reactions occur very rapidly and release large volumes of gases, creating the rapid expansion that we call an explosion. In an open area, ignited gunpowder burns with a great hissing, but, if enclosed, the gases expand outward, rupturing their container. If a single outlet is provided, most of the force of the expansion will funnel through that outlet, carrying a cannonball or other missile with it.

Gunpowder was invented in China, probably around the ninth century, and appears first in a Daoist text warning others to avoid the author's accidental destruction of his house by mixing together three seemingly innocent substances. By 950 it was being used for **flare weapons**, tubes that projected the fiery flash of a gunpowder explosion toward an enemy; a century later, it was used also for bombs, rockets, and land mines; by 1270, Mongols were using Chinese cannons to propel projectiles at enemies.

Although the use of gunpowder weapons in China was widespread in the centuries following their invention, their impact on Chinese society was surprisingly minor. The Chinese political and economic systems persisted with little disruption, and gunpowder weapons became simply some of the many devices available for use in war. In fact,

FIGURE 20.5 *Early Chinese Incendiary Device.* *This sixteenth-century drawing shows "the enemy-of-ten-thousand-men," a gunpowder device for the defense of fortified cities. A contemporary document states that it should be used "to defend remotely located small cities, in which the cannons are either weak in firing power or too heavy and clumsy to be effective weapons." This device was said to kill with its flame and poisonous smoke. Gunpowder weapons appeared first in China, but later became more important tools of war in Europe.* R. B. Fleming.

gunpowder weaponry waned in importance in China, with the result that seventeenth-century Jesuits from Europe were employed by the Chinese government to instruct in casting cannons, a skill apparently lost in the four centuries since the invention of cannons in China.

Unlike in China, the military use of gunpowder in Europe had far-reaching effects. Gunpowder came to the Arab world and to Europe by the thirteenth century. In Europe, its use quickly stimulated the construction of firearms, although it is unclear whether these were independently invented or copied from Chinese models. By 1326, guns were mentioned in an Italian manuscript, and a gun was illustrated in an English document the following year.

Clockmakers were the first European gun and cannon makers, and they transferred many of their precise technological skills directly to the making of various sorts of firearms. **Bombs,** fully enclosed vessels filled with gunpowder and ignited with a slow fuse, could be surreptitiously placed against a fortification or could be delivered from the air by a kite with a long string release. **Firepots** were pot-like vessels with modest amounts of gunpowder and fist-sized stones or metal darts that could be directed toward a light fortification or a mass of soldiers. Firepots were made larger and larger, until recognizable cannons were in use by 1346. Another modification of these firepots that appeared in Belgium by 1337 was a massing of up to 144 narrow firepots, projecting missiles the size of an egg or smaller. Mounted together on a frame, they were a potent killing system that could be fired quite rapidly. By 1374 the English had dismantled this weapon, mounted its barrels on sep-

FIGURE 20.6 *A European Siege.* *In this sixteenth-century engraving, cannons and mortars besiege a walled city. The arcs of flight of the projectiles are reminders of the importance of ballistics, a branch of applied mathematics being developed at that time.* Courtesy of Ian Hogg.

arate wooden stocks, and distributed them to foot soldiers; these were the ancestors of the modern rifle. All these weapons were unwieldy and inaccurate, but they (and their improved successors) revolutionized warfare.

The European understanding of the chemistry of gunpowder was framed by the scientific understanding of the day. Matter was seen as composed of four essential elements, and the explosive nature of gunpowder was associated with hot and dry elements. The association of sulphur with hell and volcanoes was not lost on Europeans, nor was the great heat with which charcoal burned. The role of saltpeter, a white powder that tastes salty and has no obvious connection to explosives, was less well understood. As a result, European gunpowder makers maximized the content of sulphur, actually using almost twice the optimal percentage. Saltpeter, in contrast, was minimized. These decisions were based on current understanding of

science, but their practical effect was that the explosive was about 15 percent less powerful than the optimal mixture. Only in 1790, when scholars produced a greatly different conception of the chemical reactions taking place, did Europeans adjust the formula for gunpowder to achieve maximum effect. (Chinese gunpowder makers, too, underestimated the role of saltpeter, using insufficient amounts until around 1300.)

Gunpowder had different effects on the development of various branches of European scholarship. While the science of chemistry received little impetus from gunpowder technology, the branch of mathematics and physics that dealt with cannonball propulsion was greatly stimulated. This study, **ballistics**, had begun with the catapults and other war engines of earlier periods, but their inherent inaccuracy made intensive ballistic study irrelevant. Cannons, however, could be aimed more accurately, and elevating the shot appropriately

FIGURE 20.7 *German Saltpeter Factory. Saltpeter was a critical component of gunpowder, but it was the one most difficult for medieval Europeans to acquire in quantity. Vast mineral deposits of saltpeter in South America were unavailable to them, and saltpeter in Europe had to be laboriously collected from beneath dung piles, from excrescences on mortared walls, or from low-quality mineral deposits mixed with earth. This sixteenth-century engraving shows the German process for refining mineral deposits, based on leaching out saltpeter with water that was later evaporated.*
Image Select, London.

became a major challenge. Elaborate tables and graphs of proper elevations for given charges and ball weights were compiled. These ballistic tables included the results of both trial and error and the utilization of mathematical principles.

EXAMPLES OF SCHOLARLY SCIENCE

Not every society has had scholars. There were, however, several well-established scholarly traditions in the world prior to 1500, and this section presents examples of their scholarship.

Chinese Astronomy

From the Han Dynasty onward, Chinese rulers maintained programs of astronomical research that employed dozens, sometimes hundreds, of astronomers. Two incentives generated this intense interest.

First, one means of legitimizing a royal house was through the establishment and maintenance of the calendar. The solar year consists of slightly more than 365 days, 365.2422 days to be more exact, and this means that any calendar will naturally get out of step with the stars over time. To avoid this, days were added periodically, and properly doing so was seen as a measure of the legitimacy of rule.

Second, celestial bodies were seen in a direct and unchanging relationship to the earthly and human world. Different constellations, for example, were seen as associated with different Chinese provinces, and different portions of the sky were thought to be connected to different feudal states or dynasties. Positions of stars and planets were seen as favoring or disfavoring particular kinds of activities. They were seen as the Mandate of Heaven (the deity) in physical manifestation, transmitted on to people through the stars. As stated in the *I Ching*,[6] a Chinese treatise written in the eleventh century B.C., "the heavens manifest good and evil signs through the celestial phenomena." In short, the Chinese study of celestial bodies was seen as necessary for astrology, the predicting the course of the future and the determination of divine will through the examination of celestial movements.

Given these incentives, Chinese scholars understandably were highly concerned with the prediction of astronomical events. They divided such events into one class that was inherently predictable (such as the rising of Venus) and one class that was difficult or impossible to predict (such as eclipses and supernovas). Prediction was based on the recognition of number series and their reduction to algebraic formulas. This procedure bore no implications in terms of actual positions or movements of the celestial bodies involved, and there was no official theory of movements of stars and planets. Scholars debated possibilities, but the governmental bureaucracy remained silent on the issue.

[6]*I Ching:* EE CHIHNG

IN THEIR OWN WORDS
The Chinese Heavens

Sima Qian, a Chinese scholar of the first century B.C., specialized in both astronomy and history. He summarized his view of the relationship between humanity and the heavens in the following excerpt, which sheds light on the ancient Chinese association between earthly and celestial events.

Since the beginning, when humankind came into being, rulers in successive eras have observed the motions of the sun, moon, and stars. Through the reigns of the Five Emperors and Three Kings [i.e., throughout antiquity], as the effort was continued their knowledge became clearer. [China, the land of] the ceremonial cap and belt, was considered "inside," and [the lands of] the other peoples considered "outside." The Middle Lands were divided into twelve provinces. Looking up, they contemplated the signs in the sky. Looking downward, they found analogues to these on the earth. In the sky there were the sun and moon; on earth, *yin* and *yang*. In the sky there were the Five Planets; on earth, the Five Elements. In the sky there were the lunar mansions [i.e., constellations]; on earth, the territorial divisions. The Three Luminaries [i.e., the sun, moon, and planets] are the seminal *qi*[a] of *yin* and *yang*. The *qi* [i.e., material essence] originally resides on earth, and the Sages unify and organize it. Since the time of Kings Yu and Li of the Zhou era, the ruling house of each state used different means of divination to find a way to conform to the exigencies of the time as manifested in celestial omens. From their documents and books no rules whatever for portents can be extracted. Therefore when Confucius laid out the Six Classics, he merely recorded abnormal phenomena and did not write down interpretations.

[a]*qi:* CHEE

While their techniques were largely descriptive rather than explanatory, Chinese scholars were quite successful in their predictions. By around 100 B.C., Chinese astronomers were able to predict accurately the period of Halley's comet and the occurrence of lunar eclipses. Around A.D. 400, Chinese astronomers developed a mechanical device to represent the stars in their positions in the sky, and by 1088 they had developed a water-driven clock tower to show the stars' movements. As celestial movements became more predictable, their value in astrology became lessened.

Using our distinction of technology and science, ancient Chinese astronomy was a mixture of the two. On the one hand, it sought out and described regularities in natural phenomena, making it science. On the other hand, it incorporated little interest in explaining the phenomena, instead focusing more on the practical implications for calendrics and astrology, and in that sense it was technology.

Indian Dietetics

Charaka is the traditional author of a scholarly treatise that appeared in India around 50 B.C. Charaka may have been a single individual or a

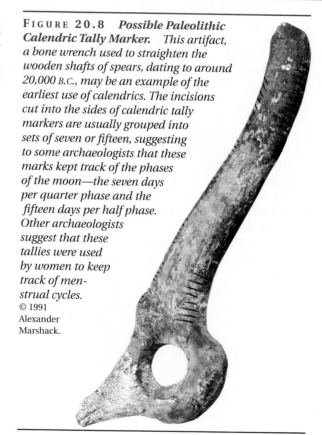

FIGURE 20.8 *Possible Paleolithic Calendric Tally Marker.* *This artifact, a bone wrench used to straighten the wooden shafts of spears, dating to around 20,000 B.C., may be an example of the earliest use of calendrics. The incisions cut into the sides of calendric tally markers are usually grouped into sets of seven or fifteen, suggesting to some archaeologists that these marks kept track of the phases of the moon—the seven days per quarter phase and the fifteen days per half phase. Other archaeologists suggest that these tallies were used by women to keep track of menstrual cycles.*
© 1991 Alexander Marshack.

composite of several, but his *Samhita*[7] formed the basis for Indian medicine in the period before 1500. Much of what Charaka codified probably had been derived earlier.

At the base of Charaka's system was a classification of five states of matter, the different combinations of which could produce various characteristics. A person's food was composed of a mixture of those five states, and one's diet affected one's person. Proper eating, therefore, was the route to proper health.

Proper eating, however, was not simple. The goal was to achieve a balance of the states of matter, but many factors affected that balance. Each person, for example, had a different constitution that was dominated by one of several states. A rajasic[8] person, for example, was dominated by a hot nature, expressed in enthusiasm, energy, impulsiveness, and greed. That person naturally should avoid foods with predominantly hot natures. On the other hand, another person's constitution might be deficient in rajasic elements and demand hot foods to achieve balance. A person suffering from chills might require additional hot foods, but a person with a fever might need to avoid them. The season, physical environment, and other factors also went into this complex mix.

How could one determine what states of matter dominated a food? The answer lay in the taste of the food, but there were no simple rules. A hot food, for example, could possess that quality by virtue of several characteristics, including irritating spiciness, acidity, or oiliness. Further, the habitat of the plant or animal that produced the food could have an effect, as with waterfowl, which are thought to be less hot than terrestrial birds. Needless to say, any food had the potential to be interpreted differently by different dieticians, and this was exactly what happened. The two millennia since the writing of the *Samhita* have seen continual debate, revision, and criticism of food classifications.

Imbalances in states of matter were considered the primary cause of disease, whether major and debilitating or minor and transitory. The chief role of physicians, therefore, was to diagnose what imbalance was causing a problem and prescribe appropriate changes. This system led to the merging of the concepts of food and medicine, and improvement could be effected either by changing the diet or by giving the patient powerful doses of substances that were not normally eaten but contained large amounts of the necessary attribute. In another society, these would have been called medicine.

This dietetic system was scientific in its explanatory nature, but it also was technological, because it had a practical goal and its efficacy was assessed on the basis of empirical results. Finally, it became part of folk culture, passing from scholars to the lay public through religious teachers.

Muslim Optical Physics

Ancient Greek scholars like Aristotle and Euclid had developed a notion that vision came about because a person's eye emitted some form of ray that shot outward and intercepted objects. When this ray encountered something, some sort of signal was sent back to the eye, where vision occurred. According to this idea, light as such did not exist in nature; it was created by the eye. This explanation held sway in European and Southwest Asian scholarship until the research of Abu Ali Hassan ibn al-Haytham[9] (965?–1039).

Ibn al-Haytham originated an alternative explanation that admitted to the existence of light independent of the eye. In his theory, any object that can be seen sends light out, either by producing it or by reflecting it. This light then travels to the eye, where it is perceived. He suggested that the mechanism of perception encompassed the eye, optic nerve, and front part of the brain. The light passed through the cornea of the eye, which focused it; it somehow was transmitted along the optic nerve; and finally it was perceived in the brain. Ibn al-Haytham's ideas are similar enough to our modern conception of vision that their monumental significance may not be easily grasped. In essence, he divorced optics from the human condition, conceiving of light as a phenomenon that exists independently of human intervention.

Ibn al-Haytham also created an innovative methodology. Rather than merely present the logic of his conception, as most of his predecessors did,

---

[7]*Samhita:* sahm HEE tah
[8]**rajasic:** rah JAH sihk

[9]**Abu Ali Hassan ibn al-Haytham:** AH boo AH lee hah SAHN IHB uhn ahl HY tohm

he set up elaborate experiments to test his ideas. In all essentials, this was hypothesis testing of the modern sort. Ibn al-Haytham's experiments were carefully thought out, and great care was put into their implementation and the recording of their results.

Ibn al-Haytham's scholarship was scientific by virtually any standard. Certainly it sought systematic explanations, and it anticipated many methods of later science. So far as we know, however, it had no connection with any technological application.

European Alchemy

Alchemy, the field of endeavor dedicated to transmuting baser metals into gold, probably developed in Hellenistic Egypt and was passed on to Dar al-Islam and finally Europe. The reasoning behind alchemy was simple enough: Nature shows abundant examples of one thing changing into another, so it should be possible to control the process. In a frequently cited example, a lamb can transform water and grass into wool and meat. Similarly, it was thought, it should be possible to turn lead into gold.

Central to alchemy was the conception of all matter being essentially the same, differing only in details. Alchemists usually worked within the framework of Aristotle's four elemental qualities—hot, cold, wet, and dry—which were believed to make up all matter. Alchemists reasoned that lead and gold shared many characteristics and had to be similar in qualities. If they could manipulate the qualities just a little, they thought, it should be possible to turn a lowly valued metal into gold, the epitome of value and purity in medieval philosophy.

In practical terms, alchemists operated by trying to reduce base metals to their simplest forms, then reconstituting them as gold. This was begun through the "stripping off" of everything except the essence of the metal, usually through some process involving heat or distillation. Then, substances were added in an attempt to add the Aristotelian qualities thought necessary to produce gold. While alchemists never achieved their goals, they developed and refined many chemical processes, including fermentation, distillation, and dissolution. The equipment they invented became useful for many later chemical and other operations.

In terms of modern scientific understanding, the goal of alchemy was unattainable. Nonetheless, it was a wedding of practical processes (technology) and theories to explain the results (science). In late medieval times, alchemy became more mystical, devoting more of its efforts to finding the elixir of life, an agent that purportedly would bring immortality. Although there had been critics of the enterprise of alchemy since the tenth century, late medieval alchemy fell from general scholarly acceptance because of its increasing mysticism.

SCIENCE AND TECHNOLOGY BEFORE 1500

The examples in this chapter illustrate some of the major relationships between science and technology in the period before 1500. Their specific details have a certain value, but more important are the patterns they reveal.

First, science and technology were not seen as wedded in the sense that they are today. Some craftspeople, such as Greek shipbuilders, worked exclusively in technology and neither contributed to nor drew upon the existing fund of scientific knowledge. Other craftspeople derived scientific principles that directed their actions, as when Saxon smiths added green withies to a forge's fire. Similarly, scholars had varying involvement with science and technology. At one extreme, Chinese astronomers directed most of their attentions to the technological implications of their work; at the other extreme, Ibn al-Haytham's optical findings apparently had no impact on technology. While alchemists' scientific theories had little impact on technology, their practical inventions supported the development of various technologies, including the manufacture of brandy and the production of certain types of perfume.

Second, in the period before 1500, there typically was a strong division of labor between scholars and craftspeople. Scholars and craftspeople had little contact in this period. Often working under royal or other patronage, scholars were members of an intellectual (and often socioeconomic) elite; craftspeople typically had less formal education, less wealth, and less prestige. Scholars communicated with one another through the writ-

FIGURE 20.9 *Roger Bacon. Bacon was a thirteenth-century English monk known best for championing the experimental method of science. He was one of the most successful scholars to find practical uses for academic ideas. Here he performs an incendiary experiment.* Science Museum, London.

ten word, but craftspeople rarely had access to these writings; the widespread illiteracy of craftspeople usually would have made access a moot point. It is difficult to envision many occasions when the two could have exchanged ideas on common problems.

The incentives motivating scholars and craftspeople were largely different, too. Scholars could enhance their personal reputations by an interesting idea or way of explaining something. Their patrons would appreciate such fame, because it reflected favorably upon them. Thus, scholars of this era most favored grand interpretations, explanations that were at a high level of abstraction and

might have no practical use. Ibn al-Haytham's remarkable theory of vision and light was an example: It illuminated scholarship, but it led to no improved technology. Craftspeople, on the other hand, were grounded in practical interests that could be translated into improved products or production methods.

Third, science in this period was very different from the science of today, and explanations in science and technology often included factors that today would be considered magical. **Magic** refers to the manipulation of the physical world through practices that have a spiritual or mystical connection, rather than a physical one. That a Hittite blacksmith should avoid sexual contact with a woman before forging an iron sword is such a magical factor, related to the efficacy of the forging only through a complex reasoning based on the sword being a masculine symbol. The sword was used by men for violent activity, and it was used for thrusting, thus relating to the male genitalia; such a potent male object could be polluted, the thinking went, if its creator were to have sexual relations with a woman and transmit her femininity. Such factors would not even be considered as part of the modern scientific explanation of how steel becomes hardened, but they were regularly invoked as explanatory factors in science and technology in this period.

This leads to a philosophical issue: Just because early science used factors that modern science considers irrelevant, does that make it nonscientific? The most important issue in science as defined in this chapter is the search for an explanation that covers a series of similar cases. Sexual contamination, as envisioned by the Hittites, would occur every time the appropriate conditions existed and, therefore, is scientific, even though it includes factors that modern scientists would consider ludicrous.

Fourth, science and technology before 1500 contained the seeds that would lead to modern science in the following centuries. The experimental method pioneered by Ibn al-Haytham attempted to codify procedures to make it unlikely that false explanations would be accepted, through accident, self-delusion, or purposeful deceit. The experimental method was laid out in Europe by Roger Bacon (1214?–1294?) and some of his contemporaries, and it increasingly became a hallmark of the modern scientific method.

SUMMARY

1. Science is the theoretical study of why and how phenomena operate, and technology is the practical design of devices.

2. The domestication of plants and animals was permitted by a rudimentary scientific knowledge of the rules of biological inheritance underlying it.

3. Iron and steel production was complex and usually included various ritual and magical practices. Scientific principles underlay these and other practices, though they were quite different from those recognized in modern times.

4. Both shipbuilding technology and the scientific study of buoyancy were quite sophisticated in Classical Greece, but there was little linkage between the two.

5. Gunpowder was developed in China and was used for weapons there; it then passed to Dar al-Islam and Europe. Scientific principles underlay the formulation of gunpowder, but they were quite unlike those recognized today and resulted in a less efficient explosive. The needs of artillery led to the science of ballistics, as accurate aiming of cannons became important.

6. Chinese astronomy was oriented mostly toward prediction of events for astrological and calendric purposes, not toward their explanation. In that sense, it was more technological than scientific.

7. Indian dietetics, based on conceptions of states of matter and their balance in the body, was scientific in theory and technological in practice.

8. Ibn al-Haytham developed a light-oriented theory of vision. This scientific breakthrough had no apparent impact on technology.

9. European alchemy tried to transmute base metals into gold. While it failed, it was a mixture of science and technology that developed processes and equipment that facilitated later endeavors.

10. Before 1500, science and technology occurred in various mixes in both scholarly and practical research.

11. The worlds of scholars and craftspeople were separate in this period, and the work of one group rarely influenced the other. Practitioners of both occupations used scientific explanations.

12. Magic was important in both technology and science in this period.

13. Science and technology in this period contained the seeds of experimentation and other elements that would come together in the modern version of the scientific method.

SUGGESTED READINGS

Cippola, Carlo M., and Derek Birdsall. *The Technology of Man: A Visual History*. New York: Holt, Rinehart and Winston, 1979. A highly readable and well-illustrated discussion of technology, particularly before 1600.

Hill, Donald R. *Islamic Science and Engineering*. Edinburgh: Edinburgh University Press, 1993. A basic survey of Islamic science and technology.

Landels, J. G. *Engineering in the Ancient World*. Berkeley: University of California Press, 1978. Really treating only Classical Greece and Rome, this small volume has an excellent section on ships and shipbuilding as well as good treatments of power sources, engineering machines, and theoretical knowledge.

Lindberg, David C. *The Beginnings of Western Science*. Chicago: University of Chicago Press, 1992. An influential synthesis that urges that premodern science not be judged by modern criteria.

Needham, Joseph. *Science in Traditional China: A Comparative Perspective*. Cambridge, Mass./Hong Kong: Harvard University Press/The Chinese University Press, 1981. A well-illustrated series of essays discussing Chinese scientific and technological accomplishments prior to 1600.

Singer, Charles, E. J. Holmyard, A. R. Hall, and Trevor I. Williams, eds. *History of Technology*. Five vols. Oxford, Eng.: Oxford University Press, 1954–58. This imposing multivolume treatment of world technology provides information and references on most topics of interest. Very authoritative and technical.

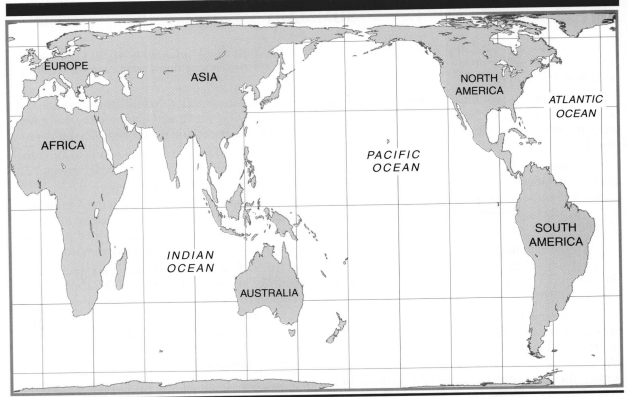

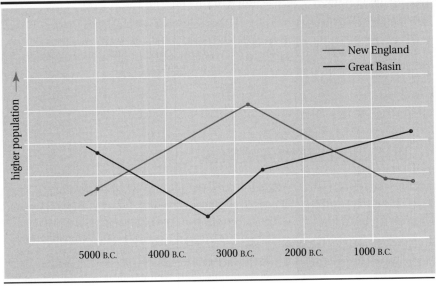

Population Change during a Dry, Warm Climatic Period. *New England and its moist forests profited as the warmth increased and extended the growing season, allowing the production of more food. The Great Basin and its desert, on the other hand, became even drier than before, limiting food and forcing depopulation. Note that the peak in New England population in this period occurred within a short time after the lowest dip in the Great Basin population.*

Population Sparks Human Change

History is often seen as the tricks that the dead have played on the living, but we may also see it as the tricks which the living play on the dead.

Although these sentiments are not attributed to one person, they have often been used by historians to tease students into thinking about the problems of historical interpretation. In this chapter, we will develop a few perspectives on the period before 1500.

DEMOGRAPHIC PERSPECTIVES

Human population growth and its resulting pressures often sparked the development of agriculture, urbanization, and significant environmental degradation. Modern human beings with brain capacities equivalent to those of people today evolved around 100,000 B.C. and began to populate the earth. Indeed, these ancestors of ours were as intelligent as anyone found today in Boston, Calcutta, or Cairo. From 100,000 B.C. onward, most of the seminal human changes arose ultimately from growing densities of people as well as from climatic and geographical factors. The increasing complexity of human relationships often sparked key developments.

527

Population Growth

Over thousands and thousands of years, human population growth has continued despite numerous periods of climatic change. Changing temperatures benefited or hindered humans depending on local conditions. In North America, the northeastern New England region saw significant population growth during a time of rising temperatures and little rainfall, but in the west, the Great Basin suffered a population decline as the desert became drier and hotter. (See the graph on p. 526.)

Looking at Figure 21.1, one sees that between 70,000 and 10,000 B.C. the global population size grew very slowly. Glaciation and warming alternated through that period until the past 12,000 years, when a milder climatic pattern reigned. In the earlier time, the population ranged between 500,000 and a few million people, but the often unfavorable climate kept population growth slow.

After 10,000 B.C., the milder climate and concentration of human populations forced people to alter significantly their economic patterns. Traditional ways of hunting and gathering no longer sufficed to feed the larger numbers. In places with suitable growing conditions and sizeable populations, agriculture appeared. People began to produce more food, and they even experimented with sowing and harvesting plants that provided storable foodstuffs. In the Americas, Africa, and Eurasia, for example, people settled in fixed locations and grew dependent on grains and vegetables like maize, sorghum, wheat, and rice.

As people in more areas began to devote more attention and energies to agriculture, the populations grew more rapidly. Figure 21.2 shows the dramatic population swell between 8000 B.C. and 4000 B.C. Total global population estimates represented by these figures range from around 5 million people to well over 86 million people in that 4,000-year span. By 4000 B.C., farming villages dotted landscapes and agricultural surpluses supported the rise of modest-sized urban centers. In Southwest Asia, Egypt, India, Mexico, and China, humans invented pottery, metallurgy, numerical systems, and written languages in response to the challenges of urban living. Pottery opened up the range of food products that could be stored and cooked. Metallurgy offered farmers better agricultural implements to increase the sizes of their harvests, soldiers better weapons with which to defend the towns, and household managers improved vessels in which to cook and store foodstuffs. Numerical and written systems afforded rulers ways with which to control their subject populations and merchants the means to keep track of their goods.

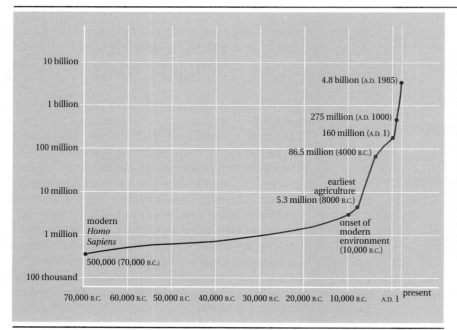

FIGURE 21.1 *World Population, 70,000 B.C. to the Present. The rate of population increase was modest throughout most of the existence of modern* Homo sapiens, *but improved environmental conditions and the development of agriculture between 10,000 and 8000 B.C. spurred rapid, exponential growth. Despite wars, plagues, and other local demographic disasters, population has continued to grow at an ever-increasing rate since that time.*

Checks on Population Growth

As people moved into cities, they also became more vulnerable to the vicissitudes of war, famine, and disease. Cities tended to attract enemy armies that desired the wealth and supplies lying within city walls. Indeed, the walls themselves are testimony to attempts by military forces to conquer cities. At the same time, living in close proximity allowed the increased spread of germs and disease. Furthermore, poor waste disposal created unsanitary conditions.

Large-scale warfare occasionally devastated cities and their surrounding regions, especially when commanders conducted sustained campaigns. The Mongol forces fought on and off in China for nearly six decades; their efforts significantly weakened farming populations and caused widespread loss of life. One scholar noted that the population of China was well above 100 million before Mongol rule and around half that about a generation after the Mongols were expelled from China. (Some of the population decrease resulted from a series of famines and epidemics not related to the warfare.) Although the total number of deaths was significantly lower, the population decrease caused by the Inca conquest of the Chanka people was a proportionally comparable to

that in China. This level of death through warfare, of course, occurred in many parts of the world.

Famine sometimes stalked city and countryside in the period before 1500. All cities were heavily dependent on agricultural products, and a drop in farming production severely threatened the well-being of urban dwellers. Floods and droughts regularly reduced harvests and led to malnutrition or famine in countryside and city alike. Warfare, especially siege warfare, also significantly reduced or severed urban access to outside foodstuffs. Even if people survived famine, they occasionally fell to diseases they contracted because of their weakened physical constitutions. Decomposing corpses and disruption of urban sanitation systems aggravated health problems.

Disease often became an efficient killer and population check. The close concentrations of people in armies seemed especially conducive to the transmission of communicable diseases. For example, two extended epidemics, from A.D. 165 to 180 and from 251 to 266, rocked the Roman Empire and demoralized the Roman leaders and commoners; the latter was known as the "crisis of the third century." The first epidemic came with returning soldiers who had fought in the eastern provinces. Not only did continual outbreaks of disease in the cities over both periods keep

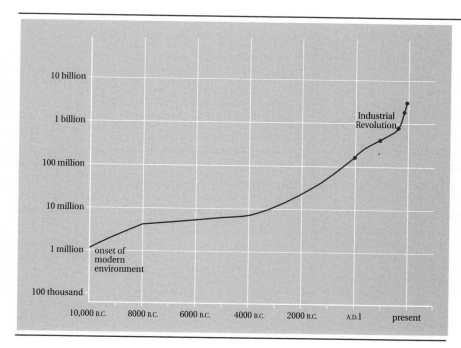

FIGURE 21.2 *World Population, 10,000 B.C. to Present. This graph is an enlargement of the latest portion of Figure 21.1. This more detailed version shows more changes in the rate of population growth, occasioned by various events and processes. The rapid population increase between 4000 B.C. and A.D. 1, for example, resulted largely from improved and expanded agriculture; the slower rate of increase between A.D. 1 and 1700 resulted largely from massive epidemics that characterized that period.*

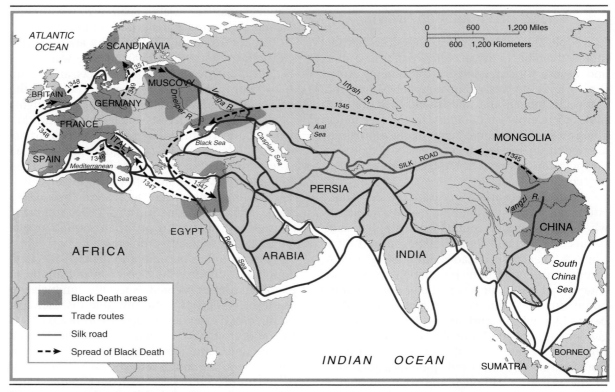

MAP 21.1 *The Spread of Black Death, around 1350.* *The occurrence of the plague and its spread from town to town along the trade routes of Asia, Africa, and Europe alerted scholars to the connection between trade and the spread of disease. Disease-carrying hosts traveled the great intercontinental roads, infecting other people as they passed from China through Central Asia and on to Europe and Africa.*

population levels lower, but the seemingly random nature of the deaths also undermined public morale. Wartime refugees also became vulnerable to malnutrition, disease, and death.

A massive epidemic, the Black Death of the fourteenth century, brought loss of life in the tens of millions of people and catastrophic debilitation to commerce and agriculture across Eurasia and North Africa. The bubonic plague seems to have initially irrupted into Chinese populations beginning in the 1320s. It spread in many parts of China until the 1350s with great loss of life. At the same time, it seems to have been carried into Mongolia and across the steppes into the Crimea. Two Central Asian areas, one inhabited by the Nestorian Christians and the other by the Uzbek Muslims, were devastated by the plague before it struck in Europe, Southwest Asia, and Northwest Africa. Travel along Chinese and Central Asian trade routes facilitated the spread of this deadly disease.

The Mongols played a key role in the spread of the plague to Europe and elsewhere. In fact, they launched one of the earliest biological warfare operations in history. The tactic came at the Mongol siege of the Genoan port of Caffra on the Crimean Peninsula in 1246. During the campaign, bubonic plague struck the Mongol forces, and before lifting the attack the commanding Mongol prince ordered that diseased corpses be launched by catapult into the city. Although many survived the siege, Caffra citizens soon contracted the plague. Thereafter, the epidemic spread by maritime trade routes through the Mediterranean and then by land and sea northward. Its southward march was effectively halted by the Sahara Desert because of the absence of people.

Alexandria, the major Egyptian port, was the next target of the plague, which soon spread along the Nile River as well as along the southern and eastern coasts of the Mediterranean Sea. The

FIGURE 21.3 *Plague in Europe.* *The Black Death ravaged Europe in the mid-fourteenth century. This painting shows a scene in Florence, Italy, where a group composed mostly of women mourns the dead; others bury shrouded bodies while priests preside over the interment. Later, the death rates from the plague grew so high in some places that these activities ceased or took on a haphazard quality.* Bibliothèque nationale/Explorer, Paris.

effects proved catastrophic for both cities and rural areas, which were left with insufficient numbers of people to support critical operations. In fact, Egyptian agriculture took ten generations to recover fully from the depredations of the epidemic.

The transmission across Europe came by a variety of trade routes, reaching the British Isles and Scandinavia and sparing parts of eastern Europe and Russia. The plague's severity varied from place to place; in England, for example, it took a century for the population to recover to pre-plague levels. Both cities and countrysides might be hard hit. Although estimates of the population loss have varied, this widespread epidemic cost more than 20 million lives by most reliable accounts. Thus, the population of many areas was severely reduced for generations by this disease. The massive death toll created labor shortages and increased wages for artisans and farmers.

Population Restructuring

Population growth affected the structure of human populations themselves. Some of this restructuring related to changes in life expectancy patterns for all groups. Other kinds of changes can be classified according to people's age or gender.

From around 100,000 to around 10,000 B.C., the structure of hunter-gatherer societies changed little. People living in groups could be expected to live into their thirties, with women enduring until their early thirties and men generally surviving until their late thirties. The large number of women dying in childbirth accounted for much of this difference.

The development of agriculture brought people into villages and effected certain structural changes. Life expectancy rates increased by about five years because of overall better nutrition and health. Gender differences still remained, owing to the continuance of deaths in childbirth for women. A related consequence was that more older people, especially older men, inhabited villages.

Once cities began to appear, between 4000 B.C. and A.D. 300, population structure changed further. General life expectancy rates remained about the same initially, gradually increasing over time. The major change came with the appearance of differentiated social groups. A gap developed and grew, for example, between the wealthy and the poor. Women from wealthy families began living longer because they received better health care, had fewer children, and did not work. Over time, the population of older people grew, especially in wealthy households. Charity expanded beyond family concerns and gradually became a focus of city governments.

Despite some urban problems, cities remained sites of opportunity for enterprising people. Not only did cities increase in size, but also they tended to exhibit remarkable resiliency in weathering the disastrous effects of warfare and disease. A chief cause of this urban ability to

bounce back demographically was the swelling or restoring of a population by migration from the countryside into the city.

URBAN TRANSFORMATIONS

Urban populations dominated political and economic life over four millennia, even though the population of nearly all states was mostly rural. Rural people sometimes played significant political and social roles, but the urban elite tended to dominate decision making in most kingdoms and empires. Merchants thrived in cities and often wielded political influence commensurate with their financial strength. In Mesoamerica, for example, merchants played key roles in political and social life.

City-states

Cities became the political center of most polities. In city-states, the city was perceived as the heart and soul of the broader polity. Over time, governments grew more professional in their staffing,

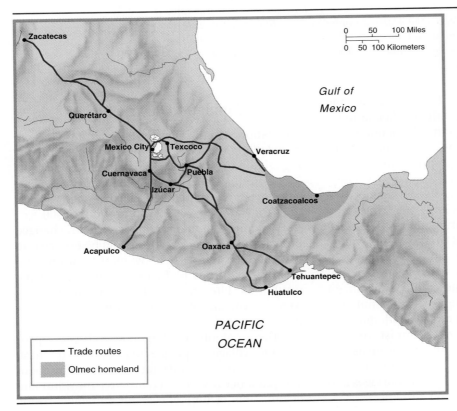

MAP 21.2 *Trade Routes in Mesoamerica around 1500.* *Trade routes of the Aztec Empire crisscrossed Mesoamerica, especially present-day Mexico. The routes connected port cities along the Gulf of Mexico with ports along the Pacific Ocean, as well as the northern parts of Mexico with Central America. Some of the routes followed trails of earlier centuries, including those of the Olmecs from the first millennium B.C.*

evaluation procedures, and ruling techniques. Officials, whatever their social or local origins, usually received an education in urban schools and closely identified with the capital's sociocultural environment.

The most common type of city-state was the pristine city-state. The Greek *polis*, for example, remained dominant for centuries in the first millennium B.C. In addition, city-states became a common pattern in the Mayan civilization of Mesoamerica during the first millennium A.D. as well as in other places and times. Although the Greeks and Mayans each had common cultural patterns and traditions, they had no lasting, overarching political structure. Each city-state retained its own identity.

Another form of city-state, the derived city-state, emerged from the breakdown of an empire. These city-states had existed in South India, for example, after the fall of the Pallava or Chola empires. When the imperial government collapsed, the capital city managed to retain control of its surrounding countryside.

Early city-states generally resembled those that survived the fall of empires. Populations of both identified primarily with their urban centers, and urban life retained its features of social stratification and economic specialization. A significant difference was that the derived city-state enjoyed the benefits of the preceding imperial infrastructure, especially a superior transportation system.

Trade and Empire

Cities tended to dominate trade relations within and between polities. They were the starting and ending points of exchanges of goods, because the significant funds necessary for long-distance trade could usually be found there. Furthermore, the large urban populations provided lucrative markets for merchants' goods, and each city established and regulated market centers. Sometimes states directly sponsored commercial activity, but, more often, they permitted organizations of merchants to finance large-scale trading ventures.

Long-distance trade in Mesoamerica began quite early. The Olmec trade, for example, ranged from the Gulf of Mexico to the Pacific coast by the first millennium B.C. The Teotihuacanos relied on obsidian as a major trade good to help build their trading network in the next millennium. The Aztecs later used roads and routes developed by their predecessors to great effect.

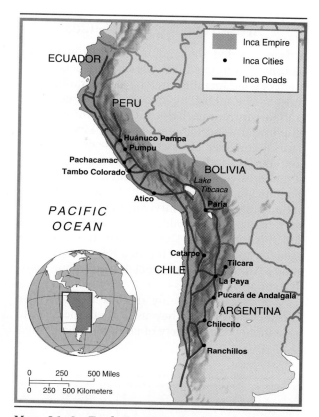

MAP 21.3 *Trade Routes in South America around 1500.* The Incas built an extensive road system that ran along the Pacific coast and wove through the Andes. Information and goods moved along the remarkable road network to all parts of western South America. Major roads passed through Cuzco, the Inca capital, located at the midpoint of the north-south highway.

In many other world areas, there has been a close relationship between trade and empire. In India, for example, Mauryas, Guptas, and Cholas all sought control of major trade routes in their rise to power. Ashoka's bloody Kalinga War in the mid–third century B.C. began over his intention of dominating land and maritime trade routes running through Kalinga, a coastal state. The Gupta conquest of the Indus Valley opened key trade routes to imperial control, as did the Chola campaigns along the southwestern coast of India. Trade revenues then played a vital role in funding lavish court styles and in financing large bureaucracies or payoffs to important local leaders. Conversely, when these revenues declined or evaporated, imperial statecraft was undermined, and, a few decades later, the empires collapsed. Similar patterns may be discerned for the Axum and Srivijaya empires in Africa and Southeast Asia.

Artisan and Merchant Guilds

Artisans tended to band together in guilds for security and lobbied officials for beneficial treatment of guild members in long-range trading ventures or in establishing market dominance. These craft organizations helped their members find employment and maintained some kind of standards for finished products, because quality goods sold better both domestically and regionally. Sometimes guilds provided limited social welfare benefits in hard times; they might help a member in times of sickness or survivors in times of a member's death. Artisan guilds also became centers for Sufi missionaries in Dar al-Islam; these mystics used the guilds as bases for their religious brotherhoods, where they found social comfort and spiritual support.

Merchants frequently organized themselves into guilds as well. They used their societies to raise money for a variety of commercial ventures.

FIGURE 21.4 *Aztec Artisan at Work.* *This codex illustration shows an artisan in Mesoamerica working with feathers, an important commodity for a people that highly valued feathered costumes. Because the state looked after the needs of its artisans, guild networks were not established during the Aztec imperial era.* Biblioteca Medicea Laurenziana.

In addition, merchant guilds lobbied for laws favorable to themselves or against exorbitant taxes. In the Byzantine Empire, for example, merchants successfully won special trading privileges, some of which were negotiated in treaties with other states. Artisans and merchants, especially those from foreign lands, frequently lived in special sections of cities and even adopted corporate governance in regulating their lives.

Some cities did not have guilds. Minoan merchants and artisans did not feel the need to organize themselves into mutual-support networks because the state provided for their needs. In addition, Aztec artisans and merchants felt no need for occupational guilds because the imperial state and kinship organizations took care of their needs, including those related to social welfare. After 1200, Southwest African kingdoms had no guilds because occupational specialists were organized along kin lines and looked after their relatives.

Urban Elites and Attitudes about Cities

Cities created large elite groups. People were needed to run state and urban governments, priests were needed to run various religious centers, and architects and artists helped design and decorate state buildings and monuments. Periclean Athens, Ptolemaic Alexandria, Ashokan Pataliputra, and Fujiwaran Kyoto were dynamic centers of elite culture and general prosperity. Seen from these lofty perspectives, life in the rural areas, especially in villages, seemed nasty, brutish, and short. Villages, of course, seldom possessed elite groups of the variety, complexity, or formal education of those found at the capitals. Exile of members of the urban elite from their cities was often regarded as a horrible punishment.

A variety of attitudes developed about cities and their inhabitants. Peasants often saw cities as centers of predatory officials or swindling merchants, and they frequently avoided travel to the cities except when compelled by economic motives. Most rural folk avoided taking complaints to the towns or cities because justice favored city folk. Pastoralists frequently viewed cities and city folk with distrust, frequently believing that cheating on commercial agreements was an urban trait. In addition, farmers rarely left their home areas; at most they might venture into regional market

FIGURE 21.5 *Peasants at Market.* *Rural folk had an ambivalent attitude toward crowded, bustling cities: The places where they were compelled to sell their produce or handicrafts were also places where they might be robbed or swindled. Pictured here are sixteenth-century peasants selling their wares in a city market.* Alinari/Art Resource, N.Y.

towns for business or the purchase of supplies. And yet, cities remained places of opportunity and fortune for people willing to take risks. Thus, a steady stream of immigrants came into the cities, especially larger political and economic centers.

ROLES AND RELATIONSHIPS

A **role** is an affiliation and a set of rights and obligations that someone assumes, and the examination of roles is a way of exploring the numerous obligations that people had in their lifetimes, especially as populations grew. All people fill multiple roles; some are of primary importance, others lesser. During one's life, roles change in number and significance; and in complex organizations related to civilizations, people have often acquired a large variety of roles.

Family Roles

Kinship involves a complexity of roles for an individual. The family is perhaps the most important social institution in history, and all people have been identified by the familial roles they have played. In fact, families had members who played multiple roles. A person might be a daughter and a mother as well as a sister or aunt, all at the same time. Through most of history, kinship has provided people with clearly defined roles and with different power associated with them. Individuals have specific identities and social places; they know who they are and often derive some form of security from that knowledge. The family or clan to which one belonged might have closely regulated one's life, yet it also might have provided some form of security against a state that demanded much from an individual. In hard times, a family or clan might also provide a kind of safety net of charity or other assistance.

Gender Roles

Within the family and the larger social environment, one's gender roles determined how a person might be treated and regarded. Tribe-level societies that practiced intensive agriculture tended to be relatively egalitarian in the distribution of political influence, social position, and economic wealth. Tribal men and women benefited more or less equally in these matters. Civilizations, on the other hand, were usually male-dominated, with females relegated to lower-status roles. Mothers were subordinated to fathers, wives to husbands, and sisters to brothers. Mother-in-law and daughter-in-law conflicts were a common pattern in families, with much friction reported as women competed for the attention of their men. During times when poor people faced economic ruin, female infanticide was often practiced. Girls were also sold into prostitution or slavery in times of hardship or to earn money.

In political realms, exceptional women might gain an opportunity to wield political power, but their position usually rested on their acceptance by males who defined the political roles. Successful women politicians might be biologically female, but they ruled like men; they were politically male. Monarchs, like Queen Hatshepsut of Egypt, even resorted to wearing false beards in order to play the male-defined role in a more realistic manner.

Women might play economic roles, but they also acted within carefully circumscribed limits. In some cases, wives became business managers, but only when their husbands died. During the Qin Empire, for example, Widow Jing became a prominent mining industrialist after her husband died. Single women seldom were permitted to start their own businesses.

Certain occupations and trades became and remained largely the preserve of women. In Greece of the Classical era, prostitution houses were run by women, and in Mesopotamia women dominated some trades, such as brewing beer. Weaving and certain forms of textile production remained in the hands of women. From China to India to Mesoamerica, women wove at home and worked in cottage industries that made cloth. Chinese empresses symbolically wove a piece of material, as did Aztec empresses. Both Chinese and Byzan-

FIGURE 21.6 *Incan Weaver.* *This Incan woman weaves cloth on a belt loom. Usually fastened to a tree, the loom was used to produce woven goods demanded by the state as annual tribute. Each family had to produce a required amount, a form of taxation. In many societies women did the great majority of this work.* Musée de l'Homme, Institut d'Ethnologie.

tine textile manufacturers employed large numbers of women. These jobs were usually extensions of traditional sex roles.

Patron-Client Relationships

The patron-client relationship was found in most societies. Rich and powerful patrons often assembled groups of supporters who were tied to them socially, politically, and economically. In exchange for loyal support on a variety of issues, the clients received financial assistance, job-seeking support, legal protection, or employment security. Frequently, these relationships centered on a specific patron, but in more complex social or political situations, a hierarchy of patrons might be established. Feudal Europe and Japan, for example, saw alliances bind clients (warriors) to lords who were themselves clients of large territorial magnates.

One type of patron-client connection involved eunuchs and flourished primarily in Eurasia. Castrated males served in the women's quarters of a

FIGURE 21.7 *Eunuchs Serving the State. Many imperial courts required the assistance of eunuchs. In this scene a key official, the chief black eunuch (lower left), escorts a prince to the place where he is to be circumcised. During the Ottoman Empire, black eunuchs became powerful because of their access to the princes and emperors whom they had befriended.* Topkapi Saray Museum.

palace and were chosen for that role because they could not impregnate the emperor's women. Sovereigns commonly employed eunuch clients as a corps of advisors in personal bureaucracies in order to circumvent regular government agencies that might resist or thwart royal initiatives. Monarchs used eunuchs as a means to control others because the eunuchs were generally loyal and easy to control. Eunuchs could not found a dynasty.

Religious Roles

When a foreign religion came to a new area (as when Buddhism came to Japan), there were two common approaches to it. The religion had either to accommodate the local beliefs or to outlaw them. Sometimes, however, missionaries converted a prominent political or social elite member to encourage their clients or subjects to accept the new religion. When Muslims came to West Africa in the ninth century, for example, they deliberately converted a few rulers and watched many in the ruler's domain convert as well.

Clergy members often assumed secular roles when tending to the needs of their congregations. Byzantine bishops, for example, handled a variety of duties for the emperor. They helped administer the laws, collect taxes, and maintain law and order in their jurisdictions. They also participated in charitable activities to help their members. In Mesoamerica, priests of the Aztec religion handled some tribute records and transactions because they could read, write, and calculate. Because many civilizations had this type of arrangement, there was no separation of church and state. Indeed, secular and religious activities often formed a seamless web.

Ethnic Identities

An additional role concerns one's ethnic identity. Many peoples saw themselves as culturally superior to peoples who did not adopt their languages and social practices. They believed these peoples to be barbarians without culture and inferior to themselves. The Ptolemaic Greek rulers of Egypt, for example, refused to intermarry with Egyptians and maintained a closely knit ruling elite.

Another feature of civilizations involved the shifting roles brought by local rule, regional rule,

FIGURE 21.8 *Crowded City Life.* *One of the night-mares of urban crowding was the disposal of human waste. This fifteenth-century French miniature shows a man using a makeshift toilet between two houses. Above him is a second-story latrine with a hole in its floor, through which human waste dropped. This lack of sanitation caused great personal discomfort and created ideal conditions for the breeding of disease.* Bibliothèque de l'Arsenal.

or imperial rule. In times of political change, a local town might find itself under a prince who then might be defeated and have his territory incorporated into a regional kingdom. Within a lifespan, that larger entity might succumb to a successful emperor who built a transregional realm. Similarly, the decline of an empire might mean a rapid return to some form of regional or local control.

ENVIRONMENTAL DEGRADATION

One of the consequences of demographic complexity found in densely populated cities was the degradation of the urban and surrounding environments. Human-waste removal presented difficult problems to city officials, and by-products of metallurgical production fouled land storage sites and nearby waterways. Deforestation, often resulting from the clearing of land for agriculture, sometimes led to erosion.

Pollution and the Environment

Tens of thousands or more of closely packed people created nightmares of human-waste disposal. Most often sewage removal or treatment was haphazard; disease flourished in towns and cities where sewage and drinking-water sources intermingled. City planners and politicians in the period before 1500 were ignorant of the causes of disease. In some Persian cities, for example, local farmers regularly gathered untreated human-waste products for use as fertilizers for their farmlands, unaware of the risks of transmitting disease.

Cities also had problems with the disposal of dead bodies, which were sources of disease. In many places, especially in Asia, people who handled the corpses and carted them to burial sites or to crematoriums suffered discrimination. Outcast groups performing these necessary societal functions could be found in Japan, Korea, and India.

Metallurgy, a major feature of civilizations, resulted in a variety of hazardous wastes. Disposal of waste by-products troubled some city managers, but most ignored the growing refuse sites or moved the factories to other places. Iron slag heaps, for example, marred the local landscape of

FIGURE 21.9 *Deforestation in China.* *This woodcut depicts Chinese logging efforts during the Ming Empire (1368–1644). Two groups of loggers chop at standing trees, while another group trims the trunk of a fallen tree. At the lower left, a supervisor addresses a group of kneeling workers. Deforestation denuded many parts of China, although at times the Chinese replanted and harvested trees as they did grains.* From *Chung-kwo pan-hua-hsuan.* Photo by Eileen Tweedy.

Nubia. Furthermore, **leaching**, the movement of chemicals as water runs off topsoil, rapidly contaminated subterranean water supplies because slag heaps typically contained extremely toxic concentrations of arsenic, antimony, lead, and radium. Ironically, waste-disposal centers have provided archaeologists with fertile grounds for amassing artifacts to understand and interpret civilizations.

Irrigation systems were developed to increase agricultural production, but they caused their own problem. Over time, salt in irrigation waters settled on farmlands, rendering them inhospitable to growing plants. One reason for the decline of the Indus River Valley civilization was overuse of irrigation, leading to a salting of the land.

Deforestation

People in this period relied heavily on wood for fuels and building materials, so densely populated places frequently denuded forest lands. China suffered the rapid loss of trees as people claimed the trees for their energy and building needs. A few ancient Chinese texts lamented the environmental destruction and the termination of a mythical era of harmonious interaction among humans, other animals, and the environment. One scholar noted that in the early Middle Ages, European cities seemed like islands in a sea of forests, but at the end of the late Middle Ages, forests appeared to be islands in a sea of towns, cities, and fields. Slash-and-burn agriculture also reduced forests and trees in many parts of the world. In addition, water runoff in deforested areas caused erosion and the silting of rivers. These effects hampered agriculture and river transport.

Agriculture Transforms Landscapes

Agricultural techniques became more complex and began to alter local environments significantly. Apart from forests falling to farmers' axes, deep-plowing techniques sometimes resulted in massive erosion. Exploitation of the Ethiopian highlands ecosystem of East Africa by the Axumite civilization brought dire consequences. Axumites harvested trees and severely reduced the forests of the highlands. The ecosystem changed dramatically over several centuries, and, when rainfall cycles became less predictable and produced more torrential deluges, mud slides carried off villages and buried parts of the capital. Key export items were also lost as forest animals retreated or disappeared. The combined losses accelerated the decline of the Axum Empire, and the region has still not fully recovered from the environmental degradation. Although this was a unique case, similar destruction by agriculture occurred all over the world.

Environmental degradation had affected numerous societies long before the Industrial Revolution of the eighteenth and nineteenth centuries. Many of the ecological problems faced in recent times have ancient historical roots.

SUMMARY

1. Modern human beings appeared about 100,000 years ago and gradually adapted culturally to their environments. Their numbers grew slowly until the development of agriculture, after which the pace accelerated rapidly.

2. Although warfare and disease reduced human populations, there was steady growth. Warfare killed great numbers of warriors and civilians. Disease proved to be an even more lethal curb on human numbers. The Black Death was by far the worst demographic catastrophe prior to the sixteenth century and killed over 20 million people.

3. Cities became the centers of city-states, federations, kingdoms, and empires. Some political trends were toward centralization, while others were toward decentralization.

4. Cities also became hubs in the trade routes that evolved into continent-wide systems by the first millennium A.D. The Mayans and Aztecs used them in Mesoamerica, while Muslims plied the caravan routes across Asia and Africa.

5. Artisans and merchants organized guilds to support their own self-interests. These craft networks helped control the quality of manufactured goods. At the same time, they offered social benefits, especially to the less fortunate of their members in troubled times.

6. City folk had their own social hierarchies and usually despised rural folk. The latter sometimes returned the scorn and distrust of urban folk.

7. A variety of roles and relationships governed the individual in society. Most related to the family and one's gender, and others related to patron-client relations, religious obligations, or ethnic identity.

8. The natural environment was dramatically changed by humankind in premodern times. Cities produced huge amounts of waste. Agriculture reduced forests, and irrigation canals also brought significant environmental alterations.

SUGGESTED READINGS

Adas, Michael, ed. *Islamic and European Expansion.* Philadelphia: Temple University Press, 1993. A series of essays examining broad issues of Eurasian history.

Chaudhuri, K. N. *Trade and Civilization in the Indian Ocean.* Cambridge, Eng.: Cambridge University Press, 1985. A major survey and interpretation of trading patterns in the Indian Ocean.

McNeill, William. *Plagues and Peoples.* Garden City, N.Y.: Anchor Press, 1976. A classic treatment of the role of disease in history.

Tuchman, Barbara. *A Distant Mirror.* New York: Ballantine Books, 1978. A survey of European history, focusing on the Black Death and its consequences.

B EFORE 1400, MOST PEOPLES WERE LARGELY ISOLATED from one another. Certainly there were trade and diplomatic contacts, and pilgrimages and wars brought some individuals into contact with foreign lands. Nonetheless, deserts, oceans, and the sheer vastness of the space between many peoples were significant barriers, given the transportation technology available at the time. Most of Africa was cut off from Europe and Asia by the Sahara Desert, and contrary currents in the Atlantic Ocean made northward voyages along the African coast difficult or impossible. Africans, Europeans, and Asians had no idea that the Americas even existed.

While there was sporadic contact in earlier periods, the contact that began with the fifteenth-century European voyages of discovery was qualitatively different. The intensity of contact produced far-reaching changes that stretched across the next three centuries. Diseases and foodstuffs were transported from continent to continent with important demographic consequences; entire populations were subjugated; and some countries grew rich by exploiting newly found lands. Improved transportation technology was partly responsible for these changes, but other factors played important roles as well.

Part Six explores the contacts following the European voyages of exploration, the changes they brought about, and the reasons that underlay increasing European domination of the world in this period. These factors are aspects of the massive and rapid change that culminates in what we call "modernity." The development of modernity is the major theme of this volume of *The Global Past*.

Throughout this volume, we use two terms that require special consideration. The **Old World** refers to Asia, Africa, and Europe, while the **New World** consists of

	INDIA	RUSSIA	PERSIA
1300			
1400			
1500		Russian Empire	
	Mughal Empire		Safavid Empire
1600			
1700			
1800			

the Americas and the Pacific islands. Some scholars object to these terms, feeling that they are based on a European perspective that is inappropriate for a global treatment of the past. We have adopted them, with some reservations, because we feel that they emphasize a fundamental distinction. The peoples of the New World and peoples of the Old World were unaware of each other's existence before the European voyages of exploration, and each had developed independently.

PART SIX

THE COLLISION OF WORLDS

All of the chapters in Part Six explore the theme of developing global interaction. Chapter 22 discusses the factors that characterize modernity and its significance to the changing world order. Chapter 23 discusses some of the most important voyages of exploration (originating in both Europe and Asia), and Chapter 24 explores the colonization that developed from the European discoveries. The exchange of ideas, items, and species between the Old and New worlds is chronicled in Chapter 25, and Chapter 26 treats the new basis of slavery and the slave trade that developed in this period, bringing Africa into global prominence and contact. Empires of western Asia, southern Asia, and eastern Europe also were in contact with new peoples in this period, and they are discussed in Chapter 27; Chapter 28 treats contemporary East Asian states and their contacts with other peoples. Finally, Issue 6 places slavery in a broader context by examining its forms around the world and over time.

TURKEY	CHINA	JAPAN	
			1300
Ottoman Empire	Ming Empire	Ashikaga Shogunate	
			1400
		Warring States Period	1500
			1600
	Early Qing Empire	Early Tokugawa Shogunate	
			1700
Late Ottoman Empire	Late Qing Empire	Late Tokugawa Shogunate	1800

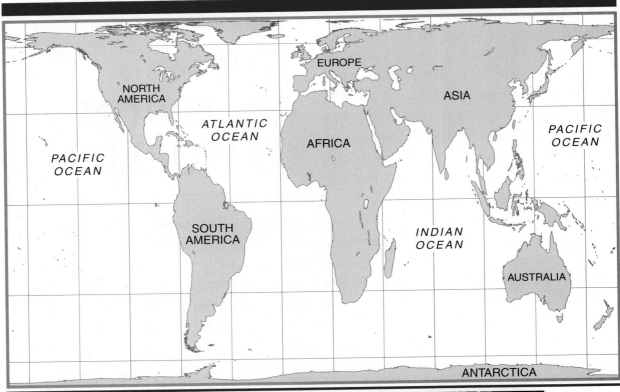

On the Edge. *Harold Lloyd, like many of his contemporaries in the 1920s and 1930s, felt caught up in the dangers of modernity. Lloyd, of course, was an actor who made a career out of generating thrills and fear among moviegoers. In this scene, he teeters on the edge of disaster, trying to cope with the hazards of a skyscraper under construction.* Corbis-Bettmann.

Exploring Modernity

If human existence were an apple, then civilization would be no thicker than its skin and the modern era would be no thicker than the insecticide on it. Human beings evolved from distant ancestors who lived more than a million years ago, and change came slowly until the invention of agriculture. Sedentary people lived in villages, towns, and eventually cities that soon became centers of civilization with characteristics such as social-class distinctions and long-distance trade.

Change accelerated, producing kingdoms and **empires**, groups of peoples and territories ruled by a single power. Over the centuries, empires rose, dominated, and collapsed, while long periods of rule by local and regional leaders alternated with domination by larger kingdoms and empires. Science and technology brought forth many important inventions and discoveries, such as metallurgy, paper, and gunpowder. In addition, religions met certain needs, and some faiths spread far beyond the places where they originated.

In this volume, we will explore the forces of change that led to modernity and the peoples who brought increasing global contact and often conflict. Modernity has accumulated some unfortunate associations, and it too often is assumed that modern societies are somehow superior to premodern societies, a judgment we will avoid. In this textbook, we will discuss modernity in terms of its characteristics. Not all of these features need be in place, but at least most of them must be present in order for a society to be considered modern.

What is **modernity**? Let us examine its features:

—a cultural outlook that focuses on progress;

—a perspective that seeks to accelerate the systematic application of science and technology to improve economic production;

—a view that shifts from a predominantly religious to a predominantly secular understanding of the world and the universe;

—governments, often nation-states, that usually seek wider participation of a broader spectrum of people in all aspects of life, especially politics;

—an increase in the determination of social status according to merit rather than birth, and the breaking of social barriers to the advancement of talented people; and

—the accelerating integration of regional economies into a global economic network that is increasingly dominated by capitalism or socialism.

Modernity slowly emerged in the western part of Europe and in Japan and by the nineteenth century across much of the world.

Progress is a crucial component of modernity. Beginning in the late eighteenth century, intellectuals developed and espoused **progressivism**, the idea that things are getting better and better. Thus, change is for the good and the result of change is always superior to the beginning. Optimism flowed from this perspective and characterized the thinking of a wide array of the ruling elite in the nineteenth century.

Part of this positive outlook developed from the systematic application of science and technology to the improvement of production. Although science and technology previously had been used to improve production, the applications had been unsystematic. In the mid–eighteenth century, Enlightenment thinkers like Denis Diderot implemented their vision of prosperity by writing the *Encyclopédie*. This reference work, illustrated with many drawings, offered information about many manufacturing techniques. Successful Japanese farmers printed and sold agricultural manuals to help increase agricultural yields throughout Japan. By the nineteenth century, German chemists developed fertilizers to help farmers, especially in Germany. One result of the great success in applying science to production was the belief that science can solve all problems.

Secularism, the practice of applying nonreligious ideas to the service of humanity, developed in the late eighteenth century and became an element of modernity. As scientists understood and explained a universe that ran according to natural laws, some people began to ignore religion as necessary to the society's functioning and well-being. A few Enlightenment thinkers espoused atheism, the belief in a godless universe, and some others gradually shrugged off spiritual concerns as irrelevant to progress. By the nineteenth century, scientists developed theories about nondivine origins of the earth and human beings. To some people, religion was outmoded and riddled with superstition. Science, they felt, had replaced religion in the modern era.

Wider participation in the nation-state became the characteristic policy in the modern age. Politicians realized that securing a broad participation of citizens in the governing process strengthened the modern state. Leaders of the American Revolution developed this concept when writing and implementing the U.S. Constitution. A significant development in that view came in the French Revolution, which created the modern military state. While other countries had elected representatives to national or local office, the franchise had been limited to the privileged and wealthy few. The French government purposely opened voting to nearly all men, and voting became a regular practice in modern France. Soon, other countries followed the French example, and people who participated in governing became enthusiastic citizens who supported their governments.

A related feature of the modern age was the opening of governmental service to people of talent. For a long time, state offices had been restricted to aristocrats and people of substantial means. Enlightenment thinkers sharply criticized this practice, arguing that many officials were incompetent. During the French Revolution, buying offices was abolished, and government service was opened to a broader spectrum of social groups. By the nineteenth century, civil service examinations were regularly used to select people for office holding. At the same time, evaluation of officials became commonplace so that ineffective

UNDER THE LENS

Japan's Path to Modernity

The Japanese played a significant role in international trade during part of the Early Modern Era, but they gradually turned inward and shut off nearly all contact with western Europeans. In that period of relative isolation (1640–1854), however, the Japanese created an integrated national market, a technologically advanced agricultural system, a prosperous middle class, a large intellectual class, and a stable polity. Most of these conditions facilitated Japan's transformation into an industrial country by the early twentieth century.

The period from 1540 to 1640 saw Japan enter international affairs in a major way. Westerners arrived in Japan in the 1540s and helped spark Japanese curiosity about Western ideas and technologies. Christianity became widely practiced, especially in the port cities frequented by Western merchants and missionaries. After the mid–sixteenth century, Japan used gunpowder technology to revolutionize warfare and began the effort to reunify a fragmented country. By 1592, Japan's rulers were looking toward Korea and China as places Japan could conquer and rule. New techniques of prospecting and retrieving silver from ores also opened significant sources of that metal for trade purposes. In fact, Japan was the second-largest producer of silver after the Americas. International trade received a significant boost from the introduction of Japanese silver in the first half of the seventeenth century.

Political and social stability concerned Japan's ruling class and triggered the closed-country policy. A small but significant number of provincial leaders and their subjects were Christians and therefore were seen as vulnerable to manipulation by Roman Catholic priests, who were usually foreign. An uprising by Japanese Christians in the mid-1630s fed the government's fears. In addition, foreigners could bring in the latest weapons and threaten political stability.

Instead of weakening Japan for future competition, Japan's isolation actually laid the foundations for modernization in the nineteenth century. Japan experienced rapid growth in its population, cities, and agricultural output. This brought urban prosperity as merchants turned to domestic trade. Roads improved and enhanced trade among cities, while peasants began producing specialized crops for urban markets. Schools multiplied in cities, towns, and villages, with the result that a significant percentage of men and women were literate by the mid–nineteenth century. Resources were carefully managed; waste products from fishing and soybean processing were used as fertilizers. Coal became a major fuel by the early nineteenth century. In all, the Japanese created the infrastructure necessary for industrialization and modernity.

---

people could be released, and effective officials could be retained or promoted. The development of universal education policies helped provide aspiring individuals with the means to take and pass civil service examinations.

Modernity brought forth increasingly integrated regional, national, and international economies. Transoceanic voyaging by Europeans expanded opportunities for trade and the prosperity that flowed from such commerce. They also benefited from the establishment of colonies as exploitative bases. Soon, Japanese and American silver circulated in China, India, and France. The

Atlantic slave trade also increased the traffic in human beings by the tens of millions in exchange for goods, like rum from the Caribbean region.

The Industrial Revolution significantly increased the number of manufactured goods and the need to develop markets for their sale. Textiles were the major goods produced in the early phase of the Industrial Revolution, and they circulated in England, on the European mainland, and in other parts of the world. The need for regular and inexpensive supplies of raw materials and markets for finished products drove imperialism, the intensive subjugation of lands and peoples by industrialized powers. In the late nineteenth century, imperialist countries like Great Britain, the United States, and Japan had carved out their empires.

A by-product of this economic and political expansion was an increasingly integrated global market system. Gradually, regional economic blocks were joined in larger economic units as imperialist nations needed to trade with other countries as well as with their own colonies. By World War I's outbreak in 1914, the globe was loosely tied together in an integrated economic system. One manifestation of this was that economic problems in one country might ripple across its national borders, affecting other coun-

FIGURE 22.1 *Thomas More's Utopia. Information about the places explored by Europeans stimulated thinkers to imagine places of ideal or farcical conditions. One model was developed by the English official Sir Thomas More early in the sixteenth century. The fictional Utopia, which means "no place," was discovered by Hythlodaeus, "the dispenser of nonsense." Thus, satirical elements were evident in More's fanciful island, which was compared with England.* Warder Collection/ET Archive.

tries. Global economic downturns became increasingly widespread in the nineteenth and twentieth centuries.

Two groups are intimately associated with modernity: the **middle class**, the class of business and professional people, and the **intellectuals**, a group whose members live by the exchange of ideas. Most civilizations have these two groups, but in the modern age they have been viewed as leaders of change. Members of these two classes increasingly believed that all barriers to what they saw as advancement had to be eliminated, and they worked hard to accomplish that goal. They increasingly advocated universal education as a primary means of advancement.

MODERNITY'S FIRST PHASE: THE EARLY MODERN ERA, AROUND 1500–AROUND 1750

Transoceanic voyaging had a profound impact on Europeans. Knowledge and wealth, for example, greatly enriched many in Europe. Trade and the systematic exploitation of peoples and resources, especially in the Americas and Africa, yielded vast riches.

European ships reached the New World in the late fifteenth century, and they first sailed in the Indian Ocean in the same century. The Americas were progressively explored, and South, Southeast, and East Asia came within the sphere of European discovery. (Australia remained out of European reach until the seventeenth century.) The global age had arrived when the crew of Ferdinand Magellan's ship successfully circumnavigated the globe between 1519 and 1522. Parts of Africa were explored by Europeans, especially beginning in the fifteenth century.

The European printing press, developed in the fifteenth century, helped the new information about the non-European world reach a wider audience because books and pamphlets could now be made more quickly, more inexpensively, and more numerously. Early in the era, Protestant Reformation leaders like Martin Luther founded breakaway religious movements, successful in part because of the large number of tracts printed in support of their ideas.

FIGURE 22.2 *Reading at Home. This sixteenth-century painting captures the sense of seriousness and wonder associated with reading. Here a woman reads aloud to an old man. Although both European men and women could read, a far greater percentage of men were literate. In some Protestant territories, reading from the Bible was an expected daily occurrence that helped to spur literacy.* Louvre © R. M. N.

Parallel developments occurred with the expansion of an intellectual class and the improvement of literacy in the cities and towns of Europe. Intellectuals using scientific methodology helped spread knowledge in areas such as astronomy, medicine, and mathematics. Through a rudimentary postal system that permitted limited correspondence, these thinkers kept abreast of recent discoveries. In the same era, popularization of various discoveries informed the wider reading public.

Measures of literacy are imprecise, but there seems to be a consensus among historians that growing numbers of urban dwellers in Europe could read during the Early Modern Era. Silent reading in the privacy of one's home became popular around the sixteenth century and led to increased reflection about ideas. At the same time, the growth of private libraries mirrored the ease of attaining books, and it was not long before library rooms were being used as meeting places. By the mid–eighteenth century, intellectuals and members of other classes met to discuss all kinds of ideas, like the perspective that social status should be based on merit.

During the Early Modern period, Europeans played an active role in the accelerating integration of regional economies into a modern global economic network. The Portuguese established strategic bases around the Indian Ocean. The English and Dutch eventually followed the Portuguese, and they enjoyed a more stable financial backing in the form of the Dutch East Indies Company and the English East India Company. All of these efforts rapidly integrated regional Asian and African markets with markets in Europe.

Towns and cities benefited from the prosperity stemming from the growth of trade and the exploitation of resources in colonies. Merchants in Antwerp, Lisbon, and London often prospered, as did the artisans who produced the necessary goods to trade abroad. Much early modern economic growth and prosperity rested on technological developments from the thirteenth to the fifteenth centuries.

A combination of inventions and improvements to existing manufacturing techniques accelerated change, especially in Italy during the Early Modern period. Wind power was harnessed by windmills, bringing a significant source of power to manufacturers. New types of spinning wheels and looms appeared and facilitated the production of textiles.

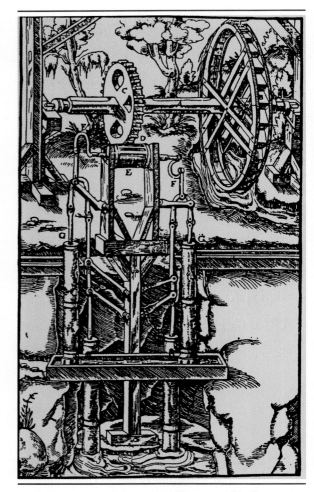

FIGURE 22.3 *Mining Machinery. This illustration from a book by Georgius Agricola, who popularized metallurgical technology in sixteenth-century Europe, shows a water-powered mining pump. Mining benefited from the application of such important inventions to the extraction process and from the need to secure metal for casting cannons and muskets.* From Georgius Agricola, *De re metallica*, 1556.

MODERNITY'S SECOND PHASE: INDUSTRIALIZATION AND WESTERNIZATION, AROUND 1750–1905

Beginning in the latter half of the eighteenth century, an industrial revolution centered in England, the Netherlands, and Flanders spread over much of the rest of west and central Europe by the mid–nineteenth century. Over the next several decades, the effects of this transformation swept across the globe, creating among many the need to Westernize.

Population growth increased markedly from 1750 to 1905. Cities of hundreds of thousands of people became commonplace in Europe. They often reeked of industrial pollution and poor sanitary conditions, but city life seemed better than rural life to many. This urbanization was the basis for industrialization.

Many other elements helped bring about the Industrial Revolution. One vital component was the application of knowledge to production techniques through Denis Diderot's encyclopedia. Underlying assumptions of this encyclopedia were that technical knowledge could be easily learned and that the skills of one industrial process might be transferred to another branch. Another assumption was that workers might be taught these things and should have some form of formal education. Monarchs influenced by thinkers of this era began calling for universal education.

In England, a companion development was the shift in the nature of patents granted by the government to reward inventors by guaranteeing them a fixed income or royalties from their discovery. This stimulated inventiveness and the application of knowledge to the improvement of manufacturing techniques.

The two most prominent social developments from 1750 to 1905 were the growth and dominance of the middle class and the emergence of an industrial workforce. These two economic classes often were hostile to each other. Union building and strikes were but two activities of the workers, while lockouts and strikebreaking were owners' responses. The guild system had been largely destroyed by industrialization, but in some places guilds gave way to unions.

The Industrial Revolution's need for resources was behind the growing power of many European countries, the United States, and Japan. They all used their industrial might to extend their control to less developed countries, fostering an imperialism that dominated global politics from 1850 to 1950. Other nonindustrialized or partially industrialized empires, such as those of China, Russia, and Austria-Hungary, could not compete and either disintegrated or fell under external control.

The ideas of democracy and liberty that flared up in the American and French revolutions were transmitted throughout the world in the nineteenth and twentieth centuries. Freedom excited many intellectuals in other parts of the world, especially those under domination by European powers. When Chinese intellectuals, for example, wished to transform their own culture, they promoted Westernization, especially democracy.

FIGURE 22.4 *The Manufacture of Soda.* *The glass industry boomed in the eighteenth and nineteenth centuries. Critical to the making of glass was the production of soda. This illustration shows the process, including the furnace where the reaction occurred (top), the vats where the soda was dissolved (center), and, finally, the method used to prepare soda for its use in the manufacture of glass. Huge factories were needed for the large-scale operations in the modern period.* After C. Tomlinson, *The Useful Arts and Manufactures of Great Britain*, Part II, Section: " The Manufacture of Soda," pp. 26, 33. London, 1848. E. Norman. D. E. Woodall.

IN THEIR OWN WORDS

A Critique of Eurocentrism in the 1990s

Late in the twentieth century, Partha Chatterjee, an Indian intellectual, wrote *The Nation and Its Fragments*, in which he examined the influence of British rule in India and Indian reactions to the British. At the same time, he subjected ideas and institutions of the West to a painstaking scrutiny and concluded that using European categories as the universal measure for various societies (Eurocentrism) severely limits intellectual discourse and understanding.

One can see how a conception of the state-society relation, born within the parochial history of Western Europe but made universal by the global sway of capital, dogs the contemporary history of the world. I do not think that the invocation of the state/civil society opposition in the struggle against socialist-bureaucratic regimes in Eastern Europe in the former Soviet republics or, for that matter, in China will produce anything other than strategies seeking to replicate the history of Western Europe. The result has been demonstrated a hundred times. The provincialism of the European experience will be taken as the universal history of progress; by comparison, the history of the rest of the world will appear as the history of lack, of inadequacy—an inferior history. Appeals will be made all over again to philosophies produced in Britain, France, and Germany. The fact that these doctrines were produced in complete ignorance of the histories of other parts of the world will not matter: they will be found useful and enlightening.

FIGURE 22.5 *Modern Art.* *Pablo Picasso loved to startle art lovers with new images. Part of a wide movement beginning in the early twentieth century, this painting of three musicians clearly reveals a different way of seeing. Some artists of the period experimented with new forms and visions, while others protested the traumas of war.* The Museum of Modern Art, New York. Mrs. Simon Guggenheim Fund.

MODERNITY'S THIRD PHASE: UPHEAVAL AND REBUILDING, 1905–PRESENT

The smug optimism implied by the idea of progress during the early years of the twentieth century was shattered by the two world wars and several revolutions that brought a ghastly loss of human life. A general questioning of modernity's costs characterized the writings of intellectuals who saw many of their friends slaughtered in World War I. Antiheroes began to appear in fiction, and intellectuals began to question the value of progress and modernity itself.

War was a major feature of the period beginning in 1905. The Russo-Japanese War ended in 1905, two world wars succeeded it, and lesser conflicts also occurred; World War II dwarfed all previous wars in the loss of human life. In addition, civil wars in Russia and China either brought to power or kept in power communist governments that slaughtered additional millions of people.

Human catastrophe and the effects of industrialization and technological development compelled many intellectuals to question seriously whether the costs of progress and modernity itself were simply too steep. Can we, many asked, speak of progress, if tens of millions of people perish in building a new political and social order? Can we still speak of modernity when the ability to take life far outstrips our ability to preserve it? Can human beings live in a world of declining resources and heavily polluted skies and waters?

The global economy became even more closely interrelated than in earlier times. By 1914, it would be an integrated global economic system. The economic collapse from 1929 to 1941 deeply affected most nations and empires. After 1945, the global economy saw general growth of competition between the capitalist and Soviet socialist systems. The Soviet system developed until the 1980s, when serious problems helped bring about a general economic collapse there from 1989 to 1991.

Another impact of the twentieth century has been environmental degradation. The capitalist and socialist economic systems have severely damaged many environments on the planet. The disposal of nuclear wastes is especially disturbing because the effects may last for generations rather

FIGURE 22.6 *Injustices Faced by Women. This political cartoon, designed by Mary Lowndes, builds on the Western world's traditional female personification of Justice. Lowndes characterized British politicians as acting unjustly by excluding women from a reform bill. By 1912, people in England and elsewhere were seriously examining the implications of keeping women from power.* Fawcett Collection.

than for years, and some environmentalists have questioned the benefits of the Industrial Revolution and the atomic age. Indeed, many are questioning progressivism and whether things are always getting better.

The increasing advancement of women and ethnic minorities is one significant twentieth-century development. It relates directly to wider social participation of more people in modern life and to the breaking of social barriers to advancement that had begun in the sixteenth century.

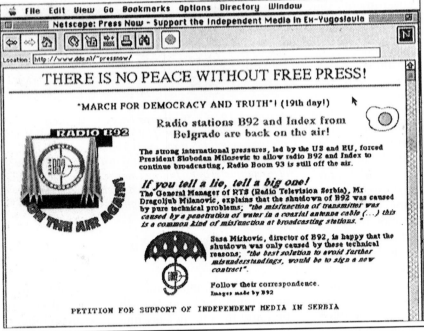

Figure 22.7 *Modern Technology and Freedom.* *This picture shows the use of computers in conveying information about political demonstrations. In late 1996, Serbs protested against their government, which had annulled elections won by opposition groups. To circulate information about these protest activities, teachers and others used the Internet. Authoritarian regimes found it difficult if not impossible to curb the flow of information because of the large numbers of computers, fax machines, telephones, and pocket radios. The communist government of Rumania once registered all typewriters held there; today such an effort would be almost impossible.* Photo by Alan Chin. Both images: New York Times Picture Sales.

In phase three of modernity, changes in travel, communication, and the economy have increased global integration. At the same time, disruptive elements like military conflicts, economic depressions, and environmental catastrophes have given governments much to consider. One theme is the questioning of progress, and another is the criticism of European ideas and values being used as universal categories. This latter debate has focused on Eurocentrism, the view that sees Europe as the measure by which everything else is judged (see "In Their Own Words," p. 552).

SUMMARY

1. Modernity, one way to characterize the era from 1500 to the present, has many important elements:

— a cultural outlook that focuses on progress;

— a perspective that seeks to accelerate the systematic application of new science and technology to improve economic production;

— a view that shifts from a predominantly religious to a predominantly secular understanding of the world and universe;

— governments, often nation-states, that usually seek wider participation of a broader spectrum of people in all aspects of life, especially politics;

— an increase in the determination of social status according to merit rather than birth, and the breaking of social barriers to the advancement of talented people; and

— the accelerating integration of regional economies into a global economic network that is increasingly dominated by capitalism or socialism.

2. The Early Modern Era was modernity's first phase, lasting from around 1500 to around 1750. Modernity's second phase of industrialization and Westernization lasted from around 1750 to 1905. Upheaval and rebuilding have characterized modernity's third phase, from 1905 to the present.

3. A transformation of Europe and Japan came in the eighteenth and nineteenth centuries and was associated with the Industrial Revolution. This shift gave many European states and Japan the power to carve out empires, some of which lasted for decades.

4. As human ingenuity perfected ways of killing, the losses from war and revolution reached tens of millions and caused many to feel disillusioned with change.

SUGGESTED READINGS

Blum, Jerome. *In the Beginning: The Advent of the Modern Age.* New York: Charles Scribner's Sons, 1994. An examination of elements of modernity that commenced in the 1840s, largely in Europe.

Chatterjee, Partha. *The Nation and Its Fragments.* Princeton, N.J.: Princeton University Press, 1993. A critique of prevailing interpretations of the history of India with wider implications for the study of global history.

Hodgson, Marshall. *Rethinking World History.* Cambridge, Eng.: Cambridge University Press, 1993. A collection of essays about Islam, Europe, and the study of global history.

McNeill, William. "The Age of Gunpowder Empires, 1450–1800," in Michael Adas, *Islamic and European Expansion.* Philadelphia: Temple University Press, 1993, 103–40. An essay about the role of gunpowder in Europe's rise in global affairs.

Mokyr, Joel. *The Lever of Riches.* Oxford, Eng.: Oxford University Press, 1990. A work examining the relationship between technological development and economic growth.

Totman, Conrad. *Early Modern Japan.* Berkeley: University of California Press, 1993. An examination of Japanese history in the Tokugawa period, including ecological and financial matters.

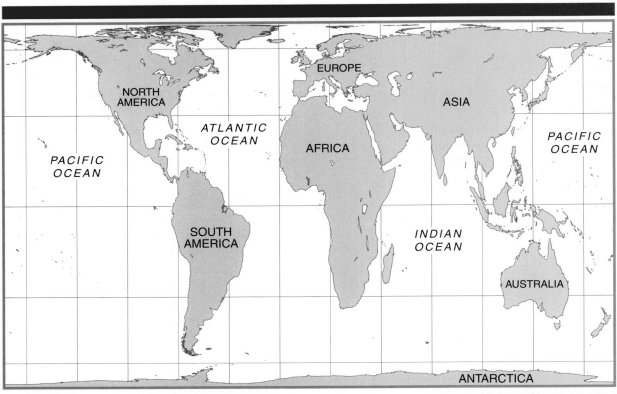

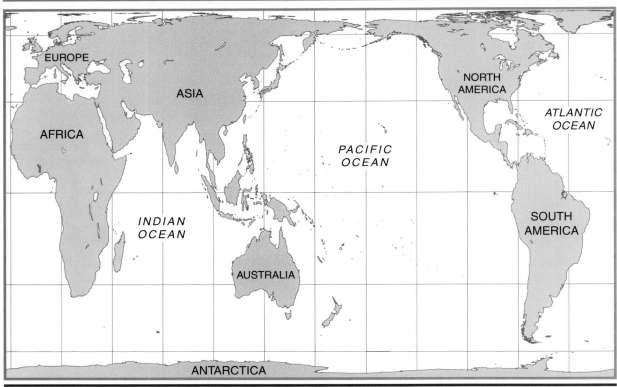

Oceanic Explorations and Contacts

1405–1780

We have traversed ... immense waterspaces and have beheld ... huge waves like mountains. ... We have set eyes on barbarian regions far away hidden in a blue transparency of light vapors, while our sails, loftily unfurled like clouds day and night, continued their course [as rapidly] as a star, traversing those savage waves as if we were treading a public thoroughfare. ...

–ZHENG HE

These words carved in stone in China celebrate the achievements of Zheng He,[1] commander of China's seven oceanic expeditions in the fifteenth century. Chinese ships, some of enormous construction, sailed and then abandoned the South China Sea and the Indian Ocean a few decades before the Europeans arrived. The Europeans, however, came to stay and reaped substantial and lasting benefits from their efforts.

Sailing across the Atlantic and Pacific oceans on a regular basis began in the fifteenth and sixteenth centuries. Before that time, the hazards of sailing for long periods kept ship captains close to shore and rarely out of the sight of land. Without a compass, for example, ships could easily get lost, and ships had to carry their own supplies. During early long-distance ocean travel, fresh water turned bad, and the absence of fruit and vegetables in the sailors' diets brought on scurvy, a dreaded disease caused by the lack of vitamin C. Fierce storms terrified crews, and ocean currents

[1] **Zheng He:** JEHNG HUH

often snagged unwary ships and took them far off their intended paths. Frequently, many ships of an expedition would be lost in stormy seas, or others would turn back home after their crews were exasperated by extended voyages away from land and a varied and healthful diet. Illness and anger fueled many mutinies, and only the most self-assured or desperate sailors continued on the lonely, unexplored routes. The Polynesians, Micronesians, and Melanesians all sailed to different island groups in the Pacific Ocean. Most of these peoples stayed south of the equator, but some Polynesians established permanent settlements in the North Pacific. The Vikings sailed the waters around Europe, venturing into the North Atlantic as far as Iceland, Greenland, and Canada. The Chinese briefly dominated transoceanic voyaging in the early fifteenth century, expending large amounts of money and even reaching Africa, but they halted and withdrew from ocean travel to concentrate on domestic issues. Many Europeans increased their interest in seagoing exploration and, by the early sixteenth century, sailed the major oceans. They also circumnavigated the earth and inaugurated a global era in history.

OCEANIC VOYAGING BEFORE 1400

Water covers much of the earth and has served as a barrier between the New and Old worlds. Polynesians and Vikings, among others, often sailed the Atlantic and Pacific in earlier times before European sailors dominated the oceans for exploration, trade, conquest, and colonization in the Old and New worlds.

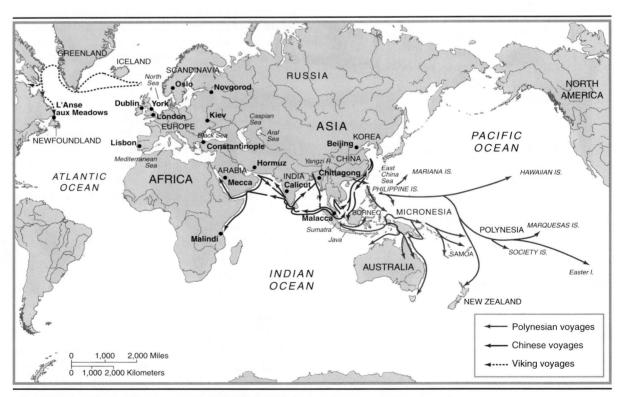

MAP 23.1 *Oceanic Voyaging before 1400.* *Polynesian, Viking, and Chinese sailors explored the waters far from their homelands, gaining knowledge of other cultures, trading, and settling in new lands. Their ships carried from a dozen to a few hundred people each, and their expeditions numbered from one hundred to nearly thirty thousand people.*

Polynesian Exploration

Beginning perhaps around 50,000 years ago, peoples from mainland Asia began exploring and colonizing islands along a path ending at the continent of Australia. Other groups, such as the Melanesians around 1500 B.C., went east to Pacific islands, like New Guinea, New Caledonia, and Fiji. Micronesians settled the more eastern and northern islands, like Palau and Guam. After 1000 B.C., Polynesians reached more remote islands, including New Zealand, Samoa, Easter Island, and Hawaii.

Polynesians achieved great navigational feats without the aid of the compass or the sextant used by other maritime peoples. Their boats were usually single- or double-hulled and often had an outrigger (a buoyant pole parallel to the hull and affixed to it by wood pieces) to stabilize the craft. The largest ships, catamarans, could carry as many as 200 people and their necessary supplies. The vessels could be propelled either by oars, in which case they needed a steering paddle or rudder, or by winds blowing into the triangular sail. With these devices, the Polynesians ventured over most of the Pacific Ocean.

To guide them, the Polynesians relied on the sun, moon, and stars as well as the flight patterns of migratory birds. On cloudy days and nights in open water, the sense of being lost must have given pause to many on board the ships. Familiar waters were mapped out and the particular places where sailors could get their bearings were noted, but new waters had no known markers to guide the explorers. Only a sense of adventure and the urge to locate new lands for colonization drove the sailors on.

Earliest human settlement in the Marquesas, Samoa, and Hawaii dates to the era from the second century B.C. to the second century A.D. The settlers fished, hunted wild animals and birds, gathered fruit, and tended gardens of taro and other tubers. The bark of trees was pounded into materials to make cloth and other products.

Polynesians also caused ecological degradation on many islands where they settled. By A.D. 500, Polynesians in Hawaii killed off nearly all flightless birds for food. Widespread deforestation of the Easter Islands brought serious erosion of agricultural fields. Saltwater marshes were used as

FIGURE 23.1 *Palm-Frond Map from the Marshall Islands.* *Various peoples of the Pacific have made nautical maps of string, twigs, or the central ribs of palm fronds. These maps show distances between islands measured in time traveled, not in actual miles, since currents and prevailing winds could cause two trips of equal distance to have very different sailing times. In its original form, this map from the Marshall Islands most likely had bits of coral and shell marking island positions. Maps similar to this probably were used by early Polynesian navigators.* Bishop Museum.

PARALLELS AND DIVERGENCES

Elements of Early Modern Sailing Technology

The Chinese and Europeans mastered the essential techniques of shipbuilding, rigging, and sailing in the fifteenth century, skills that opened the oceans to global voyaging. Over time, accurate sea charts were drawn indicating passages through straits, underwater reefs, and shoals, as well as unusual currents.

Ship construction and rigging improved significantly in the fourteenth and fifteenth centuries. Chinese ships were constructed as separate but interlocked watertight compartments, making them nearly unsinkable. Chinese sails were of square design and were made of cloth, permitting effective use of wind power. At the same time, European shipbuilders began using techniques that made lighter and larger vessels capable of carrying larger loads. They included square and triangular sails in their riggings in combinations designed to permit more effective use of wind power.

In the fifteenth century, the previously distinct northern and southern traditions of European ship design merged, producing the **full-rigged ship**, a ship of multiple sails in various positions, allowing it to take advantage of diverse wind conditions. Such ships, one type of which is the famous galleon, were superior to their predecessors in seaworthiness, size, and ability to control the direction in which they sailed. In addition, the development of the vertical stern permitted the use of a rudder that steered more precisely than the earlier steering oar, allowing the ship to avoid rocks and other obstacles. Finally, the extra space in the ship and the mounting of cannons in openings in the ship's sides made the full-rigged ship a floating arsenal that was a formidable military force used especially in India to reduce local resistance.

Both Chinese and Europeans used the compass and other navigational devices to permit sailing under all conditions. The compass was employed in sailing by the Chinese centuries before the Europeans developed it. To measure latitude, the Europeans adopted the astrolabe from the Greeks via the Muslims and adapted it, calculating the altitude of the North Star and indicating the observer's latitude.

The revival of previous cartographic knowledge also permitted the mapping of the global surface. Greek geographical works were translated into Latin by the early fifteenth century and provided models for Europeans to divide maps into grids of latitude and longitude. This made for more useful map projections and safer sailing for ships' crews.

---

sources of water for taro fields, leading to the salting of lands and rendering them unusable. Many birds on the Easter Islands were hunted to extinction for their colorful feathers.

Viking Exploration

The Norse Vikings, medieval inhabitants of the Norwegian coast, sailed the waters of the Baltic and North seas and often raided coastal settlements of continental Europe and the isles of Britain beginning as early as the eighth century. Major invasions commenced in the ninth and tenth centuries and even reached the Iberian Peninsula and places on the Mediterranean coast. The largest of the raiding vessels measured more than 100 feet long and carried as many as sixty-five fully armed Vikings; some of the fleets included as many as 300 ships. The Vikings had shallow-draft vessels for rivers as well as deep-draft ones for the oceans. The deltas of many European rivers attracted Viking settlement, and soon Viking colonies dotted much of the coastline of Europe. In England most early Viking homesteads were established along eastern shores. In addition, Vikings sailed down inland waterways in eastern Europe and Russia.

Eventually the Vikings crossed the short stretches (200 to 250 miles) of the North Atlantic to Iceland and Greenland, settling in Iceland during the first quarter of the ninth century. The only people preceding the Vikings to Iceland were Irish monks who used it for a place of retreat from worldly distractions. Greenland, about 200 miles from Iceland, attracted the attention of the Vikings in the tenth century, although European colonization did not begin there until the last two decades of the century. The Inuit had long inhabited small communities in Greenland.

The Vikings reached North America around A.D. 1000. They explored some of the coast of present-day eastern Canada and established a short-lived settlement in present-day Newfoundland. Archaeologists in the early 1960s found the remains of a Viking settlement in Newfoundland.

Norse Vikings could not sustain viable settlements in Greenland and North America. Contentious chiefs who frequently quarreled with one another ruled the Vikings, and leaders who had run afoul of more powerful chiefs ran the Viking settlements in Greenland and North America. In addition, overpopulation in some Viking lands drove some to seek lands suitable for settlement. Lands to the west were quite inhospitable to the Viking way of life, at least in the northern reaches accessible to them. Vikings were grain agriculturalists, yet no crops could be grown in the frigid lands of Greenland and adjacent North America; their houses and many of their tools were largely made of wood, but these places supported only sparse and scraggly trees. The Viking settlement in Newfoundland lasted only three years, and the Greenland settlement survived for scarcely more than a century.

Although the distances that the Vikings sailed did not compare with those of the Polynesians in the Pacific, these Europeans had sailed from the eastern to the western hemisphere, and they briefly established a small settlement in the new land. These facts attest to the sailing skills of the Vikings.

CHINESE VOYAGING IN THE INDIAN OCEAN, 1405–1433

Although the Chinese developed various navies in their history, they also maintained a strategic orientation to Inner Asia and land warfare, and centuries of conflict with various nomadic tribes from north of China helped solidify that inland orientation. In the fifth and fourth centuries B.C., northern Chinese states began building walls to protect themselves from nomad incursions, and the Qin Empire linked these walls to form the edifice now known as the Great Wall. This defensive posture against northern tribes symbolizes China's land orientation. Nevertheless, Chinese voyaging in the Indian Ocean suggests a naval tradition of consequence.

China's Emerging Naval Tradition

By the sixth century A.D., a necessity to defend their coastline and patrol their inland waterways caused the Chinese to develop a naval force. In the seventh century, a Chinese fleet defeated Japanese vessels off the Korean coast. A few centuries later, a Chinese flotilla (including paddle-wheel boats) patrolled the Yangzi River, keeping the Mongols from invading South China. When the Chinese fleet defected to the Mongols, swift conquest of the south followed.

The Mongols soon used the naval fleet to assert their political influence. Twice they attempted to invade Japan with an armada (generally of Korean ships and sailors as well as Mongol soldiers). The second attempted invasion of Japan in 1281 included a significant Chinese naval force. In the 1290s, the Mongols sailed the South China Sea, reaching the island of Java (in present-day Indonesia). Although the Mongols soon turned their focus away from maritime activities, Chinese ships continued to sail the waters of Southeast Asia.

FIGURE 23.2 *Viking Ship. This thirteenth-century seal of Bergen, Norway, depicts a Viking ship sailing the seas. While the typical Viking ship had but one dragon head on its bow, dragon heads were placed at both ends of this ship by the seal's designer, for aesthetic purposes. Bergen was a key port of trade with Viking settlements in Greenland.* Per Christoffersen, EGM-Foto. Courtesy of Rijksarkivet, Oslo.

Sailors seem to be given to superstition when facing long-distance oceanic voyaging, and the Chinese are no exception to this. Even Zheng He, a devout Muslim, actively participated in prayers and rituals honoring the Celestial Consort and the patron goddess of sailors. Originally a historical figure who lived in the tenth century, the Celestial Consort was credited with saving sailors, and worship of her spread along China's southeastern coast. The Yongle Emperor built a splendid temple to her in the early fifteenth century.

Before each voyage, Zheng He and members of the crew sacrificed goats, pigs, and cattle, and they burned incense and gave prayers for guidance and a safe return. One prayer had the words:

> As the divine swirling smoke rises, with hearts pure and true, we bow down and beseech the messengers of merit to convey by means of the incense in this burner that in this year, in this month, on this day, at this hour, we respectfully entreat the patriarchs of the imperially created compass throughout the ages: Yellow Emperor, Duke of Zhou, immortal masters of former ages divinely knowledgeable . . . Dark Raven, immortal White Crane master. . . .

> [And] patriarchs of the ages who have traversed the sea; who know the mountains, the sandbanks, the shallows, the depths, the isles, the shoals; who are conversant with the sea lanes, the mountains, the mooring waters, the constellations and guiding stars; those from past times to the present day, those who first transmitted it and those who later taught it.

> [And] the great guardian spirit generals of the 24 directions; the great spirit generals of the 24 azimuth points of the patriarch of books, the compass classic; the page boy who sets the compass directions, the spirit of the water basin, the lord of the water changing, the strongman who sets down the compass needle, the guardian spirits of the direction of the needle, the master of the lookout, and all the other immortal masters and spirit soldiers and divine emissaries—all the efficacious spirits of the incense burner.

> [And] the protectress of our ships, the Celestial Consort, brilliant, divine, marvelous, responsive, mysterious force, protector of the people, guardian of the country.

> [And] the all-seeing and all-hearing spirit soldiers of winds and seasons, the wave quellers and swell drinkers, the airborne immortals, the god of the year, and all the local tutelary deities of every place.

> Come down one and all to this incense feast, partake of this sagely vessel.

> Come rising on auspicious clouds from the ends of the earth, come down and grace our incense table . . . to protect our ships and valuables.

Certain Chinese inventions facilitated travel in waters beyond sight of land. China employed the compass in maritime activities by the twelfth century. Naval engineers had developed watertight compartments for ocean-going vessels, and at the same time, the Chinese improved anchors to be useful during storms. Indeed, with these various technological successes, Chinese merchant ships garnered the reputation of being exceptionally seaworthy, and merchants from other countries preferred to ride aboard Chinese ships, believing that the vessels would best guarantee a safe arrival at a destination.

Motivations for the Chinese Voyages

In 1403, the Yongle[2] Emperor seized power in China (see Chapter 28) and became a dynamic Ming monarch who wished to do grandiose things. One was outfitting the Ming navy to follow existing trade routes in the South China Sea and on into the Indian Ocean. The Yongle Emperor's effort, monumental in scope and scale, reflected imperial ambition and a desire to project Chinese influence

[2] **Yongle:** YOHNG leh

abroad. The program did not seek exploration, promote trade, or push colonization. It was largely symbolic, and in that way it differed from the later European voyages. Perhaps it is best understood as the idiosyncratic policy of a powerful monarch.

Another factor in China's naval voyages was the eunuchs, one of whom was Zheng He, who commanded each of the seven expeditions. Ming emperors used eunuchs for many tasks, especially ones that might incur criticism and resistance by bureaucrats who believed these tasks to be costly. The monarchs often preferred working with eunuchs, who obeyed rather than questioned imperial policies. The Yongle Emperor, for example, heavily relied on trusted eunuchs and selected Zheng He to oversee the outfitting of the armada.

The Seven Voyages

The emperor ordered the fleet to be ready to sail in 1405. Many of the empire's shipyards, including a large one near Nanjing, built the required ships. Of the fleet, the largest ships had as many as nine masts and several decks and measured nearly 200 feet across and around 450 feet in length. These ships displaced between 2,500 and 3,000 tons and could carry between 450 and 500 people. They far outsized the largest Polynesian, Viking, or European ships up to that time or into the seventeenth century. In fact, they compare in size with the largest vessels of the eighteenth century.

The fleet of the first expedition numbered over 300 ships, including more than 50 large vessels.

FIGURE 23.3 *Chinese Ship.* *This fifteenth-century multimasted sailing vessel was of the type used in the Ming expeditions led by Zheng He. Around five times as big as the ships of Columbus or Vasco da Gama, the Chinese ships carried large numbers of sailors and huge amounts of cargo. They were generally seaworthy, surviving the great cyclonic storms of the Indian Ocean.* Ontario Science Center, Toronto.

The total human cargo of the two-year voyage numbered nearly 28,000 people, in contrast to the few hundred sailors of the Polynesians and Columbus or Magellan. Although the flotilla carried a small army, they did not fight much, because its major purpose was diplomatic rather than military. Special water tankers were constructed and could supply as much as a month's drinking water. There was also one physician for every 150 sailors and many linguists to translate for the diplomats.

Zheng He's first three expeditions sailed across the Indian Ocean to India, and each time the flotilla carried many diplomatic envoys back to China to feed the ego of the Yongle Emperor. Because the fleet followed trade routes previously used by merchant ships, some commerce was conducted. Yet one must remember the low position of merchants in Confucian Chinese society. In that kind of social climate, business ventures did not receive much imperial endorsement. China's diplomatic system, in fact, demanded that the emperor return gifts of greater value than those received in a diplomatic exchange. After all, China viewed itself as superior, and that superiority carried an obligation of generosity over into the exchange of goods.

The last voyages reached the east coast of Africa and made port at Mogadishu in Somalia and Malindi farther south. One result of the voyages was the collection of animals exotic to the Chinese. The tall giraffes particularly excited the Chinese, who saw them as a kind of unicorn, a mythical beast associated with good omens for a monarch.

FIGURE 23.4 *Giraffe in China.* *The Ming sailing expeditions of the early fifteenth century brought back many exotic creatures from the regions of the Indian Ocean. This picture shows a giraffe that was transported from Africa. Chinese rulers had collected strange animals for centuries, and giraffes were considered to be among the most peculiar.* Shen Tu (1357–1434), Tribute Giraffe with Attendant, 1403–1424. Philadelphia Museum of Art. Given by John T. Dorrence.

Termination of the Voyages

Of the possible reasons for the dearth of sea voyages between 1420 and 1433, the crucial factor was the death of the Yongle Emperor in 1424. Because he had been intimately connected with the voyages, his death ended that tie and permitted critics to assert themselves with less fear of imperial retribution. In addition, factional politics played a part in the termination of the expeditions. Eunuchs, who generally supported Zheng He, frequently opposed the scholar-officials, who derided the eunuchs' lack of education and their not earning government positions through the examination system. Most scholars adhered to Confucianism, which espoused Chinese self-sufficiency; it was unseemly, they argued, for Chinese to go abroad.

Rather, the thinking went, barbarians must come to China. Scholars also opposed any hint of trade connected with the expeditions, because Confucians despised merchants. These views became more persuasive after the deaths of the emperor protecting the fleet and the influential eunuchs supporting it.

Strategic and financial considerations also played a role in halting the naval expeditions. China's Inner Asian orientation reasserted itself over time, especially after the Mongols became active in the north. (In fact, a Mongol army captured one emperor in 1449.) Ming laborers rebuilt the Great Wall in the fifteenth and sixteenth centuries. China simply could not afford a naval presence and a strong military campaign in the north. To build the great fleet, the Yongle Emperor had commandeered timber and other resources from many provinces, and the financial and material needs of the voyages severely taxed the empire's resources for defense.

Overall, China turned inward after having accomplished some remarkable naval feats decades before the Europeans arrived in the Indian Ocean. China's deliberate isolationist bent negated any influential role in global politics or relations. Coupled with the ban on overseas trade until 1567, China retired from the world naval stage at the height of its prowess. Pirates who had been swept from the seas reappeared along the China coast, and European ships arrived in China in the sixteenth century. Some Europeans became pirates or joined forces with East Asian pirates. The Chinese retreat from maritime activities was so thorough that in the late 1470s officials destroyed some records of their voyages kept in the War Ministry.

EUROPEAN EXPLORATION AND TRADE, 1434–1780

In the fifteenth century, Europeans embarked on a remarkable variety and number of exploratory voyages. Within a few decades before and after 1500, they mapped out the west coast of Africa,

PATHS TO THE PAST

The Myth of the Flat Earth

Contrary to popular belief, people in the European Middle Ages did not believe that the earth was flat. Christopher Columbus's voyage is often touted as the triumph of science over the ignorant view of medieval Christianity that the world was flat and any voyage into the unknown waters of the Atlantic Ocean would result in ships' falling off the edge into oblivion. This perception, however, was held by only a few medieval church leaders and some educated people in Europe prior to the transoceanic voyages of the fifteenth century.

How did such an error originate? The history of this little tale falls at the feet of two nineteenth-century men: Washington Irving (1783–1859), who wrote a semifictitious biography of Christopher Columbus, and Antoine-Jean Letronne (1787–1848), who wrote several works, including the four-volume geographical *Histoire de géographie moderne* (Paris, 1806). Unfortunately for later history, the sources these men used to weave their interpretations of medieval and Christian thinkers were not carefully checked by other scholars until recently, and, therefore, their imaginative embellishments were accepted as fact.

Washington Irving's biography included a completely fabricated story of a meeting with Columbus at a university. The clerics who attended supposedly declared heretical Columbus's idea that the earth was spherical. Irving's account created the encounter in order to make the biography interesting. His tale unwittingly created the basis for historical misinterpretation of medieval science. Irving's writings echoed a prejudice against medieval Christianity that had been common for centuries. In Irving's mind, Columbus represented the new science of the modern era in contrast to medieval science, and his literary scene depicted Columbus arguing the truth of a spherical earth against his oppressive persecutors. Irving wrote at the end of a scene, "Such are the specimens of the errors and prejudices, the mingled ignorance and erudition, and the pedantic bigotry, with which Columbus had to contend." Scholars believe that no such council met and no such conflict existed. The only arguments Columbus ever had concerned the accuracy of his calculations on distance.

Geography was a popular subject in the nineteenth century, and Letronne's influence as a scholar was significant. French scientific investigation often took a particularly antagonistic anticlerical stand on all issues. Letronne argued that medieval astronomers were forced to believe in a flat earth because of clerical pressure that had threatened persecution, prison, or burning at the stake. In reality this never occurred. Unfortunately, because of Letronne's influence on later geographical scholarship, the misinformation was picked up and perpetuated by scholars in other fields.

sailed throughout the Caribbean Sea, and thoroughly explored the eastern coasts of the two American continents. Diverse Europeans, including Spanish, Portuguese, English, Dutch, Scandinavians, French, and Basques, came to the New World.

What propelled these adventurers to brave the perils of oceanic crossing? Economic incentives drove many sailors into dangerous oceanic waters. Certainly many hoped to discover a new passage to India and Indonesia, whose spices were in great demand in Europe and fetched good prices. Precious metals also lured people and nations to undertake risky endeavors. The opening of new places for colonization and commerce drove many west and south from Europe. Soon, national and dynastic rivalries fed the competitive efforts to outdo the other European states.

Certainly new maritime inventions and techniques gave sailors more hope that transoceanic voyages offered a greater probability of success in returning home. The maritime compass permitted sailors to fix directions without recognizable land features on which to get a reckoning. Improved technology permitted sails that caught breezes and permitted easy maneuvering in case the wind changed direction, resulting in less chance of being becalmed. Portuguese sailors from 1434 mapped out the west coast of Africa, garnering much experience in sailing. This knowledge passed to others in the sailing community because crews of mixed nationality were common throughout this era. For example, Italians sailed with the Spanish, Scandinavians sailed with the English, and English sailed with the Dutch.

The Age of Columbus

Christopher Columbus certainly was not the first human to set foot in the Americas—he was preceded by the American Indians by many thousands of years. But his voyages made Europe aware of the Americas and initiated global integration.

Christopher Columbus sought a new way to the Indies, land of spices and immense profits. He sailed west rather than south and embarked on a risky venture that had been underwritten by the Spaniards. He outfitted three ships and a few hundred sailors, yet the consequences of his expeditions far outstripped those of the Chinese in global terms. The Europeans vied with one another to find additional lands and peoples.

FIGURE 23.5 *Entrance to a Portuguese Mansion. The Portuguese began to settle in India in the sixteenth century. This gate, built by the Portuguese, still stands in western India and features rampant lions and a coat of arms with triple-crossed lances. Portugal controlled the colony of Goa in India until the 1960s.* From K. N. Chaudhuri, *Asia Before Europe* (New York: Cambridge University Press), Plate 72, 349. Reproduced with permission. Photo courtesy of Library of Congress.

As noted earlier, Columbus actually was but one of many captains sailing from the Iberian Peninsula in the fifteenth century. The Portuguese probed along the west coast of Africa, eventually rounding the southern tip of that continent and sailing into the Indian Ocean, reaching East Africa and India in the late 1490s.

Portugal and Spain competed for new lands and wealth in the years after Columbus's first expedition. In 1493, Pope Alexander VI attempted mediation between the two countries and offered a line of demarcation between Portuguese and Spanish dominion. Envoys of the two monarchs negotiated a modification of the papal effort that was somewhat more favorable to the Portuguese. This led the following year to the Treaty of Tordesillas,[3] which divvied up the new-found lands. (The Protestant European countries ignored the division of the globe.) Brazil, claimed in 1500 by a Portuguese captain, was the only territory in the New

---

[3] **Tordesillas:** tor deh SEE yahs

World open to the Portuguese. The Spanish proceeded to explore the New World, while the Portuguese probed the Indian Ocean and sailed farther toward the islands off the Southeast Asian mainland and eventually to East Asia.

Most Spanish attention focused on Mesoamerica and South America, with the exception of Portuguese-dominated Brazil. The Spaniards undertook limited trading but concentrated primarily on exploration and conquest. One Spanish leader, Vasco de Balboa, saw a large body of water (the Pacific Ocean) from a peak in Panama. This excited him and others, because the ocean promised to be the waterway to the Indies. Some followed this speculation by sailing south and west.

The English and Dutch also undertook some tentative steps in exploration, beginning in the late fifteenth century. Some of their ships sailed along the upper coast of North America, but nothing of consequence followed in terms of exploration until the late sixteenth and early seventeenth centuries, when Henry Hudson, who sailed for both the English and the Dutch, made important explorations, including that of Hudson Bay in Canada. The French also conducted some far-ranging explorations in the Americas, but little trade or colonization occurred until the seventeenth century.

Both the Americas and Europe were strongly influenced by contact following Columbus's voyages. Millions of Native Americans perished from disease, and many others died fighting the European conquerors. Europeans grew wealthier because of the silver and gold from the New World. New foodstuffs transformed the diets of Europeans and promoted population growth.

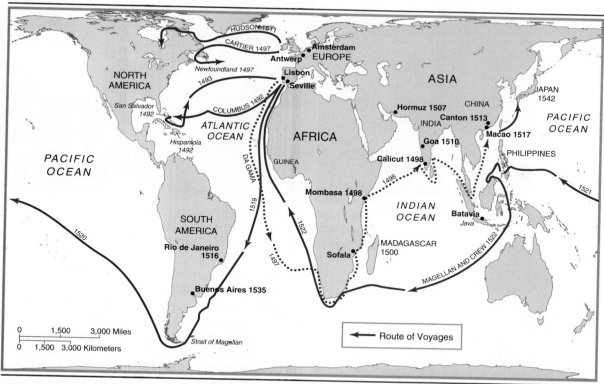

MAP 23.2 *European Voyages and Trading Posts in the Indian Ocean, 1492–1522.*
The Portuguese explored the western coast of Africa through the fifteenth century, rounding the Cape of Good Hope in 1497. Vasco da Gama, who led that expedition, sailed on to India. His feat inaugurated a Portuguese presence in the Indian Ocean that dominated trade for most of the sixteenth century via strategically placed ports. Christopher Columbus and Ferdinand Magellan sailed west and south from Europe to reach the Americas. Magellan continued on across the Pacific Ocean to the Philippines, where he was killed; his crew returned to Spain in 1522.

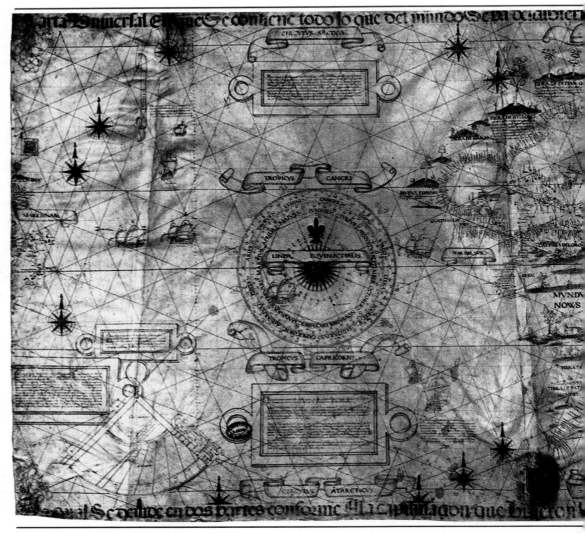

Figure 23.6 *Sixteenth-Century World Map.* *This 1529 map by Diego Ribero shows the major continents and the voyage of Ferdinand Magellan and his crew. Africa and India are rather accurately portrayed along the coasts, and the eastern coasts of*

Circumnavigating the Globe

A major turning point in global exploration began in 1519, when several ships sailing under the Spanish flag and under the command of Ferdinand Magellan reached the southern tip of South America and passed through the strait (later called the Strait of Magellan) into the Pacific Ocean. This voyage of exploration crossed the Pacific and reached various island groups, including those later known as the Philippines. By that landfall, many crew members had died and only a couple of ships remained. Captain Magellan became embroiled in a native conflict and also lost his life in the Philip-

pines. Surviving crew members sailed across the Indian Ocean, reached the Atlantic Ocean, and finally returned to Spain. They were history's first-known group to circumnavigate the earth.

This discovery sparked new expeditions by the Spanish and others who followed Magellan's westward course across the Pacific Ocean. They faced many hazards, ranging from diseases resulting from poor diet and bad water to the great storm systems of the Pacific. Survivors also had to brave contact with local peoples, some of whom were hostile.

Westward routes across the Pacific eventually became the highways between Spanish posses-

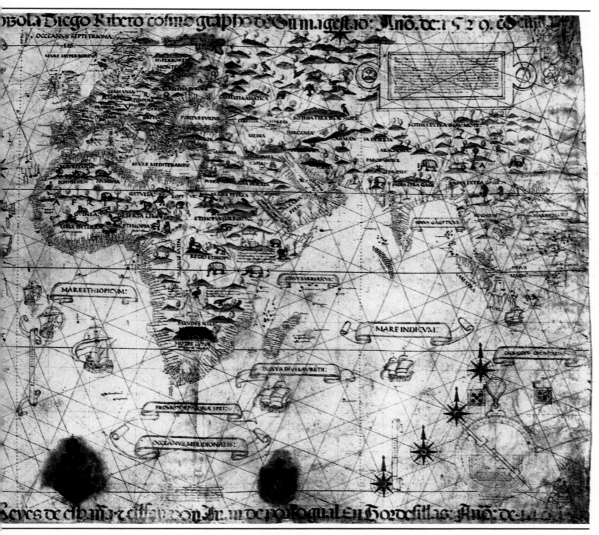

the Americas are clearly defined, unlike those in the west—a reflection of the state of mapping and European voyaging in the early sixteenth century.
Biblioteca Apostolica Vaticana.

sions in the New World and the Philippines. Soon Spanish precious metals and coins circulated across the Eurasian landmass, causing a variety of economic effects from inflation to growth of trade.

By the end of the sixteenth century, the Dutch also began to sail in foreign waters far from home. They explored the Americas, including Canada, the United States, and the Caribbean. Intrepid Dutch captains sailed to the Spice Islands (later called the Dutch East Indies and eventually Indonesia). One voyage even explored the waters off Australia in the mid–seventeenth century. The Dutch organized their explorations and trading missions in the East by chartering the Dutch East

India Company, which played a major role in the seizure of the Spice Islands for Dutch colonization and economic development.

An English ship under the command of Francis Drake, who had been authorized by Queen Elizabeth to prey on Spanish ships, also circumnavigated the globe in the latter part of the 1580s. Drake reached the Pacific from the Atlantic and successfully raided the treasure-laden Spanish ships. Rather than return to the Atlantic and face possible capture by Spanish warships, Drake headed across the Pacific. He traded in the East Indies, sailed through the Indian Ocean, and reached the Atlantic, arriving back in England to a

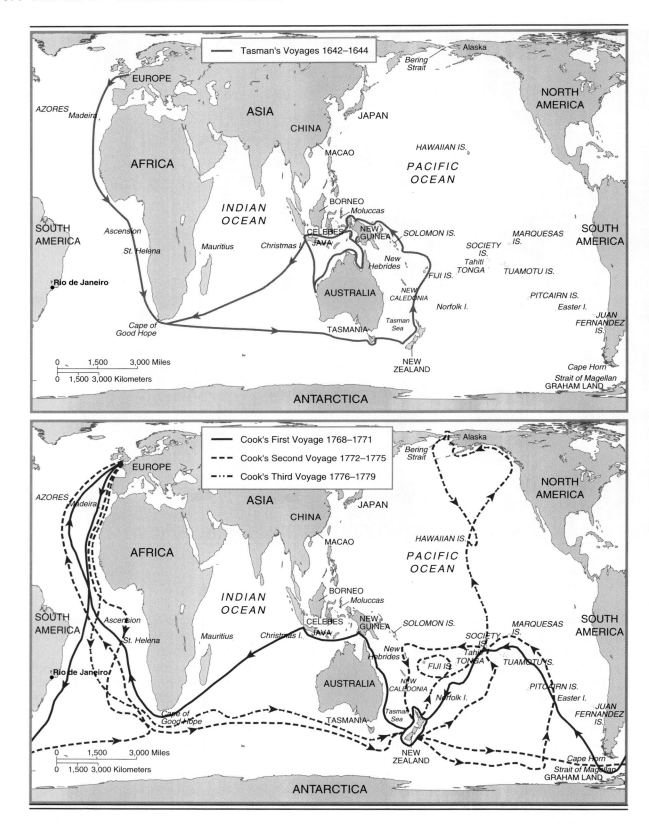

◄ MAP 23.3 *Dutch (Tasman) and English (Cook) in Australian and Pacific Waters, 1642–1780.* *In the seventeenth century, Abel Tasman sailed from the Netherlands, reaching Tasmania and New Zealand. He helped establish a Dutch presence in Asian and Pacific waters, especially in Indonesia (Dutch East Indies). James Cook arrived in those waters more than a century later and undertook much mapping and specimen collecting throughout the region. Both Tasman and Cook were nautical pioneers, advancing European knowledge and science.*

hero's welcome. This voyage excited other English captains and prompted them to emulate Drake. Moreover, the possibilities of great wealth inspired the chartering of the English East India Company, a private investment organization that funded many expeditions.

Another English explorer who circumnavigated the globe was Captain James Cook (1728–1779), and he headed three English expeditions to the Pacific that were charged by the British Royal Society to undertake scientific observations and explorations. He fully mapped the coasts of New Zealand and Australia, and his accurate maps have long been admired.

Cook's crew also included scientists who recorded various plants, animals, islands, and people. Cook landed on many islands, including Hawaii, and reached the continent of Australia. A conflict in Hawaii led to Cook's death, and reportedly King George III wept at the loss of the English scientist, cartographer, and sailor.

The Global Significance of the European Voyages

Oceanic voyaging greatly increased the contact between Europeans and others. From this activity came the beginnings of knowledge of peoples and customs in distant lands, including fanciful and dehumanizing portraits that had no factual basis.

FIGURE 23.7 *A European Perspective on the New World.* *Europeans developed fanciful images of the inhabitants of the Americas. This German colored woodcut of 1505 depicts cannibalism, a common impression that Westerners had of indigenous peoples. One can see various severed body parts, some of which are being eaten. The cannibal fantasy pervaded European literature.* The New York Public Library. Spencer Collection, Astor, Lenox and Tilden Foundations.

EUROPE	ASIA		
		1400	Zhu Di becomes Ming emperor, 1403
	Chinese voyaging, 1405–1433	–	
European voyaging, 1434–1780		–	Portuguese begin exploring African waters, 1434
		–	
		–	Columbus reaches the Americas, 1492 Portuguese arrive in Indian Ocean, 1497
		1500	
		–	Magellan begins global voyaging, 1519
		–	Cartier explores Canadian rivers, 1534–1535
		–	
		–	Drake returns to England, 1580
		1600	
		–	Henry Hudson explores Canadian waters, 1610–1611
		–	Dutch land in Australia, 1644
		–	
		–	
		1700	
		–	
		–	
		–	
		–	James Cook killed in Hawaii, 1779
		1800	

Soon new perspectives based on comparative analyses drove Europeans to reform their own societies by using non-European models.

The new information, however, also facilitated the conquest and reduction of many societies through exploitation and widespread killings. The massive Atlantic slave trade played a major role in developing American plantations and economies, and European diseases ravaged large Indian populations in all of the Americas. These developments will be covered in some detail in subsequent chapters.

Europe greatly benefited from the global exchange of foodstuffs, precious metals, and other raw materials that enriched some European monarchies and many members of the middle classes, like merchants and artisans. Indeed, a powerful economic base developed from the sixteenth century and supported European domination of much of the world in succeeding centuries.

SUMMARY

1. The Polynesians and the Vikings mastered the complex skills and technology necessary to sail in open ocean waters. Both settled distant lands, and the Vikings briefly stayed in North America. The global impact of this voyaging was limited.

2. Chinese fleets plied the Indian Ocean in the early fifteenth century. Some ships reached and explored the East African coast. Because their purpose was associated with a single emperor and was therefore idiosyncratic, they stopped soon after his death and never resumed.

3. Christopher Columbus landed in the New World while looking for a passage to India. He and his successors slowly explored the Americas, while the Portuguese sailed into the Indian and Pacific oceans.

4. Colonies were established in the New World as Europeans systematically exploited the Americas' natural resources and people.

5. Ferdinand Magellan and his crew circumnavigated the earth between 1519 and 1522. This action inaugurated a global age and was followed by voyages by Iberians, as well as by those of Dutch, English, and others.

6. Conflict sometimes characterized European relations with non-Europeans between 1500 and 1800. Some countries expelled the Europeans or kept them at bay. Other peoples in the Americas, Asia, Australia, and parts of Africa succumbed to European power.

SUGGESTED READINGS

Hugill, Peter. *World Trade since 1431.* Baltimore: Johns Hopkins University Press, 1993. A broad interpretative perspective on the interrelationship among geographical, technological, and capitalist factors in global exploration and trade.

Landstrom, Bjorn. *Columbus: The Story of Don Cristóbal Colón. . . .* Trans. by Michael Phillips and Hugh W. Stubbs. New York: Macmillan, 1966. A critical account of Columbus, depicting him as a pious but essentially greedy man.

Levathes, Louise. *When China Ruled the Seas.* New York: Simon and Schuster, 1994. A detailed account of the seven Chinese voyages in the context of China's history of maritime activity.

Morrison, Samuel. *Admiral of the Ocean.* Boston: Little, Brown, 1942. A classic and favorable account of Columbus, stressing his tireless determination, practical virtue, and nautical talents.

Mote, Frederick, and Denis Twitchett, eds. *The Cambridge History of China.* Vol. VII: *The Ming Dynasty.* Cambridge, Eng.: Cambridge University Press, 1988. This collection of essays contains an excellent section about the Ming voyages of exploration.

Smith, Roger. *Vanguard of Empire.* Oxford, Eng.: Oxford University Press, 1993. A recent examination of the technology and organization behind the European ships that sailed in the fifteenth and sixteenth centuries.

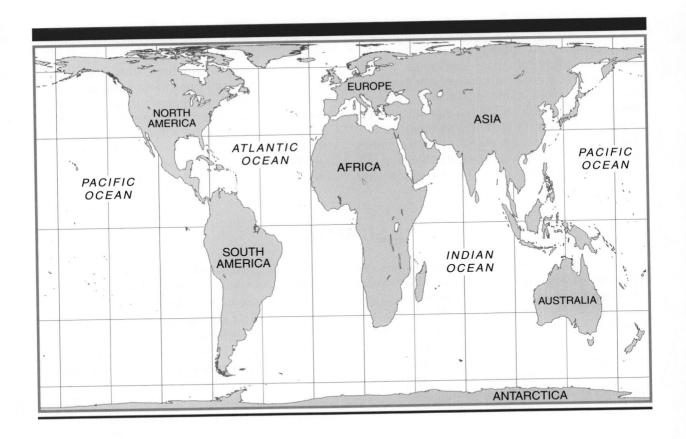

Early European Colonialism

around 1500–around 1750

Infuriated by the exploitation of India by the Portuguese who had established a toehold there in the early 1500s, Saint Francis Xavier[1] wrote acidly that colonialism consisted of "conjugating the verb 'to rob' in all its moods and tenses." One-sided and narrow as this statement may be, it emphasizes the exploitation that was created by—indeed, that was the primary reason for the existence of—early colonialism. This chapter will explore some of the motives, processes, and outcomes of the European colonial effort in the sixteenth, seventeenth, and first half of the eighteenth centuries.

The European voyages of exploration were primarily economic investments. Certainly there were scholars and a few sovereigns who held academic interests in new lands and were eager to increase their store of knowledge. Such curiosity, however, was minor in comparison to the financial advantages that the explorers and their patrons hoped to gain. Initially, the primary motive of these voyages was to find a route to India and nearby parts of Asia, thereby making direct contact with spice and silk merchants. By circumventing the Arab agents who carried the trade in the fifteenth century, Europeans reasoned that they could increase the supply of these commodities, lower prices, and make a greater profit. As it became obvious that previously unknown lands existed, European explorers and adventurers became interested in finding new sources of

[1]**Xavier:** ZAY vee ur *or* HAH vee air

575

jewels, precious metals, wood, furs, and other valuable commodities.

The spirit of economic gain that pervaded the voyages of exploration was equally prominent in the centuries that followed. Once found, it was reasoned, a new land was of little use unless wealth could be wrested from it, and this meant establishing settlements in far-flung places. To be fair, there was a diversity of motives behind the settling of foreign lands, but the one that was most common, most compelling, and most significant in the creation of policy was the economic motive. The process of establishing colonies, administering them, and extracting wealth for the home country is known as **colonialism**. While there had been colonies in earlier times, such as in ancient Greece, this was the first appearance of a distinctive hierarchic relationship between colony and home country that was to endure in some parts of the world for several centuries.

THE EUROPEAN REACTION TO NEW PEOPLES AND NEW LANDS

When explorers first brought back stories of previously unknown peoples living in the newly discovered lands, Europeans scarcely knew what to make of them. Initially, European scholars argued among themselves about whether these were truly human beings and worthy of treatment as such. This initial confusion was serious, because explorers, conquerors, and colonists were interacting with these peoples and needed guidelines for appropriate actions.

Initial Confusion

According to the book of Genesis in the Bible, Noah had three sons: Shem, Japeth, and Ham. After the Great Flood, when everyone except Noah's family had been killed, it was from these three that all the people of the world descended. According to Christian tradition, Shem was the ancestor of all Asians, Japeth of all Europeans, and Ham of all Africans. The biblical tradition left no place for other races, and the European discovery of American Indians, Polynesians, and Australians left these peoples without a biblical basis. Were they really human beings created by God? Were they simply clever beasts, sent by the Devil to confuse soldiers of God?

Further complicating matters were the unreliable reports that quickly began coming back to Europe with exploring expeditions. An enduring story was that of the sciopods[2] ("umbrella-footed people"), wild men with only a single leg, who were reported to hop along at great speed, then sit down and raise a broad foot over the head for shade. Sir John Mandeville and other travelers reported these creatures from various continents but most especially Africa. Other tales recounted winged people, headless people whose eyes and mouths were in their chests, and people with multiple arms. While most contemporary scholars discounted the least anatomically likely of these stories, the combined weight of these various accounts led scholars and others alike to believe that humanlike creatures with curious structures were to be found in the new lands. Certainly they could not be considered human, or could they?

More tales returned to Europe of fantastic beings, particularly in Africa and South America. One of these beings from Africa was huge and hairy, with a forward-projecting face and huge fangs. It walked hunched forward and beat its chest when angered. Clearly a gorilla, this creature also was imputed to have a language, to take sexual license with people who crossed its path, and occasionally to build houses or wear clothes, characteristics decidedly unlike those of the apes. These stories seemed no more unbelievable than those of winged or umbrella-footed people, and they added to the confusion of learned opinion in Europe.

What with cultured apes and monstrous people and the absence of biblical guidance, the scholars of Europe entered a prolonged debate over whether Indians (as they called all peoples from unknown lands) were truly people. The kindling of vested interest fueled this fire, because some colonial powers would have found it most convenient if the Indians had been determined to be merely clever beasts who could be exterminated or otherwise treated without human regard. The conclusion of this debate came only in 1537.

[2] **sciopods:** SY oh pohdz

The Eventual Solution

In 1493, Pope Alexander VI ruled that Indians were truly people. His reasoning lay in the facts, reported to him, that the Indians were peaceful in nature, went naked (an important criterion for the innocence of wild people), and ate no human flesh.

Unfortunately, Pope Alexander had been misinformed, and, in the years that followed 1493, it became clear that some Indians were warlike, well clothed, and cannibalistic. In fact, reports of cannibalism were typical in descriptions of new peoples, even with societies that clearly carried out no such practices, leading some modern scholars to believe that a purposeful campaign of disinformation was being undertaken. In any case, this information demanded that the pope's decree be reconsidered. After a lengthy debate in papal court, Pope Paul III confirmed Alexander's decree in 1537. As an act of faith, European Roman Catholics—the vast majority of the population in the colonizing countries at this date—now had to accept that Indians were human.

FIGURE 24.1 *Monstrous Humans from European Travel Accounts. European travelers in the fifteenth and sixteenth centuries described a variety of bizarre human beings, such as those shown here. On the left is a chest-headed being, in the center is a sciopod (umbrella-footed person) shading himself from the tropical sun with an oversized foot, and at the right is an armed and noseless cyclops. Stories of these mythic creatures gained credibility in part by being attached to legitimate accounts; this illustration comes from an edition of the travels of Marco Polo, who never mentioned any such creatures.* Bibliothèque nationale, Paris.

DIFFERING COLONIAL AGENDAS

Each country that entered the colonial arena had a different set of goals and plans of how to achieve them: colonial agendas. As circumstances changed over time, so did these agendas, producing a variety of differing colonial experiences overseas. In addition, the individuals who carried out colonial projects had their own interests and agendas, some of which were quite independent of or even in conflict with those of their home countries.

Official Agendas

Portugal and Spain were the first to become active in colonialism, dominating the sixteenth century. They were followed near the end of the sixteenth century by the French and Dutch, and the English trailed along in the seventeenth century. Each country established policies that encouraged certain types of use of the new colonies.

THE SIXTEENTH CENTURY. The Portuguese and Spanish, by virtue of their early start, were able to focus initially on the most desirable commodity: precious metals. One of the questions Columbus asked the natives of Guanahani (San Salvador) when he first set foot in the Americas was whether they had any gold. Similarly, early explorers everywhere asked the locals whether they had any gold or knew where any was to be found. The immense wealth in gold in Central America was attractive to the Spanish, who named Costa Rica ("Rich Coast") in commemoration of the gold found there as well as in Panama and Colombia. In Peru and Mexico, the Inca and Aztec Indians had hoards of gold and silver that the Spanish appropriated for their coffers.

This focus led the Spanish and Portuguese to establish themselves in such a way that they could effectively extract gold and silver for shipment home. This meant setting up settlements near or at native cities and towns, knowing that the masses of wealth would be focused there. When these treasure troves were exhausted, the towns and cities provided labor for the mines to produce more. Because the mines often were at some distance from major settlements, work parties were sent off

FIGURE 24.2 *Peruvian Implement of Gold.* *This artifact is a* tumi, *a sacrificial knife, used by the Chimú of coastal northern Peru in the early sixteenth century. It depicts a cultural hero named Ñaymlap, who has small wings projecting from his shoulders and wears an elaborate headdress and ear ornaments, all with inlaid turquoise. Objects like this were valued by Spanish conquerors primarily for their gold content, not for their artistic or cultural value. Tons of such treasures were melted down to make bars, which were easier to transport to Spain.* Boltin Picture Library.

to mine and refine the metals, which then would be sent back to the cities for shipment to the home country. This led to a settlement pattern of large, isolated concentrations of colonists surrounded by hinterlands that were composed almost entirely of native people.

This pattern typified the Americas, where conquest permitted the Spanish and Portuguese to do pretty much as they pleased. In Africa and Asia,

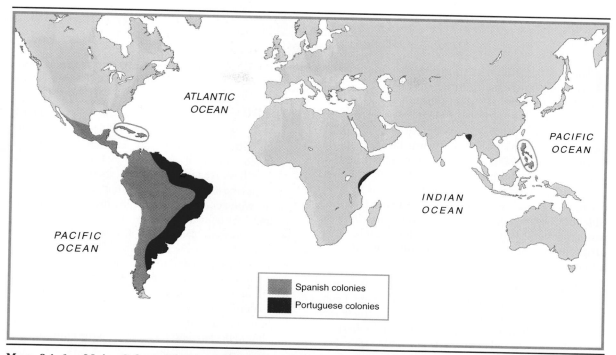

MAP 24.1 *Major Colonial Holdings in 1550.* *The European colonial system was relatively small in 1550, restricted largely to coastal areas.*

however, colonists were foreigners in lands still controlled by their native populations. As a result, in these places the colonists were restricted to small settlements or precincts within coastal cities, from which points they carried on a commerce with local businesses. The Portuguese desperately wanted access to the gold of East Africa and the silver of Iran to facilitate the Asiatic trade, but they had to trade with local producers or wholesalers, rather than merely seize it, as in the Americas. The result, however, was similar, with the majority of the colonial population restricted to a few urban settings.

An additional aspect of Spain and Portugal's colonial agenda was the desire to convert the natives to Catholic Christianity. This desire grew out of pious convictions that their faith was true and correct and that passing it on to others was the greatest favor that one could perform, even if the local people failed to recognize it. Consequently, the Spanish and Portuguese established missions, scattered throughout conquered territory, "to convert the heathen." These missions were the excep-

tions to the urban concentrations that otherwise typified these colonies, and they often formed the nuclei of settlements for the expanded settlement that was to follow in the seventeenth century.

While other countries were not particularly active in colonizing during the sixteenth century, there are noteworthy exceptions. France, Holland, and England, frozen out of the major extraction of precious metals, founded colonies in the Caribbean to serve as bases for the **buccaneers**, pirates who raided Spanish treasure ships carrying gold and silver back to Spain. Some buccaneers were commissioned by European governments as privateers, and others merely took advantage of the situation to enrich themselves on their own initiative. State-sanctioned piracy was initiated by the French in 1555 when they attacked Havana in Cuba, but the English soon eclipsed the French in this regard, establishing a colony in Jamaica and raiding widely throughout the Caribbean. The Dutch, though never so thoroughly involved, distinguished themselves in 1628 by capturing the Spanish treasure fleet with tons of gold and silver.

IN THEIR OWN WORDS

The Requerimiento

The Spanish colonial effort linked religion and the military, and nowhere is this more evident than in the *Requerimiento*[a] ("Requirement"). The *Requerimiento* was a document that *conquistadores* from 1513 forward were required to read to the Indians whom they encountered. Amazingly, this document informed Indians that they would have to renounce their own religions in favor of Christianity; if they refused, they were held responsible for their own deaths. In 1573, the *Requerimiento* was abolished by the Spanish king, part of a broader program to reduce forcible actions against the Indians.

On the part of the King, don Fernando, and of doña Juana, his daughter, Queen of Castile and Léon, subduers of the barbarous nations, we their servants notify and make known to you, as best we can, that the Lord our God, Living and Eternal, created the Heaven and the Earth, and one man and one woman, of whom you and I, and all the men of the world, were and are descendants, and all those who come after us. But, on account of the multitude which has sprung from this man and woman in the five thousand years since the world was created, it was necessary that some men should go one way and some another, and that they should be divided into many kingdoms and provinces, for in one alone they could not be sustained.

Of all the nations God our Lord gave charge to one man, called St. Peter, that he should be Lord and Superior of all the men in the world, that all should obey him, and that he should be head of the whole human race . . . and he commanded him to place his seat in Rome . . . this man was called Pope. . . . One of these Pontiffs, who succeeded that St. Peter as Lord of the world, in the dignity and seat which I have before mentioned, made donation of these isles and *terra firme* [mainland] to the aforesaid King and Queen and to their successors, our lords, with all that there are in these territories, as is con-

[a] *Requerimiento:* ray kay ree mee EHN toh

tained in certain writings which passed upon the subject as aforesaid, which you can see if you wish.

So their Highnesses are kings and lords of these islands and land of *terra firme* by virtue of this donation; and some islands, and indeed almost all those to whom this has been notified, have received and served their Highnesses, as lords and kings, in the way that subjects ought to do, with good will, without any resistance, immediately, without delay, when they were informed of the aforesaid facts. And also they received and obeyed the priests whom their Highnesses sent to preach to them and to teach our Holy Faith; and all these, of their own free will, without any reward or condition, have become Christians. . . . We ask and require . . . that you consent and give place [provide land for a church] that these religious fathers should declare and preach to you the aforesaid.

If you do so, you will do well . . . and we . . . shall receive you in all love and charity, and shall leave you your wives, and your children, and your lands, free without servitude. . . . But if you do not do this, and wickedly and intentionally delay to do so, I certify to you that, with the help of God, we shall forcibly enter into your country and make war against you in all ways and manners that we can, and shall subject you to the yoke and obedience of the Church and their Highnesses; we shall take you and your wives and your children, and shall make slaves of them, and as such shall sell and dispose of them as their Highnesses may command; and we shall take away your goods, and shall do all the harm and damage that we can, as to vassals who do not obey, and refuse to receive their lord, and resist and contradict him; and we protest that the deaths and losses which shall accrue from this are your fault, and not that of their Highnesses, or ours, nor of these gentlemen who come with us. And that we have said this to you and made this Requirement, we request the notary here present to give us his testimony in writing, and we ask the rest who are present that they should be witnesses of this Requirement.

FIGURE 24.3 *Women Pirates of the Caribbean. Piracy, sometimes state-sanctioned, flourished in the sixteenth and seventeenth centuries but was waning by the early eighteenth century. This woodcut shows Anne Bonny and Mary Read, women who sailed aboard* The Island of Providence, *an outlaw pirate vessel commanded by Captain Jack Rackam. Little is known of how these women became pirates, but they plied their trade with the same recklessness as their more numerous male colleagues, until they were captured and imprisoned in 1720.* The New York Public Library, Rare Books Division.

This raiding continued well into the seventeenth century, enriching buccaneers and serving the ends of their sponsoring countries.

While England, France, and Holland had limited interests in colonies during the sixteenth century, they still were active in exploiting the Americas as visitors, focusing on the most easily exploitable commodities: wood, fish, and furs. Their sailors arrived at the coast in ships, stayed briefly to collect the desired items, and returned home without establishing any settlements.

Northern Europe, especially Holland and England, had been running out of wood for years. The Tudor style of architecture current in this period featured thin veneers of wood that were set into stucco exteriors in lines paralleling the roof and walls of a house. In this manner, a minimum amount of wood could be used to its greatest advantage. In particularly short supply were the tall, straight trees required to make masts and spars for the fully rigged ships that had become common. The new-growth trees that dominated England were simply too small, but the forests of New England and Maritime Canada had such trees aplenty.

Similarly, the fishing banks of Europe had become depleted from decades of overfishing. The fishing banks of Newfoundland and New England, in contrast, yielded huge hauls of large fish with little effort, attracting fishermen from all over western Europe. The fish mostly were salted and packed in barrels to preserve them for the long voyage home.

Finally, Europe had made extinct or severely diminished its populations of fur-bearing animals in its zeal for furs to clothe the expanding middle class. The demand for fur remained, however, and only high-priced Russian furs could be consistently obtained. The North American continent

became a competing source. Crews on fishing boats along the North American coast frequently traded copper kettles and iron axes to local Indians in return for furs, a transaction each perceived as an incredible bargain. It was common for a fishing boat in this period to increase its profits by carrying back a few trees for mast wood and several loads of furs, in addition to its cod and flounder.

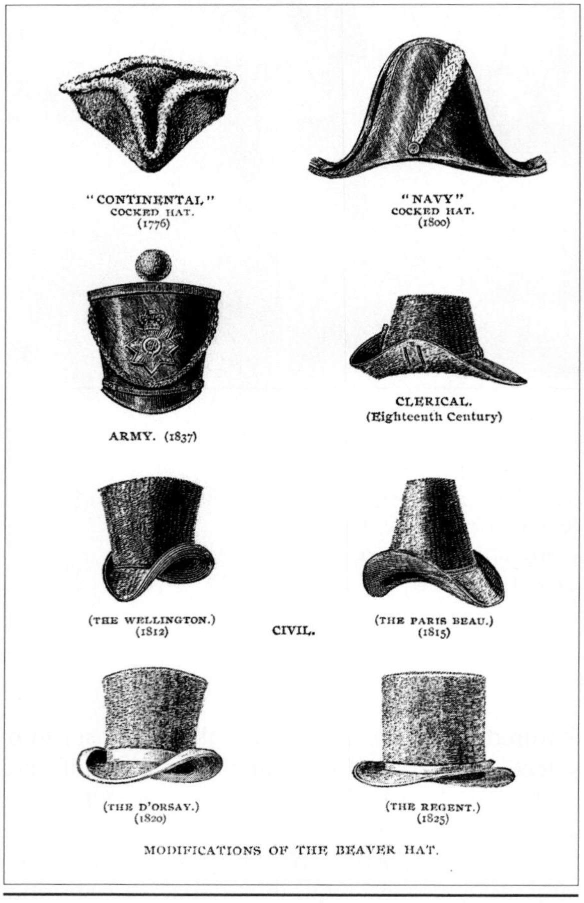

THE SEVENTEENTH CENTURY. By the seventeenth century, much of the more readily available wealth had been drained off by the Spanish and Portuguese, and they were forced to turn increasingly to less lucrative, more labor-intensive enterprises. These included mining, ranching, and growing crops.

With the richest and most accessible deposits depleted, the Spanish were forced to expend more labor in extracting mineral wealth. This meant establishing permanent settlements near major mines to serve as provisioning and entertainment centers. These mining settlements began the process of spreading the Spanish population around the colonies, away from the urban centers.

In addition, ranchers began large operations for the raising of beef and the tanning of hides. Because such ranches required vast quantities of land and could use less desirable, semiarid areas, they tended to be located at some distance from the cities that had so dominated Spanish America in the previous century. Their isolation made the ranches centers for all that the ranchers would need to survive and thrive. Ranches often had facilities for such activities as curing olives, fermenting wine, making soap, and weaving cloth.

Finally, in wetter areas, particularly along the coast, planters developed vast plantations for the growing of various cash crops, especially sugar and tobacco. While plantations provided food for local consumption, they focused primarily on crops that could be shipped to the home country and sold for great profits. Sugar was the first of these, because Europe had acquired an immense sweet tooth, increasing its per capita consumption a hundredfold between 1500 and 1650. Tobacco was a bit slower to develop as an industry, because Europeans adopted the practice of smoking only after contact with American Indians in the 1500s. Nonetheless, it was a growth industry by the early part of the 1600s, especially in Brazil.

Figure 24.4 *Beaver Hats.* *The beaver produced one of the furs most valued by Europeans, especially for hats. After trapping had destroyed the European beaver, the discovery of vast populations of beavers in North America revived the industry. This nineteenth-century engraving shows just a few of the many styles of hats that required beaver fur and fueled the North American fur trade.* Public Archives of Canada, Ottawa/Documentary Art and Photography Division (#C-17338).

FIGURE 24.5 *The Mexican Countryside under Spanish Rule.* This painting from around 1580 shows the fertile region to the south of the Valley of Mexico as it appeared to an unknown artist. The countryside is dotted with Christian churches and rich with village orchards that grew local and European fruits as well as Mexican corn and European wheat. The painting blends both native Mexican and Spanish styles, but the content focuses on the Spanish reshaping of the landscape. University of Texas, Austin. Benson Latin American Collection.

The total effect of these shifts in activities was to transform the settlement pattern of Spanish and Portuguese America. The highly concentrated pockets of colonists that had dominated the sixteenth century gave way to a broader dispersal of colonists. They remained in pockets—ranches, plantations, and missions, as well as the cities—but the pockets were far more numerous and scattered much more widely in the seventeenth century. By 1750, relatively few places in Spanish America were more than a few days' ride from a colonial settlement.

To the Dutch and English colonies, where little mineral wealth was known, the first major wave of colonists came in the 1600s. The colonies of temperate North America were seen as similar to England and Holland, though plagued with severe winters, bellicose natives, and poor soils. Nevertheless, most colonists expected to build a version of the home country there.

Tracts publicized the official colonial agenda, and one of these, written by Richard Eburne in 1624, cited the reasons why a young English man should become a North American colonist. Building the colonies would augment the power of the king of England; it would ease the population pressures felt in England at the time; it would make for lower prices on commodities in England; it would "enrich the poorer sorts hence removed"; it would improve trade; and it would "root out idleness out of this land," a great danger to the way of thinking of English Calvinists (members of a Protestant denomination).

With this in mind, colonists set about reproducing England or Holland in their colonies. The Dutch were not very successful with their North American colonies, largely because they had difficulty convincing residents of Holland that they should leave the richest and most tolerant country in northern Europe. As a result, they lost New Netherlands to the English in 1664, and it became the colony of New York. The English colonists planted their stamp on the land, founding towns and cities with names and layouts borrowed from the home country. In large measure, the English

colonies in North America—by their nature as reproductions of the home country—became economic competitors with England itself.

In the Caribbean, the English successes in buccaneering paid for the expansion of the colonies there, and the English established plantations as a way to reap the economic benefits of tropical colonial holdings. Sugar was the primary plantation crop, but dyes, cocoa, ginger, tobacco, and cotton also were important. The English toehold in Jamaica expanded to include the rest of that island, as well as St. Kitts, Barbados, and various other islands, mostly those abandoned by the fading Spanish presence. The English colonies in the Caribbean were so productive that, by 1700, they accounted for approximately 12 percent of England's imports.

The English and Dutch in Asia were limited largely to trading cities comparable to those of the Spanish and Portuguese in the previous century. The English were most interested in India and the

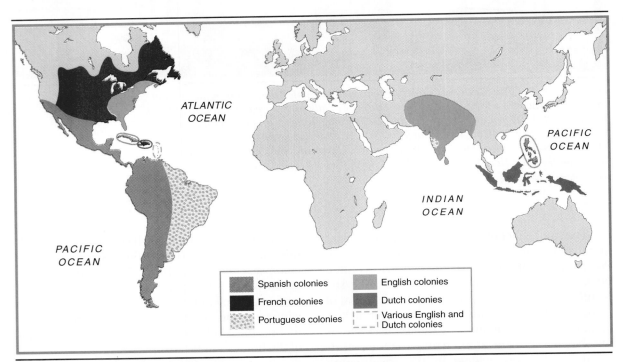

MAP 24.2 *Major Colonial Holdings in 1700.* By 1700, Europe's colonial system had expanded so that most of the Americas and various areas of Africa and Asia were within its control. Compare the size and geographical spread of colonies at this date with those at 1550 (Map 24.1).

Dutch in Indonesia, but neither conquered the local governments in this period. Rather, they carried on trade, which was especially lucrative for the Dutch.

France was not particularly successful as a colonial power but had its greatest successes in eastern Canada and the Caribbean. In eastern Canada, its attempts were driven by two-pronged efforts. First, the French were interested in establishing a trade in furs, the northern equivalent of precious metals. Second, they wished to establish a self-sufficient colony that reproduced France in North America, particularly along the St. Lawrence River. In the Caribbean, their interests were similar to those of the English and Dutch: to establish bases for buccaneers and sugar plantations.

Personal Agendas

Each country in the colonial competition had its own agenda, but the individuals who populated the colonies for them were not always moved by these state interests. Instead, most had personal agendas.

Above all else, colonists were moved by the possibility that opportunities in the new lands would bring them economic betterment. Accordingly, it is not surprising that colonists predominantly were drawn from the ranks of the poor. The first wave of Spanish colonists came primarily from Extremadura,[3] the central province of Spain that had suffered from centuries of environmental degradation. Wood supplies were devastated, soils were depleted and eroding, and travel to a new land was attractive. English colonists usually were the urban poor, lost on the streets of London with few domestic prospects and an urge to leave for the colonies. Prominent among the first wave of French colonists were impoverished petty nobles, able to claim a title but no land or wealth; they saw the colonies as opportunities to reclaim their rightful status in life.

Most of these colonists hoped to make a fortune quickly and return in triumph to their home countries. Many men left wives at home, expecting that their absence would be only for a few years. The exception was the English, who mostly realized that they were embarking on a path that

might lead to economic betterment but was unlikely to result in real wealth. Eburne, in the 1624 tract cited earlier, provides a series of arguments—many based on biblical heroines—that a man could use on his wife to convince her of the wisdom of emigrating to the colonies. Most English colonists realized that moving to the colonies, at least those in North America, meant a permanent relocation.

Another important motive for becoming a colonist was the search for a place where one could practice one's chosen religion freely. By the 1600s, the Protestant Reformation was in full swing (see Chapter 29), and some colonists sought a more tolerant place. This was an important issue in the English colonies of North America, because Calvinists were persecuted in England during the early part of this period. Once in America, the persecuted sometimes became the persecutors, and the Calvinists of the Massachusetts Bay Colony actively attacked Quakers, forcing many to move to Rhode Island. Large numbers of Dutch and Portuguese Jews moved to Brazil, hoping to escape persecution in Europe but finding conditions equally difficult in South America; most moved on to Barbados and eventually to New York.

Still another religious motive was the urge to spread Christianity. This was especially prominent among French, Spanish, and Portuguese colonists, virtually all of whom were Roman Catholic, because Catholicism traditionally has been active in seeking converts. Most colonists with this motivation were clergy, usually priests or monks, and they often showed great zeal in their ministrations. French Jesuit missionaries, such as Isaac Jogues, were eloquent in their desires to be martyred in the cause of Christ. The Catholic Church saw to it that their eloquence was publicized widely in the form of the *Relations*, printed accounts of their trials and successes in North America and elsewhere; the *Relations* served as excellent recruiting materials for the next generation of missionaries.

There was, however, another class of colonists whose emigration was not motivated by such public-spirited concerns. A certain percentage of the colonists were convicts, either sentenced to banishment in the colonies or given the choice of prison at home or freedom in the colonies. Portugal led the way, banishing prisoners to its African territories and Goa (a colony in India) in

[3] **Extremadura:** eks TREH mah DOO ruh

the early 1500s and later to Brazil. By the late 1500s France began sending convicts to the St. Lawrence Valley, and England followed in the 1600s with convicts bound for Jamaica; in the 1700s, more convicts were shipped to English colonies in Georgia and Australia. The overall number of convicts among the colonists is currently unassessed, but it probably was only a small fraction.

The reasons prompting colonists to leave their homelands were diverse and idiosyncratic. A few were escaping unhappy marriages, fleeing in the face of debt, or running from the law; some were patriots who ardently believed that massive emigration was the only solution to their countries' demographic ills; still others were religious adherents bent on finding a place to practice their religion freely or to convince natives of the truth of that religion. The vast majority, however, were calculating opportunists, confident that their chances for economic improvement were better in the colonies than at home.

THE COLONIZING PROCESS

The details differed, but the general pattern of colonizing was much the same in most of the European colonies established before 1750. The earliest toeholds grew into thriving, more balanced entities that began to compete with the home country.

The Earliest Attempts

Like exploration before it, initial colonizing usually was financed by private capital. Governments saw these endeavors as long shots, gambles with low probabilities of success, and they rarely made state money available for them. Instead, private companies typically raised the financial backing to begin a colony.

The English East India Company (established in 1600), the Dutch East India Company (in 1602), and the English West India Company (in 1621)

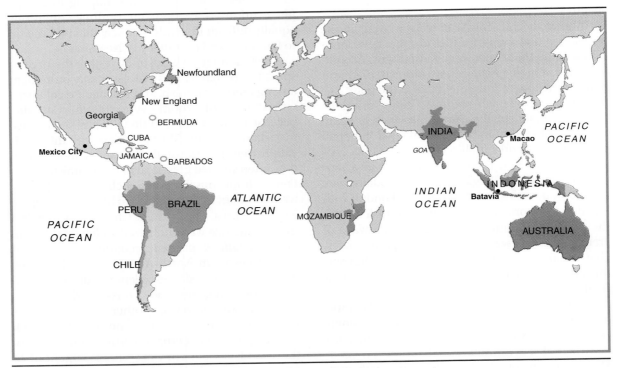

MAP 24.3   *Colonies and Colonial Towns.*   *Most early European colonies and colonial towns were located on the coasts; in the Americas, some inland areas such as Mexico were conquered and colonized relatively quickly. As European expansion progressed, colonies in the interior of continents became more common.*

UNDER THE LENS

The Many Tactics of the Dutch East India Company

The Dutch East India Company, though a private corporation, appropriated for itself many of the rights of a sovereign country. It maintained a military force, conducted diplomatic missions, and presented decrees that it expected to be obeyed. In a sense, this was not surprising, because the directors of the company were the same urban merchants that wielded great influence in Dutch government. The company and the government were but organs of the same interest group.

The military branch was the strong right arm of the Dutch East India Company, particularly in terms of naval power. When it was desirable to blockade Manila and intercept the silver shipment coming to the Philippines from Mexico, it was this branch that did the job. Similarly, when it was necessary to conquer Malacca to open the spice trade of the Malay Peninsula, the military branch undertook and accomplished the task. When the Chinese needed to be taught that they could not infringe on Dutch trading prerogatives, it was the military that sank eighty of their vessels in retribution. The inhabitants of one island famed for its nutmeg plantations were starved out by the Dutch East India Company military, effectively removing a competitor.

The diplomatic skills of the Dutch East India Company were evident in its dealings with local rulers. Through the combination of threatened force and promised reward, company operatives managed to negotiate secure agreements with local Indonesian and Malay rulers for the supply of various spices. Importantly, these agreements usually were exclusive, forbidding any trade with Europeans other than the Dutch. At the same time that they secured a plum for themselves, the Dutch precluded success on the parts of their competitors.

The decrees of the Dutch East India Company supported their trading position and were backed by the naval authority behind the company. After the effective conquest of Ceylon (present-day Sri Lanka), the company set out strict guidelines for the trade of cinnamon, including prices, monopoly (held by the company, of course), and sanctions for disobeying the decree. The rigor with which this and other decrees were enforced is testament to the military and economic might of the company.

Despite its power and successes, the Dutch East India Company was faltering by the early 1700s. Its successes had earned it a sizeable tract of land that it controlled, and this taxed even its resources. Further, errors in judgment, such as abandoning the tea trade to England as inconsequential, weakened the company's position. Finally, the Dutch government took over the duties that formerly had been granted to the Dutch East India Company, ending its period of prominence and power.

were classic examples. (An even earlier English Russia Company was founded in 1583 to handle the fur trade with Russia, but it was eclipsed by these more successful companies.) Each was a private corporation operating under crown charter. To state it differently, the state was able to determine general policy for the companies through the charters, yet the funds hazarded were private, raised by the sale of stock. The first two companies directed trade and colonizing in India and Indonesia for the English and Dutch, while the latter served the same purpose for the English in the Caribbean. All three were wildly successful, posting huge profits and establishing thriving colonial communities.

Their success, however, was their undoing. As the countries under whose charters they operated realized the magnitude of the profits to be made, they decided that the charters should be suspended, permitting the state to control directly the colonizing process. By the early years of the eighteenth century, all three companies had lost their preeminent roles in trade, which by this time was controlled directly by governments.

There were other approaches to colonization. The Spanish, for example, placed the colonizing

FIGURE 24.6 *The Portuguese Colony at Macao.* *The Portuguese secured a favorable trading arrangement with the Chinese and established a permanent colony at Macao, called "Amacao" in this engraving from around 1600. This image shows the mixture of cultural practices common to such colonies. A public cross in the center proclaims the Christianity of the Europeans, while retainers, parasols, and sedan chairs exemplify the status symbols of the local Chinese. Although it is not documented in this view, the Portuguese traders also had a distinct district that was given over for their use.* From Theodor de Bry's *Indiae orientalis* (Frankfurt, 1607). Courtesy of the John Carter Brown Library at Brown University.

process under the control of the crown, letting trade be handled by the Seville Merchants' Guild, operating under royal monopoly; the Portuguese followed a similar practice in Brazil. English colonizing in North America was through various small private companies, usually one per colony and often without royal charter.

The early colonies were largely *entrepôts*,[4] commercial centers that served simultaneously as collection centers for goods to be shipped to the home country and as distribution centers for goods coming from the home country. In places with strong native governments, such as Asia and Africa, colonies remained isolated *entrepôts* well into the eighteenth century or longer; Goa in India, Moçambique in East Africa, Batavia in Indonesia, and Macao in China were isolated European communities surrounded by native settlement.

In conquered places, however, the European *entrepôts* grew to become cities surrounded by

[4] *entrepôts:* ahn treh POHZ

other European settlements. As discussed earlier, the lure of riches drew colonists farther away from the *entrepôts*, leading to the beginnings of the next phase of colonial development.

Settling In

In conquered lands, colonists were not restricted to a limited range of commercial enterprises, and they became involved in a wide range of activities, mostly designed to make money. This economic and settlement expansion brought with it demographic and political consequences.

The earliest European colonies anywhere reflected in their demography the common belief that the colonists would be there only a short while: They were predominantly male. In Mexico City in the 1560s, Spanish men outnumbered Spanish women by a ratio of 10 to 1, and the ratios were higher in less urban places; in Batavia in 1620, there were no more than than five Dutch women; and Barbados had such a shortage of English women in 1653 that there were plans for mass importations of brides from "the lower classes" of London.

The imbalanced sex ratios in most colonies encouraged marriages and liaisons between European men and native women. In most places, such marriages were frowned upon by European colonial society, because natives were considered racially and culturally inferior; as a result, sexual liaisons or clandestine "temporary marriages" (with husbands abandoning their native wives when European women became available) were more common. These liaisons led to a new class of children of racially mixed parentage, called variously *métis*[5] (French), *mestizos*[6] (Spanish), or *mestiços*[7] (Portuguese). These mixed children usually were considered a distinct class, intermediate in status between Europeans and natives.

Different colonies took different approaches to redressing the imbalances in the numbers of European men and women. In Spanish and Portuguese America, a child with mixed parentage could be absorbed into colonial society, providing its appearance was not entirely at odds with this classification. Consequently, some children of

colonists and native women were considered European by community consent, thereby increasing the numbers of women. Elsewhere, there were programs to ship European women to colonies, as to the French Antilles in the mid-1600s. Servant girls were in great demand in the colonies, and many began arriving as the living conditions became less severe. In a few cases, such as that of the Puritan colonies of North America, the ratio of men to women was more or less equal from the start, because married couples were the preferred colonists.

FIGURE 24.7 ***Three Canadian* Métis.** *One of the consequences of the mixing of peoples in the colonial era was the creation of new racial categories. In Canada, a child of mixed Native American and European ancestry was called a* méti. *The word comes from the Old French word for "mongrel" and was originally a term of contempt, though it became an acceptable term of self-identification by the 1700s. This tintype photograph from the 1870s shows three young* méti *men whose facial features and clothing reflect their mixed ancestry.* Provincial Archives of Manitoba.

---

[5] ***métis:*** may TEE
[6] ***mestizos:*** meh STEE sohs
[7] ***mestiços:*** meh STEE sohs

On the political front, colonists were beginning to identify with the emerging colonies. In some cases, such as that of Spanish America, it was clear by 1650 that the colonies held more economic power and perhaps more political power than the home country. While Spain's economy and military might were eroding, despite being buoyed up by massive infusions of wealth from its colonies, the Spanish colonies in the Americas were growing wealthier and stronger. In other cases, the remoteness of the home country made for weaker ties; it took an average of ninety-one days for a ship from Spain to reach Mexico, and nearly two years for the trip to Chile. Individuals whose grandparents were the last of the family to have seen the home country easily could begin viewing the colony as the entity with which they identified most strongly.

Economic realities were encouraging this identification with the colony. While colonial theory held that the colony should import its manufactured goods from the home country, this often was impractical. Many items were in short supply, and residents in the home country were loath to see goods shipped overseas when their needs had not yet been met. Colonists, therefore, often were left to fend for themselves, and local industries sprang up to serve local needs.

As the colonies grew, they developed local governments. Spain imposed the viceroy system in Peru and Mexico, appointing an individual to head the civil and military governments in the place of the king. Many viceroys were inept, and all were hampered by a cumbersome governmental system imported from Spain. The English colonies were ruled by governors appointed by the crown, but they developed various forms of local assemblies to deal with internal issues. As time went by, some of these local assemblies chafed under royal restraints, building tensions between the English monarch and the colonies. These tensions eventually erupted as the American Revolution.

COLONIAL CONFLICT

Many colonies were founded in the wake of military campaigns that destroyed the native governments, and others had ongoing military conflicts between colonial and native forces. The Europeans usually claimed the right to conquer these native societies because of their "sinful ways," reducing conquest to the saving of souls. In addition, the colonies were fields where the rivalries of European powers were played out, sometimes as military actions.

Hostilities between Colonial and Native Powers

Most of the Americas came under European control either directly by conquest or indirectly by the manipulation of societies weakened by disease. The success of European military operations was founded primarily on technology and organization, coupled with the population catastrophe resulting from diseases brought by the conquerors.

MILITARY TECHNOLOGY AND ORGANIZATION. The peoples of the Americas were equipped with military weapons that were inferior to those of the Europeans they opposed. The Aztecs of Mexico, for example, wielded razor-sharp swords made of volcanic glass blades set into the edges of wooden handles; they shot arrows from bows and hurled stones from slings; they wore padded cotton armor. These weapons were pitted against Spanish cannons, muskets, and steel armor. The greater efficacy of the Spanish equipment was in part responsible for the rapid Spanish victory.

The Spanish also introduced a factor previously unknown in American warfare: war animals. The *conquistadores* rode horses, an animal unknown to the Aztec; the popular notion that the Aztecs were amazed and believed the horse and rider to be one is fantasy, but an armored horse bearing down on an Aztec warrior was still a formidable weapon. In addition, the Spanish used mastiffs, large dogs bred and trained to attack the enemy. Protected by leather armor on its sides, a mastiff would be released ahead of foot soldiers, breaking the ranks of the enemy before they could attack. The mastiffs were far more feared than horses, because they could follow a fleeing soldier almost anywhere he could go, running him down and mauling him. Many Aztecs died from wounds inflicted by mastiffs.

Military organization was another advantage of the Europeans in most places where they encountered American Indian military forces. Aztec warfare, for example, was highly regimented and ordered, but its goal was the capture of enemy

FIGURE 24.8 *Araucanian Warrior.* *The Araucanians of Chile, known today as the Mapuche tribe, were among the fiercest resisters of European colonial intrusion into the Americas. Like the Plains Indians of North America, they adopted European weapons and the horse and took advantage of their mobility to conduct hit-and-run raids on sedentary Spanish settlements.* From Felix Best, Historia de las Guerras Argentinas (Buenos Aires: Ediciones Peuser), 1960. Reproduced with permission.

soldiers to use as human sacrifices. As a result, it had evolved in such a way that it favored capturing to killing the enemy. This was effective when battling other Mexicans whose goals were the same, but it put the Aztecs at a great disadvantage against the Spanish. In other parts of the Americas, warfare was small scale and undisciplined by European standards, and Europeans had a tactical advantage there, too.

Finally, Europeans were quick to form alliances with disaffected allies and with enemies of a people they wanted to conquer. The conquest of the Aztecs, for example, was made possible in part by tens of thousands of native troops who were fighting to remove the yoke of Aztec domination from their shoulders. They did not realize, of course, that it would be replaced by a Spanish yoke. Alliance politics was played by both native

and European diplomat-soldiers, but the natives often were unaware of the scope of the European forces that eventually would come to their shores.

THE SUCCESS OF NATIVE RESISTANCE. The conquest of the Americas was neither complete nor immediate, however. While the Aztecs, possessing arguably the most powerful and well organized military in the Americas, were defeated in just two years, the Incas of Peru continued guerrilla warfare for several decades after the Spanish conquered their urban centers. In North America, the Iroquois of New York and Ontario resisted conquest for more than a century, succumbing only in the process of the American Revolution in 1781.

Successful resistance to European military conquest was most likely for nomadic or seminomadic peoples who could use their mobility as a weapon. The Apache of the American Southwest and the Chichimeca of northern Mexico are classic examples, but the Araucanians[8] of southern Chile stand out for their successful resistance. The Araucanians rapidly captured Spanish weapons, particularly the horse, pike, and musket, and learned how to use them effectively. They burned Spanish pastures, destroyed Spanish settlements, and employed Spanish tactics against the colonists. In 1586, Araucanian forces were fighting pitched battles using ranks of pikemen with bowmen among them, precisely in the Spanish manner. While the Araucanians exhausted the Spanish resources, their mobility and lack of permanent camps made it impossible for the Spanish to turn the tables on them. The Araucanians never were conquered, but in the twentieth century they voluntarily merged into modern Chilean society.

Hostilities among Colonial Powers

At the same time that colonial powers were battling native forces, they also were engaging one another in warfare. The rivalries and alliances that were in force in Europe were carried into the colonial holdings. The French and English, at war sporadically during the seventeenth and eighteenth centuries, carried their animosity into the colonies.

For the most part, these conflicts were expressed by arming natives hostile to the enemy power. In northeastern North America, for example, the French and English vied for power from the earliest colonies until 1763, when the French were defeated and forfeited most of their colonial holdings. The English armed the Iroquois, while the French armed the Huron and Algonquians; the Europeans could simply wait for their native allies to use those weapons against their traditional enemies.

Occasionally, however, active warfare broke out. The French and Indian Wars, for example, pitted French and English against one another off and on from 1689 until the eventual defeat of the French in 1763. These wars consisted mostly of frontier attacks on isolated settlements, but occasionally they erupted into full-scale battles. Though they have been given distinct names, such wars really were aspects of broader conflicts that involved Europe and all the colonial theaters.

[8]**Araucanians:** ahr oh KAYN ee uhns

ECONOMICS AND THE COLONIES

As extensions of the home countries, colonies had to solve economic problems if they were to be successful. Central to these problems was the relationship between colony and home country, one that often turned contentious. Labor and regulation of indigenous trade also were important areas of concern.

The Mercantile System

At the heart of the relationship between a colony and its home country was an ideal conception: the **mercantile system**. Defined as a relationship in which the colony provides raw materials for the home country while the home country provides manufactured goods for the colony, the ideal of the mercantile system was shared by all the colonial powers of Europe. To a greater or lesser extent, it was implemented in their actions.

In theory, the mercantile system should keep the home country strong and the colonies dependent. By providing manufactured goods to the colonies, the home country ensures that its own population is well employed, and the profits of manufacturing remain at home. The colonies, in contrast, are valuable primarily because they supply the home country with materials and an expanded market.

An example of how the mercantile system operated is provided by the **triangular trade** that the English set up. Ships left English ports laden with a variety of manufactured goods and arrived at West African ports. There they traded horses, guns, fabrics, and other items for slaves, sold by local slave traders. These slaves were carried to the Caribbean, where they were sold and the profits were used to purchase tropical products, especially sugar, molasses, rum, and indigo dye; the ship also sold iron tools, fabrics, and a wide variety of manufactured goods to the Caribbean colonists. The next stop was New England, where some of the Caribbean products and various manufactured goods from England were sold. The ship purchased furs, wood, salt cod, and other goods from New England, then returned to its English port. Each step of the way, manufactured goods flowed from home country to colony and raw materials flowed in the opposite direction.

Precious metals held a special place in the mercantile system. Because gold and silver were the foundation for all European money of this period, it was important that colonies provide these substances in whatever quantities were possible. In a very real sense, this represented an increase in wealth, resulting particularly in greater buying power in Asia.

The mercantile system was plagued by a major set of problems. To begin with, the home country was not always able to provide finished goods in the quantities needed in the colonies. This was especially true for Spain, whose sagging economic structure was taxed severely just to meet its internal needs, but it was true to a greater or lesser extent everywhere. Accordingly, it became necessary for the colonies to begin manufacturing on their own. Santo Domingo in the Caribbean began a glass industry by 1586; Bermuda began building ships by the 1630s; and Mexico instituted a major textile manufactory by the early 1600s. All of these industries were born of the need to provide for the local populace. Once these industries were begun, however, their owners chafed at the restrictions on entering the wider market, an entry that was opposed by the home country under the mercantile system. This led to resentment by colonists and many inventive ways of selling goods on the black market.

The mercantile system came to be a major point of contention between colonies and their home countries. By the middle and latter parts of the eighteenth century, economic theorists like Adam Smith (1723–1790) were criticizing the mercantile system. Smith argued that greater equality between colony and home country would stimulate the economies of both, increasing production and developing larger markets for both. He argued that this was the true benefit of foreign trade and that mercantilists had confused raw profit with overall benefit to the economic system. Such theories only fueled colonists' resentment of the mercantile system and its restrictions.

Labor

Many of the activities that colonies specialized in were very labor-intensive, demanding a great deal of labor to produce a product. Sugar manufacture, for example, required the field labor of planting, growing, and harvesting sugarcane, followed by the long process of pressing the cane and refining the fluid removed. Tobacco growing, cotton manufacture, mining, and many other colonial activities were equally labor-intensive. Colonial planters and others, accordingly, sought ways to obtain cheap labor to carry on these activities.

One way to obtain cheap labor was through slavery and related forms of servitude. Despite the initial cost of purchasing slaves, there were few ongoing expenses, and a great deal of labor could be extracted from each slave. In lowland parts of Central and South America, in the southeastern portion of North America, and in the Caribbean, slaves were the backbone of the labor force, particularly on plantations. The institution of slavery is discussed in Chapter 26 and Issue 6.

An alternative way to get cheap labor is with a labor requirement for conquered peoples. This alternative was used most extensively in Spanish America. Initially in the Caribbean and later in Mexico, Central America, and Peru, colonists implemented the **encomienda,**[9] the institution whereby Indians were required to provide labor for the Spanish for free. An individual Spaniard would be granted an *encomienda* for service to the crown, and it would state the particulars of the arrangement. It might require, for example, all the adult males of a particular native village to devote one month of labor at the direction of the holder. In essence, it was tribute rendered by the conquered to the conqueror.

Encomiendas obviously were highly desirable for Spanish colonists, because this was labor at absolutely no cost. The *encomienda* replaced slaves in some parts of Spanish America as the labor source of choice, and the *encomienda* was dominant from the early 1500s to around 1650. By the mid-1600s, various conditions developed that made the *encomienda* no longer viable. Many conscripted laborers chose to flee rather than provide the required labor, and some villages threatened revolt. The ongoing increase in the number of colonists and the dwindling number of Indians surviving introduced diseases meant that there simply were not enough Indians alive to serve the needs of the Spanish colonists in some locales.

A third source of labor, wage laborers, replaced the *encomienda* in highland Spanish America and was always dominant in the northern parts of North America—places where there were few plantations. This source of labor, however, was not

[9] *encomienda:* ehn koh mee EHN duh

FIGURE 24.9 **Encomienda** *Mining Practices in Bolivia.* *The mountain of Potosí, shown in the background of this painting, was found by the Spanish in 1545 to contain vast quantities of rich silver-bearing rock. In the foreground is a refinery where the ore was crushed and mercury was used to extract the silver. The* encomienda, *a means of imposing a labor requirement on conquered people, was used to coerce the vast amounts of labor required to mine and refine the ore—such work was both grueling and hazardous.* Hispanic Society of America.

always cheap, because wages depended on local conditions of labor supply and demand. Consequently, it was the least favored alternative for labor-intensive activities, but it increasingly was the necessary resort in the years following 1650.

Adjusting Local Commerce to European Ends

In Asia and Africa, Europeans were resisted more effectively than generally was the case in the Americas, and a different approach had to be taken by colonists there. Because riches and labor could not

simply be seized in Asia and Africa, European colonists tried to fit themselves into existing commercial networks, in the hope of gaining an advantageous position.

Portugal, for example, set its sights on the lucrative spice trade of India in the early 1500s. After a period of experimentation, the Portuguese declared in 1505 that the spice trade henceforth would be a royal monopoly conducted solely by the India House, a specially created royal office. The Ottoman Turks controlled the overland routes, so the Portuguese were forced to develop an oceanic alternative. Using silver obtained from

Brazil, Portugal purchased spices in ports along the Indian Ocean, then transported them by ship around Africa. Other sellers were largely excluded by decree, although a smuggling trade predictably emerged. Nonetheless, this and other monopolies proved a powerful tool for European colonial commerce.

The enormous infusion of American gold and silver pumped into Europe, especially Spain and Portugal, played a critical role in this redirection of trade. (Silver from Japan also played a significant, though less major, role.) Precious metals were more than mere wealth; they were the preferred medium of exchange in trade with Asia, and many Asian traders refused any other mode of payment. Prior to 1500, most of the trade between Asia and Europe had been in the hands of Arabs. They had been able to purchase spices with Iranian silver, sell the spices in Europe for various commodities, then sell those commodities in Iran and elsewhere in order to obtain more silver. After the infusion of precious metals from the Americas, Europeans were in a position for the first time to deal directly with Asian traders. Thus, they redirected major trade flows through their own hands, increasing their profits.

MISSIONS AND MISSIONARIES

Religion was mentioned earlier as a spur to colonization, encouraging some colonists to seek tolerant surroundings and others to try to convert the natives. The latter group, collectively known as missionaries, had a profound impact on some colonies.

In general, Protestants were not very active in attempting to convert natives in their colonies. A few Protestant churches, such as Quakers and Moravians, devoted significant efforts to missionary work, however. In the mid-1600s in New England, for example, Calvinists set up four **praying towns**, communities to which local Indians could come to learn the Calvinist religion, as well as other European skills and ways. The praying towns were very successful at teaching Indians the English language, technical skills (like repairing guns), and some superficial English manners, but the praying towns apparently had limited impact on Indians' religious beliefs.

Catholic approaches to conversion, in contrast, tended to be more energetic. Particularly among the Spanish and Portuguese, it was typical for several priests to set up a **mission**, a complex minimally consisting of a church, dormitories, and farm or ranch facilities. The ideal mission was self-sufficient, using converted Indians for its labor force and selling its surplus for the good of the church. Many missions approached this ideal.

Because Indians were accepted into the church as neophytes (provisional converts), they were considered committed to the mission. They were required to live there indefinitely and to perform their assigned duties. In return, they received religious and secular training, as well as various items of European technology. Leaving the mission, however, was not always permitted, and there are some cases of military-style capture and return of runaways. Alienated from their own society and often attracted to the material advantages of European technology, many neophytes and converts chose to remain at the mission; others seem to have genuinely been attracted to the religious message of the missions.

The successes of the missions in converting huge numbers of Indians in the first decades of colonization were heralded by the church. Thousands upon thousands of baptisms were conducted, and the membership of local parishes swelled. But doubts about the genuineness and persistence of conversion soon arose. In Peru in the 1560s, an end-of-the-world cult appeared among converted Indians, preaching that the diseases and catastrophes endured by the Indians were the revenge of offended ancient Peruvian gods. In eastern Mexico, priests realized that their success in conversion was due largely to the native practice of incorporating new deities into the ancient pantheon: Jesus was considered another god joining the company of older deities, such as Kukulcán[10] and Chac. To this day, Latin American Catholicism retains fragments of native religions within it.

In general, Catholic missions were most successful where they had the support of secular institutions. An isolated mission, many miles from the nearest colonial settlement, was unlikely to have sufficient material incentives to attract neophytes in the first place, and its workload might be so

---

[10] **Kukulcán:** koo kuhl KAHN

PARALLELS AND DIVERGENCES

Conversion by the Cross, the Sword, or the Copper Kettle?

Scholars continue to debate why so many native peoples in European colonies converted to Christianity. Some believe that the message of Christianity, stressing the dignity and potential salvation of the common person, was so appealing that it ensured success. Others argue that the military force that accompanied missionaries was a more compelling force. Still others contend that the material items that were associated with Christianity were the lure that attracted so many.

Certainly there is evidence that some missionaries were willing to use force or fraud to win souls. In the Yucatán Peninsula of eastern Mexico, 4,000 Indians are known to have been tortured into conversion by the military escort of Catholic priests operating there in the mid-1500s. In Portuguese colonies of Asia, orphans regularly were rounded up for mass baptism and subsequently were raised as Christians, despite complaints by local Buddhists. In Goa during the seventeenth century, beef was forcibly smeared on the lips of Hindus; contact with the forbidden meat meant that they were defiled and no longer acceptable to their faith, leaving them to turn to Christianity as the only available alternative. Anecdotes attesting to the willingness of some missionaries to call on force or fraud to coerce conversion are abundant.

But examples that seem to bear witness to the power of Christianity's message also abound. In the mid–sixteenth century, Saint Francis Xavier preached the doctrine of Christianity in the fish market of Cochin[a] in modern India, and children (coming from the despised fishing castes and having much to gain from espousing a religion that offered salvation to all) are said to have converted spontaneously. The Jesuit fathers in New France praised seventeenth-century Iroquois converts who withstood torture by enemies and refused to recant their faith. An Aztec man named Juan Diego[b] received in 1531 a vision of the Virgin María at Tepayacac[c] (present-day Guadalupe); such a vision was viewed by the priests as a sign of great faith.

Finally, many examples document the allure of technology as a major factor in conversion. Neophytes and converts were often given various material items as rewards for their faith, including copper kettles, metal knives, clothing, and guns. Among the most valued, however, were rosaries, sets of glass beads strung together in a loop with a cross attached at one end; these symbolized the sufferings of Christ, served as a memory aid in reciting prayer cycles, and were worn as personal decorations. When an Aztec, Iroquois, or Inca received a rosary, it underscored the authority of the Catholic Church, because only a powerful institution would give such a treasure to a common convert. Many converts clearly were impressed.

Which of these factors was responsible for the success of the Catholic Church in converting, to some degree, most of the Indians in the Americas and small but ardent communities in Asia? The answer probably is all three.

[a] **Cochin:** KOH chihn
[b] **Juan Diego:** WAHN dee AY goh
[c] **Tepayacac:** teh PY uh KAHK

heavy that they were scared off—and with no effective military support, neophytes could abandon the mission at will. Respect and sympathy for the natives seems to have enhanced success, and knowledge of their languages and customs also assisted. In recognition of this, several sixteenth-century Spanish and Portuguese universities established departments of American languages to train missionaries in local languages before they left for the colonies.

THE PERSISTENCE OF NATIVE SOCIETIES

There can be no doubt that the entry of Europeans as colonial powers had massive effects on native societies. Nonetheless, it would be an error to imagine that the European invasion simply wiped out local ways of life. As a simple generalization, the local elite culture was eradicated, while life among the common people sometimes went on little changed. In particular, rural people were more likely to retain their native culture than were their city cousins. Mexico provides a representative example of the changes wrought by European colonialism in the period before 1750.

For the nobility and royalty of the Aztecs, the conquest by the Spanish ended their way of life. Their sumptuous existence with palaces and servants was gone, and the nobles who survived found themselves sharing the lot of the common people. This meant earning a living through labor, losing special privileges, and submitting to the will and power of the new Spanish government. Many elite skills were lost or forgotten; native systems of court music, writing, painting, featherwork (for elaborate royal headdresses), and poetry were replaced with Spanish models. The elite simply merged with the mass of Aztec society.

For common people, however, everyday life often remained remarkably similar to what it had been before the conquest, especially in the countryside, far from Spanish influences. A farmer in a village remote from the capital carried on much as before. The same crops were planted as before, they were shared among family members as before, and a share was passed on as taxes rendered to the government as before. Christianity produced some changes, but many of the ancient native practices continued for decades, even centuries; sometimes a veneer of Christian symbolism was added to make the practices more acceptable to Spanish priests and officials.

For example, weavers continued to produce the folk costume for women and girls, consisting of some form of wraparound skirt and triangular over-the-head blouse (called a *quechquemetl*[11]). Either woven into the blouse or embroidered onto it were a series of animal figures in traditional forms. These figures represented ***nahualli***,[12] spirits of animals that would help protect the wearers from evils, whether disease or accident or spiritual

FIGURE 24.10 *Modern Mexican* Quechquemetl. *Handwoven in the village of San Francisco in Mexico's state of Hidalgo, this garment was designed to be slipped over the head and worn about the shoulders. Based on an ancient pattern and executed in threads colored with bright European dyes, the delicate embroidery depicts various birds and animals representing protective spirits.* Anawalt/Berdan Collection, Museum of Cultural History, University of California, Los Angeles. Collected in 1985.

mishap. The *nahualli*, while rejected and opposed by the Spanish clergy, nonetheless remained a potent part of religious belief for rural Mexicans, as they do in many parts of Mexico today.

No native peoples could escape the disruption of disease and conquest entirely, but it is remarkable how many ancient practices have persisted. These are particularly strong in terms of religion, local government, cuisine, and folk culture. In truth, the ancient native cultures live on in the countryside.

SUMMARY

1. Colonialism developed as a means for Europeans to economically exploit newly discovered lands.

2. Initially, Europeans were confused about the status of peoples in the Americas, Polynesia, and Australia. In 1493 and again in 1537, popes declared them human.

3. Sixteenth-century colonies in the Americas were devoted mostly to procuring precious metals;

[11] ***quechquemetl:*** kehch KAY meht
[12] ***nahualli:*** nah HWAHL lee

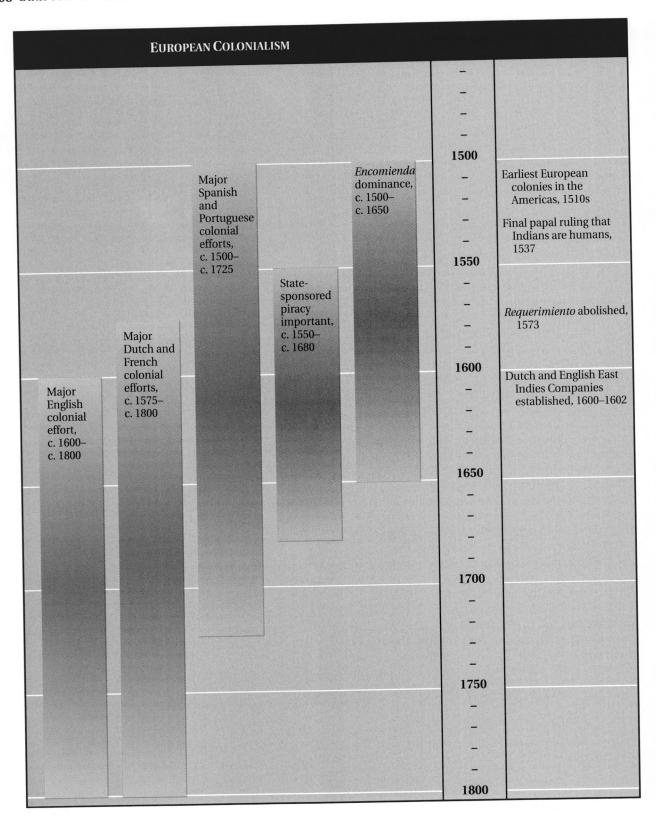

EUROPEAN COLONIALISM

Major English colonial effort, c. 1600– c. 1800

Major Dutch and French colonial efforts, c. 1575– c. 1800

Major Spanish and Portuguese colonial efforts, c. 1500– c. 1725

State-sponsored piracy important, c. 1550– c. 1680

Encomienda dominance, c. 1500– c. 1650

1500
1550
1600
1650
1700
1750
1800

Earliest European colonies in the Americas, 1510s

Final papal ruling that Indians are humans, 1537

Requerimiento abolished, 1573

Dutch and English East Indies Companies established, 1600–1602

exploitation of resources (especially wood, fish, and furs) without settlement also occurred. By the seventeenth century, colonies were more attuned to mining, ranching, and planting as means to wealth.

4. In Asia and Africa, where native peoples were not conquered in this period, European colonies were restricted to *entrepôts*.

5. The English, Dutch, and French were especially interested in reproducing the lifestyles of their home countries in colonies.

6. Individual colonists had varying motives for joining a colony, including personal economic betterment, religious freedom, the opportunity to convert natives to Christianity, and patriotic urges to aid the home country.

7. Initial colonizing usually was funded privately, often by organized companies. When profits were clearly established, control often reverted to the state.

8. Most early colonies had few women, but by 1700 they became more common.

9. By the seventeenth century, many colonists were identifying with their colony more than with the home country.

10. Both native and colonial forces used alliances to further their military ends. The superior military technology and organization of the European powers permitted them to conquer most of the Americas. European rivalries were played out in the colonies.

11. The mercantile system retained colonies in a subordinate position, providing raw materials for the home country, which in turn processed them into manufactured goods to sell in the colonies. This led to colonial resentments.

12. Labor in colonies was primarily provided through slavery, the *encomienda*, and wage labor.

13. In Asia and Africa, European colonies tried to gain wealth by adjusting native commercial arrangements to their benefits. This was made possible, in part, by the massive infusions of precious metals coming from the Americas and lesser amounts from Japan.

14. Roman Catholics were more active and effective in converting natives in their colonies, especially through missions, than were Protestants. The missions aimed for self-sufficiency and used a variety of methods to attract converts.

15. Native culture persisted following European conquests. While elite culture often was eradicated, the folk culture of common people often persisted.

SUGGESTED READINGS

Eburne, Richard. *A Plain Pathway to Plantations.* Ed. Louis B. Wright. Ithaca, N.Y.: Cornell University Press, 1962. A reprint of the original English tract of 1624, promoting colonizing overseas. Also includes insightful modern commentary.

Ethnohistory. Society for American Ethnohistory. This quarterly journal includes many seminal articles dealing with aspects of early colonialism.

Koehn, Nancy F. *The Power of Commerce: Economy and Governance in the First British Empire.* Ithaca, N.Y.: Cornell University Press, 1994. A good recent treatment of the British colonial expansion.

McClintock, Anne. *Imperial Leather: Race, Gender, and Sexuality in the Colonial Conquest.* New York: Routledge, 1995. A feminist interpretation of colonial sexual politics and its impacts.

Pagden, Anthony. *Lords of All the World: Ideologies of Empire in Spain, Britain and France, c. 1500–c. 1800.* New Haven, Conn.: Yale University Press, 1995. A recent comparison of colonialist goals, attitudes, and strategies.

Parry, J. H. *Trade and Dominion: The European Overseas Empires in the Eighteenth Century.* New York: Praeger Publishers, 1961. The classic treatment of early colonialism, reflecting the ideas of the mid–twentieth century but still largely current. Its coverage extends later than that of this chapter.

Scammell, G. V. *The First Imperial Ages: European Overseas Expansion, c. 1400–1715.* London: Unwin Hyman, 1989. An excellent overall treatment of early colonialism, emphasizing the economic basis.

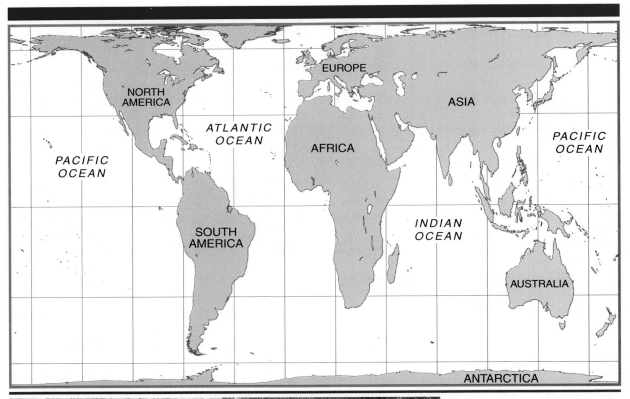

Columbus Exhibits West Indians. *Columbus captured several inhabitants of the Caribbean Islands on his first voyage to the New World and brought them back to Spain to show his patrons, the royal house of Spain.*
Mary Evans Picture Library.

The American Exchange
1492–around 1750

When members of an African family in Ghana settle down to a meal of *fetri detsi*, a sauced chicken and vegetable dish, they may know that the okra in the sauce was domesticated in Africa and that the onions have been in use there since antiquity. But they are less likely to realize that the tomatoes and chilis in the dish came from America in just the past few centuries. Similarly, when tribal Yanamamö Indians of South America's Amazon rain forest have a periodic feast focusing on banana soup, they probably are unaware that bananas came to the Americas from the Old World. The European voyages of discovery opened a door between two worlds, and a variety of things previously isolated in one hemisphere passed between the Americas and the Old World in both directions. This process is known as the **American exchange**.

There had been many other exchanges in human history. Hellenistic Greece and the Roman Empire facilitated the movement of ideas and items in the Mediterranean basin and beyond. The Mongol conquests of Central Asia and adjacent Europe opened a corridor between East Asia and Europe, fostering the Mongol exchange. The establishment of a more or less uniform Islamic culture over a vast area led to trade and travel that carried items and ideas via the Islamic exchange. These and other exchanges, however, were different in the sense that they intensified interaction that already was occurring. In contrast, the American exchange initiated contact and exchange where none had existed before.

THE BREAKING OF AMERICAN ISOLATION

Viewed in broad perspective, most of the world's land lies in two masses: Africa-Europe-Asia and the Americas. Except in the inhospitable climate of the Arctic, these masses are segregated by the great expanses of open ocean. Prior to the voyages of exploration discussed in the previous chapter, contact between these great land masses was, at best, very limited.

History, legend, and folklore are full of heroes who departed on voyages over the sea, never to return. Prince Madoc of Wales, Rata-Wai[1] of Libya, Leif Ericson of the Vikings, anonymous Phoenicians, and many others have had their champions as early seafarers who accidentally discovered the Americas. Some of these figures probably never existed outside legend, and most of the others almost certainly were lost at sea, but it remains possible that several of them may have survived to wash up on American shores. But, with a single exception, there is no compelling evidence for American landings before Columbus's.

The Vikings (Norse) of Scandinavia, however, had vessels capable of oceanic voyages by the eighth century, and their settlements in Iceland and Greenland have been studied extensively by archaeologists. The *Greenland Saga* and *Erik's Saga* were composed around 1000 and were maintained as oral accounts until they finally were written down two or three centuries later. Scholars generally accept that they were maintained carefully, because the penalty for misremembering, at least nominally, was death. The sagas describe an expedition led by Leif Ericson to what must have been America. According to the sagas, Ericson and a small group of colonists set out from Norse settlements in Greenland, sailing westward. They ultimately came to a place they called "Vinland," where they settled for three years before returning to Greenland. The dates for their expedition usually are calculated as 1002 to 1004.

The Vinland tale long has fascinated scholars, and many sites for Vinland have been suggested, chiefly in New England. Misinterpreting *vin-* as meaning grape or wine encouraged this error,

because grapes do not grow north of New England on the Atlantic coast of North America. In medieval Norse, however, *vin-* meant either berry, in general, or meadow. Using this translation, placing Vinland farther north makes sense.

In 1960, a team of Norwegian archaeologists and historians systematically explored the coast of eastern Canada, searching for a place that fit the description of Vinland. To fit the description, the place needed to have a good (though small) harbor, plenty of grassy meadows overlooking it, remains of several longhouses of the sort built by the Norse in that period, and evidence of a furnace for smelting and working iron, mined as ore from an adjacent bog. At a village in Newfoundland called L'Anse aux Meadows[2] they found just such a place, and eight summers of archaeological excavation revealed abundant evidence of an ancient Norse village.

The site produced remains of at least nine houses, a furnace for iron working, Norse-style boat sheds, domestic pigs, and abundant Norse artifacts, including iron rivets, spindle whorls (for spinning wool thread), and bronze ring-headed pins (for clasping cloaks). These items are indisputably Norse from around 1000; architectural styles and radiocarbon dating support that date. The site appears to have been occupied only for a short period, probably a few years, and all evidence suggests that this either was Vinland or another, unrecorded settlement much like it.

Why was Vinland abandoned? While it offered abundant fuel (peat from the bogs) and pasturage, it was very short on wood and other essentials of the Norse way of life. Further, the Norse had established terrible relations with the local people, whom they called **skraelings**,[3] meaning "the impoverished ones," because they had no iron tools, woven cloth, or other items of technology considered essential by the Norse. Modern scholars have identified the *skraelings* as the Inuit[4] (Eskimo). After murdering curious *skraeling* visitors, the Norse Vinlanders were harassed constantly by the *skraelings*, who would use spears to pick off Vikings whenever possible. Far from home, short on essentials, and beleaguered by

---

[1] **Rata-Wai:** RAH tuh WY

[2] **L'Anse aux Meadows:** LAHNS ee MEH dohz
[3] *skraelings:* SKRAY lihngz
[4] **Inuit:** IHN oo iht

FIGURE 25.1 *Norse Settlement in North America.* *The archaeological site of L'Anse aux Meadows in Newfoundland is probably the remains of Leif Ericson's Vinland. The grassy hummocks of this picture are what have survived of the longhouses occupied by Norse Vikings around* A.D. *1000. Abundant artifacts of Norse technology and style demonstrate that this was a Viking settlement, though the long-term effects on local Native American culture were minimal.* Parks Canada/Department of Canadian Heritage.

the natives, the Vikings found it best to return to Greenland.

The identification of L'Anse aux Meadows with Vinland is important for two reasons. First, it documents that the Norse did found a colony on the North American mainland. Second, it shows that it had almost no impact on the local people. The only cultural change brought about by Norse settlement among the Inuit of Greenland and Vinland seems to be that Inuit children began playing with toy tops that probably derived from the Norse spindle whorls. Otherwise, Inuit history and culture simply ignored the temporary intruders. To have profound effects, a colony must last longer and have greater interaction between peoples than at Vinland.

The colonies and explorations that followed the voyages of Columbus and others provided longer, more intensive contact between the intruders and the indigenous peoples, setting the backdrop for the American exchange.

THE CIRCUMSTANCES OF THE AMERICAN EXCHANGE

From the moment Columbus set foot in the Americas, the American exchange was underway. Some of the exchanges were accidental, but many were purposeful, and the circumstances of exchange had strong effects on its outcome.

First, the intensity of interaction between Europeans and Americans was an important factor in determining the degree of exchange between these peoples. Few Europeans entered some parts of the Americas, notably deserts, rain forests, and arctic regions. These areas were perceived as having few attractions, and the environments were sufficiently unhealthy or dangerous to incline Europeans to avoid them. In addition, native populations in these areas usually were dispersed and thin, making it unlikely that any Europeans there would encounter large numbers of inhabitants.

In contrast, an area endowed with rich resources and dense populations was attractive to Europeans. Wealth could be acquired in such a place, and the inhabitants there could be called upon as a labor force, as a source of information, or as an emergency support force if one needed food, shelter, or medical treatment. Central Mexico, the site of the Aztec capital, for example, was particularly attractive to the Spanish and received their early and intense attention; it also became a major theater for the American exchange.

A second factor is the purposes that spurred the European intrusion into an area. Missionaries, by definition, were agents of the American exchange, because their avowed purpose was to replace Native American religion with Christianity. In addition, many missionaries worked under the principle that Christianity could flourish only if Indians adopted "civilized" lifestyles, which to them meant European lifestyles. To greater or lesser extents, ranches, plantations, mining camps, and other European facilities also encouraged American Indians to adopt European ways. Sometimes the managers actively tried to persuade Indians to adopt European habits to facilitate the activities being carried out, as when learning the Europeans' language made communication more effective. Other times, seductive technology or styles that were perceived as sophisticated and prestigious were sufficient to entice Indians to adopt these elements of European culture.

Some Europeans actively discouraged Indians from adopting a European lifestyle. Notable here were the French fur traders in Canada, whose livelihood was anchored in a relatively intact native culture. For them to be successful, they required Indian trappers who traveled widely in their trapping expeditions and were willing to sell their furs for inexpensive European items. As many Indians began settling down near French forts, settlements, and missions in the seventeenth and eighteenth centuries, they stopped trapping, leading the traders to bemoan their own bad fortune.

The discussion thus far has focused on European traits that passed to the Americas, but the purposes of Europeans affected the flow in the opposite direction, too. Exploring expeditions, for example, often were sent out with a broad mandate to bring back information about a wide range of topics in the lands they would traverse. An explorer usually was alert to find new crops, medicines, mineral sources, and curiosities. Information on these might be presented to the public in a book recounting the expedition's adventures, and examples of items often were collected to be sent back to a sponsor in Europe. Such exploring parties were instrumental in transmitting ideas and items from the Americas to the home countries.

Third and finally, the degree of subjugation to Europeans had a profound impact on the degree of activity in the American exchange. The defeat of the Aztecs led to their status as a conquered people under the Spanish, so the only route to wealth, prestige, or power open to a Mexican native would have been through a Spanish lifestyle. Clothing, speech, housing, religion, and other aspects of culture had to meet Spanish standards if an individual were to partake of opportunities for personal advancement. Further, the thoroughness of the conquest ensured that large numbers of Spanish were living side by side with the descendants of the Aztecs, producing a fertile environment for the transmission of ideas and items in both directions.

The differing circumstances of contact were critical factors in the shape of the American exchange, affecting the items that were exchanged, the degree to which they were accepted, and the speed with which exchange took place. Among the most significant items to be transmitted from one hemisphere to the other were germs, plants and animals, technology, and ideas.

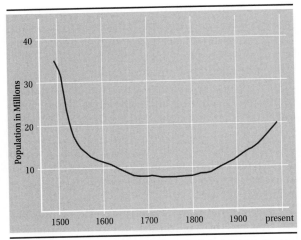

FIGURE 25.2 *Estimated Native American Population in the Americas.* *While such estimates are fraught with difficulties, an overall pattern of massive decline followed by slow rebound is evident.*

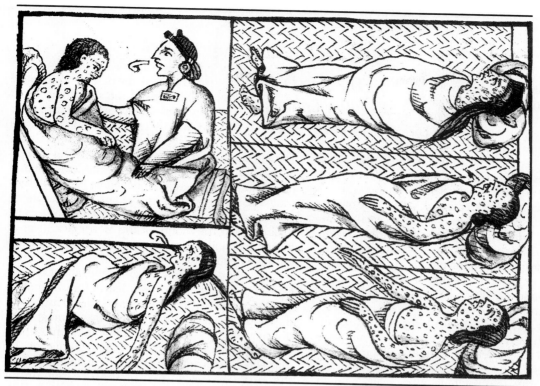

FIGURE 25.3 *Aztecs and Smallpox.* *Like other Native American peoples, the Aztecs had little natural immunity to the smallpox that Europeans unwittingly brought with them to the Americas. These illustrations by Aztec artists show victims' bodies covered in pustules and, ultimately, debilitated by the disease; the right central figure is probably deceased. The curved figures that extend from the mouths of the individuals at the left are speech scrolls, indicating that the person is speaking or (as in the bottom left image) groaning.*
Biblioteca Medicea Laurenziana.

DISEASES

Although few people realized it at the time, the first and most significant exchange between the Old World and the New World was disease. Because of an unlucky genetic history, Native Americans were particularly susceptible to Old World diseases.

People in these two hemispheres had lived in virtual isolation from each other for tens of thousands of years, and during that time they had developed slightly different genetic makeups. Some genes determine how many antibodies will be produced by the body to resist particular diseases. The Old World had been plagued by various epidemic diseases, probably since around 4000 B.C., including such killers as smallpox and influenza. In the earliest years of exposure, Old World peoples must have suffered devastating losses as those individuals lacking genes for disease resistance died. Over time, however, the mortality from diseases fell off, because an ever-increasing percentage of the survivors had genes for the production of antibodies to combat the diseases; the most susceptible to diseases had been weeded out before they were old enough to pass on their genes to their children. By the sixteenth century, the Europeans and others crossing to the Americas mostly had some level of resistance to the major deadly diseases of their era; many Europeans could be exposed to a major disease without contracting it, and still others who contracted the disease could survive it.

In contrast, Native Americans in the sixteenth century were at the same genetic point as their cousins in the Old World had been nearly six millennia before. Some had genes for combatting

UNDER THE LENS

The Merrimack Valley Epidemic, 1616–1617

The Merrimack River originates in the mountains of New Hampshire and runs through northeastern Massachusetts to the Atlantic coast. It is the third-largest river in New England, and many Indians lived along its banks in the early seventeenth century. During a few short months in the winter of 1616–1617, they were ravaged by a massive and destructive epidemic.

The Indians of the Merrimack Valley were of several tribes, loosely united into an alliance called the Pennacook Confederacy. Historical records cite the Pennacook as having around 3,000 adult males, and adult males averaged around one-fourth of New England Indian populations, leading to the standard estimate of around 12,000 persons for the Pennacook population in 1600.

In the winter of 1616–1617, three years before the establishment of the first permanent European colony in Massachusetts, a dreadful epidemic overtook the Pennacook. Descriptions recorded fifteen years later say that Indians were overwhelmed rapidly, sometimes as they walked between houses in their villages. Dizziness, high fever, and chills were the primary symptoms, and death often followed within a day or two. The first to be affected usually were the young men, but shortly after one person was afflicted, the entire village would succumb. Often the few who were well were insufficient to care for the many who were ill.

Writers of the era usually called the epidemic "the plague," but that term referred generally to any epidemic. Diagnosis nearly four centuries later on the basis of incomplete descriptions of the symptoms is not very satisfactory, but modern scholars mostly have concluded that the disease was some form of influenza. The infection of young men first was typical for epidemics in northeastern North America, because these individuals were the ones most likely to travel extensively and contact Europeans, thus becoming exposed to germs. Coastal traders from Europe came to shore near the mouth of the Merrimack River at this period, and the young men probably were trading goods—and germs—with them.

As a direct result of the epidemic, about 80 percent of the Pennacook died, leaving an estimated 2,500 survivors. This number was depleted further by the food shortages resulting from this demographic disaster that took such a heavy toll on the most productive segment of the Pennacook. Twelve of the fourteen Pennacook villages were abandoned, and the survivors regrouped in the two remaining villages.

While the most devastating, the epidemic of 1616–1617 was only one of three major epidemics that shook coastal New England before a European ever built a house there. Before a single act of hostility occurred, the Pennacook population was reduced to one-fifth its pre-Columbian level. The combined effects of disease, warfare, and cultural dislocation reduced the Pennacook to about 250 persons by 1675, and they ceased to exist by 1725.

---

smallpox and other diseases they had never encountered, but the vast majority had little or no resistance to these new diseases. As a result, Native Americans were genetically vulnerable to most Old World diseases when they were introduced to the Americas by the American exchange. Consequently, death tolls were appallingly high.

Europeans and Africans brought a remarkable array of deadly diseases with them to the Americas. Smallpox, influenza, cholera, yellow fever, bubonic plague, pneumonic plague, diphtheria, typhoid fever, measles, whooping cough, malaria, and many more Old World diseases all found their way across the Atlantic in the earliest crossings, and they found human populations biologically unprepared for them. All of these were serious diseases for Europeans, Africans, and Asians, given the state of medical knowledge of the day, but they were far more serious in American Indian communities, where 50 to 100 percent death rates were common upon first exposure to these killers. On the coasts, these diseases often came to be associated with the Europeans, but the diseases spread inland faster than the European invasion. Many of the people who died of disease in the first few decades of contact never saw a European.

Columbus's landfall on Guanahani (called San Salvador by the Spanish) provides a classic example of the insidious manner in which these diseases operated. Columbus noted no medical problems among the inhabitants of the island during his initial stay, but the next time Guanahani was contacted, it was devoid of people. Presumably all died of some disease that no one suspected was being transmitted, although a few may have survived and moved to other islands as refugees. A reasonable estimate of total population of the Americas in 1492 is 35 million, and probably 20 million people died of disease in the first half century of contact with the Old World.

The Americas had some diseases before Columbus. Aztec codices recorded epidemics, and Moche[5] art in Peru depicted individuals with erosive damage to their faces, probably the result of an insect-borne fungal disease. Analysis of skeletons and mummies shows that tuberculosis, pneumonia, hookworm, and amoebic dysentery plagued pre-Columbian Americans, just as they did Europeans, Asians, and Africans. But while the pre-Columbian Americas hardly were the disease-free paradise once envisioned by historians, they clearly had far fewer serious diseases than the Old World.

The reason pre-Columbian Americans were so fortunate lies in the nature of **disease reservoirs**, populations of animals that can contract human diseases, harboring the germs that cause them. Except in cities, human population concentrations were insufficient to harbor enough germs to keep most diseases from dying out; instead, the germs were harbored in animals in the Old World. Names of some diseases reflect this host relationship: swine flu, Asian duck flu, and cowpox (the milder form of smallpox). Other diseases also are well known for their animal carriers, as with anthrax and sheep. While the Old World had many of these disease reservoirs, few American animals were susceptible to human diseases, and epidemic diseases (if ever present) simply died out before they could become established. Even in cases where a New World animal could host a germ that attacked human beings, the scarcity of domesticated animals meant that that germ was unlikely to be in daily, intimate contact with human beings.

[5] **Moche:** MOH chay

There is a possible exception to the generalization that few dangerous diseases afflicted pre-Columbian Americans. Venereal syphilis is widely considered an American disease, though the evidence is not conclusive. Clearly, there were no major outbreaks of diseases that unquestionably were syphilis in Europe prior to 1500, and no skeletons with unequivocal syphilitic lesions have been recognized in Europe prior to that date. In contrast, many pre-Columbian American skeletons bear lesions that appear to be the result of syphilis. Further, the rapid spread of syphilis in Europe around 1500 and the very high mortality rates associated with it are suggestive of a new disease for which Europeans had little biological immunity.

FIGURE 25.4 *Pre-Columbian Pottery Depicting Leishmaniasis. While the Americas before 1492 had relatively few deadly diseases, they were not completely free of destructive illnesses. This pot from the Moche Valley of Peru dates to around A.D. 550 and shows an individual with a curiously depressed face. This person probably suffered from leishmaniasis, an insect-borne American disease that produces decomposition of the nose, palate, and lips.* Countway Library, Harvard. Courtesy of John W. Verano, Tulane University.

The American exchange was unequal in terms of the transmission of diseases and their impact. The Old World acquired only a single major disease, one that could be contracted only through sexual contact; Europeans recognized the venereal character of syphilis by 1498, so it was avoidable. In contrast, the Americas received a host of virulent, highly infectious, fatal diseases that could be transmitted through the air. Although there are very few known cases of intentional infection of American Indians with diseases, rampant epidemics were a powerful ally in the European conquest of the Americas. As P. M. Ashburn so eloquently wrote:

> Smallpox was the captain of the men of death in that war, typhus fever the first lieutenant, and measles the second lieutenant. More terrible than the conquistadores on horseback, more deadly than sword and gunpowder, they made the conquest.

PLANTS AND ANIMALS

While many plants and animals were common to both hemispheres, many also were unique to either the Old World or the New World. This is understandable, given that the Afro-Euro-Asian and American land masses had been separated for about 35 million years, after continental drift tore them apart and propelled them away from each other, opening up a depression between them into which water flowed to form an ocean. During the eons intervening between this geological event and the American exchange, there was plenty of opportunity for evolution to produce unique species on each side of the ocean.

In addition, people in each hemisphere had been domesticating plants and animals for thousands of years. The domestication process involves selective breeding, resulting ultimately in a new form with a different genetic composition from

FIGURE 25.5 *Making Indigo Dye.* *Native to India, the indigo plant was transported to and grown in European colonies in tropical America to cut the cost of the dye, which was used extensively for coloring cloth. In this eighteenth-century image, slaves tote bales of indigo leaves to a processing station for the extraction of blue dye.* Courtesy of the Charleston Library Society.

FIGURE 25.6 *Potatoes Being Fed to the Poor of Seville.* *In some parts of Europe, the virtues of potatoes were largely unrecognized for centuries after they were introduced from South America. This 1645 painting by Murillo shows poor Spanish children being fed potatoes. In Spain, potatoes were often considered a coarse food that was acceptable for the lower class, but one that would upset the more refined nature of the upper class.* Accademia de San Fernando/MAS Barcelona.

that of its wild ancestors. Domesticated species are very important in the American exchange, because these were plants and animals that already had proven their usefulness to people and had been modified to better serve human needs.

Foodstuffs

Some of the most important plants and animals that passed between the hemispheres were new foods. For most farmers in Indonesia, Poland, or Ghana, discoveries of new lands in the Americas or seizures of gold for Spanish coffers were abstract and distant, but a new food to plant was an exciting and immediate prospect. Unfortunately for scholars, most of the incorporation of American foods into Old World agriculture was done by poor, often illiterate farmers, and records of dates or circumstances of adoption often are scanty.

STARCHY STAPLES FROM THE AMERICAS TO THE OLD WORLD. Starchy crops typically form the bulk of any diet based on agriculture, and two important starchy crops came to the Old World in the American exchange: potatoes and corn. In order to entice a farmer to adopt it, a new crop had to provide significant advantages over its competitors, especially competitors that already were part of the agricultural routine. Many of the new American crops offered just such advantages.

Potatoes were developed in Peru but rapidly spread to the Old World, particularly Europe. As early as 1536, Spanish ships leaving Peru stocked potatoes as a cheap food for sailors, and some of these potatoes made their way to Spain. The earliest Europeans to grow potatoes appear to have been the Basques of north coastal Spain, around 1590; by 1650 potatoes had reached Ireland; by the early 1700s they were in Germany; by 1760 they were in Poland; and by 1790 they had reached Russia.

The attractions of potatoes were three. First, they could produce more food per acre than competing crops. In the northern European plain, where rye grain was the only starchy crop that could be counted upon to mature in the short growing seasons, potatoes yielded almost four times the amount of food per acre as did rye. Further, potatoes could grow on rye fields being left uncultivated to rejuvenate the soil, producing a crop where none was possible before, yet not depleting the soil. In the highlands of western China and Tibet, potatoes also became important in small-scale plots where other crops were ill suited.

Second, unlike any Old World starchy crop, potatoes offered such balanced nutrition that they could be eaten to the exclusion of all other foods with only minimal deterioration of health. They also were reputed to increase one's sexual potency, a not inconsequential incentive.

Finally, grain had to be harvested when ripe and kept in a barn, where it was a convenient target for plundering soldiers during the many European wars of the eighteenth century. In contrast, potatoes could be left in the ground all winter and dug as needed—no plundering soldier was going to take the time or effort to dig potatoes. In effect, potatoes were plunder-proof, protecting a farmer's harvest. This last reason almost certainly was the most important in initially encouraging the growing of potatoes in northern Europe.

These advantages spurred the widespread adoption of potatoes, and in much of northern Europe they were sometimes cultivated to the exclusion of other crops that previously had been dominant. Unfortunately, potatoes have a serious drawback that was to devastate Ireland during the potato famine that began in 1846 and ended in 1851. Unlike dependence on grains, successful dependence on potatoes requires that there never be a year so disastrous that there is no crop to harvest; potatoes can be stored only a single year, lest they sprout and rot. Consequently, long-term storage to cope with such an emergency is precluded. When a fungus arrived from America and caused the notorious blight and subsequent famine in Ireland, there were insufficient stockpiles of food to fend off starvation.

Corn was the other major American staple crop to transform parts of the Old World. Like potatoes, it could produce more food per acre than its competitors, but it had two important drawbacks. First, it lacked certain amino acids and vitamins critical for health, and an exclusive diet of corn would lead to **pellagra**, a deficiency disease resulting from a lack of niacin, a B vitamin. This meant that corn never was used to the exclusion of other starchy staple crops, avoiding the danger of a disaster like the Irish potato blight. Second, corn requires more water than wheat, so it was adopted as an alternative to wheat primarily in areas where there was abundant rainfall, areas like northern Italy and West Africa.

The spread of corn in the Old World is documented less well than that of potatoes, but it appears that corn appeared first in Spain, to which it was carried by Columbus. By 1650, it had made its way to Venice and the western parts of the Ottoman Empire. Corn made great inroads in the mountain valleys of the Balkans, and it was the fuel that sustained late-nineteenth-century Greek and Serbian independence movements centered on mountain strongholds.

Potatoes and corn benefited all those areas that adopted them, but particularly Europe and China, because their environments were most favorable for their cultivation. Populations increased with the introduction of these crops, sometimes quite markedly, as in Ireland. These burgeoning populations provided the colonists who would consolidate the European colonial conquests, particularly in the Americas. Ironically, corn and other American crops in West Africa led to increased populations, allowing the slave trade to continue longer than otherwise would have been possible, further fueling the development of the American colonies.

OTHER FOODSTUFFS. Many other foodstuffs from the Americas were transported and adopted around the world. Indeed, it is hard to imagine many of the world's cuisines without ingredients from the Americas. Thai food without its searing chilis, southern Italian food without tomatoes and zucchini, West African dishes without peanuts, village Chinese cuisine without sweet potatoes—these are practically unthinkable.

Most of these foodstuffs were important for their taste contributions rather than for their caloric value. Some, like tomatoes, made important contributions of vitamins and minerals to peasant diets otherwise short on these nutrients. Others, like chilis, became important in terms of folk medicine.

In the Americas, too, various foods from across the ocean became standard parts of the cuisine. Wheat flour tortillas in northern Mexico, olives in eastern Mexico, chickpeas in Cuba, palm oil in

Brazil, beef in Argentina, and apples in Costa Rica—all these are Old World foods that have become part of New World cuisines.

OLD WORLD FOODSTUFFS COMING TO THE AMERICAS AS THE BASIS OF LABOR. Because many of the colonial powers in the Americas saw themselves as extensions of the home country, it is not amazing that important foodstuffs were transferred from there to the colonies. By 1650, well-to-do colonists in cities throughout the American colonies could duplicate most dishes to be had in their home countries. By that date, for example, cooks in Boston could obtain apples, pears, plums, cherries, quinces, spinach, garlic, chives, cucumbers, leeks, watercress, lettuce, endive, peas, carrots, turnips, beets, onions, cabbages, and various garden herbs, all European transplants to local gardens and orchards. Still more ingredients were available as imports from England or the Caribbean.

Some foodstuffs, however, were transferred from the Old World to the Americas for reasons other than the satisfaction of European palates far from home. Wheat, bananas, cattle, and especially sugarcane (whose value was spurred by the growing appetite for sugar in Europe) all were to be the basis of plantations and ranches, many of which ran on African and Native American slave labor. Sugarcane and bananas, both tropical crops that require abundant heat and moisture, became the staples of plantations in the Caribbean, Central America, and eastern South America. Wheat and cattle could tolerate less moisture and cooler climates, so ranches and farms at higher elevations and in more temperate climates focused primarily on them. The vast lands of the Americas, once sufficient labor was found to develop them, were the grounds for the making of fortunes.

DRUGS AND STIMULANTS. Although drugs usually are not conceived of as foodstuffs, the line between the two categories is blurry. Many important foods and beverages have some effect on the mind or body, and this could cause them to be classed as drugs. Drugs and related substances were used in both the Old and New worlds before Columbus and became objects of the American exchange.

Tobacco is a plant native to America, and there were several types at the time of Columbus's voyage. Domesticated forms were grown in northern South America (where it probably was first domesticated), Central America, Mexico, and southern parts of North America; wild forms grew almost everywhere. The wild forms usually produced a more marked psychoactive effect.

Tobacco was almost always used ceremonially among Native Americans. It most commonly was

FIGURE 25.7 *English Tobacco Smoking.* *This illustration from a 1641 London broadside shows two young dandies engaging in that new practice from the Americas, smoking tobacco. The broadside author considered this behavior socially and morally degrading, calling smokers "children of spirituall fornication." Nonetheless, the habit spread throughout England and other European countries during the seventeenth and later centuries.* The New York Public Library, Arents Tobacco Collection.

smoked, either as cigars (Caribbean and adjacent areas) or in pipes (everywhere else), particularly during religious rituals and at the sealing of inter-tribal agreements; sometimes it was smoked at a greeting ritual for visitors. In South America, it also was used as snuff and as a component of enemas, both of which were part of religious rituals.

Europeans, particularly the English, encountered tobacco through greeting rituals, which were prominent among the tribes of eastern North America. The tobaccos were strong, much stronger than those in use today, and the English seemed attracted to the euphoria and other psychological effects produced. By the late sixteenth century, pipe smoking was becoming popular among the English elite, and the elite of other European countries followed shortly. The technology of tobacco use by Europeans was adopted from Americans, but its purpose was radically different: The ritual use in America was replaced with recreational use in Europe.

Alcoholic beverages were known in the Americas, though they were rare. The Iroquois of north-eastern North America made a light mead from maple sap; the O'odham[6] of the American South-west fermented a wine from the juice of cactus fruit; the Aztecs made a wine from a cactus rela-tive; and various peoples in South America made beers from corn and other starchy plants. With the exceptions of a few places in South America and Mexico, however, alcohol consumption was highly seasonal; wherever alcohol was drunk in the pre-Columbian Americas, its use was limited and highly regulated by ritual.

Europeans, in contrast, were very heavy con-sumers of alcohol. By the thirteenth century, they had mastered the technique of distillation, trans-forming wine or beer with low alcohol content into liquor with high alcohol content. They brought liquors with them to the Americas.

The introduction of liquors through the Amer-ican exchange was disastrous for American Indi-ans. Most had little or no experience with alcohol, and the few that had any experience had never encountered the potency of liquors. Without any traditional cultural rules to regulate the recre-ational use of liquor, American Indians usually learned its use from traders, who provided it free in order to secure more favorable terms in their

[6]**O'odham:** OH oh dahm

transactions; needless to say, the traders encour-aged overindulgence. Liquor became the scourge of many Indian communities, often leading to vio-lence or mishap, a problem that remains wide-spread even today.

Coca is a leafy shrub that grows high in the Andes Mountains of South America. When its leaves are mixed with powdered lime, it releases an alkaloid that induces increased stamina, a feeling of well-being, and a distorted sense of time; it also is highly addictive. The exploitative potential of this combination was recognized by the Incas, the last Andean society before the Spanish conquest, and they used it to keep miners working for long hours of arduous labor. Because miners usually could not acquire coca through any other source, they were compelled to continue working in the government-operated mines. The conquering Spanish immediately recognized the power of this substance to control miners and continued sup-plying it.

Coca in its raw form never became popular among Europeans. Once it was refined and con-centrated into a powerful narcotic, cocaine, in the 1870s, however, it became a popular drug in Europe and North America in the latter part of the nineteenth century. For several years it was believed to have only beneficial effects, particu-larly for the eyes. (This is why Sir Arthur Conan Doyle described Sherlock Holmes as a cocaine user and why, for a brief while, it was a component of Coca-Cola.) By the early years of the twentieth century, however, its role in heart attacks, strokes, schizophrenia, and brain damage was becoming recognized, and it no longer was considered benign.

The health dangers of tobacco, alcohol, and coca generally were not recognized in the early years of their adoption through the American exchange. Their perceived virtues, however, were readily appreciated by receiving peoples, and these substances have been incorporated into their cultures in varying degrees.

The Horse

The horse was imported to the Americas as the animal of choice for transportation, and herds of horses were brought to the Americas as early as the 1520s, particularly by the Spanish. Invariably, horses strayed, finding conditions to their liking

IN THEIR OWN WORDS

A Canadian Trading Frolic

In 1791, John Long published an account of his lengthy service as a fur trader in eastern Canada. Between 1768 and 1786, he had traded among various Indian tribes, but he had run short of funds and had needed to borrow money in order to return to England. His book probably was designed to help him pay off that debt. Long presents himself as an enlightened trader who was more concerned with the welfare of the Indians with whom he traded than were most of his fellows.

The excerpt presented here exemplifies several aspects of the American exchange, including technology and alcohol. Long describes this as a typical incident of trading in 1777, when a group of Ojibway Indians came to his camp to trade furs. The excerpt begins with a speech by Keskoneek, the Ojibway leader:

"It is true, Father, I and my young men are happy to see you:—as the great Master of Life has sent a trader to take pity on us Savages,[a] we shall use our best endeavors to hunt and bring you wherewithal to satisfy you in furs, skins, and animal food."

This speech was in fact intended to induce me to make them further presents; I indulged them in their expectation, by giving them two kegs of rum of eight gallons each, lowered with a small proportion of water, according to the usual custom adopted by all traders,[b] five carrots of tobacco,[c] fifty scalping knives,[d] gunflints, powder, shot, ball, &c.[e] To the women I gave beads, trinkets, &c. and to eight chiefs who were in the band, each a Northwest gun, a calico shirt, a scalping knife of the best sort, and an additional quantity of ammunition. These were received with a full yohah, or demonstration of joy.

The women, who are on all occasions slaves to their husbands, were ordered to make up bark huts, which they completed in about an hour, and everything was got in order for merriment. The rum being taken from my house, was carried to their wigwam, and they began to drink. The frolic lasted four days and nights; and notwithstanding all our precaution (securing their guns, knives, and tomahawks) two boys were killed, and six men wounded by three Indian women; one of the chiefs also was murdered, which reduced me to the necessity of giving several articles to bury with him, to complete the usual ceremony of their interment. These frolics are very prejudicial to all parties, and put the trader to a considerable expense, which nevertheless he cannot with safety refuse.

[a] Long also gives the speech in the Ojibway language, and in that version this phrase is rendered as *Nishinnorbay:* Ojibways.
[b] Diluting rum was for economic, not humanitarian, reasons.
[c] This region is too far north to grow tobacco, so it was obtained by trade.
[d] This term referred to any all-purpose knife.
[e] Et cetera.

particularly on the grassy plains of central North America and Patagonia in South America. By the latter part of the seventeenth century in North America and the middle part of the eighteenth century in South America, Native Americans had begun capturing and making use of horses. Particularly on the Great Plains of North America, the coming of the horse led to a revolution in the way of life.

Prior to this time, North American Plains tribes like the Arikara[7] and Pawnee were living a settled existence as farmers. Their sedentary villages had semisubterranean houses with sod roofs, and fields were carved out of the thick-sodded grasslands. These fields were owned by women, who organized their tending and the production of corn, squash, and beans. Bison were hunted seasonally, but this was laborious and only marginally successful on foot. There was little competition for land and only limited warfare.

With the advent of the horse, all this changed. Bison hunting from horseback was so successful that it became a year-round occupation. This, in turn, necessitated shifts in settlement, because the

[7] **Arikara:** uh RIH kah ruh

FIGURE 25.8 *Plains Indians Hunting Buffalo on Horseback.* *This detail from a painting by John Innes presents a romantic but also a fundamentally accurate picture of the use of the horse by Plains Indians in the central portions of North America. Introduced by the Spanish, horses permitted hunters to ride abreast of a buffalo herd rather than having to lie in ambush with only a single chance at success. The horse raised the status of men in Plains Indian society, placing more emphasis on the hunt and warfare.* "The Buffalo Hunt," John Innes, Glenbow Collection, Calgary, Canada.

bison shifted their haunts with the seasons, sometimes daily. Permanent sod houses were replaced with portable tepees, conical tents that could be collapsed, rolled up, and packed on a horse in a matter of minutes. Agriculture was abandoned, and the importance of women's economic roles diminished in direct proportion to the increased status of the male hunters. The horse turned these farmers into hunters, raiders, and warriors, as their increased mobility made them able to prey on people as well as on bison.

The popular image of the American Indian wearing a huge feather headdress, mounted on a horse, and chasing bison or fighting the cavalry has been immortalized in frontier art, in Holly-wood movies, and even on U.S. coinage. Like most popular images, this image is oversimplified and stereotyped, but it is a reflection of one place and time in American Indian life. The irony is that this image existed only fleetingly and as a result of the introduction of the horse by Europeans.

Phylloxera, Grapes, and the American Exchange

The glory days of the American exchange of plants and animals were before 1700, and probably 90 percent of the important species that were to pass from one hemisphere to the other did so by that date. Nonetheless, the American exchange has continued into modern times. An example is **phylloxera**,[8] an aphid from the Mississippi Valley of North America that subsists by sucking plant juices from roots. It is particularly fond of grapevines, and, when it accidentally was introduced into France in 1863, the results were devastating. Phylloxera spread through the vineyards, killing great numbers of vines. The wine grapes of France (and eventually much of Europe and beyond) were nearly wiped out. Wine production in most of the affected areas dropped by 50 percent or more, raising havoc with the economy of France and, to a lesser extent, those of Italy and Spain.

Non-Europeans may have difficulty imagining the magnitude of the problem. In many regions of France, wine making was the major industry, employing more workers and producing more income than any other. This economic disaster, coupled with huge indemnities incurred by a failed war with Prussia, helped hurl France into a serious economic crisis.

The cure for the pestilence came from America. Because there were grapes native to the same area as phylloxera, agronomists reasoned that they must be genetically resistant to the aphid. They were correct, and when the European grapevines were grafted onto American root stocks, the scourge of phylloxera was controlled. The American exchange contributed the affliction of phylloxera, but it also contributed the cure through North American root stocks.

TECHNOLOGY

Of all the arenas where the American exchange operated, the results are perhaps easiest to see in technology. New tools, materials, and methods of manufacture passed from one hemisphere to the other for a variety of reasons.

Some pieces of European technology were such improvements over traditional American technology that they were adopted readily. Almost everywhere, but especially in North America, for example, American Indians saw the advantages of guns and tried to procure them. Many colonial powers tried to curb the gun trade to Indians, often

[8] **phylloxera:** fih LOK seh ruh

with limited success, because the traders of a rival colonial power often were happy to trade guns for furs or other commodities. In New England, Indians in praying towns learned how to repair guns and manufacture many parts for them, attaining a measure of self-sufficiency.

In other cases, items were accepted but modified to improve their fit with perceived needs. For example, metalworking technology in native North American traditions before Columbus was limited, and no brass or iron was used; metals were much desired in the centuries that followed. Early trade between the English and Indians in New England included iron knives, iron hatchets, and brass kettles. While some of the kettles made their way into domestic usage as cooking vessels, many were used as fancy grave offerings; even more were cut into triangles and used as arrowheads.

Sometimes Indians adopted items not for their improvement over traditional technology but rather for the prestige associated with them. In colonial Mexico and Peru, European-style clothing bestowed a certain measure of status on the wearer; and the wearing of miscellaneous available scraps of metal armor conferred prestige but little practical advantage to seventeenth- and eighteenth-century Indians of the Great Lakes region of North America.

The process of adopting European technology was selective, and some items that might appear at first to have been advantageous were rejected. Wheeled vehicles in the Peruvian Andes, for example, were of little use, because the slopes were too steep to permit their safe or efficient use. European-style looms made little headway in Mexican home weaving, because a longstanding tradition of using backstrap looms was deeply engrained in the value system. And European grinding mills took centuries to supplant the grinding stones of Mexican households, because the cornmeal made in the mills was perceived as not tasting as good as that made by hand with a grinding stone.

Adoptions of indigenous technology by Europeans were fewer and even more selective. By and large, European technology was better suited for most colonial activities, because the colonists and most of their activities were transplants from Europe. The extensive and straight-rowed wheat fields of the Europeans were most efficiently tilled with an ox-drawn plow, not with the Indian-style

FIGURE 25.9 *Chief Tuko-See Mathla.* *Though this portrait of a leader of Florida's Seminole tribe was painted in the first half of the nineteenth century, it shows how thoroughly European technology and style had penetrated into Native American life by the eighteenth century. Tuko-See carries a rifle and wears a cast-metal medallion and gorget (a piece of armor) around his neck; his clothing is made mostly of woven European fabrics; his boots are even fastened with European laces and grommets.* National Museum of American Art, Smithsonian Institution.

FIGURE 25.10 *Louis, a Rocky Mountain Trapper.* *This painting depicts a French trapper of the early nineteenth century. Just as Native Americans had adopted European styles and technologies by the eighteenth century, Europeans on the American frontier had made similar adoptions from Native Americans. This trapper, for example, wears leather clothing, moccasins, and a native-style necklace. On the basis of material culture, it would be difficult to differentiate between this European and the Native American.* Buffalo Bill Historical Center, Cody, Wyoming. Gift of the Coe Foundation.

hoe, which was more effective with smaller, irregularly planted fields. As the conquerors, Europeans typically disdained the Indians; as discussed in Chapter 24, they felt themselves inherently superior. Consequently, Europeans and European Americans saw themselves as gaining no prestige (or other advantage) from adopting items perceived as native symbols. Indeed, wearing Indian-style hair or tattoos on the eighteenth-century American frontier usually was condemned as rustic and unsophisticated.

The primary area of adopting native technology was in frontier survival equipment. Snowshoes, fish traps, buckskin clothing, snow goggles—these items were the sort that Europeans adopted most frequently from Native Americans. This makes sense, of course, because people on the frontier, regardless of race or ethnicity, were living similar lives and meeting similar challenges. Many elements of the technology developed by American Indians over the centuries to meet those challenges were very effective and easily procured or produced by European colonists on the frontier. Any loss in prestige in the eyes of urbanites far from the frontier was a small price to pay for the increased ability to survive.

IDEOLOGIES

Diseases, plants and animals, and technology are relatively easy to recognize in the American exchange, because they have physical dimensions that can be seen, measured, and compared. Ideologies, in contrast, are difficult to trace. The same idea could have been developed independently in different places, and its presence in both Europe and the Americas does not necessarily mean that it passed from one place to the other. Further, ideas often are modified as they are transmitted from one people to another, making them difficult to recognize as coming from the same source. No doubt there are hundreds of cases of ideological exchange that remain unrecognized, but we shall focus on two examples where exchange is well documented.

Christianity

The preeminent European ideology passing to the Americas was Christianity. All of the countries with American colonies were Christian, and all imposed their creeds onto their American Indian subjects to greater or lesser extents. Missionaries are the most obvious agent of transmitting Christianity, but lay colonists also often felt an obligation to impress upon Indians the value of Christianity. The Indians, in turn, often felt that becoming Christian was a good course of action. Many Aztecs, for example, believed that the Spanish conquest occurred only because the Spanish god was stronger than the Aztec gods; consequently, it was only sensible to shift one's allegiance to the new, more powerful

deity. In New England, Pequot[9] Indians sometimes converted to Christianity to gain access to the technological training available in the praying towns. In many places, becoming a Christian conferred legal rights or prestige that made conversion desirable. The potency of these factors working together is evidenced by the predominance of Christianity among Native Americans today, especially in Latin America.

But the type of Christianity adopted in the New World was often unlike that practiced in Europe. Maya Indians of eastern Mexico, for example, went to church on Sunday and worshiped the Christian god, but they continued making offerings and conducting rituals to their traditional gods and goddesses. The cross was interpreted as both the Christian symbol of Jesus' crucifixion and the Mayan symbol of the tree of life. Among the O'odham of Arizona, Catholic churches incorporated personal altars, where corn, pollen, and other traditionally sacred objects were placed in a hybrid religion that sprang from both Christian and traditional worship. Many American Indian groups modified the version of Christianity they adopted, adapting it to accommodate existing beliefs.

Sometimes, particularly in institutions operating with slave labor, African religions also blended with Native American religions and Christianity. These non-Christian influences were guarded against by most Europeans, but they persisted in folk religion, especially in the Caribbean, parts of the American South, and Brazil. The voodoo worship of Haiti, for example, intertwines African elements (like ecstatic trance and snake ritual) with Christian elements (like cross symbolism and the role of saints) and Caribbean Indian elements (like symbolic cannibalism and the use of triangular stones).

The Idea of Confederation

In general, we would expect the conquerors to adopt few ideas from the conquered, certainly fewer than passed in the opposite direction. Nonetheless, there is a good argument that the idea of confederation and a form of governmental structure were adopted by European Americans

[9] **Pequot:** PEE kwoht

from the Iroquois Indians of New York through the agency of Benjamin Franklin.

Benjamin Franklin, the colonial writer, politician, and scientist from Pennsylvania, was one of the earliest advocates of autonomy for the English colonies in North America. In 1754, the Albany Congress, a gathering of representatives from the colonies of British North America, met with an agenda of two items: approving a treaty with the Six Nations of the Iroquois and considering Franklin's plan for a central government over seven of the colonies. Franklin was present at the Albany Congress and used his considerable powers of personal persuasion to see his plan tentatively approved by it.

The Albany Plan of Union, as it came to be known, proposed joint government by a president-general, to be appointed for the colonies by the crown, and a Grand Council. The Grand Council was to be composed of representatives of each colony, to be elected by their respective assemblies. The central government was to have been charged with the basic duties of governing, including taxing, raising armies, waging war, and making peace. If it had been implemented, it would have been the first intercolonial government. The plan required approval by the assembly for each colony involved, and these bodies rejected it unanimously.

While Franklin never stated so, many historians suspect that the Albany Plan of Union was based on the League of the Iroquois. The League of the Iroquois was a confederacy-type government of six Indian tribes and had successfully bound them together since around 1300. Clearly, Franklin was familiar with the League, because this was the government with whom the treaty under consideration at the Albany Congress had been negotiated.

At the heart of both the League of the Iroquois and the Albany Plan of Union was the concept of **confederation**—a permanent union of equal states, cooperating for their common welfare—a concept alien to European political thought of the era. Many details of Franklin's proposed confederation were remarkably similar to the details of the League of the Iroquois.

The Albany Plan of Union, for example, stipulated that voting in the Grand Council was to be accomplished by first polling the members of a delegation, deciding the vote for that delegation, then having a single vote for each colony, a system absolutely parallel to that of the League. The selection of delegates was to be accomplished in a manner parallel to that of the League, and the duties of the Grand Council were to have been the same as those for their counterpart in the League. Even the name of the ruling body was the same as that of the League.

Franklin never revealed his inspiration for the Albany Plan of Union. He did, however, in 1751 exhort his colleagues to accept some form of union by noting that the English colonies should be able to achieve this if "Six Nations of ignorant savages should be capable of forming a scheme for such a union and be able to execute it in such a manner, as it has subsisted for ages and appears insoluble." Franklin's reference to "ignorant savages" attests to the tenor of the day and gives a potent indication as to why he might have chosen not to reveal any Iroquois inspiration for his plan.

While the Albany Plan of Union never went into effect, it had a profound effect on the course of government in America, and indirectly the world. It was the first proposal for a confederation of English colonies, and many of its principles survived to become part of the Articles of Confederation, the basis of the first government of the independent United States; many of these ideas, in turn, were incorporated into the U.S. Constitution, which still structures the government of the United States. There can be little doubt that the spirit of the League of the Iroquois has extended beyond the Six Nations to help shape the American political system and from there to have major impact around the world.

WHO BENEFITED FROM THE AMERICAN EXCHANGE?

But for the debilitating effects of diseases, it is conceivable that both hemispheres might have profited from the American exchange. On the face of it, the exchange of desirable foodstuffs could only increase the food supply, the exchange of technology would facilitate labor and production, and the exchange of ideas necessarily enriched both hemispheres.

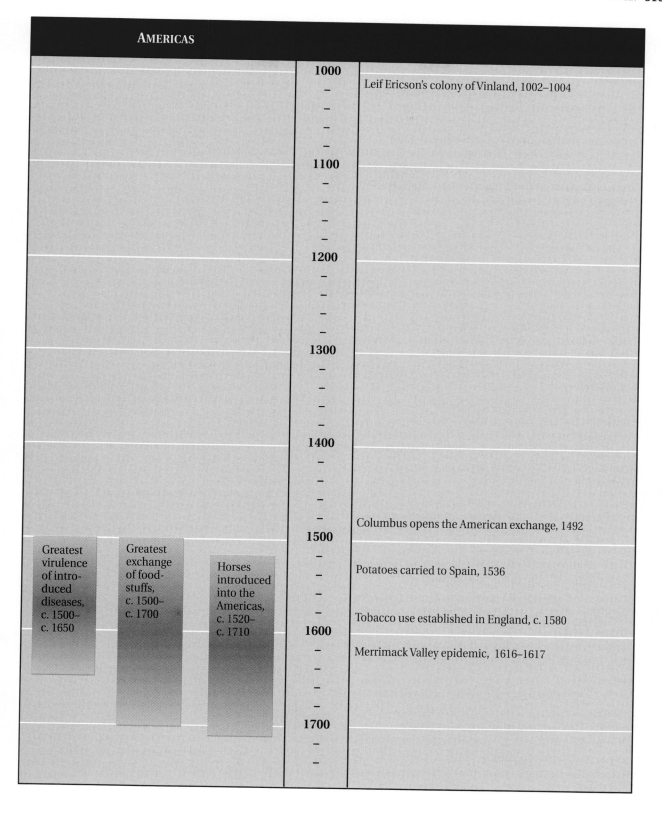

AMERICAS

Leif Ericson's colony of Vinland, 1002–1004

1000

1100

1200

1300

1400

Columbus opens the American exchange, 1492

1500

Potatoes carried to Spain, 1536

Tobacco use established in England, c. 1580

Merrimack Valley epidemic, 1616–1617

1600

1700

Greatest virulence of introduced diseases, c. 1500– c. 1650

Greatest exchange of foodstuffs, c. 1500– c. 1700

Horses introduced into the Americas, c. 1520– c. 1710

The devastation of the Americas by epidemics, however, outweighed any advantage that otherwise would have accrued to Native Americans through the American exchange. While there can be no way to know for sure, many scholars believe that the European conquest of the Americas never would have occurred if disease had not reduced populations and severely dislocated cultures there, paving the way. At the very least, Native American societies would have been better able to resist European incursions, resulting in very different events and consequences.

As events transpired, however, the primary benefits of the American exchange to Native Americans were new forms of technology and new foods. Demographic catastrophe, cultural calamity, and conquest far outweighed these benefits from the point of view of Native Americans. The Old World, on the other hand, particularly Europe, received tremendous benefits from the exchange, placing it in a position to embark on political and economic domination of the world.

SUMMARY

1. The American exchange was the transmission of diseases, plants and animals, technology, and ideology between the Old World and the Americas in the period after the European voyages of discovery.

2. While other pre-Columbian contacts between the Old World and the Americas may have occurred, only the existence of the Norse colony of Vinland is well documented. Even at Vinland the colonists had little effect on local Native American culture.

3. The type of contact between Europeans and American Indians had profound effects on the nature of the American exchange. Factors that most encouraged exchange were intense contact, European intent to modify the local cultures, and subjugation of the local population.

4. Old World diseases devastated American Indians, who had little biological immunity to them, paving the way for the European conquest of the Americas. For biological reasons, there were few American diseases that could afflict Old World peoples.

5. Potatoes and corn were the most important crops transferred from the Americas to the Old World. Particularly in Europe, they were the basis for great population growth that supplied the Americas with colonists. Other American crops like chilis became important for the tastes they imparted to cuisines around the world.

6. Most of the Old World crops transferred to the Americas were either to satisfy the tastes of European colonists or to support ranches and plantations for profit.

7. Tobacco was used in the Americas as a ritual drug, but Europeans adopted it for recreational use. Alcoholic beverages from Europe were widely sought by Native Americans, though alcohol abuse brought many problems. The Spanish continued the Inca practice of using coca to stimulate and pacify Andean miners; eventually a cocaine traffic with Europe and North America developed in South America.

8. The horse transformed the lifeways of the Indians of North America's plains. Formerly sedentary agriculturalists with a female focus to their societies, they adopted a male focus, becoming mobile bison hunters and raiders.

9. American Indians adopted various types of Old World technology for a variety of reasons, including practical advantage and acquiring prestige. European adoption of American technology was focused primarily on frontier survival tools.

10. The primary ideology to be transferred from the Old World to the Americas was Christianity. The primary transfer in the opposite direction probably was the notion of confederacy, which passed from Native Americans to European colonists in North America.

SUGGESTED READINGS

Crosby, Alfred W., Jr. *The Columbian Exchange: Biological and Cultural Consequences of 1492*. Westport, Conn.: Greenwood Press, 1972. The pioneering and classic discussion of the American exchange, still largely up to date.

———. *Ecological Imperialism: The Biological Expansion of Europe, 900–1900*. Cambridge, Eng.: Cambridge University Press, 1986. Discussion of the movements of plants and animals between Europe and colonial areas.

Ingstad, Anne Stine. *The Discovery of a Norse Settlement in America*. Oslo, Norway: Universitetsforlaget, 1977. The report of archaeological excavation and analysis at L'Anse aux Meadows, containing a wealth of detailed information and informative photographs.

Tooker, Elisabeth. "The United States Constitution and the Iroquois League." *Ethnohistory* 35 (1988): 304–36. The original and basic argument that the U.S. Constitution was inspired by the League of the Iroquois.

Viola, Herman J., and Carolyn Margolis, eds. *Seeds of Change*. Washington, D.C.: Smithsonian Institution Press, 1991. A collection of diverse essays on crops and associated economic systems transmitted through the American exchange.

Wissler, Clark. "The Influence of the Horse in the Development of the Plains Culture." *American Anthropologist* 16 (1914): 1–25. Though nearing its centennial, this remains the classic statement. Updates, primarily archaeological, are presented in an article in Viola and Margolis, cited above.

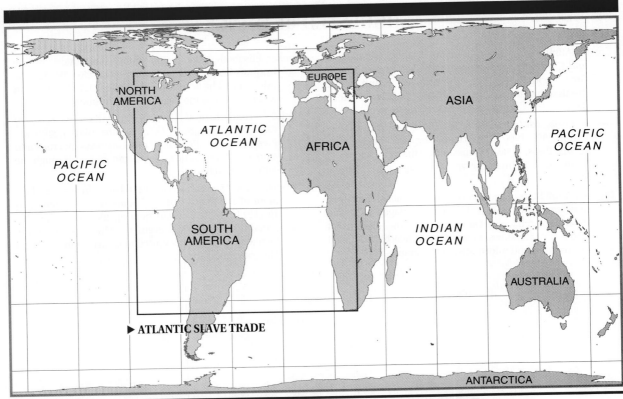

▶ ATLANTIC SLAVE TRADE

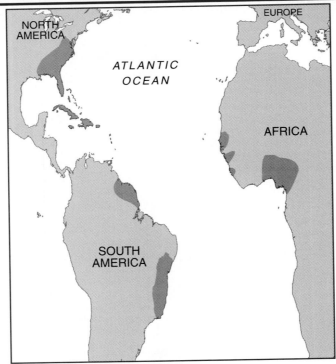

▶ ATLANTIC SLAVE TRADE

The African Slave Trade

1441–1815

By a conservative estimate, nearly 30 million Africans were captured, enslaved, and forcibly removed to foreign lands over the course of the several centuries during which the African slave trade was active. Large numbers are notoriously difficult to grasp, so a comparison may bring this figure into focus. This number is approximately the combined population of the modern cities of New York, Los Angeles, Boston, Philadelphia, Toronto, Montréal, Detroit, Miami, Washington, Chicago, Dallas, Denver, San Francisco, and Seattle. Standing shoulder to shoulder, 30 million people would span a bit over 11,000 miles, approximately the distance from Los Angeles to New York, across the Atlantic Ocean to London, and across Eurasia into central Siberia.

Slavery is defined simply as the ownership and control of other people, and it has been a common institution around the world. Indeed, by 1400 it was practiced on all the inhabited continents of the world except Australia, and its various forms are discussed in the "Issue" section for this part. The slave trade in Africa, however, was far more extensive than that anywhere else, and its significance reached around the globe.

Sub-Saharan Africa (the part of the continent south of the Sahara) was a source for slaves at least as early as 1500 B.C., though the numbers of slaves at that date were few. By A.D. 700, two corridors of slave trading had become significant. The **trans-Sahara slave trade** was that which brought slaves from sub-Saharan Africa to the Arab Berbers of

623

North Africa. From North Africa some were distributed throughout the Mediterranean and to the Byzantine Empire. This trade was plied with caravans, usually carrying about 500 slaves, crossing from oasis to oasis over the Sahara. Most of the slaves were women, described as "well educated"; most scholars interpret this phrase to mean that they were trained and skilled in traditional women's tasks, such as cooking, conversation, and companionship. The total number of slaves carried across the Sahara has recently been estimated at about 8 million people.

The other major locale for the early African slave trade was coastal East Africa. The **Indian Ocean slave trade** was that which passed through the coastal cities and northward, particularly to the sugar plantations of Southwest Asia. The first leg of the Indian Ocean slave trade was carried out primarily by Swahili traders, local Africans who procured slaves from the inland tribes and brought them to East African coastal cities, where they were sold to Arab and other maritime traders. The scale of this facet of the slave trade is not fully known. Slaves in this trade were carried to various Asian ports, but the sugar plantations of Southwest Asia were their most common destination, especially in the years 500 to 900.

The slave trade across the Sahara and the Indian Ocean was dwarfed by the development of a third corridor in the years following 1441. The **Atlantic slave trade** was that which carried slaves from Africa to Europe and the Americas via vessels sailing the Atlantic Ocean. It centered on the West African coast and was operated primarily by Europeans and their descendants in the Americas. It soon marked itself as a departure from all other forms of the slave trade in its magnitude, the degree of its brutality, and the significance of its consequences. This aspect of the African slave trade is the primary focus of this chapter.

THE NATURE OF SLAVERY BEFORE THE ATLANTIC SLAVE TRADE

Both Africans and Europeans held slaves before 1441, the onset of the Atlantic slave trade, although the numbers enslaved were far smaller than after that date. In this earlier period, there were remarkable similarities in the ways slaves were perceived, treated, and procured in both Africa and Europe.

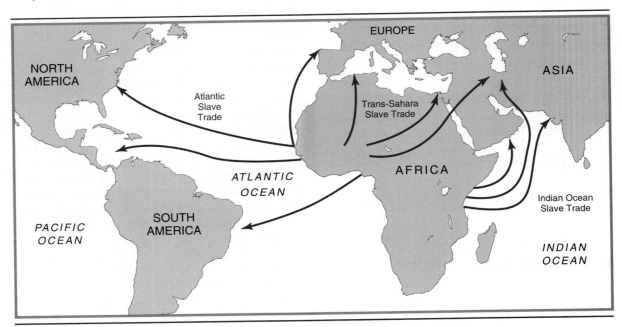

MAP 26.1 *Corridors of the Atlantic Slave Trade.* *The trans-Sahara and Indian Ocean slave trades shipped millions of Africans into foreign slavery, but both were dwarfed in magnitude by the Atlantic slave trade.*

In both places, slaves were viewed as persons whose labor was owed to their owner, but not as inanimate objects. In a fit of rage, the owner of a table could smash the table with an axe; in contrast, the enraged owner of a slave had no right to attack that slave with an axe. In either Africa or Europe, of course, a slave owner was permitted to punish slaves for wrongdoing, but the punishment was expected to be in keeping with the transgression. (The right to punish, by the way, also was accorded male heads of households over wives, children, and hired servants.) This conception of slaves as human beings with personal rights was in keeping with general conceptions of society in late medieval Europe and contemporary Africa. Both followed a hierarchic model, under which each person held obligations to social superiors, and slavery fit into this scheme well, as simply an additional tier at the bottom.

As persons, slaves could expect that their individual skills, talents, and hard work could improve their lot in life. By applying their talents, slaves could achieve greater status, better housing, more wealth, and even fame. Both in Europe and Africa, many successful slaves accumulated considerable power, sometimes owning slaves themselves. In many cases, slaves were encouraged to marry into their owners' families; a successful slave sometimes was adopted into the family, assuming the same rights as a son or daughter of the owner. **Manumission** (the freeing of a slave) was fairly common, and slaves could gain freedom through a variety of mechanisms, including a grant from the owner and purchase of their freedom with accumulated wealth.

In theory, slaves in both Africa and Europe before 1441 were to come from the ranks of those outside the mainstream of one's own society. Slaves in Africa were supposed to come from kingdoms other than one's own, and Muslims were forbidden by the laws of Islam to enslave other Muslims; in practice, these rules, though usually followed, sometimes were ignored in times of slave shortages. In Europe, slaves were supposed to come from the ranks of Jews, Muslims, or other non-Christians; in practice, however, many eastern European Christians served as slaves in western Europe, contributing their generic ethnic designation ("Slav") as the root for the modern word "slave." Several thirteenth-century papal directives decried the enslavement of white, Chris-

tian Europeans, although the practice seems to have been on the wane by the time those decrees were made.

THE BEGINNINGS OF THE ATLANTIC SLAVE TRADE

In 1434, a small technical advance in sailing technology changed the world. In that year, the Portuguese adopted the **lateen sail**, a sail on a slanted mast, which was already in use in the eastern Mediterranean. They modified it for ocean travel,

FIGURE 26.1 *Lateen Sails in Seville Harbor.* *The lateen sail revolutionized sailing between Europe and sub-Saharan Africa. In this sixteenth-century painting of the harbor in Seville, Spain, the lateen sails are furled. The yard for a lateen sail, visible on the boat in the center of the harbor channel, crosses the mast diagonally.* Museo de America, Madrid/MAS Barcelona.

and for the first time European seafarers could sail almost against the wind. Prior to this time, Europeans had no desire to sail down the west coast of Africa, knowing that incessant winds blowing toward the south made a return trip impossible. The lateen sail opened coastal West Africa to European visitors.

Antam Gonçalvez,[1] the young commander of a vessel sailing for Prince Henry of Portugal, set out for West Africa in 1441, charged with collecting a cargo of the oil and skins of sea lions. After discharging his duty, Gonçalvez wanted to curry further favor with his patron, so he decided to capture some natives of the place to bring back to Portugal. He managed to capture a man and a woman, and he later threw in with another Portuguese captain to capture ten more Africans. These twelve people became the first spoils of the Atlantic slave trade.

Many of his advisors had doubted the wisdom of Prince Henry's sailing adventures. When the first consignment of African slaves arrived, however, most changed their minds; the second cargo of 29 slaves in 1443 won over the few doubters. One contemporary raved over a commerce where so many slaves could be "captured in so short a time and at so little trouble," and Portugal threw itself into the slave trade.

At first, Portuguese slavers were raiders, mounting military expeditions to capture Africans. By the early 1450s, however, this strategy was giving way to trading with local Africans. At least one earlier expedition had turned into a small war with a profit of only 165 slaves, and it became apparent that a more economical way of procuring slaves was needed. In the decades that followed, local Africans became the suppliers for the Portuguese slave trade.

From these modest beginnings, the Atlantic slave trade swelled rapidly. The first decade of Portuguese slave raiding and trading probably saw no more than a few hundred slaves sent to Portugal, and only about 35,000 slaves are estimated to have been brought to Portugal in the entire period before 1500. This number, great as it is in human terms, is merely a trickle compared with the millions of slaves who were exported from Africa in the centuries to follow.

[1]**Antam Gonçalvez:** AHN tahm gohn SAHL behs

EUROPE TRANSFORMS THE SLAVE TRADE

Within less than a century of its inception, the Atlantic slave trade evolved into something never before seen. As its scope escalated massively, attitudes toward slaves were transformed, and treatment degenerated. Fueled by economic greed, the slave trade became a lucrative business in which human suffering was little considered as a factor in the monetary equation. As might be expected, such a financially rewarding trade fostered competition among the European powers.

The Changing Nature of the Slave Trade

Shortly after 1500, the slave trade picked up in volume and was transformed. Current historical scholarship can document that at least 14 million slaves were exported from Africa by the Atlantic slave trade in the three centuries following that date. This estimate is based on numbers calculated from ship inventories, receipts, and similar documents, so it serves merely as a minimum estimate. The task of locating and examining these documents is huge and will require many more years to complete, and even then there will be gaps where records have been lost or destroyed. Consequently, the most conservative scholars believe that future research will push the number to at least 20 million; less conservative estimates range upward to

TABLE 26.1
Documented Destinations of Slaves in the Atlantic Slave Trade, All Periods

Receiving Slaves	Number of Slaves
Europe	250,000
North America	750,000
South and Central America	6,000,000
Caribbean Islands	7,000,000
Total	14,000,000

Note that these figures underestimate the volume of the trade as a whole, because they are based on arrivals at their destinations, and significant numbers of slaves died in transit. In addition, not all documents have survived or been located by historians.

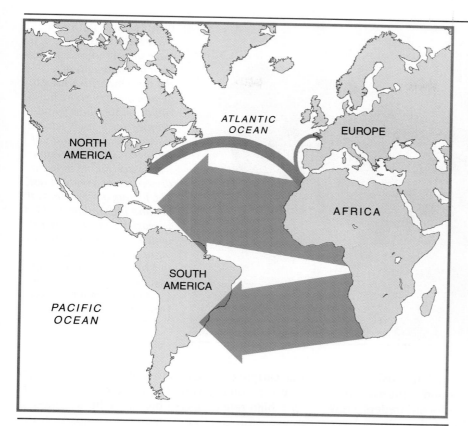

MAP 26.2 *Slave Destinations in the Atlantic Slave Trade.* *The widths of the various arrows indicate the relative volume of the trade. Tropical America was by far the greatest consumer, partly because of the short life expectancy of slaves there.*

40 million slaves or even more. No matter which figure is accurate, the number of slaves traded is staggering, amounting to an average of somewhere between six and twelve persons per hour, day and night, every day of every year.

A look at the destinations of these slaves helps explain this meteoric intensification of the slave trade. Historians disagree about details of the numbers of slaves traded, but we do have reasonable estimates of slave imports to various parts of the world (see Table 26.1). Clearly, slaves were being sent predominantly to the Americas. Less than 1.8 percent of all African slaves went to Europe (principally Portugal), and the vast majority went to South America, Central America, and the Caribbean; smaller but still significant numbers of slaves were sent to the southern parts of North America. Colonies in these places focused on agricultural plantations and were dependent on large numbers of slaves for labor; poor health conditions often resulted in early deaths for these slaves;

their places had to be taken by more slaves brought in through the slave trade. These colonies created the demand that transformed the African slave trade into the massive and brutal commerce it became.

But the European slavers had accomplices among the Africans. Coastal West African kingdoms had traded in slaves with other Africans for some time, and they were happy to exchange captives for coveted European goods. Most of the coastal states that had access to Europeans actively engaged in the slave trade; Benin and Ife were especially active. Usually Africans from these kingdoms would conduct raids on their neighbors, particularly in the savannas, to procure slaves for trade, but sometimes Africans and Europeans conducted joint ventures. In 1765, for example, an English slaver named Isaac Parker cooperated with slavers from Efik[2] (a city of the Benin kingdom) in

[2]**Efik:** AYF eek

FIGURE **26.2** *Plan of a Slave Ship. This model of a slave ship, produced in England by opponents of the slave trade, was used to demonstrate the horrific conditions on these vessels. People were densely packed side by side; the amount of space allocated per person was scarcely more than the dimension of a body at rest. The tossing of the ship, foul air, and unfamiliar food led to seasickness and diarrhea, which made the two-month voyage to the Americas an ordeal that many failed to survive.* Kingston-upon-Hull City Council, Leisure Services Department.

an expedition inland. They hid in bushes near roads and paths near villages and captured "every one they could see." The African traders grew wealthy as the result of this trade, gaining large quantities of otherwise unobtainable European goods. In fact, the rise of Benin and Ife as prominent states can be traced in part to the wealth they gained from trading slaves to the Portuguese.

After the trauma of capture, the next trial for a slave was the **Middle Passage**, the sea voyage between Africa and the Americas. (The term, which derives from the triangular trade of the English, discussed in Chapter 24, is applied because this was the middle leg of the three-part loop that began and ended in England.) Typically, slaves were packed below the decks of the ships, often so closely that it was impossible to shift position during the voyage of several weeks. While women and children usually were spared, men typically were shackled to one another at the wrists or ankles. During this passage, many slaves died of disease, unsanitary conditions, dehydration, and cruel treatment, all of which were compounded by depression, called "melancholy" by the slavers.

In some cases, slave-ship captains committed atrocities with little likelihood of punishment. One of the most infamous of these cases took place in 1781, when Luke Collingwood, a British captain,

was carrying 400 slaves to Jamaica. Realizing that he was running low on fresh water and might suffer a high rate of loss of his cargo, he schemed to transfer the loss to his insurance company. If the slaves died of thirst, the loss would be to the slavers, but if they died as a result of "the perils of the seas," the loss would be covered by insurance. Accordingly, he bound the hands of 132 of the sickest and weakest slaves behind their backs and threw them into the ocean, where they drowned. The insurance company initially refused to pay a settlement, but they were forced to do so when the British courts upheld the slave traders' claim.

Historians currently are debating the degree to which such atrocities occurred, and some historians feel that past conceptions of the Middle Passage have been influenced unduly by the political broadsides of abolitionists, whose interests were best served by publicizing the most extreme and horrific conditions. All historians agree, however, that death tolls were high and conditions were bad during the Middle Passage—the only question is how bad. Estimates for slave mortality during the Middle Passage vary from around 5 to 15 percent; for a ship carrying 400 slaves, between 20 and 60 would be likely to die during the passage. Clearly, slave traders in this period viewed their victims like fruit: merely a perishable commodity whose shipment inevitably produced losses.

It was in the early years of the 1500s that the conception of slaves changed among Europeans. Perhaps 1510 should be considered the watershed year, because this was the first time slaves were shipped to the Americas *for general sale.* Prior to this date, slaves were shipped to a particular destination and a particular owner who had ordered them for an expressed purpose, such as mining or performing domestic duties or cutting sugarcane.

From this date forward, however, slaves usually were shipped to auctioneers, who resold them to the highest bidder, as they would horses or bricks. This change signaled the shift to **chattel slavery**, the system whereby a slave was considered to have no more value than any other object and a slave's humanity and personal rights were denied.

Of course, there was great variation in how slave owners treated their slaves. Both documentary and archaeological evidence indicates that some slave owners were compassionate and others

IN THEIR OWN WORDS

In the Hold of a Slave Ship

Olaudah Equiano[a] was born in 1745, the son of a chief in the remote Ibo[b] region of the Benin kingdom, in what now is Nigeria. He had little knowledge of the wider world in 1755, when he was captured by Benin slavers who sold him to English slave traders on the coast. After years of servitude in Barbados, he purchased his freedom and devoted himself to the abolitionist cause. He published *The Interesting Narrative of the Life of Olaudah Equiano,* an account of his travels, in 1789, and it became a bestseller. These selections from that work describe the start of Equiano's terrifying passage to the Caribbean.

Quite overpowered with horror and anguish, I fell motionless on the deck and fainted. When I recovered a little I found some black people about me. . . . They talked to me in order to cheer me, but all in vain. I asked them if we were not to be eaten by those white men with horrible looks, red faces, and loose hair. They told me I was not. . . . I was soon put under the decks, and there I received such a salutation in my nostrils as I had never experienced in my life; so that with the loathsomeness of the stench and crying together, I became so sick and low that I was not able to eat, nor had I the least desire to taste anything. I now wished for the last friend, death, to relieve me; but soon, to my grief, two of the white men offered me eatables, and on my refusing to eat, one of them held me fast by the hands and laid me across I think the windlass, and tied my feet while the other flogged me severely. I had never experienced anything of this kind before. . . . I would have jumped over the side, but I could not; and besides, the crew used to watch us very closely who were not chained down to the decks, lest we should leap into the water; and I have seen some of these poor African prisoners most severely cut for attempting to do so, and hourly whipped for not eating. . . . I had never seen among my people such instances of brutal cruelty, and this not only shown towards us blacks but also to some of the whites themselves. . . . The stench of the hold while we were on the coast was so intolerably loathsome that it was dangerous to remain there for any time, and some of us had been permitted to stay on the deck for the fresh air; but now that the whole ship's cargo were confined together, it became absolutely pestilential. The closeness of the place and the heat of the climate, added to the number in the ship, which was so crowded that each had scarcely room to turn himself, almost suffocated us. This produced copious perspirations, so that the air soon became unfit for respiration from a variety of loathsome smells, and brought on a sickness among the slaves, of which many died, thus falling victim to the improvident avarice, as I may call it, of their purchasers. This wretched situation was again aggravated by the galling of the chains, now become unsupportable, and the filth of the necessary tubs [toilet tubs], into which children often fell and were almost suffocated. The shrieks of the women and the groans of the dying rendered the whole scene of horror almost inconceivable.

[a]**Olaudah Equiano:** oh lah OO day ehk wee AH noh
[b]**Ibo:** EE boh

were ruthless. The high death toll of slaves in much of the Americas, however, suggests that the greater number of slaveowners found that harsh methods served their ends best. In the South American colony of Surinam, for example, between 1676 and 1814 the standing population of slaves remained around 30,000, but this was maintained only by importing 1,500 new slaves each year; to keep the slave population constant, the entire population had to be replaced every twenty years. Clearly, life expectancy working the plantations there was very low. As elsewhere, life spans increased after the eventual abolition of slavery.

The European Scramble for Control of the Atlantic Slave Trade

The providing of slaves to the Americas was a lucrative trade, and many European powers wanted to capitalize on it. In early times, before 1600, the Portuguese had sole control of the trade. Their nautical innovations had made them the first Europeans in West Africa and had given them

FIGURE 26.3 *Slave Auction Advertisement.* Bills such as this were posted widely to advertise the auctioning of slaves arriving from Africa. This bill was posted in South Carolina in the late eighteenth century British Library.

opportunities to develop the slave trade there, and they were eager to exploit those opportunities. Setting up trading colonies along the West African coast (and, to a lesser extent, the East African coast), Portuguese traders developed strong ties with the local suppliers of slaves. Coupled with Portuguese sailing capabilities, these ties gave Portugal initial control of the Atlantic slave trade.

By the early to mid-1600s, however, the English and Dutch were starting to eclipse the Portuguese. Portuguese sailing technology by this time had spread throughout Europe, and both England and the Netherlands constructed vast commercial networks, simply outcompeting Portugal in the slave trade. By the end of the 1600s, England was the leading slave-trading nation, and the Netherlands was second. France belatedly entered the scramble in 1713 and by the middle 1700s had displaced the Netherlands as the second-largest slave trader. England, however, remained by far the leading slave-trading nation until its abolition of the trade in 1808.

It at first seems surprising that Spain had no great stake in the slave trade, given its huge colonial holdings in the Americas. In truth, though, Spain's colonies imported a bit over one and one-half million slaves, a huge number, but only a fraction of the millions of slaves traded. In part, this resulted from the fact that the economies of the Spanish colonies were attuned more toward ranches than plantations and thus were not particularly well suited to slave labor. Another factor hampering any major active involvement in the slave trade by Spain was its very limited colonial holdings in Africa, from which a slave-trading operation could be based. The Treaty of Tordesillas had defined most of Africa as too far south for Spanish colonization, and Spain's withering military strength was insufficient to permit it to ignore the treaty and seize African territory of its own for such a base.

Because of these factors, Spain purchased its slaves from slave traders of other countries. While the slave trade in Spanish holdings officially was controlled by the Spanish monarch, the actual trade was assigned to foreign traders, usually through a kind of subcontract known as the *asiento*.[3] The *asiento* permitted a foreign trader to sell slaves in Spanish lands at fixed prices, usually

[3] *asiento:* ah see EHN toh

FIGURE 26.4 *Planting Cane on a Sugar Plantation.* *Field slaves were worked hard by most plantation owners, and mortality rates were high. In this scene from nineteenth-century Antigua, slaves plant sugarcane that will later be transported to the mill in the background.* From William Clark, *Ten Views in the Island of Antigua,* 1823, by permission of the British Library.

quite favorable to the trader. The *asiento* became important around 1600, and for the next century and a half slave traders competed hotly for these economic plums. By the middle of the 1700s, Spanish sentiments were coming to favor free trade over the *asiento,* and the *asiento* was officially discontinued in 1789.

EFFECTS OF THE ATLANTIC SLAVE TRADE ON AFRICAN SOCIETIES

In general, coastal African states gained in the short term from the Atlantic slave trade, while interior states lost. Viewed in a broader perspective, however, the African slave trade was a disaster for most of sub-Saharan Africa. West Africa, the primary source of African slaves, was most adversely affected.

The coastal West African states, called "the Guinea states" by the slavers, made great economic profits from the slave trade. The slaves themselves, of course, were an important commodity that brought wealth, but so were the food stores that were sold to slave ships to support slaves and crews during the Middle Passage. The profits from this trade, however, were concentrated among the elite royal and warrior classes, thereby increasing the degree of class stratification. In addition, the enhanced resources of the warriors led to an increased reliance on warfare as a means of dispute settlement.

At the same time, the interior African states of the savanna were devastated. These had been supported by economies geared to commerce in a broad range of goods, carried on both within West Africa and across the Sahara. The commerce that had brought them prosperity was disrupted beyond repair, dynasties were toppled, and political systems broke down, usually to be replaced by governments closely tied to slaving. Droughts are a regular feature of the savanna environment, and the traditional mutual-help networks that moderated their effects were destroyed by the political unrest and economic ruin. The upshot of these changes was that regional dominance shifted from the savanna states to the coastal states.

Another major effect of the Atlantic slave trade was its impact on African demography. No region can have tens of thousands of persons plucked from it annually for centuries and not suffer. To make matters worse, those taken by slavers typically were children or young adults, the members of society who had the greatest productivity ahead of them. Recent studies have concluded that 35 percent of those taken for the Atlantic slave trade were young women, and, because women are the demographic basis for the next generation, the impact of their loss on overall population levels was significant. During the years of the slave trade, sub-Saharan African populations as a whole either declined or remained steady, despite productive new crops introduced through the American exchange, crops that spurred major population growth everywhere else.

As the Atlantic slave trade increased and African governments oriented more to it, the nature of African slavery changed. By the 1700s, slaves in many African states were treated as commodities; as in the European colonies, chattel slavery had developed. At the same time, the proportion of slaves increased dramatically. By the early 1800s, one-half to two-thirds of the people in some African states were slaves.

Islam had entered West Africa by 800, and it had become important in the precolonial trading states of West Africa, particularly among rulers and traders. Its importance continued in the sixteenth and following centuries, however, as a response to the rising tide of slavery, largely for two reasons. First, because Islam forbade the enslavement of Muslims, Africans who embraced Islam could enjoy a certain level of protection from being taken as slaves, at least by fellow Muslims. For this reason alone, many Africans converted to Islam. Second, Islam provided an orientation for governments to turn away from focusing on the slave trade. Islam encouraged civilian governments and mandated moral codes that challenged the leadership of the warrior-elites that were linked so intimately to the slave trade.

It is ironic that the Islamic states of West Africa, despite their discouragement of concentration on the slave trade, included some of the largest slaveholding communities in Africa. While religious leaders urged moderation in slave trading, favoring a balance of trade that included a broad diversity of products, individuals realized that their greatest personal profit often was to be made through slaves.

The immediate and short-term harm to Africa by the Atlantic slave trade is clear. The long-term effects have been equally damaging. Before the Atlantic slave trade, West Africa had a healthy economy based on a combination of resource extraction, manufacturing, and commerce. Political disruptions attending the slave trade destroyed most of the commerce, and local manufacturing was replaced by dependence on European goods traded into Africa. Horses and firearms were particularly sought after, the former as a symbol of warrior status and the latter as a tool for the slave trade. In the end, West Africa reduced its economy to the export of slaves and little else, placing it at an international disadvantage that many scholars see extending into the present.

SLAVE LABOR AND COLONIAL ECONOMIES

Most of the Europeans who conquered the tropical Americas had no expectations that the African slave trade would be so important to the economies of the new colonies. Initially, some envisioned using Europeans for the workforce, either as slaves (Jews and Muslims) or wage laborers. Europeans, however, soon gained a reputation as unable to survive the conditions of labor in the American tropics, and this idea was largely abandoned. Others expected to use the local American Indians as slaves. Indeed, American Indians were enslaved in various places throughout the Americas, and in Brazil the capturing of Indians for slaves was so widespread that an occupational category, *paulistas*,[4] was designated for the individuals engaged in this activity. American Indians, however, usually proved to be unsatisfactory as a labor force, because the Old World diseases that

---

[4]*paulistas:* poh LEES tahs

were part of the American exchange (discussed in Chapter 25) destroyed so many of them. European overlords had to look elsewhere for labor.

In a sense, Africa was the logical place for Europeans to look for labor. The African slave trade had been in existence for centuries, and its Atlantic branch was well established half a century before the establishment of the first colony in the Americas. In addition, European attitudes labeled Africans as inferior and therefore well suited to lives of servitude. Finally, experience with African slaves showed greater survival rates in the tropical environments of the Americas than for any other laboring group.

Nonetheless, the mortality rates for African slaves were appalling. A planter on the Caribbean island of Saint Christopher calculated in 1798 that 25 percent of the African slaves brought to his plantation died within the first few weeks of work. The greatest threats to slaves were oppressive work conditions. Mortality rates among slaves were always greatest in hot, damp lowlands, where disease and heat prostration were most dangerous. Next most lethal were the mines, followed by agricultural plantations in more healthy climates. Slaves with indoor jobs as servants fared best of all, with mortality rates approximately comparable to those of Europeans. The nature of the tasks assigned most slaves meant that many would die prematurely, and their ranks would be replenished through the slave trade.

Viewed from the perspective of the colonial powers, the slave trade was part of a broader pattern of commerce. European colonial powers, as discussed in Chapter 24, operated under the mercantile system, so one of their goals was to maximize the flow of raw materials into the home country while keeping their colonies dependent on the home country for finished goods. Another goal was to have a net surplus of money flowing into the home country. The only way to ensure the flow of imported raw materials was to provide a labor source for the colonies. The traders purchased slaves for that labor with finished goods and sold them in the colonies for either money or raw materials, which came back with them to the home country. From the mercantile view, the system was ideal.

A special place in the trade between Europe and the Americas was reserved for sugar. In 1400, most Europeans had never tasted sugar refined from cane, and the few who had done so typically used it as a medicine or a spice. (Honey and fruit juice were the only sweeteners available to them before the introduction of cane sugar into Spain by the Moors.) By the middle 1600s, however, Europeans had developed a great sweet tooth, and the demand for sugar had skyrocketed. Nowhere in Europe could sugarcane grow well, so sugar had to be imported. All the major colonial European powers had holdings in the Caribbean, and all produced sugar there. Refined and shipped in bulbous cones, sugar was used as a sweetener for various concoctions, including cocoa, newly introduced from Mexico. Reduced from the squeezings of the cane to a thick syrup, it became molasses, used primarily in the production of rum. By 1650, sugar had become a major import into Europe.

The volume and importance of sugar in European commerce directly affected the need for slaves. More than most crops, sugar required a great deal of labor. Aside from the work needed to grow the crop, its bamboo-like canes had to be cut by hand at harvesting and hauled to a mill, where they were pressed to squeeze out their juice. The juice was boiled until thick, then cooled and hardened in molds. To produce the needed quantities of sugar, huge amounts of labor were required, and that labor came from slaves.

Another crop that stimulated the use of slaves was cotton, particularly in the southeastern United States. Both picking cotton and separating the fiber from the seeds were very laborious tasks when performed by hand. The invention in 1793 of an efficient cotton gin automated and sped up the process of separating the seeds and fiber, meaning that the time spent picking cotton was the only barrier to greatly increased cotton production, which would result in greatly increased profits for plantation owners. Effective mechanical cotton pickers were not devised until the late nineteenth century, so the only solution open to the cotton planters of the early nineteenth century was to increase the number of cotton pickers. Because most cotton pickers were slaves, this meant increasing the number of slaves. It is ironic that in this case mechanization, which usually reduced the demand for labor and slaves, was a spur to increase the number of slaves on cotton plantations.

In recent years, scholars have debated whether or not slavery was an efficient system. On

FIGURE **26.5** *Sugarcane Press.* *This eighteenth-century engraving documents the details of a sugar mill for extracting sugary sap from the cane. Flowing water turned the wheel (I) at the left, which then rotated the horizontal wheel (D) in the center; the central wheel turned the rollers (C) that pressed the cane itself. Sap collected in the basin (B). This sanitized image does not illustrate such factors as the oppressive heat of the operation, the physical exertion required, and the risk of maiming accidents.* Courtesy of Dover Publications.

the one hand, it was inefficient, because one hour of slave labor usually produced less than one hour of wage-earner labor did. Further, slaves were not trusted to perform certain tasks, particularly ones that used expensive machinery, because slaves often made "mistakes" that wrecked the machinery. (One may suspect sabotage, because slaves had little reason to respect owners' property and every reason to carry on some form of resistance against the owner who enslaved them.) On the other hand, seen in terms of work produced per slave, the system was very efficient: A slave pro-

duced more in a week than did a wage earner. The reason for this apparent paradox is simply that slaves worked longer hours with fewer breaks than did wage earners. They made the system efficient by the hard labor they were forced to perform and the long hours they were forced to work. Even considering the initial investment of purchasing slaves and the ongoing costs of feeding and housing them, the system was a bargain for the slave owner. The profits were extracted from the slaves' welfare. As one planter wrote, "We grew rich because whole races died for us. For us, continents were depopulated."

African Food in America

No movement of people, no matter how brutal or dislocating, occurs without the movement of culinary traditions. Even the African slave trade brought with it a part of West African cuisine.

By the early 1700s, it was typical for African slave ships to carry huge cargoes of African foods, and their occupants usually were fed at least one African meal a day. This cultural accommodation was no act of kindness, merely a self-serving recognition that fewer slaves died if familiar foods were fed them. Manuals of the day written for slave traders explained which foods would be best for slaves from the most common areas.

Yams were especially popular, because they were cheap, stored well, were easy to prepare, and were a common food in traditional West Africa. In 1732, John Barbot recommended that slavers carry 200 yams per slave; with as many as 500 slaves in the hold of a vessel, this meant a staggering 100,000 yams. Several African foods of somewhat lesser importance also made the voyage: black-eyed peas, sesame, okra, eggplant, *ackee*[a] (a starchy fruit widely used today in the Caribbean), and watermelon (originally grown for its seeds, not its pulp). Significantly, all are foods that carried their seeds (or other plantable parts) within the edible portion and could later be propagated in the Americas.

Once in America, slaves found that some African foodstuffs were unavailable and turned to local equivalents. Common substitutions included sweet potatoes (Americas) for yams, collard greens (Europe) and wild lamb's quarters (North America) for *sokoyokoto*,[b] *craincrain*,[c] and bitterleaf greens; Asian rice for African rice; and corn or potatoes for cassava.

[a]**ackee:** ah KEE
[b]**sokoyokoto:** soh koh yoh KOH toh
[c]**craincrain:** krayn krayn

In addition to ingredients, culinary techniques and recipes crossed the Atlantic in the memories of slave women. Corn mush, a thick corn porridge, was one of the most common of slave dishes in the Americas, and it is simply African *foo foo* (cassava porridge) with corn meal substituted for cassava flour. Gumbo, an American soupy stew thickened with okra (an African vegetable), is a direct transfer from Africa, where one name for okra is "gombo." Hotpot, a Caribbean stew, is a direct transplant from West Africa.

Two African-inspired dishes in America warrant special attention: fritters and long-cooked greens. The idea of taking a soft, starchy paste (often heavily spiced) and frying it in oil is a basic and longstanding West African technique, though it was not in use in Europe until the past couple of centuries. This technique produces fritters, such as the spiced corn balls called "hush puppies." The black-eyed pea fritter Brazilians call *acarajé*[d] is identical to the Nigerian *akara*.[e] Even quintessential southern fried chicken is dredged in a spicy batter before frying, an African technique alien to the Western food tradition.

In Africa, greens are most often prepared by long cooking them with a little piece of fatty meat, then eating the greens and drinking the vitamin-rich liquid left at the end of the process. This practice was carried to the Americas, and the traditional greens and salt pork is a direct reflection of it. In folk African American society, it also was traditional to drink the "pot likker" (juices) that remained after cooking.

Over the centuries, African contributions to American cooking have made their way into culinary traditions of all ethnic groups in the Americas. What could be more American than fried chicken, more Jamaican than hotpot, more Brazilian than *acarajé*?

[d]**acarajé:** ah kah rah HAY
[e]**akara:** AH kah rah

FIGURE 26.6 *Market-place in St. Johns.* *This 1902 photograph shows the market on the island of St. Johns in the Caribbean. Such markets began at the same time as the establishment of slavery and the plantation system, and were critical as means for slaves to exchange goods. The markets' economic importance was supplemented by their social importance, since they provided a venue for meeting people, holding conversations, and making friends. For just these reasons, markets were often deemed potentially subversive and were shut down when plantation owners feared slave uprisings.* Library of Congress.

THE AFRICAN DIASPORA

The enforced dispersal of Africans during the slave trade— the **African diaspora**[5]—was the largest dispersal of its kind in history. There may never have been another migration of comparable scope, and all other massive migrations have allowed the migrants to bring with them at least some of the items, ideas, and usages that characterized their cultures. In contrast, Africans rarely could bring any physical items, and their activities as slaves were restricted in ways designed to obliterate their past. In many slave communities, for example, slave owners forbade the speaking of African languages, the use of African names, the performance

[5]**diaspora:** dy AS poh ruh

of African music or the use of African instruments, and the practice of African religions. Despite these attempts at cultural eradication, an African stamp has persisted in many aspects of life among the descendants of African slaves in the Americas.

As far as we know, no musical instruments came on the Middle Passage. Nonetheless, African music came with African slaves, and in few places is African heritage more clear than in traditional African American music. For example, the **call-and-response pattern**, wherein a leader calls a line and a chorus responds with the same or a similar line, is distinctive to West Africa and the Americas. The complex rhythmic patterns of African American music from Brazil to the American South also can be traced directly to West Africa.

The conditions of slavery encouraged the development of a special class of African American music: the work song. Work songs have strong and regular rhythms, allowing a group of workers to perform their tasks in unison. For some tasks, such as picking cotton, working at a single pace was not really necessary, but for others, such as propelling the multiple handles of a rotary mill, coordination was critical. Typically following the call-and-response pattern, work songs were sung during most group labor—fixing the work pace, coordinating movement, and buoying spirits. Variations and innovations of words and melodies were encouraged, but the rhythm was kept invariable. Slaveowners encouraged the use of work songs by slaves, one of the few cases in which an African practice was actively supported by owners.

On Caribbean plantations, Sunday traditionally was reserved as a rest day for slaves and others. By the early 1600s, slaves had established Sunday market days, when individuals (mostly women) would meet to exchange produce, handicrafts, and other items. This was a recreation of the traditional West African market, held on a regular day of the week. In the Caribbean as in Africa, women dominated this arena of commerce, using this traditional exchange mechanism to distribute homemade or home-grown items throughout the community. In addition, the market served important functions in spreading news and socializing.

While some of the African slaves brought to the Americas had practiced Islam in Africa, most had practiced native African religions or a combination of Islam and native religions. It is small wonder, therefore, that aspects of African religion were brought through the Middle Passage and thrived in the Americas. The design symbolizing the cosmos in the Kongo kingdom of Angola, for example, was (and is) placed on bowls and other vessels for preparing *nkisi*,[6] magical preparations used in religious ceremonies. It consists of a right-angle cross in the middle of a circle or oval, and the design was believed to carry great spiritual power. The same symbols have been found on ceramic pots excavated by archaeologists from slave quarters in early-nineteenth-century South Carolina; the symbol also is used on iron pots used in preparing magical medicines in modern Cuba, where it is called *la zarabanda*.[7]

FIGURE 26.7 *African Religious Symbol in America.* *This design is incised into the base of a food bowl from eighteenth-century South Carolina. Such designs are found over a wide area of exclusively slave settings. The design always appears on food bowls, never on cooking pots. The similarity of this design to a Kongo religious symbol suggests that it came to North America with slaves.* Courtesy of Dr. Leland Ferguson.

The gods of precolonial Africa survived in the spirits of **voodoo**, also known as *santería*.[8] (The word "voodoo" itself comes from West Africa, probably from the Dahomey word "vodu," meaning spirit.) Despite its reputation—gained mainly from paperback novels and "B" movies—voodoo is a religion given over primarily to healing. While its practice was forbidden under slavery, it continued underground and served as a potent link with an African past. It continues today in the Caribbean and in many areas with large populations of immigrants from there.

---

[6]**nkisi:** NKEE see
[7]***la zarabanda:*** lah sah rah BAHN dah

[8]**santería:** sahn tah REE ah

Even the notion of complex handshakes, important at various periods in African American history, is a direct transplant from West Africa. Traditionally, West African men had personal handshakes, consisting of from three to ten grips and movements in a fixed sequence. When such men met friends, these handshakes were exchanged as a greeting, much as complex handshakes may be today from Jamaica to Toronto.

The wearing of large or extravagant hats by women, another West African custom, has carried over into the Americas as well, particularly in the Caribbean and the American South. Related is the custom of wearing several hats at one time, still common in the Caribbean, although rare in the United States now.

SLAVE UPRISINGS

During most of the period of the Atlantic slave trade, few slaveowners and others of European extraction had much concern about violence at the hands of slaves. Slaves usually were forbidden to have weapons, but even more influential was the widespread belief among European Americans that African Americans were, by their nature, compliant and happy with their lot, no matter how dreadful it was. In the sixteenth, seventeenth, and eighteenth centuries, a few violent encounters on a small scale had occurred in such places as Antigua and Jamaica, and there had been individual cases of violence wherever there had been slaves. These, however, typically were dismissed as aberrations rather than as indications of a persistent or serious threat of uprising. At the end of the eighteenth century, however, this situation changed radically.

Two factors led to the most influential of all slave uprisings, the Haitian Revolution. The first was the chasm between the living conditions for slaves and those for the owner class in Haiti. Like much of the rest of the Caribbean in the eighteenth century, Haiti was overwhelmingly devoted to the raising of sugarcane and the refining of sugar. These labor-intensive tasks were performed by African slaves, who constituted more than three-quarters of the population. Conditions for slaves in Haiti were even worse than in most places,

because the ruggedness of the terrain, the poverty and exhaustion of some of the soils, and the prevalence of disease made their lot especially burdensome. In contrast, the French elite who owned and operated the sugar plantations and other businesses prided themselves on being able to maintain an opulent lifestyle far from Paris.

The second factor was the French Revolution, which began in 1789. It will be discussed in more detail in Chapter 31, but its importance in terms of Haiti is that it championed the idea that the common people could resort to violence to rid themselves of rulers who cared little for the people's desires or needs. To a Haitian slave, this could be seen as a mandate to overthrow the French owners. The oppressive and unequal conditions in Haiti were the tinder, and the French Revolution was the spark.

Fanning the flame were Haitian patriots who instigated and led violent action against the French. The first of these was Vincent Ogé[9] (around 1750–1791). A slave from birth, Ogé initiated and led an uprising in 1790; in 1791, he was captured by the French and was tortured to death after a summary trial. His martyrdom established him as a rallying symbol for his cause.

François Dominique Toussaint L'Ouverture[10] (1744–1803) then took up the responsibility of leading the uprising, which rapidly grew into a full-scale revolution for independence. Toussaint L'Ouverture had been a slave until he was given his freedom in 1789, and, although his formal education was scant, his organizational and diplomatic abilities were spectacular. Through a series of alliances and military actions, he successfully defeated most of the French forces, and the revolution was nearly won by 1801. Through treachery, the French military captured Toussaint L'Ouverture in 1802 and sent him to France, where he died in a prison cell the following year.

The final leader of the revolution, Jean Jacques Dessalines[11] (1758–1806), was a ruthless commander whose armies committed well-publicized atrocities against the French and their Haitian allies. His methods were successful, however, and

[9]**Vincent Ogé:** vehn sehn OH zhay
[10]**François Dominique Toussaint L'Ouverture:** frahn SWAH doh mih NEEK too SAHN loo vehr TOOR
[11]**Jean Jacques Dessalines:** zhahn zhahk day sah LEEN

FIGURE 26.8 *Vincent Ogé Returning to Haiti.* *The first phase of the Haitian Revolution was spearheaded by Vincent Ogé, who returned from France in 1791 after his unsuccessful plea for increased civil rights and freedoms for Haitians. Thwarted in his attempts to bring about peaceful change, he led an abortive uprising that inspired Toussaint L'Ouverture and others to launch the successful Haitian Revolution in the early nineteenth century.* Bibliothèque nationale, Paris.

Haiti achieved independence in 1804. Dessalines expelled all persons of European extraction and proclaimed himself emperor. Haiti thus became the first African American state in the Americas and only the second independent nation in that hemisphere since the European conquest. The political implications of the Haitian Revolution will be explored further in Chapter 31.

The Haitian Revolution was a chilling episode to slaveowners around the Americas. It provided evidence that African American slaves were neither docile nor contented, and it proved that they were capable of effective, well-planned, and ruthless warfare, as well as postindependence retribution against slaveowners. Slaveowners and others of European extraction feared that the Haitian Revolution would serve as an inspiration for slaves elsewhere to rise up against their owners. While no other uprisings comparable to that in Haiti developed, the events in Haiti were a potent reminder that violence was possible anywhere there were slaves. Ultimately, it was one of several factors that led to the abolition of slavery throughout the Americas.

THE END OF THE ATLANTIC SLAVE TRADE

There always had been critics of slavery and the slave trade, but the intensity of their condemnation increased sharply in the second half of the 1700s. Led by Quakers and other humanitarians, criticism focused first on the slave trade.

Statements decrying the slave trade usually were couched in idealistic terms. Quakers condemned it because it debased and harmed people, running counter to their precept of brotherly love; Enlightenment philosophers (discussed in Chapter 31) condemned it because it violated the natural rights of slaves; and humanitarian philosophers condemned it for the suffering it imposed on its victims. These religious and philosophical movements were on the rise near the end of the eighteenth century, and condemnation of the slave trade followed naturally from them.

While idealist reformers were very important in the abolition of the slave trade, they were joined by allies with less lofty motives. In the United States and various other parts of the Americas, fear of slave insurrections like that in Haiti led some to support abolition of both the slave trade and of slavery. Some slaveowners who bred slaves for sale also favored abolishing the slave trade, reasoning that limiting the supply would drive up their value on the market. The Atlantic slave trade had not been particularly lucrative in some places, such as Denmark, and relinquishing it was little concession there.

Condemnation of the slave trade initially rose to prominence in the United States, but soon the focus shifted to England. There, various commissions inquired into the horrors of the Middle Passage, and hundreds of tracts were published advocating the end of the trade. In the meantime, voices denouncing the slave trade were being heard throughout Europe and its colonies and former colonies around the world.

The first country to abolish the slave trade was Denmark, a minor player, in 1792. It was followed

FIGURE 26.9 *A Slave's Gravestone. This eighteenth-century gravestone in Jamaica memorializes Scipio Africanus, an African slave who became a Christian. While some Christian groups actively tried to convert slaves to Christianity, others feared this would lead to egalitarian aspirations, making slaves more difficult to control.* Ikon/National Trust, Trevelyan Collection.

by the United States in 1807, England in 1808, the Netherlands in 1814, and France in 1815. U.S. ships continued to carry small numbers of slaves into Cuba until this practice was outlawed in 1862. In a brief span of nine years, however, the vast majority of slave importation was made illegal.

How could the slave trade, the product of four centuries of lucrative commerce, have been eradicated in such a brief time? Certainly this was a period when humanitarian concerns were affecting public policy more than ever before. And certainly the rising literacy rate in the Western world meant that the impassioned arguments of humanitarian reformers were reaching a broader audience than they would have in earlier periods.

AFRICAN SLAVE TRADE

Adaptation of lateen sail for ocean use, 1434

Gonçalvez captures slaves in Benin and delivers them to Portugal, 1441

Portuguese dominance of Atlantic slave trade, 1441– c. 1700

Asiento in force in Spain, c. 1600– 1789

Dominance of chattel slavery in West Africa, c. 1700– 1862

English dominance of Atlantic slave trade, c. 1700– 1808

1400

1500

1600

1700

1800

1900

Haiti becomes independent following revolution, 1804

Slave trade abolished in primary trading countries, 1807–1815

Slavery abolished in most countries, 1840–1870

Humanitarian sentiment probably was the most important factor underlying the end of the Atlantic slave trade.

An additional factor, however, was the changing economic nature of European and European American society. The old elites, based on royal lineage and agrarian landholding, had dominated politics for centuries. But following the onset of the Industrial Revolution (discussed in Chapter 32), power was shifting, and the new power base was rooted in industry and had little economic need for slaves. While it would still be about half a century before slavery itself was abolished in the same countries, the abolition of the slave trade was—in part—a symptom of the emerging dominance of the industrial middle class over the agrarian elite.

SUMMARY

1. Slavery existed in precolonial Africa in a form wherein slaves retained their personal rights. The early years of Portuguese slave trading (1441–around 1500) followed this general pattern.

2. The trans-Sahara slave trade and Indian Ocean slave trade carried substantial numbers of slaves from Africa to the Mediterranean and Asia. Following 1441, the Atlantic slave trade was centered in West Africa and conducted primarily by Europeans.

3. After around 1500, the nature of the African slave trade changed: Its volume and brutality increased, and slaves increasingly were viewed as devoid of personal rights.

4. Portugal controlled the Atlantic slave trade until around 1600, when it was displaced by England, which dominated from then on, while the Netherlands and later France became important traders. Other countries had small roles in the trade.

5. In Africa, coastal states participated in the Atlantic slave trade, providing slaves for the European traders. As a result, the traders and their states became rich and politically powerful.

6. In contrast, interior African states suffered from the effects of the Atlantic slave trade. Their governments were weakened or toppled, and their populations were robbed of their most productive members.

7. Chattel slavery (slavery in which a slave's value is considered in monetary terms only) developed in West Africa after the onset of the slave trade with Europeans. Increasingly, many Africans embraced Islam in an attempt to gain the protection it offered against being enslaved by other Muslims.

8. Both interior and coastal West African states suffered in the long run from dependence on European goods and underdeveloped economies.

9. In the Americas, where most slaves were sold, high mortality rates and labor-intensive occupations created a great demand for slaves. Sugar played an especially important role.

10. The triangular trade with slave trading as its middle leg supported the goals of the mercantile system.

11. The African diaspora was the dispersal of Africans by the slave trade. Despite the massive cultural dislocation, slaves were able to retain African cultural traits, many of which survive in the cultures of their descendants today.

12. The Haitian Revolution grew out of a slave uprising and resulted in the establishment of an African American state by 1804. It shocked slaveowners and other European Americans, who feared that similar uprisings could engulf them.

13. The slave trade in the major trading countries was abolished between 1807 and 1815. Humanitarian interests probably were the most critical factor in bringing about the abolition of the slave trade, but the rise of industrialization at the expense of the interests of the agrarian elite also shifted power away from those who gained the most advantage in the use of slaves.

SUGGESTED READINGS

Allison, Robert J., ed. *The Interesting Narrative of the Life of Olaudah Equiano.* Boston: Bedford Books–St. Martin's Press, 1995. The only known account of capture as a slave, the Middle Passage, and subsequent purchase of freedom by an African. Originally published in 1789. Includes an introduction and other interpretive aids.

Curtin, Philip. *The Atlantic Slave Trade: A Census.* Madison: University of Wisconsin Press, 1969. The seminal quantitative estimates from which all modern treatments begin.

———. *Economic Change in Precolonial Africa: Senegambia in the Era of the Slave Trade.* Two vols. Madison: University of Wisconsin Press, 1975. A classic treatment of the slave trade, focusing on economics alone.

Davidson, Basil. *The African Slave Trade.* Revised and expanded edition. Boston: Little, Brown, 1980. General treatment of the African slave trade, focusing on the effects in Africa.

Ferguson, Leland. *Uncommon Ground: Archaeology and Early African America, 1650–1800.* Washington, D.C.: Smithsonian Institution, 1992. An informative synthesis on the findings of archaeology regarding slave life in the southeastern United States.

Fogel, Robert. *Without Consent or Contract.* New York: Norton, 1989. The classic account by the economist on the efficiency of the American slave system. This work caps the research that won him a 1993 Nobel Prize.

Inikori, Joseph E., and Stanley L. Engerman, eds. *The Atlantic Slave Trade: Effects on Economies, Societies, and Peoples in Africa, the Americas, and Europe.* Durham, N.C.: Duke University Press, 1992. Excellent collection of papers discussing the "winners and losers" of the slave trade.

Rawley, James A. *The Transatlantic Slave Trade: A History.* New York: Norton, 1981. A general treatment with emphasis on the quantitative reconstruction of the trade.

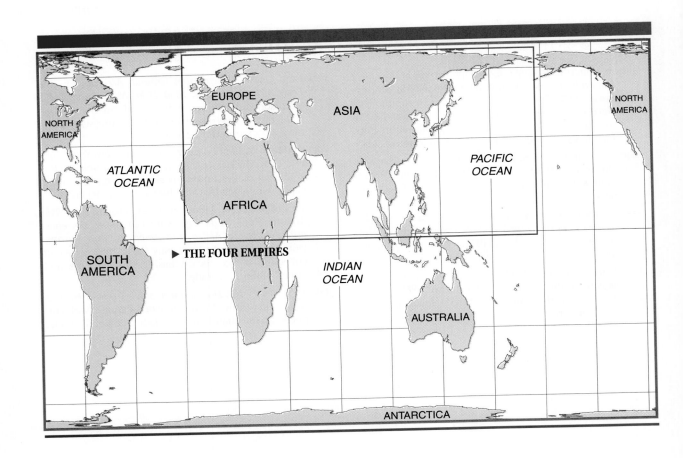

► **THE FOUR EMPIRES**

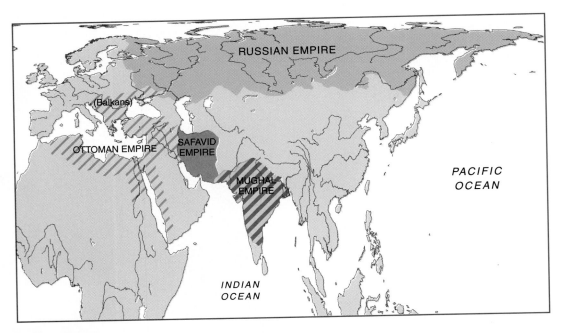

► **THE FOUR EMPIRES**

CHAPTER 27

Empires in Central Eurasia, South Asia, and North Africa
around 1350–around 1700

Several European travelers observed that they felt more comfortable in the Islamic Ottoman Empire than in the Christian Russian Empire. Perhaps those feelings reflected their familiarity with Ottoman cities, like Constantinople (modern-day Istanbul), that welcomed Europeans. Russian cities, on the other hand, had few non-Russians, who often were regarded with suspicion. Although western Europeans traveled to the Ottoman, Russian, Safavid, and Mughal[1] empires, they came as traders or advisors rather than as conquerors.

Trade and religion became dynamic elements of the Eurasian empires discussed in this chapter. The Ottoman Empire lay astride key trade routes between Europe, Asia, and Africa. The Safavid Empire controlled commercial roads between Southwest, Central, and South Asia, while the Mughal Empire dominated trade arteries in South Asia. Ottoman, Safavid, and Mughal monarchs also derived profits from maritime trade. Russian rulers had to content themselves with land trade routes within Europe but eventually conquered additional roadways between Europe and Central Asia. Islam was the dominant religion of the Ottoman, Safavid, and Mughal empires, helping their rulers to found and maintain long-lasting states. Russian rulers embraced Russian Orthodoxy, a branch of Christianity, and Russian Orthodox leaders rallied Russians to fight against invaders, like the Roman Catholic Poles in the seventeenth century.

[1] **Mughal:** MOO ghahl

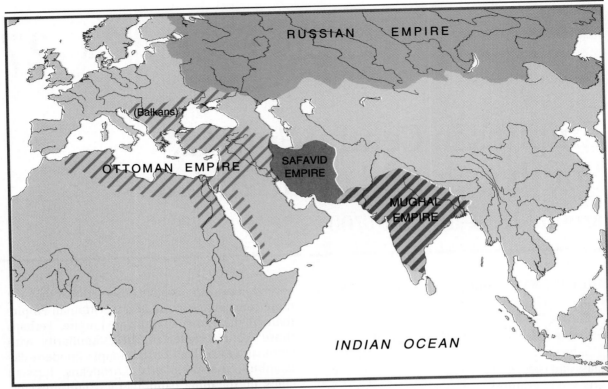

MAP 27.1 *The Four Empires, around 1700.* *The dynamic expansion of the Ottoman, Russian, Safavid, and Mughal empires brought some of them into direct contact with one another. The Ottoman Empire surrounded much of the Mediterranean Sea and covered parts of three continents. The Russian Empire controlled a vast territory, including the relatively uninhabited Siberia to its north. The Safavid Empire controlled much of present-day Iran, while the Mughal Empire united most of the Indian subcontinent.*

THE EARLY OTTOMAN EMPIRE, 1352–AROUND 1700

The Ottoman Empire began in the fourteenth century. It lasted until the twentieth century and is one of the longest-lived empires in history. One reason for this longevity was the tolerance by the Ottoman rulers of ethnic and religious differences. Religious tolerance, for example, was practiced by the Ottoman rulers, who welcomed Christians and Jews into their realm. Many served in the Ottoman government and played important social and economic roles. The Ottoman realm spanned parts of three continents, and its population reached nearly 30 million people in the seventeenth century. Although its leaders were Turks, the language of religion was Arabic and the main language of literature was Persian.

Expansion into Southwest Asia and Eastern Europe

The Mongol conquest of the Baghdad Caliphate in 1258 forced nomadic Turkic tribes, one of which was the Ottoman Turks, into the Anatolian Peninsula. Successive leaders of these Ottomans proclaimed a holy war against the Byzantine Empire in the fourteenth century; Ottoman successes brought other Muslims into the fight. A major development came in 1352 when Ottoman forces, allied with a claimant to the Byzantine throne, landed in Europe. Soon Ottoman armies began conquering the Balkan Peninsula, which lay open to expansion because of a paucity of able leaders and stable kingdoms. Imperial conquest was facilitated by the respectful treatment of Greek Orthodox Christians and by modest taxes on peasants. By 1400, the Ottoman Empire ruled parts of Islamic Asia and Christian Europe.

One significant consequence of the Balkan conquest was the formation of the **Janissaries**, warriors of European extraction who composed the elite Ottoman military force. Recruiters went into Balkan villages and selected teenage males for training as soldiers and administrators. These young men became slaves of the Ottoman **sultan**, the leader of the Ottoman Empire, and they were converted to Islam and trained as warriors or officials. Coming from Christian backgrounds and being the sultan's elite group set the Janissaries apart from other military groups. They were feared as fierce fighters.

Another feature of the Ottoman expansion into the Balkans was the forced relocation of peoples. Turkish groups were forced to resettle along and guard strategic highways that moved armies and their equipment to battle sites. Some Balkan peoples were transferred to the Anatolian Peninsula.

Capture of one sultan in 1402 caused a group of rivals to fight for control of the empire. This pattern of conflict, which often erupted early in the imperial era, led Sultan Mehmed II (reign dates 1444–1446 and 1451–1481) to promulgate the Law of Fratricide. This law made it legal for a monarch to kill his immediate male relatives who might pose a dynastic threat.

FIGURE 27.1 *Janissaries.* *The Janissaries faithfully served leaders of the Ottoman Empire for centuries. They adopted colorful ceremonial garb and were often at the forefront of heavy fighting involving the Ottoman armies. They played a crucial role in the conquest of Constantinople in 1453. In later centuries the Janissaries, like the imperial system they served, grew complaisant.* Österreichische Nationalbibliothek.

Ottoman Splendor: Mehmed, Selim, and Suleyman

In 1453, Constantinople fell to the Ottoman army under the command of Mehmed II; looting was kept to a minimum by the Ottoman sultan, who wished to keep his new capital unharmed. Known as Istanbul, the capital grew into a metropolis of around 400,000 people by 1550 and perhaps 800,000 by 1600. Mehmed was interested in Istanbul's architecture and cultural life. He oversaw the construction of the Topkapi Palace, with its immense gardens tended by perhaps 1,000 gar-

deners. Mehmed was a passionate gardener who planted exotic plants and trees. A major building complex of mosques, *medreses*[2] (colleges), libraries, and hostels was erected in Istanbul under Mehmed's direction. Funding for this center came from a large nearby market endowed by the sultan. This income ensured a permanent income for those who lived and worked in the complex; at the same time, the complex was administratively autonomous. Three hospitals were also built,

[2] *medreses:* MEH dreh sehs

Figure 27.2 *Diplomatic Embassy to the Ottoman Court.* *Italian painters sometimes worked for the Ottoman monarchs. Gentile Bellini, for example, was sent by the Venetian government to paint Mehmed II in 1480. Bias crept into the scene depicted here. Ambassadors abased themselves before the Ottoman rulers, but Bellini's painting shows a meeting of equals (center) rather than the normal submissive kneeling depicted in more accurate paintings. Note the tame deer and camels in the foreground.* Alinari/Art Resource, N.Y.

including one for women and another for non-Muslims, and each had a pharmacy.

Although *medreses* had long been in Muslim cities, they became a significant part of the Ottoman educational system. The first Ottoman *medrese* was founded in 1331 (later, Istanbul alone had 95 *medreses*), and the *medreses* of Mehmed and Suleyman I were the elite educational institutions. Famous scholars were invited to head a *medrese*; they and all students received room, board, books, and a monthly income. At the same time, top officials donated land and income for *medreses* and hostels, and men and women gave funds and lands to *medreses* and other charitable institutions.

The Ottoman sultans resumed their conquest of the Balkans and invaded lands bordering the Black Sea, where by 1500 Ottoman ships sailed unchallenged. Major trade routes in Russia and Central Asia passed into Ottoman control, and the Crimean Khanate became an Ottoman tributary state, supplying slaves for the Ottoman Empire.

Although Selim[3] I (reign dates 1512–1520) ruled only briefly, he had a significant impact on the Ottoman Empire. In 1514, his army decisively defeated the Safavid army. A few years later, Selim conquered Egypt. He also won the title of Guardian of the Two Cities (Mecca and Medina), which had been held by the ruler of Egypt. Thus, Selim became head of the Sunni sect of Islam. In addition, he was obliged to organize the annual pilgrimages (*hajj*) to Mecca, highly prestigious and profitable enterprises. Syria also fell to Selim, with Egypt and Syria soon supplying more than one-third of the imperial budget. Thus, Ottoman rulers gained access to the Red Sea, and trade routes

[3] **Selim:** SEH lihm

Ottoman expansion brought complex diplomatic relationships and often clashes with many European rulers. Thus, sultans had to cultivate diplomatic subtlety and military threat in their letters. In 1521, Suleyman I, newly ascended to the Ottoman throne, desired to conquer the island of Rhodes, a key threat to Ottoman maritime trade and an obstacle to Ottoman control of the eastern Mediterranean. In September 1521, the sultan sent an intimidating letter to the new Grand Master of the Knights of Rhodes, De L'Isle Adam.

IN THEIR OWN WORDS

A Diplomatic Exchange between Suleyman I and De L'Isle Adam

Suleyman the Sultan, by the grace of God, King of Kings, sovereign of sovereigns, most high Emperor of Byzantium and Trebizond, all powerful King of Persia, Arabia, Syria, and Egypt, Supreme Lord of Europe and Asia, Prince of Mecca and Aleppo, Master of Jerusalem and Ruler of the Universal Sea to Philip Villiers De L'Isle Adam, Grand Master of Rhodes, greeting and health: I congratulate you on your new dignity and upon your safe arrival in your estate. I hope that you will rule there in prosperity and even more gloriously than your predecessors. It rests with you to share in our favor; accept therefore our friendship, and as a friend congratulate me that emulating my father who conquered Persia, Jerusalem, Arabia, and Egypt, I have made myself master of that most important city, Belgrade. . . . I took many other strongholds and beautiful cities, destroying their inhabitants by the sword or fire, and selling the rest into slavery. Now after sending my large and victorious army home for the winter, I myself am able to return in triumph to my court in Constantinople. Farewell.

The Grand Master shrugged off the intimidation and replied in the plain language of a soldier.

Brother Philip Villiers De L'Isle Adam, Grand Master of Rhodes, to Suleyman, Sultan of the Turks, I have well understood the purport of your letter, which has been delivered by your ambassador. Your proposals of peace between us are as agreeable to me as they will be unwelcome to Cortoglu [a Turkish privateer]. That pirate omitted no efforts to surprise me on my passage from France; but having failed to stop me, as I sailed past him by night . . . he tried to carry off two merchantmen, but the galleys of my fleet drove him off and forced him to flee. Farewell.

Suleyman launched the invasion during the next summer, and after a long siege the island capitulated. Suleyman gallantly permitted the knights to depart with their weapons and possessions; he also vowed to treat the people of Rhodes well. Although a few historians question the validity of Suleyman's letter, most accept it as genuine.

---

to sub-Saharan Africa and India came under Ottoman influence.

Perhaps the height of Ottoman power came during the reign of Suleyman I, Suleyman the Magnificent (reign dates 1520–1566). He conquered Belgrade and briefly besieged Vienna in 1529. Like his predecessors, Suleyman supported the various opponents of his main European foe, the Hapsburgs, who ruled Spain, Austria, and much of Germany. Thus, Suleyman allied the Ottoman Empire with France, which vigorously opposed Hapsburg expansion policies. Suleyman gave the French special trading privileges, and soon income from this trade became a major revenue source.

Suleyman built architectural masterpieces, including the Suleymaniye, a mosque complex that still dominates Istanbul. The mosque itself had four slender minarets and a vast dome, impressing subjects and travelers alike. Its architect, Sinan[4] (around 1490–1588), has been regarded as the greatest Ottoman designer, and he grew up in the Palace School, learning his architectural trade there. Sinan built many other splendid works, like the Imperial Mosque, which was commissioned by Mihrimah,[5] one of Suleyman's daughters.

[4] **Sinan:** see NAHN
[5] **Mihrimah:** MEE ree mah

FIGURE 27.3 *Ottoman Canteen.* *Artisans were favored with financial support by the Ottoman political and social elite. This piece dates from the era of Suleyman the Magnificent in the second half of the sixteenth century. The complex gold-leaf pattern studded with jewels is meant to dazzle the viewer.* Courtesy of Topkapi Saray Museum.

Suleyman was also nicknamed the "Lawgiver." This epithet reflected the fact that the sultan issued many decrees that supplemented the traditional law of Islam. In fact, Suleyman was regarded as the model of virtue, one who was stern but just, warlike but cultured. Legal decisions were often reached by consensus after debate, and the Ottoman justice system became famed among imperial subjects for its fairness.

Class and Gender

The Ottoman leaders maintained a social system with clear distinctions. The basic one was between the rulers and the ruled. Top government officials, both in the capital and in outlying provinces, came from the Palace School. Merchants and artisans enjoyed a favorable standing in Ottoman society because of the importance given to production and trade in Islamic societies. Artisan associations, or **guilds**, not only regulated production of goods along craft lines, but they also provided important social services, like emergency loans, for their members. Some guilds even had close associations with Sufi orders and therefore assumed a religious character. Slaves from Europe and Africa also served their Ottoman masters, although Islamic law forbade the enslavement of Muslims.

Although Ottoman society was dominated by men, individual women sometimes played important roles. Muslim women generally remained confined to the **harem**, a place of forbidden entrance to adult males, except the household head. Islamic law permitted four wives to one husband, but usually only wealthy men maintained many wives and children. When a sultan was a minor or indifferent to politics, his mother allied with palace eunuchs and wielded influence, especially in the seventeenth century. Wealthy and socially prominent women had an impact through charitable activities, because Islam required all to be generous in giving to needy people. Women donated money, property, and their time to worthy causes, including educational institutions.

Arts and Literature

Although elite arts flourished, a tension developed between those who pursued or developed new ideas and those who believed in the strict adherence to Islamic law and its practices. Molla Lutfi[6] (died 1494), for example, was a famous scholar and freethinker. Because he mocked what he considered to be outmoded Islamic beliefs, Molla Lutfi made enemies among the religious leaders, who found him guilty of impiety and executed him. Ibn Kemal[7] (1468–1534), one of Lutfi's students, wrote more than 100 religious treatises and a ten-volume history of the Ottoman Empire. Other scholars wrote encyclopedias concerning political or religious matters.

From earliest Ottoman times, Muslim scholars vigorously pursued studies of mathematics and astronomy, maintaining a long tradition of expertise. In 1577, the sultan's astronomer commissioned the building of a state-of-the-art observatory that used a clock system employing European

[6]**Molla Lutfi:** MOO lah LOOT fee
[7]**Ibn Kemal:** EE bahn keh MAHL

FIGURE 27.4 *Turkish Bridal Procession.* *This seventeenth-century painting shows a bride proceeding to her wedding. Several pages, each festively attired, lead the heavily veiled bride and her companions. In most Muslim areas, women were veiled in public.*
After Tueschnor, F., *Alt-Stambuler Hof und Volksleben*, Hanover, 1925.

clock technology. Religious authorities soon objected to the observatory because it supported research that challenged some tenets of Islam and had it razed; this kind of activity drove underground research that might conflict with Islamic law. In fact, such rulings effectively ended Islamic science as religious leaders gained control.

Turkish literature and arts developed in Ottoman times and were strongly influenced by Persian literature. For example, Turkish poets were inspired by Rumi (1207–1273), one of the greatest Persian poets and mystics. Rumi founded the Mevlavi Sufi mystics, and they influenced other Turkish arts, like music and dancing.

THE SAFAVID EMPIRE OF PERSIA, 1501–1736

The Safavid Empire (named after Shaykh Safi,[8] 1252–1336) came to power and helped Persia (modern Iran) become a major player in Southwest Asia. Ismail[9] (reign dates 1501–1524), the

[8] **Shaykh Safi:** SHAYKH SAH fee
[9] **Ismail:** EESH mayh uhl

founder of the dynasty, proclaimed Shi'ism, an Islamic sect, as the ideology of the Safavid state. Conflicts between the Safavids and Ottomans soon assumed the character of a religious war, as the Ottomans were Sunni believers. Thus, the spread of Safavid rule was also the spread of Shi'ism, and strong animosities between the Sunnis and Shi'ites may be seen today.

One development connected with the collapse of the Abbasid Caliphate in the thirteenth century was the growth of folk Islam. **Folk Islam**, the religious practices of ordinary Muslims, lay beneath the surface of religious life as long as the great Islamic centers of Baghdad and Damascus flourished. With the subsequent loss of the Abbasid state in 1258, adherents of folk Islam began openly to practice their religion. Sufis attracted followings of common folk, and tombs of Sufis became sites for the faithful to visit.

Founding and Early Expansion

In 1501, Ismail (a descendant of Shaykh Safi) proclaimed the Safavid Dynasty, and early victories rallied Turkish tribes that had supported Ismail's ancestors. Having Turkish and Persian ancestry aided Ismail in building an army composed of

Turkish warriors and a government dominated by Persian officials. Ismail's success was in uniting them into a formidable whole.

Ismail used religion to weld his supporters tightly to himself. Because folk Islam permitted claiming divine status, Ismail proclaimed himself a god-emperor; he commanded absolute obedience, and his soldiers garnered a reputation for extreme ferocity. A string of victories fueled a sense of godlike invincibility and helped Ismail to forge an expansionist state.

Rather than confront the powerful Ottoman Empire and prematurely risk a defeat and total disaster, Ismail turned to other areas, which he easily subdued. The Ottoman sultan, however, knew that the Safavids presented a serious challenge to his empire; after settling internal disputes, Selim marched against Ismail, and Ottoman cannons and rifles shattered the Safavid force. Ismail escaped and ceased hostilities; having lost his ardor, he became passive after the battle against the Ottomans. Successor Safavid monarchs fought Ottoman forces, surviving several campaigns that brought loss of much territory. To stay in power, rulers permitted the growth of Turkish influence in the government and in the army. Turks under the Safavid leaders formed an elite bodyguard unit that eventually meddled in court affairs.

The Rule of Shah Abbas

Shah Abbas (reign dates 1587–1629) came to the throne at the age of sixteen years. He restructured the Safavid government and economy, recapturing land lost to the Ottomans. The first task for this **shah**, the Persian equivalent of sultan, was the

ENCOUNTERS

The Armenian Trade Connection

Among the great variety of traders in the seventeenth century, the Armenians played a significant role in the transportation and distribution of goods across wide parts of Eurasia. The cornerstone of Armenian commercial activity was the family or clan. In that sense, the Armenians are similar to the Jews of Cairo in the twelfth century or to the Overseas Chinese of Jakarta (Indonesia) in the twentieth century; each group built and sold commercial relationships on family ties.

The Armenians played crucial roles in many kinds of trade and could be found in China, the Philippines, Tibet, Russia, India, and Persia, among other places. One trademark commercial item was textiles, and one East India Company official admitted that Persian markets, under Armenian control, sold a wider variety of English broadcloth than famous stores in London. Armenians also specialized in the trade of indigo, raw silk, and wine. The prominent Armenian trade role in the Philippines came when the Spanish forbade Protestants from trading in the Philippines. This opened a place for the Armenians. Armenians traced their Christian lineage to long before the Protestant Reformation.

Because Armenians had no independent state in the seventeenth century, many had been forcibly relocated to Isfahan by Shah Abbas. From this center, the Armenians spread along caravan and maritime trade routes. One English merchant noted that

the Armenians being skilled in all the intricacies of trade at home, and traveling with these into the remotest kingdoms, become by their own industry, and by being factors of their own kindred's honesty, the wealthiest men. . . . They are a kind of privateers in trade, no purchase, no pay; they enter the theater of commerce by means of some benefactor, whose money they adventure upon, and on return, a quarter part of their gain is their own: From such beginnings do they raise sometimes great fortunes for themselves and their masters.

The families developed a training and apprentice system to bring younger members into the family businesses. Young men were trained in handwriting, foreign languages, and accounting practices. Upon reaching adulthood, they were given a sum of money to manage and were promoted according to their financial and business success. The merit-based system seemed to work for several generations as the Armenians became major players in the commercial development of the Indian Ocean region.

elimination of the Turkish guards and the conquest of their tribes. Abbas created units composed of prisoners of war from the Caucasus area; these men had settled in Persia, and most had converted to Islam. The new force became an elite element in the reorganized Safavid army; with intensive training, these soldiers became the backbone of the forces that maintained Safavid rule.

Attacks against the Uzbeks resumed in the seventeenth century, and Abbas regained the vital silk-producing regions of northeast Persia. He also asserted control over important trade routes. By 1603, Abbas felt strong enough to confront the Ottoman Turks, and he slowly won back the lands lost early in his reign. In 1622, Shah Abbas also ousted the Portuguese from Hormuz, an island fortress in the Persian Gulf. This action gave the Persians access to Indian Ocean trade, especially with the Mughals of India.

Abbas not only fought wars and reformed his government, but he also embarked on a complex series of economic reforms. Realizing that political strength rested on economic prosperity, Abbas captured vital trade routes. He built roads and refurbished old highways. **Caravanserais**, or inns where merchants could recover from arduous journeys, were founded at strategic intervals along trade routes.

The Persian capital was relocated to Isfahan, far from Ottoman areas and at the nexus of key trade routes. To promote trade, Abbas forcibly uprooted 3,000 Armenian families to settle in his new capital. These Armenians applied themselves to commerce and played a key role in the growth of trade in Persia. At the same time, the mass industrial production of ceramic wares, textiles, and carpets fueled prosperity. Silk production became a government monopoly, as did other vital industries. The royal artisans played a major role in the production of export goods. Abbas invested in trading ventures and encouraged Persian large landowners to do likewise. For diplomatic and economic purposes, Abbas maintained relations with the Mughals of India, the Crimean Tatars, and various European powers.

Arts and Literature

The relocation of the capital stimulated Isfahan's growth from a sleepy town to a world metropolis. Abbas hired architects to create monumental buildings, such as the Isfahan Mosque, the Gate-

FIGURE 27.5 *Armenian Church in Persia.* *Armenian merchants played an important economic role for the Safavid rulers. In return, they were accorded special privileges, including the construction of their own churches in Isfahan, the Safavid capital. This domed church is dedicated to Saint Astavtzatzin, the Holy Mother of God.* Courtesy of Nice Vecchione.

house, and the Royal Square. One mosque had a double dome and was built on an unprecedented scale, taking twenty years to complete. Master calligraphers decorated the building with graceful calligraphy. Chahar Bagh was an avenue nearly three miles long with fountains, cascades, trellised walls, and shaded walks with streams, flowers, and trees. People rode, walked, and conversed on this urban thoroughfare, which proclaimed Isfahan as one of the world's spectacular cities. Abbas built a Christian church for the Armenians and permitted Jews to build a synagogue.

Painters received royal patronage and much stimulation from Shah Tahmasp[10] I (reign dates

[10]**Tahmasp:** TAH uhm ehsp

1524–1576), who painted miniatures. Persians had a flair for miniature painting; long before the Safavids, outstanding Persian miniatures had been painted, some showing the influence of Chinese paintings brought to Persia by the Mongols. One famous miniaturist worked on a manuscript that contained more than 250 miniatures and consumed ten years of his life.

Shaykh-i Bahai (1546–1631) was perhaps the most admired scholar of the Safavid period. He was born in Lebanon and went to Persia. Shaykh-i Bahai mastered Persian and composed many poems in that language. He wrote more than ninety works on theology, rhetoric, Arabic grammar, mathematics, astronomy, law, and mysticism.

MUGHAL RULE IN INDIA, 1526–1707

The Central Asian ruler Babur[11] (reign dates 1526–1530) founded the Mughal Empire in India. At its height, the Mughal domain covered nearly all of the Indian subcontinent, and the Mughal emperors ruled a population of nearly 150 million people. Persian became the state language, and Persian artists, architects, and officials imparted a Persian character to an emerging Indian cultural synthesis. Although the Mughal leaders claimed Mongol and Turkish ancestry, most viewed themselves as Indians and professed Islam as their faith.

Akbar's Conquests and Administration

Akbar (reign dates 1556–1605), one of India's greatest rulers, brought Mughal rule to the western coast of India, controlled vital maritime trade routes, and expanded south to the Deccan Plateau. To overawe and protect his subjects, Akbar built four huge forts, which guarded the central area of the Mughal realm. He also massacred the population of an enemy city in 1567 to show that resistance to him could bring utter destruction.

Although Akbar came to the throne as a teenager, he and able advisors soon devised and implemented long-range solutions that brought peace and prosperity. By the age of twenty, Akbar assumed full command of his government, and one of his first actions was to marry a Hindu princess. Later he married additional wives: another Hindu, a Christian, and a Muslim. This showed Akbar's religious tolerance, according to some scholars. Akbar followed a policy of building a stable government by appointing different peoples to the administration. A Hindu commanded Akbar's army, and other Hindus served in the

FIGURE 27.6 *Persian Tile Mosaic. Persian artists of Isfahan often painted on tiles. This tile painting depicts a woman at leisure, holding a vase and being offered fruit by a servant. Gardens were often favorite sites for domestic scenes; note how the floral pattern of the woman's gown complements the flowers in the garden.* Victoria & Albert Museum.

[11]**Babur:** bah BUHR

FIGURE 27.7 *Mughal Monumental Architecture.* Akbar built a capital, Fatehpur Sikri, which was briefly occupied and later abandoned for lack of adequate water sources. This scene conveys the overwhelming majesty of the capital's main building, meant to convey the might of Akbar's rule. Among these buildings is the mosque at the tomb of Shaykh Salim Chisti, the Sufi saint who was revered by Akbar.
Roland and Sabrina Michaud/Woodfin Camp and Associates.

financial administration. They were given charge of the state's tax collection because Akbar believed that Hindu tax agents would not gouge their fellow Hindus.

Todar Mal,[12] Akbar's Hindu finance minister, devised a revenue-raising system that transformed state finances and society. Finance officials developed a survey form that took into account agricultural land size, soil fertility, and average yields of various crops (over ten-year cycles). Each crop was expressed in monetary terms, reflecting average prices in local or regional markets. Because tax receipts were to be paid in cash, peasants or their agents sold their crops in order to get tax funds. Local leaders who had dominated areas of 20 to 100 villages were forced to become state revenue

collectors in exchange for 10 percent of the tax revenues. This policy and others gave the Mughals a reputation for promoting stability and prosperity, thereby helping to prolong Mughal rule of India.

The mixture of diverse influences at Akbar's court may be seen in the patronage of various courtiers. Akbar welcomed writers in Hindi and Urdu, two languages that evolved from the admixture of Persian with local Indian dialects or languages. He also encouraged Hindu painters who specialized in drawings of India's flora and fauna. Persian poets, artists, and scientists who immigrated from Persia enjoyed imperial favor and support in and after Akbar's era.

Architectural development received great impetus during Akbar's reign. He worked on two capitals, Delhi and Agra, and planned a third. The last had to be abandoned for lack of sufficient

---

[12]**Todar Mal:** toh DAHR mahl

water to support an urban population. Akbar commanded architects and builders to construct forts, palaces, and mosques in his cities.

Akbar was illiterate, but he had books read to him, and his European contemporaries remarked on his vast knowledge and retentive memory. Avidly curious, Akbar welcomed adherents of various beliefs, including Hinduism, Christianity, and Zoroastrianism. Akbar would discuss religion with them, but, until his later years, he retained the essence of his Islamic beliefs. His realm was noted for its religious tolerance, which was especially shrewd, given that the majority of Indians believed in Hinduism.

Some of Akbar's actions and policies angered Muslims. Perhaps in deference to his Hindu subjects, he also abstained from eating beef and finally became a vegetarian. Many Muslim leaders opposed these departures from orthodox Muslim practices. Akbar's assumption of power over judging Islamic law, especially in capital offenses, caused additional grumbling by Islamic religious leaders. Part of Akbar's motivation stemmed from a case in 1578 in which a *brahman* (Hindu priest) was tried and executed for the crime of insulting the name of Muhammad. Akbar also investigated the entitlement of Muslim officials to claim state funds and found many cases of corruption.

UNDER THE LENS

Sikhism under the Mughals

Sikhism, a monotheistic religion founded in North India, began as an attempt to bridge the religious differences between Islam and Hinduism and was transformed into a religion of resistance to Mughal oppression. In the process, it appealed to commoners in northern India. By the eighteenth century, a major Sikh uprising erupted and helped bring about the decline of the Mughals, especially in the north.

The founding of Sikhism (Sikh[a] means disciple) originated with Guru (spiritual teacher) Nanak (1469–1539). Guru Nanak grew up in northern India and learned Arabic, Persian, and Sanskrit, languages associated with Islam and Hinduism. A man of great personal charisma, Guru Nanak loved to travel and walked across North India; later he went to Mecca and other cities in South and Southwest Asia. He taught that because there is one god, the creator, there is no Hindu, no Muslim. Guru Nanak welcomed all people irrespective of belief, gender, or social station. All people ate together, contrary to caste principles of strict segregation and separateness. Men and women, as well as people of different castes, shared dining facilities. Early Sikhs were exhorted to call on God's name, share earnings, and work hard.

Sikhism spread slowly through the sixteenth century, but its modest success led to persecution. Trouble for the Sikhs grew out of the succession dispute

associated with Akbar's sons. Jehangir eventually succeeded his father and executed the reigning guru, who had favored one of his brothers. This was the first of several martyrdoms that sparked the growth of Sikhism.

Aurangzeb attempted to quell Sikhism but ended up making it even stronger. Fearing the successful spread of Sikhism, especially with the conversion of Muslims, Aurangzeb arrested, tried, and executed a charismatic leader. This and other attempts at repression drove Guru Govind and the Sikhs into open resistance. Govind transformed Sikhism by turning the Sikhs into an Army of the Pure. He and his followers took the family name Singh (lion), distinguished themselves by refusing to cut their hair, by wearing a steel bracelet, and by wearing a knife or sword.

After Guru Govind's assassination, a major uprising of Sikhs engulfed much of India north of Delhi, a major Mughal city. The Sikhs were inspired by Banda, an ascetic follower of Guru Govind. Banda traveled across the northern plains preaching and welcoming all groups, including many lower socioeconomic groups. Religious fervor and hatred of elite groups drove the Sikhs to success against cavalry and cannonballs hurled against them. Cities fell to the rebels, and inhabitants who refused to convert were killed; temples were desecrated and homes were looted. Only a major effort by the Mughals in 1715 quelled the uprising, with much bloodshed and reprisal. Sikhism continued to enjoy mass support in the north.

[a]**Sikh:** SEEKH

Jehangir[13] (reign dates 1605–1627) was Nur Jahan[14] (1577–1645), who initiated many Mughal policies. Jehangir was seriously ailing for his last decade of rule, partly because of his addiction to alcohol and other drugs. Nur Jahan, in alliance with her father and brother, dominated the government, and she is regarded as one of several influential Muslim and Hindu women in the Mughal era.

Shah Jahan (1627–1658) is another Mughal ruler who merits mention. He maintained a luxurious lifestyle in which dancing, singing, and gambling entertained the court. Shah Jahan indulged himself in his harem of hundreds of wives, yet he favored one, Mumtaz Mahal, who gave birth to fourteen children. She died in childbirth, and he mourned her death by erecting a mausoleum, the Taj Mahal. One of the world's architectural masterpieces, the Taj Mahal shows a strong Persian character but also combines Hindu features and echoes the stylistic synthesis of Akbar's era.

The Reign of Aurangzeb

Aurangzeb[15] (reign dates 1658–1707), one of Shah Jahan's sons, rebelled against his father and imprisoned him until he died. Aurangzeb reacted against many previous trends in the Mughal era. He abolished the court entertainments and used religious texts to support his actions. He imposed previously revoked taxes on nonbelievers, including an assessment on Hindu pilgrims. He also revived the policy of razing Hindu temples; hundreds of architectural masterpieces fell to the destructive policies of Aurangzeb and his ardent followers.

Aurangzeb resumed the conquest of India, planning to subjugate the entire subcontinent. Because the military effort took decades, it bankrupted the treasury. Even though tax revenues had doubled from 1589 to 1689, taxes were increased to fight the wars. The contracting out of tax revenues to Muslims who purchased the right to collect the expected sums and then pocketed the excess monies brought a rapacious exploitation of Hindus, who rebelled. By his death, Aurangzeb's administration was beyond repair and eventually collapsed.

FIGURE 27.8 *Lively Discussion. This Persian miniature of the late seventeenth century depicts an unveiled woman engaged in a lively discussion with a religious teacher. Some Sufi organizations accepted women as equal members of their orders.* Museen des Kunsthandwerke, Leipzig.

At one point, Akbar created his own religion (Akbarism), which espoused one deity, the Sun God, without the need of a priesthood. He planned to unite his subjects spiritually as his government united them politically. Because of this tolerant approach to the old faiths, Akbar did not try to compel people to believe in his new one. As a consequence, the religion died with him.

Prominent families also played key roles in the Mughal government. The favorite wife of

[13] **Jehangir:** jeh HAHN gee hyr
[14] **Nur Jahan:** NUHR jah HAHN
[15] **Aurangzeb:** AH rahng zehb

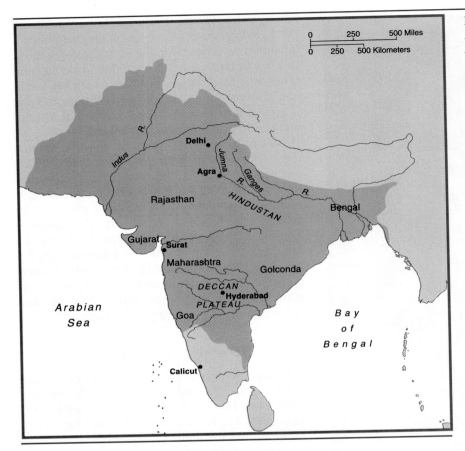

MAP **27.2** *The Mughal Empire, around 1710.* *Akbar and Aurangzeb conquered much of present-day India, Pakistan, and Bangladesh. Though pockets of resistance held out against the Mughals, especially in the west, they ruled a vast area by 1710—one that gradually succumbed to the British.*

Class and Caste

Mughal rulers presided over a traditional Islamic social structure with courtiers occupying the top of the social system, Muslim officials enjoying moderate prominence, and Muslim merchants having some prestige.

But the Mughals ruled over a majority population of Hindu subjects who were socially governed by a caste system that had endured for centuries. Although a loose, religiously defined social structure existed (the four Varna castes of *brahman* priests, warriors, commoners, and peasants), most Hindus were grouped by occupational castes (*jati*). Thus, there were scribal *jati* (lower officials), merchant *jati*, artisan *jati*, and peasant *jati*; most *jati* had regional or local identities and were largely self-regulating. The *jati* interacted economically and politically but seldom socially; members of a *jati* did not marry outside of their *jati*. One was born, married, and died within the *jati*. Thus, the Mughals ruled over two distinct social systems, which meshed at the court.

THE EMERGENCE OF THE RUSSIAN EMPIRE, 1462–1682

The Russian Empire emerged in the fifteenth century and eventually straddled Europe and Asia. Russian leaders directed a centralized state with an economy heavily dependent on the labor of serfs, peasants bound permanently to the land. Rulers of Moscow gradually became the tsars (emperors) of the Russian Empire.

Why did Moscow prevail over the other contending political entities? It was ruled by a series of leaders who usually managed peaceful successions to the throne. These far-sighted monarchs expanded their domains by all available means, including purchase and warfare, yet they understood that expansion depended on patient planning. A major success was the agreement that the Russian Orthodox Church would accept Moscow as its capital. Moscow also occupied a strategic position in northern Russia, lying between rivers along which trade goods easily moved.

The Accomplishments of Ivan the Great

The monarch Ivan the Great (reign dates 1462–1505) embarked on a series of policies to strengthen Moscow's dominance in the north. His foreign policy embodied the reconquest of western lands lost to the Lithuanians and the defeat of the khanates in the east. Ivan allied with the Crimean Khanate to defeat a Mongol-Lithuanian alliance. Victory came in 1480 and freed Moscow from two centuries of Mongol domination. Ivan fought the Lithuanian monarchy, which oppressed Russian princes under its control. Through a series of wars, many princes defected to Ivan, who claimed to rule all Russian peoples. Ivan also brought the Kazan[16] Khanate of the middle Volga River under his protection.

Aside from these diplomatic gains, Ivan conquered Novgorod and other city-states in northern Russia. Each campaign followed a carefully scripted scenario wherein Moscow's troops intervened in an internal dispute and gradually took control. Ivan understood that to conquer and rule, he must reform his government. He gained control over his officials by establishing the **service gentry**, landlords who joined his army and served in his administration. They owed their positions to Ivan and adhered to his demand for complete obedience, serving the same purpose that the Janissaries did for the Ottomans. To secure the support of the service gentry, who served away from their estates for long periods, Ivan permitted serfdom, binding peasants to the land.

Ivan established long-lasting institutions and practices. He oversaw the codification of law, which created a legal foundation for the state in 1497. In addition, a judicial system was established to dispense the monarch's justice, while other decrees directed government officials to be honest, loyal, and hardworking. Special investigating officials designated by Ivan served as a check on his subordinates.

After great personal trials, Ivan curbed the influence of his immediate family members and in-laws. He finally decided the succession in favor of his son, Basil. More than four decades of cautious rule and steady growth of Moscow's power warranted most historians to name Ivan III "the Great."

[16] **Kazan:** KAH zahn

The Reign of Ivan the Terrible

Ivan IV (reign dates 1533–1584) earned the appellation "Terrible" because he left Russians traumatized by his policies. A regency of Ivan's mother and aristocrats brought grief for Ivan, whose mother died in his eighth year. It is likely that she was poisoned; at least he suspected foul play. Aristocrat princes accorded Ivan public honor but scorned him in private. Ivan took power for himself in 1548, crowning himself tsar. In 1553, Ivan suffered a serious illness and wished to name his son heir, but he was thwarted by the princes. Finally, a suspicious Ivan turned against his top officials and aristocrats in the 1560s, launching a one-sided civil war that killed many. In the 1570s, thousands more were tortured to death, and the succession itself was affected when Ivan killed his adult son during a rage.

Ivan IV ruled effectively for many years. He reformed the government to improve its administration; a law code was published in 1550. The military was restructured and better trained in order to make it more efficient. The church was brought under governmental supervision, and church priests obeyed state law. Ivan followed his grandfather's (Ivan III) policy of expanding Russian control to the Baltic Sea, yet these early military successes united Russia's traditional enemies, Lithuania and Poland.

Ivan IV's greatest victories came in the east and southeast. The Kazan Khanate tamed by Ivan III became restive in the early 1550s, and Ivan IV launched a campaign that brought its annexation. Soon after, a second expedition conquered the Astrakhan Khanate, bringing the Volga River Valley under Russian control. A major reorientation had taken place, because now Russia, a European power, lay astride strategic Asian trade and transportation routes.

Russia's eastward expansion took a different route when the Stroganov merchant family supported the crossing of the Ural Mountains by a military force. With relative ease, Russians conquered the Siberian Khanate in the 1580s. When a group of Siberians tried to retake the khanate's capital, Ivan IV sent military support, defeating the Siberians. This opened the massive area of Siberia to Russian exploration, colonization, and exploitation. Furs, precious metals, and other materials could be easily gathered and traded. Part of the ease of Russian

Figure 27.9 *Ivan the Terrible's Reign of Terror.* *This woodcut shows the Russian tsar leading a group of subjects who are bound, awaiting punishment. Ivan is carrying the severed head of one victim, while another subject, perhaps a child, is impaled, framed by the horse's legs. In the background others are being beheaded and hanged. Thousands of people met similar deaths that were overseen by the tsar during his reign of terror.* The New York Public Library, Slavonic Division.

expansion is attributable to the many deaths caused by epidemics among Siberians, who could not withstand the diseases that the Europeans carried.

To conduct his foreign policy and expand central control of the land, Ivan IV relied heavily on the service gentry. He honored their growing appetite for permanent peasant labor by expanding serfdom. Peasants resented being bound to the land, and many fled to frontier areas in the south. The state tried to support its officials by outlawing the practice of flight and by returning apprehended serfs to their lords.

The Crimean Khanate, which had been allied with Ivan III, turned against Ivan IV, launching raids against Moscow and capturing many citizens. Perhaps 100,000 people were taken from their homes to slavery in the south. The loss of taxpayers caused a fiscal crisis, prompting authorities to raise taxes. A general depopulation resulted as many fled the ever-increasing taxes.

Ivan IV died, and, because his successor was ineffective, power devolved to capable officials who instituted reforms, reversing Ivan IV's harsh policies. Yet beneath the surface calm, the larger demographic issue of the depopulation of central Russia and the decline of tax revenues meant that any state crisis might lead to collapse. When this successor died, the line of Ivan IV ended. Rule passed to Tsar Boris Godunov (reign dates 1598–1605), an in-law of the dynastic house, but within a short time Russia found itself immersed in civil war, beset by foreign invasion, and faced with revolt by commoners.

Crisis and Revival

The Time of Troubles (1598–1613) saw Russia in collapse and chaos. The tsarist system failed to cope with its massive problems, and major social uprisings and foreign invasions imperiled Russia. Sweden took territory in the north, and Poland invaded, captured Moscow, and left a Polish ruler in charge. By 1610, it seemed that the threat of extinction haunted the Russian state. Members of the religious elite rallied the Russian people, and finally a group of landlords and merchants raised an army that defeated the foreigners. A social crisis in which the have-nots challenged the haves sputtered through various conflicts. By 1613, the people of Russia agreed that a new dynasty should rule, and they sent representatives to an assembly that elected a member of the Romanov family as the new tsar.

The first three Romanovs ruled from 1613 to 1682 and wielded power in a moderate fashion. Taxes lightly burdened the people, and foreign policies concentrated on regaining lost lands. A new law code was published in 1649, codifying the procedures and practices of serfdom for the succeeding two centuries.

Religious leaders in the 1650s and 1660s attempted to reform the Russian Orthodox ritual. Many Russians (Old Believers) viewed the changes in ritual as blasphemous and refused to accept them. This controversy in Russian Orthodoxy became political as well as religious because the state persecuted the Old Believers.

UNIFYING FEATURES OF THE FOUR EMPIRES

The Ottoman, Safavid, Mughal, and Russian empires had certain things in common, including the use of gunpowder technology, the significance of religion in defining each empire's cultural tradition, and the relative insignificance of European culture in imperial life.

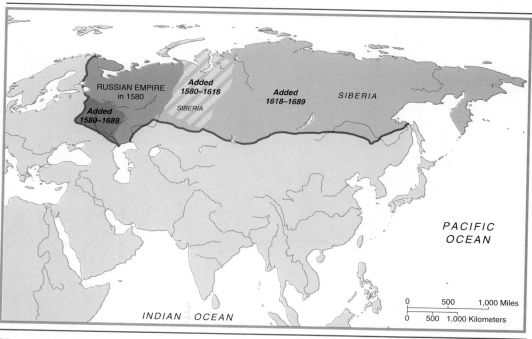

MAP 27.3 *Expansion of the Russian Empire, to 1689.* *Although Ivan the Terrible briefly added territory reaching to the Baltic Sea in the northwest, these lands could not be held until the eighteenth century. Ivan's more enduring imperial legacy was the expansion southeast to the Caspian Sea and east into Siberia, which claimed vast lands for the sprawling Russian Empire.*

The Role of Gunpowder Technology

Gunpowder technology strongly influenced the expansion of each empire. Ottoman leaders were among the first to employ cannons. They unsuccessfully battered the formidable walls of Constantinople in 1422, but more accurate and devastating cannon fire helped shatter its defenses in 1453. In 1514, Ottoman cannonballs and musket shot smashed a Safavid army poorly trained in gunpowder warfare, but Safavid commanders soon employed cannons to deadly effect against their enemies in the east. Mughal cannons devastated city walls during sieges, and Russian monarchs formed regiments of musketeers. Each empire added units of musketeers who became elite guards.

Religious Influence

Religion strongly influenced politics, social life, and the arts of the four empires. The Ottoman Turks ardently believed in Islam and often declared *jihad*, a holy struggle against their enemies, either Christian or Muslim. In the early 1500s, Egypt and Palestine were conquered, and Jerusalem, Mecca, and Medina, the three holiest cities of Islam, came under Ottoman jurisdiction. From that time, the Ottoman rulers undertook the responsibility for defending Islam, especially the Sunni sect. The major Ottoman rivals, Safavid Persians, embraced Shi'ism. This brought religious oppression in both empires because Sunnis repressed Shi'ites and vice versa. Political rivalries caused Muslim rulers to be more intolerant of other Muslims than of Christians or Jews.

Religion played a significant role in Mughal India and in Russia. Hinduism was the religion of the majority of Indians, and Islam had been in India since the eighth century. Early Mughal rulers (Muslims) practiced religious toleration, but later rulers attempted to compel all to embrace Islam. Resentment against growing intolerance by the state undermined Mughal rule in the late seventeenth century.

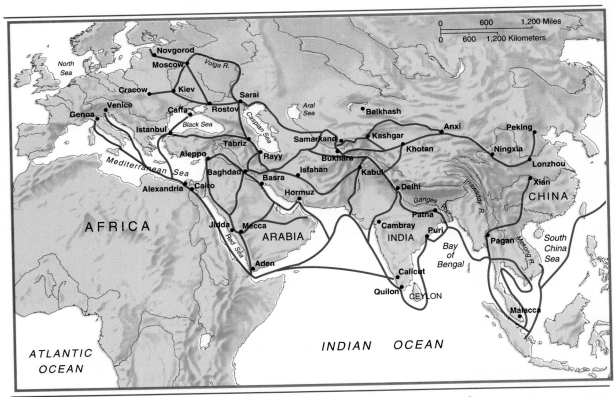

MAP 27.4 *Trade Routes of the Four Empires.* *The Mughal, Ottoman, Russian, and Safavid empires straddled vital trade routes passing from Europe and Africa through Asia. As European maritime power expanded, the land routes among the four empires became more important for intra-empire trade.*

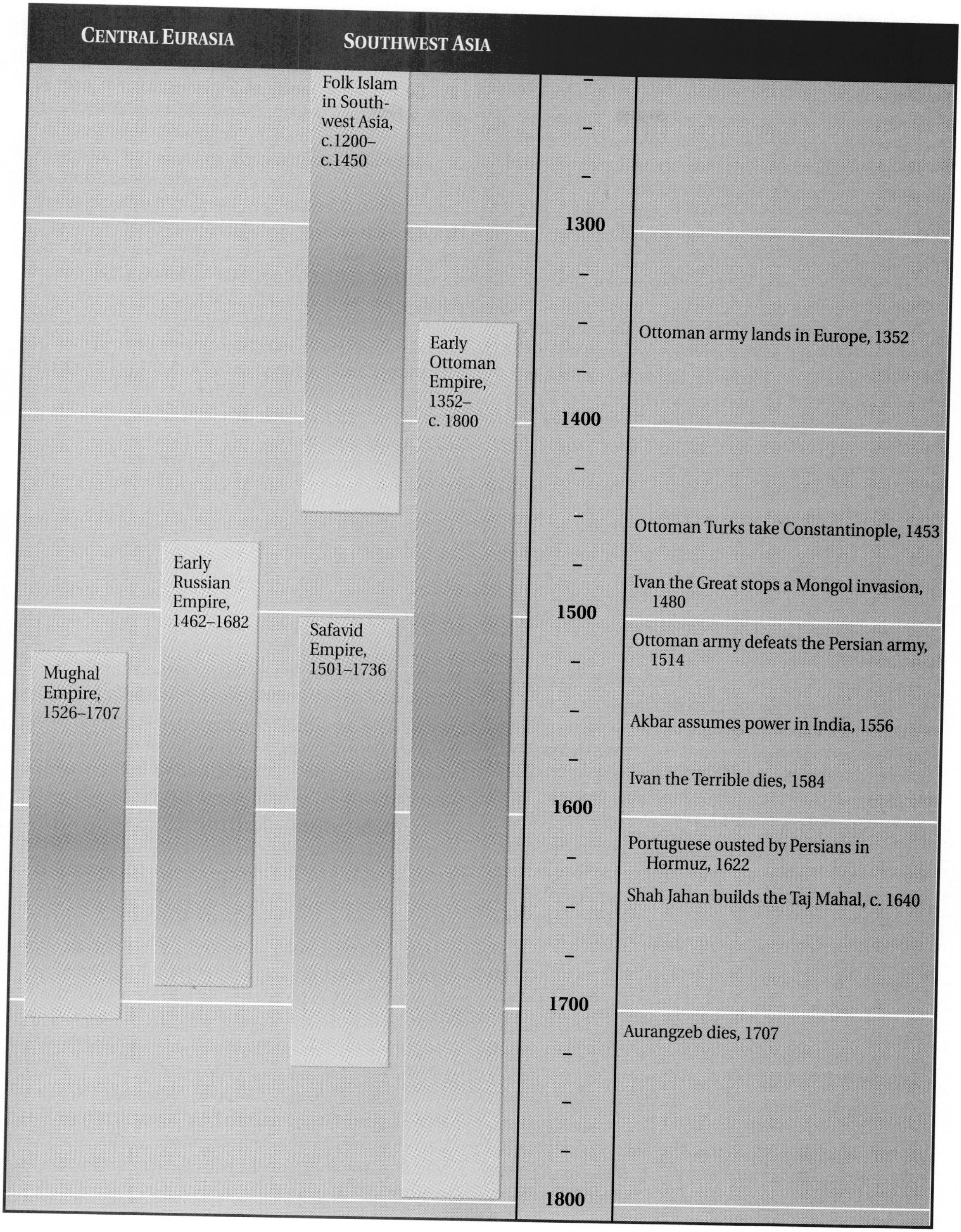

CENTRAL EURASIA	SOUTHWEST ASIA		

Folk Islam in South-west Asia, c.1200– c.1450

Early Ottoman Empire, 1352– c. 1800

Early Russian Empire, 1462–1682

Safavid Empire, 1501–1736

Mughal Empire, 1526–1707

1300

1400

Ottoman army lands in Europe, 1352

1500

Ottoman Turks take Constantinople, 1453

Ivan the Great stops a Mongol invasion, 1480

Ottoman army defeats the Persian army, 1514

Akbar assumes power in India, 1556

Ivan the Terrible dies, 1584

1600

Portuguese ousted by Persians in Hormuz, 1622

Shah Jahan builds the Taj Mahal, c. 1640

1700

Aurangzeb dies, 1707

1800

Moscow princes used the Eastern Orthodox Church to help solidify their rule by claiming to support all Eastern Orthodox adherents. During the early seventeenth century, invasion and rule over Russia by Catholic princes (Poles) brought a general rising of the Russian people led by Eastern Orthodox priests. The successful uprising had patriotic and religious overtones.

European Influence

Perhaps the most significant impact of the Europeans on the Ottoman, Safavid, Mughal, and Russian empires related to trade. Long-established trade routes brought goods to the peoples of the empires, and European merchants became important participants in trade. The Ottoman, Safavid, and Mughal monarchs played off merchants against one another, favoring those of their European allies or Europeans with whom they wished to do business. Russian rulers traded with merchants from states around the Baltic Sea but increasingly sought trade ties with the Ottomans and Safavids. Russian furs were prized by rich people of the Islamic lands and other parts of Europe, while Persian silks were worn in Russia, India, and Egypt.

Although Muslim rulers appreciated European technological and scientific advances and adopted them, their impact on Ottoman, Safavid, or Mughal statecraft was slight. Gunpowder weapons arrived in South and Southwest Asia about the same time as in Europe. Occasionally, European artisans were hired by Muslim monarchs (and Russians), but these artisans' influence was limited. Turks and Persians had traditions of excellence in astronomy and mathematics, remaining abreast of European knowledge until the late sixteenth century. After that, European scientific leadership went unheeded as most Islamic scholars confined themselves to religious and legal matters.

SUMMARY

1. The Ottoman Turks built an empire that ruled parts of Europe, Asia, and Africa. The Ottoman leaders prospered as long as they controlled most key trade routes between Asia and Europe. Rulers like Mehmed II and Suleyman I significantly expanded the Ottoman domain, and Selim I added Syria and Egypt, two vital regions.

2. Ottoman architects like Sinan designed impressive mosques and *medreses*. Important scholarly works, including encyclopedias, were written during the Ottoman era. Turkish literature showed some influence of Persian literature.

3. Ottoman society had distinct social classes, including the ruling elite, merchants, artisans, and slaves.

4. The Safavids rose in Southwest Asia, then expanded their rule over Turks and Persians. The Safavid Empire promoted the Shi'a belief system, especially in Persia.

5. Like the Ottomans, the Safavids developed trade and seized Eurasian trade routes. Shah Abbas I laid the foundations of Safavid power by building a strong economy, conquering important territory, and developing a splendid capital, Isfahan.

6. The Mughals conquered India from their base in Central Asia. A strong Persian component characterized the emerging Indian culture, which also had Turkish Islamic elements.

7. Akbar ruled effectively and created expectations of fairness that thwarted his intolerant great-grandson, Aurangzeb. Muslim classes and a caste system regulating Hindus made up Mughal society.

8. Moscow rulers created an autocratic system that relied on service gentry who needed serf support. Tsars expanded from Moscow in all directions and were most successful in the east. They fought against Polish Catholics and Russian Old Believers.

9. The Ottoman, Safavid, Mughal, and Russian empires were similar in being gunpowder-based states, in being strongly influenced by religion, and in being little influenced by European culture.

SUGGESTED READINGS

Chaudhuri, K. N. *Trade and Civilisation in the Indian Ocean*. Cambridge, Eng.: Cambridge University Press, 1985. A work that analyzes trade's impact on civilizations from 600 to 1750, using the model of Fernand Braudel.

Dukes, Paul. *The Making of Russian Absolutism*. London: Longman's Press, 1990. A standard survey of the seventeenth and eighteenth centuries.

Inalcik, Halil. *The Ottoman Empire*. New York: Orpheus Publishing, 1989 (reprint of the 1973 edition). A classic study of the first three Ottoman centuries.

Jackson, Peter. *The Cambridge History of Iran*. Volume VI. Cambridge, Eng.: Cambridge University Press, 1986. A major treatment of the Safavid era.

Riasanovsky, Nicholas. *A History of Russia*. New York: Oxford University Press, 1993. Perhaps the best Russian history survey.

Richards, John. *The New Cambridge History of India: The Mughal Empire*. New York: Cambridge University Press, 1993. An excellent examination of the Mughal Empire, including social and economic history.

Walther, Wiebke. *Women in Islam*. Trans. C. S. V. Salt. Princeton, N.J.: Markus Wiener Publishing, 1993. An examination of Muslim women, with special attention to their social position and with excellent pictures.

Wheatcroft, Andrew. *The Ottomans*. London: Viking Press, 1993. A well-illustrated survey of Ottoman politics.

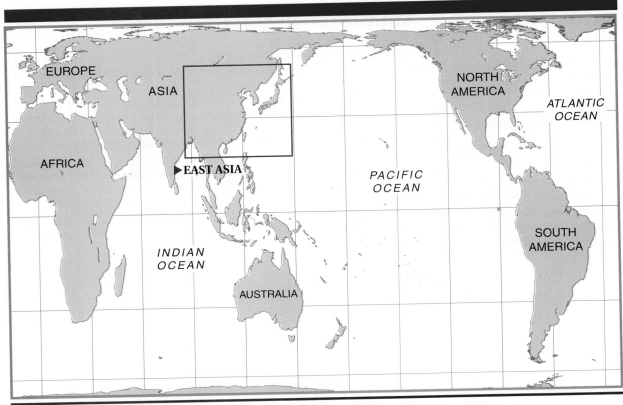

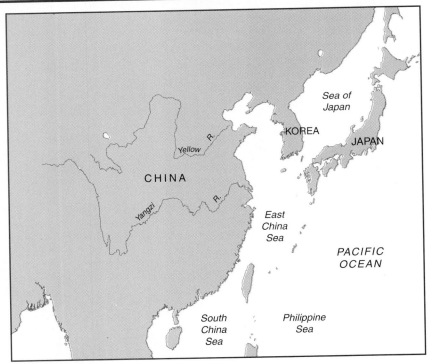

▶EAST ASIA

Colliding States in East Asia
around 1350–around 1800

In 1592, a Roman Catholic priest pored over intelligence dispatches from his contacts in Japan. They told of a large number of **samurai** *warriors gathering for an invasion of Korea and China. Tens of thousands of them were Christian Japanese soldiers, many of whom were musketeers. The massive army and naval force dwarfed the Spanish Armada, which had made a similar attempt to invade England in 1588. The Japanese military action, like that of the Spanish, failed.*

East Asian powers were in collision as states fought one another. Japan attacked Korea and China, while the Chinese invaded Vietnam or fought off the Mongols and Manchus. Europeans had only a modest impact on East Asian peoples before 1750. European traders brought guns and Christianity to the Japanese and Chinese, but soon Christianity had largely disappeared in East Asia, and the Japanese had abandoned guns.

MING EMPERORS CREATE A SINOCENTRIC WORLD ORDER, 1368–1644

A major Chinese uprising in the mid-1300s toppled the ruling Mongol Empire (1279–1368) and established the Ming Empire, which ruled for nearly three centuries (1368–1644). Early Ming rulers fashioned a stable government and created an inward-looking system of international rela-

FIGURE 28.1 *The Hongwu Emperor. This realistic portrait of the Ming Empire's founder, a former commoner, shows evidence of his having survived smallpox. The pockmarked face also helps convey the ferocity of a ruler who tyrannized his subjects and officials alike. Imperial absolutism grew as the Hongwu emperor gathered power into his own hands.* National Palace Museum, Taiwan, Republic of China.

tions. They believed that foreigners came to China to recognize the superiority of Chinese ways because China was the center of the world.

The Politics of the Hongwu and Yongle Emperors, 1368–1424

The Ming Empire, which succeeded the Mongol Empire, was founded by a commoner and orphan, Zhu Yuanzhang.[1] In order to survive, Zhu became a Buddhist monk and begged for a living, but his fortunes improved after he joined a rebel army. Within a short time, Zhu married the leader's daughter and assumed control of the force after the leader's death. Finally, Zhu Yuanzhang formed a government that administered some of China's most prosperous areas, and he gathered a core of advisors who had excellent skills in statecraft and military affairs. His Ming armies defeated all rivals, including the Mongols, and Zhu Yuanzhang was crowned and given the title of the Hongwu[2] Emperor in 1368.

The Ming government strongly reflected the founder's personality traits: suspicion about people's motives, scorn for the seemingly pretentious manners of the scholar officials, and a yearning for a return to the ways of earlier empires. The Hongwu Emperor created an inward-looking regime that shunned contact with the outside world except through a tributary system wherein emissaries bearing tribute came to China and pretended to acknowledge the superiority of its ways. Because the Chinese considered themselves superior, the emperor's return gifts had to be more valuable than those received. The Ming state formally outlawed international trade in 1372.

Administrative efficiency was severely hampered by a major purge and governmental reorganization. The Hongwu Emperor killed his prime minister and his commander of the armies. Executions and purges against suspected enemies caused perhaps 100,000 deaths; many who had connections with the prime minister and army commander suffered. These actions and the subsequent restructuring hampered the state as the emperor abolished the prime ministership, meaning that the emperor would thereafter decide all matters previously handled by the prime minister

[1] **Zhu Yuanzhang:** JOO yoo wahn jahng
[2] **Hongwu:** HOHNG woo

FIGURE 28.2 *Dragon Robe. Only the monarch or royal appointees could wear clothes with dragons on them. Dragons were the most powerful creatures in Chinese folklore, and the emperor was the most powerful of humans. People caught wearing unauthorized dragon-adorned clothing were treated as rebels and punished accordingly. This was especially true in the Early Ming era, when dragon robes came into fashion.* From Nagogawa Chusei, *Shinzoku Kibur*, 1798.

and his staff. Even the most dynamic monarch wilted under the hundreds of items demanding daily decisions. Another result of the abolition of the office of prime minister was the growing use of eunuchs to assist with various state tasks.

The Hongwu Emperor outlived his heir apparent and named his grandson to that position. When the emperor died in 1398, his grandson ascended to the throne and reigned, with several adult uncles governing parts of the empire. Within a few years many uncles had been deposed. In North China, one uncle, Zhu Di,[3] rebelled and ousted his nephew. A key ploy in Zhu Di's actions was feigning illness so that his sons, who were imperial hostages, would be released to visit their

[3] **Zhu Di:** JOO dee

father. Soon after their freeing, Zhu Di revolted and eventually took power in a bloody civil war, reigning as the Yongle Emperor (1403–1424).

Of the Ming monarchs, only the Yongle Emperor was eager to explore the known world. He championed several Chinese naval expeditions (1405–1433) that sailed the Indian Ocean, reaching the east coast of Africa. (See Chapter 23 for more information.) Yet these maritime explorations went against China's fundamental strategic outlook, which was centered on Inner Asia (Mongolia, Manchuria, and Chinese Turkestan). In fact, the Yongle Emperor's shift of the capital from the Lower Yangzi River Valley to Beijing in the north heightened China's insecurity. While Beijing was the Yongle Emperor's power base, it lay so close to the homeland of the Mongols that later Ming rulers, fearing a Mongol revival and conquest of North China, terminated the naval expeditions and rebuilt the Great Wall.

Isolation and Trade

The Ming Empire's inward orientation resumed after the Yongle Emperor's death. Ming rulers turned their backs on earlier financial policies like the use of paper money and large amounts of coinage, as well as the Yongle Emperor's promotion of external trade. Once again, Ming rulers ordered merchants to desist from trading abroad and consistently refused to trade with the Mongols. When Japanese and Chinese pirates preyed on the China coast, the monarchy forcibly moved the coastal population inland, denying the predators any resources. Despite these actions and the hobbling effect of poor monetary instruments, Chinese merchants fared well in internal trade and held their own against foreign competition. By the late sixteenth century, the massive infusion of Mexican and Japanese silver into the world economy assisted the growth of China's economy. At the same time, cities along the coast and others inland prospered because of the increasing trade. Even the government ignored its own trading ban and made profits from maritime trade.

Expanding Intellectual Horizons

The Ming era saw the development of a growing intellectual class, especially in the cities. Education was the ladder of success in providing not

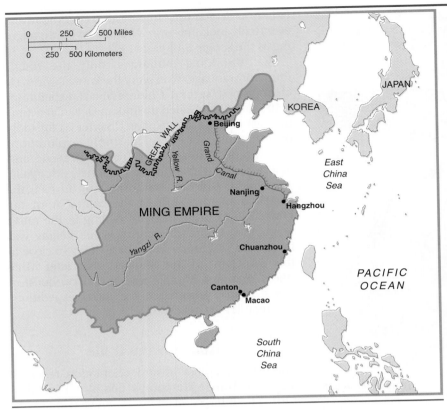

MAP 28.1 *The Ming Empire around 1600.* Although the early Ming emperors were vigorous conquerors, the territory that they and their successors ruled included only Manchuria and small lands in the west. For most of its existence, the empire was inward-looking and defensive. The Grand Canal, which had been expanded and improved by the Mongols in the fourteenth century, linked the prosperous Yangzi delta region with the capital, Beijing. Grain barges regularly plied the artificial waterway, bringing rice and other foodstuffs.

only the way to governmental service but also a way a person could enter the social elite. Thus, many went to school or learned from hired tutors.

All Ming rulers presided over an imperial examination system through which civil servants were recommended for government service. Memory was the most important element in passing the extremely difficult examinations, which required knowing by heart the Confucian classics and relevant commentaries. The Confucian ideological system became a unified political culture. The majority of officials served efficiently and provided political stability even in times of imperial incompetence. Only between 1590 and 1620, when one monarch deliberately ignored the bureaucracy, did the imperial system seriously deteriorate.

One significant intellectual and social development tied to the implementation of the imperial examination system was the expansion of social mobility. Schools sprang up in cities and towns to educate a growing number of people, some of whom read popular literary works. People, especially city folk, delightedly read short stories and novels, which were often shunned by academi-

cians as "low-brow" writings. Short-story collections became very popular. The great achievement of the Ming era, however, was the novel. Chinese novels originated from prompt books kept by storytellers who traveled within cities and told story cycles over a period of several days. Writers wove these cycles into long narratives, including historical novels like the *Romance of the Three Kingdoms*, fantasy novels like *Journey to the West*, and erotic novels like *Golden Lotus*. *Golden Lotus* mirrored society, especially in depicting Chinese women as sex objects and playthings of men.

Arts and literature were produced and supported by the intellectual class. Chinese philosophy, for example, was enriched by Wang Yangming[4] (1472–1528), who stressed that reality was as the mind perceived it. His Confucian ideas maintained a practical bent—he was a highly successful official—as seen in his adage that "knowledge is the beginning of action, and action is the completion of knowledge." Thus, book learning was the first step to knowledge.

[4] **Wang Yangming:** WONG yahng mihng

Historical studies became popular as scholars took a critical interest in their past. Chinese historiography remained a special intellectual pursuit, and Ming rulers maintained a bureau of history, where scholars prepared an official history of the Mongols, and a special office kept a record of each reign's special events for future histories. Some scholars also collected artifacts from earlier eras, and a whole field of antiquarian research opened.

FIGURE 28.3 *Scholar and Attendant. A renewed interest in Confucian ideas developed in the Ming era, and scholars became honored once again. These porcelain pieces capture the tranquil aura ascribed to persons of literary accomplishment. Ming potters excelled at making porcelain pieces that were prized in other lands, such as Persia.* Avery Brundage Collection/Laurie Platt Winfrey, Inc.

Porcelain reached a high level of development and was appreciated by collectors across the world. The famed Ming vases appeared under imperial patronage, and artisans at the imperial kilns perfected the techniques for making vases and plates. Persian potters occasionally used Chinese porcelains as models for their own pottery, which they passed off as Chinese ware.

Population Growth and Social Unrest

For much of the Ming era, a steady population increase took place, but after 1600, weak leaders and climatic changes created conditions for serious uprisings that gravely weakened the Ming government. Early population growth was based on stable political and social conditions; cities increased in size, and some urbanites enjoyed a prosperous existence.

Overcrowding became a problem by the early 1600s, especially when the weather got colder and affected food harvests. Some people migrated overseas, beginning a Chinese diaspora to the Philippines and other parts of Southeast Asia, but the numbers were too small to bring much relief. Bad weather reduced grain harvests and led to a famine and a series of devastating epidemics that killed tens of thousands of people. In addition, conditions forced some commoners to become wanderers or bandits, and widespread areas of North and Central China erupted in large-scale peasant uprisings. One revolt in north-central China saw the rapid advance of a force to the capital, and when the city gates were opened, the last Ming emperor committed suicide. The rebel, Li Zicheng,[5] failed to establish a viable government and fell in 1644 to the Manchus, a non-Chinese people who lived in the northeast.

THE EARLY QING EMPIRE, 1644–1796

The Manchus quickly overran China and established the Qing[6] Empire (1644–1912), a time of peace and prosperity. Manchu leaders adopted the traditional Chinese political system, welcoming obedient scholars who advised on how to effect a

[5] **Li Zicheng:** LEE see chehng
[6] **Qing:** CHEENG

牡丹最易近俗殆難下筆如近世工徒塗紅抹綠雖千花萬蘂總一形勢
都無神明惟北宋徐熙父子趙昌王友之倫創意既新變態斯備其賦色
極妍氣韵極厚蓋能不守陳規全師造化故稱傳神觀南田此本妍
精沒骨得其變態真可上追北宋諸賢不僅凌跨有明陳陸數子已
也壬子十月既望劍門王翚書

FIGURE 28.4 ***Flower Painting.*** *Ming and Qing artists devoted considerable time to painting flowers. Magnolias and peonies were especially favored for still-life subjects. Wang Hui painted many flowers and landscapes in the styles of famous masters who lived centuries earlier. The inscription notes the artists who influenced Wang Hui, and explains his motivation for creating such a visual perspective.* National Palace Museum, Taiwan, Republic of China.

Chinese-style state. The real power lay in the northeast, where the Manchus allied with the Chinese commander of an army near the Great Wall. This combined force swept to the capital and soon established a new dynasty.

Stability and Expansion

Between 1600 and 1800, the Manchus were blessed with able rulers. Two of them, the Kangxi[7] Emperor (1661–1723) and the Qianlong[8] Emperor (1736–1796), were outstanding leaders because they created effective administrations and significantly expanded China's territory.

The Kangxi Emperor firmly consolidated Manchu rule over China, adding new lands to the empire. He fought a civil war to extend central control over South China and defeated pirates who terrorized the local seas. Beginning in 1690, the Manchus conquered Mongolia and Tibet, increasing Chinese territory by hundreds of thousands of square miles.

Under the Qianlong Emperor, Manchu armies invaded Chinese Turkestan and crossed the Himalayas into Nepal, fighting the Gurkhas, who had been raiding Tibet. The Manchus were unsuccessful in expanding control over Burma and Vietnam, states they invaded but could not conquer. Nevertheless, the extent of Manchu influence rivaled that of all previous regimes.

Inner Asian trade routes saw increasing traffic, including growing commerce with the Russian Empire. Seaborne commerce prospered, and by the eighteenth century, Chinese wares were in great demand in Europe. Internal trade grew in the Qing era, but merchants remained handicapped by discriminatory government policies.

[7] **Kangxi:** KAHNG shee
[8] **Qianlong:** CHEE yahn lohng

Collecting and Censoring Literary Works

Maintaining the imperial examination system continued to promote education and to slowly expand the number of literate people. One group that benefited from education was women, and, while accurate numbers are difficult to determine, various evidence suggests that a modest percentage of urban women were literate by 1800. The Kangxi and Qianlong emperors presided over the gathering and organizing of vast amounts of writ-

ten materials. They also destroyed works that portrayed Manchus in disparaging terms.

The Kangxi Emperor actively employed his scholars in writing major works that would highlight imperial prestige and Manchu patronage. Soon after he began ruling, the emperor enticed several prominent scholars to work on the history of the Ming Dynasty. In addition, he sponsored another group of intellectuals who collected and published extant poems written during the Tang Dynasty, a time considered China's golden poetic age. Nearly 50,000 poems by around 2,200 poets

FIGURE 28.5 *Imperial Birthday Celebration.* *The Kangxi Emperor ruled longer than any previous monarch of China, and his birthdays were celebrated with great festiveness. Elephants and other live animals were sent to the emperor as tributary gifts from southern countries such as Vietnam and Thailand. Chinese officials and servants are distinguished from Manchus by the braids of hair that hang down their backs. A crowd gathers around the royal dais as shopkeepers look on. The foreground of this woodcut provides a glimpse into several inner courtyards.* Cabinet des Estampes, Bibliothèque nationale, Paris/Laurie Platt Winfrey, Inc.

graced the monumental collection. Among other tomes appearing in the emperor's reign was the *Kangxi Dictionary*, a vast work that recorded and defined the words used in Chinese history. These works have ably benefited scholarship ever since.

The Qianlong Emperor also promoted the gathering and categorization of massive amounts of written material. In addition, he presided over a long-lasting and widespread literary inquisition. More than his predecessors, the Qianlong Emperor was concerned about works with passages derogatory to the Manchus. He used the collection of works for a vast project, *The Complete Collection of Materials in the Four Categories* (it contained around 36,000 volumes), to peruse and censor suspicious works. More than 2,000 volumes were destroyed, and scholars who had written them were severely punished for seeming to disparage the Manchus.

Population Growth and Economic Prosperity

Perhaps the most dramatic occurrence in the Qing period was unprecedented demographic growth. The population of China in 1700 probably reached about 150 million people; by 1800, it exceeded 350 million people. Why did such a phenomenon occur, and what were its consequences? Internal peace, more widespread use of foodstuffs from the Americas, and the absence of withering epidemics all contributed to the growth. In the eighteenth

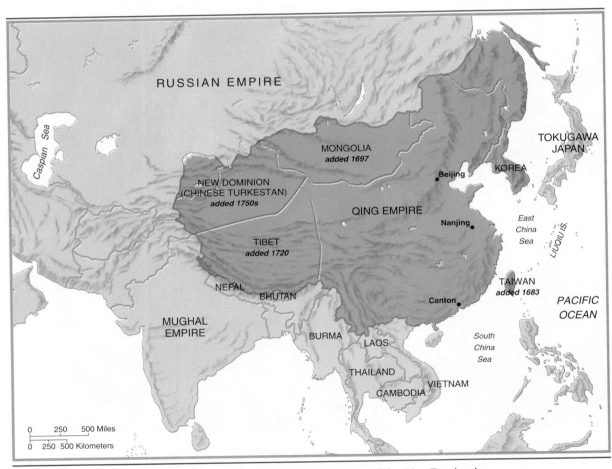

MAP 28.2 *The Qing Empire around 1770.* *The Manchu rulers of the Qing Empire significantly extended China's borders. Tibet, Mongolia, and Chinese Turkestan were added to the empire in the seventeenth and eighteenth centuries. At that time, China approximated its present borders with a territory of more than three million square miles.*

PARALLELS AND DIVERGENCES

Asian Encyclopedias before 1750

Eurasians displayed a propensity for organizing and presenting information in encyclopedic form, an attempt to bring together known information on various subjects. European examples will be explored in a later chapter; here we will examine Asian encyclopedias, including those of Chinese, Mughal, and Ottoman scholars. Asian encyclopedists generally prepared their information for officials who had to have accurate information in order to do their jobs effectively. Even encyclopedias about the Islamic sciences were primarily intended for judges and lawyers.

Ming and Qing intellectuals produced nearly 150 encyclopedias of all kinds, and they followed an encyclopedic tradition that had existed for several centuries. A major type of Chinese work dealt with political affairs; these often were written in the latter part of a dynasty, when political problems became more acute. The editors usually selected experts to write on specific problems or used the writings of former or current officials about matters of statecraft. Economic matters like administration of the salt monopoly or supervision of the silk trade also were often covered.

A seventeenth-century writer, Wang Qi,[a] wrote an important political encyclopedia and is noted for writing an illustrated encyclopedia of wide scope. The latter covered topics such as astronomy, cosmology, geography, biographies, painting, literary history, human physiology, and botany. This shows not only the author's varied intellectual interests but also those of his readers. The illustrations, of course, convey additional information, sometimes of a technical nature.

Abu'l Fazl,[b] a Mughal official, compiled an administrative encyclopedia that was widely used in the sixteenth and seventeenth centuries. He wrote in great detail on subjects such as architecture and the care and feeding of rare breeds of horses. Much of the encyclopedia's economic information came from the detailed land surveys that recorded the huge range of crops grown, their prices in different markets, data about land rights, and the availability of water resources. Modern scholars have begun to mine this and other information sources to paint a detailed picture of Mughal agriculture.

Ottoman officials made detailed land surveys and compiled encyclopedias for their officials; Ottoman scholars also contributed their own encyclopedias. Because Egyptians, Turks, and Indians also produced encyclopedias, an Islamic encyclopedist tradition existed, especially in the Early Modern Era. One group of scholars compiled an encyclopedia of Islamic sciences in order to meet the needs of religious officials who handled matters of Islamic law. Some of these sciences included practical ethics, etiquette, and other subjects tied to Muslim life and worship.

[a] **Wang Qi:** WONG chee

[b] **Abu'l Fazl:** AH buhl FAH zehl

---

century, foreign wars took place, but internal challenges to the government subsided, especially in heavily populated areas. Corn from the New World suited Chinese palates and could be grown on marginal lands; its cultivation over a larger area added significantly to the Chinese diet. The most important crops, however, were the varieties of potatoes and sweet potatoes. By the Qing period, the sweet potato had become a major component of Chinese cuisine, especially among the poor.

What effect did these changes have on politics and society? Long-term trends suggest that the amount of land available to each farming family shrank. Although new lands came under cultivation, the amount did not keep pace with the rapid demographic growth. Crowding on the land kept most peasants at the poverty level. In difficult times, people either starved or revolted. The elite also grew in number while government positions stayed relatively constant; the number of scholars taking the examinations mushroomed. When they failed to pass or enter government, discontent arose among these educated people who possessed the skills to mount political challenges.

THE ASHIKAGA SHOGUNATE, 1338–1573

The Mongols failed to conquer Japan in 1274 and 1281, but their two invasions weakened the ruling Japanese warrior government. It collapsed in the 1330s, and a dominant military leader, Ashikaga Takauji,[9] was proclaimed **shogun**, military dictator. Although Ashikaga Takauji's descendants held the title of *shogun* for more than two centuries, they ceased to wield power after the mid–fifteenth century.

The Ashikaga Shogunate (1338–1573) governed from the city of Kyoto. For the first century, *shoguns* exercised effective control, and burgeoning trade with Korea and China helped generate prosperity. Using this wealth, the Ashikaga *shoguns* supported cultural leaders.

The most powerful *shogun*, Ashikaga Yoshimitsu (reign dates 1380–1408), dominated the capital and the country. He loved fine art, subsidizing artists and architects. Perhaps the most famous surviving structure of his era was the Golden Pavilion, a private retreat of this *shogun*; its sloping roof conveys a sense of uplift and lightness. A successor built the Silver Pavilion, in many ways a counterpoint to the Golden Pavilion. The latter showed best in the sunlight, while the Silver Pavilion, located in shady areas, exuded a more subdued effect.

Drama in the Ashikaga era is reflected in the appearance of the **Noh**, a dramatic form. Noh actors wear masks to hide normal facial expressions, forcing reliance on gestures and voice intonation to convey emotion. Financially supported by various *shoguns* and *daimyo*[10] (territorial lords), Noh dramatists wrote plays for the political and social elite of Japan.

The Ashikaga state was overwhelmed by a civil war that erupted in 1467. The following decade of war devastated Kyoto and sparked a chaotic epoch known as the Warring States Period (1467–1568). The formation of provincial government centered on castle towns created by *daimyo*, who resettled their *samurai* warriors from the land to the castle towns. In exchange for the move, the *daimyo* guaranteed a fixed income for the *samurai*. In addition, village peasants farmed land, living self-sufficiently. They paid taxes to their village head, who remitted them to the *daimyo*.

JAPAN'S REUNIFICATION AND EXPANSION, AROUND 1560–AROUND 1600

A series of determined warriors envisioned and carried out the reunitification of Japan by military conquest. In addition, they promoted social, economic, and cultural policies imbued with ideas of loyalty and obedience to one's superiors. One major consequence of Japan's militarization was its attempt to conquer Korea and China, an action that ended in disaster for all parties.

The Unification Drive

Three outstanding warriors, Oda Nobunaga (1534–1582), Toyotomi Hideyoshi[11] (1536–1598), and Tokugawa Ieyasu[12] (1542–1616), forged a united Japan. Oda Nobunaga began the effort around 1560 by unifying his clan and then allying with other warlords. Oda Nobunaga defeated several opponents and occupied Kyoto in 1568, ending the Warring States Period; he formally ended Ashikaga rule in 1573. Nobunaga's assassination stopped his effort in 1582 but created the conditions that elevated Toyotomi Hideyoshi to the leadership of the national unification effort.

Toyotomi Hideyoshi was a remarkable figure, partly because of his success and partly because of his commoner origins. Only in the Warring States Period could a Japanese commoner rise to the top by ability and good fortune. In that sense he is similar to Zhu Yuanzhang, the founder of the Ming Dynasty. Toyotomi Hideyoshi's march toward unification climaxed with the defeat of the northern *daimyo*, one of whom ruled the Kanto,[13] Japan's largest plain, and Tokugawa Ieyasu was given dominion over the Kanto. In these later campaigns, 100,000 to 300,000 *samurai* were mobilized.

---

[9] **Ashikaga Takauji:** AH shee kah gah TAH kah oo jee
[10] *daimyo:* DY mee yoh

[11] **Toyotomi Hideyoshi:** TOH yoh toh mee HEE deh yoh shee
[12] **Tokugawa Ieyasu:** TOH kuh gah wah EE ay yah suh
[13] **Kanto:** KAHN toh

Toyotomi Hideyoshi conducted a land-survey program. This policy led to the measurement and registration of all arable land and told a ruler how much each *daimyo* controlled and thereby his wealth. It also focused attention on the village as the basic economic unit for the province and standardized information about potential agricultural production.

In addition, Toyotomi Hideyoshi imposed measures to foster stability in war-torn Japan. A sword hunt confiscated weapons from non-*samurai* so that ambitious people could not resort to the sword. The state prohibited people from changing their jobs, and by the Japanese modification of the Chinese four-class system (*samurai*, peasant, artisan, merchant), movement among the classes was forbidden. This policy differed from China's; there, education could provide mobility.

Japanese Expansion into Korea, 1592–1598

The final political effort of Toyotomi Hideyoshi was an invasion of Korea with the ultimate goal of conquering China and perhaps India. In 1592, more than 100,000 battle-tested *samurai* and their supporting logistical personnel landed in Korea and quickly overwhelmed Korean resistance. Chinese leaders soon realized the seriousness of the Japanese threat and mobilized armies in Manchuria, sending them to fight the invaders. A combination of Korean guerrilla warfare and a joint Chinese-Korean operation forced the Japanese south; negotiations took up several years. In addition, the Korean navy inflicted major defeats on the Japanese navy, threatening supply lines. A significant factor was the use of Korean "turtle boats," iron-clad wooden ships.

In 1598, the death of Toyotomi Hideyoshi terminated Japan's foreign adventure, leaving Korea in ruins, China in debt, and Japan relatively unscathed. Manchuria became a power vacuum where the Manchus eventually built their rival government. The Japanese treated the Koreans harshly, and carried many of them off to Japan as slaves; some Japanese brought home containers of pickled Korean ears and noses as war trophies. Korean potters and printers were compelled to move to Japan, where they helped revitalize Japanese pottery making and contributed to the printing of more books.

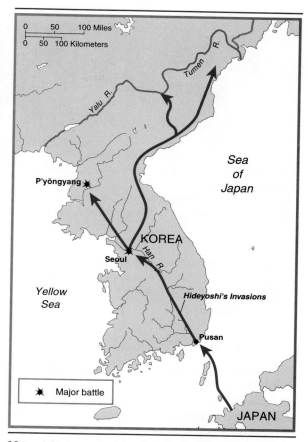

MAP 28.3 *Hideyoshi's Invasions of Korea, 1592–1598. Japan's unifier looked overseas for new realms to conquer. Since Korea stood in the path of the planned conquest of China, it suffered two massive and destructive invasions in the late sixteenth century. Korean resistance fighters and Chinese soldiers helped blunt the Japanese invasion, forcing Hideyoshi's successors to withdraw from the Asian mainland.*

THE EARLY TOKUGAWA SHOGUNATE: BUILDING MODERNITY, 1603–AROUND 1800

After the death of Toyotomi Hideyoshi, Tokugawa Ieyasu emerged as the main power in Japan when his forces defeated their opponents in 1600 at the Battle of Sekigahara.[14] Three years later, Tokugawa Ieyasu was proclaimed *shogun*, and his govern-

[14] **Sekigahara:** SEH kee gah hah rah

FIGURE 28.6 Daimyo *Procession*. Daimyo *regularly traveled to Edo and back home. Their entourages consisted of various* samurai *and servants. Lower-ranking* samurai *walked; their superiors rode on horseback. The* daimyo *himself was carried in an enclosed conveyance. Over time, the procession became more elaborate and costly, draining revenue from potential rivals to the* shogun. The Tokugawa Art Museum, Nagoya.

ment lasted for two and one-half centuries. Tokugawa Ieyasu and his successors permitted the continuance of local governments provided that the *daimyo* remained loyal.

Creating Political Stability

The Tokugawa *shoguns* were concerned about maintaining their rule and built a polity that thwarted alliances among their adversaries. All *daimyo*, for example, had to spend one out of every two years in the shogunal capital attending a variety of meetings called by the *shogun*. The other year they could return home but had to leave their wives and sons behind as hostages. All *daimyo* marriage alliances had to be approved by the *shogun*, and the size and number of castles in a province were strictly regulated. Shogunal spies also kept tabs on internal provincial administration and policies.

The shogunate had control of much economic power. Although taxes collected in the province stayed there, *daimyo* were sometimes called upon to contribute to expensive shogunal construction projects, draining monies from their treasuries. The *shoguns* and their allies controlled 60 percent of agricultural land, and the *shogun* administered the capital, Edo[15] (present-day Tokyo), and the two major cities, Kyoto[16] and Osaka.[17] In addition, mining and coinage were shogunal monopolies.

The other area of concern for the shogunate was international relations. Europeans had traded

with the Japanese since the 1540s, but they had brought Christianity and gunpowder weaponry along with trade goods. As Christianity spread through Japanese society, shogunal authorities became uneasy, fearing that Japanese Christians were more loyal to their priests, some of whom were Europeans, than to their Japanese lords. This placed the whole political and social hierarchy at risk. After a major uprising of Japanese Christians in the late 1630s, the shogunate outlawed Christianity, closed Japan to European shipping (except for a tiny Dutch outpost), and forbade Japanese from going overseas. Korean and Chinese merchants were the only other foreigners permitted to do business in Japan. These policies, which were similar to those of the Ming Dynasty, turned Japan inward and ended outside threats to stability for two centuries.

Another consequence of Tokugawa rule was the creation of large urban population centers at the new capital, Edo; at Kyoto, a large city of around 300,000 people; and at Osaka, a major trading center, also with a population numbering 300,000 people. Urban growth included the emergence of large castle towns with merchants and artisans, among others.

Caste and Gender

The Japanese borrowed the Chinese four-class system and modified it to fit their own purposes. Instead of scholars at the top, the Japanese placed the *samurai*, many of whom became scholars in the Tokugawa period. As in China, below the *samurai* were the peasants, reflecting the agrarian

[15] **Edo:** EH doh
[16] **Kyoto:** KEE yoh toh
[17] **Osaka:** OH sah kah

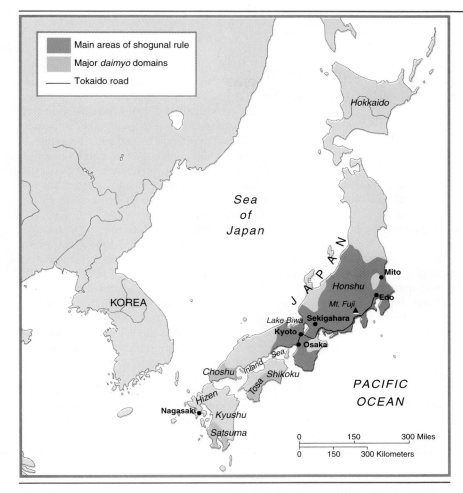

MAP 28.4 *Tokugawa Japan around 1700.* *By 1700, Japan's shogunal government had closed its doors to nearly all communication and commerce with Western diplomats and merchants. Trade with Asians was relegated to the southern islands off the coast of Kyushu. The inward-looking Japanese government had developed a political system of modest stability that lasted for over two centuries. The central government dominated the polity, permitting rival localities to survive provided they refrained from overt military challenges.*

FIGURE 28.7 *Japanese Laborers in Edo.* *Japanese woodblock art flourished in the cities of seventeenth-century Japan. Later, such work influenced European artists, especially the Impressionists. Here we see three workers sawing and stacking wood in a lumberyard. Mount Fuji sits quietly in the distance, oblivious to all human activity. Edo was an early name for Tokyo.* The Japan Ukiyoe Museum.

UNDER THE LENS
Japan Turns from the Gun to the Sword

Most empires after the fourteenth century developed and maintained gunpowder weaponry. Although some, like the Mughals and the Safavids, did not keep apace of European improvements in cannons and firearms, only the Japanese deliberately turned their backs on these weapons. They banned rifles, sidearms, and cannons from being used and permitted only a few rifles in private hands for hunting or scaring off wild birds, which threatened to eat certain crops. All of these firearms, however, had to be registered with the appropriate authorities.

A component of the unification of Japan in the sixteenth century was the introduction and spread of firearms. Oda Nobunaga, who was among the first warlords to appreciate their use, developed musketeer units. Improvements in technology brought greater firepower to bear and made the large armies of *samurai* and commoners fearsome. Toyotomi Hideyoshi and Tokugawa Ieyasu relied on gunpowder technology in their successful unification efforts.

Once Japan was united, however, governments looked askance at rifles and pistols, not to say cannons, because they threatened to disturb the peaceful order. Stability and harmony became the values most appreciated by the Tokugawa *shoguns*. Therefore, shogunal decrees forbade the carrying of the new weapons except by specially sanctioned soldiers. The *daimyo* agreed with this policy. In fact, in the late 1630s, when a revolt among Japanese Roman Catholics erupted and the rebels seized a castle, the Tokugawa government had no cannons and needed Dutch ones in order to breach the castle's walled fortifications.

Another element in the banning of firearms lay in the nature of the *samurai* elite, whose status was distinguished and was symbolized by the sword. Indeed, when Toyotomi Hideyoshi wished to distinguish the *samurai*, he forbade non-*samurai* from wearing swords. A common saying in the warrior era was that the sword was "the soul of the *samurai*." These attitudes facilitated the various governments' policies about limiting firearms. With appropriate training, commoners might shoot firearms and threaten the military monopoly of the *samurai*. That could not be permitted. Most *samurai*, therefore, eagerly supported the ban and maintained their exclusive practice of wearing their treasured swords.

---

bias of Japan's rulers; then came the artisans and merchants. Because of their desire to maintain social stability, the Japanese transformed the Chinese system into a caste order of fixed social groups without social mobility.

Japanese society was actually much more complex than the four castes, however, and aristocrats, physicians, and accountants found themselves outside the ideal structure. In addition, various pressures soon undermined the social system, despite the rulers' attempts to maintain it. The prevention of social mobility at the end of the sixteenth century briefly kept most Japanese in some form of a fixed social position, but many *samurai* became farmers or merchants in order to make a living. Other impoverished *samurai* ignored laws forbidding marriage with people of artisan or merchant background. By 1800, one's position seldom reflected that of one's grandparents.

Confucianism traditionally supported males, who dominated females in all social relationships. In fact, when the Japanese government began to promote Confucianism as an ideology conferring ideas and values of stability, the social position of women began to decline. Japanese Confucians advocated keeping women at home and under tight control; these admonitions were often supported by the *samurai* and *daimyo*. Arranged marriages became increasingly common among all social groups, and women lost inheritance rights they had previously enjoyed. Some became common laborers, and others plied traditional women's trades as well as prostitution.

One exception was the growing number of educated women. Girls joined with boys in local schools, studied in all-girl schools, or learned from private tutors. Scholars have estimated that as many as 10 percent of Japanese girls in this period could read and write.

The rapid spread of education ensured a more effective tapping of available brainpower. Increasing numbers of *samurai* became literate, as did many merchants and peasants; both males and females went to local schools. Perhaps as many as 40 percent of boys in this period were literate.

Popular and Elite Culture

The intellectual horizons of the Japanese expanded considerably in the Tokugawa period. A significant number of Japanese, especially in the cities, became literate and supported a growing output of popular culture. At the same time, traditional intellectual pursuits, like philosophy, engaged the *samurai*, who became highly literate.

Popular culture of the Tokugawa era included new dramatic forms: Kabuki plays and puppet theater plays. Both developed in the cities, catering to commoners, who watched performances that lasted for much of a day. One playwright, Chikamatsu Monzaemon (1653–1724), wrote for both theaters and is considered Japan's greatest dramatist. His play *Forty-seven Ronin* dealt with a historical incident in which forty-seven *samurai* avenged their *daimyo*'s wrongful death and caused a problem for the authorities, who could condone neither the initial murder nor the act of retaliation.

Poetry, short stories, novels, and woodblock prints also flourished in the Tokugawa era. The *haiku* poem of seventeen syllables became a popular poetic form because of its brevity and apparent simplicity. Short stories appeared in the late seventeenth century and fascinated Japanese readers, who loved their often satirical themes. Woodblock prints developed in the seventeenth century, and Japanese artists mastered forms such as nature scenes, portraits of city life, and renderings of famous Kabuki actors, receiving acclaim and imitation by later European painters.

Arts continued to flourish, too. Although few Noh plays were written, many older ones were still performed for *daimyo* and various courtiers. Confucianism was studied and commented upon by Japanese scholars, and the ideas of Wang Yangming (Oyomei in Japanese) received widespread attention, especially in the nineteenth century. One group of intellectuals strongly criticized the amount of attention given to a foreign ideology and took it upon themselves to study early Japanese institutions and ideas, which were deemed "free" from Chinese influence. A monumental history of Japan was written during much of the Tokugawa era; scholars from all over the country participated in the project, inaugurating a cross-

FIGURE 28.8 *Woman Reading. This woodblock shows a woman at ease with a book in her hand. Although the adoption of Confucianism as the ideology of the shogunate brought a decline in the status of women, many elite women learned to read and write at home. By the mid–nineteenth century, about one in ten women was literate. Japanese manuscripts are read from top to bottom and from right to left.* The Japan Ukiyoe Museum.

fertilization of ideas and a self-conscious Japanese intellectual elite.

Buddhism and Shinto, two major religions of Japan, generally maintained an entwined existence, with Shinto shrines being protected by Buddhist deities and Buddhist temples having Shinto

IN THEIR OWN WORDS

Haiku *Poetry and Commentary*

Japanese *haiku* became a distinctive poetic form in the seventeenth century and grew very popular among commoners, who loved its simple and brief message. Although most Japanese people tried their hands at *haiku*, certain masters wrote poems that have been greatly admired. Two poets, Basho[a] and Kyorai,[b] teacher and pupil, conversed about the theory and practice of composing *haiku*, and the following is Kyorai's record (including poems) of some discussions.

> The departing spring
> With the men of Omi
> Have I lamented

The Master [Basho] said, "Shohaku criticized this poem on the grounds that I might just as well have said Tamba instead of Omi or departing year instead of departing spring. How does this criticism strike you?" Kyorai replied, "Shohaku's criticism misses the mark completely. What could be more natural than to regret the passing of spring, when the waters of the Lake of Omi are veiled so enchantingly in the mist? Besides, it is especially fitting a poem for one who lives by the lake to have written."

[a] **Basho:** BAH shoh
[b] **Kyorai:** KEE yoh ry

The Master said, "Yes, the poets of old loved spring in this province almost as much as in the capital." Kyorai, deeply struck by these words, continued, "If you were in Omi at the close of the year, why should you regret its passing? Or if you were in Tamba at the end of spring, you would not be likely to have such a feeling. What truth there is in the poetry of a man who has genuinely been stirred by some sight of Nature!" The Master said, "Kyorai, you are a person with whom I can talk about poetry." He was very pleased . . .

> Will the two-day moon
> Be blown from the sky
> By the winter wind?
> —KAKEI

> Kept by the winter wind
> From falling to earth—
> The drizzling rain
> —KYORAI

Kyorai said, "I feel that Kakei's verse is far superior to mine. By asking if it will be blown from the sky, he makes mention of the two-day moon all the more clever." Basho answered, "Kakei's verse is built around the words 'two-day moon.' Take away the two-day moon and there is nothing left to the poem. It is not apparent on what you have based your poem. It is good all around."

---

shrines on their grounds. Shrines of highly venerated Shinto deities, like Amaterasu, the sun goddess, and those connected with the imperial institution became sites of pilgrimage in the eighteenth and nineteenth centuries. Millions of Japanese visited them in an outpouring of devotional passion. Fearing that many Japanese secretly continued to practice Christianity, the Tokugawa government decreed that all Japanese had to register with the nearest Buddhist temple. Authorities stamped out remaining elements of Christianity by crucifying priests and believers alike. Tens of thousands of Japanese Christians died in the ongoing persecutions. Despite these oppressive practices, a few Japanese secretly practiced the Christian faith throughout the Tokugawa period.

Consequences of Japan's Closing

The central government and the semiautonomous provinces either initiated or supported a series of efforts that led to Japan's growing economic and social integration. At the same time, significant private initiatives (often by merchants and wealthy peasants) supplemented or superseded state programs, thereby aiding agricultural productivity and accumulation of money. And although Japanese were aware of European developments in modernizing political institutions, the Japanese path toward modernity came from internal pressures and responses.

By the late seventeenth century, a small group of scholars persuaded the shogunal government to permit a few Dutch books to enter Japan. They became the basis for scholars who provided a window on the world. From the Dutch, the Japanese kept abreast of medical developments, learned about the European empires, and saw how gunpowder technology was improving. This group, by the nineteenth century, included many who urged Japan to become a colonial power.

During the seventeenth century and after, many governments took special interest in improving Japan's infrastructure. Major efforts were undertaken to build and improve roads linking Japan's major cities. Significant resources were expended to control Japan's rivers, irrigate farmlands, and reclaim lands from the sea as well as from disuse. By 1800, people easily and safely traveled to distant parts of the realm; some moved to cities, others visited sacred shrines, and a few observed how people farmed in different areas.

Between 1550 and 1650, urban growth stimulated additional changes in agriculture. By 1700, Japan had become one of the world's most urbanized societies, with three cities of 300,000 or more inhabitants and many more with populations in the tens of thousands. This development helped promote the commercialization of agriculture: Cash crops were grown specifically to sell to city folk. One of the first cash crops was cotton. Wealthy farmers enjoyed the financial security to experiment with growing cotton, and in a brief time consumer demand was driving the rapid conversion of grain fields to cotton planting. By the early 1700s, perhaps 50 percent of farmland in the Osaka area was given over to cotton fields. The seas began to be harvested on a large scale as well; drift nets were increasingly employed during the eighteenth century as sardines and other fish became increasingly commonplace in Japanese diets.

The Tokugawa era was a time of fiscal growth and maturity as the Japanese developed the basis of a modern financial system. Both the shogunate and *daimyo* developed alliances with merchant groups, giving them monopoly rights in certain trade items or protecting them from regional competitors. Despite this institutional support, many merchant groups took their own initiatives in developing markets, in seeking reliable supplies of raw materials, or in finding sources for raising money. Wholesalers, for example, fanned out in Japan to pay farmers in advance to produce specified crops or products, or they loaned money for production purposes. Some local producers grad-

ually became shipping agents for urban wholesalers and used urban capital to purchase and ship goods to cities.

New ways of raising money helped finance commercial activity. Merchants held cash on deposit, made loans, and formed joint-loan groups to spread the risk. Promissory notes secured by real estate or current accounts also went into circulation. Collectible credit drafts due in sixty days were used as collateral for loans and helped fuel a dramatic expansion of available credit. Money-changers entered financial markets to ensure transactions; maritime insurance developed by the late eighteenth century.

By 1800, self-sufficient villages long had been producing for urban markets, and there had been a general spread of agricultural technology so that production levels had improved by the nineteenth century. The central government's encouragement of blacksmiths to move into farm villages was significant because many improvements in agricultural tools came from the smiths. In addition, wealthy farmers kept journals as a record of successful experiments with tools and methods of growing crops: Some traveled to observe successful farming techniques and included them in the journals, many of which were published.

Resource Management

Human and material resource problems became serious in the Tokugawa period, and the Japanese developed a range of responses to these issues. The doubling of arable land (1550–1650) brought population growth from around 12 million people in 1650 to perhaps 28 million by 1730. Overcrowding reached severe levels and compelled the Japanese to respond. Women began marrying later and having fewer children, abortions became more commonplace, and infanticide was practiced more frequently.

Fertilizer use is another example of careful resource allocation. A trade in manufacturing by-products developed by the eighteenth century. Fish residues, along with pressed oil seeds, became fertilizers.

Clothing use illustrates another dimension of resource management in Tokugawa Japan. Japanese dress was centered on the **kimono**,[18] a

[18] *kimono:* KEE moh noh

CHINA	JAPAN		
		1300	
		–	
	Ashikaga Shogunate, 1338–1573	–	Ashikaga Takauji named *shogun*, 1338
		–	
		–	Zhu Yuanzhang founds Ming Empire, 1368
Ming Empire, 1368–1644		**1400**	
		–	Ashikaga Yoshimitsu builds the Golden Pavilion, c. 1400
		–	
		–	Japan's Warring States Period begins, 1467
		–	
		1500	
		–	Wang Yangming dies, 1528
		–	
		–	
		–	
		–	Hideyoshi dies, ending the invasion of Korea, 1598
		1600	
	Early Tokugawa Shogunate, 1603–c. 1800	–	Battle of Sekigahara, 1603
Early Qing Empire, 1644–1796		–	Japan closes its doors to most Westerners, 1640
		–	
		–	
		1700	
		–	Kangxi Emperor conquers Tibet, 1720
		–	
		–	
		–	
		1800	Qianlong Emperor dies, 1799

robelike outer garment. It was made of cloth that was cut into eight rectangular strips from a single rectangular piece. This meant that no material was wasted; children's *kimonos* were gathered at the shoulders so that they could be let out as the child grew. The sewing was by simple basting, which permitted the removal of the threads to wash the *kimono* and a quick rebasting later. When a *kimono* could no longer be worn, it was cut up for rags or diapers as needed. In a land with scarce resources, the Japanese developed techniques to conserve them efficiently.

SUMMARY

1. The Ming and Qing empires of China remained inward looking and indifferent to trade. The Qing emperors, unlike their predecessors, conquered surrounding peoples. Massive population growth based on New World foodstuffs undermined the state and led to major nineteenth-century uprisings.

2. The Hongwu and Yongle emperors set the basic patterns of the Ming Empire, including the use of eunuchs to carry out special tasks for the monarch. Moving the Chinese capital northward to Beijing intensified China's strategic focus on the Mongols and helped spur the rebuilding of the Great Wall.

3. Chinese urban life flourished and city folk often prospered. A major literary product was the novel; some novels clearly reflected social trends.

4. The Manchus of the northeast conquered and ruled China as the Qing Empire from the mid–seventeenth century. The Kangxi and Qianlong emperors ably ruled for more than a century, ordering the gathering of huge collections of scholarly works.

5. Chinese population growth in the eighteenth century created profound social strains that overwhelmed the system by the mid–nineteenth century.

6. Successive warrior governments ruled Japan. The last, the Tokugawa shogunate, ruled a unified state that coexisted with semiautonomous provinces.

7. Like the Chinese, the Japanese severely curtailed trade with Europeans and ousted Christian missionaries, who were perceived as subversive. The closing of the country enabled the uninterrupted improvement of the infrastructure.

8. Population growth helped spur the creation of large cities like Edo and Osaka. They in turn helped promote the demand for products from the agricultural sector. The commercialization of farming and the general improvement of agricultural technology and farming methods transformed the rural economy. At the same time, a whole range of financial techniques for raising capital emerged that underlay the growth of a modern commercial system.

SUGGESTED READINGS

Birch, Cyril. *Stories from a Ming Collection*. London, 1958. Representative short stories from the Ming era.

Hall, John W., ed. *The Cambridge History of Japan*. Vol. IV: *Early Modern Japan*. Cambridge, Eng.: Cambridge University Press, 1991. A history of Japan, reflecting Japanese and Western scholarship.

Ho, Ping-ti. *The Ladder of Success in Imperial China*. New York: Columbia University Press, 1964. A classic study of the Chinese imperial examination system.

———. *Studies on the Population of China, 1368–1953*. Cambridge, Mass.: Harvard University Press, 1959. A classic treatment of demographic issues in Chinese history.

Huang, Ray. *China: A Macro History*. Armonk, N.Y.: M. E. Sharpe, 1990. A thought-provoking examination of Chinese history, looking at the role of commercialization in China's modernization.

Ikegami, Eiko. *The Taming of the Samurai*. Cambridge, Mass.: Harvard University Press, 1995. A sociological examination of the transformation of the *samurai* from a warrior to a scholar caste.

Mote, F. W., and D. Twitchett, eds. *The Cambridge History of China*. Vol. VII: *The Ming Dynasty, 1368–1644*, Part I. Cambridge, Eng.: Cambridge University Press, 1988. A political examination of the Ming era by key scholars of China.

Totman, Conrad. *Early Modern Japan*. Berkeley: University of California Press, 1993. A history of the Tokugawa era, incorporating much ecological analysis.

China's Empress Dowager and Eunuchs. The Qing Empire was dominated by the Manchus, and the Empress Dowager Zixi was the most important Manchu ruler from 1862 to 1908. In this photograph taken around 1900, she sits in her royal conveyance as it is transported by eunuchs. The Manchus continued the imperial practice of employing eunuchs (the great majority of whom were Chinese) in the inner court, where the emperor's wives, daughters, and concubines lived. Unlike many of the Ming emperors, who were often under the influence of powerful eunuchs, the Manchus kept their eunuchs under strict control.
Courtesy of the Freer Gallery of Art, Smithsonian Institution, Washington. D.C.

Slavery around the Globe

In the mid–fourteenth century, King Kano Rumfa of the Hausa kingdom in what is now Nigeria appointed one slave as the head of the state treasury and another as the commander-in-chief of the military. In the mid–sixteenth century, Dutch slave owners in South Africa systematically mutilated their slaves' faces as warnings against misbehavior. How could slaves acquire so much power in Hausaland and so little in South Africa? The answer is simple: The institution of slavery has encompassed a great diversity around the world, unified only by the common fact that one person owns another. This issue explores some of that diversity, underscoring how the colonial slavery discussed in Chapter 26 is an atypical version of slavery.

The first documentary evidence of slaves comes from the Ur-Nammu tablet of Sumeria, around 2100 B.C. Most scholars believe that slaves probably were important one or two thousand years prior to this date. By 1000 B.C., slavery had appeared independently in Europe, Asia, and Africa; by A.D. 1000, it also was important in North America, Central America, South America, and the Pacific.

Slavery has been in continuous existence since its inception, and it continues today, though there are very few slaves now and institutionalized slavery is rare. Throughout this range of time and location, slavery has taken a wide variety of forms, and this section explores their areas of commonality and difference.

FIGURE I.6.1 *Ur-Nammu Tablet.* *This stone carving from Sumeria dates to around 2500 B.C. and may be the earliest depiction of slaves in the world. King Ur-Nanshe is shown twice, in oversized proportions, with his children and various attendants; the smallest figures are probably slaves.* Louvre © R.M.N./ P. Bernard.

THE CONCEPT OF SLAVERY AND ITS VARIANTS

No matter where or when it occurs, slavery has some common features that relate directly to the philosophy of owning another human being. There are, however, several variable factors that differ from case to case and are critical in determining the treatment of a slave.

The Basic Concept

Slavery can be defined by its five fundamental characteristics:

— the slave is owned by a master;

— the slave provides involuntary labor for that master;

— the slave has a low, often the lowest, position in the social hierarchy;

— the slave is acquired by purchase, capture, or birth to another slave; and

— the slave is an outsider to the master's community.

Each of these characteristics warrants a bit more discussion.

Although ownership is central to the concept of slavery, different societies have viewed the relationship between slave and owner differently. At one extreme, slaves have been seen as nonhuman objects, mere pieces of property; this is chattel slavery. At the other extreme, slaves are simply members of the lowest stratum of society who owe labor to their masters; slaves of this latter sort retain their humanity and at least some of the basic rights accorded to all people in that society. No matter how benign the relationship between the slave and owner, however, the slave is required to carry out labor at the wish of (and for the benefit of) the owner.

The slave always is near the lowest rung of the status ladder for the society in question. Although Classical Greek slaves who served as tutors and scholars, such as Epictetus, occupied a rung higher than common slaves, they still were viewed with contempt. The plays of Sophocles usually depicted slaves as sneaky, playing on an ancient Greek stereotype. Greek and Roman families expressed concern whether it was fair to a child to hire a slave tutor, because the economic savings might be offset by the possible unspecified negative effects on the child, effects that presumably would grow purely out of contact with a slave. Slaves who held high positions in governments obviously ranked high in power, but they still carried a stigma that affected their overall social position.

Normally slaves have been acquired through purchase, capture, or birth to slave parents, but there have been exceptions. Criminals could be sentenced to slavery as punishment for their crimes in many societies, including those of China, imperial Rome, and parts of West Africa. These slaves, though, were sold by the state, so they came to their eventual owner through purchase. In many societies, debtors could sell themselves into slavery, in essence their new owners purchasing them by paying their debts. Debt slavery was especially prominent in ancient Greece and Rome, eastern Europe, Southwest Asia, and the Aztec Empire. In some cases, particularly in China, destitute parents could sell children into slavery, sometimes for a pittance. Here the primary aim was to reduce the number of mouths to feed, and the money paid for the children was secondary. Nonetheless, the children were purchased, and it probably was important that money change hands to emphasize symbolically the changed status of the children.

Usually a slave comes from a group other than that of the owner. Most of the slaves of Christian Europeans were Jewish, Muslim, or nonwhite. Many scholars believe that the degradation of slavery normally is imposed only on someone from the outside, someone who could be labeled inferior on the basis of differing ethnicity, religion, or race. Sometimes, however, slaves came from the same groups as the masters, as when Benin began trading its own citizens to Europeans in times of slave shortages. When this happened, the act of assigning a person the status of slave in itself differentiated that person from the rest of the society.

In practice, there rarely is any difficulty in deciding whether or not a particular practice is slavery, although there sometimes are overlaps with serfdom and indenture, which will be discussed later. The real purpose of this definition of slavery is to focus our attention on the common core of characteristics before looking at how slavery varies from place to place.

Factors of Variation in Slavery

The variations among different systems of slavery are practically infinite, but many of the differences relate to four factors. The four factors make up a continuum, and a system of slavery may fall anywhere along it.

First, slavery may be open or closed. **Open slavery** provides realistic ways by which a slave can be freed, while **closed slavery** maintains a slave in that status for life. Open systems of slavery often permit slaves to accumulate property to purchase their freedom or standard ways to distinguish themselves (as in battle) and be granted freedom. Consequently, manumission (the freeing of a slave) is moderately common in open slavery systems. In some open slavery systems, a slave automatically is adopted into the owner's kinship group, giving the slave a place in society and paving the way to his or her eventual full incorporation into the owner's family.

In contrast, a fully closed system has no provision for the freeing of slaves. Most systems have provided some mechanism of manumission, though in some cases it was difficult to implement and, therefore, rarely used. A Brazilian plantation owner's freeing a field worker for exceptional service, for example, was unlikely, because most owners rarely had contact with these slaves and didn't know anyone's personal record. Many scholars believe that closed slavery encourages fatalism and hopelessness in slaves, thereby discouraging rebellions and escapes.

Second, slavery varies in terms of whether it extends to the descendants of slaves. Under **hereditary slavery** systems, the children of slaves also are slaves; under **single-generation slavery** systems, the parent may remain a slave, but the child is free. Hereditary slavery is an extension of closed slavery, carrying slave status beyond an individual's death, and it presumably contributes to the fatalism and hopelessness discussed earlier.

Third, as discussed in Chapter 26, slaves may be viewed as chattel (mere objects), or they may be given personal rights. At one end of this continuum, slaves lose all humanity, because society treats them as inhuman, denying them the rights that society accords human beings. At the other end, slaves are simply low-status persons who retain their basic human rights.

FIGURE I.6.2 *Roman Gravestone for Former Slaves.* *This gravestone shows portraits of Demetrius and Philonicus (most likely father and son), freedmen who previously had been slaves of Publius Licinius, a magistrate. This elite-style gravestone indicates that they were able to achieve both social and economic distinction despite their former status as slaves. It is not known exactly how they gained their freedom, but it may have been purchased by accumulated wealth.* Courtesy of the Trustees of the British Museum.

Fourth and finally, slaves may be kept for various purposes, and slaveholding societies usually have different rules for the proper treatment of slaves doing different jobs. The most common distinction is between **domestic slaves** (performing household duties) and **agricultural-industrial slaves** (providing hard labor for commercial activities). Domestic slaves usually are fewer in number and higher in status than agricultural-industrial slaves. Although agricultural-industrial slaves often produce more than the cost of maintaining them, domestic slaves usually cost more to maintain than strict economics would justify. Domestic slaves usually are luxury items whose possession confers prestige on their owner.

There are some loose correlations among these factors. Most closed systems of slavery also are hereditary and view slaves as chattel; many open systems are single-generation and consider slaves to have personal rights. Many systems of slavery that have agricultural-industrial slaves also have domestic slaves, although the opposite is not always true. These correlations are only approximate, and historical cases of slavery have combined aspects of the positions along the continuum formed by these factors into unique systems.

Slaves, Serfs, and Indentured Servants

While slavery is the best-known system of involuntary labor, it has two principal cousins with which it sometimes is confused: serfdom and indenture. The features that differentiate these three systems are subtle but significant.

Like a hereditary slave, a **serf** is a worker whose labor is owed to someone else and whose status is inherited by children, but serfs have certain personal rights and are not thought of as "owned." Serfdom is essentially a relationship between a group of laborers and a lord that guarantees certain rights for the serf and certain expectations for the lord. It is usually a manifestation of feudalism—the hierarchic relationship between a lord and vassals—and often grew out of it.

The specific rights of a serf have varied from place to place, though the central philosophy behind serfdom everywhere has been that serfs had some personal rights and could not be owned. More practically, serfs often provided a portion of their labor for their own subsistence, so in a sense they shared the profits of their own labor with their lord. Truly, their share usually was low, but they had a stake in their own activities. The very fact that their share was small meant that they could ill afford to shirk their duties.

Most serfs have been attached to a plot of land. If the feudal control of that land shifted to another lord, so did the serfs' allegiance. This relationship often is considered central to the concept of serfdom, but some serfs in medieval Europe were attached to the lord directly and could be shifted from place to place.

Indenture differs from either slavery or serfdom in that it is temporary and entered into voluntarily. It is unclear how far back in history

FIGURE 1.6.3 *East African Slave and Master.* *This photo from around 1900 documents the persistence of slavery in East Africa into the twentieth century. The slave (left) demonstrates his subordination to his master.* Keystone View Company/Library of Congress.

indenture can be traced, though it clearly existed in China in the first millennium B.C. Indenture became prominent during the era of European expansion and colonization, from about 1500 to about 1800, when individuals wanting passage to a colony but unable to afford it could sign a contract transferring rights to their labor to someone else for a specified term. In return, the person receiving the labor would provide funds for the soon-to-be-indentured servant to book passage to the colony. Indenture existed in various colonial areas, including North America, but it was most important on the islands of the Indian Ocean, where it was the primary means of obtaining labor.

In theory, slavery, serfdom, and indenture are distinct, but real cases can be remarkably murky. In the Seychelles (an island group in the Indian Ocean), for example, laborers were brought from India under indenture, but a series of laws made it difficult for indentured servants ever to complete their contracted service. Indentured servants were required to carry a ticket stating their status; if found without this ticket or in an area away from their work site, they could be jailed for a week for vagrancy. Annually, about 10 percent of indentured servants were jailed for this offense. If they were absent from work for more than six days—and, as noted, jailing was for a week—the month or sometimes the year in which they were absent was not deducted from their indenture. By accumulating offenses that prolonged servitude, an indentured servant might remain in that status for a lifetime, effectively little different from a slave.

REGIONAL SLAVEHOLDING TRADITIONS

A few examples cannot adequately represent the diversity that has existed within slavery. Nonetheless, the examples that follow, along with others in this text, will give an idea of how much variety there has been within slaveholding systems.

China

China developed slavery at least by 1200 B.C., and it was abolished only with the founding of the People's Republic of China in 1949. Chinese slavery was unique in focusing on children, usually under the age of ten years. Adolescents and young adults sometimes went into indenture to pay off debts, but entering slavery was rare. The only prominent adult slaves were concubines, whose purchase and exchange served almost as sport among the elite, and state slaves, who labored for the Han government in the early centuries A.D., making iron weapons and agricultural tools.

The reason for China's focus on children was related to the purposes to which slaves were put. There was limited agricultural-industrial slavery, and slaves usually were either domestic servants or designated heirs of the purchaser. Domestic slaves needed to be raised in an elite household if they were to be able to perform their duties with the proper polish, so they were acquired as young as was practical. Girl slaves usually were used as domestic servants, and occasionally they would be married to a son of the owner at their adulthood. Boy slaves, on the other hand, could be domestic servants or be designated as the heir of their owner. An elite man with no sons might make a slave boy his designated heir so that his line could continue, although he was more likely to adopt a relative. If a boy slave were designated as heir, he would assume virtually all the rights of a biological son. If not designated an heir by a legally prescribed age, a boy slave irrevocably became a domestic slave.

Those slaves who were not designated heirs or married to sons remained slaves all their lives, and their children also were slaves. Their tasks were not exceptionally taxing, and their lot in life was in many ways better than that of peasants. On the other hand, they were viewed as chattel, and their personal rights were highly limited.

Chinese slavery, then, was largely closed, with the exceptions of designated heirs and marriages to sons. It was hereditary and chattel-based, and it was almost exclusively domestic.

India

Slavery in India extends back at least 3,000 years and may well have existed before then. It was abolished under British colonial rule in 1844.

In North India, slaves were almost all domestic slaves, and they contributed relatively little to the physical well-being of the households in which they worked. Rather, their primary purpose seems to have been the aggrandizement of the slave owner. In South India, where most slaves were used for agricultural labor, their value rested more in economics and less in prestige. Slaves in both parts of India were considered chattel, and children of slaves automatically became slaves. Although owners could permit slaves to accumulate property in life, upon their deaths it reverted to their owners. Slaves normally could not buy their freedom, and owners rarely granted freedom as a reward for meritorious performance.

Owners were expected to care for their slaves, who were considered to be somewhat like dependent children. Owners were obligated to (and typically did) see to their general welfare, by providing appropriate living quarters and meals, health care, support and protection in old age, and funeral arrangements. Special concern was given the marriage of slaves, and owners were expected to provide spouses and to defray the costs of a wedding (much as parents were expected to do for their children). Slave owners had a strong interest in matchmaking, because the ownership of children of the match was at stake. Local rules stated whether the children would belong to the father's owner or the mother's, and special agreements could supersede the usual rule. For obvious reasons of self-interest, owners usually married their own slaves to one another, thereby reducing conflict over the children.

India's caste system, with its focus on the importance of high-caste persons avoiding tasks seen as ritually defiling, had profound effects on Indian slavery. Agricultural-industrial slaves were drawn primarily from the lowest castes, but domestic slaves had to come from higher castes because they performed ritually pure tasks like drawing water and interacting with the high-caste elite. This produced a paradox: Domestic slaves were ritually high-ranking yet socially low-ranking. A complex system of symbols and usages was developed in order to maintain this complex and seemingly contradictory status.

Also because of the caste system, outsiders were seen as unfit to handle food that was to be consumed by high-caste owners and were therefore unacceptable as domestic slaves. Consequently, slaves had to be drawn from the ranks of Indians themselves. This case is a significant exception to the general rule that slaves are drawn from different ethnic or tribal groups than those of their owners.

Slavery in India was very closed and hereditary. Although it was chattel-oriented, owners incurred a wide range of obligations to their slaves. It was primarily based on domestic slavery, though agricultural-industrial slavery was more important in the south.

The Muslim World

The areas that Islam dominated in the seventh and eighth centuries had been keeping slaves for centuries before, and the practice continued under Islam. Slaves were recruited through capture, purchase, or birth. In the first two centuries of the spread of Islam, war was common enough that capture accounted for a large percentage of slaves, but this source declined as Islam spread, because the Qur'an forbade the enslavement of fellow Muslims. In fact, the Qur'an expressly forbids the enslavement of any "people of the Book," that is, Muslims, Jews, or Christians. In practice, Muslims received the greatest protection by this proscription. Purchase of slaves was primarily through the trans-Saharan trade with West and East Africa, although a lesser trade with eastern Europe and Byzantium helped supply some areas with slaves. Law prohibited Muslims from entering slavery voluntarily to erase a debt, as well as from selling one's children into slavery.

The children of two slave parents were slaves. Marriages between slaves and free persons (usually slave women and free men), however, were common, and the resulting children usually were free. An entire dynasty of caliphs of the Mamluks (750–1258) married slave women for several centuries beginning in 1260, thereby avoiding the political entanglements of marrying women of noble families.

Slaves under Islam were used primarily as domestic servants. Enslaved women also might become entertainers or concubines, and enslaved men sometimes became business agents. Agricultural-industrial slavery was rare under Islam, with the significant exception of the sugar plantations of Southwest Asia, which were staffed by sub-Saharan African slaves through the Indian Ocean slave trade from around 500 (in pre-Islamic times) to around 900. The other major use of slaves under Islam was as military troops.

Slaves had no legal rights. They could not own property or give testimony in court. The only penalty a free person incurred for killing a slave was to provide suitable compensation to the owner. On the other hand, the Qur'an and folk sayings attributed to Muhammad preached that an owner should display kindness to a slave, and most owners probably did so. Many owners bent the rules, allowing slaves to accumulate property toward purchasing their freedom.

The freeing of slaves was fairly common. Captives could be freed by ransom, around which bargaining was considered normal. As noted previously, many slaves purchased their own freedom. Also, many owners freed slaves who showed especial loyalty, skill, or initiative.

Islamic slavery, then, was largely open. Although it was hereditary, the number of marriages between free and slave parents was great enough to reduce significantly the number of children born into slavery. Although slaves were thought of as chattel, most Muslim owners tempered that conception with kindness and relaxation of restrictions.

The Kwakiutl

Slavery, although most common in agricultural states, occasionally has thrived in chiefdoms with less complex political systems. A prime example of this is the Kwakiutl[1] of Canada's Pacific coast. There, abundant resources allowed hunters and gatherers to develop large, sedentary populations with marked class stratification.

Among the Kwakiutl, war captives often became slaves. Although the child of a slave and a free person would not be a slave, the child of two slaves would. It was considered debasing for a free person to marry a slave, so such unions were rare. As a result of capture and birth, there was a permanent slave stratum in Kwakiutl society.

Slavery for an individual among the Kwakiutl, however, was not necessarily permanent. A captive could be ransomed out of slavery by relatives at any point. Alternatively, because slaves were permitted to accumulate property, they could purchase their own freedom, essentially ransoming themselves.

Kwakiutl slaves performed a variety of labors for their owners. They were excluded from religious ceremonies, and they occasionally were sac-

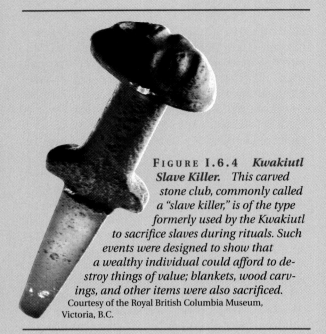

FIGURE I.6.4 *Kwakiutl Slave Killer.* *This carved stone club, commonly called a "slave killer," is of the type formerly used by the Kwakiutl to sacrifice slaves during rituals. Such events were designed to show that a wealthy individual could afford to destroy things of value; blankets, wood carvings, and other items were also sacrificed.* Courtesy of the Royal British Columbia Museum, Victoria, B.C.

rificed during rituals. Although there was no organized slave trade, slaves sometimes were exchanged along with other goods.

Kwakiutl slavery was very open, though hereditary. Slaves were chattel, but they retained certain personal rights, particularly those relating to property.

The Melanau

Slavery was prominent among the Melanau[2] of Indonesia. The Melanau chiefdom had at its apex a class of aristocrats who controlled the export of the sago palm upon which the commercial economy was based, and the labor-intensive production of sago was largely in the hands of slaves. Slavery began sometime before the eighteenth century and ended in 1948, long after Dutch law officially had abolished it in Indonesia.

Slaves among the Melanau probably were recruited by capture in earlier days, but by the late nineteenth century, when written records became common, most slaves either were born to that status or sold themselves into it in order to relieve debts. From the moment people became slaves, they were on the route to manumission. There was a fixed sequence of seven steps to manumission,

---

[1] **Kwakiutl:** KWAH kee oot uhl

[2] **Melanau:** mehl uh NOW

with increasing personal rights and autonomy as one progressed through the steps. Each step was gained by a complicated procedure involving gifts at the weddings of daughters, and the process accelerated in the later stages, as one's rights to accumulate property became greater. Slaves served as both domestic servants and agricultural laborers, and the passage from domestic to agricultural duties was an important marker of the fifth step, because the agriculturalist had greater opportunities for economic betterment. If individuals did not make it to the final step and freedom during a lifetime, their children would take up the process at the point their parents had reached before death.

Slaves had no right to regulate their own marriages, which were arranged by owners. Slaves often married free people, in which case the first child was free, the second a slave, the third free, and so forth. Slaves retained many personal rights and were not considered chattel.

Slavery among the Melanau was very open; indeed, slaves were on the track to freedom, although only some achieved it fully in a single lifetime. Slavery was hereditary, but, because children inherited the final step achieved by their parents, families moved steadily out of slavery. As with most slavery systems in chiefdom-level societies, slaves retained many personal rights.

THE SPECTRUM OF SLAVERY

Although slaves are rare in our time, they have been commonplace in human history, at least for the last five or six thousand years. Indeed, some scholars have considered slaveholding to be typical and societies without slaves as the aberration. The variety within slavery has meant that each system has had very different implications for the slave, the owner, and the society as a whole.

It is a quirk of history that we live in a time when the most well-known instance of slavery was that of the Americas in the sixteenth through nineteenth centuries, based on the African slave trade conducted by Europeans. No form of slavery is benign or beneficial to slaves, but this form was the most rapacious and brutal ever known, probably because of the huge numbers of persons involved. Almost completely closed, fully hereditary, and chattel-based, it encouraged harsh treatment, abuse, and brutality. It focused predominantly on agricultural-industrial slaves, who were considered expendable parts in a plantation machine. This system destroyed the lives and often the wills of millions of slaves. It was an extreme form of slavery, and we should not draw our picture of slavery in other periods and places from it.

SUGGESTED READINGS

Finlay, Moses I. "Slavery." In *International Encyclopedia of the Social Sciences.* Vol. 14. New York, 1968, 307–13. A brief but insightful article, the best single work on the theory of slavery.

Patterson, Orlando. *Slavery and Social Death: A Comparative Study.* Cambridge, Mass.: Harvard University Press, 1982. Argues that the essence of slavery is the alienation of the slave from any societal context.

Phillips, William D. *Slavery from Roman Times to the Early Transatlantic Trade.* Minneapolis: University of Minnesota Press, 1985. A good synthesis focusing on Europe.

Watson, James L., ed. *Asian and African Systems of Slavery.* Berkeley: University of California Press, 1980. An excellent collection of essays discussing historical systems of slavery in anthropological perspective.

ART SEVEN EXAMINES THE MULTIFACETED CHANGES that transformed Europe and other societies. Massive conflicts among European nation-states accelerated changes in society and compelled rulers to alter their polities. Later, an industrial revolution transformed economic and social systems in Europe, the United States, and Japan. And the drive for resources and markets by industrializing states led to the development of imperialism, in which Western and Japanese governments carved out empires from conquered lands in Africa, Asia, and the Americas.

Broader participation in political affairs burst forth, beginning in the seventeenth century. The English Parliament wrested power away from the monarchy and then ruled England jointly with the crown. The American and French revolutions significantly expanded the voting franchise and participation in government. These events encouraged Latin American and Asian countries to become independent. Nationalism developed in the nineteenth century and helped fuel the drive for colonies by imperialist powers.

Human beings also began to see themselves and their world in strikingly new ways. For example, people gradually saw the earth as but one planet in a vast universe, and they eventually viewed human beings as one of many species that evolved over time. Science became increasingly important.

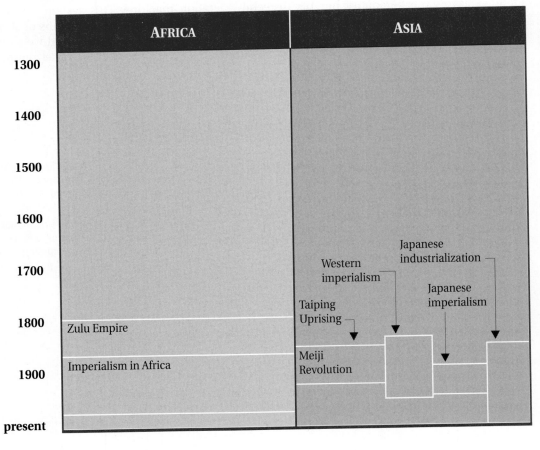

Chapter 29 examines the Renaissance in Europe, a time of expanded economic and artistic development. It also explores the Protestant and Roman Catholic reformations, a time of religious ferment and conflict. Chapter 30 probes the growth of European absolutism, when monarchs centralized their governments and gathered new power for themselves. Chapter 31 develops the concept of revolution and analyzes revolutions around the world. Chapter 32 presents the Industrial Revolution, a transformative economic process that propelled Western countries and Japan into positions of political hegemony. Chapter 33 looks at nationalism as a political force in developing Zululand and many other nation-states. Chapter 34 examines imperialism—the modern form of colonialism—which uses industrialization and nationalism to build empires, especially overseas. Chapter 35 investigates the impact of Charles Darwin, Karl Marx, and others who changed the way human beings look at themselves and their environment. Issue 7 explores the relationship between science and the masses during a time when scientific discoveries and information excited common people around the world.

PART SEVEN

EUROPE'S GLOBAL REACH

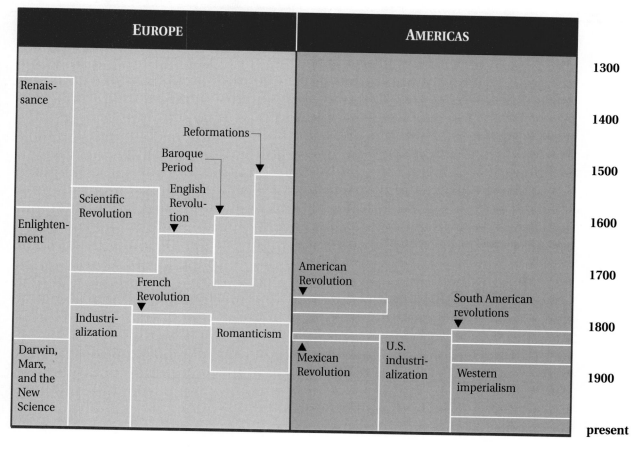

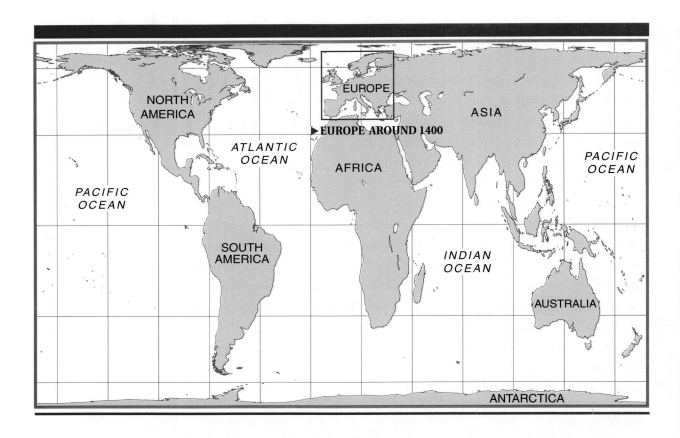

▶ EUROPE AROUND 1400

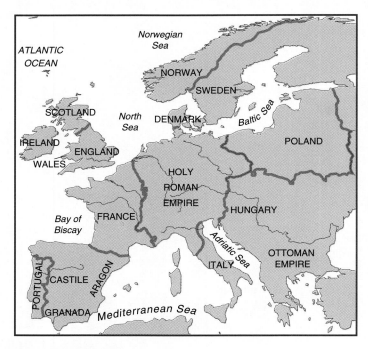

▶ EUROPE AROUND 1400

European Cultural and Religious Upheaval

around 1350–around 1650

Ortelius, a late-sixteenth-century cartographer, carried an autograph book with him on his journeys throughout Europe. He called it his "Book of Friends," and in its pages were signed the names of lawyers, diplomats, historians, poets, printers, Protestant and Roman Catholic clergy, musicians, architects, antiquarian book dealers, and botanists. The geographical range of the signatories is impressive: Spain, Portugal, Italy, Germany, France, and England are represented. The diversity of Ortelius's friendships reflects the broad spectrum of European occupations and interests from the fourteenth to the seventeenth centuries.

Life in Europe in the late fourteenth century was fraught with complexities, uncertainties, and new opportunities. As a result of plagues and wars, the European population had suffered more than 20 million deaths. The legacy of this tragedy was economic depression for some, but it allowed opportunities for others. Many survivors seized the moment to advance their social positions or introduce new ways of thinking about the world. The voyages of exploration, beginning in the late fifteenth century, challenged Europeans to expand their worldview beyond their own neighborhoods; new markets opened for European products, and new goods arrived from distant exotic places.

The changes that occurred at this time helped usher in a new era in the fourteenth century in central, western, and northern Europe. Scholars call this era the **Renaissance**, meaning the rebirth of Greco-Roman culture as an authoritative model for society. Medieval intellectual and artistic attitudes had given way to perspectives that valued the Greco-Roman period more than the immediate medieval past. This reorientation in worldview was part of a broad sociopolitical and economic process that occurred at different times, in different places, and over several centuries, from the late fourteenth through the sixteenth centuries in Europe.

Questioning of religious ideology and calls for reform, which had already begun in the Middle Ages, took on greater urgency in the aftermath of devastation from plagues and wars. Many challenged the traditional social and political structures, and arguments over basic political theories, religious tenets, and procedures for change consumed European intellectuals. Religious self-examination and reform erupted in vehement disputes and protests and eventually in the schism of the Roman Catholic Church. This period of reform and schism is called the **Protestant Reformation** by scholars. Shortly after the Protestant Reformation began, the Roman Catholic Church initiated its own reform of lax practices and abuses of privilege; this reform is known as the **Roman Catholic Reformation**.

Renaissance and Reformation attitudes did not spread to all parts of Europe, especially not to eastern Europe. For example, the Ottoman Empire and the Russian state were little affected by Renaissance and Reformation trends. But, for much of Europe, the era of 1350 to 1650 was dynamic and destructive, innovative and incendiary.

THE EUROPEAN RENAISSANCE, AROUND 1350–AROUND 1600

Ideas that the ancient Greco-Roman past was superior to the immediate medieval past emerged in Italy in the mid–fourteenth century. At the same time, economic expansion brought increased wealth into Europe, spurring patronage of the arts.

Social attitudes changed and new opportunities emerged for some people. With these economic and social changes came innovations in politics, philosophy, and the arts.

Economic Growth

Economies grew significantly in Europe during the Renaissance. Plague and war had greatly affected most of Europe, but financial devastation was not universal. Some regional commerce actually expanded because war and disease had wiped out competition. By the end of this period there were far fewer serfs throughout western Europe. Although many peasants continued to owe dues and labor services, a moneyed economy of rent payments and wages gradually supplanted the older manorial system. With tenant peasants and a growing middle class in the towns, lords tried to protect traditional rights of jurisdiction over markets and courts against the increasing power of monarchs.

European lands were sometimes reclaimed for commercial enterprises, causing a shift from farming to commercial activities. In England, for example, conversion of low-yield farms into pasturage for sheep because of a greater demand for wool brought higher profit to the lords but displaced many peasants because fewer of them were needed for animal husbandry than for crop production. Many of these dislocated peasants migrated to cities, where they became artisans and laborers or remained unemployed.

In some cases, such as that of the expansion of the wool market, commercial ventures brought increased controls on merchant activities and commercial alliances. In England, for example, the government regulated exportation of wool. All English wool had to be exported through a selected port by designated merchants, who had formed their own company. The government's payback came when the king borrowed heavily from this company to finance the crown's projects. Most of the older medieval guilds adapted to the growth in commerce by developing joint ventures. The result was the financial ruin of small, independent competitors who could not afford to match these larger capital investments.

Italian city-states had always been more commercially active than those in the comparatively agrarian areas north of the Alps because of their

MAP 29.1 *Renaissance Italy.* *Renaissance Italy was a patchwork of independent polities, many of which were fierce trade competitors. This competition sometimes resulted in aggression and warfare. Peace was usually achieved through hard-fought treaties that protected dominions over lands and trade routes.*

proximity to natural harbors and their vibrant traditions as areas of trade. Milan, for example, was known for its production of armaments and cloth. Several Italian cities became banking and insurance centers during the Renaissance. The trade network that had supported the medieval economy north of the Alps had expanded, and several major commercial centers now established financial ties with wealthy banking houses in Italy. As a result, most economies expanded rapidly. Although banking had developed in medieval Italy, standardization of policies and protection allowed for substantial economic diversity. Long and dangerous voyages led to new fiscal innovations to aid the growing commercial activi-

ties. For example, investors were encouraged by insurance that sheltered against crippling losses and by letters of credit that protected against monetary risk.

European commerce increased significantly through Jewish trade links with the vast networks of Muslim merchants in the Mediterranean. By the fifteenth century, Venice and Genoa dominated the European long-distance trade connection with Muslims in the eastern Mediterranean and acted as commercial conduits to the rest of Europe. When the Ottoman Turks disrupted eastern Mediterranean trade links and conquered Constantinople in the mid–fifteenth century, most Italian cities suffered temporary but significant revenue losses. Italian trade rebounded with new ties to Mediterranean trade and the New World trade.

Renaissance Society

Between the fourteenth and sixteenth centuries, European rural life continued as it had for centuries, with moderate changes. Cities had grown significantly. Several cities, including Venice, Milan, Naples, Paris, and London, could boast of populations totaling from 150,000 to more than 200,000. These populations created a demand for employment and goods. Most cities were divided into neighborhoods; sometimes the division was by profession, sometimes by wealth, and sometimes by religion.

European Jews had been forced to live in ghettos during the Middle Ages. Most Jews were subject to periodic acts of violence by Christians because of their religion. In many cases, authorities willingly participated in their deaths and destruction of their properties; in some cases, religious and political authorities tried to protect Jews from angry mobs. Persecutions by roaming gangs, particularly during plague years, accounted for thousands of Jewish deaths. During a plague in the city of Toledo, for example, rumors spread that Jews were poisoning the city wells, and many Jews were killed. As Renaissance trade developed in the fourteenth and fifteenth centuries, more restrictions closed many trade occupations to Jews in order to accommodate Christians. Heavy taxes kept most Jewish families in poverty, although some were able to gain funds through investments. Some Christians rejected anti-Jewish programs and supported Jews in their areas; the monarchs of the Kingdom of the Two Sicilies (southern Italy and Sicily) were recognized as tolerant rulers.

European Christians tolerated the presence of Jews in most areas and periods because of economic motives. Christians often let Jews absorb the financial burden of risky trade ventures by borrowing money and not repaying bad debts. Kings and merchants frequently confiscated Jewish wealth in fiscally lean times in order to replenish their revenues. Many Jews contributed to commercial interests with their artisan skills and merchant contacts. Others contributed to Renaissance society in the limited professions open to Jews, such as medicine.

FIGURE 29.1 *Vanities.* *This painting by the Italian artist Vittore Carpaccio depicts some of the "vanities" representative of worldly wealth that Girolamo Savonarola preached against. These Venetian women have bleached and styled hair and wear significant amounts of makeup, opulent clothing, and expensive jewelry. They are enjoying their leisure on a balcony with an attending servant and their various pets. These women happen to be prostitutes, but their attire and the setting reflect the aristocratic styles of the day. Savonarola's charismatic preaching attracted many followers who shared his abhorrence of extravagance and privilege.* Museo Correr, Venice/Art Resource, N.Y.

In all Italian Renaissance cities, important political families measured their power and influence by the number of families of lower status that supported and emulated them. Most lived near their patrons and copied their lifestyles as much as possible, leading to a pride in opulent living. Patronage of the arts was a direct result of increased economic activity.

The presence of such wealth in the face of poverty occasionally erupted in violent reaction. Girolamo Savonarola[1] (1452–1498), a preacher, led a revolt in the late fifteenth century in the city of Florence, establishing a democracy for a short period. He preached against what he saw as the immoral wealth and absurd vanities of wealthy Florentines. In huge bonfires, later given the collective name "the bonfire of the vanities," cosmetics, luxurious clothing, hundreds of pieces of art, and furnishings went up in smoke. Savonarola's radicalism eventually resulted in his arrest and execution.

Increased commercial activity certainly improved the standard of living for many in Europe, but the majority still lived meager lives. Traders in the thirteenth century could usually expect moderate growth in income, but, by the fifteenth century, competition stymied economic gains for the majority. It is tempting to assume that the grand living styles of the elite somehow raised the standard of living for everyone, but most wealthy patrons were little concerned with the plight of their poorest neighbors. To a large degree, innovations in education, philosophy, political theory, and the fine arts bypassed the poor.

THE LABOR FORCE. Labor in rural areas changed little for both men and women from the fourteenth to the sixteenth centuries. Many peasant women, however, worked in their homes as part of a cottage industry, carding, spinning, and weaving wool into cloth. Merchants then gathered the finished products for later sale in towns and cities.

Increased availability of capital through commercial activities led to an increase in paid professions in the cities. Two examples were soldiering and bookkeeping. Professional soldiers were in demand because long-distance commerce placed valuable cargoes in jeopardy. Hired by the highest bidder and given a contract, soldiers protected the

banking and shipping companies' interests. Venice employed enough soldiers to secure its seaborne empire from the Adriatic Sea to Cyprus. Professional bookkeepers found more than enough employment in banking and commercial activities. Most merchants learned to read and write as children and then acquired the necessary skills in mathematics and bookkeeping to run their own family businesses or to keep records as employees of someone else. A young man might be apprenticed to a business as a bookkeeper or even sent on to law school so that he might hire himself out as a consultant in commercial law.

The laboring class in the cities worked at numerous professions, some old and some new. For example, the sixteenth-century city of Nuremberg, a hub for northern European trade, had 140 different craft occupations. Cloth makers, potters, oar makers, carpenters, blacksmiths, and arsenal workers, to name a few, represent the variety of urban laborers. Similarly to earlier artisans, groups of specialists protected the secrets of their crafts, as when Venetian glassmakers guarded their unique knowledge of adding enamels to glass.

Many laborers in the late fourteenth and fifteenth centuries earned low wages. They toiled in the mines or in cloth production, unable to defend themselves against the exploitation of merchants and investors. No guild or other organization existed to argue on their behalf, and new joint ventures focused increasingly on company management interests rather than on employee benefits. Miners, for example, rose early in the morning and worked long hours with only a short break for a little bread and ale before returning to the shafts to pick at the veins of ore. The life of a miner proved so difficult that many received exemption from military service or taxes as compensation. In some cases, criminals served on mining teams as punishment for their crimes.

The labor force in the cities included women. A few women in the city of Venice, for example, gained employment in manufacturing. Most women working outside of the home, however, became domestic servants. Some were personal maids who helped elite women adorn themselves with the newest styles of the day. Some poorer women supported themselves in the age-old employment of prostitution, and most cities had populations of female prostitutes and special taxes on them. Venice, for example, collected lucrative

---

[1] **Savonarola:** SAHV ah nah ROH lah

prostitution taxes and became financially dependent on them. Middle-class and elite women, however, typically remained in the home and managed their households.

LITERACY AND GENDER ROLES. Literacy was limited to members of the middle or elite classes. Conduct books, such as *The Book of the Courtier* (published around 1516), outlined the proper education for young men as physical mastery of swordplay, horseback riding, hunting, and games. A "Renaissance man's" education followed the Greek ideal of both physical and intellectual training to produce a well-rounded individual. Education for both men and women followed the axiom "a healthy mind in a healthy body." Conduct books for women taught young ladies household management and the arts of dancing, singing, playing instruments, and conversing so that they might properly entertain gentlemen. Although some women received formal training in the liberal arts, most education for women continued the traditional practices of needlework, embroidery, and the reading of religious literature.

It has been observed by scholars that, in some ways, Renaissance women actually lost some of the social status that had been gained in the previous medieval period. Many medieval women had enjoyed joint business partnerships with their husbands, and some merchant wives had become accountants and financiers for their husbands' commercial enterprises. Wives of lords usually ran the manorial properties and households for their husbands, who absented themselves for court activities and military obligations. Renaissance women, however, became social casualties in changing attitudes that accepted Greco-Roman literary figures as models. For example, an ancient Athenian gender distinction was adopted that categorized women's spheres of influence as inferior

FIGURE 29.2 *Tennis. Tennis originated in France and became a popular game for the wealthy. It was played with a small ball and rackets on a green enclosed by a walled and roofed courtyard. The physical exertion required by the rigorous sport helped to achieve a well-toned body, which was part of the Renaissance ideal. Tennis was imported to England, where Henry VIII had courts built at each of his palaces.* The Folger Shakespeare Library.

and domestic, while men's spheres were thought of as superior and public. Women who had exercised authority in businesses at the end of the Middle Ages found new Renaissance attitudes limiting their influence.

SOCIAL MOBILITY. One of the most important changes during the Renaissance was the expansion of opportunities for some gain in social advancement. In England, for example, only about fifty families held official titles of nobility; their position came from wealth based on traditional taxes, dues, and rents from extensive inherited landholdings. Below the nobility were the **gentry**, a new elite status that was not officially noble, yet was higher than the middle class; it was usually associated with rural property. The gentry controlled enough land to live comfortably without the need to work actively. Many small towns sought out members of the gentry to represent them in matters dealing with the nobility, and wealthy merchants often purchased country estates, becoming gentry themselves. This kind of social mobility reflected a shift from status gained through birthright to status achieved through wealth. In contrast to England, social mobility came more slowly in parts of continental Europe. Tenants or hired laborers, however, might achieve some improved status within their social class.

Renaissance Governments

The medieval legacy of the diverse independent political power of great lords and knights, of self-governing towns with powerful guilds, and of a universal Christian society gave way to emerging centralization during the Renaissance. Monarchs, strong regional princes, and independent cities tried to establish more centralized governments by slowly weakening customary financial obligations and multiple legal jurisdictions. Centralization under monarchs occurred in Spain, France, and England.

In part, the shift toward centralization occurred as a consequence of innovations in waging war. Mass armies and cavalry replaced medieval aristocratic knights on horseback, and men with muskets replaced bowmen. Navies protected commercial enterprises with decks of cannons mounted on gunships. Kings needed the support of their commoner subjects to wage war and, con-

sequently, developed centralized policies to help govern and command them.

With this general move toward political centralization came theories that supported strong monarchies. In his essay *The Prince*, Niccolò Machiavelli[2] (1469–1527) explains that a good leader is not necessarily one who is the most virtuous. Machiavelli elaborated on the theory that an effective ruler must use any means necessary, even fear and deception, to govern. Many of Machiavelli's insights came from his astute observation of Italian politics.

Italian city-states always had strained against political control from kings, bishops, and popes, and they emerged in the thirteenth and fourteenth centuries as politically independent. These cities were commonly governed by powerful families, like the d'Medici.[3] Cosimo d'Medici (1389–1464) dominated Florence and, through an alliance with the cities of Milan and Naples, checked expansionist policies of the neighboring Papal States. Because many European ruling houses borrowed heavily from Italian financiers, several powerful Italian families extended their political tendrils into European courts. Fierce competition between cities later resulted in the emergence of five large regional polities, one of which was the Papal States under the Borgia family. By the end of the fifteenth century, the Borgias controlled the Papal States through a relative, Pope Alexander VI (reign dates 1492–1503), who used papal power against rival cities and local enemies. More a secular prince than a holy father, Pope Alexander led his family into a morass of murder plots and political intrigue that was scandalous even by Renaissance standards.

England, after the economic catastrophe of the Hundred Years War, suffered internal hostilities and civil war. One of the bloodiest contests in English history convulsed the country into a dynastic struggle. Finally, in 1485, a member of the Tudor faction became Henry VII (reign dates 1485–1509), king of England. The Tudor dynasty represents a change in English government because Henry diminished the power of the English parliament by building his power on a new royal council, whose members he handpicked from the gentry class. The royal council unequivocally established judi-

[2] **Machiavelli:** MAHK ee uh VEHL ee
[3] **d'Medici:** duh MEH dih chee

cial authority through the ruthless council of the Star Chamber, which arrested, tortured, and sentenced victims without benefit of trial. Local law was enforced through justices of the peace, who were appointed by the royal council. Henry rarely called Parliament to meet and centralized authority through his royal council, thereby keeping the nobility under control. Marriage alliances with Spain and Scotland, coupled with the support of the gentry and middle-class merchants, helped the monarchy consolidate power.

The French ruler Louis XI (reign dates 1461–1483) earned the nickname "The Spider King" because of his preference for intrigue and manipulation. A large number of the French nobility had been killed in the Hundred Years War, and Louis consolidated his power by outmaneuvering those who remained. His use of the new technologies of gunpowder and cannons blew apart the castles of the entrenched nobility. Upon his death, Louis left the area of France under the king's direct control nearly twice as large as when he inherited the crown. Louis supported middle-class interests by establishing lucrative trade treaties with other commercial centers. His interest in commercial activity brought new money into French territories and earned him the grateful support of the middle class. Succeeding French monarchs continued the policies of trying to control regional lords.

The Holy Roman Empire, consisting of most of Central Europe, was an anomaly. Consolidation there was occurring within regions rather than under the monarch. The Holy Roman Emperor since 1356 had been elected by seven major Germanic princes representing the three hundred confederated principalities and towns in the empire. By the end of the fifteenth century, however, Emperor Maximilian I (reign dates 1493–1519), a Hapsburg, exerted powerful leadership over the empire. He accomplished this task by enforcing imperial control over the assembly composed of the seven princes and representatives of the free cities of Germany. Although Maximilian waged war on Italian cities in order to reunify them with the Holy Roman Empire, he never gained political control over them. Marriage alliances, particularly with Spain, brought wealth and prosperity into the realm. The grandson of Maximilian inherited the Spanish throne (including its New World wealth and its holdings in Italy) from his mother; he also inherited the imperial crown and other lands from his father. The long history of princely power in the empire, however, limited his ability to establish long-lasting central authority.

Spain began as a patchwork of the kingdoms of Portugal, Castile, Aragon, and Muslim Granada. In the mid-1470s, the two principalities of Aragon and Castile united through the marriage between Isabella of Castile (reign dates 1474–1504) and Ferdinand of Aragon (reign dates 1479–1516). Although the realms remained separate entities, Ferdinand and Isabella were able to consolidate their power within each one. Both rulers limited the influence of the nobility in their respective assemblies. Royally appointed lawyers were members of councils that dealt with finances and justice, and royal officials replaced elected magistrates in governing cities. The expulsion of Muslims in the 1480s and Jews in 1492 from Christian-controlled areas attests to the intolerance of religious diversity by the Christians. The conquest of Muslim-held Granada in 1492 brought further religious and political unity to the peninsula. Spanish commercial interests in the New World, the expansion of previous interests into Naples and Sicily, and diplomatic marriage alliances with France, England, and the Holy Roman Empire helped to catapult Spain into European dominance.

The three kingdoms of Denmark, Norway, and Sweden were unified and ably administered by Queen Margaret of Denmark (1353–1412), who was named queen after the deaths of her husband and son. The kingdoms remained politically separate within a confederation called the Union of Kalmar but were unified under "the lady king's" authority. Although unrest plagued her successors, the Union of Kalmar lasted until 1523.

Renaissance Thought

The overwhelming social changes during the Renaissance brought intellectual and artistic change as well. Universities, which had operated since the twelfth century, shifted their emphasis to human areas of inquiry. **Humanism**, a system of thought based on the study of human ideas and actions, grew out of a developing focus on secular interests. Many of our modern colleges have schools of humanities, which are a result of the transition from the medieval focus on theology, logic, and metaphysics to a Renaissance focus on

PATHS TO THE PAST

Lorenzo Valla and Textual Criticism

The recovery of the Greco-Roman heritage meant also a recovery of ancient texts. Many had been diligently copied and preserved by studious monks throughout the medieval centuries, others had been brought into Europe in the twelfth and thirteenth centuries through Muslim contacts, and still others had come more recently through Renaissance trade networks. Many humanists became involved in the widespread search for manuscripts, while others took on the tasks of authentication and restoration of copies to their pristine condition. (Through the centuries, monks had translated texts into the Latin of their day, and the copying of copies had resulted in many scribal errors.)

Lorenzo Valla (1407–1457), an Italian humanist, attacked and criticized many medieval philosophers and historians for writing in a contemporary Latin style instead of the more formal Classical Latin style of the Roman Empire. This kind of criticism soon led to a focus on word usage, which in turn led to a study of words and their histories. This practice developed into **textual criticism**, the analysis and authentication of texts. Armed with new grammars and handbooks, critics began examining manuscripts. The most famous case of textual criticism is Valla's discrediting of the document titled *The Donation of Constantine*. In the eighth century, the papacy was threatened by the Byzantine emperor and surrounded by Germanic kings challenging papal independence. The papacy had turned to the Franks (a Germanic tribe) for aid. Upon the Frankish conquest of Italy and the liberation of the papacy from these threats, *The Donation of Constantine* was shown to the Frankish king, Pepin the Short. This edict of Constantine, the fourth-century Christian Roman emperor, placed all the western Roman territories under papal authority. In presenting this document to Pepin, the pope hoped that Pepin would not place Italy under the Frankish crown. Pepin issued an edict in his own name, establishing the independent Papal States.

In studying the document, Valla discovered that its language was not of the fourth century at all but was produced in the eighth century in order to influence Pepin. Therefore, Valla believed, the claims laid out in the document were insupportable. He called the document a forgery, and his methodology in authenticating Greco-Roman texts became a mainstay of historical analysis. Valla's discrediting of the document gave many reformers the ammunition they needed against papal authority in the Reformation period. Scholars today, however, note that an oral tradition telling of Constantine's donation had existed. This tradition was never written down until it was needed to assure papal independence from Pepin. In that sense, the document was not an intended forgery or a necessarily false statement but, to those who produced it, a transcription of a traditional belief. It was common in the Middle Ages to record folk memory and use it as legal evidence.

As a result of textual criticism, history became a discipline within the humanities that organized human events into a new narrative based on proper chronology and evidence. Later Protestant reformers used these same techniques to study biblical narrative and other Christian documents. They discovered that the apostles did not write the Apostle's Creed and that Jerome's Latin Bible had several errors in its translation from Greek to Latin. Examination of Greek texts also yielded new insights into and new Latin translations of Plato's works.

Greco-Roman subjects such as art, poetry, and philosophy. These latter subjects, concentrating on human endeavors, were considered to be more appropriate for study and became known as human studies or the humanities. The major focus of the early movement toward the humanities centered on Greek and Roman literature. Humanists believed that the Greco-Roman period was superior to the medieval era in thought and style, and they wanted to emulate ancient writers. To a certain degree, however, their emphasis on ancient Greek and Latin language and literature impeded the progression toward writing in the vernacular languages, such as French and Italian.

Petrarch[4] and Boccaccio[5] are examples of Italian humanists. Francesco Petrarch (1304–1374) studied law at Bologna and fell in love with the writings of ancient Romans like Cicero and Virgil. He wrote treatises and orations in the Greco-Roman style and attempted an epic poem. He wrote *Sonnets to Laura*, lyrical love poems to his one great love, who died in a plague. Petrarch's idealization of physical beauty and love earned him a mixed reputation: Some despised and ridiculed the new style, while others admired it. He searched out many manuscripts and encouraged other humanists to collect ancient literature, coins, and other antiquities. Giovanni Boccaccio (1313–1375) wrote the *Decameron*, which told stories about the Black Death through graphic descriptions of plague victims, in contrast to Petrarch's idealization of beauty. The focus on human experiences, shared by Petrarch and Boccaccio, caught on and became a favored topic of Renaissance literature.

Desiderius Erasmus (1466–1536), perhaps the most famous northern humanist priest, studied theology in Paris and wandered throughout Europe, quickly becoming recognized as a keen intellect. He popularized many Greco-Roman concepts in easily understood writings, and these helped to spread humanist ideas. In his 1509 work *In Praise of Folly*, Erasmus satirically exposed contemporary class pretensions. His most serious works, however, included humanist handbooks on education and interpretations of theologians of early Christianity.

Fine Arts

Renaissance attitudes inspired a new tradition of artistic support. Because the Renaissance value system expected people of wealth to sponsor the arts, Europe experienced unprecedented artistic production during the fourteenth to the sixteenth centuries. The growth of the middle class and increased wealth from commercial activities allowed all areas of the fine arts to find patrons and new avenues of expression.

LITERATURE. Michel de Montaigne[6] (1533–1592) epitomized humanist thought in his development of the literary style of essay writing. He wrote on education, friendship, skepticism, and the ideal of human beings living in a state of nature ("the noble savage"), helping to spread humanist ideas to sociopolitical theorists. He criticized certain historians: "The middle sort of historians, of which the most part are, spoil all; they will chew our meat for us." Montaigne clearly preferred to study history for himself, as any humanist scholar would. His skepticism regarding the lack of certainty in human knowledge led him to announce, "I know nothing." Consequently, his tolerance led him to decline support for either side of the religious quarrels of his day.

The Elizabethan Age in England bustled with artistic activity. The period gets its name from the influential reign of Queen Elizabeth I (reign dates 1558–1603). William Shakespeare (1564–1616) is perhaps the most significant writer of the period; his work still plays upon stages throughout the world. To a large degree Shakespeare's storylines included historical settings, but his comedic genius and psychological insight speak to the most basic of humanist issues: human nature, its emotions, and their role in comedy and historical tragedy. He captured the sentiments of many European intellectuals in these lines:

> Life is but a walking shadow, a poor player that struts and frets his hour upon the stage, and then is heard no more. . . . It is a tale told by an idiot, full of sound and fury, signifying nothing.

PAINTING AND SCULPTURE. Artists in Renaissance Europe emulated ancient styles and incorporated contemporary innovations. Lifelike statuary and painting resulted from artists' attention to the details of perspective and naturalism. The plethora of Italian painting and sculpture is perhaps best represented by two Italians, Leonardo da Vinci[7] (1452–1519) and Michelangelo Buonarrotti (1475–1564). Leonardo's numerous sketches reveal close attention to anatomical accuracy; he painstakingly duplicated human anatomy by sketching corpses and posed models. He believed that knowing the musculo-skeletal structure better prepared the artist to depict the human body realistically, even when it was clothed. Some of Michelangelo's most famous works are his frescoes in the Vatican's Sistine Chapel, restored in the late 1980s and early 1990s. These 350 biblical and Greco-Roman figures demonstrate Michelangelo's

---

[4] **Petrarch:** PEE trahrk
[5] **Boccaccio:** boh KAH chee oh
[6] **Michel de Montaigne:** mee SHEHL duh mawn TAYN
[7] **Vinci:** VIHN chee

FIGURE 29.3 *Michelangelo's* **Creation of Adam.** *This famous image, painted on the ceiling of the Sistine Chapel, depicts a scene from the Bible's Fall of Man. As with most Renaissance art, the focus is on the musculature of the figures. Adam is in repose, awaiting the spark of life (the soul) from God. He looks to God and beyond to Eve, nested under God's left arm and anticipating the moment of her birth.* Art Resource, N.Y.

artistry in depicting the human form. True to Renaissance ideals, Michelangelo examined ancient Greek and Roman works as he studied in Florence. His philosophy of art suggested that the sculpture lay encased in the marble, and his work as a sculptor was merely to free it by chiseling away the extraneous stone.

Like many Renaissance artists, Michelangelo also worked on religious topics. Art adopted and integrated Greco-Roman proportions, styles, and religious themes. Michelangelo's *David*, depicted as a young Hebrew warrior, could be mistaken for a heroic Classical Greek Apollo.

Renaissance artists' interests also led them to investigate technologies and the sciences.

Leonardo was fascinated by many scientific principles, which led to his ingenious sketches of machines. He drew flying machines, submarines, and armored cars, some of which became realities only in later centuries. During this same period, circulatory systems and musculo-skeletal structures became the focus of those who studied the "art" of healing. Universities specializing in medicine increasingly used cadavers to examine the mysteries of the human body. Adoption of Muslim medical manuals also contributed to the knowledge of medicine.

Although other European artists were already experimenting with innovative techniques of their own, Italian art styles, like literary ones, crossed

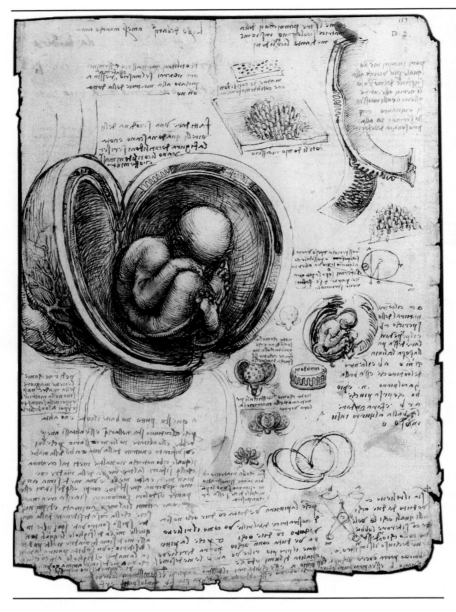

FIGURE 29.4 *Da Vinci's Embryo Illustration.* Leonardo da Vinci was one of the first artists to employ his skills in scientific illustration. Da Vinci filled notebooks with sketches of human anatomy, rock formations, machinery, plants, and birds. His inspiration came from his desire "to learn the causes of things." In this example, he studied an embryo still in the womb and made notations on the embryo's condition and environment.   The Royal Collection, © Her Majesty Queen Elizabeth II.

the Alps. Albrecht Dürer[8] (1471–1528) traveled to Venice in 1494 and returned to his home in Nuremberg heavily influenced by Italian styles. He believed that an artist should be both a humanist and a gentleman.

ARCHITECTURE. Medieval Gothic architecture's spires and towers gave way to Renaissance building designs in the Greco-Roman style, incorporat-

ing domes and columns. Palaces and villas were commissioned, new churches were built, old ones were renovated, and building facades were updated. Filippo Brunelleschi[9] (1377–1446) dominated the field of architecture in Florence, Italy. Brunelleschi and a close circle of literary and artistic friends were in charge of several building projects that displayed the new Renaissance style. The dome of Florence's cathedral was the pinnacle of

[8]**Dürer:** DOOR uhr

[9]**Brunelleschi:** broon ehl EHS kee

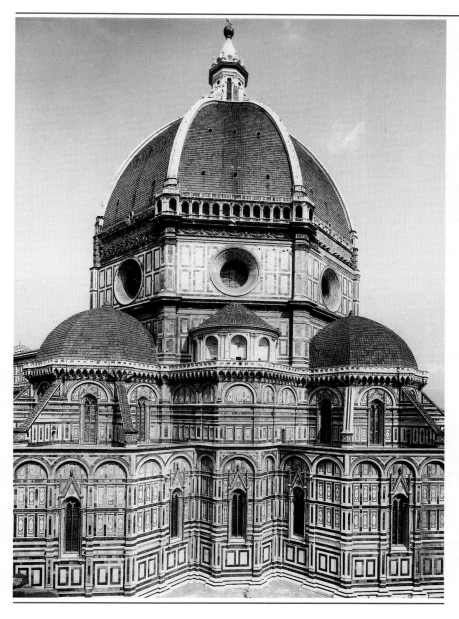

FIGURE 29.5 *Renaissance Architecture.* *Designed by Filippo Brunelleschi, the church of Santa Maria del Fiore in Florence, Italy, is an excellent example of Renaissance architecture. It employs the classical Greco-Roman styles of arches and domes and introduces the innovative pattern of symmetric geometric spaces for which Brunelleschi became famous.* Alinari/Art Resource, N.Y.

their efforts. It was patterned on the circular Pantheon in Rome, and Brunelleschi modified the design to support the expansive weight of the dome. Brunelleschi and the sculptor Donatello designed the d'Medici family burial chapel together, using Greco-Roman antecedents. In addition to other architects (including Michelangelo), Brunelleschi used Greco-Roman columns, colonnades, and capitals in his plans. Andrea Palladio was the first architect to introduce the portico, a porch with two-story columns. The portico became popular in northern Italy and in plantation-house architecture in the southern United States and the Caribbean.

MUSIC. Renaissance music delighted both the wealthy and poor in courts, cathedrals, and common meeting areas. Medieval music had developed from Gregorian chant, the single-melodic line used in the monasteries of Europe. As time passed, the chants developed polyphony, multiple lines of harmony sung together. Secular music developed in the courts of medieval Europe, where polyphonic voice lines were accompanied by horns, stringed and wind instruments, and drums. Renaissance music continued the use of multiple instruments and voices, and the music of the pipe organ became an integral part of Christian worship. Medieval science had inherited the Greek philosophical notion that nature was essentially harmonic and that music represented the very essence of the natural order of the universe; the studies of science and music brought the seeker closer to the divine. Renaissance scientists and musicians continued to see the universe as the creator's composition and music as the creator's communication.

Renaissance music borrowed heavily from music traditions of neighboring peoples around the Mediterranean basin. Courtly fanfares for kings and the elite became popular with the advent of foreign instruments, such as Muslim quarter-tone instruments that added intriguing new sounds. Increasingly complicated rhythmic patterns influenced by African styles enlivened music at various gatherings.

THE PROTESTANT REFORMATION, 1517–AROUND 1600

The Protestant Reformation shared the stage of European human endeavor with the Renaissance. Most of the reform movements of the era ended in groups splitting off from the Roman Catholic Church; these splits, called schisms, resulted from differing opinions about Christian theology. The idea of reform did not originate in this period (the early 1520s), however. There had been reform movements throughout the previous centuries in the Middle Ages, but reform in the sixteenth century had greater impact because it was swept into the current of social and political changes already taking place. The torrent of debates for religious reform soon flowed out of the cloisters and halls of cathedrals and into the streets and palaces of Europe, eroding the unity of Roman Catholicism into islands of protest and resistance.

The Renaissance concept of returning to Greco-Roman styles and precedents led many Christians to believe the practices of the early church superior to those that developed in the medieval church. In addition to examining Greco-Roman texts and early church documents, many intellectuals focused on the study of Hebrew mysticism or the study of the Hebrew language. Discontent with real or perceived worldliness in the church, the buying and selling of church offices, and mandatory donations and taxes caused tensions between the Christian laity and the clergy.

The sale of indulgences became the issue that sparked a reformation of lasting consequence. **Indulgences**, cancellation of punishments for committed sins, began in the early church as simple prayers for the dead and pleas for leniency for those who could not complete penances. By the fifteenth century, professional "pardoners" held unrestricted power to sell indulgences like vegetables at the market. Their scandalous selling of "salvation" led to such caustic poems as the following, chanted by children in the street: "As soon as the coin in the coffer rings, the soul from purgatory springs." The ensuing fight over indulgences gave Martin Luther the occasion to find his reformer's voice.

Martin Luther

Martin Luther (1483–1546), a professor at the University of Wittenberg and a monk, unwittingly began the Reformation movement in 1517 by nailing a document listing ninety-five theses (topics) to the door of a Wittenberg church. This was a common practice when someone wanted to debate issues; it acted as an invitation to anyone who desired to come and speak or listen. The issue of selling indulgences in Wittenberg was only one of many that Luther wanted to discuss, and his arguments broke no new theological ground.

What, in the pope's words, began as a "monkish squabble" quickly accelerated into a widespread debate on reform. A medieval sociopolitical atmosphere would have limited Luther's arguments to intellectual, in-house debates, the path earlier reform movements usually had taken. Because of the new technology of printing and the growth of literacy in the vernacular, Luther's ideas spread like a wildfire across parts of Europe. Copies of Luther's ninety-five theses appeared throughout Germany within three weeks of his nailing them on the church door, resulting in widespread support of his ideas.

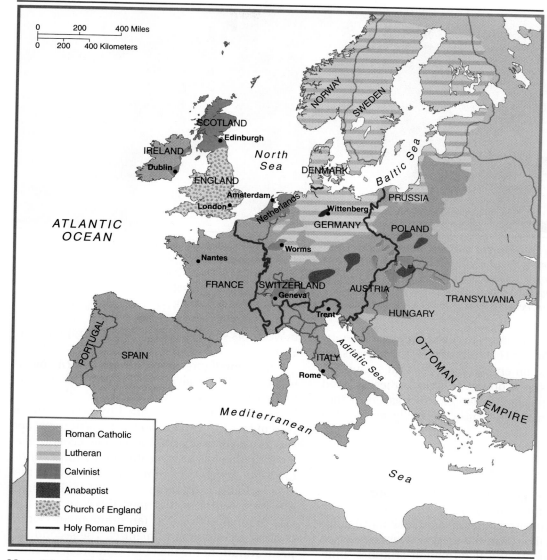

MAP 29.2 *Reformation Europe.* *This is a general map showing the dominant Christian denominations in Europe around 1600. For example, pockets of Calvinism persisted in France, while in England practices of Roman Catholicism remained. The state policy on which religious denomination would be followed sometimes changed with the death of a monarch and the ascension of the successor.*

Luther engaged in several defenses of his reformist ideas in 1520 and 1521. In the city of Worms in 1521, Luther made a final stand in his defense, refusing to recant his positions. He was outlawed under an imperial ban and excommunicated (cut off from the church). The Reformation he had begun survived as Lutheranism; its two major tenets were justification by faith alone and the subordination of all traditional statements of doctrine to the authority of scripture. These tenets challenged traditional church practices and the authority of priests, bishops, and popes.

The arguments incorporated the new Renaissance way of thinking about the past that had swept over Europe. Like others before him, Luther believed that the early church was superior in authority to the contemporary church. Luther's reading of Lorenzo Valla led him to doubt the

FIGURE 29.6 *Martin Luther.* *Martin Luther's theology focused on salvation as revealed through Scripture. Preaching, therefore, is a central part of Lutheranism, as opposed to the sacramental focus of the Roman Catholic Mass, in which preaching plays a lesser role. In Lucas Cranach's 1547 painting, Luther points to the crucifix, the vehicle for humanity's salvation; according to Lutheranism, belief in the sacrifice of Christ brings salvation.* Bridgeman Art Library, London.

validity of papal claims to supremacy over Western Christian society. His study of early theologians led him to question church practices that seemed to favor works or action over faith. Luther believed that faith, not action, led one to heaven. Luther called for major reforms, especially among the clergy.

John Calvin

Sweeping religious questioning inaugurated the rise of multiple Protestant reform movements in competition with Lutheranism. These movements developed their own theological structures based on Renaissance and Reformation attitudes. Individuals like Ulrich Zwingli (1483–1531) studied the humanist ideas of Erasmus and successfully challenged traditional theologies in Swiss territories. Humanist perspectives led to the practice of individual interpretation of scripture (regardless of educational level or ability), which challenged the role of priests as the interpreters of faith. In many areas, the Protestants fought with one another, as well as with Roman Catholics, over what constituted proper Christian belief and practice. The Anabaptists, for example, rejected infant baptism and insisted on rebaptizing all converts to their movement. Protestant dissension often led to violence and condemnation, sometimes resulting in the burning of dissenters at the stake. New reform movements sprang up all over central and western Europe.

A major figure in these new reform movements was John Calvin (1509–1564). Calvin was a French layman who had studied for the priesthood and who had continued his studies in the field of law. In 1534, Calvin left Paris to travel and speak in favor of reform. He became recognized as a reform theologian soon after his *Institutes of the Christian Religion*, a summary of Protestant theologies, found wide acceptance in 1536. Two theories were central to Calvinist theology. The first was the majesty of God (an omnipotent God in contrast to impotent humanity). The second was **predestination**, the idea that God preelects those who will receive salvation. These theories were not unique to Calvin's theology but became cornerstones of his reform doctrine. In Calvin's theology, God does not have to show any grace to humanity but magnanimously offers salvation to "the elect."

Calvin created a polity in Geneva that defined what he believed was the proper sociopolitical structure for a Christian community. The commercial city had become a refuge for Protestants fleeing France and Italy. He spelled out its political organization in the *Ecclesiastical Ordinances* of 1541. These ordinances established a mandatory public profession of faith and an oath to keep the city's Protestant-inspired laws. The city of Geneva

UNDER THE LENS
Printing and Propaganda

Printing techniques came later to Europe than to Asia. Wood-block printing, whereby text was laboriously carved into wooden blocks, had developed before the fifteenth century. By the mid–fifteenth century, Johannes Gutenberg produced one of the first European books printed with movable type, the Gutenberg Bible. Movable type consisted of a tray that held interchangeable letters that could be readily arranged and rearranged. About 3 million characters were used in Gutenberg's Bible, and about 200 copies were made. (Gutenberg purposely limited the number produced so the market would not be flooded, keeping the price high.) By the end of the century, more than 110 European cities had printing presses.

The new technology of printing made books more readily available and cut their costs. Before books were typeset, publication usually ran about 200 copies and took months to finish in wood-block formats. Most books printed by movable type, however, took considerably less time; some were printed in a matter of days. When Martin Luther published his New Testament in German, publication runs yielded about 3,000 copies. It cost roughly a week's wage for a top craftsman. This was considerably cheaper than medieval texts that would have cost hundreds of dollars in today's market, but it was still prohibitive for many.

Printed sheets, called news sheets, were posted or circulated, distributing information to an increasingly literate population in the cities. In 1493, a news sheet that was widely distributed in Rome described the voyage of Christopher Columbus. Rapid communication in the form of news sheets also disseminated reformers' religious ideas. During the Reformation, many unflattering cartoon images depicting both the pope and Luther accompanied narrative arguments. Luther specifically condoned mass propaganda techniques, especially cartoons, saying, "simple folk are more easily moved by pictures. . . ." Widespread distribution of his ideas helped fan the flames of German dissent that hastened the disintegration of Christian unity. In England, by the seventeenth century, London gentlemen sipped coffee or hot chocolate while gossiping and arguing over articles they read in *The Spectator*, a news sheet of the day.

Printing would not have had an impact on spreading either Renaissance or Reformation ideas, however, if there had not been consumers who could read the various news sheets and books. Literacy rates increased as more and more people tried to emulate elite lifestyles of opulence and the humanist appreciation of fine arts, especially literature. Latin classics, law books, and schoolbooks for teachers, doctors, and lawyers became part of the ever-increasing inventory of specialized books for sale. One publisher produced pocket-sized Greek and Latin grammars and Greco-Roman texts cheaply for the general population.

Seditious and reformist ideas could spread rapidly without a means for censure. Political and religious leaders reacted with edicts of censure against persons printing unacceptable ideas. In 1557, Pope Paul IV supported the prohibition of Protestant reform books. The *Index Librorum Prohibitorum* established the official list of books that Roman Catholics were forbidden to read or own. Protestant churches also limited the acceptable reading materials of their parishioners; Luther even presided over a book-burning. Censorship by churches and governments increased as the power of the printed word spread through mass printing.

---

was governed by a council consisting of pastors and twelve church elders. Secular powers enforced the council's decisions. Laws prohibited certain activities that were viewed as immoral, such as dancing and games. Serious doctrinal challenge could result in a death sentence; those who broke the law or denied church doctrines received severe punishment.

The city's school, established in 1559, offered the population of Geneva a Calvinist education. It taught students from elementary to advanced levels. Foreigners studied theology there and later acted as leaders for other Calvinist communities in Europe. One such reformer, John Knox, introduced Calvinism to Scotland. After building a constituency there, he established a Genevan

FIGURE 29.7 *Calvinist Church.* *Calvinist services and church buildings differed significantly from Roman Catholic ones. In contrast to the Catholic Mass, the Calvinist service (like most Protestant services) focused on the centrality of preaching the word of God from both the Old and New Testaments. Consequently, the pulpit was given a more prominent place so all could see the speaker and hear the sermon. The church interior was austere, with little or no decoration, and the congregation sat on wooden benches, sometimes segregated by gender.* German National Museum.

structure that in 1560 became known as the Presbyterian Church. Presbyterianism became the official denomination of Scotland by 1567. Through the focus on education, Calvinist reform soon spread widely, even resulting in colonies in the Americas.

Henry VIII

Protestant reform in England rode on the wave of dynastic crisis. Catherine of Aragon (1485–1536), the first wife of Henry VIII (reign dates 1509–1547), had not produced a son. Henry appealed to the pope for an annulment of his marriage to Catherine so that he might marry again in an attempt to gain an heir to the throne. Although Henry had heretofore supported Roman Catholicism against reformers, he challenged ecclesiastical authority when the application was denied by the pope (who was allied with Catherine's nephew, the Holy Roman Emperor). A royal minister convinced Henry that, as king and ruler by divine grace of God, he need not bow to the authority of the pope, even in spiritual matters. Henry convened the English parliament and used his influence to pass The Act of Supremacy of 1534. This act created the

Church of England, which recognized the monarch as its supreme head, and replaced Roman Catholicism with Anglicanism as the state religion. Henry never really wanted to break with Rome, however, and for the rest of his life he considered himself essentially Roman Catholic in theology. Nevertheless, all open opposition met with swift punishment. During Henry's reign, reform policies led to massive destruction of monasteries and churches that resisted reform and to the seizure of Roman Catholic church properties. As on the continent, the crown became the major beneficiary of confiscated church revenues.

English religious history continued to be volatile and closely associated with the political climate. Reformers in England resisted attempts by some to realign with Roman Catholicism. Henry VIII's two immediate successors alternately supported Anglicanism and Roman Catholicism between 1547 and 1558. Elizabeth I (reign dates 1558–1603) reinstituted Anglicanism during her reign but compromised on several issues of theology and church practices, shaping the development of a more tolerant Anglicanism. The queen did not allow significant changes once the compromises had been reached, and she demanded obedience. Roman Catholic and Protestant dissenters endured significant persecution, and many continued to voice their opposition to what became known as the Elizabethan Compromise.

THE ROMAN CATHOLIC REFORMATION, AROUND 1550–AROUND 1650

Reform ideas were not limited to Protestants; Roman Catholic laity and clergy also instituted the Catholic Reformation. Many within the Roman Catholic Church acted upon abuses they, too, had recognized and condemned but had not changed. By 1567, for example, Pope Pius V prohibited the sale of indulgences, but his prohibition proved too late to stem the tide of Protestant reform that the practice had set in motion. Some people who had joined Protestant movements, however, returned to Roman Catholicism because of the new reform policies. Roman Catholic reform took many paths. New emphasis was given to the private reading of

scripture, for example, while many traditional practices, like confession, remained. In addition, secular power gained greater influence as Roman Catholic kings took on the role of "champions of the faith," as had the monarchs in Protestant states. Individuals concentrated on clerical education, devotional activities, and charity; many Roman Catholic women supported hospitals and charitable programs as they sought ways to put their faith into practice.

New Monastic Orders

Spiritual renewal swept through Roman Catholicism and is perhaps best represented by the popularity of new monastic orders during the sixteenth century, focusing on the ancient ideals of service to the poor and individual spirituality. The Spanish mystics are an example of this trend. Teresa of Avila (1515–1582) founded a reformed Carmelite order in 1562. After writing of her mystical experience of Christ in *The Way of Perfection*, she traveled around Spain establishing new reformed Carmelite monasteries. She went on to write several more books, including *The Interior Castle*, which enjoyed wide readership. The combination of mysticism and reform made her an especially successful model of Roman Catholic reform and spirituality.

Another new order, the Jesuits, or the Society of Jesus, came into being as the result of the efforts of Ignatius of Loyola (1491–1556) in 1540. Jesuits became active in teaching, founding schools, and widespread proselytizing in foreign missions. In Europe, the order fostered reform and placed itself at the disposal of the papacy. No Jesuit could accept any land or title, and all members of the order were to live on charity and rely on benefactors in order to check what was viewed as the corrupting influences of power and wealth.

The Institutional Church

Pope Paul III (reign dates 1534–1549) called a general council of bishops in response to Protestant attacks in 1545, initiating the Council of Trent. The council instituted reforms, many of them inspired by humanist thought and Protestant challenges. The Holy Roman Emperor and the French king supported the reforms and worked for conciliation with Protestants within their realms. With the help of both secular and religious leaders, the council's decrees were published and its recommendations were implemented, including those condemning the buying or selling of church offices, the holding of multiple bishoprics, and the misuse of authority. Succeeding popes began to reorganize education, governance of the church, and liturgy.

The Council of Trent's actions did not reunite Christianity. There was a general reluctance by secular rulers to reentrench papal authority within the realms or territories that had already broken with Rome. State churches had already formed or were in the process of forming. The changes initiated in society as a consequence of theological reform supported schism rather than discussion and reconciliation to end conflict.

Inquisition

The initial Roman Catholic reaction to Protestant reformers had been defensive, and many early reformers had been renounced as heretics. In some areas, Catholic reform led to fear of social and political instability. As a result, reform sometimes took on a violent defense of Roman Catholicism. Inquisition had precedent in the early church and had been used against individuals and groups of heretics in the Middle Ages. During the Reformation upheaval, however, the use of inquisition became increasingly common and severe in its tactics. Earlier inquisition relied upon the punishments of fasting, pilgrimage, or imprisonment as the most common forms of eradicating heresy. Those found guilty of the most grave charges were turned over to secular authorities for execution. As political interests became more involved with religious choice during the Reformation period, however, kings and officials worked with local church officials to stamp out unacceptable religious practices. Some monarchs used reform movements as a means to centralize their authority. Under secular influence, inquisitors' use of torture and execution became more frequent.

The Spanish Inquisition is perhaps the most notorious example of secular influence on inquisition. It began under Ferdinand and Isabella in 1479, and the numbers of persons tortured may have been in the hundreds of thousands. Current estimates of those burned at the stake are about 2,000 people. Ferdinand and Isabella used the inquisition for state purposes to bond the population into one obedient realm. The Spanish

Inquisition became a formalized branch of their government, and renunciation of Roman Catholicism amounted to treason. The Spanish Inquisition first examined Jews and Muslims, who were forced to convert or be expelled, and then Protestants who sought to bring reform ideas into Spain. It was also exported to the Americas.

FIGURE 29.8 *Inquisition. Dominicans served as trained inquisitors at the court of Ferdinand and Isabella in fifteenth-century Spain. This painting by a court artist shows a scene from the life of Saint Dominic, who led an inquisition against a group of heretics in southern France. One of those charged, the man on horseback, recanted; others did not and met the fate of being burned at the stake. This image served as an inspiration to the defenders of the faith at the Spanish court and as a reminder to medieval heretics that dissenting views would not be tolerated.* Museo del Prado/MAS Barcelona.

THE RESULTS OF REFORMATION

Although sixteenth- and seventeenth-century reform movements heralded radical changes in religious expression and initiated numerous Christian sects, personal devotion to Christianity remained significant in European culture. In some cases, the search for religious truth often led to violence and religious wars. In other cases, reform brought renewed interest in basic Christian principles; religious devotion and personal piety continued to be the focus of Reformation literature. Men and women of all social classes found religious voices, and a plethora of pious works contrasted with mutual intolerance.

Social and Political Changes

One major reason these reform movements of the sixteenth century resulted in long-lasting change was the sociopolitical unrest that had been building since the fourteenth century. Church officials were associated with the aristocracy and held many revenue-gathering privileges based on medieval landholding patterns, which many commoners despised. Various social revolts had challenged the sociopolitical structures of Europe prior to the outbreak of Protestant reform. Often religious leaders, like Savonarola in Florence, rallied to the cause of social equality. Years before Martin Luther, John Ball had wandered around England preaching general social reform and had led a revolt in 1380–1381. He wrote:

> Oh good people, things do not go well in England and they will not go well until everything is held in common and there are no more serfs or lords. . . . Why should we be kept thus in bondage? We are all come from one father and one mother, Adam and Eve. How can they say or prove that they are greater lords than we are except that they make us work for what they spend?

Luther wrote treatises calling on the German princes to join the Reformation movement by breaking their ties with Rome and supporting Lutheranism in their territories. In some areas, from one-quarter to one-third of lands were under the authority of the church. Seizing the opportunity to control church lands and revenues, many of the German princes and the kings of Denmark and Sweden joined the reform movement. Eventually, each German prince chose which expression of Christianity—Roman Catholic or Lutheran—he and his subjects would follow. Subjects who did not conform could find themselves exiled.

Social Uprisings

The policies of repressive governments and self-interested lords and landlords had led to violent rebellions across many parts of central and western Europe. The only lasting changes restructured debts, from service owed to money payments; few real social reforms materialized. Social discord between the rich and the poor continued to intensify during periods of plague and war. Finally, several Protestant reformers preached open, violent insurrection, and the German peasantry revolted in 1525.

The Peasants' Revolt of 1525 exploded partly because German reformers—particularly Martin Luther—challenged the practices of Roman Catholicism. The peasants, spurred on by inspiring preachers, adopted reformist ideas. Mobs destroyed altars, crucifixes, and other furnishings and threatened the personal safety of those who resisted either social or religious reform. The leaders of the revolt put forward the Twelve Articles of 1525, which show the close interconnection of social and religious reform. The articles spell out the abolition of certain taxes and of serfdom; rights to fishing, hunting, and woodcutting; acceptable rent payments; and procedures to gain justice in the local courts. These social articles were included with religious articles, such as the right of peasants to elect the pastors of their churches and to control the use of donations made to their churches.

Martin Luther initially supported the Articles and even acted as arbitrator in the dispute. But lack of control in the movement led to random violence, and Luther withdrew his support as mobs indiscriminately burned and pillaged lords' and princes' lands. (Much of Luther's support came from the lords and princes being threatened by the mobs.) Luther wrote a pamphlet denouncing the peasants and supporting the retaliation against them. A union of princes stamped out the last remnant of the movement by 1526. Although the Peasants' Revolt was unsuccessful, many disillusioned commoners found expression for their sociopolitical grievances in the continuing reform movements.

In 1534, the French, too, endured internal religious upheaval, and persecution of Protestant reformers became increasingly severe. Massacres led to a meeting in Paris in 1559, when reformers drafted *The Articles of Faith for Reform Churches in France*, based upon Calvinist ideas. These French reformers, **Huguenots**, vowed to defend themselves if violence arose. By 1562, conciliatory gestures came from the regent of France, Catherine d'Medici, giving some freedoms to the Huguenots. Unfortunately, several massacres of reformers led to years of almost constant warfare in France (1562–1594). Claiming to foil a plot against her, d'Medici's troops and Catholic supporters killed most of the Huguenots in Paris during the Saint Bartholomew's Day Massacre of August 25, 1572. In the next few years, other French cities followed Paris's lead, resulting in the deaths of thousands of Huguenots. Restoration of peace finally came when King Henry IV (reign dates 1589–1610) signed the Edict of Nantes in 1598. Essentially a compromise for peace, the edict provided religious freedom, but with some restrictions. Henry IV and the realm remained Roman Catholic, but Protestants received guarantees of freedom of worship, the right to own property of their own, and the right to defend their property with their own troops.

Religious conflict did not end with the Edict of Nantes, however. Louis XIV tried to force religious unity in France through his perception of the state as the imperial self ("I am the State") and his idea of "one God, one king, one law, one faith." In 1685, Louis revoked the tolerant Edict of Nantes on the rationalization that no more Protestant reformers lived in France after years of restriction and forced conversions to Roman Catholicism.

Religious Wars

Religious wars seemed unavoidable as sovereigns led Protestant and Roman Catholic reformers toward state churches, and animosity toward perceived religious enemies heightened among subjects. Emotions ran high when German troops, mostly Lutheran reformers, sacked the city of Rome in 1527. More than 22,000 imperial troops,

unpaid and without a commander, killed more than 13,000 Romans. After the attack, the devastation was so great and the fear so overwhelming that the remaining citizens hid in their houses, refusing to bury the corpses being gnawed by dogs in the streets. More than 30,000 houses and several hospitals burned to the ground or were left uninhabitable. The loss of manuscripts, fine paintings, and sculptures was incalculable.

War between Protestant England and Roman Catholic Spain erupted during Elizabeth's reign, which saw the defeat of the Spanish Armada (the so-called invincible navy) and the emergence of England as a maritime force. Elizabeth had no children, and her Roman Catholic cousin Mary Queen of Scots (1542–1587) was suggested as the legitimate heir to the English throne. When Mary sought asylum from Scottish political problems at Elizabeth's court, political and religious conspirators within England and Catholic Spain soon represented Mary as a potential usurper of Elizabeth's throne. Elizabeth had Mary arrested and, with great reluctance, ordered her execution. This spurred the Spanish to hurl 25,000 men and the Armada across the channel at England in 1588. The English navy under Charles Howard, aided by stormy weather, defeated the Armada. The rest of Elizabeth's reign was marked by increased prosperity at home and commercial activity abroad unhampered by the Spanish navy.

The Thirty Years War (1618–1648), involving most of central Europe, began as a result of the Holy Roman Emperor's desire to reestablish Roman Catholicism throughout his empire. Hostilities broke out when Bohemian Protestants revolted against the emperor's Roman Catholic policies. The conflict eventually turned into a struggle over dynastic claims to the imperial crown as several neighboring monarchs entered the fray. When hostilities finally ended with the Treaty of Westphalia in 1648, many church properties became secularized and were distributed among several involved states. The monarch of each area determined which faith subjects would follow.

Women and Reform

Some women played significant roles in religious reform movements, while most found that social reform of women's roles was not part of the general call for social change occurring during the Reformation period. Martin Luther's wife, Katharina, a former nun, spent much of her time practicing basic medicine for the poor. Later in England, Margaret Fell (1614–1702) argued that women should take leadership roles in the new church her husband, George Fox, had founded. Margaret's argument in support of women's roles was based on

Old Testament precedents of women prophets, judges, and preachers. Margaret and John's church, The Society of Friends (the Quakers), had no priests, and both men and women could speak during services. Most reform churches, however, restricted the roles of women and settled into a patriarchal structure wherein men were preachers and women kept quiet in church.

FIGURE **29.9** *Woman Preaching. Some Protestant groups, such as the Quakers, encouraged women to teach and to preach in public. In many areas across Europe where social attitudes restricted women's religious roles, this practice was not met with enthusiasm. This English print satirizes a Quaker woman by showing a variety of reactions to her public speaking, ranging from amusement and skepticism to inattention.* Mary Evans Picture Library.

BAROQUE ARTS AND NEW PHILOSOPHIES

No artistic period is an island unto itself, and baroque art styles and philosophies mirrored the changes that had occurred in European society. Both the arts and philosophy reflected the Renaissance's emphasis on Greco-Roman classics, humanism, and religion and the Reformation's emphasis on sociopolitical and religious change. Artists during the baroque period (around 1550–around 1750) embraced complexity of design, paying significant attention to ornate detail. Absolutist monarchs employed the grandeur and opulence of the baroque style to demonstrate their supremacy over and superiority to their subjects. Resplendent palaces and grand halls awed and humbled court visitors. Printing technology and higher literacy rates made baroque literature more affordable and accessible. Painting and music, two examples of the fine arts, demonstrate the general changes of the period. The philosophies of Hobbes, Locke, Descartes, and Spinoza represent the influence of humanism in philosophical development.

Painting

Baroque painting shifted from the heroic grandeur of Renaissance style to a greater emphasis on ornate detail and emotion. The subjects of paintings, for example, were presented in more natural settings than in previous Renaissance presentations. Dramatic contrast of light and dark helped to focus attention on emotion. Perhaps the first baroque artist was a painter who called himself Caravaggio[10] (1573–1610), after his birthplace near

[10] **Caravaggio:** KAIR uh VAH jee oh

Attitudes toward women during the Protestant Reformation continued to change. Just as women's roles shifted within the context of Renaissance admiration of Greco-Roman models, Protestant women's roles became more restricted under the increasingly literal interpretations of Christian scripture. Although many women were highly visible in the early reform movements, Saint Paul's writings became the litmus test for the proper behavior of wives, and other biblical references were used to illustrate acceptable roles for women in society. To some extent women continued to have informal influence within Protestant groups, but their roles were increasingly restricted to being helpmates to their husbands and vehicles for procreation.

Although Martin Luther did argue that women might be allowed to preach if no man were available, his general attitude toward women can be seen in the following passage:

> Now the ones who recognize the estate of marriage are those who firmly believe that God himself instituted it, brought husband and wife together, and ordained that they should beget children and care for them . . . [Luther here explains the duties of the father—including washing diapers if need be—and then continues with the duties of the mother.] A wife too should regard her duties in the same light, as she suckles the child, rocks and bathes it, and cares for it in other ways; and as she busies herself with other duties and renders help and obedience to her husband. . . . This is also how to comfort and encourage a woman in the pangs of childbirth . . . [say to her:] "Remember that you are a woman, and that this work of God in you is pleasing to him. Trust joyfully in his will, and let him have his way with

IN THEIR OWN WORDS

Martin Luther and John Calvin Define Women's Roles

you. Work with all your might to bring forth the child. Should it mean your death, then depart happily, for you will die in a noble deed and in subservience to God. If you were not a woman you should now wish to be one for the sake of this very work alone, that you might thus gloriously suffer and even die in the performance of God's work and will." . . . We see how weak and sickly barren women are. Those who are fruitful, however, are healthier, cleanlier, and happier. And even if they bear themselves weary—or ultimately bear themselves out—that does not hurt. Let them bear themselves out. This is the purpose for which they exist.

John Calvin also spoke about the role of women in Christian society. In a commentary on Genesis, Calvin explains that women should be helpmates.

> Now, the human race could not exist without the woman; and, therefore, in the conjunction of human beings, that sacred bond is especially conspicuous, by which the husband and the wife are combined in one body, and one soul. . . . Certainly, it cannot be denied, that the woman also, though in the second degree, was created in the image of God. . . . Now, since God assigns the woman as a help to the man, he not only prescribes to wives the rule of their vocation, to instruct them in their duty, but he also pronounces that marriage will really prove to men the best support of life. We may therefore conclude, that the order of nature implies that the woman should be the helper of the man. The vulgar proverb, indeed, is, that she is a necessary evil; but the voice of God is rather to be heard, which declares that woman is given as a companion and an associate to the man, to assist him to live well.

Milan. Not everyone liked the new style; Caravaggio's popularity waned in Italy, where many patrons preferred holy subjects to be depicted in the more idealized, heroic style. Slowly tastes changed, however, and artists found fame for their applications of the baroque style; two are Peter Paul Rubens and Rembrandt van Rijn.[11]

[11] **Rijn:** RYN

Peter Paul Rubens (1577–1640) incorporated baroque presentation in such works as *The Raising of the Cross*. The figures reveal muscled bodies straining to raise up their heavy load, while foliage and a dog are painstakingly detailed in the foreground. Landscapes were another venue for Rubens to create an imposing scene. His painting *Landscape with the Château of Steen* sweeps from the detailed hunter and cart, depicted in the lower left corner, to a grand view of the countryside in all its vast splendor.

Rembrandt van Rijn (1606–1669) is a good example of the popular and influential Dutch masters of the baroque style. He was one of the most famous portrait painters in northern Europe by age 25. His religious topics have been described as vigorous and imaginative. By 1642, his fortunes had turned; his wife's death, his bankruptcy, and a paternity suit that caused him difficulty with Protestant reformers led him into depression. He began focusing on the Passion of Christ as a reflection of human suffering, producing at least ninety paintings and etchings on the theme. His work is perhaps best known for its intense realism and human emotion, often breathing life into biblical scenes that had previously been heroically idealized.

FIGURE 29.10 *Rubens's* **Descent from the Cross.** *In this seventeenth-century painting, Peter Paul Rubens uses light to increase dramatic effect; light focuses attention on Christ's body and plays on the expressive faces of the women, drawing the viewer into the painting and inviting an empathetic response. The poignancy of the scene is further enhanced by the straining of the men to lower the limp body from the height of the cross.* AKG London.

Music

Baroque musical styles evolved during the sixteenth and seventeenth centuries. Medieval and Renaissance musicians had introduced polytonality, complicated rhythmic patterns, and new instruments, but Reformation music applied new trends of scientific logic and complex mathematics to music. The hymns or chorales of the Reformation were at first based on Roman Catholic hymns but soon developed a style of their own. Statements of faith set to easily sung melodies (some even from easily recognizable bar tunes) gave voice to the religious passions of many reformers. The Roman Catholic composer Antonio Vivaldi (1675–1741) inspired communicants with dramatic emotion in his musical settings of the Mass. Four of his Mass movements exist today.

The baroque organ, a hybrid of previous organs, allowed for greater range of tonality and supported the congregational singing of reform churches. Its popularity grew under the genius of Johann Sebastian Bach[12] (1685–1750), who, with many other baroque composers, created musical masterpieces of mathematical logic that are still performed in churches and in concert halls throughout the world.

The complexities of baroque music also entertained patrons outside of the churches, in palaces and elite homes. In addition, those who frequented the theaters enjoyed the melding of music, drama, elaborate sets, and costuming in ballets, operas, and the less sophisticated but equally enjoyable stage shows. As musical entertainment became more widespread, increasing numbers of middle-class and noble patrons employed composers and performers on retainer.

New Philosophies

Political and social turmoil in the sixteenth and seventeenth centuries stimulated new theories in governance and reinforced old ones. Some theories challenged the older perceptions of political authority and the nature of humanity. New political philosophies influenced government policies concerning New World peoples and new polities and helped to inspire the theoretical changes of the Scientific Revolution, which will be discussed in Chapter 31.

[12] **Bach:** BAHK

FIGURE 29.11 *Hobbes's* Leviathan. *This engraving from the title page of Thomas Hobbes's 1651 pamphlet graphically illustrates his political philosophy. The individual subjects of the state comprise the "body politic." These subjects give their collective authority to the monarch, who rules on their behalf. The monarch holds the symbols of his secular and sacred powers, the sword and the shepherd's crook, an allusion to Jesus, the Good Shepherd.* Bibliothèque nationale, Paris.

Thomas Hobbes (1588–1679), an English tutor, wrote a controversial philosophical treatise, *Leviathan*, in which he outlined his political theory of absolutism. *Leviathan* essentially stated that sovereignty is ultimately derived from the people but then transferred to the monarch. The monarch, therefore, does not rule by divine right; yet, the monarch has absolute authority over law, revenues, military affairs, and justice. Hobbes rested his political theory on the belief that humans are driven by self-interest and fear. He theorized about how life would be lived in a purely natural state without benefit of social or political

EUROPE

European Renaissance, c. 1350–c. 1600	**1350**
	–
	– Petrarch dies, 1374
	–
	– Cosmo d'Medici born, 1389
	1400
	–
	–
	–
	–
	1450
	–
	– Niccoló Machiavelli born, 1469
	–
	– Jews expelled from Spain, 1492
	1500
	–
Protestant Reformation, 1517–1600	– Leonardo da Vinci dies, 1519
	–
	– Council of Trent, 1545 Martin Luther dies, 1546
	1550
Elizabethan Age, 1558–1603 / Roman Catholic Reformation, c. 1550–c. 1650 / Baroque Period, c. 1550–c. 1750	– Teresa of Avila founds Carmelite convent, 1562
	–
	–
	–
	1600
	–
	– William Shakespeare dies, 1616
	–
	–
	1650

controls and surmised that a condition of brutality would prevail, devoid of civilization; and to Hobbes, civilization meant European culture. In contrast to Montaigne's image of the "noble savage," Hobbes argued that natural human life would be "solitary, poor, nasty, brutish, and short." In order for people to live harmoniously and as civilized human beings, a "social contract" must be established, at least tacitly.

In opposition to Hobbes, John Locke (1632–1704) argued for constitutionalism in his *Two Treatises of Civil Government*, published in 1690. His work emphasized that the only legal government was government by consent of the governed; revolution was the natural outgrowth of a repressive government. Like Hobbes, Locke incorporated the concept of the natural state of humanity into his political theory. For Locke, a "blank slate" reflected the state of human nature. Unlike Hobbes, Locke believed in a state of nature wherein humans perform reasoned action and possess the natural rights of life, liberty, and property. Because occasional infringement of rights occurs, assent to a social contract for mutual protection is advantageous. Government, however, must be limited in its power over the governed.

In Locke's opinion, tolerance of minority opinion should be exercised for the good of all. He pleaded for religious freedom for all groups except **atheists**, people who do not believe that any deity exists, and Roman Catholics, who he believed threatened the sovereignty of the English state. Eventually his concept of freedom of speech for religious groups won wider application through those who adopted his political philosophy.

René Descartes[13] (1596–1650), a wealthy French intellectual, is often proclaimed the founder of **rationalism**, the philosophy that reason is the only valid basis for determining actions or opinions. This focus led to his axiom "I think, therefore I am," which became the cornerstone of his philosophy. According to rationalism, one's senses could delude and emotions could mislead; only the rational human mind could fathom reality. Descartes did not abandon religion; he agreed with some medieval philosophers who had argued the rationality of a creator God, but Descartes's deity did not intervene in human affairs. Because the deity had created a rationally organized universe, the human mind (seen as an attribute of God) could discover the laws of nature without the need of revelation. Thus, Descartes supported increased interest in mathematics and science and turned away from the speculative philosophies of the medieval and Renaissance periods.

Baruch Spinoza (1632–1677), a Jewish lens grinder turned philosopher, differed in his opinion of human rationality. Instead of only reason being an attribute of God, as in Descartes's philosophy, Spinoza argued that both mind and matter were infused with God. This philosophy is **pantheism**, the belief that God is present in all that God creates. It allowed Spinoza and other philosophers to view nature as worthy of scientific investigation. Like others of his day, Spinoza employed mathematical methodology to understand the rational order of the universe. Spinoza's philosophy, however, did not bode well with more traditional Jews, who did not merge God with the creation.

SUMMARY

1. Renaissance ideas had a profound influence on social attitudes, polities, and economic development. Italian cities were commercial centers and places of innovation in the fine arts. Renaissance attitudes centered on the revival of Greco-Roman culture, which became the model for Renaissance fine arts.

2. In some Renaissance urban centers, the middle class experienced rapid growth and social change, while other areas developed more slowly. Although most people were low-wage laborers,

new and more lucrative professions developed. Because of the rebirth of Greco-Roman attitudes, many elite women lost social gains they had enjoyed in the medieval period.

3. Renaissance Italian city-states tended to remain independent polities, and monarchies became more centralized in Europe. The exception was the Holy Roman Empire, which experienced regional centralization under local princes.

[13] **Descartes:** day KAHRT

4. Intellectual and artistic development was influenced by Renaissance humanist philosophy. Adoption of Greco-Roman styles and humanism in religious and political treatises influenced attitudes about the past and inspired new ways of thinking. These ideas were imported to areas colonized by Europeans.

5. The Protestant Reformation was a combination of religious and sociopolitical reform. Many lower-class revolts added to the instability of Renaissance and Reformation Europe. Rulers adopted reformist ideas to aid in their centralization policies.

6. Protestant reform was spurred by Renaissance admiration of Greco-Roman culture, which led to the belief that early church practices and theologies were superior to those of the Middle Ages or Renaissance period. The repudiation of selling indulgences spearheaded initial reform under Martin Luther. Reform spread to many geographical areas. Protestants and Roman Catholics both employed execution as a means to defend their theologies. State responses to reform varied, and in some places, like England, state leaders vacillated between Protestantism and Roman Catholicism.

7. The Catholic Reformation implemented many of the reforms that Protestants had demanded. Finally, the Council of Trent's reforms were publicized and implemented, but the Protestant Reformation had moved beyond reconciliation because of its link with sociopolitical issues.

8. Religious wars kept Europe in turmoil in the sixteenth and seventeenth centuries. France was beset by internal warfare between Roman Catholics and Huguenots; the Thirty Years War (1618–1648) began when Protestant Bohemians revolted against the Holy Roman Emperor and ended with the Treaty of Westphalia in 1648.

9. Some women played significant roles in the early Reformation, but most remained in subordinate positions. Reformation led to the acceptance of violence and schism within Christianity as a means to settle disputes.

10. Artists brought new expression to the fine arts that paralleled the changes in society. Emotion and naturalism were the hallmarks of the highly ornate baroque style.

11. New philosophies synthesized Renaissance and Reformation ideas into new political theories that supported either absolutism or constitutional monarchy. Hobbes, Locke, Descartes, and Spinoza focused on the study of nature, human rationality, and proper forms of government.

SUGGESTED READINGS

Bainton, Roland H. *Here I Stand: A Life of Martin Luther.* New York: Mentor/New American Library, 1977. A standard in Reformation history.

———. *Women of the Reformation in Germany and Italy.* Boston: Beacon, 1974. Several biographies of women and their roles in the Protestant Reformation.

Bouwsma, William J. *John Calvin: A Sixteenth-Century Portrait.* Oxford, Eng.: Oxford University Press, 1988. The standard biography of John Calvin.

Breisach, Ernst. *Renaissance Europe, 1300–1517.* New York: Macmillan, 1973. A general but thorough review of the Renaissance.

Chadwick, Owen. *The Reformation.* New York: Penguin, 1972. An old standard by a church historian.

Hale, John. *The Civilization of Europe in the Renaissance.* New York: Atheneum, 1994. A thorough treatment of the Renaissance period.

Kohl, Benjamin G., and Alison A. Smith, eds. *Major Problems in the History of the Italian Renaissance.* Lexington, Mass.: D. C. Heath, 1995. A collection of essays and documents, focusing on major issues that shaped the period.

Ozment, Steven. *The Age of Reform, 1250–1550: An Intellectual and Religious History of Late Medieval and Reformation Europe.* New Haven, Conn.: Yale University Press, 1980. An introduction to reform movements, with a focus on intellectual history.

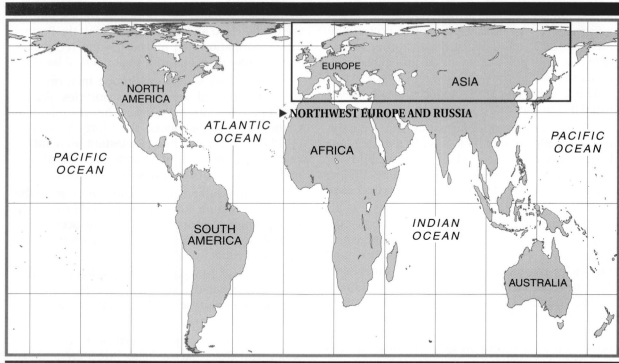

► **NORTHWEST EUROPE AND RUSSIA**

► **NORTHWEST EUROPE AND RUSSIA**

European Absolutism

1611–1740

In the world is now none that is his equal, nor has there been for centuries such a one; and indeed I doubt the future will produce his peer. Yea, truly we may call him King Gustav the wise and great, the father of the fatherland, whose like never yet reigned in Sweden, as is acknowledged not by us alone, but by men of all nations, whether friend or foe.

—AXEL OXENSTIERNA

Thus wrote Sweden's chancellor about King Gustavus Adolphus, one of the significant figures in Europe's seventeenth century. Gustavus Adolphus was the first of several monarchs who built absolutist states, which taxed their subjects most heavily in order to build strong centralized governments and large armies. It was a time of warfare and great suffering from battlefield losses, disease, and famine.

Absolute monarchs achieved varying degrees of success, because they were sometimes inhibited by long-established traditions, powerful social groups, or elite distaste for heavy taxes and the like. **Absolutism** is a system of government in which monarchs aim to achieve total control through a bureaucracy centralized along military lines. Major economic developments also accompanied the centralizing efforts of monarchs. Mining output increased substantially, metallurgical processes improved rapidly, and shipbuilding became increasingly efficient. The challenge of government was to harness these changes as efficiently and as completely as possible.

EUROPEAN ABSOLUTISM: THE BUREAUCRATIC- MILITARY MODEL

The development of absolutism in Europe was a process that often took decades to complete. It was often linked to the changing nature of European warfare, which forced governments to alter substantially their administrative systems, including tightening control of their subject peoples. Larger armies, often filled with drafted soldiers, gradually replaced mercenary forces. In order to pay and supply these military forces, monarchs gained control of their nobles and cities, which had traditions of autonomous rule. Absolutist governments grew significantly larger, extending central control over mining, arms manufacturing, and commerce.

We will define the features of the bureaucratic-military model of absolutism as:

— the adoption of a military-style chain of command for government wherein orders from the top must be promptly obeyed by all officials;

— the growing emphasis on central regulation of politics, economics, and society;

— the increasing stress on discipline, obedience, and duty in politics and life;

— the dominance of law and bureaucratic directives over customary practices; and

— the increasing use of mechanical terminology like "ship of state" to describe society and government.

Bureaucracies more successful in implementing this system were ones that harnessed social groups more fully to the all-powerful state. States that failed to implement military-style governments either exploited more intensely sources of revenue like colonies or resorted to funding ambitious strategic plans through massive loans and debt.

THE THIRTY YEARS WAR, 1618–1648

Beginning as a war defined largely in religious terms (Roman Catholic versus Protestant states) the Thirty Years War changed into a conflict pitting the armies and other national resources of the Danes, Swedes, and French against those of the Austrians and Spanish and their allies. As fighting persisted from one decade to the next, various contending governments devised means to finance and supply their armies. As bureaucracies grew in size, so did their control of economies and societies. Larger armies also meant that absolutist monarchs had the military might to cow their domestic rivals or rebels.

Central Europe had been the battleground between Protestant princes and Roman Catholic monarchs for about a century, and religious issues ignited the Thirty Years War. Conflict began when Protestant nobles of Bohemia (the present-day Czech Republic) agitated against their ardently Catholic king, Ferdinand, of the powerful Hapsburg family. The Catholic forces of Ferdinand crushed the Bohemian Protestant army, and a thoroughgoing reconversion of Bohemia to Roman Catholicism commenced. Continued successes by Catholic armies in Germany during the rest of the 1620s threatened Protestantism in Central Europe. Soon, the French perceived Ferdinand's successes as Hapsburg successes that threatened sovereign states like France, even though it was largely Roman Catholic.

While religious issues continued to be significant in the Thirty Years War, political issues assumed greater importance by the 1630s. France had begun funding Protestant armies and eventually pitted its armies against the Hapsburg forces. Fearing the growing power of Emperor Ferdinand, who threatened to dominate Germany completely, some Roman Catholic German rulers allied themselves with Protestant forces. Thus, dynastic and political concerns prevailed over religious questions in the minds of many.

France and Prussia began establishing absolutist systems in response to their need to fight wars. France's King Louis XIII and his chief minister, Cardinal Armand Jean Richelieu, jointly began devising the means to support a large French army by heavily taxing the French peasantry. Eventually, French victories over the Hapsburgs helped create the conditions for an absolutist monarchy under Louis XIV in the latter half of the seventeenth century. Although Prussia did not begin creating the conditions for absolutist rule until after the Thirty Years War, it gained new territory, and its ruler, Frederick William, needed a strong army to impose his will on the Prussians.

Three decades of warfare devastated parts of Central Europe. Some areas lost more than 50 percent of their population, and it took nearly a century for demographic growth to return to 1618 levels. Once-thriving cities and towns never recovered their prewar dynamism. Merchants and artisans, who were beginning to develop the financial and technological bases for industrialization, died from the fighting or disease. Mining and other industries, for example, declined during and after the conflict.

Political changes came through the negotiations that ended the Thirty Years War. Prussia and a few other states gained territory to offset the growth of Swedish and French power. Rulers of the surviving states determined the religion of their domains, and some states for the first time could conduct their own foreign relations. Perhaps most significant, the Thirty Years War demonstrated that ambitious monarchs needed large armies and the means to support them. With a powerful bureaucratic system, rulers could attain absolute power.

THE RISE AND FALL OF SWEDISH ABSOLUTISM, 1611–1718

Sweden became a major European power in the seventeenth century, establishing a Baltic Empire that included parts of Germany. But by the death of Sweden's monarch Charles XII in 1718, the empire lay in ruins and was never to be reconstructed. Swedish absolutism waxed and waned because it was heavily dependent on its monarchs.

Monarchs and Ministers

Because absolutism established itself gradually, we must examine it over the course of the reigns of several Swedish rulers. King Gustavus Adolphus (reign dates 1611–1632) commenced the construction of absolutist institutions, and Charles XI (reign dates 1660–1697) modified the system of government he had inherited to ensure that his wishes would be obeyed. Charles XII (reign dates 1697–1718) spent nearly two decades outside Sweden, campaigning against a variety of powers, and his prolonged absence severely undermined Swedish absolutism.

FIGURE 30.1 *Portrait of Gustavus Adolphus.* *This Swedish monarch, called by some "The Lion of the North," helped turn his country into an important European power. Gustavus Adolphus instituted numerous changes, including the establishment of an efficiently organized bureaucracy. He led his troops into Germany in 1630 and helped expand Swedish control of territories along the Baltic seacoast. The portrait conveys the sovereign's regal bearing and shrewdness.* Skokloster Collection, Styrelson, Sweden.

Gustavus Adolphus came to the throne as a teenager and developed an alliance with his chief minister, Axel Oxenstierna (1583–1654). The two men agreed that the monarchy must be strong but also that the king must rule in conjunction with Swedish nobles, especially those of the highest social ranks. Gustavus Adolphus agreed to consult regularly with the state council and the *riksdag*, an assembly of **estates** (groups of elites and other commoners). He also assented to the condition that the top bureaucratic posts should be filled with nobles who were Swedish-born. Although these limitations may have hampered other rulers, Gustavus Adolphus used his forceful character to mold institutions and people to his will. At the same time, he was committed to consultative measures by various deliberative bodies and went to great lengths to ensure a thoughtful decision-making process. This system worked well during Gustavus Adolphus's two-decade reign.

Another dimension of Gustavus Adolphus's rule was his successful military policies, which led to the foundation of a Swedish empire. Part of the reason that the king desired to have domestic harmony was to ensure stability for his intended military campaigns. In addition, Gustavus Adolphus took great pains to train and equip the Swedish army by the most modern methods. He had studied the works and methods of Maurice of Nassau, a Dutch strategist, and modified them in the course of Sweden's military campaigns. Gustavus Adolphus also gave much attention to building a military-industrial system to equip his troops with weapons and supplies.

Gustavus Adolphus's battlefield death in 1632 left the throne to his young daughter, Christina (reign dates 1634–1654), and the actual rule in the hands of Chancellor Oxenstierna and the nobles. In 1634, the bureaucracy issued a document, the *Form of Government*, proclaiming Lutheranism as the state religion, the legislative power of the *riksdag*, and the primacy of the nobles. This was an attempt by the nobles to wrest power from the monarchy. Neither Christina nor her successors ever formally accepted the document and its limitations on royal power. She took a moderate interest in government affairs once she reached adulthood but preferred engaging in intellectual debates, including some with René Descartes. Christina secretly harbored designs to surrender power and to embrace Roman Catholicism, both of which she did in 1654, to the shock of Sweden.

Charles XI completed the process of building absolutism. Shortly after he became king, Charles firmly took the reigns of power and had the *riksdag* declare the king the sole decision maker, who should consult with various councils and deliberative bodies. Ultimate lawmaking power belonged to the king, who was answerable only to God. Criticism of the king became a crime, effectively curbing freedom of expression.

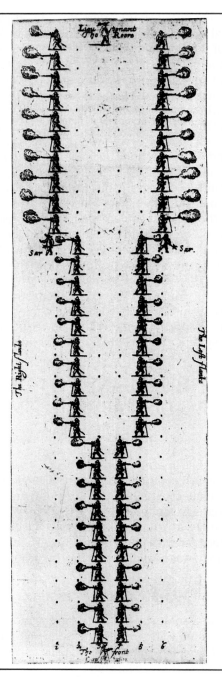

FIGURE 30.2 *Military Firepower in the Seventeenth Century.* *Maurice of Nassau helped transform military training through his writings, many of which were illustrated. This drawing shows how a particular massed formation gave a broad field of fire to the left and right. Careful and regular military training re737sulted in devastating barrages. Maurice's success on the battlefield made his writings popular with the rulers of Sweden and Prussia, as well as in the Netherlands.* Courtesy of the University of Illinois Library.

UNDER THE LENS
The Impact of Maurice of Nassau

One of Early Modern Europe's military strategists and tacticians, Maurice of Nassau, Prince of Orange (reign dates 1585–1625), offered rulers not only a means to create a superior fighting force but also a reliable way to maintain domestic order. This Dutch leader's ideas and methods spread throughout Europe in the seventeenth century; his famous manual appeared in a German edition in 1614 and by 1649 had been translated into Russian. Gustavus Adolphus carefully studied Maurice's ideas.

During his university studies, Maurice had become enamored of the ancient Romans, whose military methods he adopted. Essential to Maurice was keeping soldiers busy at all times to minimize problems of poor discipline and demoralization, especially during long siege operations. The army was divided into battalions of 550 men because this was the largest size that could respond to a single human voice. The squad of ten men acted as a single unit whether marching, deploying, or firing; soldiers became parts of a human machine that could be devastating on a battlefield. Maurice also insisted that the chain of command reach from himself down to the corporal who commanded the squad, and he established officer training schools where subcommanders learned their roles and duties.

Constant drill and weapons practice had additional advantages. Drillmasters constantly repeated the ways of using muskets, handguns, and pikes, ways that had been broken down into distinct muscular acts. Thus, when massed firing took place, the squad or battalion responded to voice commands with a minimum of error. The efficiency of the force soon became apparent on the battlefield. Later, Maurice printed an illustrated military manual for illiterates.

Political leaders realized that by using Maurice's methods, they could create a reliable and relatively inexpensive instrument for foreign and domestic needs. Constant drill and group activity established powerful psychological bonds within the units. This esprit de corps began to dominate the consciousness of the soldiers, who viewed themselves as brothers in a common cause. In addition, the soldiers saw themselves as distinct from the civilian society from which they came and could thereafter more easily follow orders to shoot their social peers or whomever their commanders chose to repress.

Because all social classes and individuals could be transformed, commoners were drafted into armies whose troops were paid at lower rates than upper-class people. These forces were inexpensive and reliable for maintaining the rule of absolute monarchs. They also facilitated the expansion of European colonies abroad.

An ongoing process of divesting land and income from the high nobles was accelerated, strengthening royal absolutism. During their heyday in power and influence in the middle decades of the seventeenth century, the high nobles amassed so much land and wealth that they became the target of criticism by the lesser nobles and commoners. In addition, these nobles and commoners allied with Charles XI to increase his power, partly so that he could carry out land reform. This land reform process undermined the power of the high nobles and brought significant revenues into the hands of the state.

Charles XII inherited the mantle of absolutism and affirmed his dominance of Sweden. His early battlefield successes maintained Swedish absolutism, but later defeats, loss of much of the empire, and Charles's death opened the gate for a time of rule by the nobles in alliance with city leaders and free peasants. The immediate cause of the dismantling of absolutism was the absence of a male or an unmarried female successor. The nobility soon filled the power vacuum.

Sweden enjoyed the services of excellent officials in the seventeenth century, and two of the best were Axel and Bengt Oxenstierna (1620–1702), father and son. The Oxenstierna family was one of Sweden's most venerable, and their kin had served Swedish monarchs for decades. Perhaps the most important official was Axel Oxenstierna, who achieved top administrative ranking about the time Gustavus Adolphus ascended the throne. The two men shaped Sweden's domestic and foreign policies through the seventeenth century. Axel

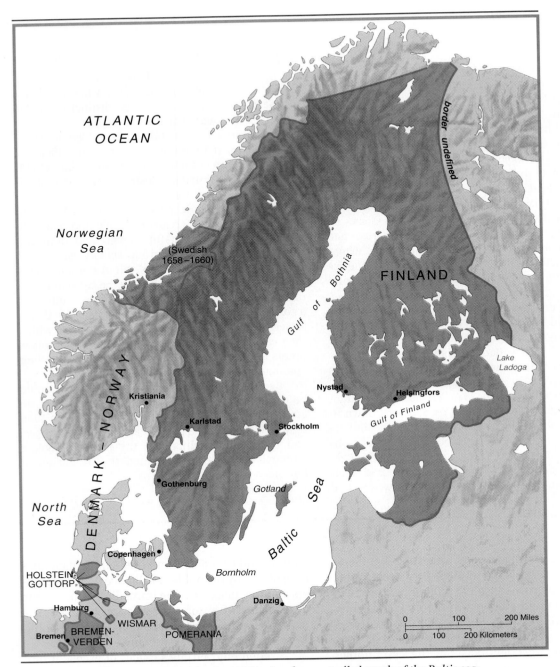

MAP 30.1   *The Swedish Empire in 1660.*   *Sweden controlled much of the Baltic sea-coast in the mid–seventeenth century. Gustavus Adolphus played a key role in expanding Swedish influence along the southern coast. Lands in Germany were lost by the eighteenth century, as were lands in the eastern Baltic region.*

Oxenstierna charted the course of alliance between high nobles and crown that prevailed in the first half of the century. His greatest contribution may have been holding the system together during the minority of Christina. Bengt Oxen-

stierna, architect of Sweden's foreign policy in the late seventeenth century, worked out a series of alliances that helped secure the empire. Yet, the great ambitions of Charles XII after 1697 unraveled this system during the eighteenth century.

The Swedish Model of Absolutism

Although various Swedish monarchs tinkered with their absolutist system, other Europeans, such as Peter I of Russia, admired and adopted parts of the Swedish bureaucratic model. Gustavus Adolphus and Charles XI fashioned an absolutism based on cameralism, a machinelike political structure that emphasized **subordination** (a chain-of-command system), **regimentation** (emphasis on discipline and obedience), and **differentiation**. The last idea was simply that each governmental bureau must concern itself with a single function; thus, finances, military affairs, or justice must each be the domain of a single department. Staffing and pay were uniform throughout the bureaucracy, and the system was grounded in a comprehensive set of laws and regulations.

This bureaucracy was fused with a national army based on conscription. The army drafted peasants who were regularly paid, highly trained, and well equipped; experienced officers, many of whom received formal educations, skillfully led this Swedish force. The combination proved formidable, as Gustavus Adolphus successfully fought the Russians and Poles to gain new territories along the Baltic seacoast. During the Battle of Lützen in 1632, Gustavus Adolphus was mortally wounded, but his soldiers rallied and carried the day against the enemy.

Socioeconomic Patterns of Swedish Absolutism

Swedish society and politics was dominated by the nobility, especially the high nobility, and they used their power to amass great amounts of land and other forms of wealth. Full-blown absolutism, however, did not develop until monarchs wrested control of land from the high nobility. Monarchs were supported by lesser nobles and by members of other estates who also allied with kings in most

FIGURE 30.3 *Swedish Iron Manufacturing.* *This eighteenth-century painting depicts a Swedish foundry where workers used simple techniques for making iron and steel. The low labor costs and exceptional quality of Swedish iron ore gave Sweden a competitive advantage in international markets. The British, especially, imported large amounts of Swedish iron, and the Dutch played a significant role in helping the Swedes develop their iron manufacturing.* National Museum of Stockholm.

political matters. Thus, Swedish absolutism had a certain appeal to a broad spectrum of people.

Mercantilism was the cornerstone of Swedish economic policy beginning with the time of Gustavus Adolphus. Industry and commerce received much attention and resources for development in Sweden. Mining, for example, was a significant industry, and copper and iron were the two most profitable metals extracted. Copper became the major revenue source, especially after the bureaucracy made it illegal to export half-processed ore. Swedes built their own ships to carry exports and sought out their own markets, and Sweden enjoyed a favorable balance of trade until the early 1700s. To support the development of Swedish industry, the state subjected workers to their employers' rules forbidding workers to move. Strikes were considered mutinous, and those who did strike were treated with great severity.

Foreigners played a large role in the development of certain industries. Dutch artisans helped create the burgeoning Swedish military industry. Louis De Geer, a prominent Dutch industrialist, enjoyed Gustavus Adolphus's confidence and helped establish a variety of armament industries. De Geer eventually moved to Sweden and was made a Swedish noble in 1641. The city of Gothenburg was rebuilt as a Dutch-style city with a large export marketplace and a canal that ran into the heart of the city.

Swedish agriculture did not maintain the developmental pace of other sectors. Although individual landownership increased, Swedish farmers did not apply much of the new agricultural technology seen in other parts of Europe. Repeated famines plagued Sweden in the late seventeenth and early eighteenth centuries.

EARLY FRENCH ABSOLUTISM, 1625–1715

The French government grew significantly larger in the sixteenth and seventeenth centuries, increasing from 4,000 officials in 1515 to 46,000 in 1665, and the financial burden of maintaining the bureaucracy along with a standing army caused unrest and suffering, especially among the peasants. Internal unification needs and the successful conduct of an activist foreign policy drove French leaders to adopt centralizing policies. A major problem, however, was that the great majority of officials had purchased their positions and could not be dismissed without compensation. They could pass their offices to their sons.

The Rule of the Two Cardinals, 1625–1661

Much of France's recovery from religious dissent and near-anarchic conditions after 1610 was owed to the policies of two chief ministers who happened to be cardinals of the Roman Catholic Church. Cardinal Richelieu (1585–1642) and Cardinal Giulio Mazarin (1602–1661) ably served their sovereigns. The two cardinals began building the foundations for French power, which loomed over Europe from the 1660s.

Although Cardinal Richelieu had become a political figure early in the reign of Louis XIII (reign dates 1610–1643), he did not wield significant power until the mid-1620s. From that point, however, he dedicated himself to increasing the influence of the monarchy and fostering internal unity, as well as to increasing his personal fortune. One problem Richelieu faced was the continuing existence of Protestant stronghold cities and areas in France. Richelieu disarmed these cities to achieve greater political unity. He also expanded monarchical influence with the creation and dispatch of royal officials or **intendants** to various parts of the realm. These loyal representatives of the king corrected local abuses and extended state reach into distant regions.

The major foreign policy challenge facing France was the growing threat from the Hapsburg family. This situation resulted from Hapsburg control of the Spanish government, the Spanish Netherlands, territory in the Italian Peninsula, and lands near France's northeast frontier. From the French perspective, the Hapsburg encirclement constituted a mortal threat, especially after the successes of the Hapsburg armies in Germany. Thus, the French government supported Protestant powers that fought against the Catholic Hapsburgs in the Thirty Years War. Danes and Swedes received financial and diplomatic support from France until the death of the Swedish king, Gustavus Adolphus, in 1632. Then, France committed itself to direct combat against the Hapsburg forces, with the French prevailing in the 1640s. The costs

MAP 30.2 *Hapsburg Possessions "Threatening" France.* *In the seventeenth century, French leaders grew increasingly worried that the Hapsburg family, a dynastic rival, might isolate and strangle France. Thus, a key aim of French foreign policy was to ensure that Spanish and Austrian possessions near France's borders be reduced or eliminated, especially in Italy and Germany. By the end of the century, French expansion under Louis XIV made these concerns superfluous.*

of supporting the war effort and the growing government triggered major French social unrest in the 1630s.

Cardinal Mazarin succeeded Richelieu and continued his predecessor's policy of strengthening France. Rather than use the system of patron-client relationships of Richelieu, Mazarin created a parallel system of power, relying on intendants as local administrators. This change alienated many other officials who benefited from the old ways, and they rebelled against Mazarin. Compounding the threat was the alliance of officials with distressed commoners in cities and rural areas. One uprising by Parisians compelled King Louis XIV (reign dates 1643–1715) to flee Paris. Louis's palace

complex and court at Versailles, located a moderate distance from Paris, became a symbol of the king's distaste for the Parisians. Cardinal Mazarin outlasted the various rebellious groups by using military commissioners and intendants to enforce obedience to royal commands. The intendant system survived.

Mazarin also taught statecraft to his young sovereign, Louis XIV. Careful schooling in the application of royal power well served the king, who ruled on his own after Mazarin's death in 1661. One of Louis XIV's first decisions concerned the personal assumption of the first minister position, as well as the royal reins of power. In addition, the overwhelming majority of top ministers

PARALLELS AND DIVERGENCES

Peasant Protests in the Seventeenth Century

The main cause of rural unrest in Europe lay in the growth of state bureaucracies, as well as in the means to fund them. New taxes, direct and indirect, triggered protests, especially when the fiscal assessments became systematic and regular. Taxes on salt, grain, and wine hit the poor quite hard, and French officials imposed a tax on each person, a tax that became a chief source of state revenue between 1630 and 1640. This assessment sparked massive peasant unrest. Quartering of soldiers also heavily burdened poor people, who deeply resented the arrogant ways of the soldiers.

Peasants had a strong sense of justice. They were convinced that their rights, going back generations, should be honored by the state and its rapacious officials. Peasants held a powerful belief in tradition and faith in the ruler's commitment to justice, so when new taxes were imposed, peasants revolted. They believed that the king was just but uninformed about the wrongdoings of his officials. Peasants also resented new obligations imposed by manorial lords who were often perceived as greedy; in addition, rural folk resisted duties proclaimed by new lords who moved into the area. In the peasants' minds, tradition had to be followed.

Even though peasant uprisings were suppressed, sometimes most brutally, the state recognized certain limits of bureaucratic power by canceling new taxes, reducing existing taxes, or abolishing restrictions on movement by peasants. Nobles, too, tread warily after a peasant outburst because the aristocrats feared for their lives, their families, and their property.

Peasant resistance centered on the village; it was their strength and also their weakness. Rural life was constantly threatened by bandits, soldiers, and officials, so village cohesiveness was a strength against outsiders. Villages were the main line of self-defense, the main taxpaying unit, the focal point of economic activity, and the center of social life for peasants. The parish church was often the village's sturdiest building, where locals gathered to resist predators. Because most farming tools could be used as weapons, a crude arsenal existed within the village community. And often it was but a short step from self-defense to rebellion. Peasant armies were also organized by village under local leadership; this gave some cohesiveness to a military force. At the same time, one village unit might refuse to fight under a commander from another village, causing disunity, especially when a defeat occurred. Thus, peasant armies were easily formed and easily dissolved.

served solely at Louis's pleasure and came from nonaristocratic origins. This was unlike Gustavus Adolphus but similar to Charles XI. Like Richelieu, Mazarin had amassed great personal wealth in feeding off the system he helped expand. Thus, the two cardinals played a vital role in strengthening France in the seventeenth century.

Louis XIV's Absolutism

French absolutism reflected the personality of the monarch who titled himself the "Sun King." Louis undertook a self-promotion campaign, including the creation of an image that, along with the dazzling court life at Versailles, awed French aristocrats. In fact, the courtliness of France was imitated across Europe. Yet Louis was not an innovator. He worked with the institutions available to him, including the bureaucracy, the courts of the nobility, and the estates of France. He controlled the patronage system and used that along with threat, persuasion, and bribery to compel obedience. Because the nobility was fragmented by the time of Louis's assumption of power, taming of the aristocrats was moderately easy.

The nature of absolutism meant that in the absence of a dynamic character such as Louis XIV at the helm, the ship of state might drift or flounder. Indeed, that happened in the eighteenth century as Louis's weaker successors failed to control

FIGURE 30.4 *Louis XIV.* *The "Sun King" set the tone for most of his fellow monarchs in the seventeenth century. Louis epitomized the absolute monarch; he commissioned artists to create impressive paintings, drawings, and tapestries as testaments to his god-like power. In this Gobelins tapestry, he sits astride his steed pointing forward while looking at the viewer. Such tapestries were an important export industry for France.* Musée de Versailles © R.M.N.

the disgruntled aristocrats. Absolutism needed a monarchical system that functioned smoothly with a strong ruler. The other legacy of Louis XIV was a firm commitment to an expansionist policy. Ultimately, this policy bankrupted France, playing a role in the unfolding French Revolution later in the eighteenth century.

In his campaign to foster French power and his own glory, Louis concentrated on dominating the internal administration. He selected capable administrators, insisting that they could be dismissed by him at any time. The great demand on resources owing to the major wars beginning in the 1660s accelerated the centralization process. Civilian militias were replaced by a central police force, and municipalities were brought under royal control, especially after the intendants gained access to and influence over municipal finances. The number of intendants was sharply increased.

By the late 1670s, the basic institutional framework and policies had been set, and Louis turned to foreign matters. His guiding principle remained the extension of French territory and influence throughout Europe and across the globe. The French army grew to a standing force of several hundred thousand; the navy swelled from a small coastal fleet to an oceanic armada of several hundred fighting vessels; and a vigorous colonization program commenced in North America, the Caribbean Basin, and India. Warring against the

Dutch, English, and others occupied nearly all of Louis's energy in his later reign.

A series of poor harvests and the heavy toll of taxation and service nearly wrecked France in the 1690s. Widespread starvation stalked the land, and the king grew unpopular. At the announcement of his death in 1715, many French subjects openly celebrated.

Financing French Absolutism: Colbert's Policies

The impetus to build a bureaucracy to enlarge and equip the military forces came from many officials, but especially from Jean Louis Baptiste Colbert (1619–1683). Although he would have preferred to create an even more centralized political system, Colbert used the intendants to double the tax revenues arriving in Paris. These funds helped build the Versailles palace complex, intended as a symbol of royal splendor that would awe the aristocrats and other subjects. The massive project took several years to complete and cost a significant fraction of the state's annual budget.

In addition, Colbert undertook a series of measures to improve the economy. He dispatched agents to hire artisans and experts in various sectors of the economy. Some came to France, although they barely offset the losses of Huguenot technicians and scientists who left France (see the discussion in Chapter 29 of the revocation of the Edict of Nantes). Colbert established the rudiments of an educational system, and he built a merchant marine force to transport French goods and to avoid tolls on Dutch and English ships. Colbert also began a modest effort to promote high-quality French export goods. The overall policy slightly improved France's economic position, but it could not forestall a serious economic crisis in the 1690s.

Social Unrest in the Age of Absolutism

The drive for a larger government and the revenues to support it triggered major outbreaks of French social protest. After taxes increased fourfold during the Thirty Years War, unrest exploded in mass actions. Dissidents maimed the livestock of

FIGURE 30.5 *The Palace at Versailles.* *Versailles symbolized Louis XIV's power and grandeur. At the same time, it represented his distrust of Parisians, who forced him to flee Paris in humiliation early in his reign. Versailles was located some distance from the French capital; Jean Baptiste Colbert, one of Louis's outstanding ministers, supervised the construction of the palace complex. The great cost of construction forced Colbert to improve tax collection and undertake revenue-raising projects.* Giraudon/Art Resource, N.Y.

FIGURE 30.6 *Peasant Discontent. This seventeenth-century painting shows peasants exacting revenge against their rulers. Soldiers who had abused peasants by eating their food, stealing their possessions, and insulting their families are caught off guard and succumb to the rage of rural folk. Although such incidents were sporadic, there were also eruptions of large-scale violence. The elite greatly feared challenges to their authority and responded ferociously to crush the unrest.* Rijksmuseum.

local aristocrats or beat local agents of the government. Haylofts and stacks burst into flame from torchings by agitated subjects, and in local carnivals people mocked members of the political and social elite by burning effigies of officials and singing ribald songs. Serious mass protests erupted in 1636 and 1637, and regional outbursts troubled the government in 1639. The most sustained unrest occurred between 1648 and 1652, when uprisings led by disgruntled officials coincided with riots by Parisians and peasants. These disturbances threatened the social and political fabric but were finally crushed.

During the 1690s, famine claimed many French subjects and consumed the attention of potential opponents of the regime. The hardest hit were peasants who were taxed to the point of desperation. Massive armed forces dampened rural unrest.

One method of co-opting potential dissenters was the elevation of talented members of the middle class into government positions. Office holding also meant rising into the aristocracy, despite efforts by the ancient noble families to divide sharply the boundaries between themselves and the new social elite. The resulting social mobility eased some tensions among the middle class, providing the state with talented bureaucrats.

The legacy of Louis XIV and the two cardinals was a centralized patchwork of contradictory parts. High taxes, large armies, and royally appointed officials increased the centralized power of the king. Yet the state's finances also depended on the sale of offices, which left sizeable portions of the government independent of the king's control. This tension between centralization and decentralization was an important structural feature of French absolutism. It was not resolved

FIGURE 30.7 *Prussian Militarism.* *Prussian absolutism depended heavily on the army. Some said Prussia was more an army with a country than a country with an army. Successive Prussian rulers built the military into an effective, well-trained instrument of power. This picture shows a training scene. Harsh discipline and constant drill were essential to effectiveness in combat. The wooden horse in the background was used as an instrument of punishment.* Bildarchiv Preussischer Kulturbesitz.

until the French Revolution did away with the sale of offices and allowed centralization to proceed unabated.

EARLY PRUSSIAN ABSOLUTISM, 1648–1740

Out of the Thirty Years War came an enlarged state, Brandenburg-Prussia (hereafter known as Prussia). A succession of three Hohenzollern sovereigns ruled Prussia between 1640 and 1740. Through shrewd statecraft and force they forged a powerful state system out of disparate and territorially disconnected parts.

Building Absolutism in Prussia

Prussian power came from strong-willed monarchs, a large army, and the building of a bureaucracy to maintain it. Frederick William, the Great Elector (reign dates 1640–1688), increased the army's size from 8,000 to 22,000 soldiers during the

Little Northern War (1655–1660). Special wartime taxes had been wrung out of recalcitrant city administrations, and the fiscal levies became permanent after the victorious monarch refused to disband his army, turning it against his urban opponents. Frederick William also co-opted the **Junkers**, the impoverished landed nobility of East Prussia, by turning the peasants who worked Junker estates into serfs. This enserfment brought agony to peasants but loyalty from grateful aristocrats who staffed the bureaucracy and army.

To support the Prussian army, Frederick William needed an efficient means to collect taxes. Reorganization of the tax system began in 1667, and Frederick William soon heavily taxed peasants and urbanites. In addition, the monarch built a bureaucracy of officials and tax collectors who were directly responsible to him. By 1713, the army had grown to 39,000 soldiers and became more battle-seasoned during combat in the early 1700s.

Frederick I (reign dates 1688–1713) gained the title King of Prussia. A significant contribution of this ruler and his wife, Queen Sophie Charlotte, was the building of many princely palaces and a dazzling courtier life centered on intellectuals, like Gottfried Wilhelm Leibnitz, who joined the faculty at the newly created University of Halle.

Prussian absolutism reached its most complete form under the leadership of Frederick William I (1713–1740), the Soldier King. The army grew to more than 80,000 soldiers and consumed around 80 percent of state revenues. Between 50 to 65 percent of the nobles in the east served in the Prussian officer corps or the bureaucracy. A military reserve system had been fashioned by organizing and training peasants for service in the event of a general mobilization. In fact, the system avoided the problem of having a larger standing army and thereby saved significant sums. Military commanders played a role in developing and

improving Prussia's roads and waterways because they wished to be able to move military units rapidly from one spot to another. One joke asserted that Prussia was more of an army with a country than a country with an army.

Frederick William I reorganized his bureaucracy along military lines. Taxing authority and material supply powers rested with the local officials who owed absolute obedience to the monarch. In addition, Frederick William I rewarded merit by permitting commoners to attain noble status through outstanding state service. He also kept officials' salaries low but augmented them with bonuses for good service. Another bureaucratic practice forbade nobles from serving as officials in their home territories to

MAP 30.3 *Prussia in 1721.* *Disparate states had been welded into Prussia by the early eighteenth century. The Prussian army and bureaucracy had played key roles in forging that unity. In the process, Prussia emerged as a significant power in European affairs, especially after 1740, during the reign of Frederick the Great.*

FIGURE 30.8 *Conscription of Jews. Prussia, like many states in Europe, treated Jews with disdain and discrimination. This drawing shows the drafting of a group of Jewish men into the Prussian army. While forcible conscription was a common occurrence, certain groups, including the Jews, were treated more harshly both in the conscription process and later while in service. Beatings were common throughout the Early Modern Era.*
Courtesy of the Trustees of the British Museum.

avoid their becoming too tied to local instead of state interests.

The system worked tolerably well but needed additional safeguards to ensure efficiency and full compliance with the sovereign's commands. Inspectors widely traveled the realm to report on the conduct of appointees in local positions. Frederick William himself journeyed around the realm to remind local officials that they served at his pleasure.

Prussian monarchs welcomed a small Protestant sect, the Pietists. **Pietism**, which became a

kind of state religion that helped centralize ideological loyalty, called for a renewal of direct religious experience. Pietists emphasized the significance of personal conversion and rebirth to a new life of active Christianity. Many areas in Europe expelled the Pietists for their refusal to submit to state laws regulating religion, but Prussia welcomed them to counter the influence of Lutheranism in the provinces: Lutherans often depended on the support of provincial nobles who might oppose state interests. Pietists became influential at educational institutions at all levels, including the universities of Halle and Königsberg. Through these intellectual centers Pietism exerted considerable sway over elite cultural life in other parts of Germany.

Social Issues in Prussia

Prussian rulers also actively encouraged the migration of numerous religious minority groups to Prussia in order to repopulate and rebuild its economy after the Thirty Years War. Perhaps 20,000 Huguenots settled around Berlin after their expulsion from France in the 1680s. Another 20,000 Protestants fled from Salzburg in 1731, and they were welcomed in Prussia. The proliferation of sects led to religious toleration in Prussia. The status of Jews remained uncertain, with some rights granted them only in the late eighteenth century. Full legal status for Jews in Prussia did not come until 1812. In many parts of Germany, Jews still experienced extreme forms of anti-Semitism and financial exploitation.

The Prussian state adopted many elements of absolutism, and its army dominated and altered the existing political and social systems. Until 1740, the army had seldom been used in extensive campaigns. In that year, Frederick II came to power and conquered the rich Austrian province of Silesia. The action embroiled Europe in a series of wars over the next twenty-three years, but Prussia survived great battle losses and emerged with enlarged territories and a full treasury. Prussian absolutism had passed a major test.

PETER THE GREAT BUILDS RUSSIAN ABSOLUTISM, 1689–1725

Peter the Great forged the basis of Russian absolutism. Within a century after his death, Russian troops helped drive Napoleon from power and secure a Bourbon restoration by Louis XVIII. Peter's legacy included a state apparatus of immense power that long outlived him, and he introduced the Western calendar, newspapers, a revised written script, and a whole complex of Western-style manners to Russia.

Peter's Youth

An examination of Peter's pre-adult years sheds light on his later actions. Peter witnessed terrifying court struggles between the families backing his mother and those backing his half-sister, Sophia. In a coup organized by Sophia, Peter and his half-brother assumed joint rule, with the actual power being placed in the regent Sophia's hands. After the ten-year-old Peter watched as soldiers murdered his relatives, he was moved into a safe haven away from Moscow.

Life outside the Kremlin's walls meant freedom from the stultifying rituals tsars performed and a chance to give free rein to his immense appetite for learning. War games fascinated Peter, and he held mock battles with real soldiers playing parts. Peter sailed local lakes, becoming enamored of naval matters. In addition, he conversed at length with Westerners, whose friendliness and knowledge excited him. In 1689, after military and policy failures by Sophia's political allies, forces loyal to Peter ousted her.

Two events, a trip to Archangel (1693–1694) and a military campaign near the Sea of Azov (1695–1696), particularly influenced Peter. In Archangel, the young tsar visited a bustling port with many ships and foreign merchants. Peter also sailed in dangerous waters, and that adventure strengthened his desire to learn more about shipbuilding and sailing. After returning from the north, Peter decided to attack the Ottoman Empire by capturing its strategic fort near an entrance to the Sea of Azov. The initial effort failed miserably, but Peter learned from the loss; after spending the winter building a new flotilla, he beat the Turks.

The Grand Tour, 1697–1698

Perhaps the most remarkable event of Peter's reign was his tour of Europe in the late 1690s. Peter traveled with a large party. This allowed him to be free in his intelligence-gathering activities. The embassy had three purposes: to collect information about how to improve Russia, to interact with top political figures in Europe, and to assess the possibilities for foreign-policy initiatives.

Peter lingered at the great shipyards of the Netherlands and England, taking the opportunity to participate in all phases of shipbuilding. Having delighted in the toil and in conversations with prominent artisans and engineers, he invited some of them to Russia to aid in a variety of technical matters.

Peter generally impressed his hosts and charmed monarchs and princes alike. The diplomatic contact afforded Peter better relations with a variety of sovereigns and a personal appreciation for the complex web of international relations in Europe. Prior to this journey, Russia's diplomatic corps often had been ineffective in representing Russia's interests. The tsar also learned that conditions seemed propitious for a dynamic diplomatic effort to strengthen Russia. Poland had become an ally, and Denmark looked north at Sweden, a great power of the seventeenth century and one that controlled much of the Baltic seacoast. In addition,

Britain and France had begun to prepare for a major war over the succession to the Spanish throne. A Russian, Danish, and Polish alliance against Sweden was forged.

The Great Northern War (1700–1721): Testing Russian Absolutism

Determined to modernize Russia, Peter knew that the task demanded a long, taxing effort. When he returned from the tour in 1698, Peter began insisting that Russians break with their traditional manners and habits. Perhaps the most famous effort involved compelling Russian men to cut off their beards to look Western. These and other policies consumed the young tsar's days until a shattering military defeat at Narva (1700) forced a transformation of Russia's political system.

FIGURE 30.9 *Peter the Great. The equestrian pose in this picture is reminiscent of Louis XIV's portrait (Figure 30.4). Peter, unlike Louis, frequently accompanied his troops into battle, and his attire is suitable to a military commander. In many ways, Peter was leading his people in a campaign to Westernize themselves. To do so, he established a military-style system that bound his subjects like serfs or soldiers.* Novosti, London.

Sweden's monarch, Charles XII, although a teenager, proved to be an adept warrior. Once Russia, Denmark, and Poland declared war against Sweden, Charles swiftly attacked Denmark. After defeating the Danes, Charles turned on Poland and won a series of victories. Then the Swedes invaded Russia, and at Narva the larger Russian army fell to the firepower of the disciplined Swedes. Charles drily noted that fighting the Russians was like shooting geese. Nearly all of Russia's commanders surrendered, and Peter, anticipating defeat, left before the battle, wishing to salvage the surviving elements and to rebuild Russia.

The staggering losses compelled the tsar to accelerate the adoption of Russian absolutism. Peter usually dressed, acted, and thought like a soldier. From his youth, army life suited the tsar's character. Militaristic discipline, loyalty, and service in a hierarchical structure could accomplish a great deal with efficient dispatch. Men and materials were quickly raised and employed.

Peter also thought in orderly and systematic ways; he believed that using logic and rationally determined methods provided the best hope of attaining lofty goals. This trait caused him to see government as a machine. Peter took great interest in laws and rules. He understood that they acted like a skeletal structure underlying the sinews and tissue of government.

The absolutist model passed its test in the Battle of Poltava in 1709. Peter had confiscated treasured Russian church bells for their metal content; to the dismay of the church hierarchy, they were transformed into new artillery pieces. Recruiters scoured the frontier regions, and their harsh methods triggered a massive uprising (1707–1708) in

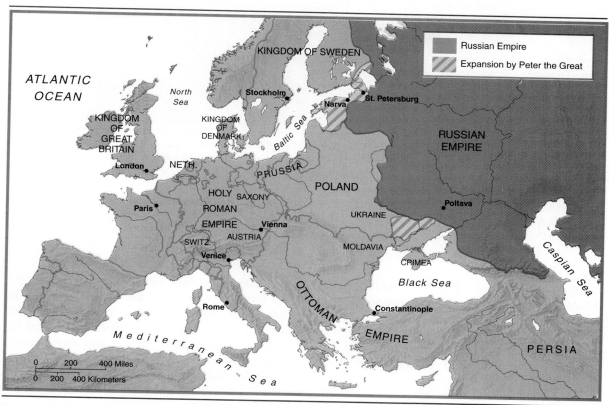

MAP 30.4 *Expansion of the Russian Empire under Peter the Great.* Peter laid the *foundations of an expanded Russian Empire by annexing lands along the Baltic coast. He also led campaigns against the Ottoman Turks and the Safavid Persians. Russia's succeeding monarchs continued his foreign policy efforts, creating one of the world's largest empires. Much of Peter's success came at the expense of Sweden.*

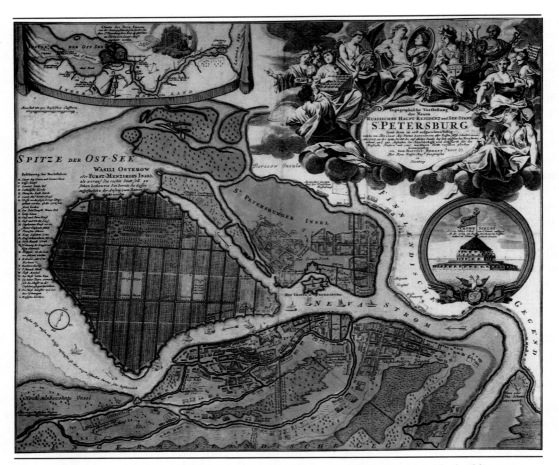

FIGURE 30.10   *Layout of St. Petersburg.*   *Great human suffering went into the building of St. Petersburg, Peter the Great's "Window on the West." Thousands of laborers died while toiling in the marshy environment of the city. This schematic, drawn around 1720 by J. P. Homann, indicates that early city plans envisioned the city being located on large islands in the Neva River. Peter was determined that the city would be built and would become a successful capital. To realize that dream, he invested considerable human and material resources.*   Courtesy of the Trustees of the British Museum.

the southern steppes. At Poltava in central Russia, Russians and Swedes fought for a second time. On this occasion, Russians routed the army of Charles XII, who fled to the Ottoman realm. At a celebratory banquet after the conflict, Peter gathered the captured Swedish officers and toasted the "lessons" that had enabled the Russian victory.

The military style soon carried over to the civilian sector. Peter spent a great deal of time and energy writing and publishing a detailed code of military law. His ideas about the state found their clearest and most complete expression in military legislation. He sought to tame and correct society by extending to it the norms of military life. Per-

haps one of the most visible products of military-like regulation could be seen in the layout of St. Petersburg, the new Russian capital, built from scratch, beginning in 1703. Peter fashioned his political center like a ship; it was meticulously planned and carefully regulated. Seemingly minor details like the dimensions of chimneys, the forms of roofs, and the placement of fences in private dwellings fell under governmental control.

Provincial administration also received the tsar's attention. There too, a military model dominated regional and local life. Each of the subnational administrative units had a military force stationed therein and attached to it. Officers assumed census-taking duties and eventually became tax collectors. In addition, military detachments were expected to assist local police forces when discontent reached major proportions. One feature of Peter's government was the large number of military figures who became bureaucrats. Discipline and obedience educated them to be loyal, hardworking officials.

Peter also revitalized the upper levels of government by applying Swedish-style hierarchies there. He created a ministry system, wherein each ministry had a specific function. The Admiralty Ministry, the War Ministry, and the Foreign Affairs Ministry constituted the first of a line of administrative structures. Peter believed that military regulation and discipline created soldiers who lived moral lives and followed modern practices. Similarly, the long-range goal of absolutism was to substitute regulation for coercion in political and social life. Peter hoped that ethical humans could emerge from his military-style system.

Transformation of the Russian Economy

Economic growth between 1695 and 1725 laid the foundations for a fiscal base that could support a major war. Mercantile policies also brought production levels to previously unimaginable highs. Once undertaken, the government's control and regulation of the iron industry conferred national self-sufficiency in iron production within five years.

Government funds and regulations helped build the factories and establishments; the state's needs for materials took first priority. Whole economic sectors came under military control, and there were factories for sail cloth, for rope, for saddles, for leather goods, and for wool. Peter insisted that manufactured products regularly be tested to ensure quality. State serfs were forced into factories as laborers, and criminals under sentences of hard labor were made to work off their sentences in manufactories.

The state, ever eager to develop strategic industries, recruited foreigners for mining and metallurgy. Indeed, an entire metallurgical complex was built in the Ural Mountains. Monopolies were frequently promised to prospectors if or when they found massive deposits of ores.

Cities like St. Petersburg were built or reoriented to meet governmental requirements. City managers collected municipal taxes, and troops lived in private dwellings in provincial cities and towns; urban centers often had to transport troops and supplies from their own resources. Horses were demanded as a kind of taxation in certain towns. The growing municipal burden forced many to flee the towns; depopulation became a major problem. Internal passports were issued in an attempt to inhibit free movement of people, and border guards turned back fleeing Russian refugees.

The merchant class was devastated by many of the tsarist policies. Peter commanded that the primary trade route from Russia to the West be shifted from Archangel to St. Petersburg. In addition, groups of merchants were forcibly moved from their hometowns to the capital. Also, as the state became more involved in the establishment of factories and other enterprises, merchants could not compete with the minimal costs of state peasant labor or with state monopolies. This expansion of state servitude doomed whole economic sectors.

Social Upheaval in Russia

Nobles were deeply affected by the new imperial laws. The main basis of the nobility was service rather than birth, and heredity was replaced by personal merit in determining social ranking. This new system gave Peter great power over the nobles; he even commanded that they could not marry until they had been educated. People from other social groups advanced into the nobility by achieving a certain level in the ranking system.

One category, state peasants, demands some consideration. This group was created by Peter to bring previously free social groups under state control and regulation. These groups included the peasants of the Russian north, the fur-tributary peasants, the single homesteaders of the south, Siberian peasants, and sharecroppers. The state peasantry, composed of more than one million adult men, became bonded to the state; their movements were curtailed and their tax obligations were increased. All too often throughout the rest of the eighteenth century, tens of thousands of these state peasants were given by tsars to their favorite courtiers. "Free" now meant fugitive or criminal, and police or army detachments regularly rounded up travelers for investigation and return to a bondage system.

IN THEIR
OWN WORDS

*Two Women
Examine Education
and Writing*

Women continued to have limited opportunities for education and personal expression in writing or other forms of artistic activity, like painting or sculpture. And the overwhelming number of women who did write or paint came from the upper classes of European society. Margaret Cavendish, the Duchess of Newcastle (1623–1673), received an excellent education and was highly regarded as a playwright and author of other literary genres. In this passage, she defends her right to write an autobiography, *A True Relation of My Birth, Breeding, and Life,* by comparing herself with other famous authors.

> But as I hope my readers will not think me vain for writing my life, since there have been many that have done the like, as Caesar, Ovid, and many more, both men and women, and I know of no reason I may not do it as well as they. But I verily believe some censuring readers will scornfully say, why hath this lady writ her own life? Since none care to know whose daughter she was, or whose wife she is, or how she was bred, or what fortunes she had, or how she lived, or what humour or disposition she was of? I answer that it is true, that 'tis no purpose to the readers, but it is to the authoress, because I write it for my own sake, not theirs. Neither did I intend this piece for to delight, but to divulge; not to please fancy, but to tell the truth. Lest after-ages should mistake, in not knowing I was daughter to one Master Lucas of St. John's near Colchester in Essex, second wife to the Lord Marquis of Newcastle; for my lord having had two wives, I might easily have been mistaken, especially if I should die and my lord marry again.

Anna Maria van Schurman (1607–1678) earned a reputation as the most learned European woman of the seventeenth century. Her father insisted that she learn alongside her brothers, and she first focused on the arts. Later, she studied ancient languages like Syriac and wrote an Ethiopian grammar. Although she was permitted the rare privilege of attending the University of Utrecht, she was required to stand behind a curtain during classes. In the work The Learned Maid or Whether a Maid May Be Called a Scholar?, Schurman states that women should be educated.

> My deep regard for learning, my conviction that equal justice is the right of all, impel me to protest against the theory which would only allow a minority of my sex to attain to what is, in the opinion of all men, most worth having. For since wisdom is admitted to be the crown of human achievement, and is within every man's right to aim at in proportion to his opportunities, I cannot see why a young girl in whom we admit a desire for self-improvement should not be encouraged to acquire the best that life affords.

Townsfolk experienced similar if startling shifts in their status. Because of a sudden imperial decree, all townspeople might wake one morning to find themselves retained as members of merchant guilds or artisan corporations. By this judgment, the number of taxpayers in an urban area significantly increased. Thus, the tax assessment on towns grew sharply, with the wealthier people paying larger shares of the town assessments. Initially, state revenues increased, but soon people fled the urban areas for the safety of the southern frontiers or the anonymity of foreign countries.

Social unrest erupted as the government's noose around its subjects' necks tightened. Acts of violence increased; the most serious challenges took place in 1707 and later, when two massive uprisings erupted in protest of the controlling policies.

WOMEN UNDER ABSOLUTISM

For women, the age of absolutism brought little change to their lives; in a few ways, opportunities seemed to lessen. Most European men believed that women should remain under male control; marriage therefore was the natural state and laws generally insisted that widows remarry. One group

EUROPE

	Events
1600	
–	Gustavus Adolphus becomes king, 1611
–	
–	Battle of Lützen, 1632
–	Cardinal Mazarin becomes First Minister, 1642
1650	Fronde begins, 1648
–	
–	
–	
–	Protestants flee French religious persecution, 1685
	Peter the Great's Grand Tour begins, 1697
1700	Battle of Narva, 1700
	Battle of Poltava, 1709
–	
–	Death of Charles XII, 1718
–	
	Protestants flee Austrian religious persecution, 1731
–	Frederick I dies, 1740
1750	
–	
–	
–	
–	

Swedish absolutism, 1611–1718

Early French absolutism, 1625–1715

Early Prussian absolutism, 1648–1740

Early Russian absolutism, 1689–1725

Thirty Years War, 1618–1648

of German women who lived by spinning pooled their wages and lived together, but the town fathers forbade all unmarried women to have their own households, forcing these women to abandon their communal life. Jewish marriages were usually arranged with the understanding that love would come later. The Jewish ideal marriage was said to be predestined in heaven, and divorce was permitted for unsuccessful unions.

Many women found their opportunities for employment limited, and when they did find work, they were usually paid much less than male workers. A few guilds were limited to women who could bequeath their tools and property to others in the guild. Louis XIV and Colbert, concerned about the lack of opportunities for women needing work, created a guild of dressmakers exclusively for them. The growing trend to license members of certain occupations also caused problems for women, and women were effectively barred from becoming licensed physicians because they were forbidden from taking university classes on anatomy and related subjects. The same thing happened to women who were apothecaries (dispensers of medicines) and midwives. In many German cities, however, custom demanded that women be midwives.

Some places in Europe and some groups permitted more participation by women in economic activities. A few Polish cities allowed women to be active in commercial ventures in the urban marketplaces; one scholar estimated that around 75 percent of traders in Polish cities were women. One measure of their financial success can be seen in the fact that in the seventeenth century about half of the loans in Danzig and Warsaw were financed by women. Because regulations often forbade women from staying at inns and therefore curtailed their travel, Jewish women relied on networks of friends to provide housing for them.

SUMMARY

1. European nation-states of the seventeenth and eighteenth centuries experimented with absolutist forms of government that included a military-style chain of command. The central government regulated politics, economics, and society, imposing discipline, obedience, and duty on officials as well as on subjects. Absolutist monarchs promoted the reliance on law rather than custom and the use of mechanical terminology in political discourse.

2. Wars often accelerated the process of gathering power in the hands of the monarch, and the Thirty Years War was a factor in the development of Swedish and French absolutism.

3. Sweden began its absolutist course under King Gustavus Adolphus, who led a coalition of aristocratic officials. Although dominance by the nobles grew after Gustavus Adolphus's death, King Charles XI reasserted royal dominance of the political system, and an ongoing land reform undermined the economic and political base of the high aristocrats.

4. French central power was built on a tension between officials who purchased their positions and officials who served only as long as the king was satisfied with their job performances. Louis XIV, France's absolutist king, dominated the nobles, but his successors could not duplicate his success.

5. Prussia built an absolutist system based on the army. Successive rulers created a bureaucracy grounded in dedicated, loyal, merit-rewarded service. Junker nobles gave loyal work in exchange for full control of the peasants who worked on their estates.

6. Peter the Great channeled his youthful fascination with foreign experts and military life into building an absolutist state, where Russian subjects either served or paid heavy taxes. Nearly every aspect of public life was state regulated and disciplined. After the warring ceased, the militarization of civil life continued.

7. Women were still regarded as inferior to men and needing to be under some form of male control. They were also frozen out of jobs by a rising professionalism that excluded them from being licensed by governments.

SUGGESTED READINGS

Anisimov, Evgenii. *The Reforms of Peter the Great*. New York: M. E. Sharpe, 1993. A compelling interpretation of Peter's era and the tsar's role in it.

Herwig, Holger. *Hammer or Anvil? Modern Germany, 1648–Present*. Lexington, Mass.: D. C. Heath, 1994. A useful survey of major issues and personalities of modern Germany.

Major, J. Russell. *From Renaissance Monarchy to Absolute Monarchy*. Baltimore: Johns Hopkins University Press, 1994. A synthesis of scholarship concerning the development of French absolutism, emphasizing the role of the nobility.

Roberts, Michael. *The Swedish Imperial Experience, 1560–1718*. Cambridge, Eng.: Cambridge University Press, 1979. A standard interpretation of the rise of the Swedish Empire.

Rosener, Werner. *The Peasantry of Europe*. Trans. by Thomas M. Barker. Oxford, Eng.: Oxford University Press, 1994. A synthesis of research about the European peasantry.

Scott, Franklin D. *Sweden: The Nation's History*. Carbondale: Southern Illinois University Press, 1988. A standard survey of Swedish history.

Wiesner, Merry E. *Women and Gender in Early Modern Europe*. Cambridge, Eng.: Cambridge University Press, 1993. A major study of women's history and issues in the Early Modern Era.

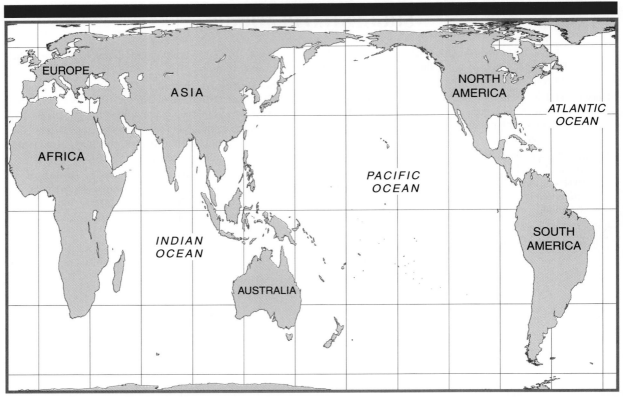

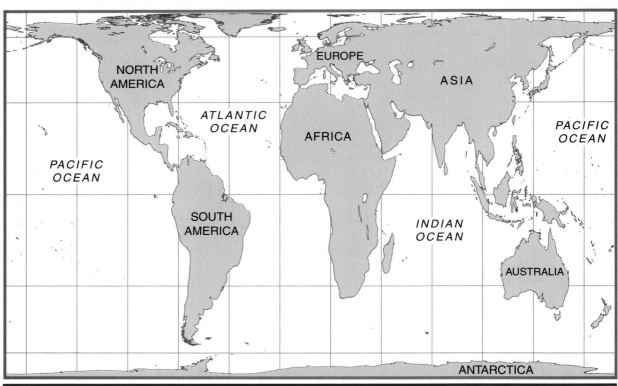

Revolutions in Europe, the Americas, and Asia

1543–1895

Charles I of England, who had been on the throne since 1625, had blundered into a bloody civil war with Parliament in 1642 and had lost, but he still had managed to persuade most war-weary Parliamentarians to accept him once again as their monarch. Army commanders, among them Oliver Cromwell, purged Parliament and put the hapless king on trial for his life in early 1649. The English Revolution of 1640 to 1689 was a long era of often violent change. Charles's execution was a turning point in the English Revolution, one of many revolutions in the seventeenth and eighteenth centuries.

From the sixteenth to the nineteenth centuries, revolutions around the world transformed people's lives. During this period, local landed elite and urban middle-class members of society gained greater participatory roles in government as the electoral franchise widened. In certain cases, even the lower socioeconomic classes contended for power, but they usually succeeded only in uniting propertied people against them.

Revolutions can change political structures, social structures, economic structures, or intellectual views of the universe and the place of humans within it. Some revolutions caused great suffering, while others transformed institutions with only moderate upheaval. A few were implemented by existing rulers, and others resulted from opposition forces seizing power and restructuring the way in which power was exercised. Abortive revolutions, such as the Taiping Uprising in mid-nineteenth-century China, also severely traumatized societies.

DEFINITIONS AND TYPES OF REVOLUTIONS

A **revolution** is a process whereby rapid and fundamental structural change occurs. It may be relatively peaceful, like the Scientific Revolution of the sixteenth, seventeenth, and eighteenth centuries or the Industrial Revolution from 1770 to 1905. More often, however, revolutions that transform societies produce great unrest, major upheaval, and massive amounts of physical violence. Revolutions are processes rather than events. Because revolutions entail significant alteration in political and social structures, time is needed to complete the transformation. A revolutionary group's seizure of power is merely a single event in the revolutionary process rather than the process itself. In that sense, it is inappropriate to speak of a single year for the American Revolution or for the French Revolution.

Revolutions may be classified into several types. A revolution that changes mainly the political structure is a **political revolution**. A revolution that alters society is usually known as a **social revolution**. The Scientific Revolution was an **intellectual revolution**, a transformation of how human beings thought about themselves and the universe around them. The Industrial Revolution (discussed in Chapter 32) was an **economic revolution**, a transformation of a country's economic structure.

Another way of looking at revolutions is in terms of the agents bringing about the revolution. A revolution implemented by the ruling elite is called an **elite revolution**, and a revolution implemented by the common people seizing power is called a **populist revolution**. Thus, for example, a political revolution may also be an elite revolution or a populist revolution.

How do revolutions compare with rebellions? A **rebellion** is an uprising by people who seek to change the leaders rather than the political structure of a country. Rebellions are invariably political and may include large-scale violence. But the aim of a rebellious group is to replace the leadership, not a polity's institutional structure.

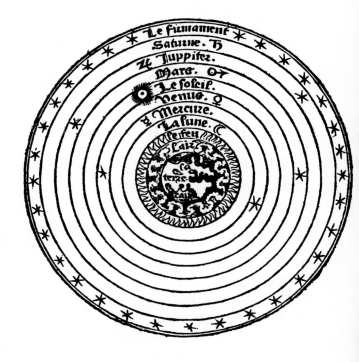

FIGURE 31.1 *The Ptolemaic Universe.* *This sixteenth-century diagram lays out the accepted interpretation of the universe as revolving around the earth. This system was elaborated by the Greek astronomer Ptolemy (A.D. 127–151) and later modified by others. Above the earth is air and then fire; above these spheres are the moon, the sun, and the five planets. If one accepts that the earth does not move, then a common-sense interpretation is that the stars and other bodies circle the earth.* Diagram from Oronce Fine, *Théorique de la huitième sphere et sept planètes.*

THE SCIENTIFIC REVOLUTION, 1543–1727

The Scientific Revolution fundamentally altered the human view of the universe and inspired new perspectives about people and ways to solve their problems. Although modern science owes much to Islamic, medieval, and Renaissance antecedents, the Scientific Revolution came when researchers abandoned the divine explanation for natural processes and explained the universe by general scientific laws. This process of secularization was a characteristic of modernity. Although important discoveries were made in most fields of science during this era, the focus in this chapter will be on two fields that experienced transformative change, astronomy and mathematics.

Nicolaus Copernicus (1473–1543) developed the first systematic critique of the Ptolemaic view of the universe, an earth-centered model of the cosmos that had held sway among European and Muslim scholars for over eight centuries. Copernicus, a Polish priest, used mathematics and logic to develop a sun-centered model of the universe, with the cosmos revolving around the sun. He believed that this more simple and elegant view was also more accurate. Much still remained to be investigated before an accurate picture of the universe emerged, but Copernicus's new perspective permitted others to think in different ways. Copernicus used different kinds of mathematics to formulate his model, and the intense use of mathematics became a feature of modern science.

Galileo Galilei (1564–1642), a professor of mathematics in Italy, improved the Dutch design of the telescope and made remarkable observations of the planets and their moons. Elaborating on fourteenth-century studies of velocity and acceleration, Galileo's research on the motion of bodies led him to conclude that heavier objects do not fall faster than lighter ones. He conducted careful experiments and helped develop the systematic and experimental method of investigating nature, using sophisticated mathematics to interpret the results. Other scientists replicated his experiments to verify the discoveries.

Advances in astronomy and other fields alarmed some members of the Roman Catholic Church. Given the religious wars of the period, new ideas were sometimes equated with heresies, and criticism of the prevailing view of the heavens might be construed as an attack on religious doctrine. For this reason, a few critics of traditional views, like Giordano Bruno, were burned at the stake for declaring that the universe was infinite. Later, when some church officials asserted that several of Galileo's teachings bordered on subversion, he yielded to the pressure and recanted certain views. More open-minded church leaders

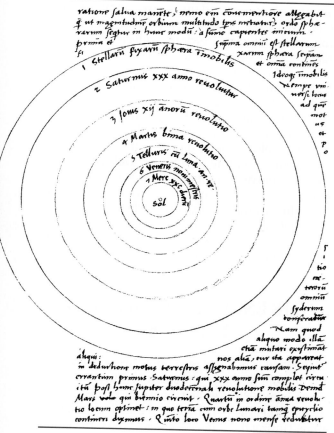

FIGURE 31.2 *The Copernican System.* *Nicolaus Copernicus's system shifted the earth from the center of the universe and placed an unmoving sun in the earth's stead. The moon circles the earth, while the earth, other planets, and stars move around the sun. Copernicus believed the orbits to be circular (they are actually elliptic). The Copernican system comes closer to representing the actual solar system than did the Ptolemaic universe, and its key achievement was to shift the earth away from the center.* Hulton-Getty/Tony Stone Images.

FIGURE 31.3 *Émilie de Breteuil, Marquise du Châtelet.* A mathematician, Émilie de Breteuil introduced Isaac Newton's work on gravity and the laws of motion to France and Europe. She translated the Principia Mathematica *into French and thereby played a key role in the history of science and in the Enlightenment, as Newton's view of a universe run by laws deeply influenced many thinkers of the era.* Private Collection/Bulloz.

between two bodies applied to humans and the earth, the planets and the sun, and all of the stars. To help explain the forces at work in his grand scheme, Newton applied his newly developed calculus, a branch of mathematics that helped spur the development of modern science. Newton published the results of his synthesis in a significant work, *Principia Mathematica*. It stands as one of the great achievements of human intellect.

Newton's ideas, especially his elegant view of a universe run by natural laws, spread to the European continent and altered how humans thought about the universe and themselves. Émilie de Breteuil, Marquise du Châtelet, played a significant role in introducing Newton's concepts to French readers. A mathematician herself, de Breteuil translated Newton's *Principia*, making it intelligible to nonmathematical readers. Her writer friend Voltaire also played a key role in popularizing Newton's ideas, arguing that human behavior might also be governed by natural laws.

One belief system, deism, gained a following during the Scientific Revolution. **Deism** asserted that the universe functioned like a machine (a clock), which was constructed by its maker. According to this theory, after fashioning the universe, which ran by natural laws, God had nothing left to do. Many deists therefore believed that God had become unnecessary.

came to accept the changing views of the universe resulting from continued scientific probing and testing. Most scientists also professed devotion to God, and they hoped to create a system that validated God in a new universal order.

Isaac Newton (1642–1727) synthesized the ideas of his predecessors into the Newtonian model of the universe, which forever replaced the Ptolemaic model. One of the unifying elements in the new scheme, gravity, had been explained by Newton, who saw that the mutual attraction

THE ENGLISH REVOLUTION, 1640–1689

A destructive political revolution swept England in the middle of the seventeenth century and concluded in 1689. Conflict between English monarchs and Parliament had been building for a long time. During the reign of James I (1603–1625) and at the ascendancy of his son Charles I (reign dates 1625–1649), the monarchy clearly enjoyed political supremacy. The monarchy could raise substantial sums of money, enjoyed significant influence in the House of Commons, and could count on the loyalty of the English people. By 1689, Parliament had ousted two monarchs from power and supported ones who agreed to limits on their authority, including Parliament's control of fiscal matters. Thus, Parliament had become a major partner in England's mixed governmental system.

Causes of the Revolution

Population growth played a key role in the crisis that precipitated the monarchy's collapse between 1640 and 1642. England's population doubled between 1500 and 1640, and the number of gentry landlords tripled. English commentators in the seventeenth century decried the huge population growth. This demographic increase contributed to long-term inflation, with rising prices steadily eroding the real wages of urban laborers. In addition, the costs of government sharply increased; one scholar estimated that in 1640 the English government would need twelve times the revenues of 1603 in order to keep pace with inflation. Stuart monarchs followed the aggressive foreign policies of their predecessors at a time when the costs of warfare were soaring.

Population pressures also increased tensions in English society. Localities became more factionalized, as seen in the rising numbers of civil litigations, heightened competition to get into college, and the growing number of contested seats for Parliament. Landlessness among the elite became more common because the growing number of male heirs in a family meant that more sons got less land or no land at all. In addition, the percentage of young people in the population grew, and males in their late teens and early twenties joined armies and demonstrated their support of the various political factions. Many turned to Puritanism, a Protestant movement that stressed discipline, sobriety, and morality to cure England's social ills.

Religion became a driving force in the English Revolution. The Stuart monarchs supported the Church of England (Anglican), including its archbishop, William Laud, who from 1637 began implementing policies that were binding on all subjects and seemed to the Puritans reminiscent of Roman Catholic practices. By restricting religious practices only to those of the *Prayer Book* of 1559, the Church of England effectively curtailed or abolished many Puritan observances. Archbishop Laud also promised to restore church lands confiscated and sold over the previous century and to curb lay control over tithes and clerical appointments. Thus, he challenged powerful secular interests. Charles I supported similar policies in Scotland, the land of his birth.

In the late 1620s, Charles I had amassed large debts and continually needed Parliament's sanc-tion to raise new monies. He also antagonized Parliament with high-handed ways, including ruling for more than a decade without its approval. Like his father, Charles believed that kings had a God-given right to rule. In 1640, a Scottish invasion of England and the collapse of the royal army forced Charles to summon a new Parliament, one that inherited the cumulative resentments from previous years. The incompetence of the monarchy in the war against Scotland added urgency to the political crisis.

Parliament's Growing Political Power, 1640–1689

Between 1640 and 1642, Parliament constituted itself as a permanent branch of government and dismantled the monarchy's independent fiscal position and many of its institutions, including the court system that sustained the king's power. John Pym, a fiery orator, often led the debates and decisions against the monarchy.

Although political problems precipitated a dynastic crisis, religious issues also drove the political debate in the legislature. Key members of Parliament believed that England should be governed jointly by the king and Parliament. Thus, arbitrary actions by Charles were seen by these Parliamentarians as threatening the tradition of joint rule. From September 1641 to March 1642, Parliament imposed a Presbyterian form of governance on the Church of England, catalogued its view of the errors of Charles from his first days as king, and placed all military appointments under its own approval. These decisive measures split the legislature and helped catalyze a body of royal adherents who pressed Charles for military action against the Parliamentarians.

The English Civil War (1642–1649) broke out, resulting in the monarch's defeat and confirmation of Parliament's dominance. Yet it also brought into being an army of Parliament that was independent of royal control, a force that slowly emerged as the power broker in English politics. The first phase of civil war set the king against Parliament (he lost), and the second pitted Parliament against a few petty provinces (they lost). Charles I was executed, and a republic was declared in 1649, lasting until 1660. Several forms of rule were attempted, but real power remained in the hands of the army and its commanders, especially Oliver Cromwell

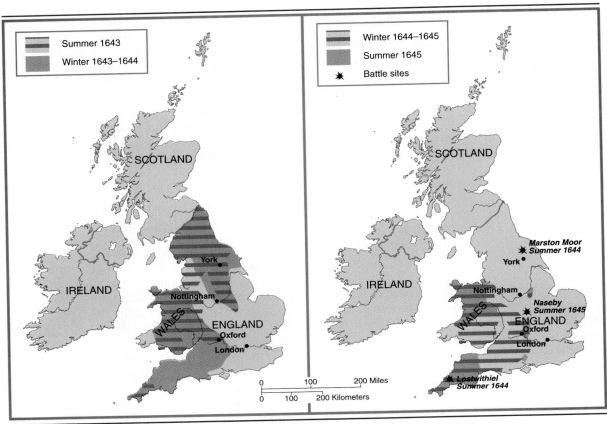

MAP 31.1   *Royalist and Parliament Areas in the English Civil War, 1643–1645.*   *East-ern areas of England generally supported Parliament while the north and west supported the crown. Gradually the north was conquered by the parliamentary army, and, by early 1645, the areas under royal control had shrunk considerably. London remained in Parliament's hands throughout, depriving the crown of a major urban base and revenues associated with it.*

(1599–1658), who was essentially a dictator between 1653 and 1658. Cromwell tried a form of direct military rule that united most of the elite against him, and after Cromwell's death, members of the political elite began plotting a return of the monarchy.

The English political elite invited Charles II, son of the executed monarch, to rule. A quarter-century of peace commenced, during which James II succeeded his brother as king. Though a converted Catholic, James was viewed as more Angli-can in his policies. The birth of a son, who would be raised Roman Catholic, ended the political calm. The English would not tolerate Catholic rule, and James was forced out by the ruling political elite. They turned to James II's Protestant daughter Mary and her Dutch husband, William of Orange.

The peaceful change showed that Parliament made and broke monarchs, confirming the suc-cess of the political and elite revolution. (Members of Parliament had already been part of England's ruling elite.)

William and Mary became joint rulers of Eng-land, but they accepted further limitations on their sovereignty to do so. The Bill of Rights was written, replacing hereditary rights by the will of the nation as expressed through Parliament. The Toleration Act of 1689, which promised freedom of worship to non-Anglican sects, provided guarantees of legal security unprecedented in England. In 1694, Par-liament issued the Triennial Act, designed to com-pel the monarchy to assemble Parliament every three years, and in the next year state censorship was ended. Thus, the English political revolution

FIGURE 31.4 *William and Mary Being Welcomed to London.* Following the fall of James II, Mary and her Dutch husband, William, became the new rulers of England. They were invited to rule partly because they were Protestants and partly because they accepted Parliament's role as a key force in English politics, which helped bring the English Revolution to a successful conclusion. Mary Evans Picture Library.

resulted in a joint rule that favored Parliament and paved the way to the evolution of a constitutional monarchy with the king or queen as a figurehead.

THE ENLIGHTENMENT

The **Enlightenment**, a movement of intellectual change that inspired thinkers in Europe and North America, began largely in the eighteenth century. It aimed to emancipate human reason from what it saw as superstition, prejudice, and the assertiveness of established religions by applying rational thought to social and political reforms. Enlightenment thinkers gathered in salons, academies, universities, reading societies, and clubs to discuss and debate ideas like natural rights, laissez-faire economics, and freedom of the individual. In this process, alliances of like-minded people were formed across elite social classes; ultimately, these

alliances played major roles in the American and French revolutions.

Some Key Enlightenment Ideas and Practices

Building on Newtonian ideas of natural laws regulating the universe, political thinkers argued that natural law was the universal foundation for all law. Natural law comes from human beings, growing out of their communal living. Such things as respect for property, honoring agreements undertaken, and the obligation to compensate for damage are elements of natural law. John Locke, one English thinker discussed in Chapter 29, used natural law to argue that the state rests on a contract between the ruler and the ruled, with each having duties to carry out to meet the needs of society. In the eighteenth century, thinkers added the idea that people have natural rights as well as duties: the right to ownership of property and freedom of

IN THEIR OWN WORDS

Enlightenment Thinkers Examine Racial Equality

Some Enlightenment thinkers used natural law to argue that all human beings are equal. They encouraged Europeans, especially explorers, to treat other peoples with dignity and respect. The following passages were written by a president of the Royal Society of London and a German naturalist and philosopher, both of whom pleaded for respectful treatment of indigenous peoples.

The president of the Royal Society recommended that members of James Cook's expedition around the world be peaceful.

> It should constantly be borne in mind that to shed the blood of these peoples is a capital crime, for we are dealing with human beings from the hand of the same almighty Creator, and are obliged to care for them as much as for the most polished European, in that they are possibly less warlike and more deserving of God's favor. They are the natural, and in a strict sense, the legal owners of the various territories they inhabit. No European nation has any right to occupy any part of that land or to settle there without their freely given consent. The subjugation of such a people cannot confer any convinc-

ing title in law, since they have not acted the part of the aggressor.

Albrecht von Haller, a German naturalist, used natural law to argue that

> Nothing is better calculated to dispel prejudice than an acquaintance with many different nations and their diverse manners, laws, and opinions—a diversity that enables us, however, with little effort to cast aside whatever divides men and to comprehend as the voice of Nature all that they have in common. However uncouth, however primitive the inhabitants of the South Seas islands may be, however remote the Greenlander may be from Brazil or the Cape of Good Hope, the first principles of the law of nature are identical in the case of all nations: to injure no man, to allow every man his due, to seek perfection in one's calling, this was the path to honor with the ancient Romans, and it is . . . the same for . . . the Hottentots [a South African tribe].

Despite these articulate and perceptive arguments for seeing a basic equality among human beings in Early Modern times, most Europeans did not follow this path. They viewed non-Europeans as inferior or even nonhuman and treated them accordingly.

---

conscience. By midcentury, Charles de Montesquieu[1] argued that the best government worked through a system of checks and balances, with no dominant branch.

Natural law was also used to promote the emancipation of women and ethnic groups, for instance Jews. As seen in Chapter 30, women had begun advocating the right to an education. Poulin de Barre[2] published a work on the equality of the sexes in 1673, and, in the seventeenth century, others began applying natural law to argue for gender equality and rights. Aristocratic women had already been elected to local governments in France, and they played prominent roles in salons. Jews also benefited from the application of natural

law to their subordinate status. Works on Jewish political rights were written in 1714 and 1781, and Jews were given full civil rights in British colonies in 1740. In Berlin, Moses Mendelssohn, a Jew, was accepted into a circle of Enlightenment writers, and he soon became a dominant figure.

In both England and France, economists like Adam Smith (1723–1790) applied natural law to economic development. Smith saw the world as a global system and believed that it should become one vast free market that would be self-regulating. Smith asserted that state intervention in economic matters was bad and should be avoided. French economists followed some of Adam Smith's ideas and stressed the importance of agriculture to economic growth. Many of these economic thinkers favored **laissez-faire**—minimal governmental interference in economic development.

[1] **Montesquieu:** mon tehs KYOO
[2] **Poulin de Barre:** POO lahn day BAH ray

The French *Encyclopédie* presented Enlightenment ideas in essay form during the latter half of the eighteenth century. Although more attention will be given to this work in Chapter 32, a few things should be noted here. Denis Diderot became editor of the *Encyclopédie* in 1746, and the first volume of more than thirty came out in 1751. Initially, it was conceived to be a French edition of a British encyclopedia, but Diderot developed a different aim. He secured the best thinkers of his age to write essays on various subjects. Voltaire (1694–1778), perhaps the most brilliant if not the most prolific Enlightenment thinker, wrote essays for the *Encyclopédie*, as did Jean-Jacques Rousseau (1712–1778), who had a significant impact on many leaders of the French Revolution. Rousseau argued that human beings are born free but are held in servitude by despotic states. He advocated government based on the consent of the governed. Jesuits tried to have this encyclopedia banned in France, but they were thwarted by Madame de Pompadour, mistress of the king.

Salons, Academies, and Societies Create Public Opinion

Ideas were important, but they needed to be discussed and widely spread in order to have a significant impact. This happened in Europe and British North America during the eighteenth century in a variety of social groups. By 1789, there were around 150 such societies in Europe alone. Ideas were disseminated even further through journals and correspondence associated with some of these organizations.

Salons appeared in France and were organized by women beginning in late-seventeenth-century Paris. Aristocratic and middle-class women invited men and a few women to have discussions about literature. After the death of Louis XIV in 1715, fundamental issues of politics, society, and economics began to be debated in the salons. Gradually, salons had an impact on the public, as they spread to the provinces as well as to Switzerland and Germany. In Berlin, for example, one popular salon was presided over by Henriette Herz, a Jewish woman.

Academies and royal societies also played a role in disseminating ideas associated with the Enlightenment. France established a society for the cultivation of the French language in 1635 and later added a society for historical studies. The Royal Society of London was founded in 1660, numbering many of Britain's most famous scientists among its members. The Royal Academy of Berlin was founded in 1701 under the auspices of Queen Sophie Charlotte to promote the welfare and reputation of the German nation. The Royal Academy developed a network of correspondents both in Germany and abroad. Many academic societies held meetings at which papers were presented, and they published journals of their proceedings. Books were reviewed in these journals, too. Some others founded more practical societies, like the Dublin Society for the Improvement of Husbandry, Agriculture, and Other Useful Arts.

FIGURE 31.5 *Enlightened Intellectual Discourse.*
This nineteenth-century painting captures the spirit of the Enlightenment by showing Moses Mendelssohn discussing religion with two guests. Mendelssohn, a Jew, was accepted into some gatherings of Enlightenment leaders. This particular scene never occurred, but reflects a challenge presented to him in 1769 to debate the superiority of Judaism over Christianity. Collection of the Judah L. Magnes Museum, Berkeley.

UNDER THE LENS
The Masons in the Enlightenment

The Masonic Order was one of the significant societies of the Enlightenment. It developed an international organization and a tolerant orientation toward other peoples and groups. Many Masonic lodges welcomed Jews as members. Indeed, a key characteristic of Masonry was equality among members.

Originally, the Masons grew out of craft guilds, especially when artisans were joined by nobles, scientists, and surveyors. Consequently, they had a broad social makeup from the beginning. Masons were committed to spreading ideas, and many of their lodges had libraries. In addition, regular correspondence was carried out among various lodges throughout Europe. In the spirit of the guilds and of the humanitarianism characteristic of the Enlightenment, Masons freely helped members in need of assistance. They nursed sick colleagues, provided burial insurance, and supported those burdened by debts.

Many early lodges were founded in England and spread rapidly across Europe in the 1720s and after. By the late 1730s, a papal decree banned Roman Catholics from being members of the Masons. A sec-ond papal decree in 1751 affirmed Catholic opposition to this society of free-thinking people. Many Masons also espoused a religion of nature that was later expressed in a song with the melody attributed to Wolfgang Mozart, himself a Mason.

Let us, then, all hand in hand be joined!
In this, our finest festive hour.
Lead us up to lustrous heights,
And banish all our earthly cares!
That union of our brothers may
Forever firm and splendid stay.

Praise and thanks to God our Master
Who our minds and all our hearts
Inspired to join in endless striving
To bring to earth His Justice, Light, and Virtue
Through the truth our hallowed weapon
May this be our godly task!

You upon our planet here,
The best of men in East and West
And in North as well as South,
Speak the truth and practice virtue,
From the heart love God and man,
Let this be our watchword still!

These organizations enjoyed success in bettering people's lives, but many people felt that more fundamental change was needed.

Reading societies became common in the latter half of the eighteenth century. These organizations were popular in Germany and France and concentrated on improving the general knowledge of the public. Members wanted to spread Enlightenment ideas through discussions and books; most had lending libraries.

REVOLUTION IN BRITISH NORTH AMERICA, 1776–1789

Like the English Revolution, the revolution in British North America brought a change of government; both were political revolutions. The first phase of this American Revolution was concerned with throwing off British rule, and the second phase dealt with the creation of a political system in the form of a limited republic. Much like the ruling class in England, wealthy landowners in America dominated politics.

Building a National Consciousness

In 1765, thirteen English colonies in North America had little in common, yet by 1776 they expressed a united resolve to declare independence from England. English colonies in what is now Canada remained loyal. Much of this nation-building effort came in response to real or imagined transgressions by England. The essential disagreement between the English and their American colonists centered on the massive debt accrued in securing the colonies from French dominion and the English government's desire to see that the settlers assumed a share of the burden.

The English government, including Parliament and king, passed a series of acts to raise funds. In addition, mercantilism supported the domination of the home country over its colonies. Goods shipped between England and the colonies had to travel on English vessels. European products destined for America first landed in England, and customs duties were collected, increasing their prices. This arrangement allowed England to profit from all trade in its colonies.

Americans found the restrictions unbearable when additional fundraising acts were passed by Parliament in the late 1760s. The colonists' cry soon became "no taxation without representation." They were unrepresented in Parliament and believed that they should not have to pay taxes they had had no say in imposing. American boycotts in response to the early acts disrupted trade, compelling England's merchants to pressure their legislators to repeal the acts. In addition, smuggling became a major and well-respected American enterprise.

One major development in the forging of an American identity was the establishment of committees of correspondence. This uniquely American development had kinship with European societies that had members who regularly corresponded with one another. Samuel Adams (1722–1803) formed an early committee during 1772 in Massachusetts, and, within eighteen months, most colonies had followed suit. These committees were clearinghouses for information about the anti-English effort.

Additional punitive acts by England drove some colonists to summon the First Continental Congress, which met for seven weeks in the late summer and fall of 1774. Delegates spent as much time socializing as debating. This proved invaluable because it helped overcome some intercolonial frictions. The First Continental Congress passed a document spelling out detailed plans to implement a general boycott against English goods. A second Congress met in May 1775 in response to hostilities that had broken out in Massachusetts during the previous month. Colonies sent representatives, who selected George Washington (1732–1799) to lead the combined colonial forces. This action consolidated the military effort because Washington, although not a military genius, possessed a flinty determination and projected a moral force.

The War for Independence, 1776–1783

The American Revolution consisted of two wars, an external war and a civil war. The external war initially involved the Americans and the English, but, in 1778, the French entered on behalf of the Americans, and Spain and Holland joined to avenge themselves on the British for earlier wars. The civil war pitted revolutionaries against loyalists, who represented perhaps 35 percent of the population but a much higher percentage of wealthy people. Conflicts occurred everywhere between the American colonists, but most seemed confined to the southern colonies. The result was

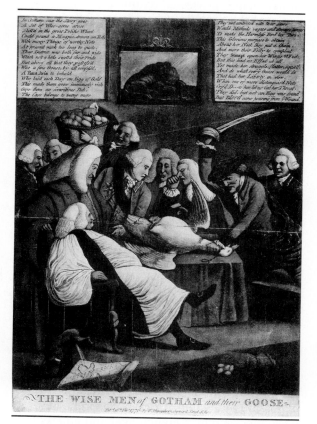

FIGURE 31.6 *Portrayal of the American Revolution.* *This British cartoon satirizes the greed of British cabinet officials who kill the goose (the non-Canadian American colonies) in order to get more than one golden egg per day. Some British were sympathetic to the cause of the American colonists.* The John Carter Brown Library, Brown University.

the expulsion of much of the loyalist population; confiscation of their property was one of the primary motivations behind their decision to relocate. This weakened the established social elite, increasing social equality.

Two writings in 1776 united many Americans in the cause of independence. Thomas Paine (1737–1809), an Englishman who recently had arrived from England, wrote *Common Sense,* a pamphlet that succinctly argued for independence. America's first bestseller, it reached a distribution of 120,000 copies. The second piece, the Declaration of Independence, has been called the most important document in American history. Largely written by Thomas Jefferson, it explained the American case for severing ties with England. Arguing from the natural-law philosophy that human beings possessed natural rights to life, liberty, and the pursuit of happiness, Jefferson put the Congress's position into a larger interpretative framework in tune with Enlightenment ideas. He showed how King George III of England violated these natural rights by a series of tyrannous misdeeds. After the Declaration was amended, it was finally adopted on July 4, 1776.

Fighting continued throughout the colonies. From 1775 to 1777, the main task of Washington and other commanders was to maintain armies in the field. With secret French assistance, the American military effort survived. Then, in the summer of 1777, an English campaign to take New York and sever New England from the rest of the separatist colonies failed, enticing the French to support the colonists openly. With the able diplomatic leadership of Benjamin Franklin, the American ambassador to France, the French committed their armed forces to the war.

Washington barely managed to keep his tattered army from disintegrating in the harsh winter of 1777–1778. He enjoyed some victories and suffered defeats in the north, while his colleagues participated in heavy fighting in the south. In 1781, the English commander, Lord Charles Cornwallis, blundered into a trap at Yorktown, Virginia. After a naval blockade by a French fleet and attacks by a combined American and French army, Cornwallis surrendered. Peace negotiations took place from 1782 to 1783, when the Treaty of Paris was signed. Independence was secured in a territory of the original thirteen colonies, including a region west to the Mississippi River, north to the Great Lakes,

and south to Florida. The British firmly held on to their more profitable colonies in the Caribbean and India.

Social Aspects of the War for Independence

People of modest means and social position yielded to merchants and landowners in the war and nation-building effort. Men of property dominated the Continental Congresses and assumed leadership of the war effort. Common people assumed a lesser political role, and the mass of women and slaves exercised little influence.

The committees of correspondence and the Continental Congresses included those who could read and write or who enjoyed substantial financial means. Many people were literate, but most depended on others to decipher written materials. Schools remained the preserve of the well-to-do, and widespread education came some decades after the war for independence. Education became a great equalizing force for common folk.

Although the Declaration of Independence included the statement that "all men are created equal," most American leaders believed in the superiority of men and whites. They believed that white males of some property were a superior group. The right to vote, for example, was extended only to those who owned property. Jefferson himself owned slaves for his entire adult life, and many other delegates also had slaves, who did not enjoy liberty and the pursuit of happiness. Earlier, in 1774, the First Continental Congress had called for the abolition of the slave trade, and many states followed its lead. Some northern states either abolished slavery or provided for the gradual emancipation of slaves; Pennsylvania formed the first antislavery society in the Americas in 1775. Because of the need to maintain unity among the colonies, references to the liberation of African Americans were stricken from the final version of the Declaration. American Indians also received no mention in the historic document. Among the various tribes, the Iroquois remained staunchly loyal to the English, while the Algonquians and the Cherokees backed the Americans.

Women, too, did not enjoy equal rights. Abigail Adams chided her husband, John, a drafter of the Declaration, not to forget the women. But the pertinent words "that all men are created equal"

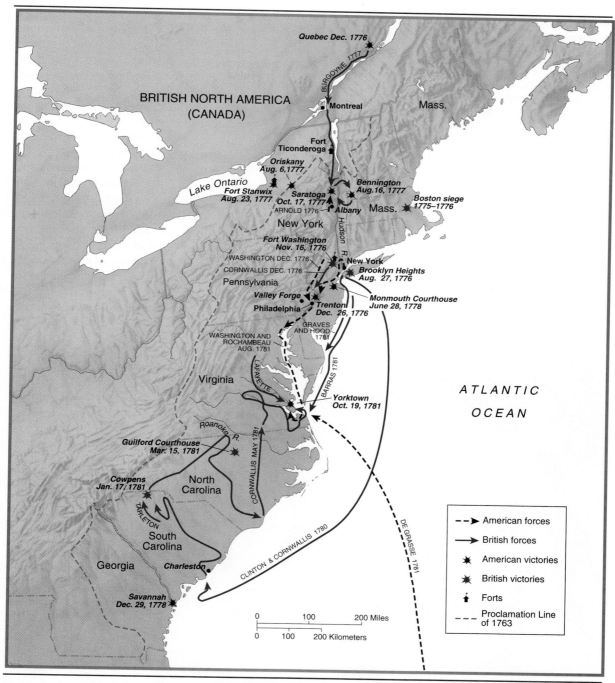

MAP 31.2 *Battles of the American War for Independence, 1776–1781.* *Many battles were fought in the American colonies, both in the north and south. A key need of the rebels was to keep military forces in the field to avoid defeat. The Battle of Saratoga was especially significant because it thwarted a British effort to sever New England from the other colonies; in addition, France thereafter gave important aid to the rebels. Another campaign of major importance was the taking of Yorktown resulting in the surrender of the British forces there. French ships played a key part in the American victory by preventing the British navy from supporting British land forces.*

suggest that Mrs. Adams's advice was ignored. Women, however, were expected to teach the values of good citizenship to their children. Women played very little role in combat activities, though a few disguised themselves as men and served in the colonial armies. Others made saltpeter for gunpowder, hid soldiers, and supported their families when their husbands were away fighting.

Creating a Constitutional Government, 1783–1789

Winning independence was only the first step in a lengthy process of nation building. The national consciousness that emerged in the early days of the independence struggle dissipated after the war. The framework of government proved to be a troubling issue because the Articles of Confederation adopted by the Second Continental Congress in 1777 failed to gain unanimous approval until 1781. It provided for a congress along with thirteen independent states. Having control of commerce, taxation, and judicial matters, the states remained suspicious of a strong, national system. Problems in the 1780s, including a failed rebellion in Massachusetts, caused men of property to work for a stronger central government. They met in 1786 and persuaded the congress to approve the gathering of a group of delegates elected by the states to amend the Articles of Confederation.

In 1787, fifty-five delegates representing twelve states convened in Philadelphia and for seventeen weeks hammered out a new governmental framework. George Washington, Benjamin Franklin, James Madison, and Alexander Hamilton decided to abandon the old system and create a new one. They fashioned a series of compromises. One body of the legislative branch was the House of Representatives, and its representation was based on population. The other body, the Senate,

FIGURE 31.7 *George Washington Addressing the Constitutional Convention.* *In 1787, delegates gathered to improve the existing political system based on the Articles of Confederation—instead, they created the Constitution. George Washington, hero of the War for Independence, was chosen head of the convention. This painting by Junius B. Stearns captures the solemnity of the meeting, which was attended by many of the Republic's leading figures, including James Madison, Alexander Hamilton, and Benjamin Franklin.* Gift of Edgar William and Bernice Chrysler Garbisch. Photo by Ron Jennings © Virginia Museum of Fine Arts, Richmond, Va.

had two representatives per state. Representatives were elected by a direct-voting process; the senators were selected by state legislatures. An executive branch was formed with a president as commander-in-chief of the armed forces. The president also came to power by an indirect election process; voters selected electors (by state), who assembled and voted. A system of checks and balances like the one favored by Montesquieu emerged, so that no one branch could dominate the others. When the new system emerged from secret sessions, it was to take effect after ratification by nine of the thirteen states.

Americans were shocked by the result of this revolutionary process, and it took several months of debate before the Constitution was approved. Supporters of the new system were known as Federalists, those who contested the outcome as anti-Federalists. James Madison, Alexander Hamilton, and John Jay wrote the *Federalist Papers* to convince New Yorkers to support the Constitution, and the essays represented some of the most significant commentaries on the new document. In 1788, after New Hampshire became the ninth state to ratify the document, preparations commenced to implement the new system. Within a year, George Washington assumed the presidency and created the instruments of government, such as the Departments of State, Treasury, and War. The House of Representatives and the Senate convened and passed the Bill of Rights, the first ten amendments to the Constitution, completing the process of forging a government that had begun in 1776.

THE FRENCH REVOLUTION, 1789–1804

Unlike the English and American revolutions, the French Revolution triggered massive violence and more significant social and political change. In 1789, France had been bankrupted by its international diplomacy. This failure coincided with growing unrest, owing to a surge of population growth. Many French thinkers admired the American struggle against England and appreciated the ideas represented in the Declaration of Independence. They longed to create a French government with similar governing ideals and practices.

Global Causes of France's Bankruptcy

Louis XIV created an absolutist state and promoted French colonialism and France's domination of Europe. These policies continued under his two successors but became more difficult to sustain. Apart from the great expenses necessary to support a large army and navy and to build a palace, increasing failure reduced the confidence of the regime's supporters. Some officials who purchased their offices were forced to pay additional sums in order to stay in power, and they became demoralized and angry at the monarchy. Economic bankruptcy and a crisis of confidence undermined the legitimacy of the traditional system.

The determination of French monarchs to rule without much consultation created an atmosphere of social and political tension. The state, for example, used the craft guilds and peasant villages as agents of regulation and control of their members. Yet these bodies inhibited the commercial and agricultural growth necessary to underwrite government programs. Taxes grew, but the taxpayers, especially members of the middle class and rural landowners, refused to pay more until they were brought into the system of governing.

Demographic Problems

Population growth exploded between 1730 and 1789, causing severe problems. Inflation increased because the outmoded agricultural system could not produce enough food to keep prices low enough for the poor. A larger population threatened already fragile food supplies. Rising prices and rents combined with lowering wages to severely pinch the poor in cities and especially in rural areas. Inflation drove up the state's expenses, but agrarian problems kept revenues low. In addition, large numbers of aristocrats and merchants enjoyed tax-exempt status, limiting the state's revenue base.

The immediate economic situation from 1788 to 1789 intensified the regime's crisis. Intermittently poor harvests in the 1770s and 1780s culminated in a disastrous grain harvest in 1788. A glut in the wine grape harvest triggered a collapse of grape prices, ruining many peasants who depended on the wine industry for all their income. The grain shortage increased the price of bread by more than 50 percent between August 1788 and February 1789. This caused sporadic and increasing levels of violence.

Collapse of the Monarchy and Upheaval, 1789–1795

Between 1789 and 1795, France saw the demise of its monarchy and the onset of internal and external war. The antiroyal and antiaristocratic nature of the revolutionary changes caused most major European states to fight France, fearing that such ideas might spread. To fight a broad array of opponents, revolutionaries mobilized nearly all adult males. By 1795, the excesses of terror by both factions had been curbed, and a new time of peace and stability dawned.

In 1788, Louis XVI had been warned that France faced economic bankruptcy if he failed to reform the government, and he had haphazardly groped for a solution to the growing crisis. By the fall of 1788, Louis had called for elections to convene an Estates General, a representative body that had not been summoned in 170 years. The Estates General was composed of three estates. The First Estate included representatives of the clergy and had many factions; it generally agreed that the existing system no longer worked. The Second Estate representatives were aristocrats. A wide range of political opinion could be found in the estate, but most wished for political change. Members of the Third Estate, everyone else in French society, had factions that desired a larger political role and more access to government positions.

Political maneuvering in the fall of 1788 brought to the fore divisions within estates, as well as among estates. Two issues centered on how many members were to represent each estate and whether the voting on issues should be by estate or by representatives. After the judicial court of Paris, a bastion of aristocratic power, ruled that each estate should have equal representation, a loose alliance of members of the three estates argued that the number of Third Estate representatives should equal those of the other two estates. Using ideas discussed in salons, they wished to reconstruct the Estates General into a national assembly. Although the king disagreed with part of the alliance's argument, he doubled the Third Estate's number of representatives.

Elections took place in early 1789 with 326 clergy selected for the First Estate, 330 aristocrats for the Second Estate, and 661 members of the Third Estate. Most of this last group were landowners and lawyers, many of whom were most hostile to the existing government and to elite members of the estates. The political struggle ended with the formation of the National Assembly in June 1789, when members of the three estates agreed to meet as a single body. A feeble monarchical response failed, and the National Assembly emerged.

Elections also stirred up commoners, who began to take matters into their own hands. Parisians stormed the Bastille, a largely abandoned prison, on July 14, 1789, thereafter celebrated as France's independence day. Rumors in the rural areas incited peasants to burn aristocratic manors and kill nobles. This uprising sparked a response in the National Assembly, where on August 4 members of the nobility and clergy renounced their special privileges.

The following year, the National Assembly produced a raft of significant changes. On August 27, 1789, they presented the Declaration of the Rights of Man and the Citizen as a statement of political principles. Among the ideas it expressed, drawn from concepts of natural law, were

— that men were born free and equal in rights;
— that states existed to protect these rights;
— that political sovereignty resided in the nation and its representatives;
— that due process of law and presumption of innocence existed;
— that all had freedom of religion; and
— that property was a sacred and inviolable right.

These Enlightenment ideals became hallmarks of the revolution. As in the American Revolution, women and slaves were not considered free or equal to free men.

In a controversial decision, the National Assembly seized church lands and other property, putting them up for sale. This action raised revenue and created a group of landholders with a stake in the success of the revolution. In the summer of 1790, the National Assembly passed the Civil Constitution of the Clergy, whereby the clergy

FIGURE 31.8 **The Tennis Court Oath.** *Jacques-Louis David became a major figure in the French Revolution through his paintings capturing famous events. Here he shows the heroism exhibited on June 20, 1789, when members of the Third Estate, along with a few members of other estates, vowed to meet as the National Assembly—the legislature of France—in defiance of the king. Most figures are given dramatic poses; some clearly are overcome with emotion.* Musée Carnavalet/Giraudon/Art Resource, N.Y.

served at the government's pleasure and had to swear loyalty to the state. Many clergy opposed these measures and rallied their parishes against the revolutionary government.

A Legislative Assembly, composed entirely of new representatives, met between 1790 and 1792, embroiling France in an external war with Prussia and Austria. Turmoil and fear of invasion propelled many radical leaders to the forefront and undermined the moderates. Maximilien Robespierre (1758–1794), for example, became increasingly influential among the lower middle classes. Robespierre headed an organization of **Jacobins**, individuals who wanted the broadest male voting

franchise, abolition of the monarchy, and price controls. Jacobin clubs followed a social pattern of the Enlightenment and evolved into a political movement.

The National Convention succeeded the Legislative Assembly in 1792 as the war worsened. The extension of the vote to most adult Frenchmen meant that the well-organized Jacobins elected many delegates. After Louis's failed effort to flee France in mid-1791, he was regarded as an enemy of the revolutionary government. He was eventually tried and convicted of treason. Louis XVI was executed in 1793, and his queen, Marie Antoinette, followed some months later.

Growing civil unrest and a poorly fought external war caused the National Convention to create a highly centralized government with much power resting in the Committee of Public Safety. This body of the National Convention instituted a national draft, implemented a merit system of military promotion, organized the supply of the army, implemented wage and price controls, and launched a reign of terror.

Terror, the deliberate use of massive force to cow or eliminate opponents, was used by revolutionists and antirevolutionists alike. It grew out of Rousseau's ideas of the general will of the people dominating the lives of individuals as well as from the French political practice of indivisible sovereignty (absolutism). Most absolutist governments had used terror to maintain control of the people. Because French absolutism had been toppled by the revolution and the revolutionaries had taken a doctrinaire political stand, control became important. In the face of the failure of state institutions to compel compliance with laws and decrees, revolutionaries resorted to terror. Fear helped discipline the army of draftees, intimidated many of the state's enemies, and furthered state control over rebellious regions. One area of western France launched a fierce resistance to the new order and suffered brutal atrocities at the hands of the revolutionaries.

In the face of terror, some people adopted grotesque forms of behavior in attempts to defuse the devastating psychological impact. A few donned human-skin clothing. A popular dance form included a peculiar drop of the head that mimicked a head falling from the guillotine. Some wore red bands around their necks, symbolizing cut throats.

In the summer of 1794, the crises had been surmounted, and the Committee of Public Safety ruled with power undreamed of a few years before. Robespierre gained power through purges sanctioned by the National Convention, but his frequent reprisals created enemies. In late July, he was voted out of office. He fell prey to the very policies he had championed and died by the guillotine after bungling a suicide attempt. The tide turned against the Jacobins and their supporters, some of whom were executed, exiled, or forced into hiding.

The revolution had fundamentally altered the political structure of France. The monarchy was abolished, feudalism was swept away, and the aris-

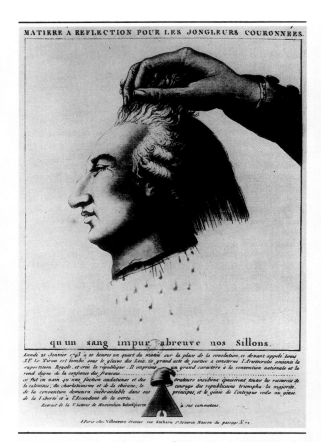

FIGURE 31.9 *The Fate of King Louis XVI. In this political cartoon, the severed head of France's former ruler is displayed over an inscription that carries a warning to the other monarchs of Europe—beware of the French example. At the bottom is an extract from a letter by Maximilien Robespierre to his constituents, saying that the execution proves the resolution of the French government and its worthiness to have the respect of the people.* Bibliothèque nationale, Paris.

tocracy was shattered; decision making resided with the people, the clergy lost their powerful political and social positions, and obstacles to central power had been swept aside.

Social Features of the Early Revolution

The opening stage of the revolution (1789–1795) brought many social changes and experiments, some of which endured. Revolutionaries followed Enlightenment ideas of reorganizing and of secularizing society. Another social consequence was the diminishment of the status of women. Finally, greater social equality among men emerged during the early revolution.

One rational innovation concerned time. The radical leaders of 1792–1794 decided to change the French calendar to show the newness of their sociopolitical experiment. They redesignated 1793 as the year 1 and renamed each of the months. The month of July, for example, was renamed Thermidore. Controlling one's reckoning of time was a powerful way to demonstrate dominance by the state. It also decisively broke with the traditional Christian numeration of years. This particular experiment did not endure and was abandoned later.

Another rational transformation concerned weights and measurements. The basis for the new system was the number ten; this was the decimal system. The meter became the standard linear measure, the liter became the standard volume measure, and the gram became the standard weight measure. This change facilitated trade because amounts and values could be easily and speedily calculated. Most of the world today uses the metric system.

Women suffered a loss of influence relative to that which they had enjoyed for decades. As early as the sixteenth and seventeenth centuries, some aristocratic women who owned property had been elected to provincial assemblies. And we have seen how some women of the aristocracy and middle class played a key role in leading salon discussions that developed French public opinion favorable to Enlightenment ideas. Jacobins and more radical revolutionaries believed with Rousseau that the eighteenth century was tainted by a "feminization" of society. A few feminists were executed by guillotine or publicly whipped as a warning to others. Women were forbidden to gather in groups of five or more, and they were banned from sitting in the galleries of the National Convention. Thus, the revolutionaries systematically drove women out of politics and back into the home to care for the young, educating their sons to be patriotic citizens.

The Directory, 1795–1799

The National Convention was transformed into a mixed government with two legislative houses and an executive branch that was elected from the upper house. The electorate was sharply reduced to around 20 percent of adult males. From 1795 to 1799, the **Directory**, a group of five men who ran the executive branch, ruled France in conjunction with the legislature. The policies of the new government favored the survivors of the elite groups; they also cut off the needy from state subsidies.

Challenges troubled the new regime, but the real threat turned out to be the army and one of its generals, Napoleon Bonaparte (1769–1821). By the end of two years in power, Directory members and local officials had become corrupt and ineffective. Finally, a coup by Napoleon toppled the Directory in November 1799.

Napoleon Bonaparte Builds a Modern State, 1799–1804

Napoleon rose to power and ruled ably until his fall in 1815. He came from Corsica and entered the French military as a teenager. By choosing artillery as a military career and by outstanding service, he became a general by his mid-twenties. The high number of battlefield deaths and desertions among officers opened the way for the rapid advancement of Napoleon and others. His alignment with the Jacobins aided his career, until their fall in the summer of 1794. Loyalty to the Directors in 1795 brought Napoleon command of the French army in Italy, where he brilliantly distinguished himself as a strategist. A campaign in Egypt in 1798, however, failed miserably and Napoleon abandoned his army in the Egyptian desert. Nevertheless, he was given a hero's welcome when he arrived back in France.

After the coup that brought him to power in 1799, Napoleon embarked on a program of stabilizing France by creating a centralized state and fashioning a hierarchical system whose officials were appointed from Paris. Bureaucrats enjoyed generous salaries and lofty status as representatives of the government in the administrative districts. Forty percent of Napoleonic high officials had been nobles under the former monarchy. Reenfranchising the aristocracy that had worked against previous regimes lent stability to the new government. A more efficient tax levy and collection system, coupled with a central bank, created a stable currency. The Code of Napoleon, a law code, fashioned a law-based government that accorded personal liberty, equality before the law, and the protection of property. It also codified the subordination of women to men. In 1802, an agreement with the pope provided for the preeminence of Roman Catholicism in France, but it insisted on state rather than papal control of the clergy. Napoleon also created a new social hierarchy based on state service. Officials were to be trained in schools, and top officials were permitted to enter the nobility. Nearly 60 percent of those who attained noble status were from the middle class, while 20 percent of the new nobles came from the lower class. To keep dissent under control, the state enforced censorship and built an effective police force.

Napoleon capped his achievements in 1804 by crowning himself emperor of France, launching a military campaign to control Europe. Despite several victories, Napoleon met major defeats in Spain, Russia, and Belgium. More than 500,000 soldiers from Napoleon's army perished in Russia alone. By 1815, Napoleon had consolidated the French Revolution, building a modern state in the process. The French Revolution was a social revolution with strong populist (early) and elite (late) elements.

REVOLUTION IN LATIN AMERICA, 1810–1824

The Napoleonic Wars indirectly affected Latin America when Napoleon ousted the Spanish and Portuguese monarchs and placed his own brothers on their thrones. These actions by the French emperor sparked the **Creoles**, the Spanish elite in Central America and South America, to fight for independence. African slaves in the French colony of Haiti also revolted and successfully established an independent government. By 1824, nearly all of Latin America lay in the hands of independent governments that ranged from republics to monarchies.

Liberation Wars

Anger against Spanish mercantilism and other colonial policies had been building among the local elite during the late eighteenth and early nineteenth centuries (see Chapter 24). Spanish control of the Latin American colonies created an environment of trade that benefited Spain rather than the colonies. This caused resentment among the Creoles, much as similar policies had angered

FIGURE 31.10 *Napoleon on His Throne.* *This portrait captures the majesty of Napoleon Bonaparte, ruler of France, in full imperial regalia. As shown, he conveys a sense of power of person. The icy stare and smooth facial features seem more like sculpture than human flesh. Before the throne is an eagle—the "emperor" of the skies and symbol of Napoleon.* Musée de l'Armée/Laurie Platt Winfrey, Inc.

North American colonists. The local elite also resented the Spanish reliance on officials sent from Spain. These officials, considered interlopers from the local point of view, quickly monopolized many top positions that had formerly been filled by locals.

Ideas from the Enlightenment filtered into Latin America and encouraged the restive members of the elite to seek redress by self-rule. Only when Napoleon's brother sat on the throne of Spain did the Creoles act.

Two key leaders in South America, Simón Bolívar[3] (1783–1830) and José de San Martín[4] (1778–1850), spearheaded independence drives. Bolívar spent most of his time in Venezuela and Colombia fighting against the Spanish royalists and occasionally against rebellious slaves who wished to be liberated. Between 1810 and 1824, the effort experienced ups and downs, and opponents ousted Bolívar's government. Bolívar also conquered Colombia and additional lands later called Bolivia (named after Bolívar) by 1824. Unlike Bolívar, who favored republican government, San Martín leaned toward monarchy. San Martín began his campaign by liberating what came to be Argentina, and in 1817, his army crossed the Andes Mountains to help liberate Chile. San Martín moved northward and conquered Peru, over which he established a protectorate. By 1822, the joint forces of Bolívar and San Martín freed Ecuador, although the two leaders bitterly quarreled over what form of government to implement.

Generally, members of the social and economic elite favored a government akin to that found in contemporary England. These conservatives feared sharing power with the slaves and the few members of the middle class, so little changed politically. Soon, however, most Latin American governments abolished slavery or promised to do so in the near future.

Brazilian and Mexican Independence

Brazil followed a different path. During the upheaval of the post-Napoleonic era, an uprising drove the Portuguese monarch from Portugal to Brazil. Because the Brazilian elite had few resentments against the monarchy, they preferred to retain a king until late in the nineteenth century. Only then did the elite topple the monarchy and implement a republic with themselves in power. In addition, because many members of the elite had plantations, slavery endured in Brazil.

Mexico saw a few abortive efforts to gain independence. The first attempts involved an uprising led by two priests. One was a Creole, Father Miguel

FIGURE 31.11 *Simón Bolívar.* *Simón Bolívar helped to liberate many South American countries. In this painting, his uniform and his tight control of the horse clearly convey a sense of command.* Courtesy of the Organization of American States.

Hidalgo y Costilla,[5] and the other was a *mestizo* (of mixed Spanish and Native American blood), Father José María Morelos y Pavón.[6] They fomented social as well as political unrest from 1811 to 1815, when the royalists and local elites finally crushed the revolutionary force of African slaves, Indians, and *mestizos*. This victorious alliance sup-

---

[3] **Simón Bolívar:** see MOHN BOH lee vahr
[4] **José de San Martín:** HOH zay day sahn mahr TEEN

[5] **Miguel Hidalgo y Costilla:** mee GEHL ee DAHL goh ee coh STEE yah
[6] **Pavón:** pah VOHN

MAP 31.3 *Revolution in Latin America, 1804–1825.* *Liberation in Latin America often came through military conquest. The Haitian Revolution began with a slave uprising against France, followed by a war of resistance. Argentina and Paraguay were liberated a few years later. Other states appeared in the aftermath of the Napoleonic wars which weakened Spain and gave hope to Latin Americans. Chile, Colombia, Peru, and Bolivia all fell to invading forces. By 1825, most of Latin America had become independent.*

ported the Spanish government until a monarch who favored the establishment of representative institutions ascended to the Spanish throne. Fearing a diminution of their political and social power, the elite supported a former royalist commander, Agustin de Iturbide,[7] who declared and won independence for Mexico. Although Iturbide formed a short-lived monarchy, rule by the social and political elite continued and dominated Mexico and much of Central America.

Thus, the revolutions in Latin America were political revolutions with an elite character. The exception was the populist social revolution in

[7] **Agustin de Iturbide:** ah GUS tyn dee ee TUHR bee deh

Haiti. Like the U.S. and English revolutions, most Latin American revolutions changed the political system and little else.

JAPAN'S MEIJI REVOLUTION, 1868–1895

Like Peter the Great of Russia, a group of Japanese *samurai* (warriors) forged an elite revolution. They transformed their political, social, economic, and cultural systems far more profoundly than did the revolutions in Europe and the Americas. The Japanese case involved more of a group effort,

PARALLELS AND DIVERGENCES

China's Taiping Uprising (1850–1864): An Abortive Revolution

History's largest uprising convulsed China in the mid-1800s, forcing the gentry elite to mobilize all of its resources to defeat the revolutionaries. Whole sections of populous Central China were devastated by the titanic conflict, and one scholar estimated that more than 20 million Chinese perished.

The Taiping Uprising grew out of the teachings of Hong Xiuquan[a] (1814–1864), who believed he was the younger brother of Jesus Christ. Hong took and failed the imperial examinations five times. After his fourth failure, Hong had a nervous breakdown and became catatonic for forty days. Later, he interpreted the event as his being taken to heaven, meeting God, and being introduced to Jesus, his older brother. According to Hong, God gave him a sword and told him to exterminate the "demons," the Manchu rulers of China.

Hong formed the God-Worshipers Society and gathered poor people by promising them a kind of heaven on earth. Hong's ideas contained a crude mixture of Christian beliefs and traditional Chinese thought. The combustible combination exploded across southern and central China during a time of massive population growth that overwhelmed the traditional social system. Hong created a shared-property system and smashed Buddhist and Confucian temples, deeply angering the gentry.

Women were elevated in social standing in the Taiping movement. In contrast to traditional Chinese practices, they could own property, hold office, take exams, choose their own husbands, and fight. A Taiping female army marched with the main force, numbering perhaps 100,000 and obeying female officers.

The Taiping rulers decreed abstinence from tobacco, alcohol, drugs, and gambling. The Taipings also decreed gender separation for all but the leaders for the new government's first several years. The policy seems directed at protecting women from rapacious men, but it also may have aimed at breaking up the family, because husbands could not even visit their wives. The Taipings wanted the complete energy and loyalty of their followers.

The Taipings moved north and picked up strength in the populated areas of Central China. Major cities, including Nanjing, China's second most important city, fell to them. Control of a prosperous area corrupted the Taipings, who lost their revolutionary momentum. In 1851, the Manchu rulers of the Qing Empire mobilized armies against the Taipings, eventually crushing them. The Taiping effort drowned in a sea of blood, and the minor changes it wrought soon disappeared.

[a]**Hong Xiuquan:** HOHNG SHOO choo wahn

---

reflecting the longstanding Japanese cultural value of consensus. Finally, the Japanese fashioned a modern, Western-style state, one that was highly centralized.

The Western Model

Japanese *samurai* had ruled Japan since the twelfth century, and a group of them continued to dominate the political system until the early twentieth century. The desire to overthrow the Tokugawa Shogunate in 1868 arose in four disaffected regions, Satsuma, Tosa, Choshu, and Hizen.[8] The effort involved a group of lower-class *samurai* who had risen to prominence by their ability rather than by birth. This clique determined that the existing, discredited shogunal government needed to be thrown out and replaced by an imperial one. Both institutions had existed in the Tokugawa era, but emperors had been powerless. These *samurai* dissolved the shogunate and shifted power to the monarchy. The teenage Emperor Meiji[9] (reign dates 1867–1912) merely sat on the throne, while power transferred to the lower *samurai* and their court allies. Rule from behind the scenes had been a traditional feature of Japanese politics.

[8] **Hizen:** HEE zehn

[9] **Meiji:** MEH jee

FIGURE 31.12 *Japanese Leaders Going Abroad.*
This image reflects the determination of Japan's leaders to learn about the world. Between 1871 and 1873, over 100 Japanese leaders and students traveled the globe, especially the West. They brought goodwill and the hope of revising unfavorable treaties imposed on Japan by Western states. Despite their failure to win equal diplomatic status, the Japanese learned much about other countries, giving them a basis on which to Westernize their own. The dress of the people mixes traditional Japanese styles with Western attire, capturing the old-new dichotomy of mid-nineteenth-century Japan.
ET Archive.

The new rulers embarked on a program of Westernization and industrialization aimed at strengthening Japan in the briefest possible time. Within the Charter Oath, a statement of principles of the new government, lay sentiments favoring studying the West and building a representative government. Behind these was the pragmatic realization that unless Japan strengthened itself, it

might perish in conquest by Westerners. Another compelling force was a nationalism fed by the sense that tiny Japan lay as a mouth-watering prize to be gobbled up by Western powers. As the rulers saw it, only an imperial government that commanded the people's loyalty could accomplish societal transformation.

After abolishing the decentralized regional governments and fashioning a highly centralized polity in Tokyo, many top leaders left Japan from 1871 to 1873 on a grand diplomatic and learning tour of the West. Soon the government established new administrative areas and appointed officials answerable only to the central government to administer them. Then, about fifty top leaders departed Japan on a diplomatic mission whose purpose included the revision of a series of unequal treaties imposed on Japan by various Western powers. The diplomatic effort failed, but the leaders learned some reasons for the economic and political dominance of the Western countries. The Japanese visited factories, legislatures, shipyards, and museums, and when they returned they committed Japan to a rapid, elite-directed transformation. This mission closely resembled that of Peter the Great in 1697 and 1698.

Social and Cultural Changes

One of the most remarkable transformations involved society. For the previous two centuries or more, one's occupation was frozen and became the determinant of one's social position. At the top, for instance, the *samurai* ruled, while at the bottom, the merchants languished. Believing that this system inhibited the development of one's individual talent, the Meiji leaders abolished this caste system. By that action, they overturned the elite status of their own *samurai* group. All people, henceforth, had to exert their own energy to succeed, and adventuresome people could flourish in business, education, and the military.

Government leaders also created a system of universal education that built on the already high literacy rates of around 40 percent for males and around 10 percent for females. The education system welcomed students of both genders and provided for a trained population to undertake the tasks necessary for building a modern Japan.

Japanese culture underwent similar dramatic changes as a small group of government officials and private people ardently promoted Western

EUROPE	AMERICAS	JAPAN		
			1500	Copernicus dies, 1543
Scientific Revolution, 1543–1727				
			1600	Galileo dies, 1642 Charles I executed, 1649
Enlighten-ment, c. 1600–c. 1780				
English Revolution, 1640–1689				Newton publishes *Principia Mathematica*, 1689
			1700	
	American Revolution, 1776–1789			Adam Smith publishes *The Wealth of Nations*, 1776 George Washington becomes president, 1789
French Revolution, 1789–1804			**1800**	Concordat with Rome, 1801 San Martín helps liberate Chile, 1817
	Revolutions in Latin America, 1810–1824			
		Meiji Revolution, 1868–1895		Iwakura embassy departs Japan, 1871 Japan wins Sino-Japanese War, 1895
			1900	

culture. Fukuzawa Yukichi[10] (1835–1901), a Japanese intellectual, traveled to Western lands and wrote a series of bestselling pamphlets and books. Indeed, he introduced whole generations of Japanese to Western ideas. The Society of Meiji Six (1873) included a mix of governmental and private individuals who met regularly and who popularized Western ideas. Translation of Western authors became a major occupation, and *Self Help*, an English work written by Samuel Smiles, sold around one million copies. Traditional Japanese works and practices experienced a temporary eclipse in the frenetic drive to Westernize.

Building a Modern State

The elite revolution unsettled many and sparked challenges to the new order. Assassination claimed a number of officials who had guided the Meiji transformation from 1873 to 1878. Planned revolts caused additional disturbances, and the most serious effort centered in Satsuma, one of the leading Meiji strongholds. Saigo Takamori[11] (1833–1877), a mighty Satsuma warrior who had led the imperial forces in 1868, became disaffected with government policy in 1873 and left politics. As the *samurai* suffered a series of blows that deprived them of elite identity, many rallied around Saigo. By 1877,

the Satsuma Uprising erupted and was defeated by the new imperial army of peasant conscripts. The counterrevolutionary uprising failed.

In 1881, government leaders decided to create a constitutional system, modeled on the German Empire, and Ito Hirobumi[12] crafted a document that would keep power in the hands of the ruling elite. About the same time, outdated Japanese legal codes were rewritten to fashion a law-based society, again patterned after that of the Germans. The new system took effect in the 1890s, and a series of political struggles between the Meiji rulers and leaders of political parties erupted. The latter successfully inserted themselves into the ruling structure, proving the viability of the Western-style polity.

The Japanese industrial effort (see Chapter 32) provided an increasingly powerful armed force. One test of the Japanese achievement came in the Sino-Japanese War (1894–1895), in which the Japanese military simply overwhelmed the Chinese. And around a decade later, the Japanese military defeated the Russians in the Russo-Japanese War (1904–1905). These victories seemed to confirm the Japanese way of revolution and began the building of a colonial empire. Japan's social revolution transformed all aspects of Japanese life and was led by the *samurai* elite.

SUMMARY

1. Revolution is a process whereby fundamental structural change occurs. Occasionally a nonviolent transformation, like the Scientific Revolution, takes place, but most revolutions are violent. Types of revolution include political, economic, intellectual, and social. Another way to analyze revolution is to determine the character of the revolutionary leadership. Thus, there are elite and populist (mass-based) revolutions. Rebellions may involve widespread violence, but they differ from revolutions in that the rebels seek to change leaders rather than structures.

2. The English Revolution transformed the government by elevating Parliament and de-

emphasizing the monarchy through civil war and political upheaval, including the execution of King Charles I.

3. The Enlightenment was an eighteenth-century intellectual and social movement that stressed the use of reason to expose and reform presumedly outmoded political, social, and religious practices. Enlightenment ideas were spread through salons, academies, and associations in the development of public opinion.

4. The American Revolution involved the winning of independence from England and the building of a centralized republican government. This revolution was dominated by landowners and merchants.

[10]**Fukuzawa Yukichi:** FOO koo zah wah yoo KEE chee
[11]**Saigo Takamori:** SY goh TAH kah moh ree

[12]**Ito Hirobumi:** EE toh HEE roh boo mee

5. The French Revolution emerged from the collapse of the enfeebled autocracy and swept away feudalism. Various revolutionary governments were installed until the modern state was founded by Napoleon Bonaparte between 1799 and 1804.

6. Latin America had a series of political revolutions whereby the propertied elite groups wrested power from the home countries and cre-ated polities that they themselves dominated. Uprisings by lower social groups were crushed. The exception was Haiti, where slaves won their independence from France and built a revolutionary order. It was a social and populist revolution.

7. Japan used an elite revolution to modernize and Westernize itself. Fundamental changes took place in society, elite culture, and politics.

SUGGESTED READINGS

Goldstone, Jack. *Revolution and Rebellion in the Early Modern World*. Berkeley: University of California Press, 1991. A fruitful synthesis of revolutionary studies in a comparative framework, emphasizing the importance of demographic growth.

Im Hof, Ulrich. *The Enlightenment*. Oxford, Eng.: Blackwood Publishers, 1994. A work stressing the Enlightenment's social context and institutions.

Keddie, Nikki, ed. *Debating Revolutions*. New York: New York University Press, 1995. A series of discussions and debates about studies of revolution.

Morgan, Kenneth, ed. *The Oxford History of Britain*. Oxford, Eng.: Oxford University Press, 1988. Essays on various periods of English history.

Spence, Jonathan. *God's Chinese Son*. New York: Norton, 1996. A recent study of the Taiping Uprising.

Stone, Bailey. *The Genesis of the French Revolution*. Cambridge, Eng.: Cambridge University Press, 1994. An analysis of the breakdown of French absolutism in terms of its failure to compete globally in colonial and economic terms.

Tilly, Charles. *European Revolutions, 1492–1992*. Oxford, Eng.: Blackwell Publishers, 1993. A recent examination of revolutions in the past five centuries.

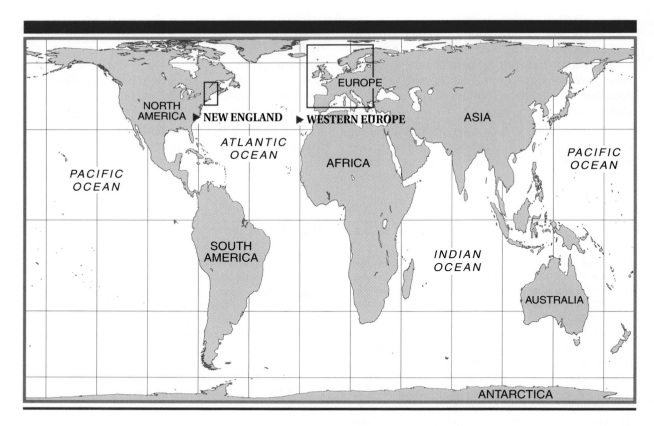

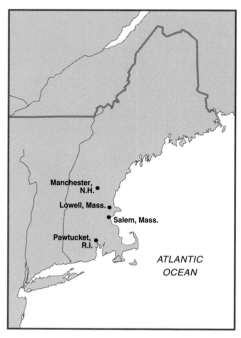

▶ NEW ENGLAND

▶ WESTERN EUROPE

The Global Industrial Revolution
around 1770–1905

In the summer of 1852, a young Mexican man began his job as a textile weaver in a crowded cloth factory outside Mexico City. Late that same summer, when water levels were at their annual lowest, a Polish farmer built a modest dam and a water-powered mill on his property; he began grinding grain and sawing lumber for his neighbors the following fall. Also in that summer, a teenage Irish woman moved to the tenements around the shoe factories of Salem, Massachusetts, and began her new job sewing soles to shoes.

Each of these lives was being transformed by a process set in motion in the eighteenth century: the Industrial Revolution. Prior to the mid–eighteenth century, goods in Europe were produced primarily by independent craftspeople. The businesses they ran, collectively termed **cottage crafts**, operated on a very small scale, used simple technology, usually employed family members for labor, and, as the phrase suggests, typically were located in the home. The vast majority of people were farmers, and the craft and service sectors composed less than 5 percent of the population. The material holdings of most people were few by today's standards, but this mode of production was able to supply society's needs.

In the mid–eighteenth century, however, Europe was on the verge of a change comparable in significance to the massive societal changes that the development of agriculture had caused. The **Industrial Revolution**, the shift to the manufacture of most goods in mechanized factories, and the changes that came in the wake of this shift, originated in England. There, around 1770, factories with large workforces of hired laborers began springing up. These factories used machines to produce far larger quantities of goods than had the earlier cottage crafts, and the wage earners employed in the factories formed part of the market that purchased these goods.

From England, the Industrial Revolution spread to western Europe and North America by the early decades of the nineteenth century. Once industry was established in a new region, it evolved along its own distinctive lines. Wages remained low in English industry, for example, while they were relatively high in the United States. Despite such differences, the Industrial Revolution had commonalities wherever it occurred.

Certainly the Industrial Revolution had roots in earlier times and was not an overnight phenomenon, but the pace of change was remarkably rapid. By 1830 or shortly thereafter, the core areas of England, western Europe, and northeastern North America had been transformed into industrial powers. Industrialization since has spread beyond these core areas, particularly to Japan and Russia.

In the core areas, the Industrial Revolution had two phases. In the first phase, lasting until about 1830, light industry dominated; textiles, shoes, and similar commodities were manufactured and sold to mass markets of consumers. While each item sold produced only a small profit, the numbers of items sold were large. In the second phase, beginning around 1830, heavy industry became important, particularly the manufacture of railroad engines, vehicles, and tracks. In part stimulated by the need to transport the products of light industry, the second phase of the Industrial Revolution shifted some of the industrial focus to expensive items that would be sold in smaller numbers. Because those large items were made mostly of steel, the expansion of the steel industry was part of the second phase. The development of the petroleum industry to fuel railroad and other vehicles also developed in the second phase.

The temptation is to see the Industrial Revolution as purely a technological development, but that temptation must be resisted. While it is true that mechanical inventions made industrialization practical, they were not really at the root of the process. Rather, intellectual and legal developments paved the way for the Industrial Revolution, while the crucial innovations were driven by economic and demographic factors. Mechanical inventions are best seen as improvements that helped the Industrial Revolution succeed, not its fundamental causes. The factories and mill towns are physical monuments to the changes that the Industrial Revolution brought, but the greatest changes were in organization, not hardware.

THE INTELLECTUAL AND LEGAL UNDERPINNINGS OF THE INDUSTRIAL REVOLUTION

Revolutions, especially economic and social ones like the Industrial Revolution, are processes, not events, and they unfold over time. Though the Industrial Revolution progressed rapidly once begun, it was preceded by several decades during which conditions gradually evolved to set the stage for the more dramatic developments that followed. Intellectual and legal developments in the core areas were critical in preparing the way for the Industrial Revolution.

Encyclopedias

Today's encyclopedias are rather bland affairs, with usually inoffensive descriptions and discussion. Early European encyclopedias, however, were politically charged and controversial, and they strongly promoted the Enlightenment ideas that were one of the driving forces of the Industrial Revolution. The Eurasian tradition of encyclopedias, discussed in Chapter 28, took root relatively late in Europe.

The first of the politically charged European encyclopedias was written by John Harris and published in 1704; it was followed in 1728 by one written by Ephraim Chambers. Both included some caustic social commentary but emphasized technical activities: how to blow a glass bottle, how to construct a cottage, how to bind a book. These early works profoundly influenced the editor of what was to be the most influential encyclopedia of all time.

Denis Diderot[1] (1713–1784) was editor of the *Encyclopédie*,[2] the massive French encyclopedia that grew out of the French Enlightenment. As editor, he had the tasks of deciding what articles to include, finding scholars to write those articles, and writing many of the articles himself. This mammoth work ran to more than thirty volumes of text and illustrations, and publication spanned the years between 1751 and 1780.

Diderot understood his task clearly, as he stated in his article on encyclopedias:

> The purpose of an encyclopedia is to assemble the knowledge scattered over the surface of the Earth, to explain its general plan to the men with whom we live, and to transmit it to the men who come after us . . . that our descendants, by becoming better instructed, may as a consequence be more virtuous and happier.

His *Encyclopédie* was to unify and present knowledge—especially knowledge about the trades—for the good of humanity. He saw trade secrets as damaging and selfish, and he and his collaborators went into the streets, shops, and wherever else necessary to research their articles. The *Encyclopédie* included articles on glass manufacture, the making of fishing nets, the production of nails, and many other craft activities. The articles often were masterful and detailed treatments, providing sufficient information for the uninitiated to be able to learn the skill discussed. Equally important,

[1]**Denis Diderot:** day NEE dee duh ROH
[2]***Encyclopédie:*** ahn see kloh pay DEE

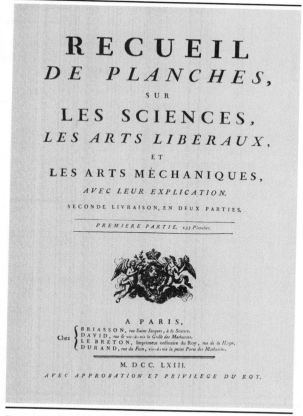

FIGURE 32.1 *Title Page of Denis Diderot's* **Encyclopédie.** *The title translates to "Collection of Plates: Sciences, Liberal Arts, and Mechanical Arts, With Their Explanation." This book and its companion volumes revealed trade secrets that were once known only to specialized artisans. The general publication of this technical information paved the way for the Industrial Revolution.* Courtesy of Dover Publications.

the *Encyclopédie* was profusely illustrated, and the illustrations provided additional technical information. The secrecy associated with the trades in Europe was gone forever.

In addition to its technical articles, the *Encyclopédie* presented essays on social and moral subjects such as the clergy, the arts, marriage, and the proper role of government. Some of the articles produced minor furors, as when the article on Geneva criticized the Puritan ways of the Swiss Calvinists there. The encyclopedists were convinced that technical advancement had to proceed in step with social advancement; it was as important to

PARALLELS AND DIVERGENCES

Japan's Agricultural Manuals

In the late eighteenth century, about the same time that the encyclopedists of Europe were collecting and publishing information on crafts and technological skills, a parallel but independent movement was taking place in Japan. There, rich peasant farmers were producing agricultural manuals to improve agricultural practices and production.

These farmers recognized that various improvements in agricultural tools and techniques were being made continually throughout Japan. These refinements, however, usually remained local, because there was no established means of disseminating the information that would allow others to take advantage of them. Accordingly, many of these farmers undertook travels throughout Japan, visiting other farmers and observing their practices. They presented their findings in text and illustrations, had copies printed, and distributed them to their colleagues.

Such agricultural manuals were crucial in spreading technical information on agriculture across Japan. The improved techniques described in these manuals were widely adopted and were instrumental in increasing agricultural production. During this period, Japan's agricultural yield per unit of area, already high, rose to among the highest in the world.

While Japan's agricultural manuals differed from the *Encyclopédie* in that they focused exclusively on farming, they bore many similarities. Both were established to spread knowledge that otherwise was difficult to obtain; both were technical in nature, emphasizing practical knowledge; both were widely distributed; and both represented a progressive faith that the future could be improved by rational efforts. The agricultural manuals were precursors to Japan's Industrial Revolution, and the productive agriculture they promoted helped bear the financial burden of Japan's industrialization in the latter part of the nineteenth century.

---

banish superstition as it was to abandon outmoded methods of making shoes.

In these social and moral articles, the encyclopedists preached an Enlightenment ideology of progress, reason, and material betterment. Underlying that ideology was a concern for the welfare of everyday people, as Diderot stated in his article on art:

> It is for the liberal arts [represented by encyclopedists] to lift the mechanical arts from the contempt in which prejudice has for so long held them, and it is for the patronage of kings to draw them from the poverty in which they still languish.

Diderot and his colleagues were preaching the kind of egalitarian ideals that three decades later would inspire the French revolutionaries.

In keeping with its thrust for simultaneous technological and social improvement, the *Encyclopédie* was peppered with political and moral views, sometimes occurring in unexpected places. The article on salt manufacture, for example, discusses the royal tax on salt immediately after citing the biological need for salt. It then launches into a condemnation of any tax levied on a necessity of life. Social and moral commentary of this sort caused the French authorities concern (rightfully, as the French Revolution later confirmed), and Diderot spent three months in jail near the beginning of the project for expressing his nonconformist views in print. His publisher began removing especially controversial statements from later volumes without Diderot's authorization, but what remained was sufficient to fuel many a heated discussion.

The *Encyclopédie* and other encyclopedias paved the way for the Industrial Revolution. First, they presented practical information on how to manufacture items. France had the most advanced manufacturing techniques of the age, and the *Encyclopédie* in particular served as a catalogue of industrial secrets for entrepreneurs throughout Europe and North America. Second, the encyclopedists advocated improved material standards of living for everyday people and saw the "mechanical arts" as the route to that improvement. The *Encyclopédie* was only one voice in a rising chorus of like-minded scholars and others.

Other Intellectual Underpinnings

The rise of encyclopedias was probably the most important intellectual support for the Industrial Revolution, but there were others. Beginning in the seventeenth century, for example, there had been an increased exchange of information between scholars and technologists, two occupational groups that, prior to this time, had communicated remarkably little with each other. Scientists of the seventeenth century also became increasingly adamant in their commitment to testing their theories, and their work became more useful to inventors.

In addition, more narrowly defined and empirically grounded questions were supplanting the grand philosophical topics of inquiry that scientists of earlier times had considered important. More narrow (but more tangible) topics, such as the chemical-combining powers of different metals, were becoming more fashionable, and these subjects had the potential to provide an inventor with information necessary to devise a new manufacturing process.

Further, increasing literacy and the development of widespread and relatively inexpensive printing permitted inventors to read the scientists' tracts, something that would have been unlikely earlier. By the mid–eighteenth century, scholarly science and manufacturing technology had become firmly wedded, and the bond became stronger as time went on.

A final intellectual input came from the English philosopher Herbert Spencer (1820–1903). Writing in the mid–nineteenth century, Spencer obviously did not affect the beginning of the Industrial Revolution nearly a century earlier, but his ideas influenced its later years strongly. Spencer developed the concept of **social Darwinism**, the idea that human society operates by a system of natural selection, whereby individuals and ways of life automatically gravitate to their proper station. According to social Darwinism, poverty is the natural condition for inferior individuals, and an inferior society will be conquered or otherwise dominated by a superior one. Social Darwinism is very much out of fashion today, but it was quite popular in the century following Spencer, and it served as a justification for all sorts of exploitation of laborers and for the extinction or domination of indigenous communities around the world.

Legal Underpinnings

Few inventors are likely to devote their energies to technological innovations if they believe themselves unlikely to benefit from them. Yet the legal systems of Europe before the seventeenth century frequently forbade inventors from using their own inventions. Monarchs (and sometimes lesser royalty) had the right to grant **monopolies**, the rights to exclusive legal use of a device. Monopolies frequently were sold by the crown to the highest bidder regardless of whether that person was the inventor, and fraud was common; sometimes royal favorites would be given a monopoly as a reward for loyalty. In this legal environment, it is small wonder that most inventors considered secrecy the best protection for an invention.

England was the first European country to abolish the old system of monopolies in 1624 and replace it with a new patent system. Under that system, an inventor had only to register a new device with the government and pay a modest fee in order to receive exclusive rights to the use of the device for a stated period. The holder of a patent was permitted to license anyone else to use the device, negotiating whatever arrangement was mutually agreeable. Other western European countries followed suit in the seventeenth century, and the United States provided for patents in its Constitution in 1789. Many scholars believe that this legal change provided critical impetus to the development of the technology that supported the Industrial Revolution.

THE DEMOGRAPHIC AND ECONOMIC BASES OF THE INDUSTRIAL REVOLUTION

While intellectual concepts, law, and technology had their impacts on the Industrial Revolution, demographic and economic factors arguably were the most important. Certainly, the reason that England was the cradle of the Industrial Revolution had nothing to do with the technology there, because equivalent or more sophisticated technology was available elsewhere. But the demographic and economic conditions in England were especially conducive to the development of the Industrial Revolution.

The Demographic Basis

In western Europe—and England in particular—population was increasing very rapidly in the eighteenth century. Average annual population increase in England, for example, was 3 percent, leading to a doubling of the population every twenty-five years. Such population growth was unusual, not having been seen since the development of agriculture and perhaps not even then. This was all the more noteworthy because large numbers of people had been leaving England and western Europe for more than a century to go to the colonies.

The reason for this population explosion was not a greater birthrate but a lower death rate. Fewer infants and children were dying, and more adults were surviving into old age, permitting women to bear children through their entire reproductive life. Several factors were behind this longevity, including an improvement in diet with the adoption of New World crops, better sanitation and medical care, and a falloff in the frequency of devastating epidemics. In addition, because most western Europeans were farmers and farming benefited from the labor of large families, there were few voluntary efforts to limit family size.

This large population meant two things for the Industrial Revolution. First, there would be plenty of labor to fuel the factories. In fact, the abnormal size of farming families led to pressures on some of the younger sons to leave the farm upon reaching adulthood, because they had little chance of inheriting it later. Second, and equally important, there was a huge market to purchase the goods that eventually would be churned out by factories once the Industrial Revolution was under way.

Another important demographic issue was mobility. A large labor pool is of little use if it is scattered all over the countryside and unwilling to move. But in eighteenth-century England there was a great willingness to migrate. It manifested itself in those who left for the colonies and in those who left for the English cities to find employment.

A final relevant demographic factor was slavery. While slaves were not a significant source of labor in eighteenth-century England, they were in the colonies from which raw materials were sent to England. The slaves underwrote the procurement system that provided English factories with cheap raw materials, such as cotton. A less exploitative system would have raised the price of raw materials, jeopardizing the economic viability of certain industries.

The Economic Basis

The Industrial Revolution had two economic prerequisites. First, if great numbers of laborers were to be lured away from farms to become factory workers, then agriculture had to be efficient enough still to provide an adequate food supply. This requirement was easily met in England, where agricultural surpluses had been commonplace for decades and where the shift from subsistence agriculture to commercial agriculture was well under way. The second prerequisite, finding sufficient capital for investment, was more complicated.

Before the Industrial Revolution, the funds needed to establish a cottage craft typically were quite modest. A factory, on the other hand, was a major investment. A great deal of money had to be assembled in order to build the facility, purchase appropriate machines, and stock up on raw materials. Furthermore, all this had to be accomplished before hiring a worker and producing a single item.

Few people could afford individually to invest this amount of money, and those who could were wealthy already and usually had little inclination to risk a substantial sum on such a scheme. The money for the Industrial Revolution, therefore, came mostly from the middle class: petty merchants, craftspeople, and clerks who had saved a bit of money and were looking for an investment. The Industrial Revolution saw investment shift predominantly from a relatively few large shareholders to a broad base of smaller shareholders. Entrepreneurs sold shares in their companies, and investors received returns in proportion to the amount of their investments. The shareholding corporation, the mechanism through which most businesses are funded today, rose to prominence in step with the Industrial Revolution.

Industrialists in the first phase of the Industrial Revolution had the advantage that many of

While massive urban factories dominated the economic scene during the Industrial Revolution, coexisting beside them was another institution: the rural mill. These rural mills were a hybrid form, drawing their organization and economics from the tradition of cottage crafts yet taking advantage of the technology of the Industrial Revolution.

A typical rural mill usually was located along a brook. A simple earthen dam created a pond, impounding enough water to run a waterwheel, while gears, levers, and pulleys transmitted the power into a small, wood-frame building. There it could be shunted to an impressive diversity of devices. After the harvest, great stone wheels ground grain into flour; in the winter, when wood was driest and farmers had the most free time for cutting it, saw blades cut logs into lumber; when a shovel needed repair, power bellows puffed a tiny forge into white heat. There were few jobs to which the rural mill could not be turned.

Typically, a rural mill could be built with materials and labor available to most farmers. The mill was made mostly from wood, and that was harvested from the land; the dam was made of earth dug from what would become the pond.

Other than appropriate land and a willingness to work, all that was required to build such a mill was a millwright's manual. The nineteenth century saw the publication of dozens of these millwright's manuals, guides giving information on how to build the mill, and they truly were spiritual descendants of Diderot's *Encyclopédie*. These manuals, usually about 100 pages long and costing a few pennies, provided sample plans, formulas for calculating the placement of the waterwheel and other elements of the mill, examples of devices for transmitting power, and hints of mistakes to avoid. They were down-to-earth and practical, and they could turn a willing reader into a competent millwright.

Few of these rural-mill operators were full-time specialists. More often, they were farmers who invested their spare time and energy in mill-building in order to supplement their income. A dollar for repairing a shovel was a bargain for both the owner of the shovel and the owner of the mill, and those dollars helped many a rural farmer rise to the respected middle class.

The owner of a rural mill usually was its sole operator, shifting attention from one task to the next, searching for clever ways to use the mill's equipment to perform new functions. Unlike the big factories, nothing was standardized here, and everything was a unique task. The rural mill truly was the heir to the cottage craft tradition, drawing on the Industrial Revolution only for its admiration of and reliance on labor-saving mechanical devices.

their facilities were modest, accommodating perhaps a few dozen workers and using relatively inexpensive machines. Still, the economic drain was substantial, and many factory managers developed ways to control their cash flow and keep the business afloat. Some companies, for example, abandoned the traditional practice of paying employees daily or weekly in favor of quarterly pay, hoping that some of the products they had made would have been sold by payday. In the meantime, workers were extended credit to buy necessities at the company-run store and be housed in company-owned tenements; in some cases, the amount owed would be deducted from the wages before they were given to the wage earner. The owners could make substantial profits on both the factory and the company store; rents usually were kept more modest as an attractant for workers.

THE TECHNOLOGICAL BASIS OF THE INDUSTRIAL REVOLUTION

If economics arguably was the heart and soul of the Industrial Revolution, machines were its bones. The day-to-day operation of a factory was dependent on those machines, and profits rose or fell with the effectiveness of the technology. Although virtually all of the machines of the

Industrial Revolution were based on principles that had been known for decades, sometimes centuries, great attention was now being given to their design and refinement.

Power Sources

Prior to the Industrial Revolution, most of the energy expended in producing goods came from human muscles. A major change came with the proliferation of a wide variety of power sources.

Simplest were the wind and water mills. With various arrangements of paddles or vanes, they were propelled forward by the current of wind or flowing water, and energy was transmitted through a central axle into a mill building. Water mills had been used in Europe since at least the first century B.C., and windmills were used there by the twelfth century A.D. Their primary use was to grind grain, but there are a few examples of mills adapted to manufacturing. A water-powered mill in France,

for example, was producing felt by 1000, as were others in Sweden and England within the following two centuries. A French water mill was used for sawing lumber in 1204, and Italian, French, and German mills made paper in the late thirteenth and fourteenth centuries. These practices were out of the ordinary and noteworthy at these dates, but during the Industrial Revolution they became common.

Especially in the United States, where many of the prime regions for industrialization were along rivers at waterfalls, water power became the primary motive force for industry. For the most part, the technology remained quite similar to that which had been known for nearly a millennium. One significant innovation, however, was developed in the middle of the nineteenth century: Rather than using water to turn a large wheel, it could be directed through a narrow jet and into an enclosed drum, where it would squirt against vanes and turn a small rotor. This device, called a

FIGURE 32.2   *Volta's Electric Battery.*   *Alessandro Volta demonstrated his electric battery to Napoleon in 1802. Volta was a theoretical scientist investigating previous conceptions of how electricity was produced. His research, however, led him to construct a device that had unexpected practical applications: the electric battery. This linkage between theoretical science and practical invention became prominent during the Industrial Revolution.*   Private collection/Bulloz.

FIGURE 32.3 *Jacquard Loom. This 1847 illustration demonstrates how just a few workers managed machines that could produce large and complicated textiles rapidly. As documented by this picture, women were prominent in the factories of the nineteenth century.* British Library.

turbine, increased the usable energy output of the water by as much as 30 percent and was especially useful along small streams or in regions where rivers shrink in the summer.

The use of water or wind power, of course, is limited to locations with the proper geographical endowment. The steam engine, however, overcame that difficulty because it could be used anywhere, including in moving vehicles. The steam engine is simple in principle. Water is heated until it vaporizes, at which point it expands and drives a piston; levers or gears transmit the energy from the piston to wherever it is needed. Greek philosophers of the fifth century B.C. invented a steam engine, but they never applied it to any practical task. Various Europeans produced more or less practical steam engines in the seventeenth and eighteenth centuries, but it was the improvements made by James Watt that produced a truly useful power source in 1782. Steam engines were variously stoked with wood, coal, or even dry animal dung.

By the end of the nineteenth century, internal combustion engines running on petroleum fuels and electric motors were becoming efficient enough to be useful. They were the only truly new power sources to be invented during the Industrial Revolution, and it is notable that they were devel-

oped only at the end of the period. The revolution, so far as power was concerned, was not in the devices themselves but in how they were used.

New Machines and Inventions

New machines to support the Industrial Revolution were as varied as the tasks they were designed to complete. There were rolling mills for making oatmeal, cotton gins for separating cotton fiber from seeds and other waste, spinning jennies for making thread, bending machines for making paper clips, rotary steam presses for printing newspapers, and even Hercules dredgers for keeping canals clear of silt. Rather than catalogue hundreds of specialized inventions, we shall examine one as an example.

In the eighteenth century, weaving patterned cloth was very laborious. It had to be made by hand, because the power looms of that era could produce only plain fabrics, all of the same thread and with no raised designs. Joseph Jacquard,[3] a French inventor, solved this problem with the **Jacquard loom**, a device that could be attached to any existing loom. To produce patterns, it was

[3]**Joseph Jacquard:** zhoh SEHF zhahk AHR

FIGURE 32.4 *Segregation of Tasks in the Industrial Revolution.* *This illustration from Diderot's* Encyclopédie *shows how the manufacture of so simple an item as a button could be split into different tasks to improve efficiency. The pair of workers at the left cut wood or similar materials into blocks, which in turn were cut into button blanks by the pair in the foreground; the trio in the background used the wheel to polish and bore perforations in the buttons.* Courtesy of Dover Publications.

necessary to raise each thread at the right moment so that cross-threads could be passed beneath it. The Jacquard loom controlled each thread individually, allowing it to be lifted at the precise instant necessary. A series of cards with holes drilled into them programmed the loom to the desired pattern. Jacquard exhibited his loom at the French Industrial Exposition in 1801 and received a medal for it. He subsequently was decorated by Napoleon and was awarded a permanent stipend by his grateful government.

The Jacquard loom exemplifies the general pattern seen in many machines of the Industrial Revolution, although it was far more successful than most. The invention really did little that was new; it automated tasks that previously had been done by hand, but the process remained much the same. In fact, the Jacquard loom differed from its predecessor only in its treatment of individual threads, rather than groups. It embodied no new scientific principles and was dramatic only in that it accelerated the weaving process.

Organizing the Workplace

The new facilities and machines required a different organization of labor from that of cottage crafts, and, in this sense, the Industrial Revolution was something entirely new. In the cottage crafts before the Industrial Revolution, a single worker normally completed the entirety of a product. Work was largely at one's own pace, and an especially productive day could be followed by a light day or even a self-proclaimed holiday. Work usually was done by one or a very few workers, and all workers probably were family members.

In the factories, many unrelated workers labored together at a pace dictated not by their own consciences but by the foreman. Work began and ended by the clock, without regard for how near one was to completing a task. Early industrialists frequently commented on how difficult it was to maintain discipline in the workplace because the workers formerly employed in crafts were so entrenched in more free-form work habits.

A major innovation in the factories was the **segregation of tasks**. Each worker had one small task to complete, and that task was repeated over and again. Making a pin in England in 1770 required eighteen distinct tasks, one person making the wire, another cutting it, another grinding the point, another making the head, another attaching it, and so on. This arrangement, alien to cottage crafts, had the virtue of efficiency. The advantage of a point-grinding machine is largely lost if a worker goes to the machine to sharpen one pin, then walks to the head-making machine to perform the next task.

The segregation of tasks was made possible by another principle of organization in the Industrial Revolution: **standardization of parts**. In cottage crafts, workers made each part as needed and fitted it to the adjacent part; in the factories, all examples of a particular part had to be the same so that any one of them could fit into its appropriate place. This meant that machines had to be designed in such a manner that it would be difficult to produce variations in their products. While the British and French pioneered the standardization of parts, it was the Americans who perfected it and made it a major element of mass production.

Another American innovation, coming into practice around 1900, was the **assembly line**. Refined by Henry Ford in his automobile plant, it consisted of a conveyor system with workers standing along it, arranged in the order in which their tasks were to be performed. Workers completed their tasks on the automobile literally as it passed by, each one executing a single, simple operation. Before the institution of the assembly line, assembling an automobile body had required 748 worker-minutes; with the assembly line, it required only 93 worker-minutes.

New Modes of Transportation

As the Industrial Revolution rumbled into its second phase in the 1820s, a crisis was brewing. Factories were hungry for the raw materials that they processed, and they spewed out large quantities of goods. Bringing in materials and distributing products became major problems in the early Industrial Revolution, but technology came to the rescue.

Thinkers as early as Isaac Newton in 1680 proposed using steam to power a carriage, and several eighteenth-century inventors built working models, but it wasn't until 1801 that a working steam-powered railroad locomotive was produced. Richard Trevithick's "Puffing Devil" was largely a circus attraction, but working steam locomotives were in service by 1829 in both England and the United States. Railroads were critical in servicing

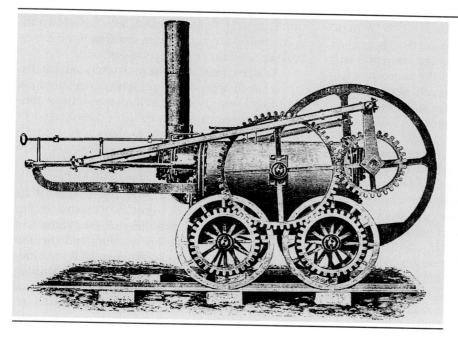

FIGURE 32.5 *"Puffing Devil." Richard Trevithick, an English inventor, designed and built the first successful railroad locomotive, which was capable of carrying seven or eight passengers at a breathtaking speed of three miles per hour. The first version, built in 1801, ran on the ground, but the difficulties of traversing uneven terrain led Trevithick to place it on rails in 1804.* From Edward W. Byrne, *The Progress of Invention in the Nineteenth Century* (New York: Russell and Russell, 1900).

many industries, especially the manufacture of iron and steel, whose raw materials and products were so heavy.

Less important, though prominent in the nineteenth century, were steamships. Working steamships were in service from 1801 on. These boats often were constructed with a very shallow draft that permitted them to operate in shallow water, so they were excellent for plying the rivers and navigation canals of Europe and eastern North America.

THE INDUSTRIAL REVOLUTION TRANSFORMS SOCIETY

The Industrial Revolution was an economic revolution whose effects were widespread and far-reaching. Economic conditions both in industrialized nations and elsewhere around the world were drastically altered, and society in industrialized nations veered in a new direction. Processes of environmental degradation that have proven difficult to reverse were also set into motion.

Economic Winners and Losers

Economically speaking, virtually all segments of society profited when a country industrialized. The investors, providing the business was managed skillfully, were likely to receive a healthy return on their investments; the entrepreneurs who established and directed the industries had the potential to become wildly rich. Many middle-class investors found themselves suddenly wealthy as the result of holding shares in a successful enterprise. Laborers, although hardly getting rich, typically found themselves in better economic shape than they had been before. Many of them had few other opportunities for wage earning, and a factory job was considered good fortune. Consumers benefited from lower prices and greater availability of previously scarce goods.

The system fed upon itself, creating increasingly favorable economic conditions for at least some of its participants. Workers who had left the farm for the factory now had more cash (though they forfeited the subsistence commodities available to farm workers), and that cash could be used to purchase goods produced by factories. The laborers for one factory were consumers of the products from all the other factories, and the growth of the labor force greatly expanded the domestic market for goods. Further, the substantial financial gains of the first phase of the Industrial Revolution provided investors with sufficient capital to fund the more expensive iron and steel factories that became prevalent in the second phase.

There were, however, economic losers in the Industrial Revolution, though the losers were predominantly not in the industrialized countries. Many of the industries of this period produced goods for a foreign market and depended on raw materials that were unavailable locally.

An excellent example comes from the cotton textile industry of England, the first major industry there and a major component of English industrial output throughout the Industrial Revolution. The climate of England, of course, cannot support cotton growing, so cotton was shipped to England, primarily from Brazil, the Caribbean islands, and southern parts of North America. Subsidized by slavery, cotton growing was lucrative for a very few growers but marginal (at best) for virtually all the laborers. Cheap raw cotton then came into England, where it was spun and woven in the factories, boosting the English economy. Two-thirds of English textile production in the first half of the nineteenth century was exported and sold at considerable profit, principally to India and Latin America, nonindustrialized regions that in some cases originally had supplied the raw cotton to England.

A clear extension of the mercantile system discussed in Chapter 24, these practices ensured the continued poverty of the colonies and other non-industrial regions. Colonies were discouraged or prohibited from attempting to alleviate their destitution by developing industries of their own and thereby becoming competitors with England.

In at least one case, England purposefully destroyed a competing industry in one of its colonies. Long a major exporter of cotton textiles throughout the southern parts of Asia, India had begun exporting textiles to England in the mid–seventeenth century. A series of wars, carefully orchestrated by the British through shifting alliances, destabilized India in the early years of the nineteenth century, destroying its textile industry and removing it as an industrial competitor.

Classes and Class Conflict

The Industrial Revolution transfigured the structure of economic classes. Between 1730 and 1830, the overall standard of living in England had improved dramatically. At the beginning of that span, the vast majority of the English population were farmers, and by the end most worked in factories or service jobs: A huge, new class of workers had been formed almost overnight. Many small investors had made sufficient money to become quite comfortable, and the ranks of the middle class had swollen. A few spectacularly successful entrepreneurs, especially in the latter half of the nineteenth century, had gained incredible wealth, becoming richer than many aristocrats.

These changes created considerable conflict. Workers and owners often found themselves at odds over working conditions and wages, and work stoppages, lockouts, and violence became more common. Labor unions of the modern kind were formed in the nineteenth century to help workers act together in their opposition to owners, though it was not until the latter half of the nineteenth century that unions were sufficiently powerful to conduct major strikes. The swarms of political upheavals in both 1830 and 1848 in part reflected the difficulties Europe was having in adjusting to the new order.

Working Conditions

Factories of the Industrial Revolution usually evoke the image of wretched working conditions, but this was far from universally true. Particularly in the early decades of the Industrial Revolution in the United States, owners went to great lengths to try to establish healthful, stimulating, and morally uplifting conditions.

Lowell, Massachusetts, is a good example. There, several textile mills opened in 1822, attracted by the falls of the Merrimack River and the favorable terrain for harnessing their power. More than just a collection of mills, Lowell included churches, assembly halls for touring lecturers and musicians, schools, a hospital, and a

FIGURE 32.6 *Lowell Hospital.* *Many American industrialists in the first half of the nineteenth century felt obligated to provide services for the welfare of their factory workers. This hospital in the mill town of Lowell, Massachusetts, provided workers with better medical care than was available to most of their contemporaries, many of whom were more financially secure. Other services included schools, churches, and concert and lecture series.*
Courtesy of the Center for Lowell History.

A s the Industrial Revolution progressed and working conditions worsened, reformers on both sides of the Atlantic Ocean began agitating for laws and regulations to improve the workplace. The plight of women and children was especially important to these reformers, and various governments commissioned studies that interviewed women and children in factories, mines, and other work venues. The following testimony was collected in 1842 by investigators looking into the conditions in coal mines. Janet Cumming, at the time eleven years old, had been working in the coal mines of Scotland for two years when she gave this testimony. The testimony is largely a quotation of her own words, but there are occasional shifts to the perspective of the interviewer. Touching accounts like this led to a series of nineteenth-century laws that limited child labor in Great Britain.

IN THEIR OWN WORDS

An Interview with an Eleven-Year-Old Coal Miner

Father gangs [assembles with other workers] at 2 in the morning: I gang with the women at 5, and come up at 5 at night; work all night on Fridays, and come away at 12 in the day. I carry the large bits of coal from the wall-face to the pit-bottom, and the small pieces called chows in a creel [basket]; the weight is usually a hundred-weight [100 pounds]; does not know how many pounds there are in a hundred-weight, but it is some work to carry; it takes three journeys to fill a tub of 4 cwt [hundred-weight]. . . . The roof is very low; I have to bend my back and legs, and the water comes frequently up to the calves of my legs; has no likening [sic] for the work; father makes me like it. . . . Never got hurt, but often obliged to scramble out when bad air [poisonous gas] was in the pit.

I am learning to read at the night-school; am in the twopenny book [beginning reading text]; sometimes to sabbath-school. Jesus was God; David wrote the Bible; has a slight knowledge of the first six questions in the Shorter Catechism.

variety of other public services. Workers in the early years were primarily young women, and special care was taken to provide them moral and practical instruction, courtesy of the company. Several other mill towns furnished comparable services.

As time passed, however, services diminished and finally were discontinued, and conditions generally deteriorated. By the late nineteenth century, work days had become longer, output quotas had increased, and safety often was sacrificed. This was the era of the sweatshop. Curiously, English factories never exhibited the good working conditions of their American counterparts, even in the early years of the Industrial Revolution. From the beginning, they were comparable to the later American sweatshops.

This pattern of benign and exploitative conditions may be explained by the geographical relationship of industry to the frontier. In England, there was no frontier to which a disgruntled worker could retreat, leaving the oppressive conditions of the factory. Workers had no alternatives, and their employers took advantage of the situation to exploit them as fully as possible. In contrast, the American frontier was within walking distance of the early factories, and workers had to be treated well if they were to stay. As the frontier advanced and the distance from the factories increased, that pressure valve no longer was available, and owners gradually turned to more exploitative practices, knowing that their employees had no viable alternatives to staying.

The dreadful conditions in factories and industrial towns led many reformers to clamor for laws regulating industrialists. Charles Dickens, himself briefly a British factory worker in his youth during the 1830s, wrote novels and stories that sometimes exposed the exploitation and greed of industry. Other social critics, such as Lewis Hine, used the newly developed technology of photography to expose the horrors of child labor in turn-of-the-century America. The combined weight of exposés and reform agitation led to laws and regulations regarding child labor, maximum length of work days, safety standards, and other aspects of labor in countries throughout the industrialized world.

The Special Role of Women, Children, and Immigrants

Especially in the early days of the Industrial Revolution, women were an important component of the workforce. A few decades later, children became a significant sector of labor, and after that, recent immigrants became important. Traditionally, none of these groups would have held a significant position in the labor force, but there were several reasons why they emerged in the Industrial Revolution.

First, these groups were considered more compliant than male, American-born adults. This was especially true of women and children, whose traditional social roles were subservient to those of adult men. All these groups were perceived as less likely to complain about conditions or to organize into labor unions, and there is some evidence that this perception was accurate. Further, in the early days of the Industrial Revolution, owners found it difficult to reshape the work habits of men accustomed to the cottage industries. By using laborers with little or no previous work experience, owners felt better able to mold them to the new requirements.

Second, these groups were willing to work for lower wages than men. In mills where both men and women worked, women's wages typically were from 40 to 60 percent lower than men's, and children's wages usually were lower still. Recent immigrants also would accept low wages, which often led to conflict with local-born workers who correctly believed that this practice undercut prevailing wage levels. A labor force willing to work for inferior wages was important in an entrepreneur's quest to extract the greatest profit from an industrial enterprise.

Effects on Cities and Countryside

The most obvious immediate effect of the Industrial Revolution was the shift of population from the countryside to cities. Many factories were located in or near cities in order to take advantage of the labor pools there, and the majority of workers became urbanites. For every worker in the city, there was one fewer farmer, and contemporary writers commented on the noticeable depopulation of the countryside.

Another important result of the Industrial Revolution, while not so immediately obvious, was

FIGURE 32.7 *Child Labor in a Carolina Cotton Mill. Lewis Hine, who photographed this scene in 1908, was a crusader against the exploitation of children in industry. Child labor was common in American factories, especially in the South, but Hine's photographic campaign drew Congress's attention to the problem and resulted in stricter and more aggressively enforced child labor laws.* Edward L. Bafford Photography Collection, University of Maryland Baltimore County.

environmental destruction. Most industries produced waste along with their products, and those wastes sometimes seriously degraded the environment. A small cottage craft could safely dump the minimal volume of waste it produced with little damage, but large factories produced much more waste, and their sustained dumping was more likely to devastate an area.

Certain industries were especially polluting. Paper mills dumped dense effluents into rivers, killing fish and contaminating waterfowl. Hat factories, important in the nineteenth century, when hats were required of socially prominent persons, employed mercury to dress the fur used in top hats, and the runoff usually was dumped in a nearby stream. One community in the Merrimack Valley had the highest rates of insanity in Massachusetts for decades, until it was realized that its residents were suffering from mercury poisoning, the result of a water supply severely polluted by its hatmaking industry. When industries used coal for metal working or producing steam for power, the landscape for miles around was sooted with black grime. There were no environmental protection laws during the Industrial Revolution, and most countries realized only in the late twentieth century how serious the dangers of pollution were.

FIGURE 32.8 *Rows of Factories in Industrial England. This photograph of factories in Burnley shows the grim result of focusing exclusively on efficiency and profit: The environment suffered massively. Not only were such working conditions depressing to workers, but the buildings they occupied were also hotter in summer, colder in winter, and more oxygen-deprived than the more spacious, less efficient structures in which they were employed prior to the Industrial Revolution.* Aerofilms, Ltd.

INDUSTRIALIZATION BEYOND WESTERN EUROPE AND NORTH AMERICA

In the modern world, political, military, and economic power are in direct proportion to the industrial strength of a country. Countries around the world have realized this since the nineteenth century, and many far beyond the original core area of the Industrial Revolution have tried to stimulate their own industrialization. They have achieved success to varying degrees, and they have modified Western-style industrialization in various ways to fit their needs and resources.

Japan

When the Meiji rulers of Japan came to power in 1868, they inherited a country on the brink of being absorbed into an expansive American trade sphere. Their predecessors had attempted to isolate Japan from the outside world, but the United States had used its military strength to force Japan into an unequal treaty that gave American nationals a privileged position in Japan. Later, other Western powers also used their military might to extract humiliating and lopsided trade agreements with Japan. Japan's industrialization was, in large measure, an attempt to build national power to the point where outsiders could not compel such unfavorable agreements.

The Meiji rulers' program to modernize Japan was based on industrial strength. Prior to this time, manufacturing had been of the cottage craft sort similar to that of Europe, and Japanese leaders began actively promoting factory growth alongside cottage crafts. Basically, quality items for domestic consumption, especially traditional items like chopsticks, continued to be made by skilled craftspeople. To complement this, factories specialized in large-scale production of inexpensive items for export and domestic use (such as cotton textiles), silk fabrics (to fill the void left when Europe's silk industry was devastated by silkworm disease in the 1870s), and armaments and other items that could be used to build the political and military power of Japan. Because Japan was resource-poor, many industries manufactured finished products from raw materials purchased abroad.

The road to industrialization in Japan was carefully guided by the government. Many top Japanese leaders had traveled to the West between 1871 and 1873 and had been impressed by Western industry and its virtues; when they returned to Japan, they were eager to promote similar developments there. These leaders recognized that Japan already possessed the elements required to support industrialization: a strong base of commercial agriculture, financial institutions for loans and investments, and coal for use as a fuel.

Government support took several forms. When sufficient capital to start an enterprise was not available in private hands, the government financed factories. When technical expertise was unavailable in Japan, the government hired foreign experts to advise in the design and establishment of factories. More than 4,000 foreign advisors were hired, paid well, and shipped back home after they had trained Japanese in their specialties. Similarly, when the problem was industrial organization, foreign experts were brought to Japan to teach European approaches. Once the industries were established, the government sold them off at bargain prices to Japanese entrepreneurs, leaving their management in private hands.

To ensure that Japanese products were competitive on the international market, the government oversaw a quality-control operation that spot-checked exports for defects and encouraged manufacturers to install quality-control procedures of their own. In the 1880s, the finance minister, Matsukata Masayoshi, implemented a program of tax incentives and other measures to encourage Japanese export of finished products.

All of these measures helped produce a powerful industrial base for Japan. Japan's trade balance was very favorable, with exports considerably greater than imports, and the military strength produced through its armament factories was demonstrated in 1895, when the Japanese military easily defeated China and began establishing its Asian empire; Japan's power was confirmed with its defeat of Russia in 1905.

While the concept of industrialization came from the West and Japanese officials were eager to borrow ideas from the West, Japan was not merely an imitator of European industry. Japanese industry acquired its own stamp, and factories were organized along a model that took the Japanese character into account. Rather than focus on indi-

FIGURE 32.9 *Tomioka Silk Factory.* *The massive factory shown in this contemporary Japanese print was an early creation of the Meiji program of industrialization in Japan. It was the first factory in Japan to apply mass-production techniques like segregation of tasks, and the first to employ women.* Tsuneo Tamba Collection, Yokohama, Japan/Laurie Platt Winfrey, Inc.

vidual workers, production teams were stressed; the family was taken as the ideal model for factory organization after about 1900. Socialized into the values of teamwork and institutional goal achievement, Japanese workers adapted well to these work teams. As in the Western tradition, women workers comprised most of the labor force, again largely because they were seen as more docile and willing to accept low wages. Men began to outnumber women in most sectors of Japanese industry only in the 1920s.

By the turn of the century, scarcely three decades after its beginning, Japan's Industrial Revolution was complete. Although Japanese industry was not as powerful as most of its European and North American counterparts, it was the strongest in Asia. In the second half of the twentieth century, Japan would become one of the greatest industrial powers in the world.

Russia

Russia did not participate in the Industrial Revolution very fully. By 1830, it was receiving imported industrial technology, primarily in the form of textile machinery. Industry had difficulty taking root, however, because there was so small a market for its products. Russian poverty was deeper than the poverty suffered by the poor elsewhere in Europe. The vast majority of Russians were impoverished serfs, and, even after emancipation in 1861, they remained too poor to purchase industrial products in quantities sufficient to support the factories. At the end of the Crimean War in 1856, Russian leaders were convinced that the lack of a strong industrial base was responsible for Russia's defeat.

Attempts were made to invigorate industry through state direction. The most successful of these began in the 1880s and lasted two decades. During that period, many armament plants were established, and a growing railroad system was used to transport raw materials and finished products. (The building of major railway systems, such as the Trans-Siberian Railroad, further stimulated industrialization.) The building of armament factories solved the market problem, because the state purchased the weapons, strengthening its international position in the bargain. Capital came partly from foreign investors but primarily from the government; high tariffs maintained the high prices of competitive foreign goods, protecting Russian products. The government monies were raised through increased taxes, causing considerable unrest, especially among the poor.

There were limits, however, to industrial growth in Russia in the early years of the twentieth century. Consistently poor agricultural yields made it imperative that attention and labor be directed to that sector, and the gap between Russian industrialization and that of western Europe continued to widen. Russian industry developed slowly until interrupted by the Russian Revolution, and the final phase of industrialization took place under socialism. As a result, it incorporated none of the entrepreneurial elements characteristic of the Industrial Revolution under capitalism.

Patterns of Industrialization outside the Core Areas

There were three patterns of industrialization outside the core area of the Industrial Revolution. Japan was successful at industrializing, probably in large part because of strenuous government intervention, astute private entrepreneurship, and the absence of neighboring industrial competitors. At that relatively early date, Western industrial powers were unable effectively to promote their

FIGURE 32.10 *Russian Armament Factory, 1916.* *This factory in Petrograd was devoted to the production of artillery pieces; the guns shown here are nearly completed. Factories like this one resulted from a government policy aimed at stimulating industry through the purchase of arms. For this reason, the Industrial Revolution in Russia followed a different course than it did in Western Europe.* RIA-Novosti/Sovfoto.

EUROPE AND NORTH AMERICA	JAPAN	RUSSIA		
Cottage Crafts period, to 1770			**1600**	
			–	British patent system established, 1624
			–	
			–	
			–	
				London Stock Exchange opens, 1697
			1700	
			–	
			–	
				Diderot publishes *Encyclopédie*, 1751–1780
			–	
Industrial Revolution: Phase 1, 1770–1830			–	Watt develops practical steam engine, 1782
			1800	Jacquard loom designed, 1801
			–	Railroads in use, 1829
Industrial Revolution: Phase 2, 1830–1905			–	
			–	American industrial working conditions begin to deteriorate, c. 1860
	Japanese Industrial Revolution, 1868–1905	Abortive Russian industrialization, 1880–1905	–	
			1900	Assembly line comes into use, c. 1900

products there, aiding Japan's success. Russia followed a second pattern. It was unsuccessful in establishing a capitalist industrial base and achieved full industrialization only through governmental involvement on the socialist model. The third pattern, that of colonies and other dependent regions, is one of little or no industrial development in this period. Home countries effectively stifled any local efforts to industrialize, maintaining the market for themselves. Industrialization would come to former colonies only a century or more later, and then it usually would be incomplete and faltering.

THE IMPACT OF THE GLOBAL INDUSTRIAL REVOLUTION

The Industrial Revolution was characterized by several elements wherever it occurred. These were:

— the use of mechanized equipment to increase output and decrease labor costs of production;

— the creation of large factories;

— mass production and standardization;

— a workplace that emphasized production, sometimes with assembly lines;

— financing that often included shareholders and stock; and

— an expanded labor force that included women, immigrants, and children.

These elements combined to form an efficient mode of organization and production that soon dominated much of the world. What made industrialization so attractive?

Above all else, industry gave individuals a chance to improve their lot. A middle-class investor might get rich by backing the right enterprise; a younger son with no future on the family farm might find an alternative career as a factory worker; a woman with few other options could support herself operating a machine. Industry gave hope for economic betterment, and for many that hope was realized, creating upward mobility in the class system.

Expansive governments, too, found industry attractive, because it went hand-in-glove with empire. An empire was an expensive business; industry could produce the wealth necessary to form and maintain it. Industry required raw materials to process; the colonies of an empire could provide them. Industry needed markets to sell its goods; empire provided colonies to expand industry's markets.

The Industrial Revolution also led to an increase in technological development. Each mechanical improvement in production processes gave its possessor an advantage over competitors, so industrialists found themselves supporting research and development in technology. Transporting goods also was a major problem for many industries, a problem that began to be solved only by the steam railroads of the second phase of the Industrial Revolution. Later, the development of internal combustion engines fueled with petroleum products led to more efficient railroads, to automobiles, and eventually to airplanes.

The cost of industrialization, of course, has been high. Nonrenewable resources are inexorably depleted; renewable resources sometimes are used faster than they can recover. Pollution has fouled our air, water, and soil. And human beings have suffered from the stresses and dangers of the factory. It is difficult to judge whether the Industrial Revolution has improved or worsened the human condition on balance, but it is clear that it has been a major force in shaping subsequent events and processes.

SUMMARY

1. The Industrial Revolution began in England around 1770; within the next fifty years it spread to the rest of western Europe and North America, where it evolved further. It was characterized by mechanization, large factories with mass-production techniques, and a reorganization of production. It largely replaced the earlier cottage craft tradition.

2. Encyclopedias laid the intellectual groundwork for the Industrial Revolution by disseminating trade secrets, advocating an improved standard of living for the working classes, and championing progressivism. Social Darwinism also played a role by providing a justification in the minds of many Europeans for exploiting colonial peoples and the poor.

3. The establishment of the patent system in Western countries encouraged inventors to focus on devising improved technology.

4. Abundant capital for investment, efficient agriculture to support industry, mushrooming population, and personal mobility all contributed to the initiation of the Industrial Revolution in England.

5. The technology of the Industrial Revolution relied on few new principles and consisted mostly of refined versions of preexisting technology. The greatest change was in the increased use of these machines, not in new technological concepts.

6. The factory required new forms of organization, including standardization of parts, segregation of tasks, and eventually the assembly line. It also required different attitudes and work habits.

7. Most segments of society profited economically from the industrialization of their countries. Colonies and other dependent regions that supplied raw materials to fuel industry, however, suffered from depressed economies as the home country thwarted their industrial development.

8. The early phase of the Industrial Revolution focused on light industry; the later phase (after 1830 in western Europe and northeastern North America) also included heavy industry.

9. The Industrial Revolution redrew class lines and intensified conflicts between classes in most places, especially between labor and management in the factories.

10. Working conditions in English and European factories were generally harsh and exploitative. Working conditions in American factories were relatively benign in the early period but became increasingly exploitative over time. This probably relates to the presence of the frontier as an escape valve in the early phase of the American Industrial Revolution.

11. Women, children, and immigrants formed major parts of the factory labor force, largely because they would work for lower wages and were considered more cooperative.

12. The Industrial Revolution hastened urbanization and created massive environmental pollution.

13. Industrialization outside the original core area has been spotty. Japan, building on a strong preindustrial base, successfully industrialized itself in the late nineteenth century under government sponsorship and through entrepreneurs. Russia's industrialization was slow until after socialism was established, so it experienced no major Industrial Revolution along capitalist lines. Most other areas did not industrialize in this era.

SUGGESTED READINGS

Chirot, Daniel. *Social Change in the Modern Age.* San Diego, Calif.: Harcourt Brace Jovanovich, 1986. A global treatment of modern industrialization, focusing on political and social impacts and written from the sociological perspective.

Dublin, Thomas. *Transforming Women's Work: New England Lives in the Industrial Revolution.* Ithaca, N.Y.: Cornell University Press, 1994. A current treatment of the role of women in the American Industrial Revolution and its effects on women's roles in society.

Fisher, Douglas. *The Industrial Revolution: A Macroeconomic Interpretation.* New York: St. Martin's Press, 1992. Examines the backdrop and consequences of industrialization in terms of economics.

Habakkuk, H. J. *American and British Technology in the Nineteenth Century: The Search for Labour-Saving Inventions.* Cambridge, Eng.: Cambridge University Press, 1962. An excellent comparative approach that presents the hypothesis of the frontier as a significant factor in shaping the Industrial Revolution on both sides of the Atlantic.

Kemp, Tom. *Industrialization in the Non-Western World.* London: Longman, 1983. Capsule summaries of the progress of industrialization in Japan, Russia/the Soviet Union, India, China, Brazil, Nigeria, and Egypt, as well as two synthetic essays. Written from the point of view of economic history.

Singer, Charles, E. J. Holmyard, A. R. Hall, and Trevor I. Williams, eds. Vol. IV of Singer, Holmyard, Hall, and Williams, eds., *A History of Technology.* Oxford, Eng.: Oxford University Press, 1958. The classic collection of synthetic essays on the technical and technological aspects of the Industrial Revolution.

Stearns, Peter N. *The Industrial Revolution in World History.* Boulder, Colo.: Westview Press, 1993. An excellent global treatment of the Industrial Revolution.

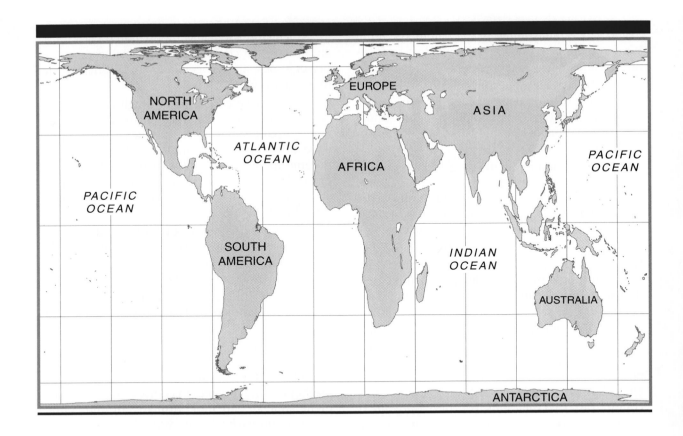

Modern Nationalism around the Globe

around 1790–1920

In 1879, columns of Zulu warriors overran an English-led army invading Zululand. Although they were using the most advanced military technology, more than 1,500 of the invaders fell to the Zulu, who were armed generally with the signature stabbing spears developed a few decades earlier. After the killing of the survivors, one Zulu force moved to take Roark's Drift, a thinly defended outpost a few miles away. The Zulu had been united into a nation by Shaka in the early nineteenth century, and they remained nationalistic and militarily potent until the Zulu War of 1879.

Like the Zulus, many peoples began to identify themselves more strongly with their government or ethnic group in the latter part of the eighteenth century. This modern nationalism was fostered by intellectuals, especially writers and scholars, who collected folktales and wrote histories. They both discovered and recreated various national pasts and traditions that inspired elite and commoners alike. Political leaders promoted nationalist movements to enhance their political power in internal unification and expansionist foreign policies.

SOCIAL AND POLITICAL ELEMENTS OF NATIONALISM

Every person plays several roles in society. One person may be a parent, spouse, community member, member of a particular occupation, and so forth. While all these roles are held at the same time, they may not be felt equally strongly. **Nationalism** is an ideology that emphasizes one's social role as a member of a nation. The nation always is characterized by a sense of ownership of the government, the nation-state. In addition, the nation usually has several characteristics:

— a common language,

— shared historical experiences and institutions, and

— similar cultural traditions, including religion, at both elite and popular levels.

In some cases, nationalism can exist even when a people does not have its own state, as with the Bosnian Serbs in the 1990s. As the fighting in Bosnia showed, nationalism has both inclusive and exclusive characteristics: The Serbs united (inclusion) and warred against the Muslims and Croats (exclusion), who also fought against each other.

Modern nationalism emerged from intellectuals and members of other elite groups, who united to enjoy common cultural activities or to defend against a common enemy. Previously, many European intellectuals of the Enlightenment had seen themselves as members of an international community, members who may have been French, German, or English but who were united by a common desire to seek universal solutions to humanity's problems. French thinkers and the French language tended to dominate intellectual discourse. Nationalists reacted against this internationalism and French cultural influence. They focused instead on the nation and their national language.

Nationalism spread to other social groups through the development of institutions like national armed forces, educational systems, extended voting franchises, and transportation networks. Often, this process emerged from policies of government officials who wished to develop a citizenry passionately devoted to the state. Newly drafted soldiers, who had been taught to revere a national flag, anthem, and history, underwent further military indoctrination to ensure that they would sacrifice their lives in the national interest. Casting votes in national elections gave people roles in forming governments and a sense of ownership of their nation-states.

Nationalism also developed in highly charged political contexts. Zulus united against other tribes and fought against Europeans, who encroached upon Zululand. Japanese leaders feared European invasion and domination, promoting nationalist slogans like "revere the Emperor and expel the foreigners." American colonists who formed the United States unified against what they perceived as tyrannical rule by Britain. Canadians united partly in fear of conquest by the United States.

Modern nationalism emerged from global interactions among peoples. During the nineteenth and twentieth centuries, Westerners and Japanese ruled indigenous peoples in empires in which the nationalistic passions of the rulers triggered nationalist movements among their subjects. These movements toppled modern empires in the twentieth century.

MODERN NATIONALISM AS AN IDEOLOGY AND POLITICAL FORCE

Nationalism has been a potent ideology and catalytic force in the nineteenth and twentieth centuries. From 1859 to 1871, nationalism played a major role in the creation of two nation-states, Italy and Germany, drastically altering the European political scene. Later, at the end of World War I, nationalism helped bring Poland, Hungary, Yugoslavia, Czechoslovakia, Latvia, Lithuania, and Estonia into being. Eventually, nationalism sparked successful independence movements in the Pacific islands, Africa, and Asia. Nationalism helped to splinter Yugoslavia and Czechoslovakia in the 1990s and eased the reunification of Hong Kong with China in mid–1997.

Early Nationalist Thought

The most developed expression of early nationalism came through the writings of Johann von Herder (1744–1803), a German. During the 1780s, Herder argued that intellectuals alone could not create nationalism; rather, they should build on elements of the common folk culture. Herder believed that a nation's past should play a vital role in the understanding of the present and planning for the future. Further, he argued, the masses should be encouraged to play a part in developing a nation's greatness. Herder and his followers condemned the French ideas and language that dominated princely courts in German-speaking areas.

Not only were French intellectuals predominant in European intellectual discourse, but French military power controlled many Europeans from 1794 to 1815. Johann Fichte (1762–1814), a major intellectual and follower of Herder, initially welcomed the French Revolution as an expression of the emancipation of the human spirit, but after the French conquered and ruled many German-speaking domains, Fichte issued his *Addresses to the German Nation* to summon a latent German spirit that he believed superior to that of the French. German nationalism was forged in reaction to French domination.

Italian intellectuals responded positively to the ideas of the American and French revolutions, but they quickly became disillusioned with the terror in France and then with the repressive rule of the French. Some Italians welcomed revolutionary ideas, like the right of a people to determine its own laws, and championed the sentiment that a nation was a unit of humanity with the right to determine its own form of political rule. Napoleon Bonaparte twice invaded Italy, and French rule helped unleash early Italian nationalism.

MAP 33.1 *Napoleon's Empire.* *Under Napoleon, the French ruled significant parts of Germany, Italy, and Spain. Their rule sometimes excited national movements of opposition to foreign domination. After the end of French control, some Germans, Italians, and Spaniards unsuccessfully attempted to establish national governments. By 1871, a united Germany and a united Italy emerged from wars of independence, wars that had connections to the national movements begun during the Napoleonic era.*

Imposition of the French language, however, provoked many intellectuals to promote cultural nationalism. Later, collapse of French rule brought in the Austrians, who opposed Italian unification as a threat to their empire.

Hatred of French tyranny captured the imagination of artists like Francisco Goya, who painted powerful scenes of Spanish patriots dying at the hands of their French rulers, conveying the horror of tyranny. Anti-French patriotic sentiments received a boost from such paintings, and they helped fuel a national mood that brought a return of the Spanish monarchy.

Gathering folktales became a way to recover and preserve the oral and written traditions of a nation, promoting nationalist identity and pride. The Grimm brothers, for example, spent many years traveling through German-speaking areas and collecting folktales and folk poetry. Wilhelm Grimm once wrote that "only folk poetry is perfect because God himself wrote it like the laws of Sinai; it is not put together from pieces like human work is." In 1812, the Grimm brothers' published endeavors began reaching a wide audience in Germany.

In a similar vein, Central European scholars followed Johann von Herder's idea that language was the glue holding a nation together. According to this idea, language was the essence of a national people and should therefore be purified by the excision of foreign words. Small groups of scholars developed grammars, compiled dictionaries, wrote literature, and edited journals. They created standard languages, like modern Czech, Slovak, Hungarian, Ukrainian, and Bulgarian, from the native tongues of peasants, servants, and shopkeepers. From these scholars also came the nationalist belief that the nation-state was the political framework for the fullest realization of the individual.

European Romanticism

Romanticism, an artistic movement of the period between 1780 and 1900, developed in Europe and spread to several countries, including those in the Americas. Romanticism, the elite artistic emphasis on feelings, imagination, and nature, often was employed as a vehicle to create national identity. European Romanticism began partly as a reaction to the Enlightenment's emphasis on reason, science, and humankind. Increasingly, Romantic writers and composers searched out their nations' folktales and folk songs to express love for the

Figure 33.1 *Spanish Resistance to French Rule. Francisco Goya made scores of etchings depicting the Spanish fight against the French from 1808 to 1813. In this scene, a Spaniard armed with a pitchfork drives away a feeble vulture. The vulture is a satire on the imperial eagle of Napoleon; the comical spectacle of its removal appears to delight the unarmed crowd in the background. Humor has often been an effective weapon against repressive governments.* Nimatallah/Art Resource, N.Y.

IN THEIR OWN WORDS

Friedrich Schlegel on Romantic Poetry

In 1798, Friedrich Schlegel and his brother often hosted gatherings of German intellectuals who criticized what they considered the bankruptcy of rationalism and championed a poetry of intuition and emotion. Among the people attending was Novalis (Friedrich von Hardenberg), who became a significant Romantic poet. Friedrich Schlegel wrote this fragment that outlined his conception of Romantic poetry:

> Romantic poetry is progressive, universal poetry. Its aim isn't merely to reunite all the separate species of poetry and put poetry in touch with philosophy and rhetoric. It tries to and should mix and fuse poetry and prose, inspiration and criticism, the poetry of art and the poetry of nature; and make poetry lively and social, and life and society poetical; poeticize wit and fill and saturate the forms of art with every kind of good, solid matter for instruction, and animate them with pulsations of humor. It embraces everything that is purely poetic, from the greatest systems of art, containing within themselves still further systems, to the sigh, the kiss that the poetizing child breathes forth in artless song. It can so lose itself in what it describes that one might believe it exists only to characterize poetical individuals of all sorts; and yet there is still no form so fit for expressing the entire spirit of an author; so that many artists who started out to write only a novel ended up by providing us with a portrait of themselves. It alone can become, like the epic, a mirror of the circumambient world, an image of an age. And it can also—more than any other form—hover at the midpoint between the portrayed and the portrayer, free of all real and ideal self-interest, on the wings of poetic reflection again and again to a higher power, can multiply it in an endless succession of mirrors. It is capable of the highest and most variegated refinement, not only from within outwards, but also from without inwards; capable in that it organizes—for everything that seeks a wholeness in its effects—the parts along similar lines, so that it opens a perspective upon an infinitely increasing classicism. Romantic poetry is in the arts what wit is in philosophy, and what society and sociability, friendship and love are in life. Other kinds of poetry are finished and are now capable of being fully analyzed. The romantic kind of poetry is still in the state of becoming; that, in fact, is its real essence: that it should forever be becoming and never be perfected. It can be exhausted by no theory and only a divinatory criticism would dare try to characterize its ideal. It alone is infinite, just as it alone is free; and it recognizes as its first commandment that the will of the poet can tolerate no law above itself. The romantic kind of poetry is the only one that is more than a kind, that is, as it were, poetry itself: for in a sense all poetry is or should be romantic.

nation and admiration for its heroes. German Romantics, for example, responded to calls by patriots to create a national culture that differed from French culture.

Friedrich von Hardenberg, also known as Novalis (1772–1801), was an important member of a group of German intellectuals who developed German Romanticism in the 1790s. Of these thinkers, Novalis perhaps best exemplifies the importance of the individual in Romanticism. In 1797, Novalis's fiancée died, an event that inspired him to write poetry that eventually brought him great popularity. Death became a central theme in Novalis's poetry, and he saw death as the purpose of life, a time of transcendent unity with God.

Humanity and nature also became central themes of Novalis's writings, leading to a mystical vision of uniting human beings with nature.

Richard Wagner[1] (1813–1883) embodied a Romantic artistic image and also nationalist tendencies in his work and life. Wagner's operas served as musical dramas, uniting art, dance, music, and poetry. He exulted in the Romantic image of the individual as genius. In his grand artistic synthesis, Wagner followed the tradition of earlier Romantics like Novalis. German history fascinated Wagner, and it came to life for him in the works he read; like other German nationalists,

[1] **Richard Wagner:** ree KAHRD VAHG ner

Wagner took a keen interest in German folktales and legends, incorporating many into his operas.

Wagner saw himself as the living embodiment of the destiny of the German nation. In 1842, upon returning to Germany from France, Wagner wrote, "I saw the Rhine [River] for the first time; with tears swelling in my eyes I, a poor artist, swore eternal loyalty to my German fatherland." He gave the operatic theater a central place in German social life. The Wagnerian opera cycle, a set of related operas, lasted for more than ninety hours of singing, dancing, and acting on the grandest scale. This led Gustav Mahler to exclaim that "If the whole of German art were to disappear, it could be recognized and reconstructed from this one work."

NATIONAL UNIFICATION EFFORTS, 1816–1877

Major unification drives occurred in Africa, Asia, Europe, and the Americas between 1816 and 1877. All were directed by ruling elites and enjoyed varying degrees of popular support in the form of nationalism. Three nations, Zululand, Japan, and the United States were challenged by external threats (invasion) or internal threats (civil war). By 1877, many countries around the world had strengthened or forged nation-states.

The Development of the Zulu Nation

In the nineteenth century, the Zulu nation had expanded into parts of southern Africa and had come upon European settlers who blocked further settlement. The confrontation helped maintain the Zulu nation by strengthening Zulu nationalism against their enemy. The Zulu spoke a common language and shared a variety of historical experiences, institutions, and cultural traditions. Conflict with Dutch and English settlers revealed the need to consolidate Zulu political and military systems for protection.

The architect of the modern Zulu nation was Shaka (reign dates 1816–1828), who assumed rulership of the Zulus when they faced the Europeans. Shaka's military genius flowered in a series of reforms. First and most important, he declared

FIGURE 33.2 *Shaka. Although this portrait titled "Chaka, King of the Zooloe" may not be an exact likeness of Shaka (few existed), it is an accurate rendering of a warrior of his time. The shield, however, may be somewhat larger than the shields carried into battle.* MuseuMAfricA, Johannesburg.

that the primary goal of warfare was to kill large numbers of the enemy. Previously, warfare had been a ritualized affair with a battle frequently ending upon the wounding of someone. Rarely would more than a few people be killed. Second, Shaka's armies were organized into formal regiments and drilled in formations and with coordinated actions. This forged a powerful bonding among the warriors, making them more likely to win large battles. Third, Shaka converted the throwing spear, a traditional weapon, into a shorter thrusting spear. His soldiers were able to advance on the enemy with shields locked, impregnable to thrown spears; then, when close enough, they rushed upon the now-defenseless

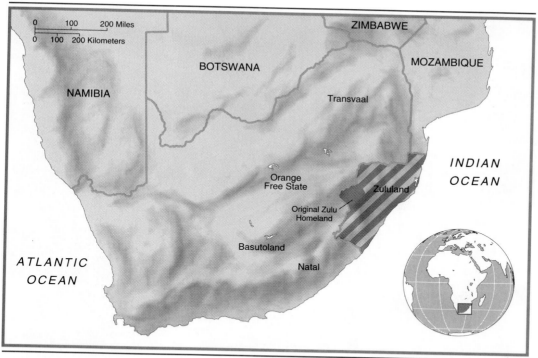

MAP 33.2 *Zulu Expansion, 1816–1879.* *Under the leadership of Shaka and his successors, the Zulus conquered and united considerable territory, creating Zululand. Zulu nationalism helped spur this expansion, which came at the expense of other tribal groups, some of whom were assimilated by the Zulus. Zulu expansion came to an end with the defeat of Zulu forces by the British in 1879. Eventually, Zululand became part of the Union of South Africa.*

foe. Fourth, Shaka assimilated conquered peoples into his own nation, ensuring a stock of women to produce food for his soldiers and a supply of men for future replacement of battlefield losses.

These reforms strengthened the Zulu nation and made it invincible against other African peoples. Indoctrination of Zulu soldiers and captives ensured a cohesive nationalism, and success in warfare lured warriors from nearby tribes, who volunteered to join the growing Zulu nation. A powerful Zululand gradually emerged, one that outlived Shaka, who was assassinated by a half-brother, Dingane.

The Zulu ambushed and killed nearly 500 Dutch colonists in 1838, incurring the wrath of the Europeans. After decades of conflict, the British finally conquered the Zulu in 1879. The Zulu legacy as a model for nationalism inspired other African peoples to undertake nationalist movements.

The Development of Japanese Nationalism

Japanese nationalism emerged from elite fears that Japan's modest size invited foreign domination. The immediate threat began when ships of Western countries entered Japanese waters in the late eighteenth century in violation of the Japanese policy of closing Japan to most Western commerce and communication. News of China's defeat by the British in the Opium War (1839–1842) alarmed the Japanese emperor, who commanded the *shogun* to strengthen Japan's defenses. This order shocked the Japanese because the emperor had hitherto been a puppet dancing to the *shogun*'s tune.

Pilgrimages to imperial shrines by commoners also indicated the revival of emperor worship. Scholars who foresaw the decline of the Tokugawa Shogunate predicted that only the imperial system

FIGURE 33.3 *Satsuma* Samurai *Fighting Imperial Troops.* *During the Satsuma Uprising, a conscript army of diverse social groups fought for the Japanese government against the warriors of Satsuma. In this print, mounted imperial troops in Western-style uniforms charge traditionally attired Japanese women armed with long-handled swords, or* naginata. *Women, however, seldom fought in armed combat during this time.* Tsuneo Tamba Collection, Yokohama, Japan/Laurie Platt Winfrey, Inc.

could rally the Japanese to defend themselves against outside threats. By 1868, a coalition of *samurai* and court nobles wrested control of the imperial palace from shogunal troops, ending the shogunate in the next few months. These new Japanese leaders used an emperor-based nationalism to legitimize their policies.

Nationalism drove many of the revolutionary changes wrought in the emperor's name. Japan's new leaders transformed the shogunal system of central and local government into a highly centralized unitary state, luring local leaders to surrender their domains to the emperor. A national army was created by conscription, undermining the exclusive *samurai* privilege of wearing swords, and imperial shrines were brought under government control. National symbols and patriotic sentiments became an essential part of the Japanese educational system. Students began each school day with a salute to the flag and a bow to the emperor's portrait.

Samurai smarted from a series of blows to their financial, social, and political bases. One large group rallied around Saigo Takamori, a former government leader, in the Satsuma Uprising of 1877. The crushing of these insurgent *samurai* in the brief civil war preserved the Japanese union and permitted the nationalist transformation to continue.

By 1894, Japan's Westernization and modernization policies achieved success. Japanese leaders embarked on a program to build an Asian empire, and the Sino-Japanese War (1894–1895) and the Russo-Japanese War (1904–1905) intensified the Japanese nationalism that led to their military successes. In 1905, some patriots rioted against their government when they learned that Japan received less than had been expected from the Russo-Japanese War's settlement. During World War I, Japan won additional territory in China, and patriots in the Japanese military plotted a takeover of Manchuria between 1928 and 1931. The success of this plot in 1932 triggered an upsurge of Japanese nationalism that eventually helped unleash World War II in Asia.

Nationalism and the Unification of Italy

Italy had been divided for many centuries. In 1859, eight separate states ruled parts of the Italian Peninsula and the islands of Sardinia and Sicily. Most of these polities had existed since the Middle Ages, and some had become powerful governments during the Italian Renaissance. In addition, France and Austria controlled parts of the Italian Peninsula.

Nationalism played a role in the unification of Italy, but nationalists who favored a republic were outmaneuvered by Count Camillo di Cavour (1810–1861), who preferred an Italian monarchy. Cavour was a nationalist who initially believed that a united Italy was an impossible dream. Yet national unity did come, between 1859 and 1871. Prior to that time, much of the intellectual foundation for an Italian nation-state had been laid. A group of thinkers, including Giuseppi Mazzini (1805–1872), founded Young Italy, a secret society to promote unification of the Italian Peninsula. Mazzini's group ardently propagandized the cause of Italian nationalism, and operas by Giuseppi Verdi helped inspire a birth of the Italian spirit.

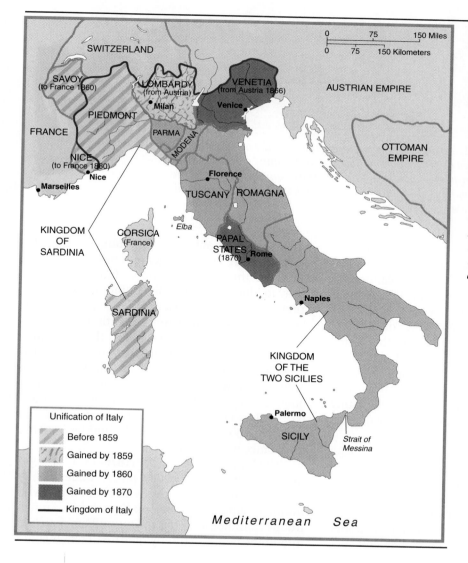

MAP 33.3 *The Unification of Italy, 1859–1871. The Kingdom of Piedmont-Sardinia unwittingly initiated the unification of Italy by seeking to expand its territories. Count Cavour allied with the French to wrest parts of northern Italy away from the Austrians. This partly successful effort spurred Italian nationalists who sought a wider unification of Italy. By 1871, all Italian territories, including the Papal States and Rome, were annexed. Sicily was added as well.*

FIGURE 33.4 *Garibaldi Landing in Sicily.* *Giuseppi Garibaldi, an Italian nationalist, formed a liberation army known as "The Thousand" to fight for the unity of his country. This scene depicts a larger-than-life Garibaldi exhorting his troops onward. His forces are welcomed and resisted. After taking Sicily, Garibaldi crossed to the Italian Peninsula and advanced northward.* Collection Bertarelli, Milan. Photo by Saporetti.

Count Cavour played a key role in the unification of Italy after he became the prime minister of Piedmont-Sardinia in 1852. Cavour planned to build Italy as an extension of his state. Efforts along those lines led to an alliance with Napoleon III (reign dates 1852–1870), emperor of France. Napoleon III desired to annex areas to the southeast of France, and Cavour managed to convince France to wage a joint campaign against Austria-Hungary in exchange for these provinces. Napoleon III's forces defeated the Austrians, liberating part of northern Italy and doubling Piedmont-Sardinia's size.

Another Italian nationalist, Giuseppi Garibaldi (1807–1882), independently led an army of patriotic soldiers to free southern Italy from foreign rule. After Garibaldi freed Sicily, middle-class Italian nationalists supported his march on Naples. Large-scale disturbances broke out there, and support for a united Italy spread across the peninsula.

These popular activities facilitated Garibaldi's effort. Fearing French anger and military action if Garibaldi threatened the pope, Cavour used his army to block Garibaldi's liberation of Rome. After intense negotiations, Garibaldi offered his conquests to the king of Piedmont-Sardinia.

Venice, which was ruled by the Austrians, became part of Italy as a result of the Austro-Prussian War of 1866. The defeat of Austria took only seven weeks and had important consequences for Italy. After Prussia's victory, the Prussian leader, Otto von Bismarck, compelled the Austrians to cede Venice to Italy, and he initiated an alliance with the Italians.

The Franco-Prussian War (1870–1871) brought the last piece of the Italian puzzle under Italian control. In order to meet the German army with his forces amassed, Napoleon III withdrew French troops from Rome. Soon, Italian soldiers marched into Rome, and the utterly defeated French could do nothing about it. Less than a year later, Rome became the capital of a united Italy, and the Vatican, a tiny area of the city, remained independent under the pope's control. Losing Rome, however, turned the papacy against the new state, hampering the program of consolidating the new state's control over Italy.

Nationalism and the Unification of Germany

German unification was facilitated by several factors, including a common language, similar cultural traditions, and the growing economic integration of Germany. Although many Germans desired to form a German nation-state, they failed to attract the requisite support of a major state, particularly Prussia. That had to await the foreign policies of Otto von Bismarck, who had his own vision of the German nation-state.

Political factors became prominent in German unification efforts in the first half of the nineteenth century. We have seen how French rule of German areas turned German cultural nationalism into political nationalism. German nationalists, however, were thwarted by Austria's Prince Clemens Metternich, who helped create a German confederation of nearly forty states under Austrian influence in 1815. Efforts by German nationalists to promote national unification were crushed by Austrian repression. During political upheavals in 1848 and 1849, when Metternich fell from power, German nationalists again failed to create a united Germany.

Economic and social factors played a more vital role in Germany's unification. In the 1830s, many German states formed the Zollverein, a free-trade alliance that included Prussia but excluded Austria. This economic organization promoted trade and economic development, which mushroomed through the rest of the nineteenth century. Another unifying element was the Prussian army's building of an integrated transportation system centering on railroad lines to be used for military purposes in wartime. Through the middle decades of the nineteenth century, musical, sporting, and cultural associations effected German cultural awareness through festivals, shooting contests, and gymnastic events. A first-rate educational system also emerged in the nineteenth century and became a focal point for German intellectuals, many of whom were ardent nationalists.

The architect of German unity was Prussia's chancellor, Otto von Bismarck (1815–1898), who circumvented the Prussian parliament and built up Prussia's armed forces. Thereafter, he used a squabble with the Danes over disputed northern territories to create an alliance with Austria, and

FIGURE 33.5
Proclaiming the German Empire. *This painting captures the spirit of celebration that accompanied the founding of the German Empire in 1871. Jubilant officers hold their swords aloft, while Otto von Bismarck, who became the empire's first chancellor, dominates the foreground. Attired in white in a sea of black uniforms, von Bismarck is the painting's central figure despite his placement below the German monarch. Much to the dismay of the French, the German Empire was proclaimed on French soil, at Versailles, the palace of Louis XIV.*
Bismarck Museum, Friedrichsruh.

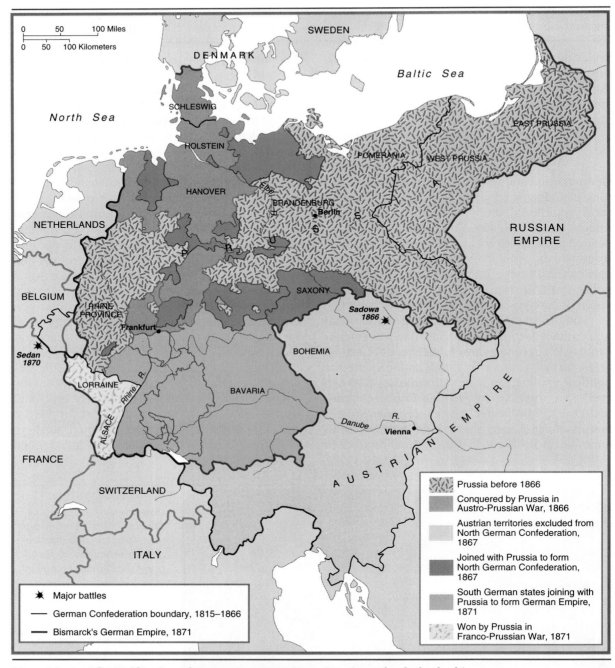

MAP 33.4   *The Unification of Germany, 1863–1871.*   *Prussia, under the leadership of Otto von Bismarck, began a policy of territorial expansion that culminated in German unification. The disputed territories of Schleswig and Holstein were wrested away from Denmark in 1863. A few years later, Prussia defeated Austria, omitting the Austrians (many of whom spoke German) from a united Germany. In 1870, France and Prussia went to war. German nationalism generated during this conflict helped push the final unification of the German states in 1871. France also lost Alsace and Lorraine to Germany, a loss that rankled the French into the twentieth century.*

their combined forces compelled the Danes to cede the contested areas. Then Bismarck deliberately provoked a crisis between Prussia and Austria over who would get the disputed territories, eventually triggering a war with the Austrians in 1866 that ended with Austria's defeat.

A major issue in Germany's unification was the composition of the German nation. Some favored a broad definition that included all German-speaking peoples; others espoused a more limited interpretation that excluded the German-speaking Austrians. A major reason for keeping out the Austrians was their rule over non-Germans (e.g., Poles, Hungarians, and Czechs). As long as Austrians insisted on keeping these peoples subject, many opposed their inclusion in Germany. More of a Prussian patriot than a German nationalist, Otto von Bismarck wanted Prussia to dominate a German state, and he had to exclude powerful Austria from the union, fearing that it could effectively challenge Prussian dominance.

To achieve German unification, Bismarck believed he needed to provoke the French into declaring war on Prussia. This could animate German nationalism to drive the remaining German states into a Prussian-dominated union. French nationalists, succumbing to some provocative diplomatic maneuvers by Bismarck, demanded that Napoleon III declare war. The remaining German states joined Prussia, whose train-transported forces quickly overwhelmed the French. Napoleon III fell into Prussian hands at the Battle of Sedan in September 1870. In early 1871, German princes and states declared their allegiance to the German monarch, and the German Empire came into being. The hapless French ceded the provinces of Alsace and Lorraine to the Germans and also paid a substantial indemnity.

Zionism: The Development of Jewish Nationalism

Zionism grew out of a reaction to the pervasive anti-Semitism in Europe at the turn of the twentieth century. Richard Wagner was but one of many intellectuals and others who hated Jews, blaming them for a variety of misfortunes plaguing Europe. A long-term economic recession from the 1870s to the 1890s, for example, provoked hatred against Jews, who were imagined to be behind the trouble.

This was a continuation of a centuries-old animosity against Jews.

Theodore Herzl (1860–1904) was a Hungarian-born Jew and journalist who covered stories involving Jews. After writing about the Dreyfus Affair, a famous French legal case that revealed deep-seated French anti-Semitism, Herzl wrote a pamphlet, *The Jewish State*, in which he argued that Jews should have their own nation-state. The

FIGURE 33.6 *Theodore Herzl. In this 1903 photo, Theodore Herzl greets people outside a synagogue. Herzl had become well known in the Jewish community for his advocacy of Zionism, the movement to create a modern Jewish state in Palestine.* The Central Zionist Archive, Jerusalem.

nationalist movement devoted to this cause, Zionism, developed, and it united Jews around the world. Zionism had a strong millennial component because some Zionists believed that the founding of a Jewish state would be the onset of the last days of the world.

Zionism flourished in eastern and central Europe in the twentieth century. Societies like the Lovers of Zion and the Jewish Colonization Association promoted Jewish settlement of Palestine, in Southwest Asia, which Jews considered to be their traditional homeland. Zionist aims grew in intensity because of the Nazi Holocaust, a deliberate extermination campaign by the German state that killed millions of Jews during World War II. Many survivors ardently believed that Jews deserved a homeland in Palestine. In 1948, the dream became a reality as the state of Israel, but the methods and passions of Zionists also helped spark Palestinian nationalism.

The U.S. Civil War

The United States underwent a major test of its unity during the Civil War (1861–1865), America's bloodiest and most convulsive conflict. Earlier, nationalism had aided in the formation of the United States, but, by mid–nineteenth century, many disagreements among states threatened the Union with dissolution. The central problem was states' rights versus those of the federal government.

Political and economic issues tied to slavery sharply divided Americans. Although many in the North morally objected to slavery and wished to abolish it, the central issue igniting the conflict was whether or not states might secede from the Union. Indeed, slavery remained in some Union states, like Maryland, until after the end of the Civil War. Southern states had long been upset by the federal government's economic policies favoring the industrialized northern states. The South's agriculture-based society needed high-tariff policies, which ran counter to the interests of other states. In addition, Southern leaders believed that the growing movement to abolish slavery in the United States could lead to an agricultural catastrophe, because they remained convinced of the need for slave labor in order to work their plantations and maintain their profits.

President Abraham Lincoln (1809–1865) strove ardently to maintain the Union. He told suspicious Southern leaders that he could live with slavery but not with disunion. These pleas fell on deaf ears, and war erupted. Northern states possessed superior material resources and industrial capabilities that gradually overcame the superior generalship of Southern generals like Robert E. Lee. At the same time, Lincoln began to conceive of a strategy for postwar rehabilitation and reconciliation. The main effort was to be victory tempered by charity, but Lincoln died from an assassin's bullet before he could implement his plans.

Nationalism sparked many Americans in the North to volunteer to fight for the Union's preservation. Soldiers in the Northern armies usually fought in state units, yet they shared a national purpose, to maintain a strong United States.

Many African American soldiers in the North had responded to the need to free their brothers and sisters from chattel bondage, and more than 186,000 African Americans served in the Union army. These African Americans played a critical role in the fighting that ultimately claimed more than a half-million lives in the North and South. Among famous African American fighting units was the 54th Massachusetts Regiment, which stormed Fort Wagner near Charleston, South Carolina.

Later, freed slaves in the South faced a difficult life with few resources to support themselves, and they benefited only slightly from the Thirteenth, Fourteenth, and Fifteenth amendments to the Constitution. These amendments officially abolished slavery throughout the United States and forbade discrimination based on race and other factors, yet the rights guaranteed by these amendments rarely were recognized after the Civil War.

Canadian Unification

Canadian political leaders decided to unite their country under British protection in the 1860s. The area of British North America had two dominant European groups, those who spoke English and those who spoke French. The latter had been brought under British control in the French and Indian War (1756–1763), and they maintained a separate identity that was encouraged by works like the *Histoire du Canada*, which was published in 1845. The author, François-Xavier Garneau,[2]

---

[2] **François Xavier Garneau:** frahn SWAH zah vee AY gahr NOH

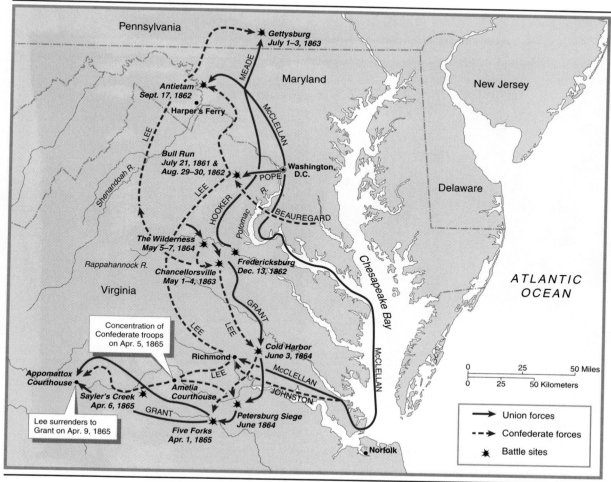

MAP 33.5 *The U.S. Civil War (East), 1861–1865.* *A major challenge to the United States began in 1861, when several Southern states seceded from the Union. Ferocious fighting followed in the next few years, leading to the deaths of hundreds of thousands. Although fighting erupted in various parts of the South and West, many of the strategic campaigns took place in the East, where the capitals of the North and South were located. A major invasion of the North, begun in 1863, was stopped at Gettysburg by Union forces. Hard fighting occurred for another year and a half until the Southern forces surrendered in April 1865.*

proved that French Canadians had a history and literature, writing a bestselling book in the process.

Canadian political leaders had been stymied in their attempts to reform the government between 1858 and 1864. They slowly realized that political deadlock created the image of weakness, attracting expansionists in the United States, some of whom had even talked about annexing parts of British North America. Two Canadian politicians, George-Étienne Cartier (1814–1873) and John Mac-

donald (1815–1891), put aside their differences to forge a united Canada. The French-speaking Cartier and the English-speaking Macdonald fervently desired to create a Canada by persuasion rather than coercion because they saw the tragedy of the bloody U.S. Civil War to their south. Macdonald promoted a Canadian experiment in cooperative nationalism, while Cartier desired that English-speaking Canadians accept policies supporting a French Canadian cultural identity.

FIGURE 33.7 *Canadian Delegates at the Charlottetown Conference.* *In 1864, delegates from many parts of Canada met on Prince Edward Island to discuss forming a Canadian confederation. Just six weeks later, a second conference in Quebec agreed to federal union. Shown in the foreground (in front of the second pillar from the left) are George-Étienne Cartier and John Macdonald, two key delegates. Meetings at Government House played a key role in the peaceful process of Canadian unity.* Public Archives of Canada, Ottawa, Documentary Art & Photography Division (C-7333).

Canadian unity developed between 1864 and 1867. A key event was the Quebec Conference, which was attended by representatives from all provinces. The delegates agreed on a federal union having central powers and provinces having autonomy, all under British protection. Representatives went to London to get British support for the Canadian proposal. Sympathetic British leaders sold the idea as a relief to British taxpayers and as an opportunity for investment. From the deliberations came the British North America Act of 1867, which created the Dominion of Canada. Prince Edward Island's inhabitants did not join until 1873, and the citizens of Newfoundland waited until 1949 for entrance into the nation-state.

Canadians enjoyed considerable autonomy within the British Commonwealth of Nations. The governor-general of Canada was appointed by London and exercised executive power on advice from the Canadian cabinet. Canadians had created a continental federation of provinces despite sharp ethnic and cultural differences. In the 1990s, however, there has been an upsurge of Quebec nationalism, centered on separating from Canada.

NATIONALISM AND THE COLLAPSE OF EMPIRES

Five major empires—the Chinese, the Ottoman, the Austro-Hungarian, the German, and the Russian—collapsed in the period between 1911 and 1918. Nationalism among subject peoples accelerated the disintegration of these empires. Out of the

MAP 33.6 *Dominion of Canada, 1867–1873.* *Canadian leaders decided to seek union in the late 1860s. They wished to forestall what they feared might be a northward expansion of the United States. Key to a union of Canada was the uniting of Quebec and Ontario, the most populous and prosperous provinces. Soon, most of the eastern maritime provinces joined the union. The British were persuaded to support this effort, keeping considerable influence in Canadian affairs. The unification process was peaceful and relatively noncontroversial.*

aftermath of this disarray came the formation of national states, many of them founded by dominant ethnic groups. Thus, the global map was redrawn dramatically.

The Collapse of China's Imperial System

The Qing Empire had been ruled by the Manchus since the mid–seventeenth century. A few million Manchus controlled the hundreds of millions of Chinese, partly through maintaining the traditional political and social systems, as well as by portraying themselves as determined defenders of Confucian values. Adopting Chinese ways and using military force had kept the Manchus in power for more than two centuries.

During the last two years of the nineteenth century, the Manchu government, headed by the Empress Dowager Cixi,[3] formed an alliance with a secret society called the Boxers. This organization of Chinese commoners, which had been both anti-Manchu and anti-Westerner, dropped the former orientation to concentrate on the anti-Western aspect. In 1900, a Boxer terrorist campaign against Westerners provoked a brief war that ended in defeat, rendering China helpless. If the Western powers had not feared a war over the division of spoils, China might have been partitioned. Utter defeat opened China to increasing foreign control.

The Boxer crisis brought a rare but temporary unity between the Chinese government and its

[3] **Cixi:** soo SHEE

PARALLELS AND DIVERGENCES

Nationalist Secret Societies

In the nineteenth century, Asians, Europeans, and Americans formed secret societies, using nationalist or racist sentiments to incite their members. Most of these groups feared repression by the ruling governments, and they acted circumspectly in order to further their plans.

Secret societies have long been important in history, and they usually have been found in places where an autocratic polity permits no political expression other than its own. In the time of modern nationalism, political aspirants formed secret organizations of intellectuals and others who hoped to ignite national movements in order to achieve nationalist goals.

The Boxers came from a long line of secret-society groups in Chinese history. Underground organizing against an existing regime goes back to at least the second century A.D. The name "Boxers" came from the Chinese designation "Society of Righteous Fists." Members frequently mastered martial-arts techniques and led their followers in antigovernment activities.

The Boxers also developed a strong anti-Western and racist bias that stemmed, in part, from the arrogant and sometimes belligerent actions of Europeans living in China. Upon learning that a growing anti-Western movement flourished in China, the Empress Dowager Cixi (reign dates 1862–1908), who despised Western meddling in China's affairs, cultivated ties with the Boxers. She encouraged their anti-Western activities in exchange for the submergence of anti-Manchu themes. In mid-1900, she allowed Boxer groups into Beijing and hoped that they might oust the troublesome Westerners. The Boxers were defeated and disappeared.

A secret society of Turkish nationalists, the Young Turks, campaigned for a thorough reform and revitalization of the Ottoman Empire. When they finally achieved their constitutional aims, the Young Turks set about oppressing the non-Turkish subjects of the realm.

Muslim brotherhoods originated as societies of like-minded men who preferred the company of fellow Muslims. By the nineteenth century, some brotherhoods turned to politics, seeking to oust Westerners from Muslim lands in Asia and Africa. When they became political, they operated in secret, fearing detection and destruction by the state. For some of them the issue was religion as well as politics, and they opposed conversions by Christian missionaries. By the twentieth century, brotherhoods became politically powerful in Arabia, Egypt, and the Sudan.

Other secret societies formed in Europe and the United States. The Italian Carbonari issued proclamations demanding Italian unity, and one Carbonari member, Giuseppi Mazzini, formed his own secret society, Young Italy, which played a role in propagandizing for Italian unification. Following the American Civil War, disaffected Southerners formed the Ku Klux Klan to intimidate the newly freed slaves, whom they considered racially inferior. Success by this racist group fueled organizations across America.

---

subjects. From 1901 to 1911, Manchu rulers attempted a series of changes, some dramatic, to reform the system. Manchus established Western-style ministries and implemented a constitutional system. Ultimately, however, all efforts collapsed along with the imperial system in 1912.

Chinese nationalism grew as imperial changes provoked political, social, economic, and cultural opposition. The government, for example, attempted to recentralize tax collections. This sparked local and provincial resistance by elite groups that depended on the tax revenues. Most important was the abolition of the Chinese imperial examination system in 1905. This profound decision ended Confucianism as the state ideology and helped sever the cultural ties between the Chinese elite and the Manchu rulers. Ethnic Chinese increasingly blamed the "blood-sucking Manchus" for China's problems. Rising nationalism helped dissolve remaining bonds of legitimacy that kept the Manchus in power. Finally, an abortive uprising in late 1911 triggered the system's collapse. Mongolian nationalism also ignited in the imperial collapse, and the independent state of Outer Mongolia emerged in 1919.

Nationalism brought down the Manchus, but it could not overcome the formidable strength of local and regional interests. In 1928, the Nationalist Party temporarily reunited China, but political ineptitude and Japanese imperialism thwarted nation building. A more lasting result had to wait

until 1949, when the Chinese Communist Party forged a new nation-state from the white heat of revolution and civil war.

The Decline and Fall of the Ottoman Empire

By 1800, the Ottoman Turks had ruled a vast empire stretching across parts of Africa, Asia, and Europe for nearly five centuries. They had provided effective rule for their subjects, who repre-

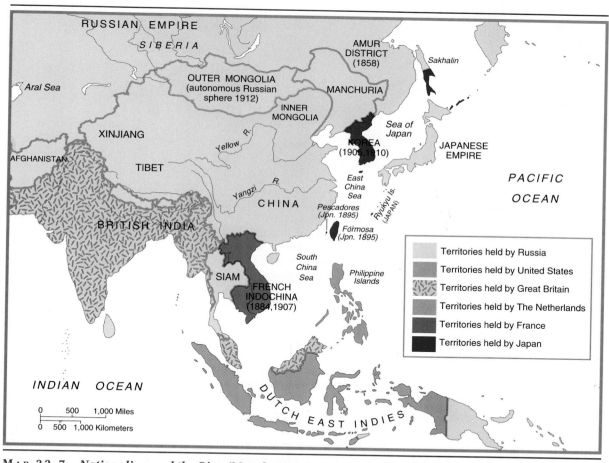

MAP 33.7 *Nationalism and the Qing (Manchu) Empire to 1912.* *The Manchus conquered and ruled China, beginning in 1644. They added Tibet, Mongolia, and Xinjiang as Chinese provinces in the seventeenth and eighteenth centuries. The Qing Empire collapsed early in the twentieth century, partly because of an upsurge in Chinese nationalism. In the collapse, Mongolia declared its independence, and Tibet and Xinjiang came under pressure from foreign powers to become independent. Both areas, however, remained under Chinese control.*

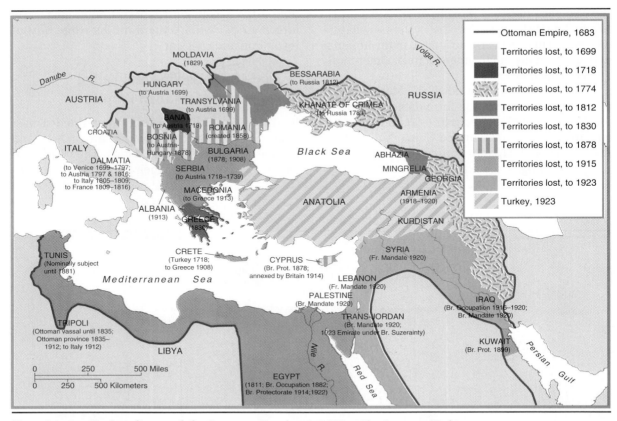

MAP 33.8 *Nationalism and the Ottoman Empire, to 1923.* *The Ottoman Turks conquered a vast domain, including parts of Europe, Asia, and Africa. They ruled a diverse group of ethnic peoples for several centuries. In the nineteenth and twentieth centuries, nationalists in the Ottoman Empire began to struggle for independence. By 1918, most of the territory ruled by the Ottoman Turks had fallen out of their control. Rising Turkish nationalism culminated in the creation of the Republic of Turkey in 1923.*

sented a diverse array of ethnic groups that were often organized like guilds. All enjoyed freedom of worship, access to their own schools and hospitals, and legal jurisdiction by the heads of their groups. Non-Muslims generally paid a special tax but were exempt from military service. Most subjects prospered under Ottoman rule.

Nationalism, however, hastened the breakup of the Ottoman Empire, especially in its European territories. Much of the nationalist pressure came in the Balkan Peninsula, which until 1829 had been controlled by the Ottomans. Balkan intellectuals began studying historical manuscripts, purifying national languages, and writing national histories. Soon, nationalists called for independence.

Russia's leaders acted as champions of the Balkan peoples, with whom they shared religious, linguistic, and ethnic ties. In the eighteenth and nineteenth centuries, Russian armies slowly wrested away control of Southeast Europe. Greeks, Bulgarians, Serbs, and Albanians revolted and appealed to the Russians and other states for assistance. At the same time, some European powers intervened to prevent Russia from assuming a dominant position. The Ottoman leaders were unable to resist the European powers, and nationalism developed in European parts of their empire.

The Ottoman Empire's decay also sparked nationalism among the Turks, a powerful ethnic group. Members of the Turkish elite despised the

FIGURE 33.8 *Young Turks Celebrating Victory. In 1908, a group of Turkish reformers wrested control from the Ottoman ruling elite. Inspired by similar movements in Europe, the Young Turk movement had been founded in the 1860s. Its activists declared that Turkey would survive only if it implemented a constitutional system. The Young Turks enjoyed a degree of success but collapsed under the challenge of nationalism.* Culver Pictures.

moribund Ottoman leadership and institutions. In 1908, one group, known as the Young Turks, forced the monarch to establish a constitutional government and ousted the ruling royalist group. They founded a state with a weak monarchy dominated by an elected parliament.

The Ottoman Empire supported the Austro-Hungarian and German empires in World War I, and it suffered the consequences of defeat: imperial collapse and territorial dismemberment. During the war, much of the empire had fallen to the British and French, and the Ottoman realm appeared near total collapse. British and French diplomats and agents had encouraged Arab nationalists, whose calls for independence were ignored after the war.

The Europeans also dictated a peace with the Ottoman ruler in 1920. This humiliating pact incited Turkish nationalists, who conquered the area of modern Turkey. In 1923, under the leadership of Kemal Atatürk (1881–1938), they declared a secular republic and negotiated a favorable settlement.

The Collapse of the Austro-Hungarian Empire

The Austrian Empire had emerged from the Napoleonic Wars with heightened influence in Central Europe. Austria, however, felt threatened by nationalism, which could undermine its multi-ethnic empire. Austria's foreign minister, Prince Clemens Metternich (1773–1859), led the effort to snuff out nationalistic fervor by ordering executions of or stiff jail terms for nationalists who stirred up people in Italy and Germany, areas of Austrian influence. Both the Italians and Germans, however, won independence and national unification by 1871.

Two other pressing concerns for Austria in the nineteenth century were Hungarian nationalism and the national tensions in the Balkan Peninsula. In 1867, the former problem was solved when Hungarians gained substantial autonomy, forming the Austro-Hungarian Empire. Hungarians won self-rulership with their own cabinet and administrative system, and Hungarian became the official language. Although this generous solution bought peace with the Hungarians, it became the model for other nationalities that demanded to rule

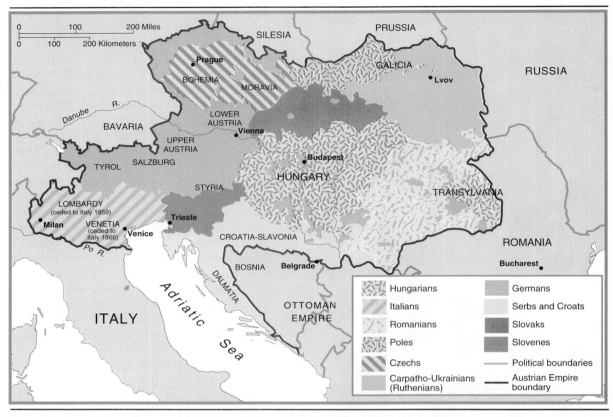

MAP 33.9 *Nationalism and the Austro-Hungarian Empire, 1848.* *Like many other empires, the Austrian Empire had been forged by the conquest and rule of diverse peoples. Nationalist agitation among the Hungarians in the latter half of the nineteenth century forced the Austrians to permit them considerable autonomy, within the new Austro-Hungarian Empire. Although this satisfied the Hungarians, many other ethnic minorities demanded similar treatment from the Austrians. Their refusal helped spark various expressions of nationalism, ultimately leading to the collapse of the empire in the aftermath of World War I.*

themselves. Thus, national tensions simmered until the outbreak of World War I.

Tensions in the Balkan Peninsula occupied the Austro-Hungarian Empire up to World War I and helped precipitate that conflict. Serbian nationalists outside the Austro-Hungarian Empire wished to destabilize the situation and provoke a war. They assassinated the Austro-Hungarian heir apparent, Archduke Francis Ferdinand, in mid-1914. After this killing, the Austro-Hungarian government demanded that Serbia give up its independence. The Serbs turned to their Russian allies for support. Soon the European alliance sys-

tem came into play and eventually brought a series of declarations of war. The ensuing conflict saw the defeat of Austria-Hungary, leading to its dismemberment and the creation of Austria, Hungary, Poland, Czechoslovakia, and Yugoslavia. Nationalism had survived the war and led to Balkan tensions that endured into the 1990s.

Nationalism and Germany

Germany had managed to contain the forces of minority nationalism in its empire, but its support of the Austro-Hungarian Empire in World War I led

UNDER THE LENS
Paderewski and Polish Nationalism

Poland had been a powerful and sophisticated nation in the sixteenth and seventeenth centuries, earning the Poles the nickname "the civilized Slavs." The eighteenth century, however, saw the gradual dismemberment and destruction of Poland as a nation, and by 1795 it had been divided among Prussia, Russia, and Austria. In 1860, Ignacy Paderewski,[a] an important figure in modern Polish history, was born in the Russian part of what would again become Poland under his guidance.

Paderewski's initial inclinations were artistic. A largely self-taught pianist, he entered a music school at the age of twelve, where he was transformed into a trombonist. He loved the piano, and, despite warnings that he never would excel at that instrument, Paderewski took it up again. By 1884, he had undertaken a piano concert tour of Europe, and his magnetic personality and musical genius made him an instant success; later tours of America also were wildly applauded, earning him greater wealth than any contemporary performer. Paderewski's stage presence, enhanced by his shock of unruly, curly redgold hair, made him the darling of the age. His stage routinely was rushed by young women wishing to touch the star; more than once he was attacked by a scissor-wielding adulator who removed a curl or two as a memento. Paderewski was once mobbed in a

[a]**Ignacy Paderewski:** EEG naht see pahd ah REHF skee

men's room when recognized by male fans, and the round of frenzied handshaking that followed left him unable to play for days.

In 1908, however, Paderewski's piano career was beginning to wind down because of persistent hand injuries that impaired his playing, and he commenced searching for alternative outlets for his energies. Paderewski turned to politics, because throughout his career he had inspired himself with the reminder that his success glorified Poland, his enslaved homeland. Beginning in 1912, Paderewski began a series of concerts and lectures—he also was a gifted orator—to raise funds to help support an independent Poland. His personal friendships with Woodrow Wilson (then president of the United States) and Herbert Hoover (later president of the United States) assisted his efforts, and the redivision of Europe following World War I restored Poland to nationhood. In 1919, Paderewski became Poland's first premier, representing his country in the negotiations at Paris that officially concluded World War I. Paderewski resigned his post under fire at the end of 1919 and returned to politics only briefly, in 1940.

Intensely patriotic, Ignacy Paderewski promoted national feelings through the arts, incorporating folk melodies and rhythms into his music and extolling Polish country life. When he turned his talents to the independence movement, his brief political career was marked by diplomacy and political acumen.

to defeat. Earlier, repression and skillful statecraft by Otto von Bismarck helped keep German politicians in check and ethnic minorities like the Poles subdued. Military defeat in 1918, however, brought the collapse of the monarchy and the loss of territory at the Versailles Peace Conference in 1919. German nationalists despised the harsh peace and subsequent loss of territory, especially the loss of Alsace and Lorraine to the French.

While educational systems in Germany and Austria-Hungary promoted German nationalism, some of the ethnic minorities resented efforts to enforce German-only language policies. The

attempted use of schools to encourage unification actually provoked nationalism among Serbs, Poles, and Czechs.

The Collapse of the Russian Empire

The tsarist Russian Empire suffered from many of the same problems that plagued the Austro-Hungarian and Ottoman empires. All presided over diverse ethnic groups and faced the growing desire of these groups for independence. Repression by the Russians, who were the dominant ethnic group, increased nationalism among the

MAP 33.10 *Nationalism and the Russian Empire, to 1920.* *The Russian tsars forged a multiethnic empire, beginning in the sixteenth century. This state, however, disintegrated during World War I, breaking into many states, among them Finland and Poland. After the Bolsheviks took power in late 1917, they began a reconquest of territories controlled by ethnic minorities. Many were retaken, becoming a part of Soviet Russia. Finland, Latvia, Lithuania, Estonia, and Poland, however, remained independent for some years.*

AMERICAS	EUROPE	ASIA	AFRICA		
				1800	Novalis dies, 1801
				–	
			Independent Zulu nation-state, 1816–1879	–	
				–	Shaka dies, 1828
				–	
		Early Japanese nationalism, 1842–c. 1910			Garneau publishes *Histoire du Canada*, 1845
				1850	
Unification of Canada 1864–1867	U.S. Civil War, 1861–1865				President Lincoln frees slaves, 1863
		Unification of Germany, 1866–1871	Unification of Italy, 1859–1871	–	Meiji Restoration begins, 1868 Franco-Prussian War begins, 1870
				–	Richard Wagner dies, 1883
	Early Zionist movement, c. 1890–1948			–	
				1900	Theodore Herzl writes *The Jewish State*, 1900
				–	
				–	
				–	
				–	
				1950	Israel founded, 1948

minority peoples, who had to use the Russian language in education and in government. In addition, ethnic Russians often got the choice political positions, even in minority areas. Vigorous efforts to convert minority groups to the Russian Orthodox faith increased tensions. These measures compelled minority peoples to abandon their native tongues, their shared histories, and their religions. Jews were especially persecuted in official riots, **pogroms**, in which bureaucrats led and incited mobs to beat up Jews and to destroy their shops and homes. All of these policies drove many into antigovernment activities.

A growing sense of Pan-Slavic identification among the ruling elite spurred Russian foreign policy. Slavs are those who speak one of many closely related languages, including Russian, Polish, Bulgarian, Ukrainian, and Serbian. Support for the Serbs remained especially important to the tsarist Russian government and brought it into conflict with the Austro-Hungarians. The Russians backed the Serbs, and the Germans supported Austria-Hungary.

After the tsarist system collapsed under the immense strain of war, the Bolsheviks, who took power in late 1917, needed a breathing space. So, in early 1918, they accepted a German-dictated peace that released Latvians, Estonians, Poles, Lithuanians, and Ukrainians from Russian control. During a bloody civil war that devastated much territory and cost millions of lives, the Bolsheviks won back most of the old tsarist domain. They failed, however, to regain control of Finland, Latvia, Lithuania, Estonia, and Poland. Only in the aftermath of the German assault on Poland and western Europe in 1940, when British and French attention was placed elsewhere, did the Soviets repossess Latvia, Estonia, Lithuania, and parts of Finland, Poland, and Rumania. A Soviet-style Russian nationalism suppressed the nationalist sentiments of these peoples.

SUMMARY

1. Nationalism is an ideology that emphasizes one's social role as a member of a nation. The nation always is characterized by a sense of ownership in the government, the nation-state. In addition, the nation usually has several characteristics:

— a common language,
— shared historical experiences and institutions, and
— similar cultural traditions, including religion, at both elite and popular levels.

Nationalism developed in the eighteenth century and was strengthened through the establishment and extension of the voting franchise, education, and military conscription pools. It also developed in response to French rule from 1794 to 1815 and to attempted suppression by leaders such as Austria's Prince Clemens Metternich.

2. The Romantic movement began in the latter third of the eighteenth century, as a reaction partly to the ideas of the Enlightenment and partly to French cultural influence in Europe. Romantics also viewed nature as alive in its manifestations and sought a mystical unity with it. Romantic composers, writers, and painters celebrated national themes, inspiration, and emotionalism.

3. Johann von Herder, Johann Fichte, and the Grimm brothers played major roles in the development of German cultural nationalism. They also inspired a group of intellectuals who believed that a national language was a key element of a nation. These people and their students standardized many modern languages of central and eastern Europe in the nineteenth century.

4. Nationalism became a force in the creation of nations like Zululand, Japan, Italy, Germany, Israel, and Canada. It also helped preserve the United States from disunion.

5. Nationalism helped the ethnic Chinese topple the Manchus in China; accelerated the demise of the Ottoman Empire and the rise of Turkey; freed many Baltic peoples, including the Latvians and Lithuanians; and precipitated two world wars.

SUGGESTED READINGS

Blum, Jerome. *In the Beginning*. New York: Charles Scribner's Sons, 1994. An account of the onset of the modern age, which Blum argues is the 1840s.

Duggan, Christopher. *A Concise History of Italy*. Cambridge, Eng.: Cambridge University Press, 1994. A recent synthesis of scholarship on Italian history.

McNaught, Kenneth. *The Penguin History of Canada*. London: Penguin Press, 1988. A standard interpretation of Canadian history.

Millington, Barry. *Wagner*. Princeton, N.J.: Princeton University Press, 1992. A recent history of Wagner's life and an analysis of his operas.

Pfaff, William. *The Wrath of Nations*. New York: Simon and Schuster, 1993. An interpretative general history of nationalism in the nineteenth and twentieth centuries.

Riasanovsky, Nicholas. *The Emergence of Romanticism*. Oxford, Eng.: Oxford University Press, 1992. An examination of the origins of Romanticism between 1796 and 1805.

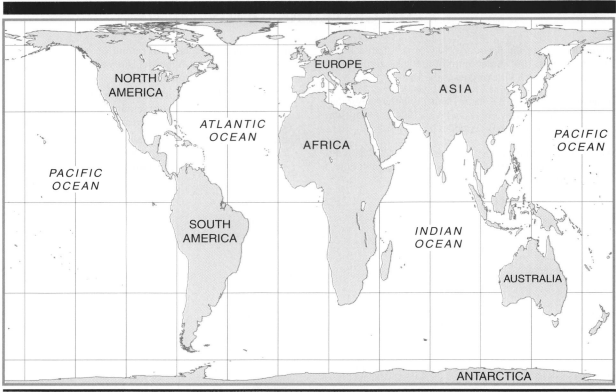

A Satirical View of China's Plight. *This cartoon depicts a prostrate Chinese dragon about to be carved up by Western powers and Japan. These imperialist countries seem ready to fight over the spoils of China's collapse, while a "noble" American eagle watches over the greedy beasts of prey. America's imperialist interests were elsewhere in Asia and focused on keeping trade open to all countries. As a consequence, the U.S. role in China was relatively passive.* From *Puck*, August 15, 1900. The Granger Collection, New York.

Imperialism around the Globe

1803–1949

Government does not depend on consent. The immutable laws of humanity require that a people shall have government, that the weak shall be protected, that cruelty and lust shall be restrained, whether there be consent or not. . . . There is no Philippine people.

U.S. Secretary of War Elihu Root enunciated this sentiment to justify imperialist policies in the Pacific Ocean during the late nineteenth century. These words could have been uttered by nearly any official during the heyday of imperialism (1870–1914), when large sections of the non-Western world fell under Western and Japanese control. Imperialist arrogance characterized policies toward subject peoples in the nineteenth and twentieth centuries.

In this chapter, attention will be focused on imperialism, the modern form of colonialism. As was seen in Chapter 24, colonialism was the process of establishing and administering colonies in order to extract wealth from them in the Early Modern Era. **Imperialism** is an economic and

833

political system of control by an industrial country needing raw materials and markets. Imperialism came later than colonialism and developed from the political leadership of industrializing nation-states. Imperialists used nationalism to garner popular support for their imperialist policies. The race to subjugate most parts of the globe intensified in the late nineteenth and early twentieth centuries, when nearly a quarter-million square miles of territory were added to empires each year. Diplomacy had averted a major war among imperialist countries until 1914, when rivalry and other factors exploded in global conflict. Many tensions and issues remained at the end of World War I, and imperialist ambitions helped ignite a second global conflict two decades later.

IMPERIALISM: INDUSTRIALIZATION, NATIONAL RIVALRIES, AND INTELLECTUAL JUSTIFICATION

Great Britain, France, Germany, Italy, Belgium, the United States, Japan, and Russia became imperialist powers in the nineteenth and twentieth centuries. The central factors behind their territorial expansion were their needs to obtain raw materials to process in their industrial machines, to find markets for the finished products, to compete successfully with rival imperialist nation-states, to control strategic places, and to drum up popular

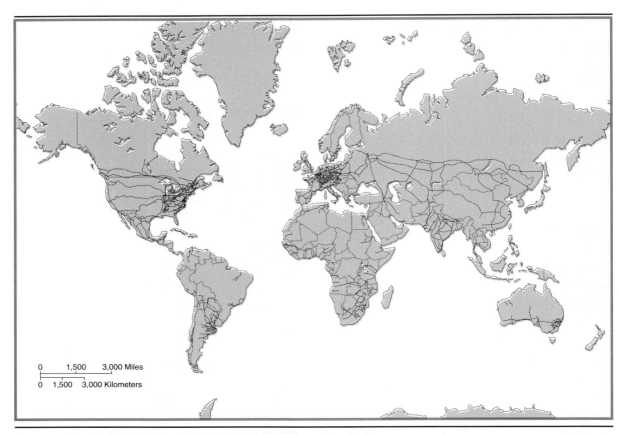

MAP 34.1 *Railroad Lines around 1900.* *Building railroads often was a way for a country to promote industrialization. Russia and Prussia used this strategy in their industrialization efforts. For imperialist countries, building railroads in their colonies improved communications and facilitated resource extraction. Troops could also be moved quickly to crush resistance movements.*

support for overseas ventures. The nation-state became the vehicle for imperialism, and national leaders saw that they could gain widespread support among their citizens by publicizing their interest in territorial expansion.

Some imperialists did not seek direct control over other countries, preferring to exercise economic domination through **client governments**, local administrations that carried out the wishes of the imperialists. They also established spheres of influence in countries or contented themselves with gaining favorable trade agreements with local governments.

Industrialization's Need for Raw Materials and Markets

As seen in Chapter 32, Great Britain industrialized in the eighteenth and nineteenth centuries; France, Germany, the United States, and Japan followed suit somewhat later. Tsarist Russia commenced an industrial program in the 1890s. All became imperialist powers during their economic transformations.

Great Britain had an extensive colonial empire before it industrialized, but it intensified and extended its economic and political sway after its industrial revolution commenced. Britain became economically dominant in Latin America during the nineteenth century and added new imperialist domains in Asia, Africa, and the Pacific basin. The possessions of Britain on the Indian subcontinent became more closely integrated into the empire at the same time.

Germany had no colonies before 1871. The formation of the German Empire in that year and Germany's rapid industrialization helped promote an overseas empire in Africa, Asia, and the Pacific region. Tensions and imperialist rivalries between Germany and other imperialist countries helped start World War I. Germany's defeat and economic problems in the 1920s fueled the crisis that eventually brought the Nazis to power in 1933. Renewed economic growth under the Nazis in the 1930s seems to have influenced Adolf Hitler's successful efforts to annex parts of Central and Eastern Europe.

The United States and Japan industrialized in the nineteenth century, and both developed overseas empires. In fact, national rivalries in Asia and the Pacific region played a role in heightening tensions between the United States and Japan. One cause of World War II was an exploding imperialist rivalry between the United States and Japan.

After spurring a massive industrial revolution in the 1930s, the Soviet Union grabbed Latvia, Lithuania, and Estonia, along with parts of Poland, Finland, and Rumania, between 1939 and 1945. Additional territories in Central and Eastern Europe were incorporated into the Soviet Empire after World War II. Although some scholars see these expansions within the historical direction of Russo-Soviet strategic planning, the fact that these acquisitions came during and after the industrialization of the 1930s supports the view that socialist imperialism was at work. In addition, all new territory soon came within the Soviet economic sphere.

National Rivalries

National rivalries intensified the efforts to develop overseas and land empires. Japan, for example, decided to vie with China and then with Russia over Korea between 1894 and 1905. The rapid dismemberment of Africa was one significant consequence of the imperialist drive for territorial control. Certainly, competition in Asia (1890s and 1940s) and Europe (1940s) helped heighten tensions between nations and helped provoke World War I and World War II.

Perceived national interests played a special role in the fierce competition to grab some territories. Hawaii lay in the mid-northern Pacific Ocean, along vital trade routes from the Americas to Asia. Control of Hawaii and Pearl Harbor, with its marvelous potential as a naval base, became a driving concern for the United States in the 1890s. About a decade later, digging and controlling the Panama Canal obsessed U.S. strategic planners. Earlier, the British decided to take control of the Suez Canal in Egypt to protect the financial interests of British investors and also to safeguard Britain's strategic passage to India.

Intellectual Justification

A variety of intellectual concepts were employed to justify the imperialists' conquest and rule. Two of the most wide-ranging efforts were the "White Man's Burden" and "Yellow Peril" slogans employed in the early twentieth century. "White Man's Burden" was a commonplace idea in Europe

FIGURE 34.1 *"Dr. Livingstone, I Presume?"* *One of the most dramatic episodes in nineteenth-century newspaper reporting was the publicity surrounding the search by Henry Stanley for Dr. David Livingstone, a missionary in Africa. A self-publicist, Stanley developed the story that captivated British newspaper readers and sparked interest in Africa. Although Livingstone was not lost, Stanley had found a story by which to make himself famous.* Mansell/Time Inc.

and the United States, and it received popular expression in the writings of Rudyard Kipling, who wrote about the responsibilities of whites toward nonwhites, whom he saw as inferior and incapable of governing themselves. The concept of "Yellow Peril" came from writers and editorial cartoonists who warned about the uniting of Asians against Westerners, rationalizing the domination of Asian lands. Westerners had to conquer Asians before Asians conquered Westerners.

Even ideas about the nature of society were used to justify imperialist expansion. Both the Soviets and the Japanese, for example, argued that their expansions came from a need to develop defensive buffer zones against enemy nation-states. The Soviets couched their rule in terms of socialist brotherhood and alliance, yet they practiced atrocities against the subject peoples. The

Japanese used the idea of one large Asian family system to argue for control of Koreans (younger brothers and sisters) and the idea of a Greater East Asian Co-Prosperity Sphere, a region under Japanese benevolent supervision, to mask their imperialist policies.

Newspapers played a significant role in the development of imperialist expansion. National education systems produced ever larger numbers of literate people, many of whom read newspapers on a regular basis. Some scholars call growth in this and other media the emergence of information capitalism because in order to sell papers, editors promoted stories that captured the public's imagination. An early example was the trek of journalist Henry Morton Stanley (1841–1904) through Africa on a search for Dr. David Livingstone. Stanley's account electrified his British readers and coined the immortal line, "Dr. Livingstone, I presume?" upon meeting with the missionary in 1871. This sensationalist account helped foster the image of deepest, darkest Africa as an alien place whose people needed to be saved.

COLONIZATION AND IMPERIALISM IN THE AMERICAS

The Americas had been colonized by various European countries beginning in the sixteenth century. By the nineteenth century, the United States and most countries in Latin America had won independence. As the United States industrialized, it became an imperialist power, focusing on territories in the Pacific Ocean and in Latin America. Britain also exerted imperialist control over countries in Latin America.

The United States and Imperialism

The United States expanded overland through the nineteenth century, establishing a network of overseas colonies from the 1890s. As the economy of the United States became more industrialized, the lure of markets and sources of raw materials attracted U.S. capitalists overseas. Capitalists have usually sought to exploit the cheap labor available in these territories.

After the War of Independence (1776–1783), the new area of colonization and settlement for the United States lay west of the Appalachian Mountains. Soon, American Indians suffered displacement by purchase, theft, and military conquest of their lands, actions of colonization by many people.

Purchase was a major means of territorial growth for the United States in the nineteenth century. The largest acquisition came in 1803 with the

UNDER THE LENS

Manifest Destiny

Well before the outbreak of the American War of Independence in the 1770s, American colonists desired to occupy the territories west of the Appalachian Mountains. Indeed, one of the causes of American anger was England's attempt to limit settlement in that region. **Manifest Destiny** was the nineteenth-century belief that the United States should expand until it controlled the Pacific coast and beyond. It became an almost religious belief for European Americans, who saw themselves destined to rule distant places and their peoples.

Manifest Destiny also related to the concept of the American frontier. Embedded within that perspective was the view that the frontier settlers must necessarily confront and overcome obstacles, including Native Americans and Mexicans. Such peoples might be killed, driven out, assimilated, or encapsulated as the need arose.

American Indian lands were often acquired through purchase, though the transaction typically was carried out through a tribal official who exceeded his authority by selling lands. In many cases, the concept of landownership was alien to the indigenous culture, and the consequences of the sale were comprehended only vaguely. Treaties also were a major route to acquiring Indian lands. Many treaties gave favorable disposition of lands to European-American settlers, and the less favorable ones were ignored by them. Relatively few lands were seized by simple force, but force often was used as an argument to encourage Indian leaders to accept purchase or treaty. The treaty system, established in 1824 but in wide use only after 1865, was designed to guarantee that some tribal lands remained for the Indian tribes.

Much of the territory in the West was purchased from various European states. The Louisiana Territory, the Florida Territory, part of the southwestern territory acquired through the Gadsden Purchase, and Alaska fit into that category. Other areas, like the Mexican Cession, were won by war. While the industrialization of the United States continued through the latter half of the nineteenth century and fueled overseas imperialism, the settling of the continental United States owed largely to more personal and less economic matters. Among the many elements persuading people to settle new places was the idea of Manifest Destiny.

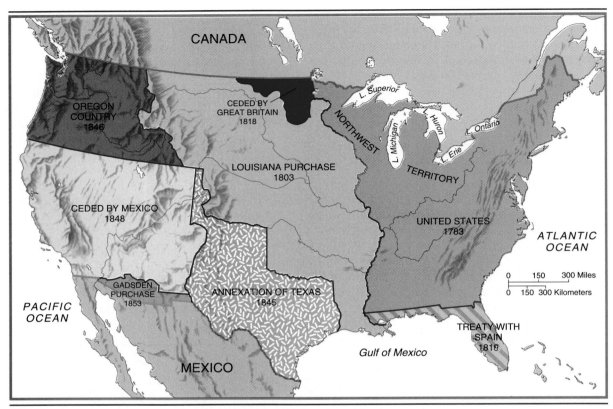

MAP 34.2 *U.S. Territorial Expansion, 1803–1853.* *The United States purchased great amounts of land during its westward expansion; two of the major acquisitions were the Louisiana and Gadsden purchases. U.S. leaders also won a significant part of the American West in a treaty settlement with Mexico after the Mexican War. These ways of expansion set the tone for the rest of the nineteenth century.*

Louisiana Purchase by President Thomas Jefferson. The French, who needed money to finance Napoleon's military schemes, sold the Louisiana Territory, which they in turn had acquired from resident American Indians by conquest and self-declaration. The United States also bought Florida from the Spanish in the early nineteenth century. That deal completed the acquisition of lands south of Canada and east of the Mississippi River. Mexico sold territory that made up part of Arizona and New Mexico, the Gadsden Purchase of 1853. In 1867, the Russians liquidated their remaining land in North America when they sold Alaska to the United States.

Conquest added more land to the United States. Most of the land from the Atlantic to the Mississippi River came to the United States from the War of Independence (1776–1783). The Mexi-

can War (1846–1848) added the Mexican Cession, including the Texas Territory and parts of the western states of New Mexico, Oklahoma, Arizona, Colorado, Nevada, and California.

Most of the remaining lands came during the Spanish-American War (1898) and its aftermath. United States industrial pressure, combined with a surge of ardent nationalism fueled by sensationalist journalism in many newspapers during the 1890s, precipitated a successful war with Spain. The United States added the Philippines, Puerto Rico, Hawaii, and Guam to its territory. Aside from strategic interests, Hawaii and the Philippines also became sources of sugarcane and pineapples, once the local resistance forces had been crushed. A resilient Filipino guerrilla movement took more than five years to defeat, costing nearly a quarter-million Filipino lives.

FIGURE 34.2 *Civilian Victims at Manila, Philippines.* *In 1945, many Filipino civilians died in the crossfire as U.S. and Japanese soldiers fought for control of Manila during World War II. Some fifty years earlier, the Philippines had seen mass graves constructed for the bodies of Filipino resistance fighters who battled American forces intent on conquering and ruling the island nation.* Wide World Photos.

The United States gained territory after the end of World War II, when Japanese possessions in the western Pacific became the United States Trust Territories. The Japanese had taken these islands from the Germans in World War I, and the League of Nations recognized Japan's claims. Later, the United Nations approved the American occupation.

Other United States interests brought direct control of new territory in Colombia. As settlement of the west intensified during the Gold Rush in the 1840s and 1850s, sea routes from the eastern to the western United States seemed more important. During the years after the Spanish-American War, President Theodore Roosevelt, an ardent exponent of naval expansion, engineered a Panamanian revolt against the Colombians. The United States recognized and guaranteed Panama's indepen-

dence in exchange for the ceding of territory in which the Panama Canal was built. American jurisdiction over the Canal Zone lasted until 1978, with a complete return scheduled for 1999.

Settlement of the continental territory followed the pattern established under the Northwest Ordinance of 1787. That decree provided for an orderly transition from territory to statehood, a process that proved highly successful. By 1912, forty-eight states had been created. Alaska became a state in 1958, and Hawaii entered the union in 1959. Puerto Rico, Guam, and the Trust Territory islands have remained outside the statehood ranks; the Philippines was granted independence in 1947.

Economic imperialism afforded the United States and other industrialized nation-states the means for indirect control of the assets of nominally independent states. Both the Monroe Doctrine of the early 1820s and the Open Door Policy of 1898 were unilateral policies by the United States with respect to Latin America and China. They asserted that these lands remain open for economic exploitation and development by all parties, especially the United States. Both gestures remained toothless, but they reflected the United States' growing economic interests in Latin America and Asia.

Economic Imperialism in Latin America

Latin America long endured the economic influence and domination of Western nation-states, especially Britain and the United States. While direct political rule remained only a short-term expedient, Western exploitation of natural resources occurred through the era. In the nineteenth century, the U.S. government increasingly considered the western hemisphere to be its special zone of influence and action. The overriding concern was the resolution of economic matters in favor of the United States.

Most Latin American countries won their independence from European colonial powers. Because wealthy members of the social elite became the ruling class of these newly independent states, they adhered to policies representing their interests. Latin American leaders struggled to revive economies that had been integrally connected with Spain and Portugal, and they decided to integrate Latin America into the burgeoning global economy.

During the nineteenth century, Britain played the most significant economic role in Latin America. The British navy ruled the seas, providing security for British ships that sailed between Latin America and Europe. Britain also possessed impressive capital resources, merchants, and insurance brokers. The philosophy of free trade stressed the importance of trade through open markets joined in a global network. This vision attracted many of the Latin American elite and offered the hope to Mexicans, Central Americans, and South Americans that they could integrate into a prosperous world structure.

The British dominated the financial exchanges in much of the western hemisphere, slowly exert-

FIGURE 34.3 *European Influence in Nineteenth-Century Chile.* *This photograph of Cape Street in Valparaiso, Chile, shows the bookstore and stationery shop of Thomas Purves, which catered to English-reading people. British economic influence was strong along the west coast of South America, and British capital dominated Latin American markets until World War I.* Courtesy of Ken and Jenny Jacobson.

PARALLELS AND DIVERGENCES

Olives, Bananas, and Sugar: Monoculture and Dependence

All farmers are faced with the same problem. On the one hand, they want to focus on the single crop that produces the best returns. On the other hand, depending entirely on one crop is risky business, because a disaster may wipe out their livelihood. Furthermore, it is not good for the soil. When farm produce is sold for cash, there is the added problem that prices rise and fall with the international market. When farmers resolve this problem by focusing on a single crop, it is called **monoculture.**

A classic case of monoculture comes from Greece of the fourth century B.C. Olive oil, the basis of much cooking in the eastern Mediterranean, was the primary export commodity of Greece, and its production was the quickest route to prosperity for farmers. Olive trees grew with little attention, rarely were there bad harvests, and the presses used to extract oil were inexpensive to construct and use. Thus, peasants converted huge land tracts into olive groves and reduced grain-growing areas. This shift vastly reduced the game population and led to erosion of the landscape but proved successful for decades. By the century's end, however, other places in the Mediterranean produced olive oil, and the market became unprofitable. Unfortunately, it was difficult for the Greeks to return the groves to grain production. Greece became dependent on expensive, imported food.

While the Greek experience was unfortunate, the problem had been self-induced. Many nineteenth- and twentieth-century monocultural disasters were fostered by imperialists. The banana industry in Central America, for example, began in earnest in 1899, when the first Honduran bananas arrived in New Orleans. Banana companies slyly tempted the newly established government of General Manuel Bonilla[a]: provide tax exemptions, and they would develop railroads, ports, and roads for Honduras. While Honduras gained an infrastructure, the main profits of the banana industry went to foreign investors, whose economic power permitted their domination of the Honduran government. Trade disruptions, such as in 1914, devastated Honduras, and fluctuations of world banana prices affected the economy immensely.

Cuba and other Caribbean islands had similar experiences with sugar. Introduced by sweet-hungry European colonial powers in the sixteenth and seventeenth centuries, sugar (and rum distilled from it) dominated all other products. This heritage persists today but with devastating results. Most Caribbean islands are politically independent, yet they import most of their food. Further, fluctuations in sugar prices severely affect their economic prosperity.

Imperialist powers fostered monoculture in their colonies, producing crops unavailable in the home country and often making huge profits. The greatest risks fell on the colonial peoples, while profits came to the investors in the home countries. The legacy of this monoculture, however, haunts now-independent countries whose economies are limited by these strategies.

[a] **Manuel Bonilla:** MAHN wehl BOHN ee yah

---

ing political control. The United States and France also had some influence in the nineteenth and twentieth centuries. Early financial efforts by Britain showed mixed results because, although the economic influence swelled, a large number of loan defaults rendered much of Latin America a high credit risk.

The economic influence of the United States rapidly increased in the latter half of the nineteenth century. While many Latin Americans appreciated the support of the United States in their independence struggles, others recoiled because the United States exercised much more control than Spain. Although U.S. investment grew about fivefold between 1898 and 1914, more than half of all foreign capital investment in Latin America still lay with the British. The United States accounted for around 15 percent of the total foreign investment in Latin America by the outbreak of World War I, but it was larger than the amounts of the French and the Germans.

From 1914 to 1949, the influence of the United States in Latin America became dominant. During this era, an inter-American system emerged and centered on the military and economic power of the United States. American military takeover of many governments in the Caribbean basin between 1912 and 1934 was justified by the need to protect the region's sea lanes. British influence sharply declined during World War I and never recovered, and when the European part of World War II erupted in 1939, the United States pressured Latin American governments into supplying war materials, basing U.S. soldiers, and signing alliances with the United States against its enemies. During World War II, the United States emerged as the dominant global power, controlling about half of the world's industrial production and two-thirds of its exports.

The political form of the inter-American system came in 1947 and 1948, when all states signed the Rio Pact, which declared that an attack on any American state was an attack on all. A year later, the Organization of American States was formed, committing its members to regular meetings, to ways of dealing with inter-American crises, and to the principles of democracy, economic cooperation, human rights, and social justice.

IMPERIALISM IN ASIA

East Asia suffered terribly from the ravages of imperialism. China and Korea fell under a Japanese imperialism, which cost millions of lives and immense loss of property. Freedom from the Japanese brought new problems and division of the Korean Peninsula and of China and Taiwan.

East Asia

Japanese leaders developed an empire in conjunction with an industrializing and Westernizing program; they believed that in order to be a modern power, Japan had to gain colonies. Fear of foreign domination also fueled Japan's imperialistic efforts. During the 1850s and 1860s, Western powers imposed a series of unequal treaties that humiliated Japan's leaders, who vowed to free Japan from foreign control. Only in the late 1890s did Japan begin to regain autonomy over its trade policies. In addition, Western imperialist threats to rule Korea and China spurred Japan's leaders to develop a long-range plan to dominate East Asia. After World War I, expansion in Manchuria and other parts of China caused Japan's leaders to pro-

tect these conquests by grabbing parts of Southeast Asia. Soon, most of Southeast Asia, East Asia, and the western Pacific Ocean had become part of the Japanese Empire.

Although the Japanese portrayed themselves as the elder brothers and other Asians as younger brothers, their policies fomented discontent among the peoples they ruled. Koreans and Chinese resented Japanese political and economic control, and Southeast Asians chafed under Japanese domination.

China had exerted political and cultural influence in East Asia through a tributary system that demanded that nations send diplomatic visits to China in exchange for trading privileges and Chinese protection. Both Korea and Japan had borrowed heavily from Chinese elite culture, especially education, family values, and hierarchical social structures.

Britain began significant trading with China in the early nineteenth century. Although the British sent diplomatic and trade missions to China in 1814 and 1834, both failed to open China to further trade and development. The Chinese sold the British large quantities of tea and other products but had little use for British imports. In order to offset this trade imbalance, the British East India Company, a private business, smuggled Indian opium into China. As a result, many Chinese became addicts. Eventually, the British government took over the company and its smuggling operation, and the British selling of opium to the Chinese continued well into the twentieth century. By the 1830s, China's drug problem mushroomed and began to cause severe economic problems for the Chinese.

These economic and social problems led to the Opium War (1839–1842) and China's defeat, commencing a long period of foreign influence and domination. Until 1894, the Chinese managed to contain the Westerners in a few treaty port areas, like Shanghai and Canton, but the Chinese government yielded to Western pressure to open more of its regions to trade. China lost control of its tariff rates, its power to try Westerners for crimes committed on its soil, and some of the revenues that had helped pay foreign debts. In the late nineteenth century, Western countries loaned the Chinese government large sums of money. The resulting indebtedness to imperialist powers formed a kind of economic imperialism shackling China.

Between 1894 and 1914, Korea and Vietnam were torn from the Chinese sphere of influence, and interior parts of China became foreign enclaves. Korea had been forcibly opened to trade by Japan in 1876, and the Japanese and Chinese governments signed an accord in 1885 to defuse tensions there. By 1894, a local Korean uprising provided the Japanese with an opportunity to extend their influence. The resulting Sino-Japanese War (1894–1895) brought China's defeat, Korean independence, and a settlement that gave Japan the island of Taiwan and a large indemnity. Other imperialist powers acquired Chinese territory in the next few years: Germany got a concession in Shandong province, Britain extended its Hong Kong lease (a prize taken in 1842) until 1997 and added new territory, Russia gained land in Manchuria, and France pressured China for a sphere of influence along the border with French Indochina.

World War I brought a reduction of Western influence in China and an increase in Japanese imperialism. The Japanese entered the war on the side of the British and the French, defeating the Germans in Shandong and adding that valuable sphere of influence. The German concession remained under Japanese control, thanks to secret deals with other imperialist powers and bribery of Chinese officials.

From 1931 to 1945, Japan launched a major effort to control Manchuria and China. Japan conquered Manchuria by 1932 and gradually expanded into China. Growing tensions provoked conflict between Chinese and Japanese soldiers in mid-1937, opening the Asian theater of World War II.

Korea gradually fell under the sway of Japanese imperialism; it was incorporated into the Japanese Empire in 1910. Harsh Japanese rule provoked intense Korean animosity. On March 1, 1919,

FIGURE 34.4 *Korean Women Demonstrating for Independence.* *March 1, 1919, was an important day in modern Korea: Around 1 million Koreans demonstrated for their freedom from Japanese rule. As this photo documents, many women were among the protesters. Though tightly constricted by custom and by the Japanese authorities, Korean women felt so strongly about their country's freedom that they took action. Overt Korean resistance, however, was ended by Japanese repression that brought numerous casualties and arrests.* Courtesy of Yushin Yoo.

around one million Koreans demonstrated against Japanese rule, triggering brutal Japanese reprisals. Soon Koreans had to learn Japanese and to adopt Japanese names. At times, so many agricultural supplies left Korea that some Koreans went hungry. Later, numbers of Korean women were forcibly taken to serve as "comfort women" for the sexual gratification of Japanese soldiers.

After World War II, Korea was divided, filling Koreans with uncertainty. The North came under control of Korean communists who were supported by Russian advisors and equipment. The South fell under American occupation and remained in turmoil, although Syngman Rhee[1] gradually amassed considerable political power. The political troubles in the South invited an unsuccessful attempt at reunification by the North Korean communists in 1950.

Southeast Asia

Western imperialism extended its control across Southeast Asia in the nineteenth century, and Japanese imperialists contended with Western rivals in the twentieth century. Although the Japanese were defeated in World War II, their last-ditch efforts to foster national movements ignited indigenous anti-imperialist movements that won independence after 1945.

The British conquest and rule of Burma (present-day Myanmar) stemmed from Britain's position in India. Leaders in India and England sought to dominate the Irrawaddy and Salween river valleys in order to enhance their trading position in Southeast Asia. Conflicts with the Burmese monarchy commenced in the 1820s and continued sporadically through the 1880s, when the country fell completely under British control.

The British exploited Burma's natural and human resources. Wood products, including the much-valued teak, were shipped to Britain for manufacturing purposes. Ivory, rubies, and jade proved valuable resources for British jewelers. As in many other parts of the British Empire, the educational system in Burma taught members of the Burmese elite Western subjects, in English. Generations of Burmese learned to speak Oxfordian English, and some studied at British universities.

The British conquered Singapore and Malaya in the early nineteenth century, ensuring open British sea lanes from the Indian Ocean to the Pacific. A major naval base was built by the British in Singapore, and it was defended by massive guns. The British also developed Malayan rubber plantations and launched tin-mining operations.

The French had been interested in Vietnam as early as the seventeenth century, but the formation of French Indochina did not occur until the nineteenth century. A desire for imperial expansion drove the French emperor, Napoleon III. He curried favor with his Catholic subjects, who wanted to convert the Vietnamese, and began the conquest of Vietnam's Nguyen[2] Empire (1802–1955). The French navy also sought port facilities for its steamships. Between 1859 and 1894, the conquest of Vietnam, Cambodia, and Laos took place. The Vietnamese resisted the French effort, but the Cambodians generally favored the French Protectorate because Cambodia was being slowly dismembered by the Vietnamese and Thais. French rule ended the dismemberment. The French Indo-China Union was forged in 1894.

The French integrated the Union into the French Empire, ruling with a formidable police and military force. Wood products were harvested and sent to France along with rubber from the rubber plantations that sprang up in the region. Much as the Burmese and Malayan elite spoke English, the Vietnamese, Cambodian, and Laotian elite spoke French. Some studied at French schools in the Union, while a few went to France for further study. During World War I, tens of thousands of Vietnamese were shipped to France as laborers. Many who returned home after the war became disaffected members of the empire because they longed for Vietnamese independence.

Japan's interest in Southeast Asia stemmed from the devastation of western Europe in 1940–1941 and the prospect of exploiting the region's resources, especially oil and rubber. The Dutch controlled the East Indies, while the French administered French Indochina and the British controlled Burma and Malaya. The Nazi conquest of the Netherlands and France, along with the Battle of Britain, opened Southeast Asia for Japanese conquest. In mid-1940, Japan forced the French to permit the stationing of Japanese troops and sup-

[1] **Syngman Rhee:** SEENG muhn ree

[2] **Nguyen:** NUH yehn

plies in northern Vietnam, and a year later, the Japanese expanded into southern Vietnam.

The United States worried about Japan's expansion and its alliance with Germany and Italy. Japan's imperialist expansion prompted the Americans to announce an embargo on oil to Japan, threatening the Japanese navy's petroleum supplies. The oil fields of the Dutch East Indies loomed on Japan's strategic horizon, but the conquest of those islands meant that the Philippines, which dominated the South China Sea lanes, had to be taken. The United States controlled the Philippines, and the U.S. naval base at Pearl Harbor, Hawaii, dominated the Pacific Ocean.

Japan attacked Pearl Harbor and launched an invasion of most of Southeast Asia. The Philippines defense system collapsed within months, and General Douglas MacArthur fled to Australia. Singapore succumbed to a jungle campaign by a Japanese general who took the naval base from the rear, thus neutralizing the powerful coastal battery that could not be turned inland. Burma and the East Indies also fell under Japanese control by mid-1942. Thailand joined the Japanese alliance. The Japanese talked about permitting local autonomy, but they acted much as the European imperialists had. By 1944, Japan, facing imminent defeat, decided to grant its Asian subjects independence. When Western countries tried to regain control of their former colonies, they met widespread resistance. Burma gained independence in 1948, and Indonesia (formerly the Dutch East Indies) followed in 1949. Independence conflicts had also commenced in French Indochina. The Philippines was granted independence by the Americans in 1947.

South Asia

Imperialist control of South Asia grew out of economic influence there through the British East India Company. It gradually replaced the moribund Mughal Empire as the dominant force in the subcontinent. Britain's patchwork array of political relationships continued into the mid–nineteenth century, when native grievances exploded in the Indian Mutiny of 1857–1858. For a brief time, the widespread upheaval threatened Britain's domination, but the Muslims and Hindus could not unite, which enabled other Indian forces to aid the British in crushing the mutiny.

Many changes stemmed from the midcentury rebellion against British rule. In 1858, Britain took over the management of India from the East India Company and, to ensure the reliability of the army in India, increased the number of soldiers from Britain. British suspicion of the Indians intensified the segregation of imperialist rulers from their subjects. Harsh rule was supported by growing racist sentiments.

British imperialism significantly changed the ecological and social makeup of North India. Widespread deforestation denuded the northern lands and devastated the lifestyles of the nomads who lived there. Some migrated to the cities, where many lived beggarly existences, while others stayed behind, eking out livings as farmers.

Famines became a regular occurrence in British India. Sometimes the cause was drought. More often, the planting of tea, cotton, and opium crops in large quantities significantly reduced the land available for grain production.

Additional suffering resulted from the systematic destruction of the Indian cottage industries. To guarantee that British imports to India did not suffer from competition from local wares, British officials enacted measures that destroyed local manufactories. These policies threw Indians out of work and forced a large number to farm. By the late nineteenth century, Indian leaders began to seek local rule or the adoption of self-help measures.

The major drive for independence came in the early twentieth century. Although leaders like Muhammad Jinnah and Jawaharlal Nehru played vital roles in the freedom struggle, perhaps the liberation effort was best personified by Mohandas Gandhi[3] (1869–1948). A man of charismatic and spiritual stature, Gandhi became a major political figure, employing mass-action techniques of *ahimsa* (nonviolence) that originated from Jain and Buddhist traditions. Gandhi also used the ideas of Henry David Thoreau relating to civil disobedience. Political fasts and other symbolic actions ignited a growing Indian resistance to British rule, leading to the independence of Hindu India and Muslim Pakistan in 1947. The two new states, however, failed to overcome longstanding religious and sectarian differences, and war erupted several times. Following the Indian lead,

[3]**Mohandas Gandhi:** moh HAHN duhs gahn DEE

FIGURE 34.5 *Indian Mutiny.* *British rule in India was based on a sense of entitlement and the ignorance of Indian customs, which created tension between ruler and ruled. When Indian soldiers turned on their officers in 1857, they began a rebellion in which both military and civilian British were killed. This lithograph, "The Massacre at Cawnpore," shows one notorious event—the killing of British women and children—that fueled severe repression. The popular revolt that had started as military mutiny forced the British government to reexamine its policies in India.* National Army Museum/ET Archive.

the other modern states of the subcontinent—Bangladesh, Bhutan, Nepal, and Sri Lanka—eventually won independence.

Southwest and Central Asia

Much of the history of Southwest Asia in the nineteenth and twentieth centuries relates to the Ottoman Empire. As was seen in Chapter 33, European portions of this Islamic state agitated for independence, and some peoples gained freedom in the nineteenth and twentieth centuries.

During World War I, the Ottomans allied with the Germans. Thus, the British, the French, and some Arab groups formed an alliance to undermine the Ottomans. One example of this coalition building was the Husayn-McMahon correspondence of 1915 to 1916, in which British diplomat

Sir Henry McMahon encouraged Arab hopes of independence. In 1916, Sharif Husayn[4] led an Arab revolt against the Ottoman Empire, and Arab forces fought alongside allied units thereafter. During the same year, the British and French negotiated an agreement that divided the Arab domain into a French-governed North and a British-administered South. This treaty showed that the two imperialist powers intended to control Southwest Asia long after the war's end.

The Ottoman rulers lost most of their Southwest Asian holdings, and the British and French assumed overlordship there. Various Arab leaders attempted to assert independence against the Europeans, but their efforts failed. During the 1920s, the British reduced their control over many

[4] **Husayn:** HOO sayn

parts of the South, but the French doggedly held on to their positions. The Saudis, one group of Arabs under Ibn Saud, conquered most of Arabia and established a monarchy. Oil discoveries in Arabia and other parts of the region highlighted its strategic importance for the oil-consuming nations in the West.

In 1917, the British government issued the Balfour Declaration, which promised a Jewish homeland in Palestine. This action recognized the importance of Zionism and the compatibility of British and Jewish interests in Southwest Asia. As early as 1865, sympathizers of the Jewish cause had established the Palestine Exploration Fund, and the Fourth Zionist Congress met in London in 1900, receiving extraordinary fanfare from the British press. World War II weakened France and Britain and transformed the political situation in Southwest Asia. By 1946, most states were either independent or soon became free. Relying on the

Balfour Declaration, many Jews planned for the creation of Israel in the former area of Palestine. In 1948, they declared the existence of Israel, provoking Arab nationalists, who sent armies that failed to destroy the new country.

Russia developed significant economic and political interests in Southwest and Central Asia, beginning in the eighteenth century. Part of the expansion stemmed from Peter the Great's war against the Persians, but a significant development began when Georgia, a country in the Caucasus Mountains region, asked for Russian assistance against the Persian and Ottoman empires. The Russians defeated the Persians and Turks, expanding further into the Caucasus region and into the Balkans. By the 1850s, Russia's aggressive moves against the Ottoman Empire alarmed the British and French, who fought against the Russians in the Crimean War (1854–1856), temporarily halting Russian expansion.

FIGURE 34.6 *Russian Troops on Patrol.* *In the nineteenth century, Russia slowly made itself the imperial master of Central Asia, fighting and conquering various Muslim states. In this 1881 drawing, a group of Russian scouts surveys acquired territory. To the east, Russian troops reached the borders of the Chinese empire, securing a temporary hold on the strategic Ili River Valley, while forces to the south halted British conquests and developed a growing interest in Afghanistan.* L'Illustration/Sygma.

During the nineteenth century, Russian imperialist interest in Central Asia precipitated an intense rivalry with the British. Part of the reason for Russia's push was the inability of Russian manufactured goods to compete in Europe, so Russians traded in Southwest, Central, and East Asian markets, where their goods were in demand. A Russo-Persian Bank and a Russo-Chinese Bank were founded to promote trade with Asian countries. Central Asian governments run by Muslim leaders opposed Russian interference. Conflicts erupted and led to Russia's conquest of much of Central Asia in the mid–nineteenth century.

Russian and British economic and strategic interests clashed in Afghanistan and Persia through the late nineteenth and early twentieth centuries. Both traded with the Afghan people. In addition, the British feared that Russian conquest would threaten their interests in India. On the other hand, the Russians saw Afghanistan as a step in their march through Central Asia. Russia and Britain, however, put aside their bitter rivalry in 1907, when they negotiated an alliance, assigning Russia a large sphere of influence in northern Persia and the British a smaller sphere in southern Persia. Russia also agreed that Afghanistan lay outside its Central Asian sphere of influence.

THE AFRICAN EXPERIENCE WITH IMPERIALISM

Between 1871 and 1912, Africa fell to European imperialism, and, by 1949, few African states had managed to regain their independence. During that time, Great Britain added nearly 4.4 million square miles of territory and 66 million people to its empire in Africa, while the French grabbed around 3.5 million square miles inhabited by 26 million people. Resistance to European domination took many forms; partially successful efforts pitted the Ethiopians against the Italians and the Zulus against the British.

North Africa

Much of North Africa fell to French, British, Italian, or Spanish domination. The French took Morocco, Algeria, and Tunisia, while the British dominated Egypt and Sudan. During the early 1900s, the British and French recognized each other's control of North African territories. The Italians added Libya to their overseas empire, while the Spanish increased their holdings in Northwest Africa (Spanish Morocco).

French influence in North Africa, based on a growing economic involvement, increased in the latter half of the nineteenth century. As France industrialized, North African markets attracted French manufacturers and financiers. In addition, many French settled in Algeria, Morocco, and Tunisia, becoming an important lobby in the French Parliament by promoting France's annexation of these territories. Another significant player promoting imperialist policies was the Roman Catholic Church, which wanted to increase missionary activities. Governments of the French republic supported overseas Catholic activities even though they pushed anticlerical policies domestically. By the 1880s and 1890s, French economic interests began seriously competing with those of the British in the eastern Mediterranean, especially in Egypt.

For much of the nineteenth century, Britain supported the Ottoman Turks in propping up their empire, and that meant maintaining a hands-off policy toward Egypt, which was in Ottoman hands. The prospect, however, of building a canal from the Mediterranean to the Red Sea meant that British ships sailing to India would not have to navigate around Africa. Although Egyptians played a major role in the Suez Canal's construction, the inflow of capital necessary to complete the work in 1870 caused severe financial problems for the Egyptians. In 1875, Britain purchased the Egyptian ruler's shares in the company that dug the canal, gaining a significant financial interest there. Political upheaval threatened British financiers in 1882, and Prime Minister William Gladstone ordered an invasion. Although never formally annexed, Egypt remained under British control until 1954.

The Sudan had often been closely linked with Egypt in the nineteenth century. In 1885, British troops commanded by General Charles Gordon were defeated by the Mahdi, ruler of the Sudan, but thirteen years later, an Anglo-Egyptian army under Lord Horatio Kitchener decisively defeated the Mahdi and his allies at the Battle of Omdurman. At the same time, French forces planted the French flag in the area of Fashoda[5] (Sudan), nearly precipitating a war between France and Britain.

[5] **Fashoda:** FAH shoh dah

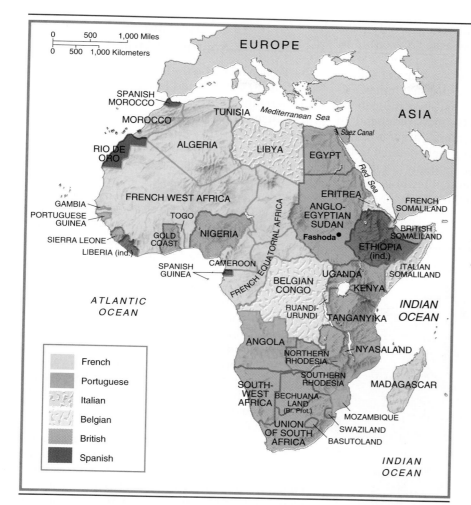

MAP 34.3 *Imperialism in Africa, to 1935.* *Although the Portuguese had established African colonies prior to the 1880s, the greatest imperialist expansion in Africa occurred within the last two decades of the nineteenth century. Great Britain and France were the major players in this territorial grab. As a consequence of its defeat in World War I, Germany lost most of its African possessions to other European countries. Most African liberation movements began after World War II.*

The French army had marched west from Ethiopia, hoping to link up with another French force coming from east-central Africa. Lord Kitchener's detachment arrived in Fashoda and asked the French to leave. After the French refused, the two commanders sipped whiskey, waiting for their governments' instructions. British nationalist public opinion grew warlike. Seeing a miscalculation, the French abandoned their claims. In 1904, the French and British negotiated an alliance that divided their respective imperial interests, keeping conflicts to a minimum.

Italy developed significant financial interests in Libya. Partly to protect these investments and also to prevent other powers from seizing Libya, the Italian government sanctioned expansion of political influence in North Africa. Between 1913 and 1943, successive Italian governments sup-

ported this colonization, initially of the coastal areas and then gradually inland. Business leaders and Roman Catholic officials supported each other in the drive to make the Libyans fully subject to Italian rule and culture beginning in the 1920s.

East Africa

Imperialist rivalries precipitated a scramble for control of East Africa. The most intense activity came in the 1880s, when the Germans, Italians, French, and British all competed for land. The Italians had the most difficult time, losing 500 soldiers to the Ethiopians in 1887 and 5,000 more in 1896 at the Battle of Adowa.[6] The latter was the greatest defeat of imperialist forces in Africa. Full-scale

[6] **Adowa:** AH doh wah

defeat and annexation of Ethiopia came only in the 1930s, when the Italians smashed the army of Haile Selassie.

German East Africa became a major battleground during World War I. British-led Indian soldiers fought against German-led indigenous troops along with some German independent units. The mixed African-German army defeated and captured four Indian regiments, much to the shock of the British. Because Germany lost the war, however, these victories counted for little. Britain took over administration of the colony.

FIGURE 34.7 *Belgian Rule in the Congo.* The *Belgian king, Leopold, ran a private empire until the early 1900s in the Belgian Congo. Even by the brutal standards of other imperialist countries of the time, Leopold's domain witnessed many atrocities. In this British cartoon, a reptilian Leopold crushes a Congolese man—a stark representation of his policies toward the Congolese people.* Mansell/Time Inc.

West and Southwest Africa

The French took over the largest amount of African lands in West Africa and primarily competed with the Germans and British for influence there. Albert Schweitzer (1875–1965) became a medical missionary in French Equatorial Africa in the early 1900s. Although imprisoned by the French during World War I for suspected German sympathies, Schweitzer returned to Africa after the war to rebuild his hospital, winning a Nobel Peace Prize in 1952. The Portuguese, Spanish, and Belgians also controlled territories in the region, while Liberia, although nominally independent, fell under control of the Firestone Rubber Company and thereby the United States.

Belgian rule of the Congo territory was ruthless, even by the standards of the day. Many Europeans deplored Belgian rule, and the horrors prompted Joseph Conrad to pen *Heart of Darkness*, a telling critique of imperialist domination of Africans. International criticism eventually forced King Leopold of Belgium to surrender his personal control to the Belgian Parliament in 1909. Conditions gradually improved, but the Congo remained a Belgian colony until the early 1960s.

The German colonies of Togo, Cameroons, and German West Africa had been set up in the mad rush of the 1880s but fell into British and French hands after World War I. The British and French divided Togo and Cameroons, while the British administered Southwest Africa.

South Africa

British control of southern Africa came after a long campaign of fighting and several military defeats and political embarrassment. Tenacity and perseverance gave the British eventual victory, and the costs forced them into a reexamination of their foreign policy early in the twentieth century.

South Africa contained a diverse mixture of African tribes, Indians, and Europeans. As seen in Chapter 33, Zulu nationalism directed by Shaka and his successors precipitated an expansion of territory, threatening the British. The Zulu War of 1879 concluded a decades-long conflict between the Zulu and the British, who suffered a defeat at the Battle of Isandhlwana before eventually winning.

FIGURE 34.8 *British Detention Camp in South Africa.* *The Boer War (1899–1902) tarnished Britain's self-image as an enlightened imperialist power. Boers, including women and children, were interned in camps like this one; about one-fifth of the prisoners died. Britain's actions during the war brought international condemnation.* MuseuMAfricA, Johannesburg.

After subduing the Zulu, the British focused on the Boers, descendants of Dutch settlers, who had been in South Africa for centuries. In the 1830s, the Boers became disgusted with British diplomatic policies, trekking northward to colonize two regions, Transvaal[7] and Orange Free State. It was a remarkable saga of a people traveling great distances in wagons similar to those that carried settlers to the western United States. Discovery of gold and diamonds in the Boer-controlled area brought fortune seekers and growing conflict. In 1896, Cecil Rhodes, who was prime minister of South Africa, sponsored an expedition of a few hundred soldiers against the Boers, hoping to expand British influence and his own prestige. Defeat of Rhodes's expeditionary force compelled Rhodes to resign, but it also compelled Britain to avenge its loss. The Boer War broke out in 1899 and lasted nearly three years, to the shock of the British, who mustered 350,000 soldiers against a Boer population of 60,000 people. Outnumbered, the Boers successfully used guerrilla tactics until Lord Kitchener responded with a scorched-earth policy that burned down Boer farmhouses and herded Boer women and children into makeshift camps. The British outlasted the Boers but were stunned by the vehement international condemnation of their conduct of the war.

SOCIALIST IMPERIALISM

Forces of nationalism and industrialization rocked the tsarist Russian Empire, bringing its collapse in 1917. The growth of a socialist state from the monarchical ruins brought a socialist imperialism. Most socialists followed Karl Marx in arguing that nationalism and imperialism stemmed from capitalism. To them, internationalism seemed more in line with the new socialist order, as expressed in the slogan "Workers of the world unite!" The experience of Soviet Russia, however, brought imperialist rule over many former Russian colonies.

Six months after the tsarist system collapsed, the Bolshevik Party under Vladimir Lenin's leadership seized power. Within months of gaining political control, the Bolsheviks blundered into a vicious civil war. During the conflict, the Bolsheviks reconquered most of the former tsarist realm.

---

[7] **Transvaal:** TRAHNS vahl

In a related war with Poland, the Soviets expected their Polish worker brothers and sisters to join them. The Bolsheviks were surprised by the nationalism of the Poles, who threw out the Soviets.

Despite the professed internationalism of the Soviets, nationalism persisted after the civil war. Seeing themselves as surrounded by hostile capitalist states, communist leaders stressed the policy of "Socialism in One Country." In the mid-1930s, Josef Stalin permitted a more open celebration of past Russian leaders, including national heroes such as Ivan the Terrible and Peter the Great.

When the Nazis attacked Poland and diverted the attention of western European countries, Soviet Russia expanded its control of other former tsarist areas. Part of Poland was annexed, the Baltic states of Latvia, Lithuania, and Estonia were occupied, and Finland was attacked. Some have argued that Soviet Russia created a defensive barrier against possible attack by the Germans, but others have noted that the Soviets continued traditional Russian expansionist policies. The annexations followed Soviet industrialization, and the new lands were integrated economically into the Soviet Union.

By the end of World War II, Soviet armies occupied parts of East and Central Europe, and, although the Soviets did not rule directly, economic imperialism continued as the Eastern Bloc countries of East Germany, Czechoslovakia, Poland, Romania, Hungary, and Bulgaria all fell into the Soviet economic sphere. Socialist imperialism governed the relationships of Europe and even Mongolia in Central Asia (after 1919).

SOME SOCIAL CONSEQUENCES OF IMPERIALIST RULE

Imperialist states came into control of other countries and brought their own institutions, practices, and ideas into the colonies, conferring subjecthood rather than citizenship on indigenous peoples. In many cases, feelings of preeminence by the rulers were supported by claims of racial supremacy, whether disguised as "the White Man's Burden" or as the Japanese view of themselves as "older brothers."

Liberation of Indian Women?

Europeans examined the position of women in many societies over which they ruled and believed that customs such as footbinding, prohibitions against widows' remarrying, female circumcision, and *suttee*[8] (the burning of Indian widows along with their deceased husbands) were barbaric and proved the inherent "inferiority" of indigenous social and cultural practices. Thus, vigorous efforts were undertaken to abolish them.

Various rulers and individuals in India, for example, also spoke against *suttee* and the practice of forbidding widows to remarry. In the seventh century, the Indian emperor Harsha had condemned *suttee* but was unable to eradicate the custom. In the eighteenth and nineteenth centuries, some Hindu sects of the lower socioeconomic groups welcomed widows. The British undertook a concerted effort to abolish *suttee* and generally succeeded in the areas under their direct control. Success fed British attitudes of superiority along with their self-image of "civilizing" rule.

Education for women in Western colonies became another arena of imperialist policy making. Missionaries established coeducational schools in Asia along with a few strictly for women. Most schools founded by imperial governments were for males only, or the grade level for girls seldom went beyond elementary school. Indians founded single-sex and coeducational schools in Bengal, where classes were taught in the regional dialect. One reason was that men wanted women to read and write only one language, their own. Indian nationalists proudly pointed out that Indian women were graduated from universities before their sisters in Britain.

While many Indian men approved of the abolition of *suttee* and of the education of women, they also fervently believed that Indian women should remain unchanged in other ways. Indian nationalists, for example, accepted change mandated by imperialist rulers in the "outer world" of political and economic relationships. On the other hand, these nationalists rejected attempts of the imperialists to transform the "inner world" of the family, where the wife was sacred. In this view, the home was not to be colonized. Although idealized as goddesses, Indian women remained under the control of men in the "inner world."

---

[8] *suttee:* SUH tee

Many Indian men feared the Western education of Indian women, especially by Western teachers. The safest way, Indian men argued, was to create schools where Indian girls were taught in the local dialect. Then there would be control over what they learned.

Rassundari Debi[a] (1809–1900), a middle-class girl, first tasted education when she was eight years old by learning arithmetic and the Bengali alphabet. The experiment died with a fire that incinerated the school but left an inner flame that would not be snuffed out. At twelve years of age, Rassundari was married, ending her chances for study and self-improvement. When her mother died, Rassundari lamented being unable to visit her and being a woman.

> I tried in so many ways to go and see my mother, but I was not fated to do so. This is not a matter of small regret to me. Oh Lord, why did you give birth to me as a human being? Compared to all the birds and beasts and other inferior creatures in this world, it is a rare privilege to be granted a human birth. And yet, despite this privilege, I have failed grievously in my duty. Why was I born a woman? Shame on my life. . . . If I had been my mother's son and known of her imminent death, no matter where I happened to be, I would have flown to her side like a bird. Alas, I am only a bird in a cage.

[a] **Rassundari Debi:** RAH suhn dah ree DEH bee

IN THEIR OWN WORDS

A Woman in Nineteenth-Century India

Rassundari always dreamed of being able to read and prayed for that skill.

> One day in my sleep, I dreamt I had opened a copy of the *Caitanya-Bhagavat*[b] [a Hindu religious text] and was reading it. As soon as I woke up, my body and mind were filled with delight. I closed my eyes and again thought of the dream, and realized what a precious gift I had received. . . . Every day I had asked the Almighty, "Teach me to read. I want to read books." The Almighty had not taught me to read, but now had given me the power to read books in my dream.

One day, Rassundari's husband left a copy of the *Caitanya-Bhagavat* for her eldest son to read. Secretly, Rassundari learned to read the holy book.

> My mind seemed to have acquired six hands. With two of them, it wanted to do all the work of the household so that no one, young or old, could find fault with me. With two others, it sought to draw my children close to my heart. And with the last two, it reached for the moon. . . . Has anyone held the moon in her hands? . . . And yet my mind would not be convinced; it yearned to read the *purana* [holy teachings].

Rassundari's sons also helped her learn to read and write, and later she wrote her autobiography.

[b] **Caitanya-Bhagavat:** KAY tahn yah BAH gah vaht

Peasant Unrest

Imperialist policies disrupted the lives of rural peoples, especially peasants. The French in Vietnam and the British in India, for example, set tax rates on individuals rather than on village communities, upsetting traditional patterns of social interaction and responsibility. In addition, tax revenues had to be paid in money rather than in crops, causing some farmers to sell their lands and move to cities, where many became indigent and homeless. The Belgians needed laborers to work the rubber plantations in the Congo and forced reluctant farmers to contribute weekly or monthly *corvée* services. Indigo plantations in Bengal and sugar plantations in Cuba severely exploited workers, causing men and women to live in near-slavery conditions.

Rural unrest developed as living conditions deteriorated, taking many forms of rural violence. One common result of growing servitude was flight, and the early exploitation of the Belgian Congo led to widespread absenteeism on the part of peasants. Isolated sentry posts around rubber plantations were overrun by peasants in the Congo, and the guards were killed. Major uprisings by Indian peasants erupted in 1857 and again in 1942, when rural folk focused their hatred on the British government. It took months and many lives for the British to restore control.

AMERICAS		ASIA	EUROPE AND AFRICA		
				1800	Louisiana Purchase, 1803 (by U.S.)
U.S. continental expansion, 1803–1898	Economic imperialism in Latin America, c. 1800–1949			–	
				–	
				–	
				–	
				–	Mexico cedes territory to U.S., 1848
				1850	
		British imperialism in South Asia, c. 1850–1948			Gadsen Purchase, 1853 (by U.S.)
				–	
				–	Alaska Purchase, 1867 (by U.S.)
			German imperialism in Africa, c. 1880–1918	–	
				–	
U.S. imperialism, c. 1890–1959		Japanese imperialism, c. 1895–1945		–	U.S. annexes the Philippines, 1898
				1900	Anglo-Russian rivalry in Afghanistan relaxes, 1907
				–	Japan annexes Korea, 1910
					Germany loses African colonies, 1918
				–	
				–	
			Socialist imperialism, 1939–1989	–	Japan's Greater East Asia Co-Prosperity Sphere, 1940
					Soviet occupation of eastern Europe, 1945
				1950	

SUMMARY

1. Imperialism is an economic and political system of control by an industrialized country needing raw materials and markets. It developed out of the Industrial Revolution and the era of modern nationalism.

2. After the United States won independence from England, the Americans continued colonizing to the Pacific Ocean and beyond. Industrialization brought U.S. control of the Philippines and economic imperialism in Latin America.

3. Latin America gained independence from Spain, Portugal, Britain, Denmark, the Netherlands, and France but had to fend off imperialist efforts to gain direct control in later decades. Latin America long suffered from economic imperialism directed by England, France, and the United States.

4. China suffered growing humiliation at the hands of the British and other Western countries until 1894. Then, Japan entered the imperialist competition and eventually dominated China from 1931 to 1945. Chinese nationalism developed from the clashes with imperialists, benefiting the Chinese communists.

5. Japan's imperialism ended in utter defeat by 1945, and a wounded Korea lay prostrate under Soviet and American influence.

6. Southeast Asia fell under Western and Japanese imperialism. Although imperialism wrought havoc, it helped generate nationalism and brought defeat for the Europeans.

7. South Asia suffered under British rule, which left the subcontinent ecologically changed and highly fragmented. Under the leadership of Mohandas Gandhi and Muhammad Jinnah, India and Pakistan gained independence.

8. The decline of the Ottoman Empire afforded the European imperialists the opportunity to replace the Turks as imperial rulers. Arab nationalism, which helped bring the change, was frustrated by the change of masters. Eventually, most Arab states won independence, but Arab nationalism was provoked by Zionism and the formation of Israel in the territory of Palestine in 1948. Russia expanded into Central Asia, seeking markets and raw materials.

9. Africa was dismembered by the imperialist powers between 1871 and 1912. Germany lost its African territories in World War I, and Italy lost its lands there in World War II. Much of Africa lay under imperialism in 1949.

10. Socialist imperialism grew out of the nationalist fervor employed in the Russian Civil War (1918–1921), and it reappeared at the end of the Stalinist industrialization effort.

11. Women in countries controlled by imperialists gained some freedoms, but they remained under male domination. Peasants often suffered under foreign rule and revolted against it.

SUGGESTED READINGS

Chatterjee, Partha. *The Nation and Its Fragments: Colonial and Post-Colonial Histories.* Princeton, N.J.: Princeton University Press, 1993. An examination of British imperialism and Indian responses to it.

Duus, Peter. *The Abacus and the Sword: The Japanese Penetration of Korea, 1895–1910.* Berkeley: University of California Press, 1995. An analysis of Japan's conquest and annexation of Korea in the context of imperialism.

Gallager, John, and Ronald Robinson. "The Imperialism of Free Trade." *Economic Review,* 2nd series, 6 (1953): 1–15. A classic argument of a creeping Western imperialism through free trade policies and treaties with Asian and African states.

Hobson, J. A. *Imperialism.* Ann Arbor: University of Michigan Press, 1971. A reprint of a classic study (1902) and critique of imperialism, one that influenced Lenin's *Imperialism.*

Kiernan, V. G. *Imperialism and Its Contradictions.* New York: Routledge, 1995. Essays from the past few decades by an important scholar of imperialism.

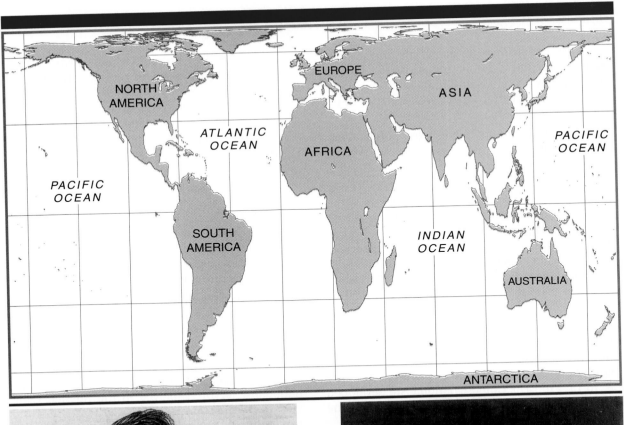

John Speke and Richard Burton. *These British geographers-explorers were fierce com-petitors in the European race to discover the source of the Nile—the place where its head-waters arose. Newspapers of the time closely followed the exploits of both men. Though his methods were less rigorous than Burton's, Speke (left) was ultimately successful.* Left: Illus-trated London News Picture Library; right: Trustees of the National Portrait Gallery.

Darwin, Marx, and Others Transform Our Views

1837 Onward

Human history is in essence a history of ideas.

This quotation from H. G. Wells reflects the pivotal position that many scholars accord intellectual history. If we accept this position, then the nineteenth century must be granted a special place in history. During that century, basic conceptions were changing in many or most academic fields, and our vision of the universe and our place in it was changing at a rate that arguably was faster than ever before or since. Certainly most intellectual disciplines can trace their modern forms directly to ideas developed in the nineteenth century.

During the nineteenth century, the fruits of the Scientific Revolution two centuries before led to drastically new ways of viewing the world. This period saw major shifts in the basic outlook, assumptions, and underlying theories in many branches of science and other scholarly fields; our understanding of how nature and people operate was elaborated into patterns that largely persist today. These new ideas, developed and debated by scholars, in turn were passed on to the general public as discoveries and theories were disseminated through books, newspapers, and other media.

INTELLECTUAL FERMENT IN NINETEENTH-CENTURY EUROPE

By the nineteenth century, the intellectual scene in Europe had become dynamic and exciting. Forces set in motion centuries before had wrought major changes in the ways that intellectuals conducted their scholarship, and more recent social changes had led scholars to question some of their most basic assumptions about the world and humanity. It was in this setting that the basic paradigms of many fields of study were reoriented.

Of considerable importance was the sheer increase in the number of professional scholars in the nineteenth century. Colleges had been around in Europe since the ninth century, but they were few and served only a small group of elite students training for particular fields, largely law, theology, and medicine. By the nineteenth century, however, higher education was expanding to include larger numbers of students and a greater variety of fields of study. Population increases of the period and the rise of the middle class fueled the upsurge in the numbers of students, and colleges and universities proliferated. In France, for example, the number of colleges and universities increased by more than 500 percent between 1750 and 1850, and there were similar increases in England, Germany, Italy, and elsewhere in Europe. This meant that more scholars were hired as professors and that more research was conducted.

At the same time that academia was expanding, it was reorganizing. In Renaissance Europe, scholars were expected to be versatile, making contributions in diverse fields. (The modern phrase "a Renaissance man" refers to someone who is knowledgeable or skilled in many areas.) Many students in the eighteenth and nineteenth centuries selected the more general liberal arts education, but increasingly large numbers chose to specialize more narrowly, focusing their study on only biology or history or mathematics. Universities began organizing into departments that reflected these academic specializations, encouraging scholars to study a more narrow field intensively. Compared with earlier times, nineteenth-century Europe had huge numbers of scholars, delving intensively into their specialized fields.

At the same time, these scholars had available to them the scientific methodology of the Scientific Revolution. The interim had seen tremendous advances in scientific knowledge, the accumulation of an impressive legion of scientific facts, and refinements in scientific method. The time was ripe to use these tools and raw materials to build new intellectual frameworks for looking at the world and society.

These scholars did not live in a vacuum, and they were profoundly influenced by the events that transpired around them. The French Revolution had spawned a new era of secularism that the succeeding decades had legitimized. Other political revolutions added to the perception of world instability, and the Industrial Revolution was in full swing, radically transforming the lives of everyone caught up in it. The pace of technological change was such that those of each generation grew up with everyday devices unknown in their parents' childhood. Omnipresent change encouraged scholars to look to new ways of seeing their disciplines, and the older tradition of looking to ancient scholars for inspiration had largely faded away. Scholars came to see progress and new ideas in a far more favorable light than had their predecessors.

Out of this setting developed a number of scholars who profoundly changed our ways of looking at ourselves. They certainly were major forces in world intellectual history, founders of the modern intellectual traditions of Western civilization.

DARWIN AND THE PLACE OF HUMANITY

Charles Darwin (1809–1882) was born into an elite, intellectual English family. Initially, he was a great disappointment to his family, who complained that he cared for nothing but "shooting, dogs, and rat-catching." His life was transformed, however, in 1831, when a family friend obtained for him a position on HMS *Beagle*.

This British vessel was setting out on a five-year voyage around the world to explore and collect scientific information, and Darwin was to be its naturalist. While he had no special training in that field, he had read widely and had always been interested in nature, and he threw himself into his position. The information Darwin gathered, coupled with his copious spare time aboard the *Beagle*, led him to formulate revolutionary ideas about the development of the various plant and animal species.

FIGURE 35.1 *HMS* **Beagle** *at the Strait of Magellan.* *The* Beagle *carried Charles Darwin around the world, carefully navigating the dangerous waters at the southern tip of South America en route to the Galapagos Islands. There Darwin studied local plants and animals, collecting much of the information that shaped his theory of evolution.* Corbis-Bettmann.

Pre-Darwinian Beliefs

At the beginning of the nineteenth century, most scientists believed that species were immutable—that is, that they could not change or evolve from one to another. This belief was founded on the everyday observation that a species always bore young of the same kind, and that there were no intermediate forms of known creatures, such as hybrids between dogs and cats. The biblical aphorism that "like produces like" was part of the fund of knowledge commonly taken for granted in the Western tradition during this period, leading most contemporary scientists to accept the immutability of species.

Another commonly held belief was that the world had been created relatively recently. There was no pressing evidence in this era to compel a scientist to believe the world was significantly older than the indications from the earliest historic documents. While only a minority of scientists at this time accepted the chronology derived from the Bible by Bishop James Ussher in the seventeenth century, which placed earthly creation at 4004 B.C., most allowed only a few tens of thousands of years for all of earthly events. A rising group of geologists (discussed later in this chapter) championed a much greater age for the earth, but they were opposed by most scholars in the early decades of the nineteenth century.

Such a short period between the beginning of the planet and the earliest historical accounts (which describe modern species of plants and animals) permitted insufficient time for the gradual development of modern species. Therefore, proponents of the short earthly chronology argued, evolution could not explain the development of species.

There was, however, a significant dissenting view, popular particularly in France. There, such scientists as Jean Baptiste Lamarck (1744–1829) and Georges Buffon[1] (1707–1788) had championed theories of **evolution**, the concept that each species developed by modification from an earlier species, now extinct. While some scientists were fascinated with this idea, neither Lamarck nor Buffon could suggest a satisfactory mechanism by which this evolution might have taken place. Rather, they suggested that new forms developed in direct response to needs. For example, if an antelope-like animal needed access to the tops of trees in order to eat the leaves growing there, individuals would strive to reach them, thus stretching their necks; these acquired traits, according to Lamarck, were passed on to offspring, and the result was the giraffe. While Lamarck and Buffon were wrong in their assumptions—experiments showed that acquired characteristics could not be passed on to offspring—they drew attention to the fact that animals and plants were adapted to the particulars of the environments in which they lived. Darwin used this insight as a crucial element in his theory of evolution.

Darwin's Theory of Evolution

As Darwin began observing plants and animals wherever the *Beagle* went, he began formulating his theory of evolution. He was particularly intrigued by the finches he found on the Galapagos Islands, off the western coast of South America. Each island was isolated from the others by winds and currents that would have made it difficult for a bird as small as a finch to have crossed from one to another, and the finches on each island were somewhat different from those on all the other islands. Yet, they all shared basic anatomy and characteristics. How could Darwin account for this?

To explain it, Darwin borrowed a concept from economics. While reading the influential *Essay on Population* by Thomas Malthus[2] (1766–1834), Darwin had been struck that every individual is in competition with every other individual. As Malthus argued, people (and animals) are such efficient reproducers that the population has the

potential to grow sufficiently to outstrip its food supply. At that point, as Malthus saw it, individuals were condemned to a miserable struggle for survival, pitted against one another in a competition that invariably would result in the death of some. According to Malthus, the struggle for scarce resources by individuals is inherent in nature.

Using this as his starting point, Darwin took the crucial next step. He argued that individuals who survive are permitted to do so by certain traits that aid their survival, perhaps greater strength or the ability to eat a broader range of foods. These traits are inherited by the offspring of the survivors and are passed on to future generations. On the other hand, animals that die out do so because they possess less advantageous traits, and those traits are weeded out of the population with their deaths. In this manner, less successful characteristics are culled from a population, and the population becomes ever better adapted to its circumstances. Darwin used the term **natural selection** to describe this notion of the most adaptive traits' persistence and others' elimination.

As applied to the Galapagos finches, for example, Darwin's theory postulated that there was a single species of finches that colonized the islands, perhaps accidentally, as a few individuals survived the rigors of traveling there from the South American mainland. As time passed, however, the peculiarities of each island shaped the finches on it. An island with very hard-shelled seeds, for example, would favor finches with stout, rugged beaks able to crack them; an island where finch food was secreted in hollows in plant stems would favor a long, slender bill, and individuals with that characteristic would be most likely to survive. The founding population of each island would have some individual variation, and natural selection would favor some variants and weed out others, leading to considerable differences between the finches on different islands.

Darwin's theory of evolution differed from all evolutionary concepts that preceded it in a crucial way. Lamarck, Buffon, and the other evolutionists before Darwin had believed that evolution was headed in some particular direction, that it was somehow improving things. Darwinian evolution, on the other hand, was not directed toward any consistent goal. As conditions changed, adaptive traits changed, and creatures that once were numerous and well adapted might become extinct

---

[1]**Georges Buffon:** ZHORZH boo FOHN
[2]**Malthus:** MAHL thoos

as selective pressures changed. While Darwin carefully avoided linking evolution to progress, this was atypical of scientists of that day, and most popular interpretations of Darwin's theories saw evolution as progressive improvement.

As he developed his theory of evolution, Darwin saw that this single concept could account for the development of all the plants and animals in the modern world, as well as all the extinct forms he argued must have existed in earlier times. This theory solved two vexing biological problems.

First, if each species had been created independently of all the others, why were there so many similarities among modern species? A giraffe, trout, parakeet, and human being are all built about the same way. They have four limbs that intersect the torso at the same skeletal points, a comparable layout of sensory organs on the head, and very similar internal organs. Other animals, such as insects, followed a different plan, but they resembled one another equally strongly. Many scientists of the day thought these unlikely to be mere coincidences; instead, they argued, somehow all vertebrates had descended from a common ancestor and all insects from another common ancestor at some time in the very distant past.

Second, geologists were unearthing a disturbing array of **fossils**, the remains of ancient creatures. Some of these fossils were quite like modern creatures, but others were very different, though still falling into general body plans comparable to those of modern creatures. Earlier scholarship had dismissed these creatures as monsters, aberrations, or failed experiments in creation, but their numbers by the nineteenth century were too great to ignore. Darwin's theory considered these fossils the remains of earlier life forms, successful for a while, yet gradually being transformed into modern species or dying out.

There were, however, difficulties with Darwin's theory of evolution. The first was time, because evolution would be a very slow process. While some scientists clung to the older idea that the earth and its creatures were less than 6,000 years old, geologists under the lead of James Hutton and Charles Lyell were demolishing it, and Ussher's chronology posed little serious impediment to the acceptance of Darwin's theory of evolution.

The second difficulty was the one that swayed most of the scientists who argued against Darwin's

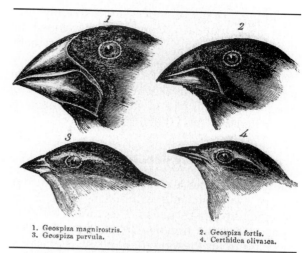

1. Geospiza magnirostris.
2. Geospiza fortis.
3. Geospiza parvula.
4. Certhidea olivacea.

FIGURE 35.2 *Four Species of Finches. Though all of the finches on the isolated Galapagos Islands are descended from the same species, they followed different evolutionary courses that adapted them for different lifestyles. The heavy-beaked species (top) ate foods that required the breaking of an outer shell or kernel, while the fine-beaked species (bottom) used their narrow beaks to pull food out from narrow crevices. Evidence like this helped Darwin to formulate his theory of natural selection.* Bibliothèque nationale, Paris.

theory. Natural selection could explain how forms could die out, but it could not explain how new forms could come about. Darwin's explanation of the Galapagos finches, for example, could explain how delicate-beaked finches could die off on an island with hard seeds, but it did not explain how that same island could develop finches with more rugged beaks than those in the founding population. Darwin recognized this shortcoming of his theory, but he never was able to devise a suitable solution. Only in the early twentieth century would theories of heredity and genetics, pioneered by Gregor Mendel and J. B. S. Haldane, finally unravel this problem. They developed the notions of heredity and genetics that underlie the modern conception of **mutation**, a spontaneous development of a new trait as a result of an error in copying the biochemicals that carry the genetic code during reproduction.

A shy person, Darwin had put off publishing his ideas. In 1858, however, another scientist, Alfred Russel Wallace, came up with the same theory. While Darwin had not published his theory, he had discussed it with colleagues and written preliminary drafts of papers. Consequently, they were aware that each scientist had developed the theory independently and that Darwin actually had collected and analyzed far more supporting evidence. Darwin and Wallace presented a joint paper in 1858, but Darwin's *On the Origin of Species* was published in 1859, and his name is associated with this influential theory.

The Scholarly Reaction to Darwin

Many scientists flocked in support of Darwin's theory of evolution, and within ten years it was accepted by most scholars. There were, however, dissenters, some troubled by the lack of a clear mechanism for the formation of new characteristics and a few concerned that evolution seemed to contradict biblical revelation. Darwin was a Christian, and he felt a certain remorse at developing a theory that he thought might undermine confidence in the spirit (if not the literal truth) of the Bible. He expressed this concern in a letter in which he detailed his agonizing over the theory, finally surrendering to its logic, at which point he noted that he felt as if he were "confessing to a murder."

Darwin's shy personality tended to shrink from controversy, and he rarely defended his theory against the attacks of critics. An early convert to evolution named Thomas Huxley, however, stepped in to defend Darwin and his theory from its earliest presentation. Huxley's strongest supporters never professed him to be shy, and he was famed for his aggressive defenses of Darwin, earning him the nickname "Darwin's bulldog."

In his early work, Darwin avoided direct discussion of human evolution. In fact, he waited to the last pages of *On the Origin of Species* to predict timidly that through evolution, "much light will be thrown on the origin of man and his history." Scientists, as well as the public, were quick to see the ramifications of Darwinian evolution, however, and much of the controversy over Darwin's theory arose out of the implication that human beings evolved from some monkey-like animal, a less than appealing notion to most nineteenth-century readers. In 1871, Darwin attacked this problem head on with his *Descent of Man*. In this book, he provided a detailed analysis of similarities between the anatomy and behavior of human beings and those of other mammals. He concluded

FIGURE 35.3 *Charles Darwin as Ape. Nineteenth-century cartoonists had a field day with the controversy that developed over Darwin's theory of evolution. This artist placed Darwin's own likeness on the body of an ape, in a parody of the author's work.* From *The Hornet*, March 22, 1871.

that "Man, with all his noble qualities . . . still bears in his bodily frame the indelible stamp of his lowly origin." The probable human ancestor, Darwin said, was "a hairy, tailed quadruped, probably arboreal in its habits, and an inhabitant of the Old World." He even went on to speculate on the way that such a creature might evolve the sentiments and morals of human beings.

Before Darwin, the European scholarly tradition had viewed human beings as noble creatures, set off from the animals by knowledge, morality, and sentiments. After Darwin, scholars were forced to see human beings as another animal, surely ennobled by intelligence but still an animal with a heritage bequeathed by its beastlike ancestors. The effects on philosophy and thinking after Darwin have been many and profound, throwing into question concepts that previously had been

---

Rarely in the history of science has there been such a reaction to a scientific theory among nonscholars as there was to Darwin's theory of evolution. By the mid–nineteenth century, a high percentage of people in Europe and North America could read, so word of Darwin's ideas spread fast. Magazines and newspapers presented simplified versions, often coupled with editorials or guest essays by opponents, and cartoonists had a field day. Usually basing their opinions purely on these second-hand accounts and commentaries, schoolteachers and members of the clergy sometimes found themselves squaring off in sermons, lessons, debates, and letters published in newspapers.

The public debate over Darwin's ideas usually was framed very differently from the scholarly debate. Most scholars of the era were primarily concerned with Darwin's failure to propose a suitable mechanism for the development of new traits in a species or to produce an unequivocal sequence of fossils that supported evolution. When these obstacles were overcome, academic opposition evaporated.

The public debate, on the other hand, was more likely to revolve on emotional issues. Those who supported Darwin often did so because of a general faith in science: Darwin's theory allowed for an orderly universe to elaborate itself without the need of divine assistance. Many opponents rejected evolution because it was contrary to the literal biblical interpretations that were current in many nineteenth-century circles; others, while not necessarily wedded to a biblical account of creation, simply disliked the idea of so noble a creature as a human having descended from the pathetic monkey or from—even worse—pond scum.

Perhaps the most dramatic confrontation of lay proponents and opponents of evolution was in the "Scopes Monkey Trial." In 1925, John Scopes, a schoolteacher in Dayton, Tennessee, was arrested for teaching Darwinian evolution in violation of a Tennessee statute. The trial attracted the best legal talent, with Clarence Darrow defending Scopes and William Jennings Bryan prosecuting him. It also attracted national attention through the press, which gave it prominent and extensive coverage. Eventually Scopes was convicted, though he was released on a technicality. The negative reaction to the statute and his conviction, however, deterred other states from enacting similar laws and led to the eventual repeal of Tennessee's statute.

---

the foundation of most Western thinking, such as divine will and the existence of the human soul. The public, too, has been greatly influenced by Darwin, some in accepting his ideas and others in criticizing them.

MARX AND THE NATURE OF SOCIETY

Within a century of Karl Marx's death, one-third of the world's people lived in countries dominated by political systems derived from his theories, and the remaining two-thirds were profoundly affected by them. Even if no other criterion were considered, Marx would have to be judged one of the most influential thinkers of the nineteenth century.

Karl Marx (1818–1883) was born in Germany to middle-class parents. He studied law and philosophy at various German universities, where his reading included the works of earlier socialists like Claude Saint-Simon[3] and Pierre Proudhon,[4] writers who had championed workers, class struggle, and the abolition of private property. He completed his doctorate in 1841, but his radical political views kept him from an academic appointment, forcing him to enter journalism as an alternative career. He wrote several articles discussing politics in the next few years, but his first important publication came in 1848, when he (along with Friedrich Engels) published *The Manifesto of the Communist Party*. From that time on, he published extensively

[3] **Claude Saint-Simon:** clohd san see MOH
[4] **Pierre Proudhon:** pee AYR proo DOH

on politics and economics, in outlets ranging from newspapers to academic journals.

Marx's ideas on society, history, politics, and economics are collectively labeled "Marxism," but that simple term belies their complexity. Not only were the ideas themselves often difficult or complicated, but they changed over time. Sometimes Marx was ambiguous, presenting conflicting ideas in different places and never reconciling them. Further complicating matters is the fact that many people have interpreted Marx since his death, sometimes producing conflicting versions of his theories. It is possible, however, to reduce Marxism to a few essential ideas that convey his main points.

1. *Historical change takes place in regular patterns determined by economics.* Marx argued that changes in ways of life are not random but are the logical outgrowths of economic systems. In particular, the **means of production**, the way that people earn a livelihood, shapes the form of government under which people will be ruled. Marx produced a scheme of cultural evolution that began with hunter-gatherers in prehistory and ended with hypothetical stages yet to come, and for each he discussed the type of government that logically would accompany the means of production.

2. *Under capitalism there is a division into antagonistic classes based on wealth.* Marx saw the major economic system of his time to be **capitalism**, that in which ownership is private and individuals compete to increase their wealth, little hampered by governmental restriction. In such a system, as Marx saw it, some individuals naturally would succeed and others would fail, leading to classes made up of individuals with similar levels of economic wealth and with common concerns. Marx was unsure how many classes there were, but he was sure that there were at least two: the **bourgeoisie**[5] (wealthy investors and their middle-class allies) and the **proletariat** (poor factory workers). The nature of society, according to Marx, ensured that these classes would be in conflict with each other, because their interests were different. In particular, the workers, having nothing to gain from their production, were alienated from their jobs; consequently, workers resented the wealth that others accumulated through their efforts.

[5] **bourgeoisie:** boor zhwah ZEE

FIGURE 35.4 *Karl Marx.* *Marx, the primary founder of communism, was one of the most influential thinkers of the nineteenth century. His ideas have influenced intellectuals in their writings and sparked revolutions that have profoundly affected world society, economics, and politics.* Corbis-Bettmann.

This class conflict was the driving force behind change.

3. *Over the long run, the profits of the bourgeoisie must decline, as must the standard of living of the proletariat.* Marx developed a complicated economic theory of constant and variable capital (items of value) that few people today accept. The logical consequence of his theory, however, was that there would be less and less material of value over time. This meant that the competition for limited capital would become greater over time, leading to increased class conflict.

4. *The state serves as an instrument of class domination.* Marx observed that the body of laws

serves largely to protect the interests of the capitalists and the bourgeoisie, tilting the odds in their favor in the inevitable class conflict. As he saw it, the main purpose of all states is to protect the status quo, hence protecting the monied ruling classes.

5. *The overthrow of capitalism and the establishment of a more fair system will have to be accomplished through revolution.* Because the legal system serves to support the current status, Marx reasoned, it will be necessary to go outside the law to change the system. Marx saw this as usually entailing a violent revolution that would replace the legal system. The new type of society would be characterized by a **socialist** economy, wherein property of all sorts would be held by everyone as a whole, and a **communist** political system that would serve the people but not support class domination. This new socialist state would be a classless system with a more equal distribution of wealth. It would be a society ruled by Marx's famous maxim: "From each according to his abilities, to each according to his needs."

6. *The revolution will need to be international and led by a communist party.* Recognizing the need for organizers, Marx argued that a communist party would need to be developed in order to lead the revolution. The revolution would need to be international, at least eventually, because national interests invariably are geared to the

---

IN THEIR OWN WORDS
The Communist Manifesto

The following excerpt is the beginning of *The Manifesto of the Communist Party*, jointly written by Karl Marx and Friedrich Engels in 1848. It introduces the factor they saw as underlying all history: class struggle.

A spectre is haunting Europe—the spectre of Communism. All the Powers of old Europe have entered into a holy alliance to exorcise this spectre: Pope and Czar, Metternich and Guizot, French Radicals and German police-spies.

Where is the party in opposition that has not been decried as Communistic by its opponents in power? Where is the Opposition that has not hurled back the branding reproach of Communism, against the more advanced opposition parties, as well as against its reactionary adversaries?

Two things result from this fact:

I. Communism is already acknowledged by all European Powers to be itself a Power.

II. It is high time that Communists should openly, in the face of the whole world, publish their views, their aims, their tendencies, and meet this nursery tale of the Spectre of Communism with a Manifesto of the party itself.

To this end, Communists of various nationalities have assembled in London, and sketched the following Manifesto, to be published in the English, French, German, Italian, Flemish and Danish languages.

The history of all hitherto existing society is the history of class struggles. Freeman and slave, patrician and plebeian, lord and serf, guild-master and journeyman, in a word, oppressor and oppressed, stood in constant opposition to one another, carried on an uninterrupted, now hidden, now open fight, a fight that each time ended, either in a revolutionary reconstitution of society at large, or in the common ruin of the contending classes.

In the earlier epochs of history, we find almost everywhere a complicated arrangement of society into various orders, a manifold gradation of social rank. In ancient Rome we have patricians, plebeians, slaves; in the Middle Ages, feudal lords, knights, vassals, guild-masters, journeymen, apprentices, serfs; in almost all of these classes, again, subordinate gradations.

The modern bourgeois society that has sprouted from the ruins of feudal society has not done away with class antagonisms. It has but established new classes, new conditions of oppression, new forms of struggle in place of the old ones.

Our epoch, the epoch of the bourgeoisie, possesses, however, this distinctive feature: it has simplified the class antagonisms. Society as a whole is more and more splitting up into two great hostile camps, into two great classes directly facing each other: Bourgeoisie and Proletariat.

monied classes. Communist and capitalist societies cannot coexist indefinitely, so the revolution would need to spread around the world.

7. *All states will wither away after the establishment of an international communist system.* Given that states existed primarily to support the interests of the bourgeoisie, there would be no need for them once classes were eliminated. Rather, the communist party, communes, and collectives would manage themselves. Marx expressed some ambiguity on just how such a system could operate without the guidance of a state.

These ideas, taken together, constitute the core of Marxism. In modern usage, "Marxism" can refer to two quite different ideologies. On one hand, it can designate an intellectual-philosophical system, wherein scholars examine historical events in terms of Marxist ideas, such as class conflict. On the other hand, it can refer to an activist political movement advocating revolution to establish a communist system. Clearly, Marx envisioned both. While most of his own writing was devoted to the intellectual ends of Marxism, he was very excited by the political upheavals of 1848, which he thought might be the beginnings of the anticipated revolution that eventually would establish communism. The government leaders who expelled Marx from France and Belgium as a subversive were correct in their assessment of his revolutionary intentions.

Marx's significance cannot be divorced from his period in history. *The Manifesto of the Communist Party* appeared scarcely fifty years after the American and French revolutions, and it was still a fresh idea in Western society that an established elite could be overthrown by a revolution and a new system could be created to replace the old one. The American and French revolutions drew the outlines of a new concept of government, and Marx's ideas colored them in.

At the same time, mid-nineteenth-century Europe was dominated by uncontrolled capitalism. Government regulation of industry and business was minimal; labor unions were yet to become potent political and economic forces; and institutions such as the graduated income tax, whereby those with greater income pay greater tax and ease the burden on the poor, had not yet been proposed or adopted. Only in later years would these responses to capitalism appear.

Marx and his period, therefore, lay in between. Philosophers had created ideas of government as a means of creating greater fairness, yet the application of most of those ideas in the economic world was still decades away. Marx and his theories provided a plan attractive both to the worker, feeling oppressed and resentful of the economic elite, and to the intellectual, attracted to the idealistic philosophy they embodied. The intellectual also saw in Marxism the first modern theory systematically to posit broad principles of regularities in history. It was this dual attractiveness that made communism a major intellectual and political force around the globe in the twentieth century.

OTHER INTELLECTUAL REVOLUTIONARIES

Darwin and Marx were not the only significant intellectual figures of the middle and late nineteenth century. Rather, every discipline had its share of seminal figures whose ideas changed their fields radically and set them in the directions that would lead to today. Just a few of those whose significance was particularly wide ranging are discussed here.

James Hutton and Charles Lyell

The biblical account of creation, with its Great Flood and other catastrophic events, was widely held to be essentially accurate by Western scholars in the seventeenth and early eighteenth centuries. This acceptance had accustomed them to the idea that events in the past were on a grander scale than the events of the modern world and led them to assume that the world had been shaped largely by such catastrophes. The school of thought that sees the past as shaped primarily by such grand events is called **catastrophism**, and for a while it dominated thinking in the geological and biological sciences.

The counterargument came from two British geologists, James Hutton (1726–1796) and Charles Lyell (1797–1875). Hutton presented many of his most important ideas in his *Theory of the Earth*, published in 1785 and revised in 1795. There, he presented **uniformitarianism**, the idea that the forces at work in nature today are similar to and on

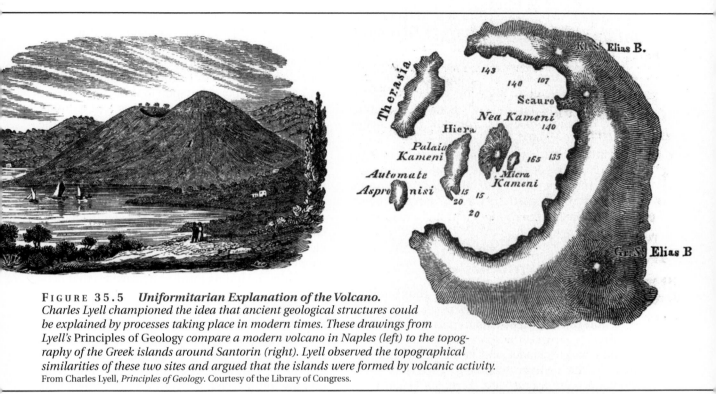

FIGURE 35.5 *Uniformitarian Explanation of the Volcano.*
*Charles Lyell championed the idea that ancient geological structures could
be explained by processes taking place in modern times. These drawings from
Lyell's* Principles of Geology *compare a modern volcano in Naples (left) to the topography of the Greek islands around Santorin (right). Lyell observed the topographical
similarities of these two sites and argued that the islands were formed by volcanic activity.*
From Charles Lyell, *Principles of Geology*. Courtesy of the Library of Congress.

a scale comparable to those that operated in the past; accordingly, because gradual processes dominate the modern scene, Hutton argued that the same sorts of processes must have been the primary shapers of the earth. Like Darwin, Hutton was reticent to become involved in academic battles, and he convinced few colleagues of his ideas. Lyell, however, enjoyed scholarly arguments, and he served as the popularizer of uniformitarianism, especially in his *Principles of Geology*, published in three volumes from 1830 to 1833. Lyell was active several decades after Hutton, and he benefited from a wealth of evidence that had come to light after Hutton's death.

Hutton and Lyell carefully examined geological deposits and realized that their structures and compositions were the same as those of deposits being formed in their own day. When they examined the evidence for ancient catastrophes put forward by the catastrophists, they found it weak and put forward uniformitarian explanations.

Archaeological evidence also played a role in the support of uniformitarianism, especially for

Lyell. Ancient stone tools had been found throughout Europe, and there was increasing evidence of their great age. French scholars reported the finding of flint tools with the bones of extinct animals at Grotte de Bize[6] in 1828. At Brixham Cave in England, similar tools and bones were found together in 1858, and these were sealed off by a cap of dripstone, limestone redeposited by the evaporation of mineral-rich waters that dripped onto the cave floor. The deposition of dripstone was well known to geologists, and it would have taken thousands of years—far more time than available with the catastrophist chronology—for the cap to have formed.

In the absence of sound evidence for massive floods and cataclysmic earthquakes as the primary forces shaping the earth, Hutton and Lyell argued that the slow processes of erosion, deposition, and the like must have been responsible. If uniformitarianism were correct—and Lyell convinced most scientists of its correctness—then the earth must be far older than the earlier scholars had calcu-

[6] **Grotte de Bize:** GROHT duh BEES

lated. Lyell was considered radical when he suggested that the earth was hundreds of thousands of years old, maybe even a million years old. Today we know that his guess was too low by a factor of several thousand, but in the 1830s it opened up a new vista for geology. Suddenly there was a great deal of time for natural processes to have produced our modern world, and new mechanisms could be entertained for those processes.

Hutton and Lyell presented a new paradigm for geology and set the stage for the development of the modern discipline. Perhaps even more important, they paved the way for Darwin's theory of evolution and the changes it brought to humanity's self-conception.

Dmitri Mendeleyev

While it had been recognized for thousands of years that different substances existed, the modern concept of elements—materials that could not be broken down into more basic substances—became part of science only in the eighteenth century. In the century following, dozens of these elements were found, and scientists began wondering whether there was any predictable relationship among them. In 1866, J. A. R. Newlands, an English chemist, presented a paper on what he called "the octave theory" of elements. He noted that if one arranged the elements from lightest to heaviest, sometimes every eighth element shared similar characteristics. Unfortunately, Newlands used an analogy to the piano keyboard and suggested bizarre chemical relationships analogous to European musical harmony; his ideas were ridiculed or ignored by his colleagues.

The next step in establishing the relationships among elements was taken by Dmitri Mendeleyev[7] (1834–1907), a Siberian-born chemist in Russia. Mendeleyev was an indefatigable worker and had established a solid reputation on diverse research concerning petroleum, egg whites, and other organic compounds. His professional life, however, was dominated by the search for order among the elements.

Mendeleyev began his study by organizing the sixty or so elements then known into a sequence based on the relative weights of one atom of each.

[7]**Mendeleyev:** mehn duh LY ehf

(While he was unable to isolate a single atom, of course, techniques were available in the mid–nineteenth century for inferring its weight.) Unlike Newlands, he assumed that this sequence was neither complete nor completely accurate. He undertook years of experimentation to verify or refine the existing data on atomic weights, as well as other characteristics of the elements. He also scoured the international literature to take advantage of work done by his colleagues, sometimes corresponding with them by the newly invented telegraph. When he felt he had adequate data, he constructed a new sequence and looked for patterns.

For the lighter elements, every eighth element shared traits. For example, the third (lithium), eleventh (sodium), and nineteenth (potassium) elements were alkali metals that had similar characteristics, including forming hydroxides that neutralized acids. As Mendeleyev moved further into the heavier elements of his sequence, he found that the similar elements were separated by various multiples of eight. Mendeleyev recognized this and compiled rules for figuring where in the arrangement each element should fall. This scheme left Mendeleyev with a table of elements arranged in order of their relative weights and with columns possessing similar characteristics; this table eventually came to be known as the **periodic table**.

Some positions in the periodic table, however, were blank, because no element then known fitted them. In 1869, when Mendeleyev first presented his ideas publicly at a meeting of the Russian Chemical Society, he suggested the existence of these missing elements. In 1871, he took the bold step of predicting not only the existence of the elements but also their natures. By following the patterns he saw among the known elements, he could predict such characteristics of these unknown elements as atomic weight, color, melting point, and ability to combine with other elements in predictable proportions to form compounds. He even went so far as to name many of these unknown elements.

Mendeleyev's 1871 paper created a sensation around the world. While many scholars were skeptical, they read the paper and were impressed with the careful work that underlay it. Soon, however, skepticism was swept aside as Mendeleyev's predicted elements began to be discovered and to conform to the characteristics he had predicted. In

ПЕРИОДИЧЕСКАЯ СИСТЕМА ЭЛЕМЕНТОВ

ГРУППЫ ЭЛЕМЕНТОВ

ПЕРИОДЫ	РЯДЫ	I	II	III	IV	V	VI	VII	VIII			0
1	I	H 1 1,008										He 2 4,003
2	II	Li 3 6,940	Be 4 9,02	B 5 10,82	C 6 12,010	N 7 14,008	O 8 16,000	F 9 19,00				Ne 10 20,183
3	III	Na 11 22,997	Mg 12 24,32	Al 13 26,97	Si 14 28,06	P 15 30,98	S 16 32,06	Cl 17 35,457				Ar 18 39,944
4	IV	K 19 39,096	Ca 20 40,08	Sc 21 45,10	Ti 22 47,90	V 23 50,95	Cr 24 52,01	Mn 25 54,93	Fe 26 55,85	Co 27 58,94	Ni 28 58,69	
	V	29 Cu 63,57	30 Zn 65,38	31 Ga 69,72	32 Ge 72,60	33 As 74,91	34 Se 78,96	35 Br 79,916				Kr 36 83,7
5	VI	Rb 37 85,48	Sr 38 87,63	Y 39 88,92	Zr 40 91,22	Nb 41 92,91	Mo 42 95,95	Ma 43 —	Ru 44 101,7	Rh 45 102,91	Pd 46 106,7	
	VII	47 Ag 107,88	48 Cd 112,41	49 In 114,76	50 Sn 118,70	51 Sb 121,76	52 Te 127,61	53 J 126,92				Xe 54 131,3
6	VIII	Cs 55 132,91	Ba 56 137,36	La 57 138,92	Hf 72 178,6	Ta 73 180,88	W 74 183,92	Re 75 186,31	Os 76 190,2	Ir 77 193,1	Pt 78 195,23	
	IX	79 Au 197,2	80 Hg 200,61	81 Tl 204,39	82 Pb 207,21	83 Bi 209,00	84 Po 210	85 —				Rn 86 222
7	X	87 —	Ra 88 226,05	Ac 89 227	Th 90 232,12	Pa 91 231	U 92 238,07					

★ ЛАНТАНИДЫ 58–71

Ce 58 140,13	Pr 59 140,92	Nd 60 144,27	61 —	Sm 62 150,43	Eu 63 152,0	Gd 64 156,9
Tb 65 159,2	Dy 66 162,46	Ho 67 164,94	Er 68 167,2	Tu 69 169,4	Yb 70 173,04	Cp 71 174,99

FIGURE 35.6 *Mendeleyev's Periodic Table of the Elements.* *Mendeleyev recognized the patterning of characteristics of elements with progressively higher atomic weights, and in 1869 produced this periodic table that predicts the existence of elements then unknown (see numbers 61, 85, and 87). Although today's periodic table is slightly larger and reflects elements discovered and synthesized since 1869, it follows Mendeleyev's essential form.* Sovfoto.

1875, a French scientist discovered gallium (Mendeleyev's "eka-aluminum"); in 1879, a Swedish scientist isolated scandium (Mendeleyev's "ekaboron"); and in 1886, a German scientist found germanium (Mendeleyev's "ekasilicon"). The discoverers of these new elements ignored Mendeleyev's names in favor of ones honoring their own nations; each of these elements' names was based on an ancient name for the country of the discoverer. Nonetheless, they all paid homage to Mendeleyev's insight. On the basis of incomplete and sometimes faulty information, he had drawn a blueprint for all the elements. Eventually the periodic table included more than one hundred elements, neatly corresponding to virtually all of his predictions.

Although the periodic table became standard fare for chemistry students, Mendeleyev remained obscure most of his life, partly because he worked in Russia, a backwater for science at that time. During one visit to the United States, he actually was introduced to a senator as Gregor Mendel, the Austrian monk who had researched the heredity of peas! His achievement, however, remains one of the most remarkable examples of pattern recognition in science.

UNDER THE LENS
Einstein's Seminal Year

Albert Einstein (1879–1955) had a very good year in 1905. He had been working in the Swiss patent office while finishing the dissertation for his doctorate in physics, which he completed in 1905. In addition, he was able to publish six papers in professional journals, three of which established his reputation as a major thinker. Recognition was not immediate, however, and he was forced to remain in the patent office until 1909, when the University of Zurich offered him his first academic appointment.

The first paper dealt with the photoelectric effect, the production of electricity by the exposure of certain substances to light. Einstein built on the theoretical work of Max Planck, demonstrating that the electric current was formed by a stream of electrons bounced out of the substance by the impact of light. This explanation, in turn, clarified the nature of light, showing that it acted both as waves and as particles.

The second paper related mass to energy in the famous equation E=mc². Prior to this time, energy and substance were conceived of as different things, but Einstein was able to demonstrate theoretically that they were aspects of the same thing. This meant that there were enormous amounts of energy locked within the atom, and this finding laid the groundwork for nuclear weapons in the 1940s.

The third paper developed the special theory of relativity, a revolutionary theory that requires considerable mathematical background to appreciate fully. Stated simply, it posits, among other things, that space and time are not separate entities; instead, they are aspects of the same thing, forming a space-time continuum. The implications of this theory are enormous, suggesting that the speed at which something moves actually affects the passage of time. Experimental verification of Einstein's theory of relativity came only in the latter half of the twentieth century.

Each of these papers had a major impact on physics. Einstein soon was honored throughout the world and was awarded a Nobel Prize for physics in 1921. He was offered prestigious posts around the world and accepted a position at Kaiser Wilhelm Institute in his native Germany. Einstein was Jewish, and his property was confiscated by the Nazi government in 1933. From that time forward he lived in the United States, becoming an American citizen.

Einstein's intellectual legacies are enormous, because he revolutionized thinking in several fields of physics. His ideas may have had their most profound effects, however, in the invention of nuclear weapons. An ardent pacifist yet determinedly opposed to the fascism of Germany in World War II, Einstein was in the grip of a dilemma. Ultimately, he urged the U.S. government to investigate how nuclear energy could be harnessed in weapons, though he later advocated restraint in the use of those weapons.

Franz Boas

Although Franz Boas[8] (1858–1942) did not found the discipline of anthropology, his effect on it was so great that he rightfully could be said to have reformulated it. Born in Germany, Boas received his doctorate in physics, but he spent his life studying people and cultures around the world.

Before he entered anthropology, Boas had been struck by the complexity of human behavior. In fact, it was the challenge of understanding this complexity that stimulated him to switch his attentions to anthropology. Boas was always distrustful of authority and cherished beliefs, and this trait fit well with the modern role of scientist as one who questioned existing ideas. Boas devised a radical revision of anthropology's assumptions, and his immensely successful teaching career at Columbia University passed his ideas along to many of the most influential anthropologists of their generation, effectively reorienting the discipline.

When Boas entered the field of anthropology in 1883, it was dominated by scholars whose ideas today would be considered racist and ethnocentric. Most anthropologists of that period believed

[8] **Boas:** BOH az

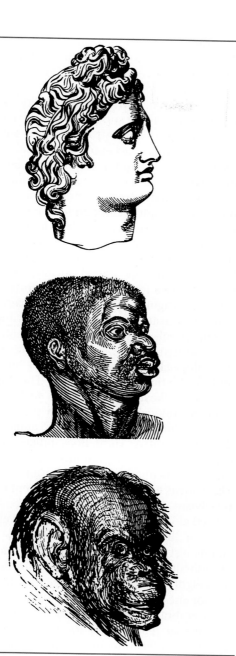

FIGURE 35.7 *Nineteenth-Century Example of Racist Science.* *This illustration dating to 1868 was designed to show a hierarchy surmounted by the idealized European; the African is relegated to a status below the European, and the chimpanzee is placed at the lowest level. The African's features have been distorted, presumably to make him appear more like the chimpanzee. Orderings of this sort were common in Western science during this period; the anthropologist Franz Boas was influential in discrediting them.* From Stephen Jay Gould, *The Mismeasure of Man* (New York: W. W. Norton & Company). Reproduced with permission.

that there were significant differences in human potential that were inborn and that race was a primary determinant of intelligence, morality, and worth. University students studying anthropology at that date read the writings of Count Joseph Gobineau[9] (1816–1882), particularly *The Inequality of Races.* This book classified humanity into four races, a relatively innocent exercise, but went on to rank these races in terms of their characteristics. Africans, for example, were described as lazy, stupid, and improvident; Asians were considered intelligent but crafty and ruled by tradition; and American Indians were said to be proud, shiftless, and only slightly intelligent. Europeans, particularly northern Europeans, contrasted with all these others: They were described as intelligent, noble, moral, and advanced.

The intellectual doctrine of racism was popular in European and American academic circles throughout the nineteenth and early twentieth centuries, though there always were dissenters. The doctrine was particularly cherished by many politicians who saw it as a moral justification for the oppression of other peoples through imperialist conquest and rule; in addition, it was invoked as a defense of the oppression of Jews, blacks, Gypsies, and other minorities at home. Given their political importance, it is little wonder that racist ideas became entrenched in intellectual tradition.

In addition to racist ideas, anthropologists of the late nineteenth century were taught that human societies could be ranked in order, from primitive to advanced—with their own society at the pinnacle of advancement, of course. The fact that an Australian Aborigine wore no clothes and had no writing was seen as the logical consequence of a faulty and childlike mind, and the culture of the Aborigine was seen as inferior to that of the civilized European. The double stigma of biological and cultural inferiority, as envisioned by these scholars, justifiably destined non-Europeans to a second-rate status. Boas was to challenge and vanquish these ideas in anthropology.

Running counter to the Eurocentric and racist ideas prominent in the anthropology of the day, Boas's ideas were rooted firmly in a conviction that all human societies had equal intelligence, creativity, talent, and potential. He conducted a wide range of studies, many of which today would be

[9]**Joseph Gobineau:** ZHOH sehf GOH bih noh

considered part of sociology or even clinical psychology, examining the intelligence of children and adults from different races. His results indicated that race was unrelated to intelligence, morality, or any other such trait. He supported this conclusion further with his field studies of other societies, concluding that they included geniuses and artists in proportions comparable to those in Western society.

But Boas went further. Not only is race unrelated to human creativity and potential, he argued, but different societies and cultures also should be viewed as equally advanced. This was a logical consequence of his first conclusion, because people of equal potential should be expected to create cultures of equal sophistication, but it challenged the long-held European assumption that Western civilization was somehow better than all other ways of life.

Boas's argument for the equality of cultures was based on three supports. First, he contended, anthropologists came from Western society and had so thoroughly accepted its cultural values that they could not easily recognize its biases. Moral judgments of other societies' behavior based on Judeo-Christian precepts were, according to Boas, one of the major factors underlying these biases. For example, Western scholars found it hard to accept that the Aztecs, who practiced human sacrifice, could have produced art as great as any in Europe. Second, he argued, societies select different emphases for their greatest efforts. The Australian Aborigines, for example, have very complex and sophisticated mythological cycles and kinship systems, while they have relatively simple technology; Germans, in contrast, have relatively simple mythological and kinship systems but complex and sophisticated technology. The high value placed by Western society on technology and military-political power assured that most other societies, judged on those criteria alone, would be deemed primitive. Third, Boas indicted anthropologists for inflexibility and arrogance in assuming that their own culture was superior to all others. These ideas encompass Boas's concept of **cultural relativism**, the notion that all cultures should be viewed as equal in sophistication and value. In the year of Boas's birth, anthropology was the staunchest scholarly advocate of inequality, both of individuals and of societies; by his death more than eighty years later, it had become the strongest proponent of equality and relativism. Anthropology's embracing of these concepts has provided intellectual justification for egalitarian policies, and the publication of popular books by such anthropologists as Ruth Benedict and Margaret Mead has brought the concepts into public consciousness.

FIGURE 35.8 *Franz Boas in the Field.* *An anthropologist, Boas spent years with the Kwakiutl tribe of western Canada. Posed like a tribesman, he wears a bark-fiber blanket made by women of that tribe. Boas's experiences in the field led him to recognize the inherent equality of all peoples and to reject the predominant racist ideas held by the academia of his time.*
National Anthropological Archives, Smithsonian Institution.

Sigmund Freud

In 1881, a woman known to history only as "Anna O." invented what today is known as psychoanalysis. She was troubled by irrational fears of various everyday things, and she consulted Josef Breuer, a prominent Vienna physician. Anna O. was graced with a forceful personality, and she insisted that Breuer listen to her recount in detail events and imaginings she had experienced since her previous visit. She called this technique "the talking cure" or "chimney sweeping," and she derived great relief through it. While Breuer was unimpressed by this case and found it merely odd, he mentioned it to a colleague who found it fascinating and exciting: Sigmund Freud.[10]

Sigmund Freud (1856–1939) was an Austrian physician who specialized in mental problems, and he believed that Anna O. had discovered a method of exploring the individual's mind. He began using her method, modifying it through the use of hypnosis or other techniques. He came to believe that patients' experiences had some strong bearing on their current mental difficulties; discovering those past events seemed to relieve the problems, yet those very events were the ones patients were most reluctant to discuss. Gradually, he developed a series of methods and concepts that formed the basis for modern psychology. While many of Freud's findings are no longer accepted, five of his basic conclusions endure as fundamental assumptions of psychology.

1. *There are hidden forces in the mind.* Previous to this, physicians had no clear explanation for phobias, manias, and other mental aberrations. Some considered them physical problems and prescribed sessions with electric machines designed to "restore mental vitality"; these machines later became a symbol of quackery in medicine. Others considered mental problems a sign of personal weakness or perversity, a behavior that could be overcome simply by the force of the patient's will. Still others were mystified by the whole phenomenon. Freud recognized that these problems were real to the patient and that they were beyond the patient's conscious control.

2. *Mental problems develop from outmoded adaptations to stress.* As Freud saw it, the mind develops ways of coping with unpleasant circumstances, and these become habitual. For example, a child who is subjected to stress will develop coping mechanisms that may be carried forward into adulthood. Once valuable, they become maladaptive for the adult and are the source of mental problems. A child, for example, might be extremely submissive to a demanding parent in an attempt

[10] **Freud:** FROYD

FIGURE 35.9 *Sigmund Freud. Freud founded the discipline of psychoanalysis in the nineteenth century and lived long enough to see it become a respected and influential field in the twentieth century. He believed that his ideas could be used to better understand historic figures and other cultures as well as contemporary patients.* Mary Evans Picture Library/Sigmund Freud Copyrights.

to gain the love the child craves; as an adult, that same person might continue submissive behavior that becomes a serious obstacle to the establishment of conventional adult relationships.

3. *The primary factor underlying mental problems is sex.* Freud saw the need for sexual gratification as the strongest instinctual urge in human

beings, and he believed that it developed very early. A child, as he saw it, inevitably formed a sexual attraction to the parent of the opposite sex, yet society's disapproval produced a sense of shame. This conflict could be coped with in various ways by the child, many of which would create deep psychological problems in later life. Many modern psychologists believe that Freud overestimated the importance of childhood sexual desires; nonetheless, this aspect of his theory has been very influential.

4. *The forces in the mind can work against one another.* The fact that patients were reluctant to discuss the things that Freud felt were most important led him to postulate that there were conceptual divisions of the mind and that they could work at counter-purposes. Eventually he elaborated this notion into three main divisions of the mind, but his great contribution was the general notion of contradictory elements within the mind.

5. *A person is likely to use a preestablished pattern to meet new circumstances.* Freud believed that people meet new challenges with old responses, ones that have proven themselves effective before. A child, for example, establishes a way of relating to its parents; as an adult, that child may continue that same way of relating to other authority figures, such as a boss, a political leader, or even a religion. Freud called this **projection** and viewed it as a complicating factor that made it difficult to trace the path from an original cause to a current problem.

Freud's historical importance lies less in the details of his specific theories than in his basic conceptions. He devised a way to look at individual human behavior that recognized the individual's past yet saw patterns of general behavior. He invented the scientific study of the human mind and provided tools for investigating it. His influence in psychology obviously was enormous, but his work also was incorporated into the studies of scholars in other fields. Anthropologists like Margaret Mead searched for evidence of Freudian processes among the Samoans and others; art historians like Arnold Hauser sought European Romanticism's Freudian roots; Freud himself devoted his last book to a Freudian analysis of Moses and the analysis's implications for theology. And finally, Freud's influence made its way to the lay public, largely through the writing of others who popularized his ideas. The fact that terms like "mania," "neurotic," and "ego" are so widely known throughout the world is a tribute to the legacy of Freud and Anna O., the woman who devised the psychoanalytic method to heal herself.

THE COMMON THREAD

The mid- and late nineteenth century was a period of incredible intellectual activity in Europe and America, and the few scholars mentioned in this chapter were chosen from the many who could have been discussed. Indeed, during this period scientists developed the ideas underlying the modern understanding of such diverse issues as thermodynamics, electromagnetism, and probability; scientific engineering, statistics, and nutrition also came into being as modern fields of endeavor.

Above all else, the scholars who transformed our understanding of these various fields reflected **scientism**, the faith that the world was predictable, that it operated according to rules and principles that could be discovered. Whether considering natural or human phenomena, these thinkers argued for patterning; this patterning, they argued, reflected processes that inexorably produced predictable results. Accident, serendipity, the unknowable—these were replaced with a confident expectation that all would eventually be unraveled and understood by science. Mendeleyev summed up the scientistic position when he wrote:

> It is the function of science to discover the existence of a general reign of order in nature and to find the causes governing this order. And this refers in equal measure to the relations of man—social and political—and to the entire universe as a whole.

While not all scholars agree so confidently that human behavior can be reduced to principles in the same manner as natural phenomena, Mendeleyev's confidence certainly was shared by Marx, Freud, and many other thinkers in the nineteenth century. The optimistic expectation of science's ability to subject nature to human control through technology has extended into the twentieth century and still is shared by many today, both scientists and the public. Faith in the natural workings of the world has encouraged an increasingly secular worldview.

EUROPE

	1750
Great expansion of European universities, 1750–1850	–
	–
	– Hutton champions uniformitarianism, 1785
	–
	1800
	–
	–
	– Voyage of HMS *Beagle*, 1831
	– Marx and Engels publish *The Communist Manifesto*, 1848
	1850
	– Darwin publishes *On the Origin of Species*, 1859
	– Mendeleyev deduces periodic table, 1869–1871
	– Boas leaves physics for anthropology, 1883
	– Freud first publishes on psychoanalysis, 1893
	1900
	– Einstein's three great papers, 1905
	–
	– Scopes trial, 1925
	–
	–
	1950

From the late eighteenth century onward, Western society was becoming increasingly enamored of progress, and scholars were no exception. Marx made progress a hallmark of his theories, because he saw humanity naturally progressing toward a more just society. Even Darwin, who tried to avoid the notion of progress, was interpreted popularly as arguing for the improvement of species.

Most nineteenth-century thinkers in the Western tradition, particularly those studying social subjects, were quite Eurocentric in their theories. Freud believed that his findings about Europeans were directly applicable to other peoples, although he believed that some "primitive" societies had arrested development, making them permanently like European children. Marx was sure that the European sequence of historical development was applicable to the rest of the world, even when there were apparent difficulties in making it fit with known facts. One of the more extravagant Eurocentrists was J. A. R. Newlands, the British physicist who believed that the chemical elements were arranged in octaves; he argued that they would combine according to laws parallel to the conventions of European music, apparently unaware that other peoples had developed radically different systems of musical harmony. The one light shining against Eurocentrism in this era was Boas, who was joined by his many students and converts.

SUMMARY

1. The nineteenth century saw the revision of many fields of scholarship in light of new methods and concepts. The greatest changes in intellectual outlooks during this period originated in Europe.

2. Charles Darwin developed the theory of biological evolution that forms the basis of the current understanding of evolution. It was based on the concepts of natural selection and the inheritance of traits from parents. The phenomenon of mutation and its importance to evolution was realized only after Darwin's death. Darwin's work inspired scholars and others to regard human beings as less separate from other animals than they had previously.

3. Karl Marx, in his writings on communism, argued that class conflict based on economic factors was the basis for political and social change. He further argued that capitalism would be overthrown by a proletarian revolution and that international communism would be established. Marx's ideas were in reaction to the unbridled capitalism of his time and the simultaneous recognition in Europe that traditional elites could be toppled by popular revolution. His ideas, though extensively modified, have remained important in many places around the world through the late twentieth century.

4. James Hutton and Charles Lyell reacted against catastrophism (the notion that massive upheavals dominated the formation of the landscape) and argued for the new paradigm of uniformitarianism (the idea that the landscape had been formed predominantly by more gradual processes similar to those at work in modern times). Their successful advocacy of uniformitarianism meant that the earth was now seen as very ancient, providing the time required for the evolutionary processes Darwin envisioned.

5. Dmitri Mendeleyev recognized the patterns inherent in the chemical elements and produced a periodic table that predicted the existence and characteristics of dozens of previously unknown elements. Subsequent research located these elements and showed his periodic table to be accurate.

6. Franz Boas argued for the equality of individuals of different races in terms of intelligence, morality, and human potential. He also contended that different cultures and societies were equally sophisticated and valuable, and condemned ethnocentric arguments to the contrary. This turned anthropology from a judgmental discipline to a champion of cultural relativism.

7. Sigmund Freud founded the fields of psychology and psychoanalysis, arguing that hidden forces in the human mind can create mental problems when outmoded patterns of behavior are continued and that many problems are caused by the conflicts surrounding sexual desires and behavior.

8. These and other scientists embraced scientism, the general philosophy that the natural and human worlds are predictable and understandable and that they follow basic principles. They sought secular laws of nature through scientific observation and experimentation.

SUGGESTED READINGS

Gillespie, David. *Genesis and Geology*. New York: Harper & Row, 1965. An excellent treatment of Hutton, Lyell, and Darwin.

Kardiner, Abram, and Edward Preble. *They Studied Man*. New York: World Publishing Co., 1961. A collection of relatively brief critical biographies of major figures in the social sciences, including Charles Darwin, Franz Boas, and Sigmund Freud. Kardiner worked with Freud, and the section on him is both extensive and authoritative.

McLellan, David. *Karl Marx*. New York: Penguin, 1982. A brief, lucid, informative summary of Marx's life, writings, and thought, as well as interpretations of Marx by political figures.

Posin, Daniel Q. *Mendeleyev: The Story of a Great Scientist*. New York: Whittlesey House/McGraw-Hill, 1948. A popularized biography of Mendeleyev, valuable because so little is available in English but frustrating because of the bulk of fictionalized dialogue diluting the historical material.

London Galvanic Generator. *Science became fashionable in the late nineteenth century, and products such as this purported medical aid sold better when touted as scientific breakthroughs.* Culver Pictures.

Science and the Masses

Carlos Alvear, a vaquero *driving cattle on the remote grasslands of Argentina, huddled over a magazine. Reading by the light of a campfire, he learned of Louis Pasteur's success in vaccinating against anthrax in far-off France. It was 1883, and the magazine was a little over a year old.*

The nineteenth-century development of Western science was unique in world history. Never before had there been so wide a literate audience and such inexpensive means of disseminating information through the printed word. In addition, the Industrial Revolution was in full swing, the notion of progress was ascendant, and the public was receptive to many of the new findings of science. Science was seen as important in its own right, but it took on greater significance because of the technology that grew from it. Under these conditions, science had a profound effect on the basic patterns of Western thought, including the sorts of explanations that everyday people found satisfying. Still, the science that made its way to the public often differed in fundamental ways from the science that was debated by scholars.

SCIENCE, WESTERN THOUGHT, AND THE WORLD

Nineteenth-century science was the product of European scholarship, but it percolated throughout Western society and into societies beyond. On

879

the one hand, lay persons in Western society came to accept the assumptions and views of science as part of their worldview; on the other hand, many educated people outside the Western tradition came to accept these ideas as they were presented through European colonial institutions.

Faith in Science Comes to Permeate Western Thought

Most Europeans and North Americans of the nineteenth century were confronted with the fruits of science in their everyday lives. The steam engine and its derivatives, the railroad locomotive and the steamship, had revolutionized transportation. Medicines, some truly efficacious and others merely making astounding claims, were heralded as scientific remedies. Mineral deposits that previously had been impractical to exploit were being mined and refined by new scientific techniques. The more colorful adventures and discoveries of scientists traveling to the far corners of the earth were reported in the newspapers and magazines of the day. These conspicuous successes brought three major changes to how everyday people saw the world.

First, faith in rational explanation increased. Science was built on the premise that everything happens for a reason and that the same cause should consistently produce the same result; the fruits of science were seen as the proof that this premise was sound. Miracles, the inexplicable, and things that happen for no apparent reason are abhorrent to the scientist, and the public increasingly came to share this scientistic view. In earlier eras, it might have been acceptable simply to throw up one's hands and declare a problem insoluble or an event the will of God, but nineteenth-century people increasingly preferred to seek a scientific explanation.

This does not mean, however, that religion was on the run in the face of the troops of science. Certainly some intellectuals argued for atheism and against organized religion, but many others found ways to integrate science and religion in their personal beliefs. In any case, few common people became embroiled in these philosophical debates. Instead, many religious people simply moved slightly more toward the pole of secular rationalism, either by explaining more things by science and relegating religion to the narrower realm of the spiritual or by developing religious views compatible with the findings of science. Perhaps miracles could happen, many nineteenth-century people suggested, but they certainly were rare and seemed to have happened more in the distant past. God created the world, they felt, but it continued to operate by itself on scientific principles, a notion similar to that of the "clockmaker God" of the eighteenth-century Deists. Literal interpretations of the Bible often were in conflict with the findings of science, and everyday people more and more came to accept the scientific explanations, considering the biblical accounts metaphorical or figurative.

Second, the position of humanity became less central. Over the centuries, the European notion of the human place in the universe consistently had been eroded by science. The earth once had been thought of as the center of the universe, around which everything else revolved; in the sixteenth century, Copernicus had proved the earth merely a planet orbiting around a star. Human beings once had been the focal point of all creation; in the nineteenth century, Darwin had made them one of many creatures that had evolved from humble beginnings, the product of luck as much as any divine plan. While still extraordinary in their cultural capabilities, human beings were being forced into a less prominent position in the worldview. This line of thinking would culminate in the twentieth century with ecological activists arguing that human beings are merely one of many species and must modify their behavior to accommodate all the others.

Third, science became the new authority, the yardstick by which things were measured. The great scientific and technological successes of the Industrial Revolution could not be denied, and it is little wonder, then, that other, less lofty accomplishments tried to bask in the light of science. Lash's Blood Purifier and Laxative, an American patent medicine of the 1870s, presumably was more effective because it was "scientifically compounded." The first Jewish cookbook published in the English language was published in London in 1846, and it described itself as a treatise on "Culinary Science." Karl Marx distinguished his ideas from their predecessors by labeling them "scientific socialism." Mary Baker Eddy founded the Christian Science Church in Boston in 1879, fusing health science and religious ideas. Even French cloth was marketed as being manufactured "according to the most scientific standards."

In one sense, this worship of science was merely the invoking of a trendy word in support of one's commercial product. But there also was a deeper reverence for science, probably an outgrowth of the ideal of progress that permeated the Industrial Revolution. Many folk beliefs were decried as mere superstition, and ruralites who believed in the evil eye were held up as examples of ignorance and backwardness by writers and others. Those who persisted in these nonscientific beliefs often kept that information to themselves for fear of being ridiculed.

Sophisticated urbanites also were subject to attack, as in the case of Sir Arthur Conan Doyle. The author of the Sherlock Holmes mysteries and

FIGURE I.7.1 *Sir Arthur Conan Doyle. The author of the Sherlock Holmes mysteries was a trained physician who was also intrigued by the occult and held seances in his London lodgings. This caricature in* Punch *lampoons Conan Doyle's beliefs, bearing a rhymed caption: "Your own creation, that great sleuth / Who spent his life in chasing Truth— / How does he view your late defiance / (O ARTHUR!) of the laws of Science?"* Mary Evans Picture Library.

a physician by training, Conan Doyle was intrigued by the occult and held seances at his London home. His beliefs earned him public attacks by prominent scientists of the day, especially Sir Arthur Keith, who published a series of scathing letters to the editors of London newspapers, leaving Conan Doyle humiliated and bitter. Others used science as a weapon with which to attack religion, as when Karl Marx and his followers described religion as "the opiate of the masses," a spurious doctrine serving to provide false hopes to the workers and peasants, making them more docile and easier to control by the state.

In nineteenth-century Europe and North America, science assumed a dominating position in society, not just for the intellectual elite but also for everyday people. The products of technology that proliferated with science during the Industrial Revolution had profound effects on everyday life, but they also served to validate the position of science as the final authority. While these objects certainly changed people's lives, it may be that the faith in science that accompanied them had even more profound effects.

Faith in Science Spreads around the Globe

The popularization of science described in the previous paragraphs was restricted largely to Western society, where the Industrial Revolution had carried the banner of science and where literacy and publishing helped spread scientific ideas. The rest of the world, however, soon was to be swept along as Western society exported its ideas abroad.

The nineteenth century was the era of European expansion, and European agents were scurrying over the globe. Governors and their agents were administering colonial governments, seeing that children were educated, because this was the first step to what they considered civilizing them. That education attempted to inculcate Western values and ideals, including science, rejecting native ideas as "primitive superstition." Missionaries, too, traveled to the colonies, attempting to convert the local people to Christianity, and that meant convincing them of the "correctness" of Western thinking, including the expunging of native magic and superstition.

Often, however, non-Western people actively sought this new scientific knowledge. Many coun-

FIGURE I.7.2 *Guyanan Missionary School.* *This school in Guyana (in northeastern South America) was run by the London Missionary Society and was designed to inculcate British values and a British-style education. On the chalkboards are maps of India and Australia—parts of the British Empire.* Archives of the Council for the World Mission, London.

tries, especially in Asia, began sending students to Western universities to receive their higher educations, and these students spread the Western findings of and attitudes toward science in their homelands. Western education and acceptance of its worldview often were viewed as signs of sophistication and actively were sought by the native elite. Some Chinese intellectuals, for example, became part of the New Culture Movement, which began in 1915. These intellectuals saw science as a hallmark of Western worldview (and therefore modernity) and welcomed it. While their viewpoint was not universal around the world, it was one reaction to Western science.

Western society had embraced science wholeheartedly, and peoples abroad came to embrace it, too, either through force or through choice. Typically, rural people were more resistant to accepting scientific thinking, often clinging tenaciously and clandestinely to their traditional beliefs. People in cities and towns, especially the elite, usually received more rigorous Western education and often became strong advocates of science and scientific thinking. To a greater or lesser extent, Western science and the faith in it spread throughout the world.

POPULAR SCIENCE

In the early part of the nineteenth century, many scientific discoveries were relatively basic, and they usually could be comprehended moderately easily by the public. As scientific knowledge accumulated and scientific theories became more complex, however, the significance of a discovery often was more difficult to appreciate. By the latter half of the nineteenth century, there were great differences between science as it was understood by scientists and science as it was understood by the masses.

Science Sells Newspapers

Newspapers and magazines were the primary means by which most people in Europe, North America, and beyond learned about new discoveries of science. Most of these publications originated in the late eighteenth or early nineteenth century as literary journals of sorts, dominated by high-toned letters on philosophy, the arts, and politics. Gradually they came to include more notices of current events and assumed a form similar to that of modern newspapers. By the mid–nineteenth century, most major cities and many smaller communities had several newspapers, all competing for readership. In order to attract that readership, newspapers emphasized topics they believed would interest their readers. The intellectual pieces often were jettisoned and replaced with sensational ones, often reporting new scientific discoveries.

But not all discoveries were equally interesting to readers, so they were not equally newsworthy. Mendeleyev's creation of the periodic table, discussed in Chapter 35, was a major advance for science and was lauded by scientists around the world, yet it never received even a mention in most newspapers. The complexities of the creation of the periodic table and the somewhat arcane nature of its significance would have made it difficult for readers to follow even a simple discussion, and they most probably would have skipped the article. Instead, the discovery of a tribe of purported cannibals or of a new planet caught the editorial eye and became known to the general public. There were three main criteria for whether a scientific subject was newsworthy.

First, the subject had to be romantic and exciting. Among the most romantic and exciting were archaeological finds of lost cities and ancient knowledge, such as Hiram Bingham's 1911 discovery of Machu Picchu in the Peruvian jungles, widely reported in the contemporary press as "the lost city of the Incas." The prediction and subsequent discovery of a new planet, Neptune, in 1846 also was a great sensation, as was the competition in 1858 among Sir Richard Burton, John Speke, and others to find the source of the Nile in East Africa. Louis Pasteur's development in 1881 of inoculation as a means of preventing anthrax was followed closely by newspapers because of its practical significance, and Pasteur was portrayed as a scientific warrior fighting disease.

Second, the scientists had to have dramatic personalities. Science was seen as a heroic enterprise, and popular sentiment demanded that it be pursued by heroic figures. Few scientists met this requirement, though those who did were lionized. Burton, for example, was a colorful scholar who spoke dozens of languages well enough to pass for a native, and he did so in order to gain access to Mecca, the holy city of Islam otherwise closed to non-Muslims; the scar from a Maasai spear that passed through his cheek only added to his reputation as an adventurer.

When scientists failed to project sufficiently robust personalities, circumstances might come to their aid. The discovery of the Egyptian tomb of Tutankhamen in 1922 was popular on the basis of the incredibly rare and valuable artifacts found

FIGURE I.7.3 *"Lord Carnarvon's Fate."* *The death of Lord Carnarvon, a member of the team that discovered the tomb and mummy of "King Tut," made front-page headlines in 1923. The drama of his death and the deaths of several co-researchers led newspapers to focus on rumors of an ancient curse rather than on the archaeological significance of their find.* Courtesy of John and Andrew Frost.

intact there, but its popular acclaim skyrocketed when various members of the expedition began dying, leading to the assertion—first put forward by the press—that a curse would kill all the members of the excavation party. (The press did not stress the facts that only a small proportion of the party died shortly after the opening of the tomb or that most of the members who died were elderly.) The incredibly well-publicized search of Henry Stanley, a reporter for the *New York Herald*, for Dr. David Livingstone in Africa in 1871 is an even more telling example. Although the *Herald* painted the picture of Livingstone as an explorer lost in the jungles of deepest Africa, he actually was resting along the shores of Lake Tanganyika following a bout of fever and was not lost at all; the "rescue mission" was prompted purely by the urge to improve newspaper circulation.

Third, and perhaps most important, a scientific discovery must be simple enough for people with limited scientific education to understand it. A more difficult discovery might be acceptable if it could be simplified by the reporter, sometimes at the expense of accuracy. Albert Einstein's theory of relativity in physics, published in 1905, was widely heralded in the press, but reporters were faced with the difficulty that most of their readers were unable to understand the theory; probably most of the reporters also failed to grasp its complexity. As a result, press coverage often praised the discovery, described it in a sentence or two with no real discussion of why Einstein believed it to be true, then proceeded to discuss the implications of "relativity" as a social concept, something Einstein never had intended.

In a real sense, the press has determined the popular reputations of scientists since the mid–nineteenth century. Those whose research or personalities led to good entertainment were the subject of extended reportage. Those whose research actually was more significant but less entertaining had to be content with the recognition of their peers.

Electrical Rejuvenation and Shocked Wheat

Many journalists of the nineteenth and early twentieth centuries saw their job as selling newspapers, not necessarily educating the public. If exotic science would sell newspapers, then maybe even greater sales could be achieved by stepping

FIGURE I.7.4 **Armageddon.** *Atlantis may have been the ancient Mediterranean island of Thera, or it may have been a literary invention of Plato and other ancient Greeks. In either case, it caught the imagination of nineteenth- and twentieth-century writers such as Ignatius Donnelly. They envisioned Atlantis as a massive and sophisticated island-state somewhere in the Atlantic, where people held lost secrets and were wiser, stronger, and better looking than anywhere else. This vision of Atlantis emphasized its demise in an apocalyptic upheaval, borrowed in part from the biblical prediction of the end of the world as depicted here. Such romantic conceptions of Atlantis have been far more popular than the more realistic (and less exotic) interpretations of scholars.* Culver Pictures.

beyond the bounds of mainstream science and publicizing ideas on the fringes of science.

The past two centuries have produced hundreds of bizarre ideas claimed by their originators as scientific breakthroughs, though rejected by the scientific community. The originators often have derided the professional scientists as too jealous to admit the worth of these new ideas, but the professionals usually have considered them simply too outlandish to merit comment. Some of the supporters of these odd ideas have been simply naïve, too poorly educated in science to recognize the weaknesses of their ideas; others have been professional con artists out to make a great deal of money; and still others have been psychologically unstable. But their ideas sometimes have appeared in seemingly reputable outlets, and they have seemed to some members of the public to be of equal stature with the findings of mainstream science.

In the 1920s in the United States, for example, the nationally distributed *American Weekly* had a column devoted to lurid pseudoscience, including arguments that the earth was flat and that electrical current fed into the body with a complicated device could prevent a person from aging. Other newspapers also publicized such exotic but peculiar findings by self-styled scientists, including a way to produce hardy wheat by "shocking" the wheat seeds with cold, the production of microscopic fish by the melting of metals, and a new theory of physics based on the mutual suction of all tangible things.

Many of these pseudoscientific ideas sound like the stuff of science fiction: the creation of life, the existence of various monsters, visits from outer space, chemicals from comets passing near the earth that affected human personalities, and the like. But they often were presented plausibly and with evidence that—if legitimate—would be persuasive. The reader with limited background in science and with a great urge to believe was likely to be taken in by at least some of these preposterous ideas. The incredible success of tabloid newspapers in the twentieth century is potent evidence that many readers are more interested in an exotic account than in scientific accuracy.

SUGGESTED READINGS

Cooter, Roger. *The Cultural Meaning of Popular Science: Phrenology and the Organization of Consent in Nineteenth-Century Britain.* Cambridge, Eng.: Cambridge University Press, 1984. A discussion of popular science, oriented around phrenology, the pseudoscientific practice of appraising personal characteristics from bumps on the head.

Daniels, George H. *Science in American Society: A Social History.* New York: Knopf, 1971. An excellent treatment of the place of science in American popular and intellectual culture.

Gardiner, Martin. *Fads and Fallacies in the Name of Science.* New York: Dover, 1952. A classic anthology of brief articles on some of the more exotic crank scientific theories. Entertaining, easy reading.

Holton, Gerald, and William A. Blanpied, eds. *Science and Its Public: The Changing Relationship.* Boston Studies in the Philosophy of Science, vol. 33. Dordecht, Holland: D. Reidel Publishing Co., 1976. Largely devoted to contemporary conditions but includes some historical material.

Nelkin, Dorothy. *Selling Science: How the Press Covers Science and Technology.* New York: W. H. Freeman, 1987. Primarily concerned with the modern situation, but contains some useful historical perspective.

I N THE FIRST HALF OF THE TWENTIETH CENTURY, there was a close interrelationship between war and revolution. World War I helped bring about the collapse of the Russian Empire and the onset of the Bolshevik Revolution. Once in power, the Bolsheviks fought a civil war and later endured World War II. The Chinese Communist Party benefited from the chaos launched by World War II. Later, it won a civil war against the Nationalist Party.

The Great Depression devastated the economies of most industrialized countries. It also helped pave the way for the German National Socialist Party (Nazis) to gain power. The success of the German and Italian national socialists encouraged other leaders to develop similar movements. Global wars, revolutions, and the Great Depression brought tens of millions of deaths in the first half of the twentieth century, causing many to despair of the future.

Chapter 36 explores the causes and the social and economic consequences of World War I. Chapter 37 analyzes revolutions in Russia and China, where two

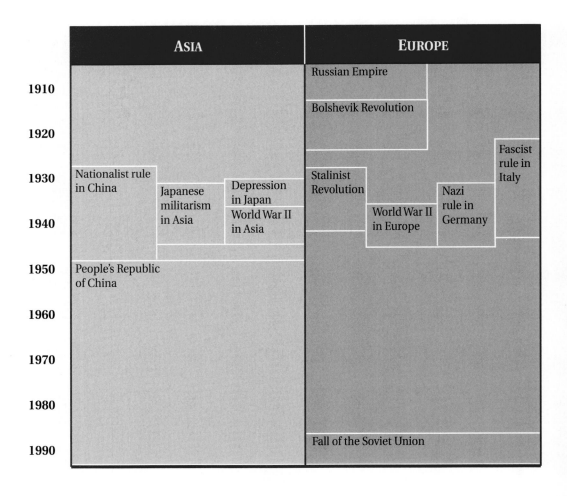

empires collapsed. Workers and peasants benefited from revolutionary governments, although many died in the collectivizations of agriculture. Chapter 38 discusses the Great Depression and the growing power of the nation-state. In many countries, periods of depression ended as states began preparing for war. Chapter 39 looks at the rise of national socialist parties. Mussolini and Hitler led the two most successful national socialist parties that set up totalitarian states. Chapter 40 examines World War II, the most destructive war in history. Coupled with the war was Hitler's determination to exterminate Europe's Jews and many other minority groups. Issue 8 examines new modes of transportation and communication that unite the world.

PART EIGHT

GLOBAL WAR AND REVOLUTION

AMERICAS	AFRICA	
World War I for United States ▼		1910
World War I for Canada	World War I in Africa	
		1920
		1930
Presidency of Franklin D. Roosevelt	Depression in the United States	Depression in Canada
	World War II in Africa	1940
▲ World War II for United States	▲ World War II for Canada	1950
		1960
		1970
		1980
		1990

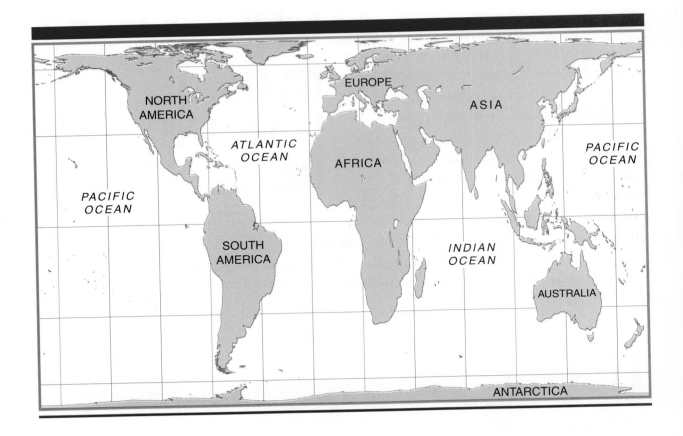

World War I and the Versailles Peace
1914–1919

In August 1914, the rectors of southern German universities issued a joint appeal about the unfolding war:

> Students! The muses are silent. The issue is battle, the battle forced upon us for German culture, which is threatened by the barbarians from the East, and for German values, which the enemy in the West envies us. And so the *furor teutonicus* [German fury] bursts into flame once again. The enthusiasm of the wars of liberation flares, and the holy war begins.

This nationalistic manifesto of 1914—tinged with racial and cultural innuendo against the Russians to the east—excited many collegians, who enlisted in the German army. The young men formed two army corps and went to the western front to fight British combat veterans in October. A ferocious battle in Belgium killed 36,000 young Germans, who were buried in a common grave in the Langemarck cemetery. This slaughter was but one among many over the next four years.

World War I (1914–1918) saw the service of 65 million soldiers from thirty-five nations around the globe. The British Empire alone raised 8.5 million combatants. Although the number of war deaths may never be accurately tabulated, most agree that perhaps 30 million people perished, about half of whom died from war-related diseases. At the same time, the German, the Austro-Hungarian, the Russian, and the Ottoman empires collapsed, and the map of Europe was redrawn by the victors at the Paris Peace Conference in 1919. Furthermore, the United States and Japan suffered little damage and earned great profits from supplying the Europeans with munitions and other materials. Because of their significant economic power, Japan and the United States emerged from the war as major players in international politics.

divide the world into empires and protectorate zones. Clashing national interests ultimately exploded in Europe in 1914, and existing alliance systems helped turn a European war into a global conflict. Japan, for example, used its alliance with the British, French, and Russians to expand into China and the Pacific Ocean region.

CAUSES AND CONTEXTS OF WORLD WAR I

Many factors played roles in the buildup to World War I. Nationalism and imperialism, for example, had promoted a brutal global competition among European states, the United States, and Japan to

Nationalism and Imperialism

Nationalist rivalries created great tensions among the imperialist states in the decades leading up to 1914 and helped precipitate World War I. The industrializing nation-states competed vigorously to impose their wills on less powerful states. Imperialist activities in Asia and Africa helped submerge

FIGURE 36.1 *Imperialist Rivalries in Africa.* *By 1905, European rivalries in Africa had begun to emerge as Germany competed with France and Britain, especially in North Africa. In this 1905 photo, Kaiser Wilhelm II leads German troops through Tangiers in a show of force. In the following year, an international conference challenged Germany's claims to Morocco. Germany's imperialist threats prompted Great Britain to ally more closely with Russia and France, laying the foundation for the Triple Entente.* L'Illustration/Sygma.

many tensions in Europe proper, and once the African and Asian states succumbed to outside domination, latent imperial rivalries erupted.

Germany felt impoverished by its lack of exploitable lands and peoples. National pride for the Germans meant competing with the British, who dominated the high seas and who had built a formidable empire that encircled the globe. One counterpressure to the increasing hostility toward Britain came from a loose coalition of German bankers, merchants, and shippers who understood that the loss of the British market for their goods and services could prove to be financially disastrous. At the same time, internal politics intensified because of the demands for greater power sharing by underrepresented groups. Many of the German elite felt that a brief and successful war might silence the internal conflict between the haves and the have-nots. Thus, the rising tide of nationalism and the monarch's determination to achieve a military settlement silenced the voices of those who wished to resolve the conflict by peaceful means.

Some German leaders favored a foreign policy that emphasized **pan-Germanism**, or unity among German-speaking peoples of all nations. Nationalist and racist ideas encouraged the interpretation of global competition in terms of racial rivalries. Not only did the Germans have to keep the Asians and Africans in their subordinate places, they also had to subdue rival Slavic groups like the Serbs and the Russians.

French nationalists sought revenge for the loss of Alsace and Lorraine to the Germans during the Franco-Prussian War (1870–1871). Alsace and Lorraine had caused trouble between the French and the Germans since the ninth century. Although France vigorously competed with Britain around the globe, fear of German power tempered French antipathy toward Britain. France did ally with Germany and Russia in the scramble for territory and influence in Asia, but the clash of French interests with those of the Germans in North Africa forged a closer relationship between France and Britain.

Britain had rarely involved itself in continental politics in the late nineteenth century, but growing German power and competition for control of the high seas compelled the British to rethink their diplomatic isolation. By 1902, they agreed to an Anglo-Japanese alliance that permitted a restationing of British naval forces in Asian waters. Britain signed an alliance with the French in 1904

and reached an understanding with the Russians in 1907.

The Russians and Austro-Hungarians feared the rising tide of nationalism in their domains. While the Russians promoted pan-Slavic policies and support for the Serbs, the German-speaking Austrians welcomed the pan-German assertions and the promises of support from Germany.

The Balkan Peninsula seethed with national tensions and plots. Serbia had gained independence from the Ottoman Empire in the late nineteenth century, but Serbs in other regions still lay under the Austro-Hungarian yoke. Other national rivalries exploded in the Balkan wars of 1912 and 1913. The settlements following these wars satisfied only a few states; the rest schemed for revenge and national aggrandizement. These tensions exploded in 1914.

The Alliance System

The global nature of World War I came partly from the alliances formed in preceding decades. Germany, France, Russia, Britain, Japan, the Ottoman Empire, Austria-Hungary, and other states formed alliance blocs that entangled the world.

The Franco-Prussian War created the German Empire in 1871 and brought German leaders new fears. Chancellor Otto von Bismarck formed his diplomatic policy around the need to isolate a vengeful France and the desire to keep close ties with tsarist Russia. Thus, Bismarck signed a treaty of alliance with the Austro-Hungarians in 1879 and another with the Italians in 1882, creating the Triple Alliance (Germany, Austria-Hungary, Italy). At the same time, he worked out a diplomatic agreement with the Russians. Things proceeded relatively smoothly until 1890, when the new German kaiser (emperor), Wilhelm II, dismissed Bismarck. The headstrong monarch had desired to conduct his own foreign policy, and his personal direction soon permitted the Russians to drift away. The kaiser never suspected that the democratic French and autocratic Russians could overcome their political differences and ally with each other.

The Triple Entente (France, Russia, Britain), allying the three major European powers, emerged from each nation's strategic insecurity and their wish to offset Germany's increasing military might. France and Russia lay on Germany's western and

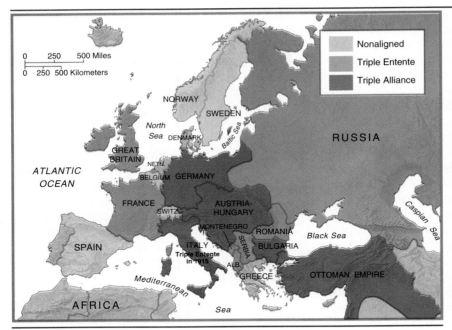

MAP 36.1 *European Alliances in 1914.* *The major European powers were knitted together in two separate alliance systems. Great Britain, France, and Russia formed the Triple Entente, members of which agreed to support each other in the event of war with other powers. Germany, Austria-Hungary, and Italy formed the Triple Alliance, although Italy refused to go to war in 1914 and switched to the other side in 1915. Other countries joined one side or the other, ensuring that the European theater would engage millions of soldiers in 1914.*

eastern borders, and, in 1890, neither had an alliance. Beginning in 1891 and concluding in 1894, France and Russia forged an alliance, despite their political differences. A significant factor in the alliance was the lure of French financing for Russia. The British and French also worked out an alliance in the early years of the twentieth century, settling their many differences. In addition, the British worked out an agreement with the Russians in 1907; the two sides resolved their imperialistic differences and agreed to cooperate against aggressive third parties.

As the Germans faced encirclement by hostile states, they drew closer to the Austro-Hungarians. After 1894, the Franco-Russian alliance threatened a two-front war, which was exactly what the German General Staff feared. To counter such an eventuality, German military planners came up with a plan to first defeat the French (as in 1870) and then turn against the Russians, who they assumed would take much longer than the French to mobilize. Timing became a critical issue for Germany's planners, who increasingly feared the Russian buildup of railroad lines and military supplies, allowing for more rapid mobilization.

Japan developed a system of alliances with various European states in the years leading up to World War I. In 1895, Japan had faced a coalition of France, Germany, and Russia that had forced the

surrender of some Japanese war gains. Thereafter, Japanese leaders endeavored to gain allies and win military and diplomatic backing for Japan's foreign policy initiatives. Japan and Britain signed an agreement in 1902 that promised mutual support in a major war, and the Russians and French later negotiated separate agreements with the Japanese. German-controlled territories in China and the Pacific tempted the Japanese, who saw them as ripe for picking in a war.

Armament Buildups in Europe and Asia

One element resulting from the Napoleonic wars, the modern military state, contributed both to the arms race before World War I and to the heavy casualties in it. Although the arms race included the massive buildup of land-based weapons and railroad networks to get them to battlefield staging areas, a striking example of armament competition came in the British and German naval race from 1900 to 1914. In the late 1890s, the German naval command decided to challenge Britain's maritime domination. This effort entailed the rapid building of a modern armada. The plan failed because Britain kept a close eye on naval competitors, and when the Germans had constructed the third-largest navy in the world the

British Admiralty accelerated its own ship-building schedule. British strategists embarked on a policy of forging alliances and drawing elements of their global navy home to the North Sea.

WORLD WAR I'S OUTBREAK AND COURSE, 1914–1918

Many European leaders expected the war to be brief, as the Franco-Prussian War (1870–1871) had been. Unfortunately for the millions of European combatants, World War I was more akin to the United States Civil War (1861–1865). Both wars were anticipated by the participants to be short-lived, both quickly reached stalemates, and both accelerated into wars of material and human attrition. Once the forward momentum of the German armies halted, weapons like the machine gun turned combat into a war of attrition that cost millions of lives.

The War's Outbreak

In June 1914, the heir to the Austro-Hungarian throne, Archduke Francis Ferdinand, fell to a Serbian assassin's bullets; this cause of World War I was linked directly to nationalism. Gavrilo Princep, the assassin, belonged to a Serbian secret society

UNDER THE LENS
World War I and Disease

World War I stands in a pivotal position in the history of disease. Inoculation had been invented some decades before, and its benefits were beginning to be recognized in industrialized countries. Further, effective medicines to halt the advance or spread of disease had been developed and distributed. Finally, the significance of germs and sterilization had become well known in Western medicine, and sickroom infection was becoming far less common. As a result of all these factors, the era of epidemics (the temporary, extensive spread of a disease) and pandemics (the prevalence of a disease in most members of a population) seemed to be coming to an end.

Ironically, the years between 1917 and 1921 saw dozens of the most devastating worldwide epidemics and pandemics, many of which claimed huge losses of life. The most devastating of these was the Spanish influenza pandemic that began in the spring of 1918. At first, its death rate was low, and it attracted little attention. By August, however, the disease had spread around the globe, and its virulence had increased. Death rates doubled and tripled in the United States, and in places like Samoa, where natural resistance was low, as many as one out of every five infected died. In the war zones of Europe and Southwest Asia, infection and death rates were high, and huge numbers of soldiers were sheltered in makeshift hospital tents. Worldwide, several million people died in a matter of two or three months. One respected historian of disease has called this pandemic probably the greatest demographic shock ever to have been suffered by the world's population.

Why was the influenza so devastating? Probably it was caused by a combination of two agents, one bacterial and one viral, that acted to produce illness far more extreme than either could alone. The tens of millions of persons who moved long distances to perform wartime service before returning home would have served as excellent carriers for these agents, and the chance encounter of the two agents would have been all that was needed to instigate the disaster. Another element in the disease's profile was its attack on young adults, who are usually spared from high mortality rates. Significant deaths among this fertile group also affected the numbers of births later.

World War I saw unprecedented numbers of people moving great distances, thanks to the advance in transportation technology. With the moving of people came the spread of germs, and many diseases spread like wildfire. Diphtheria ravaged much of North America, Britain, France, and Germany in 1917 and 1918; it probably struck other places whose medical systems were not sophisticated enough to recognize it. Cholera afflicted millions in southern Europe, Southwest Asia, and India, spreading eventually to East Asia. Anthrax had a final resurgence in Great Britain, France, and Belgium in 1919 before immunization controlled it.

FIGURE 36.2 ***Trouble in the Balkans, June 1914.*** *A key precipitant of World War I
was the assassination of the Archduke Francis Ferdinand and his wife, Sophie. Heir to the
Austrian throne, Francis Ferdinand loomed as a target for Serbian patriots. This photo, taken
shortly after the killing, shows the arrest of the assassin. With Germany's full support, Austria-
Hungary issued an ultimatum to Serbia that eventually led to the outbreak of hostilities.*
Gernsheim Collection, Harry Ransom Humanities Center, University of Texas, Austin.

that was directed by the head of Serbia's intelligence apparatus. The murder was designed to
ignite an uproar that could lead to the liberation of
Serbs under Austro-Hungarian rule.

During the weeks that followed the assassination, the alliance systems sprang into play. Austrian leaders pondered a reply to the daring assault
and consulted with German leaders, who listened
sympathetically. As early as December 1912, the
German monarch had declared himself in favor of
immediate war. After securing German backing,
the confident Austrians delivered an ultimatum to
the Serbs, who in turn sought support from Russia,
a kindred Slavic state. The Russians supported the
Serbs, bringing their French allies with them. By
late July 1914, Austrian troops began shelling Serbian positions, instigating a Russian mobilization.
This action alarmed German leaders, who had
counted on a slow Russian mobilization. Ultima-
tums and war declarations followed along the
alliance systems in the next days, and soon most
major European states were mobilizing for war.
Most scholars agree that although all belligerents

should be held accountable for the war, Germany
bears the greatest responsibility for precipitating
World War I because German leaders had advised
the Austrians to engage in hostilities rather than
seek a diplomatic resolution of the conflict.

Some European countries remained neutral at
the beginning of the war. The Scandinavian countries of Norway, Sweden, and Denmark refused to
become involved because they were near Germany
and were unprepared for war. The Dutch stayed
neutral for the same reasons. Italian leaders
decided that, because they had not been consulted
by Germany or Austria-Hungary, they need not
honor their commitment to the Triple Alliance.
Debate within Italy's leadership continued until
May 1915, when Italy finally entered the fighting,
but against Germany and Austria-Hungary. Significant consideration was given to the fact that Italy
would not be able to win new territories in the
Balkans if they did not fight. By 1918, more than
600,000 Italians had died, and Italian industry had
produced more than 20,000 machine guns and
6,500 airplanes. Italy put more and more artillery

pieces in the field, and Italian war industries grew enormous. The Italian aircraft works alone employed 100,000 workers.

Many of Europe's able-bodied men carried identity cards that told them where to assemble, while their regimental depots had long been stocked with supplies. In July 1914, around 4 million soldiers stood ready to fight, but by September, 20 million Europeans had been called up. The Germans, who depended on mobility because their war plan demanded that they first defeat the French, called up more than 4 million soldiers and transported 1.5 million equipped troops to the western front, all in less than three weeks. The French, fearing a replay of the disaster of 1870, swiftly shifted troops to the north and northwest;

even French taxis transported soldiers. The Russians surprised everyone by quickly assembling two armies at the eastern front through a railroad system built for that purpose. Ironically, when the troops and supplies reached the designated areas, human beings and horses toted most of the war material because of a dearth of transport vehicles.

Early Stalemate and Life at the Front

Desperate fighting erupted on western and eastern battlefronts, and stalemates soon resulted. On the western front, stiff and unexpected Belgian resistance delayed the German timetable and afforded the French time to organize a defensive plan. The succeeding fight in northern France stopped the

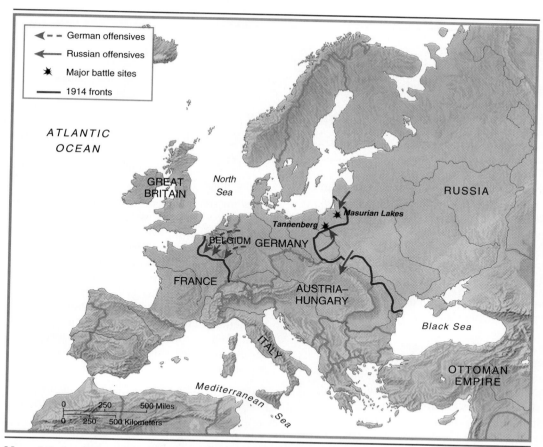

MAP 36.2 *Eastern and Western Fronts, 1914. The Germans attacked the French and British, while the Russians hammered the Germans. The fighting, which began in August 1914, quickly stalemated on both fronts, the Germans being stopped in the west and the Russians in the east. Although both fronts saw trench warfare, the eastern front saw more widespread territorial movement in succeeding years.*

German advance, and both sides barricaded themselves in a complex of trenches and bunkers that soon snaked across the war-scarred French countryside.

Stalemate on the western front evolved into a war of attrition that consumed masses of human beings and materiel. The machine gun greatly strengthened defensive lines, while the rifle afforded the infantry troops individual protection. All, however, quavered before the artillery bombardments that rained metal destruction everywhere. Whole units could be wiped out in a few hellish minutes of awesome firepower. Gas was another terrifying battlefield weapon, and among the worst of these was mustard gas. Chlorine, the principal compound in mustard gas, gave a sea-green color to the deadly mist covering the battlefields.

The slaughter continued. By September 1915, the French alone had suffered 1 million killed and wounded, and, by 1917, 1 million French had died and hundreds of thousands more were wounded. At Verdun, a heavily fortified city near the German border, the German army tried to inflict large-scale casualties upon French defenders. Earlier, German soldiers had been stopped by a spirited defense led by Henri Pétain, who declared, "They shall not pass." In 1916 and 1917, however, the French suffered more than 600,000 casualties and the Germans a similar number. Verdun's image shifted from heroic to hellish. After many of these slaughters, half of France's fighting divisions refused orders to go on the offensive, although they did agree to defend their positions. A crisis of morale threatened to engulf the combatants and bring peace through desertion rather than negotiation.

IN THEIR OWN WORDS

A British Soldier Looks at War

Life at the front frequently traumatized soldiers who faced primitive conditions with few comforts. They suffered regular artillery barrages, intermittent assaults, and gas attacks. The British war poet Wilfred Owen (1893–1918) graphically captured the terrors of war that ravaged the flower of European youth. One memorable poem by Owen, "Dulce et Decorum Est," evokes the mood of soldiers, many of whom had studied the poet Horace, to whom the Latin lines are attributed. Horace alleged that it was sweet and appropriate to fight and die for one's country.

Bent double, like old beggars under sacks,
Knock-kneed, coughing like hags, we cursed
    through sludge,
Till on the haunting flares we turned our backs,
And towards our distant rest began to trudge.
Men marched asleep. Many had lost their boots
But limped on blood-shod. All went lame; all blind;
Drunk with fatigue; deaf even to the hoots
Of disappointed shells that dropped behind.

Gas! GAS! Quick, boys!—An ecstasy of fumbling,
Fitting the clumsy helmets just in time,
But someone still was yelling out and stumbling
And flound'ring like a man in fire or lime . . .

Dim, through the misty panes and
    thick green light,
As under a green sea, I saw him
    drowning.
In all my dreams, before my helpless
    sight,
He plunges at me guttering, choking, drowning.

If in some smothering dreams, you too could pace
Behind the wagon that we flung him in,
And watch the white eyes writhing in his face,
His hanging face, like a devil's sick of sin,
If you could hear, at every jolt, the blood
Come gargling from the froth-corrupted lungs,
Obscene as cancer, bitter as the cud
Of vile, incurable sores on innocent tongues,—
My friend, you would not tell with such high zest
To children ardent for some desperate glory,
The old Lie: Dulce et decorum est
Pro patria mori.[a]

Owen earned the Military Cross for gallant action on October 4, 1918, and was killed in battle a month later, one week before the war ended.

[a] **Dulce et decorum est/Pro patria mori:** Latin for "There is no greater honor than to die for one's country."

On the eastern front, the Russians honored their commitment to the French and British by attacking East Prussia, part of Germany. Although Russian generals planned eventually to mobilize 5.3 million soldiers, military planners failed to calculate the need for massive numbers of rifles, machine guns, and artillery pieces as well as their ammunition. Consequently, poorly trained Russian soldiers invaded Germany with woefully inadequate supplies when they marched into a territory whose inhabitants systematically destroyed things that could have been used by the Russians. Commanders had few modern means of communication, relying on wireless machines over which were dispatched uncoded messages. German officers intercepted these messages and knew as much about Russian troop movements as did Russian leaders. Airplanes might have helped the Russians learn about German troop movements, but a lack of spare parts kept most of their 250 airplanes grounded. The few that flew on reconnaissance missions were mistakenly shot down by uninformed Russian soldiers who thought these flying machines must have been German. Lacking sufficient supplies and general strategic plans, the Russian armies lost nearly a quarter-million soldiers in the war's first month.

Russia's commanders achieved success against the Austrians farther south but then fell back before the Germans, who reinforced their Austrian allies. The overconfident Austrian generals had sacrificed 300,000 of their soldiers in a futile campaign against the Russians. Seeing the possibility of a Russian breakthrough into Germany, the German commander, General Paul von Hindenburg, moved an army force into the conflict and stopped the Russian advance. Heavy fighting that continued into December 1914 claimed more than 1.5 million Russian casualties and prisoners of war.

The next two years brought similar losses and a deepening crisis. Russia simply could not replace the officers killed in the early months of the war. In 1915, the Russians launched a spring offensive against the Austrians. Initially successful, it broke under a German counterattack that struck deep into Russian territory. Refugees began to flood over the land, a massive wave of humanity surviving under appalling conditions.

Soldiers on the eastern front suffered from many of the privations of their allies to the west,

FIGURE 36.3 *Trench Warfare.* *In this World War I photo, French soldiers haul the body of a dead soldier from the trenches. The morale of the stationary troops began to plummet, especially by 1916. By this time, millions of soldiers in the trenches on both fronts had endured such scenes of carnage for months, if not years.* Library of Congress.

and they often endured horrible conditions. Most lived in trenches year-round, and some had no overcoats during the war's first autumn. Others had no boots or marched with their toes sticking out of their footwear. Wounded soldiers faced operations by surgeons who often left their charges permanently crippled because of the woe-

FIGURE 36.4 *Putting One's Comrades to Rest.*
During World War I, millions died on the eastern front—
perhaps as many as 10 percent of Russia's mobilized
troops perished in battle. In this photo, a group of
Russian soldiers prepare to bury their dead. Hoover
Institution.

ful state of military medicine. Nearly one in four
who survived convalescence was mutilated for life.
One official encountered 17,000 wounded Russian
soldiers in Warsaw, lying in the cold rain and mud
without even straw matting. In the late winter of
1915, German gas attacks caught the Russians
unprepared and gasping for gas masks.

World War I's Last Years, 1917–1918

Momentous events shook politicians and soldiers
in 1917. Russia faced a systemic collapse of the
tsarist autocracy and then the seizure of power by
the Communist Party under the leadership of

Vladimir Lenin. This left an unstable situation on
the eastern front that was resolved in 1918 by the
Treaty of Brest-Litovsk, ceding major parts of the
former Russian Empire to the Germans and freeing
German soldiers for duty on the western front.

German planners saw the effectiveness of submarines in sinking British merchant ships and
weakening Britain. After earnest debates at the
highest levels, the reluctant German monarch
agreed to a policy of unrestricted submarine warfare. In February 1917, a vast increase in British
naval losses and the sinking of several United
States ships crystallized United States public opinion in favor of war. British survival was ensured by
forming convoys of merchant ships shepherded by
United States and British warships. That new effort
stymied the Germans and permitted massive
resupplying.

The major powers in the Americas entered the
war on the side of the British, French, and Italians.
This brought the western hemisphere directly into
the global conflict and provided a venue for a
demonstration of North American power, headed
by the United States. Armament factories in the
United States had supplied the Russians and
others since the outbreak of the war and now
expanded production to accommodate American
soldiers. Canadians had already fought alongside
troops from other parts of the British-led Commonwealth of Nations. More than 600,000 Canadians served in the war and 60,000 died in battle,
earning a reputation for bravery.

In 1918, the Germans made a final effort to
overwhelm the Allies on the western front and fell
back before the counterattack, suing for peace in
November. The German commanders, Hindenburg and Erich Ludendorf, gambled on a spring
offensive, before the United States could bring significant numbers across the Atlantic Ocean. German troops from the eastern front also fought on
the western front, but they could not break
through the French and British lines in a decisive
manner. Momentum turned to the Allies, who in
the summer had begun receiving large amounts of
supplies and soldiers from the United States. Hard
fighting began to wear down the Germans, whose
army barely remained intact. When the war ended,
however, Germany had been spared the devastation of other front-line countries, like France and
Italy.

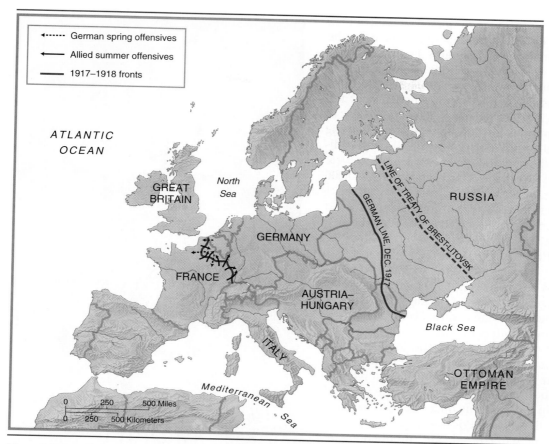

MAP 36.3 *Eastern and Western Fronts, 1917–1918.* *The eastern front began to deteriorate in 1917, when the tsarist government fell and the Bolsheviks took power with the slogan, "Peace." Fighting halted in March 1918 after the Bolsheviks ratified the Treaty of Brest-Litovsk, ending the war for Russia. The western front remained fairly static until the Germans launched a spring offensive in 1918. This campaign was halted in the summer, and the British, French, and Americans counterattacked, reaching the borders of Germany by November 1918, when an armistice was signed.*

THE HOME FRONT

As the battlefield slaughter continued, people in rear areas endured privation and suffering while contributing mightily to the war effort. Although massive amounts of supplies had been stockpiled to wage a limited war, the carnage that extended over weeks and then months compelled various countries to mobilize their human and material resources more fully. The resulting centralization efforts created governments that were taking on more control of their citizens' lives.

France

Although the outbreak of war surprised many in France and the mobilization brought a mixture of responses, patriotism blossomed in the veneration of Saint Joan of Arc, the heroine of the Hundred Years War. She became a popular symbol of French heroism in the face of defeat and suffering. Churches and schools played a growing role in rallying support for the war effort. Continued enthusiasm for the war, however, waned with defeats in 1915 and 1916. As the death toll passed

1 million persons, more despaired of the conflict. Yet most believed that the Germans must be driven from French soil, and French citizens adapted to wartime conditions over which they had little control.

The French Empire brought benefits for the French during World War I. Raw materials, of course, continued to flow to France, benefiting military and nonmilitary production alike. In addition, more than 1.9 million colonial subjects were conscripted for duty in France, and nearly 700,000 of them became combatants.

A coalition government representing most political constituencies ruled France for the first three years. In many cases, however, the military dominated the political planning. Terrible losses and worker sacrifices drove the socialists from the coalition by September 1917. Then, in November 1917, Georges Clemenceau became prime minister and restored civilian control over the army.

Economic matters overwhelmed much of the war's early decision making. The initial German onslaught captured nearly half of France's coal production and almost three-fifths of its steel capacity. To survive, French leaders were forced to intervene in the economy on a scale unseen since the French Revolution. Prices were fixed, transport systems were reorganized, and production and distribution networks were rebuilt. Shortages of labor, fertilizers, and farm machinery caused the 1917 harvest to fall 40 percent below prewar levels.

Loss of key industrial regions compelled the French government to develop a highly centralized economy. Financial investment came through loans and the printing of money, but the latter expediency fueled inflation. Although most workers supported the war, they increasingly resisted the militarylike regimentation in the factories. As living conditions deteriorated, strikes broke out around Paris. Rising prices for foodstuffs particularly incensed factory workers, who accused farmers of greediness. Workers also complained of managers' efforts to improve productivity at their expense and lengthen the work day, arguing that profits increased but not wages. Several work stoppages came in January 1917, while more erupted a few months later. Most were spontaneous, and the largest totaled around 100,000 workers.

Women formed a major component of the labor force. As men were called to the battlefields, women moved into agricultural and industrial

FIGURE 36.5 *Call to Patriotic Frenchmen.* *This poster evokes the French government's renewed commitment to the war under prime minister Georges Clemenceau. The figure of the armed French woman recalls both Joan of Arc and the female personification of Liberty leading the French people in a nineteenth-century painting by Eugène Delacroix. Prior to efforts by Clemenceau to raise his country's morale, the French had nearly dropped out of the war—especially when the death toll exceeded 1 million.* Trustees of the Imperial War Museum.

production. They soon began to dominate certain economic sectors; ordnance factories lured women from other jobs by offering higher wages. Women played a key role in the spontaneous strikes of May and June 1917 that were led by munitions and fashions-trade workers.

Human labor needs grew dramatically during the war and forced the French to recruit many foreign workers. Vietnamese from French Indochina were hired to work in France, and, by war's end, more than 100,000 had labored there. By 1918, tens of thousands of Vietnamese had served in the French armed forces, including at least one who flew with the French air force. Some Vietnamese dug and repaired trenches, while others worked on farms or in French industry. Tens of thousands of Chinese also came to France. Most Asians left after the war, but a few stayed on and became involved in political and social issues. Many Africans, especially Senegalese, came to France, either to fight or to work as laborers. Some stayed in France after the war.

The Clemenceau government vigorously pushed the war effort. Clemenceau had a cabinet minister arrested for "defeatist" attitudes and forged the discipline necessary to prosecute the war. Renewed nationalist enthusiasm provided the energy that overcame defeatist attitudes. The arrival of large numbers of soldiers from the United States bolstered the morale of the French people and troops. They helped stop the final German push in the spring of 1918 and played a key role in the counterattack that broke the German resistance. Peace came in November 1918 and was universally celebrated by the French.

Germany

Despite Wilhelm II's optimism that the coming war would be brief, the immense expenditure of resources and the years of warfare taxed the energies of the German bureaucrats. The unpreparedness of the government caused problems with food distribution that led to deteriorating living conditions and food riots as early as 1915. Two years later, large numbers of German workers began to strike, asking for better pay and improved working conditions.

German women joined the labor force in industry and agriculture to replace men who had been drafted. Adolescents, too, entered the workforce in large numbers. By 1917, more than 700,000 women toiled in armaments factories, a fivefold increase in four years. In the succeeding year, more than 100,000 women worked for the German railroads, a tenfold increase since 1914. Many of those employed by the chemical industry were women. As in France, some of these female laborers played key roles in strikes. Sociocultural attitudes against women holding regular jobs vanished under the powerful need to ensure victory.

The German Supreme Command assumed rule in the summer of 1917 as a virtual military dictatorship. The tightening of central control temporarily staved off economic collapse, but many thoughtful Germans realized that defeat loomed ahead. The military tried to forestall a major social upheaval by yielding to a representative government. The deployment of the remaining naval units in October provoked a mutiny of the sailors. By early November, workers, sailors, and soldiers set up self-governing committees, the ruling government collapsed, and Wilhelm II fled to Holland.

The Weimar Republic (1918–1933) was founded in the war's dying days, promising an open political system with a welfare state. Germany's defeat and the harsh peace that followed hampered the governing process, as did an unstable economy. At the same time, the army, bureaucracy, judiciary, educational establishment, and religious institutions from the imperial system survived. These elements inhibited the radical changes planned by many.

Around 2 million Germans died in World War I. They had valiantly served their country but participated in a losing cause. This fact led to resentment in the immediate postwar era, when politicians like Adolf Hitler played on the combined resentments and humiliations to forge an electoral base of veterans and others.

Great Britain

Large numbers of British served in World War I, including members of the empire recruited from Canada, New Zealand, Australia, Africa, and India. David Lloyd George (1863–1945) directed the British war effort. An ammunition crisis in 1915 triggered a reorganization of British industry under the leadership of Lloyd George. He implemented a military-style chain of command and promoted a policy of negotiating long-term supply contracts with factories, solving the problem for the war's duration. This approach militarized much of British industry.

Most countries imposed some form of rationing on their people, but Great Britain's need to ration was unusually acute. An island country, Britain imported many things, and German submarines blockaded the British. Thus, goods were rationed, including foodstuffs. Ration coupons were distributed and had to be taken to stores to

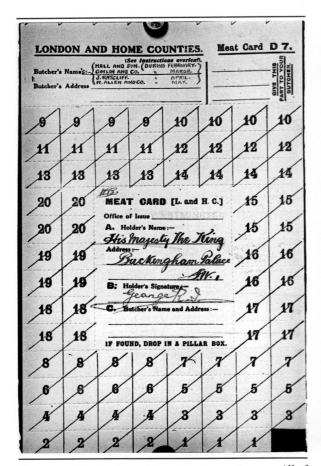

FIGURE 36.6 *Scarcity on the Home Front.* *All of Europe, and eventually the United States, faced wartime rationing. The island of Great Britain, dependent on supplies carried by ship, faced much deprivation. Shown here is the ration card used by King George V. Morale improved when the royalty endured the same hardships as other Britons.* Trustees of the Imperial War Museum.

FIGURE 36.7 *British Women at Work in a Munitions Factory.* *Thousands of women replaced men in the labor force as World War I wore on. Many women, like the factory workers pictured here, worked under extremely dangerous conditions, sometimes at the cost of their lives and their health.* Trustees of the Imperial War Museum.

be exchanged for various goods. Although a black market existed in Britain, most Britons loyally supported the rationing system.

Women were drawn heavily into manufacturing sectors of the economy. Their role was to replace the men who had been conscripted, killed, or severely wounded on the European mainland; Britain lost nearly 750,000 soldiers and suffered more than 1.5 million wounded. Around 1 million women worked in the munitions industry. Additional women served in paramilitary units in France. Yet, in the postwar era, these patriotic women found themselves increasingly displaced by the returning soldiers, many of whom enjoyed prior claims on jobs. Traditional social patterns were slowly reestablished.

Lloyd George presided over the early postwar era, when Britain's former position of global domination was altered. Britain lost ships with a capacity of nearly 8 million tons, and the national debt soared twelvefold. These and other factors changed Britain's strategic outlook. No longer could it afford massive naval armaments races with the powerful United States and Japan, which had emerged from the war with few losses and with large foreign-exchange surpluses. Thus, arms-limitation treaties in the early 1920s and early 1930s helped relieve some of the financial burden. Skillful diplomacy and political flexibility managed to slow the breakup of the British Empire and preserve British power in the postwar era.

OTHER WAR THEATERS

While the overwhelming bulk of fighting and casualties from World War I occurred in Europe, other regions saw conflict or change resulting from the war as well. The German imperial realm outside Europe totaled around a million square miles, and its ally, the Ottoman Empire, possessed significant holdings in Southwest Asia.

East Asia and the Pacific Region

When the war broke out in the summer of 1914, Japanese planners looked to China and the Pacific. Meeting their alliance commitments, the Japanese mobilized and attacked the German holdings in Shandong Province of China. Fighting was moderately costly in lives, and the German fortifications fell. Additional action in the Micronesian islands of the Pacific brought those German territories under Japanese occupation.

That Japan had larger imperialist aims may be seen in its subsequent diplomatic actions. To ensure a permanent hold on the new Asian and Pacific territories, Japanese leaders negotiated secret treaties with the British, French, and Russians. The Versailles peace talks validated Japan's claims, and continued domination resulted. The retention of areas in Shandong Province ignited Chinese popular opinion against the Japanese in 1919, helping spur Chinese nationalism.

The vulnerability of Germany's Pacific colonies invited the Australians and New Zealanders to seize those not already in Japanese hands. The German resistance proved light, and possession came with little difficulty.

Southwest Asia

While the positions of Germany's far-flung colonies limited its resistance to attack by the British and French, the Ottoman Empire's control of Southwest Asian lands was a different matter.

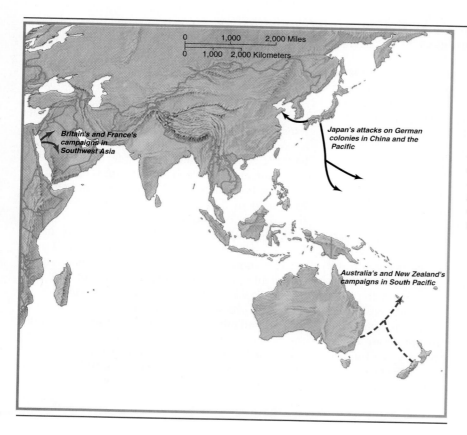

MAP 36.4 *The Asian Theater in World War I. The fighting in Asia and the Pacific was relatively brief, being largely over by 1915. The Japanese attacked German colonies in China (Shandong Province) and the North Pacific. Australian and New Zealand forces attacked German colonies in the South Pacific. Both land and sea operations were conducted in Asia.*

The Ottoman leaders joined the Germans and Austro-Hungarians in warring against the French, British, and Russians. Although the Ottoman soldiers sometimes lacked the firepower of the European forces, they were fierce fighters who fought off many advances by the European forces.

Tenacious Ottoman defensive actions held off the Russian conquest of Armenia, threw back a British attack on Mesopotamia, and limited an Arab uprising in Arabia. A major defeat for the British came in 1915 and 1916, when their forces, along with major Australian and New Zealand contingents, attacked the Gallipoli Peninsula, which was held by the Ottoman soldiers. Conceived by Winston Churchill, the campaign aimed at capturing Constantinople and driving the Ottomans from the war. Poor leadership, however, contributed to more than 150,000 casualties. By 1917, the British had assembled an army that numbered nearly 750,000 troops in the area, upsetting some who argued that Britain's primary strategic focus should be Europe rather than Southwest Asia. David Lloyd George ignored these criticisms and forged ahead on both fronts because his imperialist ambitions remained unshaken through the war years.

In 1918, the allied forces seized the offensive, and, in less than a year, the Ottoman Empire collapsed. As seen in Chapter 34, Arab support was garnered with vague British promises of Arab self-rule. By 1918, Mesopotamia had been wrested from the Ottoman Empire, Palestine had been conquered, and the Arabs of Arabia had seized their independence with significant aid from the British. In the Arabian campaign, the British adventurer and romantic T. E. Lawrence (Lawrence of Arabia) played a key role in aiding the Arabian rebel forces.

PATHS TO THE PAST
Turkey and the Armenian Genocide

Genocide is the mass killing of individuals in a deliberate attempt to extinguish a racial, ethnic, or religious group. One instance of genocide in the twentieth century was the action of the Ottoman Turks against the Armenians. Similarly to the denial of the genocide of European Jews by the Nazis, the Republic of Turkey and various organizations have, for their own purposes, discounted events that took place under the Ottoman Empire. Thus, the issue remains controversial.

When the Ottoman Empire joined with Germany in World War I, the empire had been ruled for some years by a group known as the Young Turks, who largely came from the military. An Ottoman campaign in the Caucasus Mountains against the Russians in 1914 failed miserably. Soon, the western part of Anatolia, home to perhaps 2 million Armenians, was deemed by the Turks as an area needing to be "cleansed." A complex set of actions in which hundreds of thousands of Armenians were evicted from their homes followed. Guiding the policymakers was a combination of factors, including religion (the Turks were Muslim and the Armenians were Christian), racism (the Turks strongly promoted a Turkism that was ethnically based), and wartime needs (the Turks feared an alliance between the Armenians and the Russians). Whatever the reasons, Armenian men were usually killed first and then women and children were forcibly marched to distant places. With little or no food or water, many perished along the way, and others were killed.

In the resulting carnage, several hundred thousand Armenians died. The Turkish government resettled the evacuated area with Turkish and other refugees, and many surviving Armenians were forced to convert to Islam. In a war filled with all forms of barbaric acts, the deliberate murder of a people by starvation and organized killings stands out.

Despite the attempts by apologists and revisionists who deny that this genocide took place or argue that it can be rationalized as necessary under wartime conditions, the historical memory of the Armenian Holocaust must be preserved, as all holocaust memories should be. Openness to different historical interpretations of an event does not mean that one must accept all versions as equally true. What is required is a careful examination of the relevant documents and other evidence as well as an understanding of the biases inherent in them. One might also note that Adolf Hitler confidently planned the genocide of the Jews, knowing that the world had seemingly forgotten about the Armenian genocide.

British and French imperialist ambitions determined the postwar makeup of Southwest Asia. Imperialist designs resulted in a conflict fueled by national ambitions and ethnic hatreds.

Africa

Most of the limited fighting in Africa took place in the sub-Saharan areas controlled by the Germans. In West, Central, and Southwest Africa, German resistance was limited by the small number of troops available to defend vast territories. African armed forces from Nigeria and Gold Coast helped round up Germans in Cameroon. Later, these and other armies fought in East Africa and Europe.

One region where a small, determined force held on was in Tanganyika, which remained under German control until a week after the end of the European fighting in 1918. In all, the German-led Africans occupied the attention of nearly 400,000 allied forces of Africans, Asians, and Europeans. Four Indian companies, along with their British officers, were captured by these German-led East African soldiers. Indeed, African valor and energy often lifted sagging German morale. After the war, Britain was awarded the East African territory previously held by the Germans.

Several hundred thousand Africans served in a variety of capacities during World War I. The French, for example, conscripted nearly a quarter-million sub-Saharan Africans, 157,000 of whom fought outside Africa. Some died under the most appalling conditions in Europe when French commanders neglected to provide them with winter uniforms. Large numbers of Nigerians ably fought for the British, and nearly 46,000 Kenyans died in wartime fighting.

FIGURE 36.8 *East African Troops at War. The British who commanded Indian troops in East Africa believed that their forces could easily defeat African soldiers led by the Germans. The British were shocked when their forces were captured. In this photo, a German officer directs two African soldiers.* Trustees of the Imperial War Museum.

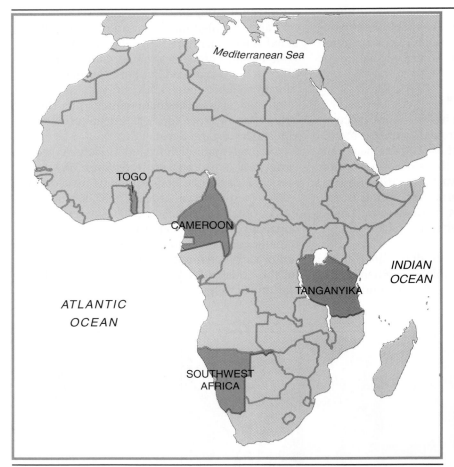

MAP 36.5 *The African Theater in World War I.* *Germany had several colonies in Africa. Those in the west were lost soon after the war began, but a stalemate emerged in East Africa until a week after the armistice in Europe. African troops— under the command of the British and French on one side and of the Germans on the other—did most of the fighting. Both sides fought well in the various campaigns, demonstrating that Africans could fight as well as Asians and Europeans.*

For the great majority of Africans, World War I meant little. Significant changes occurred in areas controlled by the Germans, but to the local peoples the war merely meant the exchange of one imperialist power for another. In some of these territories, however, tribal groups rebelled unsuccessfully against the new rulers. While the efforts failed, they foreshadowed uprisings against Western imperialism after 1945.

The Americas

The United States developed into a dominant military and economic power during World War I. The United States government followed the lead of its president, Woodrow Wilson, who advocated a nonaligned stance, even though he personally favored the British and French. Isolation worked until 1917, when unrestricted German submarine warfare helped compel the United States to enter the conflict. Wilson had become convinced that the

loss of American lives and ships signaled a call for military action.

The Germans had calculated that the United States might enter the war, but they remained confident of victory before the Americans could make a significant impact. German strategists failed to consider that the United States navy could immediately play a role in helping to defeat the submarine. It became clear to the Germans that their strategy had failed.

The United States began producing vast amounts of war materials and shipping them east. This compelled the Germans to pressure the faltering Russians to sign an agreement on the eastern front. The prospect of large numbers of United States troops on the western front made the timing of a German move vital. By early 1918, United States soldiers were arriving in Europe at the rate of 250,000 a month. These numbers weighed heavily in the fighting and accelerated the eventual German collapse.

The United States suffered little destruction or dislocation because of the war. America's economic might also increased during the war years, and Bernard Baruch, a savvy politician, played a major role in reorganizing American industry for the war effort. Not only did U.S. factories increase their industrial production, but armaments and other industries that supplied the Europeans earned large profits. In addition, the withdrawal of European countries from Latin America and other places opened new financial opportunities for United States merchants.

Latin America was little affected by World War I. Certain commodities like nitrates from Chile were traded to the combatants, spurring economic production throughout the country. Brazil, Cuba, Costa Rica, Guatemala, Haiti, Honduras, Nicaragua, and Panama declared war for political advantage and to maintain their alliances with the United States. Five others broke off diplomatic relations with the Germans, and other states remained neutral.

Canada experienced great changes from its active participation in World War I. Although the country was not physically harmed by the war, well over a half-million Canadians served, including 24,000 in the British air services and another 8,000 in the navy. Canadians suffered more killed than the U.S., and the high conscription rate heightened intra-Canadian tensions among the English and French Canadians, leading to draft riots in Quebec. Canada's prime minister insisted on and won from Britain Canadian control of the Canadian units stationed in Europe, as well as a Canadian role in wartime and peacetime issues. Indeed, Canadian nationalism grew significantly during the war and laid the foundation for an autonomous Canada.

The Canadian economy experienced major growth during the war and became more closely tied to the United States economy. Prior to the war's outbreak, Canada seemed on the verge of an economic depression. Demand created by Europe's wartime needs, however, quickly ended the downturn. Prices rose and Canada's industries developed robustly. New York City gradually replaced London as the financial center for Canadian industrialists, and United States investors significantly increased their holdings in Canada.

World War I brought the United States increased economic prosperity and growing dominance of the Americas. Before the war, the British had played the dominant financial role in Latin America and Canada. During and after the war, British investment sharply declined, while United States economic influence mushroomed.

The Germans had briefly negotiated with the Mexican government to attack the United States. In return, the Germans promised to support a return of parts of the southwestern United States to Mexico. The diplomatic effort produced no results except a heightening of tensions between the Mexican and U.S. governments. Raids by Pancho Villa across the Mexican border into the United States brought a U.S. military response that quieted the border region.

THE PARIS PEACE CONFERENCE AND THE TREATY OF VERSAILLES

The forces that haunted the outbreak of the war—nationalism, imperialism, and revolution—were in evidence at the Paris Peace Conference during the first half of 1919. During the negotiations, delegates met at many sites around Paris, and the final major settlement was signed at Versailles Palace outside Paris. All of the countries had paid a great price in lives and material; many victorious elected governments heeded their constituents' demands for revenge and compensation. Few cool-headed diplomats presided in these talks.

War Aims

France sought severe punishment of Germany and won acceptance of many of its aims, including a treaty clause blaming the war on Germany. The German army was to be severely reduced, parts of prewar Germany were to be demilitarized, and large war reparations were demanded. Having suffered hundreds of thousands of casualties and massive destruction in its territory, the French government insisted that Germany be defanged and punished. Unfortunately for French long-term interests, the domestic industrial base of Germany had been little affected by the war, nor was it reduced by the treaty.

Britain was less eager to punish Germany severely, but it also insisted on certain restraints on German power and an indemnity to help pay for the war costs. Lloyd George had been reelected

FIGURE 36.9 *Delegates to the Paris Peace Conference, 1919.* The settlement of World War I affected many parts of the world. Among these delegates from Southwest Asian and African lands is Prince Feisal (front, center), a representative of the Arabs. Behind him and to the viewer's right is T. E. Lawrence, "Lawrence of Arabia." Except for Arabia, most of Southwest Asia and Africa remained under imperialist control. Trustees of the Imperial War Museum.

prime minister on the promise of "squeezing the German lemon until its pips squeaked." An amusing word play, this slogan reflected a vengeful attitude that tainted the British negotiating position.

To many diplomats, U.S. leaders appeared to be "honest brokers" because they desired no territorial gains. They also led the most powerful state surviving the war, and their voices received a hearing. Most delegates listened favorably to President Wilson of the United States, who restated his three broad goals as the basis of a peace settlement. First, he hoped to eliminate trade barriers, interference with freedom of the seas, imperialist tensions, arms races, and secret diplomacy. Second, Wilson desired to settle European problems relating to territorial integrity, national boundaries, and nationalism. Finally, Wilson believed that an international assembly should be formed to preserve the peace won at Paris. The treaty called for the United States and the other victors to give up their own imperialist domains, but the victors' justice unmasked naked power politics.

Peace Settlements

Under the Treaty of Versailles, imperialistic control of overseas colonies simply passed from one state to another. The territories gained from Germany were mandated to the various winners. Japan got German concessions in China and Micronesia. Other Pacific islands went to Australia and New Zealand, while Germany's possessions in Africa were parceled out to a variety of states.

Europe experienced the greatest change in terms of national self-determination. Poland was re-created after more than a century. Yugoslavia was amalgamated from Serbia and other lands and peoples in southeastern Europe. Some of these groups, like the Croats and Slovenes, feared Serbian domination but were pressed into accepting the new union. Czechoslovakia was formed from territories where Czechs and Slovaks predominated, although certain German-speaking peoples also lived there. A whole string of Eastern European countries came into existence or reemerged, including Latvia, Lithuania, Estonia, Hungary, and Romania. They were supported by the war victors, forming a kind of buffer between Soviet Russia and Central Europe.

Germans felt betrayed by the treaty they were forced to accept. They were prepared to sign agreements based on Wilson's three broad proposals for peace but resented the large indemnity and the war-guilt clause. Wilhelm II and hundreds of German officers were to be tried for offenses, including war crimes. Germans disliked the fact that they were forced to withdraw to the eastern bank of the Rhine River, and they hated the loss of territory to France, Belgium, Czechoslovakia, and Poland. Germany also had to surrender the bulk of its navy, including submarines, and it had to turn over most of its machine guns, artillery, air force, and motorized transport.

The Weimar Republic leaders who had been forced by the victors to accept the peace accord became the objects of popular hatred for the betrayal. Ultranationalist groups in Germany called for a repudiation of the Versailles Treaty. When Adolf Hitler gained power in 1933, he set about scrapping the treaty's provisions and putting the German people back to work. These acts restored German pride, and Hitler benefited from German nationalism.

The League of Nations

The League of Nations suffered from the nationalist and imperialist ambitions of its most powerful members. The failure of the United States government to ratify the treaties ending the war and thereby to accept the League of Nations as an international organization undermined the League's effectiveness.

The Japanese were allocated a prominent seat in the League of Nations. At the Paris Peace Con-

ference, however, the Japanese failed to insert in the League of Nations Covenant a racial equality clause stating that all races are equal. Australians and Americans blocked the effort, and the racist sentiment behind the objection deeply offended the Japanese. Ironically, Japan's control of the Pacific islands captured from the Germans was predicated upon the racist idea that these Pacific islanders could not govern themselves. The Japanese did not seem to have minded this racist double standard.

In the two decades following the end of World War I, the League of Nations proved unable to deal with crises. Japanese aggression in Manchuria and Italian aggression in Ethiopia in the 1930s received condemnation by the League, but these diplomatic setbacks did not deter either country. In 1931, Japanese soldiers staged a violent incident, blaming it on the Chinese and using it as a pretext to conquer Manchuria. A League commission found that the Japanese had initiated the action and blamed them for the conquest of Manchuria. Similarly, Italy's conquest of Ethiopia roused the League's ire, but its condemnation had no real practical effect. Because of these and other failures, the League could not prevent the disintegration of international diplomacy and the outbreak of World War II.

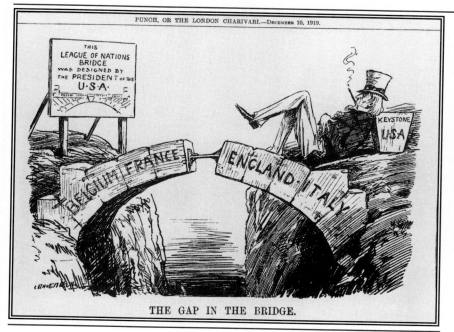

PUNCH, OR THE LONDON CHARIVARI.—December 10, 1919.

THIS LEAGUE OF NATIONS BRIDGE WAS DESIGNED BY THE PRESIDENT OF THE U·S·A·

BELGIUM FRANCE

ENGLAND ITALY

KEYSTONE USA

THE GAP IN THE BRIDGE.

FIGURE 36.10 *U.S. Reluctance Hampers the League of Nations. This British cartoon conveys the Allies' frustration when the United States opted out of the League of Nations, an organization developed by President Woodrow Wilson. Uncle Sam, looking a bit like Wilson, lazes on the keystone block for the bridge. U.S. reluctance to honor its president's commitment to the League undermined the international organization.* Library of Congress.

EUROPE	ASIA	AFRICA	AMERICAS		
				1914	Assassination of Francis Ferdinand, June 1914
				–	
				–	Russia mobilizes, July 1914
Stalemate on western front, mid-1914–early 1918	Japan wins German colonies in China and Pacific, mid-1914–1915			–	Battle of Langemark, Oct. 1914
		Allied campaigns in west and southwest, late 1914–mid-1915		**1915**	
				–	Italy joins Allies, spring 1915
Stalemate on eastern front, mid-1915–mid-1918	Campaign in Gallipoli, mid-1915–mid-1916	Stalemate in East Africa, mid-1915–early 1919		–	
				1916	
				–	Easter uprising in Ireland, Apr. 1916
				–	Lloyd George appointed Prime Minister, Dec. 1916
				–	
				1917	Romanov dynasty collapses, Mar. 1917
	Campaign in Jordan, Palestine, and Arabia, early 1917–late 1918		Unrestricted submarine warfare in Atlantic, 1917–1918	–	U.S. enters the war, Apr. 1917
				–	Bolsheviks take power, Nov. 1917
				1918	President Wilson's 14 Points, Jan. 1918
	Japanese navy patrols Mediterranean, late 1917–1918			–	Treaty of Brest-Litovsk, Mar. 1918
				–	Wilfred Owen dies, Nov. 4, 1918
Paris Peace Conference, 1919 ▼				**1919**	Armistice, Nov. 11, 1918

SUMMARY

1. Nationalism, imperialism, revolution, and alliance systems combined to create the conditions favorable for war in 1914.

2. Germany rose in 1871, created an overseas empire, and competed with the British in a naval armament race. To protect itself from a "vengeful" France, the Germans worked out the Triple Alliance with the Austro-Hungarian Empire and Italy.

3. The German treaty system and the permitting of Russia to drift away from an alliance helped push the Russians and French into a military agreement that complicated Germany's strategic problems.

4. Germany's naval armament policy caused the British to reconsider their strategic priorities. Alliances with the Japanese, French, and Russians were formed between 1902 and 1907, permitting the British to pull home elements of their navy.

5. War broke out after the assassination of Archduke Francis Ferdinand, heir to the Austro-Hungarian throne. The Germans backed their Austro-Hungarian ally, while the French supported the Russians and the Serbs. Soon, various threats and maneuvers broke into armed conflict, and, after some spectacular shifting of human beings and arms, a deadly stalemate grew into a war of attrition.

6. Each warring state became highly centralized. The unprecedented social control and war costs created severe political tensions. Russia collapsed in 1917, and Germany and her allies fell in the second half of 1918.

7. The home fronts in Europe and the Americas saw many women taking industrial jobs. Some of these women spearheaded strikes in France and Germany. Many people under colonial rule also came to France to replace the human losses in the economy.

8. Warfare also took place in Asia, the Pacific, and Africa, with the Germans losing territory while its enemies expanded their control of the new lands. The Ottoman Empire collapsed, and the Japanese Empire expanded.

9. Canada entered the war in 1914, and the United States and parts of Latin America entered three years later. With the decline of European power, the United States became dominant in Latin America and influential in Canada.

10. The great human and material losses incurred in the war heightened national desires for revenge by the winners. These pressures affected the powers who gathered in Paris during the first half of 1919.

11. The Versailles Treaty awarded German and Ottoman lands to the victors and redrew Europe's map to give the Poles, Serbs, Czechs, Slovaks, and Baltic peoples independence. The loss of territory and German-speaking peoples to other states angered many Germans and helped fuel postwar resentments.

12. A League of Nations was created, but the international organization did not easily function in a time of heightened nationalism. The absence of the United States from the organization also severely crippled it. The Japanese deeply resented the lack of a racial equality clause in the League Covenant.

SUGGESTED READINGS

Fischer, Fritz. *War of Illusions*. New York: Norton, 1975. A summation of a revisionist interpretation, blaming World War I's outbreak on the Germans.

Keegan, John. *A History of Warfare*. New York: Knopf, 1993. A general history with an excellent overview of the situation in Europe before and during World War I.

Lincoln, W. Bruce. *Passage through Armageddon*. Oxford, Eng.: Oxford University Press, 1986. An account of Russia during World War I.

Sholokov, Mikhail. *And Quiet Flows the Don*. New York: Random House, 1966. A major war novel.

Woollacott, Angela. *On Her Their Lives Depended*. Berkeley: University of California Press, 1994. A significant treatment of women in the British munitions industry during World War I.

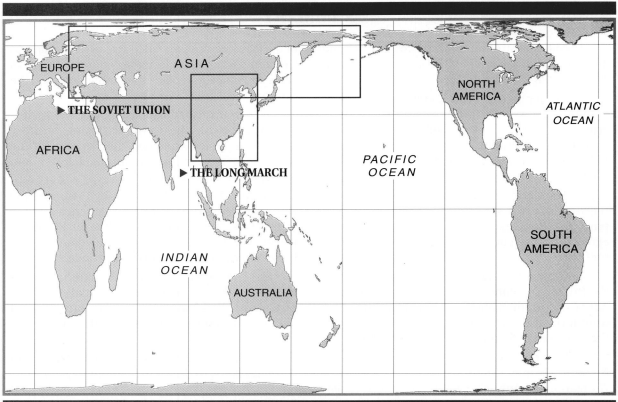

EUROPE
ASIA
▶ THE SOVIET UNION
AFRICA
NORTH AMERICA
ATLANTIC OCEAN
▶ THE LONG MARCH
PACIFIC OCEAN
INDIAN OCEAN
AUSTRALIA
SOUTH AMERICA

St. Petersburg
NORTHERN EUROPEAN PLAIN
URAL MTS.
WESTERN SIBERIAN LOWLANDS
CENTRAL SIBERIAN PLATEAU
EAST SIBERIAN UPLANDS
Moscow
Kiev
Volgograd
S I B E R I A
PACIFIC OCEAN

▶ THE SOVIET UNION

OUTER MONGOLIA
MANCHUKUO (MANCHURIA)
GANSU
KOREA
HUNAN
GUIZHOU
JIANGXI
YUNNAN
GUANGXI
GUANGDONG
BURMA
FRENCH INDOCHINA
SIAM

▶ THE LONG MARCH

Transformation of Russia and China
1905–1989

Elena stared at her charred house in the smoldering ruins of her Russian village. Only a month before, the bountiful harvest had been gathered, and she and her husband had been happy. Their debts had been paid, and they could afford a milk cow. Then the local Communist Party leader came along with a police official, saying something about moving onto a state collective farm. Yuri, her husband, and most of the others argued against Stalin's directive. Last night, they were taken away, and a scuffle between the Red Guards and the village men had caused the fires. Snow fell. What was she to do?

The tragedy of this Russian village was repeated often during the Stalinist revolution. Russians and Chinese experienced revolutions that profoundly transformed their societies. Both imperial systems collapsed because they could not adapt to the challenges of industrialization and political modernity.

UNREST AND TRANSFORMATION IN RUSSIA AND THE SOVIET UNION

War and revolution became linked processes in twentieth-century Russia. The Russo-Japanese War (1904–1905) and World War I (1914–1918) fomented massive unrest that ultimately triggered the collapse of the tsarist system in 1917. Members of the Russian Bolshevik Party under the leadership

913

of Vladimir Lenin seized power and had to fight a civil war while creating a revolutionary government. In 1941, Soviet Russia was attacked by Nazi Germany and managed to defeat the Germans, exporting revolution to Eastern Europe during and after World War II (1937–1945). Finally, the Cold War between Soviet-bloc and U.S.-allied countries led to Soviet-style revolutions in additional countries, ending in 1989, when the Soviet Empire collapsed.

Russian Unrest, 1905–1917

The tsarist system's collapse in 1917 was precipitated by many factors, not the least of which was the inflexibility of Tsar Nicholas II (reign dates 1894–1917). Serious unrest erupted in 1905, while Russia was losing the Russo-Japanese War. People lost enthusiasm for the expensive and distant war,

industrial workers longed for better working conditions, and peasants desired tax relief and more land to farm. These elements unleashed a decade of unrest and trouble for the tsar.

The massive unrest of 1905 nearly toppled the government but brought little political change. Upheaval began when a large number of unarmed petitioners met armed resistance by the government. A few people were killed at the event known as Bloody Sunday in January 1905, and the attack on peaceful subjects ignited strikes and demonstrations across the empire. Recent military defeats at the hands of the Japanese had already weakened the state's popular support. Although Nicholas finally agreed to peace talks with the Japanese and a settlement a few months later, Russia's people demanded change at home. Some wished to end the monarchy, and most wanted representative government.

FIGURE 37.1 **Russian Women Protesters.** *This photograph, taken in Petrograd in March 1917, shows hundreds of women marching for better living conditions, specifically for increased rations. Women took active roles in the political events of 1917; later, in the winter of 1918, riots by women helped bring about the collapse of the tsarist system.* VA/Sovfoto.

MAP 37.1 *Territories Lost by the Russian Empire in 1917–1918.* *The defeat of the Russian army in 1918 by the Germans resulted in the Treaty of Brest-Litovsk. Territories lost to the Germans were a significant part of European Russia, including parts of Poland, Lithuania, Latvia, Estonia, Bessarabia, Byelo-Russia, and portions of the Ukraine. These lands were heavily populated and productive for the Russian economy.*

Peace failed to stave off a confrontation between the tsar and his people, but it allowed army units in Asia to be called back to deal with the civil unrest. In October 1905, a workers' strike ignited a general work stoppage and demonstrations by laborers, students, and government officials. Within a few days, most of the empire lay idle, and the tsar contemplated his reaction. Brief consideration of a military dictatorship to drown the unrest in blood gave way to a compromise that promised an elected legislature coupled with guarantees of personal liberties. The government's offer persuaded the moderates of the opposition to compromise, and they urged the strikers to return to work. Hardliners among the workers fought back but succumbed to the massive force of the state. Workers' administrative councils, *soviets*, led the antistate effort.

Nicholas's refusal to surrender his dominant position in the system portended trouble. It took three elections before a legislature able to work with the tsar could be seated. Worker unrest resumed in 1911 and continued to plague Nicholas until the outbreak of World War I in 1914.

Wartime stresses finally unraveled the tsarist system. The initial patriotic euphoria of the mobilization evaporated with the serious defeats of Russian forces in 1914 and 1915. Nicholas foolishly assumed direct command of the Russian army, leaving the home front in the hands of Tsarina Alexandra, who was an inept administrator. In addition, she had been born in Germany, an enemy state of Russia, and the ensuing mismanagement eroded the government's remaining credibility, causing one legislator to question whether her actions reflected stupidity or treason. The hard winter of 1916–1917 and the breakdown of the transport system left a bread shortage in the capital, and a riot by irate women mushroomed into a massive protest against the tsarist system. When the government lost control of its metropolitan garrison, Nicholas abdicated and the Romanov Dynasty ended.

The next several months were a time of anarchy as the police and other agencies of control vanished. Two quasi-governmental agencies attempted to step into the power vacuum. Legislators formed the Provisional Government, which claimed to rule Russia until an elected government could be seated. A *soviet* modeled on the one of 1905 reappeared in the capital, Petrograd, and asserted that it acted in the interests of the workers and soldiers, who were mostly peasants. The Petrograd Soviet promised to support the Provisional Government, so long as the workers and soldiers received fair treatment. By August 1917, this system of dual government furthered the breakdown of authority, causing Alexander Kerensky (1881–1970), a socialist leader of the Provisional Government, to seek dictatorial power. Kerensky failed, opening the way for others to seize power.

Russia's rapid collapse had surprised everyone, including Vladimir Lenin (1870–1924), a Marxist living in exile. Lenin plotted his return to Russia upon learning of the government's demise, and he persuaded the Germans to permit him and his party to travel across Germany to Sweden. The Germans appreciated Lenin's talent for fomenting unrest, which weakened the Provisional Government. Upon arriving in Russia in April 1917, Lenin gave a speech to his Marxist supporters, known as the **Bolsheviks** (majority group). Much to the surprise of his old comrades, Lenin favored the immediate overthrow of the Provisional Government, an end to Russia's participation in World War I, the granting of seized land to the peasants, and adequate bread supplies for the cities. These proposals became central issues for the Bolsheviks,

permitting them to profit from the growing peace sentiments, peasant unrest, and anarchical conditions. The Bolshevik Party swelled in size to become a major player in Russian politics. By September, majorities supported the Bolsheviks in the *soviets* of the Russian cities.

For Lenin and other Bolshevik leaders, the central question was when to seize power. If the attempt came too early, the opposition forces might easily crush the revolutionaries; if the takeover came too late, the revolutionary situation might not sustain a Bolshevik government. In September, Lenin opted for immediate power, but his cohorts refused. After weeks of acrimonious debate, Lenin's view prevailed. On November 7, 1917, the Bolsheviks staged a coup d'état and took power.

The Bolshevik Revolution, 1917–1924

The Bolshevik Revolution transformed Russia's society, economy, and government in the midst of a terrible civil war. Much of the Bolshevik effort centered on the destruction of the tsarist socio-political-economic system and on the building of a workers' state. As counterrevolutionary groups amassed military forces, the Bolshevik government organized an army of workers for self-defense.

DESTRUCTION OF THE TSARIST SYSTEM. Among the Bolsheviks' earliest acts was the elimination or suppression of the political and economic elite. Although most aristocrats fled Russia during 1917, some remained behind. Many lost their remaining status when the Bolsheviks abolished the system of social ranks developed by Peter the Great. Some were arrested and perished in Soviet **gulags**,[1] labor camps in Siberia and northern Russia. During the civil war, fearing that the former tsar and his family might be captured by the anti-Bolsheviks, Lenin ordered the royal family's execution. Members of the middle class who enjoyed some social prominence and many clerics of the Russian Orthodox Church found themselves in the *gulags* or were shot as suspected counterrevolutionaries. Monasteries and most churches were closed or confiscated for state use. Indeed, the Bolsheviks openly avowed atheism and attacked religious beliefs of all kinds as supporting the capitalist status quo.

---

[1] **gulags:** GOO lahgs

FIGURE 37.2 *Lenin Speaking at May Day Rally.* *Lenin played a key role in overturning Russia's tsarist government in October 1917. In a speech made shortly after his return to Russia in 1917, Lenin laid the foundation for Bolshevik power; later addresses, such as this 1918 May Day speech, furthered the establishment of socialism. During Stalin's regime, photographs were doctored to remove people who had fallen out of political favor. Despite Lenin's criticism of Stalin, photos of Lenin were also altered to include Stalin at his side.* Culver Pictures.

Some workers and a few peasants joined the new government, which proclaimed itself a Marxist "dictatorship of the proletariat." Because the Bolsheviks had little or no administrative experience before November 7, 1917, they retained some tsarist officials. These, however, were supervised and controlled by Bolshevik managers. Similarly, a dire need for experienced army officers forced the new regime to grant tsarist officers army commands. Paired with each of these commanders was a party official who had the power to execute those suspected of being traitors.

One problem for the Bolsheviks concerned national elections scheduled for late November 1917. After heated discussion, elections were held, and the Bolsheviks won somewhat less than 40 percent of the vote. Later, the National Assembly held a single meeting, which was terminated by the Bolsheviks.

Protection of the Bolshevik state fell to the **Cheka**, a police force that grew to hundreds of thousands of members and undertook such responsibilities as guarding the *gulags* and frontiers. A policy of state terror instituted in September 1918 afforded the Cheka great power over the people of Russia.

The state increased enormously in size and scope during the Bolshevik Revolution. Political ministers were renamed commissars, and they gradually took charge of foreign affairs, defense,

FIGURE 37.3 *Women Being Sent to Siberia.* Imprisoned by the tsarist regime, the women in this 1905 photo are en route to Siberia. The Bolshevik government continued to use Siberia as a vast prison camp. Conditions deteriorated and larger numbers of women inmates were dispatched to Siberia under the Bolsheviks. Ullstein Bilderdienst.

and the arts. During the civil war, survival of the state necessitated an extreme form of centralized rule. The **Politburo** (political bureau) became the command center of the Bolshevik Party, numbering a half-dozen of the top party leadership, who handled daily matters. The **Orgburo** (organization bureau) handled administrative matters concerning the state apparatus, and the **Party Secretariat** dealt with organizational issues relating to the Bolshevik Party. When Soviet Russia's top administrator, Jacob Sverdlov, died during the swine flu epidemic of 1919, Josef Stalin (1879–1953) succeeded him and began to amass influence in the party and state.

CIVIL WAR AND LEADERSHIP. After coming to power, the Bolsheviks opened peace talks with German military commanders. Directing the

Soviet effort were Lenin and Leon Trotsky (1877–1940), Commissar of Foreign Affairs. Because they had an extremely weak hand, the Bolsheviks realized that they had to give up land for peace, and they decided to delay negotiations, hoping that the German proletariat would topple the German government. A twelve-day German advance had threatened the capital and the revolution. Finally, the Treaty of Brest-Litovsk (March 1918) was negotiated and presented to Bolshevik leaders; some denounced the document, which surrendered large parts of Russia's land and resources. Nonetheless, Lenin convinced a majority of party leaders to ratify the treaty.

Although the Treaty of Brest-Litovsk saved the Bolsheviks, it helped precipitate a tragic civil war. The Soviet government surrendered to the Germans more than 2 million square kilometers of land that housed 62 million people and produced a third of Russia's crops. In addition, the Soviets lost 80 percent of their sugar refineries, 73 percent of their iron mines, and 75 percent of their coal fields. One socialist faction that formerly had supported the Bolsheviks turned against them, and many opponents began to take up arms against Lenin and his party.

The Bolsheviks fought against two major groups during the Russian Civil War (1918–1921).

One opponent, the Whites, was a diverse set of military commanders and their armies, representing the aristocrats and some wealthy people. The other contending group, sometimes called the Greens, included socialists and democrats, who agreed that the land should be divided among the peasants and that there should be peace. They opposed the Bolshevik refusal to share power and the dissolution of the National Assembly. Fighting between the Bolsheviks (Reds) and Greens broke out in

MAP 37.2   *The Russian Civil War.   The Bolsheviks fought a civil war with their opponents between 1918 and 1921. During that period, the Bolsheviks lost and regained much land, many times. By the end of the civil war, however, the Bolsheviks had won back most territory lost at Brest-Litovsk. Only Poland, Latvia, Estonia, and Lithuania remained independent of Russian control.*

mid-1918 and continued for months. The Green forces collapsed after a White commander seized their political capital and their leadership. Thereafter, the civil war became a contest between the Whites and Reds. Although relatively small armies fought one another, civil war raged across Russia, claiming 7 million lives.

The Red Army was built by the Bolsheviks. Trotsky became the Commissar of Defense in 1918, traveling from front to front in an armored train. On one occasion, after a Red Army unit ran from battle, he ordered every tenth soldier shot for desertion. By the war's end, the victorious armed forces numbered about 500,000 regular combatants and several million support personnel.

Bolshevik victory was the result of several factors, including control over the Russian heartland and industry, nationalism, and the disunity of their opponents. Domination of central Russia meant an integrated transportation network, command of vital factories and supplies, and an easily defended territory. At the same time, foreign assistance (by fourteen countries) to the anticommunist forces permitted the Bolsheviks to stoke Russian nationalism. Patriotic feelings and Cheka terror silenced internal opponents, bringing cohesiveness to the war effort. By early 1921, much of the former tsarist empire had been reclaimed by the Soviet state.

In 1922, Lenin suffered a stroke. He gradually recovered and resumed some duties but left most affairs in the hands of others, including Trotsky and Stalin. Stalin's ruthless style troubled Lenin. Just when it seemed that Stalin might be forced to

UNDER THE LENS

U.S.–Soviet Relations, 1918–1922

The onset of U.S.–Soviet relations was marked by hostility and humanitarianism, elements that characterized the two countries' ties in the twentieth century. The United States intervened against the Bolsheviks in the Russian Civil War (1918–1921) and also played a major role in providing famine relief in the aftermath of that great conflict. Many of America's allies wished to see the radical Bolsheviks lose the civil war, and Japan wanted control of Siberia.

In 1918, U.S. soldiers found themselves in northern Russia late in World War I, as a part of an Allied action. They were sent to secure supplies of war materials that had been stockpiled at the ports of Murmansk and Archangel. This American expeditionary force numbered several thousand soldiers, serving with British soldiers in a joint operation. Certain American politicians also wished to keep an eye on the Soviet forces to see how they fared in the fierce civil war raging in Russia. Many U.S. troops had no idea why they had been sent to Russia, and they refused orders to fight against the Bolsheviks. After much confusion, the Americans were sent home.

A second group of Americans was shipped to Siberia in 1918; this time, they were to keep an eye on the Japanese, as well as the Soviets. Japan claimed that its forces were protecting civilians who were caught up in the civil war, but they really coveted Siberia's land and mineral wealth. Again, the American soldiers had no idea why they were in Siberia. Japanese soldiers clashed on several occasions with the Bolsheviks before finally withdrawing. Support given the anti-Bolshevik Russians by the Allies afforded the Bolsheviks the chance to use nationalism against their foes, who were derisively called "puppets of foreign imperialists." That slogan helped fuel the Bolshevik victory.

After the civil war ended, it rapidly became clear to Soviet authorities and international relief organization leaders that widespread famine stalked Russia. Calls for relief went out, and the American Relief Administration, a private organization headed by Herbert Hoover, who had performed a similar operation during World War I, provided significant aid to the starving people of Soviet Russia. By 1922, millions of tons of grain and other supplies reached Soviet Russia and were distributed with few hitches. The cooperation between Americans and Soviets saved millions of lives and showed that much good could result when both countries had common interests. Similar results occurred during World War II, when the United States supplied hundreds of thousand of trucks and gasoline to the beleaguered Soviet armies.

return some of his considerable power, Lenin suffered a new series of strokes and died in early 1924. Scientists preserved Lenin's body, which was displayed for decades as a symbol of the Bolshevik Revolution.

ECONOMIC CONTROL AND EXPERIMENTATION.

Soon after taking power, the Bolsheviks had commandeered the financial institutions, key industries, and transportation system. In certain factories, the Bolsheviks attempted worker-management programs by replacing the owners and managers with laborers. These utopian efforts lasted until a decline in factory output compelled their abandonment. During the civil war, regime survival demanded an extreme form of state control of factories. Workers were given production quotas and paid by the item, a policy they hated. After the civil war's end in 1921, strikes forced the policy's abandonment.

Agricultural production declined during the Bolshevik Revolution. Keeping their campaign promise of granting land to the peasants, the Bolsheviks decreed that lands seized by the peasants should remain in their hands. This ensured peasant support for the Bolsheviks during the civil war, because the Whites demanded that these lands be returned to the former landowners. On the other hand, the Bolsheviks seized grain from peasants during the civil war. This policy was partly dictated by declining grain supplies in cities, which were strongholds of the Bolsheviks. Armed detachments of workers fanned out into the countryside to seize grain, and these desperate measures yielded enough to feed the urban folk. The oppressive policies, however, angered the peasants, some of whom retaliated by planting less grain in succeeding years. The actions exacerbated the famine of the early 1920s. In 1921, the civil war ended and peasant uprisings compelled the state to relax its control of agriculture.

The peacetime period from 1921 to 1929 was characterized by the **New Economic Policy**, relaxation measures taken by the Bolsheviks to permit economic recovery from the ravages of warfare. Control over some factories ended, workers' wages increased, and peasants regained control of production. By 1927, most economic measures showed a return to the production levels of 1913, the last full year before World War I. The complete transformation of agriculture and industry came with the ascendancy of Stalin in 1929.

The Bolsheviks finished the destruction of the tsarist system and its social support groups. They reshaped the economy and built a modern state in the midst of a civil war. In the process, they sowed the seeds of a new revolution, one that completed the transformation of Russian life.

The Stalinist Revolution and Its Aftermath, 1924–1953

The second revolution in the Soviet Union lasted from 1924 to 1941, setting the foundation for Soviet society until 1991. Josef Stalin's shadow loomed over Soviet Russia and world affairs for much of the twentieth century. He built a powerful state by industrializing, organizing the peasants, and fashioning a massive state apparatus. By 1941, Russia was the second most powerful state in Europe after Germany, and, by 1945, it was the second most powerful government in the world after the United States. Stalin's programs and failures cost tens of millions of lives. Indeed, he may have been responsible for more deaths than any other human being.

STALIN'S PERSONAL RULE.

Between 1924 and 1929, Stalin struggled for power against top Leninists, like Trotsky. Although he was the least charismatic among Lenin's subordinates, Stalin held a great deal of power in the Politburo, the Orgburo, and the Party Secretariat. In each body, he built a faction of loyal supporters and with shrewd political maneuvering emerged triumphant in 1929 from the leadership struggle.

The Stalinists consolidated their hold on the party, although a leadership crisis developed in 1934, when a group of top Stalinists attempted to curb their leader. Later that year and until 1939, Stalin unleashed a terror against the party and other elite groups. The instrument of repression was the NKVD, a successor to the Cheka. Ruling elite members lost their lives or went to the *gulags*. The army, for example, saw the death or imprisonment of most of its top officers. As the elite echelon disappeared, a new group advanced and sometimes "claimed" the residences and even wives of the former elite.

Stalin's personal control of Soviet Russia dramatically increased. In fact, the dictatorship of the proletariat evolved from party dictatorship under Lenin to a personal dictatorship under Stalin.

IN THEIR OWN WORDS

Remembering the Stalinist 1930s

Fear stalked Soviet Russia in the 1930s. Josef Stalin collectivized agriculture, killing millions, and turned against Communist Party members and intellectuals, terrorizing them into silence. Anna Akhmatova (1889–1966) had been a published poet since 1914, writing lyric poems that charmed her readers. Marxist critics, however, disparaged her as a vestige of the past. She remained silent until 1936, when she resumed writing.

How was one to compose poems free from Stalin's security police? Her son and husband had been arrested and jailed. With a few trusted friends, Akhmatova memorized *Requiem*, her poetic portrait of the 1930s in the spirit of Dante's *Inferno*, a poetic journey into hell. She once wrote that if alive, the "late Dante would have created a tenth circle of hell." The prose-like "Instead of a Foreword," written in 1957 after much of the rest of *Requiem*, aptly sets the hellish scene.

In the terrible years of the Ezhov terror [mid-1930s], I spent seventeen months in the prison lines in Leningrad. Once someone "identified" me. Then a blue-lipped woman standing behind me, who had, of course, never heard my name, came to from the torpor characteristic of us all and asked me in a whisper (everyone spoke in whispers there), "But can you describe this?"

And I said, "I can."

Then something like a smile slipped across what had once been her face.

Earlier, in 1940, Anna Akhmatova had written the poem "Dedication," which she later published with "Instead of a Foreword" to form a powerful evocation of the Stalinist terror.

Before this woe mountains bend down,
The great river does not flow,
But strong are the prison bolts,
And beyond them are the "convicts' holes"
And mortal anguish.
For someone there blows a fresh wind,
For someone a sunset luxuriates,
We do not know, we are the same everywhere,
We hear just the fateful gnashing of keys
And the soldiers' heavy tread.
We would rise as if for early mass,
Walk through the capital turned savage,
Meet there, more breathless than the dead,
The sun is lower and the Neva more misty,
But hope still sings in the distance
The sentence . . . And immediately the tears pour,
She's already separated from everyone,
As if the life had been painfully torn from her heart,
But she walks . . . Staggers . . . Alone . . .
Where are now the involuntary friends
Of my two hellish years?
What appears to them in the Siberian blizzard,
What seems visible to them in the lunar circle?
To them I send my farewell greetings . . .

Stalin's domination of the Soviet Union continued until 1953, assuming the form of a personal bureaucracy that operated outside the regular party and state channels, and only people he personally trusted worked for him there.

STALIN'S REVOLUTION: COLLECTIVIZATION AND INDUSTRIALIZATION. According to the Marxist perspective, socialism could not be achieved until Russia had been fully industrialized. Control of the peasants became a top state priority, and the effort to subdue them merged with the harnessing of agriculture to industry. For centuries, governments of Russia feared the peasants, who constituted well over half of the population. Peasant anger had been triggered by Soviet blundering and policies favoring cities over the countryside in the 1920s. Marxists often had focused their attention on the industrial working class of the cities and treated the peasants like nascent capitalists, the enemy.

As the New Economic Policy began to break down in the mid- to late 1920s, peasants withheld their grain from the markets. Armed detachments again roamed the countryside seeking grain, and force again provoked determined peasant resistance.

The state targeted rich peasants, *kulaks*,[2] attempting to use the poorer peasants against

[2] *kulaks*: KOO lahks

them. When elements of the army and police began to surround peasant villages to force them onto state farms, peasants fought back. Soon, the label *kulak* was applied to anyone opposing collectivization. Peasants died defending their farms; others slaughtered and ate their farm animals rather than permit the state to seize them. Tens of millions of animals perished, and the animal husbandry sector of the Soviet economy did not recover from these losses until the 1950s. Peasant families were split up and parents were sent off to the *gulags*; gangs of homeless children wandered the countryside in search of food and shelter.

By 1934, agriculture had been collectivized at the cost of millions of lives. With control over the peasants and their grain, the state could purchase machinery for the industrial effort, and excessive grain requisitions starved more peasants. The Ukraine was particularly hard hit, and NKVD guards sealed off that area to prevent refugees from escaping. One scholar has estimated that 14 million people died in the human-made famine.

The Stalinist model of industrialization changed Soviet Russia. Heavy industry (like metallurgical plants) dominated the economy, receiving more than 80 percent of state capital. Planners set lofty production goals for five-year plans, and the eventual execution of 90 percent of plant managers sent the message that results were expected. In some areas, trains carrying vital raw materials for manufacturing were hijacked by factory desperados hungry to meet their quotas. *Gulags* became major work centers, their inhabitants erecting factories on and digging canals in inhospitable landscapes.

Cities were transformed during the 1930s as millions of peasants fled the countryside to work in the new factories. Later, however, the state became uneasy about all the free-wandering people, and it issued internal passports regulating movement. Once a worker found a job, the factory provided living quarters and other amenities, such as health care. Change to a new job was limited by the loss of benefits. Within a few years, most laborers in the Soviet Union worked in factories rather than on farms; most lived in cities rather than in the rural areas. The Soviet Union had developed an industrial society by 1936.

The Soviet Union avoided most early fighting in World War II but experienced catastrophic losses, beginning in 1941. Significant fighting began when Nazi Germany invaded in June 1941.

Fierce combat occupied the next four years, ending with Nazi Germany's utter defeat and the Soviet occupation of Eastern Europe. More than 30 million Soviets died, and it took years for their ruptured society and economy to recover.

As noted in Chapter 34, industrialization fostered the development of Soviet imperialism. Between 1939 and 1940, the Soviet Union seized

FIGURE 37.4 *Sentries for the Soviet State. Collectivization reduced peasants to living at near-starvation levels, and millions of people perished in the ensuing famine. To guard harvests, the government adopted severe measures of repression. These young party members are on the lookout for desperate peasants who try to steal some grain or corn from the state.* Endeavour Group U.K.

FIGURE 37.5 *Stalin Celebrating the Constitution. In late 1936, the Soviet state presented a constitution to its people. The constitution promised many freedoms, from improved civil rights to a new electoral system. Despite the fanfare organized by Stalin, the mandates of the constitution were never fulfilled, and many Russians continued to die at the hands of the Soviet police or languish in the gulags.* David King Collection.

Latvia, Lithuania, and Estonia, as well as parts of Poland and Finland. After 1943, when Soviet troops counterattacked the Nazi forces and pushed into Eastern Europe, a series of satellite governments there made up a part of the emerging Soviet Empire. The integration of the economies of these states completed the classic imperialist pattern.

STALIN'S CULTURAL INTERESTS AND IMPERATIVES.

When the Bolsheviks seized power in 1917, they began suppressing elements of the traditional elite arts, and some artists and writers eagerly supported the effort to create a new culture. The new rulers took charge of the libraries and museums, and Lenin's wife, Nadezhda Krupskaya,[3] took a personal interest in cultural matters. She oversaw, for example, the suppression of the writings of Feodor Dostoyevsky. In addition, important Russian figures, like Peter the Great and Ivan the Terrible, were interpreted in Marxist historical categories or ignored. At the same time, avant-garde poets and painters put their talents to use in service of the new revolutionary state. Over time, however, their cultural visions were censored as examples of bourgeois-decadent art.

Stalin continued some of the policies that devalued traditional art and literature. A key element of Stalin's cultural focus was in the development of **socialist realism**, a movement that stressed culture's ties to socialism. Stalin declared that literature must reflect socialist themes and arts must be more accessible to the common folk.

At the same time, Stalin promoted a revival of interest in Russia's past. A major idea behind this effort was a fear of German Nazism and the need to stress themes of Russian patriotism. One movie, *Alexander Nevsky*, focused on the thirteenth-century warrior who defeated Teutonic knights (Germans) seeking to invade and destroy Russia. The movie portrayed Germans as evil baby killers and the Russians as brave heroes repelling all enemies. The stirring musical score of Sergei Prokoviev[4] underlined the patriotic mood of the film. The titanic struggle of Soviet Russia in World War II also brought appeals to Russian nationalism.

Soviet authors and composers suffered from political persecution in the postwar era. A widespread campaign engulfed Jewish writers in the late 1940s, fomenting an anti-Semitism reminiscent of that in tsarist days. Dmitry Shostakovich[5] and Sergei Prokoviev endured alternate vilification and praise, depending on how the political winds were blowing. On one occasion, Andrei Zhdanov,[6] a top Soviet leader, summoned the two world-famous composers and proceeded to give them lessons on the piano.

[3] **Nadezhda Krupskaya:** nah DEHZ dah KROOP skay ah
[4] **Sergei Prokoviev:** SEHR gay proh KOH vee ehv
[5] **Dmitry Shostakovich:** DEE mee tree SHAHS tah koh vihch
[6] **Andrei Zhdanov:** AHN dreh ZHDAH nohv

Stalin's Legacy, 1953–1989

Soviet Russia's industrialization, along with its victory over Nazi forces, propelled it to the forefront of global politics. Control of most of Eastern Europe and parts of Central Europe enhanced the Soviet Union's power. At the same time, the Stalinist system boasted a huge bureaucracy and an authoritarian policy that punished dissent. Could the Soviets adapt to the wide-ranging and rapid changes to come?

Stalin died in March 1953, and Nikita Khrushchev[7] (1894–1971) succeeded him and served as the leader of the Soviet Union until 1964. Among Stalin's successors, Khrushchev struggled mightily to dismantle Stalinism's worst features. He opened the *gulags* and released millions of survivors, breaking decisively with the Stalinist terror. Khrushchev promoted writers like Alexander Solzhenitsyn, who criticized Stalinist excesses. In 1956, Khrushchev gave a secret speech laying bare some of the worst features of the terror, hoping thereby to discredit Stalin and Stalinists, many of whom were Khrushchev's opponents. He also attempted a series of ill-conceived economic reforms that failed. A series of foreign policy gaffes further undermined Khrushchev, who fell from power with the dismantling of Stalinism incomplete.

Leonid Brezhnev (1906–1982) succeeded Khrushchev and implemented an era of neo-Stalinist policies. Massive resources accelerated the buildup of the Soviet armed forces, aiming at the projection of Soviet power. On the other hand, Brezhnev helped develop *detente*, an easing of international tensions through goodwill gestures and negotiated arms-limitation treaties, in the 1970s. The armament buildup, however, severely weakened vital parts of the Soviet health care system. By the early 1980s, the Soviet Union was in serious demographic, economic, and political decline.

Mikhail Gorbachev[8] (b. 1929) came to power in 1985 and presided over the collapse of the Soviet system. Realizing that the Soviet Union could not survive with its aging Stalinist system, Gorbachev attempted to transform the state he inherited. Although a skilled politician who knew when to compromise, Gorbachev lacked the administrative talents and the vision to bring transformative change. He implemented policies of *glasnost* (openness and discussion), as well as *perestroika* (restructuring). Gorbachev intended to create a more humane communism and use the talents of the Soviet people to renew their system but failed. The beginning of the end came in 1989, when Eastern European states broke free from the Soviet Empire. Two years later, the Soviet Union itself collapsed after a failed coup by elements of the secret police, the army, and the party. Nationalism triumphed over imperialism. Economic collapse left unemployment and suffering in the 1990s.

CHINA'S IMPERIAL COLLAPSE AND THE TRIUMPH OF COMMUNISM

Much of the twentieth century was a time of turmoil for the Chinese people, who suffered from wars, revolutions, famine, and natural disasters. The Qing Empire collapsed in 1912, leaving unrest and political disorder. Warlordism caused havoc for Chinese society for more than a decade, and Japanese troops conquered vast regions. Later, the Chinese communists killed the gentry landlords, condemning millions. Since the late 1970s, however, the material well-being of the Chinese has improved significantly.

Imperial China's Systemic Collapse and Warlordism, 1905–1928

The gentry had long dominated Chinese life. Its position was owed to education, especially to a Confucian-based ideology that stressed hierarchical organization in the family and society. Yet China needed to modernize in order to survive in the intense international rivalries of the early twentieth century. In fact, much of China lay under foreign influence at the turn of the century, and many of its financial assets came under foreign control. To adapt, the Qing Empire decided in 1905 to abolish the imperial examination system, because its Confucian ideology seemed incompatible with the needs of modernity.

The elimination of Confucianism as the state value system brought many consequences. Confucianism supported an agrarian economy and

[7] **Nikita Khrushchev:** nih KEE tah KRUH shahv
[8] **Mikhail Gorbachev:** MEEK hayl GOHR bah shahv

despised the merchant class, retarding industrialization. Young people and women who were devalued in the Confucian system now had fewer restraints on their efforts to improve themselves.

Other Manchu reforms undermined the central government's legitimacy and hastened its collapse. One program directed more local tax monies to the national capital. This angered some provincial authorities, who took advantage of an uprising against the Manchus to secede from the empire. The Manchus also promised to implement a constitutional government, but their ineptness at handling the program spurred Chinese nationalism. Anti-Manchu forces toppled the Qing Dynasty in 1912.

Efforts to reunite China failed in the next decade or so, highlighting the profound nature of the collapse of the imperial system. Twice, ambitious individuals failed to reestablish imperial rule.

The military nature of Chinese politics from 1912 to 1928 has caused scholars to name it the Warlord Period. Militarization of Chinese politics had begun in the mid–nineteenth century. After 1912, however, force became the primary determinant of Chinese politics and was reflected in the phrase "political power grows out of the barrel of a gun." Numerous warlord regimes in various parts of China worsened the living conditions of the Chinese people. Taxes grew very heavy with burdensome special levies. Some warlords demanded that taxes for future years be paid early, and others compelled peasants to grow and harvest opium poppies. Starvation became common, and a famine from 1929 to 1932 took 3 million lives.

Peasant anger seethed in the 1920s and 1930s, fueled by gentry disinterest in traditional practices of promoting welfare policies. Landowners who previously might have aided destitute people had moved to the cities and left management of their estates to people who cursed rather than helped poor folk.

In 1915, a few intellectuals initiated a movement that helped transform the traditional elite-based culture. The New Culture Movement aimed at incorporating Western ideas, like science and democracy, into a different Chinese culture. Many of these people were given positions at Beijing University, spreading ideas through teaching as well as through writing.

On May 4, 1919, news that the Chinese delegation to the Versailles Peace Conference had agreed to Japanese demands for territorial concessions in China sparked demonstrations. Angry Chinese students, merchants, and other city folk vented their frustration against Beijing's warlord government. The resulting May Fourth Movement unleashed Chinese nationalism and political activism, and some of the New Culture Movement leaders became key figures in the May Fourth Movement.

The Bolsheviks of Soviet Russia founded the Communist International (Comintern) in 1919 to promote nationalist and socialist parties in colonies around the world. Comintern agents helped found the Japanese, Indochinese, Indonesian, and Chinese communist parties. In China, Comintern activists met May Fourth Movement leaders and others, creating the momentum to found the Chinese Communist Party in 1921.

Comintern agents also aided the reorganization of the Nationalist Party under the leadership of Sun Zhongshan (Sun Yat-sen, 1866–1925). Sun had been a leader of the movement that helped bring down the Qing government in 1912 but grew disenchanted with politics. In the early 1920s, he worked out an alliance with Comintern agents, who provided money, experts in organizational techniques, weapons, and the means to found the Whampoa Military Academy, where many of China's future leaders and military officers were trained.

By 1926, the Nationalists opened a military campaign to defeat the warlords and reunite China. Within two years, the effort commanded by Jiang Jieshi[9] (Chiang Kai-shek, 1887–1975) succeeded, and he ousted communists from his ranks and launched a terror campaign against them. Jiang used military force, and the communists did not have the means to defend themselves. The Warlord Period ended, but military affairs continued to dominate Chinese politics until 1949.

Mao Zedong and the Peasants, 1928–1947

Mao Zedong[10] (1894–1976) grew up in the Chinese countryside, the son of a well-to-do peasant. He became an intellectual and taught briefly, but his main talent was for politics. During Mao's college

[9] **Jiang Jieshi:** JEE yahng JEE yeh shur
[10] **Mao Zedong:** MOW zeh DONG

FIGURE 37.6 *Jiang Jieshi Assuming Sun Zhongshan's Mantle of Leadership.* *At the top of this poster is a likeness of Sun Zhongshan, China's leader who died in 1925. Below Sun, Jiang Jieshi raises his sword and leads his troops off to war. As commander of communist and nationalist troops, Jiang carried out Sun's dream of uniting China by force during the Northern Expedition of 1926–1928. Posters like this one helped Jiang to become the most powerful leader in the Nationalist Party.* R. B. Fleming.

days, China experienced a cultural flowering that stressed Western ideas. Mao himself was strongly influenced by these ideas and practices, helping to found the communist movement in China. As the direction of the party came from Moscow, Soviet leaders insisted on China's proletariat as the favored revolutionary class. Despite the fact that Chinese workers constituted only a tiny percentage of the population, the Chinese communists successfully developed an urban movement of workers, students, intellectuals, and women. Yet Jiang Jieshi's purge of 1927 severely crippled the communists, especially in the cities. During the mid-1920s, Mao saw that the peasants' difficult lives and their willingness to listen made them a revolutionary force. He began organizing them

and was ordered to lead them in an uprising in September 1927. It failed, and Mao with about 1,000 followers fled to eastern mountains.

THE JIANGXI REVOLUTIONARY BASE AND THE LONG MARCH. Mao joined with a group of talented military and political leaders in the local mountains. There, he formed his plan: build a base area of peasant supporters, create a revolutionary army, and seek widespread popular support. The mountains held few people, so Mao moved into Jiangxi[11] Province, where he established a base area.

Mao's land program showed key elements of his revolutionary strategy. He involved peasants in

[11] **Jiangxi:** JEE yahng shee

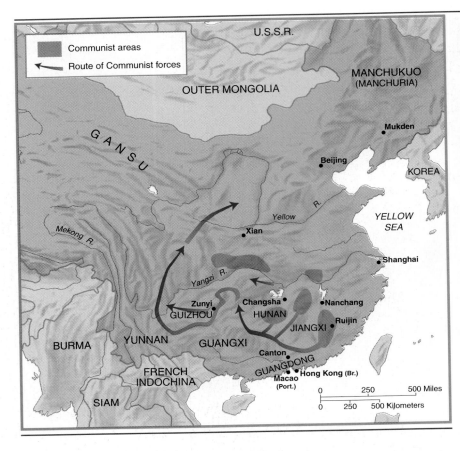

MAP 37.3 *The Long March.* The Chinese Communist Party fled the Nationalist army led by Jiang Jieshi. The Long March, an epic event that lasted a year, traversed several thousand miles. The communists crossed many remote parts of China, some controlled by ethnic minorities. They also passed through difficult terrain, including rugged mountains and seemingly forbidding marshlands. Only a few thousand people survived, but they became the party elite.

transferring land from the gentry landlords to the rural poor. In addition, the army played a key role in securing territory within which to work. After an area became secure, the communists organized the have-nots into land committees that directed the process. Communists surveyed the land and property in a village and published the results, showing who owned what. After a period of adjustment, a land committee published a list of who was to receive land and other kinds of property. Another period of adjustment followed, and then property changed hands. Each person received something, according to formulas based on age, and a family might accumulate more or less depending on its size. One section of land was reserved for the army, and its proceeds assisted war widows and orphans, as well as crippled veterans. This, of course, rooted the army firmly in the rural communities. Land transformation procedures varied somewhat over the area the communists controlled, but the general program remained intact.

Mao controlled the Jiangxi base for a few years before he was overthrown by a party faction backed by the Soviet Union. For the remaining several months of the base's existence, Mao was a kind of exile with little to do. From 1930 to 1934, the Nationalist Army, commanded by Jiang Jieshi, attempted to destroy the Jiangxi base area. Mao successfully led three campaigns against the Nationalists, and two more were commanded by Mao's Soviet-backed opponents. In the summer of 1934, the Nationalist assault on the Jiangxi base area had severely reduced the area controlled by the communists, and the land-shifting program was undone. A few months later, the whole area fell to the Nationalists. Fortune smiled on Mao because the Nationalist conquest of the base area discredited the Soviet-backed faction.

The communists broke out of the encirclement and began the Long March (1934–1935). The epic trek lasted for about a year, and the communists traversed around 6,000 miles of difficult terrain on foot. Perhaps 90,000 people began the march and fewer than 20,000 finally arrived in North China, but those who survived became a special elite in the communist movement. Top leaders formed a close-knit alliance that lasted for more than two decades. Finally, Mao Zedong became the head of the Communist Party and remained its leader until his death in 1976. He emerged from the Long March ordeal convinced of his leadership abilities and certain that with his leadership the Chinese Communist Party could accomplish anything.

The march's first phase lasted until January 1935 with many battles against the pursuing Nationalists. Heavy casualties were borne by the communists, and the capture of a district capital in a remote province gave them a brief respite. There communist leaders debated the events of the past year and the destination of the marchers. During

these meetings, a consensus emerged that gave Mao party control.

Mao led the marchers through remote parts of China to get away from the pursuing Nationalists. The communists crossed rugged mountains and a marshland 90 miles long. The marsh was dotted with treacherous bogs and a corrosive soil that inhibited sleeping on the ground. Haggard survivors emerged at their destination in the fall of 1935.

WAR AND REVOLUTION. From 1936 to 1949, the communists built a formidable movement and conquered China. In the process, they benefited from the chaotic conditions unleashed by warfare and came to power with support from China's peasantry. Indeed, the success of the Chinese Revolution depended in large part on World War II

FIGURE 37.7 *Mao Zedong. From 1935 on, the Chinese Communist Party came increasingly under the control of Mao Zedong. In this 1938 photo, Mao speaks to a group of party and army leaders in Yan'an. Following the defeat of Japan in 1945, the northern Chinese city became the communists' headquarters during their war against the nationalist government. It was during the Yan'an years that Mao wrote his major works and developed his style of mobilizing and educating the people of China.* Wide World Photos.

(1939–1945) and the ensuing Chinese Civil War (1946–1949).

On July 7, 1937, Japan and China went to war after a firefight between their forces at the Marco Polo Bridge in North China. During the war, the Chinese Communist Party refined its land policies and encouraged anti-Japanese nationalism among China's peasants. Thus, the communist movement grew from a tiny size to major dimensions largely because of active peasant support. By the war's end, the Communist Party and its army numbered about 1 million members each, and the population under their control totaled in the tens of millions.

The Chinese Civil War erupted in 1946 with heavy fighting across China. In that conflict, the communists enjoyed superior leadership, effective intelligence operations, excellent military strategy, and active peasant support. Most of this support came through the Land Law of 1947, which guaranteed peasants land and targeted the landlord class for destruction. The Nationalists fell from power, partly because inflation devastated their urban support base. During the decisive campaigns of 1948 and 1949, the Nationalists lost more than 1.5 million soldiers and never recovered.

The Chinese Communist Party and government in North China went through a program of thought reform in the early 1940s. Although an intellectual, Mao distrusted his educated peers; he identified more closely with peasantry, which he believed harbored much wisdom. To Mao, academics seemed snobbish and distant from the common people, those who could effect a revolution. In addition, Mao distrusted bureaucrats, who often tyrannized people coming to them for assistance. These beliefs lay behind the thought reform campaign of 1942 to 1944, when Mao and other top officials remolded the thinking of communist elite group members.

The thought reform process involved a painful self-examination and ultimately resulted in the release of powerful psychological forces. Small groups read and discussed common writings (mostly by Mao). Then, in an orchestrated campaign, one group member endured a session of criticism by peers. These meetings severely upset people, who feared losing face. Usually self-criticism resulted, and after verification of the sincerity of the "confession" and rehabilitation, attention shifted to the next member. Some behav-

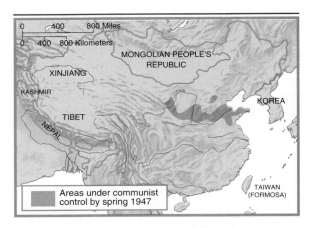

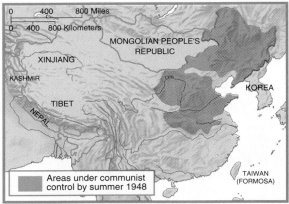

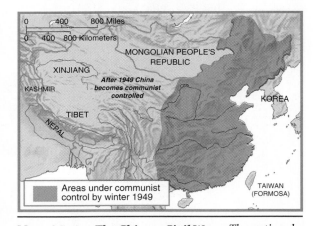

MAP 37.4 **The Chinese Civil War.** *The nationalists and communists fought a war that lasted from 1946 to 1949. Millions died and millions more were injured. The communists often controlled rural areas in Central and Northeast China. The nationalists controlled the major cities until 1948. Over time, peasant support and skilled leadership by the communists brought a victory over the nationalists. Only Taiwan remained under nationalist control after 1949.*

FIGURE 37.8 *Chinese Socialist Realism.* *After the communists established the People's Republic of China, they encouraged artists to depict examples of the tyranny of the previous government. A remarkable series titled "The Rent Collection Courtyard" appeared. In this lifesize sculpture, peasants line up to pay rent to a local landlord. Clothed in traditional garb, the peasants are observed by a figure dressed in Western clothing. While the peasants are weighed down by their burdens, the watcher, flanked by a well-fed dog, carries nothing heavier than a fan.* Sovfoto/Eastfoto.

ior modification occurred, and a kind of commonality of elite behavior emerged.

At the same time, Mao grew upset with intellectuals, who criticized the communists. Ding Ling[12] (1907–1985) was a writer who enjoyed a literary reputation before she came to the communist base in the late 1930s, where she worked in the propaganda division. By 1942, Ding Ling became uneasy about the conditions under which she worked, and she wrote literary pieces critical of male criticism of female activists and their lifestyles. The writings became controversial and helped spur Mao to deliver two addresses on literature and art. In these talks, Mao expressed the

Marxist belief that art must serve the revolutionary cause. Accordingly, literature and art must be optimistic in tone and critical of noncommunists rather than of communists. "Art for art's sake" and such ideas as the "intellectual as critic" could not be tolerated by the communists. Ding Ling underwent criticism and self-criticism before mass audiences until she was "rectified."

Elimination of the Gentry and Collectivization, 1947–1961

Beginning in 1947, the Land Law implemented a program of taking gentry property and distributing it to the poor. Although the effort ensured active peasant support of communist programs, its other

[12] **Ding Ling:** DIHNG LIHNG

aim was to wipe out gentry influence. The gentry had dominated China for centuries, and it lay in the path of the communist power hopes. Land campaigns strongly resembled those in the Jiangxi base area more than a decade earlier, except that violence occurred more often. Aroused villagers criticized and frequently killed their landlords, many of whom had tyrannized them. The process lasted into the early 1950s. Precise figures are not available, though the communists themselves admit to more than 2 million deaths. Landlord domination of society, agriculture, politics, and elite culture disappeared. Survivors of the onslaught usually had enough to live on, but their descendants were seldom permitted to forget their class origins. Destruction of the gentry left a vacuum in the countryside that was soon filled by the communists. Imperial governments had needed a few thousand officials to rule China because gentry landlords served as "unofficial officials." Communists now needed millions of **cadres**, officials and activists under party direction, to rule China.

As in Soviet Russia, the land transfers were the onset of a lengthy process to increase production. Unlike the Stalinists, however, the Maoists treated the peasants with more persuasion and less violence. The first stage of collectivization involved mutual-aid teams composed of around five families each. These units kept their family property but shared labor and draft animals. The next stage melded groups of perhaps village size (cooperatives). Land remained in private hands, though labor was shared. As labor resources increased, wells were dug and small irrigation systems were constructed. By the mid-1950s, cooperatives were merged into larger units of hundreds, if not thousands, of families. At that stage most private property was turned over to the cooperative, but peasants were permitted to keep garden plots. The massive labor pool also enabled large-scale construction projects.

In 1958, Mao became disenchanted with the pace of collectivization and the dearth of financial resources committed to agriculture. The Stalinist industrial model used by China exploited agriculture and brought into being a massive, centralized bureaucracy. In addition, Mao, who visited a rural collective that resulted from merging many cooperatives, believed that this gigantic unit of tens of thousands of people could solve many of China's economic problems. The new organization was called a **commune**, and it became the model for rural China. Mao envisioned communalism as the first stage of communism and asserted that China could move directly into communism instead of going through socialism. In other words, China—not Russia—had the potential to lead revolution on a global scale.

China's leaders backed Mao and drove the peasants into a frenzied campaign of mergers. Remaining private land was turned over to the commune, mess halls and nurseries were constructed to free women from some of their domestic duties, and top officials promoted the idea of peasants producing iron and steel in backyard foundries. Peasants melted down their iron pots and pans and bedsteads in an attempt to make steel. The effort failed, and the scrap proved worthless.

Cadres bent to the enormous pressures of their superiors, compelling peasants to work long hours to attain production targets. When lofty goals could not be reached, cadres fudged the data. As the inflated figures reached the national planners, exuberant officials proclaimed that China had reached self-sufficiency in grain output. Later, checking uncovered the deception, and the resulting embarrassment spurred bureaucrats to keep quiet and not divulge production statistics.

The policy of sparrow control best symbolizes the human failure of the Great Leap Forward, an attempt to increase industrial and agricultural production rapidly. Some communist officials decided to eliminate five types of pests, including grain-eating sparrows. People banged on metal at night, causing the panicked birds to fly until they died of exhaustion. Truckloads of sparrows were carted off by the state. What the communists learned, of course, was that the sparrows ate insects that consumed grain—and without the natural environmental check, much more grain was lost to insect pests.

Combining with human error was a rare spate of bad weather. Three years of natural calamities brought China to the brink of massive starvation by 1960. In recent years, scholars have estimated that more than 20 million people perished. As young people are more vulnerable to the afflictions of malnutrition, they suffered disproportionate losses in the early 1960s. The government finally admitted defeat and disbanded the communes. It took years for peasants to recover.

Industrialization and the Intellectuals, 1949–1978

Communist control of urban China came in 1949, and, because of the lack of personnel to run large cities, the new government retained a high percentage of Nationalist Party officials. The communists also established committees, organized city block by city block, to help control people.

The block committees gradually controlled China's cities. Composed largely of women who had adult children, these organizations informed their block members of hygienic and safety measures, helped identify prostitutes and enemy agents, and aided the government in educating people about political matters. Once in place, the committees helped eradicate prostitution, drug use and sales, various diseases, and so on. In the 1980s, they became a major part of the state effort to ensure a one-child-per-family policy by keeping tabs on the menstrual cycles of the women in their blocks. If a female became pregnant, the block committee members pressured her (if she already had a child) to seek an abortion.

The early years of the new government were spent in rebuilding war-ravaged China. Inflation was controlled until the late 1980s. Facilities were repaired, and roads and railroads were built or rebuilt as necessary.

By 1953, the state decided to industrialize. Officials followed the Stalinist model of concentrating on heavy industry, relegating agriculture to a minor economic role. After five years, China had achieved impressive production results, but problems troubled Mao and helped him decide on the Great Leap Forward program. An economic disaster, it idled about one-half of China's factories by the early 1960s. Production improved by the mid-

---

PATHS TO THE PAST

The Use of History for Political Ends in China

Chinese scholars and artists have often turned to China's past to criticize policies and monarchs who initiated them because they dared not attack their own autocrat lords. In the mid–eighth century, the poet Du Fu[a] (710–770) wrote an antiwar ballad criticizing two early Chinese rulers who had warred until their soldiers and people became destitute. Du Fu could not criticize his own sovereign, who was following similar policies.

In the early 1960s, Wu Han,[b] a playwright and deputy mayor of Beijing, wrote a play, *Hai Rui Dismissed from Office*. It concerned an honest official who lived in the sixteenth century and who had been fired because an emperor listened to Hai Rui's corrupt enemies rather than to the exemplary official. The play performed to packed houses in the capital, and rumors circulated that it was a veiled attack on Chairman Mao Zedong, who had fired his defense minister, Peng Dehuai, two years earlier. Mao had launched the Great Leap Forward (1958–1961), a dis-astrous policy that had been strongly criticized by Peng. Mao retaliated against his critic by firing him, just as the emperor had fired his honest official in the sixteenth century.

The play was performed in the early 1960s until a critic launched a broadside attack against it in late 1965. The critic accused the dramatist of criticizing Mao by using a historical event to make his point. Mao himself supported the charges and ordered an investigation. Nothing happened, and Mao surmised that a plot involving the deputy mayor, the mayor of Beijing, and others protected the playwright. These actions began the Cultural Revolution, which would convulse China for a decade.

Deng Xiaoping, who had been an ally of the mayor and deputy mayor, also fell from power in the Cultural Revolution but survived to head the People's Republic of China after Mao's death in 1976. The critic of the deputy mayor went on trial, accused of helping launch the Cultural Revolution and causing the deaths of many innocent people. He was convicted and given a life prison sentence. The play resumed production in the capital and once again played to packed houses.

[a] **Du Fu:** DOO FOO
[b] **Wu Han:** WOO hahn

1960s but slumped again in the late 1960s. A working class also emerged, with each worker controlled by a work unit that governed one's housing, food, education, and social benefits, like health care. The state also controlled the movement of its people and shifted millions of Chinese to the border regions in order to secure the areas inhabited by minority peoples.

Intellectuals suffered periods of tension at the hands of a government that needed their talents but distrusted their views. In 1956 and 1957, Mao grew troubled by the large number of bureaucrats and what he felt were their arrogant ways. He decided to use the intellectuals in a campaign to criticize officials, encouraging the intellectuals to speak out. The event known as the Hundred Flowers Campaign of 1957 slowly elicited a response by intellectuals. Although Mao believed that sharp criticisms could be exposed and blunted through debate, most institutions and practices suffered from a withering commentary. In early June, Mao turned against the intellectuals and ordered a campaign against "rightists," those who had criticized. Around 500,000 people lost their jobs and were ordered to undergo reform through manual labor. Ding Ling was charged with various crimes and subjected to a twenty-year sentence at hard labor in Northeast China.

A second major upheaval involving intellectuals erupted about a decade later. This time Mao used young students to attack officials and elite groups who held anti-Mao sentiments. The Cultural Revolution (1966–1976) convulsed China; schools closed and government offices were taken

FIGURE 37.9 *Red Guards Parading a Victim.* *During the Cultural Revolution, the Red Guards roamed China's cities, looking for enemies of Mao Zedong. This 1967 photo shows an official, accused of being an antirevolutionary, who has been forced to wear a dunce cap detailing his crimes against the people. Many officials and intellectuals were paraded and beaten by the Red Guards. By early 1967, many of China's cities were in chaos.* Wide World Photos.

FIGURE 37.10 *Deng Xiaoping and the Military.* *Like many of his contemporaries, Deng Xiaoping fought in China's wars of the 1930s and 1940s, gaining the respect and loyalty of many military commanders. During the Tiananmen days of May–June 1989, Deng called on some of these leaders to help crush the student-led protests.* Wide World Photos.

over by Red Guards claiming allegiance to Mao's dictates. Anarchic conditions led to the army's being used to restore order. In the process, Mao purged many of his enemies in the party and government, and hundreds of thousands of people died. After that time, the state took a milder view of intellectuals until 1989, when it crushed the student-led demonstrations centered on the square at Tiananmen[13] (Gate of Heavenly Peace).

Economic Growth, 1978–1989

Deng Xiaoping[14] (1904–1997), a victim of the Cultural Revolution purges, reascended the political summit in 1977 and directed an economic recovery that lasted into the 1990s. The extent of Deng's power may be measured by the fact that during the 1980s and early 1990s, he held no official position yet wielded decisive power on critical matters.

[13]**Tiananmen:** TEE yehn AHN mehn
[14]**Deng Xiaoping:** DUHNG SHEE YOW peeng

Mao's death in 1976 afforded Deng the opportunity to revive his political fortunes. Deng built a team dedicated to loosening controls over the economy. Peasants received plots of land and a state guarantee of noninterference with their use of the land. By 1985, these measures helped transform Chinese agriculture to produce more than 400 million tons of grain, an amount sufficient to feed its people. Soon special economic zones dotted China's coast, where private factories operated. China encouraged foreign investment and promoted trade, and since 1978 it has enjoyed one of the world's fastest economic growth rates, becoming one of the world's largest economies.

At the same time, Deng permitted the Chinese little political freedom. Indeed, two of his successors were replaced after tolerating individual expression and student criticism of the state. Massive gatherings in the square at Tiananmen provoked memories of the Cultural Revolution's anarchistic upheaval, and Deng ordered the Chinese army to crush the demonstration movement.

RUSSIA	CHINA		
		1900	
Russian Empire, 1725–1917		–	
		–	Upheaval in Russia, 1905
		–	
		–	
		1910	
		–	Qing Empire collapses, 1912
	Warlord Era, 1912–1928	–	Bolsheviks take power, 1917
Russian Civil War, 1918–1921	New Culture Movement, 1915–1919	–	May 4, 1919, Incident
		1920	
New Economic Policy, 1921–1929		–	
		–	
		–	
		–	Stalin in power, 1929
Collectiv-ization, 1929–1936		**1930**	
Industrial-ization, c. 1930–1941	Japanese militarism in China, 1931–1945	–	Long March begins, 1934
		–	
		–	
		1940	
		–	
Soviet Empire, 1940–1989		–	
		–	Communists take power in China, 1949
	Chinese Civil War, 1946–1949	–	Treaty of Moscow, 1950
		1950	North Korea invades South Korea, June 25, 1950
		–	Stalin dies, 1953
Political thaw, 1953–1964		–	Great Leap Forward begins, 1958
	Great Leap Forward, 1958–1961	**1960**	
		–	Khrushchev falls, 1964
Neo-Stalinism, 1964–1985	Cultural Revolution, 1966–1976	–	
		1970	
		–	Detente begins, 1973
		–	Mao Zedong dies, 1976
		–	Deng Xiaoping in power, 1977
	Market socialism, 1978–present	**1980**	
		–	Mikhail Gorbachev in power, 1984
		–	Tiananmen massacre, 1989
		–	

SUMMARY

1. The Russian tsarist system could not survive the wars of the early twentieth century and the incompetence of Nicholas II. It collapsed in March 1917, ushering in a time of anarchistic chaos that the Bolsheviks exploited.

2. Vladimir Lenin provided the strategic vision that carried his communist party, the Bolsheviks, to victory in the Bolshevik Revolution of 1917–1924. He and his fellow party members destroyed the remnants of the tsarist system and began building a socialist state. Civil war taxed the Bolsheviks and their subjects, who intensified a drive to centralize the state. After victory in 1921, Lenin relaxed state controls.

3. Lenin's death brought a party crisis of leadership that ended with Josef Stalin's victory in 1929. Stalin collectivized the peasantry and industrialized the economy. Both measures gave Soviet Russia great-power status at a cost of tens of millions of lives. Terror also purged Stalin's rivals.

4. Soviet industrialization led to socialist imperialism as the Russians claimed several Baltic states and controlled many in Eastern Europe. All economies were carefully integrated into the Soviet economy.

5. Stalin's death brought to power two reformers, Nikita Khrushchev and Mikhail Gorbachev, neither of whom successfully transformed the Stalinist system.

6. In China, Manchu rulers undermined their government by abolishing the examination system. The Qing Empire collapsed and left China in chaos with warlord rule.

7. Early efforts to create a communist movement in China's cities failed under the terrorist onslaught of the Nationalist forces commanded by Jiang Jieshi. Mao Zedong organized peasant groups to promote revolution and undertook land reform as well. He developed a successful communist strategy that led to victory.

8. The communists destroyed the gentry and collectivized China's peasants at the cost of millions of lives. The communists also gained control of China's cities, partly through the establishment of block committees dominated by women.

9. Intellectuals had been harnessed for state purposes. Mao, in particular, distrusted them, although he used them against the officials in the Hundred Flowers Campaign and in the Cultural Revolution.

10. Deng Xiaoping survived two purges and emerged as China's leader in 1977. He promoted policies of permitting individual initiative for the peasants and entrepreneurs. These programs launched China on a course of economic change.

SUGGESTED READINGS

Fairbank, John. *The Great Chinese Revolution.* Cambridge, Mass.: Harvard University Press, 1986. A classic history of modern China.

Ferro, Mark. *Nicholas II.* Oxford, Eng.: Oxford University Press, 1991. An excellent recent biography of Russia's last tsar.

Fitzpatrick, Sheila. *The Russian Revolution.* Oxford, Eng.: Oxford University Press, 1994. A social history of the Bolshevik and Stalinist revolutions.

Swain, Geoffrey. *The Origins of the Russian Civil War.* London: Longman House, 1996. A provocative study of the Russian Civil War.

Wolf, Margery. *Revolution Postponed.* Stanford, Calif.: Stanford University Press, 1985. An examination of the fate of Chinese women under the Chinese communists.

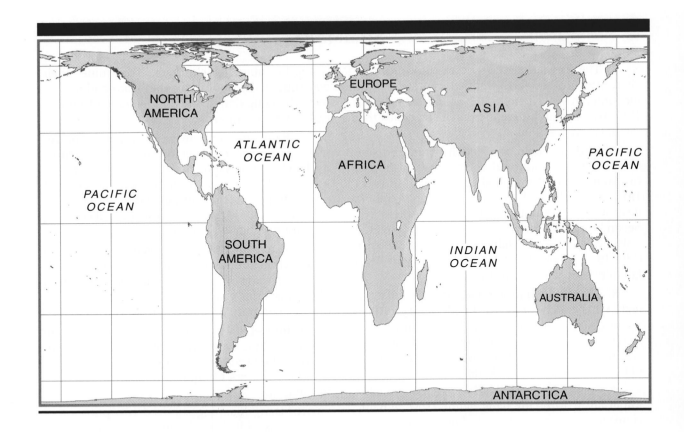

The Great Depression

1929–1941

Reiko Yamanaka had survived, barely. Her son, Jiro, had died in Asia during the last war, and her daughter, Keiko, perished from consumption (tuberculosis) and venereal disease; she had been a prostitute in Osaka, after having lost her job in a silk-spinning mill there. Last week, Reiko's husband passed away from some fever, but she knew he died of a broken heart.

So many people were out of work, and farmers suffered from falling prices. Orphans wandered silently, and old people lay in their homes, hungry like her. Japanese politicians promised help but did nothing, while a new war loomed. As a schoolgirl, she had bowed to the emperor's portrait. What could he do for her now?

In the 1930s, a worldwide depression devastated economies, governments, and societies. While some individuals prospered, many more suffered as jobs became scarce and economic return on investments plummeted or disappeared. When the economic crisis unfolded, the instinctive reaction of some countries was to protect themselves, even if that meant harming the interests of other countries. Along with the dire nature of the depression came general ignorance about its causes and how to get out of it. In fact, many early policies caused more economic problems than they solved. Only the governments of the Nazis and Soviets managed to avoid the dire consequences of the depression. While various policies in other countries made inroads against the depression, most countries emerged from the depression only during World War II.

THE DEPRESSION'S CONTEXT AND CAUSES

A **depression** is an economic downturn involving long-term production drops, widespread unemployment, and **deflation** (a steep drop in prices and wages). In many ways, the Great Depression from 1929 to 1941 was unprecedented because, while there had been business downturns in the past, they had not combined with general production losses, massive unemployment, social unrest, and a steep drop in prices. In fact, the Great Depression was a significant contraction of industrial capitalism that reached crisis proportions.

An Integrated Global Economy

Prior to 1500, regional economies had existed in different parts of the world, but when Europeans began trading overseas, economic interconnectedness grew. In the late eighteenth century, the Industrial Revolution transformed economies, bringing them into close contact with client states and colonies. Indeed, by 1929 there was an interrelationship of production and commerce with great volume and complexity that constituted a different global economic order. Unfortunately, neither political leaders nor economic experts understood this.

The Industrial Revolution brought periodic downswings and upswings in the nineteenth century. While these depressions had been recognized and commented upon as early as the 1860s, no one knew precisely what caused them or how they might be avoided. One global downturn lasted from 1873 to 1896. This deflation accompanied general increases in production with sporadic surges and drops in industrial output.

By the twentieth century, the global economy offered prospects and problems for world leaders. The integrated international economy increasingly meant that there were few independent economies. In addition, economic problems in one country affected other countries, and economic policies in one country had repercussions throughout the world. Because neither economists nor policymakers realized these relationships fully, they often followed policies that benefited their own countries at the expense of others. These leaders failed to understand that they were facing a global problem.

Connections with World War I

Although the Great Depression hit more than a decade after World War I ended, the war contributed to the depression's onset. Immense war destruction, especially in France and other parts of Europe, took many years to repair. Financial costs of the war also hindered economic recovery in Europe. Britain failed to recognize the significant losses incurred by its wartime policies. Seeking to recapture some of Britain's prewar reputation, banks returned their country to the gold standard in 1925. An artificially high value placed on British currency severely hampered exports until dire financial conditions forced the abandonment of the gold standard in 1931.

Another war-related factor involved agricultural production. Because many countries heavily committed to the fighting took resources and laborers from agriculture, they had to rely on imports of grain and other commodities. The United States, Canada, and Australia, among others, significantly increased their own production levels to supply their allies and to make profits. After the war's end, the European combatants resumed grain production without a corresponding decline in the other countries. Surpluses accumulated and drove down agricultural prices through the rest of the 1920s. Various government schemes to decrease production and raise prices failed, and between 1925 and 1929 prices for key agricultural goods dropped by 40 percent on a global scale.

Raw materials suffered similar gluts and price declines in the 1920s. Some came from shifts in wartime production and the return of traditional producers after the war; others stemmed from different factors, such as general overproduction by exporting countries.

Both Japan and the United States benefited from the industrial production vacuum owing to the war. They suffered no major war losses at home, and their healthy industries became major suppliers to the world. Prior to 1914, Japan and the United States had had unfavorable trade balances (the difference between the amount of goods a country exports and imports in a year). If the amount of exports is greater than the amount of imports, the trade balance is favorable, a condition national leaders strive hard to promote.

During World War I, Japan and the United States became major arms exporters, and they loaned money to European nations. One major development of World War I was the United States' emergence as a world power. In fact, the United States was by far the dominant economic power; it produced 40 percent of the world's industrial products, a figure more than twice the combined production of Germany and Britain. Yet the United States failed to realize that its dominant global trade position meant economic leadership and responsibility. Many U.S. policies exhibited economically nationalist tendencies, harming other nations and worsening the depression.

FIGURE 38.1 *"Black Thursday."* *This print by William Gropper starkly depicts the panic and horror of stockbrokers as they face the 1929 collapse of the stock market. Beside the tumbling ticker-tape, one man prepares to take his life rather than face further news of his ruin.* Library of Congress.

Policy Inhibitions

Political leaders around the world had little economic training and tended to be ignorant about the causes of the Great Depression and what means should be employed to end it. Even economists did not agree on the causes and remedies of the Great Depression. Furthermore, the prevailing political wisdom perceived that **inflation**, a period of sharply rising prices, was the chief cause of economic devastation. Most leaders believed that Germany's severe inflation of the previous decade had wrecked German society. Consequently, politicians and economists fought inflation in the 1930s, though deflation was actually occurring. This misperception exacerbated the economic downturn.

Another government imperative was to balance annual budgets by cutting expenditures and raising taxes. Few realized that tax increases reduced disposable income that normally might purchase products. Governmental deficits might be the price of putting people back to work.

NORTH AMERICAN, EUROPEAN, AND ASIAN DEPRESSIONS AND RESPONSES

The Great Depression affected many countries, but we will focus on the examples of a few countries in North America, Europe, and Asia. They attempted in various ways to end their depressions and rehabilitate their societies.

The Depression's Onset

Two events, the stock market crash and the passage of the Hawley-Smoot Tariff, triggered the Great Depression, and they both highlighted international ramifications of the economic collapse. The crash of the U.S. stock market in October and November 1929 ushered in psychological and financial factors of the Great Depression.

The stock market crash resulted from speculative investing and helped lead to a crisis of economic confidence. Many U.S. investors played the stock market in the late 1920s. They were lured by the general surge in stock prices and indulged in buying stocks with borrowed money, taking great risks that share prices might drop sharply. When the market declined precipitously in October, many could not pay their losses and went bankrupt. A drop of stock share prices by 40 percent between September and November 1929 also dampened consumer confidence. Because much of the United States economy was driven by the spending of private citizens, cautionary buying seriously hurt economic growth.

Passage of the Hawley-Smoot Tariff by the U.S. Congress in 1930 gravely affected foreign economies. Goods from abroad were hit by high tariffs that made them more expensive than American products. While this policy of economic nationalism may have benefited U.S. workers, it harmed America's consumers, who paid more for the goods they purchased. More important, it severely harmed those countries that relied heavily on exports for economic well-being. At the same time, this economic shortsightedness sparked similar actions by America's trading partners.

The U.S. Federal Reserve banking system, which supervised the U.S. economy, also had a role in worsening the early effects of the depression. The Federal Reserve policy of raising interest rates was designed to attract foreign investments in the United States, but it also brought deflation. As a side effect, Federal Reserve actions weakened European currencies, harming European banks and deepening the world depression.

Canada, which depended on exports of grain, raw materials, and semifinished goods, suffered from the U.S. stock market crash and the implementation of the Hawley-Smoot Tariff. Canada's maritime provinces experienced a sharp decline in the fishing industry and coal and steel manufacturing centers. The shrinking demand for Canadian grain devastated prairie states, which were later hit by drought and swarms of grasshoppers. By 1933, around 23 percent of Canada's labor force was unemployed, a staggering increase from the 3 percent unemployment rate in 1929.

Germany's Weimar Republic (1919–1933) came to power and weathered crises, many of

FIGURE 38.2 *Unemployed Workers Riding the Rails.* *Canada suffered a heavy loss of jobs during the Great Depression, and in the summer of 1935 unemployed workers organized a protest ride to Ottawa. In this photo, the riders change trains at Kamloops. The government forced the riders off the train in Regina, ending their ride with bloodshed.* Photo by the Toronto Star Syndicate.

which were economic. Part of World War I's peace settlement forced upon Weimar Germany was the payment of war reparations determined in 1921. News of the reparations triggered a massive inflation, wherein payments had to be made by wagonloads of nearly worthless money. Germany had worked its way out of the severe inflationary times of the early 1920s and relied on short-term loans to underwrite public works programs that reduced social tensions and helped economic welfare. When U.S. sources of credit dried up in 1929, partly because of the American stock market's upheaval, the main source of German money evaporated. With economic downturn and loss of external credit, German banks began to fail, and the public works programs shut down. Between 1930 and 1931, German unemployment rapidly grew by 4 million people, and a general crisis rocked the Weimar Republic.

France endured a relatively mild but prolonged depression. A devaluation of the franc (the French monetary unit) in the late 1920s kept French products competitive into 1930, a prosperous year. Furthermore, French producers were less dependent on exports than their counterparts in other countries. Thus, only about 2.6 percent of French workers were unemployed during the depression. Social unrest, however, in the form of strikes and demonstrations by political factions, festered.

Japan suffered from the economic troubles in the United States. The United States had been a major market for Japanese exports, and when economic problems hit the United States, Japan's exports plummeted. Particularly troublesome was the reduction of raw silk purchases by U.S. manufacturers. This factor brought on the Japanese depression, sparking labor unrest and terrorism by paramilitary groups that threatened the political system.

China was less hard hit by depression than Japan. In 1928, the Nationalist Army under com-

FIGURE 38.3 *Japanese Labor Unrest.* *The Great Depression hit Japan hard. In the face of mass unemployment, some workers and leftist leaders organized protest. In this 1930 photo, angry leftist workers unfurl outlawed red flags to give symbolic emphasis to their demands.* The Mainichi Newspapers.

Figure 38.4 *Franklin Roosevelt Speaking to Americans.* *President Roosevelt skillfully employed the radio as a means of communicating his message to Americans; his "fireside chats" helped bolster morale and educate people about the New Deal. Like his contemporaries, President Roosevelt sought to boost his popularity, thereby ensuring his reelection (three times) and the stability of his continuing programs.* Corbis-Bettmann.

mand of General Jiang Jieshi unified China by military conquest. Although the drop in international trade and available credit resources hurt some Chinese exporters and producers, the Chinese economy depended heavily on agriculture, a sector more sensitive to domestic than international prices. General Jiang concentrated on helping promote commercial and industrial enterprises rather than agriculture. His problems were more political than economic.

The Depression's Influence on Leadership

Franklin D. Roosevelt (1882–1945) and Adolf Hitler (1889–1945) dominated the depression years, but other leaders, like Canada's R. B. Bennett (1870–1947), played important roles in fighting the Great Depression. Although they used different means to stay in power, these three politicians pos-

sessed similarities of style and substance. The British, French, and Japanese did not have a single dynamic politician to grapple with the domestic crises brought by the depression.

Hitler, Roosevelt, and Bennett appreciated the political value of new technological developments. Hitler used airplanes in a dramatic campaign swing when he visited nearly two dozen cities in a week during national elections, and Roosevelt insisted on flying from New York to Chicago to accept the Democratic Party's presidential nomination in 1932. In a 1930 election campaign, Bennett employed his bombastic rhetorical skills to attack his opponent as timid and vacillating. After winning, Bennett played a major role in creating the Canadian Radio Broadcasting Corporation, a national radio network. Roosevelt became famed for "fireside chats" by radio, and Hitler used the radio more than fifty times in his first year in office to reassure the German people. Early in their administrations, these leaders' messages employed powerful modes of expression about the suffering of people in collective and individual terms.

Bennett's, Roosevelt's, and Hitler's management styles usually permitted their subordinates to handle specific issues. Frequently, lower officials competed against one another for the ears of the top man, and all three leaders preferred to have people and bureaucratic sectors vying with one another. In that sense, they gained unusual control over their governments.

Aid to unemployed people occupied the attention of Canada, the United States, and Germany. In 1930, Bennett summoned a special session of Parliament to vote $20 million to put people back to work. The Canadian radio network also employed writers and actors. The United States budgeted around $3.4 billion to put people to work building roads, schools, and bridges. Hitler spent even more on a per capita basis in order to fund massive public works programs that built railroads, navigation centers, and a network of highways. The Nazis used public funds for loans and tax rebates to small companies. They undertook measures to encourage consumer spending.

Economic Programs of the Depression

The United States, Canada, Germany, France, Japan, and the Soviet Union devised a series of economic programs to combat the ravages of the depression. In the process, they created more highly centralized polities that delivered welfare and other social services to their citizens.

THE UNITED STATES. Franklin Roosevelt came to power in 1933, promising a "New Deal" for Americans, a depression-fighting program of public works projects. The U.S. government preferred a loose network of management-worker alliances. The regulatory codes were more voluntary in industrial compliance, but through the Presidential Re-employment Agreement, the U.S. government set minimum wages and maximum hours. The United States also permitted the growth of unions because that brought more workers under control.

Among the American agencies created in the depression era was the Civilian Conservation Corps (CCC). It was founded to employ people in a variety of projects related to conservation issues. Men were drawn to the CCC and lived in camps governed by a military-style discipline that regimented their lives. Officers in the U.S. armed forces directed these civilians, who built bridges, repaired roads, and constructed a variety of water control projects. One major CCC effort involved planting trees by the millions, reforesting large areas of the United States.

Another agency, the Farm Security Administration (FSA), employed many people to support farmers. One of these employees was the photographer Dorothea Lange (1895–1965), who became famous for her photographs of depression scenes. Before getting the FSA job, Lange had taken sensitive and emotionally affecting photographs of the unemployed, especially white-collar workers who never expected to be out of work. A major exhibition of this work brought Lange an FSA contract. Lange photographed farm families, capturing the misery and privation of these people while giving human faces to the plight of women and children in agriculture. Many Lange photographs of the depression era have been acclaimed as masterpieces of the medium.

Roosevelt stressed the bedrock nature of rural farm life and the positive values associated with it. Like Germany, the United States organized agriculture to increase farm income. Both countries made credit easier and less expensive in the countryside. The United States tried to reduce farm production and curtail agricultural surpluses, while the Germans maximized production.

Rearmament by the United States in the 1930s provided significant funds for industry and workers. The United States spent about one-third of the initial public works budget, about $1 billion, on military projects, like aircraft carriers, cruisers, airplanes, and military airports. In response to Japanese military expansion in China and Germany's expansion in Europe, American military spending escalated to nearly $9 billion in 1939 and $34 billion in 1941. President Roosevelt believed that it was prudent to prepare for possible war.

CANADA. R. B. Bennett tried but failed to improve the lot of Canadians, especially workers, between 1930 and 1935. He got Parliament to agree, apart from the emergency funds to put people to work, to raise tariff rates by 50 percent. This policy reversed a negative trade balance and raised nearly

FIGURE 38.5 *Plight of a Migrant Family.* *In the 1930s, the American photographer Dorothea Lange was commissioned by the state of California to document the migrant farmers' way of life. Lange's photographs convey the dignity of the laborers and their families despite the harshest poverty; her work led to the creation of state-funded camps for migrants. This 1936 photograph of a worn-looking migrant mother and children was taken in Nipomo, California, during the period that Lange worked for the Farm Security Administration.* Corbis-Bettmann.

$200 million. It saved Canadian industries from bankruptcy and kept Canadian workers from losing their jobs. On the other hand, keeping prices high worsened the lives of people living on relief or on reduced incomes. Bennett created the foundations of a national bank, a national broadcasting system, and a national airlines system.

Despite these measures, the economic lot of Canadians still worsened, driving Bennett to drastic measures. In January 1935, Bennett announced a Canadian New Deal without informing his own party. The central features included a national unemployment and social insurance system, minimum wages and maximum hours in industry, a federally sponsored farm credit system, and a natural products marketing board. All were enacted by Parliament despite serious misgivings of his party members, and their enactment gave the opposition a key election issue.

GERMANY. The German economy was starting to recover from the depression when the Nazis assumed power in 1933, quickly bringing industry, labor, and agriculture under state control. The

IN THEIR OWN WORDS

Canadians Look at the Depression

Canada's leaders grappled with the problems and issues of the Great Depression in the 1930s. They put forth visions of suffering Canadians and developed analyses of the causes of the misery, as well as critiques of policies proposed to end it.

J. S. Woodsworth, member of the Canadian parliament, spoke movingly about the human catastrophe:

> In the old days we could send people from the cities to the country. If they went out today they would meet another army of unemployed coming back from the country to the city; that outlet is closed. What can these people do? They have been driven from our parks; they have been driven from our streets; they have been driven from our buildings, and in this city [Ottawa] they actually took refuge on the garbage heaps.

Prime Minister R. B. Bennett led the fight against the depression-caused suffering and offered a vision of a moribund capitalism lying in ruins:

> In the anxious years through which you have passed, you have been witness of grave defects and abuses in the capitalist system. Unemployment and waste are proof of these. Great changes are taking place about us. New conditions prevail. These require modifications in the capitalist system to enable that system more effectively to serve the people.

With these words as a preamble, the prime minister began outlining the reforms that he intended to pass before new elections were held. Inspired by the U.S. New Deal, the Canadian New Deal came into being without much consultation with his cabinet or fellow members of Parliament.

The main opposition leader, Mackenzie King, sensed an opportunity to make political hay of Bennett's seeming authoritarian manner by asking Bennett to

> tell this House whether as leader of the government, knowing that a question will come up immediately as to the jurisdiction of this Parliament, and of the provincial legislatures in matters of social legislation, he has secured an opinion from the law officers of the Crown or from the Supreme Court of Canada which will be a sufficient guarantee to this House to proceed with these measures as being without question in its jurisdiction.

King had framed the constitutional issue without having to discuss the merits of the New Deal programs. In the process, King raised questions about the prime minister's integrity in going first to the people and then to Parliament. During the ensuing campaign and election, Bennett's party lost, and most of the Canadian New Deal was repealed or called into question. Canada stumbled on to economic recovery by the end of the 1930s, especially after entering World War II.

Germans developed a state-run economy, establishing thirteen gigantic agencies that governed all sectors of industry. In addition, the Nazis broke independent unions and organized all workers into one large federation. Nazis insisted that businesses provide better housing, sports programs, and working facilities for the laborers. Slogans like the "beauty of labor" and "strength through joy" created a sense of community in factories.

Hitler and the Nazis were concerned about German consumers and their standard of living. The Nazis, for example, planned the Volkswagen (people's car) as a car that the workers could afford to own and drive. By the end of the 1930s, German citizens associated the Nazis with a secure income and an improved living standard, especially when compared with the Weimar Republic.

The German farm program resettled large numbers of farmers. In later years, plans were formulated to move huge numbers to the east (Poland and Russia). Propaganda promoted the idea that agricultural production was vital to the nation. Documentaries were made showing happy farm workers toiling in their fields.

FIGURE 38.6 *Hitler and the Volkswagen. The Nazis promoted the idea of producing and selling a "people's car," an inexpensive car that would improve standards of living and also create jobs. On May 1, 1938, Adolf Hitler unveiled the prototype; within a year or so, factories that manufactured autos had also begun to turn out tanks and armored cars.* Ullstein Bilderdienst.

FRANCE. The Great Depression in France polarized society and politics, leading to a general breakdown of effective rule and prolonging the economic crisis. The French political system lodged power in parliament rather than in the presidency. In times of general turmoil, this led to legislative deadlock. Between 1932 and 1935, for example, there were eleven different parliamentary coalitions developing fourteen separate plans to fight the depression. These legislative measures only intensified economic stagnation.

Political deadlock pressured a group of parties to form a Popular Front coalition, uniting political groups claiming to represent workers and peasants. The Popular Front governed for two years. Coalition leaders implemented a program akin to the New Deal. They encouraged workers and employers to agree to modest wage hikes and enacted legislation guaranteeing two weeks' paid holiday per year and a forty-hour work week. A price-stabilization agency was created to raise cereal prices for farmers. In addition, the Bank of France and armaments industries were taken over by the government.

JAPAN. The Japanese established and administered bureaucratic agencies that controlled whole industrial sectors and used methods similar to the Germans'. Japanese leaders also implemented a major armament program in 1931, somewhat improving the nation's economy. Japan began to enter a wartime economic environment when it conquered Manchuria in 1931 and 1932. Thereafter, larger percentages of the budget went to military needs. The Japanese government broke up unions and oversaw the general regimentation of workers for the emerging warfare state. Because Japanese nationalism became the dominant ideology in the 1930s, most workers agreed with the regimentation, and those who disagreed kept silent.

The Japanese military focused the nation's attention on farmers and their difficult plight because many officers came from the countryside. They pushed the government to offer price supports, easy credit, and other means to encourage agricultural production. When Japan annexed Korea and Taiwan, it obtained two important rice-producing areas; production of rice and other foodstuffs increased, feeding the growing Japanese military machine.

Japanese leaders encouraged migration of Japanese to Hawaii, Peru, and Brazil. During the depression, some talked of sending farmers to newly conquered Manchuria, but that proved impractical; still, large numbers of businesspeople, clerks, and laborers moved there to work in the growing number of Japanese factories.

THE SOVIET UNION. While most of the world suffered from the Great Depression, Soviet Russia industrialized, and its industrialization developed outside the global capitalist system. Between 1929 and 1941, Josef Stalin determined to industrialize the Soviet system no matter the cost. As seen in Chapter 37, he took grain from the peasantry to sell in international markets. In 1929, for example, slightly more than 1 million tons of grain was sold, and, a year later, the Soviets sold 5.4 million tons abroad. These figures, of course, underlie the Stalinist famine of the early 1930s in which millions lost their lives. Soviet Russia's industrial success invited favorable commentary from observers who traveled to Russia. In certain respects, the Soviet model highlighted the importance of industrial planning, although the great cost in human lives gave imitators pause.

The Growth of Central Power

One notable trend of the depression era was the increase in state power. Expanded governmental control over citizens during World War I had been largely undone in the postwar period. The extreme conditions of the 1930s, however, revived military-style administrations, as politicians recalled the results gained from the concentration of political power.

The U.S. presidency changed dramatically in the years of Franklin Roosevelt, who set the model for an activist presidency that achieved results through public relations and carefully crafted speeches. The White House staff grew much larger after 1933, and the executive became the strongest of the three branches of government. Indeed, Roosevelt invented the modern presidency. President Harry Truman, Franklin Roosevelt's successor, wielded much greater power than did President Herbert Hoover, Roosevelt's predecessor.

As governments took more active roles in their economies, new economic regulations and laws appeared. The combined effect, which did not fade away after the depression, was to maintain strong governmental control of certain economic sectors.

NONINDUSTRIAL COUNTRIES' PROBLEMS DURING THE DEPRESSION

Countries supplying raw materials to industrial states suffered economic losses, too. Raw materials experienced a general deflation in prices during the 1920s, making life difficult in countries dependent on income from these sources. When the depression hit, industrial states sharply reduced their purchases of raw materials. Chile, for example, went from an export trade in copper and nitrates worth 2.3 billion pesos in 1929 to one worth only 282 million pesos by 1932. This catastrophic drop devastated the Chilean economy.

Similar blows staggered other Latin American countries. The purchasing power, for example, of citizens in Argentina, Brazil, Cuba, Ecuador, Mexico, Peru, and Venezuela dropped by at least 40 percent between 1929 and 1933. Brazil, however, benefited from some fortunate circumstances that turned its economy around. Coffee production and exports played a major role in the Brazilian economy. When coffee-bean prices dropped sharply, the government and coffee growers tried various means to raise the prices. Finally, the government agreed to buy surplus coffee beans and pay some growers not to produce. These combined expenditures put more money into the economy, and because of import controls and other factors, funds were spent on local goods. This stimulated Brazilian businesses to produce and sell clothing, housewares, furniture, paper, glass, steel, and cement. By 1932, industrial production surpassed 1929 levels, and the economy grew by a healthy 8 percent a year through the rest of the 1930s.

Most countries in Latin America did not have Brazil's manufacturing base, nor did they have the raw materials to accomplish its feats. Many Latin American countries adhered to the practice of **import substitution**, relying on local businesses to fill the gaps left by the withdrawal of foreign imports. Although these measures had limited

FIGURE 38.7 *Brazilian Coffee Plantation.* *Brazil suffered moderate damage from the Great Depression. Coffee prices held steady for a time, then dropped. The government intervened and bought up the surplus coffee beans, injecting the additional money into the economy. This kept Brazilian coffee workers on the job and plantation owners out of debt. Overall, Brazil worked its way out of the economic and social dislocation.* Popperfoto/ Archive Photos.

utility in sparking economic turnaround, they did make Latin American economies more balanced in what they produced for local consumption.

The price of rubber dropped steeply before the depression. Most rubber was produced on plantations in Southeast Asia; the French oversaw output in French Indochina, the Dutch controlled the plantations in the East Indies, and the British managed rubber-producing areas in Malaya. Some rubber was also produced in Ceylon in South Asia. British plantation managers and owners responded to the low prices for rubber by striking a voluntary agreement to reduce production. This plan received support from the Dutch growers, and it worked for a time. One major problem came when the Indians in Malaya and Ceylon tapped trees outside the plantations. These indigenous entrepreneurs filled the production vacuum, much to the chagrin of Western imperialists. During the depression, price drops once again produced an agreement to reduce production. Again, Indians ignored the "tapping holiday" and increased production to make up for the price drop. The combined effect was a drop in the price of rubber from 22 cents to 3 cents per pound; British owners complained that the business was going "local." A similar government-inspired drop in cotton production in the United States to maintain world price levels saw delighted Egyptians filling the gap by increasing their production.

SOCIAL CONSEQUENCES OF THE DEPRESSION

The great upheaval wrought by the Great Depression had several social consequences. In the United States, common suffering often drew families and people closer together. Houses where tramps might find a meal were marked by those who passed through earlier. People shared what little they had, especially farm families, which always seemed willing to take in cousins or other relatives down on their luck. This seemed to happen regularly in many parts of the world. One depression-era news story told of a group of men who had been arrested for vagrancy. Rather than be troubled by the jailing, they delightedly looked forward to regular meals and a warm place to sleep.

Women responded differently to their particular needs in bad times. In many countries where women constituted a sizeable fraction of the workforce, managers kept them on because they worked for lower pay than men. In households where women were the sole wage earners, tensions rose as men found it hard to cope with role reversals.

In Germany, the Nazis took various measures to take women out of the workforce. They paid women to marry and to leave the workforce, thus opening jobs for men. Nazis also propagandized German women to stay at home and build their nests.

Divorce rates also declined significantly in many countries, as families felt forced to stay together for survival. The downside was that women and men more often remained in dysfunctional marriages and suffered the consequences.

In Asia, women suffered disproportionately from the depression. Chinese women in poor households might find themselves sold by their husbands, and Chinese children in economic deprivation faced sale to Christian missionaries for conversion, Muslims for conversion, or wealthy people for sexual gratification. Female infanticide, the killing of female infants, increased during hard times in much of Asia. Peasant girls in Japan also

FIGURE 38.8 *Peasant Girls Sold into Prostitution.* *During times of financial hardship, peasant fathers in Japan sometimes resorted to selling their daughters to prostitution houses. Money and the thought of having one less mouth to feed were powerful inducements. This practice became more commonplace during the Great Depression. The girls in this 1934 photograph have just been rescued by social workers.* The Mainichi Newspapers.

faced sale into prostitution houses or factory work by their parents.

Minority groups also bore a heavy burden in the depression years. Migrant workers, especially those of an ethnic minority, experienced discrimination because they were perceived as taking jobs away from the majority group. One reason that the Jews, whom the Nazis tried to deport from Germany in the early years of their rule, were refused welcome in Western countries was the fear that they would compete for the few existing jobs. Anti-Semitism, of course, was another reason for the rejection of Jewish immigrants.

Some American Indians in the United States were relatively better off during the depression. Life on their reservations had always been meager, so when the depression hit, the falling prices for goods permitted their money to stretch further. New Deal programs that gave relief were extended to Indians for the first time. The Navajo tribe, for example, came out of the depression in somewhat better circumstances than it had entered it.

Birth rates declined in many countries, signifying that people deferred marriage until later age. Suicide rates increased during the difficult times, and, in Japan, whole-family suicides were not

UNDER THE LENS
First You Steal a Chicken

There is a story that goes around in historical circles about a cookbook written in a time of great privation. A stewed chicken recipe, according to this story, begins, "First you steal a chicken. . . ." French historians believe the cookbook was from the siege of Paris (1871), American historians think it was from the Great Depression, and Russian historians think it was from the siege of Moscow. It may well be that this recipe was written only in the mind of an imaginative historian and that it has entered into academic folklore.

The truth remains, however, that the Great Depression was a difficult time for many Americans to eat adequately. In 1930, there were eighty-two bread lines distributing food to the needy in New York and eighty in Philadelphia; in the next three years, conditions actually worsened. Citizens in New York, St. Louis, and other cities developed orderly systems of pillaging garbage cans and dumps for edible scraps. Many rural poor were reduced to a diet consisting entirely of wild greens and berries, and the absence of these foods in winter was disastrous. At the same time, President Hoover was sticking to his philosophy that the government should not distribute handouts, leaving that chore to private philanthropy. His decision to grant $20 million to feed livestock in the southwestern drought led a U.S. representative to complain, "The administration would feed jackasses, but it wouldn't feed starving babies."

One of the ironies of the situation was that there was plenty of food in America. The federal government had been buying food to keep farmers solvent and had stockpiled huge quantities of it; in later years, surplus food would be destroyed in order to maintain price levels. Norman Thomas, a prominent socialist leader, decried the system that spawned "breadlines knee deep in wheat." The food problem of America had nothing to do with production, merely with economics and distribution.

One of the problems of the historical assessment of the crisis is that there is little agreement on its magnitude. President Hoover declared in 1931 that no American was "actually starving," yet ninety-four deaths by starvation were reported in New York City alone in that year. Prominent health specialists quarreled, some arguing that the problems with diet were due to ignorance of proper nutrition, not lack of access to food. Any examination of the problem was politically charged, and no adequate study of national health as it related to diet ever was conducted during the depression. We will never truly know even the basic facts.

One point, however, was made very clear by the depression: Whatever the dietary effects, they were being felt only by the poorest citizens. Restaurant dining, a commonsense measure of economic well-being, remained steady through the stock market crash and the years of depression, actually increasing in some places. And, while the poor struggled to get food for the table, fad diets for weight loss were the rage among the well-to-do.

NORTH AMERICA	EUROPE	JAPAN		
			—	
Great Depression in the U.S., 1929–1941			—	Stock market crash, Oct. 1929
	Great Depression in Canada, 1930–1939	Great Depression in Great Britain, 1930–1939	Great Depression in Germany, 1930–1934	Great Depression in Japan, 1931–1936	**1930**	Hawley–Smoot Tariff passed by U.S. Congress, 1930
		Great Depression in France, 1931–1940			—	
					—	Election of F. D. Roosevelt, Nov. 1932
					—	Hitler in power, Jan. 1933
					—	New Deal proclaimed, Mar. 1933
					1935	Canadian New Deal proposed, Jan. 1935
					—	Soviet Union proclaims socialism has been achieved, 1936
					—	Japan and China clash, July 1937
					—	
					—	Germany attacks Poland, Sept. 1939
					1940	
					—	U.S. rearms, 1941
					—	
					—	

uncommon. In the United States, life expectancy actually increased significantly between 1929 and 1939. Six years were added to the average American's expected life span. Improved medical care accounted for some of that growth.

Some states began to see their social mission as caring for their citizens in new ways. European nation-states were moving toward a social welfare system, and the depression era accelerated this tendency. Britain already had an unemployment insurance system and provided basic needs for the homeless and helpless. The United States prided itself on having private charities substitute for the public dole. Many Americans also espoused a rugged individualism that shrugged off charity in difficult times. The family filled a gap by taking in people. The Great Depression, however, caused a shift in thinking. President Hoover did little to help struggling people, but President Roosevelt committed the government to aiding the needy. The United States, for example, passed the Social Security Act in 1935 to pay for the retirement needs of employed people. The country thereby agreed to aid eligible workers who paid into the retirement system.

LESSONS OF THE GREAT DEPRESSION

The lessons-of-history concept sometimes is a useful teaching tool. Usually people are not sure of what might be learned from an event or a crisis. Yet the Great Depression seemed to teach economists and politicians that a quiescent, Hooverian approach to economic downturn courted disaster.

The greatest economist of the depression years, John Maynard Keynes[1] (1883–1946), actually accomplished little to alleviate the Great Depression's suffering. The ideas of his central monograph on governmental policy, published in 1936, were later followed by many leaders. During the half-century after the book's publication, Keynesian[2] policies (like deficit spending) held sway in many political circles. It might be said that no later depression of equal magnitude appeared because of these perspectives and efforts.

Another restraint on most countries was the realization that, while some mild form of protection for economic sectors might be necessary, return to the economic nationalism of the 1930s was a recipe for disaster. The Hawley-Smoot Tariff remained a symbol of protectionist stupidity to be avoided. Since World War II, international trade relations have been remarkably cooperative because more is to be gained from cooperation. Not only is there a global market, something only belatedly realized, but international trade agreements have been signed during the second half of the twentieth century to take advantage of it.

The Great Depression traumatized global societies for much of the 1930s. It followed World War I and helped prepare the way for World War II, and ferocious economic competition naturally emerged from the first and led comfortably into the second conflict. At the same time, political leaders gradually learned that massive military spending increases put many to work, alleviating the widespread unemployment of the 1930s.

SUMMARY

1. The Great Depression reflected a unique downturn in the global economy. Not only did prices plunge significantly, but production levels also sank dramatically. The crisis intensified because of economic nationalism and poor leadership.

2. Some of the problems and legacies of World War I, like the devastation it caused, the economic decline of Britain, and the recovery of the combatants' raw materials production, helped lead to the Great Depression.

3. From 1929 to 1932, government leaders tried to balance budgets and raise taxes at times when other measures were needed. In Canada, however, tariff increases raised substantial sums and kept many workers employed.

4. The stock market crash and the Hawley-Smoot Tariff helped precipitate and intensify the Great Depression. President Franklin Roosevelt

[1]**Keynes:** KAYNZ
[2]**Keynesian:** KAYN zee uhn

implemented most of the actions that helped end the depression, which lingered into the early 1940s.

5. Germany's economic collapse helped bring the Nazis to power. They and the Americans followed many similar policies to alleviate the negative effects of the Great Depression.

6. Japan devalued its currency. This policy, along with a major armament effort, pulled Japan out of the Great Depression. Both Germany and the United States also spent large sums on arming their nations.

7. Nonindustrial nations suffered in the 1930s. Many had supplied the industrial nation-states with raw materials that were no longer purchased in the 1930s. A few, like Brazil, successfully turned to production for the internal market. Local production also benefited Indian rubber producers and Egyptian cotton manufacturers.

8. The system of social welfare grew in many industrial states in the 1930s. It also played a role in the increase of political power of the nation-state.

9. The U.S. presidency became powerful during the Great Depression because of President Roosevelt's policies. A more powerful presidency is one example of the increasing centralization of industrial states.

10. Two lessons, the value of deficit spending in economic downturns and the need for international cooperation in trade matters, derived from the Great Depression and have contributed to the period of relative economic prosperity since 1945. Another lesson was that massive armament buildups helped bring countries out of their depressions.

SUGGESTED READINGS

Nakamura, Takafusa. "Depression, Recovery, and War, 1920–1945." In Peter Duus, *The Cambridge History of Japan: The Twentieth Century*. Cambridge, Eng.: Cambridge University Press, 1988, pp. 451–93. An examination of the depression in Japan.

Peukert, Detlev. *The Weimar Republic*. New York: Hill and Wang, 1992. A history of the Weimar Republic, including the depression.

Terkel, Studs. *Hard Times*. New York: Pantheon Books, 1970. An oral history of the depression in the United States.

Tint, Herbert. *France Since 1918*. New York: St. Martin's Press, 1980. A history of modern France and the Great Depression.

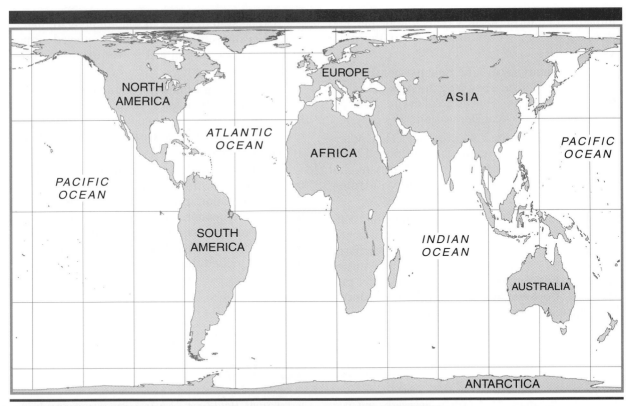

Hitler and Mussolini.
*Adolf Hitler and Benito
Mussolini represented the
two main national socialist
powers, Germany and Italy.
Although the Italians were
the first to adopt a national
socialist government, the Germans led the movement in
Europe. Hitler and Mussolini
met often to discuss political
and military matters; here they
meet in München in 1937.*
Ullstein Bilderdienst.

National Socialism around the Globe
1919–1945

On the night of November 9, 1938, Germany's Nazi government organized the destruction of thousands of Jewish-owned shops and houses. Scores of Jews were killed and hundreds more were injured. Many were arrested and shipped off to jail or concentration camps. This came to be known as the "Night of Broken Glass" (Kristallnacht) and represented the policy of the German national socialist government to eradicate Jews, first in Germany and later in Europe.

National socialism arose out of the consequences of World War I and was energized by the sociopolitical upheavals of the Great Depression. It spread globally and was one of the dominating ideologies in the European theater of World War II. National socialists desired a powerful nation-state to control the nation's economy and army in order to expand national socialism by conquest.

THE MESSAGE AND CONTEXT OF NATIONAL SOCIALISM

National socialism appealed to disparate groups through a program of great persuasiveness. **National socialism** has the following elements:

—nationalism,

—socialism,

—imperialism, and

—totalitarianism.

Of these, the first two, nationalism and socialism, are primary. National socialists believed that the nation was holy and harmonious; therefore, class conflict was evil. They were passionate nationalists, and their sense of superiority fostered racism.

National socialists were quite unlike the socialists who followed Marx's ideas. Nonetheless, national socialists shared with socialists the idea that the state should control the means of production. National socialists believed in **corporatism**, the practice of combining owners, managers, and workers in a unitary whole within a business, factory, or industrial sector. Cooperation among all business components was paramount in the national socialists' economic vision.

National socialists were ardent imperialists. They believed that the nation-state should expand. In addition, national socialists argued for colonies to reflect national glory and to provide labor and raw materials for the nation's economy.

National socialists also favored **totalitarianism**, the belief that an all-powerful nation-state should control every aspect of its citizens' lives. In national socialist ideology, the nation's unity assumed paramount importance, and everyone was subordinate to it.

National socialists condemned certain aspects of modernity. They decried what they saw as the manipulative and corrupt politics of democracy and preferred an authoritarian regime. National socialists criticized elements of modern science's view of the world, and they despised the environmental degradation and poor working conditions created by capitalism. National socialism came into existence in part as a reaction to Marxism, out of fear of Soviet Russian dominance over Europe. Marxists' espousal of atheistic ideas and their stress on class warfare and the dominance of the working class ran counter to national socialist ideology.

NATIONAL SOCIALISM IN EUROPE

Europe became and remained the primary center of national socialism in the period from 1919 to 1945. Italy and Germany developed movements that took political control and carried out national socialist policies. Other countries had minor national socialist movements.

Italian National Socialism

Italy had been a victorious power in World War I, yet its political system did not long survive the war's end. Part of the problem came with the disintegration of its ruling coalition after the war and the inability of a succession of leaders to build viable coalition governments. By 1920, political activities by new parties had become more successful.

Italian national socialism gained influence in this era partly because of the breakdown of effective government and a corresponding upheaval in the cities. The Italian Fascist Party began in the urban industrial areas of northern Italy. With a strong component of World War I veterans (57 percent of the early party members), the early Fascists fought Marxist workers in city streets in order to establish themselves as a major political movement.

Benito Mussolini (1883–1945) was the leader of the Fascist Party. Mussolini's father, a socialist, named his son after Benito Juarez, the famous Mexican revolutionary. The young Mussolini became a Marxist, calling Karl Marx his father and teacher, but broke away from Marxism because he believed it to be unpatriotic. Despite his leaving Marxism, Mussolini's movement retained strong socialist features.

Given the sociopolitical chaos of the day, Mussolini's movement grew rapidly, and its demands became more aggressive. In October 1922, he declared a march on Rome to highlight the party's power. This dramatic action paralleled the march on Rome and seizure of the government by Julius Caesar nearly 2,000 years earlier. Around 50,000 activists arrived in the capital and greatly strengthened Mussolini's bargaining position. Within weeks, he was appointed the new leader of Italy. Once he was in control, Mussolini's example inspired imitators elsewhere.

By the time the national socialists came into power, their focus shifted to the conquest and monopolization of state agencies, especially those that controlled sources of information. Soon the party found support for its program of subordinating all of Italy's problems to nationalism. That is, the Fascists created a totalitarian state. They tapped into powerful nationalist feelings among those Italians who abhorred the warring of class against class.

Over time, national socialists developed full control of the political system. Corporatism

FIGURE 39.1 *Mussolini and the "Roman Sons of the Wolf."* *By 1938, Benito Mussolini had ordered Italy's armed forces to imitate the German army's goose-step marching. Here he reviews a corps of fascist youth patterned on its German counterpart. Marching played an important part in national socialist movements, especially in Europe, and parades were used to train soldiers and to energize the country's population.* Brown Brothers.

became the guiding principle for Italian businesses and workers. Mussolini directed the takeover and the transformation, bending Italy ever more to his will. In the mid-1930s, Mussolini formed a diplomatic alliance with the Germans and later with the Japanese, countries that had influential national socialist movements of their own.

The National Socialist Movement in Germany

Germany lay in ruins after World War I. Wilhelm II had fled to the Netherlands, and the Weimar Republic was created in place of the former German government. Hampered by a war-devastated economy and a punitive peace settlement, Weimar leaders struggled to maintain power. The German Communist Party decided to take advantage of the

chaos. Workers fought in several cities and briefly managed to hold on to the local governments. In the aftermath of this violence and upheaval, the Nazi Party was formed.

Within a brief time after its founding, this national socialist group came under the leadership of Adolf Hitler (1889–1945). Born in Austria, Hitler had spent his youth as an unemployed painter of dubious talent. When World War I exploded, Hitler joined the German army, serving with distinction. After the war, he languished in southern Germany (Bavaria) until he joined and took over the leadership of the National Socialist German Workers Party (Nazi Party). For the next few years, the party was confined to southern Germany. In the period from 1920 to 1923, the party lost its military identity and began to recruit from all social groups and to establish small cells outside the south. The Nazi program also became more eclectic as the national socialists tried to appeal to many groups. Central to the platform was a virulent nationalism that placed the blame for Germany's problems on foreign countries.

Anti-Semitism became another central theme in German national socialism. From the beginning, Hitler cunningly paid lip service to rumors blaming Jews for Germany's problems, including the idea that they had been behind the severe inflation of the early 1920s. Hitler increasingly offered more radical solutions to the "Jewish question," and, when the Nazis gained control of the government, they confiscated Jewish property and intimidated Jews. Most scholars agree that these measures were calculated to produce the greatest possible effect on German popular opinion.

Franco-Belgian occupation of the Ruhr industrial region in Germany was an event that greatly increased membership in the Nazi Party. France and Belgium asserted that the Germans had failed to pay their war indemnity, and French and Belgian soldiers took control of valuable German property to support their claims. Germany's humil-

iating acquiescence to the seizure undermined the Weimar Republic and afforded the Nazis a potent political issue to exploit. Party membership grew manifold in little more than a year, and even industrial workers and miners in the Ruhr Valley supported the antiforeign policy of the national socialists.

The Nazi Party's spectacular growth persuaded Hitler to attempt a coup, which failed miserably. He planned a march on Berlin similar to Mussolini's march on Rome, but Hitler's influential allies deserted him, leading to his arrest, trial, and brief jailing. The party disintegrated in his absence. While in prison, Hitler wrote *Mein Kampf* (*My Struggle*), a book in which he outlined his political and racial beliefs.

Following his release, Hitler began rebuilding the party in the latter half of the 1920s. At the same time, the Nazis began to perfect their propaganda machine and to tailor their program to specific regions and social groups. This chameleonlike process did not seem to upset party members, although there was constant turnover in membership.

FIGURE 39.2 *Anti-Semitic Propaganda.* *Nazi leaflets like this one portrayed Jews as the source of worker and peasant servitude, thus making the Jews scapegoats for an economically depressed Germany. The left panel shows a caricatured Jewish businessman holding workers in bondage; the hammer and sickle below suggest a hidden communist agenda. The right panel promises economic freedom for workers when the Nazi Party is brought to power. Anti-Semitism was central to the Nazi ideology and culminated in the 1940s with the Holocaust, a massive attempt to exterminate Jews.* Library of Congress.

PARALLELS AND DIVERGENCES

The Roots of Nazi Racism

A prime organizing principle of Nazi ideology was its racial doctrine, which drew on a tradition of European racism and pseudo-science, serving as a justification for Nazi policies. Most peoples believe that they are the most advanced and moral, and Europeans' self-satisfied attitudes were common; the elaborate scientific edifice designed to defend them, however, was unique.

In the latter half of the nineteenth century, most German scholars were followers of Charles Darwin and his notions of biological evolution. Many also believed that his ideas could be translated directly into the social realm, following the ideas of Herbert Spencer and the social Darwinists. One influential group of German scientists, the **Monists**, carried this argument one step further, maintaining that ethnic groups were distinctive both biologically (racially) and socially, and that not all peoples were equally fit. Consequently, the most fit would naturally profit at the expense of the less fit. Some respected scientists, like Ernst Haeckel, were Monists, and the movement was highly esteemed in the German scientific community.

When this doctrine was translated into twentieth-century German political thought, it posited that Germans were the most fit of all races, and that they naturally would overwhelm the lesser races around them. Because to many Monists this was simply an application of Darwin's idea of survival of the fittest, public policies of extermination were seen as merely humane ways of speeding along the inevitable process. The Jews and Slavs, in this view, were the nearest of these lesser races, but Africans, Asians, and all non-Germanic races were thought to be inferior and eventually would become extinct. This argument had the ring of science, and it was ready-made for Nazi theorists like Alfred Rosenberg, who drew strongly on the Monist position.

The Monists borrowed their ideas from respected scientists, but they also took from branches of science that were no longer in good repute. In particular, most used **phrenology**, the now-discredited field that purported to relate physical characteristics to intellectual and moral worth. The best-known branch of phrenology claimed that the bumps on one's head revealed a person's character, but other branches made equally wild claims. Cesare Lambroso of Italy argued that careful measurements of the face could disclose criminal types; Richard Fletcher, a little-known Scottish physician, insisted that the shape of the collarbone was an indicator of one's moral nature as it related to sexuality; and Paul Broca, a biologist, claimed that brain size was a direct indicator of intelligence.

It was only a short step for Nazi theorists to turn these ideas into practical guidelines for recognizing "degenerates and inferior sorts." Nazi scientists devised formulas based on head measurements to identify Jews, Slavs, and other "undesirables." Anthropology thrived under the Nazis, largely because its practitioners devised seemingly scientific ways of recognizing targets for elimination.

Between 1930 and 1933, the Nazis achieved electoral success and power. A major factor in this era was the Great Depression. By inflaming the unrest caused by the depression, the Nazis transformed themselves from an irritant in German politics to a major political force. In January 1930, party membership numbered around 125,000; eight months later it had grown to 300,000, and by early 1933 had reached 1 million. Its increasing working-class appeal began to benefit the party in significant ways. During the election campaigns of this time, party members elected to national office increased from a handful to more than 100; in addition, the national socialists garnered around 37 percent of the national vote.

Adolf Hitler, more than Mussolini, defined national socialism. He had transcended his Austrian origins and poor education. During the years until 1930 Hitler honed his political skills, using radio and airplanes to create a flashy political product. More than one voter exclaimed that Hitler seemed to descend from the sky, like a deity. He also skillfully used the media of radio and motion pictures to dramatize the Nazi message.

UNDER THE LENS

Politics and the Media under National Socialism

The Nazis fully appreciated the power of the media in conveying the message they wished the German people to hear. Adolf Hitler himself called the radio a precondition to his victory, and he played a major role in the development of the important movie *Triumph of the Will* (1934). Less than two months after coming to power, the Nazis established a Ministry for Popular Enlightenment and Propaganda.

The radio assumed a valuable role for the National Socialist Party, both in its rise to power and in its building of a revolutionary system. Hitler wanted Germany to have the largest possible number of radios, and the number in the country increased from 4.5 million in 1933 to 16 million by 1942. Thus, Germany became blanketed by receivers carrying the Nazi message. Radio wardens were established to ensure that people had their sets on during significant radio speeches. Hitler gave about fifty radio broadcasts to the people in his first year of power, and his interpretation of events became the approved view. During parades, special microphones were stationed close to the marching soldiers in order to carry live the sounds of their goose-step footfalls. Everything was carefully choreographed.

During the normal "radio week," much time was given to musical performances, especially to light classical music by German composers. Because the somewhat soothing effect seemed satisfactory, more air time was allocated over the succeeding five years, so that around 70 percent of a weekly schedule included soothing music. Operettas by Franz Lehar and Johann Strauss led the selections played. Karl Maria von Weber's Romantic music also found a wide audience in the Nazi era. For more serious occasions, the Nazis preferred to play musical works by Richard Wagner, one of Hitler's favorite composers.

Movies, like radio, attracted the Nazi politicians, who admired propagandists in other countries. Josef Goebbels, the propaganda minister, personally paid tribute to *The Battleship Potemkin*, a Bolshevik movie directed by Sergei Eisenstein. Goebbels noted that its well-made character conveyed a powerful message likely to convert its viewers to Bolshevism.

Perhaps the most significant Nazi movie was *Triumph of the Will*, directed by Leni Riefenstahl. The idea came from Hitler's desire to present a film biography of Nazism and its leader, and he selected the title. The movie focused on a massive Nazi Party rally in Nuremberg and used it to convey the message of Nazism. Riefenstahl wrote a book about the making of the movie, detailing the immense effort that went into it. To obtain special visual effects, the city of Nuremberg had bridges, towers, and tracks constructed. The director controlled a unit of 120 people, including 16 cameramen, 22 chauffeurs to drive cars, and bodyguards. In all, well over 60 miles of film was shot. To create an overall effect, Riefenstahl chose to capture a mood rather than present a story chronologically. The impressionistic effect had a symphonic quality in which the different parts merged into a whole of sight and sound without a distracting narrative commentary. The movie received critical acclaim, even by enemies of the Nazi regime, and showed Nazi mastery of the media.

Finally, Nazi propagandists, led by Josef Goebbels, organized massive and spectacular Nazi rallies in major cities like Nuremberg.

Oratorical skill was perhaps Hitler's greatest asset. He perfected his speaking techniques in the smoky bars of Bavaria. Then he worked patiently to eliminate flaws in his delivery. He sensed an audience's mood and played to it. One film shows him standing in silence before a gathering of supporters, who chat amiably until a growing silence stills the hall. Hitler waits until he has measured them, then launches into a powerful address. He played to crowd responses by modulating his voice and using dramatic hand gestures to keep audiences enthralled.

In January 1933, the German political elite decided to manipulate Hitler and the Nazis into the government because the officials mistakenly believed that the Nazis could be easily controlled. President Paul von Hindenburg appointed Hitler to the chancellorship in 1933, but Hitler fooled the ruling politicians, who had hoped to use him for

FIGURE 39.3 *Nazi Rally.* *Nazi leaders became expert in staging rallies and events. This picture shows Hitler amidst the party faithful, accepting their salutes on September 1, 1939, the day Germany invaded Poland and drew the rest of Europe into war. This carefully staged show of nationalism included officers from all branches of the armed forces displaying their faith in Hitler as their supreme commander. Little was left to chance in these images.* Ullstein Bilderdienst.

their ends. Within months after taking power, Hitler and the Nazis had destroyed the other parties and turned state organizations to their benefit. Hindenburg's death in August 1934 facilitated Hitler's consolidation of power, permitting him to combine the presidency and chancellorship into one position, that of *führer* (leader). Chapter 38 explained how the Nazis developed their economic program and began the rearmament program after 1935. Hitler planned to shed the Versailles Treaty's controls on Germany because he realized that many Germans hated the treaty's humiliating conditions and because it limited German expansion. In violation of the Versailles Peace Treaty, Hitler unilaterally rebuilt the armed forces and reoccupied the east bank of the Rhineland. He soon began calling for the return of German peoples and former territories. Many of these efforts were tolerated by other European states, which did not wish to precipitate a confrontation. In fact, some European leaders felt that the Germans had been too severely punished.

In 1938, Germany occupied and annexed Austria, the country of Hitler's birth, and Hitler began an expansionist foreign policy. Soon after, he insisted that the Sudetenland, an area of Czechoslovakia inhabited by German-speaking people, be annexed. Germans there were provoked by Hitler to demand reunification. At the Munich Conference, attended by Mussolini, Neville Chamberlain (Britain), Edouard Daladier (France), and Hitler, the parties agreed to permit German occupation and annexation of the Sudetenland, despite the objections of the Czechs. Chamberlain and Daladier believed in appeasing Hitler and the Germans.

Neither the British nor the French wished to fight another European war like the one that had devastated their countries and had killed or crippled millions of their men.

Within the following year, Hitler demanded the return of parts of Poland. Because Hitler feared the possibility of a two-front war, he carried on negotiations with the Soviets and with the British and French. The British and French were treaty-bound to fight alongside their Polish allies, and, when they refused Hitler's demands for further appeasement, he turned to the Russians. The Nazis and the Soviets inked the Non-Aggression Pact in

MAP 39.1 *Hitler's Annexations in Eastern Europe, 1936–1939.* *Adolf Hitler came to power vowing to revise the territorial settlement imposed on Germany at the Versailles Peace Conference of 1919. Accordingly, in 1938, he annexed Austria and the Sudetenland of Czechoslovakia (with British and French acquiescence). The rest of the Czech territories and parts of Poland were annexed in 1939. Poland's fate was decided by a Soviet-Nazi pact in August 1939 and the subsequent invasion of Poland by Germany and Soviet Russia in September 1939. The latter event precipitated the European theater of World War II.*

August 1939 and attacked Poland soon after. Britain and France declared war, one that they had tried to avoid. World War II in Europe had begun.

National Socialism in Iberia

The Spanish and Portuguese national socialist groups never won significant followings. Both states saw parties come to power that co-opted their national socialist rivals. Some Spanish national socialist groups received funding from wealthy landowners and bankers, and they often received inspiration and support from Italy and

Germany. One Portuguese group, the National Syndicalist Organization, preached anticapitalism and the importance of attracting young people to the cause. About 20 percent of its membership came from students and intellectuals.

During the Spanish civil war (1936–1939), elements of the Spanish army led by General Francisco Franco (1892–1975) launched a coup against the Spanish government. Soon the Germans and Italians backed Franco, while the Soviets supported the ruling government. The Spanish civil war became a testing ground for a European war, as the Italians, Germans, and Soviets sent substan-

FIGURE 39.4 *Poster of the Spanish Civil War.* *The Spanish civil war (1936–1939) became a testing ground for national socialist armies and weapons. There they faced the forces of Spanish leftists, some of whom owed loyalty to Soviet Russia. This collage offers a leftist perspective that shows airplanes bombing the Spanish city of Madrid, taking the lives of children and destroying property. This "culture" of the national socialists is equated with fascism and terror.* Victoria & Albert Museum / Fotomas Index.

tial military aid and advisors. Although Franco's victory should have meant that the national socialists would rule, Franco refused to allow them into power. The national socialists in Spain were quickly relegated to political obscurity.

Other European National Socialist Movements

Other European countries harbored national socialist movements, but none gained a mass following. Racism proved a major theme of these parties, with the Jews and Gypsies suffering criticism and violence directed against them.

In Britain and Ireland, army veterans comprised a major element of the various national socialist movements. In both countries, national socialists adopted a variety of campaign slogans that had a constantly shifting appeal. In Britain, young people and lower aristocrats supported the British Union of Fascists. In Ireland, the rural community, especially cattle ranchers and farmers, gave the Army Comrades' Association the most support. Some Irish joined national socialist groups as a means of opposing the British, who had long been involved in Irish affairs.

Sir Oswald Mosley (1896–1980) went from England to Italy and Germany to study national socialism. Upon his return, he directed the British Union of Fascists to espouse a vitriolic anti-Semitism. He also stressed violent action, corporatism, funding of public works programs, and imperial self-sufficiency. By 1934, the British Union of Fascists had attracted around 50,000 members from most social groups and regions of Britain.

French national socialists built on conservative traditions from the nineteenth century. After World War I, the Action Française developed a program of intense nationalism that took an anti-German tone. It preached strong militarist values. Action Française was anti-Nazi, although it did favor corporatism and many Italian and German economic policies. It never assumed an important role in French politics.

The activities of the Italians and Germans helped inspire similar movements in the Netherlands and in Belgium. The dislocations caused by the onset of the Great Depression inspired change as well. Nationalism was strongly emphasized,

especially in the development of an authoritarian state. Attention was given to veterans and young people. There were many national socialist groups in the Netherlands and in Belgium, and two of the largest numbered between 50,000 and 115,000 members. The Netherlands' main party received financial support from wealthy people. It grew rapidly until the Nazis became aggressive, and, during World War II, many in the party collaborated with the Nazis.

Central and eastern Europeans not only saw the devastating effects of World War I, but they also witnessed the collapse of the Austro-Hungarian and German empires. There had been no democratic traditions in the region, and corrosive ethnic tensions predominated. There were rivalries between the Czechs and Slovaks, between the Romanians and Hungarians, between the Croats and the Serbs, and between the Jews and gentiles. Again, national socialist movements there stressed violence, appealed particularly to veterans and young people, especially students, and often strongly felt the influence of the German and Italian national socialists.

The Austrian National Socialist Party was founded in 1919 and followed Hitler's lead in most areas after 1925. Following the collapse of the Austro-Hungarian Empire in 1918, Austrian nationalism was identified with Germany and was supported by the Germans to the north. It also appealed to groups in the chameleonlike manner of the Nazi Party and attracted support from professionals in public and private businesses. Although the Austrian National Socialist Party supported union with Germany, many Austrians preferred to remain independent.

Populist attitudes predominated in national socialism in both Hungary and Romania, and students and soldiers played a critical role there. The Romanian Legion of the Archangel Michael and the Iron Guard were established in the late 1920s. They appealed to the nationalist sentiments of college and high school students, and they violently criticized and attacked the Jews for being alien to Romanian culture and values. The Hungarian Arrow Cross Party, which espoused strong anti-Semitic views, was led by army officers. In 1937 and 1938, the Arrow Cross Party gained a mass following. In 1939, the Nationalist Alliance garnered 900,000 votes and appealed to the uprooted people in urban and rural sectors.

NATIONAL SOCIALISM IN EAST ASIA

At the other end of the Eurasian landmass, active national socialist movements developed in China and Japan in the 1930s. The Chinese movement represented an effort by the Nationalist Party leader, Jiang Jieshi (Chiang Kai-shek, 1887–1975), to imitate the methods of the Italians and Germans. The Japanese developed two movements: one that appealed to army officers and soldiers, containing an element of anti-Western sentiments, and another that openly copied Italian and German models.

China's National Socialism

The primary group of national socialists in China was connected with Jiang Jieshi, head of the Nationalist Party and the leader of China. Dissatisfied with his party, which had become riddled with corruption and torn by factions, Jiang helped bring into being the Blue Shirts, an organization directly modeled on the Italian and German national socialists. The Chinese organization, however, remained a secret group in the mold of China's secret societies. Despite the clandestine nature of the movement, its influence became pervasive in the few years of its existence in the 1930s.

The military played a vital role in China's national socialism. As early as 1928 and continuing thereafter, German military missions to China were led by people with close ties to Nazi Party leaders, including Hitler himself. Because these German officers influenced the educational system of China's military academies, they indirectly inculcated the ideas of national socialism in their fellow Chinese. In addition, Chinese officers who exhibited exceptional leadership capabilities went abroad to study. Most studied and trained in Italy and Germany and witnessed national socialist rule there.

Jiang Jieshi founded the Blue Shirts in the spring of 1933. Top leaders were graduates of the Whampoa Military Academy, especially from the first three graduating classes. The first class of cadets considered themselves bound to Jiang, the commandant of the academy, as disciples to a sage. Of the survivors of the 1920s unification wars, many considered themselves a separate elite.

National revival meant everything to the Blue Shirts, who despaired at the daily reminders of China's enfeebled state. They believed that the best way to energize people was through promoting Chinese nationalism. And the best symbol for China was Jiang Jieshi. The Blue Shirts took secret vows of absolute obedience to Jiang and his commands. To create the totalitarian state, the group had to prevail over the individual and even the family. This model, of course, was adopted from the Italians and Germans.

Although foreign models were followed, the Chinese rejected many values and practices of the West. Perhaps the idea most despised by the Chinese national socialists was individualism, a term that translates into Chinese as "selfishness." The Blue Shirts violently attacked individualism, democracy, representative government, and capitalism, all of which were linked to the West. The Chinese cultural program stressed the reanimation of many positive values from China's past, to be inculcated through social institutions like schools, the National Boy Scouts Association, and special summer camps where students received three to four weeks of military training. These organizations were led by the Blue Shirts and became major recruiting grounds for them.

The New Life Movement and the Special Movement Corps also had strong Blue Shirt connections. The New Life Movement developed in the mid-1930s and stressed four main virtues: propriety, justice, honesty, and self-respect. To guide the people, Jiang issued ninety-five rules governing behavior, embodying these four virtues. The Special Movement Corps, organized in mid-1933, had about 20,000 members and was led by Blue Shirts. Central to their task in Jiangxi Province, where the Chinese communists were embedded in the Jiangxi Soviet base area, was the effort to win back people to the Nationalist Party. Local people were given small arms and limited military training. To improve their chances of gaining popular support, the Special Movement Corps investigated and rooted out local corruption and sedition. They were generally successful in Jiangxi and drove out the communists. Later, they gained some ground in Sichuan[1] Province, farther west.

Many other nationalist organizations had top leaders who came from the Blue Shirts. One of the

---

[1] **Sichuan:** SEE chwahn

FIGURE 39.5 *Mass Marriage Ceremony in China. President Jiang Jieshi sponsored the New Life Movement, a program designed to improve the lives of Chinese citizens by promoting moral conduct. This mass ceremony highlighted marriage as an institution especially sanctioned by Confucianism, a value system supported by the nationalist government. Identically attired men and women stand before a Chinese temple. Jiang used symbolic ceremonies to enhance his claim to be father of the nation.* L'Illustration/Sygma.

most crucial was the Special Services Department of the Blue Shirts. This agency acted as a counterintelligence organization and carried out assassinations. It was headed by Dai Li[2] (1895–1946), a Whampoa Military Academy cadet who developed a talent for identifying and informing on communists. He caught the attention of Jiang and joined the Blue Shirts. Soon he was put in charge of over-

seeing special tasks, including assassination. Dai Li's organization became greatly feared, and some likened him to Heinrich Himmler, the infamous head of Hitler's Gestapo (political police). Dai believed that the leader should be safeguarded, that corruption should be punished, that counterrevolutionary forces and international spies should be destroyed, and that national reconstruction should be assisted. Like the Gestapo, Dai's group terrorized many, guilty and innocent alike.

[2]**Dai Li:** DY lee

The Blue Shirts numbered only about 10,000 members and prided themselves on their elite nature. Through various organizations, however, they influenced hundreds of thousands of people. When Jiang fell into the hands of his enemies in late 1936, he negotiated with the communists and others for his release. Some have argued that one condition of Jiang's freedom was the disbanding of the Blue Shirts. Whatever the reason, the organization and many of its subagencies were abolished in 1938. Thus, Jiang lost a key support group. The Nationalist Party declined further and lost control of the Chinese mainland.

National Socialism in Japan

Although there were numerous nationalistic organizations in Japan during the 1920s and 1930s, small national socialist parties developed. Two different but related programs generated by intellectuals appeared, one in the early 1920s and the other in 1940. The first, led by Kita Ikki[3] (1883–1937), influenced a large number of young Japanese army officers and others to stage a coup in order to bring down the hated Meiji system and usher in an age of national socialist rule. The second, developed by the Showa Research Association, an elite think tank that was cultivated by Prime Minister Konoe Fumimaro,[4] enjoyed a brief influence upon Japan's elite but was overturned by key political figures.

Kita Ikki developed his brand of national socialism from native Japanese traditions and from Western socialism. Kita came from one of Japan's small islands and was born into a wealthy family with a *samurai* lineage. By the early twentieth century, he had come to appreciate socialism, writing a book that sought to bridge the gap between an emperor-oriented nationalism and socialism. After that venture, Kita twice visited China and became friends with men who had participated in the overthrow of the Manchus between 1911 and 1912.

In 1923, Kita's most important book, *A Plan to Reorganize Japan*, influenced many Japanese, especially army officers. The political program advocated a military-led coup and a period of mar-

tial law to topple the Meiji constitutional system and its ruling elite. This program offered the direct unity of the emperor with his people without the intervening layer of bureaucrats and power brokers. After three years, a representative government would be established based on universal male suffrage. Imperial lands and properties would be nationalized and given to the needy.

The economic program envisioned the retention of private property and government regulation of the economy. The purpose was to ensure efficiency and effective planning. Seven special ministries (Banks, Maritime, Mines, Agriculture, Industries, Commerce, and Railroads) would be established. They would supervise businesses that came into state hands and sell agricultural and industrial merchandise produced by state concerns. Kita urged worker profit-sharing programs and worker participation in management. There would be an eight-hour work day, binding arbitration to resolve labor disputes, and other benefits for laborers. Peasants were to enjoy a land redistribution from imperial and wealthy landowners' lands.

Kita's social program advocated treating women favorably and called for the establishment of a welfare state. Women were to have equal opportunity in the workplace and to be treated with respect. The state would punish adulterous husbands. The state also was to provide for the welfare of orphans, widows with children, people over the age of sixty, disabled people, and others who could not provide for themselves or who did not have families able to support them.

Kita's ideas profoundly influenced young soldiers, many of whom had lived in rural areas and knew of the difficult life there. Some of them were involved in assassinations of prominent leaders in the 1930s, but the event that riveted Japan's attention was the attempted coup by the First Division of the Imperial Army on February 26, 1936. Around 1,400 soldiers took over government buildings in downtown Tokyo, assassinating political and naval leaders. Emperor Hirohito's refusal to support the coup doomed it. No officials joined the effort, and the rebels were persuaded to surrender. Several leaders and Kita Ikki, who had no direct role in the coup, were tried and executed. Members of an army faction that favored the overthrow of the Meiji system were purged.

---

[3] **Kita Ikki:** KEE tah EE kee
[4] **Konoe Fumimaro:** KOH noh ay FOO mee mah roh

Another national socialist movement developed among a small group of Japanese intellectuals in the late 1930s. They had been socialists early in their academic careers, but they had moved away from Marxism and toward nationalistic positions. All of them argued for a single mass party, a powerful nation-state, government control of the economy through corporate systems, and the inculcation of an ethic that promoted service to the nation. Their proposals built on examples in Germany and Italy. These systems impressed the Japanese thinkers who viewed national socialism as the ideology of the future. They discounted the role of violence in bringing systemic change and eschewed the racist programs found in Europe. The members of the Showa Research Association wanted to establish a society that was more just, less conflict-ridden, and more efficiently administered. Unlike Kita Ikki, they did not harken back to Japan's past for models or ideas. Rather, they postulated an elite national socialism that was comprised of components from the most current ideologies. Their ideas proved to be too revolutionary and were rejected.

IN THEIR OWN WORDS

Japanese National Socialism

Japanese intellectuals were alternately attracted by or resistant to Western ideas and influences in the 1930s. While some admired Hitler and Mussolini and their movements, they also believed that Japanese national socialism had to be unique.

Members of the Showa Research Association flirted with national socialism. They wished for a single party based on occupational units, leading to a Japanese form of "one nation, one party." As in Nazi Germany, the economic order would limit profits, implement economic planning, create regional and industrial cartels, and emphasize national goals:

> The new economic structure of the . . . national defense state aims at the competition of military preparations, expansion of productivity, and . . . a mobilization of the entire personnel and material resources of the country.

> This means an epoch-making development not only in the munitions industries. Such a rapid and large-scale reorganization of the industrial structure is practically impossible under the old liberal economic structure without causing disturbances to the entire national economic structure. Therefore it is essential first of all to intensify thoroughly planned economic control.

The trend of some Japanese extremists working toward a common goal in the 1930s elicited commentary from Ryu Shintaro, a member of the Showa Research Association:

> The Social Mass [Party] now seems to stand above the contradictions [of espousing both peace and national defense]. This is a [tactical] "necessity" and it is not an earth-shaking change for Japanese social democracy. We will not argue whether [this condition] depends on the special historical and economic character of the Japanese army or on the special nature of Japanese social democracy. We cannot, however, ignore the fact that a distinct social force has newly formed. This is very different from the attitudes that European social democratic parties have taken in their antifascist movements. We will not discuss here which historical and social conditions are causing these special Japanese developments. Also we cannot judge whether these trends will lead to fascist control or social control [by the masses]. . . . At any rate, the form and shape of the "international" character of the labor movement within Japan has disappeared.

Although Japanese national socialism never developed into a full-fledged movement like those in Italy and Germany, the Showa Research Association provided the idea of a totalitarian Japanese system of one party and one nation.

NATIONAL SOCIALISM IN THE AMERICAS

National socialist ideas had a limited impact in the Americas. In North America, a few intellectuals and business leaders were attracted to the personalities of Hitler and Mussolini, and others were attracted to the economic success of the national socialists. In Latin America, military officers and soldiers became enamored of the warlike nature of the Italian and German national socialists.

North American National Socialism

U.S. imitators of the Nazi and Fascist parties could raise only a few supporters in the 1930s. The Khaki Shirts and American Vigilantes formed but were unable to attract large followings. They were led by common people who sought personal power and influence rather than the implementation of programs. Veterans had little part in these outfits, which vehemently attacked the New Deal and President Franklin Roosevelt.

Ezra Pound, the poet, and a few other intellectuals found national socialism attractive. Perhaps the most sustained and articulate espousal of such views came from Lawrence Dennis, a diplomat and financier. Dennis published *The Coming American Fascism*, wherein he rejected communism as a viable option for America because it focused on class warfare. National socialism, he felt, had the best chance of success because it promoted class harmony in the sense of corporatism found in Europe; in addition, massive public works programs could put people back to work. Dennis also reflected the common view that women should not work because marriage, he felt, was a woman's best option.

Huey Long, a U.S. politician with presidential ambitions, seemed to many to be a latent national socialist. He professed admiration for some of the European programs of national socialism and promoted large public welfare programs. Dennis believed that Long had the charisma to lead the masses in the manner of a Hitler or a Mussolini, but Long's assassination in 1935 ended that possibility. No one else developed the ideas and program to become a major U.S. political figure in the national socialist movement.

Except for a few isolated people, Canadians did not espouse national socialism. In 1935, the Social Credit Party swept to power in the Province of Alberta on a platform of mortgage relief for farmers and ranchers who suffered from the Great Depression. The party grew more anti-Semitic and restrictive of civil liberties in the 1930s. In Quebec Province, the Union Nationale came to power in 1936. It appealed to Quebec nationalism and attacked communism, gaining the support of local trade unions and religious leaders.

Latin American National Socialism

Between 1932 and 1938, there developed in Brazil a movement similar to those in Italy and Germany. This national socialist party, the Integralists, received significant funding from the Italian embassy, especially in its formative months. Integralists espoused a strong nationalism tinged with a craving for traditional values and institutions. Catholicism became a key part of their party program, as in the Iberian national socialist movements. Integralists repudiated Marxism's internationalism, its scorn for tradition, and its atheistic ideology.

Integralists vehemently fought and helped destroy a Brazilian communist movement that was funded and directed by the Comintern (Communist International). The communists in turn dominated a coalition of parties, the National Liberation Alliance. The communists and the national socialists battled each other in the streets of Brazil's major cities. The Integralists adopted the symbol of the green shirt and held highly disciplined street rallies. In crushing the communist movement in the latter half of 1935, Brazil's president declared a state of siege and ruled by decree. Mass arrests, summary trials, tortures, and executions doomed the attempted communist uprising.

The Integralists were elated by the communists' defeat. They expected to play a role similar to that of the Fascists in Italy and of the Nazis in Germany, but there was no mass movement, and, following a feeble coup attempt, the Integralists themselves faced a state crackdown. The party disappeared.

Chile and Argentina were influenced by European national socialism. Chileans formed a small National Socialist Party that clearly imitated the

FIGURE 39.6 *Interrogating a Leftist in Brazil.* *The Brazilian Integralist Party, which had national socialist leanings, regarded socialists and Marxists as enemies of the state. In this 1936 photo, a communist leader is held in restraints and guarded by a member of the security forces. Examples were made of the socialists and their allies to deter others from political activism; many were harshly punished.* Iconographia / Pulsar Images.

German Nazi Party. It had little electoral success and mainly served as a target of vehement opposition by socialists. Argentina had many paramilitary groups organized along the lines of their European national socialist counterparts. The strongest influence in Argentina was found in the military. In secret lodges, the Italian model of national socialism received some praise and imitation. The Argentinian movement, however, did not develop a powerful ideological and organizational framework.

SOCIETY UNDER NATIONAL SOCIALISM

In Italy and Germany, most groups supported the national socialists, especially when they ruled. One social phenomenon was the predominance of

men in the early national socialist movements. Soldiers and veterans seemed especially drawn to the national socialist message of the use of violence to solve problems. Many veterans from World War I could not find jobs and longed for the camaraderie and thrills they had experienced on the battlefield. Battling for national socialism seemed attractive to them.

Young people dominated the early national socialist movements in Italy, Germany, and elsewhere. War veterans, most of whom were in their twenties, were concerned about inflation and sociopolitical unrest. Young people, who had few chances to better themselves and felt cheated by circumstances, feared that the Great Depression was the start of a downward spiral that could be halted only by radical action.

The leadership core in Romanian, Hungarian, and Slovakian national socialism came from university students and from some high school students. They seemed more receptive to the relatively simple party messages and were more idealistic in seeking to bring about radical sociopolitical change. Proponents of national socialism in Japan were young army officers and their youthful soldiers. While some older people, like generals and Kita Ikki, served as models, the bulk of the activists were younger men.

Some women joined national socialist parties, but they seldom sanctioned the avowed use of violence. Significant numbers of women joined the German Nazi Party during the last years of World War II, when their percentage grew from 5 percent (1933–1936) to around 35 percent (1942–1944), or more than 2.1 million. This high percentage certainly reflects the number of men killed in wartime, but it also shows the growing influence of women on the home front, especially in businesses and industry.

While the Italian and German parties had a high proportion of middle-class elements among the core leaders, the Fascists and Nazis recruited from all social classes and all geographic regions, before and after they came to power. In that sense, they broadly represented the social makeup of their respective nation-states.

FIGURE 39.7   *On Their Way to a Book-burning.*   *These Nazis and their supporters are carrying books and other papers for destruction. A favorite method was through incineration, which sent a fiery message to intellectuals to censor their works or have them turned to ashes. Book-burnings have occurred throughout history, and the Nazi Party celebrated the destruction of literature and the diminishing of ideas they hated.*   Corbis-Bettmann.

Europe

	1910	
	–	
	–	
	–	
	–	
		Austrian National Socialist Party founded, 1919
	1920	Italian Fascist Party formed, 1919
Italian national socialism, 1922–1943	–	Mussolini takes power, 1922
		Kita Ikki publishes *A Plan to Reorganize Japan*, 1923
	–	Hitler writes *Mein Kampf*, 1924
	–	
	–	
	1930	
	–	
		Blue Shirts founded in China, 1933
German national socialism, 1933–1945	–	British Union has 50,000 members, 1934
		Social Credit Party wins power, 1935
	–	Kita Ikki executed, 1936
	–	Blue Shirts disbanded, 1938
Austrian national socialism, 1938–1945		National Alliance gains 900,000 votes, 1939
	1940	
	–	
	–	Mussolini executed, 1945
		Hitler commits suicide, 1945
	–	
	–	

SUMMARY

1. National socialism has four components: nationalism (focus on the nation), socialism (state control of the economy), imperialism (national expansion), and totalitarianism (subordination of all other elements to the nation-state). Central to many national socialist movements were the attraction of young people, veterans, and active soldiers, and resort to racist slogans, policies, and programs of violence.

2. National socialism was sparked by the aftermath of World War I and by the Great Depression. It was spurred by soldiers and young people who feared falling into poverty, as well as the Great Depression's devastation of workers and farmers.

3. Italian national socialism (fascism) owed much to Benito Mussolini. He led the party to power in 1922 and ruled a coalition of political parties afterward.

4. The Nazi Party achieved modest success up to 1923, when its leader, Adolf Hitler, attempted a coup and was briefly jailed. A second upsurge came with the Great Depression. In 1933, German leaders appointed Hitler chancellor of the Weimar Republic, and he eventually transformed Germany into a national socialist state. Hitler rebuilt the German economy and began a massive rearmament program that helped precipitate hostilities in the European theater of World War II.

5. National socialist movements were less successful in Hungary, Austria, Romania, Belgium, and the Netherlands. These national socialist organizations followed the lead of Italy and Germany, though they also had national variations.

6. Chinese national socialism came when Jiang Jieshi became enamored of the German and Italian movements. His Blue Shirts developed as an elitist Chinese-style secret society that influenced Chinese politics until they were disbanded in 1938.

7. Japan saw two movements of national socialism, one developed by Kita Ikki and the other by the Showa Research Association. The former followed many Japanese patterns and did not receive impetus from the European movements. The latter developed with Europe as a model but did not become significant in terms of government policy.

8. Latin American national socialist parties remained small and politically unimportant. They attracted some middle-class support but remained closely tied with military groups in Brazil and Argentina. They grew in imitation of European models and often were financed with European money.

9. The national socialists attracted different social groups, especially in their successful state governments. Women generally played minor roles in the national socialist movements. In some countries, intellectuals and professionals were particularly attracted to the parties.

SUGGESTED READINGS

Bracher, Karl. *Turning Points in Modern Times.* Cambridge, Mass.: Harvard University Press, 1995. A historical analysis of modern Germany, focusing on the totalitarian component of German national socialism.

Carsten, F. L. *The Rise of Fascism.* Berkeley: University of California Press, 1980. A classic treatment of fascism.

Fletcher, W. M. *Intellectuals and Fascism in Prewar Japan.* Chapel Hill: University of North Carolina Press, 1982. A look at the intellectual origins of Japanese national socialism.

Hsü, Immanuel. *The Rise of Modern China.* Oxford, Eng.: Oxford University Press, 1995. A standard history of China, emphasizing the 1930s.

Mosse, George. *Nazi Culture.* London: W. H. Allen, 1966. An important treatment of the uses that the Nazis made of culture in order to promote their message.

Mühlberger, Detlef, ed. *The Social Basis of European Fascist Movements.* London: Croom Helm, 1987. An examination of social class and national socialism.

Sternhell, Zeev. *The Birth of Fascist Ideology.* Princeton, N.J.: Princeton University Press, 1994. A look at the socialist elements in national socialism.

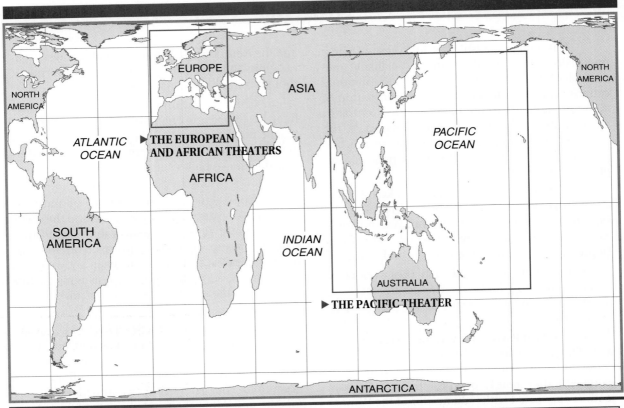

ATLANTIC
OCEAN

NORTH
AMERICA

NORTH
AMERICA

EUROPE

ASIA

▶ THE EUROPEAN
AND AFRICAN THEATERS

AFRICA

PACIFIC
OCEAN

SOUTH
AMERICA

INDIAN
OCEAN

AUSTRALIA

▶ THE PACIFIC THEATER

ANTARCTICA

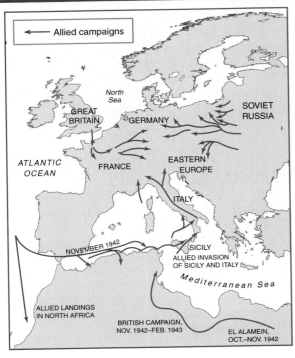

Allied campaigns

North
Sea

GREAT
BRITAIN

GERMANY

SOVIET
RUSSIA

ATLANTIC
OCEAN

FRANCE

EASTERN
EUROPE

ITALY

NOVEMBER 1942

SICILY
ALLIED INVASION
OF SICILY AND ITALY

Mediterranean Sea

ALLIED LANDINGS
IN NORTH AFRICA

BRITISH CAMPAIGN,
NOV. 1942–FEB. 1943

EL ALAMEIN,
OCT.–NOV. 1942

▶ **THE EUROPEAN AND AFRICAN THEATERS**

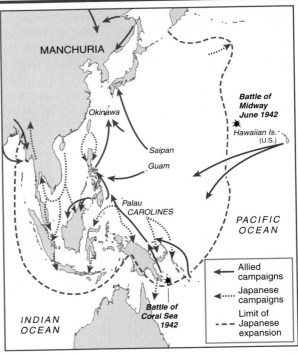

MANCHURIA

Okinawa

Battle of
Midway
June 1942

Hawaiian Is.
(U.S.)

Saipan

Guam

Palau
CAROLINES

PACIFIC
OCEAN

INDIAN
OCEAN

Battle of
Coral Sea
1942

Allied
campaigns

Japanese
campaigns

Limit of
Japanese
expansion

▶ **THE PACIFIC THEATER**

World War II and Holocausts

1937–1945

*A stench hung in the air over the ash-covered
concentration camp. Today, a Gypsy lad of barely
twenty was shot and killed for joking during the work
detail. His crumpled body lay in the pit where charred
human remains lay in smoldering piles. Among those
killed had been homosexuals, Jews, disabled people,
and senile folk. Why?*

In terms of human suffering, World War II dwarfs
all other human wars. Calculations of the loss of
life, limb, and property scarcely begin to measure
the scale of this global conflict. The number of
dead and missing double the corresponding figures for World War I and may have reached more
than 60 million people. Apart from that total,
wartime destruction uprooted millions, some of
whom moved to distant places in search of peace
or opportunity. Millions were forcibly evicted from
their homes by conquerors, paving the way for
others to resettle. Isolated examples of racist
actions involving humiliation, injury, and death
abound, but these pale in comparison to the deliberate and systematic mass murder of around 11
million Jews, Poles, Russians, Gypsies, and others
deemed unfit or troublesome.

CAUSES OF WORLD WAR II

Two main blocs fought each other during World
War II. The **Axis** included Germany, Japan, and
Italy, although other states gave minimal support

to this group. The **Allies** comprised Britain, the Soviet Union, China, the United States, and Canada, as well as less powerful countries. When France fell to the Germans in 1940, the succeeding puppet government that cooperated with the Germans was known as **Vichy France**. A group of French who were antagonistic to the Germans later formed the **Free French**, a government-in-exile. Italy was an Axis power until it fell to the Allies in 1943.

Interlocking Wars

There were three interrelated war theaters in World War II—Asia, Euro-Africa, and the Pacific. The Asian theater erupted in July 1937, when Chinese and Japanese soldiers engaged in a firefight. Although this was a small-scale engagement, hostilities soon spread until much of East and Southeast Asia became embroiled in combat.

Fighting in the European and North African theater began when Germany attacked Poland on September 1, 1939, and the loss of life in the European theater exceeded the numbers of those in the Asian theater. The Italians and Germans made North Africa a battle zone and fought with the British and Americans for control there. The United States entered the war on December 8, 1941, the day after Japanese planes carried out a devastating attack on the Pearl Harbor naval base in Hawaii. Of course, the Germans had already conquered most of Europe by then. The Euro-African theater received much attention from U.S. planners, and the American effort in the Pacific was significant. In fact, the U.S. economy sustained a two-front global war.

War Aims

Each of the major participants in World War II had its particular war aims. Many wished to expand their control of adjacent territories, while others desired to maintain their political positions. Some war aims changed as the ebb and flow of combat opened new vistas for expansion.

JAPANESE WAR AIMS. In Japan, several groups were involved in policy formulation and there was no commander-in-chief; war aims therefore often reflected a consensus derived from complex and time-consuming negotiations. At times, the army and navy could not agree on a common strategy, which limited Japan's success. The army often drove Japan's foreign policy in the 1930s and 1940s, and members of the army's high command sought to negotiate a military pact with the Germans and Italians. In contrast, Japanese naval officials feared that this foreign policy initiative might antagonize the Americans and British, both of whom had significant naval fleets in the Pacific region. Thus, until 1941, top naval leaders blocked army plans to secure that military alliance.

Germany's conquest of the Netherlands and France and isolation of Britain by late 1940 forced the Japanese to rethink their war aims. French Indochina and the Dutch East Indies enticed Japanese strategic thinkers, who desired access to the rubber and oil produced in these Southeast Asian colonies. In addition, British-controlled Malaya, Burma, and even India seemed to be vulnerable to Japanese attack. Of its potential enemies, only the United States remained strong, but Japanese leaders believed that conquest of Southeast Asia was worth risking a war with the United States. The opportunity was too significant to let pass. When Japan attacked the United States, Japanese naval and army planners intended to use the blow to negotiate a favorable settlement with the Americans. They did not wish a sustained war, because they understood that the United States possessed formidable resources.

Justification for the expansion of Japan's empire came with the idea of "Asia for the Asians." According to this view, Japanese expansion and control in Asia was a way to "help" other Asians. Although some Japanese viewed their overlordship as a tutelage effort, most scholars see it as another form of imperialist domination and exploitation.

GERMAN WAR AIMS. Adolf Hitler wanted Germany to expand to the east, but in order to do that he had to defeat and destroy Poland. Then he planned to defeat the countries of western Europe and thereafter conquer the Soviet Union. Each phase of war was to be of Hitler's choosing and timing, and each would pave the way for the next. Ultimately, Hitler intended to harness Europe's resources to defeat the United States and dominate the world. His vision was clear and closely followed.

At the same time, Hitler believed that these conflicts would deflect attention from a major war aim of cleansing Germany, Poland, and the Soviet

Union of "undesirable" racial and other groups. Not only were Jews and Gypsies to be exterminated, but many Slavs also were to be killed. A massive demographic revolution was planned.

SOVIET WAR AIMS. Josef Stalin used the various conflicts of World War II to expand Soviet power and influence. Between 1939 and 1941, he annexed Latvia, Lithuania, and Estonia, along with parts of Finland, Poland, and Romania. Although these areas were lost to German conquest between 1942 and 1944, they came back under Soviet domination when Russian armies pushed the Germans back. After 1945, the Soviet Union controlled much of Eastern and Central Europe, and Stalin took advantage of the favorable situation to expand the Soviet Empire.

"Ethnic cleansing" became a major Soviet war aim as German armies fanned out over Soviet Russia beginning in 1941. One reason for the early success of the Nazi forces was the favorable reception given them by various ethnic minorities. Recognizing this, Stalin ordered his secret police to round up and deport "unreliable" groups in the path of advancing German soldiers. Several hundred thousand Germans who had lived in the Volga River Valley for nearly two centuries were shipped to Siberia. Tatars living in their Crimean homes for centuries were deported eastward, as were many Chechens of Chechniya.

BRITISH WAR AIMS. Winston Churchill led Britain through the war years as prime minister, and his primary aim was to defeat Germany, no matter the cost. To that end, Churchill allied with Stalin, even though he hated what Stalin stood for. Churchill's other major aim was the preservation of the British Empire, and, if possible, Britain's dominant global position.

Another of Churchill's war aims was to maintain a close relationship with the United States. Both he and President Franklin Roosevelt worked hard to ensure a smooth wartime alliance. In 1940, before the United States entered the war, Churchill and Roosevelt met in the Atlantic to hammer out a United States aid package to the British. They also met several times during the war.

U.S. WAR AIMS. President Franklin Roosevelt changed his aims as situations developed. He tried to keep the United States out of the war, but when that became impossible he directed the effort to defeat Germany and Japan. Even before the United States entered the war, Roosevelt warned the Japanese against expanding into Southeast Asia, desiring to preserve the sagging European empires there. He assumed the mantle of leadership of the "Free World."

The United States insisted on "unconditional surrender" by Germany and Japan as a prerequisite to ending the war. That would free the hands of the victors to take drastic measures, if necessary, to prevent future wars.

Racism

Most countries practiced racial discrimination during the war. The United States had segregated armed forces, with African Americans, Japanese Americans, and others in separate units. In addition, Japanese American citizens were rounded up in 1942 and shipped off to camps where they were interned for the war's duration. Japanese brutally lorded it over the Koreans, Chinese, and Filipinos during their occupations. Japanese doctors carried out medical experiments on living subjects from those countries. European and North American prisoners of war suffered from sometimes barbaric forms of treatment by Japanese soldiers.

Some of the most virulent forms of racism came from the national socialists in Germany and Yugoslavia. In Germany, the Nazis aimed to systematically murder whole population groups. Reflecting longstanding animosities, Croats used national socialist policies to murder, oust, or dominate more than 350,000 Serbs. These wartime atrocities reverberated into the 1990s, when some Serbs avenged themselves on the Croats.

THE ASIAN THEATER, 1937–1945

Japan launched invasions of Manchuria, China, and Southeast Asia and made small naval forays into the Indian Ocean. For a time, the Japanese fought the Soviets and briefly considered an invasion of Siberia. They also battled United States forces in the Pacific Ocean and in the Aleutian Islands off Alaska.

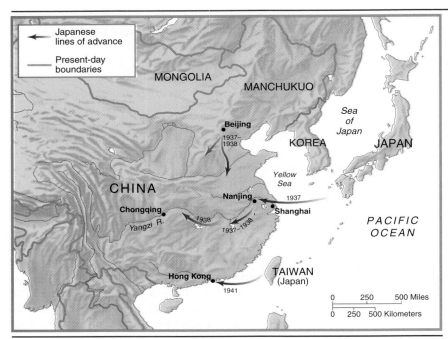

MAP 40.1 *Japanese Expansion in China, 1937–1941.* *Japan gradually expanded its influence in East Asia during the twentieth century. It annexed Korea in 1910 and took control of Germany's colonies in China in 1914. In 1931, the Japanese army began taking over territory in Manchuria. By the summer of 1937, Japanese control of China had extended into the North China Plain. Beginning in mid-1937, large-scale warfare broke out between Japanese and Chinese forces, with the Japanese expanding their control of China's cities, especially along the Yangzi River. Much of eastern China lay in Japanese hands by late 1941.*

The Japanese army directed a thrust into Manchuria, Inner Mongolia, and other parts of China from 1931 to 1937. Knowing that their government might oppose military action in China, elements of the Japanese army in Manchuria planned and executed a surprise attack on September 18, 1931. Chinese forces did not respond, and, in 1933, Japan renamed the region Manchukuo, ruling it as a puppet state. The Japanese government reluctantly supported its army and faced severe but futile criticism in the League of Nations. Japan ultimately withdrew from the League in 1933, showing it to be useless as a means of stopping aggression by a determined power.

Subsequent military campaigns brought Japan into Central China by the mid-1930s and set the stage for the beginning of World War II. China had been steadily retreating from Japanese advances because President Jiang Jieshi knew that resistance might be fatal to him. The withdrawals, however, caused Chinese nationalists to criticize Jiang so severely that by 1937 he had to resist the Japanese. When a firefight erupted on July 7, 1937, Jiang's response was to deliver a strong rebuke to the Japanese, who felt they could not back down, despite some desire to seek a negotiated settlement. Full-scale fighting broke out and continued for eight years, although the Japanese expected a quick victory, their feelings of racial superiority causing them to miscalculate resistance in China.

In 1938 and 1939, the Japanese and Soviets fought two major battles that caused great Japanese losses and a need for regrouping by their army. In the spring of 1941, Japanese and Soviet diplomats negotiated a nonaggression pact that remained in effect until August 1945.

Between May and June 1940, Nazi Germany defeated the Netherlands, Belgium, and France, opening the possibility of Japan's invasion of Southeast Asia, where the Dutch and the French had empires. Japanese planners jumped at the prospect of taking rubber plantations, tin mines, oil fields, and other Southeast Asian raw materials crucial for Japan's war machine. In July 1940, the Japanese pressured the French to permit them into northern French Indochina. This allowed the Japanese to sever key supply routes to China in hopes of compelling the surrender of the Chinese Nationalist armies. Eventually, Japanese troops moved into the southern part of the French colony, developing a base from which to threaten much of Southeast Asia, including the Philippines, a U.S. colony. At that point, the Americans announced that they intended to shut off oil supplies to Japan, making the Southeast Asian oil supplies even more valuable.

U.S. citizens watched with growing sympathy for the Chinese during the opening years of the Asian theater. Monies were raised through collections among movie theater audiences. U.S. and Canadian pilots served in China as volunteers as the famed "Flying Tigers." The U.S. government hoped that a combination of naval buildups, economic threats, and negotiations might force the Japanese to reconsider their Asian policy. Once Japan's key leaders decided on taking Southeast Asia, however, they refused to yield to pressure. The United States could avoid conflict only by accepting all of Japan's gains and its future plans.

Planning for the Japanese thrust southward took part of 1940 and most of 1941. The Japanese intended to invade Thailand and use it as a base from which to attack Malaya and Burma. To secure their sea-lanes, the Japanese had to neutralize the Philippines, bringing themselves into conflict with the United States. The initial planning aimed at attacking the Philippines itself, but the Combined Fleet's commander, Admiral Yamamoto Isoroku (1884–1943), insisted on hitting Hawaii first. The initial plan might have left open a chance for negotiations, but attacks on United States ships almost guaranteed an all-out American response.

FIGURE 40.1 *Casualty of World War II. This famous 1937 photograph shows a wounded Chinese baby amid the wreckage of a Shanghai train station after a Japanese bombing raid. The image of the crying infant underscored the war's horrors. Japan's war on China set the stage for the Asian theater of World War II, in which tens of millions would lose their lives.* UPI/Corbis-Bettmann.

FIGURE 40.2 *Catastrophe at Pearl Harbor.* *Japan's surprise attack on Pearl Harbor devastated much of America's military firepower in the mid-Pacific region and immediately drew the U.S. into World War II. Beyond the wreckage of these airplanes, smoke billows from the battleships burning in the harbor. Although most of America's battleship fleet was disabled during the attack, the Japanese missed the aircraft carriers because they were out at sea.* U.S. Navy.

On December 7 and 8, 1941, military actions unfolded over a wide front, initiated by an attack on American fortifications in Hawaii, including the naval base at Pearl Harbor. Over the next six months, Japan conquered the Philippines, Burma, Thailand, Malaya, and Indonesia. Their losses were not costly, and they gained access to vital supplies of oil, tin, and rubber. The victories also brought an overbearing arrogance, reflected in the conquerors' brutal treatment of conquered peoples. The Japanese believed that they could easily defeat the Americans and British. At the same time, the British and Americans, whose own racial prejudices had kept them from regarding the Japanese as a real threat, now saw them as almost invincible warriors. Both perspectives smacked of

racial stereotypes and inhibited successful planning. Soon, however, U.S. planners began to learn from their mistakes, revising their strategies and tactics.

In 1942, the Japanese sent a fleet into the Indian Ocean. Its purpose was to defeat the British navy there and to sever naval supply lines to the Soviets as well as to the British in North Africa. After some limited successes in Ceylon and along the Indian coast, the Japanese withdrew. The British conquered the Axis-held island of Madagascar off the African coast and used it as a base to safeguard the western and central Indian Ocean.

By and large, the remainder of operations in Asia assumed a secondary nature as focus shifted to the Pacific theater. In August 1945, the Japanese army in Manchukuo faced a massive assault by Soviet troops and collapsed quickly. Surviving Japanese officials in Harbin, a city in North Manchukuo, departed after releasing toxins from chemical and biological warfare facilities, killing large numbers of Chinese in the city. Japan's surrender in mid-August 1945 left large numbers of defeated Japanese soldiers in China.

In Southeast Asia, the Japanese had long boasted that they were better rulers than the Europeans. The Japanese did not allow their Asian colonies to rule themselves until 1945, after it had become clear that Japan was losing the war.

THE EURO-AFRICAN THEATER, 1939–1945

Adolf Hitler was the architect of the battle plan that dominated the Euro-African theater. He had come to power in 1933 and had consolidated control of the German government. At the same time, he had established a program for building the economy and rearming Germany. Hitler's determined effort propelled Germany ahead of its adversaries in Europe, and he adhered to his goals of expanding east and west. Hitler also had to be certain that the

---

PARALLELS AND DIVERGENCES

Military Codes and Ciphers

Codes have been used by military forces at least since the time of the Roman Empire to disguise the meaning of a message that might fall into enemy hands. With World War II, however, ways of making messages unintelligible to the enemy became far more important. Because radio broadcasts could not be hidden from the enemy, some means of scrambling the messages had to be devised.

Strictly speaking, a message can be rendered unreadable by two methods. With a **code**, symbols are substituted for other symbols. If "red" means to attack and "marmoset" signifies an enemy position, "red marmoset" might mean to attack that position. A **cipher**, on the other hand, manipulates the letters of the message, scrambling it so that only someone who knows the rules of manipulation can reconstruct it. A simple cipher might substitute the next letter of the alphabet for each letter of a message; with this cipher "history" would become "ijtupsz."

As military forces relied increasingly on radios, more and more effort was devoted to making codes and ciphers more complex. Their enemies, of course, devoted more and more effort to the cracking of those codes and ciphers. The German **Enigma machine** automatically produced a complex cipher of any message that was typed into it, and the Germans relied on it for much of the war. The Poles had begun to break this cipher and had produced a rough copy of an Enigma machine by the eve of the German invasion. With the invasion, the Polish machine and

information on the German cipher were spirited away to Britain, where British intelligence officers refined the Polish device and decipherment rules. One German Enigma message described the date and plans for the bombing of the English town of Coventry. Winston Churchill believed information gained by deciphering Enigma messages to be so important that he permitted the devastating bombing to go forward uninhibited, rather than reveal to the Germans that their cipher had been cracked.

The most successful of all codes in World War II was an American code used in the Pacific. It consisted of Dine,[a] the language of the Navajo Indians of the American Southwest. There were very few speakers of that language outside the United States; among the Axis powers, probably only a single German anthropology professor knew the language, and he, a Jew, had been placed in a concentration camp. The complexities of the language eluded the Japanese intelligence officers who tried to decode it, and the Navajo "code talkers" continued to operate successfully throughout the war.

Codes and ciphers remain critical to military and diplomatic communication today, especially given the sophistication of "bugging" devices. Following the lead of the Enigma machine, most ciphers today are created by computers, and their complexities are so great that only other computers can break them.

[a]**Dine:** DEE nay

German people supported his efforts, and that meant avoiding too harsh a demand on the German economy and people.

Germany's Conquest of Europe

To implement his plan, Hitler fomented trouble in the Sudetenland, a German-populated area of Czechoslovakia. After German threats, the British, who wished to avoid war, convinced the French and Italians to negotiate. The British and French ignored previous diplomatic pledges of support for the Czechs. Soon, eastern Czechoslovakia (Slovakia) was formed into a German puppet state, and the rest was annexed to Germany. Hitler turned to Poland next.

As Hitler told a conference of his generals in 1939, the aim of the Polish campaign was Poland's destruction, not merely the defeat of its army. To ensure victory, however, Hitler had to ally Germany with the British and French or with the Soviets. Britain and France refused to succumb to his wiles, so an agreement with the Soviet Union became more attractive. Both Germany and the Soviet Union had longed to dismember Poland and extend their power in other parts of eastern Europe, so they favored an alliance. In addition, the Soviet Union promised to supply Germany with raw materials to offset a British naval blockade. A nonaggression pact was worked out along with an economic agreement in late August. The Soviets and Nazis agreed to a division of territories for exploitation, with the Soviets promising to attack Poland after an initial pause.

THE POLISH CAMPAIGN. On September 1, 1939, Germany invaded Poland and swiftly crushed its army. The German combination of air strikes and

FIGURE 40.3 *World War II Poland.* *The German army struck Poland with swift, massive air attacks and mobile army units. In this 1939 photo, a German supply convoy and motor unit (right and middle) proceed toward the eastern front. While motorized units carried the vanguard to victory, horses carried much of the materials necessary to feed and rearm Germany's soldiers. On the left, Polish refugees flee the conflict on foot, carting their belongings on bicycles and horse-drawn wagons.* Wide World Photos.

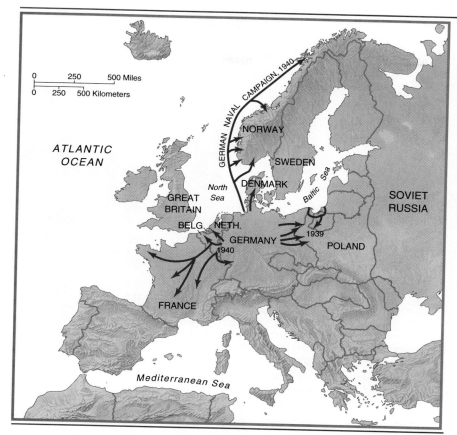

MAP 40.2 *Germany's Campaigns, 1939–1940.*
After a brief but bloody conquest of Poland (with Soviet assistance), the Germans turned to western Europe, home of their enemies, France and Great Britain. Before attacking these foes, the Germans struck at Denmark and Norway, then moved west against Belgium and the Netherlands. Finally, major German forces converged on France, nearly destroying a combined Anglo-French army. All of these countries, with the exception of Britain, surrendered by June 1940.

rapidly moving army ground vehicles (including tanks) was called ***blitzkrieg*** (lightning war). *Blitzkrieg* dominated the European theater until early 1940, when large numbers of antitank weapons began to offset Germany's military advantage. Poland collapsed under the onslaught, especially after the Soviets invaded from the east.

Both victors settled into massive campaigns of violence directed against civilian and military groups. The Soviets massacred several thousand Polish officers and other leaders at the Katyn Forest; the Germans slaughtered tens of thousands of Poles and expelled others from their homes. The purpose was to create places for Germans to settle and to begin the demographic revolution through the extermination of designated population groups. As some German army officers objected to this use of their forces, Hitler decided to transfer control of the demographic revolution to the Schutz Staffeln (SS), Germany's secret police, and to other special extermination squads.

Soviet and Nazi officials met at the end of September to redraw their original plans. The Soviets

exchanged part of central Poland for a free hand with Lithuania, a state previously considered under German protection. In 1939, Latvia, Estonia, and Lithuania agreed to allow the Soviet Union to station troops in their territories. Annexation soon followed. And in November, the Soviets launched an attack on Finland. Much to the Soviets' surprise, the Finns fought them off; 200,000 Soviets died, about eight times the number of Finnish casualties.

HITLER'S CAMPAIGN IN NORTHERN AND WESTERN EUROPE. Hitler then turned his attention north and west. Preparations took months and led to the invasions of Denmark and Norway. Both fell to German troops in early 1940; by May 10, Hitler had attacked the Netherlands, Belgium, and France. Central to the German success in most of these campaigns was *blitzkrieg*. After five days, the German tanks broke through Allied defenses and raced to the sea. This effectively divided the Allied forces, and the Germans turned to surround major British and French armies. Only a massive sea-lift rescue at Dunkirk prevented a total disaster for the

FIGURE 40.4 *Execution of Resistance Fighters.* *When the Germans defeated France in 1940, some French joined resistance forces fighting against German rule. When caught, the French patriots could expect no mercy; they were shot or otherwise executed. Resistance movements sprang up in many parts of occupied Europe.* Lapi-Viollet.

FIGURE 40.5 *Germans Surrender in Winter.* *Expecting a quick victory in Soviet Russia, German commanders had not prepared their soldiers for winter fighting. When "General Winter" struck, some freezing German troops surrendered to the better-prepared Soviet forces. This photograph shows one such result outside Moscow in the first year of the German attempt to invade Russia.* Sovfoto.

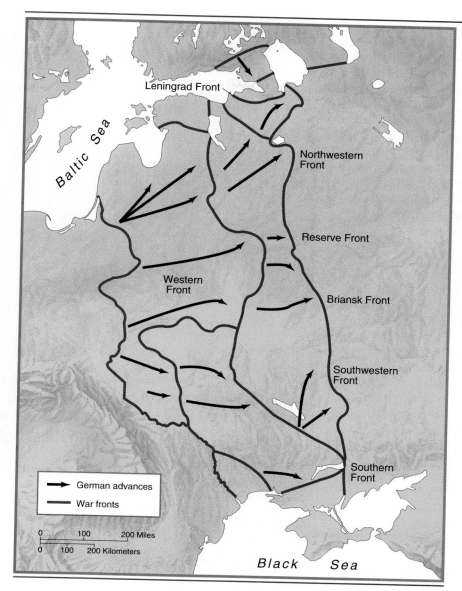

MAP 40.3 *Initial Attack on Russia, June–September 1941.* Hitler turned his attention to Soviet Russia in late 1940, planning to strike in the spring of 1941. Despite a delay of some weeks, the Germans and their allies hit the Soviet Union with a three-pronged attack, north toward Leningrad, east toward Moscow, and southeast toward the oil fields of the Caucasus Mountains. By September, many divisions of the Soviet armed forces had surrendered. As the Germans consolidated their gains and struck anew in each sector, it was only the vastness of the territory to be conquered that gave the Soviets time to regroup.

British. Britain mobilized all available vessels, including rowboats, sailboats, and ferries, to evacuate the defeated Allied soldiers. France surrendered in the latter half of June. Britain remained free but feared an invasion. Their fears were well founded, but Hitler's planned attack was called off because German troops lacked equipment and support services. Instead, Hitler concentrated on air attacks to defeat the British.

HITLER'S CAMPAIGN IN SOVIET RUSSIA. Because of their relative ease in winning the early campaigns, Hitler and the German High Command expected a brief war in the Soviet Union. Despite Germany's agreements with the Soviets, Hitler had decided that expansion farther east was critical to German security. German planners underestimated their Soviet adversary, because they believed the Slavs to be racially inferior. The western Russian area also appeared to give *blitzkrieg* forces ample opportunity for free movement to encircle and annihilate the enemy. What the Germans failed to consider was road conditions.

On June 22, 1941, Germany's invasion of the Soviet Union commenced. Stalin had ample warning that something major was about to happen because he had received countless intelligence reports about German troop movements. However, Stalin preferred not to believe the growing evidence—he felt that Germany had no reason to attack a country that already provided many of its raw materials.

The Axis army and air force attacked, and within hours the Soviet air force was virtually destroyed. Desperate Soviet pilots resorted to ramming German fighter planes with unarmed trainer aircraft. Soon, prisoners by the millions surrendered to the Germans. Although the Germans won victories, the Soviets kept fighting, and the dust of summer and the rains of autumn disabled German mechanized vehicles.

A winter counteroffensive by the Soviets threw the poorly clothed Germans back, sparing Moscow from enemy occupation. Other German forces, however, arrived at the gates of Leningrad (formerly Petrograd) and laid siege to it. For the next 900 days, the two armies contested the battleground, but the Soviets refused to be dislodged. In Leningrad, city folk bore devastating hardships, including the burning of their city and starvation. Farther south, the Ukraine fell to the Nazis in 1941, and German units drove hard to the vital oil fields beyond.

In 1942 and 1943, fronts expanded and contracted. One decisive conflict concerned the Kursk-Orel sector of south-central Russia, where the Soviets destroyed nearly 600 German tanks in one day. During the next year, the Soviets launched a massive attack all along the war front, and, by autumn, they pushed the Germans out of most of Soviet Russia and into parts of eastern Europe. By the spring of 1945, Soviet forces had entered Germany and were soon fighting in Berlin.

The Allied Campaign in the Euro-African Theater

North Africa became a battleground for several years during World War II. The British had defeated the Italians in Northeast Africa in 1940 and 1941 to secure the Red Sea and the Indian Ocean. Most large-scale engagements, however, came in North Africa, with the Italians and Germans fighting the British, Free French, and Americans. The British took the brunt of the earlier fighting as the Axis forces headed by General Erwin Rommel of Ger-

FIGURE 40.6 *Serve Mother Russia.* *This wartime poster shows a stern Motherland exhorting her sons to fight. Despite a communist ideology that condemned nationalism as a relic of the past, Soviet Russia employed all kinds of nationalistic messages to spur its citizens to defeat the invaders. Millions responded to the call to fight for victory.* Poster by I. M. Toidze, 1941, from David M. Glantz and Jonathan M. House, *When Titans Clashed* (Lawrence: University of Kansas Press). Reproduced with permission.

many in June 1942 routed the British and pushed into Egypt toward the strategic Suez Canal. The German forces were stopped and thrown back by the British, led by General Bernard L. Montgomery. Later, U.S. soldiers landed in Northwest Africa and pushed east in their first major combat of World War II. The combined forces destroyed the Axis forces in Africa by early 1943. A few

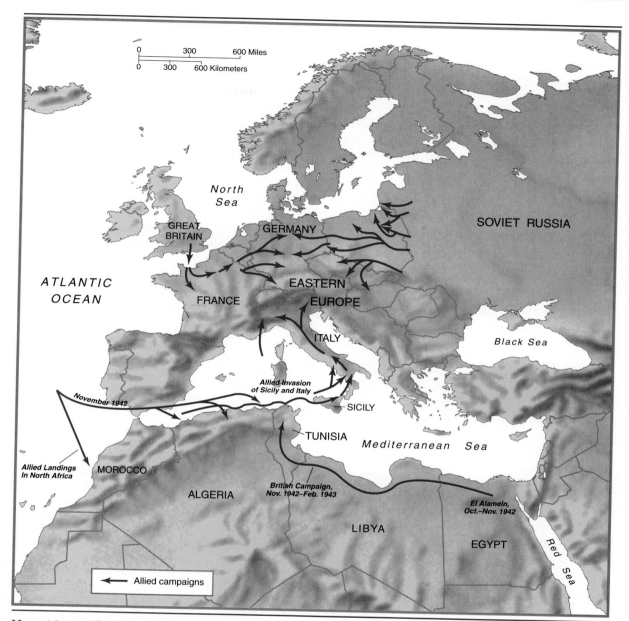

MAP 40.4 *The Euro-African Theater, 1942–1945.* *Under command of General Erwin Rommel, German and Italian forces attacked British troops in Egypt. While advancing through Egypt toward the Suez Canal, the German soldiers were stopped at El Alamein in July of 1942. Then in October, the British counterattacked and began to push back the Germans. At the same time, U.S. forces landed in northwestern Africa. By early 1943, the British and Americans had defeated most of the German and Italian forces in North Africa; they resupplied and prepared to attack Sicily and the Italian Peninsula.*

In Europe, Britain and the United States combined their forces in 1943 to attack Italy through Sicily. In 1944, they opened a second front in western Europe with an attack on German forces in France. The Soviet armed forces began a sustained push in mid-1944, and threw German forces out of Soviet Russia, pursuing them into parts of eastern Europe. By 1945, Germany was being attacked from the west and the east; resistance collapsed in May with the surrender of all German forces.

months later, the Allies invaded Italy; the Italians surrendered, but Germans in Italy resisted the Allied forces.

After a long buildup in Britain, Allied forces attacked German-occupied France on June 6, 1944, and its liberation came in the late summer. The drive on Germany commenced, and following a brief but fierce German counterattack (the Battle of the Bulge) the Allies resumed their offensive, linking up with the Soviet army at the Elbe River in April 1945. Hitler committed suicide in late April, and Germany's military leaders surrendered in May.

The fighting had been long and extremely costly throughout Europe, and the Allied powers had decided that Germany should be divided into spheres of influence to prevent another war from beginning there. At Allied conferences, Roosevelt, Churchill, and Stalin laid out the framework for the preservation of peace.

THE PACIFIC THEATER, 1941–1945

When the Japanese attacked Pearl Harbor, they inflicted great damage, but the shallow water permitted the raising and salvaging of all except one battleship, the USS *Arizona*. The United States was determined to fight rather than negotiate, and it entered the war, contrary to Japanese planning assumptions.

The swift fall of Southeast Asian countries to Japan's forces was paralleled by the Japanese conquest of island chains in the South Pacific. Here, the effort combined both army and navy personnel. A major naval strategist was Admiral Yamamoto Isoroku, who respected America's industrial might. Yamamoto had planned the Pearl Harbor attack and many other Japanese naval campaigns.

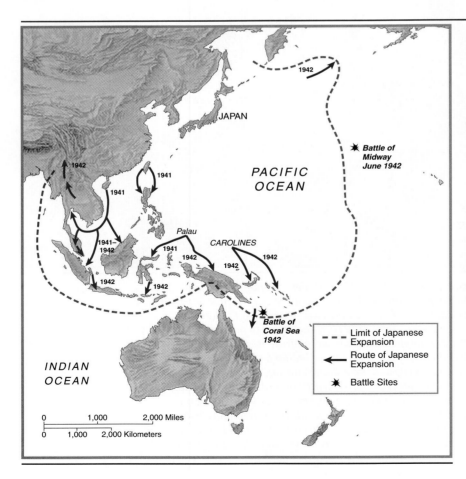

MAP 40.5 *Japanese Expansion, 1941–1942.* *Having lost their momentum in China by 1941, Japan looked to opportunities in Southeast Asia following the defeat of the French and Dutch in 1940. The Japanese desperately needed Indonesian oil after the American embargo in 1941. Japan attacked Southeast Asia and the Pacific, by land and sea, and overwhelmed most resistance until they were stopped by Allied forces at the Battle of the Coral Sea and at the Battle of Midway—thus sparing Australia and halting Japanese expansion to the central Pacific and Hawaii.*

By early 1942, the Japanese seemed invincible. They tried to sever Allied communications with Australia and contested the islands throughout the South Pacific. The Americans decided to fight a naval engagement in May 1942 in the Coral Sea. In the fierce fighting, each side lost an aircraft carrier, but the Japanese had fewer to lose. Yamamoto planned a major thrust in the east against U.S.-held Midway Island and Hawaii. Instead of concentrating his forces at Midway, Yamamoto divided them, and the Americans relied on reading the Japanese naval codes and some shrewd guesswork to win. The defeat of the Japanese at Midway saved Hawaii from invasion.

The rest of 1942 and part of 1943 were concerned with fighting in New Guinea and Guadalcanal in the South Pacific. Both engagements cost the Japanese heavily. Rather than take each Pacific island, the American strategy was to attack only strategic places, hopping over less important islands. This plan speeded up the American offensive and soon provided islands from which the Americans could bomb Japan.

Another result of the fierce fighting in the Pacific was the growing image of Japanese troops as suicidal warriors. During the battle for Tarawa, for example, the Japanese had 8 survivors from a force of 5,000. Savage fighting marked the Philippines, Iwo Jima, and Okinawa campaigns in 1944 and 1945. *Kamikaze*, suicide bombers that sank and damaged some ships, took a heavy toll on the morale of navy personnel.

Because of the image of Japanese fighters as fanatical, U.S. planners grimly estimated that the invasion of the Japanese main islands would last for months, if not years, and that it would cost 1 million Allied casualties. As the Americans had recently tested an atomic bomb, they considered the option of using it rather than invading. U.S. leaders decided to warn the Japanese that the

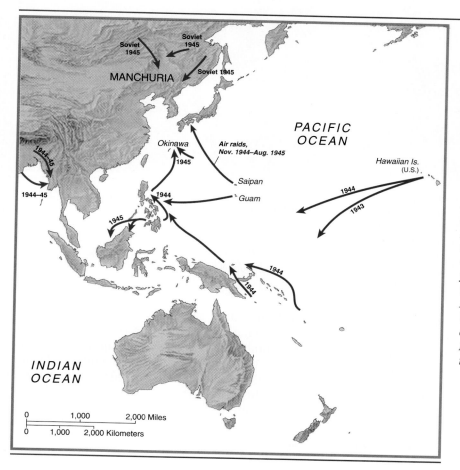

MAP 40.6 *Allied Attacks in the Pacific and Asia, 1944–1945. The Americans and British carried out a series of attacks against Japanese forces in the Pacific and Southeast Asia in 1944 and 1945. Burma and the Philippines were two main targets of the Allied forces, along with certain strategic islands in the South Pacific region. Beginning in late 1944, U.S. airplanes began bombing Japanese cities on the home islands, especially on Honshu; other Allied land and sea forces attacked and took the island of Okinawa between April and June. In August, the U.S. dropped atomic bombs on the cities of Hiroshima and Nagasaki, leading to Japan's unconditional surrender.*

FIGURE 40.7 *Destruction at Nagasaki.* *Three days after the bombing of Hiroshima, the United States released a second atomic bomb over the city of Nagasaki, killing tens of thousands of Japanese. The surrounding hills absorbed some of the blast and prevented larger death tolls, although many later died of radiation poisoning. Before the bombing, the area shown in this photo was covered with residential and industrial buildings. The skeletal structure of the Mitsubishi Steel and Arms Works and the concrete walls of a school building can be seen at the foot of the hills.* Wide World Photos.

atomic bomb would be used on them if they refused to surrender unconditionally. Nothing came in reply, so the United States dropped the first bomb on Hiroshima on August 6, 1945. More than 50,000 people died within the first ten seconds. Then, receiving no unconditional surrender, on August 9 the United States dropped a second atomic bomb, on Nagasaki. For the survivors, women, men, and children, life became a horror with the added possibility of perishing painfully from radiation sickness. The combined effects of the bombs compelled Emperor Hirohito to opt for peace. On August 15, 1945, he announced Japan's surrender to the Japanese people, most of whom heard his voice for the first time. World War II ended with more than 60 million dead and atomic weapons looming over humanity like a threatening storm cloud.

WARTIME HOLOCAUSTS

Adolf Hitler had spoken for many years about a demographic revolution to "cleanse" Germany of the population that he considered inferior. In a deliberate and horrifying effort, the Nazis used the machinery of the nation-state to accomplish their goals. During World War II, **holocausts**, mass exterminations of peoples viewed as inferior, wiped out more than 11 million people, including around 6 million Jews.

A kind of trial run of the larger genocide of Jews and others took place between 1939 and 1941 during the Euro-African theater's first phase. Under cover of war, the Nazis organized systematic efforts to identify and remove to camps certain ethnic groups and disabled or otherwise incapacitated people. Hospitals and mental institutions were asked to surrender their old, senile, diseased, or mentally disturbed patients. In a few cases, children with malformed ears and those who were bedwetters were taken. Among the 170,000 to 200,000 people exterminated were disabled veterans from World War I. Around 30,000 severe alcoholics also were killed, with more being forcibly sterilized. By 1945, between 200,000 and 250,000 people had been sterilized for a variety of reasons.

Homosexuality became a crime in Nazi Germany, and around 220,000 homosexuals perished in the concentration camps. In the Weimar Republic, which preceded Hitler's state, laws relating to homosexuality had been increasingly eased, but when the Nazis took power these decrees were rescinded and a Department to Combat Homosexuality was created. Through informers, people engaging in homosexual acts were arrested. Interest in people of the same sex brought denunciation and placement in concentration camps. Lesbians in camps generally received somewhat better treatment than gay men. In the hierarchy of the camps, male homosexuals languished at the bottom. After the war, surviving homosexuals were placed in prison and forced to complete their jail sentences.

The Nazis scoured the German population in search of people whom they considered suited to the job of mass murder on a daily basis. Some candidates could not endure the slaughter, but others replaced them. A whole bureaucratic machinery gained experience with the initial massacre, and it ran smoothly in the later stages. Among officials who accomplished the deed were many who preferred this kind of activity to serving on the front lines, while others saw themselves as involved in an important demographic revolution. A few Germans risked their lives to shelter Jews or to smuggle them out of the country.

All sorts of horrors took place in the concentration camps. Medical experiments were performed, including injecting doses of poisons to ascertain what levels were fatal. Patients were placed in vacuum chambers to see how long they could survive with no air or reduced quantities of air. Dr. Joseph Mengele devoted his camp career to experiments on twins, whom he randomly killed and performed autopsies upon. Lamp shades made of human skin were prized by camp guards. Many inmates were used for labor, but in 1941 mass exterminations of Jews began. They were gassed in groups and incinerated in specially constructed ovens.

As the Germans conquered wider regions in Europe, they implemented their program against the Jews, Gypsies, Poles, and Russians. Jews suffered the largest numbers of fatalities in the death factories. Gypsies in Germany generally suffered extermination, while those in other countries died in smaller numbers. Perhaps as many as 250,000 Gypsies perished at the hands of the Germans.

Some countries refused to turn over their Jews to the Germans. Italian officials resisted what they felt to be barbaric demands from their German allies. Only after Mussolini fell and the Germans ruled Italy did large numbers of Italian Jews die. Bulgaria and Hungary refused to send their Jews. Romania opposed the Germans after the war turned in the Allies' favor, and Denmark evacuated most of its Jews to safety in Sweden. Japan also refused to cooperate with German demands to surrender its Jewish subjects. Croats, Slovaks, and Vichy French cooperated with the Nazis.

Germans grew uneasy with periodic revelations of the mass killings, but many pretended not to know and went about their lives. Others delighted in the fulfillment of the national socialist promises of the 1920s and 1930s. One German official in the occupied Ukraine, where 1.1 million Jews died, said that the Jews had been exterminated like cockroaches. By 1945, when all of the

FIGURE 40.8 *Nazi Death Camp.* *In death camps across Nazi Europe, millions of Jews were either worked to death or gassed to death and then cremated in ovens like this one at Majdanek, Poland. Poles, Russians, Gypsies, homosexuals, and others also perished in the camps.* Ria-Novosti/Sovfoto.

camps were liberated, the full magnitude of the genocide became apparent and horrified people around the world.

SOCIAL UPHEAVAL IN WORLD WAR II

Great changes were wrought around the globe in World War II. Women were called into factories and into other occupations normally assigned to men. Families were put under strain when one or both parents were absent for long periods. Ethnic groups also felt the pressures placed on them by the stresses of wartime and massive population movements.

Society under the Nazis

The German national socialists created a racial social hierarchy. Nazis defined Aryans as "pure" Germans, with blond-haired Nordic types often being considered the elite of the Aryan category. Most "defective" peoples like the disabled, the senile, or homosexuals had been taken away or exterminated by 1941. The Germans displayed a racial hierarchy of favor among forced laborers from other countries. French workers and blonds received preferential treatment, then came Czechs, then other Slavs, and finally the Jews and Gypsies. A similar hierarchy regulated the concentration camps.

Most Germans got used to the new social structure and savored its benefits. As the war progressed and it became increasingly clear that Germany might lose, the attitude of many became "Better enjoy the war, the peace will be terrible." Indeed, until Allied troops appeared on German soil, most Germans supported the Nazis, although some Germans did resist them. Hospitals under Roman Catholic jurisdiction resisted Nazi extermination plans by refusing to release their patients. Intellectuals like Dietrich Bonhoffer wrote and spoke against the Nazis, and many were sent to prison or to the concentration camps. Military conspiracies were hatched, and one nearly managed to assassinate Hitler in 1944.

Increasing losses of young German men began to alarm the Nazis, necessitating plans to offset the shrinking of the Aryan gene pool. Some considered enticing Germans from Latin America to become breeders for the state. Others urged that multiple wives be permitted for the remaining men. Certain factions within the Nazi government actively participated in the reclassification of some Poles and Czechs who "looked" Aryan, in order to maintain adequate supplies of "breeding stock." These pragmatic compromises with Nazi racial policies flourished.

A variety of social movements emerged from German youth. Hitler Youth groups were formed in the 1930s and became a major socializing force in Nazi Germany. Hitler Youth members received paramilitary training and the inculcation of Nazi values. Another group, the "swing youth," was attracted to the swing music that came from America. The swing youth appeared in large German cities in the 1940s and were largely from the middle class, with parents serving in the government. These young people frequented dance clubs where music by German swing bands imitating the one led by Benny Goodman performed. Because swing music had been associated in the Nazis' minds with American Jews and African Americans, it was considered racially impure and was strictly prohibited. Youth in working-class areas that had been dominated by socialist parties formed gangs that often clashed with Hitler Youth groups. The Edelweiss Pirates included hundreds of people aged sixteen to nineteen years old. They came from families of skilled or semiskilled workers and confined their anti-Nazi activities to minor acts of violence. A few collaborated with the German underground to help deserters, prisoners of war, and camp escapees.

The Nazis used repression to enforce social conformity. One measure involved the Morigen Youth Concentration Camp, which was established in 1940. Young people who displayed deviant behavior, emotional inadequacies, bad tempers, or incorrigible mischievousness were sent to the camp. A brutal regimentation program attempted to rehabilitate them, but the unreformed were shipped off to the regular concentration camps for extermination.

One popular program was the National Socialist Welfare Organization. It provided relief to war widows, orphans, and people whose homes had been destroyed by Allied bombings. As the war worsened, many Germans became totally dependent on this operation.

Another area of growth during World War II was urban planning. Hitler harbored schemes for radically redrawing the urban landscapes of most cities, and a network of architects and planners emerged before and during the war. Massive state buildings were proposed, some of which came under construction. The work went on partly because of bureaucratic inertia and largely because it kept the architects and others away from the front lines, as they had to direct the erection of state buildings.

Pressing against Social Barriers: The United States

Perhaps the most significant social developments in the United States were the wartime shifts that portended postwar change. During the war, more than 7 million women entered the workforce for the first time, and others joined the war effort in all branches of the military. Although more working-class women than middle-class women took jobs, middle-class women were more likely to climb the corporate ladder. Industrial managers offered financial inducements for women from the middle class, and this practice improved wages for all. Even middle-class women, however, did not do so well as men. In addition, managers quickly learned that middle-class women refused to tolerate the harsh disciplinary measures used against their lower-class counterparts.

When the war ended, many working women went back to home life. Women who headed households, however, could not afford to lose their jobs, and lower-class women resented being fired so that a man could be hired.

Women in the armed services numbered more than 200,000 and figured in the planning for peacetime as America's legislators debated a "G.I. [Government Issue or war draftee] Bill of Rights." Some women who served in the Women's Air Service Pilots and other groups were denied benefits. Other women who were veterans took advantage of the G.I. Bill and earned college degrees, which aided their social mobility.

African American soldiers fought in segregated armed forces units. After the war, most African American veterans resisted efforts to force them back into lifestyles shaped by traditional prejudice and discrimination. A limited number earned university degrees and entrance into new professions. Racial discrimination across the United States hampered their lives. In 1943, a threatened mass march on the nation's capital brought an executive decree banning discrimination at government-funded institutions. Federal government intervention was seen as an asset by many, although a few African American leaders favored segregation as a positive thing because they believed it eliminated racial bias.

A tragic episode in American history was the internment of Japanese Americans during World War II. Many United States citizens were inflamed by fear that American citizens of Japanese ancestry would commit acts of espionage and sabotage, though no evidence then or since has substantiated that fear. Nonetheless, the U.S. government ordered that anyone of Japanese ancestry residing in "sensitive zones" (areas along the Pacific coast of California, Oregon, and Washington) be confined in special camps. Within about a month, the roundup began, and ultimately tens of thousands of Japanese Americans were placed in a dozen "relocation camps" located mostly in inhospitable deserts and frigid remote mountain areas. Those interned found their dignity shattered and their constitutionally guaranteed rights shredded; they also lost property on which, having lost their sources of income, they could no longer pay taxes. Suicide and depression followed for some internees, but others persevered until their release in 1945. There was no comparable internment of citizens of German or Italian ancestry, and most scholars believe that racism was a powerful motivation for the internment of Japanese Americans.

Limited Social Change in Soviet Russia

The most significant social change in the Soviet Union was the immense loss of life. Most Soviet families suffered tragedy owing to the war. The deaths of 30 million people or more created a serious social and demographic crisis, especially on top of the great population losses of the 1930s.

Another wartime feature was the shift of large population groups from conquered territories. The conquest of the Baltic countries brought many Latvians, Lithuanians, and Estonians to places in the east, especially to Siberia. In addition, whole populations of Volga Germans and Tatars in the Crimea were moved away because the state doubted their loyalties.

THE WAR'S ECONOMIC COSTS AND CONSEQUENCES

Perhaps more than in any previous war, the importance of military supplies and logistics outweighed other strategic factors in World War II. By this time, refinements in weapons had reached the point at which technology played a more decisive role in victory than the sheer size of armies.

The German National Socialist Economic Plan

The national socialist economic vision was realized gradually. Trade in Europe was directed by Germany, and German currency became the standard European currency. Increasingly, the state took over industries and built a large economic empire with concentration camp labor. The last war year saw the power of the Nazi Party and the SS grow rapidly. Everything was to be controlled by the state.

Hitler feared that his wars might be undermined by unrest at home, so he concentrated on moderating the wartime suffering of the German people. Although rationing began on the eve of the war, the Nazis tried to minimize its hardships, and there was no total mobilization of materials and personnel until quite late. Nazi policy had long encouraged women to leave the industrial workforce and provided such generous economic benefits that many women left their jobs during the first twelve months of the war. Some women, however, continued to work in service jobs, for instance as maids in middle-class and upper-class households. The large-scale drafting of women into the industrial sector did not come until 1943 and even then did not reach levels comparable to those in Britain or Soviet Russia.

Systematic pillaging of conquered lands and peoples, as well as the use of forced labor, permitted Germans to enjoy a moderately good living standard for most of the war. The products and materials gained often went back to Germany for state needs. Within the first war year, substantial

UNDER THE LENS

World War II in South America

Accounts of World War II usually focus on Europe, Asia, North Africa, and the Pacific, considering South America peripheral to the conflict. Nonetheless, several South American countries were directly and significantly involved in the war. For the most part, their allegiances were determined by preexisting animosities, trade links, and the sentiments of powerful ethnic minorities.

At the outbreak of war, Brazil was one of the economic powers of South America, its prosperity riding on its rubber plantations. When the global rubber industry had opened plantations in Asia in the 1930s, Brazil initially had suffered. The war cut off Allied access to much of Asia, however, and Brazil again prospered following 1941. In recognition of its crucial economic link to the Allies, Brazil declared allegiance to their cause in 1942.

Uruguay, however, was a perennial enemy of Brazil, frequently clashing with Brazil over their common border. While Uruguay officially remained neutral, it was widely recognized that its sympathies (and probably aid) went to the Axis. Paraguay, however, was a perennial enemy of Brazil and Uruguay and declared itself one of the Allies. The Chaco War, a bitter border conflict between Paraguay and Bolivia between 1932 and 1935, had made these two countries enemies; Bolivia, not surprisingly, had no wish to be allied with Paraguay and declared itself neutral, while carrying out a pro-Axis policy. This stance pleased the politically powerful German-speaking minority in Bolivia.

Argentina was the most strongly pro-Axis of the South American countries. The considerable German segment of Argentina's population, coupled with Argentina's longstanding alliance with Uruguay, pushed the country toward the Axis. Postwar investigation strongly suggests that Argentina's "Colonels' Government," led by Colonel Juan Peron, collaborated extensively with Germany. Argentina's principal rival and enemy in South America, Chile, automatically united with the Allies.

In short, much of South America was involved in World War II, either overtly or through clandestine alliances. Countries arrayed on the same side did not necessarily share political views—they were united primarily by opposition to their traditional enemies. Countries with sizeable German populations often were pro-Axis, and countries with strong economic ties to the Allies usually became staunch Allies themselves.

Although no battles of World War II were fought in South America and only token South American forces were committed to action, the resources of these countries were significant in determining the war's outcome. In a period before the development of synthetic rubber and plastic, the rubber plantations of Brazil were critical to the Allied war effort, providing tires, gaskets, and other items. Chile's nitrate mining industry also was critical, because all major explosives were based on this naturally occurring substance. The denial of nitrates to the Axis powers, which had few sources within the territory they controlled, helped shorten the war and assure Allied victory. Pro-Axis nations of South America, in contrast, could offer the Axis powers only beef, tin, and wool, less critical war materials. After World War II, some South American countries gave shelter and support to many ex-Nazis.

numbers of Poles found themselves rounded up and shipped off to German factories. There they labored in poor conditions and lived under brutal treatment by Germans. If they became seriously ill or injured, they likely faced death as "useless mouths." French, Russians, and Italians (after 1943, part of the Allies) eventually were compelled to work with the Poles to make a forced-labor "army" of perhaps 8 million people.

The Revival and Domination of the U.S. Economy

World War II gave millions of American workers jobs and ended the Great Depression in the United States. State-directed policies created a vast military-industrial complex. Even before the formal war declaration in early December 1941, large sums had been devoted to rearming the United States. Around $13 billion was spent in 1939, and more than $30 billion was spent in 1941. The war years themselves saw growth of like magnitudes. Although the American government established certain strategic industries directly, it usually contracted with private producers for war materials.

War production was spread across the United States, reflecting congressional delegations' influence and preventing industrial concentration and vulnerability to attack. Many regions received substantial federal funds to supply the nation's war needs, and economic development spread all over the country. California in particular received an enormous amount of government funds to build weapons and provide supplies, and it became a major industrial state.

Between 1941 and 1945, the American economy grew by 50 percent, with steel output nearly doubling. Shipbuilding increased by a factor of ten and included around 51 million tons of merchant marine ships to haul war supplies. The industrialist Henry Kaiser used prefabrication methods in assembling merchant ships every few days. Aircraft production also increased tenfold during the war, for a total amount of 300,000 planes (out of a total of 750,000 worldwide). In 1944 alone, the United States turned out more than 100,000 planes. Other items included more than 500 million socks, 237 million cans of insect spray, and more than 3 million hot-water bottles. The United States rearmed the British and helped supply the Soviet Union. The Soviets received nearly 400,000

trucks and 2.7 million tons of gasoline; these facilitated the Soviet push into Germany.

One other American trend involved a change in what was regarded as "women's work." Before the onset of World War II, bank tellers, office clerks, and retail cashiers had been men. During and after the war, women more frequently worked in these jobs. The federal government also employed larger numbers of women during the war.

The Soviet Wartime Economy

Of the combatants, the Soviet Union mobilized its material resources and population most completely. This was possible because the Soviet economy had been restructured previously, between 1929 and 1941, and its various sectors already lay under state control. In addition, the Soviets realized that they faced the greatest fury of Nazi Germany. The government also eased its suppression of popular expressions of fervor and encouraged the rise of patriotism.

Stalin facilitated the dismantling and relocation of factories in the path of the German onslaught. By late 1941, more than 1,500 industrial plants were up and running in or beyond the Ural Mountains east of Moscow. Some were established in areas where winter already had arrived, and dynamite had to blast the foundations for the industrial works in the frozen soil.

Soviet control of production also facilitated the standardization of most weapons systems. This meant that large numbers could be produced quickly. In addition, tanks, planes, and guns produced in the Soviet Union during and after 1942 were often superior to their German counterparts.

The Soviet Union experienced one of the most disruptive assaults in its history; perhaps only the devastation by the Mongols in the thirteenth century could rival that of World War II. The peoples of the Soviet Empire endured great privation and personal loss, yet there was a growing pride in the ability of their armies to stop the Germans. Loss, mingled with hard-won self-respect, offered some hope for a future of peace and tranquility.

Japan's Wartime Economy

Direction of the Japanese economy for military purposes had commenced in the 1930s, before the onset of fighting in the Asian theater in 1937. In the

IN THEIR OWN WORDS

Soviet Views of the Early War

Nazi armies hit Soviet Russia with hammering body blows in 1941, nearly overwhelming all resistance. A range of reactions to the invasion has been recorded, and three from 1941 appear here. The first, arising from acceptance of Soviet propaganda that had promised total victory over the Nazis, is that the attack was insane:

> "Who do they think they are attacking? Have they gone out of their minds?" . . . "Of course, the German workers will support us, and all other peoples will rise up." . . . "Our men will hit them so hard, it will all be over in a week," said one worker. "Well, it won't necessarily be finished in one week," answered another. "They've got to get to Berlin. . . . It will take three or four weeks."

The opposite was occurring. Soviet armies were being overwhelmed, and the magnitude of the crisis did not dawn on the Soviet people until July 3, 1941, when Josef Stalin spoke candidly on national radio:

> . . . the enemy continues to push forward. . . . A grave danger hangs over our country. . . . It is essential that our people . . . should appreciate the full immensity of the danger that threatens our country. . . . The issue is one of life and death for the Soviet state, for the peoples of the USSR; the issue is whether the peoples of the Soviet Union shall remain free or fall into slavery. . . . All work must be immediately reconstructed on a war footing, everything must be subordinated to the interests of the front and the task of organizing the demolition of the enemy.

Increasingly, Stalin recalled the earlier victories of Russians over enemies like Napoleon. In fact, his speech was similar to one made by Tsar Alexander I in 1812 as French forces were approaching Moscow. During the war, perhaps for the first time, Stalin became a popular figure, one identified with Soviet Russia:

> All my life I will remember what Stalin's Order meant. . . . Not the letter, but the spirit and the content of this document made possible the moral and psychological breakthrough in the hearts and minds of all to whom it was read. . . . the chief thing was the courage to tell people the whole terrible and bitter truth about the abyss to whose edge we were then sliding.

Thus spoke a soldier about his reaction to Stalin's speech. Many soldiers gave the standard battle cry throughout the war—"for the motherland, for Stalin!"

next four years, further shifting and stockpiling of resources for war intensified economic tensions. But the outbreak of war in the Pacific theater pushed Japanese production and investment to a near-total effort.

Women and Korean nationals had been induced to enter industry in order to offset the drain of Japanese men from the labor market. Women had long been participants in the manufacturing sector, and their numbers grew after the late 1930s. Production and stockpiling had given the Japanese an edge in war equipment in the early months of the war in the Pacific theater, but the overall productive capacity of the United States eventually overcame that advantage. Also, the systematic destruction of Japan's merchant marine fleet by American submarines, surface ships, and airplanes began to have an effect in the latter part of the war. American ships and planes sowed mines in the coastal waters to hamper Japan's economy.

Despite the reduced importation of raw materials, Japanese workers achieved impressive production totals as late as 1944. In 1943, Japan had produced around 20,000 airplanes, and around 25,000 aircraft rolled off Japanese assembly lines in 1944. Massive bombing raids and Allied shelling of coastal areas beginning in early 1945 contributed to the destruction of Japan's military-industrial complex.

By the war's end, most Japanese were reduced to semistarvation. Some were forced to forage for wild vegetables and tubers in the countryside. Japan's once-powerful economy was in ruins.

EUROPE AND AFRICA		ASIA AND THE PACIFIC		

			Asian theater of World War II, 1937– Aug. 1945	**1937**
				–
				–
				–
				–
				1938 Rape of Nanjing, Dec. 1937
				–
				–
				–
				–
		Euro-African theater of World War II, 1939– May 1945		**1939**
				– Hitler announces plans to exterminate Jews in Europe, Jan. 1939
				–
				– Germany attacks Poland, Sept. 1939
Holocaust, 1940–1945				**1940**
				–
				– France falls to Germans, June 1940
				–
				–
				1941
		Pacific theater of World War II 1941–1945		–
				– German invasion of Soviet Russia begins, June 1941
				– Systematic exterminations begin in Eastern Europe, Sept. 1941
				–
				1942 Pearl Harbor bombed, Dec. 1941
				–
				– German forces push toward Suez Canal, June 1942 Battle of Midway, June 1942
				–
				1943
				– German army surrenders at Stalingrad, Jan. 1943
				–
				– Russia stops German advance at Kursk-Orel, July 1943
				–
				1944
				–
				– Saipan falls to U.S., July 1944
				–
				– Major air raids on Japanese cities begin, Nov. 1944
				1945
				–
				–
				– Atomic bomb levels Hiroshima, Aug. 1945
				–
				–

SUMMARY

1. World War II, consisting of three interlocking war theaters (Asian, Euro-African, and Pacific), began in 1937 and ended in 1945. At least 60 million people died, and terrible destruction convulsed many countries.

2. The Asian theater (1937–1945) followed a six-year expansion of Japanese imperialism into China. It wrought great loss of life and injury to 21 million people. During the war, Japanese atrocities sparked nationalism among the Chinese peasants.

3. The European theater (1939–1945) grew out of Adolf Hitler's grand plan to conquer and transform Europe in his racist vision. He took power in Germany, built the economy, and waged war on Czechoslovakia, Poland, and continental western Europe. He carried out his policy of eliminating "undesirables," a dress rehearsal for the Holocaust.

4. In North Africa, General Erwin Rommel defeated British units and threatened the Suez Canal. The British rallied and pushed back Rommel, and at the same time Americans landed to the west and destroyed the German and Italian forces in 1943. Africa became the launching pad for attacks on Italy.

5. Hitler attacked Soviet Russia, expecting a quick victory. He threatened Moscow, Leningrad, and the Caucasus oil fields but failed to win despite capturing 5 million Soviet soldiers. The Soviet counteroffensive carried through to Berlin by April 1945 and helped bring the defeat of Nazi Germany in May. Hitler committed suicide shortly before Germany's surrender.

6. The Pacific theater (1941–1945) began when the Japanese attacked Pearl Harbor and sank many battleships. The Japanese swept over more Pacific islands but were halted by United States naval forces in the Coral Sea and at Midway. Heavy fighting took place in the Philippines, Iwo Jima, and Okinawa. The United States dropped two atomic bombs, on Hiroshima and Nagasaki, to end the Pacific war.

7. The Holocaust brought the deliberate deaths of 11 million people, including Jews, Gypsies, Poles, Russians, and other groups. The machinery of destruction had been set up and run between 1939 and 1941, and the mass killings increased thereafter. Each intensification came during major military operations and reflected the national socialist goal of bringing about a racial demographic revolution.

8. Women gained new prominence in many countries. In the United States, women enjoyed improved wages and working conditions.

9. During World War II, African Americans entered the United States economy and the armed forces in large numbers. Japanese Americans, Tatars, and Volga Germans were oppressed by policies of their governments.

10. The economic dimension of the war left the United States and Soviet Russia dominant. The United States in particular benefited from a vast government investment program that produced a military-industrial complex and spread economic growth around the South and the West. Germans used massive importations of forced labor and the exploitation of conquered European lands to sustain their war machine. Japan mobilized its economic resources in the 1930s and built stockpiles of war materials that helped them in the first year of the Pacific war. Defeat left Japan in economic ruins, with many starving people by September 1945.

SUGGESTED READINGS

Barber, John, and Mark Harrison. *The Soviet Home Front, 1941–1945.* London: Longman, 1991. A study of a key area of Soviet Russia during World War II.

Glantz, David, and Jonathan House. *When Titans Clashed.* Lawrence: University Press of Kansas, 1995. A study of the war between Germany and Russia, 1941–1945.

Keegan, John. *A History of Warfare.* New York: Knopf, 1993. A standard examination of World War II and of war in general.

Pyle, Kenneth. *The Making of Modern Japan.* Lexington, Mass.: D. C. Heath, 1996. A survey of Japanese history and World War II.

Weinberg, Gerhard. *A World at Arms.* Cambridge, Eng.: Cambridge University Press, 1994. A thorough examination of World War II.

Last Spike Ceremony. *On May 10, 1869, at Promontory Point, Utah, east met west at the completion of the first railroad to span North America. Locomotives of the Central Pacific (left) and the Union Pacific (right) were brought nose-to-nose and christened with champagne. Similar celebrations attended the completion of railroad networks in Europe, Asia, and South America.* Union Pacific Railroad Museum Collection.

Technology Unites the World

On May 10, 1869, a group of executives, government officials, and workers gathered at Promontory Point, Utah, to celebrate the completion of the transcontinental railroad system that spanned the United States. They ceremoniously drove "the golden spike" that completed the last section of rail, then posed for photographs. Similar ceremonies marked the openings of the Chinese Eastern Railroad (1903), the Trans-Siberian Railroad of Russia (1905), the Transandine Railroad of South America (1910), and various other railway systems around the world. These events collectively formed a milestone in the march toward global interconnectedness.

Human beings are moderately puny creatures. Without technological assistance, they are limited to traveling only a few miles a day, carrying only a few things in their arms. Through technology, however, human beings have created ways of vastly increasing the loads that can be carried, greatly expanding the distances they can be moved, and speeding up the entire process. In addition, they have devised ways of carrying messages even farther and faster.

The movement of people or goods from one place to another is **transportation**, and the movement of messages is **communication**. For most of human history, the two were coupled closely. A person walking between communities to carry a message might as well carry physical objects also, because that person had to actually travel to the second community to transmit the message. Prior to the nineteenth century there were only a few modes of long-distance communication, such as the whistling codes of Madagascar and the drums used for long-range communication in parts of Africa. These techniques, however, were uncommon and restricted the communicators to relatively simple messages. Only in the nineteenth and twentieth centuries were technologies developed that permitted wide-ranging communication without movement of people or objects.

Improvements in transportation and communication technology had dramatic effects in uniting the world. A region that previously had little contact with other parts of the world might abruptly become connected with them. Sometimes this resulted in improved quality of life, as when the opening of new trade and markets permitted increased opportunity for entrepreneurs; sometimes it resulted in destruction and misery, as when a colonial power eradicated a local way of life.

NEW MODES OF TRANSPORTATION

There are two main measures of a transportation mode's utility. **Speed** is simply how fast goods are moved, and it is clearly an important measure, especially for perishable goods. Speed also is an issue with transportation through inhospitable zones, when food and water must be carried by the travelers. The other measure, **load**, is the weight of cargo that can be transported, and it, too, has obvious importance.

A fit human being can walk at about 4 miles per hour for about half a day, carrying about 50 pounds, resulting in a practical limit of transportation by simple human power: 50 pounds, 50 miles a day. A modern jetliner, in contrast, can travel at 600 miles per hour nearly all day (with stops for refueling and crew changes), giving a daily range of about 9,000 miles; its load can be up to 150,000 pounds. Surely, transportation technology has come a long way.

Early Transportation

The earliest innovations in transportation were designed primarily to increase the load, not the speed. When animal-drawn wagons were developed in southwestern Asia around 4000 B.C., they moved at about the same speed a person could walk, but they took advantage of the greater strength of draft animals and the fact that several animals could be harnessed to a single vehicle, greatly increasing the possible load.

Early boats, too, were quite slow as late as the eighteenth century. The *Mayflower*, the ship that carried the English to Plymouth Colony in Massachusetts in 1620, averaged only a little over 2 miles per hour for the 66-day trip. The load capacity of ships, however, has increased steadily since around 500 B.C.

Faced with a desire to increase the speed of transportation, as well as the load carried, engineers and designers could take two approaches: improve the vehicle or improve the route over which it passed. Water transportation, of course, was restricted largely to improving the vehicle, because the rivers and oceans could be modified only slightly and at great expense. Nonetheless, particularly in the nineteenth and twentieth centuries, some such improvements were made.

While some modifications in land vehicles were made from the earliest times through the eighteenth century, greater improvements were made in the routes over which those vehicles passed. Road systems at various times and places have stood out for their sophistication and effect on the speed of transportation. The Roman Empire in A.D. 100 had thousands of miles of paved roads stretching throughout its domain, as did the Maurya Empire of India in the fourth century B.C., the Qin Empire of China in the third century B.C., and the Inca Empire of A.D. 1400. In each case, the road system improved speed and transportation capacity dramatically, tying together the far-flung parts of an empire. The breakup of each empire, however, led to the degeneration of its road system, and transportation in subsequent times went into decline.

Reshaping the Route: Canals

While designs and styles of wagons and other vehicles changed over the ages, the first real attempt to change the face of land transportation came about with the development of transportation canals. Canals had been used for irrigation for thousands of years, but only around the seventh century B.C. did they begin to be used for transportation as

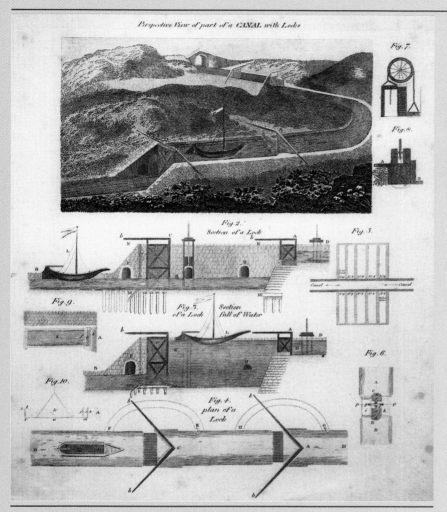

FIGURE I.8.1 *Canal Locks.*
A major problem of early canals was the regulation of water levels—a process needed to link distant points of the waterway at different elevations. The lock solved this problem, isolating a vessel in a closed dock and pumping water in or out as needed. This engineer's drawing of 1797 diagrams the apparatus.
Mansell/Time Inc.

well. At that time, Pharaoh Necho[1] of Egypt built a canal linking the Nile River and the Red Sea, major transportation routes of his era. Five centuries later, the Han Empire of China began building canals for both irrigation and transportation. Two centuries after that, the Romans built a canal connecting the Rhine River and the Zuyder Zee. Boats could carry far greater loads than wagons, and a canal permitted a boat to "sail" through land, although the construction of the canal was very costly in terms of labor.

These early canals were largely single links connecting two places, rather than a network of interconnected canals connecting many places, a **canal system**. The first major transportation canal

[1]**Necho:** NEHCH oh

system was the Grand Canal of China's Sui Empire, opened in the seventh century A.D. It was devoted solely to transportation, linking China's rich rice-producing centers with population and governmental centers so that grain tribute and taxes could be moved efficiently. The Grand Canal was refashioned by the Mongols in the fourteenth century and continued in use into the nineteenth century, by which time failure to maintain the canal plunged it into temporary disuse.

Canals in Europe apparently developed independently of those in Asia, and considerably later. Europeans had used canals from Roman times onward, but the utility of these canals was limited by the problem of connecting bodies of water at different elevations. Until the fourteenth-century invention of the **lock**, a mechanism for holding water in different parts of a canal at different elevations and moving a vessel from one elevation to the other, canal systems were impractical. Even after the invention of the lock, canal systems remained rare in Europe until the eighteenth century.

The reason lies with the huge investment required to build a canal. Private investors often were unwilling to risk such sums, even if they could afford them, and the building of major canals usually was left to governments. Canals came to be seen as sources of national pride, and they went hand-in-glove with the rise of nationalism in Europe. As land became more valuable and labor costs rose, however, planners turned increasingly toward other modes of transportation.

One special kind of canal has retained its importance through today: the canal connecting two seas. The most spectacular of these are the Suez Canal in Egypt, connecting the Red Sea and the Mediterranean Sea, and the Panama Canal in Panama, connecting the Atlantic Ocean and Pacific Ocean. The Suez Canal, completed in 1869, saved ships traveling between Asia and Europe the thousands of extra miles otherwise necessitated in rounding the southern tip of Africa. Its military significance was not lost on commanders in World War II and the Arab-Israeli War of 1967, and all sides sought to control it. The Panama Canal was completed in 1914, permitting ships to cross between the Atlantic and Pacific oceans without making the long and hazardous trip around the tip of South America.

Engine-Powered Vehicles on Sea and Land

The next great steps in transportation took place in Europe and North America, where inventors began using steam engines to power various types of vehicles. The steam engine, made practical by James Watt in 1782, could run on any fuel to boil water, using the resulting steam to power an engine. It was easy to adapt Watt's engine to turning a paddle wheel or a propeller screw, and the steamship was practical and in use by 1807.

The steam engine also was adapted to land vehicles. The first of these was the railway locomotive, in use by 1801 but truly practical only by 1829. The railroad was far faster than any contemporary

form of land transportation and could carry far greater loads. The only liability was that it could travel only on specially constructed rails, which were quite expensive to lay. Its original use, therefore, was restricted largely to moving passengers relatively short distances between cities, limiting the amount of track laid. Later, especially in the United States, entrepreneurs would extend railroads into remote areas, with the expectation that development would be stimulated by easier access to industrial and population centers. Indeed, as noted in Chapter 32, the building of railroads itself was a significant industry in the second phase of the Industrial Revolution. In some countries, particularly those of Europe, the construction of a railroad system was viewed as a source of national pride and a part of the military defense system. On the railroads of most places around the world, more efficient diesel engines that burnt petroleum for fuel eventually replaced steam engines.

The final major innovation in land transportation, the automobile, was a European invention. The earliest automobiles had been powered with steam engines, but the first successful models, invented independently by Karl Benz and Gottlieb Daimler[2] in Germany in 1885, were based on internal combustion engines that ran on petroleum products. Between 1905 and 1915, the number of automobiles in use skyrocketed. In the United States, for example, 78,000 automobiles were in use in 1905, but 2.5 million were on the roads a decade later. Henry Ford and other American industrialists began building huge numbers of automobiles in America, starting a major American industry.

The rise of the automobile was linked to good roads, and in the era between 1890 and 1915, the responsibility for building and maintaining roads shifted increasingly from local communities to regional and national governments. These larger governmental units were more committed to the development of a good road system, and roads in many parts of the world improved substantially in this period. Automobiles or trucks could reach communities that were off the railroad lines, further uniting a nation. While these vehicles carried relatively small loads, they were rapid and were not restricted to railroad tracks.

[2] **Gottlieb Daimler:** GAHT leeb DYM lur

Transportation Takes to the Skies

The final major innovation in transportation was the development of the airplane. For many years after the Wright brothers' famous test flight of an engine-driven airplane in 1903, aviation was a sport of the well-to-do adventurer. Airplanes, though fast, could carry only modest loads and were generally dangerous and unreliable; they were fit for adventures but not for everyday use.

Technical improvements, however, led to greater trust. World War I showed that airplanes could be reliable, and public sympathy encouraged their increased use. The first international passenger service began in 1919, and regular use of airplanes for the carrying of mail began in many places in the 1920s. Famous flights, such as Charles Lindbergh's solo flight across the Atlantic in 1927, enhanced the reputation of airplanes, and their major role in World War II, in which 750,000 airplanes were involved, cemented their place in modern transportation.

The development of efficient jet engines in the 1950s and early 1960s meant that air travel was by far the fastest form of transportation. Some of the more troublesome side effects of jet travel, including the shrill screech that continued throughout the flight, were eliminated or reduced by technical refinements. While jet travel has remained limited to cities with sufficiently large airports, its speed and comfort have made it the transportation mode of choice for much travel; its decreasing cost has made it affordable to a larger segment of the world's people.

FIGURE I.8.2 *The First Zeppelin. Launched in Italy in 1907, this zeppelin marked the serious development of lighter-than-air ships. Consisting of a huge canvas bag filled with a very light gas and a gondola suspended beneath the bag, the zeppelin was a viable competitor to the airplane until the 1937 explosion of the* Hindenburg *in New Jersey—a catastrophe that was recorded on film and widely publicized.* Corbis-Bettmann.

NEW MODES OF COMMUNICATION

For most of human history, communication has been almost exclusively by the spoken word, with the speaker and hearer face to face. Two major revolutions, however, have permitted people to preserve their communications over time and to project them over space.

The First Communication Revolution: The Written Word

The first major revolution in communication came about when language was first written down. This occurred independently at various places in the world, earliest in Southwest Asia around 3000 B.C., and also in Mexico, China, and Egypt. The next step in the evolution of the written word was block printing, developed in seventh-century China, where entire plates were printed at once. A thirteenth-century Korean press utilized movable type, as did the fifteenth-century German printing press. The printing press permitted for the first time the mass production of inexpensive copies of writings. The written word no longer was unique, and readers in far-flung places could read copies of the same text. Later, magazines, newspapers, and handbills would convey messages to a mass readership. Education was the only limitation on the dissemination of information.

The significance of the printing press, coupled with widespread literacy, cannot be overstated. Printing permitted large numbers of copies of a text to be produced and transported inexpensively, spreading the author's message to a large and widespread audience. Scholars could communicate their ideas to one another, even if they never had met; in this way, each could build on the findings of colleagues, speeding the growth of their disciplines. Political, religious, and social reformers could encapsulate their ideas in inspirational words and spread them to potential supporters. Everyday people could learn of foreign lands and ways, sometimes encouraging them to immigrate or experiment with new concepts of government or society. Still, speaking, writing, and printing— important as they were— remained the only major means of communication into the nineteenth century.

The Second Communication Revolution: Electronic Communications

Many inventors had dreamed of means of long-distance communication, but the first practical scheme was not put into use until 1794. Claude Chappe[3] had invented an **optical telegraph**, with slats of wood mounted atop high buildings and moved via a system of ropes and pulleys. Different positions for the slats corresponded to codes for letters, and messages could be laboriously sent along lines of sight. By 1844, Chappe's optical telegraph consisted of more than 500 stations connecting 29 French cities and spanning more than 3,000 miles.

The defects of the optical telegraph, however, were obvious. It was useless at night or during cloudy weather. The ropes could foul in the pulleys or break; winds played havoc with the apparatus. Messages had to be retransmitted many times to carry them long distances, increasing the possibility of error. Finally, it was very slow.

Many scientists began experimenting with electrical signals to carry messages. A very cumbersome and ineffective electrical telegraph was put into operation in France in 1812, and practical systems were operating in England, continental Europe, and the United States by 1837. These electrical telegraphs transmitted short bursts of electricity over a wire according to a code, and a receiver at the other end decoded the signal. Each system initially was limited to a single landmass, because wires were needed. In 1866, however, a transatlantic telegraph cable was successfully laid, linking the Americas with the Old World. By 1900, there were few places in the world without telegraph links.

In the meantime, a new technology was developing: the telephone. Alexander Graham Bell, a Scottish-born American, transmitted the first sentence over telephone wires in 1876, and the advantages of this device were immediately apparent. Two-way conversations could be carried on between speakers with no code skills, the nuances of tone could be reproduced, and the communication could proceed at a normal speed. Thomas Edison and others refined the telephone to practicality in the next two decades. By 1915, a transatlantic telephone cable was laid, linking Europe and North America.

[3] **Claude Chappe:** KLOHD SHAHP

FIGURE I.8.3 *Optical Telegraph. This mechanical device was invented during the French Revolution and put to use in 1794 to provide communication between the cities of Paris and Lille. Although it was serviceable, with different positions of the arms denoting different letters, the optical telegraph was slow, and it was ineffective in darkness, fog, or heavy rain.* Deutsches Museum, Munich.

Both the telephone and telegraph required wires connecting the communicating parties, and inventors sought ways to increase the flexibility and decrease the cost of communication by eliminating the wires. In 1886, Heinrich Hertz,[4] a German scientist, produced "Hertzian waves," the electrical waves later used for radio transmission. By the late 1890s, Guglielmo Marconi,[5] an Italian scientist, was transmitting telegraph signals, and,

in 1901, he successfully transmitted between North America and Europe.

Wireless telegraphy never had a major impact on communications, but radio transmission of voices and music certainly did. For the first time, communications could be electrically **broadcast** (sent out widely) to be received by anyone with the proper receiving device. This potential was realized first in the United States, when the Radio Corporation of America (RCA) began broadcasting music in 1920. Similar ventures proliferated in Europe shortly thereafter, though radio broadcasts in many other countries did not begin until after World War II.

Television was a logical outgrowth of radio, because most of its principles were the same. The difficulty of projecting a picture electronically was solved by 1923 by Vladimir Zworykin,[6] a Russian American scientist. The technology for television could have been implemented any time after this date, but it was not until 1939 that the first regular television broadcasts began, again initiated by the Radio Corporation of America. The popularity of radio and the general belief that the public would not be willing to pay more to receive pictures held up its introduction, and it was not until the economic boom following World War II that television took off.

The latest major communication advance can be seen as an extension of the telegraph. The **microprocessor**, the information-processing heart of a computer, converts messages into electronic impulses and can store or send these messages. Although they have many other uses, microprocessors are the innovation that has led to the "information superhighway" developed in the last years of the twentieth century: a vast network of interconnected microprocessors that can send messages from one station to another rapidly and inexpensively. Using microprocessors, a student in Houston can examine the library holdings of the University of Tokyo, a petroleum engineer in Iraq can consult professional literature otherwise unavailable in that country, and a freelance writer in India can send electronic mail to an editor in London inexpensively and rapidly.

The microprocessor, invented in 1958 by Jack Kilby and Robert Mason of the United States, consists of a chip of silicon on which are etched complex circuits that permit the microprocessor to

---

[4] **Heinrich Hertz:** HYN rihk HEHRTZ
[5] **Guglielmo Marconi:** goo YAY moh mahr KOH nee
[6] **Vladimir Zworykin:** VLAHD ih meer ZVOH ree kihn

carry out logical operations according to procedures encoded in the circuits. Every operation that a microprocessor can carry out could be accomplished—though in a more cumbersome manner—by conventional electronics. But the advantage of the microprocessor is that it can be mass produced inexpensively. The circuits are etched optically, meaning that the microprocessor is cheap enough to be widely purchased. The Univac computer, widely heralded in the 1950s, cost millions of dollars; it could be replaced in 1970 by a microprocessor that cost only $100,000; by the 1990s, a more sophisticated microprocessor cost less than a dollar. The microprocessor has been in use only for a few years, and it is not yet possible to assess the ultimate magnitude of its impact on communication.

THE IMPACT OF A SHRINKING WORLD

The march of technology has seen the inexorable improvement of the globe's transportation and communication potential. Today, a fifty-ton load can be carried across a continent in four hours by a jetliner; that same load would have taken three months for a team of more than 2,000 workers to transport in 5000 B.C.; using Southwest Asian tech-

nology of 3000 B.C., the task would have taken just as long but would have required only 100 workers; even as late as 1900, carrying the load by railroad would have taken about three days.

Prior to the nineteenth century, most transportation innovations were directed toward increasing the loads that could be carried. In the nineteenth and twentieth centuries, innovation has been directed more toward increases in speed, although loads have been increased as well. Communication advances associated with writing and printing have had major impacts on the world, but the modes of electronic communication developed since the nineteenth century have been qualitatively different. What are the impacts of these changes of the past two centuries on the world?

The economic change is obvious. As transportation has improved, the markets for goods have become broader, and items produced in one country may be found literally all over the world. This has provided some entrepreneurs with the opportunity for tremendous success, but it also has smothered others that might have been successful locally. The world trade in soft drinks is controlled largely by two American companies, and countless local beverage companies, particularly in the less industrialized countries, have been forced out of business by this competition.

These less industrialized countries, at a profound disadvantage in most economic transac-

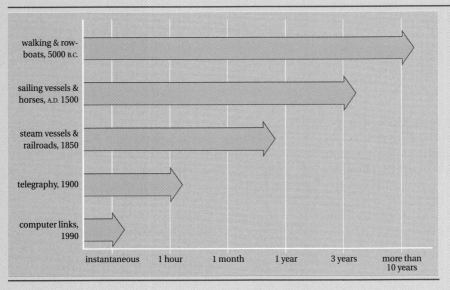

FIGURE I.8.4 *State-of-the-Art Communication.* Changing technology has had a profound effect on humans' ability to interact with one another. As we discover faster and more efficient ways of sending messages around the world, we open up new avenues for trade and cultural exchange.

tions, now sometimes find themselves with a competitive advantage over more industrialized countries, because their low labor costs may attract foreign industries searching to cut production costs. Many books are planned and laid out in New York or Boston, although often the actual printing takes place in Indonesia. Only inexpensive transportation could make such practices economically feasible.

Politically, the effects may be more complex. Improved transportation has enhanced the ability of powerful countries to use their military and economic might to coerce less powerful countries into dependent relationships as colonies, as allies dominated through military or political threat, or as countries whose economies actually are controlled by foreign corporations. On the other hand, the news media have become a powerful factor in international politics, graphically presenting conditions that, in an earlier era, would never have been recognized by the general populace. By drawing attention to abuses, the press can provide the focus for public pressure on governments.

At the social level, innovations in transportation and communication have broadened the horizons of nearly every person on the planet. There is a greater sense of shared background, interests, and skills in today's world than in any period that preceded it. Whether in Africa, Europe, or Latin America, newspapers carry many of the same stories and radios play much of the same music. This shared experience, an optimist might claim, has helped make people around the world relate to one another; a pessimist could point to intolerance and discrimination that argue otherwise. Certainly, however, this shared background, coupled with moderately inexpensive, fast, and reliable transportation, has increased the ease with which people can immigrate and successfully function in their new homes.

SUGGESTED READINGS

Clarke, Donald, ed. *The Encyclopedia of Transportation*. London: Marshall Cavendish Publications, 1974. A straightforward encyclopedia, emphasizing inventions and their operations. A good source for figuring out how a device really works.

Fabre, Maurice. *A History of Communications*. New York: Hawthorn Books, 1963. The New Illustrated Library of Science and Invention, vol. 9. A nice history emphasizing the development of writing, printing, and telegraphy, including some useful illustrations of devices.

Georgeano, G. N., ed. *Transportation through the Ages*. New York: McGraw-Hill, 1972. A series of essays on the development of roads, railroads, ships, canals, and aviation.

Smith, Anthony. *Goodbye, Gutenberg: The Newspaper Revolution of the 1980's*. Oxford, Eng., and New York: Oxford University Press, 1980. Primarily concerned with changes in newspapers brought by the electronic information revolution; also includes a brief history of newspapers.

Vance, James E. *Capturing the Horizon: The Historical Geography of Transportation since the Sixteenth Century*. Baltimore: Johns Hopkins University Press, 1986. A treatment of the geography of transportation, with considerable discussion of technological innovations and consequences.

HUMAN EXISTENCE ALWAYS HAS BEEN MARKED BY CHANGE, but the rate of change has increased over the millennia. In part, this has been caused by the inexorable growth of population. The cumulative development of technology also has been a factor, as greater technical capabilities have permitted actions with more wide-reaching consequences. Another key ingredient is the greater degree of connectedness between the parts of the world, opening the door to a wealth of transforming processes, including the fusion of ideologies from diverse cultural traditions, the expansion of economic markets, and military conflict. The twentieth century has seen the highest population levels, the most sophisticated technology, and the greatest degree of connectedness of all time, and the rate of change also has been greatest. This change has expressed itself in society, politics, economics, art, and virtually all other realms of human experience.

Baltic Demonstration. *In August 1989, citizens of Latvia and other Baltic states formed a human chain stretching across their countries to demonstrate their desire for independence*

PART NINE

ACCELERATING CHANGE

Part Nine explores aspects of this rapid change in the twentieth century, particularly after World War II. Chapter 41 discusses the Cold War era, the period of tensions between communist and capitalist countries that followed World War II. Chapter 42 examines the role of demography in the middle and late portions of the century, focusing on how and why populations have changed and what effects those changes have wrought. The part concludes with Issue 9, which considers the changing twentieth-century relationships between politics and ethnicity. These chapters and the issue provide windows on the swift and accelerating change that has characterized the twentieth century.

from the Soviet Union. This successful independence movement was one of many in the period since the end of World War II. Zoja Pictures / Gamma / Liaison International.

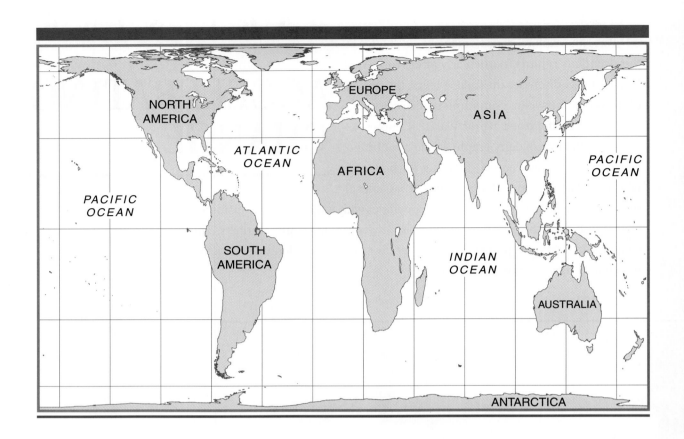

The Cold War Era

1945–1991

From Stettin in the Baltic to Trieste in the Adriatic, an iron curtain has descended across the continent.... All are subject, in one form or another, not only to Soviet influence but to a very high and increasing measure of control from Moscow.... Far from the Russian frontiers and throughout the world, Communist fifth columns are established and work in complete unity and absolute obedience to the directions they receive from the Communist centre.

—WINSTON CHURCHILL

Sir Winston Churchill's "iron curtain" speech of March 5, 1946, set the tone for a global rivalry between two coalitions of countries, the U.S. alliance and the Soviet alliance. Scholars have called this rivalry the Cold War.

The Cold War era (1945–1991) was a time not only of political rivalries but also of accelerating change. Competition and conflict between the Soviets and Americans spread to Asia, Africa, and the Americas. The rivalry was economic as well as political. The United States and the Soviet Union developed economic blocs and struggled to dominate areas with important natural resources, such as petroleum. Unchecked economic growth, however, created serious environmental problems. Massive governmental funds were poured into universities and research centers, which became vital scientific research establishments.

Scholars often use the term **First World** to describe the U.S. alliance system and the **Second World** to refer to the Soviet alliance system. The

Third World is a commonly used term to refer to the nonindustrialized countries that did not initially support either of the alliances.

THE COLD WAR, 1945–1991

The **Cold War** is the name given to the intense and multifaceted rivalry that threatened to become a hot war between the Americans and Soviets. Key elements of the Cold War are:

— sharp ideological differences,

— an arms race,

— economic competition, and

— the formation of power blocs.

A rough balance of power existed between the American and Soviet power blocs, and major war involving them was avoided.

The Central Conflict

The seeds of the Cold War were sown in the last days of World War II. Only the United States and the Soviet Union had powerful military forces and the economic strength to impose their wills on others. American armies controlled much of Western Europe and Japan, while Soviet armies dominated Eastern Europe and parts of China. Britain had been powerful in the past, but its might had been undermined by the war.

Competition between the United States and the Soviet Union produced a massive arms race. Europe became the central Cold War stage, as the Americans helped rebuild the parts of Europe under their sphere of influence, and the Soviets turned their sphere of influence into a political and economic bloc. The competition became heated, especially with the onset of an expensive arms race. In 1945, only the United States possessed nuclear weapons capable of destroying cities. By 1965, although other countries also had these weapons, the Americans and Soviets had developed intercontinental missile delivery systems. They threatened the extinction of human beings on the planet.

Clear ideological differences shaped the Cold War. The Soviets touted socialism as the most modern economic and social system, the model that would win the Cold War. U.S. leaders promoted capitalism and democracy, claiming that they represented the "Free World." In fact, both Americans and Soviets backed unsavory dictatorships in order to expand and maintain their power.

Capitalism and Soviet-style socialism dominated global economics. Although economic integration had characterized the modern age, the Cold War stalled that process through the creation of two economic networks. Limited trade passed between the two blocs, but the overwhelming economic activity of each was internal rather than external. Although the United States had rebuilt the Japanese and Western European economies, American trade goods soon struggled to compete against materials from these capitalist rivals.

Anti-imperialist struggles often became intertwined with Cold War rivalries. In Vietnam, anti-French Vietnamese independence fighters received aid from China and the Soviet Union, while the United States gave its French allies generous aid to fight communist-backed guerrillas. In Angola, anti-Portuguese resistance fighters were aided by the Soviets, and, after winning power, the new Soviet-backed regime faced anticommunist rebels backed by the United States. These are but two of many examples.

The alliance systems developed their own power blocs with direct and indirect control of other countries. The Soviets refused to tolerate independent countries within their bloc. U.S. leaders helped overthrow governments in Guatemala, South Vietnam, and the Congo (Zaire). In addition, Cold War politics not only maintained the division of Germany but also perpetuated a division of Korea (North and South) and one of Vietnam (North and South).

Spies became an important element in the Cold War, and fear of foreign agents led to repression by suspicious governments. The Soviet Union had developed a network of spies upon the Bolshevik assumption of power in 1917. The Cheka and its successor organizations (including the KGB) trained foreign intelligence-gathering officials, often competing with agents of Soviet military intelligence in ferreting out secrets from the United States and allied powers. For its part, the United States relied on the Central Intelligence Agency (CIA) and the National Security Agency (NSA) to gather information.

Political oppression was common in the Soviet totalitarian system, and the United States went through an era when communists, their sympathizers, and those suspected of being either were regularly harassed or jailed. Witch hunts were promoted in many cities and towns across America, especially in the 1950s. Innocent people's careers were ruined by the anticommunist hysteria. A U.S. senator urged the banning of books about Robin Hood because he robbed from the rich and gave to the poor; he must have been a communist, in the senator's way of thinking. One famous example

was the persecution of government officials by Senator Joseph McCarthy in the early 1950s. McCarthyism became the name given to political persecutions of this era.

The Cold War began in Europe and spread to Asia, complicating the Cold War alliance system. In 1949, the Chinese Communist Party gained control of the Chinese mainland and formed an alliance with the Soviet Union a year later. Within a decade, however, nationalist tensions and other factors shattered the Sino-Soviet agreement. Thereafter, China competed with both the United States and

FIGURE 41.1 *Wartime Allies Meet at Potsdam.* *From mid-July to early August 1945, leaders of three major Allied powers—Great Britain, the United States, and Soviet Russia— met in Potsdam, Germany, to iron out the details of peace agreements reached at the earlier Yalta conference. The resulting "Potsdam Agreement" provided, among other things, for the restructuring of the German economy and divided control of postwar Germany between the three Allies and France, another Allied country. Delegates to the conference also issued the "Potsdam Declaration," which demanded Japan's unconditional surrender. Pictured, from left to right, are Britain's newly elected prime minister, Clement Attlee, U.S. president Harry Truman, and Soviet premier Josef Stalin.* Corbis-Bettmann.

FIGURE 41.2 *Hollywood Stars Protest Government Witch Hunt.* *During the anticommunist probes of Congress, people accused of being communists were intimidated and maligned; the hunt for alleged communists in Hollywood was no exception and cost many their careers. The Hollywood stars in this October 1947 photo flew to Washington, D.C., to protest congressional tactics. Among those shown here are Richard Conte, Humphrey Bogart, Lauren Bacall, and Jane Wyatt. The hunt for communists continued despite the protest.* Corbis-Bettmann.

the Soviet Union for influence in the Third World. Vietnamese communists took control of Vietnam and eventually played off the Soviets and Chinese to become more independent from foreign domination or influence.

The Cold War in Europe

Europe was the central ideological battleground for the United States and the Soviet Union during the Cold War. As the establishment of a Soviet empire in Eastern Europe became clear, the

United States announced the Marshall Plan, an aid program to Western European countries that had experienced difficulties reviving themselves after 1945. The U.S. financial effort worked exceptionally well, and, by the early 1950s, most states had achieved a measure of growth.

Germany had been divided by the Allies during the last stages of World War II. It remained divided for decades because Europeans, especially the Soviets, wished to keep it weak, fearing a German military revival that would lead to a national expansionist state. East Germany was supported

IN THEIR OWN WORDS

A Former Communist Speaks Out

In 1948, when the Cold War was in full swing, the House Committee on Un-American Activities called Whittaker Chambers to testify about his life as an agent for the Communist Party. In the course of the committee's investigation, Alger Hiss, head of the Carnegie Endowment for Peace and former member of the U.S. State Department, had been named as a communist agent by Chambers. Between 1948 and 1950, the Hiss case riveted Americans and publicized the fact that Soviet agents had penetrated the U.S. government. Representative Richard Nixon, a member of the committee, became famous as an anticommunist inquisitor, helping him win national political office.

In the book *Witness*, published in 1952, Chambers presents his side of the Hiss case and describes the reasons for his turning against the communist side:

Almost exactly nine years ago—that is, two days after Hitler and Stalin signed their pact [Nazi-Soviet Non-Aggression Pact of August 1939]—I went to Washington and reported to the authorities what I knew about the infiltration of the United States Government by Communists. For years, international Communism, of which the United States Communist Party is an integral part, had been in a state of undeclared war with this Republic. With the Hitler-Stalin pact that war reached a new stage. I regarded my action in going to the Government as a simple act of war, like the shooting of an armed enemy in combat.

At that moment in history, I was one of the few men on this side of the battle who could perform this service. I had joined the Communist Party in 1924. No one recruited me. I had become convinced that the society in which we live . . . had reached a crisis . . . and that it was doomed to collapse or revert to barbarism.

In 1937, I repudiated Marx's doctrines and Lenin's tactics. Experience and the record had convinced me that Communism is a form of totalitarianism, that its triumph means slavery to men wherever they fall under its sway and spiritual night to the mind and soul. I resolved to break with the Communist Party at whatever risk to myself or my family. Yet, so strong is the hold which the insidious evil of Communism secures upon its disciples, that I could still say to someone at that time: "I know that I am leaving the winning side for the losing side, but it is better to die on the losing side than to live under Communism."

Chambers's words evoke his vision of a titanic struggle against evil, and his later testimony implicated members of a communist apparatus that had penetrated the government. Later, Senator Joseph McCarthy used the fear of communism to attack government officials, furthering his political career, until McCarthy was censured by the Senate for his unorthodox methods in hunting communists.

---

by the Soviets, and West Germany was bolstered by the Americans, British, and French.

Most other European states fell under the influence of a power bloc, and the forces of nationalism remained checked by the arrangement. In 1956, Hungary, a member of the Soviet bloc, tried to develop an independent defense and foreign policy, but massive force by the Soviets and their allies crushed the effort. Twelve years later, Czechs and Slovaks tried a moderate form of socialism, but, as the world tensely watched, Czechoslovakia also succumbed to invading Soviet forces. Except for a few incidents such as these, the division of Europe brought some measure of peace and stability during the Cold War era.

The military and political basis of the Cold War was in two pacts, NATO and the Warsaw Pact. NATO (North Atlantic Treaty Organization) united the United States, Canada, Britain, France, West Germany, Belgium, Norway, Italy, Greece, and Turkey in defense of Western and Central Europe. The Warsaw Pact bound the Soviet Union, Poland, Hungary, East Germany, Czechoslovakia, Bulgaria, and Romania to defend Eastern Europe. Although

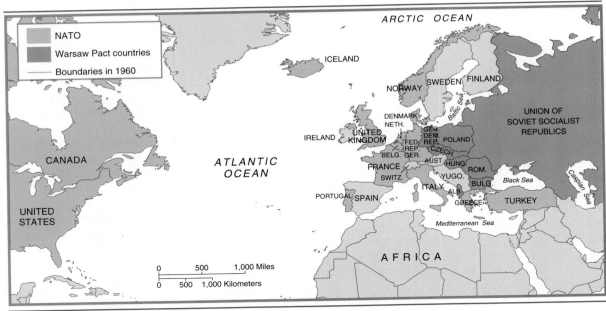

MAP 41.1 *NATO and Warsaw Pact Countries in 1960. By 1960, most of Europe as well as Turkey, Canada, and the United States were involved in NATO and the Warsaw Pact. Both the United States and the Soviet Union formed rival alliances that were characteristic of the Cold War. Although the two groups competed for significant parts of the whole world, much of their diplomatic and military planning centered on Europe.*

the two alliances concentrated enormously powerful armies in Central Europe, they never fought each other. The evolving balance of power had made warfare in Europe unwinnable.

The collapse of the Warsaw Pact came in 1989 and in a rapid manner that shocked many. After the Soviet leader Mikhail Gorbachev had been in power for a few years, some of the Eastern Europeans gambled that he would not use force to keep them in the empire. In 1989, the Berlin Wall, erected in 1961 to keep East Germans from fleeing to the West, was torn down by a popular movement. Communist governments fell in rapid succession, and newly installed national governments negotiated for the departure of Soviet troops stationed in Eastern Europe.

One of the most surprising and significant events, the reunification of Germany, came in 1990. This action not only destroyed the basis for a Soviet defense perimeter far from home, but it also resurrected a nation-state that had cost tens of millions of Soviet and Russian lives in two world wars. Although the absorption of East Germany into West Germany cost billions of dollars and caused social tensions, the united Germany has emerged as a major European power, especially economically. It threatens to rival the United States and other economic powers.

The final chapter of the Cold War came with the collapse of the Soviet Union in 1991. A failed takeover by elements of the Communist Party, the Soviet Army, and the KGB led to declarations of independence by Russia, the Ukraine, and other Soviet republics in December. Since then the fifteen countries of the former Soviet Union have bickered with one another, although some are beginning to seek some form of confederation. Russian communists and some nationalists have been calling for a reestablishment of the Soviet Union.

The Cold War in Asia

Asia became a major region of the Cold War tensions from the 1940s through the 1980s. Wars were fought in Korea, Vietnam, and Afghanistan. U.S. power suffered a serious defeat in Vietnam, and Soviet power suffered a significant defeat in Afghanistan.

FIGURE 41.3 *The "Iron Curtain" Crumbles. The Berlin Wall, erected in 1961, divided Germany, East and West, and was a visible reminder of the divisions between the American and Soviet blocs. In 1989, the wall was torn down, heralding the breakdown of Soviet power in Eastern Europe. Within a year, Germany was reunited and, soon after, Soviet Russia collapsed completely.* Alexandra Avakian/Woodfin Camp & Associates.

EAST ASIA. In 1945, Japan lay prostrate, having suffered tremendous losses in Allied bombing raids. The U.S. occupation, directed by General Douglas MacArthur, aimed to restructure Japan in order to render it incapable of fighting anew. The Americans wrote a new constitution and forced the Japanese to accept it. The constitution forbade the Japanese from having a military force, but as the Cold War developed, U.S. officials desired to rearm Japan as a major ally. The Japanese balked at acquiring an offensive military force but agreed to create a limited self-defense force.

Japan became a reliable ally with a stable political system. After political turmoil in the mid-1950s, two political parties merged, forming the Liberal-Democratic Party. It remained in power for thirty-seven years and dedicated itself to supporting the Japanese-American alliance. In addition, party leaders undertook measures to ensure economic growth, turning the Japanese economy into the world's second largest.

The Korean War (1950–1953) primarily concerned North Korea and South Korea, the United States, the Soviet Union, and China, although many other states also sent military units to fight there. Korea, a Japanese colony since 1910, had been partitioned in 1945, with the Soviets controlling the North and the United States administering the South. With Soviet backing, communist North Korea invaded the relatively democratic South on June 25, 1950. North Korea's aggression brought a military reprisal by the United Nations. The UN, planned by the Allies during World War II, had the power to wage war against aggressors. In June 1950, while the Soviet Union was boycotting the UN Security Council, the United States took advantage of the Soviet absence to push the UN to a declaration of hostilities against North Korea.

The invasion of South Korea had been a dream of Kim Il Sung (1912–1994), communist head of North Korea. Initially, Kim's battle plan unfolded with machinelike precision, but it eventually faltered. The initial thrust conquered most of South Korea, and U.S. troops and remnants of the South's army stubbornly held a small toehold along the coast. Then, General Douglas MacArthur staged an amphibious landing near Seoul, the capital of South Korea. U.S. soldiers moved out of their beachhead, threatening to cut off the retreating North Koreans. Soon, UN forces invaded North Korea, despite Chinese warnings of dire consequences.

In mid-October 1950, China's leader, Mao Zedong, felt that U.S. forces would invade Manchuria, China's newly conquered industrial base. After consultation with Josef Stalin and Kim Il Sung, as well as with China's leaders, Mao committed China to fight in Korea. Chinese forces dramatically turned the war's course. A few hundred thousand communist soldiers infiltrated the border and surprised the U.S. military leaders in November 1950. Although the Chinese pushed beyond the old border between North and South Korea, U.S. forces stabilized their lines and counterattacked. Soon, the conflict settled into a deadly war of attrition. In the summer of 1953, an armistice was signed, leading to an armed peace with both Koreas retaining about the same territory as before.

The Korean War produced several results. The Chinese had fought the Americans to a standstill and won international prestige, especially among Second and Third World countries. The Soviet Union benefited because its interests were advanced by the North Koreans and the Chinese. This kind of proxy war became attractive for both the Soviet Union and the United States.

The Korean people suffered massive casualties and immense destruction but rebuilt their country with outside assistance. With American aid, South Korea revitalized its economy and society. Military governments ruled from the early 1960s through much of the 1980s, and, although representative government suffered, the resulting political stabil-

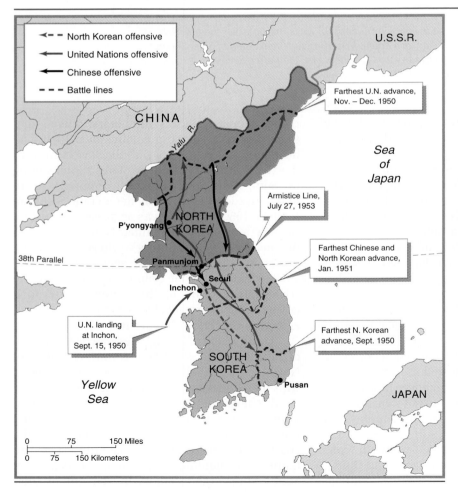

MAP 41.2 *The Korean War, 1950–1953. Korea, adjacent to Japan, China, and the USSR, became a focal point of Cold War activity during the Korean War. Although Soviet Russia did not fight in the war, its ally, China, did. The United States, a major participant in the war, used Japan as a staging area for actions in Korea. While most of the Korean Peninsula was fought over during the war, much of the conflict occurred along the 38th Parallel.*

ity helped engender general economic growth and prosperity. The North Koreans also rebuilt, but their economy did not prosper. They maintained an authoritarian government under the leadership of Kim Il Sung.

SOUTHEAST ASIA. The Cold War rivalry was complicated in Southeast Asia by the growing power of China. Another factor was the refusal of some countries, such as Burma (present-day Myanmar) to join any side. The U.S. created SEATO, the Southeast Asian Treaty Organization, a military alliance, to fight communism. SEATO countries joined the United States in the fighting in Vietnam during the 1960s.

The Vietnam War was two separate conflicts. The first war (1946–1954) was fought between the French and Vietminh. The **Vietminh** was an orga-

nization of Vietnamese communists and nationalists formed in 1941. Headed by Ho Chi Minh, a Vietnamese patriot and communist, the Vietminh took advantage of a power vacuum in Vietnam in 1945. Immediately, Vietminh agents organized independence groups, and, when World War II ended, the Vietminh launched a successful takeover from the Japanese. Vietnamese control remained until 1946, when the French returned, determined to maintain their empire.

War broke out in 1946 and lasted eight years. The Vietminh slowly took control of the countryside and gained a strategic advantage in 1949, when a Chinese communist victory in the Chinese civil war meant that Chinese material aid would be forthcoming. In 1954, the Vietminh won a major victory at Dien Bien Phu, compelling the French to admit defeat. European and Asian leaders agreed

FIGURE 41.4 *Napalmed Children.* *The Vietnam War of the 1960s and 1970s produced horrors on all sides that caused particular suffering for the people of Vietnam, especially in the South. This dramatic photograph captures the terror of Vietnamese children, some naked, fleeing from battle.* Wide World Photos.

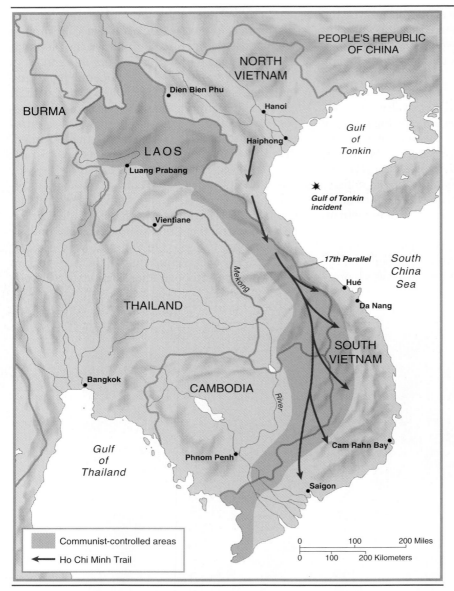

MAP 41.3 *The Vietnam War, 1961–1975.* For the United States, the Vietnam War was fought in the 1960s and 1970s—for many Vietnamese, however, fighting for their country's independence began in the 1940s and continued with few respites until 1975. The war occasionally spilled over into Cambodia and Laos, and when South Vietnam fell to the communists in 1975, Cambodia and Laos soon came under complete communist control as well. During the course of the war, China gave significant aid to the North Vietnamese, as did Soviet Russia.

at the Geneva Conference (1954) to divide Vietnam into southern (noncommunist) and northern (communist) areas and to hold national elections in two years to reunite Vietnam.

The United States refused to recognize the Geneva settlement and turned from aiding the French to entering the contest directly. The CIA, under the direction of U.S. President Dwight Eisenhower, organized a government in the South, renouncing elections. President Eisenhower later admitted that Ho Chi Minh would have won the vote. Soon, the communists organized a resistance movement in the South, the **Viet Cong**.

A second Vietnam War (1961–1975) pitted the United States and the allied South Vietnamese army against the Viet Cong and their North Vietnamese allies. A succession of U.S. presidents tried their hands at favorably settling the war in the South. Between 1963 and 1965, the collapse of the southern government and the introduction of

North Vietnamese army forces compelled U.S. leaders either to admit defeat or to use American troops to prevent the loss of the South.

The years from 1965 to 1975 saw the massive buildup of U.S. forces, a stalemate in the South, a growing antiwar movement in the United States, and the pullout of U.S. personnel. Although U.S. airplanes heavily bombed North Vietnam, American troops never invaded North Vietnam because they feared drawing the Chinese into the conflict, as had happened in the Korean War. U.S. President Richard Nixon tried a policy of turning over the conduct of the war to the South Vietnamese, but his invasion of Cambodia, which had been used as a military base by the Viet Cong, roused massive demonstrations in the United States that forced a more rapid withdrawal of American forces. A negotiated settlement between the North Vietnamese and Americans seemed to point the way to a resolution of the conflict. But a North Vietnamese attack in April 1975 triggered a rout of the South Vietnamese army a month later.

The Vietnamese communists took control of the South. They sent many Vietnamese to "re-education camps," where some died and others toiled at hard labor. They also tried a variety of socialist economic measures to rebuild the country. Most failed, despite sizeable Soviet and Chinese aid.

In 1978, the Vietnamese invaded Cambodia. Although the Vietnamese toppled the Khmer Rouge (Cambodian communists), the Vietnamese found themselves stuck in an expensive occupation. After more than a decade of fighting and supporting puppet rulers, the Vietnamese withdrew at last.

Prior to the invasion by Vietnam, Cambodians suffered three years of tyrannical rule by the Khmer Rouge (1975–1978), who rivaled the Nazis in their ferocious assault on existing institutions and people. The Khmer Rouge emptied the cities and forced cityfolk into village centers. Millions perished, including Buddhist monks, intellectuals, and other members of elite groups. In percentages, the losses dwarfed those caused by virtually all other revolutionary governments. In the 1990s, the United Nations oversaw relatively free elections, but troubles have continued to plague the Cambodians to this day.

In 1965, the Indonesian Communist Party tried to take over the Indonesian armed forces, but failure led to mass reprisals by Indonesians who saw the botched coup as a Chinese communist plot. In the aftermath, several hundred thousand people died, including Indonesian communists and Chinese-Indonesians, many of whom were killed solely because they were Chinese. Since then, Indonesia has successfully followed a Western model of economic development, using oil to facilitate industrialization.

Britain granted Burma independence in 1948 and released control over its other Southeast Asian colonies somewhat later. Behind these actions was the realization that powerful national movements wanted self-rule and that armed resistance to them generally was futile. In Malaya, however, the British fought a communist insurgency by playing on the fact that some liberation fighters were of Chinese ancestry. Using ethnic rivalries and Cold War rhetoric to their advantage, the British defeated the insurgency. Nevertheless, the British abandoned the region by the mid-1960s, realizing that their global empire was lost.

SOUTH ASIA. Although the dominant force in South Asia was the antagonism between the Muslims and Hindus, Cold War rivalries surfaced there as well. India and Pakistan became rivals in the subcontinent, especially over the question of who should administer Kashmir, a strategic border territory mostly under Indian control. Indo-Pakistani Wars (1947–1948 and 1965) were fought with no decisive results. In 1971, internal upheaval in Pakistan exploded into a war in which East Pakistan (separated by 1,000 miles of Indian territory from West Pakistan) won independence, declaring itself the nation of Bangladesh. India fought on behalf of Bangladesh in order to split up and weaken its rival, Pakistan.

The Cold War came to South Asia when India allied itself with the Soviet Union and Pakistan allied itself with the United States. As the Chinese and Soviets became more estranged, the Indians and Soviets drew closer. In 1962, India and China fought a brief war in the Himalaya Mountains region, a war the Chinese won. Pakistan had already developed a military alliance with the United States and became closely tied with the Chinese. Pakistan also became a major base for anti-Soviet activities during the Afghanistan War (1979–1989).

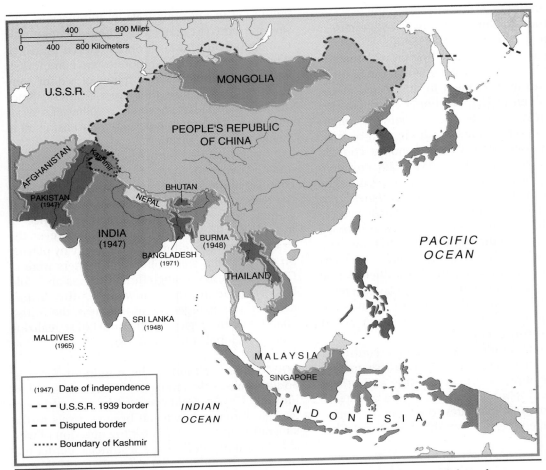

MAP 41.4 *South Asia in 1972.* *The British rule of South Asia and ultimate withdrawal in the late 1940s raised the problematic issue of the partition of India and Pakistan. These two South Asian powers fought several wars between 1947 and 1971. With the help of India, Bangladesh (formerly East Pakistan) broke away from West Pakistan in 1971. Since then, other countries have avoided foreign conflicts, although Sri Lanka has experienced a prolonged civil war.*

SOUTHWEST AND CENTRAL ASIA. The Cold War also intruded into Southwest and Central Asian politics. Many Islamic countries accepted Soviet aid in the 1950s and 1960s to offset U.S. aid to Israel. Egyptian President Gamal Abdul Nasser (1918–1970) threw out U.S. advisors and welcomed the Soviets. That meant abandoning the Western economic model and influence, as well as accepting Soviet aid and military advisors. Many countries chose Nasser's option, although Nasser's successor, Anwar Sadat, tossed out the Soviets in 1977, bringing Egypt back into the Western orbit. Syria and Iraq also developed close ties with the

Soviets in the 1960s; they suffered when the Soviet Union declined and collapsed in the 1980s and 1990s.

A central concern for many Arab states was the state of Israel. As seen in Chapter 33, Zionists (Jewish nationalists) pursued the dream of a Jewish homeland in Palestine. After a time of immigration in the early decades of the twentieth century, Jewish leaders pressured the British government to have land assigned to them. Terrorism and guerrilla warfare forced the British to accede to the formation of Israel. Arab states, however, fought Israel in 1948, the first of several conflicts. Israel won in

FIGURE 41.5 *Palestinian Refugees Awaiting Deportation.* *The creation of the state of Israel in Palestine in 1948 led to war and the dislocation of large numbers of Palestinians. Over the following decades, most of them lived in makeshift refugee camps. During the 1960s, the Palestine Liberation Organization was formed to take back Palestine through the use of armed force.* Burt Glinn/Magnum Photos.

1948 and again in 1956, 1967, and 1973. The 1973 conflict brought Soviet threats of military intervention. In response, the United States went on a full nuclear alert, at a level just short of launching an attack on the Soviet Union. Since 1973, Israel has managed to negotiate a peace settlement with Egypt (1977) and to ease tensions with the Palestinians and Jordan. The United States has mediated in these agreements.

Iran strove to be a major power in Southwest Asia. It had substantial petroleum supplies and a thriving economy, but when an Iranian government nationalized British oil holdings in 1951, British and U.S. leaders began a policy of undermining Iran. Eventually, the government fell. In 1953, Shah Muhammad Reza Pahlavi, Iran's ruler, embarked on a program of modernizing Iran and arming it with Western weapons. Repression, especially against the religious hierarchy, fomented unrest that toppled the shah in 1979. The religious leadership that came into power abrogated the U.S. alliance and also destroyed communist influence. The Republic of Iran went its own diplomatic way in the 1980s and 1990s, and it became embroiled in a war with Iraq that lasted through the 1980s, resulting in millions of casualties.

Central Asia has been home to Muslims since at least the seventh century, and they number in the tens of millions of people of diverse ethnic backgrounds. In the nineteenth century, the Russian government conquered much of the region, leaving only Afghanistan under British control. During the collapse of the Russian Empire in 1917, many Central Asian states declared independence. However, the Soviets reconquered much of Central Asia. After the British left, the Soviets supported an unstable regime in Afghanistan.

The Soviet Union invaded Afghanistan in 1979 and soon found itself embroiled in a major conflict not unlike America's Vietnam War. Afghans have prided themselves on their independence and resistance to foreign rule. When the Soviets attacked, many Afghans fought back. After United States leaders provided surface-to-air missiles and

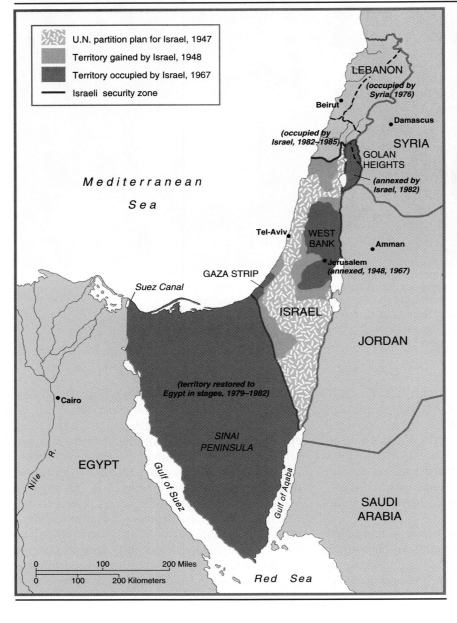

MAP 41.5 *The Arab-Israeli Wars and Peace, 1948–1982.* *Since its founding in 1948, Israel has fought a series of wars with its Arab neighbors. In the process, Israel has annexed significant territories and returned some conquered lands to Egypt in exchange for peace. During these conflicts, hundreds of thousands of Palestinians were rendered homeless and were forced to live in refugee camps. More general peace settlements in the region await the 1990s and beyond.*

FIGURE 41.6 *Afghans Celebrating on a Soviet Tank. Although heavily outgunned by the Soviet army, the Afghans managed to defeat their northern neighbor, leading to eventual Soviet withdrawal. U.S. military aid improved the Afghans' chance of success. In this 1980 photo, a group of Afghan soldiers celebrate the capture of an enemy tank.* Alain Mingam / Gamma/ Liaison International.

other military assistance, the Afghan resistance fighters began to inflict heavy casualties on the Soviets, who began seeking a way to end the conflict. By 1989, the Soviets withdrew and their puppet government collapsed, and successor governments have proved unable to rule the country effectively.

The Cold War in Africa

Africans suffered from Cold War rivalries. The Soviets viewed Africa as an area for the penetration of its influence, and they hoped to appeal to the anti-imperialist African nationalists. As new states cre-

ated one-party governments and adopted socialist economic policies, the Soviet Union gave military and economic aid to them. Angola, a former Portuguese colony, received Soviet aid, especially to fight off a rebel movement backed by the Americans. The United States had little interest in Africa until the Soviets began to appear there. Soon, however, the United States gave foreign aid, including military assistance, to African states. China gave help to a few African countries as well. When the Cold War ended, U.S. and Soviet aid vastly decreased, leaving many of the African states impoverished.

Kenya had been under British rule for many decades. In the 1940s and 1950s, the Kikuyu Uprising (the Mau Mau) fought against the British imperialists. The struggle lasted from 1952 to 1956 and then subsided until the British finally surrendered their control in the early 1960s.

One-party government characterized Kenyan politics, and the Kenya African National Union (KANU) represented a merging of the country's major parties. KANU's top leaders promoted their nationalist, pragmatic, and socialist goals. They created a mixed economy of state-run industries, along with those under private ownership. Similarly, when KANU developed its land policies, it preferred to have people purchase lands from the white settlers rather than undertake a nationalization and redistribution of land. The economy prospered until the late 1970s, when a recession hit most African countries. Social changes, like promoting universal education and improving the status of women, were introduced by KANU.

France controlled Algeria for more than a century, and more than 1 million French lived in that North African country, constituting Algeria's ruling class. In 1954, Arabs and Berber tribes revolted against French rule, and the fighting continued for seven years. Complicating matters was the fact that many French in Algeria detested the French government, fearing it would back the native Algerians. A brief uprising among the French in Algeria fizzled after the French president, Charles DeGaulle, took stern measures against it.

The Algerians overthrew the French, and the new Algerian government followed socialist policies to improve the well-being of its people in the 1960s and 1970s. Some prosperity came with the development of Algeria's oil reserves. In the 1990s, the rise of Islamic fundamentalist movements has complicated political life for the ruling elite, and repressive acts against the fundamentalist Islamic leaders have sent them underground. Elections that would likely have been won by the fundamentalists were canceled, leading to a bloody civil war.

The Cold War in Latin America

Latin Americans also became involved in Cold War rivalries. The United States had a long history of supporting dictators who adhered to its political and economic agendas. In Guatemala, a reforming government that threatened to overturn the existing sociopolitical status quo was toppled by the United States in the early 1950s. A precipitant to U.S. action was the nationalization of substantial property owned by the United Fruit Company, a U.S.-based business.

In 1959, revolutionaries overthrew the U.S.-backed Cuban regime and established a Marxist state headed by Fidel Castro. Two years later, a U.S.-supported invasion of Cuba failed. In October 1962, U.S. leaders had learned that the Soviets had built a missile base in Cuba; U.S. leaders viewed having Soviet missiles ninety miles from the U.S. mainland as intolerable. The Cuban Missile Crisis threatened to unleash nuclear war between the Cold War rivals. Although diplomats negotiated a

UNDER THE LENS

A Folk Hero of the Cuban Revolution

Ernesto "Che" Guevara (1927–1967) became a popular figure among revolutionaries and a cult hero among many young people in the 1960s and 1970s. Educated as a doctor in his Argentine homeland, Che roamed Latin America in search of a revolutionary struggle. He was in Guatemala when the United States helped overthrow the government, which had proved too anti-American. Later, Che Guevara joined with Fidel Castro to seize power in Cuba.

During the early 1960s, Che wrote extensively on revolution in Latin America. Following the lead of China's Mao Zedong, a man whom Che admired, he believed that the peasantry was the most important social force for revolution in Latin America. Thus, the countryside rather than the city should be the place where the revolutionaries should build their armies. Guerrilla warfare was to be the means of struggle to take power in the Third World. Once in control, the revolutionaries should use art and literature as vehicles to further the transformation of society, inspiring the people to change themselves. To promote that end, Che Guevara helped undertake a massive and successful campaign to spread literacy among the Cuban people.

Once in power, Che led an economic planning agency in Cuba. Very soon, he faced the task of motivating Cuban workers to help develop the economy. In the process, he hoped to transform people into socialists through the use of moral incentives. Through the popular education system, people were taught to help others for the good of society rather than for themselves. At the same time, Che Guevara did not rule out the use of material incentives to motivate people. But he believed that making material rewards the driving force in achieving economic aims corrupted people and led to class stratification, weakened communal solidarity, and distorted income equalization. This, of course, led away from socialist ideals.

By the mid-1960s, Che Guevara became disenchanted with the direction of the Cuban Revolution, leaving Cuba for new revolutionary pastures in Latin America. Fidel Castro, the Cuban leader, wanted to build communism in Cuba, relying heavily on the Soviet Union to accomplish that task. Che Guevara criticized the subordination of Cuba to a great power. He also believed that revolution within any one country had to take place in the context of revolutionary struggles and revolutions within the entire Third World. Thus, he was less interested in the Cold War as a struggle between the Soviet Union and the United States.

Che's romantic spirit brought him to South America. By the mid-1960s, he had been rumored to have been sighted in numerous places, and he had helped launch several unsuccessful revolutionary movements. Finally, in 1967, soldiers of a counterinsurgency campaign in Bolivia found and killed him. Che Guevara, who had inspired millions in life, became a martyr to revolutionary causes around the globe.

peaceful resolution of the crisis, the near-disaster sparked interest in tension-reducing measures. Soon, a series of arms-reduction treaties was signed by Soviet and U.S. leaders.

In the 1970s, the Sandinistas, a Marxist revolutionary movement in Nicaragua, overthrew a corrupt dictatorship backed by the U.S. government. The new state was recognized and aided by many Western European countries and the Soviet bloc. During the 1980s, however, elements of the U.S. government supported anti-Sandinista forces, despite specific congressional laws prohibiting intervention. U.S. President Ronald Reagan saw the illegal activity as part of the larger Cold War confrontation between the Soviet Union and the United States. The abandonment of covert U.S. aid and an election that ousted the Sandinistas reduced tensions there.

ECONOMIC TRANSFORMATION AND CRISIS

The Cold War severely taxed the U.S. and Soviet economies but provided growth for other countries. Third World countries, especially those in Africa, suffered from lack of outside investments; Cold War aid often provided critical funds though it stressed military rather than civilian projects.

The U.S. role in the Vietnam War (1961–1975) rent the United States' economic and social fabric. By the late 1960s, the United States could not fight a war and maintain an expensive welfare system implemented by President Lyndon Johnson. In 1971, President Richard Nixon responded to the deteriorating economic situation by freezing wages and prices, as well as taxing imports. In 1973 and 1979, two significant increases in petroleum prices rocked the U.S. economy. Anger with America's Cold War policies triggered massive antiwar demonstrations, galvanizing important segments of society. In addition, African Americans, Native Americans, women, and homosexuals challenged prevailing social practices, like racial and sexual discrimination.

In the 1980s, President Ronald Reagan accelerated a defense-spending program begun by his predecessor, President Jimmy Carter. This effort helped stimulate an economic boom that was enhanced by a mushrooming of export growth. By the mid-1980s, Reagan negotiated major arms-reduction programs with his Soviet counterpart, Mikhail Gorbachev, to reduce the formidable costs of the arms race.

U.S. Cold War activities benefited the Japanese economy. The Korean War, for example, turned Japan into a major military supplier for the U.S. army. The Toyota automobile company was nearly bankrupt when the United States placed orders for thousands of Toyota trucks, helping the company prosper. Japanese manufacturing output grew 50 percent from 1950 to 1951. The Vietnam War of the 1960s and 1970s also benefited the Japanese economy, which supplied some of the military needs of the U.S. army.

By the 1980s, Japan boasted the second-largest economy in the world and annual trade surpluses of around $100 billion. Large multinational corporations such as Mitsubishi and Sony produced Japanese goods that dominated many regional and national markets, leading to Japanese pride in their economic power. Many Japanese viewed the United States as a declining power, at least until the Japanese economy hit a prolonged slump in the early 1990s. American policy and investment had helped shape Japan into a major world power and ally.

Although some South Asian countries were among the poorest in the world, their economies gradually have developed, reducing poverty in the area by the 1990s. India initially concentrated on state-controlled industrial growth and received economic aid and technical assistance from the Soviet Union. It had achieved modest levels of economic growth by the 1990s. After 1991, major efforts were undertaken to open India to market forces, and economic growth has accelerated, especially in computer technology. Pakistan has been less successful in industrializing and has had to rely on financial assistance from abroad.

ENERGY AND THE ENVIRONMENT

The twentieth century became the era of petroleum because of the widespread use of the internal combustion engine. In addition, petroleum by-products, such as plastics and various chemicals, have permeated modern societies, with the result that human beings have become dependent on oil.

FIGURE 41.7 *OPEC's Growing Power.* *The Organization of Petroleum Exporting Countries (OPEC) gained great influence in the 1970s and 1980s. Its members controlled a large proportion of the world's petroleum and began to set higher prices than ever before. Most industrializing and industrialized countries that relied on oil imports were hard hit; Japan was particularly vulnerable because it imported 99 percent of its petroleum needs. This 1980 American cartoon reflects the perspective that OPEC was ruining the new year with its policies.* © 1984, Pat Oliphant. Distributed by the Los Angeles Times Syndicate.

The industrial potential of petroleum had been discovered in the mid–nineteenth century, and its refinement made kerosene a popular fuel in the latter half of that century. The internal combustion engine created a demand for a new source of fuel. The British navy, for example, decided in favor of oil over coal for its ships' power in the years leading up to the outbreak of World War I. World War II soldiers and sailors relied even more heavily on oil, as evidenced by the Japanese drive to Indonesia's oil fields in 1942 and the Germans' fight for the oil fields in the Caucasus Mountains.

Western countries often enjoyed monopolistic control over many Third World nations' oil fields until the early 1970s. Then Arab nations banded with some other major oil-supplying countries to form a **cartel**, a group that produces a significant percentage of a material, that cooperates to fix production levels and prices, and that dominates international distribution of the material. This cartel, the Oil Producing and Exporting Countries (OPEC), controlled much of the global supply of oil and raised prices sharply on two occasions, in 1973 and in 1979. These steep increases caused severe

budgetary problems for oil-consuming nations and sparked inflation. At the same time, many OPEC nations became wealthy, and they recycled these dollars back into Europe and the United States. Hard hit were Third World countries that also needed oil but had few funds to pay for their energy supplies.

The Persian Gulf War of 1991 showed the importance and dangers of petroleum production. Iraq had longstanding claims to Kuwait, which Iraq's Saddam Hussein seized in 1990. Because Iraq and Kuwait claimed a significant fraction of global oil reserves, this triggered a United Nations military response. After assembling a formidable armed force, including personnel from Saudi Arabia, Egypt, Britain, and others, U.S. leaders initiated a massive bombing campaign as a prelude to a ground offensive that lasted four days. Kuwait was freed, and much of the Iraqi army lay in ruins. Huge oil fires and spills gave the night landscape the look of a hellish inferno and horribly fouled the Persian Gulf. A deliberate act of ecocide had been committed by the departing Iraqi forces.

Although oil has remained supreme in the world, other energy sources, like coal, atomic energy, natural gas, wind power, and geothermal power, have become more widespread in usage. Coal has remained a common fuel in many parts of the world, although burning it causes air pollution. Atomic energy also became a major supplier of energy through power plants in the First and Second worlds.

Atomic energy couples great opportunities with serious liabilities. Power generation by this means often has proven expensive, but the needs of various industrial states, like those of Japan, encouraged the building and use of nuclear power plants. Japan lacked coal and oil resources and turned to nuclear power generation to supply some of its energy needs. One problem with nuclear facilities is their vulnerability to attack by terrorists. Another is the possibility that peaceful uses of atomic energy might produce enough fissionable material to construct atomic weapons. The Iraqis, for example, were in the process of building nuclear weapons but fooled inspectors about their intentions, and the North Koreans raised tensions in the Korean Peninsula by refusing to permit international inspectors to analyze materials produced by their nuclear power plants

in 1995. Another problem with nuclear power plants has been the possibility of meltdowns of their reactors. In 1986, for example, a power plant at Chernobyl in the Ukraine exploded, spewing nuclear-contaminated materials across much of Europe. Nuclear waste disposal has been another serious problem.

A list of environmental issues began to dominate politics from the 1960s. People had become concerned about overpopulation, environmental degradation, and the waste of natural resources. Environmental sensitivity markedly increased in the 1960s and has brought change. Kenya, for example, has expended a significant amount of resources in enforcing its Wildlife Protection Act. Hunting safaris that seriously reduced the wild-animal population have been replaced by controlled tourist ventures with people wielding cameras rather than rifles. Local Kenyans have been lured into working in the tourist industry, lessening the attraction of poaching.

Industrialization has caused significant environmental degradation, especially since 1945. Industrial-waste sites in the United States have cost billions of dollars to clean up. In Japan, the Minamata disease caused by poisoning of rivers by industrial wastes was perhaps the first named

FIGURE 41.8 *Victim of Environmental Poisoning in Japan.* *A mother bathes her seventeen-year-old daughter who was born blind and physically disabled as a result of mercury poisoning. A local chemical plant dumped metal wastes into the water supply of Minamata Village; cases of environmental poisoning in the region became known as Minamata disease.* W. Eugene Smith/Black Star.

environmental affliction. Human beings who drank the untreated water began to display symptoms of severe nerve damage. Soviet-bloc countries had vast areas of industrial pollution from East Germany to the Ural Mountains.

Some environmentalists have warned people and their governments that the widespread use of fossil fuels has unleashed unprecedented amounts of carbon dioxide into the atmosphere. The layer of carbon dioxide permits the sun's energy through but traps it, as in a greenhouse. Thus, the earth's temperature will rise over time. If this process continues unchecked, they argue, an increase of the earth's temperature by a few degrees will cause disastrous weather and environmental changes. Other scientists have challenged these models, pointing to problems in accurately measuring the globe's temperature.

Air pollution has caused serious problems around the world since 1945. Industrial countries reported unusual levels of human respiratory problems and environmental degradation, and most cities felt some effects due to air pollution. Mexico City has had serious smog problems since the 1970s. Athens and Rome have watched the corrosive effects of smog on longstanding cultural treasures, like the Acropolis and the Colosseum.

SCIENTIFIC DISCOVERIES

World War II governments organized their scientists and technicians around a variety of war-related projects, and the onset of the Cold War fostered widespread state-funded scientific investigation. Although diverse countries were involved in massive scientific projects, the Cold War rivalry meant that the United States and the Soviet Union dominated.

World War II was a time when inventions like radar and airplanes were considerably improved. The U.S. government's most significant effort, the Manhattan Project, symbolized what a mobilized government might accomplish. The project's purpose was to develop an atomic bomb, and the United States spent around $2 billion to accomplish that task. It gathered and organized hundreds of scientists and technicians. They developed an atomic bomb that was exploded as a test in New Mexico in July 1945. For a few years, the United States monopolized this new weaponry, but the Soviets tested an atomic bomb in 1949. A few years

later, both countries had detonated hydrogen bombs, much more destructive weapons.

A second war effort involved the development of rocketry, and the Germans invested much capital and human resources in that project. Late in the war, German rockets were launched against Britain, bringing limited death and destruction; more significant, they inspired great fear and anxiety among the British. U.S. and Soviet officials collared some of the top German missile scientists, and both powers' missile programs benefited from the knowledge derived from the Germans. When atomic bombs were attached to intercontinental missiles, they became strategic weapons systems of awesome destructive power.

Rockets facilitated the exploration of space. The Soviet Union surprised the world with the launching of *Sputnik*, the world's first human-made satellite, in October 1957. That event spurred the American educational system completely to revise its scientific and mathematics programs. Government funds flowed to these areas, and elementary and secondary schools developed a new emphasis on science and mathematics. Graduate schools reduced the amount of time necessary to earn a doctorate degree in order to train scientists more quickly. In addition, the U.S. government worked hard to overtake the Soviets in missile delivery systems. The arms race heightened fear of war and brought the creation of civil defense systems. American and Soviet schoolchildren underwent regular air raid drills during periods of the Cold War.

In the early 1960s, U.S. President John Kennedy challenged the American people and scientific community to land U.S. astronauts on the moon and return them safely before the end of the decade. A huge financial outlay and large-scale organization of scientists and engineers supported the moon race. Despite problems, American astronauts reached the moon on July 20, 1969, planting the U.S. flag there. The mood of America in the late 1960s, however, turned against such large-scale projects that seemingly did not benefit ordinary people. Although some additional programs of great size continued to receive money, only projects related to military needs were awarded consistent funding.

The federal government also spent considerable amounts of money on scientific research in universities across the United States. These funds helped provide the financial means for investigative projects, but they also helped foster a government-university complex that troubled many. Some feared the loss of the independence of university governance and academic freedom. Antigovernment feelings that surfaced in the 1960s and 1970s, fueled by concerns over the Vietnam War, caused soul-searching among academic scientists who lived off federal funds.

Other scientific and technological discoveries appeared outside government settings. Private industry spent large sums on research and development in the United States, and the Japanese and Germans began to outspend Americans in the 1980s. The International Rice Research Institute in the Philippines used U.S. and other funding to produce dwarf varieties of rice. These rice plants have higher yields of grain and sturdier stalks, preventing preharvest breakage under the weight of the grains. Now about one-fourth of the world's rice comes from these varieties. Yields increased about 100 percent per unit of area. These varieties, though, require chemical fertilizers and pesticides, putting them out of reach of many small farmers. These dwarf plants were primarily developed from 1967 to 1974.

SOCIAL CHANGE IN THE COLD WAR ERA

The pace of social change accelerated after 1945. Around the world, interest groups agitated for greater equality of opportunity in political, economic, and social arenas. In the ensuing decades, some of their goals were partly achieved, exemplifying the democratizing trend of modernity.

Expanded Suffrage and Office Holding

Voting rights and office-holding opportunities for women and ethnic minorities grew rapidly after World War II. Although women and some minorities had gained access to political systems in the nineteenth and early twentieth centuries in the West, most in other parts of the world had to wait until after 1945 to vote or to hold office.

In the West, women gained the franchise in the early twentieth century; office holding came somewhat later. Norway, for example, permitted women to vote in national elections by 1907, the same year they could vote in Wyoming, the first

U.S. state to adopt female suffrage. Despite a lengthy struggle for the vote on the national level, the final, successful push for the vote came in World War I, when the extensive war-related service of women in the United States and Europe earned the respect of many men, who hastened the amendment process. U.S. women got the right to vote after the passage of the Nineteenth Amendment to the U.S. Constitution in 1920.

Since 1920, not only have women voted, but they have run for office. Although women have been elected as prime ministers in Norway, Iceland, Israel, and Britain, their numbers in office still represent far less than their percentage of the population. Margaret Thatcher of Britain held office through the 1980s, becoming one of the longest-ruling prime ministers in modern British history.

Asian women gained the right to vote after World War II. Japanese women, for example, got the vote only during the U.S. occupation (1945–1952). Women have run as candidates for

FIGURE 41.9 *Prime Minister Indira Gandhi.*
Indira Gandhi succeeded her father, Jawaharlal Nehru, as leader of India and governed from 1966 to 1977 and from 1980 to 1984. She and many other women emerged as national leaders during the Cold War era. Wide World Photos.

Japan's House of Representatives, and a few have held office in the period since 1945. South Asians not only have given women the vote, but they have elected several women as heads of state. Indira Gandhi of India was elected as prime minister in 1966, remaining a powerful leader until her assassination in 1984. She promoted significant policies, including family planning to moderate India's rapid population growth. Benazir Bhutto won the prime ministership in Pakistan in 1988, becoming the first woman to head an Islamic state in the twentieth century. A military dictatorship ruled Bangladesh for most of its existence, but in free elections in 1989, Kaleda Zia was elected prime minister, and she held office for a brief time. Sirimavo Bandaranike assumed power in Sri Lanka after her husband's assassination in 1959, and she remained the dominant political figure in the 1960s and 1970s.

African women got the vote in the postindependence period, but because many states in Africa were dictatorial, the vote meant little. In addition, African women continued to hold limited economic and political power. When male-dominated nation-states passed economic laws or other measures, women's interests were generally ignored. Land reform in Ethiopia during the 1970s, for example, gave land to male family heads only; similar patterns were found in Cameroon, Mozambique, and elsewhere. North African states frequently have been guided by Islamic precedent, so women only gradually received the right to vote. They have not been able to gain much influence through elective office.

The matter of one's sexual preference in terms of office holding has been controversial in industrial states during the post-1945 period. Controversy arose as homosexuals openly espoused their sexual preferences when running for office. Election of homosexuals to high office in the United States has increased in the 1980s and 1990s. The U.S. Congressional Gay-Lesbian Caucus, for example, had more than twenty members in 1994. First World countries have been more tolerant of overt homosexual activity and office holding than those in the Third World.

Ethnic-minority participation in the electoral process has increased dramatically around the world, especially in the industrial world. African Americans were given the right to vote by an amendment to the U.S. Constitution in 1868. That constitutional guarantee, however, meant little in the South and other areas because restrictive measures often effectively kept African Americans from voting until well into the twentieth century. One strategy used to limit African American voting was the **poll tax**, a fee imposed on each voter. Many African Americans could not afford to pay the sum. Others failed to pass literacy tests that were given only to African Americans.

Voting restrictions continued until the American civil rights movement of the 1960s. Pressure put on Congress by large marches and rallies, including a massive march on Washington, D.C., led by the Rev. Martin Luther King, Jr., resulted in the passage of the Voting Rights Act of 1964, sweeping away state requirements that effectively kept many African Americans from voting. Other laws have been passed, and Supreme Court decisions have confirmed and extended these rights to all ethnic minorities. Out of one voting rights act in 1988 came the creation of electoral districts designed to facilitate majorities of certain ethnic minorities. Thus, members of these ethnic groups were more likely to win elections to the House of Representatives. The Supreme Court threw out some of the new districts in 1996. In addition, voter-registration drives have aimed at turning ethnic voting blocs into powerful political forces.

Between 1948 and 1991, South Africa followed *apartheid*, a legal system of racial segregation and discrimination enforced by a minority white government. Black Africans were forced to submit to white rule while living under state-sponsored repression and poverty. In the early 1990s, Nelson Mandela, a major leader of the African National Congress (ANC), was released from years of imprisonment for his political beliefs. Mandela's release signaled the start of political reforms led by South Africa's prime minister, F. W. de Klerk. In the spring of 1994, South Africans of all races were permitted to vote freely for the first time: The ANC and Mandela were swept into power.

Toward Universal Education in the Third World

Universal education had generally been achieved in the First and Second worlds by 1945. After 1945, newly liberated countries in Asia and Africa adopted national goals of universal education. They saw education as the means to train people for the workforce, to improve people's chances of social advancement, and to implant ideas and val-

FIGURE 41.10 *South Africa's Leaders Meet. Nelson Mandela (center), F. W. de Klerk (right), and Mangosuthu Buthelezi (left) were frequently at odds in the negotiations that brought a representative government to South Africa in 1994. After freedom was achieved, these men sometimes posed for pictures to show their unity. While violence accompanied the fall of apartheid, peaceful actions and gatherings prevailed, giving hope for the future of South Africa.* Juhan Kuus/Sipa Press.

ues important to the nations' rulers. At the same time, families began demanding educational opportunities for their children because they realized that schooling could be a major road to advancement of the individual and thereby the family. Although universal education was often a government's stated goal, discrimination against women in societies in Africa and elsewhere meant that they seldom attained educational levels comparable to those of men.

The central government usually supplied the funds to create the educational infrastructure. In a few cases, like Kenya, a local system of education emerged. The Harambee Self-help Movement there permitted communities to build local schools with minimal governmental involvement.

One source of private education has come from religious schools. In parts of Africa and elsewhere, these schools were holdovers from imperialist times when Christian missionaries established schools. Many of these institutions carried over into independence. Muslim schools, often with religious leaders as teachers, flourished with little government support. Secular subjects have been taught in these schools, and, in countries like Pakistan, government decrees have insisted that basic Islamic principles and religious tenets be instilled in the students.

Public and private schools frequently followed Western education models and subject matter. The curriculum, usually Western, emphasized science and mathematics. In some extreme cases, such as in the Guyana educational system, students had to take London-based exams which had geographic detail about Britain that was alien and of little interest to Guyanans. Sometimes more latitude was permitted in literature and other humanities in using non-Western materials.

Expanding educational opportunity has been part of the process of democratization, one of the elements of modernity. Education has become the ladder to success for all people, but especially for women and minorities. People feel more ownership in governments that permit them to vote, hold office, and earn an education. That, in turn, helps officials govern more effectively.

ASIA	E. EUROPE	W. EUROPE / N. AMERICA		
			1940	
			–	
			–	
			–	Berlin airlift begins, 1947
Vietnam War, 1946–1955		NATO, 1949–present	–	Israel founded, 1948
Korean War, 1950–1953			**1950**	
			–	
			–	
	Warsaw Pact, 1955–1989		–	Hungarian Uprising, 1956
			–	Suez crisis, 1956
			1960	
Vietnam War, 1961–1975			–	Sino-Indian War, 1962
			–	Kenya becomes independent, 1963
			–	Six-Day War, 1967
			–	Tet Offensive, 1968
			1970	Soviet troops invade Czechoslovakia, 1968
			–	Indo-Pakistani War and Bangladesh independence, 1971
			–	
			–	
			–	Ayatolla Khomeini takes power, 1979
War in Afghanistan, 1979–1989			**1980**	Soviet troops land in Afghanistan, 1979
Iran-Iraq War, 1980–1988			–	
			–	
			–	
			–	Berlin Wall torn down, 1989
			1990	Reunification of Germany, 1990

SUMMARY

1. The Cold War (1945–1991) lasted nearly fifty years and involved the great-power rivalry between the United States and the Soviet Union. The Soviet collapse in 1991 ended the Cold War.

2. Europe became the major place of Cold War rivalry. The Soviet Union suppressed uprisings in Hungary (1956) and Czechoslovakia (1968). A more relaxed Soviet policy in the late 1980s led to the independence of the Soviet bloc countries and Germany's reunification in 1990.

3. The Korean and Vietnam wars became battlefields of the Cold War and showed the limits of American power.

4. India and Pakistan, traditional rivals, became involved in Cold War politics, with India supporting the Soviet Union and Pakistan backing the United States.

5. A major conflict in Southwest Asia revolved around the formation of Israel in 1948. Arabs and Israelis fought many wars over who should control Palestine. In Central Asia, the Soviet Union failed in its effort to control Afghanistan during the 1980s.

6. African states threw off imperialist rule, gaining independence after 1945. Kenya and Algeria, for example, overthrew British and French colonial rule.

7. U.S.–Latin American relations were often tense, especially when United States leaders brought down a government in Guatemala and supported antigovernment Cuban and Nicaraguan forces.

8. The Cold War stretched the U.S. and Soviet economies to the breaking point, but it helped spur economic development in Japan and Western Europe. Many Third World economies heavily relied on foreign aid and suffered aid reductions when the Cold War ended.

9. Science benefited from government funding and organization, especially in projects like the atomic bomb program of the 1940s and the space exploration effort of the 1960s. Cold War rivalries, especially in military affairs, helped funds flow to scientific projects.

10. Petroleum became the dominant fuel of the twentieth century. Atomic energy offered another means to produce power but presented potential problems, including nuclear accidents and waste disposal.

11. Environmental degradation has become a major concern since the 1960s. Industrial pollution has fouled skies, and the careless disposal of industrial wastes has contaminated drinking water.

12. The growth of an environmental movement in the 1960s paved the way for a variety of government programs and policies.

13. Social change accelerated after 1945, bringing expanded voting rights and office holding to women. Ethnic minorities and homosexuals also benefited politically from more tolerant attitudes. Racial equality legislation passed in many countries, and universal education became a reality for millions.

SUGGESTED READINGS

Carson, Rachel. *Silent Spring*. Boston: Houghton Mifflin, 1962. A classic treatment of the overuse of pesticides, an environmental problem that kills many animals.

Goncharov, Sergei, John W. Lewis, and Xue Litai. *Uncertain Partners*. Stanford, Calif.: Stanford University Press, 1993. A revisionist interpretation of the Korean War in the light of Sino-Soviet relations.

Liss, Sheldon. *Marxist Thought in Latin America*. Berkeley: University of California Press, 1984. A standard treatment of Latin American socialist movements and leaders.

Nafziger, E. Wayne. *Inequality in Africa*. Cambridge, Eng.: Cambridge University Press, 1988. An examination of the economic policies of African governments in the Cold War era.

Walker, Martin. *The Cold War*. New York: Henry Holt, 1993. A survey of global history since 1945.

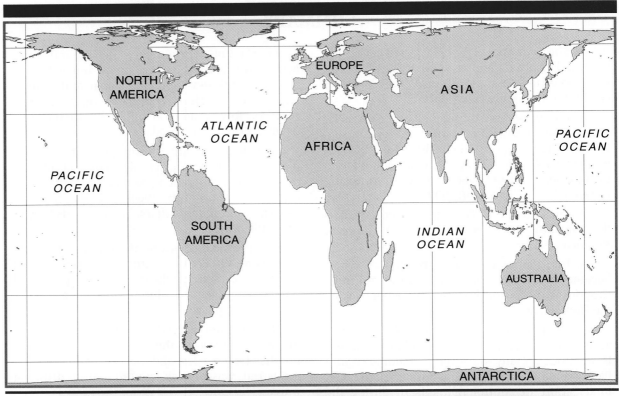

A Mother and Her Children at Ellis Island. *Ellis Island was the primary point of arrival for immigrants entering the United States in the first decades of the twentieth century.* Brown Brothers.

Populations in Change

1945 Onward

In 1976, Pol Pot became the prime minister of Cambodia, a fertile Southeast Asian country of about 9 million people. In the following three years, Pol Pot's government oversaw the killing of at least 1 million and possibly as many as 3 million persons who were judged questionable in their loyalty to the state. Such "sins" as having a college education, speaking a foreign language, or wearing eyeglasses were considered signs of intellectualism (and potential disloyalty) and could lead to execution. One to 2 million persons died of widespread famines and the privations of forced labor; 1 million fled to Thailand. In all, about half of the population died or left Cambodia within three years.

The Cambodian case is unusual in its magnitude, but it is only one of many major population dislocations that have occurred around the world in the period since the end of World War II. The study of population, its changes in size and composition, and its movements is known as **demography**. The period beginning with the final years of World War II has been remarkable in the scale of demographic changes and the rapidity with which these changes have taken place.

One major factor in these changes is technology. Technological changes, particularly in food production and medicine, have helped extend human life; parallel changes in military technology have made possible the mass killing of huge numbers of people in a brief span of time. Improved, less expensive modes of transportation have made long-range migration more feasible.

A second factor is the sheer size of the human population by the twentieth century. The population in 1945 probably was about two billion people, far greater than at any previous time. With such a huge population, the number of adults of parenting age exceeded that of any earlier time, and the potential number of children born on any day was much higher than ever before. Population has continued to grow throughout the twentieth century, reaching a staggering 6 billion persons today.

These and other factors have combined to produce massive population changes in the latter part of the twentieth century, sending ripples through all aspects of life. Political policies, economic decisions, social policies, and wars around the world all have been shaped by changes in the size, composition, and location of population.

POPULATION SHIFTS IN THE WAKE OF WORLD WAR II

Some of the demographic effects of World War II have been documented in Chapter 40. The genocidal campaigns directed against Jews and other groups of people had major demographic effects, reducing their numbers by as much as half. In addition, battle and bombing casualties sometimes were high, producing significant decreases in population. Many other demographic effects of the war, however, related primarily to the movements of people over space.

The first major postwar population shift occurred in 1945, when millions of prisoners of war, political prisoners, and forced workers were liberated from Nazi German camps by allied military forces. Most returned to their home countries or regions, though some, particularly Jews, elected to move to places with less painful memories. Many Jews immigrated to Palestine shortly after World War II, and many others moved to the United States, Canada, and Great Britain.

A second major population shift was the expulsion of millions of ethnic and national Germans from Eastern European countries. Some came from families that had been living in these areas for generations, while others had moved there only in the 1930s, after German annexation of parts of Poland, Czechoslovakia, Austria, and Hungary; others were occupation forces in Roma-

nia and Croatia. The total number of Germans displaced by these actions was more than 12 million.

The expulsion of these Germans created a vacuum into which flowed millions of non-Germans, some of whom had been displaced during earlier German expansion. Nearly 2 million Czechs, forced eastward into Slovakia a decade before, surged back to their homeland; 3 million Poles who had sought refuge in eastern Poland and points farther east returned to western Poland. Millions of other Eastern Europeans moved westward into the lands these other Slavs had vacated.

A final major population shift occurred in the Baltic countries of Lithuania, Latvia, and Estonia. Traditional enemies of the Soviet Union, these countries were divided in their loyalties during World War II. Many who had fought against the Soviets migrated to Sweden, creating a flow of nearly a quarter of a million immigrants. Others stayed in these Baltic states, while another quarter of a million migrated to Poland or other parts of the Soviet Union.

In total, about 28 million Europeans migrated from one country to another in the aftermath of World War II. In Asia, Africa, and the other theaters of war, population movements were far less massive, although there were war-related migrations in China involving millions of civilians. Japanese occupations in Asia and the Pacific had included relatively little transfer of civilian Japanese populations to conquered regions, although the retreat of military forces at the end of the war involved about 3 million military personnel. Similarly, World War II in Africa had been focused on the northern parts of the continent, and the arid environment there had deterred major movements of people.

POPULATION MOVEMENTS TO BOLSTER POLITICAL CONTROL

Several major population movements in the postwar era were for political purposes. Some of these were voluntary, often in response to the creation of new countries and often with the blessing of one or more governments. Others were engineered by governments to consolidate their political control, transplanting huge numbers of people against their wills.

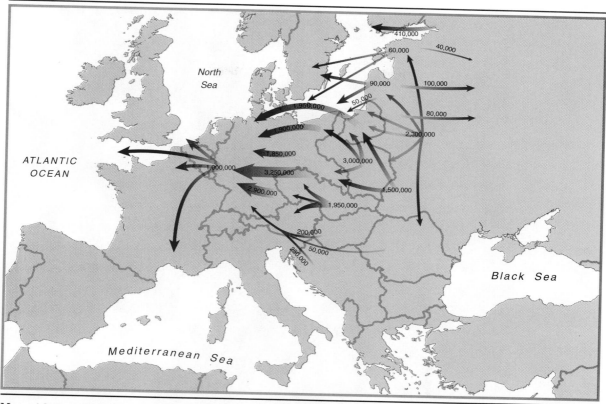

MAP 42.1 *Major Population Movements in Post–World War II Europe.* *Following World War II, European countries underwent major population changes. Returning troops, refugees, and forcibly resettled peoples constituted most of these migrations.*

Voluntary Migration

Much of the voluntary migration following World War II consisted of members of one religious group moving to a state where they would dominate. Political and economic concerns have prompted most of the remainder.

INDIA AND PAKISTAN. Great Britain annexed the various Indian states into the British Empire following their conquest in 1757. Prior to this conquest, there had been no politically unified India, and separate states differed in government, religion, language, and social customs. The religious differences between Hindus and Muslims were strong, and these surfaced overtly in 1912. Indians had charged the British governor with arbitrary conduct against them, and the British were attempting to mollify the Indians by granting them elected seats to the British government's legislative council in India. In response to pressure from both

Muslims and Hindus, the British agreed that some of the seats would be allocated to Muslims and some to Hindus.

The drive for Indian independence began among Hindu intellectuals, who established the Indian National Congress (INC) in 1885. In 1906, Muslim intellectuals founded the Moslem [Muslim] League, also dedicated to gaining independence from Britain. From the beginning, however, these groups were in conflict, because the INC envisioned an India dominated by the Hindu majority, while the Moslem League wanted to see India divided into separate Muslim and Hindu states.

These interests came to a head during World War II. In 1942, the INC and its leadership, Jawaharlal Nehru[1] and Mohandas Gandhi,[2] demanded immediate independence and threatened civil disobedience (and perhaps more violent

[1] **Jawaharlal Nehru:** jah WAH hahr lahl NAY roo
[2] **Mohandas Gandhi:** moh HAHN duhs GAHN dee

FIGURE 42.1 *Mass Relocation during the Partition of India. This photograph by Margaret Bourke-White shows Sikhs in bullock-drawn carts making their way to India from what had become Pakistan in 1947. Indian troops such as the soldier on horseback (middle, left) were given the task of protecting the Sikhs from possible violence during their migration.*

Margaret Bourke-White, *Life* Magazine, © Time Inc.

action) if it were not forthcoming. By this time, some renegade factions of the INC had raised the Indian National Army and actively were fighting alongside the Japanese against the British. Afraid that the INC would ally India with the Axis powers, the British outlawed the INC until the war ended. In the meantime, the Moslem League and its leader, Mohammad Ali Jinnah,[3] reiterated allegiance to the British and were permitted to continue operations throughout the war. During this period when the INC was illegal, the Moslem League prospered, gaining considerable political prestige and power.

[3] **Mohammad Ali Jinnah:** moh HAH mehd AH lee JIH nah

In 1946, the British offered independence to India; and, recognizing the strength of the Moslem League, the INC reluctantly agreed to a division of the country in 1947. The predominantly Muslim provinces were in the far eastern and far western parts of the country, while the predominantly Hindu portions were in the vast central area. The central area became India and the eastern and western parts became the single state of Pakistan. (In 1971, eastern Pakistan became a separate country, Bangladesh.)

The major problem was that two rich states, Punjab and Sind, had totally mixed populations. Not only was there no clear majority there, but members of the Hindu, Muslim, and Sikh religions lived side by side throughout these states, with no simple spatial distributions by religion. Consequently, no simple partition was possible. Nonetheless, they were divided more or less arbitrarily into Indian and Pakistani portions, and civil violence was immediate and massive. An estimated 500,000 persons were killed during the partition of these states. A few million Muslims remained in areas controlled by Hindus, and smaller numbers of Hindus stayed in Muslim-controlled areas; both governments made special efforts to protect these minorities. Nonetheless, great numbers were unwilling or afraid to remain, and about 15 million people began the harrowing trek to the east or west.

A migration of this sort means more than merely leaving a familiar place. Migrants also leave behind lands owned personally or by their families, sacred shrines, jobs, and friends. The economic, religious, and social fabric of people's lives is torn irreparably.

ISRAEL AND PALESTINE. Other significant migrations of the same era were brought about by the creation of the new state of Israel. The British Empire included Palestine, the land around Jerusalem, sacred as the Holy Land for Jews, Christians, and Muslims. In the nineteenth century, Palestine had a predominantly Arab Muslim population with minorities of Christians and Jews.

In the late nineteenth century, intellectual European Jews conceived of Zionism, the nationalistic quest to establish a Jewish state in the Holy Land. From the last two decades of the nineteenth century onward, Jews from Eastern Europe began migrating to Palestine. Most merely sought to escape persecution in Europe, but some were Zionists intent on establishing a stronger Jewish claim for Palestine. The trickle of Jewish immigration grew to a flood by the 1920s and increased further in the 1930s, when Jews escaping Nazi Germany came to Palestine by the tens of thousands. In 1890, the percentage of Jews in Palestine

FIGURE 42.2 *Jewish Settlers in Israel, 1949.* *This family has migrated from Europe to Israel, where they will be farmers. Their future farm is marked at this stage by only a banner bearing a religious quotation in Hebrew.* Corbis-Bettmann.

was under 5 percent; by 1922, it had risen to 22 percent; by 1936, it was 29 percent. In 1946, on the eve of the establishment of the state of Israel, it had reached 32 percent. All of these figures reflect percentages in Palestine as a whole, though Jewish populations were concentrated in the parts of Palestine that eventually became Israel. (For comparison, Jews in 1997 constituted about 85 percent of the population of the area of former Palestine, that is, both Israel and areas of Palestine under Israeli control.)

In 1946, the British government announced its intention to withdraw from Palestine. The following year, the United Nations agreed to turn most of Palestine into the Jewish state of Israel; the remainder of Palestine would be merged with Transjordan to become the Arab state of Jordan. Although Arab Palestinian leaders rejected this agreement, David Ben-Gurion, a Zionist leader and first president of Israel, announced the creation of Israel on May 14, 1948, the day the British withdrew.

Fighting between the Jewish and Arab factions ensued immediately. Palestinian Jews received financial aid from Jewish communities around the world and from some Western governments; Palestinian Arabs received military aid from neighboring Arab states, including troops from Syria, Egypt, Jordan, Lebanon, and Iraq. The better-equipped Israeli forces were successful in resisting the more numerous Arab army, and Israel occupied much of the former Palestine. Israeli forces carried out systematic destruction of Arab villages, and Arabs continued guerrilla warfare; massacres of civilians occurred regularly on both sides. War broke out again in 1956, 1967, and 1973, and each time Israel expanded its occupied territories; these areas remain legally disputed today. Palestinian Arabs opposed the existence of Israel until their parliament reversed this opposition in 1996.

From the Arab viewpoint, Israel was seen as an intrusive state, claiming land that had belonged to Arabs for centuries. Because it was illegitimate, its violence against Arabs was unlawful; therefore, it was appropriate to return violence. From the Israeli viewpoint, God had given this land to the Jews, and Israel was a legitimate state. Consequently, it was legitimate to use force to defend it. These conflicting viewpoints persist largely into today.

As a result of the military conflict in Palestine, two-thirds of the Muslim and Christian Arabs in former Palestine left or were forced from their homes by the better-equipped Jewish forces. These displaced people sought and received refuge in neighboring Arab countries, and, as with any refugees, their suffering and loss was intense. The subsequent wars created even more Palestinian refugees, and major portions of the population lived as refugees for more than a generation.

From the 1960s onward, the Palestinian Liberation Organization (PLO) and its leader, Yasser Arafat, spearheaded Palestinian diplomatic missions, labor and consumer strikes, and terrorism to gain the creation of an independent Palestinian state. In 1994, a negotiated agreement between Israel and the PLO led to partial autonomy of a new Palestine, composed of some of the disputed lands occupied by Israel and comprising a portion of the pre-Israel Palestine.

Since the creation of Israel, Jewish immigration has continued to be a potent force. Immigration from Europe and North America was strong in the 1950s, then fell off in the 1960s and 1970s. A small surge came in the early 1980s with the coming of *felashas* (Ethiopian Jews) fleeing oppression in their home country. Immigration swelled massively in the late 1980s as the Soviet Union allowed Russian Jews to emigrate; the collapse of the Soviet Union further spurred Jewish immigration to Israel. Israeli leaders have used immigration as a political tool, settling Jewish immigrants in areas previously dominated by Arabs in order to secure a stronger claim to those lands.

Arab migration in Palestine and Israel has been of smaller scale and not always voluntary. Arab migration was strongest in the early years of Israel, when many left areas that had become Israel; about 1 million Arabs remained in Israel. Israeli policies of exiling Arab dissidents created a small but significant increase in the numbers of Arabs leaving Israel in the 1970s, 1980s, and early 1990s. Estimates of the numbers of Arabs displaced in Palestine range from just under 1 million to as many as 3 million persons.

VOLUNTARY MIGRATION ELSEWHERE. In the last decades of the twentieth century, civil wars wracked many countries, creating masses of refugees worldwide. In many cases, the successful faction committed atrocities against the losers or seized their property; in those and other cases, fears of such atrocities or seizures motivated thousands of refugees to flee their home countries. Many of these conflicts had an ethnic basis, and no one

---

IN THEIR OWN WORDS

Zionism and Arab Dislocation

Zionism arose from the insecurity of Jewish life in Europe. The dangers of discrimination, expulsion, and extermination led many Jews to seek a new homeland in Palestine. This was a nationalist quest, but many recent scholars have viewed it also as imperialism, taking a territory by force and subjugating the native inhabitants. Early Zionists supported this project with racist stereotyping of Arabs, as shown in this extract from a 1918 letter from Chaim Weizmann,[a] a prominent Zionist:

> The Arabs, who are superficially clever and quick witted, worship one thing, and one thing only—power and success. . . . The Arab, quick as he is to gauge a situation, tries to make the most of it. . . . The *fellah* [peasant] is at least four centuries behind the times, and the *effendi* [urbanite] . . . is dishonest, uneducated, greedy, and as unpatriotic as he is inefficient.

By implication, a Zionist claim to Palestinian lands would improve their management.

Those who implemented the Jewish seizure of Arab lands after the United Nations decree were well aware of the magnitude of population displacement that would be necessary to achieve their ends; however, they felt it was justified by the "rightness" of their goals. Moshe Dayan,[b] a high Israeli military official, reflected those attitudes in a statement in 1969:

> We came to this country which was already populated by Arabs, and we are establishing a Hebrew, that is, a Jewish state here. In considerable areas of the country [about 6 percent] we bought the lands from the Arabs. Jewish villages were built in the place of the Arab villages. . . . There is not one place built in this country that did not have a former Arab population.

Hundreds of Arab villages were systematically destroyed by Israelis, creating hundreds of thousands of Arab refugees.

An anonymous Arab woman provided the following statements about the events following the attack and destruction of her village in 1948:

> We slept in the village orchards that night. The next morning, Umm Hussein and I went to the village. The chickens were in the streets, and Umm Hussein suggested that I go and bring some water. I saw Umm Taha on my way to the village courtyard. She cried and said: "You had better go and see your dead husband." I found him. He was shot in the back of the head. . . . I stayed in Kabri [her village] six days without eating anything. I decided to leave and join my sister, who had fled earlier with her family to Syria. . . .

Not all Israelis supported these seizures of land. Hannah Arendt, an Israeli scholar, interpreted these events as follows:

> After the war [World War II] it turned out that the Jewish question . . . was indeed solved—namely by means of a colonized and then conquered territory—but this solved neither the problem of the [Arab] minority nor the stateless. On the contrary, the solution of the Jewish question merely produced a new category of refugees, the Arabs, thereby increasing the number of the stateless by another 700,000 to 800,000 people.

[a] **Chaim Weizmann:** HY eem VYZ mahn
[b] **Moshe Dayan:** MOH shuh DY ahn

---

could claim neutrality when political affiliation and ethnicity were viewed as essentially the same thing.

Refugees from Vietnam, Cambodia, El Salvador, Haiti, Ethiopia, and Rwanda, to name but a few, sought sanctuary in unprecedented numbers during these decades. Usually war or political oppression drove refugees to migrate, but sometimes persistent and systematic religious or ethnic discrimination was the cause. Christians in India, for example, have frequently complained that they are discriminated against in job hiring and other economic activities and that they sometimes are harassed and beaten.

Many of these came to the United States, France, and Great Britain, because those countries were allies in their cause or former colonial powers controlling the country before its independence.

FIGURE 42.3   *Vietnamese Boat People.   Conditions in Vietnam deteriorated in the late 1970s, and many thousands of refugees fled by boat to neighboring countries. The refugees shown in this 1979 photograph are part of a group of 573 persons who spent forty-five days on a Malaysian beach until local authorities, considering them illegal aliens, ordered the refugees and their boats to be towed out to sea.*   J. Pavlovsky/Sygma.

Others, often poorer people who could not afford the cost of fleeing to distant lands, sought shelter in neighboring countries, frequently at great risk to their personal safety.

For the most part, these refugees have become productive members of the country to which they migrated, but their presence sometimes has caused resentment among the long-time citizens. There are costs attendant to coping with a large flood of immigrants, including the providing of education and services. Sometimes these services must accommodate linguistic and cultural systems alien to the host country, and sometimes the long-time citizens fear that new immigrants will compete for scarce jobs or will form a criminal element. Racism also can create major barriers for those coming to foreign shores, and violent anti-immigrant groups have proliferated in Western Europe in the wake of increased immigration. Immigrants who may have endured the loss of everything in their native countries may find a different set of miseries in their adopted land.

A distinctive sort of voluntary migration, very different from that discussed here, took place in many parts of the world when former colonies and parts of empires were granted their independence. Some citizens of the former colonial power preferred to return to their home countries, often out of fear of violent freedom movements. In Kenya, for example, British colonists fled the Kikuyu (Mau Mau) Uprising in 1952, afraid that nativist orientation would lead to their deaths if Kenya gained independence. In other cases, racism or fears of economic instability led individuals to return to their home countries. In parts of East Africa, Indians and Pakistanis also fled newly independent countries for fear of violence or loss of their property. Although the numbers of such immigrants were relatively small, their departure often had significant effects on the newly independent countries, because they often controlled considerable capital that, if invested in the new country, could have smoothed the economic transition to independence.

Government-Mandated Migration in China and the Soviet Union

The examples just given have included cases where an individual deciding not to migrate might suffer considerable personal risk and economic hardship. Nonetheless, the individual had to make a choice, and some individuals elected to remain where they were. The cases that follow, however, are examples of migrations ordered and carried out by governments in order to consolidate their political power. In these cases, decisions were made by government officials, and the individuals destined to move had little or no say in the matter.

The People's Republic of China found itself in an awkward position in the 1950s: Its interior provinces were overpopulated, and some of its outer provinces had substantial majorities of ethnic non-Chinese. Tibet, for example, had been claimed by China since 1928 and had been seized by Chinese military forces in 1951. The majority of the citizens of Tibet were ethnically Tibetan, and the Chinese recognized the potential for an active freedom movement there. To avoid this, they mandated that millions of ethnic Chinese from the Chinese heartland move to Tibet. These numbers were great enough that ethnic Tibetans were swamped with ethnic Chinese, thereby reducing the likelihood of a successful independence movement. Comparable forced migrations of ethnic Chinese to the provinces of Xinjiang[4] and Inner Mongolia also took place.

[4]**Xinjiang:** SHIHN jee ahng

Similarly, the Soviet Union saw potential for independence movements in the eastern Prussia region (formerly part of Germany) and in the Baltic states of Lithuania, Latvia, and Estonia. To reduce the likelihood of independence movements, the Soviets forcibly moved several million ethnic Russians there and expelled many ethnic Germans, effectively diluting local political sentiments. Similar forced population movements were conducted by the Soviets in Central Asia and the Ukraine.

Such movements are relatively rare in history, largely because few governments have such complete political control that the populace will tolerate massive dislocations. These involuntary migrations are usually a sign that a powerful, totalitarian state is engendering considerable loyalty among the citizens of its core territories.

POPULATION GROWTH IN THE POSTWAR WORLD

Throughout the period of human existence, long-term population growth has been the rule, not the exception. In the latter half of the twentieth century, however, a new phenomenon has emerged. For the first time, large segments of the human population have reduced population growth drastically, sometimes creating stable or even decreasing population levels. At the same time, other population segments have grown at rates unprecedented in history.

The Demography of Population Growth

Whether or not a population grows is based on a simple equation: If the number of people surviving to maturity is the same as in the previous generation, the population is stable. Higher survivorship means population growth, and lower survivorship means population decline. Throughout most of history there has been a slow but steady increase in population, as each generation slightly outstripped its predecessor. The reason that population increase was not faster lay primarily in death, not birth.

In most of history, women typically have borne children more or less constantly throughout their childbearing years, many women bearing a dozen or more children. Incentives for parenting large numbers of children included having plenty

UNDER THE LENS

China's One-Child-per-Family Policy

Under the leadership of Mao Zedong, China had been tolerant of its rapid population growth. The rejection of traditional values during the Cultural Revolution, especially from 1966 to 1969, led to a new promiscuity, however, and China's rulers became concerned. It is unclear whether birth rates actually rose significantly as a result of this relaxation of traditional sexual restraints, but it drew attention to what Chinese leaders increasingly were seeing as a dangerous demographic problem.

By 1980, Deng Xiaoping, China's new leader, was convinced that a sharply increasing population would be disastrous for China. He believed that there would be insufficient jobs to employ everyone and that government funds needed for the economic transformation of China would have to be diverted to support the additional population. Accordingly, he decreed China's one-child-per-family policy.

This policy mandated that, except for thinly populated areas on the periphery of the country, every family should be restricted to one child. To encourage conformity to this mandate, the government conducted advertising campaigns to popularize the idea and provided birth control devices and abortions to put it into practice.

Enforcement of the policy was largely by persuasion. Block committees (civilian neighborhood leadership groups) were the source of the persuasion; they monitored mothers' menstrual cycles and encouraged their families to pressure them to have abortions if they became pregnant with a second child. The effect of this persuasion is difficult for most people outside Chinese society to appreciate, but the extreme value placed on conforming to the community's expectations made this a potent convincing force for Chinese women. Little formal punishment was prescribed, but children after the first were denied medical, educational, and other benefits normally provided by the state.

One stumbling block to the policy was the long-standing cultural value on male children. Parents whose first child had been a girl often were reluctant to accept that they would have no male descendant. Though illegal, female infanticide became more common, paving the way for a possible son. In attempts to overcome this bias toward male children, billboards and other advertising pictured happy parents with their single girl child.

The one-child-per-family policy has been quite successful at slowing population increase. By the 1980s and 1990s, however, problems related to its success were beginning to be evident. Services attuned to children, such as schools, were being underutilized, and it was recognized that caring for aged parents—traditionally shared by several children—would have to be assumed by a single offspring, providing that person survived long enough to do so. While the Chinese government has recognized the gravity of these problems, it has continued to implement the one-child-per-family policy and has done little to alleviate the problems it has spawned.

of offspring to assist with agricultural duties and having children to care for the parents in old age. In many societies, kinship has been reckoned through the male line, so male children took on great importance; having sufficient numbers of boys to ensure that one of them would live to maturity to carry on the family name and inherit property was incentive to enlarge families. Less frequently discussed by scholars but equally important was the general lack of reliable and safe means of birth control until recent years. The upshot is that most families had lots of children.

Having many children, however, did not guarantee that they all would survive to maturity. In fact, having a large family often strained the family finances to the point that food became scarce from time to time, the undernourished children became more susceptible to disease, and several children might die at once during an epidemic. Historical demographic studies around the world have shown that the average number of children surviving to adulthood rarely exceeded three per family. When taking other factors into consideration, such as premature deaths of mothers during childbirth

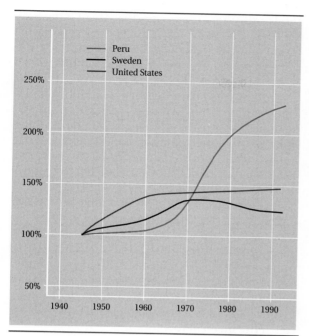

FIGURE 42.4 *Population Growth Curves. There are three basic patterns of human population growth in modern times. The most common pattern is that of Third World countries, where population growth tends to be continuous, as exemplified by the curve for Peru. A second common pattern, represented by population growth in the United States, is typical of most industrialized countries and shows a plateau as the population becomes more or less stabilized. A rare pattern, shown in the curve for Sweden, characterizes a few industrialized countries where population has actually decreased in recent years.*

and members of the society who never had children, the number of children per couple surviving to maturity averages 2.2, resulting in a modest rate of about 10 percent growth per generation.

Postwar Population Stability in the Industrialized World

World War II had brought many changes on the social front in the industrialized countries (the First and Second worlds), and these had profound impacts on practices affecting demography. The waging of World War II had revolved around industrial output, and the country with the greatest number of sophisticated tanks or airplanes and the fuel to power them was most likely to be suc-

cessful. Because armies were predominantly composed of men, women were left to staff the effort on "the home front," and many factories were operated predominantly by women.

After the war, many of these women returned to domestic life, but some stayed on in the workforce. With the economic boom of the 1960s came expectations of luxuries that previously had been out of reach. In order to ensure the availability of a new car, a nice house, a swimming pool, or a vacation in Venice, many women entered the workforce, and families with both husband and wife working became increasingly common.

The demographic consequence of this was that it became inconvenient for a family to have children, because this might require that the wife leave her job, reducing the family income and placing those luxuries out of reach. At the same time, the cost of raising a child was increasing, especially because it was becoming more of an expectation that a child would attend college. In addition, the number of families engaged in agriculture had been steadily declining through the century, and the emphasis on industry during and following the war further decreased the number of farming families. While numerous children were an economic advantage on a farm, economically they were a liability to industrial and service workers.

The "baby boom" that lasted from the late 1940s to the late 1950s in many parts of the industrialized world tapered off, and birth rates fell off drastically. Until the postwar era, birth rates had remained more or less constant in the industrialized countries, and population growth had been high. In the postwar era, however, birth control had major impacts on birth rates for the first time. Various devices and techniques had been available for decades, but the development and popularization in the early 1960s of oral contraceptives, popularly known as "the pill," made birth control simple, unobtrusive, and inexpensive. Some religious leaders praised this new technology on moral grounds, believing it would diminish the population growth that they saw as threatening global welfare.

There were, however, dissenting voices criticizing birth control. The Roman Catholic Church, in particular, condemned all birth control technology as morally wrong and forbade its use by its adherents. Evangelical Christians and some Muslim fundamentalists joined their condemnation, as did some secular leaders, such as Mao Zedong. Surveys throughout the period in most industrial countries, however, showed that huge numbers of women (including Catholics and Muslims) used oral contraceptives. Various groups advocating the limitation of family size, such as Planned Parenthood and Zero Population Growth, became prominent and influential during this period.

With the reduced economic incentive for large families and the technology to keep birth rates low easily and inexpensively available, population in industrialized countries in the years following 1960 grew at much slower rates than before. Most industrialized countries reached a more or less stable population level by 1980, and some northern European countries actually were slightly decreasing in population. Previous economies, with their emphasis on small-scale agricultural production, would have been devastated by this demographic situation, but the industrial economies of the late twentieth century were able to thrive in this environment. The gradual shift during the last decades of the twentieth century to more information-based occupations was even more tolerant of a low rate of population growth, because even fewer numbers of workers were needed.

Population Growth in the Third World

While industrialized nations in the postwar era were trimming population growth, quite the opposite was occurring in the nonindustrialized countries of the Third World. There, population was growing faster than ever before, creating major economic, political, and social problems.

Countries of the Third World continued to be based primarily on small-scale agriculture. As a result, a family with many children continued to have advantage. Women seldom held jobs outside the domestic sphere, and there were few industrial jobs to entice them. Not only were there few incentives to limit the number of one's children, but birth control devices to do so were rare, unfamiliar, and often expensive. Under these circumstances, it is little wonder that birth rates remained high in most Third World countries.

Death rates for infants and children, however, began to drop rapidly in the postwar Third World. Improved communications technology, particularly television, had promoted wider knowledge of the Third World among the citizenry of industrialized countries, and that citizenry became more aware of the appalling health conditions in much of the rest of the world. With the economic prosperity that began in the late 1950s, industrialized countries set up an unprecedented number of programs to aid Third World people. Governments, churches, and private organizations began hundreds of programs to bring modern medicine and improved nutrition to remote corners of the world. The advances in medicine that had helped control disease among troops in World War II, as well as new advances churned out by public and private research organizations, were brought to cities and villages in Latin America, Africa, Asia, and the Pacific Islands. Probably the greatest impact came from preventative medicine, with immunization and education programs vastly decreasing childhood deaths from disease. The bringing of these medical treatments to the Third World is often called **the medical revolution**.

At the same time, scientific research was creating new strains of crops, new fertilizers, and new pesticides specially designed for Third World conditions. These technological advances, known collectively as **the green revolution**, sometimes doubled or even tripled the annual agricultural output of a community. The vastly increased food supplies made possible by the green revolution tremendously decreased hunger and the concomitant susceptibility to disease in the Third World.

The green and medical revolutions together substantially reduced infant and child death rates throughout the Third World. In countries like Guatemala and Nigeria, the likelihood that a child would survive to adulthood increased from around 30 percent to more than 80 percent. In effect, the next generation might be more than twice the size of the parents' generation, meaning at least a doubling of national populations every generation. Putting this in perspective, the rate of population increase became about twenty times that of the years preceding the green and medical revolutions. A plummeting death rate and an unchanged birth rate spelled rates of population increase unparalleled since the beginning of agriculture.

These rates of population growth produced both benefits and severe problems for the countries in which they occurred. On the positive side, families had to endure fewer deaths, and there

FIGURE 42.5 *Medical Care in the Third World.* *This American nurse of the organization Médecins Sans Frontières (Doctors Without Borders) provides medical assistance to Africans in Sierra Leone. Such volunteer programs from industrialized countries complement efforts by Third World countries to provide their citizens the benefits of medical advances.* Courtesy of Doctors Without Borders.

were plenty of children for agricultural tasks and carrying on the family name. The many problems, however, soon began to cause trouble.

As children grew to adulthood, they needed land to carry on their farming way of life. In earlier times, the numbers of surviving children eligible for inheritance was small, and a combination of clearing excess lands and dividing the ancestral lands could accommodate them. But with perhaps six or seven daughters (or sons, depending on the rules of inheritance) competing for the land, this strategy would leave inheritors with chunks too small for efficient farming. This meant the clearing of increasing amounts of land, often leading to deforestation, erosion, extinction of species, and general environmental degradation.

As agriculture became less attractive, more and more rural villagers found themselves drawn to the cities. Jobs often were perceived as abundant there, though the reality was quite different. The departing colonial powers that had ruled most Third World countries took much of the capital necessary for industrial development with them. Consequently, few Third World countries had significant increases in urban jobs, yet the population in the cities was growing faster than anywhere else. Shanty towns, wretched and unhealthful squatter districts inhabited by demoralized citizens with few options, grew up around many cities. Most who had gone to the city had given up any claim they might have held to agricultural lands and had no place to return to.

In the 1970s, there was great concern in the industrialized nations over unbridled population growth in the Third World. Books with provocative titles like *The Population Bomb* argued that this unchecked growth eventually would lead to various global problems, including inadequate food supplies, a degraded environment, and military conflict over land. One fear in some industrialized countries was that floods of immigrants would try to flee deteriorating conditions in their home countries, seeking a better life. Increasing numbers of applicants for immigration in many industrialized countries fueled this fear. Popular opinion in most industrialized countries was that people in the Third World should be educated to the problems of rapid population growth and assisted with the control of their birth rate.

In Third World countries, however, this sentiment usually was greeted with distrust. Many of these countries had only recently emerged from colonial control and believed that the population-control movement might be merely a trick on the part of the industrialized powers. If a country's strength is in its people, an attempt by outsiders to encourage a country to reduce its population growth could be seen as an attempt to keep the Third World weak, thereby avoiding possible threats to the dominance of the industrial powers.

In addition, religious objections to birth control continued, further reducing the effectiveness of the population-control movement. The opposition of the Catholic Church in predominantly Catholic Latin America and Islam in predominantly Muslim parts of Africa were especially significant. The Reagan and Bush administrations of the United States in the 1980s and early 1990s severely curtailed government foreign aid for birth control and forbade the use of aid for some measures to slow population growth, including voluntary abortion. These decisions had a major impact,

FIGURE 42.6 *Shanty Town in Jakarta, Indonesia.* *The growth of downtown Jakarta has engulfed many shanty towns around it. This 1979 photograph shows wealth and poverty juxtaposed within the urban landscape. In the shadow of a skyscraper, this single-family house will survive only a few more years before the family will be forced to relocate.*
Stuart Franklin/Magnum Photos.

PARALLELS AND DIVERGENCES

Foreign Migrant Workers

Migrant workers are laborers who travel from place to place to find work. Many leave their home country, either temporarily or permanently, because jobs are few. Migrant workers are most numerous when one country has surplus labor and limited jobs, while a neighboring country has a need for cheap labor. As a result, foreign migrant workers often are exploited, earning low wages for demanding or dangerous work. Still, they participate because they have few or no options to make equivalent wages in their own country.

A classic example of the long-term use of foreign migrant workers comes from the copper mines of South Africa. Until 1994, South Africa was ruled by a white minority that also controlled the economy of the country, including its mines. Work permits regularly were given to vast numbers of Zambians and other foreign nationals who were willing to work in the mines for lower pay than most South Africans would accept. The dust from copper mining is a low-grade poison, and miners suffered endemically from headaches and internal disorders; the risk of cave-ins and other disasters was moderately high, especially given that safety precautions historically were not strenuously enforced. The miners worked long hours with few holidays, and they were away from their homes and families for months or years at a time.

What made Zambians work in the copper mines? This employment was available to them, and it permitted them to earn more than any equivalent opportunity at home. Most of these miners were single young men in their late teens or twenties, and they intended to work only three or four years, enough to establish some savings so that they could start a business at home. Many were thwarted in this dream, however, because the costs of living in a copper camp could be high, and most workers sent a considerable portion of their paycheck to their families at home, leaving precious little for their savings. Sometimes ill health, brought on in part by the conditions in the mines, forced them to return to Zambia no richer than before.

The institution of the foreign migrant worker appears around the world when a relatively rich country is near a relatively poor one and there is access between them. Mexican farm workers in the United States, Algerian farm workers in France, Turkish laborers in Germany, and Ethiopian domestic servants in Kuwait—all are examples of the combined effects of overpopulation and unequal distribution of employment opportunity and wealth. And in all cases, there are dangers that migrant workers will be exploited by local employers who recognize their vulnerability and that they will be resented by local workers who see them as competitors. Cesar Chavez (1927–1994) organized the United Farm Workers Union in California in response to such problems in 1962 and after a multiyear strike was able to obtain better wages and working conditions for grape pickers. Similar unions have developed in many places around the world.

---

because the United States had been the primary world provider of such foreign aid. All in all, programs instituted by the industrialized countries had little effect in limiting population growth in the Third World through the 1970s and 1980s.

By the late 1980s, however, the negative effects of increased population were more evident in many Third World countries, inclining their leadership to become less hostile to attempts at population control. In 1994, at the historic Cairo Conference on Global Population, many Third World countries reversed their previous opposition and agreed that steps would have to be taken to reduce their birth rates in order to avert disaster.

FAMINE, CIVIL WAR, DEATH, AND DIVISION IN AFRICA

Along with rapid population growth in the continent as a whole, parts of Africa since World War II have experienced a series of demographic dislocations. These have included large numbers of deaths and vast movements of people, brought about largely by the combined factors of drought and ethnic factionalism.

The **Sahel**[5] is the semiarid region immediately to the south of the Sahara, cutting through Soma-

[5] **Sahel:** sah HEHL

FIGURE 42.7 *Famine in the Wake of Drought.* *The Sahelian drought and political upheavals that accompanied it led to mass starvation. This 1992 photograph from Somalia shows an emaciated corpse on a wheelbarrow, awaiting preparations for burial.*
James Nachtwey/Magnum Photos.

lia, Ethiopia, the Sudan, Chad, Niger, Nigeria, Mali, Burkina Faso, and Senegal. It is there that the great African drought occurred. The Sahel is naturally quite dry, so it is marginal for agriculture and much of it is used for cattle pastoralism. Increasing populations in the Sahel have led to more intensive land use, which in turn has led to the killing off of natural vegetation, more rapid runoff of rainfall, and increased erosion.

A natural downturn in rainfall between 1968 and 1974 created a major drought, intensified by the environmental degradation induced by human overuse of the land. A second period of drought from 1983 to 1985 produced even more disastrous results. Since the beginning of these droughts, the desert has eaten up the Sahel at a rate ranging from 5 to 30 miles per year, making parts of these formerly productive lands essentially worthless for human uses. During the drought, agricultural and pastoral production throughout the Sahel was considerably diminished, and local food production was devastated. While this drought would have caused hardship under any circumstances, the political situation exacerbated the suffering and led to tremendous loss of life.

The drought and consequent food shortages caused unrest throughout the Sahel, and some political players were quick to take advantage of it. Aspirants to power sometimes fanned the fires of discontent, hoping to undermine the power of the ruling faction; leaders of the ruling faction sometimes diverted aid to members of their own tribe at the expense of other tribes. And various opportunists hijacked international aid shipments of food for sale and personal gain.

This situation led to widespread starvation in some regions, and when disease struck it had more devastating effects because of the undernourished

THIRD WORLD COUNTRIES

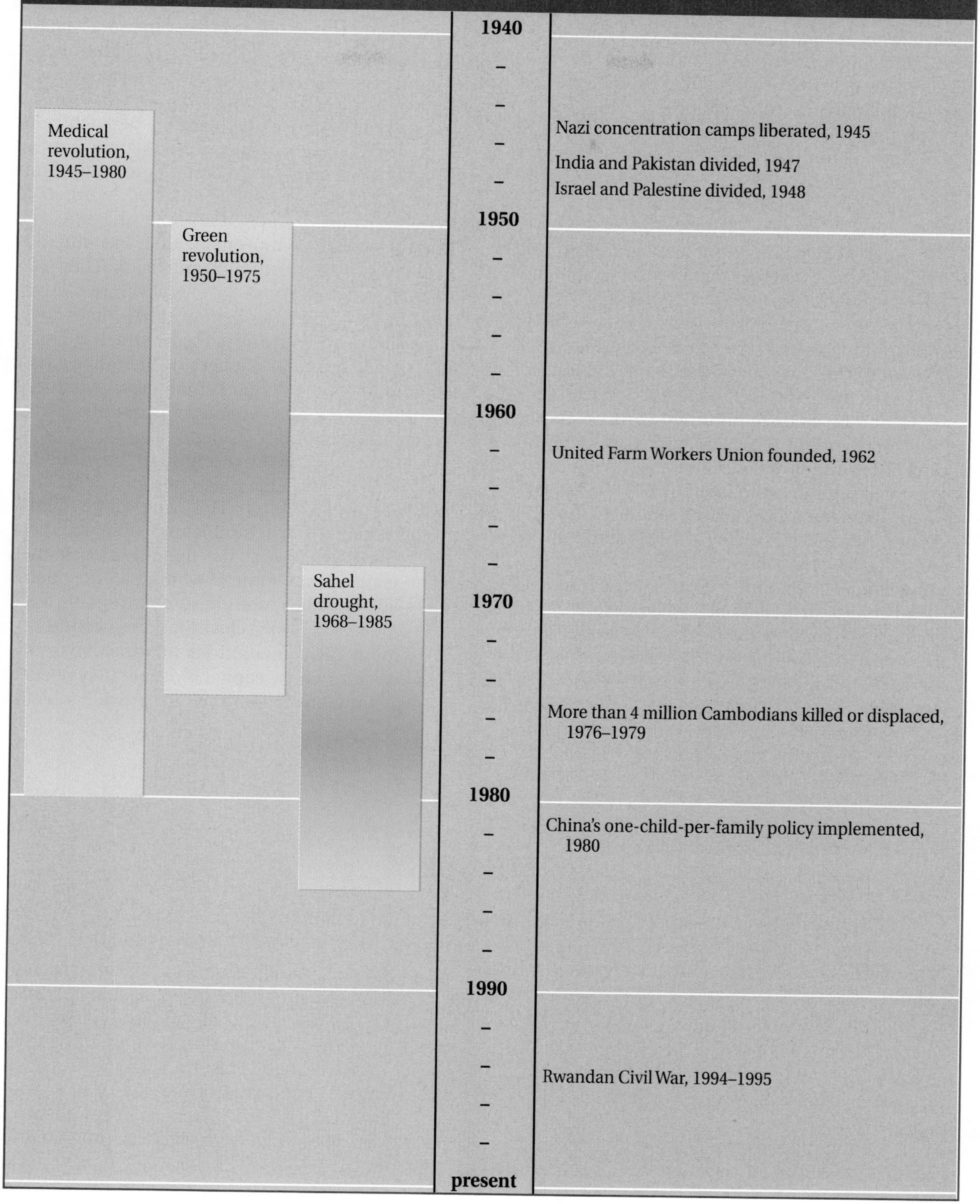

Medical revolution, 1945–1980

Green revolution, 1950–1975

Sahel drought, 1968–1985

1940	
–	
–	
–	Nazi concentration camps liberated, 1945
–	India and Pakistan divided, 1947
	Israel and Palestine divided, 1948
1950	
–	
–	
–	
–	
1960	
–	United Farm Workers Union founded, 1962
–	
–	
–	
1970	
–	
–	
–	More than 4 million Cambodians killed or displaced, 1976–1979
–	
1980	
–	China's one-child-per-family policy implemented, 1980
–	
–	
–	
1990	
–	
–	Rwandan Civil War, 1994–1995
–	
–	
present	

condition of its victims. The total number of deaths resulting from food shortages is unknown but clearly reaches more than a million. Further, civil wars in Somalia, Ethiopia, the Sudan, and Chad claimed hundreds of thousands more lives. These wars encouraged refugees to seek shelter with their fellow tribe members, who could be expected to be political allies. This often meant the crossing of borders, and there was considerable international flux of populations in the Sahel, often lasting well beyond the period of the drought.

Intertribal conflicts and demographic dislocations have not been restricted to the Sahel, however. In 1994, Rwanda, in Central Africa, was plunged into a violent civil war that was fought along ethnic lines. In the weeks that followed, at least 100,000 civilians were killed in a rampage of atrocities from both sides. Violence, disease in the wake of thousands of unburied corpses, and general deterioration of living conditions forced Rwandans of both factions to flee the country. In the most rapid refugee flight of its scale in history, more than three-quarters of a million Rwandans massed on and crossed over the borders with Tanzania and Congo-Zaire within days of the onset of violence. In a country of over 4 million people, nearly one-fourth had been killed or forced to flee in the first two weeks of the civil war, and the numbers rose in subsequent weeks and months.

Conditions in Rwandan refugee camps in Congo-Zaire were very difficult. Food and medical supplies were in short supply, doctors and nurses were few and overworked, sanitary conditions were compromised by the masses of people in restricted areas, and factional fighting was common. Although reliable estimates are not available as of early 1997, it is clear that large numbers of Rwandans died from disease and violence in these camps. In late 1996, political developments in Congo-Zaire led to the opening of a corridor through which Rwandan refugees could pass to Rwanda in safety. Over the course of only three days, nearly half a million refugees returned to Rwanda from Congo-Zaire in a massive but orderly population movement that was attended by remarkably little suffering and death. There was another wave of returning refugees from Congo-Zaire in early 1997, as Zairian rebel forces (who shared ethnicity with one of the Rwandan factions) threatened Rwandan refugees of the other ethnic faction. (In May 1997, the Zairian rebels overthrew the government and renamed the country as the Democratic Republic of Congo.)

The forces of factionalism, sometimes abetted by natural disasters, have kept portions of Africa in civil war and turmoil. The long-range demographic effects of such troubles are difficult to foresee, but it is clear that the fighting has claimed millions of victims, some of whom had the talents and skills to help guide these countries through their troubles. It also is clear that these conditions make many African countries unattractive to foreign investors whose capital is desperately needed to help stimulate economies and provide jobs for citizens.

SUMMARY

1. Demography is the study of population in all its aspects. The pace and scale of demographic change have increased dramatically since World War II.

2. Major population movements took place in Europe immediately following the end of World War II. Captives from Nazi Germany were released, Germans in eastern Europe were expelled, Slavs in eastern Europe moved into regions from which Germans had been expelled, and citizens of the Baltic states moved to Sweden and Poland. In total, about 28 million people moved from one country to another immediately following the war.

3. Voluntary migration, especially along religious lines, was important in establishing political control in states created after World War II. This was true in the case of India and Pakistan and in the case of Israel and Palestine. Many of these voluntary movements were of refugees fleeing violence. In the 1970s and later, large numbers of people seeking refuge from civil wars migrated to new countries.

4. Government-mandated population movements in China and the Soviet Union settled members of the majority ethnic group in outlying regions of their countries in order to forestall independence movements by ethnic minorities.

5. In postwar industrialized countries, birth control measures have reduced the birth rate to keep it in line with increased survivorship, the result of improved medicine and food supplies. These countries have had essentially steady population levels without growth.

6. In Third World countries, the medical and green revolutions have decreased child mortality, leading to rapid rates of population increase. The resulting overpopulation has led to environmental degradation and to various social and economic problems. Initially distrustful of efforts by industrialized countries to assist in limiting their birth rates, Third World countries in the 1990s recognized the problem and became more receptive to possible solutions.

7. Ethnic strife in Africa has resulted in widespread conflict, sometimes spurred by natural disasters. These conflicts often have resulted in great loss of life and major refugee flight.

SUGGESTED READINGS

Cornell University Workshop on Food, Population, and Employment. *Food, Population, and Employment: The Impact of the Green Revolution.* New York: Praeger, 1971. A detailed treatment focusing on the sociopolitical effects of the green revolution. Though fairly old, its information and conclusions remain current.

Fraser, T. G. *Partition in Ireland, India, and Palestine: Theory and Practice.* New York: St. Martin's Press, 1984. A treatment of these countries' national partition processes, applying a general model.

Koehn, Peter H. *Refugees from Revolution: U.S. Policy and Third-World Migration.* Boulder, Colo.: Westview Press, 1991. General treatment with an interpretation critical of U.S. policy in the 1980s.

Piore, Michael J. *Birds of Passage: Migrant Labor and Industrial Societies.* Cambridge, Eng.: Cambridge University Press, 1979. An elegant treatment of the general issues, drawing primarily on U.S. examples.

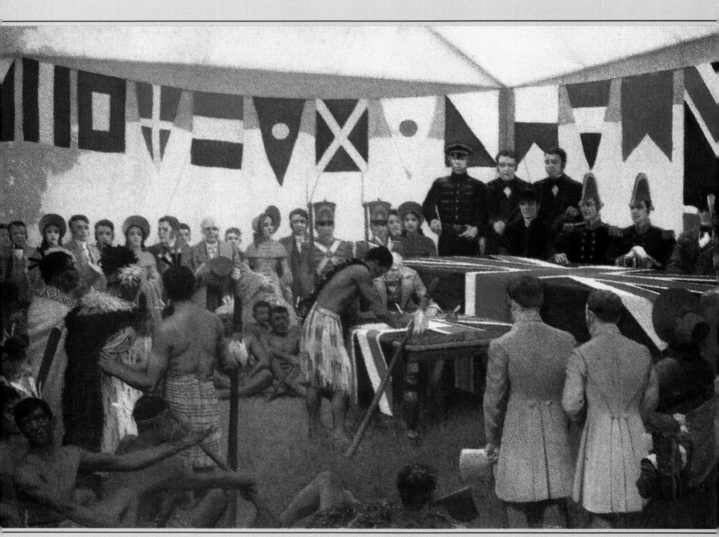

Signing of the Treaty of Waitangi. *Although the Maori were conquered by the British Empire, they maintained a significant presence and demanded the protection of their rights as the native peoples of New Zealand. Such protection was promised by the Treaty of Waitangi, signed in 1840 by Chief Tamati Waka Nene and Governor William Hobson; the treaty, however, was ultimately a failure.* Eileen Tweedy/ET Archive.

Ethnicity and Politics

When the legislative body that governs Papua New Guinea opened its 1996 session, it was composed of members representing more than a dozen parties, each with a core constituency defined by ethnicity. The ruling group consisted of a coalition of several of these parties that shared certain interests. No single ethnic group was able to dominate either society or government, a condition increasingly common in the modern world.

Ethnicity has been a factor in most politics throughout history. In the past century or so, however, the complexion of global politics has changed, placing ethnicity in a central position as never before.

THE MONOETHNIC STATE

The early civilizations, with the possible exception of that of ancient Egypt, were populated largely by citizens who viewed themselves as quite similar to one another. They spoke the same language, worshiped the same gods, followed the same customs, and—most important—considered themselves members of the same named group. Such a self-identified group that shares culture is called an **ethnic group**, and in some places ethnic groups are conventionally called "tribes." A state whose citizens are mostly from the same ethnic group or tribe is called a **monoethnic state**.

It was understandable that most early civilizations would be monoethnic states, because they

1061

were relatively small and isolated, developing in a more or less homogeneous region. As military technology and political organization evolved, however, states expanded their borders, overflowing into regions occupied by other ethnic groups. Sometimes these groups were absorbed into the dominant ethnic group, as when local tribes became part of the Inca following their conquest in fifteenth-century Peru. Other times, these groups retained their ethnicity but were denied full participation in society, as when the Normans who invaded England in 1066 denied Anglo-Saxons access to offices and various business enterprises, or when Anglo-Australians denied Aborigines the rights to vote or hold property. (Eventually the Normans and Anglo-Saxons in England merged to form a single composite English ethnicity; Aborigines have received the rights to vote and hold property but remain far less politically powerful than other Australians.) Minority ethnic groups can exist in a monoethnic state, but they must remain subordinate to the dominant ethnic group.

Nationalism, treated in detail in Chapter 33, fostered monoethnic states in Europe and lands under European control in the eighteenth and nineteenth centuries. The emphasis on a common past and culture, a great common purpose, and a national identity encouraged this development, but there was a serious problem. Many of these countries included substantial numbers of other ethnic groups. Efforts were made to bond some of them to the dominant ethnicity, as when Nazi German scholars went to great lengths to show the similarities in skull shapes between Germans and Czechs of the Sudetenland, arguing that these similarities indicated a previously unrecognized ethnic kinship. In other cases, ethnic groups were denied the vote, the right to own property, and other privileges accorded "regular" citizens; in this manner, South Africa's official *apartheid* policy of the 1960s through the 1980s set blacks apart from white citizens by law.

THE MULTIETHNIC STATE

The **multiethnic state** incorporates two or more ethnic groups into its citizenry and extends full privileges to them. Multiethnic states have developed in three main ways: as a result of the breakdown of empires, as the result of immigration from disparate places, and as a development out of colonial holdings.

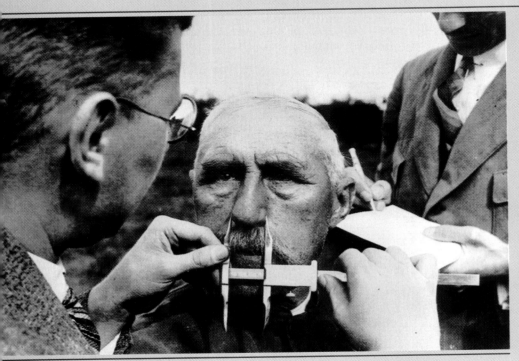

FIGURE I.9.1 *Nazi Skull Measurement. Anthropologists had measured skulls for decades, but under Nazi Germany the measurements took on a new purpose: the classification of individuals into ethnic groups to determine their fates. This photograph from 1936 shows two scientists from the League for Propagation of Racial Knowledge measuring a man to determine his "true" ethnicity. In later years, such measurements could lead to classification as a member of an "undesirable" group (Jew, Gypsy, or Slav) and to imprisonment or execution.* Ullstein Bilderdienst.

The Imperial Legacy

An empire, by definition, is a state that expands its political control over other peoples. Not every empire, however, is a multiethnic state, because some empires withhold political, economic, and social privileges from conquered peoples, reserving them only for the dominant ethnic group. The Roman Empire before the third century A.D., for example, had levels of citizenship for males and accorded some citizens rights withheld from others; only citizens of the highest level were granted the right to vote, various economic privileges, and the right to run for office. Consequently, the Roman Empire—despite its ethnic diversity—was not a multiethnic state.

Other empires, however, have been clearly multiethnic in their organization. The Aztec Empire of Mexico, for example, incorporated various ethnic groups into itself with full privileges. Some of these were allies and others were conquered peoples, but either way they maintained their distinctive ways of life and identification as Mixtec,[1] Tototepec,[2] or Mexica. This identification, of course, meant that loyalties sometimes were split, as when Tototepec rebelled against Aztec imperial rule, leaving its citizens to decide whether their personal loyalties lay more with Tototepec or with the Aztec Empire.

Lands of Opportunity

A second mechanism of multiethnic state formation is through large-scale immigration from diverse sources. This process began essentially with the European voyages of discovery of the fifteenth century and the subsequent colonial occupation of captured lands.

The European explorers of this era recognized little or no prior claim to land on the part of the American, African, Australian, or Pacific island peoples living on it. Indeed, a primary purpose of these explorations was to claim new lands for whatever European power was sponsoring the voyage. As a result, Europeans often viewed these new lands as "open," without inhabitants and, therefore, ready for immigration. In a more real sense, the demographic disasters that befell the native inhabitants shortly after the European

arrival resulted in so much death that some places became truly open.

Some of these new lands were largely closed to immigration from individuals who were not citizens of the colonial power controlling them. In some cases, laws permitted immigration only by citizens of the home country. In other cases, opportunities were seen as sufficiently meager that immigrants from elsewhere were unlikely to choose to go there.

Other lands, however, were perceived as rich and attractive and drew immigration from many sources. Foremost among these was the United States, but Canada, Australia, Argentina, Brazil, and South Africa also drew heavy multiethnic immigration from Europe. Wave after wave of immigrants flocked to these countries, creating multiethnic populations of great diversity. Some ethnic groups, particularly non-Europeans, suffered official discrimination and were not accorded full privileges in the early years of these countries, but all now have official policies granting all citizens equal rights. With the granting of equal rights (in theory, at least), these countries became multiethnic states.

The Legacy of Colonialism and Imperialism

The final major route to a multiethnic state was along the rocky paths of colonialism and imperialism. Those lands unlucky enough to be conquered and controlled as colonies usually became multiethnic through one of two processes.

In the Americas, many colonies became multiethnic states by virtue of the distinction between Europeans and Native Americans. The names differ from country to country, but the general pattern remains the same: Those of pure or nearly pure European extraction are of one ethnic group, those of nearly pure American Indian extraction are considered another group, and those of mixed parentage are a third group. These three ethnic groups constitute the multiethnic aspect of American multiethnic states derived from colonies.

Why are there not several ethnicities for American Indians? Certainly there were many tribes at the time of European contact, and each viewed itself as a separate ethnic group. The demographic disasters of contact with Europe, however, reduced the numbers and power of American Indian

[1] **Mixtec:** MIHSH tehk
[2] **Tototepec:** toh toh TEH pehk

groups incredibly. As a result, American Indians in the twentieth century largely have banded together for mutual support. This merging of various tribes into a single interest group is known as **pan-tribalism**. While the economic, social, and political conditions of many American Indians are not good, pan-tribal political efforts have produced considerable gains in the past few decades, especially in North America and eastern South America. Successes have included return of lands, monetary settlements, and return of sacred items from museums. Another result of pan-tribalism has been the limitation of conflict among Native American ethnic groups over political power.

In Africa and Asia, the process of forming multiethnic states has followed a different course. In these continents, the division of the land into colonies was based on principles that made sense to the European conquerors, not to the local peoples. One tribe might be divided by a colonial boundary, and any colony was likely to have many tribes within it. When these colonial boundaries became national boundaries following independence, this meant that each country was a fragile coalition of tribes (many historically hostile to one another) and that tribal units sometimes were divided between countries. Because tribes largely equated with political parties, the political mix of any country was likely to be volatile.

Take Nigeria as an example. The boundaries of the British colony were established by the maneuverings of the British, French, and Germans, all of whom had colonies in West Africa in the latter half of the nineteenth century. Areas were thrown together into a single colony because the British could claim and hold them. This meant that tribal areas of the Hausa, Fulani, Yoruba, Kanuri, and Ibo were united into a single colony. Many of these groups were mutually antagonistic; portions of the tribal lands of most of them extended into adja-

FIGURE I.9.2 *Meeting of the Amazonian Peoples. This pan-tribal meeting held in Pará, Brazil, in 1995 was designed to build the solidarity of members of various Amazon Basin tribes, many of whom previously had been hostile to one another. Such meetings stress the common problems currently faced by all tribes, particularly the struggle to hold on to their territories in the face of encroachment by logging and mining interests.* Ricardo Azoury/Pulsar.

FIGURE I.9.3 *Zulu Rally in South Africa.* *These members of the Inkatha Freedom Party, an ethnic-based political party dominated by the Zulus, carry spears and shields. The function of these "cultural weapons," however, is primarily symbolic of the Zulu identity.* Oosterbroek Ken / Gamma/Liaison International.

cent colonies that were held by the French or Germans. The only glue holding the colony together was the colonial power.

Political movements between the end of World War II and the early 1970s left nearly all of Africa and Asia independent. What formerly had been colonies now were countries. Because the glue that once had held a colony together was missing, it was left to these new countries to try to form cohesive multiethnic states from the materials bequeathed them by colonialism and imperialism.

THE REASSERTION OF ETHNICITY IN INTERNATIONAL POLITICS

The years since World War II have seen ethnicity move to the fore as a factor in politics. Ethnically based political parties are active in every country that holds free elections. Civil wars are fought between rival ethnic groups, and multiethnic states are partitioned to produce monoethnic states. Some of the most dramatic of these developments have taken place as a result of the independence of former colonies and the breakup of the former Soviet Union.

Ethnic Politics in Former Colonies

In most of Africa and parts of Asia, political parties are highly identified with particular ethnic groups. In South Africa, for example, the first all-race election held in 1994 featured the African National Congress and the Inkatha[3] Freedom Party as major participants. Each party, however, drew its primary support from a single tribe or group of tribes; the Inkatha Freedom Party was supported by Zulus, and the African National Congress by a coalition of other tribes. The Moslem League and Indian National Congress, discussed in Chapter 42, were ethnically based parties instrumental in securing independence for Pakistan and India. Modern political parties in both countries draw much of their support from constituencies based on ethnicity and caste status.

These parties sometimes have formed the nuclei for hostile forces in civil wars. The 1994 civil war in Rwanda, for example, was a more violent and well-publicized version of conflict that had been ongoing in that country since 1962. The ruling party in 1994 was dominated by the Hutu tribe, but the leadership was inclining toward greater inclusion of the minority Tutsi tribe in its power structure. Upon the death of the Rwandan presi-

[3] **Inkatha:** ihn KAH tuh

dent, rumored to have been engineered by members of his own party antagonistic to his inclusion of Tutsi in the government, government (Hutu) and rebel (Tutsi) forces opened hostilities. The fighting in the weeks that followed was savage and marked by abundant atrocities committed by both sides. Refugee camps were shelled, pedestrians were hacked to pieces with machetes, and victims were dragged from their homes and shot in the street. What appeared on the surface to be random violence, however, actually was shaped mostly by longstanding tribal animosities.

The Rwandan example is by no means unique. The Congo (later known as Zaire) was wracked by a devastating civil war between 1962 and 1965. The Ibo tribe fought with government forces between 1967 and 1970 in an unsuccessful attempt to secede from Nigeria and establish Biafra as an independent state; in 1966 alone, seven military takeovers transferred power from one ethnically based party to another in Africa. The secession of Bangladesh from Pakistan (through a guerrilla war), the ongoing independence movement of Kashmir in India, and the ongoing insurgency in the Kachin region of northern Burma (Myanmar) attest that ethnically based political movements have been important in Asia as well.

The nature of the colonial experience in Latin America, as discussed earlier, has led to fewer ethnically based political movements of the sort common in Africa and Asia. In 1994 and 1995, however, a pan-tribal organization of Mayan Indians in the Chiapas region of Mexico took over several government buildings and carried on military operations for weeks before they settled into diplomatic negotiations with the federal authorities. This movement, however, was not aimed at autonomy or at the seizing of political control; instead, it was a highly visible means of publicizing government mistreatment of the Indians and forcing the Mexican government into political concessions.

The Ethnic Basis of the Breakup of the Soviet Union and Yugoslavia

In the late 1980s, regional sentiments in the republics comprising the Soviet Union were surfacing, and the Baltic republics of Lithuania, Latvia, and Estonia had declared their independence. In 1991, bowing to overwhelming sentiment, the government under Mikhail Gorbachev declared that the republics were free to decide whether they wished to continue in union with one another. Within a few months, the Soviet Union had been disassembled and transformed into over a dozen independent states. Many of those were monoethnic states with small minority populations, while others had sizeable minority ethnic populations and were taking steps in the 1990s to suppress or control those minorities in order to establish monoethnic states.

FIGURE I.9.4 *Soviet Army Seizes Lithuanian Television Station.* *In 1991, when Lithuania declared its independence from the Soviet Union, Soviet troops responded with massive force and on January 12–13 opened fire on unarmed protesters outside the national radio-television station in Vilnius; the army captured the building, killing thirteen persons and seriously wounding 100. The Lithuanian independence movement, however, persisted and eventually achieved its goal.* Pascal Le Segretain/Sygma.

Throughout the former Soviet bloc, countries formerly welded together from smaller units have elected to split apart. Czechoslovakia voted to divide itself into the Czech Republic and Slovakia; the northern provinces of the Georgian Republic have continued military attempts to secede, as has Chechniya; and Armenia and Azerbaijan have continued to dispute their common boundary on the basis of ethnic distributions. These and many other splits and conflicts are rooted in ethnic issues long submerged under Soviet control.

Like the Soviet Union, Yugoslavia was a union of distinct ethnic groups held together by an authoritarian central government. In 1991, however, Yugoslavia dissolved as all its component states but Serbia and Montenegro seceded. Several years of bitter war ensued, particularly among Christian Serbs, Muslim Bosnians, and Christian Croats. Savage at times, the war has been marked by massacres of civilians and prisoners, the persistent blocking of food convoys destined for starving civilians, and widespread devastation. The United Nations and other international organizations made repeated diplomatic attempts to end the fighting and even resorted to military action to enforce cease-fires. By 1997, these efforts had achieved a tenuous peace and a fragile alliance between Croats and Bosnians, but it is unclear whether the region's peace will last.

ETHNICITY AND POLITICS IN THE TWENTY-FIRST CENTURY

It is ironic that, as twentieth-century transportation and communications are linking the world together in a way never before possible, the world is becoming politically more fragmented. The lesson to be learned is that mere contact is not enough to unite peoples politically. The might of major European powers was all that kept antagonistic ethnic groups together under colonial rule, just as Soviet power held together many multiethnic polities that now threaten to split apart. Now that these powers are diminished, how will people choose to organize themselves?

Max Weber, the early-twentieth-century sociologist, asserted that there were two conditions under which a group of people might voluntarily band together. First, they might see the mutual benefit in resisting some outside force; he called this the **associative bond**. Second, they might simply wish to be with others who shared beliefs, values, and customs; this was the **communal bond**. The associative bond favors multiethnic states, coalitions of equals founded on common need; the communal bond favors monoethnic states, states in which similarity is enforced by the absence or subordination of ethnic minorities. The absence of minorities can be brought about by careful placement of borders to encompass ethnic regions; alas, "ethnic cleansing" and other programs of extermination or relocation also have been used.

In the twenty-first century, countries will be straining between the conflicting benefits of these two kinds of bonds. On the one hand, larger, multiethnic states have greater resources and ability to cope with problems, including external aggression; they sacrifice the comfort of shared culture, however, forcing their citizens to adjust to one another's idiosyncrasies. On the other hand, smaller monoethnic states provide a strong body of shared beliefs and identity at the expense of the practical advantages of the larger, more diverse polity. At the end of the twentieth century, many people have opted for emphasizing the communal bond and the monoethnic state. The future may see a continuation of this decision or a return to the associative, multiethnic state.

SUGGESTED READINGS

Ingham, Kenneth. *Politics in Modern Africa: The Intertribal Dimension.* London: Routledge, 1990. A treatment of the tribal factor's significance in African politics, with abundant examples. Written before the demise of *apartheid* in South Africa and the massive (1994) intertribal conflict in Rwanda.

Kellas, James G. *The Politics of Nationalism and Ethnicity.* New York: St. Martin's Press, 1991. A general, theoretical treatment of the issue of ethnicity and politics, taken from the social science perspective.

Other information can be drawn from current newspapers and news magazines; it is almost certain that one or more similar conflicts will be active at any moment.

THIS VOLUME OF *THE GLOBAL PAST* HAS examined a great number of events, processes, ideas, and persons shaping world history in the past five centuries. When looking at these specifics, it may be difficult to see the long-term patterns of which they form a part. Part Ten points out some of these larger patterns, drawing attention to significant trends, cycles, and new directions.

Chapter 43 examines the arts and how they reflect their times. What do cartoons or murals say about changing political attitudes in the world? How did World War II affect French and Japanese films? How did blues singers fuse dissimilar artis-

tic traditions to create new art forms? Chapter 43 will explore these and other questions in its quest to show how art reveals insights into society.

Chapter 44 tackles the major theme of this text: how the world has become progressively more integrated over the past five centuries. It provides insights into the grand pattern of history for the modern era, helping us anticipate what the future may bring.

PART TEN

PERSPECTIVES

Technology in the Modern Era. *Fermenters like this one are used for the production of insulin, Interferon, and other medicinal drugs. Today's high-tech facilities mass-produce medicines through biochemical processes dependent on microorganisms existing in nature. One of the paradoxes of the modern era is that sophisticated procedures and technologies often rely on basic, natural processes.* Dan McCoy/Rainbow.

***Cartoon of* The Rite of Spring.** *When Igor Stravinsky's ballet* The Rite of Spring *opened in Paris in 1913, its radical innovations caused riots. This cartoon by Jean Cocteau, a writer, painter, and great supporter of experimental theater, shows a caricature of Stravinsky at the piano, flanked by puzzled-looking theatergoers.* V & A Picture Library.

Guerrilla Girls. *This New York–based coalition of artists uses art to express political protest; wearing gorilla masks, they hang posters to protest sexism and racism in the art world.* Deborah Outline.

The Arts as Mirrors of the Modern World

"Art mirrors life." The name of the author of this quotation has been lost over the years, but the truth of the sentiment persists. Artists are the products of the forces that shape society at large. If this were not true, each artist would follow her or his own idiosyncratic creative urges, and there would be no styles distinctive to an age or nation.

Instead, we see the intimate linking of artists to their worlds. Successful artists choose themes relevant to their times, and they often select modes of expression that reflect the social, economic, and political realities of their environment. Even those artists who try to insulate themselves from the influences of the outside world are still shaped by them, because their ideas and concepts are molded by their culture.

As a result, the arts reveal society. They expose its strengths, its weaknesses, its sources of pride, and its fears. In effect, they are a mirror in which society, with all its beauty and blemishes, is reflected. Sometimes looking at society through the arts can reveal deep-seated concerns that are less obvious when viewed by different means.

FOLK ARTS, FINE ARTS, AND POPULAR ARTS

For convenience, the arts often are divided into three categories. **Folk arts** are those that have long traditions and are learned in informal settings, as

1071

when a parent teaches a child a folk song. Folk arts usually are viewed as received knowledge by the people who practice them, and innovation often is discouraged. As a result, they often are very conservative, changing only slowly. Folk art typically is perpetuated by amateur artists. The painting of hex signs on barns by Pennsylvania Germans is an example of folk art.

Popular arts are the forms of art that receive wide distribution and are appreciated by large numbers of people. The popular arts have exploded in the twentieth century, thanks to technology that permits huge numbers of people to experience art electronically. Radios, televisions, videocassette recorders, audio systems, film projectors, high-quality photoreproduction equipment, and a wealth of other devices permit billions of people daily to appreciate arts that otherwise would be available only to a few people in live performances or in art galleries. Popular artists usually are professionals, and the genre is very subject to crazes, fads, and brief periods of popularity of an artist or work. Doo-wop music of the 1950s, a form of a cappella rock-and-roll singing with lush melodies and close harmonies, is an example of popular art.

Fine arts are the elite wing of the arts, appealing mostly to a small group of enthusiasts, many of whom have academic training in the arts. Praised as intellectual and sophisticated by their proponents, the fine arts sometimes are disparaged as snobbish and pretentious by their detractors. The fine arts usually are produced by highly trained artists who simultaneously are part of an academic establishment and are rebelling against it. Many fine arts of the nineteenth and twentieth centuries reflect the attempts of the artists to break with traditional forms and create new, distinctive, modern forms. Fine artists usually are professionals, though their limited audience means that they rarely attain the financial rewards or fame of the popular artists. A Beethoven symphony is an example of the fine arts.

These distinctions are for convenience only, and the categories overlap somewhat. Count (William) Basie, the famous jazz musician, also wrote classical music, bridging the gulf between the popular and fine arts. Grandma Moses (Anna Mary Robertson Moses), the rustic painter of rural New York, achieved great fame and popularity, yet her art was essentially folk in character. Despite the vagueness of the boundaries of these categories, the terms frequently are useful in discussing the arts.

In their different ways, folk arts, popular arts, and fine arts all reflect the concerns, attitudes, and values of the time and place in which they were created. This chapter examines four themes that recur again and again in the arts of the modern period: nationalism, innovation, alienation, and fusion.

NATIONALISM

The rise of the modern nation-state created a demand for expressions of nationalism, and art became a major vehicle for these expressions. The modern nation-state demanded not just loyalty from its citizens; it demanded that they have greater loyalty to the nation-state than to any other ideology, polity, or entity. If the nation-state were to overcome the competing demands of a citizen's region, religion, family, and ethnic group, it required strong symbols that would remind citizens of their obligations to the nation-state. Art has proven particularly good at providing those symbols, particularly through expression in the popular and fine arts.

We saw in Chapter 33 how the nineteenth-century Romantic movement in the European fine arts fostered nationalist feelings. Drawing on stories, music, and themes prominent in folklore, it fostered distinctive national styles of music, dance, visual arts, painting, drama, and literature. While styles changed and Romanticism went out of vogue, national styles of musical composition continued. One of the best examples comes from the United States, where Aaron Copland (1900–1994) produced a body of overtly nationalist music during the middle decades of the twentieth century. His "Billy the Kid" drew on the story of the famous outlaw, using themes and rhythms from cowboy music; "Appalachian Spring" evoked the passing of winter in the mountains of the eastern United States, using themes from folk tunes; and "Rodeo" produced a rollicking image of steer ridin' and bronco bustin'. Copland's style had little of the emotion and exoticism of Romantic music, but he retained the emphasis on national style that had arisen with Romanticism.

National Anthems

A **national anthem** is a song that is adopted by a nation as a symbol, used at official occasions and often protected against desecration by law. While some countries and rulers were associated with particular songs prior to this date, the year 1795 marks the adoption of the first official national anthem. At that date, revolutionary France adopted "La Marseillaise"[1] as its national anthem. Originally titled "War Song for the Army of the Rhine," this song got its name from a band of revolutionaries from Marseilles in 1792. From there, it became a rallying chant of the revolutionaries, and—with new and less violent words—it was officially adopted as the national anthem of France.

Most other Western countries adopted national anthems during the nineteenth century, a period of nationalistic fervor, and these anthems became sources of great pride. Fine arts composers extracted musical quotations from them to represent countries, as when Peter Ilyich Tchaikovsky[2] included snatches of "La Marseillaise" in his "1812 Overture," indicating the Napoleonic army entering battle against the Russians. *Casablanca*, an American film set in a nightclub during World War II, includes a moving scene in which French and Germans sing their national anthems at the same time, each trying to drown the other out in obvious symbolism of their national antagonism.

During the Bolshevik Revolution, the Soviet Union adopted "Internationale" as its national anthem. This song previously had been a rally anthem of communists throughout Europe, calling for an international communist revolution, and it was logical to adopt it, given the Soviet Union's communist ideology. In 1943, however, the Soviet Union was in the midst of international conflict and feared defection of some of its member states during World War II; an anthem that emphasizes an ideology shared internationally is not the best symbol for a nation struggling to survive. Accordingly, the Soviet Union dropped "Internationale," replacing it with a new anthem called "Unbreakable Union of Free-born Republics," which remained in place until 1989. After the breakup of the Soviet Union in 1989, however, the "unbreak-

FIGURE **43.1** *Anthem of Victory.* *Evelyn Ashford, an American gold medalist in track at the 1984 Olympics, is emotionally overwhelmed during the playing of "The Star Spangled Banner" at the medal ceremony. National anthems are powerful artistic symbols often used to evoke nationalism.* David Madison/Duomo.

ability" of the Soviet Union no longer was a credible theme, and individual states developed their own anthems, often resurrecting ones in use before 1917. Russians, however, were unable to agree on a replacement, as national competitions failed to provide an acceptable new anthem. Just before the 1996 Olympic Games, Russia hastily adopted a national anthem titled "Patriotic Song" so that gold medal winners would have an anthem to accompany their medal ceremony. As of early 1997, however, this anthem had no words, because there was

[1] **La Marseillaise:** lah MAHR say yehz
[2] **Tchaikovsky:** chy KOFF skee

no agreement on whether they should be militant or pacific, regionalist or international.

Japan also came to the end of the twentieth century with its national anthem in doubt. "Kimigayo,"[3] the Japanese national anthem, uses millennium-old words from an anonymous poem, coupled with a melody written in the 1870s. It was first performed for the Emperor Meiji's birthday in 1880, and it became the national anthem in 1893. "Kimigayo" was a potent rallying force during World War II, and it came to be associated with Japanese imperial expansion. During the 1980s and 1990s, Japanese political factions disputed the appropriateness of "Kimigayo" as a national anthem, ultranationalists favoring its retention and socialists wanting no anthem that reminded them of wartime imperialism.

Former colonies gaining their independence, especially since World War II, usually have adopted national anthems immediately. Most often these have been based on folk songs from the dominant ethnic group in the country. When the country has been based on a more or less equal coalition of ethnic groups, the song usually has been written on commission by a professional composer and has not used folk themes.

Revolutionary Posters

With the Bolshevik Revolution in Russia came a new form of art: the revolutionary poster. (See full-color illustration on p. A-32.) These posters were printed by revolutionary groups before and during the seizure of power, and the communist government printed them afterward. Between 1918 and 1921, more than 3,600 revolutionary posters were printed. They were posted at conspicuous places around cities and towns, inspiring support for the revolution, the revolutionary government, and its policies. In later years, the style of socialist realism created in the Bolshevik Revolution was adopted by communist revolutionary movements around the world.

This was not the first time that posted notices had been used in a revolution or other upheaval. Indeed, handbills with written messages had been posted during the French Revolution, the American Civil War, and at various occasions before then. The Russian posters, however, differed from their predecessors in the degree to which their art

commanded attention. More than a century had elapsed between the French and Bolshevik revolutions, and printing had improved considerably. Even though printing in Russia was a bit less sophisticated than elsewhere in Europe, it was capable of mass producing fairly complex, multi-colored posters. These posters featured art and bright hues and were far more arresting than the posters of previous eras. In addition, Russian revolutionaries pioneered the mass distribution of posters as a means of inspiring support.

The Russian poster drew on Russian folk art for some of its inspiration, but more direct input came from political cartoons that appeared in the satiric journals thriving between 1905 and 1907. These journals, mostly underground operations critical of the tsarist government, sprang up in large numbers following the 1905 massacre of citizens by tsarist troops on "Bloody Sunday" but were suppressed effectively by 1908. Their artists, however, were available when posters began being produced a decade later.

From these sources, the poster artists developed a distinctive series of styles. Most frequent were dramatic presentations of heroic or tragic figures in emotion-evoking poses. A woman and child might be seen cowering before blood-crazed tsarist troops; a heroic worker might be seen seizing a flag and carrying it forward in the storming of a position; a grandmother might be seen stolidly harvesting wheat to feed the soldiers at the front. These scenes were selected carefully to play upon the sentiments of the Soviet people and to encourage them to sacrifice for the cause.

Such posters were a departure from public art in the tsarist period. In that period, generals and royalty were the typical subjects of public art. With the revolution, the emphasis shifted to common people performing their parts in the successful operation of Soviet society. True to the communist ideal, workers were the most important group, and a great variety of occupations was portrayed. Women appeared prominently in many posters, providing role models for women who might otherwise have felt uncomfortable applying for work in a factory or as a miner.

The widespread use of posters extended well past the violent overthrow of the government and lasted throughout the process of revolution. During the establishment of the Soviet government, posters focused particularly on political and economic themes, using these to inspire support.

[3] **Kimigayo:** kee mee GY oh

FIGURE 43.2 *Diego Rivera Mural.* *In the early twentieth century, Diego Rivera and his fellow Mexican muralists decided that art should be rendered on public walls, where it would be available to both the poor and rich alike. This mural by Rivera presents a panorama of Mexican history from pre-Columbian to modern times.* Enrique Franco-Torrijos.

During periods of internal or external military challenges, posters tended to place greater emphasis on military and political issues. During calm times when the government was trying to promote social and economic development of the society, economic and cultural themes were dominant. The use of posters as a recognized arm of the state continued in the Soviet Union through the late 1970s, although they had lost much of their impact by the 1950s.

Mexican Mural Art

Mural art—the painting of pictures on walls—stretches back into Mexican prehistory, at least back to around A.D. 350. Modern Mexico shares this interest in wall painting, and many walls throughout Mexico bear marvelous murals. The tradition of mural painting is not unbroken from antiquity, however, and the twentieth-century boom in mural art traces back only to 1922.

The Mexican Revolution beginning in 1910 was a reaction to the elitist, antipeasant, anti-Indian policy of the Mexican government. By 1917, the revolutionaries had replaced the government, and there was a feeling that true social change would follow. In this atmosphere, a group of artists in 1922 decided that they should stop painting pictures on canvas to be sold to rich people; instead, they should paint scenes glorifying the common people of Mexico and the national past, and these should be painted on public walls, where all could appreciate them. Painters like Diego Rivera[4] (1886–1957) and José Orozco[5] led the way, and thousands of murals were the result.

[4] **Diego Rivera:** dee AY goh ree VAYR ah
[5] **José Orozco:** hoh SAY oh ROHS koh

UNDER THE LENS

Pre-Columbian Mexican Murals

Ancient Mexican Indians faced the walls of their temples and palaces with plaster and placed beautiful murals there. The best-preserved of these are at the ancient city of Teotihuacán, just north of Mexico City, and at the ancient Mayan site of Bonampak.

At Teotihuacán, the dry climate has preserved murals dating back to around A.D. 350. In these murals, physicians heal the sick, athletes play the ritual ball game that was both entertainment and worship, and fortunate souls cavort in the heaven of Tlaloc, the rain god. In the heaven scene, some people dance with linked hands, others play games with marbles, and swimmers frolic in abundant water. Trees, flowers, and butterflies are everywhere, and over it all rules the conventionalized representation of Tlaloc, with his blue feather headdress.

At Bonampak, different styles prevailed, and scenes were mostly of the rendering of homage. Subject peoples form lines to present tribute to a ruler, and rulers present offerings to the gods. Unlike the cavorting Teotihuacán figures, most of the Mayans stand rigidly upright with a standardized formal pose. This pose reveals a profile with a forehead that slants back, a curved nose, and a pendulous lip. These characteristics were used by the ancient Mayans to distinguish themselves from other ethnic groups in their paintings.

The Mexican muralists of the twentieth century created a new mural style, but they self-consciously incorporated elements from these ancient styles into their works. Diego Rivera's medical murals juxtapose ancient medical practices from Teotihuacán with modern medical clinics; the ancient gods from Tlaloc's heaven mingle and talk with Jesus and Christian saints, and their faces include both the slanted Mayan ones from Bonampak and the angular ones from Teotihuacán. His characters have ornamental curves emanating from their mouths, speech scrolls that were the conventional symbol representing vocalizations in ancient Mexican art. And personified Death, with a hollow skull and flowing robes, often stalked the inhabitants of murals, reflecting the prominence of death in both ancient Mexican and medieval Spanish folk culture. For Rivera and his contemporaries, the use of both Native American and Spanish imagery was critical to the creation of a national style of mural art.

The murals are in varying styles, but they have many common characteristics. All are more or less realistic, in recognition that highly abstract styles might be difficult for untrained citizens to appreciate. Themes emphasized a distinctive Mexican past and present, underscoring that the challenges of today are little different from those of the Mexican past.

These murals have inspired generations of Mexican muralists, and the tradition has flowed over the border into areas of the United States with large Mexican American populations. Diego Rivera and others painted murals in Chicago and San Francisco, and these inspired Mexican American artists to produce murals in the same style. The early murals are a blend of fine and popular art, but many of the later murals are truly folk art, with untrained amateurs producing beautiful and culturally meaningful works of art for passersby to appreciate. At both periods the murals have served to stimulate a sense of national and ethnic pride.

Fighting Ducks and Blazing Buzzards

The potential of films for fantasy was quickly appreciated by filmmakers, and the first animated cartoons appeared in the 1890s. They truly came into their own as popular formats in the 1930s, when depression-era melancholy in the Western countries could be chased away by an afternoon at a cinema, which necessarily included at least one cartoon. In the United States, Walt Disney, Warner Bros., and a few others produced the vast majority of cartoons, and they were widely distributed to theaters. Since then, they have been broadcast over television thousands of times, finding new generations of audiences.

One of the mainstays of American commercial cartoon films was unrestrained yet impotent violence. A pudgy fellow might be shot from a cannon and flattened against a brick wall, but after a suitably humorous sequence of reconstituting himself, he would be as good as ever. Cartoon characters were shot, stabbed, minced, blown up, and crushed on a regular basis, but their demises always were short-lived. In fact, it was critical to revive the characters to avoid distressing the younger members of the audience.

When the United States entered World War II, however, some cartoon films changed drastically.

FIGURE 43.3 *Satire of Hitler. This poster, titled "And Yet It Moves!," is a collage by John Heartfield, a German artist so disenchanted with Nazi Germany that he moved to England and adopted an English name. Its portrayal of Hitler as a sword-wielding ape on top of the world illustrates both Heartfield's contempt for Nazism and the power of art to make a political point.* Kunstsammlung, Stiftung Archiv der Akademie der Künste Berlin (Heartfield Archiv).

No longer mere entertainment, they became vehicles for promoting patriotism and national pride through the use of war plots. In some cartoons, characters made jokes about ration books, victory gardens, and other wartime emergency measures; these were interspersed throughout stories that otherwise were of the same nature as before the war. But other cartoons depicted the war itself, either directly or through a metaphor, and in these cartoons violence took on a more serious aspect.

Cartoons depicted Germany's Adolf Hitler and Japan's General Tojo fairly regularly, and, after plot maneuverings, these cartoons invariably ended with a bomb falling on the villain. Other cartoons showed peaceful families of ducks swimming along or flying in V-shaped formations. Unprovoked, a squadron of buzzards would swoop down on them, sometimes firing machine guns or dropping bombs, and sometimes killing ducks. The buzzards typically would be shown with German-style helmets or with swastika armbands. After a suitable period of carnage, a hero would emerge, take to the air, and shoot down the villainous buzzards. They dropped, usually in flames.

These cartoons violated a basic convention of the genre: the invulnerability of the characters in the face of violence. Innocent victims sometimes died, and the villains almost always did. There were no resurrections in these cartoons, and viewers must have been moved by this. In the name of patriotism, cartoons were turned into propaganda vehicles to fuel support of the Allied cause in World War II.

Samurai Films in Japan

Historic dramas are a longstanding genre in Japanese drama, set in periods before the Meiji industrialization and Westernization of Japan. The film versions of these dramas, ***jidai-geki***[6] in Japanese, became popular in the 1950s and continue so through today. Most of these films are set in the shogunate period and portray proud *samurai*, down on their luck but retaining their honor. They are presented a virtuous task to complete, and the film depicts their attempts to do so.

One of the most famous of these films is *The Seven Samurai*, directed by Akira Kurosawa[7]

[6] ***jidai-geki:*** JEE dy GEHK ee
[7] **Akira Kurosawa:** ah KEE rah koo roh SAH wah

(b. 1929) and produced in 1952. In this film, a peasant village is terrorized by nearly 100 bandits who are trying to exact tribute, and the peasants try to hire *samurai* to protect them. The amount they can offer is too little to attract the *samurai*, who are, however, moved by the peasants' plight, and seven *samurai* set out to defend the village. As the plot advances, the *samurai* (assisted by the peasants, whom they have trained) fight skillfully and bravely, and the number of bandits is reduced; but so is the number of *samurai*. Finally, in a climactic scene, the *samurai* destroy the remaining bandits, but only two *samurai* survive. They muse that they may have won that day but that the fighters are always the losers.

Jidai-geki reflect many facets of postwar Japan. They underscore the tragedy of violence, but even more they present an image of a glorious and honorable past, desirable at the conclusion of an unsuccessful and brutal war. By stressing pre-Western themes, they are an act of passive rebellion against the Allied occupation of Japan from 1945 to 1952; the stress on violent military action contrasts markedly with the demilitarized government forced upon Japan by the terms of surrender in World War II.

Reggae's Message

Jamaica, the Caribbean country widely known for its resorts and foreign tourists, also is a country of abject poverty. Out of that poverty arose a form of popular music that was initially nationalistic but since has become an anti-imperialist symbol around the world.

In the 1950s, Jamaica had its home-grown African American music, calypso. It had a long tradition as a folk music, but it came to be associated with the sedate version played for tourists in expensive resorts. In the 1960s, influenced heavily by American rock-and-roll artists, many young Jamaicans developed a new form of music: reggae.[8] **Reggae** is a form of African Caribbean music, heavily influenced by American blues and rock and roll, with a distinctive rhythm that emphasizes the second beat of a measure.

The rhythm is catchy and good to dance to, but the appeal of reggae goes far beyond its musical virtues. The home of reggae is Trenchtown, a poor neighborhood of Kingston. There, such reggae artists as Bob Marley (1945–1981), Peter Tosh (1944–1987), and Bunny Wailer (b. 1945) adopted a political philosophy and lifestyle to accompany their music.

The sociopolitical wing of reggae was **Rastafarianism**, a movement dedicated to revitalizing pride in African heritage among Jamaicans and achieving racial equality. The first Rastafarians ("Rastas," for short) appeared in 1930, when Haile Selassie[9] was crowned emperor of Ethiopia, becoming the first native African national ruler since the conquest of Africa by European imperialists. Emperor Selassie was known as Ras Tafari ("Governor Tafari") before being crowned emperor, and it is from this title that Rastafarians derived their name. Rastafarians saw his ascension to the throne of Ethiopia as a symbol of the coming political and economic freedom for Africans in Africa and abroad.

The political climate of the 1960s transformed Rastafarianism. Drawing on freedom movements in Africa, the civil rights movement in the United States, and radical political movements (particularly in the United States), Rastafarians became more pressing in their demands. They believed the Jamaican government to be a relic of imperialism and Jamaica to still be in a neocolonial status, a place where ethnic minorities were systematically exploited and accorded little power in governance. Accordingly, they called for expanded political freedoms, economic development leading to financial independence, and recognition of Jamaica's African heritage.

These demands were championed by performers who had achieved superstar status in Jamaica (and sometimes abroad) through their reggae. Concerts might draw more than 100,000 fans, and the power of charismatic performers to move crowds is well known. The Jamaican government became very concerned that Rastafarianism might be a threat to security. At the same time, reggae lyrics began incorporating overt political messages, such as these phrases from "Get Up Stand Up" by Peter Tosh:

> Get up stand up, stand up for your rights.
> Get up stand up, don't give up the fight.
> . . . .
> And half the history has never been told.
> And now that children have seen the light
> They're gonna stand up for their rights.

---

[8] **reggae:** RAY gay

[9] **Haile Selassie:** HY lee sah LAHS ee

Such apparent calls to resistance and sometimes violence scared the government and police of Jamaica. Attempts to reconcile differences and mollify reggae activists were largely successful, although one performer, Peter Tosh, resisted these attempts. After several threats and one earlier attack, Tosh was murdered. While the police concluded that the murderer was an unidentified burglar, many people believe this was a political assassination.

In addition to their political views, Rastafarians advocated a form of life based partly on a return to nature. The supreme spirit, Jah, was said to inhabit all things, and reverence demanded that devout Rastafarians respect all living things. There were rules for the proper roles of men and women, advocacy of the use of marijuana (*ganja*) as a ritual drug, and expected standards of dress, including the signature male "dreadlocks," long hair crushed together into braidlike strands.

Reggae went through many changes in the late 1980s. Both Bob Marley and Peter Tosh, the greatest stars of the genre, had died, and a new generation of artists had arrived. The newer artists were less interested in political action and Rastafarianism, and the militant aspect of reggae abated.

FIGURE 43.4 *Bob Marley in Concert.* *Bob Marley (1945–1981), Jamaican singer, songwriter, and guitarist and the best known of all reggae artists, performs in front of a portrait of Haile Selassie. Selassie, also known as Ras Tafari, was the Ethiopian emperor who inspired Rastafarianism, a religious-cultural movement that originated in 1930s Jamaica. Marley's music expressed his commitment to Rastafarianism and the politics of nonviolence; the scale of his success brought his message to an international audience.* Peter Simon.

But the global influence of reggae remains. In a small village in Bolivia, on an Indian reservation in Arizona, along the street in any African city—a visitor can still hear the first wave of reggae with Marley, Tosh, and Wailer. While reggae no longer is the most popular style of pop music in Paris or Berlin, it is prominent throughout most of the Third World.

What is the attraction? First, this is Third World music. It was developed, written, and performed by individuals unaffiliated with the United States or any other industrialized power. While it arose out of nationalism, it has evolved into an agent of internationalism. Second, in many cases, it fuels African pride with its focus on Ras Tafari, its overt African orientation, and its African American performers. Even among non-African communities of the Third World, the focus on oppressed ethnic minorities is welcome. Third, it reflects values that resonate in many Third World societies: reverence for the land and living things, faith in a god, and a rejection of aspects of Western-style society. Fourth, the overt message of pride and the achievement of equality strikes a chord among many people around the world. Reggae is the international music of the oppressed.

INNOVATION

The pattern has recurred over and over again in nineteenth- and twentieth-century Europe, just as it had (to a lesser extent) in the seventeenth and eighteenth centuries. An artist in one of the fine arts has striven to develop a new style, a new message, or a new mode of expression. Finally succeeding in doing so, the artist presents this new kind of art to the world and is savaged by critics and public alike. The new art has succeeded too well in its goal: It is so different from its predecessors that consumers are unable to appreciate it.

Examples of this phenomenon abound in the fine arts of the Western tradition. One critic declared in 1854 that Franz Liszt, the great Romantic composer, was an ignoramus who clearly was unaware of what constituted the "correct" structure for a sonata, completely missing the point that Liszt was trying to reformulate the genre of sonatas to make it more flexible. When impressionist painting first appeared in France of the 1870s, it was ridiculed as "just a batch of daubs and paint blobs"; impressionists were forced to organize their own shows because established galleries would not handle their works. In 1913, a ballet called "The Rite of Spring" was produced in Paris; it was created by some of the greatest artists of the age, with music by Igor Stravinsky, choreography by Vaslav Nijinsky, and sets by Erté. Despite the all-star production team, the ballet was interrupted by laughter and catcalls from the audience, resulting ultimately in a riot between supporters and detractors. Critics maintained that the music was inharmonious and without discernible melody and that the dancing was merely awkward jumping around.

What these and many other cases have in common is that these artistic ideas, works, and movements were reviled when they were new but since then have been praised and declared great. The genius in these works led to their acceptance by critics and public alike, but only after some time had passed, allowing these people to become accustomed to their artistically radical new ideas.

What led artists to such drastic breaks with tradition, breaks that made their works initially unpalatable and unpopular? Three factors probably are most responsible:

— increased value placed on creativity, imagination, and intellectual stimulation;

— the progressive ideology; and

— artists' desires to distinguish themselves.

The increased importance of creativity, imagination, and intellectual stimulation often meant that some of the elements traditionally valued in art had to be sacrificed. Beauty, for example, had been a traditional yardstick of artistic success, but the innovators of the nineteenth and twentieth centuries increasingly were ready to jettison attractiveness if doing so meant a more creative, imaginative, or stimulating piece. In essence, the mental process of figuring out a work of art became increasingly dominant over the emotional process of enjoying it.

The progressive ideology of the nineteenth century contributed to this process as well. The basic tenet of progressivism is that improvement naturally arises out of change; consequently, any action that produces change is a step toward improvement. Innovation for innovation's sake was promoted by this ideology. In fact, innovation came to be perceived by many elite devotees of the arts as the litmus test for good art.

Finally, artists came to see themselves in a somewhat different light from their predecessors. In earlier centuries, artists were conceived first and foremost as skilled practitioners, persons whose manual and visual skills permitted them to produce well-crafted works of beauty; in the nineteenth century, artists began to be seen more as intellectual creators who devised new approaches to creating art. Being a mere practitioner of art was to risk being labeled as uncreative or derivative. The way to make one's name was to create a new style, not just to create works within a previously established style.

The fine arts in the past two centuries therefore have placed an ever-increasing value on innovation among artists, even at the risk of producing art that has little or no audience. Few in the public have the appropriate training to appreciate some cutting-edge works of art, and most have little interest in working hard to appreciate a work of art that may be neither attractive nor easily understandable. As a result, many modern musical compositions have never been played to an audience, galleries showing avant-garde paintings may have few visitors, and the circulation of modern poetry magazines remains small. In this sense, the fine arts have become attuned to a smaller intellectual elite than at any time in the previous five centuries.

The arts in the twentieth century became far more stylistically diverse than in any earlier time. Greatly divergent approaches were tolerated and encouraged. At the same time that Stravinsky was experimenting with dissonance and unusual rhythms, Edward Elgar was composing lyrical melodies and lush harmonies along more traditional lines; while Pablo Picasso was reducing people and objects to geometric forms, Georgia O'Keefe was painting realistic animal skulls in the desert setting of the American Southwest. This diversity makes it impossible to select a few examples that adequately represent the diversity of art in this period. Nonetheless, the examples that follow provide some idea of the range of innovation that has been tolerated and encouraged in the past century.

John Cage, the Prepared Piano, and the Organization of Sound

Prior to the twentieth century, classical music had seen its innovators, but the differences between their innovative music and that against which they were reacting, seen from the perspective of today, were quite small. In the twentieth century, however, the degree of difference between traditional forms of classical music and avant-garde forms became far greater. Some composers, such as Arnold Schoenberg, rejected the time-honored European system of harmony or even any system of harmony; others, like Lou Harrison, abandoned traditional modes of rhythm and its notation; still others, like Erik Satie, incorporated unusual sounds, like those of typewriters and shower hoses, into their music. One of the most innovative of these avant-garde composers was John Cage.

John Cage (1912–1992) was the son of an inventor, and he often considered himself an artistic inventor. After a brief stay in college, he dropped out to travel in Europe. He was largely self-taught in music and was acknowledged as extremely well read in a wide variety of fields, ranging from architecture to fungal botany. He first published musical compositions in 1932, and he remained productive through the rest of his life.

Cage was perfectly capable of writing beautiful music in more traditional styles, and some of his early works were of this sort. He preferred, however, to stretch the borders of music with new sounds, new ideas, and new forms. In fact, he redefined music as "the organization of sound," opening the door to all sorts of sounds not usually conceived of as musical.

Cage's first radically new piece was "Bacchanale," written in 1938 for what he called the **prepared piano**. The pianist was instructed to place various articles among the strings of the piano, resulting in buzzing, clunking, and whirring sounds during the performance. These sounds were largely unpredictable, varying from performance to performance, and most listeners found them unattractive. Cage's point, however, was not to make beautiful music but to make interesting music, and one way to make it interesting was to integrate new sounds into it.

In 1942, Cage published "Credo in Us," a percussion piece that incorporated either a radio or a record player, producing unpredictable sounds that interwove with the more programmed percussion rhythms. He carried this idea further in 1955 with "Speech," wherein several radios were tuned to different stations, and the resulting chance combination of sounds constituted the musical performance. Perhaps his most controversial work came in 1952 with "4'33"," a performance of 4 min-

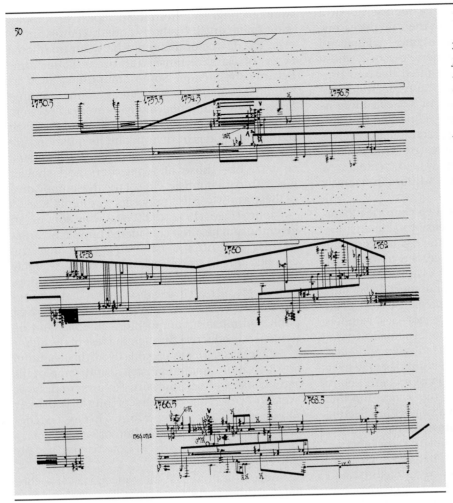

FIGURE 43.5 *John Cage Score.* This page from Cage's *34'46.776* shows his disdain for convention. While the staffs and notes are reminiscent of those in standard musical usage, the score cannot be read traditionally, forcing the performer to interpret what is intended. Such purposeful confusion makes the piece radically different each time it is played. ©1960 by Henmar Press Inc., 373 Park Avenue South, New York, N.Y. 10016.

utes and 33 seconds in which a performer sat on stage with any instrument, as silent as possible.

Needless to say, Cage received considerable negative reaction to many of his works. Some critics ridiculed him, and his concerts drew sparse audiences. Much of his music was damned because it required no skill to perform (and, some said, none to compose), and his detractors accused him of indulging in stunts in order to attract public attention. Yet he is considered a major figure in modern classical music. What makes John Cage worth examining?

Cage said, in effect, that there has been enough beautiful music composed. He was interested, rather, in expanding the world's vision of music beyond the attractive to include, potentially, every sound, no matter how ugly, dissonant, or grating. By having an audience listen to supposed silence, he felt that they would realize the wealth of sounds occurring during what is conventionally considered soundlessness. Because all sounds were equal to Cage, it mattered little that these sounds were ordinary or unattractive or outside the musician's control.

What mattered above all else to John Cage was to do something new. Attractiveness of the piece was to be sacrificed for raw originality; Cage's music was designed to appeal not to the spirit or to the senses but to the mind. As he wrote about his music, "Whenever I've found that what I'm doing has become pleasing, even to one person, I have redoubled my efforts to find the next step." To

Cage, music was a means of stretching the mind to experiment with new ideas, a set of progressive inventions, each farther from the starting point than the last. The result was a body of music intentionally placed as far from the historical continuum of fine arts music as the composer could put it, marking a major break in the Western musical tradition.

Abstract Expressionism

One of the more influential of twentieth-century fine art painting styles was **abstract expressionism**, a style characterized by an attempt to abandon previous artistic conventions and to emphasize the spontaneous, personal, free, unstudied, and intuitive aspects of art. Sometimes this meant abandoning planning and control and permitting chance to play a significant role in the production of the painting, much as chance played a role in some of Cage's music.

Abstract expressionist painters emphasized abstraction, the reduction of an image to simpler elements the artist considers most essential. The subjects of abstract expressionist paintings might be real objects or persons, but they are presented in a manner that makes them difficult to recognize. Alternatively, an abstract expressionist painting might be nonrepresentational, making no effort to depict anything more than a design.

There were two primary schools of painting within abstract expressionism. One, **action painting**, featured slashes of paint intersecting on a canvas; the other, **field painting**, used featureless and often overlapping masses of colors. Action painting was the earlier and led to field painting.

The pioneer of action painting was Jackson Pollock (1912–1956). Pollock was born in Idaho and raised in southern California, and some critics commented that his paintings had the grandeur and scale of the American West. He attended art school in New York and learned technique there,

FIGURE 43.6 *Jackson Pollock in Action. Jackson Pollock, an abstract expressionist known for his use of spontaneous techniques, would often hurl gobs of paint with his hands or sling paint from a brush whipped near the canvas. In this 1949 photo, Pollock experiments with different media.* Martha Holmes, *Life* Magazine, © 1949, Time Inc.

but his art remained relatively unaffected by contemporary artistic styles.

Pollock's early work in the 1930s depicted places and things, mostly people, in manners that were easily recognizable. By the 1940s, however, he increasingly was distorting his representations, and by the late 1940s he had abandoned all attempts to depict physical objects. Instead, he practiced action painting, hovering over large canvases and hurling dollops of paint at them from a swung brush. The resulting lines of paint intersected one another at various angles, partly determined by Pollock's planning but increasingly determined by chance. A sarcastic comment in the press dubbed Pollock "Jack the Dripper."

Pollock's devotion to action painting grew in part out of his absorption with violence. He was fond of barroom fisticuffs and idolized the semi-violent rebel-heroes of 1950s American films, such as Marlon Brando in *On the Waterfront*. By hurling paint, he felt that he was playing out his personal involvement with violence. Because art, in Pollock's conception, was a purely personal experience, the result had to be interesting to the artist.

And others found Pollock's art interesting. Many critics raved over it, some proclaiming him the greatest living artist. While most of the public was mystified by his art, wealthy clients bought it in quantities that permitted him a comfortable livelihood.

The second school of abstract expressionism, field painting, was pioneered by Willem de Kooning[10] (1904–1997). Born in the Netherlands but living most of his life in the United States, de Kooning discovered abstract expressionism and began working in it in the 1950s. His version was more cerebral and planned than Pollock's, prompting Pollock to say to de Kooning: "You know more, but I feel more."

Most of de Kooning's art depicts things, usually people, though they are reduced to masses of color. (See full-color illustration on p. A-32.) Sometimes a painting will be simply masses of flat color, emphasizing pure design and depicting nothing. His art usually is conceived of as more quiet and deliberate than that of Pollock.

Abstract expressionism was popular only from the late 1940s to the early 1960s, but it left a mark

[10] **Willem de Kooning:** WIHL ehm duh KOHN ihng

on modern painting. Just as Pablo Picasso's abstract art had taken a turn away from traditional painting styles of the 1920s, abstract expressionism signaled a radical departure from the evolution based on earlier forms, opening the door for all sorts of future innovations. Further, it marked the beginning of serious attention to American painters in international art.

Free Verse

Of all the forms of Western literature, poetry in the sixteenth and seventeenth centuries clearly was the one most constrained by conventions of structure and form. Poems were of various named kinds, such as the English sonnet and the ballad, each of which was expected to meet certain requirements. An English sonnet, for example, was supposed to have fourteen lines, divided into three sets of four lines and a concluding pair; each of these sets of lines was expected to present a complete idea; each line was to have a meter, specifically to be made up of ten syllables, with every other syllable accented, starting with the second; the lines were supposed to rhyme with a pattern of *abab-cdcd-efef-gg*, wherein each letter represents a particular ending syllable of a line. These combined requirements placed sonnet writing under a daunting set of restrictions.

Poets from the seventeenth century onward tinkered with poetic forms, creating new ones, modifying old ones, and occasionally working outside the forms. It was only in the nineteenth century, however, that some poets stepped outside the forms altogether and created **free verse**: poetry that self-consciously avoided the traditional conventions of meter, rhyme, and structure. The first free verse was written by Walt Whitman (1819–1892), the American poet, in *Leaves of Grass*, published in 1855. Whitman introduced stanzas like:

> Has anyone supposed it lucky to be born?
> I hasten to inform him or her, it is just as lucky to die, and I know it.

Such verses flew in the face of traditional poetry: They had no rhyme, no discernible pattern of accented syllables, and irregular numbers of syllables per line. This freedom from predetermined structure is the essence of free verse.

IN THEIR OWN WORDS

"There Are Some Men"

Leonard Cohen is a contemporary Canadian poet who writes in free verse and other styles. The poem presented here, "There Are Some Men," is a tribute to a deceased friend written in free verse. It has five stanzas, each with a different number of lines; lines vary from two to ten syllables and have no regular pattern of accents; there is no rhyme. By rejecting these elements, Cohen frees himself to focus on creating a personal statement, individual in every particular, to memorialize his dead friend.

There are some men
who should have mountains
to bear their names to time.

Grave-markers are not high enough
or green,
and sons go far away
to lose the fist
their father's hand will always seem.

I had a friend:
he lived and died in mighty silence
and with dignity,
left no book, son, or lover to mourn.

Nor is this a mourning-song
but only a naming of this mountain
on which I walk,
fragrant, dark, and softly white
under the pale of mist.
I name this mountain after him.

As might be expected, Whitman's poetry was seen as radical and was greeted with considerable initial critical condemnation. The idea of free verse, however, was greeted with enthusiasm by some poets and critics, including Gustave Kahn, a French poet who in the 1880s coined the term and wrote a manifesto of how free verse would remove the fetters of poets. By 1900, free verse was well established and accepted among poets and poetry lovers, and it permitted new generations of poets to stretch the limits of the medium.

Generalizations are difficult with a medium as diverse and unconstrained as free verse, but it is fair to say that most free verse writers use the freedom from repetitive structure to create emphasis. A single word that stands out from the rest of the poem, for example, takes on special significance and begs the reader to pay special attention to it. This poem by E. E. Cummings, published in 1923, illustrates this well:

Buffalo Bill 's
defunct
          who used to
          ride a watersmooth-silver
                              stallion
and break onetwothreefourfive pigeonsjustlikethat
                    Jesus
he was a handsome man . . .

Other poets have taken the idea of arranging words into visually interesting patterns even further, as when the words of a poem create the visual image of a bird's feather or a man smoking a cigar. Modern poets continue to develop new devices for presenting their art.

ALIENATION

Traditionally, the arts were expected to be uplifting, to provide a beautiful insight into reality. Consequently, the subjects and themes of art were primarily pleasant, attractive, and enjoyable. In the second half of the twentieth century, this changed dramatically. Literature and drama often focused on antiheroes, characters who had a certain charisma but were less than exemplary in their behavior or morals. Increasingly, stories ended unhappily and good characters remained unrewarded for their virtue. A cynic might contend that this view of life is more realistic than the one traditionally propounded, but it also represents a reorientation of the arts.

Many critics see this as a reflection of profound alienation in the twentieth century. Dissatisfaction with the wars, inequalities, and tragedies

FIGURE 43.7 *Scene from* Une Si Jolie Petite Plage. *This typical example of* film noir *features jaded cynics confronting one another and their collective depression. This genre developed out of the profound alienation of the era following World War II in Europe.* Museum of Modern Art, Film Stills Archive.

of the past has led many people to reject whatever they view as part of the historical baggage of the century. "Beatniks," "hippies," "punks," and others have been explicit about their alienation from and rejection of the societies they inherited, but other artists usually have encoded their rejection into their work.

Postwar Films

The medium of the film is ideally suited to popular arts. On the one hand, creating a film is a fairly expensive endeavor; on the other hand, the finished film can be easily reproduced for mass viewing. The two factors, coupled with the historic allure of the film to audiences, have made films in the twentieth century an ideal way to project ideas to a mass audience or to draw on that audience's sympathies and anxieties. While many of the filmmakers after World War II were trained in the fine arts, their films—largely for economic reasons—were typically directed toward mass audiences.

LE FILM NOIR. France had developed a successful film industry prior to World War II, an industry that had turned out a wide range of films, including historical dramas, comedies, sex farces, and the like. The devastation of war and enemy occupation, however, had throttled the French film industry, and, in the 1950s, France was trying to rebuild it. In this rebuilding period, many of its talented directors turned to a new genre.

This genre, known as ***le film noir***[11] ("the dark film"), focused on the dark, pessimistic, and gloomy side of life. One film of this genre is *Une Si Jolie Petite Plage* ("Such a Pretty Little Beach," 1948), directed by Yves Allégret.[12] The standard film blurb (used in movie descriptions in television guides) for this film describes it as follows:

> A murderer returns to the small seaside town where he spent his childhood, befriends the maid at the hotel, and after a few days kills himself.

[11] *le film noir:* luh feelm nwahr
[12] **Yves Allégret:** eev ahl ay GRAY

There is little that is cheerful in *film noir*. While many *films noirs* were critical and box-office successes in France, their gloomy nature was less popular with moviegoing audiences abroad.

Film noir is a logical outgrowth of **existentialism**, a philosophical movement linked to such thinkers as Jean-Paul Sartre[13] (1905–1980). Existentialism posits that the greatest problem facing anyone is existence itself, that reason and good intentions will not be enough to explain why things happen as they do, and that anguish at the failure to control the course of one's life is to be expected. Although its intellectual roots go back to prewar times, existentialism attained its greatest appeal in postwar France.

The appeal of existentialism to a war-ravaged France is obvious: It freed the victims from the obligation of trying to understand why they had suffered so greatly. According to existentialism, suffering is the natural state of humanity, and one's personal suffering—while perhaps intense and devastating—is only one share of the great misery of humanity as a whole. *Film noir* focused on and glorified suffering, making it the central theme. The pervasiveness of existentialism in the French film industry of the 1950s is evidenced by the fact that French critics of the period referred to *film noir* as "realism." *Film noir* gave audiences a means to acknowledge and accept their misfortune, providing an outlet for alienation.

GODZILLA AND MONSTER ISLAND. Just as in France, the film industry in Japan during the 1950s was trying to rebuild from the devastation of World War II. One of the successful genres of films developed in Japan during this period was the monster film. These films in almost every way are the opposite of the *samurai* dramas of *jidai-geki*. While *jidai-geki* are dramatic and very serious, monster films are light and usually provide abundant humorous moments. *Jidai-geki* typically attract the most acclaimed actors in Japan, while monster films usually attract less famous and less esteemed actors. While *jidai-geki* often are written with considerable literary skill, monster films are more likely to be written quickly and with little attention to symbolism or eloquence, lending them a "cartoonish" feel.

[13] **Jean-Paul Sartre:** zhahn pohl SAHR truh

But monster films still tell a great deal about postwar Japan. The most famous of them all, *Godzilla* (1956), features a dinosaurlike monster that is freed by an earthquake from a lava flow where it has been trapped for unknown eons. It then descends on Tokyo for no apparent reason, wreaking havoc as it goes. All attempts to destroy Godzilla fail, and it continues its rampage, making loud honking noises and tearing down buildings and power lines. Eventually, however, Godzilla simply goes away. Later films in the same series reveal other monsters, many of which live on Monster Island, and they take on varying positive and negative roles as they attempt to destroy Japan or protect it from other monsters. Many of these monsters were prompted to violence by American nuclear testing in the Pacific; in later years, some were aroused by air pollution, global warming, or increased ultraviolet radiation resulting from the humanly induced breakdown of the atmospheric ozone layer.

Japan is the only country to have felt the effects of nuclear weapons in war, and the Japanese have a unique appreciation of the magnitude of destruction that they produce. Monster films offer another version of utter destruction, sometimes unleashed by natural forces but more often released by unwise human use of the planet. Once set in motion, these processes cannot be controlled by human technology or effort. On the one hand, monster movies reflect a fatalism, recognizing that devastation may occur at any time; they reflect an alienation born of nuclear destruction, military defeat, and humiliation. On the other hand, they serve as a warning that human actions can easily result in unforeseen and destructive consequences.

Punk Rock, Grunge Rock, and Their Allies

From the 1960s onward, popular music has included some form of music that springs from the alienation and uncertainties of modern life. These have been variously known in different periods as "punk rock," "grunge rock," and other terms; the details of style have changed over the years, but the message has remained the same: The world is horrible, so all that is left is to have a good time.

These forms of music are not particularly distinctive musically, developing out of mainstream

FIGURE 43.8 *Sid Vicious and Johnny Rotten of the Sex Pistols.* *Alienation has been a significant theme since the middle of the twentieth century. The Sex Pistols, from their name to their musical style to their performance style, epitomized alienation in the mid-1970s and influenced the music of the 1980s. Their 1976 debut record, "Anarchy in the U.K.," brought punk rock into the mainstream, initiating the public to a genre known for its controversial expression of discontent.* Richard E. Aaron/Sygma.

rock and roll. They usually are characterized by heavy rhythms, simple melodies, and limited harmonies; singing styles are usually powerful, rasping, and coarse, with more interest in emotional effect than in raw beauty. As with so much modern art, the idea is not to produce a beautiful product but to produce an interesting product.

Dominant themes of the lyrics include sex, drugs, and violence, often reflecting a sense of despair. In essence, they say that we all will die soon, so we might as well experience as much sensory pleasure as possible, saving nothing for an uncertain future. Some lyrics focus explicitly on the probability of joblessness, nuclear war, or failed personal relationships. One minority form of this music advocates white supremacy and some-

times violence against other races. Probably no other form of art reflects the alienation of its creators so clearly as this one.

FUSION

As transportation and communication technology have improved over the last few centuries, the world's peoples have been in unprecedented contact with one another. Great distances separating places of residence no longer mean that people will have no knowledge of one another; immigrant communities around the world help make that contact face to face. The artistic result of this contact is **fusion**, the incorporation of ideas from various ethnic and national traditions into art. Fusion has been taking place for centuries, but the twentieth century has seen a quantum jump in the magnitude of fusion in the arts, including folk, popular, and fine arts.

"I Got to Sing the Blues"

No music has been more influential worldwide than that fusion of African and European music which developed in the American South in the centuries following the arrival of African slaves in the American colonies. We have no idea what name was given to this music by its originators in the seventeenth century, but it was ancestor to the blues, jazz, and rock and roll.

When African captives were brought to the Americas as slaves, they brought many elements of their culture with them. Because music was a prominent part of West African life, music was an important piece of culture carried in the minds of slaves. In the Americas, some African songs could be transferred directly, particularly rhythmic work songs that could be used to coordinate group activities in agricultural labor. Slaveholders forbade the practice of African religions by slaves, so African ritual songs had to be recast, but many doubtless resurfaced as Christian hymns and spirituals. New songs were invented using African principles, and some songs blended African and European elements.

There were common elements derived from Africa in most of these songs. Most had powerful rhythms, sometimes incorporating complex syncopations. Many employed call-and-response, an African principle whereby a soloist sings a line and a chorus sings a variant on it. Many melody lines generally ascended and then descended over a couplet or verse, again following a typical African pattern. Some of the harmonies of this music came straight from Africa, but others were borrowed from English or Scottish folk music. (The European population of the early colonial American South was largely of English or Scottish origin.)

Musically speaking, much stayed the same with the conclusion of the U.S. Civil War and the emancipation of the slaves in the United States. African American work parties still went to the fields and still sang the same types of songs; spirituals and hymns remained a prominent part of

Christian devotion; and after-work entertainment continued to include music. There was, however, a significant change that had a profound effect on the development of African American music in the South: the barrelhouse.

A barrelhouse was no more than a bar, but in the segregated South of the late nineteenth and early twentieth centuries, a bar could serve only European American or African American customers. The barrelhouses run by and for African American patrons included music by semiprofessional entertainers, and barrelhouses became hotbeds of musical innovation. This setting saw the development of the **blues**, a form of African-inspired music characterized by distinctive rhythms, repetitive structure, and melody lines that generally descended from initial high notes.

Folk artists became popular artists as some found that they could eke a meager living off their music. Blues artists with such colorful names as Leadbelly, Blind Lemon Jefferson, Frankie Jaxon, Ma Rainey, and Cripple Clarence Lofton toured the African American barrelhouse circuit. The life was tough, working late hours in an establishment that focused on drinking and attracted many of the less savory elements of the community. Many a blues performer ended up murdered or in jail.

It was the blues of the barrelhouses that found its way to the cities and sparked the development of **jazz**, a more polished, innovative, and orchestrated outgrowth of blues. While blues focused on inexpensive instruments (guitars, spoons or other rigged-up percussion instruments, and voices), jazz used the whole range of instruments of the popular dance orchestras of the day, especially horns and woodwinds. Blues relied on repetition of moderately simple melodies and harmonies with complex rhythms, but jazz introduced greater complexity of melody, harmony, and especially structure. The greater complexity of jazz often meant that its performers had to be able to read music, while few blues artists had this skill. Both blues and jazz remained true to their African origins, retaining complex rhythms and call-and-response patterns.

Like blues, jazz originally was restricted essentially to African American performers. Jazz's rise in urban areas during the 1910s and 1920s, however, meant that the whole ethnic spectrum of America was exposed to it through clubs, records, and radio. By the 1930s, Americans of European and Asian extraction had joined the ranks of jazz performers. Europeans also listened to jazz, and all major European cities had their jazz clubs; many African American performers found the less racially charged atmosphere of Paris preferable to that of Macon or Memphis. Asia and Africa, particularly South Africa, also had some jazz clubs, although fans there were more likely to listen to jazz on records.

The birth of jazz did not mean the death of the blues. Rather, the blues persisted, largely in rural areas. After World War II, there was something of a revival of interest in blues that led to the development of **rhythm and blues**, an electrified and polished version of the blues, which developed into **rock and roll** in the 1950s. Early rock-and-roll music was mostly written and performed by African American entertainers, but versions (known as "covers") were performed by white musicians for white audiences. Cover versions typically had less prominent rhythms, less strident vocals, and a less emotional feel. Over the decade of the 1950s, however, covers became increasingly less common, and European American and African American versions of rock and roll gradually converged. This became especially so with the introduction of strongly blues-oriented British musicians like Eric Clapton and John Mayall in the 1960s. Rap music of the late twentieth century is a joint outgrowth of rock and roll and the African American oratorical tradition.

Born in the era of sophisticated transportation and communication systems, rock and roll spread

PATHS TO THE PAST

Leadbelly

Huddie Ledbetter was born in 1889 in Louisiana and became a folk blues artist who adopted the stage name of "Leadbelly" and eventually played the African American barrelhouse circuit. By the time of his death in 1949, he had accomplished something very unusual for an African American in that era: He had successfully crossed over into popularity in mainstream American music. While his music has been widely heralded for decades, his life is more controversial.

Some facts are clear. In 1918, he was convicted of manslaughter in a barroom brawl and sent to prison in Louisiana. Paroled in 1925, he was in a Louisiana prison again in 1930 and was paroled again in 1934. He went to New York City in that year and became a sensation as a performer and recorder of his own blues songs. He died a pauper in Bellevue Hospital in 1949.

Beyond these facts, however, it is difficult to find the real Leadbelly. His biography was written by John Lomax, the folk-song collector who managed him. In it, Leadbelly appears as an arrogant, hard-drinking, womanizing, violent man who was attracted to the life of a blues musician because it permitted him to indulge these vices. Lomax is portrayed as his would-be reformer, negotiating Leadbelly's release from prison in Louisiana and trying to assist him in adjusting to New York.

Leadbelly himself rejected this version of his life, saying, "Lomax did not write nothing like I told him." Subsequent historians have raised further doubts. Many of Leadbelly's songs were published under Lomax's name, and it appears that Leadbelly may have been exploited by Lomax and others appearing to befriend him. Certainly Lomax's involvement led to his financial success, while Leadbelly remained impoverished. Leadbelly's imprisonment clearly stemmed from a killing he committed, but it is equally clear that justice fell harder on African American men in the South in that era than on their white neighbors. As to the details of Leadbelly's character, different acquaintances have recorded different impressions.

Out of all this emerges a picture of the blues artist in a difficult world. Doubtless, some artists were attracted to the life because of the freedoms and license it provided, just as others rejected it for the same reasons. It would be difficult, however, to find a single blues artist who never had been cheated, exploited, or manipulated by management. And the life expectancy of the most prominent blues artists of this era was scarcely fifty years, suggestive of a hard life with dire consequences.

around the world. At the end of the twentieth century, virtually every country in the world has its own version of rock and roll. Some versions, like Puerto Rican *salsa*, Afro-Caribbean *zouk*, and Kenyan *benga*, have had influences on popular music internationally.

All of the forms of African American music have served a variety of purposes. Spirituals and gospel music engendered a feeling of community and have been a source of comfort for generations of the devout. The blues, sung as folk music on a back porch after work, provided a psychological release for individuals who were suffering from bad times. Many blues songs and some jazz had risqué lyrics that often carried a sexual meaning to the initiated. These must have provided entertainers with a chuckle, especially when white audiences failed to catch the hidden meanings of "smoking a cigarette" or "what it is that tastes like gravy (I'll betcha don't know)." And all of these forms of music gave professional musicians some level of economic mobility, providing them with a profession that permitted creative work and at least a hope of financial return.

Picasso and African Art

Pablo Picasso (1881–1973) was one of the most innovative and influential artists of the modern era. Predominantly a painter, he developed several styles, but his early work is of greatest interest to us here. Born in Spain, Picasso began his formal art training in Barcelona in 1896 but soon moved to Paris, where he became a sensation.

FIGURE 43.9 *African Influence on Picasso's Art.* *Modernist works by Pablo Picasso, such as his 1907* Bust of a Woman or a Sailor *(left), were profoundly affected by African masks that the painter first saw in the museums of Paris. On the right is a sickness mask from the Pende people of Congo-Zaire. The unmistakable relationship between such masks and his abstractions of human faces was acknowledged by Picasso himself. Left:* Art Resource Inc., N.Y. *Right:* ©1994 Africa Museum, Tervuren, Belgium. Photo by Roger Asselberghs.

In Paris, Picasso became entranced with West African masks. Made of wood and designed to be worn during ceremonies, these masks were well represented in Parisian museums, and Picasso studied them intently. He was particularly taken by the way a mask would effect a purposeful geometric distortion of a face. An almond-shaped mask, for example, elongated the face, then sharpened its features, especially at the forehead and chin. Picasso recognized that this kind of distortion of figures could produce interesting visual art, and many of his earlier works were devoted to this. These works were the first step toward the abstraction (simplification and distortion) that was to typify most of Picasso's work in his later years.

Picasso's use of African inspiration occurred in an era when Western artists still considered non-Western art to be "primitive" or simple. Part of Picasso's genius was his recognition that it was merely different. He tapped that difference to enrich his own artistic work, stimulating artists ever since to follow his lead.

Cuban Culinary Fusion

Cooking is not usually considered an art, though chefs regularly refer to the "culinary arts." Nonetheless, it is a creative expression that is as much shaped by its environment as any other art, and it profitably is considered a popular art form, one that frequently shows ethnic fusion.

As Cuban immigrants have streamed into southern Florida (mostly following the communist takeover there in 1959), Miami has become the capital for a new style of food, known variously as "Nuevo Cubano"[14] ("New Cuban") or "Cuban Fusion." Miami's population is equally divided between Latin American immigrants, mostly from Cuba, and native-born Americans of various ethnicities. Restaurateurs began developing Cuban Fusion cuisine in the 1980s, and it is widely eaten now by both Cuban and other Americans.

Cuban Fusion dishes draw on traditional Cuban cooking but are different in several ways. They are generally lighter and less filling than traditional Cuban foods, and they use a wider variety of ingredients. In addition to the black beans, spices, and fruits of Cuban cooking, Cuban Fusion uses luxury items of European cooking, such as caviar, lobster, and salmon; in addition, various Thai and other influences are clear, such as seasoning with fish sauce and garnishing with coriander leaf.

Cuban Fusion cooking can be a delight to the palate, but it has a strong symbolic meaning as well. To the hundreds of thousands of Cuban immigrants in Florida, it says that they are Americans now and have a joint heritage. To the rest of America, it says that Cubans have become a vibrant part of the ethnic mix of the modern United States.

SUMMARY

1. The arts are shaped by the time and setting of the artists who produce them. Consequently, they provide insight into history and society.

2. Folk art is produced by traditional, amateur artists; popular art is produced professionally for a mass audience; fine art is produced professionally for an elite audience.

3. Nationalism has been strongly reflected in the arts from the mid–nineteenth century onward, including in national anthems, revolutionary posters, Mexican mural art, animated cartoons, and Japanese *samurai* films. Romanticism and national styles in fine art music of the Western tradition also have reflected nationalist sentiments. Reggae has a more international message, appealing to oppressed peoples everywhere.

4. Innovation in the fine arts has become increasingly important since the late nineteenth century. Reasons for this have been an elevated evaluation of creativity, imagination, and intellectual stimulation; progressive ideology; and artists' desires to distinguish themselves. This sometimes has meant sacrificing traditionally valued elements such as beauty.

5. John Cage focused on interesting organization of sound, rather than traditional styles of music. Abstract expressionism, as practiced by Jackson Pollock and Willem de Kooning, created highly abstract paintings that contained random elements. Free verse, as pioneered by Walt Whit-

[14] **Nuevo Cubano:** NWAY voh koo BAHN oh

man, abandoned traditional structures of poetry. All of these are examples of artistic innovation.

6. *Film noir* in France, Japanese monster films, and punk (and related) music are examples of the effects of alienation after World War II.

7. Blues, jazz, rock and roll, and fusion cooking are examples of fusion in folk and popular art. Picasso's inspiration by African masks is an example of fusion in fine art.

SUGGESTED READINGS

Armes, Roy. *French Cinema*. New York: Oxford University Press, 1988. Chapter 8 deals with French realism and *film noir*.

Gaugh, Harry F. *Willem de Kooning*. New York: Abbeville Press, 1983. Good critical treatment of de Kooning's art, with good reproductions and some biography.

Govenar, Alan. *Living Texas Blues*. Dallas: Dallas Museum of Art, 1986. A short book tracing the history of blues in Texas, though it is generally applicable to the history of blues everywhere.

Kostelanetz, Richard, ed. *John Cage*. New York: Praeger, 1970. A collection of essays by and about John Cage.

Landau, Ellen G. *Jackson Pollock*. New York: Harry N. Abrams, 1989. There are many Pollock treatments, and this is one of the better combinations of biography, criticism, and good reproductions.

Manuel, Peter. *Popular Musics of the Non-Western World*. Oxford, Eng.: Oxford University Press, 1991. Compendious reference on local and international folk and (especially) popular music styles.

Nicholas, Tracy. *Rastafari: A Way of Life*. Garden City, N.Y.: Anchor Press, 1979. A simple account of Rastafarian beliefs and activities during the first wave of reggae.

Rodríguez, Antonio. *A History of Mexican Mural Painting*. New York: G. P. Putnam's Sons, 1969. Excellent treatment, focusing on Mexican murals in the twentieth century.

White, Stephen. *The Bolshevik Poster*. New Haven: Yale University Press, 1988. By far the most compendious collection and analysis of Bolshevik posters, containing far greater variety than any other treatment.

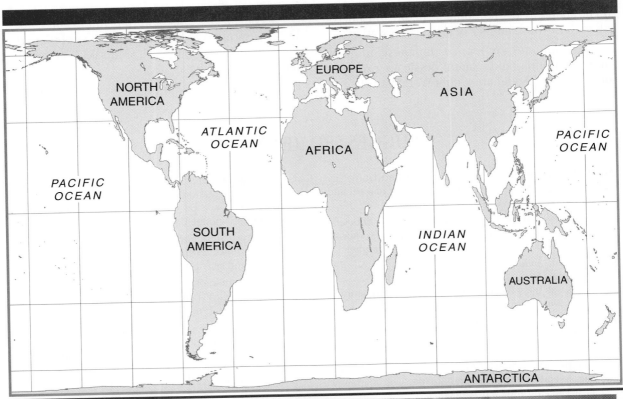

Kuwaiti Oil Fields Aflame. *Iraq invaded Kuwait in 1990, hoping to present the global community with a situation that could not be reversed. A military alliance of Europeans, Americans, and others ousted the Iraqis less than a year later. As the Iraqi Army pulled out, it set ablaze the oil refineries and fields. This act of ecocide, the deliberate destruction of an ecosystem, caused extensive, long-term damage to the surrounding environment. In this picture, an American soldier watches the inferno.* Jim Lukoski/Black Star.

World Integration

In 1988, United Nations peacekeeping soldiers won the Nobel Peace Prize for their humanitarian operations around the world since 1945. This recognition reflected the importance of the United Nations as an international organization dedicated to global rather than national issues. In that sense, the United Nations represents the trend toward world integration in a time of resurgent nationalism.

A fundamental tension between integration and separateness has characterized the modern era. Throughout the modern era, transportation and communication technology have fostered greater connectedness and integration, including commercial links. At the same time, other factors have favored maintenance of local, ethnic, religious, or national identity.

ECONOMIC INTEGRATION AND CHALLENGES

Global economic integration has been a developing process, especially since the sixteenth century. By the early twentieth century, economic relationships had become interdependent, and unilateral actions by a country today often have international consequences. These consequences extend beyond the economic sphere to include political and environmental effects, sometimes global ones.

Economic Integration

Between 1500 and 1750, economic relationships increasingly spanned continents and oceans. The English, for example, established the Russia Company to develop better trade links with Russia, and the East India Company was formed by the English to conduct trade with India, China, and the Americas. The Dutch founded the East Indies Company to promote trade with peoples of the islands of Southeast Asia and Japan. The African slave trade was a significant example of trade between Africa, the Americas, Asia, and Europe. Underlying the growing economic connections were improvements in sailing technology that permitted goods to be more speedily transported.

Regional trade alliances, usually centered on empires, were also formed. Ottoman rulers developed impressive trade links within the area they controlled, as did the Mughals in India. And the Ottomans, Mughals, and Safavid Persians conducted significant interempire land trade. The same could be said about the Ming and Qing empires of China. These decisions by rulers of land empires increasingly left oceanic trade to Europeans, who also had better technology with which to navigate the oceans.

After 1750, the Industrial Revolution propelled the British and other industrializing nations to seek sources of raw materials and markets for finished products. Industrialization also brought increasing wealth and power to industrialists and their countries. Trade agreements were negotiated between Western countries and China, for example, extending trade links to new markets.

In the nineteenth and twentieth centuries, a developing international trade network sparked a standardization process. The metric system, for example, became increasingly accepted as the standard for weights and measures. Similarly, the British pound, which had become the major global currency in the nineteenth century, gave way to the U.S. dollar by the 1920s. French, which had been the accepted language for international diplomacy, has given way to English, which has also become the globally preferred language for scientific discourse, computer networking, and air-traffic control.

After 1500, economic growth and integration spurred the emergence of a prominent middle class in Europe. Merchants and bankers directed the economic transformation, while lawyers, clerks, and physicians benefited from the increasing opportunities to make a reasonable living. During the Industrial Revolution, the middle class became important not only economically but also socially and politically. Opportunities for members of the middle class to enrich themselves were greater in cities; chances for improvement were more limited in rural areas, where land use was often restricted to only a wealthy few.

Urbanization flourished as cities grew in numbers and in spatial area. Cities became more prominent as centers of economic activity, especially during the Industrial Revolution. Pittsburgh, Osaka, and Manchester, for example, developed into commercial and manufacturing centers. Railroad lines, highways, and airports increasingly integrated cities like these into a global trade network.

Beginning in the twentieth century, a series of political and economic crises rocked the international trade system, threatening economic integration. World War I weakened the economic power of the Europeans while strengthening the United States and Japan. Imperialist powers relied on their colonial domains as market areas free of international competition. World War II shattered the economic strength of most Western countries and Japan. Only the United States and the Soviet Union emerged with the economic power to establish trade blocs.

Since 1945, world trade has mushroomed, benefiting many countries, but national economic interests have unsettled the international economic order. Dominant economic countries in the aftermath of World War II concluded that economic prosperity depended on financial stability and cooperative planning. In 1945, U.S. and world leaders sponsored the Bretton Woods Conference, which set global currency exchange rates based on gold and the U.S. dollar. By 1967, a General Agreement on Tariffs and Trade had been negotiated and provided a fairly stable international trade network. With these mechanisms, a better-integrated trade system developed. In the 1980s and 1990s, a second General Agreement on Tariffs and Trade (GATT II) was negotiated, opening up national markets more than ever before.

On the other hand, regional economic blocs, such as the European Economic Community (EEC) and the North American Free Trade Agree-

PEROT FOOTBALL

BLOCK IT!

NAFTA

PROTECTIONISM 93 93

FEAR 90 90 90

WICKS
© THE SIGNAL 1993

FIGURE 44.1 *NAFTA Cartoon.* *The North American Free Trade Agreement caused controversy in American politics with many groups opposing the treaty. This cartoon captures the appeal of Ross Perot, a major NAFTA opponent who played on fears of losing jobs to promote protectionist trade policies. Perot's efforts failed as NAFTA passed in the U.S. Senate.* Rothco.

ment (NAFTA), have fostered more narrow economic interests. In 1951, a few Western European states began merging their economies, with the vision of eventually creating one economy. In 1958, the Treaty of Rome came into force, creating the European Economic Community. The EEC's economic output had exceeded that of the United States by 1980. Prime Minister Margaret Thatcher appreciated the financial benefits of British membership in the EEC. Although the British had stayed aloof from the EEC, the Thatcher government pushed hard to join the EEC and pushed for a single market with common manufacturing standards, trade regulations, and professional qualifications by 1992. Other European countries hoped to join the EEC but were excluded until the 1990s. NAFTA merged the markets of Canada, the United States, and Mexico. It was successfully negotiated in 1993, barely passing ratification by the U.S. Senate and offering modest economic gains since then. Thus, there has been tension between national and regional economic interests.

Challenges to Economic Integration

Although growing economic integration has characterized the era since 1500, special-interest groups have decried economic competition, asking for protection. **Protectionism** is the practice of sheltering local industries and businesses from international competition, and it has characterized national economic policies for much of the modern era.

Protectionist thought and economic practices developed in Europe during the seventeenth and eighteenth centuries. Mercantilist countries believed that they had to export more than they imported, and their leaders usually adopted high tariff rates, making cheap foreign goods more costly and protecting local products. As noted earlier, in the late seventeenth century, English textile manufacturers faced heavy competition from Indian cotton goods. After the manufacturers pled their case in mercantilist terms, high tariffs were slapped on the Indian imports, destroying the competition.

In the nineteenth century, many countries continued to practice protectionist policies. Russia, for example, used high tariffs to protect local industries, especially in the 1890s. The Chinese and Japanese lost control of their tariff policies because of the unequal treaties they were forced to sign with Western countries.

Protectionism reached a high point during the Great Depression. Country after country imposed high tariffs to shelter their national industries, motivated by the rise of nationalism. Although a few businesses were shielded, many others went bankrupt when their export markets dried up as high tariffs elsewhere ballooned the prices of manufactured goods. Their actions, taken to protect national self-interests, worsened the global situation. Indeed, the general trend was a shrinking global trade system, disrupting economic integration.

Since 1945, protectionist policies have been more subdued. Many countries concluded that the trade conflicts of the Great Depression hurt all countries and attempted to develop trade programs with more open markets. Although countries like Japan and South Korea have adopted mercantilist policies that protected certain industries, they have generally begun opening their markets to foreign trade competition. GATT II has further encouraged that opening trend.

The Soviet Union and China developed economic systems that lay largely outside the international economic order, hindering global economic integration. A significant part of the competition between the Soviet Union and the United States during the Cold War era was economic. In that sense, economic rivalry disrupted the general economic integrative trend. With the collapse of the Soviet Empire in 1991, however, prospects for greater economic unity on the global level have increased. In the late 1970s, China also opened its economy to international trade and investment, and Chinese leaders have eagerly sought membership in GATT and other global economic organizations. The Chinese economy has been the world's fastest-growing economy in the latter decades of the twentieth century.

In the 1980s and 1990s, a few U.S. leaders have worried about the loss of U.S. jobs and businesses from international competition, and they have fought the various trade agreements, such as GATT and NAFTA. U.S. trade unions have been very uncomfortable with policies promising low tariffs and easy access to the U.S. market. Although not a few jobs have been lost to economic competition from other countries such as Japan, the general trend has been toward significant job growth in the United States from a burgeoning export effort by U.S. businesses. For example, the U.S. and Japanese economies are so enmeshed that a trade war would have dire consequences for both.

The forces of economic integration and national interest have struggled with each other throughout the modern era. While most leaders recognize that national and global interests are linked, it is equally clear that they are not always identical. A policy may improve conditions within a country yet harm the global system; conversely, a policy may improve the world economy at the expense of national economic welfare. As a result, the tension between forces favoring and opposing economic integration produces periods when one or the other is dominant.

Environmental Consequences of Economic Integration

The increased pace of economic development and integration in the modern era has brought environmental problems with accelerating severity. Agriculture's spread and commercialization played a major role in the deforestation of continents and the erosion of soils. In addition, industrial pollutants have deeply affected people and ecosystems across political boundaries. Resource depletion has affected many countries, and the inadvertent modification of the earth's climate has threatened many people.

In the sixteenth, seventeenth, and eighteenth centuries, European colonists transformed the landscape of North America and Indonesia. Eastern North America was largely forest in 1500, but, by 1800, the massive stands of trees had largely been cleared for agricultural purposes. In Indonesia, many tropical rain forests were cleared for agricultural farmland.

Multiple factors have led to the clearing of forests around the globe, especially in the Third World, causing concern among environmentalists. Apart from agriculture, grazing by livestock has prevented reforestation in parts of the world. Demand for wood products, especially for the construction of houses, has led to heavy logging. Mining has also been a significant factor in reducing forests. The vast loss of forests troubles people who not only fear the destruction of unique ecosystems but who also lament the extinction of animals and medicinal plants. Once again, economic national interests conflict with international interests. Third World countries, for example, need to industrialize but are hindered by international commitments to preserve natural resources.

Air pollution has grown significantly with industrialization, and careless economic policies have caused problems that cross national borders. Fossil fuels, especially coal, have been notorious polluters of the air. In addition, they have caused acid rain, corrosive rainfall that kills trees and fouls lakes. Canada, for example, has suffered from acid rain coming from the United States, while Finland has endured acid rain problems coming from Poland. Massive fossil fuel burning in the nineteenth and twentieth centuries has also contributed to the **greenhouse effect**, the concentration of carbon dioxide in the upper atmosphere, which lets in and traps heat from the sun. This leads to global warming, which some scientists have shown to be a serious environmental problem.

The diminishing ozone layer in the upper atmosphere has also given great concern to environmentalists and citizens alike. Certain industrial gases, such as chlorofluorocarbons (CFCs), bind with ozone, reducing the amount of atmospheric ozone. Because ozone helps prevent harmful ultraviolet rays from entering the atmosphere, the reduction of the ozone layer can have serious health consequences, including increased incidence of skin cancer. In 1987, most countries finally agreed to reduce significantly their CFC emissions by the end of the twentieth century, showing international cooperation in attacking environmental problems.

Nuclear accidents, tests, and waste disposal have also caused problems that cross borders. In 1986, a Soviet nuclear plant exploded at Chernobyl, spewing nuclear radiation into the atmosphere and across Europe. Many Europeans suffered severe health problems because of this accident. U.S., Soviet, French, and Chinese nuclear

FIGURE 44.2 *Deforestation in Brazil.* *Destruction of the Amazon became a major environmental issue in the 1980s and 1990s. Evidenced here are the ravaging effects of strip mining, which has leveled a large section of the oxygen-producing rain forest. Such unchecked waste alarmed many in Brazil and around the world.* Antonio Ribeiro / Gamma/Liaison International.

FIGURE 44.3 *Catastrophe at Chernobyl.* *In 1986, a Soviet nuclear power plant in the Ukraine caught fire, releasing into the atmosphere massive amounts of radiation that caused death and disease. Although Soviet leaders initially denied any problems, they quickly reversed this policy and allowed critical reporting of the disaster.* Novosti, London.

tests have also caused serious air pollution by radiated particles that dropped over other countries. Environmentalists have become alarmed by the casual disposal of nuclear wastes, especially in the ocean. Toxic effects from nuclear materials can contaminate areas for thousands of years.

Other environmentalists have publicized the problem of overfishing in the oceans. Many countries have built and dispatched giant fishing fleets around the world, and they have developed major industries and created large numbers of jobs. Overfishing has already significantly reduced the numbers of edible fish. Fishing communities along the western U.S. coast have dwindled in size because of the absence of salmon in ocean waters. Thus, national interests can also disrupt people's livelihoods around the globe.

POLITICAL INTEGRATION

Since the end of the nineteenth century, internationalism has also begun to gather adherents who have reacted strongly against the conflicts brought by nationalism. Ideologies such as Marxism have developed partly in reaction to nationalist activities. Furthermore, cooperative unions, such as the League of Nations, the United Nations (UN), the Organization of American States (OAS), the Organization of African Unity (OAU), and the Arab League, have been formed to address issues beyond narrow national interests. At the same time, nationalists have decried international agencies and adherents, causing serious tensions.

Nationalism has been perhaps the most powerful political force in the nineteenth and twentieth centuries. It was a driving force, for example, behind the formation of Germany and Zululand. Nationalism also undermined the Russian Empire and helped oust imperialist powers ruling in Asia and Africa. In that sense, nationalism acted against integrationist trends and tendencies.

Some internationalist ideologies have developed in reaction to nationalism. Karl Marx saw nationalism as a by-product of the capitalist system and therefore doomed to disappear as the socialist system began to take hold internationally. His vision focused on class, especially the working class, and he argued that workers would eventually

FIGURE 44.4 *Protests against Fishing Ban.* *As some fishing grounds became severely depleted, various governments imposed bans on fishing. While many protesters at this 1996 demonstration in New England recognized the need to be more environmentally sensitive, their livelihood was dependent on fishing. Furthermore, they resented the fact that other governments ignored the bans and allowed their fleets to continue fishing.* © 1996 Josh Reynolds.

see that the ties binding them together cut across national boundaries. Marx encapsulated his vision in a memorable line from his *Communist Manifesto*: "Workers of the world unite."

Although world leaders had flirted with forming international organizations, the real impetus for international cooperative unions came only in the aftermath of the two world wars. The League of Nations was formed in 1919 to help implement the conditions of the Versailles Peace Treaties and to provide a body that would discuss problems affecting the international community. The League, however, failed to prevent World War II and disintegrated. The United Nations was formed in 1945 to deal with international crises and was more successful than the League. Neither body,

however, could do much in the face of determined opposition by a major world power.

Regional bodies of cooperation have also come into existence in the twentieth century. The Organization of American States was formed in 1948 to deal with inter-American issues. In the 1950s and 1960s, it generally supported the United States' positions on diplomatic matters, prohibiting Cuba from participating in OAS activities. The Arab League came into existence in 1945 to discuss and mediate matters relating to Arab states. Its headquarters remained in Egypt until 1979, when Egypt signed a peace treaty with Israel. Then, Egypt's membership was suspended and the headquarters was transferred to Tunisia. The Organization of African Unity (OAU), a union that appeared

FIGURE 44.5 *Meeting of the OAU.* *The Organization of African Unity formed out of the need to discuss common issues in the aftermath of the collapse of imperialism in Africa. Many delegates to the OAU are dressed in Western clothing while others are wearing more traditional attire.* Laurent van der Stockt/Liaison International.

in 1963, has more than fifty African member states. All of these bodies are examples of political integration.

Thus, a kind of dynamic equilibrium has evolved in which international and national forces vie with each other. Sometimes one or the other has been temporarily ascendant, but, at least, a major world war has been averted, and some degree of political integration has been maintained.

RELIGIOUS INTEGRATION

Contrary to economic and political trends toward integration, religions have generally resisted integrating tendencies. Except for a few instances of ecumenism (bridging religious differences), the trend has been toward retaining and increasing differences.

Islam and Christianity became even more dynamic in converting peoples and encouraging migration of the faithful overseas in the Early Modern Era. Roman Catholic missionaries achieved considerable success in the Americas and the Philippines and more limited results in India, China, and Japan. Muslims were somewhat successful in spreading Islam in the Indian subcontinent, especially during the Mughal Empire. Their most successful proselytizing came in Indonesia and the southern Philippines and was directed by mystics and merchants. Thus, a major trend has been the development of religious communities through proselytizing and migration across widely disparate areas.

At the same time, Islam and Christianity were shaken by sectarian disputes. Shi'ites have persecuted Sunnis and Sunnis have persecuted Shi'ites in Southwest Asia. The Protestant Reformation and the Roman Catholic Reformation brought a

FIGURE 44.6 *Mourning Khomeini's Death. Millions of Iranians mourned the loss of the Ayatollah Khomeini, the religious leader who imposed a fundamentalist form of Shi'a Islam. Mass outpourings of grief were held in public places in the capital of Teheran and elsewhere.* E. Rad / Gamma/Liaison International.

split in Western Christianity. Religious wars convulsed parts of Europe in the sixteenth and seventeenth centuries.

Ecumenical trends have developed since 1945, but they have been limited in scope and have often been found at the grassroots level. Pope John XXIII (reign dates 1958–1963) promoted ecumenism during his papacy, though his successors have been less committed to it. Although some talks between Protestant and Catholic groups have been ongoing, little significant change has resulted.

More important has been the growth of religious fundamentalism, especially in Protestantism and Islam. **Fundamentalism** is the religious belief that posits strict adherence to practices supported by a literal interpretation of sacred texts. In a real sense, religious leaders have always claimed to be acting according to scripture. But religious fundamentalism in the twentieth century has evolved partly from the challenges of secularization. Re-

ligious fundamentalists have also frequently opposed ecumenical tendencies. Although fundamentalists have usually been a small percentage of a larger religious community, their skill at political organizing has given some of them significant influence.

WHITHER INTEGRATION?

One of the justifications of studying history is that we can learn from experience and thereby shape our futures more effectively. It is fitting, therefore, to conclude this book with an attempt to predict what the future will bring. With a mixed picture about current prospects for global integration, such a projection is challenging.

Despite protectionist tendencies in many if not most nations, the benefits of continued economic integration have become most compelling. With the signing of GATT II and NAFTA, powerful constituencies favoring opening trade have been encouraged. More international agreements will be negotiated and implemented. Perhaps some kind of agreement between the EEC and NAFTA will be proposed. Certainly, some form of NAFTA will bind the Americas early in the twenty-first century. At the same time, the close enmeshing of national markets will mean that serious trade disruptions would have a rippling effect through many countries' business and consumer sectors. Integration will make it more difficult for protectionists to implement trade-restricting policies. Global pressures to adopt environmentally friendly economic policies should increase tensions in the twenty-first century, as Third World countries continue to pursue national self-interest.

Just as the economic integration of Germany paved the way for its political integration, global economic integration will facilitate more political cooperation and decision making on an international level. Regional political associations might perhaps have a better chance of developing political unions. EEC countries, for example, have already used their close economic ties to begin developing common political institutions, a European Parliament. The United Nations will continue to be forceful when its interests coincide with those of powerful countries. At times, however, one or more strong countries will continue to thwart UN efforts in international disputes.

Religious tendencies will continue to run counter to integrative trends. Although limited attempts at religious ecumenism will continue, the pervasive direction will be toward maintaining sectarian differences. Religious bureaucracies will be very reluctant to share power with religious leaders from other sects. Furthermore, when religion becomes a part of the nationalist ideology, a powerful fundamentalist political force emerges, thwarting religious and political integration.

SUMMARY

1. Economic integration has been a general trend since 1500. The Industrial Revolution became the driving force behind global economic growth and closer economic ties. In the nineteenth and twentieth centuries, standardization became a major consequence of economic integration as first the British pound and then the U.S. dollar became the preferred international currencies. The metric system gradually became the accepted format for weights and measures, and English became the language of science, diplomacy, and air-traffic control.

2. The development of the noncapitalist Soviet bloc and China undermined global economic integration for most of the twentieth century, but the breakup of that autonomous system has meant better economic integration.

3. Economic integration has also meant that environmental problems can stretch beyond a country's borders. Massive deforestation of North America and Indonesia has occurred, while mining, agriculture, and housing construction have reduced forests around the world. Acid rain generated in the United States has harmed Canada's forests and lakes, and unrestricted use of chlorofluorocarbons has reduced the ozone layer's screening of ultraviolet radiation, increasing health problems such as skin cancer.

4. Tensions between internationalism and nationalism have developed in the modern era. International ideologies such as Marxism have focused on class rather than on the nation. International and regional cooperative unions, such as the United Nations, the Organization of American States, the Arab League, and the Organization of African Unity, have formed to promote discussion and solution of common problems.

5. Religious integration has been spotty at best. Although Christian and Islamic missionaries have actively spread their faiths, sectarian disputes sapped both religions. Religious fundamentalism has tended to highlight differences rather than commonalities among religions, and fundamentalists have become powerful by organizing political interest groups.

SUGGESTED READINGS

Franck, Thomas. *Nation against Nation*. Oxford, Eng.: Oxford University Press, 1985. A history of the United Nations, focusing on its relations with the United States.

Kaplan, Lawrence, ed. *Fundamentalism in Comparative Perspective*. Amherst: University of Massachusetts Press, 1992. Essays about Christian, Islamic, and Jewish fundamentalism.

Schama, Simon. *Landscape and Memory*. New York: Knopf, 1995. An analysis of nature in history, providing a historical context for environmental concerns in the late twentieth century.

Weston, Anthony. *Back to Earth*. Philadelphia: Temple University Press, 1994. A reassessment of the environmental movement and its future role in political movements.

Glossary of Terms

A

absolutism   a system in which monarchs aim to achieve total control through a bureaucracy that is centralized along military lines

abstract expressionism   one of the most influential of fine-art painting styles in the twentieth century, characterized by an attempt to abandon previous artistic conventions and to emphasize the spontaneous, personal, free, unstudied, and intuitive aspects of art

acropolis   a high area in early Greek cities that served as a gathering place for safety against raids

action painting   a twentieth-century school of painting within abstract expressionism that was pioneered by Jackson Pollock; it emphasized the artistic process and featured intersecting slashes of paint across the canvas

African diaspora   the enforced dispersal of Africans during the slave trade

Afrocentrism   the view that Africa is the primary location of important cultural innovations that subsequently spread into Western civilization and were adopted around the world

agora   a central market area in early Greek cities

agricultural-industrial slaves   slaves who provide hard labor for commercial activities

ahimsa   the Jain doctrine of causing no harm to any living soul

alchemy   the field of endeavor dedicated to transmuting baser metals into gold

Allah   the Islamic deity

Allies   one of the two main blocs of united world powers that fought in World War II; it was composed of Britain, the Soviet Union, China, the United States, and Canada, as well as smaller countries

alloying   the mixing of metals to produce a metal with characteristics different from those of any of its components

alphabetic writing   writing that uses a limited number of symbols to represent the component sounds of a language

American exchange   the process by which a variety of species, ideas, and technology that were previously isolated in one hemisphere passed between the Americas and the Old World

Ancient Style   a form of prose that developed during the later Tang Empire of China (763–907) that required essays to be clear and simple

animism   the worship of deities thought to reside in natural forces and objects such as rivers, trees, and mountains

annealing   heating and gradually cooling a metal to reduce internal stresses and make it harder and more durable

anthropomorphism   the practice of attributing human characteristics, such as physique or temperament, to deities or other nonhuman entities

apartheid   a legal system of racial segregation and discrimination enforced by a minority government; between 1948 and 1991 it was legal in South Africa, where it was enforced by a white minority government upon the black majority

Apedemak (ah PEH deh mak)   the local Nubian lion god

applied mathematics   the mathematical study of measurement and prediction, used to solve real-world problems

aqueduct   an artificial channel that carries drinking water

archaeology   the study of the human past, primarily through material remains

archons (AWR kahnz)   officials who ran the day-to-day government in early Athens

Areopagite Council (air ee OH pah gyt)   a group of aristocrats who governed ancient Athens

asiento (ah see EHN toh)   a subcontract that permitted a foreign trader to sell slaves in Spanish lands at fixed prices that were usually quite favorable to the trader

assembly line   an American innovation, refined by Henry Ford in his automobile plant, that consisted of a conveyor system with workers standing along it, arranged in the order in which their tasks were to be performed

associative bond   one of the two conditions asserted by the sociologist Max Weber under which a group of people might voluntarily band together, in this case for the mutual benefit of resisting some outside force. See also **communal bond**

astrology   the prediction of the future on the basis of the alignments of stars and planets

Atlantic slave trade   trade that carried slaves from Africa to Europe and the Americas via the Atlantic Ocean

avatar   an incarnation of a Hindu god

Axis   one of the two main blocs of united world powers that fought in World War II; it consisted mainly of Germany, Japan, and Italy

ayllu (EYE yoo)   a cabinet of advisors appointed by the ruler of the Inca Empire

B

ballistics   the branch of mathematics and physics that deals with the propulsion of projectiles

band   a group of around 30 to 200 people living together with little or no formal government; a band derives food from hunting, fishing, and the gathering of plant foods

Bantu expansion   the spread of Bantu speakers, with their distinctive artifacts, iron technology, language, and culture, throughout most of sub-Saharan Africa

barter   the trading of one item for another

Bering Land Bridge a stretch of dry land that once connected North America and Asia, allowing people to migrate by foot to the Americas

bias factors that affect one's ability to observe and understand

biological evolution the concept, advocated by Charles Darwin in *On the Origin of Species*, that one species of plant or animal can (and did) change into another over long periods of time

bipartite universe the universe of the Hopis, who believe in two independent, similar worlds—one for the living Hopi and one for the spirits

blitzkrieg literally translated as "lightning war," the term used for the German combination of air strikes and rapidly moving army ground vehicles during World War II

block printing the carving and inking of a page of text onto a wooden surface in order to reproduce many copies

bloom a rocky mass of impure iron formed by smelting iron ore

blues a form of African-inspired music that developed in the American South; it is characterized by distinctive rhythms, repetitive structure, and melody lines that generally descend from initial high notes

Bo a vassal group in Zhou China that ruled small territories

Bolsheviks Marxist supporters of Vladimir Lenin in early-twentieth-century Russia

bomb a fully enclosed vessel filled with gunpowder and ignited with a slow fuse

bourgeoisie (boor zhwah ZEE) wealthy investors and their middle-class allies

brahmans the caste of Aryan priests in ancient India

broadcast to send out a message widely to be received by anyone with the proper receiving device, such as a radio

buccaneers pirates who raided Spanish treasure ships that were carrying gold and silver back to Spain from the Caribbean

Buddha Prince Siddhartha Gautama, who lived in imperial India from around 563 to 480 B.C. and who is believed by Buddhists to be "the enlightened one"

bureaucracy a hierarchy in which officials represent the state and its ruler in many interactions

bushido a code of behavior for Japanese *samurai* that required self-denial, indifference to adversity, and generosity to the less fortunate

C

cadres officials and activists under party direction in the People's Republic of China

calendar system a system of dates and years that is based on astronomy

caliph an Islamic political and religious leader

call-and-response pattern a song pattern, common to West Africa and the American South, in which a leader calls a line and a chorus responds with the same or a similar line

calpulli (kahl POO lee) the residential district of Aztec commoners, in which land was held at least partly in common; also the people who live in such a district

canal system a network of interconnecting artificial waterways linking many places

canon law church laws regulated by church officials in Christianity

capitalism an economic system wherein ownership is private and individuals compete to increase their wealth, mostly unimpeded by government restriction

caravanserais inns where merchants could recover from arduous journeys along trade routes in Dar al-Islam

cartel a group, producing a significant percentage of a material, that cooperates to fix production levels and prices and dominates international distribution of the material

cast iron molded and somewhat refined iron that remains brittle and soft

caste a hierarchical system of social categories in India that determines one's status, occupation, rights, and duties

casting producing shaped objects by melting metal and pouring it into a mold, where it hardens

catastrophism a school of thought that sees the geological past as shaped primarily by major events such as earthquakes and floods

central places places where people from surrounding communities go to procure goods and services unavailable in smaller settlements

century an ancient Etruscan and Roman military organization, consisting of 100 soldiers

ceremonial center a place with little or no permanent population that is reserved for religious activities

chattel slavery a system in which a slave is considered to have no more value than any other object and in which his or her humanity and personal rights are denied

Cheka a police force with hundreds of thousands of members that protected the Bolshevik state and, in 1918, undertook responsibilities that included guarding the *gulags* and frontiers and implementing a policy of state terror

chiefdom a group of around 1,000 to 10,000 people organized under a leader with true coercive power and having several layers of wealth, authority, and prestige, often with named classes and many different occupations

chinampas Aztec fields, formed by dredging nutrient-rich mud from lake bottoms and piling it in shallow water

chivalry a code of behavior for European feudal knights that encouraged honesty, courtesy, and the defense of the defenseless

cipher a method for making the meaning of a message unintelligible to an enemy or outsider by scrambling the letters so that only someone who knows the rules of manipulation can reconstruct the message

circuses large arenas for races and major sporting events in the Roman Empire

city-state an urban system, including a city and its surrounding supportive villages and farms, that is united under a single government

civet a musky substance, derived from the civet cat and used in perfumes

civilization the final stage of cultural evolution, characterized by dependence upon agriculture, long-distance trade, state government, occupational specialization, urbanism, and class stratification

class a segment of society with a distinctive level of wealth, prestige, and power

class stratification the condition under which members of a society have differential access to resources and power

client governments local administrations that carried out the wishes of imperialistic governments

closed slavery a system of slavery that maintains a slave in that status for life

coca the plant from which cocaine is extracted; it grows abundantly in the Andes

code a method for making the meaning of a message unintelligible to an enemy by substituting certain symbols for others

codex (plural: **codices**) a handwritten book; the term is usually reserved for Mesoamerican, Islamic, and European examples

cola nut a nut, indigenous to sub-Saharan Africa, that can be chewed before a meal to stimulate appetite and digestion, or ground into a powder and used as a condiment

Cold War the intense and multifaceted rivalry that threatened to become an actual war between the United States and the Soviet Union from 1945 to 1991; key elements of the Cold War included sharp ideological differences, an arms race, economic competition, and the formation of power blocs

colonialism the process of establishing colonies, administering them, and extracting their wealth for the home country

colossal heads large Olmec sculptures probably representing rulers

comitatus (koh mee TAH toos) a Germanic friendship structure that compelled kings to rule in consultation with their warriors; warriors owed advice, political support, and military allegiance to their kings

commandery a large administrative district of the Qin Empire

communal bond a condition asserted by the sociologist Max Weber under which a group of people might voluntarily band together, in this case for the desire to be with others who share beliefs, values, and customs. See also **associative bond**

commune a model of economic organization in Mao Zedong's rural China that involved merging many cooperatives

communication the movement of messages from one place to another

communism a political system that aims to serve the people without supporting class domination

confederation a permanent union of equal states that cooperate for their common welfare

Confucianism the most significant philosophy in Chinese history; founded by Confucius (551–479 B.C.), it stressed a human-centered, moral-based life

consul a military leader in ancient Rome who held the power to command the troops and to execute the law

Contemplative Daoism the most mystical and anarchistic philosophy of China's Classical Age, asserting that the best government is no government and the best social conventions are no social conventions

corporatism an element of national socialism involving the practice of combining owners, managers, and workers in a unitary whole within a business, factory, or industrial sector

corvée **labor** the practice of requiring healthy men to contribute their labor for about one month out of every year for the good of the state

cottage crafts the collective term for small-scale, home-based businesses run by independent artisans

covenant a contractual agreement between a people and their deity whereby the deity agrees to bless and protect the people in return for worship and devotion

Creoles the Spanish elite in nineteenth-century Central and South America

cultural evolution the idea that there is a general tendency over time for cultures to become more complex

cultural relativism a concept developed by Franz Boas that all cultures should be viewed as equal in sophistication and value

culture the learned behavior and values that characterize each human group

cuneiform (koo NAY ih form) an ideographic system of writing with some alphabetic (or syllabic) elements that developed in Sumeria around 4500 B.C.

cyclical time a conception of time in which a sequence of stages is seen as repeating forever

Cynicism a philosophy, popular in ancient Greece, that called for a return to the simple life of the early Greek city-state; its followers idealized the life of poverty, wearing rags and eating only what was given to them

D

daimyo (DY mee yoh) a Japanese territorial lord who was a retainer of a *shogun* in feudal Japan

Dao (DOW) in Daoist philosophy, the path or the way; metaphorically, the origin of all things

Dar al-Islam the Islamic territory during the height of Islamic expansion, culturally connecting Asia, Africa, and Europe

deffufa (duh FOO fuh) a massive mudbrick tower near the city of Kerma in central Nubia that was used for storing goods

deflation a steep drop in prices and wages

Deism a belief system that gained a following during the Scientific Revolution; it asserted that the universe functioned like a machine that ran by natural laws, and consequently its maker, God, had nothing left to do

Delian League   a coalition formed in Greece following the Persian Wars in order to provide for the common defense and the liberation of any Greeks who remained under Persian control

democracy   a political system that places government in the hands of all its citizens or their elected representatives

demography   the study of population and its changes in size, composition, and movements

depression   an economic downturn involving long-term production drops, widespread unemployment, and deflation

descriptive model   a model that focuses on how a process operates

detente   the easing of international tensions through good-will gestures and negotiated arms-limitation treaties that was developed by the Soviet leader Leonid Brezhnev and the American leader Richard Nixon in the 1970s

dharma (DAHR mah)   the Buddhist concept of cosmic law, truth, and proper living through ethical conduct and social responsibility

diaspora (dy AS poh ruh)   the forced migration and dispersion of a people

differentiation   as applied to government, the idea that each governmental bureau must concern itself with a single function

Directory   a group of five men who ran the executive branch of the French government and ruled the nation in conjunction with the legislature from 1795 to 1799

disease reservoir   a population of animals that can contract a human disease and harbor the germs that cause the disease

domestic slaves   slaves who perform household duties

dynastic succession   a succession of rulers from the same family

E

economic revolution   a transformation of a country's economic structure

economic trade   trade conducted in order to obtain an otherwise unavailable item

Eightfold Path   the Buddhist concept for the correct path that one must follow in order to eliminate desire and suffering; it includes correct views, aspirations, speech, conduct, livelihood, effort, mindfulness, and meditation

elite culture   the cultural elements distinctive to the upper classes

elite revolution   a revolution implemented by the ruling upper classes

empire   a state that controls a large area that encompasses societies culturally different from itself; also, a group of states or territories that is ruled by a single power

encephalization index   a measure of the average brain size for a species, adjusted for its body size

enclave   a distinct area of a city in which a segregated population group lives

enclosure   the conversion of low-yield farming areas into pasturage for livestock in England

encomienda (ehn koh mee EHN duh)   the institution that required American Indians to work for the Spanish colonists without compensation

Enigma machine   a machine that automatically produced a complex cipher of any message that was typed into it; it was used by the Germans in World War II

Enlightenment   an intellectual movement that championed the centrality of human reason and inspired eighteenth-century thinkers in Europe and North America

entrepôt (ahn truh POH)   a colonial commercial center that served simultaneously as a collection center for goods to be shipped to the home country and as a distribution center for goods coming from the home country

Epicureanism   a Greek philosophy of the fourth century B.C. that was based on the belief that the senses are the foundation for all knowledge

estates   groups of elite and other commoners who formed the assembly of the *riksdag*, which consulted with the king in seventeenth-century Sweden

ethnic group   a self-identified group or "tribe" of people that has in common a culture and, sometimes, a language

ethnocentrism   the belief that one's own ideas, values, culture, and cherished behavior patterns are socially, morally, or religiously correct and superior to others

eunuch   a castrated human male

Eve hypothesis   the theory that all human beings evolved from a single female ancestor in the last 100,000 years

ever-normal granary system   a system of the Qin-Han Empire of China whereby the government collected grain from various regions of the empire into warehouses and redistributed it to the people as required

evolution   the concept that each species developed by modification from an earlier species

exchange   any process by which goods flow between people; also a period of transmission of ideas, species, and technology

existentialism   a philosophical movement linked to such thinkers as Jean-Paul Sartre that posits that the greatest problem facing anyone is existence itself; it attained its greatest appeal in post–World War II France

explanatory model   a model that focuses on the motivations or underlying causes of a process

F

fact   a description of an event or action that is generally agreed to be true on the basis of present evidence

faunal succession   a method for dating a deposit by dating the fossil within it

female infanticide   the killing of female infants, a practice that usually increases during hard times

feudalism   a decentralized sociopolitical structure in which a weak monarchy attempts to control the lands of the realm through reciprocal agreements with regional leaders

feudalization of the church   the process, in medieval Europe, through which church lands fell into the hands of kings and great lords, who then made vassals of bishops and granted properties to the church

fief   a gift of land awarded to a regional leader by the king, who in return received an oath of loyalty and military support

field painting   a school of painting within abstract expressionism that was pioneered by Willem de Kooning and used featureless and often overlapping masses of color

filial piety   honor to one's parents; a vital part of Confucius's teachings

filioque clause   a particular clause ("and the Son") in the Christian Nicean Creed that contributed to serious disagreement between the Roman Catholic Church and the Eastern Orthodox Church

le film noir (luh feelm nwahr)   literally, "the dark film"; a film genre that was developed in France in the 1950s and focused on the dark, pessimistic, and gloomy side of life

fine arts   the elite wing of the arts, produced by highly trained artists

firepot   a potlike weapon filled with gunpowder, stones, and darts, which was used in fourteenth-century Europe

First World   the U.S. economic and political bloc of allied nations during the Cold War

flare weapon   a tube that projected a flash of gunpowder and was first used in China in the tenth century

folk arts   those arts that are typically perpetuated by amateur artists; have long, unchanging traditions; and are transmitted in informal settings, such as from a parent to a child

folk culture   the cultural elements embraced by the lower classes

Folk Islam   the religious practices of ordinary Muslims, connected with the collapse of the Abbasid Caliphate in the thirteenth century

fossils   the remains of ancient plants and animals

Four Noble Truths   the basis of Buddhism, stating that (1) life is suffering; (2) suffering has a cause; (3) the cause is desire; (4) desire and suffering may be eliminated by following the correct path

Free French   an exiled government, founded by a group of French who were antagonistic to the Germans during World War II

free verse   poetry that self-consciously avoids the traditional conventions of meter, rhyme, and structure; it was pioneered by the American poet Walt Whitman in the nineteenth century

full-rigged ship   a ship with multiple sails set in various positions, allowing the vessel to take advantage of diverse wind conditions

fundamentalism   the religious belief that posits strict adherence to practices supported by a literal interpretation of sacred texts

fusion   the incorporation of ideas from various ethnic and national traditions into art

G

Ge'ez (GHEE ehz)   the script used to write the language of Axum

genocide   the mass killing of individuals in a deliberate attempt to extinguish a racial, ethnic, or religious group

gentleman   the ideal Confucian type; a person of noble character who treats others humanely, helps the weak and the poor, reviews and criticizes his own actions daily, and radiates moral force

gentry   a new elite social class formed in England during the Renaissance; it was not officially noble, yet was higher than the middle class and usually associated with rural property

genus   a taxonomical category of moderately to closely related species

geography   the study of the ways in which people have used the planet's land and resources

ghetto   originally, the Jewish section of an Italian city; any segregated enclave in cities around the world

glasnost   policies of openness and discussion implemented in the Soviet Union by Mikhail Gorbachev in the 1980s

great art style   an art style that occurs over a broad geographic area and is the dominant and often the only style within a culture, other than family-based folk art

green revolution   technological advances in agriculture, such as drought-resistant crops, new fertilizers, and pesticides, that doubled or even tripled the agricultural output of a community and decreased hunger in the Third World during the post–World War II era

green withy smelting   the process employed in pre-Roman Britain of making steel by adding fresh twigs to molten iron shortly before pouring it out

greenhouse effect   the concentration of carbon dioxide in the upper atmosphere that traps heat from the sun, leading to global warming, which some scientists have warned is a serious environmental problem

guild system   a hierarchical organization of merchants and artisans that regulated production of goods and worked for the common political, economic, and social interests of its members

gulags (GOO lahgs)   labor camps in Siberia and northern Russia beginning in the Bolshevik Revolution

Gung   blood relatives of the ruling house in Zhou China

H

hagiography (HAW jee AHG ruh fee, *or* HAY gee AHG ruh fee)   in Christianity, the laudatory biography of a saint

hajj   the pilgrimage made by Muslims to Mecca

harem   a place of confinement for elite Muslim women, where all adult males except for the head of the household are forbidden to enter

Hellenes   the Greek name for the Greeks, from about the seventh century B.C.

Hellenization   the spread of Greek culture

helots   war prisoners of ancient Sparta who were farmers, were restricted in their rights, and were constantly guarded by Spartan soldiers

hereditary slavery   a system of slavery under which children of slaves are also slaves

hijra (HEEJ rah)   the migration of Muhammad and his followers from Mecca to Medina in 622

history   the study of the human past, primarily through the interpretation of documents

holocaust   mass extermination of a people viewed as inferior

hominid   any member of the family of animals that includes human beings

hoplite   a citizen-soldier in ancient Greece

Huguenots   French Calvinists beginning in the sixteenth century

humanism   a system of thought based on the study of human ideas and actions

humoral medicine   the philosophy that bodily substances have inherent qualities that must be balanced in order to maintain health

I

icon   a representation of a holy person

iconoclast   one who destroys holy images

iconophile   one who venerates holy images

Ideals   Plato's changeless, eternal, and nonmaterial forms in the mind of the Platonic god

ideograph   a hieroglyph representing an entire word or complex idea

ideographic writing   a form of writing in which each symbol represents an idea, irrespective of the pronunciation of the spoken word

ideology   the complex of ideas and philosophy that directs one's goals, expectations, and actions

immortal   the ideal type in Contemplative Daoism; an entity that lives in the mountains, possesses magical attributes, subsists on simple foods, drinks dew from plants, is able to fly, and cannot be destroyed

imperial   referring to an empire

imperialism   the process of forming, extending, or maintaining an empire; an economic and political colonial system of an industrial country needing raw materials and markets

import substitution   the practice of relying on local businesses to fill the gaps left by the withdrawal of foreign imports

Inca   the ruler of the Empire of Tawantinsuyu; also commonly used to describe the empire itself or its people

indenture   a temporary position entered into voluntarily by impoverished individuals who transfer the rights to their labor to someone else for a specified term in exchange for transportation, lodging, monies, or other necessities

Indian Ocean slave trade   the trade in slaves that passed through the coastal East African cities and northward, particularly to Southwest Asia

indulgences   cancellation of punishments for committed sins; the sale of indulgences in Roman Catholicism was one of the abuses that led to the Protestant Reformation

Industrial Revolution   the shift to the manufacture of most goods through mechanized factories and the changes that came in the wake of this shift; it originated in eighteenth-century England

inflation   a pattern of sharply rising prices and wages

inquisition   originally, an inquiry into what was being taught or preached by lay preachers in medieval Christianity; later, the inquiry by a designated church official into whether anyone held "correct" beliefs

intellectual class   the social class that lives by the exchange of ideas

intellectual revolution   a transformation of how human beings think about themselves and the universe around them

intelligence   the ability to learn, reason, and create; one of the characteristics of human beings

intendants   royal representatives of Louis XIII of France who were appointed by Cardinal Richelieu to correct local abuses and extend state reach into distant regions

interpretation   an inference that is consistent with the facts and extends knowledge beyond them by the use of logic, analogy, or some other method of reasoning

intrinsic growth   the increase in population as a result of families' having more than two children who survive to adulthood and become parents

investiture   the medieval European procedure whereby lords awarded land grants and symbols of secular and holy office

irrigation   the practice of bringing water to agricultural fields through canals or similar devices

J

Jacobins   a European political group during the Enlightenment who wanted the broadest male voting franchise, abolition of the monarchy, and price controls

Jacquard loom (ZHAHK ahr)   a device, invented by Joseph Jacquard in eighteenth-century France, that could be fitted onto any existing loom, accelerating the process of weaving patterned cloth

Janissaries   warriors of European extraction who composed the elite Ottoman military force

jati   a social classification system of India's imperial age, in which an individual's social status was defined by birth and ritual position, which included one's job

jazz a polished, innovative, and orchestrated outgrowth of blues that developed in American cities and used the whole range of instruments of the popular dance orchestras of the day, especially horns and winds

jidai-geki (JEE dy GEHK ee) the film versions of the historic Japanese dramas, set in periods before the Meiji industrialization and Westernization of Japan and often depicting *samurai* attempting to complete virtuous tasks

jihad (jee HAHD) an Islamic holy war; a holy struggle by the Islamic Ottoman Turks against their Christian or Muslim enemies

Junkers the landed nobility of East Prussia

K

k-selection the reproductive pattern practiced by animals that have few young and invest a great deal of care in each one

kachinas inhabitants of the Hopi spirit world

kami (kah MEE) an early Japanese local deity, usually associated with fertility

kamikaze Japanese suicide bombers who sank and damaged some Allied ships by crashing into them during World War II

karma the Buddhist belief that the residue of a person's actions attaches to the person's soul

kimono (KEE moh noh) a robe-like Japanese outer garment

kivas (KEE vuhz) underground rooms where Hopi men conduct private ceremonies of ritual devotion to the spirits in order to ensure rainfall

kraal a government capital in southern and southwestern Africa

kshatriyas (kuh SHAH tree ahs) the caste of warriors in ancient India

kulaks (KOO lahks) originally, wealthy Russian peasants; eventually, anyone opposing collectivization during Stalinist rule

L

lactose intolerance the genetic inability to digest the sugar (lactose) in milk

laissez-faire (LEH say FAYR) minimal governmental interference in economic development

lateen sail a sail from the eastern Mediterranean that was adapted by the Portuguese; its slanted mast made it possible to sail almost against the wind

leaching the movement of chemicals through soils, caused by water runoffs

Legalists philosophers and bureaucrats in Warring States China who believed that government must be powerful both militarily and economically

li a code of honorable or righteous behavior for Chinese feudal warriors

liege the lord, usually the king, with the greatest feudal claim on a vassal in the European feudal system, which allowed a vassal to serve many lords

lifeways typical behaviors for a society

linear time a conception of time in which time passes inexorably forward with no repetition of cycles

load a measure of a transportation mode's utility that measures the weight of the cargo that can be transported

lock a mechanism invented in the fourteenth century for holding water in different parts of a canal at different elevations and moving a vessel from one elevation to another

logic the methodology of using systematic reasoning to discover truth

long ship a long, narrow ship of the Classical Greek period; such ships were fast but unstable

lords of the land Southwest African men who simultaneously were leaders of their kinship groups and priests who dealt with spirits that inhabited various spots in their lineage territories

lugal a war leader elected during periods of emergency in ancient Sumeria

M

magic the supposed manipulation of the physical world through practices that have a spiritual or mystical connection, rather than a physical one

Magna Carta a charter signed by King John of England in 1215 that reiterated traditional English aristocratic rights, one being to participate in the rule of England

Mahabharata (mah hah BAH rah tah) the world's longest poem and one of the epic works of Indian civilization

maharaja a great ruler in India

Mandate of Heaven an idea begun in ancient China by Zhou rulers, who argued that the former Shang rulers had lost their legitimacy and that the time for a new regime had come; later it became synonymous with popular support

manifest destiny the nineteenth-century belief, popular among European Americans, that the United States should expand until it controlled the Pacific coast and beyond

manioc a starchy, calorie-rich root crop that is widely grown in Mesoamerica; it is also known by its Spanish name, *yuca*

manorialism a self-sufficient economic system based on a lord's feudal manor with agricultural workers who are often bound to the land

manumission the freeing of a slave

means of production the way that people earn a livelihood

medical revolution the bringing of medical treatments such as immunization to the Third World in the post–World War II era

medreses (MEH dreh sehs) colleges built in cities of the Ottoman Empire

mercantile system a relationship in which a colony provides raw materials for the home country and the home country provides manufactured goods for the colony

Mesoamerica an area in pre-Columbian Mexico and Central America where certain distinctive cultural traits were present: corn-squash-beans agriculture, pyramids as bases for temples, a hieroglyphic writing system, a common calendar, a distinctive ball game, and human sacrifice

metallurgy the set of skills, practices, and knowledge that relate to the working of metals

microprocessor the information-processing heart of a computer, which converts messages into electronic impulses and can store or send these messages

middle class the intermediate socioeconomic class between the elite and commoners, composed of business and professional people in modern societies

Middle Passage the sea voyage in the Atlantic slave trade between Africa and the Americas

migrant workers laborers who travel from place to place to find work

military model of government a centralized political system with a chain of command, emphasizing strict obedience

"missing link" a hypothetical human-ape that could bridge the evolutionary gap between modern human beings and our proposed apelike ancestors

mission a complex (designed for the religious conversion of native peoples) consisting of a church, dormitories, and farm or ranch facilities

missionary a person who purposely sets out to preach, teach, and persuade individuals or groups consciously to accept the belief system or theology of the missionary's religion

model a picture of how or why a general process works

modernity a cluster of changes occurring after about 1500 in western Europe and Japan and by the nineteenth century across much of the world; it was characterized by a focus on progress, the application of science and technology, a secular understanding of the world, wide participation in government, determination of social status according to merit, and increasing economic domination by capitalism or socialism

Monists an influential group of German scientists in the late nineteenth century who expanded the idea of Social Darwinism, maintaining that ethnic groups were distinctive both biologically (racially) and socially and that not all peoples were equally fit

monoethnic state a state whose citizens are mostly from the same ethnic group or tribe

monoculture a practice whereby farmers focus on a single crop

Monophysite a form of Christianity whose adherents believe that Jesus has a single, unitary nature, not the dual natures of man and God that mainstream Christianity claims

monopolies the rights to exclusive legal control of an invention, a device, or trade

monotheism the belief that only one god exists

monumental architecture large and impressive buildings and similar structures erected at public expense

Moors North Africans of mixed Berber and Arab parentage

mosque a Muslim place of worship

multiethnic state a state that incorporates two or more ethnic groups into its citizenry and extends full privileges to them

mural art the painting of pictures on walls

mutation a spontaneous development of a new trait as a result of an error in copying the biochemicals that carry the genetic code during reproduction

N

nagashi an individual who led several clans during the rise of the Axum kingdom in Ethiopia

nahualli (nah HWAHL lee) animal spirits that the Aztecs believed would protect them from evil

national anthem a song that is adopted by a nation as a symbol, used at official occasions, and often protected legally against desecration

national socialism twentieth-century ideology that includes elements of nationalism, socialism, imperialism, and totalitarianism; national socialists, who believed that the nation is holy and harmonious and that all class conflict is evil, desired a powerful nation-state to control the nation's economy and an army in order to expand their ideology by conquest

nationalism an ideology that emphasizes one's social role as a member of a nation, often with a common language, shared historical experiences, and similar cultural traditions

natural selection a biological theory developed by Charles Darwin, which posits that, over time, a species' most adaptive traits are passed on and others are eliminated

navala the essence of the Hopi spirit world, which could migrate to the Hopi world in the form of rain

New Economic Policy economic relaxation measures taken by the Bolsheviks during the peacetime period from 1921 to 1929 to permit economic recovery from the ravages of warfare

New World the area consisting of the Americas and the Pacific islands

nirvana for Buddhists, the state at which existence ceases and the soul no longer needs to be reborn

nkisi (NKEE see) magical preparations used in religious ceremonies in the Kongo kingdom

Noh a Japanese dramatic form that originated in the Ashikaga Shogunate era; actors wearing masks rely upon gestures and voice rather than on facial expression to convey emotion

nomarch the governor of a provincial area in ancient Egypt

nome a provincial area in ancient Egypt

noneconomic trade trade conducted to cement friendships and other ties

Nuclear America the area in the Americas, composed of Mesoamerica and Peru, that first developed complex societies

nzimbu (NZIHM boo)   a type of shell that was the official currency of the kingdom of Kongo

O

oasis   an island of lush vegetation in a desert, usually fed by a spring

obsidian   the delicate volcanic glass required in making the fancy and sharp Mayan tools

occupational specialization   the division of labor into specific jobs

oikos (OY kohs)   the ancient Greek household unit, which consisted of the family, land, slaves or tenants, buildings, and livestock of a single farmer

Old World   the area consisting of Asia, Africa, and Europe

Oldowan tools   tools comprised of a piece of stone with one to five flakes removed to form a sharp edge; these crude and early tools, fashioned by *Homo habilis*, were unearthed in the Olduvai Gorge in Tanzania

oligarchy   rule by a few influential members of the elite

open slavery   a system of slavery that provides realistic ways by which a slave can be freed

optical telegraph   the first practical means of long-distance communication, involving slats of wood mounted atop high buildings and moved by a system of ropes and pulleys

Optimate Party (AHP tih mayt)   the ancient Roman traditionalists who supported aristocratic control through old family alliances and senatorial contacts

oracle bones   bones used in ancient China to predict the future; the earliest evidence of Chinese writing remains on these bones

oral accounts   stories and descriptions of the past preserved by word of mouth

ore   compounds in which a metal is chemically bonded to other elements

Orgburo   the organization bureau that handled administrative matters concerning the state apparatus during the Bolshevik Revolution

"out-of-Africa" theory   the argument that the evolution to modern *Homo sapiens* took place only once and in Africa; from there, according to this view, modern people spread to the rest of the world, outcompeting earlier local hominids, who became extinct

outcaste   the lowest hereditary social group in India, which performed polluting tasks, such as waste removal

P

paddy-field method   a very productive method for growing rice that was perfected in the Chinese Song era; wet-field rice was cultivated through the use of dams, irrigation ditches, sluice-gates, and the treadle water-pump

Paleo-Indians   the earliest native Americans

paleomagnetic dating   a method for dating fossils by reading their preserved magnetic fields and comparing them with known magnetic fields at different dates

pan-Germanism   an ideology favoring unity among German-speaking peoples of all nations

pan-tribalism   the merging of various tribes into a single interest group

pantheism   the belief that divinity is present in all creation

papal monarchy   the central administrative bureaucracy of the Roman Catholic Church that rivaled those of European kings in the period from roughly the end of the eleventh to the end of the thirteenth century

Parthenon   the temple of Athena in ancient Athens

Party Secretariat   the office that dealt with organizational issues relating to the Bolshevik Party

pastoralism   the herding of domesticated animals

patriarch   a bishop of one of five particularly important Christian cities (Jerusalem, Antioch, Alexandria, Rome, and Constantinople)

patricians   the wealthy class in early Rome

patron deity   a particular god or goddess believed to protect a city and to be superior to all other deities

pax Romana   the long period of peace during Augustus's reign from 31 B.C. to A.D. 14

peasant   a farmer who works lands owned by the family or a landlord

pellagra   a deficiency disease resulting from a lack of niacin

perestroika   the policy of restructuring implemented in the Soviet Union by Mikhail Gorbachev in the 1980s

period   a span of time, defined by scholars for convenience, during which conditions, events, and lifeways remained more or less similar and were distinctive from those of preceding and succeeding periods

periodic table   Dmitri Mendeleyev's table of elements arranged in order of their relative weights and with groupings possessing similar characteristics

Peru   a cultural area in pre-Columbian South America consisting of the highland and coastal portions of modern Peru, as well as the adjacent highland and coastal areas of Ecuador, Bolivia, and Chile

phalanx (FAY langks)   a block of infantry soldiers in ancient Greece consisting of as many as 100 men lined up in rows as many as eight deep

pharoah (FAIR oh)   an ancient Egyptian king who embodied all authority and was believed to be god incarnate

philosophy   the pursuit of wisdom or knowledge

phrenology   a now-discredited field of science adopted by the Monists that purported to relate physical characteristics to intellectual and moral worth

phylloxera (fih LOK seh ruh)   an aphid from the Mississippi Valley of North America; it subsists by sucking plant juices from roots and devastated French wine grapes in the nineteenth century

physical remains   material items that are left behind by past peoples and preserved

Pietism   a small Protestant sect that was sanctioned by the Prussian state and emphasized direct religious experience, personal conversion, and rebirth

plating the production of a thin layer of one metal on another; usually a less valuable metal is plated with a precious one

plaza a flat open area between buildings

plebeians the commoner class in early Rome

pochteca (pohch TEH kuh) Aztec merchants who also served as diplomats and spies

pogrom an official riot in which bureaucrats led and incited mobs to persecute Jews in Europe

polis (plural: **poleis**, POH lee ihs) an early Greek city-state

Politburo the political bureau that became the command center of the Bolshevik Party in Soviet Russia

political revolution a revolution that changes mainly the political structure of a country

polity a state government

poll tax a fee imposed on each voter and sometimes implemented as a strategy to prevent certain impoverished minority groups from voting

polytheism the worship of many gods

pontifex maximus the chief priest in the ancient Roman government

popular arts the forms of art that are typically perpetuated by professionals, are subject to fads, and receive wide distribution to large numbers of people

Populares Party (pahp yoo LAHR ehs) a political party in ancient Rome that manipulated the citizens' votes in exchange for reforms and handouts

populist revolution a revolution implemented by the common people's seizure of power

potassium-argon dating a method for dating a rock by measuring the amount of argon in it

praying towns in colonial New England, Calvinist communities where local Indians could come to learn the Calvinist religion as well as European skills and ways of life

predestination the idea that God preelects those who will receive salvation; a cornerstone of Calvinist theology

prepared piano a term coined by the composer John Cage to describe the process in which a pianist was instructed to place various articles among the strings of the piano, resulting in largely unpredictable buzzing, clunking, and whirring sounds during a performance

primary source a document that was written by a participant in or an eyewitness to the event, activity, or process being described or analyzed

primates the order of animals that includes human beings, apes (such as gorillas, chimpanzees, and orangutans), and monkeys

principate system an imperial monarchy in Rome that was established by Caesar Augustus and was based on traditional titles and offices

progressivism the idea that things are getting better and better and that change is likely to bring improvement

projection a systematic mathematical transformation that provides rules for drawing a two-dimensional map from three-dimensional data

proletariat factory workers

prophet a person believed to have been called by a deity to act as its representative

proselytizing the activity of preaching to, teaching, and persuading individuals or groups to accept a particular belief system or theology

protectionism the practice of sheltering local industries and businesses from international competition; it has characterized national economic policies for much of the modern era

Protestant Reformation a period of religious protest that began in 1521 and resulted in the fragmentation of the Roman Catholic Church and the creation of Protestant sects

pueblo a multiroomed masonry house in Hopi culture that sometimes reaches two or three stories high

purchase trade that uses currency

pure mathematics the abstract study of numbers, logic, and spatial forms

Purposive Daoism a philosophy of China's Classical Age, favoring minimal social regulation, limited government, and patience in personal relationships

Q

quinoa (KEE nwuh) a grain from the amaranth plant that was an important part of the ancient Peruvian diet

Qur'an (KOOR ahn) the holy book of Islam

R

radiocarbon dating a method for dating materials that were once alive by measuring the amount of radioactive carbon within them

raffia a fabric made of palm fiber that was manufactured in the kingdom of Kongo and elsewhere

raja a common term for the monarch in Indian history

Ramayana (RAH mah yah nah) an epic poem from ancient Indian civilization

Rastafarianism the sociopolitical wing of reggae, and a movement dedicated to revitalizing pride in African heritage among Jamaicans and to achieving racial equality

rationalism the philosophy that maintains that reason is the only valid basis for determining actions or opinions

rebellion an uprising by people who seek to change the leaders rather than the political structure of a country

reciprocity with the spirits mutual obligation between the human Hopi world and the spirit world

reggae (RAY gay) a form of Afro-Caribbean music developed by Jamaicans in the 1960s that is heavily influenced by American blues and rock and roll, with a distinctive rhythm that emphasizes the second beat of a measure

regimentation in Sweden, an emphasis on discipline and obedience in government and life

reincarnation   the belief that people have past and future lives

Renaissance   an era of artistic, sociopolitical, and economic change that occurred in Europe from around 1350 to around 1600; it was characterized by an interest in Classical Greco-Roman forms

revolution   a process of rapid and fundamental structural change

rhetoric   the art of argument

rhythm and blues   an electrified and polished version of the blues (a musical form) that developed after World War II with a revival of interest in the blues

rock and roll   a form of music that developed from rhythm and blues in the 1950s, when it was mostly written and performed by African American entertainers

role   an affiliation and a set of rights and obligations assumed by a person in a particular social context

Roman Catholic Reformation   a reform movement within the Roman Catholic Church that began shortly after the Protestant Reformation

Roman exchange   traditional commercial products, previously unavailable commodities, styles, and ideas that coursed through the Roman Empire and its trading partners in great volumes

Romanization   the emulation of Roman ways

Romanticism   an artistic movement originating in Europe and spreading to the Americas between 1780 and 1900; it emphasized feelings, imagination, and nature and was often employed as a vehicle with which to create a national identity

round ship   a slow, sturdy, spacious ship of the Greek Classical period

S

sacbes (SAWK bayz)   earthen roads raised above the surface of the jungle floor in Mayan civilization

Sahel (sah HEHL)   the semiarid region immediately to the south of the Sahara Desert, site of the great African drought, including parts of Somalia, Ethiopia, the Sudan, Chad, Niger, Nigeria, Mali, Burkina Faso, and Senegal

samanta **system**   a system in seventh-century India that granted semiautonomous rule to recently conquered territories and their rulers

samurai   a professional warrior in feudal Japan; literally, "one who serves"

Sanhedrin (san HEE drihn)   the religious council and highest seat of Jewish justice in Jerusalem until A.D. 90

saqia (SAH kee uh)   an ox-powered waterwheel used to lift water from the Nile to agricultural fields in the Nubian kingdom of Meröe

satrap (SAY trap)   a governor of an ancient Persian province

satrapy   a province in ancient Persia

savanna   a semiarid grassland with occasional trees

schism   a split; often used to refer specifically to a religious split caused by differences of opinion

scholasticism   a medieval philosophy involving the use of reason to develop faith and understanding of the created universe

science   the quest to understand natural phenomena and to learn how and why things work as they do

scientism   the belief that science is the primary, if not sole, reality of human existence; the faith that the world is predictable and that it operates according to rules and principles that can be discovered

Second World   the Soviet economic and political bloc of allied nations during the Cold War

secondary source   a document in which information that has been gathered from primary sources is analyzed and digested, providing an interpretation of the event or process

secularism   an ideology arguing that nonreligious ideas should be the organizational basis for society

sedentary   a term that describes people who live in a single, permanent settlement

segmentary opposition   a widespread African approach to political organization in which each individual, as a member of a series of hierarchic groups based on kinship and village residence, is politically loyal to the largest hierarchic group that can array itself against the antagonist in a conflict

segregation of tasks   a major innovation of the Industrial Revolution whereby workers had only one small task to complete, and that task was repeated over and over again

Senate   a council of ancient Rome that advised the government leaders, over whom it exerted considerable influence

serf   a worker whose labor is owed to someone else, usually a feudal lord, and whose status is inherited by children, but who also retains certain personal rights and is not conceived of as "owned"

service gentry   landlords who joined the army and served in the administration of Ivan the Great of fifteenth-century Russia

shadouf (shah DOOF)   a technology devised in ancient Egypt, consisting of an upright support with a swinging lever that was used to lift buckets of water from irrigation canals

shah   a ruler of Muslim Persia; the leader of the Persian Empire

Shi'a (SHEE ah)   a prominent Islamic sect

Shih   a vassal group in Zhou China that often fought for the higher lords or served as officials

shoen (shoh ehn)   private estates in eighth-century Japan and after

shogun   military dictator of Japan

shogunate   a military overlordship and the dominant governmental structure in feudal Japan

shovel-shaped incisors   front teeth with side edges that curl slightly backward, a genetic trait distinctive to East Asians and American Indians

shudras (SHOO druhs)   the class of menial workers and indigenous peoples in ancient India

sign   a marker that indicates meaning but is not arbitrary

Sikhism (SEEK ihz um)   a monotheistic religion founded in sixteenth-century northern India; it began as an attempt to bridge the religious differences between Islam and Hinduism and was transformed into a religion of resistance to Mughal oppression

single-generation slavery   a system of slavery under which the children of slaves are free

Skepticism   a philosophy popular in ancient Greece that was based on the belief that there is no ultimate pattern by which to order one's life

skraeling (SKRAY lihng)   a Norse word meaning "impoverished one"; it was used to describe the Inuit, whom the Vikings encountered in Vinland

slavery   the ownership and control of other people

smelting   the rendering of ores to derive pure metals from compounds

Social Darwinism   the idea that human society operates by a system of natural selection, whereby individuals and ways of life automatically gravitate to their proper station; the concept was developed by the nineteenth-century English philosopher Herbert Spencer

social history   the study of everyday life in the past

social revolution   a revolution that alters society

social sciences   the disciplines that study human culture and behavior

socialism   a type of economy wherein property of all sorts is held by everyone as a whole

socialist realism   a movement that stressed culture's ties to socialism, and a key element of Josef Stalin's cultural focus

sophists   itinerant paid instructors in ancient Greece whose teaching emphasized advancement in the professions of politics, law, teaching, and playwriting

source analysis   a set of procedures developed by historians to determine whether a particular document is legitimate and accurate

soviets   workers' administrative councils that led the antistate effort during political unrest in Russia in the early twentieth century

Spanish Inquisition   an inquisition that became a formal branch of the government in fifteenth-century Spain

speed   a measure of a transportation mode's utility, based on how fast goods are moved

stages   patterns of cultural characteristics that are common to societies of a similar level of complexity

standardization of parts   a principle of organization in the Industrial Revolution in which all examples of a particular mechanical part had to be the same so that any one of them could fit into its appropriate place

state government   a government with strong leadership, a supporting bureaucracy, and a supportive ideology

steel   a hard and useful metal formed by the chemical bonding of iron and carbon

stela parks   elite Axumite cemeteries with tall stones as markers

stelae (singular: **stela**)   large stones with low-relief carvings on their flat surfaces

steppe   grasslands, particularly in Inner Asia

Stoicism   a Greco-Roman philosophy beginning in the fourth century B.C. that was based on the belief that human happiness grows out of self-control and the performance of duty, rather than from the mere pursuit of pleasure

subinfeudation   the practice of reapportioning regional lands to leaders of smaller areas in a feudal system

subordination   a chain-of-command system

sub-Saharan Africa   the area south of the Sahara Desert

Sudanic-type state   a form of government in West and Central Africa after 700 in which the state was ruled by a divine king who was believed to be descended from the creator god

sultan   an Islamic ruler, outside of Persia; the leader of the Ottoman Empire

sumptuary laws   regulations stating what clothing and ornaments may be worn by members of each social class

survival of the fittest   the concept that individuals with traits that aid in their survival will live long enough to pass those traits on to their offspring, and individuals with undesirable traits will be weeded out because those traits will lead to their deaths before they have the opportunity to pass the traits on to offspring

sutra   a treatise, in poetry or prose, on some issue in Buddhism

suttee (SUH tee)   the Hindu practice of burning widows on the funeral pyres of their husbands

symbol   in linguistics, an arbitrary marker that stands for something else

syncretic   a descriptor applied to a newly formed religion that uses elements of both an earlier, traditional religion and a newly introduced religion

system of correspondences   a complex Hopi system of symbols that relates cardinal directions, colors, types of clouds, ritual items, lightning, plants, animals, and many other things to each other

T

tax farming   the selling of tax-collecting authority by the state

technology   the production of material items; the study of making devices that serve a purpose

tef   a milletlike grain that was domesticated by Ethiopians

terror   the deliberate use of massive force to cow or eliminate opponents; it was used by revolutionists and antirevolutionists in late-eighteenth-century France, among other places

textual criticism   the analysis and authentication of texts

theme (THEHM eh)   in the Byzantine Empire, an area administered by generals exercising both military and civil power

theocracy a form of government that recognizes a deity as the head of the government and a high religious official as the interpreter of that deity's will

Third World the nonindustrialized countries that did not initially support either of the Soviet or U.S. alliances during the Cold War (1945–1991)

tlatoani (tlah toh AH nee) the Aztec emperor

totalitarianism a belief that an all-powerful nation-state should control all aspects of its citizens' lives

trans-Sahara slave trade the trade that brought slaves from sub-Saharan Africa to the Arab Berbers of North Africa

transportation the movement of people or goods from one place to another

trellis theory the argument that modern *Homo sapiens* evolved locally from preexisting *Homo erectus* populations

triangular trade a trading system linking England, West Africa, and the Caribbean, involving sugar, rum, slaves, and manufactured goods

tribe a community with leadership by example, usually consisting of 100 to 2,000 people who have settled in a single, permanent village and get most of their food through the growing of crops

tribunes the representatives of the plebeians, elected after the plebeian boycott in ancient Rome

tribute the rendering of goods to a powerful individual or state by a subordinate

trireme (TRY reem) a long ship of the Greek Classical period with three banks of rowers that could travel fast and steadily

tropical rain forest a dense tangle of low-latitude trees and undergrowth with abundant water

turbine a device consisting of an enclosed drum that was developed in the nineteenth century to harness water power; it replaced the waterwheel and increased the usable energy output of running water by as much as 30 percent

tyranny originally, the usurpation of rule by an individual who has widespread support and is brought into power by citizens in opposition to oppressive oligarchical control in ancient Greece

U

uniformitarianism the idea that the forces at work in nature today are similar to and at a scale comparable to those that operated in the past

Upanishads ancient Sanskrit discourses that speculate about the nature of reality

upright bipedalism the ability to walk on two legs, characteristic of the earliest known hominids and possibly developed in response to the need to carry infants away from danger

urbanism the condition in which the settlement system in a region consists of some relatively large settlements that are internally diverse and that serve as central places

urbanization the development of cities

usury loaning funds out at a particularly high interest rate

V

vaishyas (VAY shee ahs) the caste of commoners in ancient India

varna an Aryan social classification system of India's imperial age

vassal a military retainer of the king in a feudal system; vassals usually took an oath of loyalty to the king in return for control of lands given to them by the king

Vedas (VAY duhs) a series of religious and historical works transmitted orally by the Aryans until they were transcribed around 500 B.C.

verticality the strategy of farming at different elevations in order to grow a variety of crops that thrive in different climates

Vichy France the puppet government that cooperated with the Germans following the fall of France during World War II

Viet Cong a communist-led resistance movement in the south of Vietnam formed in opposition to the noncommunist, U.S.-established government there

Vietminh an organization of Vietnamese communists and nationalists formed in 1941 and headed by Ho Chi Minh, a Vietnamese patriot and communist

voodoo a religion originating in precolonial West Africa and given over primarily to healing; also called *santería*

W

wampum shell beads of different colors that the Iroquois strung together to form pictorial belts

well-field system the manorial system in Zhou China, in which the plots were laid out like a tic-tac-toe schematic (#), resembling the Chinese character for "well"

were-babies a common motif in Olmec art consisting of human babies with fangs and jaguar paws

world religion a religion that has gained significant numbers of adherents across broad geographical expanses; world religions include Judaism, Hinduism, Buddhism, Christianity, and Islam

wrought iron a form of refined iron that is harder and less brittle than cast iron but remains somewhat malleable

Y

yanakuna (yah nah KOO nah) in the Inca Empire, a class of people who were lower than commoners; usually translated as "slaves"

Yasa (YAH sah) a binding legal code promulgated by the Mongol leader Chinggis Khan and derived from Mongol customs, ancestral traditions, and additional decrees

yin **privilege** the exemption of high officials' sons from civil service examinations during the Chinese Sui and Tang eras

Z

la zarabanda (lah sah rah BAHN dah) a Cuban magical symbol (a right-angle cross in the middle of a circle)

ziggurat a tiered temple near the center of a Mesopotamian city

ACKNOWLEDGMENTS

Chapter 1

Excerpt from *His Five Letters of Relation to the Emperor Charles V* by Hernando Cortés, edited and translated by Francis Augustus (A. H. Clark, 1908).

Excerpt from *The War of Conquest, How It Was Waged Here in Mexico* by Bernardino de Sahagún, edited and translated by Arthur J. O. Anderson and Charles E. Dibble (Salt Lake City: University of Utah Press, 1978).

Excerpt from *The History of the New Indies and Spain* by Diego Durán (New York: Orion Press, 1964).

Chapter 2

Excerpt from the Iroquois creation myth, as told to Russell Barber.

Chapter 3

Excerpt from *The Florentine Codex, Book 9,* edited and translated by Arthur J. O. Anderson and Charles E. Dibble. (Santa Fe: School of American Research; Salt Lake City: University of Utah Press, 1978). Copyright © 1982 by the School of American Research. Reprinted by permission.

Chapter 4

Excerpt from *The Code of Hammurabi,* translated by Robert Harper (Chicago: University of Chicago Press, 1904).

Chapter 5

Excerpt from *Anthology of Chinese Literature,* edited by Cyril Birch. Copyright © 1965 by Grove Press. Used with the permission of Grove/Atlantic, Inc.

Chapter 6

Excerpt from *A Forest of Kings: The Untold Story of the Ancient Maya* by Linda Schele and David Freidel (New York: William Morrow and Company, 1990).

Chapter 7

Excerpt from *The Aeneid of Virgil,* translated by Allen Mandelbaum. Translation copyright © 1971 by Allen Mandelbaum. Used by permission of Bantam Books, a division of Bantam Doubleday Dell Publishing Group, Inc.

Excerpt from *The Odyssey of Homer,* translated by Richmond Lattimore. Copyright © 1965, 1967 by Richmond Lattimore. Copyright renewed. Reprinted by permission of HarperCollins Publishers, Inc.

Chapter 8

Excerpt from *The Letters of Pliny the Younger,* translated by B. Radier. Copyright © 1969 by B. Radier. Reprinted with the permission of Penguin Books, Ltd.

Chapter 9

Excerpt from *The African Past: Chronicles from Antiquity to Modern Times,* edited by Basil Davidson (Boston: Little, Brown and Company, 1964), pp. 55–56. Copyright © 1964 by Basil Davidson. Reprinted with the permission of Curtis Brown, Ltd.

Chapter 10

Excerpt from *Translation of the Edicts of Ashoka* by Romila Thapar. Copyright © by Romila Thapar. Used by permission of Oxford University Press, Inc.

Chapter 11

Excerpt from *Han Agriculture* by Hsu Cho-yun. Copyright © 1980 by University of Washington Press. Reprinted with permission from the publisher.

Chapter 12

Excerpt from *Say I Am You,* edited and translated by John Moyne and Coleman Barks (Athens, GA: Maypop Books, 1994), pp. 22–23. Copyright © 1994 by Coleman Barks. Reprinted with the permission of Coleman Barks.

Chapter 13

Excerpt from *Medieval Women Writers* by Katharina M. Wilson. Copyright © 1984 by University of Georgia Press, Athens. Reprinted with permission from the publisher.

Chapter 14

Excerpt from *Four Huts: Asian Writings on the Simple Life,* edited and translated by Burton Watson (Boston: Shambhala Publications, 1994), pp. 73–77. Copyright © 1994 by Burton Watson. Reprinted with the permission of Shambhala Publications, Inc., Horticultural Hall, 300 Massachusetts Avenue, Boston, MA 02115.

Chapter 15

Excerpt from *The African Past: Chronicles from Antiquity to Modern Times,* edited by Basil Davidson (Boston: Little, Brown and Company, 1964), p. 78. Copyright © 1964 by Basil Davidson. Reprinted with the permission of Curtis Brown, Ltd.

Chapter 16

Excerpt from *The Florentine Codex, Book 9, Chapter 3,* edited and translated by Arthur J. O. Anderson and Charles E. Dibble (Santa Fe: School of American Research; Salt Lake City: University of Utah Press, 1978). Copyright 1982 by the School of American Research. Reprinted by permission.

Chapter 17

Excerpt from *Change in Byzantine Culture in the Eleventh and Twelfth Centuries* by A. P. Kazhadan and Ann Wharton Epstein, University of California Press, Berkeley.

Chapter 18

Excerpt from *An Introduction to Chinese Literature* by W. C. Liu. Copyright © 1966 by Indiana University Press. Reprinted with the permission of Indiana University Press.

Chapter 19

Excerpt from *The History of the World Conquerer* by Allah-ad-din Atha-Malil Juvaini, translated by John Andrew Boyle. Copyright © 1958 by the President and Fellows of Harvard College. Reprinted with the permission of Harvard University Press.

Chapter 20

Excerpt from "The Chinese Concept of Nature" by Mitsukuni Yoshida in *Chinese Science: Explorations of an Ancient Tradition,* edited by Shigeru Nakayama and Nathan Sivin. Copyright © 1971 by the Massachusetts Institute of Technology Press. Reprinted with permission of the Massachusetts Institute of Technology Press.

Chapter 22

Excerpt from *The Nation and Its Fragments* by Partha Chatterjee. Copyright © 1984 by Princeton University Press. Reprinted with permission of Princeton University Press.

Chapter 23

Excerpt from *When China Ruled the Seas* by Louise Levathes. Copyright © 1997 by Louise Levathes. Used with permission of Oxford University Press, Inc.

Chapter 24

Excerpt from *Major Problems in American Indian History,* edited by Albert Hurtado and Peter Iverson (Lexington, MA: D. C. Heath, 1994), pp. 83, 84.

Chapter 25

Excerpt from *Voyages and Travels of an Indian Interpreter and Trader* (Toronto: Coles Publishing).

Chapter 26

Excerpt from *The Interesting Life of Olaudah Equiano,* edited by Robert Allison. Copyright © 1995 by Bedford Books.

Chapter 27

Excerpt from *Suleiman the Magnificent: Scourge of Heaven* by Antony Bridge (New York: Dorset Press, 1987).

Chapter 28

Excerpt from *Sources of Japanese Tradition* by William DeBary. Copyright © 1958 by Columbia University Press. Reprinted with permission of the publisher.

Chapter 29

Excerpt from *Readings in Her Story: Women in Christian Tradition,* edited by Barbara J. MacHaffie (Augsburg Fortress Publishers, 1992).

Chapter 30

Excerpt from *Women and Gender in Early Modern Europe* by Merry Wiesner-Hanks. Copyright © 1993 by Cambridge University Press. Reprinted with permission of the publisher.

Chapter 31

Excerpt from *The Enlightenment* by Ulrich Im Hof. Copyright © 1993 by Blackwell Publishing. Reprinted with permission of the publisher.

Chapter 32

Excerpt from "Human Documents in the Industrial Revolution in Britain" by Royston Pike in *Working in America: A Humanities Reader,* edited by Robert Sessions and Jack Wortman (Notre Dame, IN: University of Notre Dame Press, 1992).

Chapter 33

Excerpt from *The Emergence of Romanticism* by Nicholas Riasonovsky. Copyright © 1992 by Nicholas Riasonovsky. Used with permission of Oxford University Press, Inc.

Chapter 34

Excerpt from *The Nation and Its Fragments* by Partha Chatterjee. Copyright © 1984 by Princeton University Press. Reprinted with permission of Princeton University Press.

Chapter 35

Excerpt from *The Communist Manifesto* by Karl Marx and Friedrich Engels. English Translation in 1888 by Samuel Moore.

Chapter 36

Excerpt from A *History of Warfare* by John Keegan. Copyright © 1993 by Alfred Knopf. Reprinted with permission of Random House, Inc.

Excerpt from *The Collected Poems of Wilfred Owen,* edited by C. Day Lewis. Copyright © 1964 by New Directions Books, p. 5. Reprinted with permission of New Directions Books.

Chapter 37

Excerpt from *In a Shattered Mirror: The Later Poetry of Anna Akhmatova* by Susan Amert. Reprinted with the permission of the publishers, Stanford University Press. Copyright © 1992 by the Board of Trustees of the Leland Stanford Junior University.

Chapter 38

Excerpt from *The Penguin History of Canada* by Kenneth McNaught (London: Penguin Press, 1988).

Chapter 39

Excerpt from *The Search for a New Order* by W. M. Fletcher. Copyright © 1982 by the University of North Carolina Press. Used by permission of the publisher.

Chapter 40

Excerpt from *The Soviet Home-Front* by John Barber et al. (London: Longman, 1991).

Chapter 41

Excerpt from *Witness* by Whittaker Chambers. Copyright © 1952 by Random House. Reprinted by permission of Random House, Inc.

Chapter 42

Excerpt from *The Origins of Totalitarianism* by Hannah Arendt. Copyright © 1951 and renewed 1979 by Mary McCarthy West. Reprinted by permission of Harcourt Brace & Company.

Excerpt from "*Ha-Aretz,* April 4, 1969" in *The Question of Palestine* by Edward Said (New York: Vintage Press, 1979).

Excerpt from "The Zionist Occupation of Western Galilee, 1948" by Nafez Nazzal in *Journal of Palestinian Studies* 3 (3): 70, 1974.

Chapter 43

Excerpt from *The Spice Box of Earth* by Leonard Cohen. Copyright © 1961 by Leonard Cohen. Reprinted with the permission of the author, c/o Peter S. Shukat, Esq., Shukat and Hafer, New York.

Global Change from Prehistory to the 1500s

Full-Color Maps

These color maps are here for your reference. We hope you will have reason to consult them over the course of your study of world history. You might use them to remind yourself of dates and locations in which certain civilizations thrived. They might cause you to notice which cultures flourished simultaneously and which bordered one another. At times, you might find yourself comparing these maps to the map of the world today and thinking about the historical influences on the world we now live in. We also hope you turn to this appendix whenever you need to find a good map quickly.

On each two-page spread you will find maps that illustrate the changes that came to one geographical area over the period of time covered in Chapters 1–21. These areas are Southwest Asia, India, East and Southeast Asia, the Americas, Europe, the Mediterranean, and Africa. The final map illustrates the spread of world religions from 450 to 1450.

Southwest Asia and the Mediterranean, around 2700 B.C.–331 B.C.

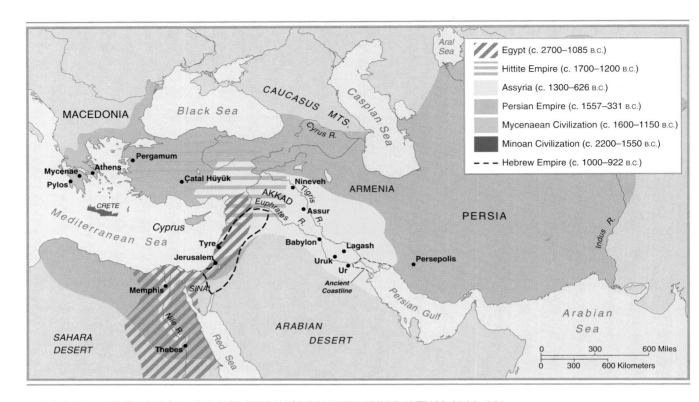

Map Legend:

- Egypt (c. 2700–1085 B.C.)
- Hittite Empire (c. 1700–1200 B.C.)
- Assyria (c. 1300–626 B.C.)
- Persian Empire (c. 1557–331 B.C.)
- Mycenaean Civilization (c. 1600–1150 B.C.)
- Minoan Civilization (c. 2200–1550 B.C.)
- Hebrew Empire (c. 1000–922 B.C.)

▶ **ANCIENT SOUTHWEST ASIA AND THE EASTERN MEDITERRANEAN, 2700–331 B.C.**

Ancient Southwest Asia (Ch. 4) saw the rise of numerous states, some of which developed into empires. In some cases these empires united several cultural groups and civilizations. The Persian Empire stretched from the Indus River Valley (Ch. 5) to Egypt, uniting various peoples under one polity and controlling major trade routes. Alexander, a Macedonian general, conquered the Persian Empire, creating an empire that was vast but short-lived (Ch. 8). Unity dissolved after Alexander's death, creating a patchwork of smaller polities. These areas would never again be united under a single state.

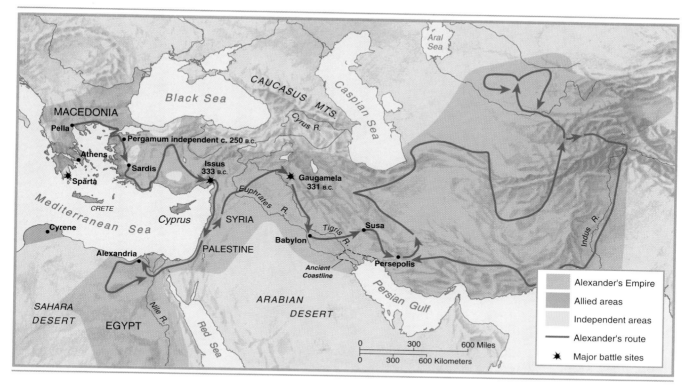

▶ **ALEXANDER'S EMPIRE AND THE SUCCESSOR STATES, 334–331 B.C.**

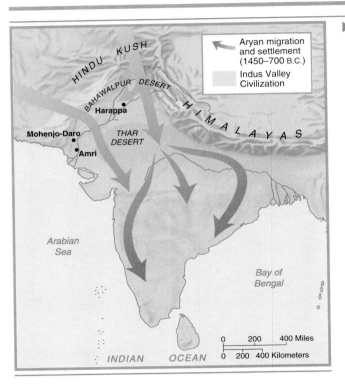

▶ **INDUS VALLEY CIVILIZATION AND ARYAN MIGRATION AND SETTLEMENT, 2500–700 B.C.**

▶ **INDIA, 320 B.C.–A.D. 550**

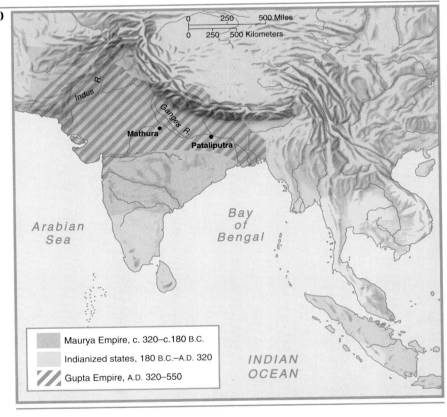

South and Southeast Asia, around 2500 B.C.–A.D. 1350

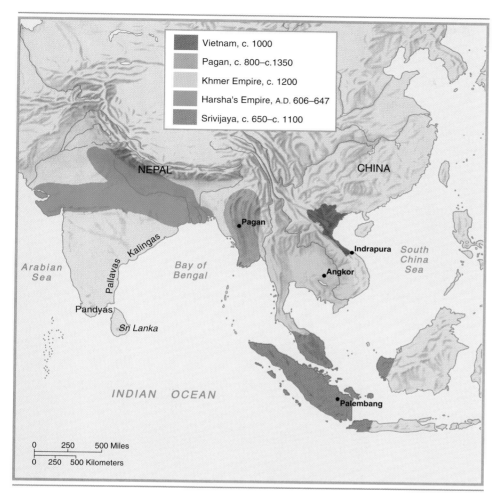

Legend:
- Vietnam, c. 1000
- Pagan, c. 800–c.1350
- Khmer Empire, c. 1200
- Harsha's Empire, A.D. 606–647
- Srivijaya, c. 650–c. 1100

NEPAL

CHINA

Pagan

Indrapura

South China Sea

Angkor

Arabian Sea

Kalingas

Pallavas

Bay of Bengal

Pandyas

Sri Lanka

INDIAN OCEAN

Palembang

0   250   500 Miles
0   250   500 Kilometers

▶ **REGIONAL STATES IN SOUTHEAST ASIA, AROUND 606–1350**

INDIA SAW THE EARLIEST STATE FORMATION IN South and Southeast Asia (Ch. 14). The Indus Valley civilization flourished for centuries, then collapsed. Only after the Aryan migrations from Southwest and Central Asia did Indian states form, especially in the Ganges Valley. The Maurya, classical-age Gupta, and Harsha empires ruled over large sections of India (Ch. 10). After the seventh century, regionalism became the dominant trend. State building also began in the early centuries A.D. in Southeast Asia. By 1200, major states had appeared on mainland and inland Southeast Asia (Ch. 14). The Burmese, Khmer, Vietnamese, and Malays had established viable polities.

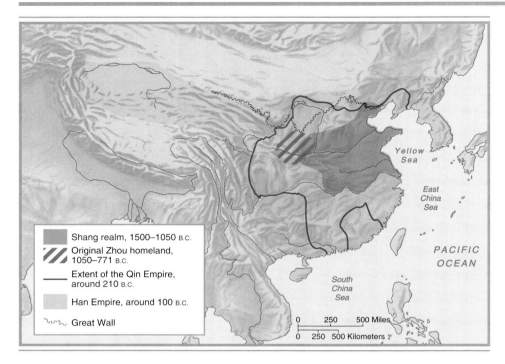

Shang realm, 1500–1050 B.C.
Original Zhou homeland, 1050–771 B.C.
Extent of the Qin Empire, around 210 B.C.
Han Empire, around 100 B.C.
Great Wall

Yellow Sea
East China Sea
PACIFIC OCEAN
South China Sea

0   250   500 Miles
0 250 500 Kilometers

▶ ANCIENT AND EARLY IMPERIAL CHINA, 1500–AROUND 100 B.C.

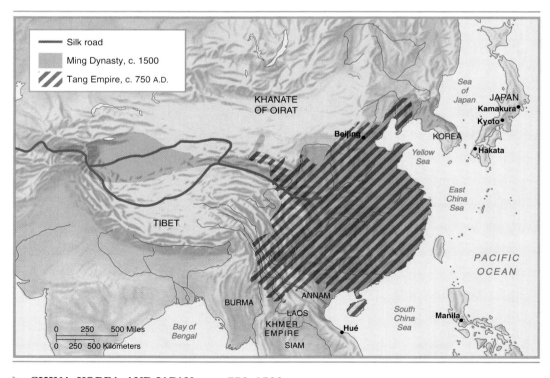

Silk road
Ming Dynasty, c. 1500
Tang Empire, c. 750 A.D.

KHANATE OF OIRAT
Sea of Japan
JAPAN
Kamakura
Kyoto
Beijing
KOREA
Yellow Sea
Hakata
East China Sea
TIBET
PACIFIC OCEAN
BURMA
ANNAM
LAOS
KHMER EMPIRE
Hué
South China Sea
Manila
SIAM
Bay of Bengal

0   250   500 Miles
0 250 500 Kilometers

▶ CHINA, KOREA, AND JAPAN, A.D. 750–1500

East and Central Asia, around 1500 B.C.–A.D. 1340

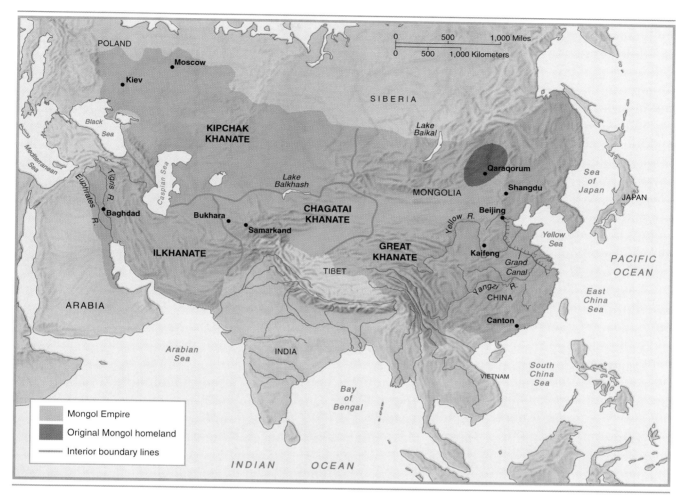

▶ **THE MONGOL EMPIRE AROUND 1206–1340**

S UCCESSIVE DYNASTIES EXPANDED CONTROL of areas making up part of modern China (Ch. 5). The Shang realm included much of the Yellow River Valley and the North China Plain. The Zhou territory included lands once controlled by Shang and expanded southward to the Yangzi River. Qin emperors added new domains, especially to the south, while the Han Empire controlled part of Korea, Southwest China, and areas to the west. By 762, Chinese control over the western region had been lost, regained, and lost again. By 1500, nonwestern lands ruled by Tang emperors (Ch. 18) were retained by their Ming counterparts (Ch. 28). The Mongols (Ch. 19) conquered and ruled a vast domain, covering most of Asia and a small part of Europe. This was one of the few times general unity was achieved in Asia.

The Americas, around 4000 B.C.–A.D. 1532

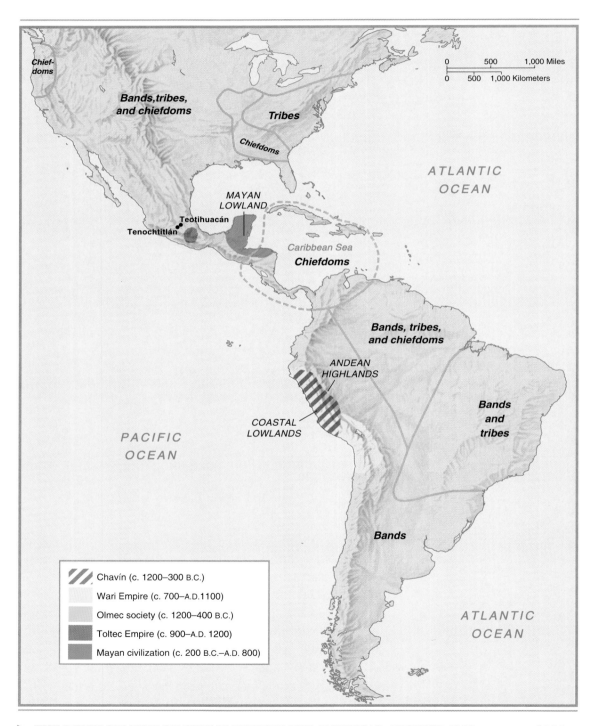

Chief-doms

Bands, tribes, and chiefdoms

Tribes

Chiefdoms

ATLANTIC OCEAN

MAYAN LOWLAND

Teotihuacán

Tenochtitlán

Caribbean Sea

Chiefdoms

Bands, tribes, and chiefdoms

ANDEAN HIGHLANDS

Bands and tribes

COASTAL LOWLANDS

PACIFIC OCEAN

Bands

ATLANTIC OCEAN

500   1,000 Miles
500   1,000 Kilometers

Chavín (c. 1200–300 B.C.)

Wari Empire (c. 700–A.D.1100)

Olmec society (c. 1200–400 B.C.)

Toltec Empire (c. 900–A.D. 1200)

Mayan civilization (c. 200 B.C.–A.D. 800)

▶ THE DEVELOPMENT OF CIVILIZATION IN THE AMERICAS, AROUND 4000 B.C.–A.D. 1200

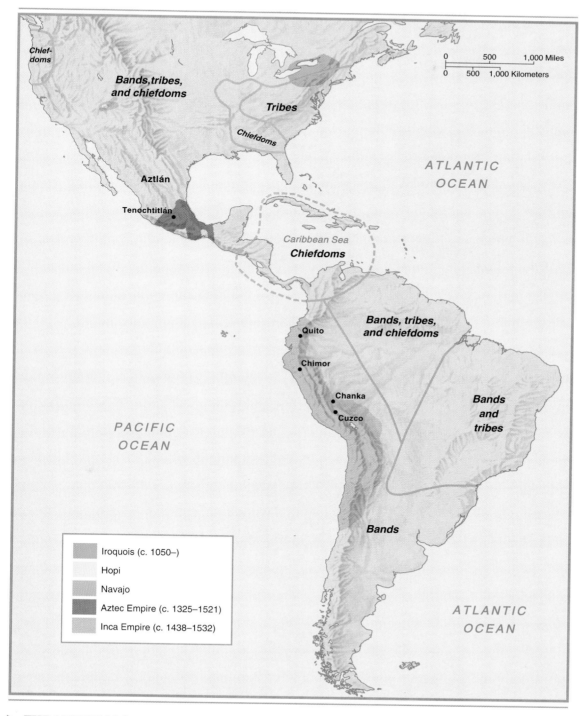

D URING MOST OF THE PERIOD WHEN THE Americas were isolated from the rest of the world, they were organized into regional and local political units. There were periods, however, when interregional empires developed. The largest empires, those of the Aztecs and Incas (Ch. 16), were in the latest period. Other peoples, like the Maya (Ch. 6), were unified by similar culture but were divided into many antagonistic states.

Iroquois (c. 1050–)
Hopi
Navajo
Aztec Empire (c. 1325–1521)
Inca Empire (c. 1438–1532)

▶ **THE AMERICAS ON THE EVE OF EUROPEAN CONTACT, AROUND 1300–1532**

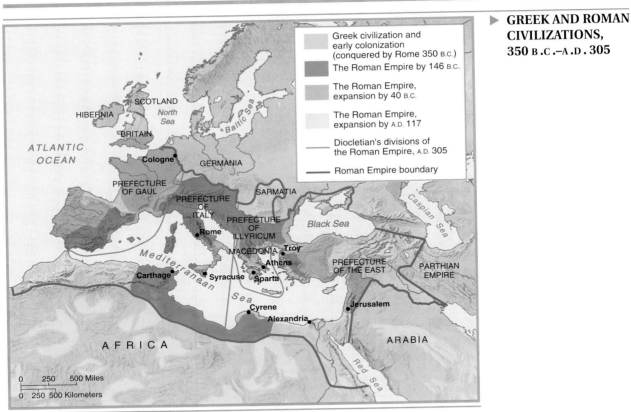

GREEK AND ROMAN CIVILIZATIONS, 350 B.C.–A.D. 305

Greek civilization and early colonization (conquered by Rome 350 B.C.)

The Roman Empire by 146 B.C.

The Roman Empire, expansion by 40 B.C.

The Roman Empire, expansion by A.D. 117

Diocletian's divisions of the Roman Empire, A.D. 305

Roman Empire boundary

SCOTLAND
HIBERNIA
North Sea
BRITAIN
ATLANTIC OCEAN
Baltic Sea
Cologne
GERMANIA
PREFECTURE OF GAUL
PREFECTURE OF ITALY
SARMATIA
Rome
PREFECTURE OF ILLYRICUM
Black Sea
Caspian Sea
Mediterranean Sea
MACEDONIA
Troy
Athens
Sparta
PREFECTURE OF THE EAST
PARTHIAN EMPIRE
Carthage
Syracuse
Cyrene
Alexandria
Jerusalem
AFRICA
ARABIA
Red Sea

0 250 500 Miles
0 250 500 Kilometers

EUROPE, SOUTHWEST ASIA, AND NORTH AFRICA, 500–843

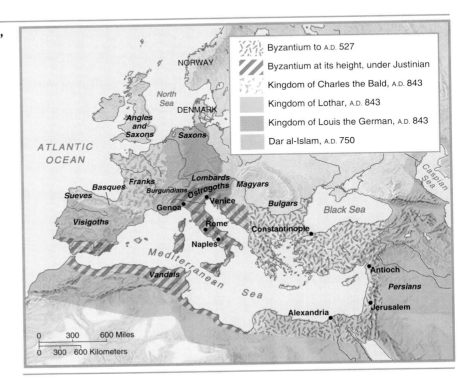

Byzantium to A.D. 527

Byzantium at its height, under Justinian

Kingdom of Charles the Bald, A.D. 843

Kingdom of Lothar, A.D. 843

Kingdom of Louis the German, A.D. 843

Dar al-Islam, A.D. 750

NORWAY
North Sea
DENMARK
Angles and Saxons
Saxons
ATLANTIC OCEAN
Franks
Basques
Burgundians
Lombards
Ostrogoths
Magyars
Sueves
Genoa
Venice
Bulgars
Black Sea
Visigoths
Rome
Constantinople
Naples
Mediterranean Sea
Vandals
Antioch
Persians
Alexandria
Jerusalem
Caspian Sea

0 300 600 Miles
0 300 600 Kilometers

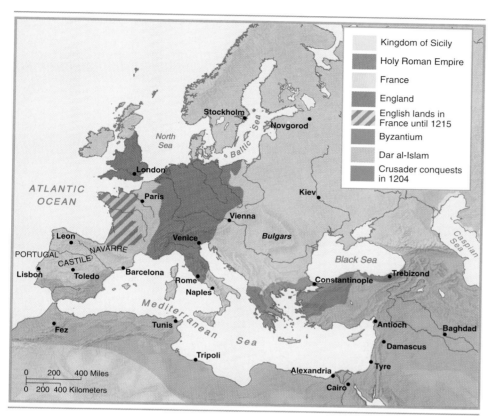

Legend:
- Kingdom of Sicily
- Holy Roman Empire
- France
- England
- English lands in France until 1215
- Byzantium
- Dar al-Islam
- Crusader conquests in 1204

▶ MEDIEVAL EUROPE, BYZANTIUM, AND MUSLIM STATES, AROUND 1200

THE HISTORIES OF EUROPE, SOUTHWEST ASIA, and North Africa were united for a significant period during the Roman and Byzantine empires (Ch. 17). Trade flourished in the homogeneous political zones during peacetime, and goods and ideas flowed freely among cultures. Regional polities emerged as migrating peoples challenged political unity. After a period of transition between the fourth and fifth centuries (Ch. 13), the Roman Empire (Chs. 7 and 8) broke into a patchwork of Germanic states in the west and the new state of Byzantium in the east. After the rise of Islam in the seventh century (Ch. 12), North Africa and most of Southwest Asia remained united under Dar al-Islam but divided into regional polities.

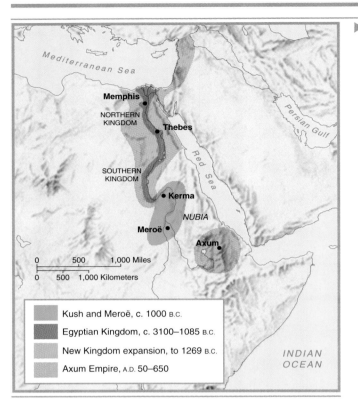

► **ANCIENT AFRICAN CIVILIZATIONS,**
3100 B.C.–A.D. 650

Kush and Meroë, c. 1000 B.C.

Egyptian Kingdom, c. 3100–1085 B.C.

New Kingdom expansion, to 1269 B.C.

Axum Empire, A.D. 50–650

► **AFRICA AND DAR AL-ISLAM,**
AROUND 50–1200

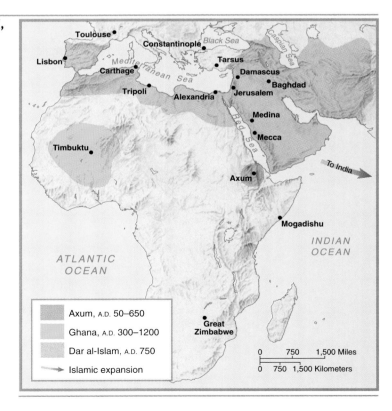

Axum, A.D. 50–650

Ghana, A.D. 300–1200

Dar al-Islam, A.D. 750

Islamic expansion

Africa and Dar al-Islam, around 3100 B.C.–A.D. 1550

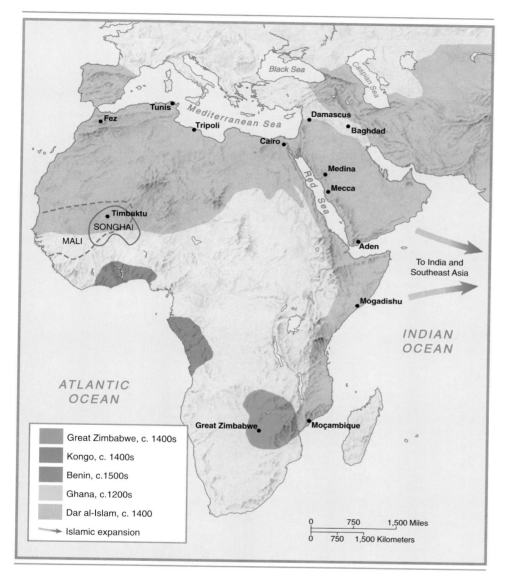

Great Zimbabwe, c. 1400s
Kongo, c. 1400s
Benin, c.1500s
Ghana, c.1200s
Dar al-Islam, c. 1400
Islamic expansion

▶ **LATER AFRICA AND DAR AL-ISLAM, AROUND 1100–AROUND 1550**

THE EARLIEST CIVILIZATIONS IN AFRICA DEVELOPED in the northeastern part of the continent (Ch. 9). Later, internal developments and the influence of Islam stimulated the origin of many civilizations south of the Sahara Desert (Chs. 12 and 15). The spread of Islam led to the development of Dar al-Islam (Ch. 12), those lands that shared Islamic culture.

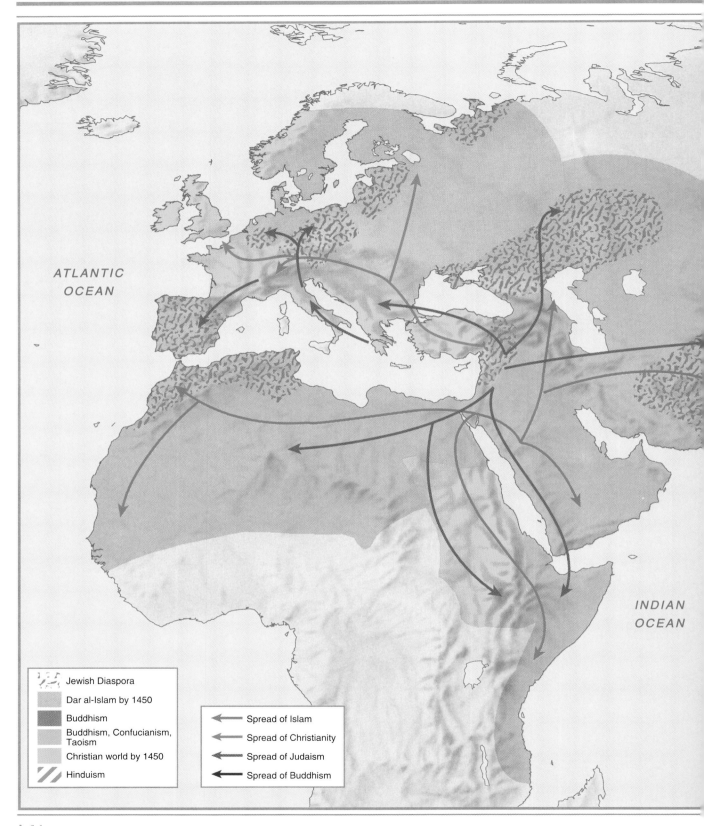

ATLANTIC
OCEAN

INDIAN
OCEAN

Jewish Diaspora

Dar al-Islam by 1450

Buddhism

Buddhism, Confucianism,
Taoism

Christian world by 1450

Hinduism

Spread of Islam

Spread of Christianity

Spread of Judaism

Spread of Buddhism

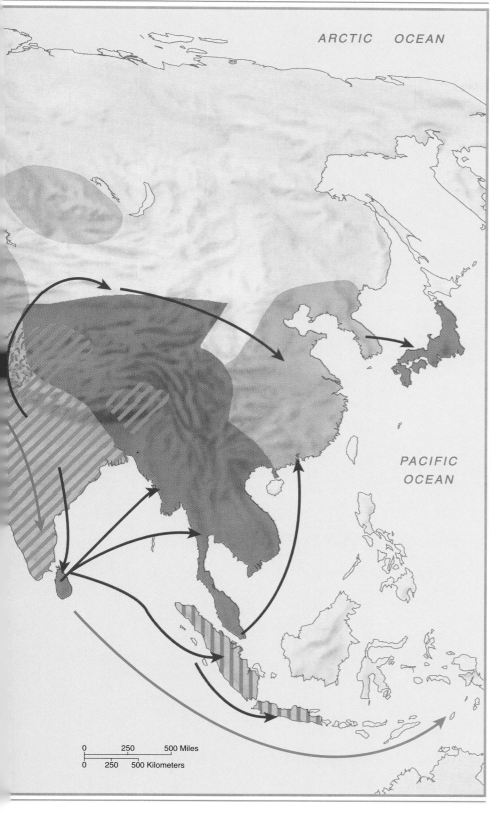

The Spread of Religions in Eurasia and Africa, around A.D. 450–1450

T HIS MAP SHOWS the major avenues of world religions' spread from their points of origin into new areas (Issue 4). Religions expanded through conquest, missionary activity, and exchange of ideas. In many cases, more than one religion spread into a geographical area. For example, both Buddhism and Islam were introduced, at different times, into Southeast Asia. The map shows the predominant religions in each area by about 1450; for example, both India and China had Christian populations, but their numbers remained small.

ARCTIC OCEAN

PACIFIC OCEAN

0   250   500 Miles
0 250 500 Kilometers

Global Change from 1500 to the Present

Full-Color Maps and Art

These color maps are here for your reference. We hope you will have reason to consult them over the course of your study of world history. You might use them to remind yourself of dates and locations in which certain civilizations thrived. They might cause you to notice which cultures flourished simultaneously and which bordered one another. At times, you might find yourself comparing these maps to the map of the world today and thinking about the historical influences on the world we now live in. We also hope you turn to this appendix whenever you need to find a good map quickly.

On each two-page spread you will find a collection of maps that illustrate the changes that came to one geographical area over the period of time covered in Chapters 22–44. The areas covered are Asia, Russia and the USSR, the Americas, Europe, and Africa. On the final page you will find two full-color examples of twentieth-century art.

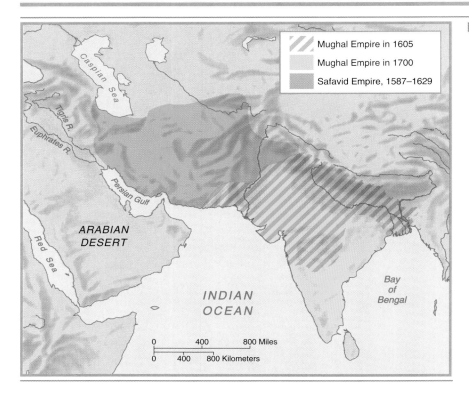

► **INDIA AND PERSIA, 1587–1700**

Mughal Empire in 1605

Mughal Empire in 1700

Safavid Empire, 1587–1629

► **THE QING (MANCHU) EMPIRE, 1644–1912**

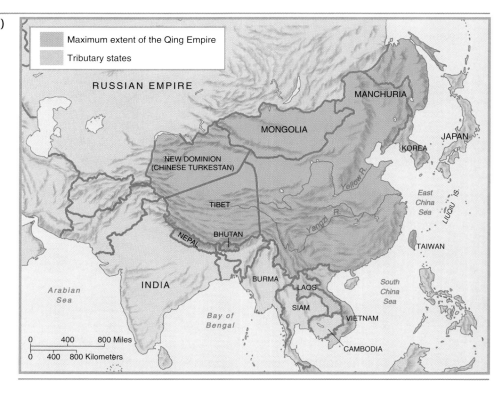

Maximum extent of the Qing Empire

Tributary states

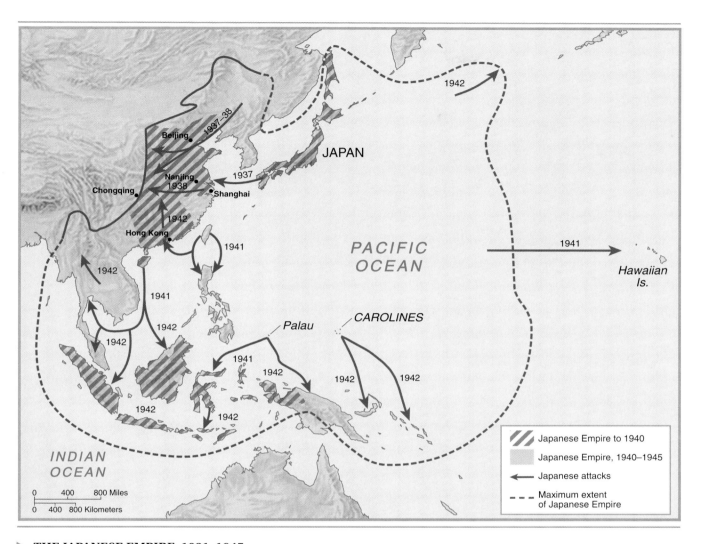

▶ **THE JAPANESE EMPIRE, 1931–1945**

ASIA, THE LARGEST CONTINENT, HAS SEEN A variety of empires in the last several centuries. In 1500, only the extreme western and eastern parts of Asia were under imperial rule (the Ottoman Empire and the Ming Empire in Ch. 28). Two hundred years later, the Ottoman (pp. A-20–A-21), Russian (p. A-22), Safavid, and Qing empires controlled most of the Asian landmass and its peoples (Chs. 27 and 28). From 1700 to 1900, imperial decline and European expansion through colonialism and imperialism overwhelmed the Safavid and Mughal empires. Most of Southeast Asia, too, fell under European imperialist rule. Japan became imperialistic in the 1890s and gradually took control of most of East and Southeast Asia, by the 1940s. Since 1945 (Ch. 40), these empires have dissolved, leaving in their wakes a complex array of independent states, many of which center on distinct ethnic groups. Nationalism has been a force for national unification and imperial dissolution.

BESSARABIA
(to Russia 1812)

MOLDAVIA
(1829)

HUNGARY
(to Austria 1699)

AUSTRIA

TRANSYLVANIA
(to Austria 1699)

KHANAT
OF CRIM
(to Russia 1

BANAT
(to Austria 1718)

CROATIA

ROMANIA
(created 1858)

ITALY

BOSNIA
(to Austria-
Hungary 1878)

DALMATIA
(to Venice 1699–1797;
to Austria 1797 & 1816;
to Italy 1805–1809;
to France 1809–1816)

BULGARIA
(1878; 1908)

Black Sea

SERBIA
(to Austria 1718–1739)

MACEDONIA
(to Greece 1913)

ANATOLIA

ALBANIA
(1913)

GREECE
(1830)

TUNIS
(nominally subject
until 1881)

CRETE
(Turkey 1718;
to Greece 1908)

CYPRUS
(Br. Prot. 1878;
annexed by Britain 1914)

LEBANON
(Fr. Mandate 1920

Mediterranean Sea

PALESTINE
(Br. Mandate 1920

TRIPOLI
(Ottoman vassal until 1835;
Ottoman province 1835–
1912; to Italy 1912)

LIBYA

EGYPT
(1811; Br. Occupation
1882; Br. Protectorate
1914;1922)

Danube R.

Nile R.

0   150   300 Miles
0   150   300 Kilometers

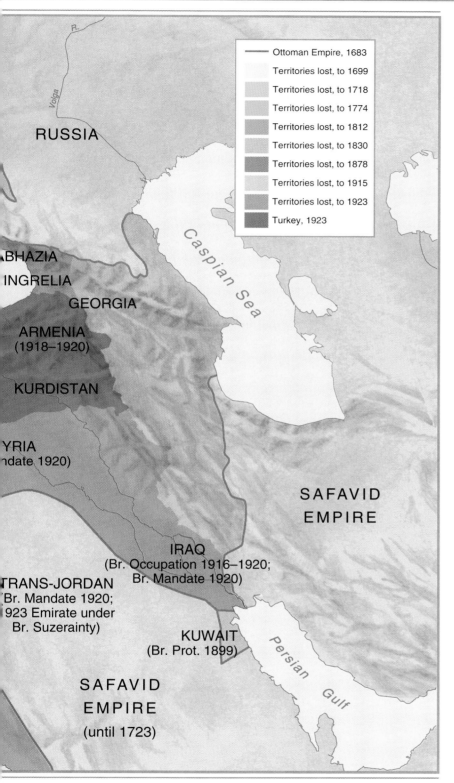

RUSSIA

Volga R.

Caspian Sea

ABHAZIA

INGRELIA

GEORGIA

ARMENIA
(1918–1920)

KURDISTAN

SYRIA
(Mandate 1920)

SAFAVID
EMPIRE

IRAQ
(Br. Occupation 1916–1920;
Br. Mandate 1920)

TRANS-JORDAN
(Br. Mandate 1920;
1923 Emirate under
Br. Suzerainty)

KUWAIT
(Br. Prot. 1899)

Persian Gulf

SAFAVID
EMPIRE
(until 1723)

——	Ottoman Empire, 1683
	Territories lost, to 1699
	Territories lost, to 1718
	Territories lost, to 1774
	Territories lost, to 1812
	Territories lost, to 1830
	Territories lost, to 1878
	Territories lost, to 1915
	Territories lost, to 1923
	Turkey, 1923

The Ottoman Empire, 1683–1923

A T ITS HEIGHT, the Ottoman Empire spanned three continents and ruled over 30 million people. One reason for the empire's longevity was its religious and ethnic toleration of its diverse citizenry, which included Asian Muslims, European Christians, and Jews. While the empire offered Muslims some advantages (like exclusion from a special tax), for the most part people of all backgrounds and faiths enjoyed shared freedoms.

By the early eighteenth century, however, stirrings of nationalism (Ch. 33) began to threaten the empire's foundations. Ethnic groups within the empire began to unite, often with support from Russia or European nations. During the nineteenth century, many independent nations emerged in the territories formerly under Ottoman control; by 1918, most of the original empire had been chipped away. The Ottoman Empire suffered additional losses as a result of its defeat in World War I; peace dictated by the Allies left little land and much resentment. This rage spurred Turkish nationalism and led, in 1923, to the establishment of the Turkish Republic and the end of an empire that had lasted almost five hundred years.

Russia and the Soviet Union, 1580–1989

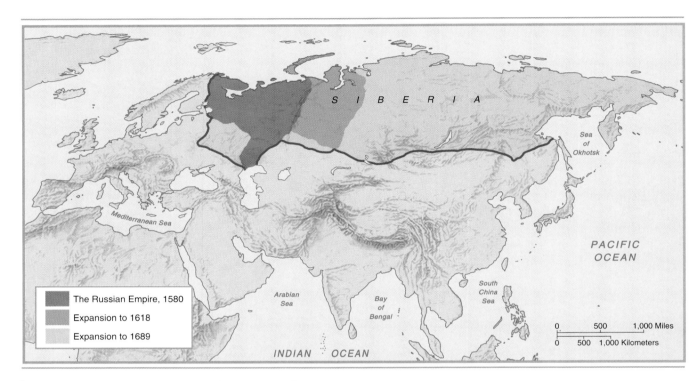

The Russian Empire, 1580

Expansion to 1618

Expansion to 1689

▶ **THE EXPANSION OF THE RUSSIAN EMPIRE, 1580–1689**

ORIGINALLY A EUROPEAN COUNTRY, RUSSIA BEGAN expanding into Asia in the mid–sixteenth century (Ch. 27). Siberia became the main avenue of expansion in the seventeenth century, with Russians reaching the Pacific Ocean during that era. Much of Central Asia was added in the nineteenth century. Although the Bolsheviks decried the previous colonial policies of the tsarist government, they reconquered most of the former imperial realm, adding Mongolia as a client state in 1919 (Ch. 37). The Soviet Empire held together until 1991 but by 1992 had dissolved into fifteen different states (Chs. 41 and 42), with Russia holding much of the territory it held in 1689.

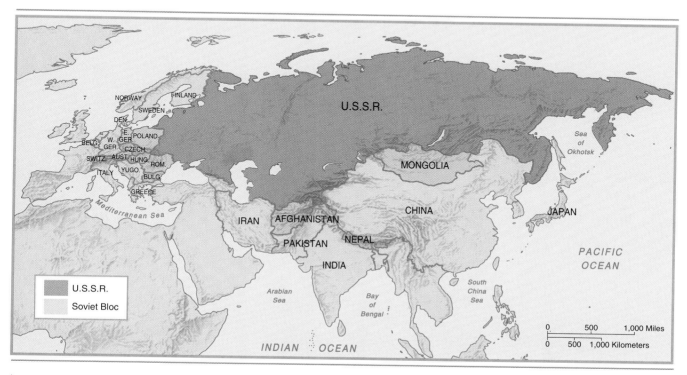

▶ **THE SOVIET UNION, 1945–1989**

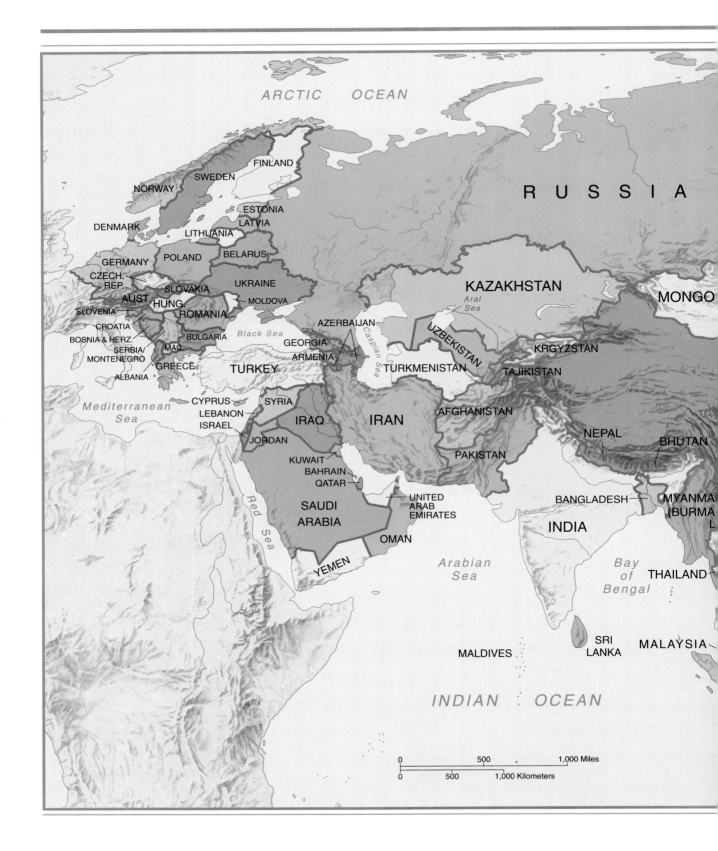

ARCTIC OCEAN

RUSSIA

FINLAND

SWEDEN

NORWAY

ESTONIA

DENMARK

LATVIA

LITHUANIA

GERMANY

POLAND

BELARUS

CZECH.
REP.

SLOVAKIA

UKRAINE

AUST.

HUNG.

MOLDOVA

SLOVENIA

ROMANIA

CROATIA

BOSNIA & HERZ.

BULGARIA

SERBIA/
MONTENEGRO

MAC.

GREECE

ALBANIA

Black Sea

KAZAKHSTAN

Aral
Sea

AZERBAIJAN

GEORGIA

ARMENIA

UZBEKISTAN

KRGYZSTAN

Caspian Sea

TURKMENISTAN

TAJIKISTAN

MONGO

TURKEY

CYPRUS

SYRIA

Mediterranean
Sea

LEBANON

ISRAEL

IRAQ

IRAN

AFGHANISTAN

JORDAN

KUWAIT

BAHRAIN

QATAR

SAUDI
ARABIA

Red
Sea

PAKISTAN

UNITED
ARAB
EMIRATES

NEPAL

BHUTAN

BANGLADESH

OMAN

INDIA

YEMEN

MYANMA
(BURMA
L

Arabian
Sea

Bay
of
Bengal

THAILAND

MALDIVES

SRI
LANKA

MALAYSIA

INDIAN OCEAN

0   500   1,000 Miles

0   500   1,000 Kilometers

A-24

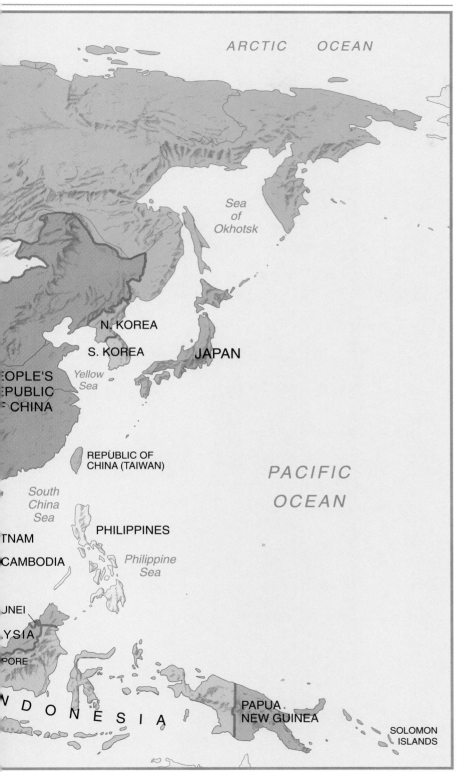

ARCTIC OCEAN

Sea of Okhotsk

N. KOREA

S. KOREA

JAPAN

:OPLE'S
:PUBLIC
:CHINA

Yellow Sea

REPUBLIC OF CHINA (TAIWAN)

PACIFIC OCEAN

South China Sea

TNAM

:AMBODIA

PHILIPPINES

Philippine Sea

JNEI

YSIA

PORE

DONESIA

PAPUA NEW GUINEA

SOLOMON ISLANDS

Asia and Eastern Europe Today

Before World War II, many states in Asia and Eastern Europe were larger and more ethnically diverse. With war came displacement and death for millions of soldiers, civilians, and refugees. These conditions, and the social change they brought, have had tremendous short-term effects on the political map of the area (Issue 9 and Ch. 44). A stream of Jewish refugees settled in Southwest Asia, altering the region's ethnic balance. The establishment of Israel in 1948 did not resolve tensions between Arabs and Jews. Fighting in this region continues today.

India earned independence from British rule shortly after World War II to discover its own religious fragmentation. Two more countries, Pakistan and Bangladesh, have also emerged in South Asia. The ongoing Kashmir independence movement suggests that there may be more changes ahead.

As Russian power in Eastern Europe declined, ethnic ties flourished. Lithuania, Latvia, Estonia, Slovakia, Slovenia, Bosnia and Herzegovina, Serbia, and the Czech Republic are all less than fifty years old. These new states' borders were drawn to reflect the ethnic makeup of each region, though the continued fighting in the former state of Yugoslavia proves that social disputes cannot be settled by territorial divisions. With the breakup of the Soviet Union from 1989 to 1991, numerous countries (like Ukraine and Georgia) have emerged in Southwest and Central Asia.

The Americas, 1700 to the Present

T HERE WERE major popu-
lation movements from
the Old World to the New
World (Chs. 24–26) following
its discovery by Europeans in
the fifteenth century. The
colonial peopling of the Americas brought millions of
settlers, largely replacing the
Native American population.
The great surge in population
movement, however, came in
the nineteenth and twentieth
centuries, when transpor-
tation became more available
and less expensive. Reconstruction of migration
statistics is notoriously unreliable, and these figures are
only approximations.

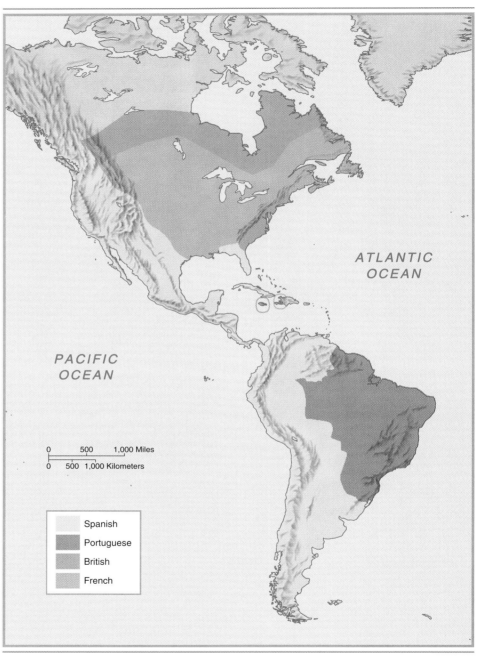

ATLANTIC
OCEAN

PACIFIC
OCEAN

| 0 | 500 | 1,000 Miles |
| 0 | 500 | 1,000 Kilometers |

Spanish
Portuguese
British
French

▶ **COLONIAL OWNERSHIP OF THE AMERICAS, 1700–1763**

From		To North America	To Mexico and Central America	To the Caribbean	To South America
Western Europe	Iberia	1	6		2.5
	Italy	11	1		1.5
	other countries	32	1		6
Eastern Europe		17	.2		.2
West Africa		6	2	5	12
East Asia	China	.2	.1		.2
Southeast Asia		3	.2		.1
Southwest Asia	Iran	.6			
	Arabia	.6	.1		
South Asia	India/Pakistan	.5		.1	

ESTIMATES (IN MILLIONS)

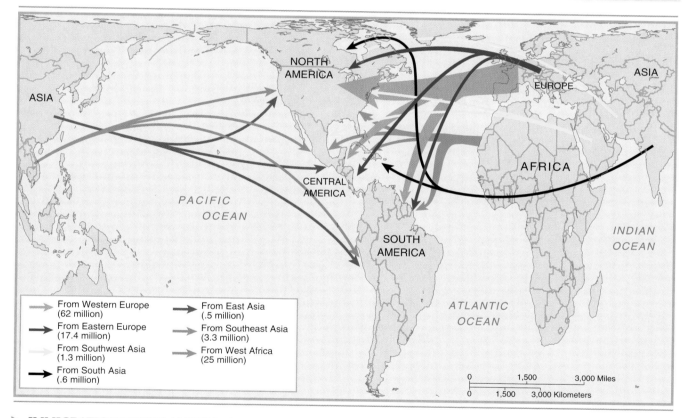

From Western Europe (62 million)

From Eastern Europe (17.4 million)

From Southwest Asia (1.3 million)

From South Asia (.6 million)

From East Asia (.5 million)

From Southeast Asia (3.3 million)

From West Africa (25 million)

▶ **IMMIGRATION TO THE AMERICAS, SINCE 1500**

Europe, 1560–1989

EUROPEANS HAVE ENDURED a variety of political systems in the centuries since 1500. By 1660, the Ottoman and Holy Roman empires could claim jurisdiction over large numbers of Europeans, and the hold of the Holy Roman Empire over its peoples was tenuous at best. The Swedes fashioned a Baltic empire that collapsed early in the eighteenth century (Ch. 30). The next major empire was created by Napoleon Bonaparte's conquests in the early nineteenth century (Ch. 31). It lasted until 1814 and was succeeded by the Austrian and Russian empires. Rising nationalist tensions in the Russian, Ottoman, and Austro-Hungarian empires helped precipitate World War I (Ch. 36), during which the Triple Entente (France, Russia, and Great Britain) fought Germany and Austria-Hungary. In World War II (Ch. 40), Britain and the Soviet Union allied (with the United States) to fight Germany and Italy. Central European states seemed to be allied and fighting against western and eastern European states in both wars. During the Cold War (Ch. 41), the Soviet Union and the United States formed alliance systems (the Warsaw Pact and NATO) that involved many European states. Since 1991, these military alliance systems have either collapsed or searched for a new purpose, but economic alliances and connections have continued to flourish and deepen.

▶ **EUROPE, 1560–1660**

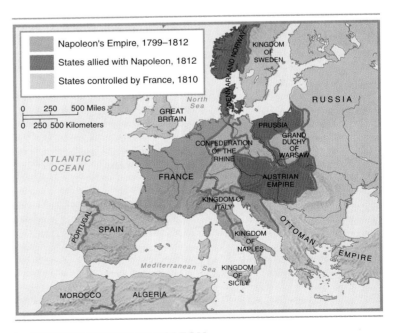

▶ **EUROPE UNDER NAPOLEON**

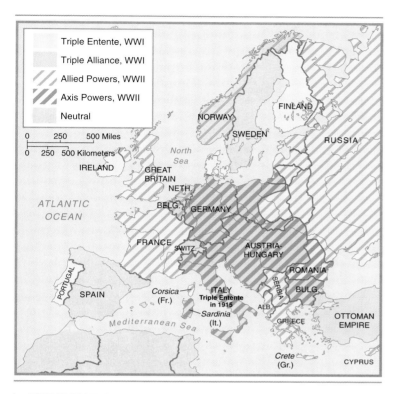

▶ **EUROPEAN ALLIANCES IN WORLD WARS I AND II**

▶ **COLD WAR EUROPE, 1945–1989**

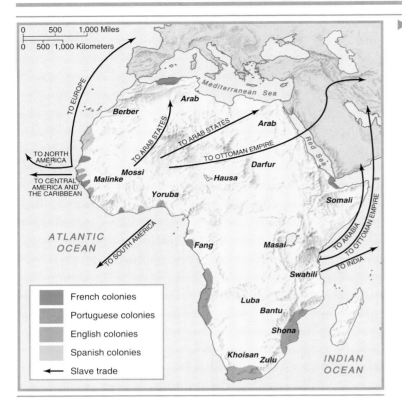

► **AFRICA TO 1800**

French colonies
Portuguese colonies
English colonies
Spanish colonies
← Slave trade

► **IMPERIALISM IN AFRICA, 1880–1914**

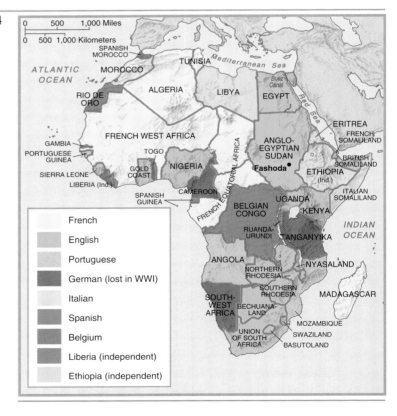

French
English
Portuguese
German (lost in WWI)
Italian
Spanish
Belgium
Liberia (independent)
Ethiopia (independent)

Africa, 1800–1997

A T THE BEGINNING OF THE NINETEENTH CENTURY, European colonial powers were just establishing toeholds in most of Africa (Ch. 26 and Issue 6), though power rested primarily with native governments. By the end of that century, most of Africa had fallen to imperialist countries such as France, Britain, Belgium, and Germany (Ch. 34). Some territories passed from the possession of one European power to another, especially with the settlements following World War I. These territories remained under foreign domination until the late 1950s and after. By 1990, Africans had wrested control of their lands, gaining independence.

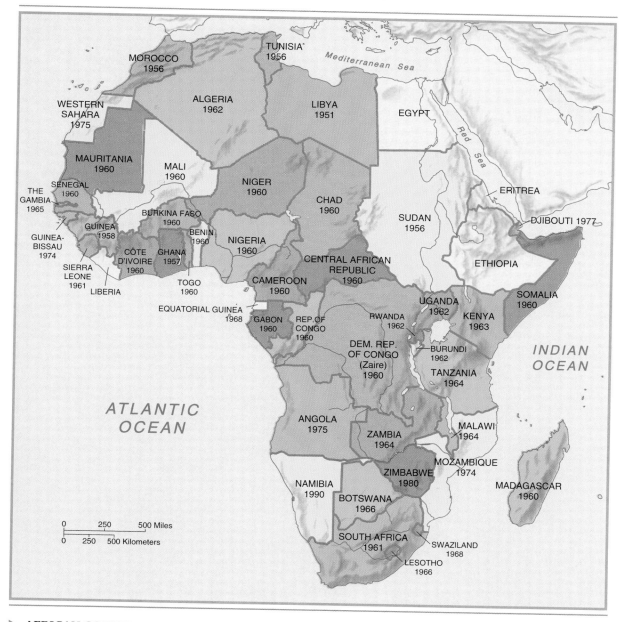

▶ **AFRICAN COUNTRIES EARN INDEPENDENCE, 1951–1997**

Two Examples of Modern Art

MODERN ART has grown out of the Western art tradition and reflects that heritage. At the same time, it has diverged significantly from traditional goals. These two works demonstrate elements of tradition (use of art for nationalistic or patriotic purposes) and divergence (use of abstraction for novel effects).

In 1920, Dmitri Moor's striking poster entitled "Have You Volunteered?" (right) challenged viewers to join the Russian revolutionary cause. The Bolshevik Party had seized power in Russia in 1917, and by 1920 the country was engaged in a major revolution. Red—used in the clothing of the Red Army soldier and the factory behind him—symbolizes the communist ideology and suggests the importance of the workers as the backbone of the Bolshevik movement. Many workers volunteered for the Red Army, bringing it to victory by 1921.

Unlike most abstract expressionist art, this 1964 work (below) by the Dutch-born painter Willem de Kooning depicts a particular subject, in this case a woman. Rather than record detail, however, de Kooning transforms the woman's image into layers of rich color that overlap one another.

Right: Courtesy of Stephen White, University of Glasgow. *Below*: Hirshhorn Museum and Sculpture Garden, Smithsonian Institution. Gift of Joseph H. Hirshhorn, 1966. Photo by Lee Stalsworth.

▶ **RED SHIRT POSTER**

▶ **WILLEM DE KOONING'S** *WOMAN, SAG HARBOR*

Index

I-1